# THE SHAPE
# OF THE
# LITURGY

# THE SHAPE
# OF THE
# LITURGY

BY

## DOM GREGORY DIX
### MONK OF NASHDOM ABBEY
### D.D., OXON

Bloomsbury T&T Clark
An imprint of Bloomsbury Publishing Plc

## BLOOMSBURY
LONDON · OXFORD · NEW YORK · NEW DELHI · SYDNEY

**Bloomsbury T&T Clark**

An imprint of Bloomsbury Publishing Plc

Imprint previously known as T&T Clark

| | |
|---|---|
| 50 Bedford Square | 1385 Broadway |
| London | New York |
| WC1B 3DP | NY 10018 |
| UK | USA |

**www.bloomsbury.com**

**BLOOMSBURY, T&T CLARK and the Diana logo are trademarks of Bloomsbury Publishing Plc**

First published 2005
Reprinted by Bloomsbury T&T Clack 2015, 2016, 2017

Introduction © Simon Jones 2005

© 1945 Dom Gregory Dix
First published January 1945
Second edition 1945
This edition first published 2005
Reprinted 2007 (twice), 2009, 2010, 2011, 2012, 2015

**British Library Cataloguing-in-Publication Data**
A catalogue record for this book is available from the British Library.

ISBN: HB: 978-0-8264-7942-6
PB: 978-0-5676-6157-9
ePDF: 978-0-5676-6328-3
ePUB: 978-0-5676-6329-0

**Library of Congress Cataloging-in-Publication Data**
A catalog record for this book is available from the Library of Congress.

Typeset by Integra Software Services Pvt. Ltd.
Printed and bound in Great Britain

TO
THE REVEREND FATHERS AND BRETHREN
OF THE
SOCIETY OF S. JOHN THE EVANGELIST
AT COWLEY

# CONTENTS

PAGE

INTRODUCTION TO THE 2005 EDITION - - - - - xii

INTRODUCTION. THE PURPOSE OF THIS ESSAY - - - xxxi

CHAPTER

I. THE LITURGY AND THE EUCHARISTIC ACTION - - 1
The Liturgy and its Shape—The Liturgical Tradition

II. THE PERFORMANCE OF THE LITURGY - - - - 12
Saying and Doing—Public and Private—The 'Church'—The Worshippers

III. THE CLASSICAL SHAPE OF THE LITURGY—I. - - 36
THE SYNAXIS
Synaxis and Eucharist—The Synaxis, or Liturgy of the Spirit

IV. EUCHARIST AND LORD'S SUPPER - - - - - 48
The 'Four-Action' Shape of the Eucharist—The Last Supper—The Meaning of the Last Supper—The Primitive Eucharist—The Lord's Supper or Agape—The Separation of the Eucharist from the Agape

V. THE CLASSICAL SHAPE OF THE LITURGY—II. - - 103
THE EUCHARIST
The Pre-Nicene Eucharist—The Greeting and Kiss of Peace—The Offertory—The Rinsing of the Hands—The Imposition of Hands on the Elements—The Eucharistic Dialogue and Prayer—The Amen—The Lord's Prayer—The Fraction—The Communion—The Ablutions

VI. THE PRE-NICENE BACKGROUND OF THE LITURGY - 141

VII. THE EUCHARISTIC PRAYER - - - - - - 156
i. The Roman Tradition—The Eucharistic Prayer of Hippolytus. ii. The Egyptian Tradition—Prayer of Oblation of Bishop Sarapion. iii. The Syrian Tradition—The Liturgy of SS. Addai and Mari—The Liturgy of S. James—The Rite of Jerusalem in the Fourth Century—The Rite of Antioch in the Fourth Century

VIII. BEHIND THE LOCAL TRADITIONS - - - - 208
The Present State of the Question—The Primitive Nucleus of the Prayer—The Second Half of the Prayer—A Critical Reconstruction of the Traditional Theory

CHAPTER PAGE

IX. THE MEANING OF THE EUCHARIST - - - - 238

Consecration and Sacrifice—The Eucharist as *Anamnesis*—The Eucharist as Action—The Eucharist as Manifestation—Eschatology —'The Spirit' and Eschatology—Eschatology and the Eucharist— 'The Spirit' and the Eucharist

X. THE THEOLOGY OF CONSECRATION - - - - 268

The 'Liturgy' of the Celebrant—The Function of the Prayer in the Eucharistic Action—Fourth Century Ideas of Consecration— S. Cyril's Doctrine of Consecration and the Rite of Jerusalem— The Invocation of the Spirit—The Invocation as effecting the 'Resurrection'—The 'Eastern' and the 'Western' ethos—The Tradition of Asia Minor?—The 'Great Entrance' and the Preparation of the Elements—The Invocation in the modern Eastern Rites Additional Note:—The Eastern Teaching on the Invocation

XI. THE SANCTIFICATION OF TIME - - - - - 303

From a Private to a Public Worship—The Coming of Monasticism and the Divine Office—The Development of the Christian Calendar: (*a*) the Pre-Nicene Calendar; (*b*) the Post-Nicene Calendar—The Organisation of the Propers—Saints' Days in the Post-Nicene Calendar—The Fourth Century and the Liturgy

XII. THE DEVELOPMENT OF CEREMONIAL - - - - 397

Vestments—Insignia—Lights—Incense—Summary

XIII. THE COMPLETION OF THE SHAPE OF THE LITURGY - 434

*A. The Fusion of Synaxis and Eucharist. B. The Completion of the Shape of the Synaxis.* The Introduction. i. The 'Far Eastern' Introduction; ii. The Egyptian; iii. The Greek; iv. The Western: *a.* At Rome; *b.* Outside Rome: Milan; Spain; Gaul—The Lections and Chants—The Prayer after the Sermon. *C. The Junction of Synaxis and Eucharist.* The Invention of Litanies—The Veil and the Screen—The Creed—The Prayer 'of the Day'—Offertory Chants—Offertory Prayers—The 'Names' and the 'Diptychs'. *D. The Completion of the Shape of the Eucharist.* In Egypt—In Syria —In the Byzantine Rite—In Africa—The Roman Communion Blessing—In Spain—In Gaul—The Roman Post-Communion —The Western Conclusion. *E. The 'Third Stratum'*

XIV. VARIABLE PRAYERS AT THE EUCHARIST - - - - 527

In the Eastern Rites—In the Western Rites—The Preface and Sanctus in the West—The East and the West

XV. THE MEDIAEVAL DEVELOPMENT - - - - - 546

*A. The Development of the Eastern Rites. B. The Development of the Western Rites.* The French and Spanish Rites—The Italian Rites—Gelasian Sacramentary—Leonine Sacramentary—Italian Local Rites—Gregorian Sacramentary—The Western Synthesis— The Reforms of Charlemagne—The English Influence—The Work of Alcuin—The End of the Gallican Rite—The Adoption

# CONTENTS

CHAPTER                                                                    PAGE

of Alcuin's Missal—The Western Missal—Mediaeval and Post-
Mediaeval Developments—Uniformity—The Mediaeval Present-
ation of the Liturgy—Lay Religion in the Dark and Middle Ages
—Lay Communions—Later Mediaeval Eucharistic Devotion—
Mediaeval Liturgy
    Additional Note:—Mediaeval Eucharistic Devotions for Layfolk
and the Protestant Conception of the Eucharist


XVI. THE REFORMATION AND THE ANGLICAN LITURGY    -    613
    The Post-Mediaeval Crisis—The Reformation—Archbishop
Cranmer—Cranmer's Liturgical Work—The Anglican Settlement
    Additional Note:—The Present Liturgical Position in the Church
of England


XVII. 'THROUGHOUT ALL AGES, WORLD WITHOUT END'    -    735

INDEX    •    •    •    •    •    •    •    •    •    •    •    754

NOTE

A table showing the Development of the Synaxis to c.AD800
will be found overleaf.

# DEVELOPMENT OF THE SYNAXIS TO *c.* A.D. 800

Original nucleus thus: (A), (B), etc.
'Second Stratum' thus: (α), (β); (§); (1), (2), (3)
Later elements in each rite bracketed thus: [ ]
Date when particular items were added is given where known

|  |  |  | (Monophysite) | | |
|---|---|---|---|---|---|
| I | | | | II | |
| Ps-Denys | E. Syrian | Armenian | W. Syrian | Coptic | Gk. St. Mark |
| (α) *Censing* | ? | (α) *Censing* | (α) *Censing*<br>5th c. | (A) GREETING<br>(§) *Prayer*<br>[ (α) *Censing*<br>? 6th c. ] | [ (α) *Censing*<br>? 6th c. ] |
| — | — | — | — | — | — |
| — | — | [ (1) *Entrance*<br>*Chant*<br>(Monogenes<br>? cent.) ] | — | — | [ (1) *Entrance*<br>*Chant*<br>(Monogenes) ] |
| — | — | [(A) GREETING)] | — |  | (A) GREETING |
| — | — | — | — |  | (§) *Prayer* |
| — | — | (β) *Psalm 'of day'*<br>= *Hymn* | — | (2) *Litany* |  |
| — | [ (3) *Hymn*<br>⟨Trisagion<br>before<br>8th cent⟩ ] | [ (3) *Hymn*<br>(Trisagion) ] | ⟨Trisagion<br>after<br>Epistle⟩ | ⟨Trisagion<br>after<br>Epistle⟩ | [ (3) *Hymn*<br>⟨Trisagion<br>? cent.⟩ ] |
| — | — | [(2) *Litany*)] | — |  | — |
| (β) *Hymn*<br>(Psalms) | (β) *Hymn*<br>(Psalms) | (β) *Hymn*<br>(Psalm) | — | — | — |
| — | — | — | — |  |  |
| — | — | — | — |  |  |
| — | — | — | — |  |  |
| (B) LECTIONS | (B) LECTIONS | (B) LECTIONS | (B) LECTIONS | (B) LECTIONS | (B) LECTIONS |
| ? | (C) CHANTS<br>between (B) | (C) CHANTS<br>between (B) | (C) CHANTS<br>between (B) | (C) CHANTS<br>between (B) | (C) CHANTS<br>between (B) |
| (D) SERMON | (D) SERMON | (D) SERMON | (D) SERMON | (D) SERMON | (D) SERMON |
| (E) DISMISSALS | (E) DISMISSALS | (E) DISMISSALS | <(E) DISMISSALS> | (E) DISMISSALS | <(E) DISMISSALS> |

See Chapter 13, pages 434–472

Items known to have existed but since disappeared bracketed thus: < >
The sign '—' means that this element is altogether absent in the history of the rite
A blank means that this item is found at some other point in the rite

| III | | IV | | | |
|---|---|---|---|---|---|
| *Byzantine* | *Gk. St. James* | *Roman* | *Milanese* | *French* | *Spanish* |
| [ (α) *Censing* 6th c. ] | [ (α) *Censing* ? 6th c. ] | — | — | — | — |
| [ Enarxis Litanies introduced ? 8th c. ] | — | — | — | — | — |
| (1) *Entrance Chant* (Monogenes A.D. 536) ⟨ (A) GREETING attested c. A.D. 400 ⟩ | (1) *Entrance Chant* (Monogenes A.D. 536) (A) GREETING | (1) *Entrance Chant* (Psalm c. A.D. 430) | (1) *Entrance Chant* (Psalm ? 6th c.) | (1) *Entrance Chant* (Trisagion with Kyries 6th c.) (A) GREETING | (1) *Entrance Chant* Psalm [ Trisagion added c. 7th c. on great feasts ] |
| — | (2) *Litany* (Jerusalem 5th c.) | (2) *Litany* (c. A.D. 495) | (2) *Litany* | — | (Litany after Epistle) |
| | | | or | | |
| (3) *Hymn* ( Trisagion c. A.D. 440 ) | (3) *Hymn* ( Trisagion before A.D. 470 ) | (3) *Hymn* ( Gloria c. A.D. 500 ) | (3) *Hymn* ( Gloria with Kyries 6th c. ? ) | (3) *Hymn* ( Benedictus 6th cent. ? ) | (3) *Hymn* ( Gloria c. 9th cent. ) |
| — | | — | — | — | — |
| — | — | — | — | — | — |
| | | (A) GREETING | (A) GREETING | [ ? (A) GREETING after 7th cent. ] | |
| — | — | ($) *Prayer* | ($) *Prayer* | ($) *Prayer* | [ ($) *Prayer* c. 10th cent. ] |
| | | | | | (A) GREETING |
| (B) LECTIONS | (B) LECTIONS | (B) LECTIONS | (B) LECTIONS | (B) LECTIONS | (B) LECTIONS |
| (C) CHANTS between (B) | (C) CHANTS between (B) | (C) CHANTS between (B) | (C) CHANTS between (B) | (C) CHANTS between (B) | (C) CHANTS between (B) |
| (D) SERMON | (D) SERMON | (D) SERMON | (D) SERMON | (D) SERMON | (D) SERMON |
| (E) DISMISSALS | (E) DISMISSALS | <(E) DISMISSALS> | (E) DISMISSALS | <(E) DISMISSALS> | (E) DISMISSALS |

# INTRODUCTION

T HE number of articles written on significant anniversaries of the
publication of *The Shape of the Liturgy*[1] bears eloquent witness to
the unparalleled impact and long-lasting influence which Dom
Gregory Dix's 'fat green book', as he affectionately referred to it,
has had over liturgical scholarship and revision in the last sixty years.
Described by Keith Watkins in 1965 as 'a permanent contribution to
our understanding of Christian worship',[2] by the time it celebrated its
Silver Jubilee, Kenneth Stevenson acclaimed its author as 'one of the
greatest liturgical scholars which the Church of England has produced'[3]
and *The Shape* as 'a most remarkable book ... which will go down in
history as the greatest piece of liturgical writing of an Anglican this
century'.[4] Twenty-five years later, as an increasing number of scholars
were less certain than they once were of the conclusions Dix had drawn
from his evidence, *The Shape* was nevertheless acknowledged by Paul
Bradshaw to be 'one of the most influential books in the field during the
second half of the twentieth century',[5] while Pierre-Marie Gy
recognized Dix to be one of the main 'awakeners' and leaders of a
generation of young Anglican and Roman Catholic liturgists.[6]

It goes without saying that, over the sixty years of *The Shape*'s life, a
number of important alternative hypotheses have been suggested,
several of which we shall return to in the course of this introduction.
But let it not be said that Dix was unaware of his own limitations.
Even after the fourteen years of research and fourteen months of
writing which culminated in the publication of this *magnum opus*, he
had the humility to recognize that, in course of time, 'details will be
corrected; considerable gaps will be filled in; some things will appear

---

[1] First published in January 1945, a second edition appeared in August of the same
year.
[2] Keith Watkins, 'The Shape of the Liturgy: A Twentieth Anniversary Review',
*Encounter* 26 (1965), p. 75.
[3] Kenneth Stevenson, 'Dom Gregory Dix: a Silver Jubilee', *Studia Liturgica* 12 (1977),
p. 207.
[4] Stevenson, *Gregory Dix: Twenty-Five Years On*, Grove Liturgical Study 10
(Nottingham: Grove Books, 1977), p. 23.
[5] Paul Bradshaw, 'The Homogenization of Christian Liturgy – Ancient and
Modern', *Studia Liturgica* 26 (1996), p. 1.
[6] Pierre-Marie Gy, 'Re-Visiting Dom Gregory Dix after Fifty Years', *Worship* 70
(1996), p. 4.

in a different proportion'.[7] Rejecting the label a 'History of Liturgy', he intended *The Shape* to be 'useful' for the non-specialist,[8] 'a book for the intelligent Christian ... who is anxious to acquire a practical acquaintance with the subject as it now stands'.[9] In this task, he surely succeeded. What he could never have imagined, however, was the way in which *The Shape* heralded a new era in the study of liturgy, and that, despite the important developments in liturgical scholarship which have taken place since 1945, sixty years on the imprint of Dix's *Shape* can still be traced in the eucharistic liturgies of many Anglican Provinces as well as other Christian denominations: a tribute, indeed, to what John Robinson described as 'not only ... a superb piece of English prose, but ... a masterly presentation ... of what the living organism of the Liturgy has been and is'.[10]

Although, unsurprisingly, *The Shape* is no longer regarded as the standard liturgical reference work it once was, its place on the bibliographies of students of liturgy throughout the English-speaking world is still justified, and the very fact that Bradshaw's most recent work on the origins of the Eucharist begins with an attempt to refute four aspects of *The Shape*'s principal thesis[11] is evidence enough of a *tour de force* still to be reckoned with.

The introduction to this new edition of Dix's great work will attempt to assess the influence of its scholarship over the past sixty years, discussing the significance of the imprint of *The Shape* in a number of contemporary eucharistic rites and drawing attention to significant areas where Dix and contemporary liturgical scholarship have parted company. Since it is not possible, within the confines of this study, to comment on all of *The Shape*'s major hypotheses, the central thesis of the fourfold shape of the Eucharist will be our principal focus. Before that, however, let us put *The Shape* in context, by looking briefly at its author and what motivated him.[12]

### *Behind* The Shape

George Eglington Alston Dix was born in London on 4 October 1901. Educated first in Eastbourne and then at Westminster School, Dix

---

[7] *The Shape*, p. 743.
[8] *Ibid.*, p. ix.
[9] *Ibid.*, p. 736.
[10] John Robinson, *Liturgy Coming to Life* (London: Mowbray, 1960), p. 21.
[11] Bradshaw, *Eucharistic Origins*, Alcuin Club Collection 80 (London: SPCK, 2004), p. vi.
[12] For a detailed survey of Dix's life and work, see Simon Bailey, *A Tactful God* (Leominster: Gracewing, 1995).

went up to Merton College, Oxford[13] in 1920 to read history and left three years later with an Upper-Second class degree. After a short period of ordination training at Wells Theological College, he returned to Oxford in October 1924 to be ordained as tutor and lecturer in modern history at Keble College. Dix's stay at Keble was short-lived, and after just two years he moved to the Benedictine Abbey at Pershore, shortly before the Abbey itself moved to Nashdom in Buckinghamshire. At his clothing as a novice, Dix took the name Gregory, and it was as part of this Religious Community that Dix remained until his untimely death in 1952.

If any one aspect of community life at Nashdom is pertinent to our present study, then it is surely its worship. This Anglican Benedictine community, like its monk and sometime Prior, Dom Gregory, defined itself very clearly as Anglo-Papalist. With its Latin mass and offices from the Roman Missal and Breviary, a very clear statement was being made about its ecclesiology. By the rites and ceremonies of its daily round of worship, Nashdom Abbey self-consciously asserted its Catholic identity within the Church of England. As Simon Bailey points out:

> It was not an unfortunate accident that the only model for the Benedictine life was the Roman Catholic one. It became a very deliberate offering of the fullness of that life, from the Roman world, placed in the Church of England.[14]

It is against this background that *The Shape* needs to be read. Although, for two years during the Second World War, Dix reacquainted himself with Anglican rites as he looked after his brother's parish in Beaconsfield, his spiritual home was at Nashdom, and it was from this liturgical *milieu* that Dix called for reform of the Prayer Book, agonized over failed attempts at its revision, and articulated a number of ideas which were to become the fundamental building-blocks of the Liturgical Movement. *The Shape*'s most famous purple passage, 'Was ever another command so obeyed?'[15] speaks of an unbroken continuity in the celebration of the Eucharist, and this was obviously Dix's own personal experience as a priest, even more so as a priest of the Roman Rite:

[13] The present writer has the good fortune to have as his study part of the set of rooms once occupied by Dix's tutor, William Garrod. Dix returned to Merton in 1948 to receive a DD, the University's recognition of his contribution to liturgical scholarship.
[14] Bailey, *A Tactful God*, p. 40.
[15] *The Shape*, p. 744.

This very morning I did this with a set of texts which has not changed by more than a few syllables since Augustine used those very words at Canterbury on the third Sunday of Easter in the summer after he landed.[16]

That said, Dix is not uncritical of elements of the Roman Mass. Reflecting on the use of offertory prayers, he criticizes those which anticipate the effects of consecration and communion at the offertory, among which he names the invariable prayers in the Roman missal.[17] Equally, when discussing the language of the liturgy, he blames the liturgical use of Latin in the medieval period for excluding 'the great mass of the people from intelligent participation in the church services'[18] and, elsewhere, having outlined the deficiencies of the 1662 Prayer Book and its need for reform, he is able to say that Anglicans 'have an immense advantage over the dissenters in that we have a liturgy, and over the Roman Catholics in that it is in the vernacular'.[19]

Many readers will find it hard to reconcile the Romish habits of the monk at Nashdom with the patristic purity of the author of *The Shape*, whose zeal for reform was partly driven not only by a critique of the individual piety of the Reformation, but also of the medieval church in which he believed corporate worship at the Eucharist had declined 'into a mere focus for the subjective devotion of each separate worshipper in the isolation of his own mind.'[20] As Stevenson suggests, Dix pushes his point too far when he states that, 'the history of Protestantism itself indicates that they were the chief and most permanent sufferers by the accumulated mistakes of the mediaeval Latin church'.[21] But with such an historical perspective, it is hardly surprising that Dix stood alongside the liturgical reformers of the twentieth century who looked to the early Christian centuries for inspiration in the process of revision. Indeed, the desire to steer liturgical revision in the Church of England along a particular path, namely to the pre-Nicene Church, was part of *The Shape*'s *raison d'être*. When Dix asks the following questions at the beginning of Chapter 8, he is in no doubt as to what the answers must be, and spends another 550 pages making sure that his confidence is shared by the reader:

---

[16] *Ibid.*, p. 745.
[17] *Ibid.*, pp. 119f.
[18] *Ibid.*, p. 618.
[19] *Ibid.*, p. 732.
[20] *Ibid.*, p. 599.
[21] *The Shape*, p. 639; Stevenson, 'Dom Gregory Dix: A Silver Jubilee', p. 213.

Can we hope to find in the primitive church, say in the second century, coherent universal principles which can guide our own ideas about liturgy? Was there anything ... in what is vaguely called 'the early church' which might serve as a standard or model by which the perplexities of Prayer Book revision in twentieth century England might be lessened?[22]

But what of the monk at Nashdom? The apparent tension which seems to exist between Dix's own liturgical practices, his criticism of the Latin mass and his advocacy of Prayer Book reform can, perhaps, be reconciled, through the lens of ecclesiology. As Papalists, the place of the Pope and reunion with Rome were obvious priorities on the ecclesial agenda of every monk at Nashdom but, perhaps, especially so for Dom Gregory, whose journey towards life oblation was marked by frequent uncertainty as to whether he should convert to Roman Catholicism.[23] For an Anglican such as Dix, the legal requirement to use rites 'authorized or allowed by Canon'[24] or questions of liturgical preference, were always going to be trumped by the Roman Mass, whatever its deficiencies, as the only rite which truly expressed and embodied the full communion with the Pope and, thereby, the Universal Church, for which Dix and his community longed. For the Roman Rite as for the Prayer Book, the ecumenical liturgical movement, which Dix influenced to such a great degree, presented the opportunity for liturgical convergence and possible reunion within the Eucharistic shape of the primitive church.

### The Shape of the Eucharist

With this background in mind, let us now consider Dix's principal thesis, the fourfold shape of the Eucharist. Distancing himself from the view of earlier scholars who had argued that:

> there was a single primitive type or model of the rite, not only of outline or shape of the rite as a whole (which is true) but also of its central formula, the 'great eucharistic prayer', originally the only prayer which the service contained.[25]

Dix puts the case forcefully for what is, in effect, a modified form of this theory, which maintains a common origin as the source of later

---

[22] *Ibid.*, p. 208.

[23] Bailey, *A Tactful God*, pp. 48ff.

[24] From the Church of England's *Declaration of Assent.*

[25] *The Shape*, p. 4. Bradshaw refers to this as the 'Philological Approach'. See P. Bradshaw, *The Search for the Origins of Christian Worship*, 2nd edition (London: SPCK, 2002), pp. 1ff.

eucharistic rites, but sees this being expressed in the shape of the liturgy rather than its verbal content. Thus, in his Introduction, he is able to state with confidence that:

> It is true that by careful analysis there is to be found underlying most of these varying rites and all of the older ones a single normal standard *structure* of the rite as a whole. It is this standard structure which I call the 'Shape' of the Liturgy.[26]

The original 'Shape', Dix identifies as the 'seven-action scheme' of Jesus at the Last Supper, in which Jesus took bread; gave thanks over it; broke it; and distributed it, saying certain words; and after the meal took the cup; gave thanks over it; and distributed it, saying certain words. Over the course of time and 'before the first three gospels or I Cor. began to circulate with authority',[27] the meal which separated bread from cup disappeared and the 'seven-action scheme' was transformed into a fourfold shape:

> With absolute unanimity the liturgical tradition reproduces these seven actions as four: (1) The offertory; bread and wine are 'taken' and placed on the table together. (2) The prayer; the president gives thanks to God over bread and wine together. (3) The fraction; the bread is broken. (4) The communion; the bread and wine are distributed together.
>
> In that form and in that order these four actions constituted the absolutely invariable nucleus of every eucharistic rite known to us throughout antiquity from the Euphrates to Gaul.[28]

It is difficult to over-estimate the influence which this simple and apparently self-evident thesis has exerted over liturgical scholarship and revision; a thesis which, in recent years, has attracted more comment and criticism than any of *The Shape*'s other hypotheses. For Dix, the identification of this shape as the universal and invariable template for early eucharistic practice provided the perfect starting-point for criticism of the Church of England's own eucharistic provision as well as the criteria for its reform.

In this Introduction we will limit our comments to three aspects of the shape theory: the existence of a sevenfold action and the likelihood of its transformation to a fourfold shape; the extent to which the fourfold shape can be said to be the invariable model for the Eucharist; and the relationship between the dominical 'taking' and the liturgical 'offertory'.

[26] *The Shape*, p. xi.
[27] *Ibid.*, p. 49.
[28] *Ibid.*, p. 48.

*From Seven to Fourfold Shape*

Although Bryan Spinks has indicated that the New Testament accounts of the Last Supper reveal a ninefold rather than sevenfold shape,[29] a more damaging criticism of Dix's thesis is Bradshaw's suggestion that there is no evidence at all that a Christian community ever celebrated the Eucharist according to a sevenfold shape, with bread and cup rituals separated by a communal meal. Dix himself describes the Last Supper as the 'source' of the Eucharist rather than its 'model'.[30] However, drawing a parallel with the relationship between the celebration of the Passover and the Exodus from Egypt, Bradshaw argues convincingly that it is unlikely that early Christian communities ever saw 'Do this in remembrance of me' as an instruction for exact repetition and that it was more likely to have been interpreted as a command to eat and drink in remembrance of Jesus whenever they ate a ritual meal together.[31]

Developing his thesis that the earliest period of the Church's history is characterized by liturgical variety rather than uniformity,[32] and influenced by the work of Andrew McGowan,[33] Bradshaw advocates various patterns of primitive eucharistic celebration, including bread and cup rituals taking place at the beginning of a meal,[34] the cup ritual preceding the bread ritual[35] and wineless Eucharists.[36] Although many of Bradshaw's theories raise possibilities of the existence of a number of practices, rather than providing concrete evidence for their performance, he has nevertheless successfully undermined Dix's thesis that pluriformity of meaning was held together by uniformity of structure, and that eucharistic worship which does not conform to a predetermined shape must be identified with the *agape*.[37]

In the light of the general pluriformity of primitive Christianity, early eucharistic meals may have varied not only in theological emphases between the different traditions but also in the very form of the meal itself, variations that we cannot easily dispose of by

[29] Bryan Spinks, 'Mis-Shapen. Gregory Dix and the Four-Action Shape of the Liturgy', *Lutheran Quarterly Review* 4 (1990), 167. Spinks counts Jesus' words, 'This is my body', 'This is my blood' as two additional actions.
[30] *The Shape*, p. 48.
[31] Paul Bradshaw, 'Did the Early Eucharist ever have a Sevenfold Shape?', *Heythrop Journal* 43 (2002), p. 73.
[32] Bradshaw, *Search*, p. x.
[33] In particular, Andrew McGowan, *Ascetic Eucharists*, (Oxford: OUP, 1999).
[34] Bradshaw, *Eucharistic Origins*, (London: SPCK, 2004), pp. 45ff.
[35] Bradshaw, 'Did the Early Eucharist ever have a Sevenfold Shape?', pp. 74f.
[36] Bradshaw, *Eucharistic Origins*, pp. 51ff.
[37] See, for example, Dix's treatment of the *Didache*. *The Shape*, pp. 90ff.

consigning those that do not fit our ideal to the supposed category of an *agape* rather than a Eucharist ...: for some communities, *agape* was the name given to their eucharistic meal.[38]

According to Bradshaw, Dix's belief that the move from the sevenfold to the fourfold shape was connected to the separation of the eucharist from the meal around which it was celebrated,[39] would have involved 'a diverse collection of local congregations all being willing to make the same radical shift'.[40] Rather he suggests that, following the pattern of meals at Qumran, where bread and wine were blessed together before the community began eating, and later rabbinic law which allowed the blessing of wine before a meal to replace the same blessing after eating, it would not have been unusual for first century Jewish-Christian communal meals, such as the Eucharist, to have begun with a blessing of bread and wine. Then, when the meal dropped out of the eucharistic celebration, since it was already common to bless bread and wine together at the beginning of the meal, a change in practice far less drastic than the telescoping of a seven action scheme was required to reveal the fourfold shape.[41]

Although Bradshaw's thesis is, without doubt, more plausible than Dix's, it could be argued that his argument is pushed further than the evidence or, rather, lack of it, will allow. For example, *Didache* 9–10 is cited as an example of thanksgiving over the cup followed by thanksgiving over the bread preceding a communal meal.[42] Although this is certainly one interpretation of the material, there are sufficient ambiguities and complexities within the two chapters of this ancient church order to cast doubt upon it. An alternative approach is offered by Alan Garrow, who believes that what are described here are two separate accounts of the same liturgical event: 'a full meal, followed by a prayer that creates a connection between the past full meal and the forthcoming eucharistic meal'.[43]

Whereas Bradshaw considers the rubric 'Concerning the broken bread' (Greek *klasma*) in *Didache* 9.3 to be 'an odd choice when presumably the bread had not yet been broken',[44] Garrow interprets it as meaning precisely what it says. Since the breaking of bread would most likely have taken place at a full meal, he suggests that this has

---

[38] Bradshaw, *Search*, p. 70.

[39] *The Shape*, p. 50.

[40] Bradshaw, 'Did the Early Eucharist ever have a Sevenfold Shape?', p. 74.

[41] *Ibid.*, pp. 74f.

[42] For a more detailed analysis of this text, see Bradshaw, *Eucharistic Origins*, pp. 24ff.

[43] Alan Garrow, *The Gospel of Matthew's Dependence on the* Didache, *JSNTS* 254 (T&T Clark, 2004), pp. 25f.

[44] Bradshaw, *Eucharistic Origins*, p. 24.

already happened before the thanksgiving over the cup and the bread in Chapter 9, thus presenting a series of events which are mirrored exactly in Chapter 10.[45] Garrow's thesis is, of course, as much a challenge to Dix's labelling of *Didache* 9–10 as an *agape*[46] as it is to Bradshaw's view that these two chapters are evidence of the blessing of bread and wine before a communal meal, as practised in Qumran. What is certain is that from whatever route the fourfold shape emerged, from the time of Justin its imprint can be clearly discerned in the majority of eucharistic rites in east and west, and so it is to this fourfold shape which we must now turn.

## The Fourfold Shape

Dix's thesis that the four dominical acts of taking, giving thanks, breaking and distributing constituted the invariable model of the liturgical Eucharist takes us to the heart of *The Shape*, although such a theory had been expressed before 1945. Eight years earlier, in the essay he contributed to Gabriel Hebert's *The Parish Communion*, Dix had written of the Eucharist having four *momenta*.[47] Dix's contribution to such a collection was, itself, an indication that he saw this theory to have practical implications for liturgical revision. And Hebert himself had highlighted 'the four Biblical verbs: He took bread, blessed, brake, gave it to them', in his *Liturgy and Society* in 1935.[48]

Although Spinks believes the fourfold shape theory to be flawed and unreliable,[49] the majority of scholars are still more likely to agree with Colin Buchanan who, whilst objecting strongly to Dix's equation of the first dominical act with the liturgical offertory, nevertheless believes the four-action shape rightly to enjoy widespread acceptance.[50] The principal areas of disagreement in the past sixty years have centred around the interpretation of the 'taking' and the invariability of the fourfold shape. The latter has already been referred

[45] Garrow also highlights the structural, verbal and conceptual similarities between the prayer forms in these two chapters. Garrow, *Matthew's Dependence on the* Didache, pp. 26f. See also Alistair Stewart-Sykes, 'The Birkath Ha-Mazon and the Body of the Lord: A Case Study of *Didache* 9–10', *Questions Liturgiques* 85 (2004), pp. 202ff, who accepts Garrow's basic thesis, but suggests that the meal is sandwiched between the cup and bread rituals.

[46] *The Shape*, pp. 90ff.

[47] A. Gabriel Hebert (ed.), *The Parish Communion* (London: SPCK, 1937), p. 100.

[48] Hebert, *Liturgy and Society* (London: Faber, 1935), p. 40.

[49] Spinks, 'Mis-Shapen', p. 161; see also, John Fenwick and Bryan Spinks, *Worship in Transition* (Edinburgh: T&T Clark, 1995), pp. 48ff.

[50] Colin Buchanan, 'Gregory Dix – The Liturgical Bequest', *Churchman* 114 (2000), p. 275.

to in the previous section. As someone searching for a model for
liturgical revision over which there could be ecumenical agreement, it
suited Dix's purposes very well to emphasize an invariable pattern of
eucharistic celebration in the primitive church. However, whereas it
can be said with some confidence that most of the ancient eucharistic
rites known to us are modelled on a fourfold shape, the available
evidence does not support *The Shape*'s conclusion that it constituted
the 'absolutely invariable nucleus of every eucharistic rite known to us
throughout antiquity'. As Bradshaw makes clear, such a theory can
only be sustained

> by very selective use of the evidence – by denying that primitive
> Christianity was as pluriform as modern New Testament and
> historical scholarship suggests and by ignoring meals that were
> patterned otherwise.[51]

That said, Bradshaw's important critique does not diminish the
significance of the fact that the majority of rites known to us are
modelled in this way, nor does it render the fourfold shape an
illegitimate pattern for contemporary liturgical revision.

Some, however, have objected to the fourfold shape on the basis
that it gives equal weight to each of the actions. Although it is true to
say that Dix attaches great importance to the actions within the shape,
and spends some time in a detailed analysis of each of them, he never
says that he invests them with equal significance.[52] Indeed, the first
and third actions may well have become weighed down by doctrinal
and liturgical controversies, but that does not justify their removal
from the shape, even if their significance is only considered to be
utilitarian. Spinks' 'two actions' constitute, without a doubt, the
centre of the eucharistic action, 'eating and drinking which is
paramount, and thanksgiving, the omission of which would be
churlish',[53] but it is not possible to give thanks over the bread and
wine unless they have been taken; nor can bread be distributed unless
it has been broken. If Dix's thesis is to be revised, then rather than
reducing it to a twofold shape it may be more prudent to follow
Richard Buxton who, in commenting on Justin's account of the
Eucharist, suggests that

[51] Bradshaw, *Search*, p. 140.
[52] Spinks, 'Mis-Shapen', p. 167. In this view, Spinks follows G. Michell, who states
that in the primitive period neither the offertory nor the fraction were accorded the
prominence which they subsequently attained. G. A. Michell, *Landmarks in Liturgy*
(London: DLT, 1961), p. 41.
[53] Spinks, 'Mis-Shapen', p. 167.

it is probably better to see it as two major actions, namely thanksgiving and reception, accompanied by two minor ones that are there for purely utilitarian reasons, whatever symbolic reasons became attached to them later on.[54]

### The Taking and the Offertory

The action which has attracted most discussion is the 'taking' and Dix's interpretation of it as the liturgical offertory. Here, in particular, it is important not to forget that, for a priest of the Roman Rite, offering and sacrifice are fundamental to a proper understanding of the Eucharist. A considerable amount of *The Shape* is given over to this subject which, notwithstanding Dix's own theological preferences, seems to have been misunderstood by some of his later critics.

In brief, Dix believes that, from the earliest history of the church, the liturgical tradition has interpreted the 'physical necessity' of taking bread and wine before they are blessed as being 'a ritual act with a significance of its own'. As the first of the dominical acts, he sees it as an integral part of the eucharistic action, rather than a practical preliminary to it.[55] For Dix, the available evidence which points to eucharistic practice in the second century is unanimous in revealing

> the same general understanding of the eucharist as an 'oblation' (*prosphora*) or 'sacrifice' (*thusia*) – something offered to God; and that the substance of the sacrifice is in every case in some sense the bread and the cup.[56]

It is not possible for this study to consider these sources in any great detail. Spinks and Buchanan have argued separately that the handing over of bread and wine by the people, either before the Eucharistic Prayer, as in the West, or at the beginning of the service, as in the East, is a purely functional action, and that their preparation was the function of deacons rather than the laity.[57] They accuse Dix of using this early evidence to support and develop a theology of the offertory, whose popularity and influence spread in England as a result of the Parish and People movement in the twentieth century. We have

[54] Richard Buxton, 'The Shape of the Eucharist: A Survey and Appraisal', in Kenneth Stevenson (ed.), *Liturgy Reshaped* (London: SPCK, 1982), p. 85.

[55] *The Shape*, p. 110.

[56] *Ibid.*, p. 112.

[57] Spinks, 'Misshapen', pp. 168ff; Colin Buchanan, *The End of the Offertory – An Anglican Study*, Grove Liturgical Study 14 (Nottingham: Grove Books, 1978), pp. 5ff. From their respective theological positions, it is probably true to say that Dix is as guilty of Buchanan's charge of 'finding an "offertory" in every rite' (p.14), as Buchanan is of finding an equally ubiquitous absence of one.

already referred to Dix's essay in Hebert's *The Parish Communion*, in which he wrote

> The Offertory is, then, the most striking expression of that common priesthood which is shared by the laity, whereby singly and collectively they offer to God a real sacrifice of 'themselves, their souls and bodies' to become the Body of His Son.[58]

Spinks and Buchanan may well be justified in asserting that Dix read more of his own eucharistic theology into the rites of Justin Martyr and the so-called *Apostolic Tradition* of Hippolytus than the evidence of the texts themselves will allow. However, that in itself is not sufficient grounds to remove this action from the shape, to discredit the subsequent development of offertory theology, to call into question the appropriateness of its use today, or indeed to raise doubts over whether the evidence of Justin's *First Apology* can be called as a witness to the origin of the offertory,[59] however it might be interpreted, whether or not it is a self-conscious development of the taking at the Last Supper.

Particular theological concerns have been expressed at the identification of the bread and wine with those who are offering them. 'Into that loaf of bread', says Robinson, 'goes the whole working life of the world ... And in the bottle of wine we have the symbol of all life's joy and leisure, everything given to make glad and free the heart of man'.[60] Both Buchanan and Spinks object to such an interpretation and call to their defence an essay by Michael Ramsey on the Parish Communion in which the then Bishop of Durham criticizes the offertory procession as 'shallow and romantic pelagianism'.[61] Although Ramsey does, indeed, use these words with reference to the offertory, this is not the whole of his argument. Rather, he is concerned that sacrificial language and imagery associated with the offertory *and* the post-communion should not be disconnected from the one sacrifice of Christ.

> The idea of sacrifice is taught in many parishes in connection with the offering of bread and wine in the offertory and ourselves, our souls and bodies, in the prayer after the Communion.
>
> By itself, however, this sort of teaching about sacrifice can be a

---

[58] Hebert (ed.), *The Parish Communion*, p. 114.

[59] Stevenson, for example, sees 'the offertory beginning in Justin'. Stevenson, 'Dom Gregory Dix: A Silver Jubilee', p. 211.

[60] Robinson, *Liturgy coming to Life*, p. 62.

[61] Buchanan, *The End of the Offertory*, p. 31; Fenwick and Spinks, *Worship in Transition*, p. 128. See also, B. A. Mastin, 'Jesus said Grace', *Scottish Journal of Theology* 24 (1971), pp. 449–56.

shallow and romantic short of Pelagianism. For we cannot, and we dare not, offer aught of our own apart from the one sacrifice of the Lamb of God.[62]

It is difficult to see how such a comment could have been aimed at Dix, since he, too, is concerned that no action within the fourfold shape should be interpreted in isolation from the others. Thus, 'the offertory, the prayer and the communion are closely connected moments in a single continuous action, and each only finds its proper meaning as part of the whole'.[63] Having emphasized the relationship between the offertory and the sacrifice of Calvary, Dix goes on to make an important distinction between the offering of the bread and wine at the offertory and the offering which takes places within the Eucharistic Prayer:

> The offertory is not, of course, the eucharistic oblation itself, any more than the last supper was itself the sacrifice of Christ. It is directed to that oblation as its pledge and starting-point, just as the last supper looks forward to the offering on Calvary. The offering of themselves by the members of Christ could not be acceptable to God unless taken up into the offering of Himself by Christ in consecration and communion.[64]

Here there appears to be no disagreement between Dix and Ramsey. As the offertory prayers of the modern Roman Rite make clear,[65] the gifts are not offered by men and women as symbolic representations of their life and work before they are first acknowledged to have been given to humanity through the goodness and generosity of God the creator.[66] Thus, it is God who takes the initiative at the offertory and the church which offers the bread and wine back to him, praying that when they are offered again during the Eucharistic Prayer, the self-offering of the people will be one the self-offering of Christ in the bread of life and cup of salvation.

---

[62] Michael Ramsey, *Durham Essays and Addresses* (London: SPCK, 1956), p. 18.

[63] *The Shape*, p. 110.

[64] *Ibid*, p. 118.

[65] Blessed are you, Lord, God of all creation. Through your goodness we have this bread / wine to offer, which earth has given and human hands have made. It will become for us the bread of life / our spiritual drink.

[66] Buchanan seems to ignore this creation reference when he says that: 'To emphasize *our* provision of them [the elements] is to distort the simplicity of the central concept in the sacraments – that God affirms and uses his created order as a means of his grace'. Buchanan, *The End of the Offertory*, p. 38.

## The Shape *Today*

Let us conclude our brief overview of the influence of *The Shape* by considering the extent to which the outline of Dix's fourfold shape is visible in contemporary liturgical revisions. Frustrated by the attempts at Prayer Book revision in 1927/8 and the inadequacies of the Interim Rite,[67] Dix was concerned that *The Shape* should not only excite interest in liturgical study, but also provide criteria for liturgical reform. Ironically, the first rite to bear the marks of *The Shape* was *The Order for the Lord's Supper* of the Church of South India (CSI), the union of whose constituent denominations Dix vociferously opposed.[68] Here, at last, was a Eucharistic rite which clearly embodied the fourfold shape and was widely admired by liturgists from various traditions. Thomas Garrett, a member of the CSI Synod Liturgy Committee, makes clear that

> what we lacked in knowledge we made up for in enthusiasm, some of it inspired by the timely publication of Dix's *The Shape of the Liturgy*, an undoubted *preparation liturgica* for the Church of South India, albeit one which we hope we have taken with a grain of salt.[69]

In this first fruit of Eucharistic revision, approved by the CSI Synod in 1950, the title 'offertory' is used to describe the first dominical act, in which bread, wine, money and gifts in kind are brought to the altar.[70] The offertory prayer concludes with a quotation from 1 Chronicles 29.11, 'All that is in heaven and earth is thine, and of thine own do we give thee'. Like the modern Roman Rite, it acknowledges that what is offered to God already belongs to him, but also makes clear that this is only possible in union with Christ's own self-offering: 'we come to thee through him, unworthy as

---

[67] The 'Interim Rite' proposed a bringing together of the 1662 Sursum Corda, Preface, Sanctus, Prayer of Consecration and Prayer of Oblation into one single Eucharistic Prayer. It was inspired by proposals put forward by Walter Frere in his *Some Principles of Liturgical Reform* (London: John Murray, 1911). This pattern was eventually given official authorization in 1966 by the Schedule of Agreed Amendments to 1662 known as Series 1. For Dix's criticism of the Interim Rite and 1927/8, see *The Shape*, pp. 666f and pp. 699ff.

[68] For a more detailed account of Dix's opposition to what he considered to be a schismatic alliance, see Bailey, *A Tactful God*, pp. 121ff.

[69] Tom Garrett, *Worship in the Church of South India* (London: Lutterworth Press, 1958), p. 13.

[70] The inclusion of a liturgical offertory does not remove further manual acts during the Eucharistic Prayer. As the introduction to the rite makes clear, 'At the words "took bread", the presbyter shall take the paten with the bread into his hands. At the words "took the cup", he shall take the cup into his hand'. The Church of South India, *An Order for the Lord's Supper* (Oxford: OUP, 1954), p. vii.

we are, and we humbly beseech thee to accept and use us and these our gifts for thy glory'.[71]

In the wider Anglican Communion, appreciation of *The Shape* and admiration for the CSI's new rite were two of the principal driving forces behind Resolution 74 of the 1958 Lambeth Conference, which urged that 'a chief aim of Prayer Book revision should be to further that recovery of the worship of the primitive Church which was the aim of the compilers of the first Prayer Books of the Church of England'. However, in the Church of England, it was not until the Draft Order of Holy Communion in Series 2 (1966) that Dix's influence was clearly felt.[72] The titles used for individual sections of the rite revealed that the Eucharistic action was now clearly understood as being divided between The Preparation of the Bread and Wine, The Thanksgiving, The Breaking of the Bread, and The Sharing of the Bread and Wine. Although the controversial word 'offertory' had deliberately been avoided, one of the prefatory notes indicated that the rubric at this point in the service, 'Then shall bread and wine be placed in order upon the holy Table',[73] permitted a variety of practice: 'both an Offertory Procession of lay people from the congregation, and also the simplest placing of the bread and wine upon the holy Table'.[74]

The work of the Liturgical Commission between Series 2 and the 1980 authorization of the *Alternative Service Book* (*ASB*) attempted to clarify some of these ambiguities by making an even more obvious distinction between the preparation of the gifts and the taking of the bread and cup.[75] That being the case, the *ASB* rubrics did not altogether rule out an offertory, since the curiously worded note 33, 'The president may praise God for his gifts in appropriate words to which all respond **Blessed be God for ever**' permitted the use of the Roman offertory prayers, without actually printing them. Such an 'offertory' was, however, associated with the preparation of the gifts rather than the dominical taking, which was now a rarely performed but mandatory part of the service, required by a rubric which asked the president to 'take the bread and cup into his hands and replace them on the holy table' before beginning the Eucharistic Prayer.

---

[71] *Ibid.*, p. 10.

[72] Buchanan notes that the Liturgical Commission he joined in 1964 was 'composed largely of Dix's contemporaries … reflecting … quite a few of his actual findings'. Buchanan, 'Gregory Dix – The Liturgical Bequest', p. 262.

[73] The Liturgical Commission of the Church of England, *Alternative Services: Second Series* (London: SPCK, 1965), p. 155.

[74] *Ibid.*, p. 147.

[75] See Buchanan, *The End of the Offertory*, pp. 36f.

Thus, the desire to disconnect the preparation of the gifts from the taking gave rise to a new liturgical action, often performed in silence. From the visual perspective of the congregation, it is difficult to see how, in such circumstances, the practical preparation of the altar, with or without associated prayers, could be distinguished from this imitation of the dominical taking. Indeed, visually, the latter often appeared strange and stilted, as if the priest was comparing the weight of the two vessels![76] If the justification for such a gesture was to preserve the fourfold shape, then this was a form of Dixian fundamentalism which would not have found favour with the author of *The Shape*, for whom the taking took place at the offertory, as the table was being prepared.

By the time the *ASB* was replaced by *Common Worship* at the turn of the millennium, Dix's influence was still clearly visible. A new note, entitled 'The Taking', refers explicitly to the fourfold shape, but muddies the water by locating the taking either after the preparation of the table or during the Eucharistic Prayer, thus permitting the Eucharistic rite to be modelled on a modified form of *The Shape*, in which preparation of the altar and the dominical taking are clearly distinguished, or on an adapted form of the Prayer Book tradition, which associated both the taking and the fraction with the institution narrative within the Prayer of Consecration:

> In Holy Communion the Church, following the example of the Lord, takes, gives thanks, breaks and gives. The bread and wine must be taken into the president's hands and replaced upon the table either after the table has been prepared or during the Eucharistic Prayer.[77]

In an appendix, *Common Worship* also prints a version of the Roman offertory prayers, alongside several others, under the title 'Prayers at the Preparation of the Table'.[78] Although the provision of any such text goes one stage further than the *ASB*, in each prayer the verb 'to offer' has been replaced by 'to set before you'. It is possible, however, that, despite moving away from the language of offering, the Church of England alternative is more of a synonym of its Roman counterpart than some have taken it to be. Indeed, 'to set before you' has

[76] For a more detailed consideration of some of the practical implications of taking the elements, see Benjamin Gordon-Taylor and Simon Jones, *Celebrating the Eucharist* (London: SPCK, 2005), pp. 62f.

[77] The Church of England, *Common Worship: Services and Prayers for the Church of England* (London: CHP, 2000), note 17, p. 333. It is interesting to note that, within Order 1, similar flexibility is not permitted for the fraction.

[78] *Ibid.*, pp. 291ff.

something of the sense of pledge and starting point that Dix was trying to articulate.

A brief survey of recent Eucharistic revisions in other parts of the Anglican Communion reveals that it is not just in England that the fourfold shape is alive and well.[79] In 1985 the Canadian *Book of Alternative Services* referred explicitly to 'the fourfold "shape" of the liturgy' and to Dix's *Shape* in a footnote,[80] as well as expressing a very strong symbolic connection between the preparation of the gifts and 'the offering of ourselves and the whole creation to God'.[81] Four years later, the new rite of the Church of the Province of Southern Africa expressed Dix's views on the offertory even more clearly when it printed a slightly adapted from of the Roman offertory prayers (retaining the verb 'to offer') under the heading 'The Taking of the Bread and Wine'.[82] The New Zealand rite of the same year was a little more ambiguous than its South African contemporary, referring to the presiding priest *taking* 'sufficient bread and wine which may be brought forward by representatives of the congregation' under the heading 'The Preparation of the Gifts', after which it printed a single prayer, based on the Roman offertory texts, which despite referring to the bread and wine being shared rather than offered, nevertheless included a petition for God to 'accept and use our offerings for your glory'. [83]

More recently, the 2004 revision of the Church of Ireland Prayer Book makes a very careful distinction between the various actions which occupy the space between the Peace and the Eucharistic Prayer. Under the title 'Celebrating at the Lord's Table',[84] two rubrics refer to the table being prepared and the gifts of money being brought forward and presented. The instruction to *place* the bread and wine on the table (if it has not already been done) comes under a sub-heading 'At the Preparation of the Table', and may be accompanied by one of four optional prayers (including 1 Chronicles 29.11, 14). A

[79] For an assessment of the influence of the fourfold shape over other denominations, see Fenwick and Spinks, *Worship in Transition*, pp. 127ff.

[80] The Anglican Church of Canada, *The Book of Alternative Services* (Toronto: Anglican Book Centre, 1985), p. 180.

[81] *Ibid.*, p. 177.

[82] The Church of the Province of Southern Africa, *An Anglican Prayer Book* (London: Collins, 1989), p. 116.

[83] The Anglican Church in Aotearao, New Zealand and Polynesia, *A New Zealand Prayer Book* (HarperSan Francisco, 1989), pp. 419f. The same prayer was also included in the most recent Australian revision: The Anglican Church of Australia, *A Prayer Book for Australia* (Alexandria, NSW: Broughton Books, 1995), p. 127.

[84] The title used for this part of the service in the report of the fifth International Anglican Liturgical Consultation. David Holeton (ed.), *Our Thanks and Praise: The Eucharist in Anglicanism Today* (Toronto: Anglican Book Centre, 1998), p. 284.

further subheading 'The Taking of the Bread and Wine' represents the imitation of the first dominical act, unmistakably separated from what has gone before, and which may be accompanied by 1 Corinthians 5.7b-8a in the form of a versicle and response.[85] The new Irish rite is, perhaps, the most coherent and articulate expression of a reformed version of Dix's fourfold shape, removing the possibility of using any prayers which have their origin in the offertory of the Roman Rite, and highlighting the ritual taking by providing a text to accompany it, albeit one which, in other Anglican rites, is more commonly used as an invitation to communion. Such clarity is not achieved by the Church in Wales, whose latest revision places two alternative texts under the rubric: 'The priest takes the bread and the cup'. The second option uses the Roman offertory prayers unchanged, whereas the first clearly refers to the elements being taken:

We celebrate together the gifts and grace of God.
We take this bread,
we take this wine,
to follow Christ's example
and obey his command.[86]

Despite this confusion, it is interesting to note that of the three recent liturgical revisions in the British Isles, only the Welsh rite has moved from a four-action to a two-action shape, in accordance with the recommendations of the fifth International Anglican Liturgical Consultation in 1998. The report of that meeting states that: 'The assembly offers praise and thanksgiving over the bread and wine, and partakes in the body and blood of Christ'.[87] This has been achieved by the Church in Wales by including the taking within 'The Thanksgiving' and the fraction within 'The Communion', whereas the English and Irish rites maintain a very self-conscious fourfold shape.

### *Whither* The Shape?

In 1977 Stevenson rightly observed that the influence of Dix's four-action shape on liturgical revision had been immense, and that 'it could almost be said that every rite that has been compiled since manifests the work of Dix in its revised structure'.[88] Almost thirty years

[85] The Church of Ireland, *The Book of Common Prayer* (Dublin: Columba Press, 2004), p. 208.
[86] The Church in Wales, *An Order for the Holy Eucharist* (Norwich: Canterbury Press, 2004), p. 35.
[87] Holeton (ed.), *Our Thanks and Praise*, p. 284.
[88] Stevenson, *Gregory Dix: Twenty-Five Years On*, p. 24.

later it is quite remarkable to observe how Dix's influence upon liturgical revision appears to be no less significant, and if recent revisions are anything to go by, shows little sign of abating.

Dix begins his final chapter on an optimistic note, identifying hopeful signs of a renewal of interest in the study of liturgy in post-war Britain.[89] The blossoming of liturgical scholarship since that time is due in no small part to enthusiasms kindled by Dix's *Shape*. For those approaching *The Shape* for the first time, it is hoped that this introduction will whet the appetite to use Dix's 'fat green book', not as a liturgical encyclopaedia, but as a means of exciting interest in the study of Christian worship, allowing the poetry of Dix's expansive prose to communicate the author's enthusiasm and sense of wonder at the mystery which is his subject. Although, over the last sixty years, scholars have become less convinced by the certainty with which Dix draws conclusions from his evidence, *The Shape*'s enduring value lies, not in providing its readers with right answers, but in encouraging them to ask right questions, and thereby to continue the exploration in which Dix was engaged, the exploration of the origin, development, meaning and future shape of humanity's response to a command never so obeyed.[90]

Such enduring value was appreciated by Edward Ratcliff in one of the first reviews of *The Shape*, an enduring value in which Dix's readers can have confidence today:

> Perhaps enough has been said to indicate the learning and richness of the book. It may be that, with the passage of time, some of its statements and theories will have to be modified or recast and others discarded; but this in no way detracts from its value and importance. It is replete with instruction for the professed liturgical student; and the beginner and the casual reader alike may open it in confidence that, unlike all but a few of existing 'Introductions', it will teach them the right questions to ask, and, where its own answers are not final, it will suggest the direction in which correct answers are to be sought. *The Shape of the Liturgy* should materially assist the much-to-be-desired reshaping of English liturgical studies.[91]

Simon Jones
Merton College, Oxford
May 2005

---

[89] *The Shape*, p. 735.
[90] *Ibid*, p. 744.
[91] Edward Ratcliff, 'Review of Gregory Dix, *The Shape of the Liturgy*', *Theology* 48 (1945), p. 131.

# INTRODUCTION

## THE PURPOSE OF THIS ESSAY

THE origin of this essay was a paper read at their request before the Cowley Fathers during their General Chapter in August 1941. I have ventured, therefore, in this different form to offer it again to the members of the oldest, the most respected and in more ways than one the greatest of our Anglican communities of priests.

The re-writing of the original very condensed paper for a less specialised public involved, I found, much more expansion and alteration than I at first intended. It seemed worth while to take this trouble with it because it set out information which I was told would be interesting and useful to many people, if it could be put before them in a way reasonably easy for non-specialists to understand. To a pragmatic Englishman that word 'useful' is always a temptation to embark on lengthy disquisitions, and I found that I had succumbed before I knew it. The subject of the paper—the structure of actions and prayers which forms the eucharist—has, of course, a permanent interest for christians. But it is beginning to be recognised that this has a much wider and deeper significance than its ecclesiastical or even than its purely devotional interest. It is only within recent years that the science of Comparative Religion has fully awakened to the value of the study of 'ritual patterns' for the appreciation of any given system of religious ideas and its necessary consequence in human living—a 'culture'. The analysis of such a pattern and the tracing of its evolution opens for the historian and the sociologist the most direct way to the sympathetic understanding 'from within' of the mind of those who practise that religion, and so to a right appreciation of the genius of their belief and the value of their ideas and ideals of human life. We christians have naturally been a little shy of making this new approach to the understanding of our own religion; at least it has been little studied up till now in England. Yet, rightly used, it should lead to a deepening and enriching of our own christian faith, a new sensitiveness and balance and discrimination in our belief and practice; and also—what is urgently needed—a new comprehension of the causes of our differences between ourselves. This, and not a despairing agreement to ignore them, is the only effective first step to their removal.

Of all christian 'ritual patterns' that of the eucharist is by common consent central and the most important. True, it is neither christian nor scientific to isolate it altogether from those which embody the christian conception of the eternal responsibility of each individual soul (technically, baptism, confirmation and penance), or from those which express the social, organic quality of fully christian life (the sacrament and idea of different 'orders' in the church, and the perpetual round of the divine office as a representative worship).[1]

Nevertheless, so far as this world is concerned, these others are directed towards and centre upon the eucharist, and their results are largely expressed in the eucharistic action. It is accordingly the ritual pattern of the latter which is the most revealing of the essential christian understanding of human life.

The book which has emerged from the process of re-writing the original paper, after delays due to the claims of other work and the difficulties of wartime publishing, is quite different from the one I had expected. This is a not uncommon misadventure with authors, and in itself a fact of no interest; but the change had better be explained. The paper was written by an Anglican for Anglicans; it dealt with a troublesome contemporary Anglican problem, from the ordinary Anglican standpoint and assumptions. Even so it was found impossible to state clearly what this specifically Anglican problem involves, to explain its causes or to discuss it usefully, without relating it to a much wider background. Herein lies the change between the paper and the book. The latter remains quite obviously something written by an Anglican, and I am happy that it should be so. But I recognise that what was the background of the paper has become the substance of the book, and that the domestic Anglican problem has assumed a more scientific proportion to the subject as a whole.

That is as it should be The most isolated christian—say a celtic anchorite (the nearest equivalent to a christian Robinson Crusoe)—in so far as he is specifically christian, does not come to God like the pagan mystic, as the alone to the Alone. Even if he does not use a traditional formula like the Lord's prayer or the 'Glory be to the Father', he prays within a whole framework of christian ideas received from others. When his prayer is most spontaneous and from his own heart, the belief according to which he prays, the general type of his prayer and much—probably most—of his actual phrasing are still largely drawn from what he has learned from others—his teachers, christian services he has attended in the past, his mother, his bible, many different sources. Ultimately it all comes to him, even the use of his bible, from the tradition of prayer evolved in the worshipping church. And it is with local churches as with individuals. Behind each of them stands the classic tradition of christendom, making its influence felt all the time, even if only by their attempts to react against it. Behind the Church of England, for instance, and her present official eucharistic rite, there stretches the vast tradition of performing the eucharist in much more ancient and more numerous churches for fourteen centuries before Archbishop Cranmer was born. We cannot cut ourselves off from this immense experience of the eucharist in the past, even if we

[1] Unction and matrimony stand a little apart, but they can be attached to these two groups.

would. It has moulded and contributed to our own in all sorts of ways, far
more numerous and complicated and subtle than we readily recognise.
And in so doing it has largely created both our present advantages and our
present difficulties, so that we can neither fully profit by the one nor
effectively remedy the other without some understanding of their causes.
This inescapable solidarity of all christians in their prayer, even of the
most resolute and exclusive sectarians with whom it is utterly unconscious, is
a striking and at times ironic lesson of christian history. It is inseparable from
the nature of christianity itself, and rooted in the biblical view of religion,
that of the Old Testament as well as the New. It is not surprising that it
finds its most obvious and universal expression in the history of what is the
climax of christian living, that christian corporate worship whose centre
and gauge from the beginning has been the eucharist.

From one point of view the eucharist is always in essence the same
thing—the human carrying out of a divine command to 'do this'. The
particular eucharistic rite we follow is only a method of 'doing this'. It
might seem strange at first sight to the conventional 'Martian enquirer'
that there is not one single way of 'doing this', absolutely identical throughout christendom; and that none of the many ways of 'doing' it has anywhere
remained the same from the days of the apostles until now. On the contrary,
this simple bond of christian unity has a peculiarly complicated and
ramifying history of variation. It is true that by careful analysis there is to
be found underlying most of these varying rites and all of the older ones a
single normal or standard *structure* of the rite as a whole. It is this standard
structure which I call the 'Shape' of the Liturgy. But it somewhat discon-
certingly appears that this standard Shape or sequence of the Liturgy has
in at least one major particular been altered from the pattern originally laid
down at the last supper; and that this alteration was nowhere undone from
the first century to the sixteenth, and even then only in one or two groups
which have won no general approval. Apart from these isolated groups that
standard Shape has everywhere remained unchanged for more than
eighteen hundred years, overlaid yet never refashioned. But within that
rigid framework the eucharist has adapted itself perpetually with a most
delicate adjustment to the practical conditions and racial temperaments
and special gifts of a multitude of particular churches and peoples and
generations.

Here, I suggest, is something of the greatest significance as a clue to
what is authentically christian in life and thought. That standard structure
or Shape of the Liturgy can be shewn to have had its first formation in the
semi-jewish church of the apostolic age. But it has persisted ever since, not
because it was consciously retained as 'apostolic' or even known to be such
—it was not even recognised to be there—but only because it fulfilled
certain universal *christian* needs in every church in every age, not only for
outstanding saints but for the innumerable millions of plain nameless sinful

christian folk, for whom in different ways the eucharist has always been the universal road to God.

The intricate pattern of local variety overlaid on the unchanging apostolic core of the rite is the product of history. It is the proof that the christian liturgy is not a museum specimen of religiosity, but the expression of an immense living process made up of the real lives of hosts of men and women in all sorts of ages and circumstances. Yet the underlying structure is always the same because the essential action is always the same, and this standard structure or Shape alone embodies and expresses the full and complete eucharistic action for all churches and all races and all times. The action is capable of different interpretations, and the theologies which define those interpretations have varied a good deal. But they can vary only within certain limits while they interpret one and the same action. When-ever and wherever the eucharistic action is changed, *i.e.* whenever and wherever the standard structure of the rite has been broken up or notably altered, there it will be found that some part of the primitive fulness of the meaning of the eucharist has been lost. And—in the end—it will be found that this has had equally notable results upon the christian *living* of those whose christianity has been thus impoverished. It may sound exaggerated so to link comparatively small ritual changes with great social results. But it is a demonstrable historical fact that they are linked; and whichever we may like to regard as the cause of the other, it is a fact that the ritual change can always be historically detected before the social one. To take two cardinal instances: There is an analysable relation between the *non-com-municant* eucharistic piety which begins in the later fourth century and certain obvious weaknesses and special characteristics of the christianity of the dark and middle ages, which first shew themselves in the fifth century. There is again a clear relation between, on the one hand, certain special tendencies of Latin eucharistic piety in the later middle ages which come to full development in the sixteenth century all over the West, and on the other that post-renaissance individualism, first in religion and then in living, which has had such outstanding consequences upon the general situation of Western society in the eighteenth, nineteenth and twentieth centuries.

It is the 'ritual pattern' of the eucharistic action which is here studied, as it is 'done' by this standard structure of the Shape of the Liturgy. This involves approaching the whole matter not so much from the standpoint of the theologian (though one cannot ignore theology in dealing with it) nor yet directly from that of the pure historian (though history supplies the bulk of the material), but from that of the liturgist. Since I am thus attaching a label to myself, I hope I may be allowed to explain what I con-ceive the word to mean. It means neither an antiquarian collector of litur-gical curiosities for the sake of their own interest, nor yet an expert in modern ecclesiastical rubrics, but merely a student of Comparative

Religion, who is himself a believing christian, exercising his science especially on the practice of worship in his own religion.[1] It is true that that practice—and especially the standard structure or Shape of the Liturgy —was not formed and is not maintained by theories and scientific analyses at all, but by the needs and instinct of ordinary christians living in the most direct contact with history and under its pressures. That is part of the practical value to ourselves in an age of confusion of an analytical study of it. A book on this subject need not be a particularly difficult book, though if it is to be thorough it must needs be a long one, because it deals with something which underlies and accompanies the whole history of Western civilisation for nearly two thousand years, with which it has continual mutual interactions.

What I have tried to understand, therefore, is not only when and how, but *why* that standard structure or Shape of the Liturgy took and kept the Shape it has. There is necessarily a good deal of history in this book but (I hope) no archaeology for archaeology's sake, which is unfortunately what most people seem chiefly to expect from liturgists and their works. The very word 'liturgy' has, I know, a distinctly archaeological and even 'precious' sound in many people's ears. (I regret that I cannot find another which will quite serve its purpose.) What are called 'liturgiologists' are apt accordingly to be treated by English churchmen with that vague deference accompanied by complete practical disregard with which the Englishman honours most forms of learned research. From the ecclesiastical authorities they usually receive kindness tempered with a good deal of suspicion, as experts in some mysterious and highly complicated theoretical study, whose judgement it may be expedient to satisfy if that can be done without provoking a qualm in the Diocesan Conference, but whose labours have in any case no practical bearing on what goes on in the ordinary parish church. Liturgists have no particular reason to be pleased with the mandarin-like position thus accorded them. They are in reality only students of what actually goes on and has gone on in every parish or other church in christendom and went on before there were special buildings called churches, ever since thirteen men met for supper in an upper room at Jerusalem— the 'common prayer' of christians. And precisely in so far as their studies are scientifically conducted they are capable of useful and important practical applications.

Yet it must be admitted that the liturgists have largely had themselves to thank for the reverent disregard with which their labours are so generally treated. They persist in presenting their subject as a highly specialised branch of archaeology with chiefly aesthetic preoccupations, as though the

---

[1] The technique of the liturgist must be fully as 'scientific' in its methods as that of the *religionsgeschichtliche schule* in Germany. But I think it will be obvious to anyone carefully studying their works that they lost much in insight into their material by not sharing the belief of those who produced it.

liturgy had evolved of itself in a sort of ecclesiastical vacuum remote from the real life and needs of men and women, who have always had to lead their spiritual lives while helping to carry on the whole muddled history of a redeemed yet fallen world. Archaeology is no doubt fascinating to specialists but it is a recondite business. And though beauty is an attribute of God and as such can be fittingly employed in His worship, it is only a means to that end and in most respects not a directly necessary means. The ordinary man knows very well that prayer and communion with God have their difficulties, but that these arise less from their own technique than from the nature of human life. Worship is a mysterious but also a very direct and commonplace human activity. It is meant for the plain man to do, to whom it is an intimate and sacred but none the less quite workaday affair. He therefore rightly refuses to try to pray on strictly archaeological principles. And so he feels quite prepared to leave what he hears called 'The Liturgy' to be the mystery of experts, and is content instead humbly to make the best he can of the substitute (as he supposes) good enough for him and his like, *viz.* taking part in 'worship' as he finds it in the customary common prayer at his parish church, grumbling a good deal if the clergy alter the service with which he is familiar so that he cannot follow it for himself. This, of course, happens to be 'The Liturgy' in some form. And this attitude of the layman seems to me, if I may say so, not only justifiable but also very 'liturgical' in the strict sense of the word. It has been the normal attitude of the good layman in every age of the church, and it is easy to shew that it has been among the strongest forces making for the maintenance of the liturgy from the very beginning.

The position of the clergy in the matter is different. The cleric has a professional or technical interest in 'worship' as such because it is his special business, an interest which the layman does not, or certainly need not, share. The cleric is therefore much more disposed to consider and to experiment with novel ideas in this field. Further, the parochial clergy have a pastoral responsibility to help their people to worship as well as possible, for the greater glory of God and the profit of their souls. It says something for their sense of duty that over most of christendom during the last century various practical changes in public worship (*e.g.* in church music) which are now universally admitted to be improvements and generally adopted, have been introduced almost entirely through the efforts of the parochial clergy and ministers, not seldom in the face of opposition from the laity and without encouragement from higher ecclesiastical authority.

This is natural enough. The clergy have a conscientious responsibility for the *quality* of worship, and the laity of necessity follow rather than lead in such questions. But one might well have expected that the lead everywhere would come from the official chief pastors of the church. In theory it should be so, and in the ancient church it largely was so in practice. But the unfortunate fact is that all over christendom, ever since about the twelfth or thirteenth century, the higher ecclesiastical authorities have largely been absorbed in administrative routine.[1] It can hardly be hoped that the administrative mind will ever be either in sufficiently immediate touch with the contemporary spiritual needs of ordinary individuals or sufficiently at leisure for constructive thought, to be able to make very striking contributions in this field. It is much the same case everywhere.[2] Doubtless most christian leaders regret their own preoccupation with machinery. It is an obvious danger, against which the church was obliged to take precautions in the first years of her existence.[3] But now that these are no longer very effective, it is unfortunately true that all over christendom the most valuable contribution to the progress of ideas which can ordinarily be looked for from authority is the adoption without too much obstruction and delay of useful ideas promoted chiefly by the subordinate clergy. Nevertheless, a survey of the history of christian worship everywhere reveals the encouraging fact that though the action of authority can usually delay, it can also often hasten and almost never finally prevent movements of thought and changes of practice which have a real theological motive. The usual interval which elapses between the efforts of the pioneers and their recognition by authority seems to be, on the average, between seventy years and a century, though Rome—exceptionally conservative—has often taken anything between one hundred and five hundred years to legalise long accepted changes in her own discipline of worship.[4] Apart from such

[1] Probably the feudalisation of the episcopate and the complication of business by the systematising of canon law were responsible for this sterility in the West, while the transformation of the Eastern churches into a bureaucracy in the later Byzantine period and subsequent Turkish oppression have had much the same effect in the East.

[2] A great French prelate was discussing with an Anglican the parallel development (*mutatis mutandis*) within their respective churches of certain liturgical ideas which have both devotional and social applications. 'Et vos évêques anglicans?'—asked the Frenchman—'Que pensent-ils de tout cela?' 'Oh! Votre éminence connait assez bien les évêques. Quand une idée quelconque s'énonce nouvelle, tous les évêques se mettent à la condamner immédiatement.' 'Ah! Oui. C'est par force d'habitude, n'est-ce-pas? C'est leur métier.' 'Mais si ça persiste et devient moins impopulaire, peu à peu on trouve que les évêques se taisent. Enfin, tout d'un coup, on trouve les évêques en tête.' 'Alors, c'est chez vous comme partout. Mais maintenant, en quelle phase se montrent-ils, vos évêques?' 'Maintenant, éminence'—(hopefully—this was in 1936)—'nos évêques commencent à se taire.' 'Admirable! En France ils ne sont pas encore toujours aussi prudents. Mais si on gagne les curés, c'est tout ce qu'il faut pour la marche des idées '

[3] Acts vi. 2 *sqq.*

[4] Among innumerable modern illustrations one might give, here are a few: The *Motu proprio* of Pope Pius X in 1910, adopting the principles of the reform of church music first advocated at Solesmes in the 1840's; the extension by Popes Leo XIII and Pius XI of the cultus of the Sacred Heart, propagated ever since the seventeenth century by the Jesuits and others; the provision in the proposed Anglican revision of the *Prayer Book* in 1928 for the 'Harvest Festivals' inaugurated by Hawker of Morwenstow seventy years before; the adoption in the Scottish *Book of Common Order* in 1938 of liturgical reforms advocated forty years before by McCrie and other presbyterians. (This appears to be almost a record for speed in such matters. The Moderator and other administrators hold office only for one year.)

exceptions and the avowed liturgical revolutions of the sixteenth century, the interval of at least two generations seems to have been fairly constant all over christendom since the thirteenth century.

There have appeared in modern times a number of movements for the deepening of the christian idea and practice of worship—the *Zoe* movement among the Greek Orthodox—the 'Liturgical Movement' in the Roman Church, and another going by the same title in Scottish Presbyterianism— the 'Wesleyan Sacramental Fellowship'—sporadic Lutheran movements before the war (the best known but not the most interesting being that with which the name of F. Heiler was associated)—and the various off-shoots of the 'Oxford Movement'[1] in England which began in the last century. There is an obvious relation between them all throughout christendom. They have met with slightly varying degrees of official patronage and hindrance, and about the same intensity of popular mis-understanding, wherever they have appeared. But on the whole it can be said that in every case their most solid support has come from the younger parochial clergy and ministers. In the Roman Church on the Continent, where the movement has made the greatest practical headway (despite certain mistakes of tactics and presentation, which gave an impression of concern with inessentials) a great deal of valuable study and guidance has been afforded by the religious. But even there the effective impact on the life and devotion of the church has been chiefly due to the efforts of the parochial clergy and a nucleus of keen lay support, with the bulk of the laity slowly adapting themselves to the new ideas, and the bishops (with certain great exceptions) following—acquiescently, apathetically or reluc-tantly as the case might be—safely behind. So, at all events, the situation before the war was described to me by more than one scholar or prelate who should have known. Continental catholics have something else to think about at present, and the situation may well have changed when they can give their attention to it once more.

In England there has been the additional handicap of a great lack of literature on the subject which can be covered by the useful French term *haute vulgarisation*—I mean books which will meet the needs of the thought-ful and educated christian, cleric or layman, who is not and does not intend to become what he calls a 'liturgiologist', but who is aware that ideas are stirring on this subject. Such a man may have a natural desire to under-stand without prejudice what it is all about, but roughly and without too much technical jargon and stretches of untranslated dead languages. Above all he wants to know its bearing on his own christian life and prayers and his ordinary worship in his parish church. I have tried to keep in mind this need and desire, and to serve such a reader with what is neither a manual

[1] In this respect it is more properly described as the 'Cambridge Movement'. It was the 'Cambridge Ecclesiological Society' which led the way in changes in wor-ship expressive of the changes in theology advocated at Oxford.

of 'liturgiology' nor a book of devotion, but an explanation of what is after all a technical and somewhat complicated subject put in as untechnical a way as the matter seems to allow. I assume only that he wishes to understand it from a certain practical point of view, that of the worshipping christian, with a serious interest in the subject but no great background of technical knowledge.

I must admit that the book has been swollen more than I like by the need to cite at some length the historical evidence which is the basis of the explanation. Probably this will not detract from its interest for most readers, and in any case it could not be avoided. Modern research has greatly altered this groundwork of the subject in recent years, but it has done so almost unnoticed and piecemeal. The standard manuals in English are without exception disfigured by obsolete information, and the new and more scientific investigations are scattered broadcast in scholarly periodicals and monographs in many languages. In the circumstances there seems to be a need for a book which with the aid of some new material and fresh investigations will give a coherent statement of the new view of the subject as a whole. I have tried to do this in outline, and as such I have hopes that even scientific students of liturgy will find some things to interest them here.

The book having taken this form, it must largely avoid the specifically Anglican interests of the paper from which it began. It is true that I have added a chapter on certain changes made in the Anglican rite at and after the Reformation, and also some considerations on the difficulties of the liturgical situation in Anglicanism at the present time. That is because I conceive that no Anglican could do otherwise at present, if he wishes to serve his own church. But it will be found that I have not prejudiced my attempt to explain by the advocacy of any particular proposals. Two years in a parish since the war began have left me with an intense sympathy for the lay communicant and his parish priest in facing those difficulties, which are ultimately not of their making. They have also left me with strong doubts as to whether any of the current proposals, official or otherwise, are based on a sufficiently searching analysis of what those difficulties really are, or why they have come to be felt as difficulties. Yet until some such analysis has been established and understood we are not likely to get on to the right road to a solution. In any case, there are already advocates enough before the church. It is the vocation and justification of scholarship not to plead a case but to discern and illuminate the problem for the jury.

Sixteen out of seventeen chapters, however, deal with a wider theme, even if some marks of their origin are still upon them. These things are the common inheritance of all the baptised, the legacy of our common Mother before our family quarrels had grown so sharp and tragic. It would be an additional reward for fourteen months of writing and fourteen years of study if that on which I have laboured to serve my own brethren should help others also to love God better through their own liturgies. Many different rites are drawn on here, and though I do not pretend to think that they have all the same meaning, they are all, I believe, alike at least in one respect. No liturgy is simply a particular 'way of saying your prayers', which would be only an instrument for one department of life. Prayer expresses a theology or it is only the outlet of a blind and shallow emotion; and like all prayer a liturgy must do that. But because it carries prayer on to an *act*, every eucharistic liturgy is and must be to some extent the expression of a conception of human life as a whole. It relates the individual worshipper to God and His law, to redemption, to other men, to material things and to his own use of them. What else is there in life?

In this period of the disintegration and attempted reconstruction of thought about our secular society, the individual's relation to society and his need for and securing of material things are the haunting problems of the age. There is a christian pattern of a solution which is expressed for us and by us at the eucharist. There the individual is perfectly integrated in society, for there the individual christian only exists as a christian individual inasmuch as he is fully exercising his own function in the christian society. There his need of and utter dependence upon material things even for 'the good life' in this world is not denied or even ascetically repressed, but emphasised and met. Yet his needs are met from the resources of the whole society, not by his own self-regarding provision. But there the resources of the society are nothing else but the total substance freely offered by each of its members for all. There, too, is displayed a true hierarchy of functions within a society organically adapted to a single end, together with a complete equality of recompense.

But the eucharist is not a mere symbolic mystery representing the right order of earthly life, though it is that incidentally and as a consequence. It is the representative act of a fully *redeemed* human life. This perfected society is not an end in itself, but is consciously and wholly directed to the only end which can give meaning and dignity to human life—the eternal God and the loving and conscious obedience of man in time to His known will. There the eternal and absolute value of each individual is affirmed by setting him in the most direct of all earthly relations with the eternal and absolute Being of God; though it is thus affirmed and established only through his membership of the perfect society. There the only means to that end is proclaimed and accepted and employed—man's redemption through the personal sacrifice of Jesus Christ at a particular time and place in human history, communicated to us at other times and places through the church which is the 'fulfilment' of Him. That is the eucharist. Over against the dissatisfied 'Acquisitive Man' and his no less avid successor the dehumanised 'Mass-Man' of our economically focussed societies insecurely organised for time, christianity sets the type of 'Eucharistic Man'—man giving thanks with the product of his labours upon the gifts of God, and daily rejoicing with his fellows in the worshipping society which is grounded in eternity. This is man to whom it was promised on the night before Calvary that he should henceforth eat and drink at the table of God and be a king. That is not only a more joyful and more humane ideal. It is the divine and only authentic conception of the meaning of all human life, and its realization is in the eucharist.

GREGORY DIX

NASHDOM ABBEY
  BURNHAM, BUCKS
    *Corpus Christi* 1943

## NOTE TO THE SECOND EDITION

A new edition having been called for within three months of the first publication, I have taken advantage of it to correct a few misprints which had escaped my notice and a number of minor slips. There has been no time to take account in this edition of a certain amount of fresh evidence which has been most kindly put at my disposal by various scholars, for which I am grateful, and to which I hope to adjust my own findings at some future date. But I am happy to say that such expert criticism as the book has already received suggests that this will affect no more than details and isolated points, leaving the general presentation of the subject here substantially unchanged.

GREGORY DIX

NASHDOM ABBEY
  *St. Benedict's Day* 1945

# CHAPTER I

## THE LITURGY AND THE EUCHARISTIC ACTION

### THE LITURGY AND ITS SHAPE

'LITURGY' is the name given ever since the days of the apostles[1] to the act of taking part in the solemn corporate worship of God by the 'priestly' society[2] of christians, who are 'the Body of Christ, the church'.[3] '*The* Liturgy' is the term which covers generally all that worship which is officially organised by the church, and which is open to and offered by, or in the name of, all who are members of the church. It distinguishes this from the personal prayers of the individual christians who make up the church, and even from the common prayer of selected or voluntary groups within the church, *e.g.* guilds or societies. In the course of time the term 'The Liturgy' has come to be particularly applied to the performance of that rite which was instituted by our Lord Jesus Christ Himself to be the peculiar and distinctive worship of those who should be 'His own';[4] and which has ever since been the heart and core of christian worship and christian living—the Eucharist or Breaking of Bread.

The profound reasons for this centring of the general christian experience on the eucharist will be touched on later. Here it is enough to say that all eucharistic worship is of necessity and by intention a *corporate action*— '*Do* this' (*poieite*, plural). The blessed Bread is broken that it may be *shared*, and 'we being many' made 'one Body'; the blessed Cup is delivered that it may be a '*partaking* of the Blood of Christ'.[5] It is of the deepest meaning of the rite that those who take part are thereby united indissolubly with one another and with all who are Christ's, '*because*' (*hoti*) each is thereby united with Him,[6] and through Him with the Father, with Whom He is One.

This understanding of the rite, as essentially a corporate action, is clearly expressed in the very first christian description of the way in which it was performed. Writing at the close of Domitian's persecution, in the autumn of A.D. 96, S. Clement of Rome reminds the Corinthian church: 'Unto the high-priest ( = the celebrant-bishop) his special "liturgies" have been appointed, and to the priests ( = presbyters) their special place is assigned, and on the levites ( = deacons) their special "deaconings" are imposed; the layman is bound by the ordinances for the laity. Let each of you, brethren, make eucharist to God according to his own order, keeping a good conscience and not transgressing the appointed rule of his "liturgy".'[7]

Writing from one apostolic church to another at a date when some of

[1] Acts xiii. 2.     [2] I Peter ii. 5.     [3] Eph. i. 22, 23.
[4] John xiii. 1.     [5] I Cor. x. 16.     [6] I Cor. x. 17.
[7] I Clem. 40, 41.

the actual disciples of the apostles must have been still living (even if he were not such himself) Clement in the preceding context seems to imply that these 'appointed rules' for the 'liturgies' of the different 'orders' are of divine institution, apparently from our Lord Himself. Be this as it may, here in the first century the eucharist is emphatically a corporate action of the whole christian body, in which every 'order' from the layman to the bishop has its own special 'liturgy', without the proper fulfilment of each of which the worship of the whole church cannot be fulfilled.[1]

The eucharist is here the vital expression towards God of what the church fundamentally *is*, a corporate 'holy priesthood to offer up spiritual sacrifices acceptable to God through Jesus Christ'.[2] If such a conception of the rite as a united and uniting action towards God of the whole church is to be realised, there are needed three things:

(*a*) If the whole eucharist is essentially one action, the service must have a logical development as one whole, a thrust towards that particular action's fulfilment, and not merely a general purpose of edification. It must express clearly by the order and connection of its parts what the action is which it is about, and where the service as a whole is 'going'. It is this logical sequence of parts coherently fulfilling one complete action which I call the 'Shape' of the Liturgy.

(*b*) The structure of the service itself ought somehow to express the particular function of each 'order' in the church, its 'special liturgy' in Clement's phrase, and bring this into play in fulfilling the corporate action of the whole.

(*c*) For a corporate action there must be in the minds of all a common agreement at least on what the action itself *is* on which they are solemnly engaged together. Agreement on what it *means* is less absolutely necessary, even if very desirable.

It is the sequence of the rite—the Shape of the Liturgy—which chiefly performs the eucharistic action itself, and so carries out the human obedience to the Divine command 'Do this'. It is the phrasing of the prayers which chiefly expresses the *meaning* attached to that action by the theological tradition of the church. Both are essential parts of eucharistic worship. But they have an independent history, even though they are always combined in the tradition of the liturgy.

### The Liturgical Tradition

In considering the primitive history of the eucharist we have to keep in mind continually the circumstances of a church life whose conditions were

[1] The laity are an 'order' in the church no less than the 'holy orders' of the clergy, and were anciently required to undergo a three years' preparation and training before they were allowed to enter it by baptism and confirmation. Under the shadow of persecution in a heathen world this would appear more obvious than in times when the christian laity could be confused with the general body of ratepayers.
[2] 1 Peter ii. 5.

profoundly different from our own. The New Testament documents, in sharp contrast with the fulness of Old Testament directions for worship, contain no instructions as to the form of the eucharistic rite, or detailed accounts of its celebration, beyond the brief notices of its institution. There are a number of N.T. allusions to its existence, and S. Paul regulates certain points in connection with it for the Corintnians. But such information as the N.T. offers is theological or disciplinary rather than liturgical, *i.e.* it deals with the meaning and effects of the rite and the spirit in which it is to be performed, rather than the actual way in which it is to be performed which the N.T. everywhere takes for granted. This is quite natural. The eucharist had already been at the heart of the religion of christians for twenty years before the first of these New Testament documents was written. It had trained and sanctified apostles and martyrs and scores of thousands of unknown saints for more than a century before the N.T. was collected and canonised as authoritative 'scripture', beside and above the old jewish scriptures. Christians of the first two or three generations naturally tended to see their own worship in the light of their bible, *i.e.* of these jewish scriptures of the O.T., which had formed the only bible of Jesus and the apostolic church, for which the altar of sacrifice on Mt. Moriah was the centre of all human life, the link between the world and God.[1] The results of this were not more than superficial, a matter of metaphors and illustrations, though the Old Testament in this way formed a useful barrier to the infiltration of purely pagan conceptions into eucharistic theology, in the period before christian thought in the gentile churches was mature enough to protect itself. But it is important for the understanding of the whole future history of the liturgy to grasp the fact that eucharistic worship from the outset was not based on scripture at all, whether of the Old or New Testament, but solely on *tradition*. The authority for its celebration was the historical tradition that it had been instituted by Jesus, cited incidentally by S. Paul in 1 Cor. xi. and attested in the second christian generation by the written gospels. The method of celebrating it, the primitive outline of the liturgy, was from the first prescribed, not by an authoritative code, but by the tradition of custom alone.[2]

One remarkable feature of the N.T. allusions to the eucharist is the rich

[1] *Cf. e.g.* the Ep. to the Hebrews or 1 Clem. 41 above, or other documents. The tendency in some form was universal.

[2] This final authority of custom over the liturgy continued down to the sixteenth century, when in the West the command of positive law begins to supersede custom. Thus *e.g.* the 'Uses' of Sarum, etc. are superseded in England by the 'enactment' of a rite prescribed in detail by a parliamentary statute. The same thing happ ned in the Church of Rome at the same period—*cf.* the language of the Bull *Quo Primum* 'imposing' the reformed missal of Pius V. The principle is the same; there is only a difference in the legislator. In the East, despite frequent interference with the liturgy by Byzantine emperors from the fifth to eighth centuries, custom is to this day nominally authoritative for the liturgy. But there custom has acquired a more rigid force than it had in the West making it virtually equivalent to positive law.

variety of meanings they already find within the single rite of the broken Bread and the blessed Cup. It is the solemn proclamation of the Lord's death;[1] but it is also the familiar intercourse of Jesus abiding in the soul, as a friend who enters in and sups with a friend.[2] It fulfils all the past, as the 'true'[3] and the 'secret'[4] manna, the meaning of all sacrifice,[5] the truth of all Passovers.[6] But it also looks forward to the future beyond the end of time, as a mysterious anticipation of the final judgement of God,[7] a foretaste of the eternal Messianic banquet of heaven,[8] a 'tasting of the powers of the world to come.'[9] It foreshadowed the exultant welcome of His own at that Second Coming,[10] for which those who had first lost their hearts to Him in Galilee looked so wistfully all their years after, that the echoes of their longing murmured on in the eucharistic prayers of the church for centuries. By the time the New Testament came to be written the eucharist already illuminated everything concerning Jesus for His disciples—His Person, His Messianic office,[11] His miracles,[12] His death[13] and the redemption that He brought.[14] It was the vehicle of the gift of His Spirit,[15] the means of eternal life,[16] the cause of the unity of His church.[17] This is not an exhaustive analysis of New Testament teaching about the eucharist. Nor do I suggest that all these passages are intended to be directly about the eucharist (they are not) but that in all of them the experience of the eucharist is at least colouring and affecting the author's presentation in some cases even of other matters, which is what is significant for our purpose. They shew that the church had found in the eucharist an entire epitome of 'the Gospel' before our four gospels had been written.

This fact of a great variety of meanings found within the single rite of the eucharist by the apostolic church of the first generation had important consequences for the future of the liturgy, though it has been curiously little appreciated in modern study. The theory still generally accepted in liturgical text-books is that there was a single primitive type or model of the rite, not only of outline or shape of the rite as a whole (which is true) but also of its central formula, the 'great eucharistic prayer', originally the only prayer which the service contained.

The fact is that the liturgical tradition of the text of the eucharistic prayer in the great historic rites—Syrian, Egyptian, Roman and so forth—only begins to emerge into the light of secure and analysable evidence in

---

[1] I Cor. xi. 26.    [2] Rev. iii. 20.    [3] John vi. 52.    [4] Rev. ii. 17.
[5] Heb. xiii. 10.    [6] I Cor. v. 7; Luke xxii. 18.    [7] I Cor. xi. 30, 31, 32.
[8] Luke xxii. 30.    [9] Heb. vi. 5.    [10] I Cor. xi. 26.
[11] John vi. 33, 35, 48.
[12] The accounts of the feeding of the multitude are obviously 'coloured' by the eucharist.
[13] 'It was not the death upon Calvary *per se*, but the death upon Calvary as the Last Supper interprets it and gives the clue to its meaning, which constitutes our Lord's sacrifice. The doctrine of sacrifice (and of atonement) was not read *into* the Last Supper; it was read out of it' (The present Bishop of Derby, in *Mysterium Christi*, ed. G. K. A. Bell, London, 1930, *p.* 241).
[14] John vi. 51.    [15] I Cor. xii. 13b.    [16] John vi. 53 54.    [17] I Cor. x. 17.

the third-fourth century, and even then there are big gaps in our knowledge. In the *later* fourth century, when our knowledge is more definite, we find three facts which can be taken as certain: (*a*) The outline of the rite—the Shape of the Liturgy—is everywhere most remarkably the same, after 300 years of independent existence in the widely scattered churches. (*b*) The content of the eucharistic prayer is by then also to some extent the same in arrangement and even in certain phrases. But (*c*) the great historic families shew strongly marked peculiarities of their own. It is the combination of the first two ascertained facts together with the discounting of the third which has led to the assumption that all eucharistic rites, not only in their outline but in the formula of their eucharistic prayer, are originally derived from a single 'apostolic' model.

I believe that this assumption, which has been the accepted view on the matter ever since the seventeenth century, has caused a serious misunderstanding of the early history of the eucharist, and among ourselves has been an indirect cause of some of our liturgical difficulties. Now that research is beginning, tentatively but with increasing success, to push back our knowledge of the liturgy into the period *before* the later fourth century, the evidence is beginning to wear a different appearance. The outline—the Shape—of the Liturgy is still everywhere the same in all our sources, right back into the earliest period of which we can as yet speak with certainty, the earlier half of the second century. There is even good reason to think that this outline—the Shape—of the Liturgy is of genuinely apostolic tradition. On the other hand, the further back we trace the contents of the eucharistic prayer, the more remarkable are the differences which begin to appear between the various groups of churches; though, as I have said, the different traditions of the prayer revolve always around the same essential action, and it is possible, even probable, that they were all originally rooted in a single type. This is not to say that there was an original 'apostolic' fixed *text* of the eucharistic prayer; there is no evidence of that. But because the eucharistic action was everywhere the same, the prayer which expressed the meaning of that action had necessarily certain fixed characteristics, though these were phrased and expressed in a great variety of ways by different churches.

The explanation is that the pre-Nicene[1] church faithfully reflects in its eucharistic practice the conditions of the most primitive period of christian history, the period before the canonization of the New Testament, before the great intellectual structure of doctrinal orthodoxy had reached more than a rudimentary stage, before the nascent canon law had established any but the vaguest effective organisation above the local churches, which

---

[1] Pre-Nicene = the period before the first General Council of Nicaea A.D. 325. The final toleration of Christianity by the Roman empire dates from A.D. 312-321. So 'pre-Nicene' roughly means the period of the persecutions, during which christian worship was always a *private* not a public worship.

were therefore largely self-administered in their internal daily life under their own bishops. But the vigour of this local life of the churches must not conceal from us the fact that they conceived of themselves not as a 'federation' but as a 'unity'.

Every local church had received the *rite* of the eucharist—the way of performing it—with its first evangelisation. This is important. It means that the living tradition of the liturgy as the heart of its corporate life went back into the very roots of every apostolic church, in a way that its theological tradition *about* the eucharist, which was necessarily in large part the product of experience and reflection, could not go back. Some interpretation of the rite there must have been from the outset, given by the founders when they taught their first converts about the eucharist and celebrated it among them. But that interpretation was not then given as a complete and final thing. For the N.T. allusions to the eucharist shew by their variety that there was no complete and fixed interpretation in the apostolic age, but only a rapidly growing and wonderfully rich experience by individuals and churches of the many meanings the single rite could have. The single primal fact of the rite had been given by Jesus without commentary, beyond the identification of the elements with His own sacrificial Body and Blood. It was left to the church to explore for herself the inexhaustible depths of its meaning; and from the first every local church was joyfully at work on doing so.

And even the developed local tradition of the *meaning* of the eucharistic action—which was what was expressed in the local tradition of the eucharistic prayer—could not be an entirely static thing, because the prayer was not yet a fixed formula. Within a customary outline the celebrant-bishop was to a considerable extent free to phrase the prayer as seemed to him best.[1] Thus the local tradition of the prayer in any church could grow from many sources besides the teaching of the original founders—from the prayers and meditations and happy (or less happy) inspirations of subsequent bishops; from the devout study by them or by others of the Old Testament scriptures, and later on of the new christian writings; or by deliberate borrowings from other churches far or near. Over the lapse of a century or two the corporate religious experience of the eucharist by a local church would insensibly demand some expression in its prayer, and would in turn be largely moulded by the ideas this expressed. Here the particular genius of races and languages played a quite recognisable part. And as the church at large from the second to the fourth century penetrated more deeply into the meaning of revelation, and so theological science grew, we can actually trace, even in the scanty and fragmentary surviving evidence, the continual repercussions of general theological advance on the phrasing of all eucharistic prayers, by a process of ceaseless liturgical

[1] *Cf.* Justin Martyr, *Apology*, I. 67 (*c.* A.D. 150); Hippolytus, *Ap. Trad.*, x. 4, 5 (*c.* A.D. 215).

revision carried on independently in every local church.[1] Liturgical texts were becoming more fixed in the fourth century, but the traditional freedom of phrasing allowed to celebrants ensured a certain elasticity in the prayer at least until well after A.D. 350 in most places.[2]

The eucharistic prayer was, however, the only thing in the rite which was thus pliable, because it was the 'president's' own 'special liturgy', in Clement's phrase, *i.e.* that part of the worship of the corporate body which he contributed to the whole eucharistic action, and which he recited alone. It was comparatively easy for one man to add new phrases to a traditional framework, or to compose a wholly new prayer and read it from a manuscript. But the deacons and the people did their parts by custom and by rote; and to change these, which were as much their 'special liturgies' as the celebrant's prayer was his, was a much more difficult matter. Thus there is a constant tendency for the people's responses, the deacon's proclamations, etc., which form the framework in which the celebrant's prayer (or prayers, as the rite developed) is set, to remain more archaic than the prayers themselves.[3] Theology is a progressive technical science, and remains therefore always the professional preserve of the clergy and the interest of a comparatively small educated *élite* of the laity. Liturgy, on the contrary, is a universal christian activity, and so a *popular* interest; and therefore always remains a very conservative thing. It was the fact that the eucharist as a whole was a corporate act of the whole church which everywhere maintained the rigid fixity of the outline of the liturgy, through the conservatism of the laity. Changes in this outline only began when the rite as a whole had been partially 'clericalised' by becoming something which the clergy were supposed to do *for* the laity, and the laity for the most part had lost their active share in its performance. It was the fact that the eucharistic prayer was always precisely the one thing which the clergy did perform (and were there to perform) by themselves on behalf of the whole church, which made it always the most mutable thing in the rite. But even in the prayers themselves the silent pressure of the conservatism of the

[1] Hippolytus' eucharistic prayer (c. A.D. 215) in some of its phrases expresses his own peculiar theology of the Trinity; the opponents of this theology, even if they used a prayer of that type, would not have used those particular expressions. So the prayer of Sarapion (Egypt c. A.D. 340) reflects the third century 'Logos-theology' of the Egyptian school, but with a fourth century explicitly anti-Arian turn, which can only be due to his own revision of the old prayer of his church of Thmuis; and so on.

[2] The church of Rome was always conservative, and early tended to fixity of forms. By A. D. 450 the addition there of an adjectival phrase to the fixed traditional form of the prayer by S. Leo the Great becomes a matter of remark and worthy of record. Yet the Roman canon has suffered one great upheaval since his day, probably under S. Gelasius (A.D. 494–6) and, oddly enough, without any record being preserved of what was done; and there was a further revision c. A.D. 600.

[3] *E.g.* the people's response at the end of Sarapion's eucharistic prayer (A.D. 340) is the one already traditional at that point in Egypt, but it does not grammatically fit the end of his particular prayer. We have an instance of the same thing among ourselves in the survival of the people's responses before and after the gospel by continuous *popular* tradition, where the official rite no longer provides for them at all.

worshippers (in whose name, after all, they were uttered) often maintained very ancient phrases and features down to comparatively late dates, with which contemporary theology could not always easily come to terms, and which it constantly attempted to modify or to explain away.

Throughout the pre-Nicene age these local eucharistic prayers were continuously developing, dear to the people from local tradition and lifelong personal associations and the habits of devotion, and hallowed by the memory of great saints and martyrs who had observed or ordained them.[1] In an age when scripture, doctrinal tradition, ecclesiastical machinery of all sorts, and so much else which we can take for granted, were not yet such firm elements in the framework of church life and christian thinking as they are with us, the liturgy was the great channel of the life of the church, on which all else depended. The fixed traditional outline of the rite, everywhere and always the same, maintained and expressed the church's cohesion. The 'living voice' of the liturgical ministry, teaching through the traditional yet free medium of the prayer and through the liturgical sermon (which had, as we shall see, a rather different function from that which it has with us), guided the church's faith and thought and inner life, to a degree we find it hard to recognise.

The fourth century brought imperial recognition of the christian religion and the end of persecution, and with that the possibility of a world-wide instead of a local framework of organisation. There was now the opportunity and the desire for the comparison and exchange of traditions between the churches, for their mutual enrichment and imitation, on a scale unknown before. The Shape of the Liturgy was still everywhere the same. And now the greatest differences between the churches in what did differ in their rites, the contents of their eucharistic prayers, begin to a certain extent to be 'ironed out', as it were, by a mutual adjustment. The patriarchates of Antioch and Alexandria in the East, and the rather different sort of pre-eminence of Rome in the West, take on a more solid organisation. The rites of their daughter churches tend to assimilate themselves to those of the patriarchal ones in each case, even where there was no direct pressure from the presiding sees to do so. And between these great groupings there is assimilation, though each retains marked characteristics of its own. We can actually trace a number of verbal borrowings in the eucharistic prayer by Egypt from Syria, and by Syria from Egypt, and by Rome perhaps from both; and there is at least one instance of a reverse of influence from Rome upon the other two, directly or indirectly.[2] In the fourth or early fifth

---

[1] Cf. e.g. the letter of Polycrates, bishop of Ephesus c. A.D. 195 (ap. Eusebius, Ecclesiastical History V, xxiv, 2) for the pride which churches already took in their local customs and the local saints to whom they were attributed, before A.D. 200. By then the last living links with even the sub-apostolic age—men like the nonagenarian bishop Pothinus of Lyons, martyred c. A.D. 180—were being broken, and there was beginning to be a 'christian antiquity' to study and to revere.
[2] Cf. p. 264.

century it looked as though there were a real possibility that the political unity of the christian world would eventually bring with it a large measure of liturgical uniformity too. It is an instance of that effect of political history upon the liturgy of which we have another in sixteenth century England, when the new royal centralisation of English life into a much more conscious national unity destroyed the old local 'uses' of England in favour of one national uniform rite.[1]

But with the collapse of effective political unity in the old Roman empire, a reverse tendency begins in the fifth century. East and West go their own ways, overlaying the partial uniformity reached in the fourth century with a fresh series of different developments, this time in the outline as well as in the prayers of the rite. This second flourishing of local varieties after the fifth century goes much further in the West than in the East, because the West becomes much more completely disintegrated politically. This made contacts between provincial churches and between the provinces and the central church of Rome more difficult and infrequent.[2] Only when Charlemagne once more brings the West in large part under a single political control, round about A.D. 800, do we find another impulse towards uniformity arising, this time under direct imperial encouragement. This dies away once more into a renewed growth of purely Western local variations (less pronounced this time) as the Carolingian empire breaks up again in the later ninth century.

In the East the continued unity of political rule in the shape of the Byzantine empire continued to foster the tendency towards liturgical uniformity. But the rite which eventually prevails in the East is again the rite of the *political* capital, Byzantium (Constantinople), which had hoisted itself into the position of a new patriarchate, at first beside and then dominating the older patriarchates of Alexandria and Antioch. By the thirteenth century this Byzantine rite had virtually ousted the old patriarchal rites of Egypt and Syria from their own churches among the Orthodox.[3]

---

[1] In England the state hastened the process by force, whereas in the fourth century it was natural and voluntary. But it would probably have happened in England at some point in any case; had the state not intervened; leaving perhaps isolated local peculiarities in some places, like the Lyons use in France, or that of Milan in Italy, or those of Toledo or Braga in Spain and Portugal, as interesting survivals.

[2] The attempt to keep them up was nevertheless made in matters of liturgy. *E.g.* the Council of Vaison in Gaul (A.D. 529) prescribes conformity to the use of *Kyrie eleison* in Gaul, as it had recently been introduced at Rome and in most other western churches. But the attempts at uniformity were spasmodic, and died away as the political confusion grew worse during the sixth century.

[3] The liturgy of Alexandria finally gave way to that of Byzantium among the Egyptian Orthodox churches under Byzantine pressure in A.D. 1193, but it had been considerably 'Byzantinised' before that. In Syria the Greek rite of S. *James* was still occasionally used in the thirteenth century, but its use even on the feast of S. James finally died out altogether. It was revived for use on S. James' Day once a year at Jerusalem in 1905, not with the old Jerusalem text, but in the Byzantinised form in which it had survived once a year as a curiosity in the island of Zante.

Only the political revolt of racial groups in Syria and Egypt preserved the old patriarchal rites in the vernacular as symbols of political independence, in schismatic churches which began rather as instruments of nationalist aspiration than in genuine theological differences. Thus was completed the development of a single uniform liturgical use throughout the *Orthodox* East, which has come in the course of time to influence very considerably even the rites of the dissidents.[1]

In the Latin West modern ease of intercourse between the churches has brought about much the same state of affairs in spite of political disunity. The early mediaeval 'third crop' of local varieties which arose after the ninth century has been steadily assimilated to the current Roman rite, though relics of them are now carefully preserved in certain places (Milan, Lyons, Braga, etc.). Elsewhere in the West, as a consequence of the Protestant Reformation in the sixteenth century, there has arisen what from our point of view must be considered as a large 'fourth crop' of local variants of the basic Western type, in the rites of the Reformed bodies. It is true that those who use them do not as a rule think of them in this way. Their compilers were far more concerned to follow what they regarded as 'scriptural warrant' than anything in the liturgical tradition against which they were in revolt. But the Reformers themselves thought largely in terms of the Western tradition within which they had been trained. In consequence their rites all reveal under technical analysis not 'primitive' characteristics at all, nor anything akin to the special Eastern tradition, but a marked dependence on the basic Western liturgical tradition at a particular stage late in its development. In saying this I am well aware of the theological differences which distinguish the Protestant 'Supper' from the Roman Catholic 'Mass'. Nevertheless, when strictly liturgical ethos and characteristics are in question, it is a fact that the former is really only a group of varieties of the latter, or better, a group of rites derived from the latter, and markedly dependent upon it for some of their special features.

So we have reached the position to-day of two main types of liturgy, Eastern and Western, by the elimination of a large number of other rites, some of them at least as ancient as the two which have survived. The present main Eastern type has developed from the fourth century rite of the Eastern 'holy city' Jerusalem, as remodelled and expanded in the Eastern political centre, Constantinople. The present main Western type has developed from the fourth century rite of the Western 'holy city',

---

[1] The vernacular is the badge of the dissident churches of the West as it was in some measure in the East. But the rites they maintain in the West are not *ancient* local rites adopted as badges of national independence under a theological cover (as in the East), but products of the genuine theological revolution of the Reformation; though political differences had a great influence here, too. The tendency of the followers of the catholic revival in nineteenth century Anglicanism to 'Romanise' in their use of the Anglican liturgy is exactly parallel to the tendency of the later Copts and Jacobites to 'Byzantinise' their own rites, by the introduction of the *Prothesis*, the *Monogenes*, the Great Entrance, and other purely Byzantine features.

Rome, as remodelled and expanded in the Western political centre, the nucleus of Charlemagne's empire in Gaul and the Rhineland. The most important formula, the eucharistic prayer, in these two types seems to have been sufficiently similar in the second and third centuries for us to be able to postulate an original similarity, at least of general type in the first century.[1] But the two rites are now very different from each other after a separation of 1,600 years, even in striking features of what anciently was uniform everywhere, the Shape of the Liturgy. Yet under this later growth the Eastern and Western types of rite both still maintain what may be called the classical form of the eucharistic action—that fixed outline, the core of which descends from the time of the apostles, and which it is our purpose to study.

[1] *Cf.* p. 231 *sqq.*

# CHAPTER II

## THE PERFORMANCE OF THE LITURGY

### SAYING AND DOING

IF such an abstraction as 'the general conception entertained by the typical Anglican priest or layman of what the eucharist fundamentally is' can be analysed, it will be found, I believe, that he thinks of it primarily as something which is *said*, to which is attached an action, the act of communion. He regards this, of course, as an essential constituent part of the whole, but it is nevertheless something attached to the 'saying', and rather as a consequence than as a climax. The conception before the fourth century and in the New Testament is almost the reverse of this. It regards the rite as primarily something *done*, of which what is said is only one incidental constituent part, though of course an essential one.

In pointing such a contrast there is always a danger of making it sharper than the realities warrant. But in this case I am confident that the contrast is really there. The modern conception is not characteristic of any one 'school of thought' in modern Anglicanism, or indeed confined to Anglicanism at all, but is true of modern Western devotion as a whole, catholic and protestant alike. We all find it easy and natural to use such phrases as, of the clergy, '*saying* mass', and of the laity, '*hearing* mass'; or in other circles, 'Will you *say* the Eight?' or '*attending* the early Service'. The ancients on the contrary habitually spoke of '*doing* the eucharist' (*eucharistiam facere*), '*performing* the mysteries' (*mysteria telein*), '*making* the synaxis' (*synaxin agein, collectam facere*) and '*doing* the oblation' (*oblationem facere, prosphoran poiein*). And there is the further contrast, that while our language implies a certain difference between the functions of the clergy and the laity, as between active and passive ('*taking* the service' and '*attending* the service'; '*saying*' and '*hearing*' mass), the ancients used all their active language about 'doing' the liturgy quite indifferently of laity and clergy alike. The irreplaceable function of the celebrant, his 'special liturgy', was to 'make' the prayer; just as the irreplaceable function of the deacon or the people was to *do* something else which the celebrant did not do. There was difference of function but no distinction in kind between the activities of the various orders in the worship of the whole church.

This contrast between the modern Western and the ancient and primitive conception of the liturgy as something 'said' and something 'done' could be carried, I think, a good deal deeper, into the realm of the whole psychological approach to the rite, and would prove illuminating in many directions. It would explain, for instance, what is to us very striking, the complete absence from the original outline of the rite of anything in the nature of 'communion devotions'. The ancient approach did not preoccupy itself at all with devout feelings, though it recognised that they would be there. It concentrated attention entirely on the sacramental *act*, as the expression of a will already intent on amendment of life, and as the occasion of its acceptance and sanctification by God; and so far as the liturgy was concerned, it left the matter at that, in a way which our more introspective devotion would probably find unsatisfying, though it served to train the saints and martyrs of the age of persecution.

It was in the Latin middle ages that the eucharist became for the first time essentially something 'said' rather than something 'done' (the East has never accepted such a change). It had long been a thing in which the people's share was primarily to attend to what the clergy 'did' on their behalf, rather than something in which they took an equally vital and active share of their own. (This change began in the East, in the fourth-fifth centuries, and spread to the West from there.) We need continually to be on our guard against taking our own essentially 'late' and specifically 'Western' and 'Mediaeval' approach to eucharistic worship as the only or the original understanding of it. As Anglicans that is necessarily ours (I am not trying to be paradoxical) because the Anglican *devotional* tradition is exclusively grounded on the Western and Mediaeval devotional tradition. This is not a matter of 'party'; under all the party-labels and theological catchwords this devotional tradition is quite remarkably homogeneous, and betrays its origins at once under historical investigation.

Take, for one instance among many, the practice of kneeling to receive communion. This is universal among Anglicans, and its abandonment would cause as much disturbance and surprise among 'Evangelical' as among 'Anglo-catholic' or 'Moderate' communicants. It is the posture deliberately adopted by many 'protestant' clergy by contrast with the universal catholic tradition that the priest stands to communicate. Yet the practice of kneeling by anybody for communion is confined to the Latin West, and began to come in there only in the early Middle Ages. The ancient church universally stood to receive communion, as in the East clergy and laity alike stand to this day; the apostolic church conceivably reclined in the oriental fashion, though this is uncertain. Yet the Church of England fought the Puritans most vigorously on the point when they would have stood or sat; and the 'Black Rubric' stands in the Prayer Book to this day to witness by its provisions that she did so not so much on theological grounds as out of deference to a devotional instinct which is entirely a product of the Latin middle ages.

Or take again the devotions our manuals commonly contain as 'Preparation for communion'. The 'Seven Prayers ascribed to S. Ambrose' are by Abbot John of Fécamp, of the early twelfth century. The prayer 'Almighty and everlasting God, behold I approach the sacrament of Thy only begotten Son . . .' is by S. Thomas Aquinas of the thirteenth century. The prayer after communion 'Most sweet Lord Jesus, pierce my soul with the wound of Thy love . . .' is by his contemporary, S. Bonaventura, and so on. There is nothing new or specially 'Anglo-catholic' about the use of these and other mediaeval prayers by Anglicans. Versions of some of them are to be found in Sutton's *Godly Meditations upon the Most Holy Sacrament of the Lord's Supper* (1630) and in *The New Manual of Devotions*, of which the twenty-eighth edition was published in 1822. One of them has furnished a prayer to the well-known manual of Bishop Walsham How. Others were used in part by Bp. Simon Patrick of Ely in his *Christian Sacrifice*, first published in 1671 and republished four times in the eighteenth century.[1] They are not used out of reverence for their authors; they are generally printed anonymously. Their only appeal is that they express faithfully what the devout Anglican communicant wants to say. And what he wants to say was said for the first time by the Latin Middle Ages.

It is not among the 'Anglo-catholics' but among those who would regard themselves as the more traditionally Anglican groups that we find the notion most strongly held that the 'simple said service' is the most satisfactory method of conducting the eucharist—*i.e.* the mediaeval Latin acceptance of 'low mass' as the *norm*. Never before then had there been 'a simple said service'; and the net effect of its introduction was virtually to exclude the people from all active share in the liturgy, so that it finally became a thing 'said' by the clergy, which the people's part was to 'hear'. It is, indeed, our mediaeval Latin past which accounts for much in our devotional tradition which we are all of us apt to mistake as 'protestant'. If you believe that the liturgy is primarily a thing 'said', your part in it if you are a layman is chiefly to 'hear'. It is because we have carried this notion to its logical conclusion, that we get those periodical outbursts of irritation among the laity about the 'inaudibility' of the clergy; and quite reasonably, if we consider the implications of our devotional tradition. 'Hearing' is virtually all that we have left to the laity to do.

It was the conviction that the laity ought to *see* the consecration of the sacrament which originally sent the Anglican clergy round to the awkward 'North End'. (Incidentally, there are implications in the whole notion that 'consecration' is a thing to be effected by the clergy, while the laity merely 'watch' and 'hear', which the student of mediaeval doctrine and, especially, mediaeval practice will recognise as familiar.) But the idea in itself that the laity should *see* the consecrated sacrament is not new in the sixteenth century. Doubtless it was given then a new theological pretext. But devotionally it is only an echo of the mediaeval layman's plea, 'Heave it higher, Sir Priest!' when he could not see the elevated Host at the consecration.

---

[1] *Cf.* also his translation of hymns by S. Thomas Aquinas *On the morning before Communion*, publ. A.D. 1721. *Cf.* also the devotions by S. Anselm and S. Bernard (twelfth century) recommended by Stanhope in 1701 and republished several times before the last edition in 1918.

This may sound fantastic until one looks for a moment at a devotional tradition which has not descended through the Latin middle ages. In the East the layman early came to feel that he ought *not* to see the consecration. The veil which hid the whole sanctuary at that moment was already coming into use in North Syria in the later fourth century. It spread widely, and was later reinforced elsewhere by a solid screen of masonry and painting, the *ikonostasion*, whose purpose was to *prevent* the laity from doing precisely what the Western Elevation was introduced to help them to do—to see the sacrament at the consecration. This development was not forced upon the Eastern laity by the clergy; it was and is their own strong feeling about the matter, that they ought not to see the consecration. A devout and highly educated Orthodox layman, a former cabinet minister, has told me of the profound shock he received when he first attended an Anglican celebration (done, apparently, quite 'decently and in order') and witnessed what he called our 'strange publicity' in this. This is only the result of another devotional tradition than that of the Latin middle ages, which has formed and moulded our own, even when we seem to be most strongly reacting against it.

This question might be carried much further. But it is sufficient here to have indicated that there is a considerable difference between our own fundamental conception of the eucharist and that of the primitive church, and also where our own conception has its roots. Of course our own practice retains strong traces of the older way of regarding things, *e.g.* in the plural phrasing of our prayers. And we need not condemn or renounce our own devotional tradition just because it is Western and mediaeval in origin. It is not in itself any more or any less desirable to pray like the third century than like the thirteenth, provided always that we know what we are doing. But if we are to penetrate to the universal principles which underlie all eucharistic worship, we must be able for the moment to think ourselves out of the particular devotional approach which is our own, and to free ourselves from the assumption that it is the only or the original approach. Otherwise it must operate as a barrier to all clear understanding of other and older traditions, and so impoverish our own possibilities in worship.

The first main distinction, then, which we have to bear in mind, is that the apostolic and primitive church regarded the eucharist as primarily an *action*, something 'done', not something 'said'; and that it had a clear and unhesitating grasp of the fact that this action was *corporate*, the united joint action of the whole church and not of the celebrant only. The prayer which the celebrant 'said' was not the predominant thing in the rite. It took its place alongside the 'special liturgies' of each of the other 'orders', as one essential in the corporate worshipful act of the whole church, even as the most important essential, but not to the exclusion of the essential character of the others.

### Public and Private

The second main distinction we have to bear in mind is this: We regard christian worship in general, not excluding the eucharist, as essentially a *public* activity, in the sense that it ought to be open to all comers, and that the stranger (even the non-christian, though he may not be a communicant) ought to be welcomed and even attracted to be present and to take part. The apostolic and primitive church, on the contrary, regarded all christian worship, and especially the eucharist, as a highly *private* activity, and rigidly excluded all strangers from taking any part in it whatsoever, and even from attendance at the eucharist. Christian worship was intensely corporate, but it was not 'public'.

Our own attitude is the result of living in a world which has been nominally christian for fourteen or fifteen centuries. The attitude of the ancient church did not arise, however, from the circumstances of a non-christian world, for it was adopted before opposition began, and continued in circumstances when it would have been quite easy to modify it. The fact is that christian worship in itself, and especially the eucharist, was not by origin, and is not by nature intended to be, a 'public' worship at all, in the sense that we have come to accept, but a highly *exclusive* thing, whose original setting is entirely domestic and private. This has had abiding results on its performance. Even in a nominally christian world, the eucharist has always retained some of the characteristics of a private domestic gathering of 'the household of God'.[1]

Let us look for a moment at its beginnings. It was instituted not in a public place of worship but in an upper room of a private house, in circumstances arranged with a seemingly deliberate secrecy,[2] among a restricted company long selected and prepared. In the first years after the Ascension we do indeed still find the apostles and their followers frequenting a public worship, but it is the jewish public worship of the temple and the synagogue, in which they still felt at home. Their specifically christian worship is from the first a domestic and private thing. They met in one another's houses for the Breaking of Bread.[3] There was no christian *public* worship in our sense at all.

The jews did not exclude non-jews from attendance at their public worship in the synagogues, where they encouraged them, or from the outer court of the Temple where they at least tolerated them. But the rules which excluded all who were not jews, either by race or by a thorough-going 'naturalisation' as proselytes, from all *domestic* intercourse with jews were strict. It was because of the specifically domestic character of christian worship and especially the eucharist, that the admission to it of gentiles who had not passed into the church through judaism provoked the crisis between S. Paul and the jewish christians which we can discern in

[1] Eph. ii. 19.        [2] Mark xiv. 13.        [3] Acts ii. 46.

the N.T.,[1] though we cannot trace the details of its settlement. In the circles and period from which our documents come the whole question was over and settled before they were written, and no longer excited a living interest. Perhaps the question never was properly settled in principle but simply ended by the march of events. The proportion of gentiles to jews in the church changed with extraordinary swiftness, so that within forty years of the Last Supper what had begun as a small and exclusive jewish sect had become a large and swiftly growing but still rigidly exclusive gentile society which retained a small jewish wing.

This left the question of whether christianity was to develop into a public worship still an open one. In Syria the jewish christians clung with a pathetic loyalty to their double allegiance for centuries, and maintained a jewish public worship either in the ordinary synagogues or in public synagogue assemblies of their own. But to the gentile churches the matter presented itself differently. The breach between them and the jewish synagogues took place at different moments in different churches, though probably nowhere outside Palestine did any connection last for more than a few years at most. A few months or even weeks generally saw S. Paul and his converts expelled from all connection with the local jewish community. But even before this happened, their christian and eucharistic worship was already a domestic thing, wholly their own. Yet their exclusion from the synagogue would leave the local christian church with no public worship at all, in the face of all the needs of missionary propaganda. The state was not yet officially hostile, and it would have been comparatively easy to organise some sort of public worship, open to all who might chance to enter. There was, for instance, a time when S. Paul was 'lecturing daily in the school of one Tyrannus' at Ephesus[2] which might well have proved the starting point of such a development, and doubtless there were many such moments. What decisively prevented any such idea was the rigidly exclusive and domestic character of specifically christian worship, and especially of the eucharist. Thus early christian worship developed along its own inherent and original line of exclusiveness even in the gentile churches.

It was not that the church did not desire converts; she was ardently missionary to all who would hear, as jews and pagans were quick to complain. But propaganda meetings were rigidly separated from 'worship', so that they were not even accompanied by prayer. They were confined to the announcing of the christian message by the reading of the scriptures and oral instruction, and then all who were not already of the 'laity' by baptism and confirmation—even those who were already convinced of the truth of the gospel but had not yet received those sacraments—were invariably turned out before prayer of any kind was offered, let alone the eucharist. Thus christianity was able to dispense with the erection of any sort of special buildings for its worship for at least a century and a half, and con-

[1] Acts x.–xv.; Gal. i. and ii., etc.      [2] Acts xix. 9.

centrated itself instead in those 'house-churches' which meet us everywhere in the N.T. and the 2nd century. In these the exclusive and domestic
character of its eucharistic worship was entirely at home, and their atmosphere also informed the spirit and the arrangements of the liturgical worship at the *synaxis* or *syneleusis*, the non-eucharistic 'general meeting' of
the whole local church. It was this originally domestic spirit of christian
worship as much as anything else that preserved the clear understanding
of its corporate nature. The understanding of this began to fade at once
when it was transformed into a 'public' worship in the great basilicas of
the fourth century.

Nevertheless, the exclusive character of eucharistic worship still continued to manifest itself, though in a different way, after it had taken on the
new character of a truly public worship in a nominally christian world. In
the first three centuries to be present at the eucharist virtually meant being
a communicant. The christian had a personal qualification for being
present, baptism and confirmation. Before receiving these sacraments he
was required to make an explicit statement that he shared the *faith* of the
church in the revelation and redemption by Jesus Christ.[1] Without this he
could not be of that 'household of faith'[2] whose domestic worship the
eucharist was. It was the indiscriminate admission to baptism and confirmation of the infant children of christian parents when all society began to
turn nominally christian which was at the root of that decline of lay communion which set in during the fourth and fifth centuries. This reached
its lowest point in the West in the seventh century, and was met by the
establishment of a rule during the ninth century that laymen *must* communicate once a year at Easter at the least. In the East, where even this minimum rule was not formally established, many devout laity ceased altogether to communicate for many years, while continuing regularly to
attend the liturgy. The clergy strove everywhere to avert this decline of
communion. Sermons abound in the works of the Fathers, especially in
those of the West, entreating and exhorting the laity to communicate more
frequently, but in vain. The infrequency of lay communion continued
everywhere so long as society at large remained nominally christian. Even
the heroic measures taken at the English Reformation to force the laity to
more frequent communion, by the odd device of making it a statutory
duty of the citizen, and by forbidding the clergy to celebrate at all without
three lay communicants at the least, quite failed of their object. The chief
practical results of these measures were a certain amount of profanation of

---

[1] This is, of course, still retained in the Book of Common Prayer. *Cf.* the questions and answers before baptism, 'Dost thou believe' the Apostles' Creed? 'All this
I stedfastly believe.' 'Wilt thou be baptised in this faith?' *Cf.* also the bishop's
question of candidates for confirmation, '. . . acknowledging yourselves bound to
*believe* and to do all those things which your Godfathers and Godmothers then undertook for you?'

[2] Gal. vi. 10.

the sacrament as a political qualification for public office, and the prevention of celebrations by the lack of lay communicants.

There seems to be a deep underlying reason for this universal refusal of the laity in all churches to receive holy communion with any frequency. The *domestic* character of eucharistic worship, which had been lost to sight by the officials of a church long dominant in social life, continued obscurely to assert itself in the feeling of the laity that communion was somehow not intended to be 'for everybody'. And since 'everybody' was now equally qualified in theory by having received baptism and confirmation, the only line of demarcation which remained was that between clergy and laity. Between the seventh century and the nineteenth all over christendom the clergy were normally the only really frequent communicants. The de-christianisation of society in general in the nineteenth and twentieth centuries has once more marked out the practising christian laity as members of 'the household of God',[1] and so included them again within that 'exclusiveness' which the eucharist has always been instinctively felt to demand. That seems to be why the laity in all communions alike have begun during this period to respond for the first time to the exhortations which the clergy never entirely ceased to make to them to communicate more often.[2]

We have now to describe the form and arrangement of this domestic gathering of 'the family of God, which is the church of the living God'.[3]

### The 'Church'

Until the third century the word 'church' (*ecclesia*) means invariably *not* the building for christian worship[4] but the solemn assembly for the liturgy, and by extension those who have a right to take part in this. There were of course plenty of other meetings of groups of christians in one another's houses for prayer and edification and for the *agape* or 'Lord's supper' (not

---

[1] Eph. ii. 19.
[2] The dependence of frequent lay communion on the existence of openly non-christian surroundings, at least in the West, is very remarkable indeed when it is examined historically. And it continues. I remember the late Cardinal Verdier telling me that in France, where *la communion fréquente* has been preached perhaps more successfully than anywhere else in our generation, the results in practice were still largely confined to Paris, the big towns and certain districts. Elsewhere, where a peasant population mostly *retains* the social tradition of catholicism in daily life, the old rule of lay communion at Easter only is still general, despite vigorous propaganda in favour of frequency.
[3] 1 Tim. iii. 15.
[4] It used to be said that the first use of *ecclesia* for a building occurs in the *Chronicle of Edessa* (a small 'native' state on the frontier of the empire in N.E. Syria) for the year A.D. 201, when 'the *ecclesia* of the christians' there was damaged by a flood. But the authenticity of this passage in this chronicle has been challenged. In any case Edessa was the first state officially to adopt christianity as the religion of all its citizens; its first christian king is said to have been baptised in A.D. 206. The tendencies which produced church buildings elsewhere in the late third and fourth centuries were therefore at work in Edessa in the later second century.

to be confused with the eucharist). But these gatherings were never called
'*ecclesia*', 'the general assembly and church of the first-born',[1] as the
Epistle to the Hebrews terms it, but *syneleuseis* or 'meetings'. The distinction between them lay partly in the corporate all-inclusive nature of
the *ecclesia*, which every christian had a right and a duty to attend; whereas
the *syneleuseis* were groups of christian friends and acquaintances. The
phrase is constant in early christian authors from S. Paul onwards that the
*ecclesia* is a 'coming together *epi to auto*', (or *eis to hen*) not merely 'in one
place', but almost in a technical sense, of the 'general assembly'. But above
all what distinguished the liturgical *ecclesia* from even the largest private
meeting was the official presence of the *liturgical* ministry, the bishop,
presbyters and deacons, and their exercise there of those special 'liturgical'
functions in which they were irreplaceable. 'Without these it is not called
an *ecclesia*'.[2]

We get a vivid little side-light on such 'private meetings' of christian
groups for prayer and instruction in the contemporary record (from shorthand notes taken in court) of the cross-examination of the christian layman
S. Justin, during the trial which ended in his martyrdom (A.D. 165).

'Rusticus, Prefect of Rome, asked: "Where do you meet?" Justin said,
"Where each one chooses and can. Do you really suppose we all meet in
the same place (*epi to auto*)? It is not so at all. For because the God of
christians is not circumscribed by place, but is invisible and fills all
heaven and earth, He is worshipped and glorified by the faithful anywhere." Rusticus the Prefect said, "Tell me, where do you meet, or in
what place do you collect your disciples?" Justin said, "This is my second
stay in Rome, and I have lodgings above one Martin by the baths of
Timothy; and the whole time I have known no other meeting-place
(*syneleusis*) but this. And if any one desired instruction from me, I have
been accustomed there to impart to him the teachings of the truth."
Rusticus the Prefect said, "Well then, are you a christian?" Justin said,
"Yes, I am a christian." '[3]

This confession sealed Justin's fate, and the Prefect turns at once to the
examination of the little group of six men and one woman arrested with
him in his lodgings, who also confessed and shared his martyrdom. But
Justin in his answers is deliberately hedging behind the word *syneleusis*, to
avoid imperilling the *ecclesia* by revealing its meeting place. Ten years
before his arrest he had described in his *Apology* (65) how the catechumen
was brought from the private instructions in which he had been prepared
for baptism to where 'the brethren have their *synaxis*' (public meeting)
for the eucharist and first communion; and how (67) 'On the day which is
called Sunday there is a general (*epi to auto*) meeting of all who live in the

---

[1] Heb. xii. 23.
[2] S. Ignatius (second bishop of Antioch in Syria, martyred c. A.D. 115), *Epistle to
the church of Tralles*, iii. 1.
[3] *Acta Justini* iii.

cities or the countryside', for the liturgical synaxis and eucharist under the bishop.

It was at the *ecclesia*—in 'the church'—alone that a christian could fulfil his personal 'liturgy', that divinely-given personal part in *the* corporate act of the church, the eucharist which expressed before God the vital being of the church and each of its members. The greatest emphasis was always laid upon the duty of being present at this, for which no group-meeting could be a substitute. Thus S. Ignatius writes to the christians of Magnesia in Asia Minor, 'as the Lord did nothing without the Father . . . so neither do you anything without the bishop and presbyters. And attempt not to suppose anything to be right for yourselves apart (from others). But at the general meeting (*epi to auto*) let there be one prayer, one supplication, one mind, one hope, in love and joy unblameable. . . . Be zealous to come together, all of you, as to one temple, even God; as to one altar, even to one Jesus Christ. . . .'[1] So he writes to the church of Philadelphia, 'Be careful to observe one eucharist, for there is one Flesh of our Lord Jesus Christ and one Cup unto union in His Blood; there is one altar, as there is one bishop together with the presbytery and the deacons'.[2]

We shall meet again this insistence on a single eucharistic assembly of the whole church, bishop, presbyters, deacons and laity together. This always remained the ideal, until it was finally lost to sight in the later middle ages. But the growth of numbers and the size of the great cities early made it impossible to fulfil it in practice; and Ignatius already recognises that the bishop may have to delegate his 'special liturgy' to others at minor eucharistic assemblies: 'Let that be accounted a valid eucharist which is either under the bishop or under one to whom the bishop has assigned this'.[3] The last church to abandon the tradition of a single eucharist under the bishop as at least an ideal was the church of the city of Rome. There the Pope's 'stational mass' at which he was assisted by representatives of the whole clergy and laity of the city continued as the central eucharistic observance right down to the fourteenth century, and did not wholly die out until 1870. Of course there were other celebrations simultaneously in the 'Titles' or parish churches. But for centuries it was the custom at Rome to despatch to each of these by an acolyte the *fermentum*, a fragment from the Breads consecrated by the Pope at 'the' eucharist of the whole church, to be placed in the Chalice at every parish eucharist, in token that each of these was still in Ignatius' phrase, 'under the bishop', as the 'liturgy' of the presbyter to whom 'the bishop had assigned' it.

The fact that the whole church or a very large part of it was expected to be present at the weekly Sunday *ecclesia* forced the church from the outset

---

[1] Ignatius, *Ep. to Magnesians*, vii. 1 and 2 (A.D. 115).
[2] Ignatius, *Ep. to Philadelphians*, iv. 1.
[3] Ignatius, *Ep. to Smyrnaeans*, viii. 1. (N.B. The bishop or his delegate is not yet thought of as the 'celebrant' of the eucharist, which is the act of the whole church 'under' the presidency of the bishop.)

to hold this in the houses of its wealthier members, for there alone could it be accommodated in a domestic setting. Certain families of Roman nobles had been attracted to the church, and even, perhaps, furnished martyrs for the faith, before the end of the first century. And fortunately the great Roman mansion of the period offered in its traditional lay-out certain arrangements not found in the tenements in which the mass of the population lived, which precisely suited the needs of the church.

The domestic apartments of the noble family were a modern addition to the traditional scheme of old Roman houses, and lay at the back of the palace. With typical Roman conservatism the front half of the patrician great house in the first century retained for its public rooms the exact ground-plan of the peasant's hut of the first Latin settlements twelve or fifteen hundred years before, though, of course, immensely enlarged and embellished. The entrance hall (*vestibulum*) led to a large pillared hall, the *atrium*, which was always lighted by skylights or open to the air in the centre. This formed, as it were, a broad nave with narrow aisles. At the further end from the entrance, and generally forming a dais up one or two steps, was a further room, open along its whole front to the *atrium*; this inner room was known as the *tablinum*. The central part of this (forming a sort of chancel) was separated from its side-portions, the *alae* or 'wings' (= choir-aisles) by low walls or pierced screens. Behind the *tablinum* a further door led to the private apartments and domestic quarters of the house.

The *tablinum* represents the original log-cabin of the primitive settler, with a lean-to (the *alae*) on either side. The *atrium* was the old fore-court or farmyard, roofed over—(*atrium displuviatum* = 'fore-court sheltered from the rain' was its full name)—and the rooms which opened off it at the sides represented the old farm-buildings and sheds of the steading. But the intense conservatism of the Roman patricians preserved more than the mere plan of their ancestral huts; it rigorously kept up the memory of their primitive fittings. Let into the floor of the *atrium* was always a large tank of water, the *impluvium*, representing the original well or pond beside which the farm had been built. Between this and the entrance to the *tablinum* there stood always a fixed stone table, the *cartibulum*, the 'chopping-block' outside the door of the hut.

The *tablinum*, the original home, was revered as the family shrine, even though it was also used as a reception room. There in a pagan household was the sacred hearth; there stood the altar of the *Lares* and *Penates*, the ancestral spirits and the gods of hearth and home. There at the marriage of the heir was placed the nuptial bed from which the old line should be continued. When the whole patrician clan met in family conclave or for family rites, there was placed the great chair of the *paterfamilias*, the head of the clan, and around him sat the heads of the junior branches, while the younger members and dependents stood assembled facing them in the *atrium*. On the walls of the *alae* and the *atrium* were hung the trophies and portraits of generation upon generation of nobles who in the past had brought honour to the name and house.

Here ready to hand was the ideal setting for the church's 'domestic' worship at the eucharist, in surroundings which spoke for themselves of the noblest traditions of family life. The quaint old images of the household gods and their altar must go, of course, along with the sacred hearth and its undying fire. All else was exactly what was needed. The chair of the *pater-familias* became the bishop's throne; the heads of families were replaced by the presbyters, and the clansmen by the laity, the members of the household of God. Virgins and widows and any others for whom it might be desirable to avoid the crowding in the *atrium* could be placed behind the screens of the *alae*. At the back near the door, where the clients and slaves of the patrician house—attached to it but not of it—had once stood at its assemblies, were now to be found the catechumens and enquirers, attached to the church but not yet members of it. The place of the stone table was that of the christian altar; the tank of the *impluvium* would serve for the solemn immersion of baptism in the presence of the whole church. When the 'candidates' ( = 'clothed in white') emerged, they could dry in one of the side rooms; and then, clothed in the white linen garments they received after baptism in token that they had entered the kingdom of God[1], they were led straight to the bishop to receive the unction of confirmation. This was what actually made them members of the 'order' of laity, with whom they would henceforward stand in the *ecclesia*. The dining room of the house (*triclinium*) which usually opened off the *atrium* could be used when needed for the christian 'love-feast' (*agape* or 'the Lord's supper'; by the second century this had lost its original connection with the eucharist, if indeed it had much connection with it even in later apostolic times).[2]

The only addition to the furnishings of such a house which christian worship required was a raised pulpit or reading-desk from which the lector could make the lessons heard, and on the steps of which the soloists could stand to sing. (Hence the name 'gradual' for the oldest chant of the liturgy, the psalm between the epistle and gospel lections, from *gradus* = 'a step'). Beside the lectern at vigil services was placed a large lamp-stand or else a great taper, to give light to the lector. It was the business of the deacon as the general 'servant of the church' to place this ready burning, or to light it and bless it, when it was required. This blessing of the lamp is a survival of jewish practice into christian worship. The chief continuing survival of this originally utilitarian ritual is seen to-day in the paschal candle of the Roman rite, which the deacon still lights and blesses beside the lectern at the beginning of the Easter vigil service on Holy Saturday.[3]

[1] *Cf.* Rev. iv. 5; vii. 9; xix. 14.          [2] *Cf. p.* 260.
[3] The symbolic blessing of fire which now precedes the deacon's blessing of the vigil light is a late (eleventh cent.) intrusion into the Roman rite, from Gallican

Thus christian worship was normally carried out during the centuries of persecution, not by any means in the secrecy and squalor which is popularly associated with 'the catacombs', though in the strict privacy and seclusion which Roman tradition attached to the home. The surroundings might indeed have about them not a little grandeur in the great atrium of a Roman palace with its marbles and mosaics and rich metal furnishings. We get a vivid little picture of the possibilities of such domestic worship even in much less impressive surroundings from the official report of the seizure of the christian place of worship at Cirta[1] in North Africa, at the beginning of the last great persecution in A.D. 303. It happens to have survived because the report of the occasion officially filed in the municipal archives was put in as evidence in a *cause célèbre* in the African courts half a generation later.

'In the viiith consulship of Diocletian and the viith of Maximian on the xivth day before the Kalends of June (May 19th, 303 A.D.) from the official acts of Munatus Felix, high-priest (of the emperor) for life and Warden of the Colony of the Cirtensians.

'Upon arrival at the house where the christians customarily met, Felix, high-priest etc. said to the bishop Paul: "Bring forth the scriptures of your law and anything else you have here, as has been ordered by the edict, that you may carry out the law." Paul the bishop said: "The lectors have the scriptures, but we surrender what we have got here." Felix, high-priest etc. said to Paul the bishop: "Point out the lectors or send for them." Paul etc. said: "You know who they all are." Felix etc. said: "We do not know them." Paul etc. said: "Your staff know them, that is Edusius and Junius the notary clerks." Felix etc. said: "Leaving aside the question of the lectors, whom my staff will identify, surrender what you have here." Paul the bishop sat down, with Montanus and Victor of Deüsatelium and Memorius the presbyters, the deacons Mars and Helios standing by him, Marcuclius, Catullinus, Silvanus and Carosus the subdeacons, Januarius, Maracius, Fructuosus, Miggin, Saturninus, Victor and the other sextons standing present, and Victor of Aufidum writing before them the inventory thus:

> 2 golden chalices
> *item* 6 silver chalices
> *item* 6 silver dishes
> *item* a silver bowl
> *item* 7 silver lamps
> *item* 2 torches
> *item* 7 short bronze candlesticks with their lamps
> *item* 11 bronze lamps with their chains

sources, of a ceremony already in use at Jerusalem before the end of the fourth century. The original Roman beginning of the vigil is the practical one of getting a light to hold the service by.

[1] Now Constantine, in Algeria.

*item* 82 women's tunics[1]
*item* 38 veils
*item* 16 men's tunics
*item* 13 pairs of men's slippers
*item* 47 pairs of women's slippers
*item* 18 pairs of clogs[2]

Felix etc. said to Marcuclius, Silvanus and Carosus the sextons, "Bring out all you have here." Silvanus and Carosus said: "We have brought out everything which was here." Felix etc. said: "Your answer has been taken down in evidence." After the cupboards in the bookcase were found to be empty, Silvanus brought out a silver casket and a silver candlestick, which he said he had found behind a jug. Victor of Aufidum said to Silvanus: "You would have been a dead man if you had not managed to find those." Felix etc. said to Silvanus: "Look more carefully, that nothing be left here." Silvanus said: "Nothing is left, we have brought it all out." And when the dining room (*triclinium*) was opened, there were found there four baskets and six casks. Felix etc. said: "Bring out whatever scriptures you have got, and comply with the imperial edict and my enforcement of it." Catullinus brought out one very large book. Felix etc. said to Marcuclius and Silvanus: "Why do you only bring out a single book? Bring out all the scriptures you have got." Catullinus and Marcuclius said: "We have no more because we are subdeacons. The lectors keep the books." Felix etc. said to them: "Identify the lectors." They said: "We do not know where they are." Felix etc. said to them: "If you don't know where they are, tell us their names." Catullinus and Marcuclius said: "We are not informers. Here we stand. Command us to be executed." Felix said: "Put them under arrest." '

The account goes on in the same meticulous photographic detail, recorded in the shorthand of the public slave standing behind Felix, to recount the search of the lectors' houses. Every word, every action is pitilessly noted, so that each man's exact responsibility can be fixed if the record ever has to be produced in court; how one lector was a tailor; how the schoolmaster, evidently the copyist of the local church, was found with two books and some loose quires still unbound; how the wife of one of the lectors surrendered six books lest her absent husband be accused of hiding them; and how the public slave nicknamed 'The Ox' was sent in to search her house and see if he could find more, and reported 'I have searched and found nothing.' The veil of the centuries seldom wears so thin as in that piercing moment when Paul the bishop silently sat down, for the last time, on his episcopal throne; and his presbyters came and sat around him as usual, and the deacons took their stand on either side—almost automatically—as they had done so often at mass, to watch the heathen high-priest

---

[1] These and the following items are for use at solemn baptism.
[2] I have no idea what these were for. Perhaps for baptism, or possibly some christian had left them there to be called for later.

pile together before their eyes the sacramental vessels which their own hands had handled. And the level voice of the clerk Victor of Aufidum making the inventory goes on—'Two gold chalices—six silver chalices—six silver dishes— . . .'

They sat through it all in silence, even when the two subdeacons made their gallant useless refusal to betray men whose names were already perfectly well known. What could they have said? To have surrendered the scriptures and the sacred vessels was 'apostasy', still for clerics (though not for laymen) the irremissible sin, for which there was no possible penance. And they knew it; Felix knew it; even the grinning public slaves knew it. They had saved their lives—but they had all irremediably forfeited their orders in that quarter of an hour. I know no more moving picture of the inner meaning of the persecutions than that shamefaced helpless group of apostate African clergy with the uncouth Berber names—the men who were not martyrs—as the public slave saw them across the shoulders of their enemies and jotted down their actions on that hot May afternoon sixteen centuries ago.

What is more to our immediate purpose, the church of Cirta was a small church in an unimportant provincial town. It had not yet needed to build itself a basilica as many of the more thriving churches had done or begun to do in the later third century, but still worshipped in the old way in a converted private house. The majority of its clergy were quite evidently 'of the people.' But they had a collection of church plate which few parish churches in England at the present day could rival.

Though outside Rome the domestic setting was not always so apt, the arrangements did not greatly vary. When in the third century times grew easier in most places, and church buildings became needful and possible, the model usually seems to have been furnished by the private house and not the pagan temple or the jewish synagogue.[1] When the end wall of the *tablinum* no longer masked the domestic half of the house it was found more convenient to build it in a semi-circle, following the curve of the presbyters' seats. But this was in fact a development which had already been anticipated in some private houses in the second century, which already have semi-circular *tablina*. The plan of the basilica with an apse which was thus formed had been coming into general use for various public buildings for some time. The *alae*, which even in private houses often

[1] The first exception is found in Constantine's churches at Jerusalem and Bethlehem, built between A.D. 320 and 330, which were modelled on Syrian pagan sanctuaries. But the only certainly pre-Nicene christian church in the East yet found, at Dura-Europos in Mesopotamia (c. A.D. 230), was a converted private house. For other types see G. Bagnani, *Journal of Roman Studies* ix (1919), pp. 78 sqq.; G. Leroux, *Les Origines de l'edifice hypostyle* (Paris, 1913), pp. 318 sqq.; R. Viellard, *Les Origines du titre de S. Martin aux Monts à Rome* (*Studi di antichità cristiana*, iv), Rome, 1931; and, for the different history of the North of Europe and the Central and Northern Balkans the work of J. Strzygowski, esp. *Early Church Art in Northern Europe* (London, 1928).

extended in a right angle beyond the oblong sides of the *atrium* (*cf.* plan) would one day grow into transepts. The extension of the *tablinum* would form the great choir and sanctuary of the cruciform Gothic churches. The constructional difficulties of joining four separate pitched roofs at a centre were solved by the capping of the whole building, in the East with a dome, in the less skilful West with a tower. There in the briefest outline is the history of the ground plan of the christian church. But its roots, like the roots of the worship it was built to shelter, are in the home and not in the temple.

At Rome the old domestic worship of the house-churches in a sense survived even the definitive end of the persecutions. In the fourth century some of the old christian families in whose homes the 'church' had been sheltered for so long, made over their mansions to house the new christian public worship. Interior changes were made in the way of knocking down party walls and so on. More appropriate decorations were laid on. The portraits of grim Etruscan and Latin ancestors were replaced by mosaics of the Old Testament worthies and the christian saints, the forerunners and most distinguished members of the 'household of God'; or, as at S. Paul's outside the walls, by medallions of the whole line of Roman bishops, the successive heads of the christian family. But the structure of the old houses remained. Thus the Roman basilica of SS. John and Paul still presents the exterior façade of the third century palace of the Senator Byzantius with its windows filled in; and on the roof is still the fourth century tiling, laid on when he gave it to be adapted for the new public way of worship. So at the basilica of S. Clement excavations have revealed three stages one above the other. Below the ground is what seems to be part of the first century Roman palace from which in January A.D. 96 the prince Titus Flavius Clemens, the father of the heirs-presumptive to the imperial throne, went out to die for the 'foreign superstition' to which his wife Domitilla certainly, and he himself probably, had given their allegiance. Here S. Peter is reputed to have preached, and here certainly Pope S. Clement before the end of the first century must have done his 'liturgy' at the eucharist in the way of which he wrote to the Corinthians.[1] Above this house of memories has been found the fourth century basilica of which S. Jerome writes, and which saw the condemnation of the doctrines of the British heretic Pelagius in the years when Rome was falling and the barbarians were at last within the gates. Above that again, on the same site and plan, is the lovely twelfth century church we see to-day, furnished with much that was preserved from the earlier fourth century church.

### The Worshippers

'As we have many members' says S. Paul, 'in one body, and all members have not the same office; so we being many are one body in Christ, and are

[1] *Cf. p.* 1.

every one members one of another; having spiritual gifts (*charismata*) differing according to the grace (*charis*) that is given us.'[1] 'Office' or 'function' in the body of Christ can only be fulfilled by a special spiritual effect (*charisma*) of the grace (*charis*) of the 'Spirit' of Christ. The 'orders' in the church exercised their 'spiritual gifts' each in its own 'office' or 'liturgy', to complete the living act of the whole Body of Christ towards God. That, briefly, is the eucharist and its performance.

The arrangement of the 'church' or 'assembly' was simple; the bishop sat upon his throne, which was covered with a white linen cloth, in the *tablinum*, facing the people across the altar; the presbyters sat on either hand in a semi-circle; the deacons stood, one on either side of the throne, the rest either at the head of the people before the altar or scattered among them maintaining order; some of the subdeacons and their assistants, the acolytes, guarded the doors; the others assisted the deacons in their various duties. The laity stood, facing the bishop, the men on one side, the women on the other. The catechumens and strangers stood by themselves at the back.

When this arrangement of the assembly was first adopted is unknown. But it must have been well within the first century, for not only is it the absolutely universal later traditional arrangement, but it is clearly reflected in the symbolism of the heavenly 'assembly' of the church triumphant—the real 'assembly' of which all earthly churches are only symbols and foreshadowings—in the visions of the Revelation of S. John, which was published probably in A.D. 93. In this book everything centres upon 'the golden altar which is before the throne of God'. Before it stands the multitude, 'which no man can number', of the redeemed. Everywhere are the ministering angels. And the four and twenty elders of heaven have their seats in a semi-circle around the 'great white throne of God and the Lamb', as the earthly presbyters have their seats around the white-clothed throne of the bishop. It seems probable that it is the symbolism of the book which has been suggested by the current practice of the church in the first century and not *vice versa*, because the arrangement described was that which was traditional in churches which disputed the inspiration and canonicity of the Apocalypse (about whose authority and authorship there was doubt even in the third century).

Thus when S. Ignatius speaks of the bishop as 'enthroned as the type of God, and the presbyters as the type of the college of the apostles, and the deacons entrusted with the deaconship of Jesus Christ'[2] he is referring to that same eucharistic ordering of the church which we find already presupposed in the Apocalypse.

The particular comparisons which Ignatius finds apt here for the three orders, and which he repeats some twenty times in seven short epistles, strike modern students as a surprising choice. When we think about it we

---

[1] Rom. xii. 4–6.        [2] Ignatius, *Epist. to the Magnesians*, vi. 1 (A.D. 115).

can readily recognise the force of likening the deacons, whom he elsewhere describes as 'the servants of the *ecclesia*'[1], to our Lord, Who was among us 'as he that serveth',[2] even though that is hardly our normal way of regarding the diaconate. But, doubtless under the influences of ideas about the Apostolic Succession, we should in practice probably be more likely to compare the collective *episcopate* than the collective presbyterate to the 'college of the apostles'—a comparison which Ignatius never makes, and of which he apparently has no idea. And while we recognise in theory that the individual bishop has the final pastoral and priestly responsibility for souls throughout his diocese and that the parish priest is only his delegate, yet bishops are in practice so remote from the spiritual life of their flocks that it is the individual presbyter of whom we naturally think as representing to his people the pastoral and priestly office of our Lord, the true Shepherd and High-priest of all christians. But there is in the difference between our usage and that which Ignatius represents (and which is by no means confined to him among early writers) much more than a mere consequence of the exchange of functions between bishop and presbyter, which came about in the fourth century with the growth of numbers and the consequent impossibility of direct episcopal pastoral care for a large diocese.

The comparison which Ignatius does make, of the bishop to 'God the Father', is apt to strike us as strange if not extravagant. It has no parallel at all in our conception of the relation of any of the three orders to the church. But it is the whole point of his illustration, and the difference of outlook involved is significant of a profound difference in our way of regarding the church, and consequently amongst other things the eucharist.

In the idea of Ignatius, and of the primitive writers generally, it is *the church as a whole*, and not any one order in it, which not so much 'represents' as 'is' Christ on earth. Our Lord had repeatedly identified Himself with *all* who should be His. The recognition of Him in His members is to be His own supreme test for His followers at the judgment: 'Inasmuch as ye did it unto one of the least of these My brethren, ye did it unto Me.'[3] S. Paul had systematised this teaching of our Lord Himself into the doctrine of the church as 'the Body of Christ', and all christians as His 'members in particular'. The primitive church took this conception with its fullest force, and pressed it with a rigour which is quite foreign to our weakened notions. The *whole church* prayed in the Person of Christ; the *whole church* was charged with the office of 'proclaiming' the revelation of Christ; the *whole church* offered the eucharist as the 're-calling' before God and man of the offering of Christ. All that which He has done once for all as the Priest and Proclaimer of the kingship of God, the church which is 'the fulfilment of Him'[4] enters into and fulfils. Christ and His church are

[1] *Ep. to Trallians*, ii. 1.
[2] Matt. xxv. 40.
[3] Luke xx. 27. lit. 'he that deaconeth.'
[4] Eph. i. 23.

one, with one mission, one life, one prayer, one gospel, one offering, one being, one Father. Such a conception left little room for regarding one order in the church, whether bishop or presbyter, as in any exclusive sense the representative of Christ *to* the church; even though the deacons might be described as 'entrusted with the ministry' of Christ in the special aspect of its humility. On this view the church as a whole represents or rather 'is' Christ. 'Do you all follow your bishop', writes Ignatius to the church of Smyrna, 'as Jesus Christ followed the Father.'[1]

If the bishop had a special representative function it must therefore be as the 'father of the family' of God, 'from whom the whole family in heaven and earth is named.'[2] (So we find the real point of the requirement for a good bishop that he must be, 'One that presideth well over his own family keeping his children well-ordered in all good behaviour; for if a man know not how to preside over his own household, how shall he bear the care of the *ecclesia* of God?'[3]) It was, in our still surviving phrase, as 'father in God' that the bishop sat enthroned as 'the image of God'[4] and the 'type of the Father';[5] to whom his presbyters were bidden to 'defer, not so much unto himself, but unto the Father of Jesus Christ, the bishop of all';[6] whom if a layman disregarded, 'he doth not so much deceive this bishop who is seen, as deceive himself about that One Who is invisible.'[7] Even in the act of distributing holy communion, where if anywhere we should feel that the bishop-celebrant most obviously filled the place of our Lord Himself, the primitive church was able to see the matter otherwise. In the Johannine conception of the eucharist, '*My Father* giveth you the true bread from heaven.'[8] And it is in fact this Johannine conception, and not the Synoptic concentration on the Body and Blood, which reveals itself in the oldest formula of administration which has come down to us: 'And when the bishop breaks the Bread, in distributing to each a fragment he shall say: "The Bread of Heaven in Christ Jesus." '[9]

But however clear the understanding of the whole matter in this way might be, there was in practice another side to it. The throne of the bishop was in reality—as the Apocalypse expressed it—'the throne of God *and* the Lamb.'[10] The bishop represented God revealing, but also God redeeming. He had really a double relation to his church, and a twofold 'liturgy' as prophet and priest, of which only one half could be quite satisfactorily attributed to him as the representative of the Father. This comes out clearly in the terms in which S. Hippolytus describes the special 'office' or 'liturgy' of the bishop in a work written *c.* A.D. 230. The language of this

[1]Ignatius, *Ep. to Smyrnaeans*, viii. 1.    [2]Eph. iii. 15.
[3] 1 Tim. iii. 4 and 5.
[4] *Clementine Homilies*, iii. 62. (A fourth century Syrian work.)
[5] Ignatius, *Ep. to Trallians*, iii. 1.    [6] Ignatius, *Ep. to Magnesians*, iii. 1
[7] Ignatius, *Ep. to Magnesians*, iii. 2.    [8] John vi. 32.
[9] Hippolytus, *Ap. Trad.*, xxiii. 5. (Rome, *c.* A.D. 215.)
[10] Rev. xxii. 3.

writer can be shewn to agree entirely with the conceptions held by S. Clement *c.* A.D. 96, though the latter never clarifies his notion of the episcopate quite in this way by a brief definition. Hippolytus writes, 'Peing found successors of the apostles, and partakers with them of the same grace (*charis*) of high-priesthood and the teaching office, and reckoned watchmen of the church.'[1] Hippolytus here regards priesthood and teaching as the two aspects of the special grace of the Holy Ghost given in episcopal consecration.[2] But it was more than a mere matter of practice that the bishop's 'liturgy' of teaching was exercised actually sitting upon the throne, while that of priesthood was fulfilled away from the throne and standing at the altar; even though as priest he still faced the people as God's representative, and did not stand with his back to them as their leader. The bishop unmistakeably spoke *to* the church for God as prophet and teacher; but he spoke *for* the church to God in the eucharistic prayer, however clearly it might be understood that the eucharist was the act of the whole church. There was here an aspect of his office which would one day make of the eucharist in practice something which was rather the act of the celebrant on behalf of the church than the act of the church as a whole.

The power of prophecy no less than the power of priesthood was conveyed in the bishop's ordination. Passages are numerous which refer to this special grace of 'teaching' as a unique sacramental endowment of his office, and not as an exercise of such intellectual powers as he might possess. 'We ought', advises Irenaeus, 'to hearken to those elders who are in the *ecclesia*, to those who have the succession from the apostles, who with the succession in the episcopate have received the *unfailing spiritual gift of the truth* (*charisma veritatis certum*) according to the *Father's* good pleasure. But others who are outside the original succession, and who hold meetings where they can, we ought to hold suspect as being either heretics and men of evil doctrine, or else as creating a schism and self-important and self-pleasing, or again as hypocrites, doing what they do for the sake of gain and vain-glory.'[3] It was as an *inspired* teacher 'according to the *Father's* good-pleasure' that the bishop taught from the 'throne' or *cathedra*—the official 'chair' of his church which he shared with no one else but inherited from all his dead predecessors back to the first apostolic missionaries to that church. The bishop's 'throne' is not so much a seat of government (he is not the 'ruler' but the 'watchman' of his church according to Hippolytus' definition above) as a 'teacher's chair'; 'for the *cathedra*', says Irenaeus, 'is the symbol of teaching.'[4]

The bishop's chair is nevertheless 'the throne of God *and* the Lamb',

---

[1] Hippolytus, *Philosophumena*, i. 1. (Rome, *c.* A.D. 230.)
[2] *Cf.* the very similar language used in his prayer for the consecration of a bishop. *Ap. Trad.*, iii.
[3] Irenaeus of Lyons, *c.* A.D. 180. *Adv. Haer.*, iv. 26. 2. (Note the old distinction between the *ecclesia* and other gatherings.)
[4] Irenaeus, *Demonstration of the Apostolic Preaching*, ii.

because the bishop is by his office both prophet and priest. It is true that as
prophetic teacher he chiefly represents the Father, God revealing Himself.
But even here it is by the Son that the Father reveals Himself—'Jesus
Christ, the unerring mouth in Whom the Father hath spoken',[1] as Ignatius
says. It is remarkable that he goes on immediately for almost the only time
to compare the bishop with the Son: 'Remember in your prayers the church
which is in Syria, which hath God for its bishop in my place. Jesus Christ
alone shall be its bishop—He and your love.' As teacher of the church the
bishop presided throughout the synaxis from his throne. As high-priest
(not priest) he presided over the eucharist at the altar. Here comparison of
the bishop's 'liturgy' with the office of the Son became, as we have seen,
inevitable. What we have already said forbids us to make too rigid a distinction between his representation of the Father at the synaxis, and of the
Son at the eucharist respectively. But once the celebrant had come round to
the front of the altar[2] the tendency was to regard him first as the leader and
then as the representative of the 'priestly people of God'; and finally as the
exclusive celebrant, and in his own person the representative of Christ to
the people.

When the time came for the church openly to signify in the ornament of
her new church-buildings the inner meaning of her symbolism, the throne
of the bishop in the apse was still recognised as representing 'the throne of
God and the Lamb.' But there was a natural reluctance to figure above it
the Person of the invisible Father, though it is surprising how many of the
old mosaics do contain somewhere, under the form of a Hand pointing
from a nimbus or some such symbol, a reminder of this aspect of the
primitive office of the bishop who sat below.[3] But inevitably the representation concentrated on the figure of the Son, Who is 'the express image'
of the Father.[4] Here the traditions of East and West began to diverge. In
the East it is the figure of Christ the *Pantocrator* ( = Ruler of all things)—
'unto Me all power is given in heaven and in earth'[5]—as 'the image and
glory of God',[6] which dominates the mosaic decorations of the apse above
the throne—still God revealing. In the Western basilicas it is more usually
the figure of the Lamb of God—God redeeming—which is set above the
throne in the apse. He is at first represented in His triumphant nuptials
with the church,[7] later on as 'the Lamb slain from the foundation of
the world.'[8] By a not unnatural development this latter was eventually trans-

<hr/>

[1] *Ep. to the Romans*, viii. and ix.
[2] This change took place in the East at large between the fourth and fifth centuries, and in the West in the eighth–tenth centuries. It had originally no particular
reason beyond that of fashion and convenience.
[3] The last survival of the early tradition is found in mediaeval England, where a
painting of the Three Persons of the Trinity often occupied the apex of the chancel
arch, which is architecturally the same feature of the building as the arch of the
apse in a basilica.
[4] 2 Cor. iv. 4 and Heb. 1. 3.          [5] Matt. xxviii. 18.
[6] 1 Cor. xi. 7.          [7] Rev. xix. 7.          [8] Rev. xiii. 8.

formed into a 'realistic' crucifix.[1] As the long Romanesque and Gothic choirs grew out of the short apse of the basilica, and the art of mosaics declined in the West, the crucifix came to be set as a carved figure within the arch and not above it—the great Rood of our mediaeval churches. There are no breaks in the liturgical tradition in these things—only a continual evolution. Those who have most deeply pondered the different genius of the Eastern and Western rites of the eucharist will most readily seize the significance of these two different evolutions in the central *motif* of the decoration of the church, alike for eucharistic theology, for liturgical ethos and for devotional approach to the sacrament itself. But this divergence of symbols is in itself only a symptom and not a cause of divergent theological tendencies, which were there in the Eastern and Western churches from at least the third century. The important point for our immediate purpose is that in East and West alike the later symbolism represents a *change* from the original conception of the bishop's office as representative of the Father.

*The Presbyters.* We have seen that Hippolytus calls the bishop 'the watchman' or 'guardian' of the church, but not its ruler. Government is in fact the special province of the corporate Sanhedrin of presbyters of which the bishop is president. He has initiative, leadership, the prestige of his office, and a responsibility for the well-being of the church in every way. But administrative decisions largely depend upon his carrying most of his presbyters with him. The bishop is ordained as prophet and priest. The presbyter is ordained 'to share in the presbyterate and govern Thy people in a pure heart'[2] in concert with the bishop and all his fellow presbyters. As such he has need of 'the Spirit of grace and counsel' which the prayer at his ordination asks for him, for the government of the People of God even on its mundane side is not a merely secular office (*cf.* the Judges of Israel). But *qua* presbyter he has no strictly liturgical functions at all, whereas the bishop has almost a liturgical and sacramental monopoly as '*high*-priest' of the whole 'priestly' body, the church. Though Clement, to carry through his analogy of the eucharistic assembly with the sacrifices of the Old Testament, styles the presbyters 'priests', he is careful not to say that they have a 'special liturgy' like the bishop or the deacons, but only their own 'special *place*', in the semi-circle of seats around the throne.[3] Yet

---

[1] Realistic representations of the crucifixion are not, as is sometimes supposed, a Western innovation. They appear for the first time in christian art in S.E. Asia Minor during the sixth century and spread thence to the West by way of Constantinople during the eighth–ninth centuries, becoming common in the West only during the twelfth–thirteenth centuries. The crucifix crowned and robed seems to be a compromise between the old Eastern figure of the *Pantocrator* and the new Eastern figure of the crucifix. It is found in the West chiefly in the tenth–eleventh centuries.

[2] Hippolytus, *Ap. Trad.*, viii. 2 (Prayer for the ordination of a presbyter). Rome, c. A.D. 215. *Cf. Ap. Trad.*, iii (Prayer for the consecration of a bishop).

[3] I Clem. 40, cited *p*. I.

when sub-division of the eucharistic assembly became necessary by growth of numbers, a presbyter was the obvious delegate for the bishop's liturgical functions at the minor eucharists. And we have seen that such were already necessary even in Ignatius' time (c. A.D. 115), though the first explicit mention of a presbyter celebrating apart from the bishop is found only in the middle of the third century in the Decian persecution at Carthage.[1] The fact that the presbyter could be called upon to preside at the eucharist in the absence of the bishop led to his being given a share in the bishop's eucharistic 'liturgy' at the *ecclesia* when he was present with the bishop. During the second century, between Clement and Hippolytus, we find that a custom had grown up that presbyters should 'concelebrate' with him, joining with him in the imposition of hands on the oblation after the offertory and consecrating Breads upon the altar beside him, or at their places in the apse behind him, on glass patens held up before them by the deacons, while the bishop said the eucharistic prayer.[2]

Yet it is true that the presbyter only acquires liturgical functions by degrees, and then rather as the bishop's representative than as his assistant. It is in the fourth century, when the peace of the church and the immense growth of numbers had made it impossible for bishops in most places still to act as the only ministers of all sacraments to their churches, that we find the real change taking place in the functions of the presbyter. He becomes the permanent liturgical minister of a separate congregation, to whom he normally supplies most of those 'liturgies' of sacraments and teaching for which the pre-Nicene church had habitually looked to the bishop. After the middle of the fourth century we begin to find a change in the language used about the presbyter. He is referred to no longer as an 'elder', but as a 'priest' (*hiereus, sacerdos secundi ordinis*). The old feeling that the bishop is the real high-priest of his whole church still forbids the application to the presbyter of exactly the same term of 'high-priest' (*archiereus, sacerdos* without qualification). Thus 'priesthood', which had formerly been the function of all members of the church with the bishop as 'high-priest', becomes a special attribute of the second order of the ministry. On the other hand, the presbyterate by thus being split up into a number of individual liturgical deputies of the bishop has lost its old corporate character, and with it its old corporate governmental authority. The bishop absorbs more and more of its administrative authority, but in return parts with his liturgical monopoly. The only sacramental function he retains in his own hands is the bestowal of 'order' in the church—confirmation which admits to the order of the laity, and ordination which admits to the orders of deacon, presbyter or bishop.

*The Deacon.* The accepted derivation of this order from 'the Seven' who organised poor relief in the apostolic church at Jerusalem is uncertain, but they are certainly of apostolic origin.[3] They come into sight rather as the

---

[1] St. Cyprian, Bp. of Carthage, *Epistle* v. 2.          [2] *Ap. Trad.*, xxiv. 2.          [3] Phil. i. 1.

bishop's personal assistants in his liturgical and pastoral functions, but also as an order with functions of its own. It is as such that they minister the Chalice while he distributes the Bread, and read the gospel upon which he is to comment in his sermon. They are, as Ignatius describes them, 'not merely ministers of food and drink, but the servants of the *ecclesia*.'[1] As such, they have certain definite 'liturgies' and take quite a prominent part in the service, especially by announcing to the assembly what is to be done at each fresh stage of its progress. But by immemorial tradition they never directly address God on behalf of the church; that is the 'liturgy' of the bishop. The deacon, even in 'bidding' the prayers of the church, speaks *to the church*, not to God.

The 'minor orders' of subdeacon, lector, acolyte, which already existed about the year A.D. 200, were not yet reckoned definitely as 'orders' with an ordination by laying on of hands for a special grace of the Holy Ghost. They were 'appointments' made by the bishop to a particular duty which if necessary could be performed by any capable layman. The special character of the 'holy orders' which bishop, presbyter and deacon received is precisely the power and authority to fulfil a function in the *ecclesia* which a member of the general body of laity could not fulfil. In a regulation about the official 'widows', who formed both a special body of intercessors and a special object of charity in the church, Hippolytus lays it down: 'Let the widow be appointed by word only and let her then be reckoned among the (enrolled) widows. But she shall not be ordained, for she does not offer the oblation nor has she a "liturgy." But ordination is for the clergy on account of their "liturgy." But the widow is appointed for prayer, and this is (a function) of all.' [2]

We return, therefore, to the conception of the eucharist as the act of the whole Body of Christ through its many members, each with its own 'office', to use S. Paul's phrase, with which we began. It is the Spirit of Christ in the Body of Christ which alone empowers the members to fulfil their own special offices in that vital eucharistic act which is the life of the church. The layman receives this Spirit for his 'liturgy' by confirmation, the cleric for his special function by ordination. But to both alike it is the gift of grace to live their own part in the life of the Body; and this life is expressed corporately in what happens in the *ecclesia*. 'There are diversities of gifts, but the same Spirit; and there are differences of ministries but the same Lord; and there are diversities of operations but it is the same God which worketh all in all.'[3]

[1] Ignatius, *Ep. to Trallians*, ii. 1.      [2] Hippolytus, *Ap. Trad.*, xi. 4 and 5.
[3] 1 Cor. xii. 4–6.

# CHAPTER III

## THE CLASSICAL SHAPE OF THE LITURGY: (I) THE SYNAXIS

### Synaxis and Eucharist

THE primitive core of the liturgy falls into two parts—the *Synaxis* (a Greek word which means properly simply a 'meeting') and the *Eucharist* proper (or 'thanksgiving'). These were separate things, which had a different origin. The synaxis was in its Shape simply a continuation of the jewish synagogue service of our Lord's time, which was carried straight over into the christian church by its jewish nucleus in the decade after the passion. The eucharist on the contrary was of directly christian development; though this, too, had a jewish background in the passover sacrifice-meal, in the *kiddûsh* or religious meal of the household with which the sabbath and the great feasts began, and more particularly in the common meals with a devotional purpose held by jewish religious brotherhoods (*chabûrôth*). But whatever its jewish setting and pre-history may have been the christian eucharist as such derived from the last supper.

Originally synaxis and eucharist were separable, and either could be and frequently was held without the other. It happens that our earliest account of christian worship in any detail, in S. Justin's *Apology* (c. A.D. 155), describes the eucharist twice over. Once (67) it is preceded by the synaxis, and once (65) it is preceded only by the conferring of baptism. The next earliest witness, S. Hippolytus, in his *Apostolic Tradition* (c. A.D. 215) also describes the eucharist twice, once preceded by the consecration of a bishop (ii. and iii.) and once preceded by baptism and confirmation (xxi. and xxii.), but in neither case accompanied by the synaxis. In the fourth century they were still distinct and easily separable. In some churches down to the sixth century the typical eucharist of the year, that which commemorated the last supper, was still celebrated at dusk on Maundy Thursday without the synaxis (which had already been celebrated earlier in the day at noon followed by the eucharist) and began, as we should put it, with the offertory.[1] Even to this day the Roman missal affords on Good Friday an almost perfect specimen of the old Roman synaxis of the second century, followed on this occasion not by the eucharist but by the fourth century Syrian rite of the Veneration of the Cross and the second century service for communion from the reserved Sacrament.[2]

[1] *Cf. p.* 441.
[2] *Cf.* G. Dix. *The Mass of the Presanctified* (Church Literature Association, London).

However, despite their separate origin and different purpose, the synaxis normally preceded the eucharist in the regular Sunday worship of all churches in the second century. From the fourth century onwards the two were gradually fused, until they came everywhere to be considered inseparable parts of a single rite. We shall find that both their original distinction and their later fusion had at the time a true appropriateness to the contemporary situation and mission of the church in the world. Nevertheless, each part always retained the essentials of its own character, though less distinctly in the East than in the West. Thus it comes about that all over christendom the first part of the eucharistic action still revolves around the book of the scriptures[1] and not around the chalice and paten at all. Historically this still testifies to the purely jewish pre-christian origin of this part of the rite, though we shall find that there is a deeper reason than mere historical conservatism. Even so late a composition as the English Prayer Book of 1662 still never mentions holy communion at all until half the service which it calls 'The Administration of Holy Communion' is over, yet few communicants ask themselves why so strange a thing should be. But such is the force of unconscious liturgical tradition, even where it has suffered so considerable a disturbance as that involved in the recasting of our liturgy at the Reformation.

### The Synaxis, or Liturgy of the Spirit

The jewish synagogue service, which was the root from which the apostolic synaxis sprang, consisted of public readings from the scripture, the singing of psalms, a sermon and a number of set prayers. Rabbinic scholars are in disagreement as to whether the prayers came first or last in the synagogue of the first century A.D., and there is no direct evidence from that period as to what prayers were in use, though some extant jewish forms probably go back to this date. In the third century the jews undoubtedly placed them in a group at the beginning, and this may have been the original practice of the synagogue. But in all christian churches from the earliest moment at which we have definite evidence[2] the prayers were universally placed last, after the sermon, and have remained there ever since. This was evidently a fixed christian tradition. Either the later jewish practice differed from that usual in the jewish circles from which the apostolic church emerged; or conceivably, the christians deliberately changed the position of the prayers from motives we shall understand in a moment. If so, the change must have been made early and probably by apostolic authority, for later christian tradition to be so universal and firm on the point.

[1] Now bound up for convenience with the eucharistic prayers in the form of a missal or altar-book in the West, but still separate in the East.
[2] S. Justin, c. A.D. 155, for Rome; the *Didascalia* and Origen in the first half of the third century, for Syria and Egypt.

The original unchanging outline of the christian synaxis everywhere was as follows:—

1. Opening greeting by the officiant and reply of the church.
2. Lesson.
3. Psalmody.
4. Lesson (or Lessons, separated by Psalmody).
5. Sermon.
6. Dismissal of those who did not belong to the church.
7. Prayers.
8. Dismissal of the church.

(9. On occasions a collection for the poor, the expenses of the church, etc., was made. But this was rather a separate duty of church life, which might for convenience be performed at the 'meeting', than a part of the synaxis itself.)

1. *Opening Greeting and Reply.* This was in a sense only a polite method of 'calling the meeting to order' and indicating that proceedings were about to begin. But the 'meeting' was after all one with a religious purpose, and the greeting took a religious form. It is found all over christendom in one of two forms: 'The Lord be with you', or 'Peace be unto you' (or 'to all'). Both are of jewish origin (*cf.* Ruth ii. 4, John xx. 19) and came into christian use from the beginning. The jewish Talmud remarks of the first that 'It was used of old time when a man would recall his companions to remembrance of the Law.'[1] As such it is probably an inheritance from the original jewish-christian worship of the first days of christianity, in which the immediately following first lesson would be taken from the Law of Moses. The other form, 'Peace be unto you', is the ordinary oriental greeting 'Salaam' (Heb. *Shalom*). It had a special and beautiful significance in christian worship as the first greeting of the Risen Lord to His own (John xx. 19). By a delicate distinction it later came to be reserved in the West to the bishop, as the direct personal representative of our Lord to his own church, while the presbyter was restricted to the less significant form referring only to the lessons about to be read. The reply of the church, 'And with thy spirit', suggests by its 'semitic parallelism' that it, too, came originally from jewish usage, of which there may be an echo in 2 Tim. iv. 22. But it was interpreted by christians as an acknowledgement of the special grace of the Holy Ghost received by the celebrant at his ordination for his ministry[2], which at the synaxis was to proclaim and interpret the Word of God set forth in the scriptures now about to be read.

[1] Tractate *Berakoth, Tos.* vii. 23.
[2] *Cf. e.g.*, Theodore of Mopsuestia (Asia Minor *c.* A. D. 400) *Catecheses* vi. ed. Mingana, *p.* 91. The use of 'The Lord be with you' is still officially restricted to those in holy orders. It may be suggested that it was the inappropriateness of *the reply*, interpreted in this sense, to those not ordained, which originally suggested the prohibition of their using the greeting.

2, 3 and 4. *The Lessons and Psalmody.* The jewish practice was to read first from the Law of Moses as the most revered of their scriptures, and then, after psalmody, one or more lessons from the Prophets or other books. The christians came to adopt an ascending instead of a descending order of importance in the reading of the lessons,[1] which was also roughly the chronological order of their original writing. The christians read first one or more lessons from the Old Testament,[2] then from the apostolic writings, and finally from the gospel which records our Lord's own sayings and doings. The 'Word of the Lord' finds its completeness in the 'Word made Flesh.' In large gatherings at least, if not always, the lessons were chanted to a simple inflection rather than read. This was partly in order to secure that they should be heard distinctly, and partly to give them solemnity as the Word of God to the church, and through the church to the world. This custom also had been known in the jewish synagogues, even if it was not necessarily always observed in small country places.

Between the lessons came the singing of psalms or other canticles from scripture (a chant known in later times as the 'gradual' from its being sung by the soloists from the 'steps' of the raised lectern), a custom which must have been familiar to our Lord and His apostles, since it was universal in the synagogues of their day. It served as a relief for the attention of the hearers. But it also offered the opportunity by intelligent selection for a devotional comment on the scripture just read which would bring home its point to the minds and hearts of the hearers. Such rare examples as we have of really early 'comment' in this way by the chant on the lesson show an apt and ingenious understanding of the devotional use of the scriptures.[3] Dignity and attractiveness were given to this musical side of the service by entrusting much of it to special singers who sang elaborate solos. But the corporate nature of the rite was not lost sight of, and a part was usually reserved for the whole congregation to join as chorus in a simple refrain. Until the fourth century the psalmody appears always to have been in this form in the church, elaborate solo and simple chorus, and never, as it is usually with us, by two alternating choruses. The earlier christian form was that which had been employed in the synagogue, where the signal for

[1] Justin, *Apol.*, i. 67 suggests that this had not yet been adopted when he wrote c. A.D. 155.

[2] Among the O.T. lessons the Law of Moses seems for a while to have retained something of its jewish pre-eminence over the other O.T. scriptures in christian eyes, and therefore was read after them in the new ascending order. Later the church adopted a purely chronological scheme in reading the O.T., placing the Law first and the Prophets, etc., after; thus returning to the jewish order, though for a different reason. So on Good Friday, the Roman rite, which retains for this day a second century form of synaxis, reads Hosea before Exodus. But on Holy Saturday, the lessons of which were arranged in the fourth century, the Law is read before the Prophets. There are now many different strata in the liturgical cycle, the product of 2,000 years of history, and each of them has its own characteristics.

[3] *E.g.* the use of Ps. xc. 1–12 as a comment on Hos. vi. at the paschal vigil, which was the Roman use in the third and probably in the second century.

the people's refrain was the cantor's cry 'Hallelujah', whence the 'Alleluias' still found in the gradual at the liturgy. The method of psalmody to which we are accustomed may have been used in the jewish temple, but it did not come into christian use apparently until A.D. 347–48, when it began to be employed by a confraternity of laymen at Antioch, and from there spread rapidly over christendom.[1] The use of the psalter 'in course' (*i.e.* right through in regular order, and not as selected psalms to comment on other scriptures) in christian services is one of the by-products of the monastic movement of the fourth century.

5. *The Sermon.* The delivery of the sermon was as much the bishop's 'special liturgy' and proper function at the synaxis as the offering of the eucharistic prayer was his 'special liturgy' at the eucharist. As we have seen, the bishop at his consecration received a special 'gift of grace' (*charisma*) for the office[2] not only of high-priest of the church's prayers and offerings, but also of quasi-inspired 'prophetic teacher'[3] of the church's faith. He is the church's mouthpiece, as it were, towards man as well as towards God. Except in emergencies, therefore, he was irreplaceable as preacher at the synaxis, the solemn corporate 'church', even by the ablest of his presbyters. The great Origen himself gave great scandal in the third century by presuming to preach as a presbyter at the synaxis at Caesarea, though he did so at the invitation of the local bishop. And the feeling died hard. At the end of the fourth century the people of Hippo objected to their aged bishop's delegation of the sermon at the synaxis even to that prince of popular preachers, S. Augustine. It was the 'special liturgy' of the bishop's 'order', without which the action of the whole church in its synaxis was felt to be incomplete. The presbyters and other christian teachers might expound their ideas at other gatherings to as many as would hear them, but the synaxis had a different character from even the largest private gathering of christians. It was the solemn corporate witness of the whole church to the revelation of God recorded in the scriptures. At this the bishop, and the bishop only, must expound the corporate faith which his local church shared with the whole catholic church and the whole christian past, back to the apostles themselves. It was this, the unchanging 'saving' truth of the gospel, and not any personal opinion of his own, which he must proclaim in the liturgical sermon, because he alone was endowed by the power of the Spirit with the 'office' of speaking the authentic mind of his church.

There is a passage of S. Irenaeus which sheds so much light on the conception of the liturgical sermon in the second century that it is worth quoting here, despite its length:

'Having received this office of proclamation and this faith aforesaid, the

---

[1] *Cf. p.* 328.      [2] Rom. 12. 5.
[3] So the christians of Smyrna describe their late bishop Polycarp, the disciple of S. John, in A.D. 156 (*Mart. Pol.* 16).

church, though she be spread abroad over all the earth, diligently observes them as dwelling in a single household; and she unanimously believes these things, as having one soul and the same heart; and she concordantly proclaims and teaches and hands down these things, as having but one mouth. For, though the tongues of earthly speech differ, yet is the force of tradition ever one and the same. And the churches which have been planted in the Germanies have received no different faith and taught no otherwise, nor those in Spain, nor those among the Gauls, nor those in the East, nor those in Egypt, nor those in Libya, nor those that are in the centre of the world (Italy). But as the sun, God's creature, is one and the same for all the world, so does the proclamation of the truth everywhere shine and enlighten all men who are willing to come to the knowledge of the truth. And as among those who preside over the churches he who is very skilled in teaching says nothing else than this—for no man is above his own teacher—so he who is but a poor teacher yet does not omit the contents of the tradition. For since their faith is one and the same, neither does he who can say a great deal about it actually add to it, nor does he who can say but little diminish it.'[1]

It was this 'tradition' of faith, the unchanging revelation shared by all generations of christians alike, which the bishop proclaimed in his sermon, basing himself on the scriptures just read. He preaches therefore, in his official capacity, *sitting* upon the throne behind the altar which was his 'teacher's chair', as the representative of God revealing Himself to the world.

6, 7 and 8. *The Dismissals and Prayers.* Thus far the synaxis had been in fact what it was in name, a 'public meeting', open to all who wished to attend, jews, pagans, enquirers of all kinds, as well as to the catechumens preparing to be received into the church by baptism and confirmation. The church had a corporate duty to preach the gospel to the world and to witness to its truth. But prayer was another matter. Thus far there had been no prayer of any kind, but only instruction.

The church is the Body of Christ and prays 'in the name' of Jesus,[2] *i.e.* according to the semitic idiom which underlies the phrase, 'in His *Person.*' 'The Spirit of adoption whereby' the church cries to God in Christ's Name, 'Abba, Father'[3] with the certainty of being heard, 'Himself makes intercession'[4] with her in her prayers. The world had a right to hear the gospel; but those who have not yet 'put on Christ' by baptism[5] and thus as 'sons' received His Spirit by confirmation[6] *cannot* join in offering that prevailing prayer. All who had not entered the order of the laity were therefore without exception turned out of the assembly after the sermon.

[1] *Adv. Haer.* I. x. 2. S. Irenaeus, disciple of Polycarp, the disciple of S. John, was bishop of Lyons c. A.D. 180–200.
[2] John xiv. 13. [3] Rom. viii. 15. [4] Rom. viii. 26. [5] Gal. iii. 27.
[6] Gal. iv. 6.

The catechumens who had accepted the faith, but had not yet been added to the church by the sacraments, first received a special blessing from the bishop. The following text of this, from Egypt in the fourth century, is the earliest we possess, and probably goes back considerably behind the date of S. Sarapion (c. A.D. 340) under whose name it has come down to us. The deacons first proclaimed loudly: 'Bow down your heads for a blessing, O ye catechumens', and then the bishop raising his hand in the sign of the cross blessed them: 'We raise our hand, O Lord, and pray that the divine and lifegiving Hand be raised for a blessing unto this people;[1] for unto Thee, eternal Father, have they bowed their heads through Thine only begotten Son. Bless this people unto the blessing of knowledge and piety, unto the blessing of Thy mysteries; through Thy only-begotten Son Jesus Christ, by Whom glory and might be unto Thee in the Holy Ghost now and throughout all ages. Amen.'

The deacons now proclaimed: 'Let the catechumens depart. Let no catechumen remain. Let the catechumens go forth'; and when these had gone, cried again: 'The doors! The doors!' as a signal to those of their number, or their assistants, who guarded the doors, to close and lock them against all intrusion. Then the church corporately fell to prayer.

First a subject was announced, either by the officiant (in the West) or the chief deacon (in the East), and the congregation was bidden to pray. All prayed silently on their knees for a while; then, on the signal being given, they rose from their knees, and the officiant summed up the petitions of all in a brief collect. They knelt to pray as individuals, but the corporate prayer of the church is a priestly act, to be done in the priestly posture for prayer, standing. Therefore all, not the celebrant only, rose for the concluding collect.

The following is the scheme of the old Roman intercessions still in use on Good Friday.

'*Officiant:* Let us pray, my dearly beloved, for the holy church of God, that our Lord and God would be pleased to keep her in peace, unity and safety throughout all the world, subjecting unto her principalities and powers,[2] and grant us to live out the days of a peaceful and quiet life in glorifying God the Father Almighty.

'*Deacon:* Let us bow the knee. (*All kneel and pray in silence for a while.*)

'*Subdeacon:* Arise.

'*Officiant:* Almighty everlasting God, Who hast revealed Thy glory unto all nations in Christ, preserve the work of Thy mercy; that Thy church which is spread abroad throughout all the world may continue with a firm faith in the confession of Thy holy Name: through . . .'

There follow prayers for the bishop, the clergy, and 'all the holy people

---

[1] The bishop prays with uplifted hand as representing the Father here.
[2] *I.e.* the forces of Satan, Rom. viii. 38; Eph. vi. 12.

of God';[1] for the government and the state; for the catechumens; for the needs of the world and all in tribulation (a particularly fine collect, which has inspired one of the best of the official Anglican prayers for use in the present war); for heretics and schismatics; for the jews, and for the pagans. These prayers probably date from the fourth and fifth centuries in their present form, but may well be only revisions of earlier third century forms.

Or we may take an Eastern scheme from the Alexandrian liturgy, probably of much the same date as these Roman prayers.[2]

'*The deacon proclaims first:* Stand to pray. (All have been 'standing at ease' or sitting on the ground for the sermon.)

'*Then he begins:* Pray for the living; pray for the sick; pray for all away from home.

'Let us bow the knee. (*All pray in silence.*) Let us arise. Let us bow the knee. Let us arise again. Let us bow the knee.

'*The people:* Lord have mercy.'

(The officiant's prayers in their original form have been lost in this section of the intercessions;[3] but the deacon's proclamations continue:)

'Pray for fair winds and the fruits of the earth; pray for the due rising of the waters of the river; pray for good showers and the harvest of the land.[4] Let us bow the knee, etc.

'Pray for the safety of men and beasts; pray for the safety of the world and of this city; pray for our most christian emperors. Let us bow, etc.

'Pray for all in captivity; pray for those that are fallen asleep; pray for them that offer this our sacrifice (*i.e.* for their intentions); pray for all that are in affliction; pray for the catechumens. Pray! Let us bow,' etc.

The text has also been preserved of what appears to be substantially an even older set of Alexandrian intercessions, now known as 'The three great prayers', which now follow this diaconal litany and are still used at several points in the Coptic rite. It runs as follows:

'*Deacon:* Pray for the peace of the one holy catholic and apostolic orthodox church of God. (*The people prostrate and say:* Lord have mercy.)

'*Officiant:* We pray and beseech Thy goodness, O Lover of mankind: remember, O Lord, the peace of Thy one holy catholic and apostolic church which is from one end of the world to the other: bless all the peoples and all the lands: the peace that is from heaven grant in all our hearts, but also graciously bestow upon us the peace of this life. The emperor, the armies, the magistrates, the councillors, the people, our

---

[1] This prayer is interesting as still recognising the laity as an 'order': 'Almighty everlasting God by whose Spirit the whole body of Thy Church is governed and sanctified; hear us as we pray for all its orders (*pro universis ordinibus*), that by the gift of Thy grace Thou mayest be faithfully served by all its ranks (*omnibus gradibus*).'
[2] Brightman, *Liturgies Eastern and Western*, 1896, p. 158 sq.
[3] A much expanded later version of them will be found L.E.W., p. 166.
[4] These petitions reflect the local needs of Egypt, where winds from the desert may bring sandstorms fatal to the crops, and all life depends on the annual rising of the waters of the Nile.

neighbours, our comings in and our goings out, order them all in Thy peace. O King of peace, grant us peace, for Thou hast given us all things: possess us, O God, for beside Thee we know none other: we make mention of Thine holy Name. Let all our souls live through Thine Holy Spirit, and let not the death of sin have dominion over us nor all Thy people; through, etc.

'*Deacon:* Pray for our Patriarch, the Pope and Father *N.*, Lord Archbishop of the great city of Alexandria. (*The people prostrate and say:* Lord have mercy.)

'*Officiant:* We pray and beseech Thy goodness, O Lover of mankind: remember, O Lord, our Patriarch, our honoured Father *N.* Preserve him to us in safety many years in peaceful times, fulfilling that holy pontificate which Thou hast Thyself committed unto him according to Thy holy and blessed will, rightly dividing the word of truth, feeding Thy people in holiness and righteousness; and with him all the orthodox bishops and presbyters and deacons, and all the fullness of Thy one only holy catholic and apostolic church. Bestow on him with us peace and safety from all quarters; and his prayers which he maketh on our behalf and on behalf of all Thy people (*here he shall put on an handful of incense*) and ours as well on his behalf, do Thou accept on Thy reasonable altar in heaven for a sweet-smelling savour. And all his enemies visible and invisible do Thou bruise and humble shortly under his feet, but himself do Thou keep in peace and righteousness in Thine holy church.

'*Deacon:* Pray for this holy assembly (*ecclesia*) and our meetings.[1] (*The people prostrate and say:* Lord have mercy.)

'*Officiant:* We pray and beseech Thy goodness, O Lover of mankind: remember, O Lord, our congregations. Grant that we may hold them without hindrance, that they may be held without impediment, according to Thy holy and blessed will, in houses of prayer, houses of purity, houses of blessing. Bestow them on us, O Lord, and on Thy servants who shall come after us for ever. Arise, O Lord God, and let all Thine enemies be scattered; let all them that hate Thine holy Name flee from before Thy face, but let Thy people be in blessings unto thousands of thousands and ten thousand times ten thousand, doing Thy will by the grace of Thine only-begotten Son Jesus Christ our Lord; through Whom . . .'

These Egyptian prayers are obviously similar in places to the old Roman prayers we have just glanced at, and the general scheme is the same. But this ancient universal scheme has already adapted itself to the particular genius of the different churches. The Roman prayers express exactly the old Roman temperament. They are terse, practical and vigorous, expressing pointedly and precisely what they wish to say without rhetoric or ornament of any kind beyond the polish and sonority of their Latin. The

---

[1] This is the ancient distinction between the solemn 'assembly' (*ecclesia*) and the private meetings (*syneleuseis*).

Egyptian prayers are more 'flowery' in their devotion, though just as obviously sincere. They repeat themselves and cite scripture and poetise their requests; and one notes that tendency to elaboration for elaboration's sake (*e.g.* in the triple prostration) which has led to the complication of all Eastern liturgies. But all this is only to say that the East is not the West, and that in using the same ideas each will do so in its own way, which is in the long run the chief secret of that which differentiates the catholic church from the sects.

The important point to notice here is that in the early fourth century it is not only the position of the intercessions in the Shape of the Liturgy and the main points of their contents which are the same in East and West; that might have been expected. But all christendom was then still at one on the way in which the public intercession should be offered—by a corporate act involving the whole church, in which nevertheless each order—laity, deacon and officiant (bishop or presbyter)—must actively discharge its own separate and distinctive function within the fulfilment of the 'priestly' activity of the whole Body of Christ. It offers to God not only itself in its organic unity, but all the world with its sorrows and its busy God-given natural life and its needs. There is here a very revealing contrast with our own practice in this matter of liturgical intercession—the long monologue by the celebrant in the 'Prayer for the Church Militant' and the rapid fire of collects at the end of Morning and Evening Prayer. With us the deacon's part has completely disappeared, and the people's prayer—the *substance* of the old intercession, which the clergy's vocal prayers and biddings originally only led and directed—has been reduced to a single word, 'Amen.' If the truth be told, many of the more devout of our laity have come to suppose that intercession is a function of prayer better discharged in private than by liturgical prayer of any kind, so unsatisfying is the share which our practice allows them. The notion of the priestly prayer of the whole church, as the prayer of Christ the world's Mediator through His Body, being 'that which makes the world to stand', in the phrase of an early christian writer, has been banished from the understanding of our laity. Their stifled instinct that they, too, have a more effective part to play in intercession than listening to someone else praying, drives them to *substitute* private and solitary intercession for the prayer of the church as the really effective way of prayer, instead of regarding their private prayer as deriving its effectiveness from their membership of the church. So their hold on the corporate life is weakened and their own prayers are deprived of that inspiration and guidance which come from participating in really devout corporate prayer. The old method derives from the profoundly organic conception of the church which possessed the minds of the pre-Nicene christians. Our own is the product of that excessive clericalism of the later middle ages, whose conceptions of public worship were riveted upon the Anglican devotional tradition by the mistakes of the sixteenth century, and which we now take for granted. Then and now its result upon the devout laity is to provoke an excessively individualistic conception of personal prayer.

By the middle of the fourth century the universal use of this pre-Nicene method of corporate intercession was beginning to disappear, a process in which the Antiochene invention of the 'Litany' form played an undesigned part (*cf. pp.* 477 *sqq.*). Another fourth century innovation, this time first attested in the church of Jerusalem, was the transference of the intercessions themselves from the old position after the sermon to a point within the eucharistic prayer, a change which other churches imitated in various different ways. The resulting duplication of the intercessions in some rites and their shifting in others is the first serious complication of the old clear universal Shape of the Liturgy.

But before these fourth century Syrian innovations the synaxis everywhere ended with the intercessions offered in the way we have described. If the eucharist were not to follow, the congregation dispersed, either with a dismissal by the deacon or, in some fourth century churches, with a blessing by the bishop.

When the eucharist did follow the synaxis, these intercessory 'prayers of the faithful', as they came to be called, though part of the synaxis, were attended exclusively by those who were about to be present at the eucharist. The catechumens and enquirers who had been present at the lections and sermon were dismissed before the prayers began. The intercessions thus came to be regarded rather as the opening devotion of the eucharist than as the conclusion of the synaxis. When the misleading names 'mass of the catechumens' for the synaxis, and 'mass of the faithful' for the eucharist, began to be attached to the two parts of what had now been fused into a single rite, the 'prayers of the faithful' were by a natural mistake included in the latter. But the earlier evidence is clear enough that they were originally the conclusion of the synaxis and not the beginning of the eucharist. Everywhere the synaxis celebrated apart from the eucharist ended with these prayers, as did the evening synaxis (corresponding to evening prayer or vespers) when this was first instituted as a public service, probably in the fourth century. The eucharist when celebrated alone normally began with the offertory.[1] It is as part of the synaxis and not as the beginning of the

---

[1] The exception in pre-Nicene times was the baptismal eucharist, at which both Justin (*Ap.*, i. 65) and Hippolytus (*Ap. Trad.*, xxii. 5) interpose these prayers between the initiation of the new christians by baptism and confirmation and the offertory of the eucharist at which they forthwith made their first communion. This was a special case of which the purpose seems to have been to allow the neophyte to discharge at once all the functions and enjoy all the privileges of the 'order of laity', into which he had just been admitted. The special restrictions on the catechumen took three forms: he might never receive the kiss of peace from the faithful; he might not pray with the faithful; he might not eat with the faithful. (They are derived, of course, from the jewish restrictions on *domestic* intercourse with non-Israelites, which were the same.) The catechumen receives the kiss of peace from the bishop immediately after receiving the chrism of confirmation, which conveyed the gift of the Spirit; he forthwith prays with the church in the intercessions, exer-

eucharist that the intercessory prayers must be taken when we come to consider the Shape of the Liturgy as a single whole.

cising his 'priestly' ministry as a christian; he then makes his communion after joining in the offering of the eucharist, his supreme function as a member of the 'priestly' body, which is also the highest form of 'table-fellowship' with the faithful. Hippolytus does not insert the prayers before the offertory on the other occasion at which he describes the eucharist without a preceding synaxis—at the consecration of a bishop (*Ap. Trad.*, ii and iii). In Justin *Ap.*, i. 67 the prayers come before the offertory as the conclusion of the preceding regular Sunday synaxis.

## CHAPTER IV

## EUCHARIST AND LORD'S SUPPER

### THE 'FOUR-ACTION' SHAPE OF THE EUCHARIST

THE last supper of our Lord with His disciples is the source of the liturgical eucharist, but not the model for its performance. The New Testament accounts of that supper as they stand in the received text present us with what may be called a 'seven-action scheme' of the rite then inaugurated. Our Lord (1) took bread; (2) 'gave thanks' over it; (3) broke it; (4) distributed it, saying certain words. Later He (5) took a cup; (6) 'gave thanks' over that; (7) handed it to His disciples, saying certain words.[1] We are so accustomed to the liturgical shape of the eucharist as we know it that we do not instantly appreciate the fact that it is not based in practice on this 'seven-action scheme' but on a somewhat drastic modification of it. With absolute unanimity the liturgical tradition reproduces these seven actions as four: (1) The offertory; bread and wine are 'taken' and placed on the table together. (2) The prayer; the president gives thanks to God over bread and wine together. (3) The fraction; the bread is broken. (4) The communion; the bread and wine are distributed together.

In that form and in that order these four actions constituted the absolutely invariable nucleus of every eucharistic rite known to us throughout antiquity from the Euphrates to Gaul.[2] It is true that in the second and third centuries, if not already in the first, a number of more or less heretical groups took exception to the use of wine and celebrated their eucharists in bread alone or in bread and salt; or if they retained the cup, it contained only water. In the former case, of course, their rite had still a 'four-action

---

[1] This is the account in Matt., Mark, and 1 Cor. Variant texts of Luke xxii. yield respectively (1) the above scheme or else a 'ten-action scheme' with two cups (according to whether the first cup of xxii. 17 is reckoned part of the actual rite or not); (2) a different 'seven-action scheme', with a single cup before the bread; (3) a 'four-action scheme', with no cup. The most recent full discussion of the original form of the text of this chapter is that of Dr. F. L. Cirlot, *The Early Eucharist*, 1939, *p.* 236 *sq.* His conclusion (which to me only just fails to be convincing) is that the so-called 'longer text' has the best chance of being what S. Luke wrote, as affording the most probable starting-point for the development of each of the variants. For the older view that the textual evidence supports the originality of the 'shorter text' (as was held by Westcott and Hort) *cf.* Sanday, Hastings' *Dictionary of the Bible*, ii. 636a *sq.* (to which, if I may venture a personal opinion on a matter outside my competence, I still, rather hesitatingly, incline.)

[2] The rite of *Didache* ix. and x. is often claimed as an exception. On the reasons for regarding this as intended for the *agape* and not for the eucharist proper (which is treated of separately in *Did.* xiv.) *cf.* Dom R. H. Connolly, *Downside Review*, LV. (1937), *p.* 477 *sq.*; F. E. Vokes, *The Riddle of the Didache*, London, 1938, *p.* 177 *sq.*; *Dictionnaire d'archéologie chrétienne et de liturgie*, xi. 539 *sq.*; *cf.* also *pp.* 90 *sqq.* below

shape'—offertory of bread, prayer, fraction, communion. In the case of those who used a cup of water—a practice which was at one period rather commoner even within the church than has been recognised by all scholars —though these groups had departed from tradition so greatly as to change the contents of the cup, yet they still did not offer, bless or distribute it separately from the bread. Thus even these irregular eucharists adhered to the universal 'four-action shape' of the liturgy, of whose unquestioned authority in the second century they afford important evidence.

This unanimity with which the early liturgical tradition runs *counter* to the statements (certainly historically true) of the New Testament documents that our Lord took, blessed and distributed the bread separately from the cup, and broke the bread before He blessed the cup, is curious when one comes to think of it. The change from the 'seven-' to the 'four-action shape' can hardly have been made accidentally or unconsciously. It was a change in several important respects of traditional jewish customs which our Lord Himself had scrupulously observed at the last supper, and which the church remembered and recorded that He had observed. Even in such a point as the position of the fraction—liturgically always placed after the blessing of the cup, and not before it as in the gospels—it would have been easy to conform to the N.T. accounts while leaving the convenient 'four-action scheme' practically intact, as *e.g.* our Prayer Book of 1662 has done.[1] Yet no tendency to do so appears before the later middle ages either in the East or the West.[2] Evidently, liturgical practice was not understood by the primitive church to be in any way subject to the control of the N.T. documents, even when these had begun to be regarded as inspired scripture (*c.* A.D. 140–180).

This liturgical tradition must have originated in independence of the literary tradition in all its forms, Pauline or Synoptic. And it must have been very solidly established everywhere as the invariable practice before the first three gospels or 1 Cor. began to circulate with authority—which is not the same thing as 'existed', nor yet as 'were canonised'—or some

[1] Cranmer orders the fraction in 1549, but has no directions at all as to where it is to come, though the 1549 rubrics seem to exclude it at the consecration of the bread. It was probably assumed to come in the traditional place after the Lord's prayer. The 1552 and the Elizabethan Books are silent as to whether there is to be a fraction. Our present practice is officially an innovation in 1662, though it had been the Caroline practice (at least of Cosin) twenty years before it was authorised by the present rubric.

[2] In the fourteenth–fifteenth century the Copts invented the custom of placing a fraction at the words of institution over the bread as well as at the traditional point before communion. At about the same time a similar idea began to appear in the West; see the evidence collected by V. Staley, *The Manual Acts* (Alcuin Club 1927) though he draws the wrong inference from it. There is no positive evidence for the authorisation of a fraction at this point in the West before the sixteenth century, and then it was confined to N. France; though the practice had to be forbidden by Archbishop Pole in England in Mary's reign. It seems to have been a temporary fashion all over christendom in the fifteenth–sixteenth centuries, which died out again in most places, but happened to 'catch on' among Copts and Anglicans.

tendency would have shewn itself somewhere to assimilate current practice to that recorded as original by witnesses so accepted. This change
from the 'seven-' to the 'four-action scheme', made so early and by such
unquestionable authority that all christian tradition without exception for
1,400 years was prepared to ignore the N.T. on the point, must be connected in some way with the severance of the eucharist proper from its
original connection with a meal, a development which raises very peculiar
problems which we shall have to treat in some detail.

### The Last Supper

Our Lord instituted the eucharist at a supper with His disciples which
was probably *not* the Passover supper of that year, but the evening meal
twenty-four hours before the actual Passover. On this S. John appears to
contradict the other three gospels, and it seems that S. John is right.[1]
Nevertheless, from what occurred at it and from the way in which it was
regarded by the primitive jewish christian church it is evident that the last
supper was a jewish 'religious meal' of some kind. The type to which it
best conforms is the formal supper of a *chabûrah* (plural *chabûrôth*, from
*chaber* = a friend).

These *chabûrôth* were little private groups or informal societies of friends
banded together for purposes of special devotion and charity, existing
within the ordinary jewish congregations, much like the original 'Methodist'
societies within the Church of England before the breach with the church
authorities developed.[2] More than one modern scholar, as well jewish
as christian, has remarked that in jewish eyes our Lord and His disciples
would have formed just such a *chabûrah*, only distinguished from hundreds of other similar societies by its unusually close bond and by the
exceptionally independent attitude of its leader towards the accepted
religious authorities. The corporate meeting of a *chabûrah* regularly took
the form of a weekly supper, generally held on the eve of sabbaths or

[1] The best discussion of the problem in English is that of Dr. W. O. E. Oesterley,
*Jewish Background of the Christian Liturgy*, 1925, pp. 158–192. *Cf.* especially his
argument that S. Paul and the second century church took for granted the Johannine
chronology of the passion (p. 183 *sq.*). This, the almost universal conclusion of
modern investigators, has, however, recently been challenged in Germany, and it
is only fair to say that the question is not yet finally settled.
[2] The question of the function and even of the existence of these *chabûrôth* in the
first century has been disputed. It seems certain that among the pharisees they
were chiefly concerned with a scrupulous observance of the laws of killing and
ritual 'cleanness'. (*Cf. Jewish Encycl.*, vi. 121 *b*.) But there are indications of a wider
and more purely social character assumed by such societies in some circles, not
least in the regulations recorded in the tractate *Berakôth* for their common meals.
Nevertheless, those who disbelieve in the existence of this earlier type of *chabûrôth*
have only to omit the word from this chapter and accept the regulations cited as
governing any rather formal evening meal in a pious jewish household; and they
will not, I think, then disagree with their application to the last supper in the form
here put forward.

holy days, though there was no absolute rule about this. Each member of the society usually contributed in kind towards the provision of this common meal. The purpose of the supper was chiefly mutual recreation and social intercourse, though the business of the society was also managed on these occasions. Given the special religious background of such a society, religious topics—of perpetual interest to all jews—normally formed the staple subject of conversation at any such meal.

The customs which governed such suppers are quite well known to us from rabbinic sources.[1] They were largely the same as those which were carried out at the chief meal of the day in every pious jewish household, though they were probably observed with more formality and exactness in a *chabûrah* than at the purely domestic meal of a family.

No kind of food was partaken of without a preliminary 'giving of thanks'—a blessing of God for it, said over that particular kind of food when it was first brought to the table. The various formulae of blessing for the different kinds of food were fixed and well-known, and might not be altered. Many are recorded along with much other interesting information about the *chabûrah* supper in the jewish tractate *Berakoth* ( = blessings) of the *Mishnah*, a document compiled c. A.D. 200 on the basis of authorities of the second and first centuries A.D. and in some cases of even earlier date.[2] Each kind of food was blessed once only during the meal, the first time it appeared. (Thus *e.g.* if a particular kind of vegetable were served with the first course, it would not be blessed again if it appeared also with the second.) *Hors d'oeuvres*, or 'relishes' as the rabbis called them, might be served before the meal proper began, and over these each guest said the blessing for himself, for they were not yet reckoned 'one company'.[3] If wine were served with these, it was likewise blessed by each one for himself. But once they had 'reclined' for the meal proper, the blessings were said by the host or leader alone for all, except in the single case of wine.

After the 'relishes', if such were served (which were not counted as part of the meal) the guests all washed their hands, reciting meanwhile a special benediction. After this point it was not allowed for late-comers to join the

---

[1] All the chief discussions of these are unfortunately in German. The most important is in J. Elbogen *Der Jüdische Gottesdienst, etc.*, Frankfurt, 1934. (*Cf.* also the same author's article *Eingang und Ausgang des Sabbats, etc.* in the vol. *Festschrift für I. Lewy's 70 Geburtstag*, ed. Brauer & Elbogen, Breslau, 1911, p. 173 *sq.*) Among other important German discussions (by christians) are those in H. Lietzmann, *Messe und Herrenmahl*, Bonn 1926, p. 202 *sq.*, and K. Völker, *Mysterium und Agape*, Gotha 1927, pp. 3 *sqq.* (both of which are regarded by jewish experts as brilliant but inaccurate). In English *cf.* Oesterley, *op cit.*, p. 167 *sq.*

[2] *Berakoth* is conveniently accessible in English in the admirable translation by Lukyn Williams (S.P.C.K. 1921) of which I cite the pages as well as the ordinary ref. numbers to *Berakoth*. Rabbi Köhler has collected a large number of these ancient benedictions from this and other sources in *Jewish Encycl.*, iii. p 8 *sq. s.v.* 'Benedictions'.

[3] *Berakoth. Mishna*, vi. 6 ; *Tosefta*, iv. 8. (E.T., p. 48.)

*chabûrah* meal, because the meal proper began with the handwashing and 'grace before meals', and only those who shared in this could partake. There might be up to three preliminary courses of 'relishes' before this grace, but after the grace came the meal proper.

At all jewish meals (including the *chabûrah* supper) this grace took always the following form. The head of the household, or host, or leader of the *chabûrah*, took bread and broke it with the words 'Blessed be Thou, O Lord our God, eternal King, Who bringest forth bread from the earth'. He then partook of a fragment himself and gave a piece to each person at the table.

The meal itself followed, each fresh kind of food being blessed by the host or leader in the name of all present the first time it appeared. By an exception, if wine were served at the meal each person blessed his own wine-cup for himself every time it was refilled, with the blessing, 'Blessed art Thou, O Lord our God, eternal King, Who createst the fruit of the vine'.

At the close of the meal an attendant brought round a basin and a napkin (and sometimes scent) and hands were washed again.[1]

Finally came the grace after meals—'*the* Blessing' or 'Benediction' as it was called, without further description. (I propose in future to call it 'the Thanksgiving' for purposes of distinction, but the same word, *berakah* = 'blessing' was used for it as for the short blessings, *e.g.* over bread or wine above, or other foods.) This was a long prayer said by the host or father of the family in the name of all who had eaten of the meal. It was of strict obligation on all male jews after *any* food 'not less than the size of an olive' or 'of an egg'.[2] But on any important family occasion, and at a *chabûrah* supper in particular, a little solemnity was added by its being recited over a special cup of wine (which did not receive the usual wine-blessing) which was known quite naturally as 'the cup of the blessing' (for which we shall use here S. Paul's phrase 'the cup of blessing'). At the end of 'the Thanksgiving' this was sipped by whoever had recited the prayer, and then handed round to each of those present to sip. Finally, at a *chabûrah* supper, the members sang a psalm, and then the meeting broke up.

The text of 'the Thanksgiving', which formed the grace after all meals, may be given thus:

'*The host begins:* "Let us give thanks . . ." (if there should be an hundred persons present he adds "unto our Lord God")[3].

'*The guests answer:* "Blessed be the Name of the Lord from this time forth for evermore."

---

[1] If scent were used it was poured on the hands of the guests, who then wiped them on the hair of the attendant! *Ibid. Tosefta*, vi. 5 (*p.* 68).

[2] *Ibid. M.,* vii. 3; *T.,* v. 14 (*p.* 60).

[3] *Ibid. M.,* vii. 5 (*p.* 62). The text of this invitation was made to vary a little according to the size of the company addressed. The rules for these variations are given in this passage of *Berakoth.*

'*The host:* "With the assent of those present—(they indicate their assent) —we will bless Him of Whose bounty we have partaken."

'*The guests:* "Blessed be He of Whose bounty we have partaken and through Whose goodness we live."

'*The host:* "Blessed art Thou, O Lord our God, eternal King, Who feedest the whole world with Thy goodness, with grace, with loving-kindness and with tender mercy. Thou givest food to all flesh, for Thy loving-kindness endureth for ever. Through Thy great goodness food hath never failed us: O may it not fail us for ever, for Thy great Name's sake, since Thou nourishest and sustainest all living things and doest good unto all, and providest food for all Thy creatures whom Thou hast created. Blessed art Thou, O Lord, Who givest food unto all.

' "We thank Thee, O Lord our God, because Thou didst give as an heritage unto our fathers a desirable, good and ample land, and because Thou didst bring us forth, O Lord our God, from the land of Egypt, and didst deliver us from the house of bondage; as well as for Thy Covenant which Thou hast sealed in our flesh; for Thy Law which Thou hast taught us; Thy statutes which Thou hast made known unto us; the life, grace and loving-kindness which Thou hast bestowed upon us, and for the food wherewith Thou dost constantly feed and sustain us, every day, in every season and at every hour. For all this, O Lord our God, we thank Thee and bless Thee. Blessed be Thy name by the mouth of all living, continually and for ever; even as it is written 'And thou shalt eat and be satisfied, and thou shalt bless the Lord thy God for the good land which He has given thee'. Blessed art Thou, O Lord, for the food and for the land.

' "Have mercy, O Lord our God, upon Israel Thy people, upon Jerusalem Thy city, upon Zion the abiding place of Thy glory, upon the kingdom of the house of David Thine anointed, and upon the great and holy house that was called by Thy Name. O our God, our Father, feed us, nourish us, sustain, support and relieve us, and speedily, O Lord our God, grant us relief from all our troubles. We beseech Thee, O Lord our God, let us not be in need either of the gifts of men or of their loans, but only of Thine helping hand, which is full, open, holy and ample, so that we may not be ashamed nor confounded for ever and ever . . ." '

The text above is that still found in the jewish *Authorised Daily Prayer Book*.[1] The current text adds other things before and after, which are known to be of comparatively recent date, and even this central series of benedictions has probably undergone some expansion and revision since the first century A.D. The petitions of the last paragraph must have been recast (if the whole section was not added bodily) after the destruction of the Temple in A.D. 70. But all jewish scholars seem to be agreed that at least the first two paragraphs in substantially their present form were in use in

[1] Compiled by Rabbi S. Singer, with notes by the late Israel Abrahams (London, 1932, *p.* 279 *sq.*).

Palestine in our Lord's time. The short bread- and wine-blessings given before, which are still in use, are found verbally in *Berakoth*.[1] All three forms—the bread and wine blessings and the first two paragraphs of the Thanksgiving—can be taken as those which our Lord Himself habitually used as a pious jew.[2]

This, then, is the general jewish background of the last supper, which the New Testament accounts presuppose almost at every word (especially is this true of that in 1 Cor. xi.). It is a *chabûrah* supper, such as our Lord and His disciples were accustomed to hold regularly, held on this occasion twenty-four hours before the passover of that year. It is a meal held with some little formality and ceremony because it has a religious significance of its own.

First come the 'relishes',[3] with a cup of wine, in which our Lord does not join them—'Take this and divide it among yourselves, for I say unto you, I will not drink of the fruit of the vine until the Kingdom of God shall come' (Luke xxii. 17). It is a sideways allusion to the wine-blessing which each of them is at that moment saying for himself—'Blessed be Thou, O Lord our God, eternal King, Who createst the fruit of the vine'.

Then supper begins in the usual way, with the invariable grace before meals. Our Lord takes bread and breaks it, just as He had always done before, just as every jewish householder and every president of any *chabûrah* took it and broke it at every supper table in Israel throughout the year. He 'gives thanks' over it, but the words of His thanksgiving are not recorded. Of course not! Why should they be? Every jewish child knew them by heart: 'Blessed be Thou, O Lord our God, eternal King, Who

---

[1] *M.*, vi. 1 (*p.* 43).

[2] This is the most convenient point to mention the '*Kiddûsh*-cup', another common cup additional to the 'cup of blessing', which has a place in the supper ritual on sabbaths and holy days. *Cf.* Oesterley, *op. cit. pp.* 167 *sq.* and 184 *sq.* He would find a place for it at the last supper, chiefly on the ground that reminiscences of the prayer with which it would be blessed ('passover-*Kiddûsh*') have affected christian eucharistic prayers. This is possible, but if true would not necessarily prove that 'passover-*Kiddûsh*' was used at the last supper itself. In fact, unless the last supper was the actual passover supper of that year (and Oesterley himself has come near demonstrating that it was *not*) there is no reason to suppose that any *Kiddûsh* prayer or cup found a place in it, since it was not a sabbath or holy day, to which *Kiddûsh* was restricted. Jewish practice has varied a good deal at different periods as to where this prayer and the accompanying cup should come in the course of the meal on days when it was used, from before the breaking of bread at the beginning to before or after the 'cup of blessing' at the end. If it was used at the last supper, it might account for the cup of Luke xxii. 17; but it seems so unlikely that the last supper fell on a holy day, that this is more likely to be an ordinary cup of wine served with the 'relishes' before supper began. In any case, the '*Kiddûsh*-cup' was not confused in jewish practice with the 'cup of blessing', though both were common cups blessed by the host. They received different blessings, were associated with different ideas and came at different points in the meal.

[3] It seems to be some traditional recollection of this preliminary course which makes all three synoptists place the 'breaking of bread' after the beginning of the supper. In jewish practice this ceremony of breaking bread was always reckoned the *start* of the meal itself.

bringest forth bread from the earth.' And He distributes it in the usual way to His 'friends' (*chaberim*), as He had done so often before. But this time there is something unusual, not in the ritual but in an enigmatic remark He makes as He gives it to them: 'This is My Body which is for you. Do this for the re-calling of Me' (1 Cor. xi. 24).

As is well known, there is a school of modern critics which believes that our Lord had no particular intention that what He did at the last supper should ever be repeated by His disciples, or that at least He spoke no word which revealed such an intention.[1] In particular the command to 'do this for the re-calling of Me' at this point, in connection with the distribution of the broken bread at the beginning of the meal, which is recorded only by S. Paul (1 Cor. xi. 24), has been widely regarded as in any case unhistorical. As we shall be dealing with the point at length a little later it is sufficient here to point out that whatever the command to 'do this' may or may not have meant, it *could not* in our Lord's mouth have been simply a command to break and distribute bread at the beginning of a common meal, for the simple reason that *this is precisely what they will in any case all of them do in future, inevitably and invariably, every time they sit down to supper on any evening with any other jew in Israel*. The breaking of bread, in that exact way, and with that 'thanksgiving', is *of obligation* upon every pious jew at every meal. Nor could S. Paul in reciting the 'tradition' of 1 Cor. xi. 24 possibly have supposed that 'Do this' was a solemn command merely to continue the rite of breaking bread. He was perfectly well aware that this practice did not depend for its repetition upon our Lord's command at all, but was ingrained habit with every decent jew. He himself remembered to do it, almost automatically, with a hasty mouthful snatched in the middle of a shipwreck.[2]

---

[1] In Germany this view, which was elaborately supported by Jülicher and Spitta in the last century, is now taken almost as axiomatic by most Lutheran scholars, who no longer trouble to argue the question very seriously, *cf. e.g.*, Lietzmann, *op. cit* p. 249 *sq.* For a still more radical view, *cf.* K. L. Schmidt, *Die Religion in Geschichte und Gegenwart* (1926) i. 6 *sq.* In England its originator in an extreme form seems to have been P. Gardner, *The Origin of the Lord's Supper*, London, 1893. *Cf.* the same author's *The Religious Experience of S. Paul*, London, 1910. Of recent expositors, Dr. H. D. A. Major more or less resumes Gardner; Dr. J. W. Hunkin, now bishop of Truro, has put forward an extreme form of the theory (resembling closely that of Schmidt) in an essay included (rather oddly, in the circumstances) in the volume entitled *The Evangelical Doctrine of Holy Communion* (ed. A. J. Macdonald), Cambridge, 1930. (*Cf.* esp. *pp.* 18 *sqq.* and 37 *sq.*) For a careful statement of a less radical view, *cf.* Dr. A. E. J. Rawlinson, now bishop of Derby, in *Mysterium Christi* (ed. G. K. A. Bell, bishop of Chichester), London, 1930, *p.* 235 *sq.* There are other English expositions of the same position, but these contain all that is of any importance to the study of the question.

[2] Acts xxvii. 35. The remarkable thing, which caused the author of Acts to record the incident, was not that S. Paul 'broke bread and gave thanks' before eating, but that he did so 'in presence of them all', heathen though most of them were, which was a form of 'table-fellowship'. But even S. Paul does not distribute his bread to the heathen, though it has no connection with the eucharist. It was simply the ordinary 'grace before meals'.

If the command 'Do this' does not mean that our Lord supposed He
was instituting a *new* rite, what does it mean? The emphasis must be on
the other half of the sentence—'for the re-calling of Me.' He is not instituting a new custom, but investing a universal jewish custom with *a new and
peculiar meaning for His own chabûrah*. When they 'do this'—as they will
assuredly do in any case—it is to have for them this new significance. He
will no longer be with them at their future meetings. He is going to His
death before to-morrow night, and He knows it now, though He had so
longed to keep this Passover with them.[1] But that does not mean that the
*chabûrah* will never meet again. On the contrary, the impression of all
those months and years with Him will not simply be effaced as though they
had never been by to-morrow night. The *chabûrah* will meet again, somewhere, some time. And whenever it does meet, it will inevitably begin its
supper by 'breaking bread', as all *chabûrôth* do. But *when* that particular
*chabûrah* 'does this'—after to-morrow—they will not forget His words on
this occasion!

Something like that His words must have conveyed to the apostles when
they heard them for the first time, and very puzzled they must have been.
There was not very much in the words 'This is My Body which is for
you', spoken without comment *and heard without knowledge of the words
He was going to say as He handed them the cup after supper*, to give them any
particular clue as to what the *new* meaning for them of this ordinary action
was to be.

After this enigmatic remark supper proceeds as usual, though with a
quite unusual sadness, and after a while with a growing and terrible feeling
of tension. There were the incidents of Judas' sudden departure and the
sorrowful prophecies of betrayal and denial and desertion, and all the rest
of the story that we know so well. At last the meal is over, and the time for
the final rinsing of hands has come. It is probably at this point, rather than
at the rinsing before the meal, that Jesus makes His only change in the
absolutely normal procedure of any *chabûrah* supper—one that He Himself calls an 'example' which they should in future imitate.[2] Instead of
leaving this menial office to the youngest or 'the attendant' whose duty it
was,[3] He Himself, their 'Master and Lord' (*Rabban* and *Maran*, the
loftiest rabbinic titles of reverence) takes the customary towel and basin,
and with heartbreaking humility washes not their hands but their feet. He
comes, apparently, to Peter last of all, probably because Peter was the
eldest of them all, and 'when there are more than five persons present'
it is good manners to begin this rinsing of the hands with the youngest
and end with the eldest.[4] Then He reclines once more upon the 'first

[1] Luke xxii. 15.                                      [2] John xiii. 15.
[3] *Berakoth, Tos.*, vi. 5 (*p.* 68). The 'attendant' might be a member of the *chabûrah*,
even a rabbinical student.
[4] *Ibid.* v. 6, *p.* 50.

couch', and the talk continues, gradually becoming a monologue, for a long time.

It is growing late; it was already well after sunset when Judas went out.[1] It is time to end this meeting with the 'Thanksgiving', the invariable long benediction said after all meals. But to-night because it is a *chabûrah* supper, this is to be said over the 'cup of blessing' standing ready mixed upon the table.[2] Water was customarily mixed with wine for drinking in any case, and unmixed wine was reckoned more suitable for washing in than drinking.[3] In the case of the cup of blessing this addition of water was so much the custom that rabbi Eliezer ben Hyrcanus (*c.* A.D. 90) reckoned it a positive rule that the Thanksgiving could not be said over it until it had been mixed, though the majority would not be so absolute.[4]

On this occasion all is normal. 'After supper He took *the* cup' (1 Cor. xi. 25)—it needed no more description for S. Paul than does '*the* cup' at the end of supper at most places in the *Mishnah*, though elsewhere he gives it its rabbinic name, 'the cup of blessing'.[5] 'And gave thanks and gave it to them' (Mark xiv. 23; covered by S. Paul with the words, 'Likewise also the cup'). Again the words of His 'Thanksgiving' are not recorded for us. Why should they be? They were as familiar to every jew as the Lord's prayer is to us. 'Let us give thanks', He began. And when they had intoned their responses, 'Blessed art Thou, O Lord our God', He chanted, 'eternal King, Who feedest the whole world with Thy goodness . . .', and so to the end of the sonorous phrases they all knew by heart. 'And', after the Thanksgiving, 'He gave it them and they all drank of it' (Mark xiv. 23) exactly as usual, exactly as every other *chabûrah* drank of the cup of blessing at the end of its meeting for supper. And then, while the cup is passing from one to another in silence, He makes another startling incidental remark: 'This cup is the New Covenant in My Blood. Do this, whenever you drink it, for the re-calling of Me' (1 Cor. xi. 25).

I do not want to labour the point, but once more 'Do this' is not and *cannot* in any circumstances be interpreted as a command simply to bless and partake of the cup of blessing at the end of their *chabûrah* meals in future, in the sense of ordering them to repeat something they would otherwise never have done. Nor could S. Paul possibly have supposed that it was, since every *chabûrah* in Israel normally did it every week. Once again it is the attaching of a *new meaning* to something which they will

---

[1] John xiii. 30.
[2] *Berakoth, Mishnah*, viii. 2. 'The school of Shammai say: Men wash their hands and afterwards mix the cup. And the school of Hillel say: Men mix the cup and afterwards wash their hands'—an instance of the precision with which all the details of the *chabûrah* supper were regulated. (Shammai and Hillel lived *c.* 10 B.C.) A considerable interval could elapse between the actual end of supper (marked by the hand-washing) and the final 'Thanksgiving'; *cf. ibid.* viii. 3 on 'Tidying the room'; and viii. 8 on what to do if the Thanksgiving gets forgotten altogether.
[3] *Ibid. Tos.,* iv. 3 (*p.* 45).     [4] *Ibid. Mish.,* vii. 8 (*p.* 64).
[5] 1 Cor. x. 16.

quite certainly repeat from time to time without any command from Him
—less often than the breaking of bread at the beginning of the meal, but
still frequently in any case. (Wine was cheap and easy to get; there is no
instance of a *chabûrah* meal without at least this one cup of it, and no
rabbinic regulation as to what is to be done in its absence.)[1]

But this time part, at least, of His new meaning must have been quite
shockingly plain to the apostles at the first hearing of the words. He has
just been thanking God in their name in the Thanksgiving over the cup
'for *Thy Covenant* which Thou hast sealed in our flesh', and all the tremendous things that meant for the jew—the very essence of all his religion.
And now, whenever this particular *chabûrah* meets again for all time to
come—'This cup is the *New* Covenant' sealed 'in My Blood. Whenever
you drink (the cup of blessing in My *chabûrah*) do so for the re-calling of
Me'. 'And when' like every *chabûrah* at the close of its meeting 'they had
sung a psalm, they went out' (Mark xiv. 26)[2].

What our Lord did at the last supper, then, was not to establish any new
rite. He attached to the two corporate acts which were sure to be done when
His disciples met in the future—*the only two things which He could be sure
they would do together regularly in any case*—a quite new meaning, which
had a special connection with His own impending death (exactly what, we
need not now enquire).

The double institution in bread and wine has a vital bearing on the whole

---

[1] It is puzzling to account for Lietzmann's statement that the early Jerusalem
church 'very seldom' used wine at its *chabûrah* meals in later years (*op. cit. p.* 250)
because our Lord in His wanderings through the land had habitually taught them
to use water. To say the least of it, this consorts singularly badly with the accusation,
'Behold a gluttonous man and a wine-bibber!' (Luke vii. 34). Lietzmann is, of course,
making out a case, essential to his theory of eucharistic origins, that S. Paul is
chiefly responsible for the regular addition of the cup to the original Jerusalem rite
of the 'breaking of bread' only. But that it seems unnecessary to take such special
pleading seriously, I would undertake to produce at least ten pieces of evidence that
wine was commonly procurable even by the poorest in first century Palestine, and
that abstinence from it was regarded as the mark of professional ascetics like the
Essenes and the Baptist, from whom our Lord always dissociated Himself.

[2] I leave this interpretation of the last supper as it stood (but for one readjustment
where I was plainly wrong) in my draft before I came on the very similar explanation given by Dr. Cirlot, *The Early Eucharist, p.* 155 *sq.* I am much reassured to
find that his fuller discussion reaches substantially the same conclusions from a
somewhat different basis. We seem to have read much the same ancient and modern
literature, but so far as I remember my own starting points were two: the remark of
Sanday, Hastings' *Dictionary of the Bible,* ii. 637*a*: 'The institution of the Eucharist
appears to have connexions both backwards and forwards—backwards with other
meals which our Lord ate together with His disciples, forwards with those common
meals which very early came into existence in the Apostolic Church'; and side by
side with that, this from Dr. Oesterley (*Jewish Background, etc., p.* 172): 'The circle
of friends formed by Christ and the Apostles constituted a *chabûrah.* According to
John xv. 14 our Lord refers to this in the words, Ye are my friends (*chaberim*) if ye
do the things which I command you'. Given those two broad hints and a certain
knowledge of *chabûrah* customs, the explanation above seems to arise straight out
of the N.T. facts; though it has escaped the notice of all New Testament scholars
among us until Dr. Cirlot. My own debt to him in the rest of this chapter is considerable, but difficult to assess exactly.

future history of the eucharist. The breaking of bread at the beginning of the supper was something which happened at every meal, even when a jew ate alone. Had our Lord instituted His new meaning for the bread-breaking only, the eucharist would have developed into a *private* rite, something which a christian could do by himself just as well as in company with his brethren (like taking holy water or making the sign of the cross). But the 'cup of blessing' was something which marked a *corporate* occasion, which was the special sign of a *chabûrah* meeting. It was the inclusion of the cup within the new significance which made of the eucharist something which *only the church* could do; and every single reference to the celebration of the eucharist in the New Testament from Acts ii. 42 onwards proves that the point was understood from the first. The institution in bread alone might have sufficed to 'provide holy communion' (like a priest communicating himself from the reserved sacrament when in the absence of a congregation he cannot celebrate). The association of the bread with the cup provided the basis from which would spring the whole *sacrificial* understanding, not only of the rite of the eucharist but *of our Lord's 'atoning' death* itself, in time to come.

Our Lord, then, at the last supper actually commanded nothing new to be done, but reinterpreted what He could be sure would go on in any case. With the recognition of this, quite nine-tenths of the properly historical difficulties which to unprejudiced scholars have seemed formidable in the New Testament accounts of the institution of the eucharist by our Lord Himself lose their foundation. For, so far as I understand them (and I think I have read all the expositions of them of any importance) they one and all depend in the last analysis upon the venerable assumption that *the jews* who first told and recorded the 'tradition' in 1 Cor. xi. 24, 25, were under the impression that the breaking of bread and the blessing of a cup would never have been continued by the apostles but for some special command of Jesus to do so. I call this assumption 'venerable' because it is made by S. Cyprian in Africa in the third century, and even by S. Justin at Rome in the second. I submit that it is natural enough in *gentile* writers as soon as the church had lost all living touch with the normal jewish practice of piety (say after A.D. 100). But it is nothing less than preposterous to attribute such a misconception either to S. Paul the ex-pharisee (who shews himself quite at home in the technical terms of *chabûrah* practices) or to the rigidly judaic church of Jerusalem in the decade after the passion. And from one or other of these the 'tradition' in 1 Cor. xi. must, by common consent, be derived.[1]

[1] It is also a somewhat chastening reflection on modern critical scholarship that the most radical critics in this matter have all continued to accept without question the untenable interpretation of 'Do this' devised by the second and third century Fathers—so much are we all creatures of tradition! And this despite the fact that the main outlines of *chabûrah* customs (which were unknown to these Fathers) are well known to modern scholars. This failure to criticise their own assumption in

We are here concerned with New Testament criticism not directly but only as it affects the history of the liturgy. We have therefore a certain right to assume the historical truth of the institution of the eucharist by our Lord exactly as the New Testament documents record it. Nevertheless, the public questioning of this fact by more than one of our present Anglican bishops has been so well known (not to say painful) to so many Anglicans, especially among the clergy, that I hope I may be forgiven if I carry the matter somewhat further.

The eucharist or breaking of bread is everywhere in the N.T. a rite for which christians 'meet together', and which individuals or fractional groups do not perform for themselves. This is natural since it is by origin and in essence a *chabûrah* rite, something which is impossible outside the corporate meeting of the society. From the jewish point of view, this rite actually constitutes the formal meetings of the society as such, and distinguishes them from casual or partial assemblies of its members. Again, for certain members of a *chabûrah* habitually to separate from the common supper to hold a supper of their own, and especially habitually to offer the Thanksgiving over a separate cup of blessing, would be in jewish eyes to constitute a separate *chabûrah*.[1] Thus the rule that the essence of schism is 'breach of communion' may be said to go back not merely to the origins of christian eucharistic worship, but actually behind that into its jewish pre-history. The *chabûrah* supper is thus emphatically a corporate occasion, which by rabbinical rule required at least three participants for its proper performance.[2] But the breaking of bread and the saying of the Thanksgiving over the cup were by jewish custom performed by the 'president' alone, who received certain special privileges in the other parts of the meal in consequence.[3] The president of the meal is indeed referred to more than once simply as 'he who says the Thanksgiving', just as, conversely, the christian Justin in the second century refers to the bishop who 'eucharistises' the bread and wine as 'the president' (*prokathēmenos*) without further description. There is here the germ of a precedence and authority arising out of the liturgical 'presidency' of the christian *chabûrah* supper which is of quite special importance in the origins of the episcopate, though I am not aware that it has yet been adequately taken into account in the discussions of that much disputed question.

The origin of the eucharist as essentially a *chabûrah* rite also affords what seems a sufficient answer to the theory that whatever our Lord may have done at the last supper (which can hardly, on this theory, be des-

---

the matter is the more remarkable in the case of scholars like Lietzmann, Rawlinson and Hunkin, who actually talk about the *chabûrah* as a well-known institution at the time, and give it a large place in the *subsequent* development of the eucharist.

[1] Cf. *Berakoth*, M., iii. 7 and 8 (*pp.* 63 *sq.*) where 'companies' (of the same *chabûrah*) supping in separate rooms of the same house must join for the Thanksgiving.

[2] *Ibid.* vii. 1 and 4, *pp.* 59 and 62.          [3] *Ibid. Tos.*, v. 7, *p.* 50.

cribed as 'instituting the eucharist', since there was in His mind no thought of a future rite) was concerned only with the breaking of bread, while the sacramental use of the cup is an addition by S. Paul upon the model of hellenistic mysteries[1]. In this form, without the cup, the rite is supposed to have been originally practised at Jerusalem. This theory is really based on the abnormal 'bread-eucharists' found in certain apocryphal 'Acts' of various apostles, and on the traces of 'bread-and-water eucharists' even within the catholic church in the second and third centuries. But it enlists also the 'shorter text' of Luke xxii,[2] as the only authentic account of all that happened at the last supper, preserved for us by 'that careful historian S. Luke'. The case is strengthened by the apparently technical use of the phrase 'the breaking of bread' *alone* to describe the whole rite in the Jerusalem church in the 'pre-Pauline' years.[3]

To take the evidence in the same order: (1) There is no single scrap of the evidence for 'bread eucharists' or 'bread-and-water eucharists' outside the New Testament[4] which can conceivably be dated earlier than *c.* A.D. 150;[5] *i.e.*, it is all later than the rise of that wave of ascetic enthusiasm which culminated in a whole group of similar movements classed together by modern scholars as 'Encratite'; some of these were outside and some remained inside the church. But all alike rejected, amongst other things, the use of wine; and to their fanaticism on the subject we can reasonably attribute the disuse of wine in these cases at the eucharist. All the apocryphal 'Acts' which furnish the evidence for these peculiar eucharists also teach the 'Encratite' view of sexual intercourse. It also seems quite unscientific to attribute a weight to the tradition represented by these relatively late documents comparable (let alone superior) to that of the statements of 1 Cor., Mark and Matt., which are at all events first century evidence. There is no other matter on which their evidence on the history of the apostolic age has secured similar respect from serious scholars. In any case, they shew themselves in some points (*e.g.* in the 'four-action shape' of their 'bread-and-water eucharists') dependent on the developed ecclesiastical tradition.

(2) What of the 'shorter text' of Luke xxii? This exists in several different forms. That which is best attested, the oldest form of the 'Western

---

[1] This is the theory put forward with learning and ingenuity by Lietzmann (*op cit. pp.* 249 *sqq.*) and with more *naïveté* by Dr. Hunkin, *The Evangelical Doctrine, etc. pp.* 19 *sqq.*

[2] This omits both the words '. . . which is given for you. Do this,' etc. over the bread in *v.* 19, and all mention of the cup of blessing after the meal, together with any trace of a 'Blood-Covenant' saying by our Lord in any connection, *i.e.* the whole of Luke xxii. *vv.* 19*b* and 20 in the Authorised Version.

[3] Acts ii. 42, 46.

[4] Collected by Lietzmann, *op. cit. p.* 240 *sq.* Dr. Hunkin altogether omits this—the only solidly established part of the evidence.

[5] The earliest is either in the Leucian *Acts of John*, or perhaps that of the original version of the *Acts of Judas Thomas*. The *Acts of Paul and Thecla* (*c.* 165 A.D.) offer the earliest evidence for 'bread-and-water eucharists' held by people certainly inside the catholic church, and Cyprian *Ep.* 67 about the latest.

text' (D, *a*, *ff²*, *i*, *l*) must certainly have existed in the early second century, as did also the 'longer text'. The 'Western text' reads very oddly, thus: (19ª) 'And He took bread and gave thanks and brake it, and gave unto them saying, This is My Body. (21) But behold the hand of him that betrayeth Me is with Me on the table.' Various attempts seem to have been made both in ancient times (*e.g.*, by *e*; *b*; *Syr. Sin.*; *Syr. Cur.*) and by some modern scholars to amend the impossibly harsh transition from 19ª to 21. But it looks as though all the ancient alternative forms of the 'shorter text' are secondary, despite the attempts made to defend some of them by various contemporary scholars.

We can, I think, dismiss the attempt to explain away the 'shorter text' in all its forms as a deliberately manufactured version made in very early times to support the Encratite practice of wineless eucharists. Such a mutilation would hardly have omitted the words 'which is given for you. Do this for the re-calling of Me' over the *bread*, unless it was made with excessive carelessness.

It seems sufficient at this point (in view of what we shall say later) to point out that whether this be what S. Luke wrote or not, it cannot as it stands be a complete account of what happened at the supper. From the first the eucharist was always a *corporate*, not a private observance. These 'bread eucharists' themselves are everywhere represented as essentially a rite of the christian society and not for the christian individual. But our Lord *could not* have been understood to be giving such a corporate meaning to the bread-breaking alone *without associating the breaking of bread in some way with the cup of blessing* at the end of the meal, since it was the use of the cup of blessing alone which distinguished the *chabûrah* meal from an ordinary meal, and not the breaking of bread, which happened every time any pious jew ate, even alone. It cannot be entirely accidental that it is S. Luke alone, the only gentile writer among the New Testament authorities, who ignores the special importance and place of the cup of blessing at a *chabûrah* meal from the jewish point of view.[1]

(3) What, finally, of the clinching point, the use of the term 'breaking of bread' alone to describe the whole rite of the eucharist in the Jerusalem church? Does that by its mere form *exclude* the use of the supposedly 'Pauline' cup? The argument from silence could hardly appear more fragile. But in any case Acts xx. 11 describes S. Paul's celebration of the eucharist at Troas, in what purport to be the words of an eye-witness. And

---

[1] This does not account for the existence of the 'shorter text'. I hesitate to put forward a personal view on a matter in which I have no real competence. But it does look as though the 'shorter text' in its 'Western' form were that from which all the other extant variants developed as attempts to amend it. Yet I cannot persuade myself that it represents exactly what the author originally wrote. Rather, we have to do with a textual corruption almost at the fountain-head, which means that the problem is insoluble with our present materials. This is a very unsatisfactory conclusion. Nevertheless, if we do not know certainly what an author wrote, we can hardly hope to discern what he meant.

there we read that 'going back upstairs he *broke bread* (*klasas arton*) and ate'. The same phrase in the same book cannot by its mere wording *exclude* the use of the chalice at Jerusalem and *include* it in the practice of S. Paul.[1]

These pre-Pauline eucharists at Jerusalem inevitably figure rather largely in 'liberal' speculation, but—apart from what S. Paul himself has to tell us about them—exactly how much do we know about them? From Acts ii. 42 and 46, read in the light of Acts xx. 7 and 11,[2] we can be sure of two things: (1) that some sort of eucharist was held corporately in the Jerusalem church from the earliest days; (2) that it was held in private houses. As to the form of the rite Acts supplies no tittle of information. We can speculate about that, if we wish, on the basis of the 'Petrine' or 'deutero-Petrine' tradition underlying Mark xiv. (which is clearly verbally independent of 1 Cor. xi. 24, 25). But as regards the form of the rite, Mark xiv. will yield only something entirely similar to the 'Pauline' rite of 1 Cor. xi. That is the sum total of our knowledge concerning the earliest eucharist at Jerusalem—apart from what S. Paul has to say about it, which proves on analysis to be quite considerable.

The most important thing which S. Paul says is that he believes that his 'tradition' about the last supper in 1 Cor. xi. comes ultimately 'from the Lord'. He must therefore, in the nature of things, have supposed that at some point it had passed through that primal group of Galilaean disciples who formed the nucleus of the Jerusalem church, and who had been in any case the only actual eye-witnesses of what occurred at the last supper. He had himself had intermittent but direct contact with some of these men, and was in a position to check for himself their acquaintance with the story as he had received it. In view of the importance which he ascribes to the eucharist in 1 Cor., it is hard to believe that he entirely neglected to do so ; but that he did check it requires to be proved.

That he can merely have invented the whole story as he tells it in 1 Cor. xi. is quite incredible. Apart from any question of his personal integrity— which is not irrelevant—there was that opposition party 'of Cephas' in Corinth itself,[3] ready and willing to raise an uproar about any such

[1] I am sorry if I appear here to be wasting ink upon rather childish arguments. But they are those set forward by Lietzmann in his in some ways very valuable study (*pp.* 238 *sq.*) which is by way of becoming quite a standard work among English writers. Having used it with admiration and profit for the last thirteen years, and drawn attention in print more than once to its importance, I may be allowed to suggest that acceptance of it cannot be uncritical. In almost every chapter, particularly towards the end, there are conclusions which are quite staggering in their arbitrariness when they are checked by the alleged evidence, which is not always adequately cited.

[2] The phrase to 'break bread' is fairly common in jewish sources in the general sense of to 'have a meal'. It is only when read in the light of the occasion at Troas (xx. 7) which is clearly liturgical, that ii. 42 and 46 can be held certainly to include the eucharist.

[3] Even if S. Peter had not recently been at Corinth in person. The visit seems required by the situation there, and is actually attested by the earliest document we possess from the Corinthian church, the letter of Denys of Corinth to Soter of

deliberate misstatement, which would ruin the whole effect of the epistle. Nor does it really save the apostle's credit to suppose that he had hypnotised himself into believing that a story emanating from his own imagination was factual history, and that 'I received by tradition (*parelabon*) from the Lord that which I also handed on as tradition (*paredōka*) to you' really means 'I had by revelation from the Lord' in trance or vision 'that which I handed on to you as historical tradition.'[1] He certainly did put confidence as a rule in his own mystical experiences, but he himself would not have men to be at the mercy of such gifts.[2] Such a theory does not in fact tally with the apostle's usage of words. He uses precisely the same phrase in this epistle of a whole series of *historical* statements about our Lord which does unquestionably proceed from the original apostles and the Jerusalem church. 'When I first taught you I handed on to you as tradition (*paredōka*) what I had received as tradition (*parelabon*) how that Christ died for our sins . . . and that He was seen by Cephas, next by the twelve. Then He was seen by above 500 brethren at one time . . . then He was seen by James, next by all the apostles.'[3] In the face of such evidence the 'Vision theory' really should not have been put forward as a piece of scientific scholarship; these are the resorts of a 'criticism' in difficulties. As Harnack once remarked, the words of S. Paul in 1 Cor. xi. 24 'are too strong' for those who would deprive them of their meaning.

The responsibility for the historical truth of the 'Pauline' tradition of the last supper, rests therefore—or was intended by S. Paul to rest—not on S. Paul but on the Jerusalem church, and ultimately on Peter and those others at Jerusalem who were the only persons who had been present at the supper itself. If one considers carefully the contents of the supposedly 'Petrine' tradition in Mark xiv. (which is verbally independent of 1 Cor. xi.) S. Paul's reliance on this derivation seems justified. 1 Cor. expresses that tradition in a more primitive form, roughly at the stage when S Paul first learned it—within ten years at the most of the last supper itself, perhaps within five. The account in Mark xiv. expresses the same tradition in the form which it had reached when Mark was written, ten years or more later than 1 Cor. and thirty years at least after the last supper. As one would expect, the earlier account is the more directly factual, more concerned simply with 'what happened'. The later one is still accurate in essentials, but compared with that in 1 Cor. xi. it has 'worn smoother' in the course of time, and become to some extent 'ecclesiasticised' in its interest.

Rome (c. A.D. 160). The greatest hellenistic historian of our time, Eduard Meyer, has gone so far as to say 'How the fact that Peter visited Corinth has ever come to be questioned passes my comprehension' (*Ursprung und Anfänge des Christentums*, iii. 441).
  [1] This is the theory put forward (rather less baldly) by P. Gardner, *The Religious Experience of S. Paul, pp.* 110 sq.
  [2] *Cf.* 1 Cor. xiv.
  [3] 1 Cor. xv. 3–6; *cf.* S. Paul's usage *ibid.* xv. 1 Gal. i. 9; Phil. iv. 9; 1 Thess. ii. 13; iv. 1, 2; 2 Thess. iii. 6.

If the tradition of 1 Cor. can be traced back to Jerusalem, as I think can be proved in a moment, the fact has this much importance, that we can dismiss without further ado the whole theory, now somewhat old-fashioned, of any influence of hellenistic pagan mysteries upon the *origins* of the eucharist. James the Just and his fellows had no secret leanings towards Mithraism! But in any case no hellenistic influence of any kind would have produced a rite so exactly and so unostentatiously conforming to the rabbinical rules of the *chabûrah* supper as the 'tradition' of 1 Cor. xi. 24, 25 actually does. When it is examined in this light one primary characteristic becomes undeniably clear. Even if it is not true, at all events it was *invented by a jew to be believed by jews*, and not by gentiles at Antioch or Ephesus or Corinth. I do not propose to elaborate on this, which is really a matter for New Testament scholars and not for a liturgist. But I will mark two points:

(1) The way in which the words in connection with the cup are introduced: '. . . for the re-calling of Me. *Likewise also the cup*, after supper, saying . . .'. There is here no mention of 'taking' or 'blessing', or that they drank, or of what cup '*the* cup' may be. I submit that only in circles perfectly familiar with *chabûrah* customs could things be taken for granted in quite this allusive fashion—with 'likewise' standing for 'He took and gave thanks'; with the emphasis on 'after supper', which sufficiently identifies 'the' cup as the 'cup of blessing'—but only for those who know that this final cup is the distinctive thing about a *chabûrah* meal; with no statement of the contents of the cup and no mention of the Thanksgiving said over it, because these things go without saying—but only for a jew.

(2) The double instruction to 'Do this for the re-calling of Me' is at first sight remarkable, and seems a curious wasting of words in so elliptic an account. The historical truth of the tradition that our Lord said it even once would be challenged by probably the majority of scholarly protestants, and is doubted by many Anglican writers who in principle would be disposed to allow that our Lord probably did say something like 'This is My Body', and 'This cup is the New Covenant in My Blood', in connection with the bread and the cup at the last supper. For instance, Bishop Rawlinson seems very representative of that type of Anglican scholarship which used to be called 'liberal catholic' when he writes: 'The reiterated words "Do this in remembrance of Me", "Do this as often as ye drink it in remembrance of Me" . . . were perhaps not spoken by Jesus—it is at least conceivable that they may have come to be added in the course of liturgical practice by way of explicit authorisation for the continual observance of the rite. . . . When all has been said which along these lines may rightly be said, the solid core of the tradition (the elements, for example, which are common to Mark xiv. and to S. Paul) persists as an unshakable narrative of fact, a story quite uninventable. The Lord Jesus, on the eve of the Crucifixion, actually did take bread, blessed it by the giving of thanks,

and said "This is my body", and proceeded, taking a cup, to say "This is my blood of the Covenant", or "This is the Covenant in my blood." [1]

It is clear from this that Dr. Rawlinson is further towards the traditionalist side than Dr. Hunkin (whose N.T. criticism is almost entirely negative) in seeking to defend the substantial truth of the institution of the eucharist by our Lord Himself. Yet it is scarcely surprising that this line of argument has failed to make much impression on the consensus of scholarship in Germany, or even in this country outside that very narrow circle which combines the ecclesiastical with the academic. Such a treatment of the evidence may look like a way of deliverance to the scholar who is also a devout ecclesiastic, anxious to serve truth but also desirous of saving if he can the mainspring of all eucharistic devotion. But it is hardly likely to impress the scientific historian, who is concerned above all to test the quality of his evidence. If the whole tradition has been vitiated by such motives on so important a point so near the source, as this admission of the spuriousness of the reiterated instructions how to 'do this' in 1 Cor. xi. concedes, then the substantial genuineness of the adjacent words 'This is My Body' and 'This cup is the New Covenant in My Blood' is not going to be put beyond question by bringing in a *later* attestation of the same tradition by Mark xiv. If one appeals to historical criticism as the final arbiter of religious assent or disbelief—as the 'liberal catholics' very courageously tried to do—then to historical methods in their rigour one must go. The genuine liberal is justified in rejecting the liberal catholic's selective treatment of the evidence as insufficiently faithful to scientific historical methods, and biased by the motive of saving the essentials of the traditional theology of the sacrament from the wreck of its traditional justification. From his point of view the liberal catholic's head may be in the right place, but his catholic heart has failed him at the critical moment.

When the time comes for a just appreciation of the liberal catholic achievement[2] it now seems likely that the decisive cause of the breakdown

---

[1] *Mysterium Christi*, p. 240. *Cf.* for other examples of at least acceptance of the same line of treatment, Sir W. Spens in *Essays Catholic and Critical* (ed. E. G. Selwyn, 1st ed. 1926), 3rd ed. 1938, *p.* 427, and (I suspect) Dr. N. P. Williams' essay in the same volume, *pp.* 399 *sq.* Dr. Williams admits: 'We may concede at once that the main weight of this hypothesis [*sc.* that our Lord Himself instituted the eucharist with the intention of founding a permanent rite] must rest upon the command which He is believed to have given, "This do in remembrance of Me".' But he devotes the greater part of his essay to what is in effect an attempt to establish an alternative basis for the 'hypothesis'. It does not seem unfair to conclude that he also regards the words 'Do this etc.' as sufficiently doubtful to be no longer an entirely sufficient warrant in themselves for the rite. Plenty of other examples are available of this tendency to 'drop' the words 'Do this' as indefensible. It had become virtually the accepted fashion among Anglican theologians after 1920.

[2] I would venture in passing to suggest to my own theological contemporaries and juniors that if the time has already come for the verdict as to the fact, we are not yet in a position to pass sentence, but have still to consider the circumstances in mitigation. Some of the published judgments seem very harsh, even when one makes allowance for the exasperating impenitence of some of those concerned. Our pre-

of its attempted synthesis between tradition and criticism will be found all along the line to lie less in its theology (which was usually trying to be orthodox) than in its history. Here it accepted without criticism certain assumptions common to the whole nineteenth century philosophy of history, which have now been discarded as untenable by secular historians.[1]

So here, the historical problem was actually both less complicated and more urgent than the 'liberal catholics' allowed. Once it is recognised that the reiterated instructions to 'do this' *could not* have been intended by our Lord (if He gave them) or understood by S. Paul or any other first century jew to be simply commands to repeat the breaking of bread and the blessing of a cup at a common meal (because the disciples would go on doing these things in any case) but must have reference to the *new meaning* these normal jewish actions were henceforward to bear for them—once this is recognised, the words 'do this' become indissolubly linked with the words 'This is My Body' and 'This cup is the New Covenant in My Blood'. The alleged motive for any 'spiritually-inspired' addition of the words 'do this etc.' *alone* to an otherwise sound tradition ('by way of explicit authorisation for the continual observance of the rite') disappears, and we are confronted with the alternatives (*a*) of deliberate invention of the whole 'tradition' of 1 Cor. xi. 24, 25, or (*b*) of genuine reminiscence.

From the point of view of strictly historical method, the crucial test of this tradition lies in the occurrence of the words 'Do this for the remembrance of Me' *twice over*, in *v.* 24 in connection with the bread as well as in *v.* 25 in connection with the cup. For consider! As soon as the eucharist has become an established rite, even as soon as it is known to consist of a special meaning connected with the *bread and* wine, the words 'do this etc.' in connection with the bread at once become unnecessary. But at the last supper the apostles could not know at all what was coming. When the bread was broken at the beginning of the meal the words in connection with the cup were still an hour or more in the future—'after supper'. The two things were by no means closely connected in jewish custom; as we have seen, the one took place at all meals, the other only on special occasions. If our Lord wished to connect the breaking of bread at the beginning of the meal and the cup of blessing at the end of it—both together to the exclusion of all that came in between—in a new meaning connected with His own death, then at the last supper and *on that occasion only, it was necessary to say so at the breaking of the bread as well as in connection with the cup*.

decessors really were facing a much more difficult situation than some of our 'neo-Barthians' and 'neo-traditionalists' seem to recognise.

[1] It was weakened also by a frequent technical inadequacy in its application to particular problems of the ordinary historico-critical methods, arising from the fact that most of the writers concerned were trained as philosophers or theologians rather than as historians. It was, for instance, his complete mastery of historical technique which distinguished the work and conclusions of a scholar like the late C. H. Turner from those of the 'liberal catholic' school.

Once the new special connection between these two actions had been
made in the minds of the disciples, even on the first occasion after the last
supper on which they held their *chabûrah* meal together, the words 'Do
this for the re-calling of Me', in connection with the bread at all events,
became entirely unnecessary. As soon as it was certain that the *chabûrah*
was going to continue to meet regularly—say soon after Pentecost—these
words really became unnecessary in both cases. Even the longer text of
Luke xxii. (the only authority other than 1 Cor. xi. to insert them at all)
does so only with the cup, and there they appear to have been inserted in
deliberate imitation of 1 Cor. xi. 25. The gospels of Matt. and Mark, put
together more than a generation after the event, during which time the
eucharist has been continuously the very centre of the life of the christian
*chabûrah*, quite naturally omit them altogether. Their accounts of the last
supper are not intended as *mere* reports of what occurred at the supper;
they are designed to furnish the historical explanation of the origin of the
established 'ecclesiastical' rite of the eucharist with which their readers are
familiar.[1] They can and do take it for granted that the eucharist is something which has continued, and in details they reflect current liturgical
practice. Thus the Syrian Gospel of Matt. (alone) has added the gloss that
the partaking of the eucharist is 'for the remission of sins', which we shall
find to be an abiding and peculiar characteristic of Syrian eucharistic
prayers. So Mark has altered 'This cup is the New Covenant in My Blood'
to 'This is My Blood of the New Covenant' to secure a closer parallel to
'This is My Body'. The original form of the saying in 1 Cor. xi. 25 is
inspired directly by the original circumstances of the *chabûrah* supper,
where the bread is separated from the cup by the whole intervening supper,
making a close parallelism unnecessary. There the cup of blessing and the
Thanksgiving just said over it for the '*Old* Covenant' are the immediate
objects of the apostles' attention at the moment of our Lord's speaking.
Hence, 'This *cup* is the *New* Covenant in My Blood.' The later Marcan
form bespeaks long and close association of the bread and cup together in
christian understanding and practice, by its very assimilation of 'This is
My Blood' to 'This is My Body'. The tradition as to what happened at the
supper is still correct in essentials in both gospels, but it has been partially
'ecclesiasticised' in its interest; it has an explanatory as well as a strictly
historical purpose.

But in this Matt. and Mark differ from the 'tradition' which lies behind
1 Cor. xi. 24, 25. However S. Paul may be using it in his epistle, that was

---

[1] There seems to be real justice so far as concerns Matt. and Mark in K. L.
Schmidt's remark (*op. cit. col.* 9) that 'We have before us in the accounts of the last
supper a piece of tradition which in the general setting of comparative religion one
can call an "aetiological cult-narrative" which serves the purpose of explaining a
cult action customary in the society, or else a "cult-legend" '. (The question is
'which?') Though S. Paul in 1 Cor. xi. is *using* his 'tradition' in precisely this
aetiological way, its *substance* in itself is something else, a narrative.

originally put together with no other motive than of recording exactly what our Lord did and said at that supper, regardless of its 'point' for any later situation. It is pure *recollection*, or it would never have retained those words 'Do this for the re-calling of Me' over the broken bread, *absolutely necessary at that point on that one occasion, and absolutely superfluous on any other.*

Nevertheless, the historian is entitled to press the theologian a little further yet. Those superfluous words 'Do this for the re-calling of Me' are in the text of I Cor. xi. 24 for one of two possible reasons: either because they are true, they were actually spoken; or else because someone—a jew familiar with *chabûrah* practice—has deliberately (and quite brilliantly) thought himself back into the circumstances which could only have occurred on that *one* occasion. The hypothesis of accidental elaboration in good faith is certainly excluded. But what of deliberate invention?

Ancient inventors of legends were not as a rule so ingenious. But in any case the theory that at Jerusalem, in the society of Peter and those other ten witnesses who had been present at the supper, an entire fabrication could gain credence and be foisted off on S. Paul without their connivance seems altogether too fantastic to be discussed. And if *all* those who actually were present at the supper were party to a conspiracy to deceive, then there never was any means of convicting them of falsehood, either for S. Paul or for the modern student.

Those christians, however, who may feel bound to defend this hypothesis ought first to address themselves to three questions, which so far as I know (and I think I have read all the relevant literature) they have never hitherto faced seriously in all that they have written either in England or abroad. (1) How did these orthodox jewish-christians first come to associate their absolutely normal *chabûrah* supper so specially with the idea of a *death*, an idea which is utterly remote from all connection with the *chabûrah* meal in judaism? (2) If their *chabûrah* meeting was exactly like that of dozens of other *chabûrôth*, and had originally no special connection with the last supper of Jesus, why did it first come to be called 'the *Lord's* supper', and in what sense did they first come to suppose that it was specially 'His'? (3) How did these exceptionally pious jews first come to hit on the idea of *drinking human blood* (even in type or figure)—to a jew the last conceivable religious outrage—as the sign of a 'New Covenant' with a God, Who, with whatever new understanding of His character and purpose, was still unhesitatingly identified with the Jehovah of the Old Testament?[1] Indeed, could any authority less than known and certain

---

[1] In saying that liberal speculation 'has not seriously faced' these questions, I do not mean that they have not recognised their existence, but that they have not as yet produced any answers worthy of the name. Dr. Hunkin, for instance, expends a series of fifteen—no less!—accumulated 'conjectures' in surmounting the third (*op. cit. pp.* 18–20). The decisive point is passed thus: 'It was an easy step to take the wine as representing the Lord's blood; not indeed a step that would have been

words of our Lord Himself have ever established such an idea in the face
of the persisting inhibitions exemplified in Acts x. 14; xi. 8; xv. 29; etc.?

The Jerusalem church displayed many of the conservative virtues. But
those who like to think that that old bottle actually generated the new wine
will find little encouragement in the somewhat questioning reception it
offered to new ideas when they were put before it by SS. Peter and Paul.

### The Meaning of the Last Supper

The 'liberal' investigation of the New Testament conducted during
the last two generations with such immense thoroughness and ingenuity
usually found itself arriving at the disconcerting conclusion that on every
point of importance the primitive church was more vitally creative for the
future history of christianity than was Jesus of Nazareth Himself. It is the
irrationality of such results which more than anything else has brought
about the various contemporary revolts against the whole liberal outlook
in theology. These are directed not so much against its methods, which are
being superseded rather than discarded, as against its basic assumptions
and the conclusions to which they inevitably led; for it is now plain that
despite all the deference to critical methods which liberal scholars sincerely
endeavoured to pay, their conclusions were as often dictated by their pre-
suppositions as by their actual handling of the evidence.

So in this case. The liberal thesis about the origins of the christian eucharist was that it had little or no direct connection with the last supper of
Jesus, Who if He did then perform any symbolic action and utter any symbolic words in connection with bread (and a cup also, which is even more

natural to a Jew, but a step not difficult to imagine in a cosmopolitan community
like the Christian community at Antioch' (*p.* 19). So it was as easy as that! But
unfortunately there subsist certain difficulties in that case, requiring further 'con-
·ectures' which are not made by Dr. Hunkin, but which I will venture to supply.
Presumably Barnabas, the jewish levite specially sent from Jerusalem to take charge
of the Antiochene church (Acts xi. 22), warned his assistant Saul of Tarsus 'They
may not like this very much at Jerusalem'. But S. Paul, who though 'of the straitest
sect of the pharisees' did not share this jewish prejudice about blood, had got hold
of a cock-and-bull story about the last supper off the Antiochene gentile converts;
into which story the *chabûrah* customs had been so cunningly worked that it completely convinced Barnabas that that was how it must have happened; drinking
blood was not really a new idea at all, but what the Jerusalem church had meant all
along. And so when Peter came down to Antioch Barnabas convinced him, too, that
that was really what had happened at the last supper. And when Peter and Barnabas
and 'all the jews' at Antioch disagreed violently with Paul (Gal. ii. 11–13) actually
about the question of 'table-fellowship' (which involved the eucharist) in that particular church, they none of them felt any longer that there was anything 'unnatural to a jew' about this strange idea that S. Paul had taken up with there, and
did not think of mentioning the matter to him. And it was their silence on this
occasion which led him to tell the Corinthians that he had 'received' the whole
story 'by tradition from the Lord'. (I choose this particular example of liberal
scholarship, not to single it out as exceptional—it seems typical of the methods which
have been pursued in some cases to elucidate the whole question—but because any
reader can easily check the whole matter for himself in this case.)

strongly doubted) could not have had in mind anything more than the immediate occasion. At the most, all He did was to give a vivid forewarning to the reluctant minds of His disciples in the form of an acted parable of the certainty of His own immediately impending death. 'The main intention in the mind of our Lord was a twofold intention; first to encourage in His disciples the hope of the coming of the Kingdom; and second to bring home to them the fact that His own death was, in the mysterious purpose of God, necessary before the Kingdom could come.'[1] He was giving no instruction for the future. It is argued that He mistakenly hoped that His own death would forthwith precipitate the end of time itself and of all this imperfect world-order in an apocalyptic convulsion which should inaugurate the world to come. How could He, then, have been legislating for a future religious society stretching across continents He had scarcely heard of for centuries which He hoped would never be? All else, all that we mean by the eucharist, is the result of accident, of mistakes made in all good faith, and of the 'mystical experience' of those who had known and loved Him only at second hand, all remoulded by the more sinister influences of Mediterranean folk-religion. The eucharist, the perpetual rite of the New Covenant, the supposed source of the holiness of saints and of the fortitude of martyrs, the comfort of penitents, the encouragement of sinners, for which tens of thousands of men have died and by which hundreds of millions have lived for twenty centuries from the arctic circle to the equator —this is the creation not of Jesus at the last supper, but of anonymous half-heathen converts to the primitive church in the twenty years or so between the last supper and the writing of 1 Corinthians.

This is a theory which has its historical difficulties, but which goes some way towards relieving a certain awkwardness about the existence of the material rite of the eucharist and its historical place in the very centre of the christian religion. This had already been felt in more ways than one among the Reformed Churches, for centuries before the nineteenth century liberal movement in theology arose to give it explicit avowal and to provide relief. After all, the Quakers have a certain appeal to logic on their side against other protestants. If one holds that the essence of the christian religion is 'justification by faith *alone*', material rites like baptism and the eucharist, even though their retention in some form is more or less enforced by reverence for scripture, by tradition and by the needs of human nature, are apt in time to degenerate into embarrassments to the theory, and 'optional appendages' to the practice, of a subjective ethical piety. But in its actual expression the difficulty of the liberal theologians is not so much protestant as nineteenth century secularist. When Eduard Meyer wrote that 'The thought that the congregation . . . enters into a mystical or magical communion with its Lord through the receiving of bread and wine . . . can never have been uttered by Jesus Himself',[2] this atheist

[1] Hunkin, *op. cit. p.* 18.    [2] *Ursprung und Anfänge des Christentums*, i. 179.

jewish historian used terms with which we have been made familiar by more than one modern Anglican bishop. He spoke for once not out of his historian's insight into the first century, but out of a deep prejudice which characterised nineteenth century thought in general, in which he had grown up. This assumed a discontinuity between 'matter' and 'spirit' so absolute that 'dead matter can never become the vehicle of spiritual reality'.

Such a dualism was utterly remote from the thought of the first century, both jewish and hellenistic.[1] The sacramentalism of primitive christianity became undeniably plain to liberal theologians more than fifty years ago. The Old Testament was then being misread as a fundamentally Lutheran document by an altogether one-sided emphasis on its prophetic element, under the influence of German theology, even by leading Anglican scholars;[2] while the other jewish evidence was grossly neglected (despite the labours of individual scholars like R. H. Charles). In the circumstances it seemed a reasonable process to attribute the origin of the christian sacraments to 'early pagan infiltrations' from the hellenistic mystery-cults, in which sacramentalism was supposed to have flourished. And S. Paul, by the accident that he was born at Tarsus (and despite his pharisaic training at Jerusalem) was available as a target for the accusation that 'though ready to fight to the death against the Judaising of Christianity, he was willing to take the first step, and a long one, towards the Paganising of it.'[3]

The alleged parallels between primitive christian and contemporary pagan sacramentalism have in fact reduced themselves to unimpressive proportions under recent investigation. But Meyer as an historian, in the sentence quoted above, might also have reflected that there could have been no absolute historical impossibility that Jesus the jew ever uttered such a thought, if only because many contemporary jews of a certain spiritual intelligence—including the incurably rabbinic Saul of Tarsus—thoroughly believed that He had. We have seen that the historical evidence, critically treated, in no way compels the belief that He did not utter it. On the contrary, it establishes what I would venture to call the certainty that the story that He did so did not originally proceed from a hellenistic source at all. Whether it be true or false, it comes as it stands from a rigidly and above all an entirely unselfconsciously and traditionally jewish background, which can hardly be other than the early Jerusalem church, with its nucleus of Galilaean disciples who had actually been present at the supper.

[1] On the 'emphatically and radically non-dualistic' character of jewish thought 'even to excess', and the 'rudimentary and germinal sacramentalism' which 'not only existed but flourished as an essential part of the jewish religion, from the O.T. into Rabbinism', cf. the very valuable first lecture of F. Gavin, The Jewish Antecedents of the Christian Sacraments, London, 1928.

[2] E.g. Gore, in denying the existence of a jewish sacramentalism (The Holy Spirit and the Church, p. 92) is merely echoing Bousset, Die Religion des Judentums in späthellenistischer Zeitalter, pp. 199 sq. without independent investigation.

[3] W. R. Inge, Outspoken Essays (1st Series), p. 228.

Considered in itself this evidence also indicates—what is not surprising—
that the ordinary canons of historical criticism hold good in this case. As a
rule (failing the direct attestation of eye-witnesses, which is almost always
lacking to the classical historian) the earliest and most directly transmitted
account of an incident in ancient history will be found to furnish the best
information. The tradition repeated by S. Paul in 1 Cor. xi. 24, 25 is
'fresher', more factual, more authentic than the later, more 'ecclesiasticised', accounts in Matt. and Mark, which have passed through a longer
and more complicated process of oral transmission before they came to be
written down. If S. Paul's evidence on what Jesus said and did at the last
supper is 'second-hand', that of the gospels is likely to be 'third-' or 'fourth-
hand' by comparison. S. Paul's evidence on the last supper is in fact just
about as strong as ancient historical evidence for anything at all is ever
likely to be, stronger indeed than that for almost any other single saying of
our Lord considered in isolation.

Nevertheless though the 'liberal' theory when it is critically examined
may be pronounced in its essentials mistaken and even perverse, it holds a
valuable element of truth. The last supper and what our Lord said and did
at it must be set upon a much wider background, if we are to understand
not only what it meant but what it effected. To this end I venture to set
out a rather lengthy extract from the conclusions of a book which I personally have found the most illuminating single product of New Testament
criticism in any language which has appeared in our time.

'Nowhere in the N.T. are the writers imposing an interpretation upon a
history. The history contains the purpose, and is indeed controlled by it.
That is to say, the historian is dealing in the end with an historical figure
fully conscious of a task which had to be done, and fully conscious also that
the only future which mattered for men and women depended upon the
completion of his task. The future order which it was the purpose of Jesus
to bring into being, depended upon what he said and did, and finally upon
his death. This conscious purpose gave a clear unity to his words and
actions, so that the actions interpret the words, and the words the actions.
The same purpose which caused the whole material in the tradition
[which lies behind the composition of our present written gospels] to
move inexorably towards the crucifixion, forced the theologians [S. Paul,
S. John, Hebrews] to concentrate upon his death in their endeavour to
expose the meaning of his life. . . . The purpose of Jesus was to work out
in a single human life complete obedience to the will of God—to the
uttermost, that is, to death. . . . The whole tradition agrees in depicting
his obedience to the will of God as entirely unique, isolated and creative;
he consciously wrought out in flesh and blood the obedience demanded by
the O.T. scriptures and foretold by the prophets. His obedience springs
from no mere attempt to range Himself amongst the prophets of Israel, or
amongst the righteous men of old, or amongst the best of his contem-

poraries, but from the consciousness that, according to the will of God, the whole weight of the law and the prophets had come to rest upon him, and upon him only. . . . But the obedience of Jesus was also a conscious conflict. It was a contest with the prince of evil for the freedom and salvation of men and women. Upon the outcome of this contest depended human freedom from sin. . . . The whole N.T. rings with a sense of freedom from sin. But this freedom rests neither upon a spiritual experience nor upon a myth, but upon a particular history which lies in the immediate past, and to which the original disciples had borne witness . . . Jesus Himself did not think of His life and death as a human achievement at all. Language descriptive of human heroism is entirely foreign to the N.T. The event of the life and death of Jesus was not thought of as a human act, but as an act of God wrought out in human flesh and blood, which is a very different matter. The event was conceived of as a descending act of God, not as the ascending career of a man who was successful in the sphere of religion. . . . Primitive christianity came into being because the christians believed what he had said and done to have been the truth. The whole spiritual and moral power of the primitive church rested ultimately not upon a mystical experience, but upon its belief that what Jesus asserted to have been the purpose of his life and death was in very truth the purpose of God.'[1]

This seems altogether justly observed. But how came the primitive church to its *understanding* of 'the purpose of His life and death'? That Jesus Himself from the first attributed a Messianic significance to His own life and death is a fact which permeates every strand of the records about Him. But the evidence is no less unanimous that up to the moment of the Crucifixion He had not yet fully conveyed His own understanding of Himself and His purpose to the members of His *chabûrah*. If Acts i. 6, 7 is to be believed, they had not grasped it even after the resurrection. One thing is certain. The interpretation was not suggested to them by the mere *memory* of the events themselves. There was nothing whatsoever about the execution of a condemned criminal by the most shameful death a jew could die—however piteous, however undeserved—which could suggest for one moment to a jew the all-redeeming sacrifice of a New Covenant, superseding that of Sinai. Yet the sacrificial interpretation of that death, the Messianic interpretation of that life of apparent frustration, is no mere Pauline importation into christian doctrine. It is something which quivers and flames behind almost every verse of the New Testament, which dominates every theme and strand of that uniquely complex collection. There is a single creative interpretation of the whole Old Testament behind all that is written in the New—our Lord's own interpretation of it.

[1] Hoskyns and Davey, *The Riddle of the New Testament*, 1936, pp. 216 sq. I am indebted to the Rev. F. N. Davey and Messrs. Faber & Faber for permission to make this long citation.

But this interpretation is only implied in the first three gospels, and plainly stated for the first time in the apostolic writings. He saw His own office as Messiah and foresaw His own death as its direct consequence. But during the ministry the bare fact of His Messiahship is treated as a deadly secret; its mode of achievement, by His own death, was spoken of only towards the end and with great reserve. Sacrificial language of indisputable plainness about that death is attributed to Him only at the last supper. At the supper and even after the supper the apostles did not yet understand. But at the supper He had taken means that they would understand in time. And the place of understanding would be at the table of the eucharist, which He then fore-ordained.

For the last supper was not strictly a eucharist, but its prophecy and promise, its last rehearsal. It was only the last of many meetings of His old *chabûrah* held in the same form; it was still outside the Kingdom of God, which He Himself had not yet entered until after the next day's final taking of it by violence.[1] But at this meeting the old accustomed rite is authoritatively given, not a new institution, but a new meaning; a meaning it cannot bear on this occasion, but will hereafter. There could be no 're-calling' before God of an obedience still lacking complete fulfilment; no Body sacramentally given or Blood of the New Covenant, until Calvary was an accomplished fact and the Covenant-Victim slain; no 'coming again to receive them unto Himself' until He had 'gone away' in humiliation 'to prepare a place for them'; no entering into the Kingdom of God and 'the world to come', until the 'prince of this world' had found that he 'had nothing in Him', even when His life was sifted to the uttermost by death.

But though our Lord at the supper gives the present rite an entirely future meaning, His whole mind and attention is riveted neither on the present nor on the future, but on something altogether beyond time, which yet 'comes' into time—the Kingdom of God, the state of affairs where men effectively acknowledge that God is their King.[2] Kingship to that oriental mind meant oriental despotism—as David or Solomon or Herod were kings, absolute unfettered masters of men's lives, limited only by their own natures and characters and purposes, and not by any rights that others might have against them. The goodness of God is the only law and constitution of God's Kingship, and because that goodness is absolute the Kingship is absolute too. Jesus lived and died in unflinching and conscious obedience to that despotic rule of goodness,—as the 'slave' of God, the *pais theou*, or as we translate it, the 'servant' of Isaiah lii.–liii. As such He knew the goodness of that Kingly rule; into that slavery He will initiate His own, for that is what the coming of the Kingdom of God among men means. In that Kingdom He will drink new wine with them, and eat with

---

[1] Luke xxii. 16, 18.
[2] This is always of 'the age to come' in this world; for in no individual is it ever complete while he is in this world, except only in Him.

them of the eternally fulfilled passover of a deliverance from worse than Egyptian bondage.[1]

But the only way to the final coming of that Kingdom is by His own hideous death to-morrow, and they have understood little or nothing of that way.[2] They have only blindly loved Him. His death would prove to uncomprehending love only the final shattering of the hope of that Kingdom's ever coming. Even the amazing fact of His resurrection, seen simply as the reversal of Good Friday, could provide no *interpretation* of what had happened, no prevailing summons to them to take up their crosses and follow Him into the same unreserved surrender to the Kingship of God. Above all, it could provide no earthly fellowship within that Kingdom with Himself beyond death. 'Having loved His own that were in the world, He loved them unto the end.' And so at the last *chabûrah* meeting there is the fore-ordaining of the eucharist, which provided the certainty that in the future they would come to understand and enter into—not His death only—though that gives the clue—but His life also, His Messianic function and office, His Person and the Kingdom of God itself—learn by experiencing these things, by 'tasting of the powers of the age to come.'[3] And the means are to be two brief and enigmatic sentences attached by Him—quite unforgettably—to the only two things they are quite sure in the future to do again *together*. By attaching these sayings exclusively to the corporate rite of the *chabûrah* and not to any individual observance or to the personal possession of any particular spiritual gift, He had effectively secured that this understanding, when they reached it, should be corporate —the faith of a church and not the speculation of individuals.

But at the last supper itself all this is still in the future; it is the sowing of the seed of the eucharist, not its first reaping. At the supper His *chabûrah* could not understand the new meaning He intended *them* in the future to attach to the old rite of the bread and the cup, for that which it interpreted was not yet accomplished. It was the giving of a triple pledge; to Himself, that what He had to do to-morrow He would accomplish; to them, that 'I appoint unto you a kingdom, as My Father hath appointed unto Me; that ye may eat and drink at My table in My Kingdom';[4] to His Father, that the cup for all its bitterness should be drunk to the dregs. To our Lord's whole life the last supper has the relation of an offertory to a liturgy, whose preceding synaxis consists in the scriptures of the Old Testament and the sermon of His life and ministry; whose consecration is on Calvary and oblation in the resurrection and ascension; and whose communion is the perpetual 'coming' with power to His own. They did not yet understand, but with Him, by Him, at the eucharist that uncomprehending *chabûrah* would become the primitive jewish church, which proclaimed from the first, not His survival of death but 'Let all the house

[1] Luke xxii. 16, 18.  [2] John xiv. 5.  [3] Heb. vi. 5.
[4] Luke xxii. 29, 30.

of Israel know assuredly that God hath made that Jesus Whom ye have *crucified*, both *Lord and Christ*.'[1] That is an interpretation of Calvary which they could not have learned from the resurrection alone, but only from the meaning attached to Calvary at the last supper seen in the light of the resurrection. The last supper is not a eucharist, for the eucharist is intended to be the response of the redeemed to the redeemer, the human obedience to a Divine command, the human entrance into understanding of a Divine instruction—'as oft as *ye* shall drink it.' The primitive church and not its Lord first celebrated the eucharist, in the necessity of the case. But the primitive church did not create the eucharist. It would be less untrue to say that the eucharist created that primitive church which preached the paradox of '*Messiah crucified*, the power of God and the wisdom of God.'[2]

There is more—much more—than this in what happened at the last supper, but at least there is this. Without opening the general question of our Lord's foreknowledge, on which pre-suppositions vary, we may say that it is not at all a question of whether our Lord could be legislating for a vast future religious society, but of whether He could and did intend to initiate that present religious society, His *chabûrah* of which He was the acknowledged founder and leader, into His own understanding of His own office, and especially of His own death which explained the rest. The whole record of His ministry is there to prove that He did so intend. They had not grasped it, but He could and did provide that they should do so in the future. The Messianic, redeeming, sacrificial significance which the whole primitive jewish church unhesitatingly saw, first in His death, and then in His Person and whole action towards God, is the proof that this meaning was grasped by·that church primarily through the eucharist, which arose directly out of what He had said and done at the last supper. There, and there alone, He had explicitly *attached* that particular meaning to His own death and office. As the bishop of Derby has brilliantly discerned: 'The doctrine of sacrifice (and of atonement) was not . . . read *into* the last supper; it was read out of it.'[3] And it was meant to be.

How long the primitive church continued to celebrate its eucharist at 'the Lord's supper', with a complete *chabûrah* meal between the breaking of bread and blessing of the cup on the model of the last supper, is not certainly known. But it is possible that the length of that period has been over-estimated by modern students, who usually place the separation of the eucharist from the meal round about A.D. 100 or even later.

---

[1] Acts ii. 36.     [2] 1 Cor. i. 23.

[3] *Mysterium Christi*, 1930, p. 241. Dr. Rawlinson believes that 'it is just possible' that S. Paul may have been the first christian to see 'what our Lord meant by the last supper' (p. 240). But this understanding of the death of Jesus as the atoning sacrifice of the Messiah surely goes much further back into the primitive christian tradition than S. Paul. *Cf.* C. H. Dodd, *The Apostolic Preaching and its Development, passim;* Hoskyns and Davey, *op. cit. pp.* 103 *sq.*, etc.

At the end of the second century we find two separate institutions, already traditionally called 'the eucharist' and 'the agape' or 'Lord's supper', existing side by side in the same churches, celebrated under different circumstances, by different rules, for different purposes, at different times of the day. It is evident that though they are clearly distinguished, both are ultimately derived from the *chabûrah* supper; and it is, I think, also clear how their separation has been effected. The eucharist consists simply of those things in the *chabûrah* supper to which our Lord had attached a special new meaning with reference to Himself, *extracted* from the rest of the Lord's supper, to which no special christian meaning was attached. The agape is simply what remains of the *chabûrah* meal when the eucharist has been extracted. This appears when we examine their forms.

### The Primitive Eucharist

We have seen that the universal 'four-action shape' of the liturgical eucharist consists essentially of four parts: offertory, prayer, fraction and communion.

(1) *The offertory*. Each communicant brings for himself or herself a little bread and wine, and also very frequently, other small offerings in kind of different sorts, oil, cheese, vegetables, fruit, flowers, etc.[1] These latter were placed upon or beside the altar, where they were blessed in a special clause at the end of the eucharistic prayer—a clause which maintains its place at the end of the Roman canon to this day, the *per Quem haec omnia*.[2] This is simply a survival of the custom of providing the *chabûrah* supper out of the contributions in kind by its members, though in the case of the bread and wine another meaning was given to the offering by the church before the end of the first century.

(2) *The prayer*. When the eucharist was extracted from the *chabûrah* supper, the disappearance of the intervening meal brought the breaking of bread at its beginning and the Thanksgiving over the cup of blessing at its end into conjunction. The traditional brief jewish bread-blessing in itself had no special connection with the *chabûrah* meeting, but was simply the ordinary grace before all meals, with reference to the supper that followed. It consequently went along with the supper, and re-appears at the agape, not at the eucharist. The long Thanksgiving at the end of the meal was always regarded as and called in jewish practice '*The* Blessing' for all that had preceded it. It was also specifically the blessing for the 'cup of blessing' itself (which did not receive the ordinary wine-blessing). Accordingly it now becomes '*The* Blessing' or '*The* Prayer' of the eucharist, said over the bread and wine together.

[1] Hippolytus, *Ap. Trad.*, v., vi., xxviii.
[2] *Cf.* the place of the blessing of chrism etc. on Maundy Thursday, the blessings of grapes and so forth in the Leonine Sacramentary, and other surviving traces of the practice.

That this was so can be seen from its special name, 'The Eucharist' (-ic Prayer), *hē eucharistia*, 'The Thanksgiving', which is simply the direct translation into Greek of its ordinary rabbinic name, *berakah*. To 'bless' a thing and to 'give thanks' to God for a thing over it were synonymous in jewish thought, because in jewish practice one only blessed a thing *by* giving thanks to God for it before using it. There were thus available two Greek words to translate the one Hebrew word *berakah*: *eulogia* = a 'blessing', or *eucharistia* = a 'thanksgiving'; according to whether one put the chief emphasis on the idea of the thing for which one thanked God, or of God to Whom one gave thanks for the thing. Accordingly we find these two Greek words used apparently indifferently in the N.T. as translations of this same Hebrew verb. Thus Mark (xiv. 22, 23) in successive verses says that our Lord 'blessed' (*eulogēsas*) the bread and 'gave thanks' over (*eucharistēsas*) the wine, where a jew would have used the word *berakh* in both cases.[1]

S. Paul tends to use *eucharistein* rather than *eulogein*, even in cases where not 'the eucharist' but ordinary 'grace before meals' is certainly intended, *e.g.* of meat bought in the market;[2] though he uses *eulogein* especially of the eucharist itself.[3] Outside the gospels and S. Paul *eucharistein* does not appear in the N.T. Evidently terminology took a generation to settle down. The word 'eucharist' came in the end to be applied technically (*a*) to the christian sacramental prayer, then (*b*) to the whole action or rite of which that prayer furnished the formal verbal expression, and (*c*) finally to the elements over which the prayer was uttered and on which the rite centred. This seems to be due not to the language of scripture, which supplied no decided rule, but to the accident that the usual form in which the jewish word *berakah* was taken over into Greek christian usage was *eucharistia* when the change from the 'seven-' to the 'four-action shape' of the liturgy was made in the first century. (But for this we in England to-day might have spoken habitually of 'Celebrations of the Holy Eulogy', instead of the 'Holy Eucharist'.) The inference is that the terminology was not framed by S. Paul.

In making the exceedingly important change in the structure of the rite which resulted from leaving out the supper, the church scrupulously retained everywhere the old jewish invitation of the *chabûrah* president to his companions to say 'the Thanksgiving'—'Let us give thanks unto the Lord our God'. This is phrased in that particular form which was restricted by the rabbis to occasions when 'one hundred persons are present',[4]

---

[1] But it is at least an interesting point that the bread-blessing translated literally into Greek would begin *eulogētos ho kyrios*, whereas the opening words of the Thanksgiving in Greek would be *eucharistēsōmen toi kyrioi*. There may be a lingering tradition of the actual formulae used by our Lord behind the apparently casual choice of words in Mark xiv. 22, 23.

[2] 1 Cor. x. 30.                    [3] 1 Cor. x. 16.

[4] *Berakoth*, M., vii. 5 (*p.* 62).

*i.e.*, more than a merely private party. Thus accidentally did gentile christianity preserve evidence that the original jewish church had regarded the eucharist as an official and corporate actiòn of the whole church (*ecclesia*), and not a rite which any group of christians could perform at a private meeting (*syneleusis*). To this invitation in jewish practice those present 'made assent'. No jewish formula for this has been preserved, but the 'semitic parallelism' of the traditional christian response, 'It is meet and right', seems obvious enough. This survival of the special 'invitation' which prefaced the Thanksgiving of a *chabûrah*, together with the name *eucharistia*, would in itself suffice to link the christian 'eucharistic prayer' over the 'cup of blessing' with the *berakah* over the 'cup of blessing' which closed the *chabûrah* meal. And the case does not seem to be weakened when we look at the contents of the two prayers.

In the jewish Thanksgiving over the cup of blessing (*p.* 53), the first paragraph, 'Blessed be Thou . . .' contains the obligatory 'blessing' or 'glorifying of the Name'. But it is primarily a thanksgiving for God's bounty in giving earthly food, and its chief reference is to the meal which has just been taken. This reference disappears, therefore, from the christian eucharistic prayer along with the meal. But the second paragraph has a different bearing: 'We give thanks unto Thee . . .' for the entrance into Canaan, for the deliverance from bondage, for the Old Covenant established by the Law, for 'the life, grace and loving-kindness which Thou hast bestowed upon us, for the food wherewith Thou dost sustain us continually'. When we come to look at the earliest christian eucharistic prayer, it is possible to see in its opening clauses this type of thanksgiving repeated, but transposed into a christian key. 'We give thanks unto Thee' for the entrance into what the second century delighted to think of as the 'New Canaan', the sacrament, in connection with which the newly confirmed partook of symbolic milk and honey when they made their first communion;[1] for the deliverance from the bondage of the devil and sin, achieved by the incarnation and the passion; above all for the New Covenant set up through the rite of the last supper.[2] The christian prayers naturally go on to new and specifically christian developments which hinge upon this last point. But there seems to be at least a possibility that the form and theme of the first half of some of the christian prayers have their origin in this second paragraph of the *berakah*, when the substance of their contents is considered carefully.[3]

(3) *The fraction.* The bread was originally—at the *chabûrah* meal and the last supper—broken simply for distribution and not for symbolic purposes,

---

[1] *Cf.* Hippolytus, *Ap. Trad.*, xxiii. 2. At the baptismal eucharist is to be offered not only bread and wine, but 'milk and honey mingled together, in fulfilment of the promise to the Fathers, wherein He said, I will give you a land flowing with milk and honey; which Christ indeed gave, even His Flesh, whereby the faithful are nourished like little children . . .' *Cf.* Tertullian, *de Res. Carn.*, xxiii.
[2] *Cf. p.* 216.    [3] *Cf. pp.* 220 *sqq.*

immediately after it had been blessed. So in the liturgical 'four-action' shape of the rite, it is broken at once after the blessing (by the *eucharistia*, along with the wine) for communion which follows immediately. But though there is nothing in the record of the last supper to suggest that our Lord made any point of the broken bread representing His own Body 'broken' on the cross (and in fact the fourth gospel makes a strong point of the fact that His Body was not broken)[1] the symbolism was bound to suggest itself to somebody. The reading 'This is My Body which is broken (*klōmenon*) for you' in 1 Cor. xi. 24, adopted by the A.V. alongside the other (more strongly attested) ancient interpolation 'given for you', is the proof that this symbolism of the fraction as representing the passion was explicitly adopted in some quarters in the second century.

(4) *The communion*. It appears to have been the universal tradition in the pre-Nicene church that all should receive communion standing. This was the posture in which the cup of bles ing was received at the *chabûrah* meal, though the broken bread was received sitting or reclining at table. Presumably the change in posture for receiving the bread was made when the meal was separated from the eucharist. The jews stood for the recitation of the *berakah* and to receive the cup of blessing, and this affected the bread, too, when its distribution came to be placed between the end of the *berakah* and the handing of the cup.

Communion ended the rite, just as the handing of the cup was the last of those points in the *chabûrah* meeting to which our Lord had attached a special meaning. The psalm which ended the *chabûrah* meal therefore reappears at the agape, not at the eucharist. There was thus no 'thanksgiving' at the end of the primitive eucharist. The *berakah* was itself a 'Thanksgiving' and this was the meaning of *eucharistia* also. The idea of a corporate 'thanksgiving for the Thanksgiving' could only come to appear reasonable after the church had lost all contact with the jewish origins of the rite. Even then the tradition was for centuries too strong to be set aside that the *berakah* or *eucharistia* was the *only* prayer in the rite, which must express in words its whole meaning—from the offertory to the communion. It is only in the fourth century that a corporate thanksgiving after communion begins to make its appearance in eucharistic rites in Syria and Egypt; and even then in the great historic rites it always remains a very brief and formal little section, appended, as it were, to the eucharistic action, which really ends at its climax, the communion. A single sentence of dismissal, probably said by the deacon, appears to have been the only thing that followed the communion in the pre-Nicene church. Here again the influence of its origin appears to have marked the Shape of the Liturgy permanently throughout christendom, down to the sixteenth century.

Such was the structure of the pre-Nicene eucharist in its 'four-action shape', the bare elements of those parts of the *chabûrah* rite to which our

[1] John xix. 36.

Lord had given a new christian meaning, extracted from their setting in a supper. Without anticipating the discussion of the date when this 'four-action shape' was reached we can at least say that the separation of the eucharist from the meal must have been made at a date when the jewish origins of the rite were still completely understood, and by men to whom they were very dear, or they would hardly have preserved the traces of them so reverently.

### The Lord's Supper or Agape

We have said that the 'Lord's supper' or agape in the second century presents us with a religious meal retaining all the features of a *chabûrah* supper from which the christian eucharist had been removed. The Western rules for its celebration in the second century are best known to us from the *Apostolic Tradition* of Hippolytus; Tertullian also informs us concerning some details of the African observance.

Hippolytus introduces the subject by insisting on the obligation upon all of fasting frequently, especially the presbyters, virgins and widows. But 'the bishop cannot fast except when all the laity fast. For there will be times when some one wishes to offer ⟨a meal⟩ to the church, and he cannot be denied.

'(*a*) And ⟨the bishop⟩ having broken the bread must on all occasions taste of it, and eat with such of the faithful as are present. And they shall take from the hand of the bishop one fragment (*klasma*) of a loaf before each takes his own bread, for this is the "blessed bread" (*eulogion*). But it is not the eucharist, as is the Body of the Lord.

'(*b*) And before they drink let each of those who are present take a cup and give thanks (*eucharistein*) and drink; and so let the baptised take their meal.

'(*c*) But to the catechumens let exorcised bread be given, and they shall each for themselves offer a cup. A catechumen shall not sit at table at the Lord's supper.

'(*d*) And throughout the meal let him who eats remember (*i.e.*, pray for) him who invited him, for to this end he (*i.e.* the host) petitioned that they might come under his roof . . .

'(*e*) If you are all assembled and offered something to be taken away, accept it from the giver ⟨and depart⟩ and eat thy portion alone.

'(*f*) But if ⟨you are invited⟩ all to eat together, eat sufficiently, but so that there may remain something over that your host may send it to whomsoever he wills as the superfluity of the saints, and he ⟨to whom it is sent⟩ may rejoice with what is left over.

'(*g*) And let the guests when they eat partake in silence without arguing. But ⟨let them hearken to⟩ any exhortation the bishop may make, and if any one ask ⟨him⟩ any question let an answer be given him. And when the bishop has given the explanation, let every one quietly offering praise remain silent till he [?the bishop] be asked again.

'(h) And if the faithful should be present at a Lord's supper without the bishop but with a presbyter or deacon present, let them similarly partake in orderly fashion. But let all be careful to receive the blessed bread from the hand of the presbyter or deacon. Likewise a catechumen shall receive ⟨from him⟩ the exorcised bread. If laymen ⟨only⟩ are present without a cleric, let them eat with understanding. For a layman cannot make the blessed bread. But let each having given thanks (*eucharistēsas*) for himself eat in the Name of the Lord.

'(i) If at any time any one wishes to invite the widows, let him feed them and send them away before sunset, even though they are advanced in years. But if he cannot ⟨entertain them at his house⟩ because of the circumstances, let him give them food and wine and send them away, and they shall partake of it at home as they please.'[1]

All this is exceedingly interesting by reason of its obvious jewish derivation.

(a) The bishop still 'says grace' in the customary jewish fashion, and this is still the start of the christian *chabûrah* meal. (b) It is curious to find the old rabbinic exception in the case of wine (*viz.*, that all blessings were said by the president alone on behalf of all present, except only in the case of wine) still observed at Rome c. A.D. 215 after more than a century of gentile christianity. (c) The old jewish rules against table-fellowship 'with men uncircumcised'[2] have been transferred by the church to any form of table-fellowship 'with men unconfirmed'. (Circumcision and confirmation are both termed the 'seal of the covenant', under the Old and New Covenants respectively, in the New Testament.) This is the origin of the rule that only the *confirmed*, not the baptised, may be communicants. The catechumens, however, though they are not yet of the Body of Christ, are adherents of the church, and not excluded from its charity. Though they may not receive of the bread broken in fellowship, they receive what better befits their condition, not yet freed from the power of sin and the devil, exorcised bread; and they bless each their own cup of wine for themselves, as gentiles drinking in the presence of a jewish *chabûrah* were permitted to do by jewish custom.[3] They stand apart from the church's table, but they can receive the hospitality of its christian host.

There is no 'Thanksgiving' said at the end of this meal over a 'cup of blessing', because this item of the *chabûrah* rite has been transferred to the eucharist, where it has become the 'consecration prayer'. However, the Lord's supper in Hippolytus is in this more logical—and probably more

---

[1] *Ap. Trad.*, xxv.; xxvi. 1–13; xxvii. The text of this passage is in some uncertainty, and I am dissatisfied with details of the restoration in my ed. *pp.* 45 *sq.* I offer the above as an improvement, from a fresh study of the oriental versions. In all essential points this seems more or less secure.

[2] Acts xi. 3.    [3] *Berakoth, Tos.*, v. 21 (*p.* 73).

primitive—than that of some other churches. For in Tertullian[1] we hear of prayer at the end of the meal, and also in the East. The absence of the cup of blessing is in itself sufficient to indicate that this is not a 'fossil eucharist' of any 'primitive' type, as Lietzmann supposes. From this point of view the individual blessing of wine cups by each participant is no substitute for the eucharistic chalice. The 'Thanksgiving' over 'the cup of blessing' had always in jewish custom been said by the president alone for all the rest, a usage which descended directly to the recitation of the eucharistic prayer by the bishop-celebrant. The blessing of a separate cup by each participant for himself reproduces the jewish practice with regard to ordinary cups of wine drunk in the course of the *chabûrah* meal.

But though this Lord's supper or agape thus represents exactly what remained of the *chabûrah* meal when the primitive eucharist had been extracted from it, it is nevertheless in one respect a changed institution. It is no longer a communal supper of the church which all christians can attend in their own right, but a private party to which the guests can come only by the invitation of their host, whose bounty they are expected to repay by their prayers, as the jewish guest had been expected to do.[2] Indeed, on occasion the 'Lord's supper' is now a dignified name for what is not much more than a distribution of charitable doles (*cf. e, i,* above). On the other hand its origin in the common meal of the church seems to be indicated by the fact that the lay host cannot as such 'say grace' for his guests, a function naturally reserved to the clerics at a *church* meal, but which at a private though still definitely religious meal of laity only one would expect to be transferred to the host. Here, on the contrary, in the absence of any cleric at all, each guest is to 'eucharistise' his meal for himself (*cf. h*). Doubtless the presence of some of the clergy, if not of the bishop himself (which is taken as normal) was about as usual at these religious meals in the second century as their attendance at the parochial 'Christmas parties' of pre-war days was with us; and the cleric present naturally 'said grace'. But the fact that a layman *cannot* say grace for others suggests that originally this Lord's supper was a definitely 'ecclesiastical' occasion at which the clergy were indispensable, as the only people entitled to act for the church corporately. Eastern evidence does not necessarily hold good for Roman origins; but Ignatius of Antioch, almost exactly a century before Hippolytus, had written, 'Without the bishop it is not lawful . . . to hold an agape.'[3]

In Hippolytus, therefore, the meaning of the Lord's supper has somewhat decayed by its getting, as it were, into private hands, instead of being a communal meal. Doubtless the exceptional size of the Roman church from the early second century, when its members, already many hundreds

---

[1] *Cf. infra.*
[2] *Berakoth, Tos.,* vii. 2 (*p.* 75). 'What does a good guest say? Remember the householder for good.'
[3] *Smyrn.,* viii. 2.

strong, could not in practice assemble for a common meal, had led to this change. But it retains the marks of its origin in the indispensable part assigned to the clergy, the jewish bread- and wine-blessings performed strictly according to ancient jewish rules, and the religious—not to say rather lugubrious—behaviour expected of all concerned.

Tertullian's information as to the rite in Africa is much less detailed. 'We do not sit down to supper before we have tasted something of prayer to God. We eat as much as hunger requires; we drink as much as befits temperance. We take our fill as men who are mindful that they must worship God even by night; we talk, as men that know their Lord is listening. After water for rinsing the hands and lamps have been brought in, each is called forth into the midst to sing to God as his knowledge of the scriptures or his own invention enables him, which is a test of how much he has drunk. Prayer equally marks the end of the banquet.'[1] The 'foretaste' of prayer appears to be a cryptic reference to the distribution of blessed bread. The bringing in of the bason and lamps were a *chabûrah* custom, but they were also common customs at the evening meal all round the Mediterranean. The singing of psalms after dinner, like the concluding prayer, may be *chabûrah* survivals, but they are natural in any case. Wine was drunk, but we hear nothing of a common cup. This, however, is mentioned as an element in the African agape by Cyprian.[2]

In the East we hear rather more about the Lord's supper, or the 'church's supper' as it is sometimes called, than we do in the West, and there the institution lasted longer as a normal observance. Doubtless the small country churches found it much easier to keep up the custom of meeting for a common meal than the larger town churches, and in the East christianity generally spread out to the countrysides much earlier than in the West, where until the fourth century it remained almost exclusively an urban religion.

The fullest information about the Eastern form of the agape is found in the present text of some versions of the *Apostolic Tradition*, into which it has been interpolated from some oriental source.

(*a*) 'When the evening is come, the bishop being present, the deacon shall bring in a lamp. The bishop standing in the midst of the faithful before he blesses it (*eucharistein*) shall say: "The Lord be with you all". And the people also shall say: "With thy spirit". And the bishop also shall say: "Let us give thanks unto the Lord"; and the people shall say: "It is meet and right. Greatness and exaltation with glory are due unto Him." And he shall not say: "Lift up your hearts" because that shall be said ⟨only⟩ at the oblation. And he prays thus, saying:

' "We give thanks unto Thee, O God, through Thy Son Jesus Christ our Lord, because Thou hast enlightened us by revealing the incorruptible light.

<hr>

[1] *Apologeticus* 39.        [2] *Ep.*, lxiii. 16.

' "We therefore having finished the length of a day and having come to the beginning of the night, and having been satisfied with the light of the day which Thou didst create for our satisfaction, and since we lack not now by Thy grace a light for the evening, we sanctify Thee and we glorify Thee; through Thine only Son our Lord Jesus Christ, through Whom to Thee with Him ⟨be⟩ glory and might and honour with the Holy Ghost now and ever and world without end." And they shall all say "Amen."

(b) 'And having risen after supper, the children and virgins shall sing psalms by the light of the lamp.

(c) 'And afterwards the deacon holding the mingled cup of the oblation (or of the meal) shall say the psalm from those in which is written "Hallelujah." [After that the presbyter has commanded, "And likewise from those psalms."] And afterwards the bishop having offered the cup as is proper for the cup, he shall say the psalm "Hallelujah." And all of them as he recites the psalms shall say "Hallelujah", which is to say: "We praise Him Who is God most high: glorified and praised is He Who founded all the world by His (lit. one) Word."

(d) 'And likewise when the psalm is completed, he shall give thanks over the ⟨bread⟩, and give of the fragments to the faithful. (And they shall take from the hand of the bishop one fragment of a loaf before each takes his own bread.)'[1]

This is not by Hippolytus, but it is now found in full in the Ethiopic version (only) of his work. Though it gives us an Eastern and not a Roman form of the rite, it is not necessarily much, if at all, later in date than Hippolytus' genuine work. It had already found its way into the fourth-fifth century Greek text of the *Apostolic Tradition* which was the remote original of the present Ethiopic version, and also into the very good MS. of Hippolytus which lay before the compiler of the *Testament of our Lord* (c. A.D. 400). It was found also in the text which was used to form the *Canons of Hippolytus* (c. A.D. 600?), and perhaps was known to the compiler of *Apostolic Constitutions* Bk. viii. (c. A.D. 375). To have affected so widely the fourth century text of Hippolytus all over the East this passage must have been originally introduced during the third century—*i.e.* within seventy or eighty years of Hippolytus' death—and it therefore offers satisfactory evidence as to the rite of the agape in the East before Nicaea. It is unfortunate that the *Testament*, the *Canons* and the *Constitutions* only reproduce part of the passage, which throws us back on the Ethiopic version for our knowledge of the text as a whole. For this latter is only a mediaeval translation made from an Arabic translation made from a Sahidic translation of the Greek original, and it has naturally become a little 'blurred' in the process. However, in view of the complicated history

---

[1] *Ap. Trad.*, xxvi. 18-32. The last sentence is a repetition of Hippolytus' genuine direction at xxvi. 2.

of the text, we may well be thankful that it is still as intelligible as it is, for it is of the greatest interest.

The lighting and blessing of a lamp for the evening meal had a place of its own in jewish domestic piety, where it signalised the beginning and end of the Sabbath on Friday and Saturday evenings. It had also a special connection with certain festival observances. In every strict jewish home for more than two thousand years the lighting of the sabbath lamp has been and is still one of the privileges of jewish mothers; and to this day the lights of the *Habdalah* and *Hannukah* as well as the Sabbath retain their place in jewish observance. The ordinary jewish blessing to be said at the lamp-lighting was 'Blessed art Thou, O Lord our God, eternal King, Who createst the lamps of fire',[1] and the question of whether the word 'lamps' here should be singular or plural was debated between the schools of Shammai and Hillel, *c.* 10 B.C. The bringing in and blessing of the lamp played a part in the *chabûrah* supper, and the exact point at which this should be done formed another subject of discussion between these two rabbinic schools;[2] but it appears that they were agreed that it should come after the meal was concluded in any case. Here it comes before.

As is well known, the jewish practice survived into christian worship in the ceremony of the *Lucernarium*, the blessing of the evening lamp with a thanksgiving to God for the day, which was still found all over christendom from Mesopotamia to Spain in the fourth century, and survives to this day in the East and at Milan and Toledo. One of the most famous and lovely of early christian hymns, *Phōs hilaron* (best known to us in Keble's magnificent translation, 'Hail gladdening light of His pure glory poured', A. & M. 18) was written to be sung at this little christian ceremony, whose survival in the blessing of the paschal candle we have already noted.[3]

When we look back at (*a*) we find that it is only an early form of the *Lucernarium*. The deacon, as 'the servant of the church', brings in the lighted lamp, which the bishop (in this form of the rite) is to bless. (In some places the deacon did so.) The blessing is done with a form obviously modelled on the ordinary christian 'eucharistic' prayer, retaining the old jewish notion that one blessed persons and ʳhings by giving thanks to God for them over them. The first sentence, though it is not in any way verbally derived from the jewish lamp-blessing, may be described as in substance a christian remodelling of it. The remainder of the prayer is a thanksgiving for the past day, beautiful in its simplicity and directness, which ends with that 'seal' of the Name of God without which in jewish and early christian teaching no *eucharistia* or *berakah* could be valid.

(*b*) raises the question of the order in which the proceedings are here described. It is most usefully discussed a little later.

(*c*) The Ethiopic translator has evidently got into a certain amount of

---

[1] *Berakoth, M.,* viii. 6 (*p.* 70).   [2] *Ibid.* viii. 5 (*p.* 68).
[3] *Cf. p.* 23.

confusion over the 'Hallelujah' psalms. (I am inclined to strike out the sentence about the 'presbyter', bracketed in the text, as an intrusion.) But the main point of what he is trying to say is obvious enough. At the festal supper on the greater jewish feasts, Passover, Pentecost, Tabernacles, New Moons and some others, it is still the jewish custom to recite the *hallel* (Psalms ciii.-cxviii. taken as a single psalm; often called the 'Egyptian *hallel*' to distinguish it from the 'Great *hallel*'—Ps. cxxxvi.). This is partly monotoned and partly chanted by a 'reader'. In the latter chanted part (Ps. cxviii.) it is still customary for the congregation to alternate with the reader's solo in a chorus, consisting now of the repetition of Ps. cxviii. 1, 'O give thanks unto the Lord, for He is good, for His mercy endureth for ever.' Though the refrain suggested in the text is different, it is evidently the same custom of the recital of the *hallel* with a chorus-refrain in one part of it, which is being described. We know that the custom of reciting the *hallel* at supper is older in jewish practice than our Lord's time, at all events at Passover;[1] and on other feasts it is at least as old as the second century.[2] Since the *hallel* was a purely festal observance and the last supper did not take place on a jewish festival, it is unlikely to be the 'hymn' of Mark xiv. 26; but its occurrence here at the agape is certainly something which descends from the primitive jewish church.

(*c* and *d*) We have already noted[3] that on festivals there was another common cup blessed and partaken of, besides the cup of blessing, both at a *chabûrah* meeting and at the ordinary family meal of a pious jewish household. This was the *kiddûsh*-cup. It received a special blessing, incorporating the ordinary wine-blessing, but also including clauses making special reference to the festival or sabbath which was being observed. A variable blessing of the cup of this kind may be indicated in our text by the phrase 'as is proper for the cup'. The point in the meal at which the *kiddûsh*-cup was blessed and handed round has varied at different periods in jewish practice; but the most thorough discussion of the matter, that of Elbogen, arrives at the conclusion that in the first century A.D. it preceded the breaking of bread at the beginning of the meal, though he has not convinced all jewish experts on this.[4] Here, however, it is certainly the equivalent of the *kiddûsh*-cup which is in question at this christian 'Lord's supper'. This recitation of the *hallel* marks it out as a festal occasion, to which the *kiddûsh*-cup was restricted; and the cup of blessing *never* preceded the breaking of bread, but always marked the end of the meal, of which the bread-breaking marked the beginning.

(*b*) We are now in a position to discuss the arrangement of the parts of this christian observance in the light of jewish custom. Where exactly is the meal proper intended to come in this text? The jewish order would have been *kiddûsh*-cup (probably), bread-breaking, supper, blessing of

---

[1] *Pesachim, Mishnah*, x. 6.    [2] *Sukkoth, Tos.*, iv. 1.    [3] *Cf. p.* 54 *n* 2.
[4] *Cf.* F. L. Cirlot, *op. cit. pp.* 7 *sqq.*

lamp. The christian order almost reverses this. But if the single sentence (b) were omitted, or regarded as placed out of order to explain the purpose for which the lamp is provided, there would be no mention of the meal until after the bread-breaking, and we should have an ordinary jewish *chabûrah* meal on a festal occasion (only without the 'cup of blessing' or the accompanying Thanksgiving) but with the lamp-blessing at the beginning instead of at the end. The Ethiopic editor evidently thought the meal ought to come after the bread-breaking, since he has gone on to repeat Hippolytus' genuine directions about this at the end of this interpolated passage from his special Eastern source. The point is not of great importance, though the close connection between the jewish and christian customs is shewn by the fact that some scholars have thought that the christian account might conceivably be corrected by the jewish rules.

I do not myself believe that this is necessary. It may equally well be that we have to do with a deliberate christian rearrangement, due to the removal of the 'cup of blessing' and the accompanying Thanksgiving (the climax of the jewish rite), by their transference to the eucharist. The christian *chabûrah* meal has been given a new climax by the transference of the *kiddûsh*-cup and 'grace before meals' to the place of the cup of blessing and 'grace after meals'. The lamp-blessing, 'left in the air' by the transference to the eucharist of the Thanksgiving, with which in jewish custom it was closely connected, has been given a new 'Thanksgiving' of its own, and has changed places with the *kiddûsh*-cup to supply an opening devotion. Be this as it may, and it seems an obvious and complete explanation of the facts, all the elements of this christian Lord's supper, whatever their right order, are individually derived from the *chabûrah* rite on festal occasions. The *hallel* and the *kiddûsh*-cup are not derived from the last supper itself, but are an independent survival of jewish festal customs into gentile christian practice. They witness to the joyful spirit in which the apostolic church kept its Lord's supper,[1] and perhaps to the fact that when it had been separated from the eucharist it was customarily reserved for festivals, perhaps Sunday evenings. Otherwise the tradition of incorporating *hallel* and *kiddûsh* into the agape would hardly have arisen.

From our immediate point of view the two important points to be borne in mind are (1) That the Eastern form of the agape or Lord's supper, unlike the Roman, certainly included a common cup, whose blessing preceded that of the bread; (2) That this cup derives not from the cup of blessing (the eucharistic chalice) but from the *kiddûsh*-cup, which marked festal occasions and was not used at the last supper. The pointed omission of the 'cup of blessing' (never confused in jewish practice with that of the *kiddûsh*) and the Thanksgiving—the invariable sign of a *chabûrah* meeting—

[1] Acts ii. 46.

D.S.L.

from the supper of the christian *chabûrah* after the separation of supper
and eucharist, points to the deliberate intention of the jewish apostolic
church to differentiate the Lord's supper from the rite of the 'New
Covenant', ordained by our Lord at the last supper. The later gentile
church would not be likely to make these careful jewish distinctions.

What is probably a rather earlier set of Eastern directions for the agape
is found in chapters ix. and x. of the little second century christian work,
the *Didache* or 'Teaching of the xii Apostles to the Gentiles.' It runs as
follows:

ix. 1. 'Concerning the thanksgiving (*eucharistia*) thus give ye thanks
(*eucharistēsate*):

2. 'First, concerning the cup: "We give thanks (*eucharistoumen*) unto
Thee, our Father, for the holy vine of David Thy servant, which Thou
didst make known unto us through Jesus Thy servant; to Thee be the
glory for ever."

3. 'Concerning the broken ⟨bread⟩ (*klasma*): "We give thanks unto
Thee, our Father, for the life and knowledge, which Thou didst make
known unto us through Jesus Thy servant; to Thee be the glory for ever.
(4) As this broken ⟨bread⟩ was scattered upon the tops of the mountains
and being gathered became one, so gather Thy church from the ends of the
earth into Thy kingdom; for Thine is the glory and the power through
Jesus Christ for ever."

5. 'Let no one eat or drink from your thanksgiving (*eucharistia*) but
those who have been baptised into the Name of the Lord. For concerning this also (*kai*) the Lord said, 'Give not that which is holy unto the
dogs.'

x. 1. 'And after you are satisfied thus give ye thanks:

2. ' "We give thanks unto Thee, holy Father, for Thy holy Name,
which Thou hast made to tabernacle in our hearts and for the knowledge
and faith and immortality which Thou hast made known unto us through
Jesus Thy Son; to Thee be the glory for ever. (3) Thou, Master Almighty,
hast created all things for Thy Name's sake and hast given food and drink
unto men for enjoyment, that they might give thanks unto Thee (*eucharis-
tēsōs n*): but on us Thou didst graciously bestow spiritual food and drink
and eternal life through Thy Son. (4) Before all things we give thanks
unto Thee for that Thou art mighty; Thine is the glory for ever. (5)
Remember, O Lord, Thy church, to deliver it from all evil and perfect
it in Thy love, and gather it from the four winds, which has been sanctified
unto Thy Kingdom, which Thou didst make ready for it; for Thine is the
power and the glory for ever."

6. ' "Let grace come and let this world pass away. Hosanna to the God
of David. If any is holy, let him come; if any be not, let him repent. Maranatha. (Our Lord, come!) Amen."

7. 'But allow the prophets to give thanks as much as they will.'

What are we to make of this? A generation ago in Germany it was taken for granted by most protestant scholars[1] that these prayers and rubrics concerned not the eucharist proper but the agape. Since then there has been a change of opinion, shared by Roman Catholic scholars including Duchesne and Batiffol, which English scholarship has followed without much independent criticism, affected chiefly, one suspects, by Lietzmann's theory of eucharistic origins. It is now commonly held that we have here a specimen of a jewish rite in the actual process of being turned from a non-sacramental meal into a eucharist in the later sense. I confess that the older view seems to me much the more probable. The author of the *Didache* knew the liturgical eucharist as well as the agape, and describes it under quite different terms in chapter xiv. thus:

1. 'Every Lord's day of the Lord (*sic*) having come together break bread and give thanks (*eucharistēsate*), first confessing your sins, that your sacrifice may be pure. (2) Every one that hath his dispute with his companion shall not come together with you, until they be reconciled, that your sacrifice be not defiled. (3) For this is that sacrifice which was spoken of by the Lord, "In every place and season offer unto Me a pure sacrifice; for I am a great king, saith the Lord, and My Name is wonderful among the Gentiles."[2] (xv. 1) Choose for yourselves therefore bishops and deacons ...'

This is the eucharist as the second century church generally understood it, celebrated by the liturgical ministry of bishops and deacons, with its preliminary arbitration on quarrels that the church may be one. It is held on Sunday, and the word twice used here for 'come together' is that sometimes employed for the special liturgical 'coming together' by other first and second century authors. Three times over the writer insists that this eucharist is a 'sacrifice', and he quotes a text of Malachi which is employed by Justin Martyr (*Dialogue*, 116) at Rome c. A.D. 150 with reference quite certainly to what we mean by the eucharist.

When we look back to the alleged 'eucharist' of ix. and x. none of this seems to be in the writer's mind at all. On the contrary, this appears quite clearly to be the agape when it is compared with what we know from other sources about that rite in the East. There is a cup, but it precedes the bread, as in the Eastern agape rite we had previously considered. And the blessings for both, though they are in no way verbally derived from the jewish wine- and bread-blessings (except that both christian and jewish wine-blessings contain the word 'vine', which is not very surprising) are at least framed upon the same model, in that they are brief 'blessings of God' and not of the wine and bread themselves. The Thanksgiving after the meal is a little closer to the jewish Thanksgiving though even here no direct point of contact can be made. But there is at least the sequence of

---

[1] *Cf. e.g.* F. Kattenbusch, *Realencyklopädie für prot. Theol.* (1903) xii. 671 *sq.*; P. Drews, *Z.N.T.W.*, 1904, *pp.* 74 *sq.* There were even then notable exceptions, including Harnack, but this was the general position.
[2] Malachi i. 11, 14.

the three ideas: (a) thanksgiving for earthly food; (b) thanksgiving for the 'spiritual food and drink' (of the eucharist proper) which is of the essence of the New Covenant; (c) prayer for the church. These recall the three jewish paragraphs of (a) thanksgiving for earthly food; (b) thanksgiving for the Old Covenant, with its essence in the Law and Circumcision; (c) prayer for jewry. But there is in this rite no cup of blessing accompanying the Thanksgiving, which is precisely the distinction between eucharist and agape. And when the substance of the prayers—beautiful in themselves— is considered, is it possible to see in them anything whatever but grace before and after meals?[1] The *Didache* knows and quotes the gospel of Matt. It is surely incredible that the author could have ignored the close connection of the eucharist proper with the passion established in Matt. xxvi.

What, then, are we to make of the word *eucharistia*, etc., so repeatedly used of this cup and bread? It seems to me to prove exactly nothing. We have already seen that in early christian usage *eulogein* and *eucharistein* are used indifferently to translate the single Hebrew verb *berakh*, and these prayers are undoubtedly what a jew would have called *berakoth*, for all their christian content. S. Paul uses *eulogein* of consecrating the eucharist proper, and *eucharistein* of blessing meat bought in the public market. By the time of Hippolytus terminology is settling down; the 'blessed bread' of the Lord's supper is *eulogion*, clearly distinguished from 'the Lord's Body' of the eucharist. But even he is not quite consistent. When there is no cleric present at a Lord's supper to 'eulogise' the bread, the laity are each to '*eucharistise*' the food for themselves.[2] Earlier terminology had shewn the same continual lack of precision. Justin speaks of the christians worshipping God 'with a formula of prayer and thanksgiving (*eucharistia*) for all our food' (*Ap.* I. 13), almost verbally the phrase which he employs for the consecration of the liturgical eucharist (*Ap.* I. 66). The bishop in the Ethiopic agape-rite above 'eucharistises' a lamp; 'eucharistic' prayers for the consecration of chrism, bishops, virgins and all sorts of things and persons are to be found in the Roman Pontifical to this day. The mere word *eucharistia* in an early christian document does not at all establish that the subject concerned is 'the eucharist' in our sense.

Finally, there is the prohibition (ix. 5): 'Let no one eat or drink of your eucharist but those baptised in the Name of the Lord.' We have already seen from Hippolytus that the catechumens (and other pagans *a fortiori*) might not have 'table-fellowship' with the church at the agape any more than at the eucharist. And here, as a matter of fact, the *Didache* gives an

---

[1] K. Völker, *Mysterium und Agape*, pp. 135 sq. strains the sense almost to breaking point to find a spiritual or quasi-sacramental meaning in them. I confess I remain completely sceptical when I look at the text. They get no nearer to being 'sacramental' than does the bishop's lamp-blessing in the Ethiopic rite of the agape above: 'We give thanks unto Thee, O God, through Thy Son Jesus Christ our Lord, because Thou hast enlightened us by revealing the incorruptible light'.

[2] *Ap. Trad.*, xxvi. 13 (*cf.* above, *p.* 83 *h*).

almost open indication that its author has in mind something *other than* the eucharist proper. He writes of his blessed cup and bread, 'For concerning this *also* the Lord said, "Give not that which is holy unto the dogs" ' (Matt. vii. 6). The 'blessed bread' of the agape is holy, though not eucharistic.

We conclude, then, that *Didache* ix. and x. are entirely in line with what we know of the Eastern agape in pre-Nicene times, as *Didache* xiv. is entirely representative of second century ideas about the liturgical eucharist. The book was written as a guide for the laity, not for the clergy, and elsewhere gives detailed regulations only on things which the laity may do for themselves. These little agape prayers may be taken as the exact Eastern equivalents of Hippolytus' general direction to the laity when met without a cleric at the Lord's supper to 'eucharistise' the food each one for himself, and then 'eat in the Name of the Lord'. Prophets, as specially inspired persons, even though laymen, are not bound to use the set forms; just as the bishop, in virtue of his prophetic *charisma*, is not bound to follow a set form in the eucharistic prayer proper.

This is the agape or Lord's supper as celebrated privately by a party of christian friends. But in the third century in the East it could still be a corporate and official observance of the whole church. In a Syrian work written *c.* A.D. 250, the *Didascalia Apostolorum*, the author, speaking of the reception to be accorded to christian strangers visiting another church, lays it down that 'If it be a bishop, let him sit with the bishop; and let him accord him the honour of his rank, even as himself. And do thou, O bishop, invite him to discourse to thy people; for the exhortation and admonition of strangers is very profitable, especially as it is written: "There is no prophet that is acceptable in his own place." And when you offer the oblation, let him speak. But if he is wise and gives the honour [*i.e.* of celebrating the eucharist] to thee, at least let him speak over the cup'.[1] Here we have evidence of the feeling that the bishop is the only proper prophetic teacher and priest of his own church, who ought not in any circumstances to be replaced at the eucharist by anyone else, however distinguished, when he is present. It witnesses also to the bishop's 'discourse' or exhortation at the agape, of which Hippolytus speaks. And it mentions the use of a cup in the East as an important element in that rite, just as in the Ethiopic order (*c*) and in the *Didache* (ix. 2).

The last text of any importance or interest on the Lord's supper or agape which we need consider comes from an Egyptian rule for virgins leading an ascetic life in their own homes, in the days before the religious life for women in convents had been fully organised. It is traditionally ascribed to S. Athanasius, an attribution which has been both questioned and defended by modern scholars without decisive reasons on either side. But it appears to be Egyptian and of the early fourth century. It runs thus:

[1] *Did. Ap.*, ii. 58. Ed. R. H. Connolly, 1929, *p.* 122.

'After None take thy food having given thanks to God over thy table with these words:

' "Blessed be God, Who hath mercy upon us and nourisheth us from our youth up; Who giveth food unto all flesh. Fill our hearts with joy and gladness that at all times having a sufficiency in all things, we may superabound unto every good work, in Christ Jesus our Lord, with Whom unto Thee is due glory, power, honour and worship, with the Holy Spirit unto ages of ages. Amen."

'And when thou sittest down to table and comest to the breaking of bread, sign thyself thrice with the sign of the cross, and say thus "eucharistising": "We give thanks (eucharistoumen) unto Thee, our Father, for Thy holy resurrection (sic). For through Thy servant Jesus Christ Thou hast made it knɔwn unto us. And as this bread which is upon this table was scattered and being gathered together even became one; so let Thy church be gathered together from the ends of the earth into Thy kingdom, for Thine is the power and the glory, world without end. Amen."

'This prayer at the breaking of bread before thou eatest thou shouldst say. And when thou settest it down upon the table and art about to sit down, say the "Our Father" right through. The aforesaid prayer, "Blessed be Thou, O God", we say when we have eaten and rise from the table. But if there are two or three virgins with thee, they shall "eucharistise" over the bread that is set forth and offer the prayer with thee. But if there be found a woman catechumen at the table, let her not pray with the faithful, nor do thou in any case sit to eat thy bread with her. Nor shalt thou sit at table to eat with careless and frivolous women without necessity. For thou art holy unto the Lord and thy food and drink has been hallowed (hēgiasmenon). For by the prayers and the holy words it is hallowed (hagiazetai)'[1]

The eucharistia 'Blessed be God' (which despite the misleading opening rubric turns out to be for the end of the meal) appears to be remotely derived from the first paragraph of the old jewish berakah after meals. The breaking of bread is simply the old jewish grace before meals, with a prayer similar to that found in Didache ix. There is, however, no obvious trace of a use of the Didache elsewhere in this work and the text of this prayer differs verbally a good deal from that of the Didache. It is possible that we have here an independent use of a traditional prayer for the agape rather than a direct literary quotation, though the Didache was certainly in circulation in fourth century Egypt. The rule against catechumens praying or eating with the faithful is still in full force for the agape as for the eucharist. There is no cup at all, for the virgins are vowed to an ascetic life and avoid the use of wine. There is no distribution of the broken bread, for the virgins each 'eucharistise' and offer the prayer to-

[1] dub. Athanasius, de Virginitate, 12, 13. (Certain features of the Greek suggest a translation from Coptic.)

gether, just as the laity, met at the Lord's supper without a cleric, are bidden to do by Hippolytus a century before. What is interesting is to find the whole technical terminology of the liturgical eucharist, 'eucharistising', 'hallowing', 'We give thanks unto Thee . . .', 'breaking the bread', 'the bread set forth' (*prokeimenon*—the regular word for the liturgical oblation) —still unhesitatingly applied to this obviously purely domestic meal of women alone, in the fourth century when there can be no question of any confusion of ideas between agape and eucharist. It is a warning not to build theories on the 'eucharistic' terminology applied to the agape in earlier documents.

We are now in a position to come to our conclusions about the Lord's supper or agape, and its relation to the eucharist. There is no evidence whatever that these are really parallel developments of the same thing, a 'Jerusalem type' of non-sacramental fellowship meal, and a 'Pauline type' of eucharistic oblation, as Lietzmann and others have supposed. Both derive from the *chabûrah* supper. But the eucharist consists of those two elements in the *chabûrah* customs to which our Lord Himself at the last supper had attached a new meaning for the future with reference to His own death. These have been carefully extracted from their setting, and continued in use apart from the rest of the *chabûrah* meal for obvious reasons. The Lord's supper or agape consists precisely of what was left of the *chabûrah* meal when the eucharist had been removed. In fact we may say that while the eucharist was derived directly from the last supper and from nothing else, the agape derived really from the *previous* meetings of our Lord's *chabûrah* before the last supper, though the separation between them was not made in practice before a generation had passed. And just as the *berakah* at the end of the supper, the only prayer of the jewish rite which was transferred to the new christian rite, furnished it with its new name by direct translation into Greek as *eucharistia*, so what was left of the supper seems to have furnished the Greek name of the Lord's supper. Dr. Oesterley seems justified in his suggestion 'that the name *Agape* was intended as a Greek equivalent to the neo-Hebrew *Chabûrah* . . . which means "fellowship", almost "love".'[1]

The permanent mark of the separation of the two rites was the complete absence of the 'cup of blessing' and the accompanying *berakah* from all known forms of the Lord's supper or agape. In this the christian continuation of the *chabûrah* supper differed notably from its jewish parent, where these two things were the central point and formal characteristic of a *chabûrah* meeting. The transference of just those two elements in the supper ritual to which our Lord had assigned a new meaning connected with His own death to a new and separate rite is in itself a strong indication of the way in which the liturgical eucharist was regarded by those who first made the separation. This is especially striking when we consider the

[1] *Jewish Background of the Christian Sacraments*, p. 204.

significance of the phrase 'the New Covenant in My Blood' in connection with the second paragraph of the *berakah* about the Old Covenant, which was rewritten in terms of the new christian meaning to form the christian eucharistic prayer. In the circumstances, the disappearance of these two all-important items from the christian *chabûrah* meal would be a quite sufficient differentiation between the two somewhat similar rites of the agape and the eucharist for jewish christians, but probably not for gentile converts from paganism. This, as well as the care and delicacy with which the separation was made, needs to be taken into account in considering by whom and when the 'four-action shape' of the eucharist was organised, a point which remains to be discussed.

### The Separation of the Eucharist from the Agape

At first sight S. Paul's evidence in 1 Cor. xi. appears to be decisive that the eucharist and agape were still combined in a single observance when that epistle was written. But upon closer inspection this interpretation, though still, I think, the most probable, becomes less certain than is generally supposed. The difficulty is partly due to the difficulty of deciding how far S. Paul's use of quasi-technical terms is already in line with that which became normal in the second century; and partly to the tantalisingly obscure way in which he refers to the actual practices at Corinth to which he is objecting, which he and his correspondents could take for granted, but which are by no means easy for us to make out.

S. Paul has just been rebuking the Corinthian peculiarity of allowing women to pray unveiled and concluded that 'we have no such custom, nor have the churches of God', as a decisive reason against it (*v.* 16). 'With this watchword' he continues 'I praise you not that you hold your liturgical assemblies not for the better but for the worse.' His converts, to whom he had taught the rite of the New Covenant, have evidently made some change in their method of celebrating it, which they thought to be an improvement, but to which he takes serious objection. But, 'First, when you hold your assembly in the *ecclesia*, I hear there are quarrels among you, and I partly believe it' (*v.* 18). Having dealt with this, he comes to the main point. 'Therefore when you assemble as the *ecclesia* it is not to eat the Lord's supper, for each one greedily starts on his own supper at the meal, and one goes hungry and another gets tipsy'. Having regard to the fact that the 'Lord's supper' in the second century means the agape *apart from* the eucharist proper, and that the first phrase can perfectly well mean 'When you assemble as the *ecclesia* it is not *possible* to eat the Lord's supper', it would be legitimate to understand this as meaning that the *ecclesia* is not the right sort of occasion at all for celebrating the agape, but only for the eucharist; *i.e.* the two rites have already been separated and the innovation of the Corinthians consisted precisely in combining them again. Such an interpretation would be strengthened by the following verse 'Have you not houses to eat and drink in?' (*i.e.*, the home is the right place for the agape). 'Or do you despise the *ecclesia*' (*i.e.*, the liturgical assembly) 'and put to shame them that have nothing? What shall I say? Shall I praise you for this? I praise you not' (*v.* 22). Then follows (23–5) the 'tradition' concerning the last supper, followed by the application (26): 'Whenever you eat this bread or drink this cup, ye do solemnly proclaim the Lord's death till He come. Whoever shall eat this bread or drink the cup of the Lord unworthily, shall be guilty of the Body and Blood of the Lord. Let a man therefore test himself and so eat of the bread and drink of the cup; for he that eateth and drinketh unworthily eateth and drinketh judgment unto himself, not discerning the Lord's Body.' There follow the proofs of this in the Corinthians' own experience of the result of unworthy communions. He concludes: 'Wherefore, my brethren, when ye come together to eat, wait for one another; and if anyone is hungry, let him eat at home.'

The difficulty is that S. Paul uses indiscriminately the same words 'eat' and 'drink' for partaking of the sacramental species and for the satisfying of hunger at a full meal. It would be equally reasonable to interpret this last sentence as meaning either 'Wherefore, my brethren, when ye come together to eat (this bread and drink this cup) wait for one another, and if anyone is hungry let him eat (a proper meal) at home'; or, 'when ye come together to eat (the combined eucharist and agape) wait for one another; and if anyone is hungry (and cannot wait) let him eat (a preliminary meal) at home.' I do not see how on the basis of the text as it stands, considered simply in itself, either interpretation can be shewn decisively to be wrong.[1]

But there are wider considerations to be taken into account. Whatever may have been the precise innovations which the Corinthians were so proud of,[2] it is plain that the secular and social aspects of the communal supper had largely obscured for them its religious and sacramental elements. Among the jews, with their long tradition of the *chabûrah* meal as a definitely religious occasion, introduced and closed by observances of piety, with every separate kind of food, every cup of wine, and every convenience (such as the lamp and the hand-washing) solemnly hallowed with its own benediction, such a meal could preserve both its aspects of social

---

[1] The same ambiguity attaches to the account of the celebration of the eucharist by S. Paul at Troas, Acts xx. 7 *sq.*.

[2] Dr. Cirlot (*op. cit. pp.* 27 *sq.*) suggests that they had reintroduced the *hors d'œuvres* and wine before the bread-breaking at the beginning of the meal, on Palestinian precedent, which S. Paul had discarded as unnecessary in gentile churches; and that some Corinthians had taken advantage of this 'preliminary snack' to satisfy hunger after a hard day's work by bringing their own *hors d'œuvres* on a very lavish scale. The body of the meal, on both jewish and gentile precedent, would be communally provided, and the difficulties of 'one going hungry and another getting tipsy' in this part of the meal would be less likely to arise.

fellowship and Covenant-rite in some sort of balance. But gentile churches had no such previous training in their background. Even the meetings of the nearest gentile equivalents, the hellenistic *hetairiai* or 'clubs', though they had usually a religious association, were by no means always occasions of what we (or a jew) would call 'piety'. The religious aspect of the matter was, as a rule, not much more than a pretext for merry-making; and the kind of devotion called out by the unethical deities—with certain important exceptions—to whose cult these pagan banquets gave a social recognition was not as a rule likely to commend itself either to the jewish or the christian sense of religion. If S. Paul had introduced at Corinth the eucharist still combined with the agape, it is easy enough to see how his unsteady new gentile converts could come to lay the emphasis on the more human aspect of the observance, to the neglect of the special meaning attached to the bread-breaking at the beginning and the cup at the end. It is much more difficult to see how if they were from the first familiar with the eucharist as a Covenant-rite already isolated from the supper they could so quickly forget its solemn meaning, even if they had had the idea of reviving the jewish *chabûrah* practice by combining the sacramental rite and the supper once more. On these grounds, rather than because of any absolute irreconcilability with the text of 1 Cor. xi., we must reject all the forms of the theory that at the time of the writing of that epistle the eucharist was no longer associated with the agape in a single observance.[1]

The matter seems to be rather different when we come to examine the later accounts of the last supper in Matt. and Mark. S. Paul is unconsciously relating what he has to say about the specifically eucharistic bread and wine to their place in the supper, *e.g.* '*After supper* He took the cup', and so forth. Matt. and Mark, though they note that the historical institution of the rite took place at a supper, are no longer concerned to do this. They concentrate on the two things which later liturgical practice *isolated* from the supper in the eucharist, and neglect all else. They do not even state where and when in the meal they came, or whether together or at an interval. No one would gather from either account that anything occurred in between. They are writing primarily for gentile readers, to whom the details of jewish custom would be unfamiliar and perhaps not particularly interesting. But they are also writing for christian readers, and it rather looks as though the interrelation of eucharist and supper to one another was no longer familiar or interesting to christians. There is, too, the further point that both have changed 'This cup is the New Covenant in My Blood' to 'This is My Blood of the New Covenant', apparently to secure a closer parallel to 'This is My Body'; which suggests that the two 'words' are in much closer connection than when they came at opposite

[1] In different ways this has been defended by scholars of very different allegiances, *e.g.* Mgr. Batiffol and K. Völker.

ends of the supper. Neither argument is decisive, indeed, either separately would seem rather trivial. But they both point in the same direction.

The next point is the introduction of the word 'agape' as a technical term for the christian common meal (whether with or without the eucharist). This occurs in the New Testament only at Jude 12 (and perhaps also in 2 Pet. ii. 13 if *apatais* be not the true reading) where certain heretics are denounced as 'blemishes feasting with you in your *agapai*.' There is here no apparent reference to the eucharist, but only to a christian 'feast'. The new term had presumably been introduced to describe a new observance, the supper apart from the eucharist. But this is found only here, among the later *strata* of the New Testament, in the second christian generation.

In the next generation the new word has become a technical term used by distinction from 'the eucharist' to describe the observance, now becoming traditional, of the supper altogether apart from the liturgical eucharist. Writing to the Smyrnaeans, Ignatius (*c.* A.D. 115) warns them: 'Without the bishop let no one do any of the things which pertain to the *ecclesia*. Let that be accounted a valid eucharist which is under the bishop (as president) or one to whom he shall have committed (it). Wheresoever the bishop may be found, there let the whole body be, as wherever Jesus Christ may be, there is the catholic church. It is not allowed without the bishop either to baptise or to hold an agape.'[1] Ignatius is not laying down a new principle, but insisting on the liturgical basis of the bishop's authority in his church. Without the exercise of his 'special liturgy'— either personally or by deputy—there cannot be a valid eucharist, for the 'Body of Christ', the church, is not organically complete without him, and therefore cannot 'offer' itself or fulfil itself in the eucharist. Anyone *can* baptise or hold an agape 'without the bishop'; there is no question of 'validity' in such a case, but 'it is not allowed' to do so, for unity's sake and for discipline. These are things which 'pertain to the *ecclesia*' and the whole life and unity of the *ecclesia* centre in the bishop as the representative of the Father and the special organ of the Spirit. 'Apart from the bishop' and the lesser liturgical ministers 'it is not even called an *ecclesia*' (*i.e.* a *liturgical* assembly), as Ignatius says elsewhere. The agape here is an observance as well known as baptism or the eucharist, and independent of either.[2] The new Greek term, *agape*, has established itself as the translation of *chabûrah*, just as in Ignatius *eucharistia* is the accepted technical translation of *berakah*. The *eucharistia* is the *berakah* apart from the *chabûrah* supper, and the *agape* is the *chabûrah* supper without the *berakah*.

We need not pursue the question further. Justin, the next christian author, describes the eucharist but does not mention the agape. Yet it

---

[1] *Smyrn.*, viii.

[2] Lightfoot in his note (*ad loc.*) takes the view that eucharist and agape were still combined. But he produces no instance of agape used to denote both supper and eucharist combined, and none such exists. On the contrary, they are here distinguished.

must have continued uninterruptedly throughout the second century if only as a private observance—at Rome as well as elsewhere—for so much jewish custom in connection with it to have been handed down by tradition to the days of Hippolytus and other later writers. In the form of charitable 'treats' for the poorer christians it lasted into the fifth century in most churches, and in association with old pagan customs of funeral feasts it is not wholly extinct to this day in the East,[1] and in Abyssinia, while its more indirect survival in the *pain bénit* of French churches (which are a survival of unconsecrated offertory breads) is well known.

The word *agape* by the end of the second century had acquired for Tertullian in the West just as much as for Clement of Alexandria in the East the purely christian technical sense of a religious supper apart from the eucharist, just as clearly as the word *eucharistia* had acquired for them both the equally technical sense of the rite of the New Covenant, the bread and cup pronounced to be the Lord's Body and Blood, celebrated apart from a supper. If we can fix with any precision the period in which these two words were first accepted among christians generally as conveying their particular technical meanings, which do not by any means suggest themselves from ordinary Greek usage, then we shall have established the date of the separation of eucharist and agape. The two technical terms would not have existed without the need for distinguishing the two things. 'The Lord's supper' would have sufficed to describe them in combination, as it had for S. Paul.

In Ignatius (c. A.D. 115) the word *eucharistia* has everywhere without doubt its technical meaning of a *rite*. This strengthens the conclusion that when he tells the Smyrnaeans that neither 'eucharist' nor 'agape' is to be celebrated apart from the bishop, he means two different rites, and that 'agape' no less than 'eucharist' is here a technical term, as it also appears to be in Jude 12. The abrupt use of the word without explanation in both documents argues a general familiarity with it, and since the term implies the thing, the agape apart from the eucharist must have been familiar, in Syria and Asia Minor at all events, by A.D. 100. If we may take it that the two rites had not been separated when S. Paul wrote 1 Cor. xi. (c. A.D. 54) —he never uses either *eucharistia* or *agapē* as terms for a rite—we have thus a period of about fifty years in which we must place both the separation of the two rites and the establishment of that 'four-action shape' of the eucharistic liturgy which was universal in the second century and ever after.

The direct evidence will not allow us to press the question any closer, but in estimating the probabilities there are certain points to be weighed.

---

[1] For a late collection of prayers for the agape in this form used among the Nestorians cf. Dom M. Wolff, *Ostsyrische Tisch- und Abendmahlsgebete, Oriens Christianus*, III. ii. 1 (1927), *pp. 70 sq.* For the better known traces of the agape in the Eastern Churches see *Tischgebete und Abendmahlsgebete in der Altchristlichen und in der Griechischen Kirche*, E. v. der Goltz, Leipzig, 1905 (*T.U.* xxix. ii).

(1) The conditions which dictated the separation were much more likely to arise in gentile churches with their pagan background than among jewish christians. We have seen that they arose very quickly at Corinth, despite the fact that S. Paul had personally instructed the original converts there on the meaning of the eucharist, and had exercised supervision over that church afterwards. What of gentile churches which had no such advantages—those, say, founded by converts of his converts? Christianity spread with extraordinary swiftness among gentiles in the years A.D. 40–60. The need for such a reform might become pressing and general in quite a short time. (2) The separation, whenever it was made, was made with great delicacy and considerable knowledge of jewish customs, by men who cherished the jewish past. One has only to consider such things as the retention of the host's invitation to offer the *berakah* and the guests' assent before the eucharistic prayer; or the retention of the bread-breaking at the agape despite its duplication of that at the eucharist, because this was the invariable jewish grace before meals; while the 'cup of blessing', the invariable jewish accompaniment of the *berakah* at a *chabûrah* meal, was not retained at the agape because the latter was not in the same sense 'the' *chabûrah* rite for the christians, and the *berakah* itself had been transferred to the eucharist. These things speak for themselves. They were done by jews, and accepted by all at a time when the gentile churches still looked to jewish leaders in their new faith. That stage did not last long after A.D. 70 so far as we can see. (3) There is the further consideration of the universal and unquestioning acceptance of the 'four-action shape' in the second century, when most things were being questioned by the scattered churches, without oecumenical leaders, without generally accepted christian scriptures and with only undeveloped standards of orthodoxy of any kind. There was then no tradition whatever of a 'seven-action shape'—such as the N.T. documents, already in circulation and reverenced though not yet canonised, proclaimed as original. (4) There are the further indications, very slight in themselves, that when Matt. and Mark were written (A.D. 65–80) the exact relation of the eucharist to a meal was only of academic interest to christians.

It is impossible to do more than indicate the probabilities—perhaps only the possibilities—of the case. But these do point back to the apostolic age itself as the period of the formation of the 'four-action shape' of the liturgy —after the writing of 1 Cor. but before the writing of the first of our gospels. And if we must look for a place whence the new separate rite of the 'eucharist', and the new name for it, spread over all the christian churches— this is much more hazardous—there is Rome, the church of Peter the apostle of the circumcision and of Paul the apostle of the gentiles, in the capital and centre of the world, which 'taught others', as Ignatius said, and had 'the presidency of charity'. With a strong jewish minority in a Greek-speaking church, the need for Greek equivalents to *berakah* and *chabûra* as technical terms would be felt there as soon as anywhere, much sooner than in purely gentile or purely jewish churches. This is not much more than speculation. But what is fact is that the Roman Clement is the first christian writer to describe (1. 40) the liturgical gathering of the christian church for its 'oblations', not at a supper table but in what later became the traditional arrangement of the *ecclesia*, with the words 'Let each of you, brethren, in his own order make eucharist (*eucharisteito*) to God.'

# CHAPTER V

## THE CLASSICAL SHAPE OF THE LITURGY: (II) THE EUCHARIST

IN this chapter we shall study what may be called the skeleton of that 'four-action shape' of the eucharist whose first century origins we have just investigated. We shall examine this here, so far as may be, simply in its sequence rather than in its meaning. We have seen that the liturgical eucharist, as it emerged from its association with a meal in the 'Lord's supper', consisted always of four essential acts, all of which were derived from the jewish customs of the *chabûrah* supper: (1) The offertory, the 'taking' of bread and wine, which in its original form in the four-action shape was probably derived from the bringing of contributions in kind for the *chabûrah* meal. (2) The prayer, with its preliminary dialogue of invitation, derived directly from the *berakah* or thanksgiving which closed the *chabûrah* meal. (3) The fraction, or breaking of the bread, derived from the jewish grace before all meals. (4) The communion, derived from the distribution of the broken bread at the beginning and the cup of blessing at the end of the supper of every jewish *chabûrah*. The liturgical eucharist consisted simply of those particular things in the ordinary *chabûrah* customs to which our Lord at the last supper had attached a new meaning for the future. These had been detached from the rest of the *chabûrah* ritual and perpetuated independently. To these the primitive church added a preliminary greeting and kiss, and a single final phrase of dismissal. This is the whole of the pre-Nicene eucharist.

### The Pre-Nicene Eucharist

The proceedings began, like those of the synaxis, with a greeting exchanged between the president and the *ecclesia*. And just as the greeting at the synaxis, 'The Lord be with you', had reference to the first item of the liturgy, the lesson from the Law, so the greeting at the eucharist referred directly to the first thing at the eucharist, the kiss of peace. At the eucharist the holy church is alone with God and not mingled with the world (represented by the enquirers and the unconfirmed catechumens present at the synaxis). And so the invariable formula at the beginning of the eucharist is not 'The Lord be with you' but 'Peace be unto you', the greeting of the Lord to His own.[1] By the fourth century, if not before, this had been elaborated a little in most churches on this particular occasion, to 'The peace of God be with you all' (in Syria), or 'The peace of the Lord be always with you' (in the West). The church answered, as always, 'And

[1] John xx. 19.

with thy spirit'. And again, because at the eucharist the holy church is separated 'out of the world',[1] the wish can be fulfilled. The peace of Christ is 'not as the world giveth', but from *within*. And so the persecuted church manifested its peace within itself by the exchange of the kiss of peace enjoined in the New Testament, the bishop with the clergy around the throne, and laymen with laymen and women with women in the congregation.[2]

One or more deacons now spread a linen cloth which covered the whole altar. This preparatory act, which is mentioned at this point, before the offertory, by more than one early writer,[3] soon received various mystical interpretations, such as that which saw in it a likeness to the preparation of the linen grave-clothes for the Body of the Lord on the first Good Friday evening.[4] But it is in reality a merely utilitarian preparation, 'spreading the table-cloth' when the table is first wanted, to receive the oblation. The Eastern rites have now removed it to the very beginning of the liturgy and changed the old plain linen cloth for the elaborately embroidered two silk cloths of the *antiminsion* and the *eilēton*. But it still survives in the Roman rite at its original point, as the spreading of the plain linen corporal by the deacon before the offertory of the bread and wine. In some such homely form this little ceremony must go back to the very beginnings of the liturgical eucharist.

These are preliminaries. The eucharist itself now follows, a single clear swift action in four movements, with an uninterrupted ascent from the offertory to the communion, which ends decisively at its climax.

The bishop is still seated on his throne behind the altar, across which he faces the people. His presbyters are seated in a semi-circle around him. All present have brought with them, each for himself or herself, a little loaf of bread and probably a little wine in a flask. (By a touching local custom at Rome after the peace of the church, the orphans of the choir-school maintained by the charity of the Pope, who had nothing of their own to bring, always provided the water to be mingled with the wine in the chalice.) These oblations of the people, and any other offerings in kind which might be made, the deacons now bring up to the front of the altar, and arrange upon it from the people's side of it. The bishop rises and moves forward a few paces from the throne to stand behind the altar, where he faces the people with a deacon on either hand and his presbyters grouped around and behind him. He adds his own oblation of bread and wine to those of the people before him on the altar, and so (presumably) do the presbyters. (It may be that at this point the bishop and presbyters rinsed their hands with a ewer held by a deacon, even in pre-Nicene times, though the custom is first attested only by S. Cyril of Jerusalem in A.D. 348.)

[1] John xvii. 6.  [2] Hippolytus, *Ap. Trad.*, xviii. 4.
[3] *E.g.* Optatus of Milevis, *adv. Donatistas*, vi. 2 (Africa *c.* A.D. 360).
[4] Theodore of Mopsuestia, *Catecheses* v. (*ed.* Mingana, *p.* 86), Asia Minor *c.* A.D. 410 (*cf. p.* 282).

The bishop and presbyters then laid their hands in silence upon the oblations. There followed the brief dialogue of invitation, followed by the bishop's eucharistic prayer, which always ended with a solemn doxology, to which the people answered 'Amen.'

The bishop then broke some of the Bread and made his own communion, while the deacons broke the remainder of the Bread upon the table, and the 'concelebrant' presbyters around him broke Bread which had been held before them on little glass dishes or linen cloths by deacons during the recitation of the prayer by the bishop. (It may be that even in pre-Nicene times the bishop invited the church to communion with the words 'Holy things for the holy', but again this custom is first certainly attested by Cyril of Jerusalem in the fourth century, though there may be an allusion to it by Hippolytus at Rome in the early third century.[1])

There followed the communion, first of the clergy, seemingly behind the altar, and then of all the people before it. Nobody knelt to receive communion, and to the words of administration each replied 'Amen.'

After the communion followed the cleansing of the vessels, and then a deacon dismissed the *ecclesia* with a brief formula indicating that the assembly was closed,—'Depart in peace' or 'Go, it is the dismissal' (*Ite missa est*), or some such phrase.

The faithful took home with them portions of the consecrated Bread from which to make their communions at home on mornings when the liturgy was not celebrated. The deacons—after the third century their assistants, the acolytes—carried portions of the Bread to all who could not be at the Sunday *ecclesia*. Other deacons (in later times acolytes) carried portions of the Bread consecrated at the bishop's eucharist to be placed in the chalice at each of the lesser eucharists celebrated under the presidency of presbyters elsewhere in the city. This was done in token of their communion with him, and as a symbol that the bishop remained the high priest and liturgical minister of his whole church, whether actually present with him at the eucharist or not.

Such was the pre-Nicene rite. It remains to consider it in detail.

## 1. *The Greeting and Kiss of Peace*

Like that which opens the synaxis, the greeting is not in itself much more than an intimation that the proceedings are now formally beginning, though since the *ecclesia* is emphatically a religious assembly, this takes a religious form, connected with the kiss of peace which it introduces.

The greatest pains were taken to see that this latter did not degenerate into a formality. We have noted, *e.g.*, the insistence of the *Didache* on the necessity of reconciling any fellow-christians who might be at variance with each other before they could attend the eucharist together, or 'your

[1] *On the Pascha*, iii., rebuking those who 'do not come with holiness to the holy things'.

sacrifice is defiled'.[1] The unity of the church as the Body of Christ, which ever since S. Paul's day had been understood to be of the essence of the sacrament[2], can be violated by personal disputes among its members as well as by a formal ecclesiastical schism, whose token as well as reality lies in the holding of a separate eucharist apart from the catholic communion. It was the duty of the bishop and presbyters to mediate in all such disputes between members of their own church, and regular sessions were held for this purpose by what was virtually a christian *sanhedrin* of elders (presbyters) under the christian high-priest (the bishop). The Syrian *Didascalia of the Apostles* orders them to 'Let your judgments be held on the second day of the week, that if perchance any one should contest the sentence of your words, you may have space until the sabbath to compose the matter, and may make peace between them on the Sunday.'[3] There is no little pastoral shrewdness in the extensive suggestions this document makes about the conducting of such 'courts christian', by the application of some of which our own ecclesiastical courts might be a good deal improved.

Besides adjusting disputes between parties the bishop and presbyters had to judge accusations against individuals, for the penalty of grave or notorious sin was excommunication. The senior deacon formally acted as accuser in such cases, a function which still survives among the various duties of Anglican archdeacons.

By the terms of the gospel itself every christian was bound to accept the arbitration and discipline of the *ecclesia* upon pain of excommunication.[4] It is one of S. Paul's chief reproaches against the Corinthians that they had forsaken this evangelical discipline to go to law with one another before the courts of the pagan state.[5] Pagans were not admitted either as witnesses or accusers before these christian tribunals;[6] still less could they be judges. The primitive church took with the utmost seriousness the 'separateness' of the holy church in its inner life from the pagan world out of which it had been redeemed. The corporate discipline of the personal lives of its members was a part of the supernatural life of the church as the Body of Christ, in which the world could have no part at all.

It is a striking instance—one among many—of the way in which the liturgy was regarded as the solemn putting into act before God of the whole christian living of the church's members, that all this care for the interior charity and good living of those members found its expression and test week by week in the giving of the liturgical kiss of peace among the faithful before the eucharist. In the East in the third century the deacon from beside the bishop's throne cried aloud, while the kiss was actually being exchanged, 'Is there any man that keepeth aught against his fellow?'— as a final precaution so that even at the last moment the bishop might

[1] *Did.*, xiv. 2, *p.* 91.        [2] I Cor. x. 17.
[3] *Didascalia Apostolorum*, ii. 45, *ed.* Connolly, *p.* 111 (Syria, ? before A.D. 250).
[4] Matt. xviii. 17.        [5] I Cor. vi. 1.
[6] *Didascalia Apostolorum*, ed. cit. *p.* 109.

make peace between them.[1] By the fourth century this question had become stereotyped into the warning by the deacon, 'Let none keep rancour against any! Let none (give the kiss) in hypocrisy!' which survived in some of the Eastern rites for centuries, even after the actual giving of the kiss had been abandoned. In connection with the offertory and the kiss of peace which preceded it, more than one of the fathers cites Matt. v. 23, 'If thou art offering thy gift unto the altar and there rememberest that thy brother hath aught against thee . . .'[2] Whatever its original application in the gospel, the liturgical offertory was the only christian observance to which it could be literally applied.

The kiss of peace as a sign of respect or friendship was as ancient among the jews as Isaac's blessing of Jacob and the latter's reconciliation with Esau. The church inherited it from judaism in her ceremonial in more than one connection. Thus it was given to a newly consecrated bishop at his enthronement, not only by his clergy but by every confirmed member of his new church, before he offered the eucharist with them for the first time as their high-priest.[3] The bishop himself gave the kiss to each new christian whom he admitted to the order of laity by confirmation, immediately after signing him on the forehead with the chrism which conveyed the gift of the Spirit.[4] Here again the kiss is the symbol of that 'fellowship of the Holy Ghost', of which the 'communion' of the church is only the consequence and the outward sign. Until that moment the neophyte had never been permitted to exchange the kiss of peace with any of the faithful,[5] because he was not yet of the Body of Christ, and so had not yet received the Spirit, and by consequence could neither give nor receive the peace of Christ.

In our Lord's time among the jews the kiss was a courteous preliminary to any ceremonious meal, whose omission could be a cause for remark.[6] As such it may well have been in use at the Lord's supper in the early days at Jerusalem, if not at the last supper itself. S. Paul refers to it more than once as a token of christian communion, but without direct reference to the eucharist, though its use at the liturgy in his day can hardly be doubted.[7] In the second century and after, the kiss had its most frequent and significant christian use as the immediate preparation for the eucharist, the

---

[1] *Ibid. p.* 117.
[2] *Cf.* Irenaeus, *adv. Haer.*, iv. xviii. 1; Cyril of Jer., *Cat.* xxiii. 3, etc.
[3] Hippolytus, *Ap. Trad.*, iv. 1.      [4] *Ibid.* xxii. 3.      [5] *Ibid.* xviii. 3.
[6] Luke vii. 45.
[7] Rom. xvi. 6; 1 Cor. xvi. 20; 2 Cor. xiii. 12; *cf.* 1 Pet. v. 14. Lietzmann (*op. cit.* p. 229) draws a striking picture. 'We are at Corinth at a meeting of the congregation. A letter from the Apostle is being read out and draws near its end. . . . And then rings out the liturgical phrase, "Greet one another with the holy kiss. All the saints kiss you also in Christian communion"—and the Corinthians kiss one another— "The grace of our Lord Jesus Christ and the love of God and the fellowship of the Holy Ghost be with you all!"—"And with thy spirit" answers the church. The letter is ended and the Lord's supper begins.' (This over-strains the evidence a good deal, but it probably represents something like the truth.)

token of that 'unity of the Spirit in the bond of peace' which for S. Paul is the very foundation of the fact that there is 'One Body'.[1]

Justin is the first author who actually states that the kiss is the preliminary to the offertory,[2] where we find the kiss placed also by Hippolytus at Rome some sixty years later.[3] It was evidently a fixed and settled part of the liturgical tradition that it should come at this point of the rite at Rome as elsewhere in pre-Nicene times. It illustrates the fragmentary and haphazard nature of the evidence with which we have to deal that the kiss does not happen to be mentioned again in Roman documents for almost exactly two hundred years after Hippolytus; and that then we find its position has been shifted in the local Roman rite from before the offertory to before the communion, a position where it had an equal appropriateness, but which was contrary to all primitive precedent.

It seems likely that in making this, the only change (as distinct from insertions) in the primitive order of the liturgy which the Roman rite has ever undergone, the Roman church was following an innovation first made in the African churches, where the kiss is attested as coming before the communion towards the end of the fourth century.[4] By then the African churches had also adopted the custom (? from Jerusalem) of reciting the Lord's prayer between the fraction and the communion. Coming as it did in the African liturgy as the practical fulfilment of the clause '. . . as we forgive them that trespass against us', the kiss acquired a special fittingness as a preliminary to communion. This was less obvious in the contemporary rite of Rome, where the use of the Lord's prayer in the eucharistic liturgy (at all events at this point) does not seem to have come in until the time of S. Gregory I. (c. A.D. 595). When Rome thus tardily followed the rest of christendom in adopting this custom, the *Pater noster* was inserted, not as in Africa after the fraction, but as at Jerusalem, between the eucharistic prayer and the fraction. The Roman kiss of peace was thus permanently separated from that clause of the Lord's prayer which had first attracted the kiss to this end of the rite from its original position before the offertory.[5]

---

[1] Eph. iv. 3 and 4.          [2] *Ap.* I. 65.          [3] *Ap. Trad.*, iv. 1.
[4] Augustine, *Ep.* lix. (*al.* cxlix.), *cf. Sermon* vi.
[5] In Africa c. A.D. 400 the order was eucharistic prayer, fraction, Lord's prayer, kiss, communion. At Rome it was eucharistic prayer (Lord's prayer introduced by S. Gregory), fraction, kiss, communion. It is one instance of a variation brought about by the independent adoption of the same customs by different churches at various times, of which we shall meet many instances. The only difficulty is to be sure when Africa first inserted the Lord's prayer into the eucharist. Elsewhere it is first certainly attested by S. Cyril at Jerusalem in A.D. 348. But certain phrases of S. Cyprian's have led many authors to take it for granted that it was already used after the eucharistic prayer at Carthage in the third century. To me it seems that this is precisely what both Cyprian and Tertullian do *not* say, or even hint at, in their very full treatises on the Lord's prayer. Tertullian mentions the kiss in the liturgy c. A.D. 210 as 'the seal of prayer' (*de Orat.* 18). But it is impossible to be sure whether by this he means of the Lord's prayer (in or out of the eucharist) or of the intercessory prayers at the end of the synaxis (which immediately preceded the kiss when synaxis and eucharist were celebrated together) or of the eucharistic prayer.

In any case Rome appears to have adopted this new position for the kiss before the communion not very long before A.D. 416, when the matter is brought to our knowledge by a letter from Pope Innocent I to his neighbour, bishop Decentius of Gubbio, urging that other Italian churches near Rome (which still retained the kiss in its original position before the offertory) ought to conform to current Roman practice on this and other points. The Pope gives the rather odd reason for placing the kiss in its new position, after the fraction, that 'by the kiss of peace the people affirm their assent to all that has been done in the celebration of the mysteries.' Had he said, as S. Augustine had done, that the kiss of charity is a good preparation for communion it would have been more convincing.[1]

In the East also the primitive position of the kiss has been altered, though not to the same position as at Rome; and the evidence suggests that the Eastern change was made before it was made in the West. The kiss is found *after* the offertory, instead of before it, at Jerusalem in A.D. 348. But at Antioch it still remained in its original position in the time of Chrysostom[2] (c. A.D. 385). The Jerusalem customs must have been spreading northwards in Syria in Chrysostom's time, however, for not only does the Antiochene rite of the fifth century place the kiss *after* the offertory as at Jerusalem, but in the (generally Antiochene) rite of Mopsuestia in southern Asia Minor as described by its bishop Theodore (c. A.D. 410), the kiss there also has been transferred to after the offertory[3]. (This is not the only Jerusalem custom which Mopsuestia had by then adopted.) At some point in the fifth or sixth century the new Jerusalem fashions were adopted at Constantinople, and from that royal church spread far and wide over the East. Only the native churches of Egypt still keep the kiss in its original place before the offertory.

In the West the Mozarabic rite in Spain adopted the Byzantine position for the kiss along with a certain amount of other Byzantine practice, probably in the sixth century, as a result of the temporary occupation of Spain by Byzantine forces under Justinian. Before the ninth century Milan

In the vision of the contemporary martyr Saturus, told in his own words in the *Passion of Perpetua, etc.* 12, the kiss seems to be the end of a synaxis, not the preliminary to communion. But in the nature of things such evidence cannot be conclusive. On the whole it seems more likely than not that in pre-Nicene times African practice, like that of Rome, conformed to the universal use elsewhere and placed the kiss before the offertory.

[1] This letter has been strangely misunderstood by modern commentators who, with their minds full of the competition of the Roman and 'Gallican' rites in the seventh century—there is no evidence that the latter existed as a recognised entity in A.D. 416—attempt to persuade us that Pope Innocent is here defending antique Roman customs against the encroachments of 'Gallican' novelties even in his own province. I fear the Pope is doing nothing so respectable. On the contrary, he is trying to force Roman innovations on old-fashioned country churches in Italy, which had kept to the old ways once common to Rome and themselves.

[2] *de Compunctione*, i. 3, and so in *Ap. Const.*, viii. But *Ap. Const.*, ii. places it after the offertory, as at Jerusalem.

[3] Theodore, *Catecheses*, v. (*ed.* Mingana, *p.* 92).

had followed Rome in placing the kiss itself before the communion, though to this day the Milanese deacon still proclaims *Pacem habete*—'Have peace (one with another)'—at the ancient place before the offertory. In the Celtic churches, to judge by the *Stowe Missal*, the kiss came at the Roman and African place, before the communion. I know of no evidence as to when these remoter Western churches adopted this Roman custom, but it must have been very early, for there is no tradition of any other usage among them.

So it comes about that while vestiges, at least, of the apostolic kiss of peace are still found all over catholic christendom (except in the Anglican rites) it now stands in its primitive position only among the Copts and Abyssinians.

## 2. *The Offertory*

Some 'taking' of bread and wine before they could be blessed would seem a physical necessity in any eucharistic rite. But such a mere necessary preparation for consecration is not at all the same thing as the offertory of the liturgical tradition, which is itself a ritual act with a significance of its own. It is an integral and original part of the whole eucharistic action, not a preliminary to it, like the kiss of peace. This is not to say that its significance has always been sharply distinguished from that of what followed upon it. The offertory, the prayer and the communion are closely connected moments in a single continuous action, and each only finds its proper meaning as a part of the whole. Nevertheless, from before the end of the first century the offertory was understood to have a meaning of its own, without which the primitive significance of the whole eucharist would be not incomplete but actually destroyed.

The first extant document which describes the offertory in any detail is, once more, the *Apostolic Tradition* of Hippolytus, and even this leaves one important point obscure. 'To (the bishop) then let the deacons bring up the oblation (*prosphora*), and he with all the presbyters laying his hand on the oblation shall say "eucharistising" thus . . .' and there follow the dialogue and prayer.[1] The bread and wine are here called 'the oblation' *before* they have been 'eucharistised' by the bishop's prayer. Elsewhere in the same work they are so called even before they have been 'brought up' by the deacons or so much as brought into the *ecclesia* at all. Those about to be baptised and confirmed are told 'It is right for every one to bring his *prosphora*' with him to his initiation, to offer for himself at the 'midnight mass' of Easter which followed.[2] This is a point of some importance in discerning the particular sense in which the offertory was originally regarded as an 'offering.'

Attempts have been made to see in this idea of the bread and wine as something 'offered' to God a quite recent development in Hippolytus'

[1] *Ap. Trad.*, iv. 2.          [2] *Ibid.* xx. 10.

time, due to a resurgence of jewish influence.[1] There is no evidence for such 'judaising' in the later second century, and in point of fact Hippolytus' description of the offertory and the terms it uses takes us no further than that of Justin at Rome sixty years before him. Justin says, 'When we have ended (the intercessions) we salute one another with a kiss. Then bread is "offered" (*prospheretai*, perhaps better translated here 'presented') to the president and a cup of water mingled with wine.'[2] Justin does not mention the deacons by their title here, or the imposition of hands on the oblation, but in so summary a description for pagan readers there is no particular reason why he should. He does use the technical term *prospheretai*, and if its sense is here ambiguous, he is certainly not unaware of its technical meaning. In another work intended for christian readers he interprets the words of Malachi i. 11—'In every place incense shall be offered unto My Name and a pure *offering*' as referring to the eucharist. He explains the last words as 'The sacrifices which are offered (*prospheromenōn*) to God by us gentiles, that is the bread of the eucharist and cup likewise of the eucharist.'[3] Thus though he habitually prefers the term 'sacrifice' (*thusia*), which he uses some half-a-dozen times over of the eucharist, to that of *prosphora*, he is quite clear that there is a real 'offering' in the rite, specifically of the bread and wine; and he uses this technical word for the liturgical offertory.

Sixty years again before Justin in the last years of the first century A.D. Clement had written from Rome that the 'bishop's office' is to 'offer the gifts' (*prospherein ta dōra*).[4] Does this mean that what for Hippolytus a century and a quarter later was the 'liturgy' of the deacon at the offertory had been performed in Clement's day by the bishop? Not at all. In Hippolytus' prayer for the consecration of a bishop, the 'liturgy' of the bishop's 'high-priesthood'—(the office of the bishop is thus described by Clement also)[5]—is defined precisely as in Clement's epistle, as being 'to offer to Thee the gifts (*prospherein ta dōra*) of Thy holy church.'[6] But in Hippolytus' prayer for the ordination of a deacon his functions are defined with equal precision in relation to those of the bishop, as being 'to bring up (*anapherein*) that which is offered (*prospherein*) to Thee by Thine ordained high-priest'.[7] The Greek terminology concerning the oblation (*prosphora*) is throughout the pre-Nicene period quite clear, and does not (as a rule) vary from one writer to another. The communicant 'brings' (*prosenegkein*) the *prosphora*; the deacon 'presents' it or 'brings it up' (*anapherein*); the bishop 'offers' (*prospherein*) it.[8] The *prosphora* itself is at all points 'the

[1] G. P. Wetter, *Altchristlichen Liturgien* (t. ii. *Das christliche Opfer*. Göttingen, 1922–5) is the chief statement of this view. Lietzmann (*op. cit. pp.* 181 *sqq.*) takes a somewhat similar line, but *pp.* 226 *sq.* appears to follow a rather different argument. (It is almost incredible, but neither argument mentions Justin or Clement.)
[2] *Ap.* I. 65.    [3] *Dialogue*, 41.    [4] I *Clem.* 44.
[5] *Ibid.* 40.    [6] *Ap. Trad.*, iii. 4.    [7] *Ibid.* ix. 11.
[8] *Cf.* Canons 1, 2 and 3 of the Council of Ancyra, *c.* A.D. 314.

gifts of Thy holy church', but the 'liturgies' of each order in connection with it are proper to each order and not interchangeable.[1] It is the special eucharistic 'liturgy' of each order which distinguishes it and constitutes it a separate 'order' in the organic Body of Christ. Thus Hippolytus can lay it down: 'Let a widow be instituted by being named only and then let her be reckoned among the enrolled widows. But she shall not be ordained (by the laying on of hands) for she does not offer the oblation nor has she a "liturgy". *But ordination (cheirotonia) is for the clergy on account of their "liturgy".* But the widow is instituted for prayer and this is ⟨a function⟩ of all ⟨christians⟩.'[2]

It is worth noting that Clement implies that our Lord Himself had laid down how He wished the 'oblations and liturgies' at the eucharist to be performed, and emphasises the fact that these latter are different for the different 'orders' (tagmata).[3] Whatever we may think of the truth of his first statement, it certainly implies that such arrangements and ideas went back at Rome for a considerable time before Clement wrote (A.D. 96)—long enough for even the leader of the Roman christians to have forgotten when and how they originated. Such ideas and arrangements in their precision are very hard indeed to fit in with a eucharist celebrated in combination with a supper. They presuppose in their elaboration the liturgical eucharist and the arrangement of the *ecclesia* in a liturgical assembly, not at a supper table. There is here an indication that at Rome—at all events—the ordinance of the liturgical eucharist apart from the agape was achieved in the first, the apostolic, christian generation.

This unique series of documents, Clement, Justin, Hippolytus, enables us to say with confidence that at Rome terminology, practice and general conception concerning the eucharist had varied in no important respect between the last quarter of the first century and the first quarter of the third. Rome was generally regarded elsewhere during this period as the model church, especially because of its conservatism, its fidelity to 'apostolic tradition' by which other churches might test their own adherence to the same standard.[4] For other local liturgical traditions we have unfortunately no such chain of evidence. All we can say is that every one of these local traditions at the earliest point at which extant documents permit us to interrogate it, reveals the same general understanding of the eucharist as an 'oblation' (prosphora) or 'sacrifice' (thusia)—something offered to God; and that the substance of the sacrifice is in every case in some sense the bread and the cup. We can detect certain differences of interpretation

[1] There were difficulties about finding different words in Latin to represent *prosenegkein, anapherein* and *prospherein*, but the three 'liturgies' of the orders were as clearly distinguished by Latin authors as by Greek.
[2] *Ap. Trad.*, xi. 4 and 5.                    [3] *1 Clem.* 40, 41.
[4] *Cf. e.g.* Irenaeus, *adv. Haer.*, iii. 3, 2—which, whatever else it may mean (if anything) in the way of 'jurisdiction', certainly regards the Roman church in this light of a standard or norm for other churches in fidelity to tradition.

within this general conception; but to the conception itself as thus stated there is no exception whatever in any christian tradition in the second century and no hint of an alternative understanding of the rite anywhere. This is an important principle, which it is worth while to establish in detail.

To take the Eastern traditions first: For Ignatius, *c.* A.D. 115, the earliest Syrian writer extant, the eucharistic assembly of the church is *thusiasterion* 'the place of sacrifice', and 'he who is not within it is deprived of the bread.'[1] We have already noted the threefold application of the word *thusia*, 'sacrifice', to the eucharist by the (probably) Syrian *Didache* (xiv.) at a later point in the second century. If this be not Syrian, then it must be regarded as the earliest evidence on the eucharist in Egypt. But if the *Didache* is Syrian, then the earliest Egyptian writer on the eucharist whose evidence has survived is Clement of Alexandria (*c.* A.D. 208). He denounces those Encratite heretics 'who use bread and water for the oblation (*prosphora*) contrary to the rule of the church'.[2] The early liturgical tradition of Asia Minor and the apostolic churches there is quite unknown to us (one of the most serious of all the many handicaps under which the study of early liturgy has to be carried on). It seems probable, however, that we get some inkling of this Asian tradition at second hand from S. Irenaeus of Lyons *c.* A.D. 185, who had learnt his faith from Polycarp, bishop of Smyrna forty years or so before Irenaeus wrote his book *Against the Heresies*. He is most conveniently treated among Western writers. But if he witnesses to it, the tradition of Asia differed nothing in essentials, though perhaps something in interpretation, from that which we find elsewhere. It is a confirmation of this agreement, though a regrettably late one, that the first statement on the general conception of the eucharist from an Asian author, by Firmilian, bishop of the important church of Caesarea in Cappadocia in A.D. 256, speaks of an erratic prophetess in Cappadocia *c.* A.D. 220 who had 'pretended to consecrate bread and do the eucharist and *offer the sacrifice* to the Lord' with a novel but not unimpressive sort of eucharistic prayer.[3]

In the West, we have already glanced at the Roman evidence of Clement, Justin and Hippolytus, and the next witness there is Irenaeus in Gaul, with his Eastern upbringing and Roman associations. He speaks of our Lord as 'Instructing His disciples to *offer* to God the first-fruits of His own creation, not as though He had need of them, but that they themselves might be neither unfruitful nor ungrateful, He took that bread which cometh of the (material) creation and gave thanks saying, This is My Body. And the cup likewise, which is (taken) from created things, like ourselves, He acknowledged for His own Blood, and taught the new *oblation* of the New Covenant. Which the church learning by tradition from the apostles, throughout all the world she *offers* to God, even to Him Who provides us with our own

[1] Ignatius, *Eph.* v. 2.           [2] *Stromateis*, I. 19.
[3] *ap.* Cyprian, *Ep.* 75, 10.

food, the first-fruits of His own gifts in the New Covenant. . . . We ought
to make *oblation* to God and be found pleasing to God our creator in all
things, with a right belief and a faith unfeigned, a firm hope and a burning
charity, *offering* first-fruits of those things which are His creatures. . . .
We *offer* unto Him what is His own, thus fittingly proclaiming the communion and unity of flesh and spirit. For as the bread (which comes) from
the earth receiving the invocation of God is no more common bread but
eucharist, composed of two realities, an earthly and a heavenly; so our
bodies receiving the eucharist are no more corruptible, having the hope of
eternal resurrection. . . . He wills that we *offer* our gift at the altar frequently and without intermission. There is therefore an altar in heaven,
for thither are our prayers and *oblations* directed.'[1]

Unmistakably, Irenaeus regards the eucharist as an 'oblation' offered to
God, but it is as well to note the particular sense in which he emphasises
its sacrificial character. Primarily it is for him a sacrifice of 'first-fruits',
acknowledging the Creator's bounty in providing our earthly food, rather
than as 're-calling' the sacrifice of Calvary in the Pauline fashion. It is true
that Irenaeus has not the least hesitation in saying that 'The mingled cup
and the manufactured bread receives the Word of God and becomes the
eucharist of *the Body and Blood* of Christ';[2] and similar teaching is to be
found in the passage above. There is, too, the significant addition of the
words 'in the New Covenant' to 'the first-fruits of His own gifts'. Irenaeus
is clear, also, that the death of Christ was itself a sacrifice, of which the
abortive sacrifice of Isaac by his own father was a type.[3] But when all is
said and done, he never quite puts these two ideas together or calls the
eucharist outright the offering or the 're-calling' of Christ's sacrifice.

It is conceivable that the particular errors of the Gnostic sects he is
directly combating (which all taught that the material creation is radically
evil) have something to do with the emphasis which Irenaeus lays on the
eucharistic offering as the 'first-fruits of creation'. But it seems also that
this is only an emphasis on an authentic strain of primitive tradition, which
lies behind his teaching that 'we offer unto Him that which is His own',
'the first-fruits of His own gifts.' This does not happen to be represented
in the New Testament in direct connection with the eucharist. But there
are in the New Testament passages like 'Giving thanks (*eucharistountes*) at
all times for all things in the Name of our Lord Jesus Christ to God the
Father',[4] and 'Through Him, therefore, we present a sacrifice (*anaphero-
men thusian*) of praise continually to God',[5] which by their very language-
would suggest such an understanding of the eucharist. The same idea is
expressed to this day in the Roman canon: 'We offer to Thy glorious
majesty *of Thine own gifts and bounties* . . . the holy bread of eternal life

---

[1] Irenaeus, *adv. Haer.*, iv. xvii. 4—xviii. 6.
[2] *Ibid.* v. ii. 3.       [3] *Ibid.* iv. v. 4.
[4] Eph. v. 20.       [5] Heb. xiii. 15.

and the cup of perpetual salvation.' What is striking is that the same idea
almost in the same words is still found also at the same point of the
eucharistic prayer of the *Liturgy of S. Basil*, which probably comes
originally from Asia Minor.[1] Such a coincidence in the later liturgical
traditions of Rome and Asia Minor (which had little later contact with
each other) with the teaching of a second century father who had close
relations with both these regions can hardly be accidental. We must not
forget, either, that the jewish *berakah*, from which all eucharistic prayers
are ultimately derived, did ʒive thanks to God for His natural bounty in
its first paragraph, as well as for the blessings of the Covenant in its second.

In Africa, Tertullian soon after A.D. 200 is quite explicit that the eucharist
is a *sacrificium*;[2] that the material of the sacrifice is the *oblationes* brought
by the people;[3] and that 'the bread which He took and gave to His disciples
He made His own very Body by saying (*dicendo*) This is My Body.'[4]
But only once does Tertullian come near Irenaeus' central thought of the
christian sacrifices as being taken from created things, when he reminds
Marcion (who regarded matter as the work of an imperfect 'Creator'
different from the God and Father of our Lord Jesus Christ) that our
Lord 'to this day has not repudiated the water of the Creator wherein He
cleanses His own; nor His oil, wherewith He anoints His own (in confirmation); nor the mingling of honey and milk wherewith He feeds their infancy;
nor bread, whereby He makes His own very Body to be present. Even in
His own sacraments He has need of the beggarly elements of the Creator.'[5]

Yet though the conception and the terms of sacrifice are applied by
Tertullian to the eucharist, we get no theory of the nature of that sacrifice
from him. It is only with Cyprian in the next generation (*c.* A.D. 255) that
the African doctrine is fully stated. For him, as for Tertullian, the matter
of the sacrifice is the oblations brought by the people. Thus he rebukes a
wealthy woman 'who comest to the *dominicum* (Lord's sacrifice) without a
sacrifice, who takest thy share (*i.e.*, makes her communion) from the sacrifice offered by the poor.'[6] But for Cyprian the whole question of *how* the
eucharist is constituted a sacrifice is as clear-cut and completely settled as
it is for a post-Tridentine theologian: 'Since we make mention of His
passion in all our sacrifices, *for the passion is the Lord's sacrifice which we
offer*, we ought to do nothing else than what He did (at the last supper).'[7]

There is no reason whatever to suppose that Cyprian was the inventor
of this way of defining the eucharistic sacrifice, or in any intentional way
its partisan. But he proved its most influential propagator. Cyprian is the
most attractive of all pre-Nicene authors, and so far as the West was concerned always the most widely read in later times. His explanation of the

[1] Brightman, L. E. W., *p.* 329, *l.* 6.      [2] *de Orat.*, 18.
[3] *de Corona*, 4.
[4] *adv. Marcion.*, IV. 40.      [5] *Ibid.* I. 14.
[6] *de Op. et Eleemos.* 15; *cf. Epp.* i. 2; xii. 2; xxxiii. 1, etc., etc.
[7] *Ep.* lxiii, 17.

sacrifice has a simplicity which recommended it to popular devotional thought, and that sort of logical directness and unity which has always appealed to Western theologians. It is not surprising that what may for convenience be called the 'Cyprianic' doctrine of the sacrifice came to prevail in the West, almost to the exclusion of that line of thought which is prominent in Irenaeus. The teaching of Cyril of Jerusalem led to a similar development along the single 'Cyprianic' line of thought in later Eastern teaching about the eucharistic sacrifice, though the Easterns hardly reached the same precision in their understanding of the matter as the later Westerns.

It would be misleading, as I see the matter, rigidly to divide early eucharistic teaching into an Eastern or 'Irenaean' and a Western or 'Cyprianic' doctrine, or to suppose that Irenaeus himself was importing anything alien or novel into current Western teaching in his own day, in his emphasis on the 'sacrifice of first-fruits'. There is an older witness than either Irenaeus or Cyprian to the original balance of Western eucharistic doctrine—Justin. He speaks of the eucharist as the 'pure sacrifice' of christians, 'as well for the "re-calling" (before God, *anamnēsis*) of their sustenance both in food and drink, wherein is made also the memorial (*memnētai*) of the passion which the Son of God suffered for them.'[1] Irenaeus and Cyprian each develop one half of this double interpretation of the eucharist, not in opposition to but in isolation from the other. But it is an interesting fact that the earliest Western eucharistic prayer, that of Hippolytus, a professed follower of Irenaeus, already makes the 'Cyprianic' doctrine the more prominent of the two aspects of the matter a generation before Cyprian wrote. Evidently Irenaeus is emphasising a side of tradition which theologians generally were beginning in his day to leave out of account. But there is the enduring witness of the Roman canon and of the *Liturgy of S. Basil* that in the East and in the West alike the 'Irenaean' doctrine did not wholly die out, though it passed out of current theological teaching. The liturgical tradition, partly through its conservatism and partly by its unspecialised appeal and practical interest for the rank and file of christians, does as a rule succeed in remaining broader in its scope than the tradition of theology. It preserves in combination different ideas, some of which theological theory sometimes prefers to ignore for the sake of securing neat and smooth explanations.

The detailed consideration of the doctrine of the eucharistic sacrifice in the various early local traditions has led us away from our immediate subject, the offertory in practice, as an integral part of the eucharistic action. But the establishment of the fact that this whole action was everywhere regarded as in some sense the offering to God of the bread and wine is not

---

[1] *Dialogue* 117. *Cf. Ap.* I. 13 and 67. There is a similarity of language (*eph hois prospherometha*) in these two passages to that of Hippolytus *Ap. Trad.*, iv. 11 (*prospheromen . . . eph hois*) with an important difference of meaning.

at all irrelevant to the interpretation of its initial movement, the offertory, by which that meaning was directly expressed in the rite.

Irenaeus applied to the liturgical offertory the words of our Lord about the widow's mite—'That poor widow the church casts in all her life (*panta ton bion*, Luke xxi. 4) into the treasury of God.'[1] Thus he stated epigrammatically the essential meaning of this part of the rite. Each communicant from the bishop to the newly confirmed gave *himself* under the forms of bread and wine to God, as God gives Himself to them under the same forms. In the united oblations of all her members the Body of Christ, the church, gave herself to *become* the Body of Christ, the sacrament, in order that receiving again the symbol of herself now transformed and hallowed, she might be truly that which by nature she is, the Body of Christ, and each of her members members of Christ. In this self-giving the order of laity no less than that of the deacons or the high-priestly celebrant had its own indispensable function in the vital act of the Body. The layman brought the sacrifice of himself, of which he is the priest. The deacon, the 'servant' of the whole body, 'presented' all together in the Person of Christ, as Ignatius reminds us. The high-priest, the bishop, 'offered' all together, for he alone can speak for the whole Body. In Christ, as His Body, the church is 'accepted' by God 'in the Beloved'. Its sacrifice of itself is taken up into His sacrifice of Himself.[2] On this way of regarding the matter the bishop can no more fulfil the layman's function for him (he fulfils it on his own behalf by adding one *prosphora* for himself to the people's offerings on the altar) than the layman can fulfil that of the bishop.

The whole rite was a true corporate offering by the church in its hierarchic completeness of the church in its organic unity, so much so that the penalty of mortal sin for members of every order was that they were forbidden to 'offer', each according to the liturgy of his own order. The sinful layman was 'forbidden to offer',[3] just as the unfrocked deacon was forbidden to 'present',[4] and the deposed bishop was forbidden to celebrate (*prospherein*) where we should have said 'forbidden to receive communion.' The primitive layman's communion, no less than that of the bishop, is the consummation of his 'liturgy' in the offering of the christian sacrifice.

The offertory in the original view of the rite is therefore something much more than a ceremonial action, the placing of bread and wine upon the altar by the clergy as an inevitable preparation for communion. It is as the later liturgies continued to call it—even when it had lost all outward signs of its primitive meaning—the 'rational worship' by free reasonable

---

[1] *Adv. Haer.*, IV. xviii. 2.                    [2] *Eph.* i. 6.
[3] Cyprian, *Ep.* xvi. 14.
[4] *Cf.* Council of Ancyra, *Can.* 2. Suspended deacons are 'to cease from all their holy liturgy, that of presenting (*anapherein*) the bread or the cup, or proclaiming' (*sc.* the 'biddings' in church). *Cf. Can.* 5, repentant but suspended laymen may be present at the eucharist ' without a *prosphora* ', and *therefore* without communicating.

creatures of their Creator, a self-sacrificial act by which each christian comes to his being as a member of Christ in the 're-calling' before God of the self-sacrificial offering of Christ on Calvary. 'There you are upon the table', says S. Augustine to the newly confirmed communicants at the Easter liturgy, 'there you are in the chalice.'[1]

In the primitive rite this self-offering was expressed by *action* in the offertory, simply by the silent setting of the church's offerings by the church's servants (the deacons) upon the altar, which in the early symbolism was itself thought of as representing Christ.[2] The recital of an offertory *prayer* by the celebrant, accompanying and in some sort expressing the meaning of this action of the church (and in much later thought usurping its importance in the rite), does not appear to have been thought of anywhere much before the end of the fourth century.[3] It is of a piece with the usual conservatism of the Roman rite that even after such a prayer had been introduced at Rome, it should have been whispered—as it is to-day—not said aloud, in deference to the tradition that the real offering was the *act* of the people through the deacons, from which nothing should distract attention.[4] The celebrant's part at the most was to 'commend' the oblation made by the church to God, not to make it himself. Our Lord's 'taking' of bread and wine at the last supper was done without comment; and it is this action of His, done by the whole church, His Body, which the liturgy perpetuates in the offertory.

The offertory is not, of course, the eucharistic oblation itself, any more than the last supper was itself the sacrifice of Christ. It is directed to that oblation as its pledge and starting-point, just as the last supper looks forward to the offering on Calvary. The offering of themselves by the members of Christ could not be acceptable to God unless taken up into the offering of Himself by Christ in consecration and communion.

Nevertheless, though this distinction can readily be made in theory, it is one which is easier to see than to express by the actual prayers of the liturgy. The primitive rites had nothing corresponding to an offertory prayer at the moment of the offertory, but the meaning of the offertory

---

[1] Augustine, *Serm.* 229.

[2] Heb. xiii. 10; Ignatius, *Magnesians*, vii; Optatus of Milevis, *contra Donatistas*, vi. 1.

[3] The earliest reference to such a prayer which I have noted is in the letter of Pope Innocent I to Decentius (A.D. 416) where 'the prayer which commends the oblations to God' seems to refer to something on the lines of the offertory *secretae* of the later sacramentaries, where such a 'commendation' is their normal tenor. (It was not necessarily a variable prayer in A.D. 416.) *Cf. p.* 500 *sq.*

[4] *Cf.* for the East, Theodore of Mopsuestia, *Cat.* V. (*ed. cit. pp.* 87 *sq.*). 'These things (*sc.* the offertory by the deacons) take place while all are silent . . . every one must look at the bringing up and spreading forth of such a great and wonderful object with a quiet and reverential fear, and a silent noiseless prayer. . . . When we see the oblation on the table . . . great silence falls on those present'. Theodore's idea of the offertory has certain novel developments, but this much is traditional. *Cf. p.* 283.

was nevertheless formally expressed in words in 'the' prayer, the eucharistic prayer itself. 'We offer to Thee' says the earliest known formula of the eucharistic prayer, that of the Western Hippolytus, 'the bread and the cup'. 'We *have* offered the bread' says the next earliest, that of the Eastern Sarapion, looking back to the offertory action and interpreting it. Such clauses of the eucharistic prayers, detached in this way from the action they define, are apt to seem to our modern Anglican notions[1]—which have been moulded by one particular mediaeval Western emphasis—quite out of place in what we call the 'prayer of consecration', a phrase which really states only one aspect of the matter. The *'eucharistic'* prayer was originally intended to embrace in its single statement the meaning of the whole rite, from the offertory to the effects of receiving communion.

One may go further, I think, and say that a survey of the actual offertory prayers which later came into use all over christendom suggests that an opposite difficulty was found in framing such prayers, *viz.*, to avoid using phrases which are equally out of place by anticipating the effects of consecration and communion at the offertory.[2] The offertory prayers which ultimately depend on the Syrian liturgical tradition save themselves from this mistake by turning their attention to the offerers rather than the offering, though they betray their late date by identifying the 'offerers' with the clergy and especially the celebrant, rather than with the church as a whole.[3] But the very remarkable, not to say disconcerting, notions which were already being attached to the offertory by popular devotion in the East by about A.D. 400,[4] are an indication of the difficulties which can arise even when the liturgical tradition itself is discreet. The genuinely Roman offertory prayers, the *secretae*, never became a public—an audible —part of the rite. They are as a rule sober, if rather vague, 'commendations' of the people's offerings to God, whose terms amply repay careful examination.[5] If more attention had been paid to their careful theological language in the middle ages, fourteenth-fifteenth century Latin teaching would have been less open to objections, and sixteenth century protestant reactions might have been less indefensibly sweeping.

But elsewhere, where the new notion of 'offertory prayers' was accepted with less reserve, the results are not fortunate. Thus the invariable prayers at the offertory of the host and chalice in the present Roman missal (which

---

[1] I do *not* mean specifically 'Anglo-catholic.'

[2] Certain liturgists, enthusiasts for the modern 'liturgical movement' (*cf. e.g.* Dom Vandeur, *La Sainte Messe, notes sur la Liturgie,* 1924) have gone so far as to accept as right such an anticipation at the offertory, to which they have given the curious name of 'le petit canon'. It need hardly be said that such exaggerations are as destructive of the real interpretation of the eucharist as the previous neglect of the meaning of the offertory against which such writers are in reaction. There have been signs of a similar lack of balance in one or two Anglican writers, anxious to emphasise the 'sociological values' of the offertory. These are there, and it is right that they should be brought out; but not at the expense of the essential meaning of the rite as a whole.

[3] *Cf.* p. 495.          [4] *Cf.* p. 284 *sq.*          [5] *Cf.* those on p. 496.

are tenth-eleventh century 'Gallican' intrusions into the original Roman offertory) speak of the unconsecrated bread and wine as 'this immaculate victim' and 'the cup of salvation', precisely as the Roman canon speaks of them after consecration. Other Gallican offertory prayers are equally confusing from the standpoint of theology. The old Egyptian offertory prayer (whose language suggests a date towards the end of the fourth century) runs thus: 'Master Lord Jesus Christ . . . make Thy face to shine upon this bread and this cup, which we have set upon Thy table. Bless them, hallow them, sanctify and change them, that this bread may become indeed Thy holy Body and the mixture in this cup indeed Thy precious Blood. And may they become to us all for participation and healing and salvation.'[1] This is nothing less than a complete anticipation of the whole eucharistic prayer at the offertory. The truth is that offertory and consecration and communion are so intricately connected as parts of a single action that it is exceedingly difficult to express their meaning separately. The primitive church was not on the wrong lines in putting its whole interpretation of the rite into the single formula of 'the' eucharistic prayer.

All this, however, leaves one important practical point obscure, as unfortunately it is left by the available evidence. We know that all over christendom the layman originally brought his *prosphora* of bread and wine with him to the *ecclesia*; that was a chief part of his 'liturgy'. We know, too, that the deacons 'presented' these offerings upon the altar; that was a chief part of their 'liturgy'. What we do not know, as regards the pre-Nicene church generally, is when and how the deacons received them from the laity.

From the fourth century and onwards East and West differed considerably on this point in practice, and the difference is ultimately responsible for all the most important structural differences between the later Eastern and Western rites. In the East in later times it was the custom for the laity to bring their oblations to the sacristy or to a special table in the church before the service began (*i.e.*, as a rule before the synaxis). The deacons fetched them from there when they were wanted at the offertory (the beginning of the eucharist proper). This little ceremony soon developed into one of the chief points of 'ritual splendour' in the Syrian-Byzantine rites, and became the 'Great Entrance'. In the West the laity made their offerings for themselves at the chancel rail at the beginning of the eucharist proper. Each man and woman came forward to lay their own offerings of bread in a linen cloth or a silver dish (called the *offertorium*) held by a deacon, and to pour their own flasks of wine into a great two-handled silver cup (called the *scyphus* or the *ansa*) held by another deacon. When the laity had made their offerings, each man for himself, the deacons bore them up and placed them on the altar.

The difference between these two ways of receiving the people's

[1] Brightman, L. E. W., *p.* 148; *cf. p.* 124

offerings may seem a mere question of convenience, something quite trifling; and so in itself it is. But if any young liturgical student seeking a useful subject for research should undertake to trace the actual process of development of structural differences between the Eastern and Western rites since the fourth century (and it needs more investigation than it has received), he will find that they all hinge upon this different development of the offertory in the two halves of christendom. And if he should go further and seek to understand the much more sundering differences of *ethos* between the two types of rite (and without that he will never understand the religion of those who use them, or learn anything worth knowing from either) he will find himself on point after point being led back by his analysis to this trivial original difference between East and West in their treatment of the people's offerings, between receiving them in the sacristy beforehand and receiving them at the chancel at the offertory. There is this much to be said for the impossible ideal of rigid uniformity of rite, that without it christians unconsciously grow to pray and so to believe somewhat differently, and mutual charity becomes increasingly difficult. There are differences of ideas about the liturgy (and so about the one eucharist) lying behind the contrast of the long and complicated Byzantine *prothesis* with the mere laying of a host upon the paten by the Western sacristan without prayer or ceremony of any sort whatever—just so that it shall be there when the priest uncovers the vessels. We find on the one hand the gorgeous Eastern 'Great Entrance' while the choir sings the thrilling *Cherubikon* and the people prostrate in adoration, and on the other the pouring of a little wine into the chalice by the Western priest at the altar with a muttered prayer while the choir sings a snippet of a psalm and the people sit. There is a difference—to take another sort of instance—between the *reasons why* the East came to substitute a 'holy loaf' for the domestic bread of the people's offering as the actual matter of the sacrament, and the West (centuries later) brought in the unleavened wafer, thin and round and white[1]. All these differences and a dozen others, which are not simply of ecclesiastical practice and rite, but of commonly held ideas about the eucharist, and above all of eucharistic *devotion* in the minds and hearts of the ordinary churchgoing christians of the Eastern and Western churches—all of them eventually find their roots in this little difference between the collection of the offerings beforehand in the sacristy in the East and the collection of them at the offertory in front of the altar in the West. Which is the original practice, or were there always two?

It is rather noticeable that neither Justin nor Hippolytus in their

---

[1] Incidentally, will not someone produce a thesis or tractate or treatise on the very illuminating development of this difference? All modern treatments of the matter which I have seen carry us very little further in point of mere quantity of information than Mabillon's seventeenth century dissertation *de Pane Eucharistico* in his *Analecta Vetera*, and in real understanding of the matter no further, if as far.

accounts of the Western offertory says anything which would suggest the existence at Rome in the second and third centuries of that oblation 'of the people by the people' before the altar which is such a striking feature of all the Western rites in the—let us say—fifth century. On the other hand, the Syrian *Didascalia c.* A.D. 250 says of the deacons, 'Let one stand continually by the oblations of the eucharist; and let another stand without by the door and observe those that come in. And afterwards when you offer let them minister together in the church.'[1] This does suggest that in Syria in the third century the people's *prosphorae* were handed in to a deacon before the service began; and therefore that the subsequent Eastern practice already existed *in Syria* in pre-Nicene times. Further than that I cannot see that the evidence available takes us. But Dom Bernard Capelle and a number of other Benedictine scholars have argued of late years that the whole subsequent Western practice originated as a local Roman development in the fourth century, and that the Eastern practice is the original one of the whole pre-Nicene church.

It may be so, but I confess that I am inclined to be sceptical. It is not at all the case that we have positive evidence of a change of Roman practice on this matter during the fourth century, but simply that we have no evidence at all anywhere from the pre-Nicene period as to how the layman's oblation came into the hands of the deacons, apart from the passage of the *Didascalia* just cited. This does, I think, imply the later Eastern practice in pre-Nicene Syria. But that does not by any means imply that it was then universal, even in the East. If there were then other customs at the offertory in other churches, it would not be the only point on which early Syrian peculiarities eventually spread widely, and even prevailed everywhere after the fourth century.

The first direct evidence for the subsequent Western practice is comparatively late; but then so is that for the Eastern practice, apart from the inference I have drawn from this passage of the *Didascalia*. Except for this one statement I do not recollect that any Eastern writer attests the existence of the subsequent Eastern practice at the offertory in his own rite before S. John Chrysostom at Antioch in Syria, in a work written probably about A.D. 387.[2] It happens that the first witness to the Western oblation of the people before the altar is S. Ambrose at Milan in a work written almost at the same time, to whom this practice is well-known and normal.[3] In Africa the practice appears to have been known to S. Augustine at Hippo, though his evidence as to how the oblations of the people reached the altar is not absolutely decisive. It is certainly attested as the custom there by Victor of Vita in the fifth century.[4] It is taken for granted by

[1] *Didascalia Apostolorum*, ii. 57 (*ed. cit. p.* 120).
[2] *de Compunctione*, i. 3. The reference though indirect seems certain. Cyril of Jerusalem does not describe the offertory.
[3] *Expos. in Ps.* cxviii, *Prol.* 2.
[4] *Victor Vitensis*, ii. 17.

Caesarius of Arles as the normal custom in the early sixth century in S.E. France, the first information from Gaul that we possess about the offertory. But in view of this author's habitual 'Romanising' his evidence might be discounted by some. It is, however, specifically insisted on as the traditional custom in Gaul by the exceptionally representative Council of Macon in A.D. 585.[1] It is an indication of the nature of the evidence available that none of these authors mentions the intervention of the deacons in the collection of the oblations in the West; and that all of them are earlier than the first mention of the Western custom at Rome where it is supposed to have originated. It is just such practical details which every one of the faithful knew by practice that ancient authors naturally take for granted.

But there is more to be said yet. The supposed 'Roman' custom must at one time have existed in Egypt. The deacon's thrice-repeated command to the people to bring up their offerings at the offertory still keeps its old place in the Coptic rite,[2] though for many centuries now the actual offertory has been made in Egypt at the Byzantine place, before the liturgy begins. There is evidence, too, that the 'Roman' custom prevailed in the fourth century in Asia Minor.[3] Looking at the matter closely, and despite the lack of pre-Nicene evidence which handicaps both theories in the same way, it seems unlikely that the later 'Western' rite of the offertory first arose in the fourth century. It is too deep-rooted in the ideas of the pre-Nicene fathers about the meaning of the people's oblation for that (cf. Irenaeus sup.). And it is too widespread in the East as well as the West at too early a date to be a local Roman innovation. Rather it seems (though the early evidence is too fragile for certainty either way) that there were in the pre-Nicene church two different practices, not in the moment but in the manner of the offertory, and that the Syrian practice differed from that in other churches. That a Syrian peculiarity should later have come to prevail all over the East is not unexampled. That the considerable structural variations between the Eastern and Western rites should have developed out of this trifling original difference in the treatment of the people's offerings may be surprising, but it is only an indication of the fundamental importance of the offertory for the understanding of any eucharistic rite.

[1] Council of Macon, can. 4; Caesarius, Serm. 265 (ap. S. Augustine Spuria). P. L. 39, 2238.
[2] Brightman, L. E. W., p. 164, l. 8.
[3] Cf. Brightman, L. E. W., p. 164, l. 8 for Egypt, and p. 525, l. 9 sq. for Asia Minor. These pieces of evidence have been challenged by E. Bishop ap. Homilies of Narsai. ed. Connolly, pp. 116 sq., it seems on insufficient grounds, though he is right in his criticism of Brightman's actual statements. But e.g. the story about Valens' offering in Gregory Naz. Orat., xliii. 52, even if it was not of bread and wine but money, as Bishop contends, was offered at the offertory, after the sermon, not before the liturgy began, and at the sanctuary rail, not in the sanctuary—which points to the subsequent 'Western', not 'Eastern', practice having prevailed at Caesarea of Cappadocia in the later fourth century.

### 3. *The Rinsing of the Hands*

The rinsing of the celebrant's hands before the eucharistic prayer is first mentioned by S. Cyril of Jerusalem in A.D. 348. After the fourth century this custom is found in all rites in connection with the offertory; but the utilitarian origin which has been suggested for it—to remove any soiling which might have resulted from the handling of the various oblations at the offertory—will not bear examination. The hands of the deacons who had actually disposed the oblations were left unrinsed. It was the hands of the bishops and presbyters, which had so far not come in contact with the oblations at all, which were washed, while the deacons ministered ewer, bason and towel. S. Cyril himself protests that the action is purely 'symbolic', in token of the innocence required of those who serve the christian altar (Ps. xxvi. 6), and not utilitarian, 'for we did not come into the *ecclesia* covered with dirt'.[1]

It seems such a natural little ceremony that one is rather surprised not to find it mentioned before Cyril, and outside Syria not before the end of the century. But the 'lay-out' of the evidence suggests that it is just one of those symbolic and imaginative elaborations of the rite which became natural as soon as the eucharist took on something of the nature of a 'public' cultus during the fourth century, but for which the directness and intensity of pre-Nicene concentration on the sacramental action in its naked simplicity offered no encouragement. Of such developments the Jerusalem church under S. Cyril was, as we shall see, very much a pioneer, though the rest of christendom was soon quite ready to copy them.

If the *lavabo* be older than Cyril's time, we can perhaps look for its origin (if such a natural gesture need have a particular origin) to that washing of the hands customary among the jews before 'the Thanksgiving' at the end of a meal, of which our Lord Himself made just such a symbolic use.[2] This rinsing, according to the rabbis, was not so much of utilitarian as of religious importance. The Israelite might not offer prayer without ablution, as the priests of the Temple might not approach the altar to 'liturgise' without it.[3] The *berakah* in a sense offered the preceding meal to God, and so might not be offered by one who was uncleansed. All these customary ablutions reappeared in early christian practice, whether by direct derivation from judaism or by natural instinct we cannot say. Thus the bishop approached his own 'liturgy' at the altar with the same symbolism as the jewish priest, and the christian layman washed his hands before even private prayers.[4] As soon as christian churches began to be erected with legal approval, fountains were provided in the forecourt for

---

[1] *Cat.* xxiii. 2. *Ap. Const.*, viii. also insists on the purely symbolic meaning, and places the lavabo *before* the offertory.
[2] John xiii. 4.                                    [3] Exod. xxx. 20.
[4] Hippolytus, *Ap. Trad.*, xxxv. 1, 8, 10; Tertullian, *de Oratione*, 13. Both disapprove a little of the practice, but they record it.

these ritual ablutions of the laity before entering for the liturgy.[1] Their remote derivatives are to be seen in the holy-water stoups at the doors of catholic churches to-day, which combine, however, the half-utilitarian notion of the early christian ablutions before prayer with the similar but wholly religious notion of 'lustration' or purification. The *lavabo* of the celebrant before offering the eucharistic prayer, which is intended to symbolise purity of heart rather than to procure it, to this day retains the original christian emphasis.

### 4. *The Imposition of Hands on the Elements*

Hippolytus' rubric that after the oblation has been set upon the altar by the deacons the bishop 'with all the presbyters laying his hand on the oblation' shall proceed to the eucharistic dialogue, is not, so far as I know, paralleled elsewhere.[2] The practice bears a certain resemblance to that of the Old Testament in the case of a sin-offering on behalf of 'the whole congregation (*ecclesia*) of Israel'. There 'the congregation shall offer a young bullock . . . and bring him before the tabernacle . . . and the elders of the congregation shall lay their hands on the head of the bullock before the Lord and the bullock shall be killed before the Lord'; after which the 'anointed priest' is to make propitiation with its blood 'before the vail' and at the altar.[3] But a more probable origin for this imposition of hands on the oblation lies in the analogy of other such impositions of hands described by Hippolytus: (i) by all the bishops present on a bishop-elect, before that imposition by one bishop alone with the prayer which actually consecrates the elect to the episcopate; (ii) by the bishop on the heads of the candidates before baptism, with an exorcism; (iii) by the bishop on the heads of the candidates before confirmation, with a prayer for their worthiness to receive the gift of the Spirit about to be bestowed by anointing with chrism.[4] The gesture, which is a natural and universal token of blessing, would appear to be employed in all these cases to signify a preparation of *persons* to receive sacramental grace. There is nothing similar accompanying blessings of *things* (a somewhat novel extension of the idea of blessing *c.* A.D. 200) elsewhere in Hippolytus. Yet the eucharistic oblation in some sort represented the persons of the offerers, and might perhaps be treated in the same way. Or it may be outright simply a gesture for the blessing of the oblations themselves, and so the fore-runner of those signs of the cross over the oblations at this point which are found in all later rites. Its mention is in any case a confirmation of the fact that the

---

[1] *Cf. e.g.* Eusebius, *Eccl. Hist.*, x. iv. 40 (*c.* A.D. 314). Western examples are found at about the same time.

[2] *Ap. Trad.*, iv. 2. The somewhat similar custom in the Milanese offertory appears to be of early mediaeval origin.

[3] Levit. iv. 13 *sq.*

[4] *Ap. Trad.*, ii. 3; xx. 8; xxii. 1. *Cf.* xix. 1 (on catechumens).

second century church saw in the offertory a ritual act with a religious significance of its own, not merely a necessary preliminary to consecration and communion.

The presbyters clearly join in this as 'concelebrants' with the bishop. Their office had originally in itself no properly liturgical but only administrative functions, as is clear from a comparison of the early prayers for ordination with those for the bishop and deacon. But from their deputising as liturgical presidents in the absence of the bishop, they had come in the second century to acquire such functions in conjunction with him at the eucharist when he was present.[1]

### 5. The Eucharistic Dialogue and Prayer

As we have seen, the jewish *berakah* was preceded by a dialogue between the president and members of the *chabûrah*, from which the christian eucharistic dialogue is clearly derived.[2] As reported by Hippolytus[3] *c.* A.D. 215 this is already (with one slight change) in exactly that form in which it is still found in the Roman and Egyptian rites. But in the rest of the East it has been to some extent elaborated in later times. In the Byzantine rite the Pauline greeting 'The grace of our Lord Jesus Christ etc.'[4] has been substituted for 'The Lord be with you', as a kind of blessing of the congregation. This is not mentioned by S. Cyril of Jerusalem, but variants of a slightly different form are found in the Antiochene liturgy of *S. James* and in that of *Apostolic Constitutions*, viii. The present Byzantine form is found in the Antiochene writings of S. John Chrysostom *c.* A.D. 390, and also in the East Syrian liturgy of *SS. Addai & Mari*. It would seem therefore that the substitution of 2 Cor. xiii. 14 for 'The Lord be with you' at this point is a custom which originated at Antioch sometime in the later fourth century, and which spread thence to all countries which followed a generally Syrian type of rite. It has never been adopted outside the Syrian tradition.

The second ℣ and ℟ 'Lift up your hearts', 'We lift them up unto the Lord' appear to be of purely christian origin; the ℣ is more idiomatic in Greek than in Latin, the ℟ is more idiomatic in Latin than in Greek, which may be a sign of where they were invented. But they are found in all the Greek liturgies as well as the Latin ones, and are indeed first attested in Greek, by Hippolytus. They are quite certainly part of the primaeval

---

[1] This development was no doubt assisted by the fact that they had inherited from the jewish presbyters of the Sanhedrin the duty of joining in the episcopal imposition of hands at the ordination of new presbyters (not, of course, at the consecration of bishops). The presbyterate was, in both the jewish and christian view, a *corporate* body, of which the 'high-priest' (jewish and christian) was from one point of view only the president. They did not join in ordaining the deacon because the latter was the bishop's *liturgical* assistant, a sphere in which the presbyters originally had no share.

[2] *Cf. pp. 79 sq.*          [3] *Ap. Trad.*, iv. 3.          [4] 2 Cor. xiii. 14.

core of the liturgical eucharist; and their character is another slight indication that the first formation of the 'four-action shape' of this took place in bilingual Rome, and spread thence all over christendom.

They were confined strictly to use at the sacramental eucharist, unlike the other parts of the dialogue,[1] and the reason is not far to seek. They are intended to remind the *ecclesia* that the real action of the eucharist takes place beyond time in 'the age to come', where God 'has made us sit together in heavenly places in Christ Jesus, that in the age to come He might shew the exceeding riches of His grace in His kindness towards us through Christ Jesus.'[2] We shall discuss this more at length later. Here it is sufficient to have noted their eschatological character. Once again, the later Syrian rites have elaborated the primitive formula, while the Roman and Egyptian ones have kept to the original simplicity. Cyril of Jerusalem already has 'Lift up your minds' for 'your hearts'; and S. Euthymius, who wrote at Jerusalem about a century later, has 'Lift up your minds and hearts'. This has become the ordinary Syrian form. The reply is similarly 'improved upon' in some of the Syrian rites, *e.g.*, We lift them 'unto Thee, O God of Abraham and of Isaac and of Israel, O glorious King', in the liturgy of *SS. Addai and Mari*.

The third $\mathbb{V}$ and $\mathbb{R}$ in Hippolytus, 'Let us give thanks (*lit.* make eucharist) unto the Lord', 'It is meet and right', are clearly derived from the invitation of the president of the *chabûrah* before reciting the *berakah* after supper and the 'assent' of his company. Hippolytus' form is that laid down by the rabbis 'when there are ten in company' at the *chabûrah*. The form of the Roman rite, '. . . unto the Lord our God', which was followed by Cranmer, is that which was prescribed among the jews when there were an hundred present.[3] The survival of this $\mathbb{V}$ and $\mathbb{R}$ at this point would alone suffice to identify the christian eucharistic prayer with the jewish *berakah*.

I do not wish to suggest that the Syrian rites alone have had the trick of amplifying the primitive dialogue. Here for instance is the form it takes in the Mozarabic rite:

*The Priest.*    I will go unto the altar of God.
*People.*        Even unto the God of my joy and gladness.
*The Deacon.*    Lend your ears unto the Lord.
*People.*        We lend them unto the Lord.
*The Priest.*    Lift up your hearts.
*People.*        We lift them up unto the Lord.
*The Priest.*    Let us give worthy thanks and praises unto our God and Lord, the Father, the Son and the Holy Ghost.
*People.*        It is meet and right.

It is difficult to see what is gained by such changes as these, beyond elaboration for elaboration's sake. It is worth noting that the Roman rite in

[1] *Cf. e.g. p.* 85.        [2] Eph. ii. 6, 7.        [3] *Berakoth, M.*, vii. 4 and 5

the West and the Egyptian rite in the East still often coincide in such details, though there has been little contact between the Egyptian and Roman churches since the fifth century. This is because both have kept close to the original universal tradition. The Syrian rite in the East and the Gallican rites in the West tend to diverge not only from the Egyptian-Roman tradition but from one another (despite certain superficial agreements due to direct cultural and political contacts) because each has independently elaborated upon the original universal tradition.

As we shall be dealing with the eucharistic prayer separately in chapter seven, all that need be said here is that though Hippolytus' words at iv. 2, 'with all the presbyters',[1] might possibly be construed to mean that the presbyters are to say the prayer with the bishop as well as lay hands upon the oblation with him, other passages in the *Ap. Trad.*, especially the careful safeguarding of the bishop's right to phrase the eucharistic prayer as he thinks best, and even perhaps to do so *ex tempore*,[2] seem to make it clear that the bishop alone uttered the prayer. This was his 'special liturgy', and had been since apostolic times. Just as the president of the *chabûrah* alone said the *berakah* while the members of his society stood around the table in silence, so the christian president said the *eucharistia* while all the members of his church stood grouped in silence around the altar. S. Paul appears to witness to the absolute continuity of practice in this recitation of the eucharistic blessing by one alone for the rest, when he deprecates the celebrant's uttering the *eucharistia* 'in the Spirit' (*i.e.*, in the babbling. of the unintelligible 'tongues' under the stress of prophetic excitement), 'Otherwise how shall he who occupies the position of a private person (*i.e.* the layman) say Amen to thy *eucharistia* seeing he understands not what thou sayest? ... In the *ecclesia* I had rather speak five words with my understanding that I might teach others also than ten thousand words in a "tongue".'[3]

### 6. *The Amen*

By an Anglican tradition which dates from the seventeenth century a special importance attaches to the 'Amen' of the laity at the end of the Prayer of Consecration, as being their share in the 'consecration' itself, the verbal exercise of their 'lay-priesthood'. Whatever the justification for this notion, it was certainly not derived from Archbishop Cranmer, who deliberately omitted any direction for the laity to respond 'Amen' to this prayer in 1552, in which he was followed by the Elizabethan and Jacobean revisers. The response of the people was not reinserted officially until 1662, though it appears to have been said in practice by the people in Charles I's time, with the encouragement of the 'high church' divines of the period.

---

[1] *Cf. p.* 110.          [2] *Ap. Trad.*, x. 3–5.          [3] I Cor. xiv. 16 *sq.*

Without wishing to depreciate the patristic scholarship of the Carolines, which was as a rule more extensive than deep, it must be pointed out that whatever the value and importance in itself of the practice to which they gave currency, the idea upon which they based it is by no means a safe guide to the intention of the primitive church in attaching the importance it did to the 'Amen' after the eucharistic prayer. The bishop's 'liturgy' of 'offering the gifts' exercised through that prayer was the peculiar function of his 'order'. The primitive ideal of corporate worship was not the assimilation of the office of the 'order' of laity to those of the other orders, but the combination of all the radically distinct 'liturgies' of all the orders in a single complete action of the organic Body of Christ. The primitive church attached an equally great importance to the 'Amen' of the communicant after the words of administration at communion, which the Carolines did not attempt to restore in English practice, though they reappear in Laud's Scottish Book of 1637. It is obvious, I think, that these two 'Amens' cannot have precisely that significance which the Anglican 'high church' tradition attached to the 'Amen' after the consecration, as an 'assent' by the laity to the prayer of the clergy. In all three cases 'Amen' was originally rather a proclamation of faith by the laity for themselves than a mere assent. It was in fact as much a part of the 'eschatological setting' of the eucharist as the cry 'Lift up your hearts' before the prayer began.

The word 'Amen' is Hebrew and not Greek. It was left untranslated in the liturgy after *c.* A.D. 100 because its full meaning proved to be in fact untranslatable, though attempts seem to have been made in the first century to press the Greek *alēthinos* ( = 'genuine') into use as a substitute.[1] The Hebrew root 'MN, from which 'Amen' is derived, meant originally 'fixed', 'settled', 'steadfast', and so, 'true'. 'The Hebrew mind in its certainty of a transcendental God, fixed upon Him as the standard of truth. ... The inability of the Hebrew mind to think of the character or nature of God apart from His actions in the world caused them to think of His truth, not as static, but as active or potentially active. God must, God would, manifest His truth to the world, for His nature demanded a vindication of itself. ... So the truth of Jehovah came to be sighed for in exactly the same way as His mercy and His righteousness. When they were revealed, when He finally acted, the Messianic age would have dawned.'[2] It is entirely in accord with this that in the jewish translation of the Old Testament into Greek, the Hebrew 'Amen' is almost always translated by 'Would that it might be so!' (*genoito*).

We can now see what the most strongly eschatological book of the N.T. means when it applies the word as a title to our Lord Himself, 'These things saith the Amen, the faithful and true witness, the source of the creation of God.'[3] In Him the truth, mercy and righteousness of God *have*

[1] *E.g.* Rev. iii.7
[3] Rev. iii. 14.
[2] Hoskyns and Davey, *op. cit., p.* 35.

*been* revealed; in Him God *has* acted; in Him the Messianic 'age to come' *has* dawned. Or as S. Paul puts it, 'In Him (Jesus) all the promises of God are yea, and in Him is the Amen by us to the glory of God.'[1] In Him is vindicated the eternal faithfulness of God to His promises; in Him, too, is the perfect human response to the everlasting living 'Yea' of God. In Him, as members of His Body, we too know and accept and proclaim the 'truth-fulness' of God, to His glory. That is the coming of the Kingdom of God among men. The word was perpetually upon our Lord's lips—'Amen, Amen, I say unto you . . .'—not less than sixty-three times in the gospels. As a German scholar has brilliantly remarked, 'In the "Amen" before the "I say unto you" of Jesus the whole of Christology is contained in a nut-shell.'[2]

When, therefore, the christian church inherited the jewish custom of responding 'Amen' to the 'glorifying of the Name of God' at the close of doxologies and other prayers, it nevertheless did so with a considerable change of emphasis. What for the jew was a longing hope for the future coming of God's truth, was for the christian a triumphant proclamation that in Jesus, the Amen to the everlasting Yea of God, he had himself passed into the Messianic Kingdom and the world to come. It was the summary of his faith in Jesus his Redeemer, and in God his Father and King. As such it was the fitting conclusion to the last words of the christian scriptures;[3] and an equally fitting response alike to the eucharistic prayer and the words of administration, where that redemption and that father-hood and kingship find their full actuality within time. As the conclusion of the doxology which closed the eucharistic prayer with the proclamation of the revealed majesty of One God in Three Persons, it prolonged and endorsed the tremendous affirmation 'unto all ages of ages' (or as we customarily translate it 'world without end') with an echo of the timeless worship of heaven.[4] On the whole it is not surprising that the second generation of gentile christians despaired of translating a word of such depth of meaning by the Greek *alēthinos*, with its purely negative conno-tation of 'what is not false', and disdaining the now superseded future reference of the Septuagint *genoito*,—'would that it were so'—ended by retaining the jewish word in which our Lord had Himself affirmed 'Amen, I say unto you' the truth of God.

### 7. *The Lord's Prayer*

The first positive evidence for the use of the Lord's prayer at the end of the eucharistic prayer is found, once again, in S. Cyril of Jerusalem (A.D. 348). It is absent from the rite of *Ap. Const.* viii. and not mentioned in Chrysostom's writings at Antioch a generation later. It was therefore

---

[1] 2 Cor. i. 20.
[2] H. Schlier, *Theologisches Wörterbuch* (ed. Kittel) I. 341 (1932).
[3] Rev. xxii. 21.                    [4] Rev. xix. 4.

not a general Syrian custom in Cyril's time. At about the same period it appears to be missing from the Egyptian rite as represented by Sarapion. In the West it is mentioned by S. Ambrose in his *de Sacramentis*[1] vi. 24, about A.D. 395 at Milan. At about the same time it is first mentioned in Africa by S. Augustine, who early in the fifth century says that 'almost the whole world now concludes' the eucharistic prayer with this.[2] The exception he has in mind is probably Rome, where the innovation does not seem to have been accepted until the time of S. Gregory I (*c.* A.D. 595).[3] It is to be noted that in the West the position of the prayer varied slightly, a sure sign that it was accepted at different times by different churches. In Africa it came between the fraction and the communion; at Rome, when it was at length admitted, it was placed in the Jerusalem position, immediately after the eucharistic prayer itself, before the fraction. At Milan it appears to have been placed within the eucharistic prayer itself, at its close, but followed by the doxology of the eucharistic prayer and the 'Amen'. It is to be noted that while at Jerusalem the bishop and people recited the prayer together, in the West it appears to have been treated as a part of the eucharistic prayer and therefore recited by the celebrant only, the people responding with the last clause, or simply with 'Amen'. Certainly this was the case in Africa in S. Augustine's time,[4] as it was later at Rome and in Spain. In France the Syrian custom of a general recitation was adopted at some point before the end of the sixth century, but 'it is practically certain that this was not the original custom anywhere in the West.'[5]

### 8. *The Fraction*

Oddly enough Justin does not mention the fraction, and our first description of it is from Hippolytus. In describing the first communion of the newly confirmed he clearly states that the bishop 'breaks the bread'.[6] But in describing the ordinary Sunday eucharist he says: 'On the first day of the week the bishop, if it be possible, shall with his own hand deliver to all the people, while the deacons break the bread.'[7] The explanation of this apparent contradiction is to be found, it seems, in the description of the rite of the Papal mass in the *Ordo Romanus Primus* of the seventh-eighth century. There the Pope still breaks the Bread for his own communion and that of the clergy around him but (to save time?) the deacons who are his chief liturgical assistants break the Bread for the communion of the people

---

[1] That this work, the attribution of which to Ambrose has long been disputed, is really his *cf.* Dom R. H. Connolly, *Downside Review*, lxix. (Jan. 1941), *pp.* 1 *sq.*
[2] Augustine *Ep.* 59.
[3] So I interpret S. Gregory, *Ep.* ix. 12, in conjunction with John the Deacon, *Vita Greg.* ii. 20. But some have supposed that he only shifted the position of the prayer at Rome from the African position after the fraction to before it.
[4] Augustine, *Serm.* 58. 'It is recited daily at the altar and the faithful *hear* it'.
[5] W. C. Bishop, *The Mozarabic and Ambrosian Rites* (Alcuin Club Tracts, xv. 1924) p. 40.
[6] *Ap. Trad.*, xxiii. 5.            [7] *Ibid.* xxiv. 1.

while he makes his own communion. It is also to be noted that according to Hippolytus the concelebrant presbyters are also to 'break the Bread' which has been held before them on patens by the deacons during the bishop's recitation of the prayer, and distribute this to the people. This practice is also found surviving in the Papal mass 500 years later in the *Ordo Romanus Primus*.

The original purpose of the fraction, both at the jewish 'grace before meals' and at the last supper, was simply for distribution. But symbolism laid hold of this part of the rite even in the apostolic age. It is clear from 1 Cor. x. 17 that in S. Paul's time the fragments were all broken off a single loaf before the eyes of the assembled communicants. This is the whole point of his appeal for unity in the Corinthian church. This was still the case in the time of Ignatius who writes of 'breaking one bread' (or 'loaf', *hena arton*), again as the demonstration of the unity of the church.[1] Before the end of the second century, however, this symbolism had lost its point and another was *substituted* for it, in some churches at least, that of the 'breaking' of the Body of Christ in the passion.

The separation of the eucharist from the supper did, of course, have the effect of concentrating attention much more upon its character as a 're-calling' of the Lord's death, though this was not a new idea of its purpose. What led to the change of symbolism in the fraction was probably the practical fact that the bread was no longer broken from a single loaf but from several, rather than any change in the theoretical understanding of the rite. The increase in the numbers of communicants would have something to do with this, though the loaf could within limits be increased in size. But the custom of taking the bread for the sacrament from the people's offerings probably had more effect. These were numerous but small; when the eucharist was combined with a meal most of them would be eaten as common food, along with the other offerings in kind from which the supper was provided. But when the meal was separated from the liturgy, and yet the individual offerings of bread and wine were continued, the custom of consecrating more than one of the little loaves would impose itself, though it was not necessarily accepted by every church at the same time. But when it was, a fresh symbolism would be required, and that of the 'breaking' in the passion was natural.

There is not, however, the slightest suggestion of this in the N.T. Matt. and Mark give as the only words over the Bread 'Take, eat, this is My Body.' John expressly denies that 'a bone of Him' was broken. What S. Paul seems to have written in 1 Cor. xi. 24 was 'This is My Body which is for you' (*to hyper hymon*). But the desire for a symbolism in connection with the Bread parallel to that of the Blood 'shed for many'[2] led to the

---

[1] Ignatius *Eph.* xx. 1.
[2] Mark xiv. 24; Matt. xxvi. 28. Not represented in the earlier account in 1 Cor. xi. 25.

filling up of S. Paul's phrase variously in different churches, as '. . . is broken (*klōmenon*) for you', or '. . . is given (*didomenon*) for you', according to whether the emphasis was placed on the fraction or the distribution in local liturgies. The form 'which is broken for you' is already found in the Roman tradition of the prayer according to Hippolytus *c.* A.D. 215, but is not represented in Justin at Rome sixty years before. It is possible that the original reading of Hippolytus' text was 'which *will be* broken for you', phrased in the future as in the earliest extant Latin text of the Roman eucharistic prayer.[1] This points to an early recognition of the fact that the last supper was not a eucharist properly speaking, because Calvary was not yet an accomplished fact.

Other churches adopted the form 'which is given for you' or, as in Egypt, 'which is broken and distributed (*diadidomenon*) for you'; and in course of time liturgical practice thus had a reflex action on the MS tradition of the text of 1 Cor. xi. So *e.g.*, the unique reading of this verse in the very important sixth century MS. of the N.T. *Codex Claromontanus* (D) '. . . which is broken in pieces (*thruptomenon*) for you', is otherwise found only in a liturgical text, that of the eucharistic prayer in *Ap. Const.*, viii.—proof positive of the way in which the liturgical traditions of local churches reacted on the text of the scriptures. From our modern standpoint one would rather have expected that the influence would be the other way. But in fact no ancient liturgical institution narrative is known which is simply a quotation from the scriptures. They all adapt and expand our Lord's words as reported in the N.T., sometimes very boldly. It was not so much that any superior historical authority was supposed to lie behind the continuous tradition of the recitation in the liturgy—that is a modern way of looking at the matter which would hardly have suggested itself then. There was only a strong sense that the liturgical tradition which had arisen before the scriptural narratives were canonised had its own independence, and also its own control in the shape of custom.

Cranmer used this ancient liberty in compiling the institution narrative of the rites of 1549 and 1552, which is a conflation from the various scriptural accounts. He could not foresee that by including the non-scriptural word 'broken' in the words of institution over the bread he would give occasion to the revisers of 1662 to commit the blunder of transferring the fraction from its original and universal place before the communion to a point in the middle of the eucharistic prayer. By this not only is its proper purpose as a preparation for distribution (as at the last supper) obscured by a non-scriptural symbolism, but its original character as one of the great successive acts which have together made up the 'four-action' structure of the eucharist ever since sub-apostolic times (at the latest) has been partially destroyed in our rite.

The fraction was always the point in the rite which offered most

[1] S. Ambrose, *de Sacramentis*, iv. 5.

opportunity for symbolic development. After the fourth century various complicated arrangements of the broken Bread upon the altar were evolved in the Eastern and Gallican churches, some of which were not free from superstition.[1] A more innocent and meaningful custom, which arose earlier, was that of placing a fragment of the broken Bread in the chalice, 'to show that they are not separable, that they are one in power and that they vouchsafe the same grace to those who receive them', as Theodore of Mopsuestia explains in the first account of this practice which has come down to us.[2] But it is certainly older in some form than Theodore's time (c. A.D. 400). It seems to me likely (but not demonstrable) that its historical origin lay in the custom of the *fermentum*. This is the name given to that fragment of the consecrated Bread brought from the bishop's eucharist to that of the presbyter celebrating the sacrament at a lesser *ecclesia* elsewhere, in token of the bishop's eucharistic presidency of his whole church. It seems that the *fermentum* was placed in the chalice by the presbyter at this point. The custom of the *fermentum*, which goes back at least to the early years of the second century, died out comparatively early in the East, probably in the fourth century; though it lasted on at Rome to the eighth or ninth century. It seems possible that when the Bread from the bishop's eucharist ceased to be brought to the Eastern presbyter to be placed in his chalice, a fragment from the Bread consecrated by the presbyter himself may have been substituted, in unthinking continuance of the old custom; and then a new symbolic meaning (in itself valuable) was afterwards found for its new form, as so often happened in liturgical history.

It was also at this point that in later times the *sanctum*, a fragment reserved from the eucharist consecrated at the last mass in that church, and brought to the altar at the offertory[3] to symbolise the perpetual identity of the sacrifice offered in the eucharist, was placed in the chalice and consumed. But this is a later custom which is not heard of before the sixth century.[4]

Having broken the Bread the bishop, in the fourth century and after, held it aloft and invited the church to communicate with the words 'Holy things unto the holy.' It is not quite easy to represent the full meaning of this in English. The Greek *hagios* and the Latin *sanctus* mean not so much

[1] Cf. the specimens collected by Scudamore, *Dict. of Christian Antiquities* (ed. Smith), I. 687 sq., s.v. Fraction.
[2] *Cat.* vi. (ed. cit. p. 106). The whole passage is interesting as shewing that the rather elaborate form of the ceremony now found in the Eastern rites with a 'signing of the Bread with the Blood' as well as the placing of a fragment in the chalice was already fully developed at Mopsuestia, though no author before Theodore so much as mentions it. Cyril of Jerusalem does not mention the fraction at all, so that we cannot say that this particular elaboration originated at Jerusalem, but it has that sort of style. Certainly it appears to be of Syrian origin.
[3] So in Gaul. At Rome it was brought to the altar at the introit. The custom does not seem to be known in the East.
[4] The first mention of it seems to be Gregory of Tours, *de Gloria Martyrum*, 86 (c. A.D. 580).

what is *in itself* 'good' (which is the connotation of the English 'holy') as what 'belongs to God.' It is, for instance, in this sense that S. Paul speaks of and to his Corinthian converts as 'chosen saints' (*hagioi*) in spite of their disorders and quarrels. Perhaps the bishop's invitation can be most adequately rendered as 'The things of God for the people of God'. This places the whole emphasis where the early church placed it, on their membership of the Body of Christ and His redemption of them, and not on any sanctity of their own.

The words of this invitation are first recorded by Cyril of Jerusalem,[1] to which he says that the people replied '(There is) One holy, our Lord Jesus Christ.' The same formula of response, insisting very beautifully on the uniqueness of our Lord as the source of all human goodness, is found in the liturgies of *S. James, S. Basil, Ap. Const.* viii., *S. John Chrysostom, SS. Addai & Mari,* and the Armenian liturgy; it is also quoted by S. Gregory of Nyssa and S. Cyril of Alexandria as used in their day. But an alternative form of response quoted by Theodore of Mopsuestia,[2] 'One Holy Father, one Holy Son, one Holy Ghost' has found its way at some point into the Egyptian liturgies of *S. Mark* and *S. Cyril*.

This verbal invitation and its response do not seem to be attested at all in the West during the fourth and fifth centuries and never became general there. This suggests that the seeming reference to them in Hippolytus *On the Pascha* iii. is due to an accidental similarity of phrase and not to contemporary use of them in the third century Roman rite.[3] Like so many other details which are picturesque and touching in the developed liturgies, this is probably an innovation of the fourth century church of Jerusalem which was soon copied so widely as to appear a general tradition.

### 9. *The Communion*

This is the climax and completion of the rite for all pre-Nicene writers. Justin in his description says little about its details save (twice over) that communion was given by the deacons with no mention of the bishop and presbyters.[4] However this may be (and it strikes me as authentic early practice) Hippolytus insists more than once that the bishop shall if possible give the bread to all the communicants 'with his own hand', assisted by the presbyters. The presbyters also are to minister the chalice, 'or if there are not enough of them the deacons'. This may mark a rise in the liturgical importance of presbyters during the sixty years since Justin, due chiefly to the need for multiplying celebrants. But it may equally possibly be only a little mark of a special jealousy which Hippolytus the presbyter felt for the

---

[1] *Cat.* xxiii. 19.          [2] *Cat.* vi. (*ed. cit. p.* 110).
[3] I am glad of this opportunity of withdrawing my remarks on this point in *The Parish Communion*, p. 102, *n.* 4.
[4] *Ap.* I. 65, 67.

liturgical privileges of the order of deacons which comes out more than once in the *Apostolic Tradition*.

At all events the deacons retained a special connection with the administration of the chalice, even at Rome, and also the right to administer the reserved sacrament under the species of Bread, which is assigned to them by Justin. The Council of Nicaea (A.D. 325) in its eighteenth canon felt obliged to interfere energetically to forbid deacons in certain churches to administer communion to presbyters even at the public celebration, or to make their communion before presbyters and even before the bishop-celebrant. Evidently the deacons retained in some churches[1] their primitive position as the exclusive 'servants of the tables'[2] of the church. They were ordered for the future to receive their communion from the hands of the bishop or presbyters and after those orders; and not to sit among them in the *ecclesia* but to stand, as anciently, in token of their office as mere liturgical assistants to the higher orders.

From this period dates the beginning of the slow atrophy of the diaconate as a real 'order' in the church, especially in the West. Its proper functions in the eucharist came eventually to be regarded as purely ceremonial, to be discharged by a priest in deacon's vestments if a deacon were not available—an idea quite foreign to the notion of 'order' in the primitive church. The diaconate itself degenerated into a mere period of preparation for the responsibilities of the priesthood. The older idea of the diaconate as an 'order' in its own right was retained in the East, and also in the Roman Curia after it had disappeared in most Western churches. It is from local Roman practice that the Anglican 'archdeacon' (in practice now always in bishop's or presbyter's orders) derives the peculiar attributes and functions attached to his title, as the bishop's closest assistant in the administration of his diocese.

Hippolytus' fullest description of the administration of holy communion is in his account of the eucharist which followed upon the reception of baptism and confirmation by the catechumens. The new christians on that occasion received not only from the ordinary eucharistic chalice of wine and water, but also from a chalice of water only—'for a sign of the laver that the inner man . . . may receive the same ⟨cleansing⟩ as the body', as he explains—has this a connection with the 'living water' of John vii. 38? —and from a third chalice of mingled milk and honey (in sign of their entry into the 'promised land'; cf. p. 80, n. 1). His account of the actual communion runs thus:

'And when the bishop breaks the bread in distributing to each a fragment he shall say "The Bread of heaven in Christ Jesus." And he who receives shall answer, "Amen."

---

[1] Alexandria appears to have retained this custom of deacons giving communion to all both in Bread and Wine down to the fourth century.

[2] Acts vi. 2.

'And the presbyters—but if they are not enough the deacons also—shall hold the cups and stand by in good order and with reverence, first he that holds the water, second he who holds the milk, third he who holds the wine. And they who partake shall taste of each cup thrice, he who gives it saying: "In God the Father Almighty", and he who receives shall say: "Amen." "And in the Lord Jesus Christ", and he shall say: "Amen." "And in the Holy Spirit ⟨which is⟩ in the Holy Church"; and he shall say "Amen." '[1]

There are several points here. First, as to practice: We know from other evidence that communion was received standing, and that the clergy received before the laity. It seems that the ministers stood before the altar and that the communicants moved from one to another of them, instead of the ministers passing along a row of communicants as with us. The same practice is implied by S. Cyril of Jerusalem in the fourth century.[2]

Secondly, there are the words of administration. Those modern theorists who are fond of repeating that the so-called words of institution at the last supper are really words of administration find no support in the practice of the primitive church. On the contrary, that church in this the earliest full account of the eucharist places the words of institution as the central thing in the eucharistic prayer. For the words of administration it uses formulae which rather pointedly avoid the emphasis of the synoptic gospels on the Body and Blood of Jesus as such, in order to take up the Johannine allusion to 'that Bread which cometh down from heaven and giveth life unto the world . . . he that eateth of this Bread *shall live for ever*'. It is another way of insisting that, as Ignatius of Antioch had put it a century before, the eucharistic Bread is 'the drug of immortality, the remedy that we should not die';[3] or as Irenaeus says 'Our bodies receiving the eucharist are no more corruptible, having the hope of eternal resurrection'.[4] We shall find this primitive insistence on 'the Spirit that quickeneth' in the eucharist[5] carried on after the fourth century chiefly in the Eastern liturgies, but with this great difference—that, in the fourth century and after, the Eastern theologians recognised in the 'Spirit' energising in the eucharist only the Third Person of the Blessed Trinity; the pre-Nicene centuries interpreted it with the New Testament rather of 'the latter Adam Who was made a quickening Spirit',[6] the Second Person of the Trinity Who gives Himself in the eucharist as on Calvary 'for the life of the world"[7]— the 'One Spirit into' which, says S. Paul, 'we have all been made to drink'.[8]

The threefold formula at each of the cups at the baptismal eucharist was presumably used on other occasions at the partaking of the eucharistic chalice alone. It forms the perfect climax of the rite, describing as it does the mutual compenetration of God and the soul in holy communion.

[1] *Ap. Trad.*, xxiii. 5 sq.  [2] *Cat.* xxiii. 22.
[3] Ignatius, *Eph.*, xx. 1.  [4] Irenaeus, *adv. Haer.*, iv. 18, 5.
[5] John vi. 63.  [6] I Cor. xv. 45.  [7] John vi. 51.  [8] I Cor. xii. 13.

This primitive recognition of what the communicant received in holy communion as 'Spirit' did not in any way exclude a thoroughgoing recognition of the fact that the consecrated Bread and Wine 'is (*esti*) the Flesh and Blood of that Jesus Who was made Flesh'.[1] No words could well be stronger, but they are echoed in their realism by every second century writer on the eucharist. It was by receiving His Body and Blood that one received the 'Spirit' of Christ. So Hippolytus concludes his eucharistic prayer with the petition 'that Thou wouldest grant to all Thy saints who partake (of the Body and Blood in holy communion) . . . that they may be fulfilled with holy Spirit.'[2] Or, as he explains his theory of communion more at length in another work: 'They are guilty of impiety against the Lord who give no care to prepare for the uniting of their bodies with His Body which He gave for us, that being united to Him we might be united to holy Spirit. For it was for this reason that the Word of God gave Himself wholly into a Body and was made Flesh, according to the phrase of the gospel—that since we were not able to partake of Him as Word, we might partake of Him as Body, fitting our flesh for His spiritual Flesh and our spirit to His Spirit so far as we can, that we might be established as likenesses of Christ . . . and through the commingling with the Spirit your members might become members of the Body of Christ, to be cherished in sanctity.'[3] Without entering on the very remarkable topics touched on in this passage, it is at least clear that Hippolytus' general theory is that one partakes of the 'Body' in order to receive of the 'Spirit' of Christ; and that by 'Spirit' in this context he means the Word of God, the Second Person of the Trinity rather than the Third. It is the energising of the heavenly and ascended Christ in His members on earth through His 'Spirit' thought of almost impersonally, which is here conceived as the 'effect' of holy communion. Making allowance for a certain clumsiness of phrasing due to an undeveloped terminology, I do not think that the modern communicant, or even theologian, really conceives the essence of the matter very differently, or that Hippolytus' statement of it would have been questioned by any one in his own day.[4]

But this primitive language was destined to be replaced by one more familiar to us in the fourth century, perhaps in the third. By then in East and West alike the words of administration had acquired a synoptic instead of a Johannine form: 'The Body of Christ', 'The Blood of Christ'—to each of which the communicant still replied, 'Amen.' Doubtless this was in part due to a closer grasp of Trinitarian theology by the church, which led to a greater insight into the Person and mission of God the Holy Ghost. The primitive and scriptural terminology which spoke of the heavenly Christ as 'Spirit' began to be discarded as confusing, or reinterpreted—not without some difficulty—as applying to the Third Person. This led again to

[1] Justin *Ap.* I. 65.
[2] *On the Pascha*, iii.
[3] *Ap. Trad.*, iv. 12.
[4] *Cf. pp.* 266 sq.

reinterpretations of the archaic language of the liturgical tradition by novel theological theories. But besides this transfer of meaning in terminology, there was, it appears, a certain change of thought, more subtle to trace but even more profound in its results, which had a great part in the matter. The old eschatological understanding of the eucharist as the irruption into time of the heavenly Christ, and of the eucharist as actualising an eternal redemption in the earthly church as Body of Christ even in this world, was replaced by a new insistence on the purely historical achievement of redemption within this world and time by Christ, at a particular moment and by particular actions in the past. We shall discuss this difficult matter more at length later. Here it is sufficient to have noted that such a change in the general way of regarding the eucharist does mark the period in which the words of administration underwent a change from a Johannine to a synoptic form, and that the two facts appear to have some relation to one another.

### 10. The Ablutions

The end of the communion marked the real end of the rite. But just as the preparing of the table by the spreading of a cloth at the beginning was done in the presence of the *ecclesia*, so the cleansing of the vessels at the close took place publicly before the dismissal. Just so the tidying of the room after the meal had been one of the prescribed customs at a *chabûrah* supper in judaism.[1] No detail of the rite was too homely to be accounted unfitting at the gathering of the household of God. Even after a formal corporate thanksgiving had come to be appended as a devotional 'extra' to the original rite of the eucharist in the fourth century, the ablution of the vessels in most churches retained its original position before the thanksgiving. In the Constantinopolitan rite they still remained in this position in the ninth century, where they are mentioned in the *Typicon* of the Patriarch Nicephorus.[2] Similarly in Egypt the canonical collection of Ebnassalus (Safi'l Fada 'il ibn 'Assal, thirteenth century) cites a constitution of the monophysite patriarch of Alexandria, 'Abdul Masitz (A.D. 1046–c. 1075) which indicates that in his time the ablution of the vessels in Egypt still took place after the communion and before the thanksgiving. But in Syria as represented by the liturgy of *Apostolic Constitutions*, Bk. viii., the custom had already come in before the end of the fourth century of not consuming the sacrament at the communion, but removing it to the sacristy (or the 'table of preparation') in the vessels before the thanksgiving, and performing the ablutions there after the service was over. After the tenth century this custom was generally followed in the East. Presumably the original reason was connected with reservation; but this removal of the elements to the sacristy for the thanksgiving does balance

[1] *Berakoth*, viii. 3 (*p.* 67).
[2] *Monumenta Jur. Eccl. Graec.*, ii. 341.

the other Syrian peculiarity of keeping the elements in the sacristy until they were actually wanted at the offertory.

The effect was the same in Syrian and non-Syrian rites alike; the sacramental elements were not upon the altar except during the vital sacramental action itself—from the offertory to the communion. Even when a thanksgiving had been appended to it, the church instinctively marked off the original apostolic core of the eucharist from all the devotional accretions which later ages have added to it in this simple but very effective way.

It must have been at this point of the rite, before the ablutions, that the faithful received some of the consecrated Bread to carry home with them for their communions on weekdays, and the deacons and acolytes received those portions which they were to convey to the absent and to the presbyteral eucharists elsewhere. But reservation in general is a subject only indirectly connected with the liturgy, and I have thrown what remarks I have to offer about it into a separate additional note.[1]

. . . . . .

Such was the pre-Nicene eucharist, a brief little rite which in practice, even with quite a number of communicants, would probably not take much longer than a quarter of an hour or twenty minutes. Even of the items we have considered here it seems to me more probable that two— the *lavabo* and the Lord's prayer—are fourth century additions rather than genuinely primitive constituents of the Shape of the Liturgy, though the question is open to discussion. Yet its brevity and unimpressiveness must not blind us to the fact that the celebration of the eucharist was throughout the pre-Nicene period not only the very heart of the church's life and the staple of the individual christian's devotion, but also the perpetual object of a quite hysterical pagan suspicion, and from time to time of formidable police measures by an efficient totalitarian state. It is important from more than one point of view to understand clearly just how the mere practice of its celebration was regarded both by christians and by their opponents in this period. It will be convenient to study this in the next chapter, before going on to consider the eucharistic prayer and the inward or theological meaning of the rite.

[1] This has been published separately under the title of *A Detection of Aumbries* (Dacre Press, London 1942) and is not here reproduced.

# CHAPTER VI

## THE PRE-NICENE BACKGROUND OF THE LITURGY

WE have said that despite its extreme structural simplicity there was no ideal of squalor or poverty about the pre-Nicene celebration of the eucharist. The list of church plate at Cirta and many other such indications are a sufficient guarantee of that. The baptistery attached to the house-church at Dura-Europos (c. A.D. 230) was painted from floor to ceiling with pictures of scenes from the Old and New Testaments, and a similar decoration of the assembly-room of the church had just been begun when the building was destroyed. There could be a considerable degree of splendour about the setting of the *ecclesia* in a great Roman patrician house, and even where this was lacking attempts were evidently made to supply some dignity. There was no puritan cult of bareness for its own sake.

There was, too, an element of ceremony in the celebration and a good deal of moving about. The rite was viewed essentially as an action, and a number of people cannot combine to take different parts in a corporate action without some such element of ceremony, in the sense of organised and concerted movement. It was a large part of the deacon's 'liturgy' by his 'proclamations' to direct and give the signal for these movements. There was, too, an element of solemnity; the bishop's prayer was probably chanted as the jewish prayers had been chanted. The use of the informal speaking voice for any part of the eucharist appears to be an innovation of the Latin churches in the early middle ages; for the eucharistic prayer itself it was not known before the Reformation. One cannot make much of the use by pre-Nicene writers of *dicere* (to say) in connection with the prayers. The ancients habitually used this word of a *recitative, e.g. dicere carmen* (*lit.* = 'to say a song'). Probably the immemorial preface-chant of the West[1] represents approximately the way in which the whole eucharistic prayer was originally recited there. Very similar intonations are traditional for the public prayers of the liturgy all over the East.

When all is said and done, the impression left by the early evidence about the celebration of the eucharist is one not so much of simplicity as of great *directness*, as became a deliberately 'domestic' act. There was no elaborate or choral music at the eucharist as at the synaxis; no special vestments or liturgical ornaments or symbolism, nothing whatever to arouse the emotions or stir the senses or impress the mind—just a complete and intense concentration upon the corporate performance of the eucharistic action in its naked self, without devotional elaborations of any kind whatever.

[1] In its 'ferial' not 'festal' form. The latter is known to be a later elaboration.

It is very easy for us to romanticise the life and worship of the primitive christians. What was conventional in the social setting of their day has for us the picturesqueness of the strange and remote; what was straightforward directness in their worship has for us the majesty of antiquity. It is a useful thing occasionally to transpose it all into the conventions of our own day and look at the result.

Suppose you were a grocer in Brondesbury, a tradesman in a small way of business, as so many of the early Roman christians were. Week by week at half-past four or five o'clock on Sunday morning (an ordinary working-day in pagan Rome) before most people were stirring, you would set out through the silent streets, with something in your pocket looking very like what we should call a bun or a scone. At the end of your walk you would slip in through the mews at the back of one of the big houses near Hyde Park, owned by a wealthy christian woman. There in her big drawing-room, looking just as it did every day, you would find the 'church' assembling—socially a very mixed gathering indeed. A man would look at you keenly as you went in, the deacon 'observing those who come in',[1] but he knows you and smiles and says something. Inside you mostly know one another well, you exchange greetings and nod and smile; (people who are jointly risking at the least penal servitude for life by what they are doing generally make certain that they know their associates). At the other end of the drawing-room sitting in the best arm-chair is an elderly man, a gentleman by his clothes but nothing out of the ordinary—the bishop of London. On either side of him is standing another man, perhaps talking quietly to him. On chairs in a semicircle facing down the room, looking very obviously like what they are—a committee—sit the presbyters. In front of them is a small drawing-room table.

The eucharist is about to begin. The bishop stands and greets the church. At once there is silence and order, and the church replies. Then each man turns and grasps his neighbour strongly and warmly by both hands. (I am trying to represent the ancient by a modern convention. The kiss was anciently a much commoner salutation than it is with us in England, but it implied more affection than does merely 'shaking hands' with us.) The two men by the bishop spread a white table-cloth on the table, and then stand in front of it, one holding a silver salver and the other a two-handled silver loving-cup. One by one you all file up and put your little scones on the salver and pour a little wine into the loving-cup. Then some of the scones are piled together before the bishop on the cloth, and he adds another for himself, while water is poured into the wine in the cup and it is set before him. In silence he and the presbyters stand with their hands outstretched over the offerings, and then follow the dialogue and the chanted prayer lasting perhaps five minutes or rather less. You all answer 'Amen' and there follows a pause as the bishop breaks one of the scones

---

[1] *Didascalia*, ii. 57.

and eats a piece. He stands a moment in prayer and then takes three sips from the cup, while the two men beside him break the other scones into pieces. To each of those around him he gives a small piece and three sips from the cup. Then with the broken bread piled on the salver he comes forward and stands before the table with one of the deacons in a lounge suit standing beside him with the cup. One by one you file up again to receive in your hands 'The Bread of Heaven in Christ Jesus', and pass on to take three sips from the cup held by the deacon, 'In God the Father Almighty and in the Lord Jesus Christ and in the Holy Spirit in the holy church', to which you answer 'Amen'; then you all file back again to where you were standing before. There is a moment's pause when all have finished, and then most of you go up to the bishop again with a little silver box like a snuff-box into which he places some fragments of the Bread. You stow it in an inside pocket, reflecting perhaps that Tarcisius was lynched six months ago for being caught with one of those little boxes upon him. There is another pause while the vessels are cleansed, and then someone says loudly 'That's all. Good morning, everybody.' And in twos and threes you slip out again through the back door or the area door and go home—twenty minutes after you came in. That is all there is to it, exter-nally. It would be absolutely meaningless to an outsider, and quite un-impressive.

But perhaps it did not all end quite so easily. You might very well never walk back up Maida Vale again. Perhaps the bishop stopped to speak to someone on the front-door steps as he went out, and was recognised by a casual passer-by who set up a great shout of 'Christian! Christian!' And before anyone quite realised what was happening a small jostling crowd had collected from nowhere and someone had thrown a brick through one of the windows; doors and windows were opening all down the street and there was a hubbub of jeers and yells, till a policeman arrived majestically, demanding 'Wot's all this 'ere?' 'It's those ——— christians again!' shouts someone, and the policeman gets out his notebook and looks severely at the bishop standing with the two deacons just behind him at the foot of the steps. 'Wot's all this about?' And then in response to the accusing shouts of the elbowing crowd there comes the deadly challenge from the policeman, 'Is that right that you're a christian?' And the bishop admits he is a christian. 'There's another of them', says someone, pointing at one of the deacons. 'There's a whole gang of them in there.' The deacons briefly admit their faith, and the policeman looks doubtfully at the house. It's said that they always come quietly, but one never knows. He blows his whistle, more police arrive, the house is entered, and soon afterwards twenty-two people, including the bishop and his deacons and the little grocer from Brondesbury, are marched off to the station.

The proceedings are by summary jurisdiction, as in the case of a raid on a night-club with us. They are all charged together 'with being christians', *i.e.* members of an unlawful association. Each is asked in turn whether he pleads guilty or not guilty. If he answers 'guilty', his case is virtually decided. The magistrate is perfectly well aware of the christian rule of never denying their religion. Someone's courage fails at the critical moment and he falters 'Not guilty.' Then there is a simple further test to be applied. At the side of the court-room is hung a picture of the king. 'Just go and kneel in front of that picture and say "Lord have mercy upon me", will you?' says the magistrate. (The offering of the conventional pinch of incense or few drops of wine before the statue of the deified emperor, which was the routine test for christianity, involved no more religious conviction than such a ceremony as I have invented here.) Some of the accused go through the prescribed test with white faces and faltering lips. One goes to the picture to do so and his conscience suddenly gets the better of his fear; he knocks the picture off the wall in a revulsion of nervous anger. He is hustled back to the dock and the picture is hung up again. The magistrate, a reasonable man, again asks each of those who have pleaded guilty whether they will even now go through the little ceremony. They all refuse. There is no more to be done, no possible doubt as to the law on the matter: *non licet esse christianos;* 'christians may not exist.' The legal penalty is death, and there is no ground of appeal. As a rule there is no delay. Unless they were reserved for the arena, sentences on christians were usually carried out on the same day. So in our modern analogy fifteen christians were hanged that afternoon at Wandsworth. On other occasions the policy of the administration might have caused private instructions to be issued to the magistrates that the law against christianity is not to be too strictly enforced for the present; a sentence of the 'cat', penal servitude for life and transportation would have been substituted for the death-penalty. Whether this was really much more merciful may be doubted. The imperial lead-mines in Sardinia, for instance, which were the usual convict-station for Roman christians in such a case, must have been even more like Devil's Island than Botany Bay. Most of the prisoners died within two or three years.

We shall not begin to understand what the eucharist meant to christians until we have estimated this background of real danger and intense hatred in a setting of absolutely normal daily life. It is true that organised and official persecution by the state was by no means continuous, that there were long periods when the central government was otherwise occupied, and wide regions where the local authorities were inclined to turn a blind eye to the existence of christians, provided these did not thrust themselves upon their notice. But there were other periods and equally wide regions where official persecution raged with violence for years together. For two hundred years, from Nero to Valerian (roughly A.D. 65–260), christian worship was in itself a capital crime. For another fifty after that, the law against christian assembly relaxed; but to be a christian was, by an illogicality, still brought under the capital charge of *laesa maiestas*. There is the opinion of Ulpian the jurist and the actual contemporary court-record of martyrdoms to prove that even in this period of peace in the latter half of the third century martyrdom was still only a matter of whether you happened to be accused. No one ever knew even in a period when the government was quiescent when persecution might not break out in the form of mob-violence, or what trivial cause might bring upon a man the inescapable official challenge 'Art thou a christian?' Callistus trying to recover a commercial debt from jewish debtors finds them making this charge against him in the prefect's court to avoid payment; and within an hour or two he has been scourged and sentenced for life to the deadly Sardinian mines.[1] Marinus, the soldier accused of christianity by a comrade envious of his promotion to centurion, is dead three hours after the accusation has been lodged.[2] Both these typical stories are reported by contemporaries from periods which rank more or less as times of toleration. We can and should distinguish between the intermittent hostility of the government and the unorganised and unpredictable malignity of the mob or of private informers. But when all has been said that is true in mitigation of the severity of ancient persecutions, for two hundred and fifty years from Nero to Constantine to be a christian was in itself a capital crime, always liable to the severest penalty, even when the law was not enforced. It remains a demonstrable historical fact from contemporary records that during this period thousands of men and women were killed, tens of thousands more suffered grievously in their fortunes and persons, and hundreds of thousands had to put up with the opposition of their families and the suspicion and ostracism of their neighbours for half-a-lifetime and more. And the storm centre throughout the whole period was undoubtedly the eucharist.

When we regard what actually took place in the early eucharistic rite, the fear and hatred it inspired over so long a time seem ridiculous. Yet it is an uncanny fact that there is still scarcely any subject on which the imagination of those outside the faith is more apt to surrender to the unrestrained nonsense of panic than that of what happens at the catholic eucharist. As a trivial instance, I remember that my own grandmother, a devout Wesleyan, believed to her dying day that at the Roman Catholic mass the priest let a crab loose upon the altar, which it was his mysterious duty to prevent from crawling sideways into the view of the congregation. (Hence the gestures of the celebrant.) How she became possessed of this notion, or what she supposed eventually happened to the crustacean I never discovered. But she affirmed with the utmost sincerity that she had once with her own eyes actually watched this horrible rite in progress; and there could be no doubt of the deplorable effect that solitary visit to a Roman Catholic church had

[1] Hippolytus, *Philosophumena*, ix. 11.
[2] Eusebius, *Eccl. Hist.*, VII. xv. 1.

had on her estimate of Roman Catholics in general, though she was the soul of charity in all things else. To all suggestions that the mass might be intended as some sort of holy communion service she replied only with the wise and gentle pity of the fully-informed for the ignorant.

I mention this peculiar opinion of a good and sensible woman because it illustrates well enough a frame of mind among the ancient pagans which was at once a cause and a result of christian secrecy about the eucharist. The gruesome stories of ritual murder and cannibal feasts which have been told since the stone age—when, no doubt, they had their justification—about all unpopular associations, received a fresh impulse from misunderstandings of indiscreet christian talk of receiving 'the Body and the Blood'. The dark suspicions of orgies of promiscuous vice or even organised incest, which the nasty side of men's imaginations is always willing to credit about mysterious private gatherings, were stimulated by talk of 'the kiss' and of 'brothers' and 'sisters'. The point is that these charges against the christians were taken with the utmost seriousness by multitudes not only of the cruel and foolish and ignorant but of normally humane and sensible men. When the heathen slaves of a christian master broke down under the torture always employed in the Roman courts to ensure the truthfulness of a slave's evidence—such was the extraordinary reason seriously maintained for the practice—and proceeded to 'confess' their knowledge of such goings on among the christians, it may have added to the disgust with which the decent pagan regarded all mention of the eucharist, but hardly at all to the strength of the general conviction that the holding of the *ecclesia* ought to be stopped by the authorities at all costs. One has only to read, for instance, the account by an eye-witness at Lyons in A.D. 177 of the pathetic occasion in the persecution there when after just such a 'confession' by heathen slaves the *apostate* christians were mobbed by the crowd as self-confessed 'polluted wretches' (*miarous*), to realise just what associations the very word 'eucharist' would have in the mind of any decent Lyonnais for the next thirty years, or what sort of hysteria a rumour of the holding of christian worship would be likely to work up in the city.

The imperial government was a great deal better informed than the populace. It regarded the church as a potential political danger for precisely the same reasons as any other totalitarian government is bound to do so. At times it took vigorous measures to protect itself against this danger, and it is an instance of Roman governmental capacity that whenever it did so it showed a clear understanding of the problem which confronted it. Active measures were always directed not so much against the holding of christian beliefs as against the expression of that belief in the *worship* of the *ecclesia*. Those officials, for instance, who actually carried out the persecution under the emperor Decius (A.D. 250–251) must have been perfectly well aware from their behaviour that of the thousands of christian apostates who offered sacrifice under threat of instant martyrdom, the vast majority remained sincerely convinced christians in belief, even though by the failure of their courage at the moment of trial they now faced life-long exclusion from christian communion. The persecutors were not concerned to produce sincere believers in the deity either of the emperor or of the Olympian gods, but to put an end to the illegal meetings of the christian *ecclesia*. They could be content with the merest pretence of conformity because they could rely on the discipline of the church itself to exclude from the *ecclesia* all who had in any way compromised. The government's attack was pressed all the time upon worship, by striking especially at the clergy with martyrdom or penal servitude, by the confiscation of all property upon which christian worship was proved to have taken place, and by a variety of other measures, all designed to make impossible the holding of the *ecclesia*. But there was no parallel attempt by a counter-propaganda to discredit christian beliefs or to defend pagan ones.

The church being what it was, the act of taking part in the common worship could be accepted by church and state alike as the effective test of christianity. From the point of view of the state it was deliberate treason (*laesa maiestas*). From the point of view of the church the corporate action of the eucharist in the *ecclesia* was the supreme positive affirmation before God of the christian life. There was no place on either view for that modern 'christianity' which owns no allegiance to the church and her worship. To the state an academic belief which did not express itself in worship carried no danger of christian allegiance. To the church belief which did not express itself in worship would have seemed both pointless and fruitless. Christian belief was the condition of admission to that worship, explicitly required before baptism and confirmation, which alone admitted a man to pray with the church, let alone communicate. On the other hand, for a confirmed christian to allow himself to take any part whatever in non-christian worship was 'apostasy', a public declaration that he renounced that faith in Christ as his redeemer which was his passport to worship. Down to A.D. 252 apostasy involved perpetual exclusion from the *ecclesia* in this world and damnation in the next, unless perhaps the lapsed christian might hope to move the mercy of God after death by a life-long penance outside the corporate life of the church. The state was content to accept the logic of the christian principle that religious belief can only be finally and adequately expressed by *worship*. When the well-organised Decian persecution encouraged apostasy by making compliance easy, and reaped an immense harvest of lapses, it must have seemed that the church was about to be strangled in her own inviolable discipline.

The church met the crisis by a revolutionary change in that discipline, which the government does not seem to have anticipated. In the teeth of bitter opposition from the zealots everywhere, the bishops restored to membership of the *ecclesia* all apostates who showed the sincerity of their repentance by undergoing a period of penance. The lapsed flocked back in thousands, and the correspondence of S. Cyprian contains abundant evidence with what eagerness they sought to resume their christian life, not as believers—they had never ceased to be that—but as *worshippers*. For the christian as for the persecutor the liturgy formed the very life not only of the church corporately but of the individual soul. It was a statesmanlike move, probably the only one which could have enabled the church to survive the second wave of persecution which the baffled government at once launched against the christian revival under Valerian (A.D. 254–9). The state was eventually distracted by foreign war, and had to own itself unable to stamp out the *ecclesia*. An edict of Gallienus conceded permission to the christians freely 'to use their *ecclesiai*', the property in which was restored to them (A.D. 260).[1]

This was a virtual concession of freedom of worship, but it left the legal position ambiguous. Christian worship was no longer in itself a crime, and the church became a tolerated if not a legally recognised association. But christianity was not a legal religion, and the individual christian could still be charged with high treason.

For the next forty years the state simply turned its back upon the fact that the church existed, though everyone was aware that 'the christian question' would have to be faced one day. But the forty years of uneasy toleration which ended the third century brought a considerable increase in christian numbers, which together with the liberty of assembly now permitted, began to force upon the church a more regular organisation of her worship. We find special church buildings for this purpose beginning to be erected in many towns and even in some quarters of Rome itself during this period. In Asia Minor especially the church came to number quite a large proportion of the population and could come more into the open. At Nicodmeia, the Eastern capital, where high officers of the court and even members of the royal family were attracted to the church, the christian bishop's cathedral is said to have been the most imposing public building in the city before the end of the third century.

Elsewhere, christians were usually an unpopular minority, and worship had to be conducted with more discretion. But everywhere (as we have seen at Cirta) it was now an open secret where christian worship was held and who the christian clergy were. When the last tempest of persecution arose under Diocletian A.D. 303–13—the longest as well as the fiercest the church ever had to face—it was again upon christian worship that it pressed most fiercely. That worship was itself now much more open to attack by reason of its new semi-public organisation. This time, too, there was a real attempt to refute christian teaching by intellectual propaganda, and a systematic destruction of christian literature. The virtual prevention of corporate worship except in the most furtive fashion for nearly ten years

---

[1] *Cf.* the text of the edict, *ap.* Eusebius, *Eccl. Hist.*, VII. xiii. 1, which clearly means houses, not 'churches' in our sense.

and the gradual extinction of the clergy by martyrdom or apostasy did on this occasion reduce the church to the direst extremities, in a way no previous persecution had ever done. The edicts of toleration put out in 313 by the emperors Maximin and Maximian, and comprehensively ratified and enforced by the new christian emperor Constantine in the following year, came only just in time to save her from complete disorganisation. The West was now finally free from organised persecution by the state, but the Eastern provinces still had to endure it intermittently for another five years

It will be seen that popular and official persecution of the church had very different motives. The state feared the church; the populace disliked the christians. The state wished to make apostates; the mob as a rule preferred martyrs. It is a constant feature of the genuine *Acta* of the martyrs to find the magistrate arguing and pleading with the prisoner to deny his faith and fulfil the formal test of sacrifice, even delaying and straining the law sometimes to secure something which will pass for a denial, while the mob howl for the prisoner's death.

The Roman judicial standard was on the whole a high one. There is evidence that many of the magistrates did not enjoy the duty of enforcing the law against christians, and recognised its futility and injustice. But though the administration might often be disposed to avoid charging men with christianity, the law placed a fatal weapon in the hands of both the hostility of the mob and private enmity. Once the accusation of christianity had been brought to his notice the magistrate was bound to take cognisance of it. And once a man was put that fatal question 'Art thou a christian?' there was no other way but apostasy or sentence. The magistrate and the martyr were alike helpless. It was always open to a magistrate more energetic or fanatical than his fellows to set the law in motion himself within his jurisdiction. But except when instructions were received from the central administration to 'tighten things up', this appears to have been comparatively rare; and the general practice of changing the local magistrates annually usually ensured a brief duration to such local official action.

It is plain from second and third century christian literature that the great permanent danger to the christians came from the mob. As Tertullian puts it, 'They think the christians are at the bottom of every disaster to the state and every misfortune of the people. If the Tiber floods the city or the Nile fails to flood the fields, if there are portents in heaven or earthquakes on earth, if famine comes or plague, they clamour instantly "Throw the christians to the lion." So many, to one lion?'[1]

Thus the church could not meet the charges of cannibalism and incest, which the man in the street honestly believed about the eucharist, in the only way which might have been effective—though it did not convince my grandmother—by holding the rite with absolute publicity. This was partly at least because the state made the holding of christian worship in itself a

[1] Tertullian, *Apologeticus*, xl.

capital crime. In any case she would probably have been reluctant to do this in a pagan world, because the eucharist expressed in its very essence and idea the 'separateness' of the holy church from 'the world that lieth in wickedness.'[1]

There was thus left only the alternative of denying the charges as often as possible in the course of propaganda, and enduring their consequences when this failed—as it invariably did—to convince the public. Justin in the famous 'Open Letter to the Government' which is known as his *First Apology* tried the expedient of describing just what was done at the eucharist with a disarming frankness, which to a modern reader must seem a convincing (and rather skilful) demonstration of its entire harmlessness. Yet it had no effect whatever on contemporary opinion. In his second manifesto of the same kind issued a year or two later, Justin himself obviously despairs of achieving much by this method of reasonableness, and adopts a much more indignant and defiant tone.

Tertullian used instead the method of a biting irony. But it is obvious throughout the book that though he addresses the administration he is really trying to counter the popular rumours about orgies at the eucharist, which are having a very serious effect. He twits the officials with the fact that they have never been able to discover the scantiest factual evidence for these charges—'how many babies any particular person has eaten, how many times he has committed incest, who the cooks were. . . . What a boast for any governor, if he had actually caught a man who had eaten a hundred babies!'[2] But his argument on these things is really addressed not to the officials, who did not take these charges seriously, but to the public which did. 'Suppose these things are true for the moment. I only ask you who believe that such things are done to imagine yourself eager for the eternal life they are supposed to secure. Now! Plunge your knife into an innocent baby that never did anyone any harm, a foundling. Perhaps that is some other christian's office. Well, any way, stand looking down on this human being gasping in death almost before it has lived; wait while its new little soul escapes; catch its gurgling blood and soak your bread in that. Then gulp it down with pleasure! Then lie down and point out where your mother is to lie and where your sister. Take careful note, that when the dogs (chained to the lampstand) plunge all in darkness you may make no mistake. You will have done a sacrilege if you fail to commit incest. By these mysteries and this confirmation you shall live for all eternity. Tell me, now, is eternity *worth* that? . . . Even if you thought so, I deny that you would want it on those terms. Even if you did want it, I deny that you *could* bring yourself to gain it thus. Why then can others, if you cannot? Why can you not, if others can? We are different from you in nature, I suppose—dog-headed men or sciapods? We have a different sort of teeth, or feel a different lust? You believe men can do these things? Then pre-

[1] 1 John v. 19.                    [2] Tertullian, *Ap.*. ii

sumably you can do them. You are a man yourself, just like a christian. If you know you could not bring yourself to do them, then do not believe that others can. . . . I suppose when someone wants to be initiated in this way he first goes to the high-priest of these mysteries, to find out what preparations he must make. And he tells him, "Oh, you will need a baby, a *teeny* baby, which does not understand death and will smile under your knife; and bread in which to catch its squirting blood . . . and above all, you must bring your mother and your sister." What if they will not come, or the convert has none? What about christians who have no near feminine relations? I presume he can be no rightful christian unless he be a brother or a son?"[1]

Of course this sort of firework did no more good than Justin's calculated *naïveté*. Indeed Tertullian's whole *Apology* is so much in the nature of a devastating counter-attack on paganism all along the line that it seems more calculated to infuriate any conventionally-minded pagan who happened to read it than to soothe his alarm at the alleged revolutionary opinions and morals of the christians. But the lurid background of suspicion and calumny about the eucharist and ill-will towards those who took part in it has to be borne in mind in considering the importance that christians attached to its celebration and the reasons why they clung to this ill-famed rite.

These men and women did not run continual risks to attend it merely because there they remembered with thankfulness in a specially moving way the death of Jesus which had redeemed them. They could do that anywhere and alone; some of them did it most of their waking hours. Nor was it simply that in the eucharist alone they could satisfy a personal longing for God by receiving holy communion. As a matter of fact if a devout third century christian on his deathbed could have reckoned up all the communions he had ever made, he would probably have found that the large majority had been made from the reserved sacrament at home, quite apart from the liturgy. These desires of christian personal devotion could be and were satisfied in private in comparative safety, without the dangers and scandal which centred round the eucharist. There was, indeed, a rather striking absence from the primitive eucharistic rite of any devotional practice which was calculated to arouse or feed a subjective piety—no confession of sins or devotions in preparation for communion, no corporate thanksgiving even, nothing but the bare requisites for the sacramental *act*. It was a burning faith in the vital importance of that eucharist *action* as such, its importance to God and to the church and to a man's own soul, for this world and for the next, which made the christians cling to the rite of the eucharist against all odds. Nothing else could have maintained the corporate celebration of the liturgy through the centuries when the *ecclesia* was outside the law.

For these christian men and women were very normal. They were

[1] Tertullian, *Ap.*, viii.

not impossibly heroic. Their answers in the dock often shew that they were very frightened. Even when they were most defiant their rudeness is often a mark of fear. Few men could look forward to the appalling tortures which the courts in the later second century sometimes took to applying—'to make them deny their crime' as Tertullian bitterly remarked, 'not like other criminals to confess it'—without considerable perturbation. Many of them apostatised when it came to the final test, often most of them. The world, the flesh and the devil were as active and deadly with them as they are with christians nowadays. And so was another enemy whose assaults on the church of the martyrs we often ignore though we know its deadening effects on ourselves—routine, the mere fact that one has been trying to be a christian for quite a long time and little seems to come of it. The parable of the Sower was just as true then as now. But these normal men and women were prepared with open eyes to accept the risks and inconveniences they undoubtedly did encounter, just to be present at the eucharist *together and regularly*. I submit that it casts a flood of light on their beliefs about the eucharist and the nature of the church and christian salvation generally, that they attributed this desperate importance not so much to 'making their communion' as to taking part in the corporate action of the eucharist.

It was to secure the fulness of this corporate action that a presbyter *and a deacon* had to be smuggled somehow into the imperial prisons, there to celebrate their last eucharist for the confessors awaiting execution; and S. Cyprian takes it as a matter of course that this must be arranged.[1] To secure this for his companions as best he could, the presbyter Lucian lying with his legs wrenched wide apart in the stocks of the prison at Antioch celebrated the mysteries for the last time with the elements resting on his own breast, and passed their last communion to the others lying equally helpless in the dark around him.[2] To secure this a whole congregation of obscure provincials at Abilinitina in Africa took the risk of almost certain detection by assembling at the height of the Diocletian persecution in their own town, where the authorities were on the watch for them, because, as they said in court, the eucharist had been lacking a long while through the apostasy of their bishop Fundanus, and they could no longer bear the lack of it. And so they called on a presbyter to celebrate—and paid the penalty of their faith to a man.[3] To secure this was always the first thought of christians in time of threatened persecution. 'But how shall we meet, you ask, how shall we celebrate the Lord's solemnities? . . . If you cannot meet by day, there is always the night', says Tertullian, bracing the fearful to stay and meet the coming storm [4] Even when a church had been scattered by long persecution, the duty was never forgotten. 'At first they drove us

[1] Cyprian, *Ep.*, v. 2.          [2] *Boll. Acta SS.*, Jan. 7th, iv. 14.
[3] *Cf.* the contemporary *Acta Martyrum Abilinitinensium*.
[4] Tertullian, *de Fuga in Persecutione*, 14.

out and . . . we kept our festival even then, pursued and put to death by all, and every single spot where we were afflicted became to us a place of assembly for the feast—field, desert, ship, inn, prison', writes S. Denys, bishop of Alexandria, of one terrible Easter day *c.* A.D. 250, when a raging civil war, famine and pestilence were added to the woes of his persecuted church.[1]

Literally scores of similar illustrations from contemporary documents of unimpeachable historical authority are available of the fact that it was not so much the personal reception of holy communion as the corporate eucharistic action as a whole (which included communion) which was then regarded as the very essence of the life of the church, and through that of the individual christian soul. In this corporate action alone each christian could fulfil for himself or herself the 'appointed liturgy' of his order, and so fulfil his redeemed being as a member of Christ. For my own part I have long found it difficult to understand exactly how the eucharist ever came to be supposed by serious scholars at all closely comparable with the rites of the pagan mysteries. The *approach* is so different. In the mysteries there is always the attempt to arouse and play upon religious emotion, by long preparation and fasts, and (often) by elaborate ceremonies, or by alternations of light and darkness, by mystical symbols and impressive surroundings, and pageantry; or sometimes by the weird and repulsive or horrible. But always there is the attempt to impress, to arouse emotion of some kind, and so to put the initiate into a receptive frame of mind. As Aristotle said, men came to these rites 'not to learn something but to experience something.' The christian eucharist in practice was the reverse of all this. All was homely and unemotional to a degree. The christian came to the eucharist, not indeed 'to learn something', for faith was presupposed, but certainly not to seek a psychological thrill. He came simply to *do* something, which he conceived he had an overwhelming personal duty to do, come what might. What brought him to the eucharist week by week, despite all dangers and inconveniences, was no thrill provoked by the service itself, which was bare and unimpressive to the point of dullness, and would soon lose any attraction of novelty. Nor yet was it a longing for personal communion with God, which he could and did fulfil otherwise in his daily communion from the reserved sacrament at home. What brought him was an intense belief that in the eucharistic action of the Body of Christ, as in no other way, he himself took a part in that act of sacrificial obedience to the will of God which was consummated on Calvary and which had redeemed the world, including himself. What brought him was the conviction that there rested on each of the redeemed an absolute necessity so to take his own part in the self-offering of Christ, a necessity more binding even than the instinct of self-preservation. Simply as members of Christ's Body, the church, all christians must do this, and they can

[1] Dionys. Al. *ap.* Eusebius, *Eccl. Hist.*, VII. xxii. 4.

do it in no other way than that which was the last command of Jesus to His own. That rule of the absolute obligation upon each of the faithful of presence at Sunday mass under pain of mortal sin, which seems so mechanical and formalist to the protestant, is something which was burned into the corporate mind of historic christendom in the centuries between Nero and Diocletian. But it rests upon something more evangelical and more profound than historical memories. It expresses as nothing else can the whole New Testament doctrine of redemption; of Jesus, God and Man, as the only Saviour of mankind, Who intends to draw all men unto Him by His sacrificial and atoning death; and of the church as the communion of redeemed sinners, the Body of Christ, corporately invested with His own mission of salvation to the world.

Despite all the formalism and carelessness and hypocrisy which a social tradition of the general attendance at the eucharist of all who have been baptised involves, and has always involved, in catholic countries, there is this to be said: that no personal subjective devotion on the part of select individual communicants can manifest Christ as the redeemer of *all* men and of *all* human life, either to themselves or to the world or before God. Nor can the corporate being of the church as His one Body with many members be fulfilled in an action from which the greater part of the baptised and confirmed members are regarded or regard themselves as tacitly excluded.

We do well to approach the mystery of Christ's Body and Blood with the profoundest reverence and searching of heart. Yet a eucharist where the table is 'fenced', even only by the consensus of christian opinion, a eucharist at which frequency has come to be regarded as a special preserve of the clergy and 'the devout', and at which the majority of practising christians are present only on comparatively rare occasions—this has just as much ceased to be the scriptural and primitive eucharist as has the most unprayerful and conventional non-communicating attendance at Sunday mass by the tradesmen of a Sicilian country town.

The unfamiliarity of a vast proportion of 'C. of E.' christians with the eucharist may have begun with a false notion of reverence. It has ended by destroying the true understanding of the eucharist even among many of those who still frequent it. The clergy will all have encountered those choice souls who actually prefer to 'make their communion' only in the peace of a week-day celebration, where three or four leisured people can scatter themselves widely all over the church, and avoid disturbance by the larger congregation at 'the 8 o'clock' on Sunday. It would probably surprise the clergy to find how widespread this self-centred devotion is among the laity, and how many regular communicants would prefer to fulfil their personal religious needs in this way if their situation gave them the week-day leisure. This is not much better than a parody of devotion to the eucharist, which our practice and teaching have somehow succeeded in implanting as the ideal. Behind it lie centuries of the mediaeval distortion of the eucharist as the focus of a subjective individual piety. In reality it is the very action of Him who came 'to die not for that nation only, but that also He should *gather together in one* the children of God who were scattered abroad.'[1]

[1] John xi. 52.

# CHAPTER VII

## THE EUCHARISTIC PRAYER

LET us look back for a moment. We have seen that the eucharist is primarily an action, our obedience to our Lord's command to 'Do this'; and that this action is performed by the Shape of the Liturgy, the outline of the service viewed as a single continuous whole. We have also seen that the *meaning* of this action is stated chiefly in the great eucharistic prayer, which formed the second item of that 'four-action shape' of the eucharist which has come down almost from apostolic times. Since this prayer was originally 'the' prayer, the only prayer in the whole rite, it was there that the whole meaning of the rite had to be stated, if it was to be put into words at all in the course of the service. We have also noted that, while the tradition as to the outline of the rite was always and everywhere the same, there was no such original fixity about the content and sequence of this prayer. Its text was subject to constant development and revision, so that it varied considerably from church to church and from period to period, and even (probably within narrower limits) from celebrant to celebrant.[1]

In this chapter we shall set out the oldest specimens of ancient local traditions of this prayer which have come down to us, together with other material which throws light upon them.

The traditions we shall chiefly consider now are three—those of Rome, Egypt and Syria, for Rome, Alexandria and Antioch were the three most important churches in pre-Nicene times. But there were other traditions of the prayer elsewhere, some of them equally ancient, in North Africa, Spain and Gaul in the West, and in the apostolic churches of the Balkans and Asia Minor in the East. Unfortunately, by the accidents of history it happens that no texts of the eucharistic prayers of these churches have survived from pre-Nicene times, or indeed from any period at which their evidence can usefully serve for even a tentative comparison with the really ancient material.[2] Our survey is thus bound to be very incompletely representative of the whole liturgical wealth of the pre-Nicene church as it actually existed, and the reader may reasonably wonder how it would be

[1] In pre-Nicene times the normal celebrant was, of course, the bishop, who certainly always had freedom to phrase the prayer as he wished within the traditional outline. But there is evidence to show that when a presbyter deputised for the bishop he was not more restricted. It was a freedom belonging to the celebrant, not to the episcopal office, though doubtless presbyters tended to copy their own bishop to a large extent.

[2] The Visigothic and Mozarabic rites of Spain, the *débris* of the Gallican rites of Gaul and the Byzantine liturgy of *S. Chrysostom* are all products of such changed circumstances of the church, that even if material is still to be found in them which is as old as the fifth century—which has yet to be proved—it is not possible to compare it closely with the material we shall be using here.

affected if these lost traditions could be included. I believe that the answer is 'very little in principle and a great deal in detail', because of the form of the conclusions to which the extant material actually leads. The missing traditions of the prayer, if they could be recovered, would probably shew in its structure and phrasing a diversity equal to, or even greater than, those which survive. Such little evidence as we have about them suggests that they were verbally as independent of the prayers which we do know as these clearly are of one another. On the other hand this fragmentary evidence, and still more the incidental statements about the eucharist in the writers from these churches, suggest equally strongly that their fundamental understanding of the rite, that 'meaning' of it which their eucharistic prayers sought to state, was the same in all essentials as that found in the prayers which have survived. Diversity of form and a fundamental identity of meaning seem to have been the marks of the old local tradition everywhere.

### (i) *The Roman Tradition*

We begin once more with the *Apostolic Tradition* of Hippolytus, the most important source of information we possess on the liturgy of the pre-Nicene church. This invaluable document contains the only pre-Nicene text of a eucharistic prayer which has reached us without undergoing extensive later revision. We have to be on our guard, however, against interpreting all the other evidence exclusively in the light of this single document (which raises almost as many fresh problems as it solves, from one point of view), just because it is in this way of such unique interest and importance. In itself it represents only the local tradition of Rome, though at an early stage, before developments had become complicated.

After the opening dialogue, already sufficiently commented, Hippolytus' prayer runs thus:

(a) We render thanks unto Thee, O God, through Thy Beloved Servant Jesus Christ, Whom in the last times Thou didst send ⟨to be⟩ a Saviour and Redeemer and the Angel of Thy counsel; Who is Thy Word inseparable ⟨from Thee⟩;

(b) through Whom Thou madest all things and in Whom Thou wast well-pleased;

(c) Whom Thou didst send from heaven into the Virgin's womb, and Who conceived within her was made flesh, and demonstrated to be Thy Son, being born of Holy Spirit and a Virgin;

(d) Who fulfilling Thy will and procuring for Thee an holy people, stretched forth His hands for suffering (*or* for the passion) that He might release from sufferings them who have believed in Thee;

(e) Who when He was betrayed to voluntary suffering (*or* the passion) in order that He might abolish death and rend the bonds of the devil and tread down hell and enlighten the righteous and establish the ordinance and demonstrate the resurrection,

($f^1$) taking bread ⟨and⟩ making eucharist to Thee, said: Take, eat; this is My Body, which is [*or* will be] broken for you.

($f^2$) Likewise also the cup, saying: This is My Blood which is shed for you.

(*g*) When ye do this ye do [*or* make ye] My 'anamnesis'.

(*h*) Now, therefore, doing the 'anamnesis' of His death and resurrection

(*i*) we offer to Thee the bread and cup

(*j*) making eucharist to Thee because Thou hast made us worthy to stand before Thee and minister as priests to Thee.

(*k*) And we pray Thee that [*Thou wouldest send Thy Holy Spirit upon the oblation of Thy holy church*][1] Thou wouldest grant to all who partake to be made one, that they may be fulfilled with ⟨the⟩ Holy Spirit for the confirmation of ⟨their⟩ faith in truth;

(*l*) that we may praise and glorify Thee through Thy Servant Jesus Christ through Whom honour and glory ⟨be⟩ unto Thee with ⟨the⟩ Holy Spirit in Thy holy church, now and for ever and world without end.

℟ *Amen.*[2]

We may analyse the structure of the prayer thus:

(*a*) Address: Relation of the Father to the Eternal Word.

(*b*) Thanksgiving for Creation through the Word.

(*c*) Thanksgiving for the Incarnation of the Word.

(*d*) Thanksgiving for Redemption through the Passion of the Word.

(*e*) Statement of Christ's purpose in instituting the eucharist.

(*f*) Statement of His Institution of the eucharist.

(*g*) Statement of His virtual command to repeat the action of (*f*) with a virtual promise of the result attaching to such repetition.

(*h*) Claim to the fulfilment of the promise in (*g*).

(*i*) Offering of the elements

(*i*) constituting obedience to the command in (*g*), with an interpretation of the meaning understood by this obedience.

(*k*) Prayer for the effects of communion.

(*l*) Doxology.

This prayer was written down more or less verbally in this form at Rome *c.* A.D. 215, but the author emphatically claims that it represents traditional Roman practice in his own youth a generation before. It appears certain

---

[1] This clause is more likely (on the textual evidence) to be a fourth century addition than part of Hippolytus' third century text. *Cf.* my edition of *Ap. Trad.*, London, 1937, *pp.* 75 *sq.*

[2] *Ap. Trad.* iv., 4 *sq.* (Words in ⟨ ⟩ are not in the original, but supplied to help the sense in translation).

that some of the phrasing in *a–e* is of his own composition, and represents his own peculiar theology of the Trinity; and it is at least possible that the wording of other parts of the prayer is from his own pen. But this does not make it improbable that the *structure* of the prayer as a whole (including *a–e*) and some of its actual wording were really traditional at Rome. The following parallels from the writings of Justin Martyr (Rome *c.* A.D. 155) all occur in professedly eucharistic passages, and some are even more remarkable in Greek than in English for the resemblance of their phrasing to that of Hippolytus.

(*a*) The bishop 'sends up praise and glory to the Father of all through the Name of the Son and the Holy Ghost' (*Ap.* I. 65).

(Jesus is the 'Beloved', the 'Servant', the 'Saviour', the 'Redeemer' and the 'Angel of God's counsel' in a number of passages in Justin, though none of them are explicitly about the eucharistic prayer; the Word is 'not separable' from the Father (*Dialogue*, 128) but again this is not explicitly connected with the eucharistic prayer.)

(*b–d*) The eucharist was instituted 'that we might at the same time *give thanks* to God *for the creation* of the world with all that is therein for man's sake, and for that He has *delivered* us from the evil wherein we were born, and for that He *loosed* ⟨*the bonds*⟩ of powers and principalities with a complete loosing by *becoming subject to suffering according to His own will*' (*Dialogue*, 41).

(*c*, *d*, *g*) 'As by the Word of God Jesus Christ our Saviour was made flesh and had flesh and blood for our salvation, so also we have been taught that this food "eucharistised" by a formula of prayer which comes from Him . . . is the flesh and blood of that Jesus Who was made flesh. For the apostles in the memoirs which are by them, which are called "gospels", have recorded that thus it was commanded them ⟨to do⟩: that Jesus took bread and gave thanks and said "Do this for the *anamnesis* of Me: This is My Body"; and likewise took the cup and gave thanks and said "This is My Blood" ' (*Ap.* I. 66).

(*h*) 'The offering of fine flour ordered ⟨in the Old Testament⟩ to be offered on behalf of those who were cleansed from leprosy was a type of the bread of the eucharist, which Jesus Christ our Lord ordered to be done [*or* 'sacrificed'] for an *anamnesis of His passion* which He suffered on behalf of men, whose souls have ⟨thereby⟩ been cleansed from all iniquity' (*Dialogue*, 41).

(*i*) '*The sacrifices which are offered* to God by us gentiles everywhere, *that is the bread of the eucharist, and the cup* likewise of the eucharist' (*Dialogue*, 41).

(*j*) The bishop 'sends up eucharists (thanksgivings) *that we have been made worthy of these things by Him*' (*Ap.* I. 65). 'We ⟨christians⟩ are the true high-priestly race of God . . . for God accepts sacrifices from no one but by the hands of His own priests' (*Dialogue*, 116).

(*k, l*) These have no verbal parallels in Justin's allusions to the eucharist like the above, though the same sentiments are to be found at large in his works.

We can thus at the least say that there is nothing whatever in the specifically eucharistic teaching of Hippolytus' prayer which would have been repudiated by Justin sixty years earlier.

How far, then, does the tradition represented by Hippolytus' prayer go back? I shall suggest later that at least the general *structure of the first part* of Hippolytus' prayer was an inheritance from the days of the jewish apostles at Rome, which the Roman church with its usual conservatism had maintained more rigidly in the second century than some other churches. We shall find that this prayer as a whole is more 'tidy' in arrangement and more logical in its connections, less confused by the later introduction of inessentials, and more theological and precise in its expression of what is involved in the eucharistic action, than the others we shall consider. Here it is necessary only to draw attention to the careful articulation of its central portion (*e–j*).

The only point of any difficulty which arises in interpreting this prayer is the question of the exact bearing of (*e*). Is it to be understood as stating that our Lord went to His 'voluntary passion' in order that He 'might abolish death' etc.; or does Hippolytus mean that He *instituted the eucharist* in order that 'He might abolish death', etc.? Grammatically the sentence could mean either; and though to our way of thinking the former meaning may seem much more obvious, it seems from other passages in Hippolytus' works that he did think of holy communion precisely as the means whereby Christ intended to bestow on us these benefits of His passion. Thus he speaks of communion as 'the food which leads thee back to heaven, and delivers from the evil powers and frees from hard toil and bestows on thee a happy and blessed return to God.'[1] Similarly, commenting on Luke xxii. 15 ('With desire have I desired to eat this passover with you before I suffer') Hippolytus remarks, 'This was the passover which Jesus desired to suffer for us. *By suffering He released from sufferings* (*cf.* Prayer (*d*) above) and overcame death by death and *by a visible food bestowed on us His eternal life.* . . . Therefore He desired not so much to eat as He desired to suffer *that He might deliver us from suffering by* ⟨our⟩ *eating*.'[2] In the face of these and certain other expressions which Hippolytus uses elsewhere, it seems unnecessary to argue further. Hippolytus regards holy communion as the means by which Christ 'abolishes death' and 'rends the bonds of the devil' in the faithful communicant. It is a means of 'enlightenment' and a 'demonstration of the resurrection' (*cf.* John vi. 53–57). The institution at the last supper 'establishes an ordinance'—a phrase in itself difficult to interpret of the passion.

The institution narrative of (*f*) is in fact the pivot of the whole prayer as

[1] *On the Pascha,* v. 2.     [2] *Ibid.* vi. 5.

it stands. It is the climax or point of all that precedes, and the starting point of all that follows. The command and promise it contains (g) are the justification for all that is done and meant by the church at the eucharist. This is carefully defined in (h), (i), (j), as (1) the offering of the bread and cup (2) which is the 'priestly' action of the church, and therefore a sacrifice (3) because it is the *anamnesis* of His own death and resurrection commanded by our Lord to be 'done'; or as Justin (*sup.*) calls it, 'What Jesus Christ our Lord commanded to be done for an *anamnēsis* of His passion, which He suffered on behalf of men whose souls have (thereby) been cleansed from all iniquity.' In other words, the eucharist was regarded in the second century as the divinely ordered '*anamnēsis*' *of the redeeming action* of our Lord. A good deal therefore turns on the word *anamnēsis*, which we have so far left untranslated.

This word, which the Authorised Version translates as 'Do this *in remembrance* of Me' in the New Testament accounts of the institution, is more common in Roman writers in connection with the eucharist than elsewhere in pre-Nicene times. As we shall see, it does not appear in the parallel sections of some traditions of the prayer. It is not quite easy to represent accurately in English, words like 'remembrance' or 'memorial' having for us a connotation of something itself *absent*, which is only mentally recollected. But in the scriptures both of the Old and New Testament, *anamnēsis* and the cognate verb have the sense of 're-calling' or 're-presenting' before God an event in the past, so that it becomes *here and now operative by its effects*. Thus the sacrifice of a wife accused of adultery (Num. v. 15) is 'an offering "re-calling" her sin to (God's) remembrance' (*anamimnēskousa*); *i.e.* if she has sinned in the past, it will now be revealed by the ordeal, because her sin has been actively 're-called' or 're-presented' before God by her sacrifice. So the widow of Sarepta (1 Kings xvii. 18) complains that Elijah has come 'to "re-call" to (God's) remembrance (*anamnēsai*) my iniquity', and therefore her son has now died. So in Heb. x. 3, 4, the writer says that because 'it is not possible that the blood of bulls and goats should take away sins' (in the sight of God), the sacrifices of the Old Testament were no better than a 're-calling' (*anamnēsis*) of the offerers' sins before God. And though in this passage there is some indication that *anamnēsis* has here partly at least a psychological reference to the Israelites' own 'conscience' of sins, it is plain from the passage as a whole that it is primarily before God that the sins are 're-called' and 'not purged' or 'taken away'. It is in this active sense, therefore, of 're-calling' or 're-presenting' before God the sacrifice of Christ, and thus making it here and now operative by its effects in the communicants, that the eucharist is regarded both by the New Testament and by second century writers as the *anamnēsis* of the passion, or of the passion and resurrection combined. It is for this reason that Justin and Hippolytus and later writers after them speak so directly and vividly of the eucharist *in the present* bestowing on the

communicants those effects of redemption—immortality, eternal life, forgiveness of sins, deliverance from the power of the devil and so on—
which we usually attribute more directly to the sacrifice of Christ viewed
as a single historical event *in the past.* One has only to examine their
unfamiliar language closely to recognise how completely they identify the
offering of the eucharist by the church with the offering of Himself by our
Lord, not by way of a repetition, but as a 're-presentation' (*anamnēsis*) of
*the same* offering by the church 'which is His Body.' As S. Cyprian puts it
tersely but decisively in the third century. 'The passion is the Lord's
sacrifice, which we offer.'[1]

These three points may be said to stand out from our cursory examination of the Roman eucharistic prayer: (1) The centrality in its construction
of the narrative of the institution as the *authority* for what the church does
in the eucharist. Its importance in this respect is greatly emphasised by
being placed out of its historical order, after the thanksgiving for the
passion. (2) What is understood to be 'done' in the eucharist is *the church's
offering and reception of the bread and the cup,* identified with the Lord's
Body and Blood by the institution. This 'doing' of the eucharist is our
Lord's command and a 'priestly' act of the church. (3) The whole rite 're-
calls' or 're-presents' before God not the last supper, but the sacrifice of
Christ in His death and resurrection; and it makes this 'present' and operative by its effects in the communicants.

## (ii) *The Egyptian Tradition*

We have no pre-Nicene text of the eucharistic prayer from Egypt. The
earliest document of this tradition which has come down to us is a prayer
which is ascribed in the unique eleventh century MS. to S. Sarapion,
bishop of Thmuis in the Nile delta from before A.D. 339 to some date
between A.D. 353 and *c.* A.D. 360. Whether the ascription to Sarapion
personally be correct or not (and it is quite possible, despite certain difficulties) the prayer is undoubtedly Egyptian, and in its present form of the
fourth century, from before rather than after *c.* A.D. 350. But there are
strong indications that this extant form is only a revision of an older
Egyptian prayer, whose outline can be established in some points by comparison with eucharistic passages in third century Egyptian writers.[2] We
shall not go into this reconstruction in any detail here. Our business is
only to establish summarily certain differences from the third century
Roman prayer of Hippolytus, and also certain very important similarities
of ideas, which seem to belong to the third century Egyptian basis underlying the present text, as well as to the present text itself.

[1] *Ep.* 63, 17.
[2] For certain parts of the prayer this was done in some detail, *Theology,* xxxvii.
(Nov. 1938), *pp.* 261 *sq.*

### Prayer of Oblation of Bishop Sarapion.

($a^1$) It is meet and right to praise, to hymn, to glorify Thee, O uncreated Father of the Only-begotten Jesus Christ. We praise Thee, O uncreated God, Who art unsearchable, ineffable, incomprehensible by any created substance. We praise Thee Who art known of Thy Son the Only-begotten, Who through Him art spoken and interpreted and made known to every created being. We praise Thee Who knowest the Son and revealest to the saints the doctrines concerning Him: Who art known of Thy begotten Word and art brought to the sight and understanding of the saints ⟨through Him⟩.

($a^2$) We praise Thee, O Father invisible, giver of immortality. Thou art the source of life, the source of light, the source of all grace and truth, O lover of men, O lover of the poor, Who art reconciled to all and drawest all things to Thyself by the advent (*epidēmia*)[1] of Thy beloved Son. We beseech Thee, make us living men; give us a spirit of light, that we may know Thee, the true ⟨God⟩ and Him Whom Thou hast sent, Jesus Christ; give us ⟨the⟩ Holy Spirit that we may be able to speak and tell forth Thine unspeakable mysteries. May the Lord Jesus speak in us and ⟨the⟩ Holy Spirit and hymn Thee through us.

($b^1$) [For Thou art far above all principality and power and rule and dominion and every name that is named, not only in this world but also in that which is to come. Beside Thee stand thousand thousands and ten thousand times ten thousands of angels, archangels, thrones, dominations, principalities, powers: by Thee stand the two most honourable six-winged Seraphim, with two wings covering the Face and with two the Feet and with two flying, and crying 'Holy'; with whom receive also our cry of 'Holy' as we say

($b^2$) Holy, holy, holy, Lord of Sabaoth; full is the heaven and the earth of Thy glory.

($c$) Full is the heaven, full also is the earth of Thine excellent glory. Lord of powers, fill also this sacrifice with Thy power and Thy partaking: For to Thee have we offered this living sacrifice, this unbloody oblation.]

($d^1$) To Thee have we offered this bread, the likeness of the Body of the Only-begotten. This bread is the likeness of the holy Body, because the Lord Jesus Christ in the night in which He was betrayed took bread and brake and gave to His disciples saying: Take ye and eat, this is My Body which is being broken for you for the remission of sins. Wherefore we also making the likeness of the death have

---

[1] This is a regular Egyptian word for the incarnation. Originally it meant the state entry of a governor into his province. It was also used for the 'appearances' of pagan gods.

offered the bread, and beseech Thee through this sacrifice to be
reconciled to all of us and to be merciful, O God of truth;

($d^2$) [and as this bread had been scattered on the top of the mountains
and gathered together came to be one, so also gather Thy holy
church out of every nation and country and every city and village
and house and make one living catholic church.]

($d^3$) We have offered also the cup, the likeness of the Blood, because the
Lord Jesus Christ taking a cup after supper, said to His own disciples: Take ye, drink; this is the New Covenant, which is My Blood,
which is being shed for you for remission of sins. Wherefore we have
also offered the cup, offering a likeness of the Blood.

($e^1$) O God of truth, let Thy holy Word come upon (*epidēmēsato*) this
bread that the bread may become Body of the Word, and upon this
cup that the cup may become Blood of the Truth;

($e^2$) and make all who partake to receive a medicine (*lit.* drug) of life, for
the healing of every sickness and for strengthening of all advancement and virtue, not for condemnation, O God of truth, and not for
censure and reproach.

(*f*) For we have called upon Thy Name, O Uncreated, through the
Only-begotten in ⟨the⟩ Holy Spirit.

(*g*) [Let this people receive mercy, let it be counted worthy of advancement, let angels be sent forth as companions to the people for bringing to naught of the evil one and for the establishment of the church.

(*h*) We entreat also on behalf of all who have fallen asleep, of whom also
this is the 're-calling' (*anamnēsis*)—(*There follows the recital of the
names*)[1]—sanctify these souls,.for Thou knowest them all; sanctify
all who have fallen asleep in the Lord and number them with all Thy
holy powers and give them a place and a mansion in Thy kingdom.

(*i*) And receive also the eucharist of the people and bless them that have
offered the oblations (*prosphora*) and the eucharists, and grant
health and soundness and cheerfulness and all advancement of soul
and body to this whole people.]

(*j*) Through Thy Only-begotten Jesus Christ in ⟨the⟩ Holy Spirit:
(℟ *of the congregation*) As it was and is and shall be unto generations
of generations and world without end. Amen.

This is much longer than Hippolytus' prayer, but from the point of view
simply of eucharistic teaching it says no more than the terse and direct
theological statements of the Roman prayer, and it says it less precisely and
adequately. A variety of new themes have found their way into the contents, but they obscure the simple outline found in Hippolytus without
adding anything essential to the scope. The structure may be analysed thus:

(*a*) *Address*. This is much more elaborate than that of Hippolytus, but is

---

[1] This rubric is in Sarapion's text.

concerned with the same subject, the relation of God the Father to God the Son (to the exclusion in each case of the Holy Ghost). The first paragraph directly repudiates the teaching of Arius that the Son does not know the essence of the Father and is a creature. This makes it clear that it has been re-written (or perhaps added bodily before the second paragraph) during the second quarter of the fourth century, when the Arian controversy was at its height. If the older formula contained anything equivalent to Hippolytus' thanksgivings for creation, incarnation and passion, only the faintest traces remain, in the references to 'every created being' and 'the advent' of the Son, with no allusion to the passion at all.

(b) *Preface.* What seems to have altered the character of (a) is the intro-duction of the sanctus, and of the preface introducing it. The note of 'thanksgiving' and the word itself have disappeared from the address, which has become a sort of theological hymn leading up to the preface. Omitting certain very interesting theological changes in (b) which can be shown to have been made in the fourth century,[1] we note only that the use of the sanctus at the Alexandrian eucharist, preceded by a preface closely resem-bling Sarapion (b), can be traced in the writings of Origen at Alexandria c. A.D. 230.[2] This is the earliest certain evidence of the use of this hymn in the liturgy. Earlier citations of the words of the angelic hymn from the scriptures by Clement of Rome and Tertullian do not necessarily reflect a use of it at the eucharist, and it is absent from Hippolytus' liturgy and from some other early documents. It is also noticeable that while the later Alexandrian *Liturgy of S. Mark* shews little trace in other parts of its eucharistic prayer of being descended from a prayer at all closely resembling that of Sarapion, in the one point of the wording of its preface *S. Mark* exhibits only small verbal variations from the text of Sarapion (b). The simplest explanation of these various facts is that the use of the preface and sanctus in the eucharistic prayer began in the Alexandrian church at some time before A.D. 230, and from there spread first to other Egyptian churches, and ultimately all over christendom. If this be true, Sarapion's (b), though an integral part of the text in its present (fourth century) form, is an interpolation into the original local tradition of the prayer at Thmuis, as is indicated by its having been borrowed almost verbally from the liturgy of Alexandria. We have no means of judging when this Alexandrian para-graph was first incorporated into the liturgy at Thmuis, whether as part of that revision which formed our present text of the prayer—which is certainly responsible for the present form of (a) and may quite well have included a recasting of the whole opening part of the prayer (Sarapion was a close friend and prominent supporter of S. Athanasius, bishop of Alex-andria from A.D. 328–373)—or by some earlier revision at Thmuis during the third century. But at Thmuis the preface has received no local develop-ment or variation worth mentioning from the Alexandrian text, which in

[1] *Cf. Theology*, xxxvii. (Nov. 1938), *pp.* 271 *sq.*       [2] *Ibid*

the conditions of the period suggests that its incorporation was not of long standing when the present revision was made.

(c) *Prayer for the acceptance of the 'living sacrifice'*. This section is difficult to interpret. At first sight it marks an abrupt transition from the worship of the sanctus to the offering of the eucharistic oblation of the bread and the cup. The phrase 'the unbloody sacrifice' is used by fourth century writers (first by Cyril of Jerusalem A.D. 348) to mean the specifically eucharistic offering of the consecrated bread and cup; and a prayer having a definite reference to the consecration of the bread and cup, at this point *before* the recital of the institution, is a peculiar characteristic of some later Egyptian eucharistic prayers.

Nevertheless it is open to doubt whether this was the original application of (c), even if by Sarapion's time it had already come to be interpreted in this sense. There is a certain difficulty in the prayer that God would 'fill this sacrifice' with *His* 'partaking', which is awkward on any interpretation, but especially so if (c) be really a prayer about the bread and the cup. And there is an unexpectedness about the phrase 'this *living* sacrifice' applied to the elements on the altar at this stage of the prayer without any sort of warning, even allowing for the fact that the idea of a 'moment of consecration' had hardly developed in the fourth century (as the next section of the prayer sufficiently indicates). But it would be a good deal easier to understand if it has a connection with the previous petition, 'we beseech Thee make us *living* men'. In this case the 'living sacrifice and unbloody oblation' of (c) will have reference to the 'sacrifice of praise' offered in the hymn of the sanctus, and not to the eucharistic offering which follows. It is at least worthy of notice that in a pre-christian jewish work (c. 100 B.C.) *The Testament of the xii Patriarchs*, the angels in heaven are said to offer 'a rational and unbloody oblation' to God,[1] and it is in this angelic worship of heaven that the congregation has just been joining by the sanctus. Similarly a second century christian writer, Athenagoras,[2] speaks of 'the lifting up of holy hands' by christians as 'an unbloody sacrifice and rational liturgy', clearly with reference to prayer and praise rather than to the eucharist as such. In this case Sarapion (c) would represent originally a prayer for the acceptance of the sacrifice of praise offered in (b),[3] much as (d¹) contains a prayer for the acceptance of the eucharistic sacrifice of the bread and wine offered in the preceding sentence; and as (i) is a prayer for the acceptance of 'the eucharist of the people' offered in the whole preceding prayer.

Such an interpretation of (c) eases the abruptness of the main transition of thought, which comes not between (b) and (c), but between (c) and (d). The transitions are not very well managed anywhere in this prayer, but it seems easier at this point if there is a passage of ideas from the offering of

---

[1] *Testament of Levi*, iii. 6.
[2] *Legatio pro Christianis*, xiii. *Cf.* also Eusebius, *Hist. Eccl.*, X. iv. 68.
[3] *Cf.* also the Alexandrian preface on *p.* 218.

the worship of the sanctus as a 'living sacrifice' of praise, to the offering of the eucharistic 'sacrifice of the death'. This carries with it the implication that (c) (which thus depends on the sanctus) is also an interpolation into the original form of the rite of Thmuis. A good deal has been built on the application of (c) in this prayer to the eucharist by some writers; but it does not really seem to make much difference to the specifically eucharistic theology of the prayer to exclude (c) from consideration in this respect.

(d) *The Offering and Institution.* As a preliminary to understanding this section it is best to dispose of ($d^2$), which completely destroys the symmetry, otherwise obvious, between ($d^1$) and ($d^3$). The unsuitability of describing the corn from which the eucharistic bread has been made as having been originally 'scattered on the tops of the mountains' among the mud-flats of the Nile delta makes it plain that this is not an authentic product of the native tradition of the prayer at Thmuis, but a rather unimaginative *literary* quotation. It is in fact borrowed from the prayers for the agape found in *Didache* ix.[1] (In the Syrian or Transjordanian setting in which the *Didache* was probably composed, cornfields on the hill-tops occasion no surprise.) As an elaboration of ($d^1$), ($d^2$) is still a rather glaring 'patch', which has not yet produced a similar elaboration of ($d^3$). This suggests that it had not very long found a place in the prayer when the present recension was made. It may even have been introduced as a 'happy thought' by the last reviser, since it virtually duplicates matter found more in place in (g), which is itself an addition to the original outline of the prayer.

By contrast with Hippolytus, Sarapion in (d) fuses the formal statement of the offering of the elements with the narrative of the institution, which Hippolytus keeps distinct (*cf.* Hipp. (f) and (i)). Sarapion also states explicitly that the actual offering has already been made at the offertory, which Hippolytus leaves in the background. We have already seen the reason for this in the fact that 'the' prayer had originally to put into words the meaning of the whole rite, of what precedes as well as of what follows. Thus Sarapion can say 'We have offered' (before the prayer began) even though the whole prayer is itself headed in the MS. 'Prayer of Offering' or 'Oblation'. Finally, even more plainly than in Hippolytus, the narrative of the institution is here pivotal for the whole prayer, as the supreme authority or justification for what the church does in the eucharist—'This bread is the likeness of the holy Body *because* the Lord Jesus took bread', etc.

(e) *Prayer for Communion.* This section forms a single whole, even though it falls into two distinct parts. It is a prayer for communion, the first part of which is concerned with the means and the other with the effects. In contrast with Hippolytus, where the institution narrative is taken as *implicitly* identifying the bread and wine with the Body and Blood of Christ by virtue of His own promise, Sarapion's prayer shews a new desire for an *explicit* identification. This desire is found in other fourth century writers also, but

[1] *Cf. p.* 90.

hardly before that time. The way in which, e.g., ($d^3$) goes out of its way to emphasise this identification of the bread and wine with the Body and Blood by the institution narrative itself, with the peculiar formula '. . . drink, this is the New Covenant, *which is* My Blood' (instead of 'in My Blood', Luke xxii. 20), suggests that at one time the Hippolytan understanding of the force of the institution narrative had prevailed in Egypt also. It was only later that it was felt to need reinforcing by an explicit petition for the identification of the elements with the Body and Blood, such as we get here in (*e*).

However this may be, Sarapion is not unique in the fourth century in feeling this, or in the way in which he expresses himself, by a prayer for the 'advent' (*epidēmēsato*) of the Word, parallel to His 'advent' (*epidēmia*) in the incarnation (*cf. a²*). S. Athanasius in the same period in Egypt writes: 'When the great prayers and holy supplications have been sent up *the Word comes upon the bread and the cup and they become His Body.*'[1] The same idea is found in a number of Ethiopic rites which are of Egyptian connection, if not actual origin. Outside Egypt S. Jerome in Syria sixty years later speaks of bishops as those who 'at the eucharist pray for the advent of the Lord',[2] and similar language is used in Asia Minor in the fourth century, and later still in Italy, Gaul and Spain.[3] This introduction of a prayer for 'the coming of the Lord', the Son, the Second Person of the Trinity, is a straightforward conception, which only makes explicit the ideas originally involved in the reference to the incarnation and in the institution narrative in earlier versions of the prayer. The implications of these references had already been made plain by writers like Justin in the second century.[4] But the introduction of such a petition alters to some extent the balance of the prayer as a whole, by weakening the position of the institution narrative as the central pivot of the whole prayer.

Even in so early a specimen as that of Sarapion, the prayer of ($e^1$) is definitely 'consecratory' in form, and thus prepares the way for the conception of a 'moment of consecration' within the eucharistic prayer as a whole. This conception was eventually accepted by East and West alike, though they chose different 'moments' to which to attach the idea. It was by a third development, a sort of theological refinement upon this secondary stage of any sort of explicit prayer to reinforce the old identification of the elements with the Body and Blood through the institution narrative, that the Greeks evolved during the fourth and fifth centuries the 'tertiary' stage of a prayer that specifically the Holy Ghost, the Third Person of the Holy Trinity, would (in some sense) 'make' the elements into the Body and Blood of Christ. This became for them the 'moment of consecration'; a

---

[1] *Fragment vii. ad Baptizandos*, P.G. 26. 1935.
[2] *In Soph.* iii. P.L. xxv. 1377.
[3] *Cf. Theology*, xxviii. (Apr. 1934), pp. 197 sq.
[4] *Cf. e.g. p.* 159 (c, d, g).

'moment' which the West, when it adopted the idea from the East, continued to place at the old pivot of the prayer, the institution narrative. Had the West wished to follow the East in divorcing the 'moment' from the institution, it could have found one at the prayer *Quam oblationem* of the Western canon *before* the institution narrative, which is just as much 'consecratory' as is $(e^1)$ in Sarapion. Rome therefore reached this secondary stage of a petition for consecration apart from the institution; but remained there, without advancing to the 'tertiary' stage of the Eastern prayer for the sending of the Holy Spirit. Sarapion's prayer in $(e^1)$ thus foreshadows the parting of the ways between later Eastern and Western liturgical ideas.

$(e^2)$ Having prayed for the means of communion, Sarapion prays for its effects. Here it is noticeable that whereas Hippolytus' prayer for the communicants confines itself to purely spiritual effects, that of Sarapion recognises that the sacrament is a 'drug' or 'medicine' of life, for the body as well as the soul. We need not suspect that this difference represents a 'rapid decline of spirituality between the days of persecution and those of the established church of the fourth century', as one English writer has suggested. (Sarapion himself felt the full force of the Arian persecution of the catholics, and probably died in exile.) It is quite true that Hippolytus *at this point* says nothing of the eucharist as concerned with the human body; but in his section $(e)$ he has quite clearly stated that one purpose of the institution of the eucharist is 'to abolish death' etc., which amounts to much the same thing, though put in a different way. In point of fact, Sarapion rests on old Egyptian tradition in what he calls the eucharist here. Clement of Alexandria, *c.* A.D. 190, had pictured our Lord as saying to the soul: 'I am thy nourisher, giving Myself as bread, whereof he that tastes shall never more have experience of death, and daily giving Myself for the drink of immortality.'[1] We shall see in the next chapter that these ideas go back right through the second century into the New Testament itself. The Roman canon follows the tradition of Hippolytus in that it prays only for spiritual benefits for the communicants—that 'they may be filled with all heavenly benediction and grace', a conservatism which is followed by our Prayer Book 'Prayer of Oblation'. But our words of administration—'preserve thy *body* and soul'—have gone back to the wider view of the effects of communion, by contrast with the Roman words—'preserve thy soul unto everlasting life'. In more discreet language our form contains Sarapion's teaching that the eucharist is a 'drug' or 'medicine of life' for the body as well as the soul.

$(f)$ *The Invocation.* We have already spoken of the great importance attached in the primitive christian and the pre-christian jewish tradition to the 'glorifying of the Name' of God at the close of the *berakah* or *eucharistia*, the 'Thanksgiving' at the end of supper. We have a further hint in this clause of the part played by this conception. The prayer in $(e^1)$ and

[1] *Quis dives salvetur?* 29.

(*e²*) for the identification of the elements with the Body and Blood of Christ and for their eternal effects upon the bodies and souls of the communicants—*the* petition of the whole eucharistic prayer—is here understood as being efficacious chiefly '*because* they have called upon the Name of God'. So again, Clement of Alexandria, citing an even earlier Egyptian writer *c.* A.D. 160, with whom Clement does not disagree on this point, says: 'The bread is hallowed by the power of the Name of God, remaining the same in appearance as it was ⟨when it was⟩ taken, but by ⟨this⟩ power it is transformed into spiritual power'.[1]

Whatever the danger of approximating to mere magic in such ideas, we have to recognise that the special efficacy of prayer 'in the Name of God' or 'of the Lord Jesus' is clearly found in the New Testament, not only in the teaching of the apostles—and in their practice, *e.g.*, in the matter of exorcisms—but also in the teaching of our Lord Himself.[2] There is no clear dividing line to be drawn between the application of such ideas to the sacrament of the eucharist, and to that of baptism, whether this be given 'in the Name of' the Holy Trinity or, as primitively, 'in the Name of the Lord Jesus'. We accept it placidly in the case of baptism out of use and wont, because the church happens to have retained it in its full primitive significance in baptism. We are startled at it in the case of the eucharist, because there the church early overlaid it with other ideas. But in the time of Sarapion it had not yet entirely lost its primitive force in the eucharist, and it is likely that this clause was deliberately retained out of a lingering sense of the importance of the old conception, when the intercessions which follow in the present (fourth century) text were first interpolated at this point in the prayer.

(*g*), (*h*), (*i*) *The Intercessions, for the Living, the Dead and the Offerers.* These are an addition to the original outline of the prayer, of a kind which was made in most churches at some point within the prayer before the end of the fourth century. When the eucharist was celebrated apart from the synaxis in the pre-Nicene church there was a real loss in the absence of any intercessions whatever. There was a natural desire to replace them in some way; and it is quite possible that in some churches the custom arose during the third century of treating the intercessory 'prayers of the faithful', which really formed the close of the synaxis, as a sort of invariable preliminary to the eucharist, even when this latter was celebrated without the rest of the synaxis. (But Sarapion's own arrangement in his collection of prayers still puts the intercessions at the opposite end of the book to the prayers of the eucharist proper, in an altogether separate service.)

The alternative was to insert some intercessions at a fresh point within the eucharist itself. The rigidity of the primitive outline, which permitted of only one prayer at the eucharist, 'the' eucharistic prayer, necessitated their being included somehow within that, whatever confusion to its primi-

---

[1] *Excerpta ex Theodoto*, 82.          [2] *E.g.* Mark ix. 39; John xiv. 13, etc.

tive shape and purpose this might cause. Even when the two services were celebrated together, there was a natural desire to associate a prayer for the 'special intentions' with which the eucharist was being offered as closely as possible with the act of offering, and this would lead to the same result. The existence of some prayer for the communicants towards the close of the prayer (in all the traditions with which we are acquainted) led in some churches to the development of this part of the prayer to cover other objects of intercession as well, as here at Thmuis, and also at Jerusalem, where it is probable that the practice started. In the fourth century such a position for intercessions acquired the further sanction of the idea of the special efficacy of prayer in the presence of the consecrated sacrament, which we shall find attested by S. Cyril of Jerusalem in A.D. 348.[1] But Jerusalem in the fourth century, and especially S. Cyril, are in the forefront of 'liturgical advance', and there is no sign of this further special development of ideas in Sarapion.

Alexandria and Egypt generally adopted another notion, that the special intentions of the sacrifice ought to be named *before* it was actually offered. We find accordingly that the Alexandrian intercessions were inserted into the opening of the prayer, before the sanctus. At Rome the intercessions for the living settled down at the beginning of the prayer (but after the sanctus), and those for the dead (originally only inserted at masses for the dead) at the end. Elsewhere other points were chosen; *e.g.*, at Edessa they were interpolated after the sanctus and the first half of the eucharistic prayer, immediately before the consecration.[2] There was no uniformity about this, because each church began to copy others in 'modernising' its liturgy at different moments and under different influences, inserting now the preface and sanctus, now intercessions for the living, now commemorations of martyrs and so on, at whatever point in its own local tradition of the prayer seemed most fitting; and in doing so it borrowed now verbally, now only in ideas, now from one source, now from another, or added native compositions and elaborations of its own as the liturgical gifts and knowledge of its successive bishops permitted.

The general result, when the synaxis and eucharist came to be fused into a single rite, celebrated as a normal rule without a break, was a duplication between the old intercessions, the 'prayers of the faithful', at the close of the synaxis, and the new intercessory developments within the eucharistic prayer. The old 'prayers of the faithful' tended after a while to atrophy in most rites, or even to disappear altogether, as at Rome and in the Syriac *S. James*.

The chief points of interest in Sarapion's intercessions are: (*h*) The description of the eucharist as the *anamnesis* of the dead—clearly in the same sense as at Rome of 're-calling' something *before God*. But the word is not applied to the eucharist as the *anamnesis* of the passion in Sarapion, though

[1] *Cf. p.* 199.          [2] *Cf. p.* 179 *n.*

it is found in this sense in Origen in third century Egypt. In (*i*) the prayers for the offerers are of interest as the earliest Egyptian evidence for the custom of each communicant bringing his or her own *prosphora* for themselves. To be one of 'the people' (laity), to offer the *prosphora* and to partake of communion, were still all virtually the same thing in Sarapion's time in Egypt, to judge by the way the petitions in ($e^2$), (*g*), and (*i*) repeat one another in their prayers for 'advancement'. In the later Alexandrian intercessions also, those for the dead immediately precede those for the 'offerers'.

(*j*) *The Doxology.* In the present text this is reduced to meagre dimensions. Probably the interpolation of the intercessions has eliminated an older fully developed form at (*f*), which marked the conclusion of the prayer. That (*j*) does *not* preserve the original conclusion postponed to the end of the interpolated intercessions, seems clear from the fact that the traditional people's response 'As it was' etc., does not attach itself to Sarapion's conclusion either grammatically or in sense, though it is appended in the MS.

Comparing the whole prayer with that of Hippolytus one may say that though it is more than probable that Sarapion ultimately derives from a prayer on the *berakah* model, and though there are certain points of contact between Hippolytus and Sarapion in structure, it has in any case lost touch with its original type much more than has the older Roman prayer. Additional themes like the sanctus and the intercessions have complicated and obscured the outline so much that no clear verdict could be given on this question of derivation from the *berakah* from the study of Sarapion's prayer taken alone. And certainly there has been no borrowing between the Roman and Egyptian prayers in the course of development. In the central part of the prayer [Sarapion (*d*)–(*f*) = Hippolytus (*e*)–(*j*)] the differences of phrasing and arrangement are very marked indeed, considering that both prayers are dealing with exactly the same subject.

But this obvious independence of the two traditions only brings into greater relief their agreement on the substance of those points which we noted as outstanding in Hippolytus' statement of the meaning of the eucharistic action:

(1) The bread and the cup are explicitly stated to be 'offered' to God—though in Sarapion separately, in Hippolytus together. (2) Sarapion explicitly calls this a 'sacrifice', as Hippolytus calls it a 'priestly' ministry; the meaning is the same though the statement is diverse. Though the eucharist is not called 'the *anamnēsis* of the passion', as in Justin and Hippolytus, it is called 'making the likeness of the death'. And (3) as in Hippolytus, the pivotal importance of the narrative of the institution in the prayer, as the ground of the eucharist's effective 're-calling' before God of the sacrifice of Christ, does not in any way obscure the fact that it is Calvary and not the Upper Room which is thus 're-called'.

## (iii) *The Syrian Tradition*

In Syria the church of Antioch claimed and was accorded a primacy from, at the latest, some while before the end of the second century. But for a variety of reasons this was never so effectively exercised as was that of Alexandria over Egypt. Despite a cleavage of race and language between the native Copts and the large population of immigrant Greeks, Egypt had been a self-conscious unity under the leadership of Alexandria for centuries before the coming of christianity. The unchallenged supremacy of the Alexandrian bishop over all the churches of Egypt only gave christian expression to an enduring political and geographical factor in past Egyptian history. But from pre-historic times Syria has always been a mosaic of different races, cultures, religions and languages, which no political framework has ever held together for long. The welter of Canaanite tribes of very diverse racial origin which the Hebrews under Joshua succeeded in overcoming in the hills of Southern Syria is typical of the pre-historic background of the whole country. It is equally typical of its history that the invading Israelite confederacy should promptly have disintegrated into its original tribal units under the Judges; and even after it had been welded into a single state under Saul and the House of David, should have split again after less than a century into the rival states of Israel and Judah. The North and East of Syria were no less prone to division than the South throughout their history—until only yesterday, when the four separate republics of French Syria and the two states of Palestine and Transjordan under British mandate still divided a country which seems geographically destined to be a unity, but which is racially and culturally one of the least united in the world.

During the century c. 250–150 B.C., the Seleucid kings of Antioch made the most promising of all the many attempts to unify Syria, on the basis of the introduction everywhere of Greek language and culture. They hoped this would be a general solvent of all the diverse local traditions, and act as a cement for the motley elements over which they ruled. They were thwarted by the stubborn adherence of large parts of the population to their ancient cultures, of which the resistance of the jews of the South under the Maccabees is only the most obvious and violent example.

The Seleucids failed in their main object, but they had a good deal of incidental success with their chosen means, the introduction of that form of later Greek civilisation which we call 'Hellenism.' Henceforward Syria was riven by a new division, running right across all its old fractions, that between hellenism and the old native cultures, which diverse though they were, may be classed together as predominantly semitic. This new cleavage does not run along racial lines, for the vast majority of the hellenists were not immigrants but hellenised Syrians. Nor was it primarily geographical, though naturally Antioch and the great coast towns were strongholds of hellenism, as the hinterland was of the native tradition. But there were large purely oriental quarters in Antioch itself and whole Aramaic-speaking districts in its neighbourhood; on the other hand there were at times strong Greek influences at work in Edessa and Damascus, inland cities which were normally centres of semitic culture; while some of the smaller cities on the Eastern frontier were completely hellenised. The backbone of the semitic tradition was the peasantry of the countrysides, as the peak of hellenism was found in the towns. But there were Greek-speaking country districts, while some towns, especially in the East—Edessa, Palmyra, Damascus—were strongly semitic by tradition, and others like Aleppo and Emesa (Homs) formed a sort of debatable land between the two cultures. In short, Syria was an older underlying patchwork of races, languages, traditions and religions, with a recent and different patchwork of hellenism and the surviving native cultures superimposed upon it. The underlying patchwork is *local*, but the only line of division one can draw between hellenism and the oriental traditions is purely *cultural*. By A.D. 300 a man might be a Syrian (which could mean racially a mongrel of half-a-dozen different strains) and yet as hellenised and westernised in speech and mind and habit of life as an inhabitant of Athens or Alexandria or even Rome. And his next-door neighbour might be equally Syrian by blood and remain as completely oriental in culture and language and thought as his fore-fathers a thousand years before. Or he might be bilingual, with some sort of footing in both worlds. First Rome and then Byzantium inherited the hellenising policy of the Seleucids; and while these European powers ruled the land, Antioch, which had been founded as the capital of hellenism in Syria, remained the administrative and ecclesiastical capital. With the return of semitic ascendancy after the Arab conquest in the seventh century, dominance returned to the old semitic centre of Damascus, to which both the Arab rulers and the christian patriarchs transferred their courts. Henceforward Antioch slowly declined into insignificance.

The patriarchate of Antioch saw itself as the christian heir to the Seleucid tradition of the leadership of all Syria in the path of hellenism; and with only two brief exceptions (under the heretical patriarchs Paul of Samosata in the third century and Severus in the sixth), it identified itself with the 'royalist' hellenising movement throughout its history. But in adhering to this policy the patriarchs had to face in the ecclesiastical field just those same centrifugal tendencies and obstinate local traditions which faced every attempt at political centralisation. When Bishop Juvenal of Jeru-salem in A.D. 451 succeeded after twenty-five years of manoeuvring in extracting from the general council of Chalcedon formal recognition of his see as an independent patriarchate over Palestine, he only added a christian chapter to the long story of the wars of Israel with Syria which punctuate the Books of the Kings, and are continued by the revolt of the Maccabees against the Seleucids. And besides this inveterate separatism of the South there were other pockets of local resistance to all Antiochene or hellenistic domination, less strongly marked but in the end equally tenacious. Against the overwhelming political power of Rome or Byzantium these local patriotisms could only express themselves in terms of ecclesiastical resistance, under the pretext of doctrinal heresy culminating in schism. But these dissident churches drew their strength from racial and cultural forces far more than from theological nicety. Apart from a whole succession of obscure and fantastic popular movements like that of the Messalians in the fourth century (most of which were hardly sufficiently christian to be classed as heresies) we have to reckon, first, with the great East Syrian revolt against Antioch in the fifth century, which adopted the banner of the Nestorian heresy; and secondly, with its doctrinal opposite, the West Syrian revolt of the sixth century which called itself Monophysite; and thirdly, with the Maronite schism in the Lebanon of the eighth century, which took the excuse of Monothelitism. We need not here concern ourselves with the doctrinal pretexts. The real dogma of all the rebels was 'anti-Byzantinism' or 'anti-hellenism' as the 'orthodoxy' of Antioch was always in practice 'Caesaro-papism.' Between them the royalist patriarchate and the nationalist schisms shattered Syrian christianity as a living force, and left it permanently weakened to face the pressure of mohammedan political conquest. To-day more than three quarters of the descendants of the old christian inhabitants of Syria are mohammedans, and the christian remainder is so riven into fragments as to be a negligible missionary power. The islamic populations of Syria and Egypt no less than their schismatic churches are permanent monuments of the long attempts of the church of Constantinople to dominate the christian world in the interest of the Byzantine emperors.

It is not surprising that this background of abiding cultural division and local separatism should have left its mark on the liturgy. But the liturgical divisions of Syria, by a series of historical accidents, do not entirely coincide with those of ancient ecclesiastical politics or present doctrinal allegiance. In the field of liturgy we can distinguish four main influences which cross the present sectarian divisions in a most confusing way:

(1) The old rite of the church of Antioch itself, which is very imperfectly known;

(2) The other early West Syrian liturgical traditions, which we shall ignore;

(3) The East Syrian tradition, centred in Edessa;

(4) The South Syrian tradition of Jerusalem.

(1) What may be called the 'patriarchal' rite of Syria was the so-called *Liturgy of S. James*. It is generally taken that, as it stands, this is *not* the old local rite of Antioch, which is known to us only obscurely from a number of sources, of which the most reliable are hints to be found in the Antiochene

writings of S. John Chrysostom (c. A.D. 360–397).[1] S. *James* as it stands is closely connected with the fourth century rite of Jerusalem, which was adopted by the Antiochene church at some point in the fifth century—when is uncertain. It had not yet happened when S. John Chrysostom left Antioch in A.D. 397, and it is reasonable to suppose that it did not happen after A.D. 431, when Bishop Juvenal of Jerusalem greatly embittered relations between Jerusalem and Antioch by claiming not merely independence (which he successfully asserted twenty years later) but jurisdiction over Antioch itself for his own see. The unique position of Jerusalem as the 'holy city' and above all its prestige as a model of liturgical observance were such during the turn of the fourth and fifth centuries as to cause the adoption of Jerusalem customs to a greater or lesser extent by other churches all over christendom. It is not surprising that it should have influenced its own patriarchal see in these respects with especial force at this time. At all events, Antioch to some extent adopted and adapted the Jerusalem *Liturgy of S. James*, probably between A.D. 400 and 430, and made it the patriarchal rite so far as Antiochene influence extended.

Strangely enough, though the patriarchs of Antioch thus introduced the Jerusalem rite into North Syria, they did not themselves remain faithful to it, and ultimately abandoned its use altogether. In pursuit of their usual hellenising policy they had begun (? in the seventh century) to use a version of the Greek *Liturgy of S. Basil*, as at least an occasional alternative to their own rite of *S. James*. After some centuries of increasing 'Byzantinising', they ended in the thirteenth–fourteenth century by dropping all trace of their own Syrian rite in favour of the full rite of Byzantium, upon which power the Antiochene orthodox patriarchate had by then become helplessly dependent. Thus *S. James*, though the patriarchal rite of Antioch, is neither a 'pure' descendant of the original rite of the Antiochene church, nor the rite which has been used by its patriarchs for the greater part of their history.

(2) North-West Syria followed its patriarchs in adopting *S. James*, but with one important reservation. While the structure and framework of *S.*

---

[1] To this, or before this, most liturgists would add the *Clementine Liturgy* of *Apostolic Constitutions* viii., with the admission that its editor has adapted the Antiochene rite to an unascertained extent to suit his own personal ideas. Dr. Baumstark and Dom Engberding have both hinted—the subject has not been pursued further than that—that light might be thrown on the old Antiochene rite by a study of certain Maronite peculiarities, especially in the Maronite *Liturgy of the Apostles*. This line of approach certainly offers more hope of a successful reconstruction of old Antiochene practice (on some points and taken in conjunction with other sources) than that process of taking *Ap. Const. au pied de la lettre*, while formally voicing a mild suspicion of the author's good faith, which has hitherto formed the chief English contribution to the debate. I have a suggestion of my own to make below as to the old Antiochene rite. And I strongly suspect that the rite taken as the basis of his work by the compiler of *Ap. Const.* was not that of Antioch itself but of some other North Syrian city, a rite of the same general type, but with traditions of its own.

THE EUCHARISTIC PRAYER 177

*James* everywhere came into use, the text of its eucharistic prayer never achieved the same prescriptive authority in N.W. Syria as the rest of the rite. Some seventy alternative eucharistic prayers are known from this region, composed at all periods from the fourth-fifth centuries down to the fifteenth. In other words, the working authority of the Antiochene patriarchate was never sufficiently strong in the nearest parts of its own territory, even before the great revolts of the sixth century, to break down the old tradition that every church could follow its own usage in the phrasing of its eucharistic prayer, and that celebrants could remodel this within certain limits at their own discretion. The general outline of these prayers follows that of *S. James* fairly closely as a rule. But some of them exhibit very interesting and probably ancient variations, and have been only roughly adapted to fit the *S. James* type; while even those prayers which follow it more closely are verbally independent compositions on the same theme rather than mere imitations.

But by the time of the Monophysite schism (sixth century) *S. James* had obviously become the standard West Syrian tradition. For a while after that royalists and schismatics used the same rite, until the royalists came to think of it as a badge of local particularism and abandoned it for the rite of Constantinople. This left it to the exclusive use of the Monophysites, among whom it now survives in an Arabic translation, though before the seventeenth century it was generally used in an ancient Syriac version (which is still in use in a few christian villages round Damascus). The Syriac appears to have undergone more than one revision since the sixth century, sometimes to bring it into greater conformity with Byzantine innovations, sometimes in complete independence of these. Even in their hostility to Byzantium the provincials could not help being more than a little impressed by the Byzantines' own valuation of themselves as the source of all that was 'correct' in matters ecclesiastical. They were consequently always apt to adopt the latest Byzantine customs after more or less delay, and so gradually to Byzantinise their own rites. Modern and mediaeval Monophysite MSS. of *S. James* differ textually from one another more considerably than those of any other rite—another symptom of the permanent lack of central authority in matters liturgical in Syria.

(3) North-East Syria seems never to have adopted *S. James*, having gone off into Nestorianism and independence too early to have been much influenced by its adoption by the patriarchs of Antioch. Instead, this part of the country adopted as its standard liturgy the ancient rite of the church of Edessa, the Liturgy of *SS. Addai and Mari* (the traditional 'apostles' of Edessa). This may well be connected originally with the second century rite of Antioch, whence Edessa had received the faith; though this is no more than a very reasonable conjecture. Edessa was a semi-independent state on the Eastern Roman frontier, a strong centre of semitic culture and tradition, though theologically it also acted as a channel for the diffusion

of Greek ideas to the purely unhellenic regions around and east of itself. Even Nestorius, whose teachings the later school of Edessa professed to follow, was an ecclesiastic of Antioch who became patriarch of Constantinople; and his teachers Theodore and Diodore, who were venerated as Nestorian 'doctors', were likewise thoroughly hellenised, even though all three were from inner Syria and probably racially non-hellenic. The Edessan liturgy has therefore undergone some infiltration of hellenic ideas even in the earliest texts now available.

But it is of unique interest and importance none the less, because it is basically still a *semitic* liturgy,[1] the only remaining specimen of its kind. It is cast in a different idiom of thought from that of the eucharistic prayers of the hellenistic christianity which had developed out of S. Paul's missions to the hellenistic world north and west of Syria. Its special importance lies in this—that any agreement of *ideas* with these hellenistic prayers which may be found to underlie the marked peculiarities of *SS. Addai and Mari* helps to carry back the eucharistic tradition of the church as a whole behind the divergence of Greek and Western christianity generally from that oriental world to which the original Galilaean apostles had belonged. The obscure history of the Syrian liturgies has a special interest just because it illustrates that contrast between the whole mind and thought of the hellenic and semitic worlds which rarely meets us with any definiteness in christian history outside the pages of the New Testament. We shall therefore conclude this chapter by examining two Syrian eucharistic prayers which are expressions of the two aspects of Syrian tradition, those of the more semitic *Liturgy of SS. Addai and Mari* and of the more hellenistic *Liturgy of S. James*. There is much to be learnt from their different ways of expressing what is fundamentally the same liturgical tradition.

### The Liturgy of SS. Addai and Mari

(*a*) Worthy of praise from every mouth and of confession from every tongue and of worship and exaltation from every creature is the adorable and glorious Name [of Thy glorious Trinity, O Father and Son and Holy Ghost,]

(*b*) Who didst create the world by Thy grace and its inhabitants by Thy mercy and didst save mankind by Thy compassion and give great grace unto mortals.

(*c*[1]) [Thy majesty, O my Lord, thousand thousands of those on high bow down and worship, and ten thousand times ten thousand holy angels and hosts of spiritual beings, ministers of fire and spirit, praise Thy

---

[1] The credit for drawing attention to the importance of *SS. Addai and Mari* in this and other respects belongs to the Rev. E. C. Ratcliff, whose reconstruction of its original form is to be found in a brilliant essay in the *Journal of Theological Studies*, xxx, *pp.* 23 *sq.* Though I have ventured to differ from him in certain details, I am, like all other students, indebted to his essay for my understanding of this liturgy.

Name with holy Cherubim and spiritual Seraphim offering worship to Thy sovereignty, shouting and praising without ceasing and crying one to another and saying:

(c²) Holy, holy, holy Lord God of Hosts; heaven and earth are full of His praises and of the nature of His being and of the excellency of His glorious splendour. Hosanna in the highest, and Hosanna to the Son of David! Blessed is He that came and cometh in the Name of the Lord! Hosanna in the highest! And with these heavenly hosts]

(d) We give thanks to Thee, O my Lord, even we Thy servants weak and frail and miserable, for that Thou hast given us great grace past recompense in that Thou didst put on our manhood that Thou mightest quicken it by Thy Godhead,

(e) and hast exalted our low estate and restored our fall and raised our mortality and forgiven our trespasses and justified our sinfulness and enlightened our knowledge, and, O our Lord and our God, hast condemned our enemies and granted victory to the weakness of our frail nature in the overflowing mercies of Thy grace.[1]

(f) And we also, O my Lord, Thy weak and frail and miserable servants who are gathered together in Thy Name, both stand before Thee at this time

(g) and have received by tradition the example which is from Thee,

(h) [rejoicing and glorifying and exalting and commemorating and performing this (great and fearful and holy and life-giving and divine) likeness of the passion and death and burial and resurrection of our Lord and our Saviour Jesus Christ.]

(i) And may there come, O my Lord, Thy Holy Spirit and rest upon this oblation of Thy servants, and bless and hallow it that it be to us, O my Lord, for the pardon of offences and the remission of sins and for the great hope of resurrection from the dead and for new life in the kingdom of heaven with all those who have been well-pleasing in Thy sight.

(j) And for all this great and marvellous dispensation towards us we will give Thee thanks and praise Thee without ceasing in Thy church

---

[1] At this point the modern Anglican editors have inserted the narrative of the institution from 1 Cor. xi. 23–5, apparently because they could not conceive of a eucharistic prayer which did not contain such a feature, and thought this the most appropriate point at which to insert it. It is found in no MS. here or elsewhere in the prayer, and the Nestorians themselves seem to have no tradition of interpolating it at any point. In Malabar in the fifteenth century they were accustomed to do so *outside* the prayer, just before the fraction—a sufficient indication that the rite did not originally contain it within the prayer. Apparently *Addai and Mari*, like the 'Fragments of a Persian Anaphora' from the same region published by Bickell, never included a narrative of the institution. As we shall see, its absence was made good in another way. After (e) the MSS. all insert an intercession, but this is clearly an interpolation of a relatively late date, part of which had not yet been inserted so late as the tenth century. For the 'Persian Anaphora' *cf.* the revised text, *ed.* R. H. Connolly, *Oriens Christianus*. N.S., xii.–xiv. (1922–4), *pp.* 99 *sqq.*

redeemed by the precious Blood [of Thy Christ], with unclosed mouths and open faces lifting up praise and honour and confession and worship to Thy living and life-giving Name now and ever and world without end.

℞ *Amen.*

Before commenting in detail on this prayer there are two general observations of some importance to be made. (1) So far as can be ascertained the biblical text which underlies the scriptural citations in this prayer is not a Greek text, but one of the Syriac versions—which, it is not possible to distinguish. It would appear certain, therefore, that unlike most other Eastern vernacular rites, *Addai and Mari* was not originally a translation from the Greek, but was composed in Syriac.

(2) Whatever may be the case in the opening address of the prayer and certain phrases elsewhere, the body of this eucharistic prayer is undoubtedly addressed not to the Father but *to the Son*. Phrases such as 'Thou didst put on our manhood' (*d*), and 'the example which is from Thee' (*f*), are quite inapplicable to the First Person of the Trinity; and 'Thy . . . servants who are gathered together in Thy Name' is a reference to Matt. xviii. 20—'Where two or three are gathered together in My (our Lord's) Name, there am I in the midst of them.' However surprising the idea of a eucharistic prayer to the Son may seem to us, it was not very unusual in antiquity. Besides the Egyptian *Liturgy of S. Gregory* and another Egyptian eucharistic prayer published by Hyvernat, there are three Ethiopic liturgies all addressed to the Son. In Syria itself the Monophysite *Second Liturgy of S. Peter* and two lesser Maronite liturgies are directed to the Son, as is *part* of the eucharistic prayer of the Syriac *S. James* itself,[1] which is followed in this by nearly all the sixty or seventy lesser Syriac liturgics. Evidently there was a strong tradition on this point in Syria generally. In the West there are distinct traces of such a custom having once been common in Mozarabic and Gallican eucharistic prayers; and the repeated condemnation of the practice by two North African councils at the end of the fourth century proves that it was not unknown there either. The fact that *SS. Addai and Mari* is addressed to the Son is thus only a proof of antiquity, and not an exceptional peculiarity.

(*a–c*) *Address, Memorial of Creation, Preface and Sanctus.* It seems fairly clear that the preface and sanctus, which have no connection with what precedes and follows, are an interpolation, and that *Addai and Mari* (like Hippolytus) originally did not contain any such feature. 'Came and cometh' in the Benedictus is found also in the Syriac *S. James*, which may give us a clue as to whence the whole passage was borrowed (*cf.* p. 188). What is more difficult to decide is the authenticity of (*a*) and (*b*). The address to the Trinity has obviously been rewritten, but Mr. Ratcliff has pointed

[1] *Cf. p.* 190 n.

out that (a) 'Worthy . . . of confession from every tongue . . . is the Name
. . . of Thy . . . Trinity' is reminiscent of Philippians ii. 9–11, where, however, 'the Name' is the Name of Christ. It seems, therefore, probable that
the interpolation of the sanctus has led to the re-writing of (a) in *Addai and
Mari* (much as we saw that it has done in Sarapion); but in *Addai and Mari*
this has been effected by the substitution of an address to the Trinity for
an older address to the Son. In this case the phrase 'Thou didst save mankind by Thy compassion' finds a natural explanation.

(d–e) *Thanksgivings for Incarnation and Redemption.* There is nothing of
much importance to be said about these clauses, except to draw attention
to the parallel with Hippolytus (c) and (d) of the memorials of the incarnation and redemption in *Addai and Mari* (d) and (e). There is also
some similarity of language between *Addai and Mari* (e) and Hippolytus
(e), but the real parallel with Hippolytus (e) in thought is in *Addai and
Mari* (i).

(f) *The Presence.* This is the first important structural difference of
*Addai and Mari* from Hippolytus. Part of what is put *after* the institution
narrative in Hippolytus (j) ('because Thou hast made us worthy to stand
before Thee') *Addai and Mari* places *before* its own equivalent to an institution narrative. We have already noted the implication of the allusion to
Matt. xviii. 20, 'Where two or three are gathered together in My Name,
*there am I in the midst of them.*' In the reference to 'standing before Thee'
in *Addai and Mari*,[1] there is probably an allusion to Luke xxi. 36—'pray
. . . that ye may be worthy . . . to stand before the Son of Man.' Behind
all this section (f) of *Addai and Mari* lies the New Testament idea of the
eucharist as an anticipation of the second coming and last judgement.
(In scriptural language to 'stand before' God has often the sense of 'to
appear for judgement'.) But it is all put by way of allusions which are
unfamiliar to us, though doubtless conveying their meaning with sufficient
clearness to those who used and framed the prayer.

(g) *The Institution. Addai and Mari* has no explicit institution narrative,
but it has an equivalent to it in this brief allusion to what happened at the
last supper. The important point to notice is that structurally it plays
precisely that pivotal part in the whole prayer which the extended narrative
plays in other prayers. It states the *authority* for performing the eucharist
and justifies the petition for communion which is about to follow. The
difference of treatment from Hippolytus and Sarapion should not be
allowed to obscure this fundamental similarity between the two types of
prayer.

(h) *Statement of the Purpose of the Eucharist* ( = Hippolytus (h) ). This
section of *Addai and Mari* in its present form has in any case been re-
written, since it suddenly refers to our Lord in the third person, instead of
addressing Him directly like the rest of the prayer. The whole connection

[1] Perhaps also in that of Hippolytus (j).

of thought between (g), (h) and (i) is very confused and difficult to follow.
Mr. Ratcliff, emphasising the parallel between 'example' in (g) and 'likeness' in (h), is disposed to omit the words 'great and fearful and holy and
life-giving and divine' in (h) as a later expansion, but to retain the rest of
(h) as an original part of the prayer. Interpreting 'the great and marvellous
dispensation' of (j) as 'the passion and death and burial and resurrection'
mentioned in (h), he would exclude (i) altogether from the original form of
the prayer. He regards its interpolation—at all events in this position—as
a later insertion made to bring *Addai and Mari* more into line with Greek
Syrian liturgies (*cf. S. James*, j¹, j², *p.* 191).

I confess that I cannot, as at present advised, quite accept this reconstruction, for a variety of reasons. First, this does not help us as regards
the sudden 'switch' in the address of the prayer from the Son to the
Father, about which Mr. Ratcliff offers no suggestion; nor does it mend the
halting construction of the whole sentence. It is impossible to be dogmatic
in such a case, but it seems to me that the real interruption to the sequence
of thought in the prayer lies precisely in this clause (h), with its sudden
wordiness and change of address, and its equally abrupt mention of the
specific events of 'the passion, death, burial and resurrection' which the
prayer has carefully avoided mentioning ·everywhere else. (*Cf. e.*) The
prayer as a whole is concerned with the eternal *effects* of redemption
mediated by the eucharist, not with the historical *process* of the achievement of redemption in time. If (h) be omitted, the grammar, sequence and
intention of the prayer become clearer. The 'example which is from Thee'
(g) then justifies the petition for communion in (i); the allusion to the last
supper (g) explains 'the oblation' of the church in (i). As we shall see, there
is a close connection of thought between (g) and (i) which would make
them complementary in any form of the prayer. I conclude, therefore, despite the acknowledged authority of Mr. Ratcliff on the history of the Syrian
liturgy, that it is (h) which is an interpolation inserted to bring *Addai and
Mari* more closely into line with Greek Syrian liturgies; and that (i) is an
integral part of the prayer in anything like its present form. Some indication of the importance of the point is that with the elimination of (h) there
disappears the only direct reference in the whole prayer to the passion and
resurrection of our Lord.

(i) *Prayer for Communion.* The interpretation of this section is technically
a somewhat delicate matter. It is natural that those scholars who accept
the theory that some petition that God would 'send' the Third Person of
the Holy Trinity to 'make' the elements the Body and Blood of Christ[1] was
an essential part of every primitive eucharistic prayer, should be disposed
to see here only one more example of what they conceive to have been the
universal primitive practice. It is equally natural that those scholars who
believe such an *epiklesis*-petition to have been a Greek invention of the

---

[1] *I.e.* the petition known as the *epiklesis*, exemplified *e.g.* in *S. James*, j¹, *p.* 191.

fourth century should be inclined to treat the whole section as a later interpolation intended to bring *Addai and Mari* into line with Greek fourth century developments.

Both ways of regarding it seem rather too simple to fit all the facts of the case. On the one hand, (*i*) is hardly an *epiklesis* at all, in that it does not actually pray for any sort of conversion of the elements, but for something quite different, namely for *the benefits of communion*. It is in fact a petition for those benefits exactly parallel to the clauses we have already found forming the essential petition of the eucharistic prayer before the doxology in Hippolytus (*k*) and in Sarapion (*e²*). On the other hand, the terms in which *Addai and Mari* frames this petition are so obviously primitive (and, I would add, so obviously un-Greek), resting as they do upon that jewish eschatological doctrine which tended to be lost to sight in gentile christianity after the second century, that one must hesitate a good deal to regard (*i*) as any sort of *late* invention. As regards its later *transference* from somewhere else in the rite to this point, this is a possibility. But we cannot eliminate this section without cutting out of the prayer as a whole every element of petition whatsoever, which is in itself an improbable form for such a prayer to take after the second-third century.

Finally, while I agree that there is no vestige of evidence in any Greek or Latin author outside Syria during the first three centuries that the Holy Ghost was recognised as playing any part whatever in the consecrating of the eucharist (which in that period is invariably ascribed to the Son), there is one Syrian piece of evidence[1] that 'Holy Spirit', in some sense, was recognised as playing some part in the consecration by Syrian churchmen during the third century, if not earlier. *Addai and Mari* is not a Greek or Latin document but a Syriac one, and it is best considered in relation to its own special background of semitic Syrian thought and altogether apart from the ideas of the Greek and Latin churches. We can therefore leave the whole controversy about the Greek *epiklesis* on one side for the moment, and consider this clause of *Addai and Mari* simply in what it says itself— 'May there come, O my Lord, Thy Holy Spirit and rest upon this oblation . . . and bless and hallow it that it be to us . . . for the pardon of offences . . . and for the great hope of resurrection from the dead and for new life in the kingdom of heaven . . .' What exactly is the meaning of '*Thy* Holy Spirit' here, in a prayer addressed to the Son?

A quotation from the standard work on jewish theological doctrine, which is remote from all suspicion of partisanship on questions of christian liturgy, will give us the clue. 'Christians speak of God's being in their churches, and of the presence of the Holy Spirit in their religious assemblies or with the individual in secret prayer, without meaning anything different. In Jewish literature also the "Holy Spirit" frequently occurs in connections in which "the Presence" (*shekinah*) is elsewhere employed

[1] *Cf. p. 278.*

without any apparent difference of usage . . .'[1] There are certain limitations to be observed in this jewish equating of 'the presence' of God with 'the spirit' of God. But it is clear that in the Old Testament 'the spirit of the Lord' which brings superhuman strength, wisdom, insight, etc., is not intended to represent a personal agent, but a force—in the older stories often almost a physical force. In general 'the spirit of the Lord' is rather a manner of conceiving of God Himself as active in a thing or person, than even a divine attribute. 'The spirit of the Lord' seems to refer particularly to God's presence as *energising* (and is therefore especially connected with the excitement of prophesying); while the much rarer term 'the holy spirit', though equally impersonal, seems to refer to God's presence as 'brooding' or 'resting' on a thing or person, like 'the cloud' of the *shekinah* resting upon the Mercy Seat. Thus in a well-known verse of the fifty-first Psalm, 'Cast me not away from *Thy presence*' is equated with 'Take not *Thy holy spirit* from me'. In the Mishnah there is a tale of a gathering of rabbis at Jamnia, at which a mysterious voice was heard saying, 'There is here a man who is worthy that the holy spirit should rest upon him, but that his generation is not worthy'. The Talmud in telling the same story substitutes 'the presence' (*shekinah*) for 'the holy spirit', apparently with no consciousness that it is making any change. Cases are even known in which different MSS. of the same jewish work use the terms *shekinah* (presence) and *ruḥ-hakodesh* (holy spirit) indifferently in copying the same sentence.

Nor was this conception of 'holy spirit' as virtually meaning the 'presence of God with power' confined to judaism. Without entering here into obvious cases of its appearance in early christian writers, it is enough to point out that it was taken up into the usage of the jews who wrote the christian New Testament. Thus S. Paul can say of the risen and glorified Lord in heaven now 'energising' on earth through His members, 'The Lord is that Spirit'.[2] And a modern New Testament scholar can sum up a discussion of the Pauline doctrine of the Mystical Body with the words: 'The Spirit is the element or power whereby the glorified Body or Person of Jesus *is present* to us and inflows upon us.'[3]

If we may take it that in the very archaic prayer of *Addai and Mari* the words '*Thy* holy spirit' applied to the Son are to be understood as the virtual equivalent of 'Thy presence' or 'the power whereby Thy glorified Body is present to us', in the fashion of the Old and New Testament writers, the whole construction and meaning of the petition become perfectly clear and straightforward. The prayer is addressed to the Son, Who is reminded of His own 'example' given at the last supper. 'May Thy glorified Body or Person come upon this oblation of Thy servants to bless and hallow it that it may be to us *the means of sharing here and now in Thy glorified life*'. Such at least seems to be the only reasonable interpretation

---

[1] A. F. Moore, *Judaism*, I. *p.* 437. (*Cf.* III. *n.* 167, *p.* 134.)     [2] 2 Cor. iii. 17.
[3] G. M. Farrer in *The Parish Communion*, *p.* 80 (italics mine).

of the actual things for which the petition as it stands makes request. I venture to think that this is not a 'later' but a very early conception indeed of the results of receiving holy communion, exactly in line with that conception of the whole eucharist as an anticipation of the second coming of our Lord which began to die out in most churches before the end of the third century, or even earlier.

Two small points remain to be noted. First, it may be asked why a petition for the 'coming' of our Lord—the Word—in (e.g.) Sarapion should be a later development of the prayer, while in *Addai and Mari* it seems to be an integral part of the structure. Development varied from church to church, but I think we can see one reason in this case in the different form of reference to the last supper in the two prayers. In Sarapion, as in Hippolytus, the quotation of our Lord's words of institution *sufficed to identify* the church's bread and wine with the Body and Blood of our Lord's promise, by their actual recitation—'This bread is the likeness of the Body *because* the Lord Jesus took bread saying . . . This is My Body . . .', as Sarapion puts it. But where, as in *Addai and Mari*, the reference to what took place at the last supper was in the form of a mere allusion, there was needed further verbal expression of the identification of the church's offering with what our Lord Himself had pronounced it to be. This is expressed by *Addai and Mari* in its usual allusive style by the prayer addressed to the Son, 'May there come, O my Lord, Thy presence upon this oblation of Thy servants.' Some such petition would be felt to be necessary in eucharistic prayers upon this particular Syrian model from a very early date, in a way not so pressingly felt where an institution *narrative* could be understood to supply the identification.

Secondly, all that Hippolytus expresses about the nature of the eucharist by calling it the 'priestly ministry' of the church, and Sarapion expresses by calling it a reconciling 'sacrifice' and by 'offering the likeness' of the Body and Blood, is expressed in *Addai and Mari* by the one word, 'this *oblation* of Thy servants', which from the context is clearly the bread and the cup. For all its great differences of form and arrangement *Addai and Mari* witnesses quite sufficiently to the one universal interpretation of the eucharist as sacrifice, even though the hellenistic liturgies have developed this idea more explicitly, as *Addai and Mari* in turn develops other aspects (*e.g.* the second coming) which these leave in the background.

(*j*) *The Doxology*. Here again an attempt has been made to redirect the prayer to the Father, by the insertion of the words 'of Thy Christ'. But we have already learned from (*f*) that 'Thy Name' in which the communicants are 'gathered', and which in (*j*) is 'glorified', is the Name of Jesus, so that the interpolation is obvious. The doxology here is not an ascription of praise to the Three Persons of the Trinity—nothing so theological! It is simply a 'glorifying of the Name' in the old jewish fashion, and a remarkably beautiful one. We may compare it with the very ancient (possibly pre-christian) jewish prayer known as '*Half-Kaddish*' which in the synagogue ritual marks off the close of separate parts of the service: 'Magnified and hallowed be His great Name in the world which He created according to His will. May He establish His Kingdom in your lifetime and in your days, and in the lifetime of all the house of Israel speedily and in a near time. May His great Name be blessed for ever and to all eternity.' In *Addai and Mari* the world *has been* 're-created' by the precious Blood, and the Kingdom *has been* established; the communicants are within it even in this world and they already bless and magnify 'the living and life-giving Name' of Jesus for evermore in 'new life in the kingdom of heaven with' all the saints, for 'the great and marvellous dispensation' of redemption. The eucharist itself is here the direct fulfilment of the old jewish eschatological hope.

*Addai and Mari* is obviously peculiar among eucharistic prayers, both in its subtle allusiveness to so much in the New Testament background of the eucharist which other early prayers leave undeveloped, and in its strange ignoring of elements which they explicitly state. To come upon a eucharistic prayer which from beginning to end in its original form has no mention of God the Father or of the Holy Trinity, of the passion of our Saviour or His resurrection, which does not so much as use the words 'bread' and 'wine' or 'cup', or 'Body' and 'Blood', or speak the Name of 'Jesus' is in itself remarkable. No less unusual is the omission of any explicit mention of 'partaking' or 'communion'. All these things are no doubt latent there and taken for granted; but they are not of the framework of this prayer, as they are of the framework of prayers that have been inspired by the systematic Greek theological tradition. *Addai and Mari* is a eucharistic prayer which is concentrated solely upon the *experience* of the eucharist, to the momentary ignoring of all other elements in christian belief and thought. *Maranatha!* 'Our Lord, come!' (or perhaps 'has come'), the ecstatic cry of the first pre-Pauline aramaic-speaking disciples, is the summary of what it has to say.

These things need to be taken into account in estimating the age of this prayer, for the substance of which the later second or early third century hardly seems too early a date. However that may be, it is obviously archaic enough in form and feeling to be comparable with the prayer of Hippolytus from the opposite end of the christian world and the opposite pole of christian thought. It is not only in their contents that the two prayers form a contrast, so that what each develops and insists upon the other leaves unsaid or barely hinted at. It is in their whole background of thought and genius that they are different. Hippolytus, for all the relics of old jewish form, is thoroughly hellenic in its attempt to frame its statement of the essential meaning of the eucharist in rational relation to the whole christian revelation. *Addai and Mari* is equally semitic in the intensity of its absorption in the eucharistic experience, and in its concentration upon eschatology to the exclusion of philosophising.

But when one has recognised the great differences not only of structure but of mentality which lie behind them, and which demonstrate their wholly independent history, the underlying agreements are the more striking. One need only refer back to the three points we noted as distinctive of the substance of Hippolytus' prayer to see at once that they are found, perhaps with a different emphasis, but unmistakeably the same points, in this wholly different semitic tradition. (1) The institution at the last supper is central in the construction of the prayer, as the *authority* for what the church does in the eucharist. The difference in the fulness of reference between the two prayers does not in the least affect the pivotal nature of the reference in both cases. (2) The essence of the eucharist—what the church does in the eucharist—is the *oblation* of the bread and the cup. This is identified with the Lord's Body and Blood by His own promise and command, to which *Addai and Mari* makes a bare but sufficient allusion in the reference to 'the example which is from Thee.' (3) The whole rite 'recalls' before our Lord, not the last supper, but the redemption He has wrought for mankind, and makes this present and operative by its effects in the communicants.

In *Addai and Mari*, by contrast with Hippolytus, the emphasis is not on the historical process of redemption by the passion and resurrection, but on its eternal results. That is ultimately the great difference of idea between them; and even this idea, which is emphasised in *Addai and Mari*, is found in a subordinate position in Hippolytus (*e*).

### The Liturgy of S. James

We have already spoken of the history of this rite, of which the present text both in Greek and Syriac descends from an Antiochene (? early fifth century) edition and expansion of the fourth century rite of Jerusalem. This older Jerusalem form is known to us only from the account of it given by S. Cyril of Jerusalem to the newly confirmed, who had just attended it for the first time, in Easter week A.D. 348. The Greek *S. James* will be cited as Jg and the Syriac as Js, and the summary by S. Cyril as C. In the original the passages of C which we reproduce here are absolutely continuous (*Catechesis*, xxiii. 5–11), though they have to be broken up here in order to relate them to the text of Jg and Js, which has been expanded after S. Cyril's time. Jg and Js have been revised independently of each other, now one, now the other representing a better text. I follow as a rule Jg, for convenience, noting only some of the variants of Js. Words between † . . . † are not in Js. Matter underlined in Jg is derived from C.

*Jg (and Js)*

**Preface and Sanctus. (a)**

*People:* It is meet and right.

*Priest:* Truly is it meet and right, fitting and our bounden duty to praise Thee, to hymn Thee, to bless Thee, to worship Thee, to glorify Thee, to give thanks unto Thee, Maker of all things visible and invisible, †the treasury of eternal good, the source of life and immortality, the God and Lord of all,† Whom the heavens praise and the heaven of heavens and all the power thereof, the sun and moon and all the choir of the stars, earth, sea and all that in them is, †the assembly of the heavenly Jerusalem, the church of the first-born whose names are written in the heavens, the spirits of the righteous and prophets, the souls of the martyrs and apostles,† angels, archangels, thrones, dominations, principalities, virtues—dread powers, Cherubim with many eyes and the six-winged Seraphim who with two wings cover their faces and with two their feet and with two they fly, and cry one to the other with ceaseless voices and unsilenced praising the hymn of victory of Thine excellent glory, with clear voice singing and shouting, glorifying and crying and saying:

*People:* Holy, holy, holy, Lord of Sabaoth

Full is the heaven and the earth of Thy glory.

Hosanna in the highest.

Blessed is He that [*Js adds* came and] cometh in the Name of the Lord!

Hosanna in the highest.

*C xxiii. 5–6*

5. 'Next you say, It is meet and right. For when we make eucharist (*i.e.* give thanks) we do a thing which is meet and right. For He doing not what was meet but above what was meet gave us free benefits and made us worthy of such good things.

6. 'Then we make mention of the heaven and the earth and the sea, of the sun and moon, the stars and all creation rational and irrational, visible and invisible; angels, archangels, powers, principalities, virtues, dominations, thrones, cherubim with many faces, as though we said with David 'O magnify the Lord with me' [Ps. xxxiv. 3]. We also make mention of the Seraphim, whom Isaiah in the Holy Spirit saw standing around the throne of God, with two wings covering the Face [*i.e. of God*] and with two the Feet and saying, Holy, holy, holy, Lord of Sabaoth. For therefore do we say this praise of God which we have been taught by the Seraphim, that we may become partakers in the praises of the armies of the heavens.'

*Address.* (*b*) *Priest:* Holy art Thou, O King of the ages and Lord and giver of all holiness; and holy is Thine only-begotten Son our Lord Jesus Christ, by Whom Thou madest all things; and holy is Thine all-holy Spirit, Who searcheth all things, even the deep things of God;

*Memorial of Creation.* (*c*) Holy art Thou, ruler of all things, almighty, good, awful, merciful, most chiefly shewing pity for the work of Thy hands, Who didst make man from the earth in Thine own image and likeness,

*Memorial of Fall and O.T.* (*d*) Who didst bestow freely upon him the delight of paradise, and when he transgressed Thy command and fell from thence, Thou didst not despise nor forsake him in Thy goodness, but didst chasten him as a merciful father; Thou didst call him by the law and instruct him by the prophets;

*Memorial of Incarnation.* (*e*) Lastly Thou didst send Thine only-begotten Son our Lord Jesus Christ into the world that He might by His coming renew and raise up Thine image ⟨in mankind⟩. Who coming down from heaven and being incarnate of ⟨the⟩ Holy Ghost and Mary the Virgin Mother of God, lived among men and wrought all things for the salvation of our race.

*of Passion.* (*f*) And being about to accept His willing and life-giving death by the cross, sinless on behalf of us sinners,

*of Institution.* (*g*) In that night in which He was betrayed, or rather gave Himself up for the life and salvation of the world, took the bread into His holy and undefiled and blameless and immortal hands, and looking up to heaven and showing it to Thee His God and Father, gave thanks and hallowed and broke and gave it to His holy disciples and apostles, saying:

[*The deaconsclaim:*    For the remission of sins and for life eternal]

Take, eat; This is My Body Which is broken for you and given for the remission of sins.

[*The people:* Amen.]

Likewise after supper He took the cup and mixed it of wine and water, and looked up to heaven, and showed it to Thee His God and Father, and gave thanks and hallowed and blessed and filled it with holy spirit and gave to His holy and blessed disciples saying:

Drink ye all of it: This is My Blood of the New Covenant Which is shed for you and for many and given [*lit.* shared out] for the remission of sins.

[*The people*: Amen.]

Do this for My *anamnesis* ; for as oft as ye do eat this bread and drink this cup, ye do proclaim the death of the Son of Man and confess His resurrection till He come.

[*The deacons:* We believe and confess.

*The people:* Thy death, Lord, we proclaim and Thy resurrection we confess.]

*Anamnesis.* (*h*) [1]And we sinners making the *anamnesis* of His life-giving sufferings, His †saving cross and† death and †burial and† resurrection on the third day from the dead and session at the right hand of Thee, His God and Father, and His second glorious and fearful coming, when He shall come to judge the living and the dead, when He shall reward every man according to his works—spare us, O Lord, our God—or rather according to His own pitifulness,

*First Offering of Sacrifice and Prayer for Communion.* (*i*) we offer unto Thee, O Lord, this fearful and unbloody sacrifice, beseeching Thee tha. Thou deal not with

[1] Js has in this passage 'Making the *anamnesis* therefore O Lord of Thy death and Thy resurrection on the third day from the dead', and so addresses the prayer to the Second, not the First Person of the Trinity, down to the beginning of (*j*[1]).

us after our sins nor reward us after our iniquities, but according to Thy leniency and Thine unspeakable love towards mankind overlook and blot out the handwriting that is against us Thy suppliants; and of Thy free grace bestow on us Thy heavenly and eternal gifts that eye hath not seen nor ear hath heard nor hath it entered into the heart of man ⟨to conceive⟩, but which Thou hast prepared, O God, for them that love Thee; †and cast not away Thy people because of me and my sins, O Lord Thou lover of men†; for Thy people and Thy church entreat Thee.

[*The people:* Have mercy upon us, O Lord God the Father almighty.]

*1st Invocation.* (*j*¹) Have mercy upon us, O God almighty, †have mercy upon us, O God our Saviour, have mercy upon us, O God, after Thy great mercy† and send forth upon us and upon these gifts that lie before Thee Thine all-holy Spirit, the Lord and life-giver; that shareth Thy throne with Thee, O God and Father, and with Thine only-begotten Son; that reigneth with Thee, of one substance and co-eternal; that spake in the law and in the prophets and Thy New Testament; that came down in the likeness of a dove upon our Lord Jesus Christ in the river Jordan and remained upon Him; that came down upon Thine holy apostles in the likeness of fiery tongues †in the upper room of the holy and glorious Sion in the day of holy Pentecost.†

*2nd Invocation.* (*j*²) Send down, O Lord, upon us and upon these gifts that lie before Thee Thy self-same Spirit the all-holy that hovering with His holy and good and glorious coming He may hallow and make this bread the holy Body of

*C xxiii.* 7–11

7. 'Next, having sanctified ourselves with these spiritual hymns, we entreat God that loveth mankind to send forth the Holy Spirit upon the gifts that lie before ⟨Him⟩—[*The Holy Ghost elsewhere in C is described as:* 'Who came down upon the Lord Jesus Christ in the likeness of a dove, Who energised in the law and the prophets' (*Cat.* iv. 16); *and as:* 'The Holy Ghost, Who spake in the prophets, and at Pentecost came down upon the apostles in the likeness of fiery tongues here in Jerusalem in the church of the apostles on the hill' (*Cat.* xvi. 4).]

—that He may make the bread the Body of Christ, and the wine the Blood of Christ.

Christ [*The people:* Amen.] and this cup the precious Blood of Christ [*The people:* Amen.]

*2nd Prayer for Communion.* (*k*) that they may be unto all that partake of them for the forgiveness of sins and for eternal life, unto the hallowing of souls and bodies, unto fruitfulness in good works, unto the establishment of Thy holy catholic and apostolic church which Thou hast founded upon the rock of the faith that the gates of hell should not prevail against it, delivering it from all heresy and scandals of them that work iniquity, preserving it until the end of time;

*2nd Offering of Sacrifice.* (*l*) We offer unto Thee, O Lord [*Js adds:*] this same fearful and unbloody sacrifice

*Intercessions.* (*m¹*) on behalf of Thy holy places, which Thou hast glorified by the epiphany of Thy Christ and the visitation of Thine all-holy Spirit, and chiefly for the holy and glorious Sion the mother of all churches, and for Thy holy catholic and apostolic church throughout all the world; do Thou now bestow upon her, O Lord, the rich gifts of Thine all-holy Spirit.

(*m²*) Remember, O Lord, especially within her our holy fathers and bishops throughout the world, rightly dividing in orthodoxy the word of Thy truth.

(*m³*) Remember, O Lord, according to the abundance of Thy mercy and Thy pity me also Thy humble and unprofitable servant and the deacons that stand around Thy holy altar and grant unto them a blameless life, preserve unblemished their diaconate and make them worthy of a good degree.

(*m⁴*) Remember, O Lord, the holy and royal city of God (*i.e.* Antioch) and

For whatever comes in contact with the Holy Ghost is hallowed and transformed.

8. Next, after the completion of the spiritual sacrifice, the unbloody worship,

over this sacrifice of propitiation we entreat God for the common peace of the churches;

for the good ordering of the world;

every city and region and them of the orthodox faith that dwell therein, ⟨remember⟩ their peace and safety.

($m^5$) Remember, O Lord, our most pious and Christ-loving emperors, the pious and Christ-loving empress, all their servants and armies, and ⟨grant them⟩ help and victory from heaven; lay hold upon shield and buckler and stand up to help them [*Jg adds from the Byzantine rite:* †subdue unto them all the warlike and savage peoples that delight in war; convert their minds, that we may pass a peaceable and quiet life in all piety and godliness.

($m^6$) Remember, O Lord, them that travel by sea and by land, and christians that sojourn in strange countries; those of our fathers and brethren that are in bondage and in prisons, in captivity or exile, in the mines, in torture or in bitter slavery†]—

($m^7$) Remember, O Lord, them that are diseased and sick and them that are possessed by evil spirits and speedily help and deliver them, O God.

($m^8$) Remember, O Lord, every christian soul that is afflicted and distressed, and that needeth Thy mercy and help, O God; and convert them that are in error.

($m^9$) †Remember, O Lord, those of our fathers and brethren that labour, and serve us for Thy holy Name's sake.

Remember, O Lord, all men for good, have mercy upon all, O Lord, and be reconciled unto us all.†

[*Jg here inserts a Byzantine interpolation, and then resumes its own text with:*]

($m^{10}$) Vouchsafe also to remember, O Lord, all them that have been pleasing unto Thee from the beginning of time in

for the emperors; for the army and the allies;

for them that are sick;

for them that are afflicted; and, in a word, for all that are in need of help we all ought to offer this sacrifice.

9. Next, we call to remembrance all them that have fallen asleep before us; and

their several generations, our holy fathers, the patriarchs and prophets, apostles and martyrs

first the patriarchs, prophets, apostles and martyrs,

(*m*[10a]) [(*The following passage is introduced from the Byzantine liturgy*) confessors and holy teachers, and every righteous soul perfected in the faith of Thy Christ. (*The following is not Byzantine, but interpolated:*) Hail, full of grace, the Lord is with thee; blessed art thou among women and blessed is the fruit of thy womb, because thou didst bring forth the Saviour of our souls.

(*Byzantine:*) Chiefly our all-holy, undefiled and blessed-above-all, the ever-virgin Lady Mary the Mother of God; saint John, the glorious prophet forerunner and baptist—(*The following is not Byzantine, but is not found in Js, and is taken from the Jerusalem diptychs*) †the holy apostles Peter and Paul, Andrew, James, John, Philip, Bartholomew, Thomas, Thaddaeus, Matthew, James, Simon, Jude, Matthias; Mark and Luke the evangelists; the holy prophets, patriarchs and righteous; saint Stephen, first of deacons and first of martyrs; and all Thy holy saints from the foundation of the world.† (*The original text of Jg resumes thus*):—]

(*m*[10] *continued*) not that we are worthy to make mention of their blessedness, but that they too, standing beside Thy fearful and dreadful judgment seat may in their turn make mention of our wretchedness, and we may find grace and mercy before Thee, O Lord, for succour in our time of need.

that God by their prayers and intercessions would receive our supplications.

(*m*[11]) [*Js only*] Remember also, O Lord, our holy bishops who have gone to their rest aforetime, who interpreted for us the word of truth, who from James the

Next, also for our holy fathers and bishops that have fallen asleep before us archbishop and apostle and martyr even to this day have preached to us the orthodox word of truth in Thine holy church . .

[*Jg and Js*] Remember, also, O Lord the God of the spirits of all flesh, them that we remembered and them we have not remembered of the orthodox †from righteous Abel unto this very day.† Do Thou Thyself refresh them †in the land of the living, in Thy kingdom, in the joy of paradise† in the bosoms of Abraham and Isaac and Jacob our holy fathers, whence pain and grief and tribulation have fled away, where the light of Thy countenance surveyeth all things and shineth perpetually.

(*m*¹²) [*Jg only, Byzantine:* †And grant us to make a christian end and to please Thee, and direct our lives without sin and in peace, O Lord, Lord; and gather us together under the feet of Thine elect when Thou wilt and as Thou wilt, only that it be without shame and without iniquity.†]

*Prayer for Pardon.* (*n*) Through Thy only-begotten Son, our Lord and God and Saviour Jesus Christ; for He alone has appeared upon earth without sin, through Whom both to us and to them in Thy goodness and love of mankind. [*The people:* remit, forgive, pardon, O God, our offences, voluntary and involuntary, those we know and those we know not of,] by the grace and pitifulness and love of mankind of Thy only-begotten Son;

and in a word of all who have fallen asleep among us, believing that this is the greatest aid to their souls, for whom the entreaty is made in the presence of the holy and most dread sacrifice.

10. And I want to convince you of this by an example. For I know many people say: If a man leave this world in sin, what is the good of remembering him in the prayer? But, truly, if a king were to banish men with whom he was angry, and then those who were not like them were to make a crown and offer it to him on behalf of those who were being punished, would he not grant them some relaxation of the punishment? In the same way, we offering prayers to God for the dead, though they were sinners, do not make a crown, but we offer Christ sacrificed for our sins, propitiating God that loveth mankind on their behalf as well as on our own.

*Doxology.* (*o*) With Whom blessed be Thou and glorified with Thine all-holy and good and life-giving Spirit, now and for ever and world without end. [*The people:* Amen.]

[*Js substitutes this doxology:* that in this as in all things Thine all-honoured and blessed Name may be glorified and magnified, with the Name of our Lord Jesus Christ and Thine Holy Spirit, now and ever and world without end—*which is a* '*glorifying of the Name*'. Cf. *Addai and Mari* p. 180.]

(*p*) *Priest:* Make us worthy, O Lord that lovest mankind, with freedom and without condemnation, <u>with a clean heart, with soul enlightened and with un-</u>ashamed face and holy lips, <u>to dare to call upon Thee, our holy God and Father in</u> heaven and to say: Our Father . . .

11. Next, after these things we say that prayer which the Saviour taught His own disciples, and with a clean conscience we call upon God our Father, saying, Our Father . . .

After our discussion of the contents of the prayers previously considered there is no need to comment closely on *S. James.* The reader will be able to see for himself just how fully and yet how independently (*g*) (*h*) and (*i*) in *S. James* once more illustrate those three points which we originally noted from the prayer of Hippolytus as containing the essential statement of the meaning of the whole eucharistic action.

But this is in *S. James* as it is given here, which is substantially a fifth century edition. There are obviously problems concerning the relation of this to (1) the summary of the rite of Jerusalem given by S. Cyril in his *Catecheses, c.* A.D. 350, and (2) the old fourth century rite of Antioch. A full discussion of these problems would involve entering into technical questions of the greatest interest to a specialist but not essential to the purposes of the general reader, and involving many complications. It seems better therefore only to point out quite cursorily some indications of the history underlying the present text of *S. James.*

### The Rite of Jerusalem in the Fourth Century

S. Cyril's summary of the eucharistic prayer opens with a preface of which the greater part is recognisable in *S. James* (*a*), taken over verbally into its text. There is a curious detail, however, in Cyril's phrasing which is *not* taken over by *S. James,* but which suggests that the Jerusalem preface was originally borrowed from the Egyptian tradition of Alexandria (where the use of the preface and sanctus was probably first developed). The third century Alexandrian writer Origen in treating of the two seraphim in Isaiah vi., in close connection with the eucharistic preface and sanctus, makes it clear that he interprets Isaiah vi. 2 as meaning that the two seraphim 'had each six wings; with twain he covered the Face *of God* and with twain he covered the Feet *of God* and with twain the seraph (itself) did fly'.[1] Accordingly we find the seraphim in Sarapion's preface (Sar. *b*[1]), 'With two wings covering *the* Face' (*to prosōpon*), *i.e.* of God. By the time of S. Athanasius the Alexandrian church had altered this to the usual later form, '*their* faces' (*ta prosōpa*), as we find in the text of S. *James*, and as is attested at Antioch in the later fourth century by S. Chrysostom.[2] But Cyril of Jerusalem, like Sarapion, still keeps to the third century Egyptian interpretation, a sign of the quarter from which the Jerusalem rite had originally borrowed the use of the preface and sanctus.

After the sanctus comes the great puzzle in Cyril's account of his eucharistic prayer. 'Next (*eita*), having sanctified ourselves with these spiritual hymns (*i.e.* the sanctus), we entreat God to send forth the Holy Spirit . . .' Is it really possible that in the Jerusalem rite the invocation of the Spirit followed *immediately* after the sanctus, with no thanksgiving for creation, incarnation and passion, no narrative of the institution or *anamnesis* clause, or anything else, between? That is what he appears to say, but the statement has appeared so improbable to successive commentators and liturgists that they have all tried hard to make him say something else. So, *e.g.*, Brightman:[3] Cyril 'is only expounding the salient points of the rite, and for the purposes of his exposition the whole passage between the sanctus and the intercession would be a single paragraph with the form of invocation for its essential point.' He then goes on to try to find passages elsewhere in Cyril's writings which 'may be assumed to represent the contents of the (missing) paragraph.'

I confess I am sceptical of such methods of dealing with a writer who elsewhere shews himself so faithful a summariser. Brightman fails to find a single phrase other than scriptural quotations common to Cyril and that part of the text of S. *James* which we here label (*b–i*). One observes, too, that 'next' (*eita*) is one of Cyril's habitual transitions, and that it invariably means with him what it says—'next'. Thus (xxiii. 4 and 5), after commenting on 'Lift up your hearts' and 'We have them with the Lord', Cyril says, '*Next*, the priest says "Let us give thanks unto the Lord" . . .' (and after a comment on this) . . . '*Next*, you say "It is meet and right".' So in his account of the eucharistic prayer (*p.* 192), '*Next*, after the completion of the . . . sacrifice, we entreat etc. . . .', where the intercessions do actually come 'next' in the text of S. *James*. '*Next* we call to remembrance all them

[1] Origen, *de Principiis*, iv. 3. 14.   [2] *de Poenitentia*, ix. 1.
[3] L. E. W., *p.* 469.

that have fallen asleep', where there is good evidence that the clause commemorating the saints did come 'next' to the petition 'for all that are in
need'; and so on. Everywhere else in *Catechesis* xxiii. when Cyril seems to
omit even a few words of the rite from his commentary he appears to
insert not 'next' (*eita*) but 'after this' (*meta tauta*) before resuming his
summary. I find it difficult to assume that in this one case by 'next' Cyril
meant 'After a great part of the prayer has been said.' And if he did mean
that, why associate the invocation so closely with the sanctus: 'Next, *having
sanctified ourselves with these spiritual hymns*, we call upon God, etc. . . .'?
He is going through the contents of the prayer for the benefit of those who
have just attended the eucharist for the first time in their lives, for whom
such skipping about would be quite unnecessarily confusing. On the whole
it seems much more likely that Cyril means what he says, and that the
invocation in the fourth century Jerusalem rite followed immediately upon
the sanctus, however unexpected such an arrangement may be to us, with
our modern presuppositions as to the 'proper' arrangement of a consecration prayer.

This invocation is of a type we have not hitherto met. There is no room
here for the old Syrian equivalence of 'spirit' with 'presence'. What is
intended is unmistakably a prayer for the descent of the Holy Ghost, the
Third Person of the Holy Trinity, as at Pentecost. Whether the elaboration
on the office of the Holy Ghost now found in (*j*[1]) of *S. James* stood in
Cyril's rite or not,[1] his sixteenth and eighteenth *Catecheses* make it clear
that he held the doctrine of the full Personality and Godhead of the Holy
Ghost with a precision and clarity not very common among his contemporaries. (The Godhead and consubstantiality of the Third Person of the
Trinity were authoritatively promulgated only in A.D. 381 by the Council
of Constantinople, after more than a generation of controversy and confusion on the matter.)

Not only is the invocation itself in Cyril given a precision of address
which is lacking in that of *Addai and Mari* (*i*), but the petition which follows in Cyril—'that He may *make the bread the Body of Christ*,' etc.—has
been given a different turn to that of the old Syrian invocation in *Addai and
Mari*, 'that He may bless and hallow it, that it may be to us for the pardon
of offences', etc., which is really a prayer for the *benefits* of communion.
That of Cyril is a prayer for the *means* of communion. In Cyril a new idea,
that of the 'transformation' or 'conversion' of the elements, finds clear
liturgical expression.

This is not wholly a revolution. Second century writers like Justin,
Irenaeus and Hippolytus could write that 'the food which has been made
eucharist *is* the Flesh and Blood of that Jesus Who was made Flesh';[2] the

---

[1] I should suggest that it did not. The passages from his fourth and sixteenth
*Catecheses*, which offer somewhat similar material, could quite as well be due to an
independent use of scripture as to reminiscences of liturgical phraseology.
[2] Justin, *Ap.* I. 66.

reserved sacrament 'is the Body of Christ',[1] 'the cup and the bread receive the Word of God and *become* the Body and Blood of Christ'.[2] But there is a real step, even if it be an inevitable one at some point or another, from such language to the formulation of a theological theory as to *how* the identification of bread with Body, wine with Blood comes to be—a theory about 'the effects of consecration'. And that step is taken for the first time in the fourth century, and among extant writers for the first time explicitly by S. Cyril of Jerusalem.

It is true that the idea of such a petition is at least half developed in the eucharistic prayer of his older contemporary, Sarapion: 'O God of truth, let Thy holy Word come upon this bread *that the bread may become* Body of the Word . . .' The idea of the necessity or desirability of such a petition was 'in the air', as we say, in the first half of the fourth century, perhaps in some circles in the third century. But Sarapion's language is still linked with older ideas (*cf.* Irenaeus, 'The cup and the bread receive the *Word* of God'). This is, one might say, the product of 'popular' rather than 'scientific' theological reflection upon the mystery of the eucharist—that the Word Himself, the Second Person of the Blessed Trinity, Whom the communicant receives in communion, should be invoked to 'come upon' the elements (in some sense), as He took to Himself the Body formed in the womb of Mary. But Cyril gives clear-cut expression in his liturgy to a different theological theory, which is more evidently a product of the schools: 'to send forth the Holy Spirit that He may make the bread the Body of Christ . . . for whatsoever comes in contact with the Holy Spirit is hallowed and transformed.' After that the way is clear, on the one hand for the development of the idea of a 'moment of consecration', and for the Eastern identification of that 'moment' with the invocation—in Cyril's rite no other possibility could suggest itself—and on the other for a clearer definition of doctrines of 'conversion' or 'transformation' of the elements, issuing ultimately, by a process of selection, in a particular metaphysical explanation—transubstantiation.

After the invocation Cyril's rite appears to 'complete the sacrifice' (in his own phrase) by an act of offering, as found in the text of S. *James* (*l*). It then proceeds to the intercessions, on the ground that 'this is the greatest aid to their souls, for whom the entreaty is made *in the presence of the holy and most dread sacrifice.*' Once more here is a novelty, or rather two novelties. The idea of the special efficacy of prayer in the presence of the Blessed Sacrament (developed long afterwards in the Teutonic countries of the West in such practices as 'Exposition') is here revealed as an originally Eastern notion. So far as I know nothing similar had been said by any author before Cyril. From at least the later second century it had been customary everywhere to offer the sacrifice for particular objects, but the

[1] Hippolytus, *Ap. Trad.*, xxxii. 2.
[2] Irenaeus, *adv. Haer.*, iv. 18. 4.

matter had not been further defined. Once again there is not exactly any-thing wholly revolutionary in what Cyril says, but again there is a logical and (to my mind) a theological step in the process of developing an accepted practice into a theological theory. And again Cyril is the first whom we know to have taken that step.

The other novelty lies in the use of the word 'most dread' (*phrikodestatos* = literally, 'what makes one's hair stand on end') of the consecrated sacra-ment. This 'language of fear', which Cyril uses in one or two other places, is unexampled in any previous writer treating of the eucharist. Scrupulous care against accidents to the sacrament had been insisted on by earlier writers;[1] they emphasise on occasion that we should 'fear' to make an unworthy communion.[2] But they suggest nothing corresponding to 'fear' or 'dread' of the consecrated sacrament as such. This idea of the 'awfulness' of the sacrament, however, soon became a commonplace with Syrian writers (notably Chrysostom) from whom it passed into the Eastern litur-gies, though it never took much hold in the West. Again Cyril stands out as the representative of an innovation destined to a long future, not wholly out of connection with the past, but distinctly something new. When we add that Cyril is the first writer to mention the commemoration of saints in the eucharistic prayer (and he has a theological theory about that, too) we begin to understand the sort of man and the sort of rite in the sort of church we are dealing with. The church of Jerusalem in the fourth century is 'very advanced' and S. Cyril is 'a very extreme man', with no over-whelming reverence for old-fashioned churchmanship.

Is such a prayer as his summary seems to describe—preface and sanctus, followed at once by a consecratory invocation, offering, intercessions and Lord's prayer—a possibility? Or must we believe with the older liturgists that Cyril's summary omits without trace half the contents of his eucharis-tic prayer? The reader has the whole of the textual evidence before him. For my own part I believe that he means what he says and has adequately described the whole of his rite.

If so, can we see how such a rite, of so unexpected a form, could come into existence? What has happened to the old 'thanksgiving' section which opened the traditional form of the prayer in other churches?

We have already seen that the introduction of the preface and sanctus from Alexandria had in effect destroyed the 'thanksgiving' opening in Sarapion's prayer at Thmuis. The introduction of the preface and sanctus has done the same thing in the present Roman canon. Sarapion's prayer has filled up its place with its theological hymn ($a^1$ and $a^2$) and its prayer about 'the living sacrifice' (*c*). It seems entirely possible that the introduc-tion of the Alexandrian preface and sanctus at Jerusalem should have had

[1] Tertullian, *de Corona* 3; Hippolytus, *Ap. Trad.*, xxxii. 2, 3; Origen, *in Exod. Hom.*, xiii. 3.
[2] E.g. Origen *in Psalm* xxxvii; *Hom.*, ii. 6.

the same sort of result as at Thmuis, but that there the gap was not filled up at all, as it was not filled up at Rome.

But, it may be said, at Thmuis and at Rome the disuse of the 'thanksgiving' section still left intact the institution-narrative and what followed. Why are these missing, along with the 'thanksgiving', at Jerusalem? There was in any case no stereotyped line of development in the different churches in the course of such changes; but a particular answer suggests itself in this case. At Rome and Thmuis the reference to the last supper formed a considerable part of the prayer—a *narrative*. In Syria, if *Addai and Mari* be any guide, it was a mere *allusion* to the last supper, which, however pivotal in the structure of the prayer, was from the first supplemented with some sort of petition. Such an allusion *could* be dropped more easily than a full narrative in the course of an extensive alteration of the traditional prayer, provided that the petition to which it pointed was retained and elaborated in such a way so as to include somehow the allusion to the last supper.

This seems to be roughly what has happened at Jerusalem. If we look back at *Addai and Mari* for a moment (*p.* 179), after the allusion to the last supper as 'the example', there comes the petition (*i*) for 'holy spirit' (*i.e.* 'presence') with the 'offering' of the elements (in the phrase 'this oblation of thy servants'). This issues into the petition 'to bless and hallow it', developing into a prayer for the benefits of communion ('that it may be to us for the pardon of offences,' etc.). If we look at Cyril's rite now, it seems that the invocation has been rephrased so as to include *the force of both* the reference to the last supper *and* the vague invocation of 'holy spirit' on 'the oblation'. The change of the petition from 'bless and hallow it that it may be to us for the forgiveness of sins and eternal life', to the exact theological notion 'that the Holy Ghost may make the bread the Body of Christ' etc. does recall the last supper by its terms (bread, Body, wine, Blood) in a way that the petition in *Addai and Mari* (*i*) fails to do. The offering of the sacrifice in the brief phrase of *Addai and Mari*, 'this oblation', has been made more explicit in Cyril; and the prayer for the communicants has become Cyril's unprecedentedly developed intercessions.

I feel bound to point out that the last three paragraphs are in themselves mere speculation, as no other page in this book is speculative. Yet I think it may be claimed that these are 'scientific' speculations about facts, in the sense that though we are not able to make a connection between *ascertained* earlier facts about the third century rite of Jerusalem (of which nothing is known) and the account of it given by S. Cyril, we have to relate Cyril's rite, unusual as it appears at first sight, quite closely to the general Syrian liturgical background. If his terminology be closely examined, it will be recognised, I think, by anyone methodically acquainted with the development of such things, that it is unmistakably post-Nicene in its key-words. This means that it is in large part a product of some revision not more than twenty years before Cyril commented upon it for the catechumens in

A.D. 348. Though each separate item has been equipped with a basis of an up-to-date theological theory, which has largely dictated the actual form of each item in the revised prayer, it would not be quite fair to describe the fourth century rite of Jerusalem as a mere collection of the latest ideas from all over the place, put together into a liturgy without any regard whatever for local tradition. Things did not happen quite in that way in the church before the sixteenth century. For all its superficially novel form, the Jerusalem liturgy is still integrally related to earlier Syrian tradition as this is exemplified by *Addai and Mari*. (In saying this I do not mean to suggest that *Addai and Mari* as such was in use at Jerusalem in the third century, but merely that something on the same lines may be taken as by far the most probable form of the earlier Jerusalem use.) In Cyril the old semitic eschatological tradition of the Syrian eucharistic prayer has been hellenised and 'theologised' and transformed, with an obvious desire to be up-to-date and correct. But it is still fundamentally Syrian even in the form in which he describes it. The great influence which the rite of Jerusalem was destined to exert directly and indirectly on all the Eastern rites (and even on some Western ones) during and after the fourth century renders this a fact of outstanding importance.

How far does Cyril's rite still conform to those basic ideas which so far we have found reproduced so faithfully but in such various ways by the prayers we have studied? There is one difference which stands out—the prayer has been given an entirely new pivot instead of any reference to the last supper—the invocation. But even here the elaboration of its terms to include the words 'bread', 'Body', 'wine', 'Blood', does something to restore the loss. Yet this seemed to other Eastern churches which adopted the Jerusalem form of invocation insufficient to satisfy the traditional sense of the necessity of some clearer allusion to the last supper. We shall find in a moment *S. James* supplying an institution-narrative from another source, and this is typical of all the Eastern rites which adopted this peculiar Jerusalem form of invocation. In Cyril's rite there was no option but to regard the invocation as the 'moment of consecration', an idea which was coming in during the fourth century in the East. Elsewhere, by retaining the old institution-narrative or allusion alongside the newly adopted 'consecratory invocation', the Eastern rites laid the foundation of that liturgical and theological duality (not to say confusion) in their theory of the consecration and the eucharistic prayer, which all the efforts of their theologians from Chrysostom to Cabasilas and Mark of Ephesus have never quite succeeded in explaining, or explaining away. It has its roots not in theological theory but in liturgical history.

As regards the other two points, the eucharist is still explicitly something 'offered' to God, though it is no longer stated to be 'the bread and the cup' which the church offers, but 'this fearful and unbloody sacrifice'. It is not easy to say whether the rite is regarded more particularly as the representation of the last supper or of Calvary, because all explicit mention of either event is lacking throughout the whole prayer—a survival of the same sort of Syrian 'allusiveness' as we have found in *Addai and Mari*. If the terms of the invocation recall the last supper, the phrase at the end of the intercessions, 'we offer Christ immolated for our sins, propitiating God . . .', recalls the sacrifice of the Cross. But there is nothing here corresponding to the explicitness of the *anamnesis* of Christ's death and resurrection in the prayer of Hippolytus, or of the 'likeness of His death' in Sarapion.

But the most important difference between the Roman and Egyptian prayers and those of Syria lies in the absence from the latter of all *mention of 'partaking'*, of actually receiving holy communion. *Addai and Mari* shares this omission with Cyril, but at least in *Addai and Mari* there is a prayer for the benefits of communion in its invocation petition (*i*). Even this has gone from the Jerusalem rite, in the elaboration of its invocation to include the reference to the last supper. No doubt the idea of receiving communion is there in the background, and the practice is presupposed for all present at the liturgy, as Cyril himself makes clear.[1] But this does not alter the fact that the idea of communicating has been ousted from all explicit mention in the eucharistic prayer by the one-sided emphasis on the offering of the sacrifice for various objects, whereby 'we offer Christ immolated for our sins, propitiating God for them as well as for ourselves' (xxiii. 7). This is the key-phrase of Cyril's commentary. A Western massing priest a thousand years later might have been more familiar with this terminology of the fourth century Eastern father than were his own third century predecessors. Again there is here something which one cannot exactly call a revolution. One can parallel both halves of this statement in substance—separately—in the third and even in the second century. But once more Cyril has taken a logical and probably a theological step in advance, not only in combining them, but in framing his exposition of the eucharistic action *exclusively* in terms of this thought-out theological theory of sacrifice, with no adequate mention of the theology of communion. One can see where things are going along this line—straight to the non-communicant eucharistic piety of the Byzantines and of the later middle ages in the Western church.

To sum up S. Cyril's liturgy, its ideas are still connected with those of the pre-Nicene past in more than one way, but they are no longer identical with them. They are, however, quite representative of new developments which would carry very great weight in the later fourth and fifth centuries, the period which was decisive in the formulation of later liturgical tradition.

[1] *Cat.* xxiii. 21, 22.

## The Rite of Antioch in the Fourth Century

This must be very summarily treated here because a thorough discussion would involve complicated textual questions concerning the relation of *S. James* to the liturgy of *S. Basil*, which is not in question in this chapter. It would also require detailed textual comparisons with certain passages in the Antiochene writings of S. John Chrysostom (c. A.D. 370-397) and other evidence. But a number of points can be briefly indicated.

*S. James (a)*. In this preface section of *S. James* everything seems to be satisfactorily accounted for by the text of the Jerusalem preface in Cyril until we reach the words 'with ceaseless voices and unsilenced praisings the hymn of victory' which are not represented in Cyril. It is at least worth noting that these particular phrases are cited from the liturgical preface at Antioch by S. John Chrysostom before *S. James* had been adopted there.[1]

*(b-c)*. These sections are not cast quite in the form of a 'thanksgiving', but rather of a brief review of sacred history. It would be difficult to give the 'thanksgiving' form directly to a narrative which included the Fall. But a mention of Eden and the Fall and the O.T. dispensation generally in this part of the prayer appears to be an Antiochene peculiarity; it is found only in liturgies which derive from the Antiochene tradition.[2] It is again worthy of notice that a similar mention of Eden and the Fall and the Law and the Prophets in this part of the eucharistic prayer is found in Chrysostom's Antiochene writings.[3]

There is a relationship between *S. James (b-c)* and the equivalent parts of the liturgy of *S. Basil*, which is not close enough to describe as 'borrowing' on either side but which is nevertheless unmistakeable in places. It might well be accounted for by their being independent versions of the same original tradition.

*S. James (f, g, h)*. But this relation is different when we come to the institution-narrative and *anamnesis* section of *S. James*. There (after a momentary divergence in *f*) the texts of *S. James* and *S. Basil* are identical, except for the most trifling verbal changes. One rite has directly borrowed off the other, and it appears to be *S. James* which is dependent on *S. Basil*. A full institution-narrative was certainly already to be found in the Antiochene rite in the time of Chrysostom, who attributes to it a central importance in the rite.[4] So far as they go, his quotations agree with the present institution-narrative of *S. James (g)*, but this could be due to a common use of 1 Cor. xi. as the basis of the account. There seems to be no trace of an *anamnesis* section in Chrysostom, and all account of an *anamnesis* is

---

[1] *Cf.* the evidence collected in Brightman, L. E. W., *p.* 479, *ll.* 46 *sq.*
[2] Its appearance in the mediaeval text of the Alexandrian liturgy of *S. Mark* is due to a later (? sixth century) revision. It does not appear in the fourth-fifth century text of *S. Mark* found in the Strassburg Papyrus No. 254.
[3] Brightman, *op. cit. p.* 479, *ll.* 22 *sq.*
[4] Brightman, *op. cit. p.* 479, *ll.* 50 *sq.*

missing from the verbose description of the rite of Mopsuestia (of Antiochene type) by his contemporary Theodore. If *Addai and Mari* be an adequate guide, it was precisely the institution-narrative which would need amplifying and the *anamnesis* section which would have to be supplied from somewhere else in an old Syrian tradition, if this were being brought up to date in accordance with most other Greek liturgies in—say—the fourth or fifth century. This would account for the borrowing here in *S. James*.

One notices the eschatological emphasis of the latter part of (*h*) in *S. James* (*cf. Addai and Mari f*), including the vivid touch—'Spare us O Lord our God'—which represents the last judgement as actually taking place. Evidently the Syrian tradition which understood the eucharist as an anticipation of the second coming had not weakened when this prayer was composed.

*S. James* (*i*) goes on to offer the sacrifice in a single phrase, and then to pray for the forgiveness of sins and 'Thy heavenly and eternal gifts', in substance though not in phrasing very much as in *Addai and Mari* (*i*).

It seems worthy of attention that if a doxology were appended after the words 'them that love Thee', we should have in *S. James* (*b–i*) a *complete eucharistic prayer*, parallel in content to but verbally independent of the eucharistic prayer of Hippolytus. Such a prayer would also have a good many points in common with *Addai and Mari*. But here there would also be the big differences that *S. James* (*b–i*) contains a complete institution-narrative and an *anamnesis* (probably derived bodily from *S. Basil*) but *no* invocation of 'holy spirit' in any form (up to this point). None of this matter (*b–i*) is derived from Cyril's Jerusalem rite, but some of it has distinct points of contact with the scattered allusions to the fourth century rite of Antioch in Chrysostom.

*S. James* (*j, h*). However, *S. James* in its present form goes on to add an invocation—in fact, as we have seen, two. One of these (*j²*) evidently contains matter derived from the Jerusalem rite described by Cyril. The other (*j¹*) is in a form which there is some reason to believe was in use in the region of Antioch in the later fourth century, since it reappears in substance in the invocation of the liturgy in *Ap. Const.*, viii.[1] It is also clear from Chrysostom that an invocation of some kind was already in use at Antioch in his day, though it seems impossible to make out the text from his allusions.[2] But one notes that both invocations in *S. James* come *after* the point at which the analogy of other rites would lead us to expect such an invocation to be placed (*i.e.* one would expect an invocation in *S. James* (*i*), following the words 'beseeching Thee' in its first sentence).

*S. James* (*k*). In (*k*) *S. James* produces a second prayer for the communicants in the same terms, 'for the forgiveness of sins and for eternal life', as

[1] Brightman, *op. cit. p.* 21, *ll.* 3 *sqq.*
[2] Brightman, *op. cit. pp.* 474, *l.* 20 and 480, *ll.* 1 *sqq.*

that in *S. James* (*i*). With *S. James* (*k*) we may compare the prayer for the benefits of communion in *Addai and Mari* (*i*). But the brief allusion in the latter to 'Thy church' has been expanded in *S. James* (*k*) into a rudimentary intercession for 'Thy holy catholic and apostolic church'. There is evidently a good deal of duplication in all this part of the rite; there are two invocations, two prayers for the benefits of communion, two offerings of the sacrifice, two prayers for the 'holy catholic and apostolic church', and so on.

*S. James* (*l, m, n*) are mostly taken over from the fourth century Jerusalem rite.

One general inference which seems to impose itself from this brief survey is that the fourth century Jerusalem rite was fused with the fourth century rite of Antioch to produce the 'patriarchal' rite of Antioch (the present *S. James*) rather by way of addition to the Antiochene local tradition than by way of substitution for it. Considerable fragments of the supposedly 'lost' old rite of Antioch are to be found embedded in the present text of *S. James*.

Their discernment, however, is likely to be a more complicated matter than the mere subtraction of what can be detected as 'Jerusalem' material by comparison with Cyril. There seems to have been more than one stage in the process of compilation to form the present text of *S. James*, and the details of the process can hardly be accurately disentangled in the present state of the materials. In this connection I would draw particular attention to the place of the '*non*-Jerusalem' invocation material in ($j^1$) and ($j^2$) (which has attracted to itself the similar material derived from the Jerusalem rite). Instead of coming in (*i*) where on the analogy of other rites we should expect it, it is placed as a sort of appendix to the body of the remains of the old Antiochene eucharistic prayer, *after* the point at which one would look for a doxology to the old Antiochene prayer. This is interesting, because Mr. Ratcliff has pointed out[1] that there are traces of a third century Syrian practice of placing an invocation of the Spirit *outside* the eucharistic prayer proper, immediately before the fraction. If the present order of *S. James* preserves (as it seems to do) the outline of the old Antiochene rite, this may have been the original position of the invocation when it was first introduced at Antioch. Strange as it may seem to us with our presuppositions, such a position is really not an unnatural one. The Nestorians of Malabar in the later middle ages inserted the institution-narrative, which their own rite (*Addai and Mari*) did not contain at all, in that very place just before the communion. They had come to realise that other churches valued and used it and they wanted to include it somehow in their rite, but there seemed no suitable position for its insertion within the structure of their own traditional eucharistic prayer. When many Syrian churches were making such an invocation the central pivot of their rite, Antioch, the

[1] *Art. cit. p.* 31.

mother church of Syria, might well feel that something of the kind ought somehow to find a place in its own rite, and yet be unwilling at that time to disturb its own traditional arrangement of the prayer in this particular matter. A 'supplementary' position for new items, after the eucharistic prayer proper and before the communion, is a common form of compromise attested in all rites. (The position of the Lord's prayer is an obvious example.) In course of time such supplements are always apt to be fused into a single whole with the original body of the prayer, or at least to be treated as inseparable from it, by mere invariable association (cf. the position of the Lord's prayer at Milan, between the conclusion of the eucharistic prayer and its doxology).[1]

Be that as it may, the evidence of duplication and conflation in all this part of the eucharistic prayer of S. James seems undeniable. Whatever the exact explanation, we have here plain traces of the complicated sort of process by which during the fourth-fifth centuries the great historic rites gradually assumed their final form.

[1] Cf. p. 131.

## CHAPTER VIII

## BEHIND THE LOCAL TRADITION

THE reader has now seen something of the evidence for a great diversity in the local traditions of the eucharistic prayer during a period which may be roughly defined as from about A.D. 200 to 400. Had the last chapter included even a summary analysis of other prayers, such as the Eastern liturgies of *S. Basil* (from Asia Minor) and *S. Mark* (from Alexandria) or the Roman canon, all of which contain a good deal of older material overlaid by fifth and sixth century revision, the impression of a great early diversity in eucharistic prayers would have been strengthened, and the range of ideas found in them would have been extended. We have also seen how towards the close of the fourth century, as a result of continual local revisions and mutual borrowings, eucharistic prayers everywhere were beginning to shew a general structural similarity and even a partial identity of phrasing.

It will be one of the most important technical tasks of liturgical studies in the next ten years to pierce this later superficial uniformity and to recover the fragments of genuinely ancient local traditions beneath.[1] But this is a task which is only beginning to be attacked with properly scientific methods, and it would be out of the question to attempt here even a sketch of the problems which will have to be re-examined in detail by experts before we shall have reached the stage of solidly established conclusions. That would require a book in itself, and one of a much more technical character than this can claim.

Yet it seems necessary, even in a book for the general reader and at the present stage of research, to attempt to give some sort of answer to the main question: Can we hope to penetrate through this (fourth–fifth century) period of growing uniformity, and behind that through the period of the unordered growth of local traditions (in the third–fourth century) back to some sort of original uniformity? Can we hope to find in the primitive church, say in the second century, coherent universal principles which can guide our own ideas about liturgy? Was there anything, for instance, in what is vaguely called 'the early church' which might serve as a standard or model by which the perplexities of Prayer Book revision in twentieth century England might be lessened? That is the sort of question which the plain churchman or the practical bishop wants to put to the liturgical stu-

[1] The pioneer work in English along these lines is a small book by the present chancellor of Lincoln cathedral, Dr. J. H. Srawley, on *The Early History of the Liturgy* (Cambridge, 1913). It is unfortunately out of print, but is still sometimes available second-hand. This is still the best technical introduction to liturgical studies available in English.

dent, and to which (so it seems to me) he is entitled to expect a plain and practical answer—and to which (so it seems to him) he does not always get one. I hope I shall not seem to be trying to evade the question if I begin by pointing out the conditions in which such a plain and practical answer has to be framed at present, especially by an Anglican.

### The Present State of the Question

The early evidence on the eucharist is both fragmentary and complicated. Not only its interpretation but its discovery is often a matter needing a very delicate discernment. The pre-Nicene church was a secret society, which deliberately intended to seclude knowledge of its liturgy from all but its own tested members. It is as a rule only by hints and allusions that liturgical matters are referred to by writers of the first three centuries in works which deal primarily with other aspects of the christian religion. (There are exceptions, like Hippolytus' *Apostolic Tradition*, but these are few.) To those who frequented the christian rites such allusions were enough to illustrate the author's meaning; to others they would convey little or nothing—and the modern student is often among the 'others' for practical purposes. It is not surprising, though it is unfortunate, that for two centuries experts have interpreted this sort of evidence in different ways, and that different general theories have dictated two different types of answer to this main question which the plain christian wants to put. The two schools may be distinguished here as the 'traditionalist' and the 'critical'. Without going at all deeply into the controversy between them, it is necessary to say a little about their respective theories.

Beginning so far as modern times are concerned with the German scholar Probst about 1860, the traditionalists have for nearly three generations now been proclaiming to such of the public as take an interest in these things that a primitive standard type or model of the eucharistic prayer did exist, and that its form is not difficult to reconstruct. The attempt to demonstrate its existence and explain its meaning has preoccupied most of the more 'popular' literature (if that adjective is applicable to any of the productions of liturgists) on the subject for at least sixty years past. Some writers of this school have contended that there existed a 'lost *text*' of the eucharistic prayer, of apostolic or sub-apostolic origin, from which all the historic rites were developed by a process of expansion or perversion. The greater part of the traditionalists, however, impressed by the evidence for a general custom of more or less free phrasing of the eucharistic prayer by the celebrant, have sought rather to establish the idea that there was a normal or standard *outline* or framework of the prayer, to which all such prayers ought to conform, and to which, they argued, the majority of such prayers have conformed since very early times. This authentic model the earlier representatives of this school mostly found to be best represented by the Byzantine or North Syrian type of prayer, whose earliest complete example is the eucharistic prayer of the liturgy in the *Apostolic Constitutions, Bk. viii.*, from the region of Antioch *c.* A.D. 375. More recently they have concentrated their attention on the eucharistic prayer of Hippolytus, which is now known to have been one of the sources used by the compiler of the *Apostolic Constitutions.*

This theory is currently associated in England with the name of that very distinguished liturgical scholar the late Bishop Walter Frere, C.R., whose last book, *The Anaphora* (S.P.C.K., 1938), may be taken as its latest and most brilliant exposition. But the theory is in reality much older than Frere's rehabilitation of it, and far from being a peculiarly Anglican thesis. It was first put forward in a fully developed form by the French liturgist Pierre Le Brun in his *Explication de la Messe* in 1726, but in essentials it goes much further back. It is, for instance, the basis of the anti-protestant polemics of the first editor of the *Apostolic Constitutions,* the Spanish Jesuit Francisco Torres in the sixteenth century. In a naïve form it can be traced back into the roots of the middle ages, to the Carolingian liturgists of Gaul in the ninth and tenth centuries.[1]

In modern times it has attracted the support of three outstanding representatives of German scholarship in three successive generations: Probst (Roman Catholic), Paul Drews (Lutheran), and Dr. Anton Baumstark (Roman Catholic), besides a large number of lesser names not only of the German but also of the French and Italian liturgical schools (*e.g.* Dom Cagin). In Anglican liturgical study this has been the dominant theory at least since the compilation of the second Scottish Prayer Book in 1764. Its influence here may be traced chiefly to the work of Bishop Thomas Rattray, whose essay on *The Ancient Liturgy of the Church of Jerusalem* was published in the year after his death, 1744. It is sometimes said that this was the theory generally held by the English Caroline divines of the seventeenth century, but this is true only with such qualification as to be virtually untrue.[2] The fact is that the Carolines, like the Non-Jurors after them, took only an unscientific interest in the early *history* of the liturgy, and did not advance to the stage of producing serious theories about that, though they had plenty to say about its theology.

Whether its influence in England began in the seventeenth or the eighteenth century, the traditionalist theory has long enjoyed here two great practical advantages for its propagation. As the established and dominant theory, it has affected nearly all the elementary manuals and text-books, so that every fresh exposition of it could always appeal to that

[1] It is surprising how many theories which pass for 'modern' in the liturgical schools have their source in these very interesting, ingenious and systematic liturgical writers of the dark ages. Their only drawback is that they knew so little and said so much about the practice of the primitive church.
[2] *Cf. e.g.* the evidence collected by Brightman, *Church Quarterly Review,* civ. July 1927, *pp.* 242 *sq.*

general background of liturgical knowledge which most of the clergy had picked up in the course of their professional training. And in itself it offers a clear and attractive theory which anyone interested can grasp without much difficulty, and which can be illustrated effectively by much of the evidence from the fourth and fifth centuries.

Over against the traditional school, however, there stands not so much a 'school' as a long succession of some of the greatest names in the history of liturgical scholarship—Tommasi in the seventeenth century, Forbes of Burntisland and Ceriani in the nineteenth, Brightman, Armitage Robinson and Lietzmann in the twentieth, and above all, Edmund Bishop (perhaps the greatest of all liturgists)—all of whom have either explicitly rejected the traditional theory as seriously misleading, or at least based their own studies on a quite different understanding of the evidence. Some of them (e.g. Bishop and Ceriani) had hinted at the possibility of a radical dualism in liturgical origins. In our own day Lietzmann has boldly developed this into the idea that there were from the first two quite different types of liturgy in the church, different not only in form but in essential meaning, which he would derive respectively from the Pauline and the judaising churches of the apostolic age. The critical school (if such they can be called) have differed considerably among themselves in their positive state-ments,[1] but they at least agreed in this, in rejecting both the form and the basis of the traditional theory of a single primitive type of prayer. They all emphasised the signs of a very great variety in the outline of the eucharistic prayer before about A.D. 350.

Unfortunately, excepting Lietzmann, every one of these names is that of a writer who was very much a 'scholar's scholar'. Their most important contributions on this particular subject are mostly, either like those of Tommasi and Forbes, incidental statements found in works on other aspects of liturgy which are now unprocurable even at second-hand, or else printed as articles buried away in back numbers of theological periodicals which are not very commonly available.[2] And just because their criticisms of the accepted theory are based chiefly on the earlier evidence which is particu-larly difficult and complicated to handle, their work as a rule shows little consideration for the wayfaring man. The scholar's caution and perception of *nuances*, his wariness of the over-simplification of complex questions, his distrust of short-cuts to results, are all qualities necessary for the pursuit of truth. But they do not make for easy reading, and these writers suffer from all these virtues. It is possible to detect in them a sense (eminently reason-

---

[1] *Cf. e.g.* Brightman's criticisms of Armitage Robinson; *Theology*, ix. (July 1924) pp. 33 *sqq.*

[2] The most accessible in English are an article by Armitage Robinson in *Theology*, viii. (Feb. 1924), pp. 89 *sq.*, and an appendix by Edmund Bishop to Dom R. H. Connolly's edition of *The Liturgical Homilies of Narsai*, Cambridge (*Texts and Studies*, viii. 1), 1909, pp. 126 *sqq.* Both are outstanding pieces of scholarship; the latter in particular is magisterial. But neither is at all easy reading for the uninitiated.

able in the state of the evidence until just the last few years) that the main questions of eucharistic origins were by no means ripe for positive solution; and they do not as a rule give more than hints of where they believe the true solutions to lie. The only attempt at a general exposition of a 'critical' thesis which has ever been made, Lietzmann's *Messe und Herrenmahl* (Bonn, 1926), fully justified this caution. It is spoiled, for all its brilliance, by not a few extravagances.

It is not surprising, I think, that confronted on the one hand by a long-established theory which is attractive and lucid in itself, and which can account for an impressive selection of what passes for 'ancient' evidence (though it is almost entirely post-Nicene); and on the other hand by what seemed to be a recondite and chiefly negative criticism, the bulk of what might be called 'interested but not expert' opinion in Anglican clerical circles should have tended for many years past to accept the traditionalist thesis without much hesitation. Such outright rejection of it as there has been was derived from attachment to present Anglican liturgical practice, or from post-Tridentine doctrinal sympathies among a certain section of 'Anglo-catholics', much more than from reasons of history or technical liturgical study. The results of this state of affairs became obvious and practical in 1927–28.

We are not here concerned at all with the question whether the proposed new Anglican canon drawn up then was or was not desirable in itself, but simply with the fact that it was the product of a particular technical theory about the early history of the liturgy which had been in debate among scholars for two centuries before 1928, and which at the least had been shewn to be open to serious historical criticism. This does not seem to have been clearly understood by the majority of the bishops when they put forward their proposals, and not at all by the church at large when these were being considered. It was soon obvious that the criticisms of this element in them made by scholars of the calibre of Armitage Robinson and Brightman greatly surprised and disconcerted men like Bishop Headlam of Gloucester, who were lending intelligent support to the proposals, but who on technical questions of liturgy could speak only as amateurs, as was plain from their replies.

Yet the constructive weakness of the critical school of liturgists was illustrated once more in this, that though they made many incidental suggestions for the practical improvement of the proposed rite, they produced no easily understood criticism of its form or general justification for their own ideas, and no alternative scheme as a whole. In the event their criticisms were ignored by authority as 'unhelpful'—a verdict which had in it a certain rough-and-ready justice, but little wisdom, as the issue proved.

This same attitude of surprise tinged with resentment was noticeable in these same interested but inexpert circles ten years later, at the very cool reception accorded to Frere's book on *The Anaphora* by the reviewers (mostly competent liturgical scholars) almost without exception in the learned periodicals of all countries. It was inevitable from the form in which Frere had cast his book that discussion in England should reawaken some of the polemics about 1928. It was quite unnecessarily unfortunate that camp-followers on both sides tried to involve a matter of pure scholarship in questions of personalities and ecclesiastical politics. But apart from the small groups which acted in this way, there was a large body of thoughtful Anglican opinion which was genuinely puzzled that such a book should be received by scholars as *The Anaphora* undoubtedly was, with a virtually unanimous rejection of its main thesis, accompanied by respectful compliments on the manner of its presentation.

Frere himself, as his last letter to me shewed, was by no means unprepared for this reception. He was quite aware that with the advance of knowledge and method in the last twenty years the historical difficulties which confront the traditional theory of a single original type of eucharistic prayer had grown more and more formidable, and that he was probably the last living scholar of the first rank to maintain it in anything like its traditional form.[1] The truth is that the book is a skilful rearguard action, an attempt to recast the traditional theory in such a way that it should still be tenable in face of the growing critical difficulties. It is proper to say that, in the judgment of most of those qualified to pass an opinion, his attempt in the particular form in which he made it must be held to have failed; though it was well worth making and in some things has pointed the way to a truer solution. But in view of the way in which the whole matter has sometimes been handled it seems right to insist here that it is only incidentally connected with the name of Bishop Frere or the proposals of 1927–28,[2] and not at all with doctrinal or ecclesiastical allegiance. It is part of a technical debate among liturgical scholars which had been proceeding at intervals for some two centuries before 1928, though in the opinion of most competent scholars it is now in sight of a conclusion. The theory which Frere embraced originated with the Roman Catholics Torres and Le Brun, and has numbered among its modern defenders Roman Catholics, Lutherans and Anglicans just as indifferently as it has numbered them among its critics.

It will have been worth while reflecting a little at length on this episode if it makes clear the difficulty at the present moment of giving 'plain and practical' answers about the primitive eucharistic prayer, of the kind which I for one believe that liturgical science ought to be able to give. The traditional theory did give such an answer, but there is good reason to fear

[1] Even the veteran Dr. Baumstark has modified his support of it considerably of late years.
[2] The actual form of the *epiklesis*-clause in these proposals, on which discussion has centred, was not of Frere's making at all. It was composed by a well-known 'evangelical' bishop, and Frere, though he accepted and defended it publicly for reasons of policy, was prepared in private to criticise its wording somewhat strongly.

that it was a very misleading answer. On the other hand, the critical school, while it has made good its thesis of a great diversity in pre-Nicene eucharistic prayers and overthrown the traditional theory that the Syrian type of eucharistic prayer represents the original universal type, has found nothing very coherent to put in its place as a plain and practical guide for the modern church. Yet to say, as some scholars have implied of late, that we cannot rightly look to the primitive church for such guidance, because it had not itself achieved any intelligible principles in liturgy, would be, I believe, to consent to a mere reaction against the traditional theory which is not warranted by the evidence. And it would rob the science of liturgy not only of all practical value to the church, but of its chief interest in the eyes of all but a few specialists who might continue to make it their hobby.

Yet if the question continues to be put in the way in which the traditional theory has for so long encouraged the ecclesiastical public to put it, 'Can we find in the primitive church a model or standard for a modern eucharistic prayer?'—the answer of the liturgists will be, 'Certainly not, if what we are required to pursue be any form of the mediaeval or modern myth of a single apostolic or sub-apostolic *text* of the prayer'. Such a text never existed, and it is hard to see any complete scheme of a common arrangement in the immense variety of the early material, as this is now slowly coming to light. Yet the pre-Nicene church was quite well aware of what it supposed itself to be doing when it celebrated the eucharist. It should be quite possible to discover and interpret its liturgical principles truly, if only we look for the kind of principle which was then recognised, not those which the fourth and fifth century fathers in their very different situation, or the Byzantines and the mediaeval Latin church, or Tudor and Stuart statesmen, successively elaborated for themselves. Whether pre-Nicene liturgical principles, if we can discover them, will be of much use to us in our very different circumstances is a matter which might require further consideration when we find out what they were.

For the liturgical scholar the technical question resolves itself into this: Does that great variety which has been discerned in the eucharistic prayers of the early fourth century, and which seems to increase as we penetrate back into the third, does that go back all the way to a beginning in the apostolic age in a sort of liturgical anarchy? Or is there some element of truth in the discredited traditional theory of an original uniformity, by which we may find general principles which will interpret the apparent confusion of these prayers? This book has been written partly in order to shew that there is.

### The Primitive Nucleus of the Prayer

What was fixed and immutable everywhere in the second century was the outline or Shape of the Liturgy, what was *done*. What our Lord insti-

tuted was not a 'service', something said, but an action, something done—
or rather the continuance of a traditional jewish action, but with a new
meaning, to which he attached a consequence. The new meaning was that
henceforward this action was to be done 'for the *anamnesis* of Me'; the consequence was that 'This is My Body' and 'This cup is the New Covenant
in My Blood'. Apart from these statements, the formulae which Jesus had
used at the last supper, the jewish grace before and after meals, had referred
exclusively to the *old* meaning. Beyond these brief statements, both the
new meaning of the action and the words in which to express it were left to
the church to find for itself, and there was nothing to suggest that this was
a process to be completed by the first christian generation.

We have seen that the church in reflecting upon this legacy from her
Lord was soon led to disencumber this jewish action from everything in
its traditional jewish setting which could obscure its new christian meaning,
and so to form the rite of the eucharist apart from the supper. The universal scheme of this, that 'four-action shape' in which the prayer formed the
second item, went back to the end of the first century, perhaps to the last
years of the apostolic generation itself. From the uniformity of this outline
everywhere and the early identity of the dialogue introducing the prayer,
one would infer that the new form of the rite, together with its new name
of 'the eucharist', spread all over christendom in the last quarter of the
first century from a single centre, which—if we must try to locate it—is
most likely to have been Rome.

What would form the chief content of 'the' prayer, which originally
afforded the only possibility of giving verbal expression to the meaning of
the rite as a whole?

First, the name 'eucharist', '*thanksgiving*', governed the whole rite from
beginning to end. Secondly, this expressed the *old* meaning with which our
Lord Himself had 'done this' at the last supper. Thirdly, this was something carried over from the very roots of the eucharist in the *chabûrah*
supper into its new christian shape, by the retention of the dialogue of host
and guests ('Let us *give thanks* unto the Lord our God') as well as by the
derivation of the eucharistic prayer from the jewish *berakah* ( = 'thanksgiving'). Fourthly, this jewish *berakah* itself, traditional at the last supper
and the primitive Jerusalem eucharist when this was still celebrated as
the beginning and end of a meal, contained elements which looked beyond that mere thanksgiving for food which would soon come to seem
quite inadequate as the fulness of the new christian meaning began to be
understood.

When we look back at this *berakah* (*p.* 53) and place beside it the consensus of the second century evidence as to the contents of the christian
prayer, we can perhaps see a parallel of thought which does not seem
to me to be either fanciful or accidental, though others must judge for
themselves.

Its first paragraph opens with the usual formula of address to God in such blessings: 'Blessed be Thou, O Lord our God' etc. Besides the specific 'thanksgiving' for the meal (which would be irrelevant to the 'four-action shape' of the eucharist) it contains a 'blessing' or 'glorifying of the Name' of the kind obligatory in all jewish blessings.

It is, however, the second paragraph which is of most importance to us now.

| *Jewish grace* | *Justin and Hippolytus* |
|---|---|
| 1. Thanksgiving 'because Thou didst give as an heritage unto our fathers a desirable good and ample land.' | 1. Thanksgiving 'for the creation of the world with all that is therein for man's sake.' (Justin, *Dialogue*, 41.) |
| 2. Thanksgiving for redemption from Egypt and deliverance from the house of bondage. | 2. Thanksgiving for redemption from 'the iniquity wherein we were born' (Justin, *ibid*.) 'release from sufferings . . . rend the bonds of the devil.' (Hippolytus, *c, d, e*.) |
| 3. Thanksgiving for 'Thy Covenant . . . Thy Law . . . the life, grace and loving-kindness which Thou hast bestowed upon us.' | 3. Thanksgiving for the New Covenant: 'that we have been made worthy of these things by Him' (Justin, *Ap*., I. 65); 'procuring for Thee an holy people' (to replace the old Israel). (Hippolytus, *d*.) |
| 4. Thanksgiving for 'the food wherewith Thou dost continually feed us.' | 4. 'Taking bread and giving thanks said: "Take, eat; This is My Body . . ." ' |
| 5. The paragraph concludes 'For all this, O Lord our God, we thank and bless Thee; blessed be Thy Name by the mouth of all living continually and for ever'—a second glorifying of the Name. | 5. Besides the opening address and 'Naming' of God (as Father and Son and Holy Ghost in most liturgies) we have already seen the importance of the concluding 'glorifying of the Name' in all rites, stated by Hippolytus to be obligatory. (*Ap. Trad.*, vi. 4.) |

It is quite open to anyone to say that the parallels here are both too vague and too subtle to be anything but accidental. Yet if a prayer had been handed down in a tradition by a process of more or less free reproduction extempore Sunday by Sunday for a century through a long line of celebrants, the most that could be expected to maintain itself would be a series of themes in a certain connection. And this particular series of themes, apparently in approximately the same order, is found as matter of the eucharistic prayer at Rome in Justin *c*. A.D. 155 and in Hippolytus fifty years later. The same themes, in approximately the same order, are found too in other traditions, *e.g.* at Antioch and Edessa; though we cannot in these other cases prove that they were in use in the second century, as we can at Rome. Such a widespread use suggests a very early diffusion. And some explanation is required for the fact that the allusion to the last supper in most rites[1] is curiously placed, coming out of its historical order, *after* the thanksgiving for redemption by the passion.

Despite certain difficulties,[2] it does seem that those who believe that there was an original authoritative outline of the prayer could make out (by a comparison of traditions) an overwhelmingly strong case for regarding this series of 'Thanksgivings' as the original opening of the prayer (after the preliminary 'Naming' of God), especially if its derivation from the second paragraph of the *berakah* be admitted. The traditional school have tended for some reason to ignore this series of 'Thanksgivings'.[3] But I will venture to prophesy that this will eventually prove to be their fortress, which the critics will be unable to capture.

The connection—if such there be—between the jewish and christian thanksgiving is one of ideas and form only, not of phrasing. The *berakah* has been entirely re-written in terms of the New Covenant. It concentrates in a remarkable way on the work and Person of our Lord, even where, as by Hippolytus, it is addressed to the Father and not to the Son, as in *Addai and Mari*. The series is, in fact, in itself an *anamnesis* of Him, as our Lord had ordained.

On the other hand, if this 'Thanksgiving series' (following the preliminary 'Naming' of God) formed the original opening of the prayer, it was from quite an early date—let us say vaguely the late third or fourth century—not the only form such an opening could take. An opening sequence of 'Thanksgivings' does not appear at all in the only extant examples of the old Egyptian tradition, *viz.*, Sarapion, and the authentic text of the liturgy of *S. Mark* as found in the Strassburg papyrus (fourth-fifth century).

[1] The exceptions are Cyril at Jerusalem, Sarapion in Egypt and the present Roman canon. Each of these is essentially a fourth century representative of its own tradition. It can be shown that in the case of Syria and Rome Cyril and the canon are independent 'modernisations' of their respective traditions in this particular matter by that very 'go-ahead' period; and that old Syrian and Roman tradition did place the mention of the last supper after that of redemption (*cf.* Hippolytus and *Addai and Mari*). It cannot be shewn, but it is likely, that Sarapion represents the same process at work in Egypt.

[2] One of these is the 'Thanksgiving for Creation'. It might be possible to argue from the whole of the evidence as now known that this is a later addition, originating in the long disputes at Rome over the Gnostic doctrine that creation was in itself evil and not an act of the goodness of God, a doctrine which this 'Thanksgiving' as found in Justin and Hippolytus seems intended to challenge. But these controversies might have led only to a change or increase of emphasis on this point in the Roman prayer, not to the insertion *de novo* of the idea itself into the scheme everywhere.

[3] They are passed over by Frere in three lines in *The Anaphora*, *p.* 25.

D.S.L.

As this text has not hitherto been given, but will now be necessary to the argument, we may say that a collation of this papyrus, where it is legible, with the mediaeval Greek and Coptic texts of *S. Mark* reveals the following as having been the opening of the Alexandrian prayer in the later fourth century:

(1) *Address:* 'It is truly meet and right, holy and fitting and expedient for our souls, O Living God, Master, Lord God the Father almighty, to praise Thee, to hymn Thee, to bless (*eulogein*) Thee, to confess Thee night and day,

(2) *Creation:* 'Thee, the creator of heaven and all that is therein, the earth and all that is on earth, the seas and rivers and all that is in them; Who didst create man according to Thine own image and likeness. Thou didst make all things by Thy Wisdom, Thy true Light, Thy Son our Lord and Saviour Jesus Christ:

(3ª) *Preface* (1st half): Through Whom unto Thee with Him and with the Holy Ghost, we give thanks (*eucharistountes*) and offer the reasonable sacrifice of this bloodless worship, which all nations offer unto Thee from the rising up of the sun even unto its going down, from the north even unto the south; for great is Thy Name among all nations and in every place incense is offered unto Thy Holy Name, and a pure sacrifice, offering and oblation,

*[Here the intercessions are interpolated. The preface resumes:]*

(3ᵇ) *Preface* (2nd half): 'For Thou art far above all principality and power and rule and dominion and every name that is named . . .' [*and so through the rest of the preface to the sanctus, almost verbally as in Sarapion* b¹; *cf. p.* 163].

There is here no sequence of the 'thanksgiving' themes. But it is conceivable that something of the sort once stood as the opening of this Egyptian tradition as well as of all others. *S. Mark* (2) looks like a survival of the 'creation theme' following the preliminary 'Naming' of God, even though it is cast rather in the form of a 'praising' for creation than a 'thanksgiving' for it (*cf.* Sarapion a¹ and a²). This latter word does not appear in *S. Mark* until we reach (3), and not at all in Sarapion till the end of the prayer (*i*). It looks as though this 'thanksgiving' (it is convenient to retain the word, even though it is not quite accurate in the case of *S. Mark*) for creation, which is rather pointless as it stands, was once followed by others for the incarnation, redemption, etc. on a scheme comparable to that of Hippolytus and *Addai and Mari*; and as though the later members of the series had been ousted by the preface and sanctus. But it is to be remembered that the preface and sanctus were already found in the Alexandrian rite *at some point* by the time of Origen *c.* A.D. 230, and that there is nothing to suggest that their use was then a recent innovation.

It is usual to regard the preface and sanctus as a peculiar development of the 'thanksgiving series' opening of the prayer. But the fact remains that it appears in practice not as a development of it but as an alternative to it, a sort of liturgical cuckoo, which ends by taking the place of the 'thanksgivings' whenever it is admitted into the prayer. Only in the prayers of the Antiochene type has a successful effort been made to fuse both forms, by prefixing the preface and sanctus (borrowed from Egypt *via* Jerusalem) to the old Antiochene 'thanksgiving series' (*cf. S. James, pp.* 188 *sq.*); and even there, if the wording of *S. James b, c, d,* be examined, it will be found that the prefixing of the sanctus has led to the elimination of the actual 'thanksgiving' form of the clauses. The word 'give thanks' has been replaced by the form 'Holy art Thou', etc. When the preface and sanctus were adopted by other churches, as at Jerusalem and at Rome, it displaced altogether in their rites that sequence of 'thanksgivings' which *Addai and Mari* and Hippolytus assure us was the pre-Nicene tradition of Syria and Rome alike, but of which Cyril at Jerusalem and the present Roman canon know nothing.

It seems probable when we look at *S. Mark* that something of the same sort happened in the first instance at Alexandria itself, where, so far as we know, the preface and sanctus originated. But there the first member of the old Alexandrian sequence of 'thanksgivings', that for creation, survived when the following 'thanksgivings' for the incarnation, redemption, etc. were eliminated in favour of the preface and sanctus. Perhaps that for creation survived in *S. Mark* chiefly through the difficulty of disentangling it from the 'Naming' of God in § 1. The opening of *S. Mark* (in §§ 1 and 2 taken together) constitutes a 'Naming' of God as Father and Son, to the exclusion of the Holy Ghost, of the type found as the opening of Hippolytus and Sarapion But it would be difficult to extract the creation theme from the text of *S. Mark* as it stands, while leaving this 'Naming' as a coherent sentence. If we are right in supposing that a series of such thanksgivings once came between that for creation in *S. Mark* 2 and the preface and sanctus in 3, it would seem that the combination of preface and sanctus with the sequence of 'thanksgivings' differed at Alexandria from that found at Antioch. At Antioch in *S. James* the preface and sanctus come first. At Alexandria in *S. Mark* the preface and sanctus appear to have come *after* the sequence of 'thanksgivings'. I will hazard a suggestion as to why this should be so in a moment.

To revert now to the general question, Was there an original uniform type of eucharistic prayer? We have found something of which traces appear to be present in all the early traditions, *viz.*:—An opening address and 'Naming' of God, followed by a series of 'Thanksgivings' or 'Praisings' on a sequence of themes beginning with creation, incarnation and redemption. (We need not at this point try to decide exactly where this sequence ended, and whether it originally included a reference to the last supper or

not. The universal existence of such a sequence is sufficient for our immediate purpose.) But it is when we pass beyond the possible contents of this
sequence of themes into the second half of the prayer that the difficulties
in the way of establishing the existence of any original universal model of
the prayer become really formidable.

The evidence we have already surveyed represents the traditions of the
three leading pre-Nicene churches of Syria, Egypt and Rome, and includes
all the most ancient evidence extant, except that to be derived from certain
heretical gnostic writings. When one has eliminated from the second half
of each of these prayers all that can safely be ascribed to later local developments and to borrowings, it is not easy to detect any single scheme upon
which they all arrange their parts and ideas.

To take but one instance, though a cardinal one: Three ideas which
Hippolytus keeps distinct and arranges in three successive statements
(*fg, h, i*)—the recital of the institution, the *anamnesis* of 'His death and
resurrection' and the offering of the bread and the cup—Sarapion in
Egypt expresses inextricably entangled with one another in his section *d*
(with no mention of the resurrection). *Addai and Mari* in Syria contains
the first and the last, but in its earlier form, apparently, not the second.
But it expresses them differently again, by the barest allusions, in connection with other ideas, in *g* and *i*. One can trace in the second half of all
these prayers the recurrence of some ideas which are the same in substance,
but differently handled and differently arranged. The one obvious point of
arrangement in which they all agree in their second halves is that all end
with a doxology or 'glorifying of the Name'.

Thus the later traditions of the prayer all show a similarity of arrangement in their first half, the 'Thanksgivings'. Especially impressive is the
identity of the series of themes everywhere. But they shew great diversities
of content and arrangement in their second half. The inference is that
any original material common to them all covered only the first half and
the concluding doxology.

Is it possible to conceive of a primitive type of eucharistic prayer which
consisted simply of a 'Naming' of God, followed by a series of 'Thanksgivings' for the New Covenant and concluding with a 'glorifying of the
Name'? It would be without much which later ages considered essential to
such a prayer. But at all events one can see how it could be called '*the
Thanksgiving*'. And after studying the themes of the 'Thanksgivings' as they
are actually handled in the various traditions, one can see how they could
be regarded precisely as 'the *anamnesis*', the solemn 're-calling' before
God, of the work and Person of Jesus Christ. Finally, for my own part, I
can see how such a prayer as a whole could be derived directly from that
jewish *berakah* which was used at the last supper, and in the jewish apostolic
church. Such an outline of the prayer could very well be a part of that
fixed 'four-action shape' of the liturgy by which the *chabûrah* ritual was

so delicately adapted to the new christian form, and which took over amongst other things the very dialogue which immediately preceded and introduced the *berakah*.

This is all quite possible, but a little evidence is worth a great deal of plausible speculation. Can we find any examples of this type of primitive prayer? The two oldest prayers we have, Hippolytus and *Addai and Mari*, can both be dated in substantially their present form soon after A.D. 200, and these are both prayers which have a fully developed 'second half'. It will therefore be of little use seeking beyond the second century for an unexpanded prayer. Second century evidence is scanty and hard to interpret, but we can only examine once more our three traditions.

Let us look back at the Alexandrian liturgy of *S. Mark*, with (1) its 'Naming' of God; (2) thanksgiving for creation; (3) preface and sanctus. If—it has not been demonstrated and the reader must judge for himself of the probability of the hypothesis—but *if* in S. Mark a series of similar 'thanksgivings' for incarnation, redemption, etc., originally stood between the present thanksgiving for creation (2) and the preface (3)—then one begins to see the point! 'Through Whom unto Thee with Him and with the Holy Ghost'—but this is the normal introduction of a *concluding doxology*, a '*glorifying*' of the Name (*cf.* Hippolytus *l*). 'For great is *Thy Name* among all nations, and in every place incense is offered unto *Thy holy Name* . . . For Thou art far above . . . every *name* that is *named* . . .' and so to a climax with the seraphim 'ever shouting and crying' as they '*hallow and glorify*' the dreadful holiness of the Name of God—'Holy, holy, holy, Lord of Sabaoth; full is the heaven and earth of Thy glory!' And then did the people answer, 'As it was and is and shall be unto generations of generations and world without end. Amen'—as they still answered at the end of Sarapion's prayer out of immemorial tradition, though in his day an immense interpolation now divided the sanctus from their response, and his actual ending no longer invited the traditional reply?

We seem to have stumbled on the 'lost' doxology of the old Egyptian tradition (*cf. p.* 172), and a remarkable one it is. But its position carries with it the implication that what follows it, the bulk of the prayer as it now stands—precisely the equivalent in contents of the 'second half' of Hippolytus and *Addai and Mari*—is an addition to the original nucleus. I do not want to overpress the case, and I will put what appears to me to be the explanation in the form of questions, the answers to which can be weighed by the reader for himself.

In the original Alexandrian prayer was there a series of 'praisings' (on the same general scheme as the 'thanksgivings' in Hippolytus and other traditions) of which only the first for 'creation' now survives, followed by a 'glorifying of the Name' with a climax in the sanctus? Is the remainder of the prayer another example of the successive *appending* of new items in a supplementary position between the original body of the prayer and the communion? (*Cf. S. James, pp.* 205 *sqq.*, the Lord's prayer in all rites, the *Agnus Dei* in the Roman rite, etc.) Is the 'telescoping' of the original nucleus (so that the 'praising for creation'—its original beginning—now comes immediately before the preface and sanctus—its original ending) a result of the gradual fusion of these supplements with the original *eucharistia*, and perhaps due to a desire to shorten a prayer becoming unwieldily long by successive additions? Is the strange abruptness which marks the transition from the sanctus to the rest of the prayer in Sarapion *c* (an abruptness found equally in the transition after the sanctus in *S. Mark*) explained by the fact that the rest of the prayer was not originally connected at all with the sanctus? (Are the awkward transitions from one section to another throughout the latter part of the prayer of Sarapion to be explained as the marks of successive additions which have never been properly fused together?) Does the phrase, 'We offer the reasonable sacrifice of this unbloody worship', coming where it does in *S. Mark* (3), explain the original application of the phrase, 'to Thee we *have* offered this living sacrifice, this unbloody oblation' (inserted by Sarapion *c* at a point *after* the sanctus) to the angelic worship, as already suggested on *p.* 166? Have we in *S. Mark* traces of an original *eucharistia* of 'praisings', preceded by a 'Naming' of God and ending with a glorifying and hallowing of the Name, as the *root* of the Egyptian liturgical tradition?

Let us now look at the earliest evidence about the contents of the Roman eucharistic prayer, that of Justin, *c.* A.D. 155. It is worth while studying his language carefully.

(*a*) 'The president ... sends up praise and glory to the Father of all things through the Name of the Son and the Holy Ghost, and makes thanksgiving (*eucharistian*) at some length that we have been made worthy of these things by Him. And when he has finished the prayers and the thanksgiving (*tas euchas kai tēn eucharistian*), all the laity present shout assent saying 'Amen'.... And when the president has eucharistised (*eucharistēsantos*) and the people have shouted assent ...' (there follows the communion). (*Ap.*, I. 65.)

(*b*) 'For we do not take these as common bread or common drink. But as by the Word of God Jesus Christ our Saviour was made Flesh, and had Flesh and Blood for our salvation—so, we have been taught, by a word of prayer which comes from Him, the food which has been "eucharistised" ... is the Flesh and Blood of that Jesus Who was made Flesh. For the apostles in the memoirs which came from them, called "gospels", have recorded that thus it was commanded them—that Jesus took bread and gave thanks and said, "Do this for the *anamnesis* of Me; this is My Body"; and likewise took the cup and gave thanks and said, "This is My Blood" ' (*ibid.* 66).

(*c*) 'The president sends up prayers together with thanksgivings (*euchas*

... *eucharistias*) to the best of his powers, and the people applaud, saying 'Amen" ' (*ibid.* 67).

(*d*) ... 'the bread of the eucharist, which Jesus Christ our Lord commanded to be offered for the *anamnesis* of the passion which He suffered on behalf of men for the cleansing of their souls from all iniquity; that we might at the same time give thanks to God for the creation of the world with all that is therein for man's sake, and for that He has delivered us from the wickedness wherein we were born, and overthrown the powers and principalities with a perfect overthrow by becoming subject to suffering according to His own counsel' (*Dialogue*, 41).

These are the only passages in Justin which appear to deal directly with the contents of the eucharistic prayer (though not the only ones dealing with eucharistic theology). (*a*) and (*c*) are obviously summaries of the briefest sort; (*b*) may or may not refer to something actually found in the prayer as Justin knew it, but the description of the account of the institution as a 'word' or ' "formula" of *prayer* which comes from' Jesus suggests that it had liturgical associations for Justin. (*d*) is not directly stated to refer to the actual contents of the prayer. But it expresses the meaning of the eucharist, which is what the prayer was intended to do; and it does so in terms so strikingly similar (for a summary) to those of the first part of Hippolytus' prayer that we need have no hesitation in taking it in this sense.

One might be tempted to infer from Justin's use of the phrase 'prayers and thanksgivings' in (*a*) and (*c*) that the eucharistic prayer as he knew it contained an element besides 'thanksgivings', something analogous to the second half of the prayer in Hippolytus. But in view of the order in which he places them, 'prayers' before 'thanksgivings', this can hardly be pressed. It might even be argued that in (*a*) the word *euchas* 'prayers' refers back to the intercessory 'prayers' (*euchas*) before the offertory, mentioned two lines before our quotation begins, where Justin had omitted to mention that the laity replied 'Amen' to these 'prayers', an omission which he is now repairing. But the expression a 'formula of prayer and thanksgiving' (*logoī euchēs kai eucharistias*) is found elsewhere in Justin (*e.g. Ap.*, I. 13) apparently as an elegant variation meaning quite vaguely 'a thanksgiving to God'. It seems unwise to assume that he had in mind any rigid distinction in using the two words. In (*a*) the phrase 'When he has finished the prayers and the thanksgiving' is repeated as 'When the president has eucharistised (given thanks)', not 'prayed and eucharistised'.

For the rest one cannot but be struck by the fact that the emphasis in describing the president's prayer is *entirely* on the element of 'thanksgiving'. It is possible to recognise in the beginning of (*a*), 'praise and glory to the Father of all things through the Name of the Son and the Holy Ghost', the opening Address and 'Naming' of God. At once after this comes 'he makes thanksgiving... and when he has finished.., the thanksgiving' the people answer, Amen. So far as the language here goes it would be difficult to say that it suggests any element between the 'thanksgiving' and the Amen.

It is quite true that we have already established (*p.* 159) that there is nothing in the contents of the second half of Hippolytus' prayer which would not have been accepted by Justin sixty years before him. But this is not necessarily quite the same thing as saying that it was all in the prayer in Justin's day. It was precisely ideas which were already believed and accepted about the eucharist which people would come to feel ought to be incorporated in the prayer which expressed the meaning of the eucharist. The expansion of the prayer may quite well have taken place in the generation between Justin and Hippolytus, a period about which we know very little, but in which the ideas about the eucharist which they have in common were presumably commonly held in the Roman church. Bating for the moment the question of the institution narrative, which requires separate discussion, all that we can safely say is that Justin's language is quite consistent with the idea that the Roman prayer in his day consisted only of an Address and 'Naming' of God followed by a series of 'Thanksgivings' for creation, redemption, etc., and nothing more. If his prayer contained other elements, he has not mentioned them.

As regards the Syrian tradition, we are hampered by a total lack of orthodox documents between Ignatius, *c.* A.D. 115, and the *Didascalia, c.* A.D. 250. From Syria we have the *Acts of Judas Thomas,* which were perhaps composed in the second century.[1] But if so, they have been heavily revised in the third–fourth century, and it is unfortunately the liturgical material which shews some of the clearest traces of revision. There is, however, a document of the same kind, the *Leucian Acts of John,* from Asia Minor, which M. R. James was prepared to affirm comes from 'not later than the middle of the second century'. We may cite a eucharistic prayer which this puts into the mouth of the apostle, as illustrating at an early stage the eucharistic tradition of Asia which in later times shews more affinities than any other with that of Syria, for which second century evidence is totally lacking.

(*a*) 'We glorify Thy Name, which converteth us from error and ruthless deceit:

'We glorify Thee Who hast shewn before our eyes that which we have seen:

'We bear witness to Thy loving-kindness which appeareth in divers ways:

'We praise Thy merciful Name, O Lord.

---

[1] The original date and language of this document have been much disputed. It is possible, even probable, that the original Syriac author of the second century would have passed for orthodox in his own surroundings, and that the gnostic flavour of the text is chiefly due to a later reviser.

(b) 'We give thanks to Thee, Who hast convicted them who are convicted of Thee:

'We give thanks to Thee, O Lord Jesu Christ, that we are persuaded of Thy grace which is unchanging:

'We give thanks to Thee, Who hadst need of our nature that should be saved:

'We give thanks to Thee that Thou hast given us this sure faith,

(c) 'For Thou art God alone, both now and ever.

'We Thy servants who are assembled with good intent and are gathered out of the world (*or* risen from death) give thanks unto Thee,

'O Holy One!'[1]

It would be very unwise to attempt any reconstruction of the content of the early Eastern eucharistic prayer from this gnostic farrago. But one can detect in most gnostic liturgical practice a steady retention of the orthodox forms while reinterpreting their meaning in gnostic terms and rewriting their formulae in gnostic jargon. Here I draw attention only to the form of this eucharistic prayer. It is addressed not to the Father but to the Son, as is that of *Addai and Mari*. It opens (a) with a 'glorifying of the Name'; it consists (b) of a body of four 'Thanksgivings', the number we found in the parallel between the *berakah* and the second century Roman evidence; and it ends (c) with the statement 'We give thanks unto Thee, O Holy One' (*hagie*), as there is reason to believe that the original Egyptian form ended with a 'thanksgiving' (*S. Mark* 3a) leading up to the 'hallowing' of the sanctus. It is fair to say that the same document contains elsewhere (§ 109) another eucharistic prayer in which this structure is less clearly apparent, though it seems at bottom the same.

But it appears safe on the evidence of the prayer above to assert at least that eucharistic prayers of the structure which we have been led to suppose existed in Egypt and at Rome in the early second century were not unknown in the Eastern churches also at that date.

### The Second Half of the Prayer

We turn now to what is a more tangled matter, the arrangement of the 'second half' of the prayer as this is found in the various traditions. We are met at the outset by the question, where exactly does this second half begin? There is a broad distinction between the series of Thanksgivings and what follows, but where does the dividing line come? In all the traditions the 'second half' may be defined as lying between an allusion to the last supper (either a full institution narrative or a mere mention) and a concluding doxology. The latter is universal and traceable to the primitive nucleus. Is some reference to the last supper also traceable to this nucleus?

[1] *Acts of John*, E.T., 85; M. R. James, *Apocryphal New Testament, p.* 250.

It is difficult to say. On the one hand, such a reference is found in some form in all the traditions. The jewish *berakah* in its final thanksgiving for the earthly 'food wherewith Thou feedest us continually' contains something which might easily have suggested a thanksgiving for the heavenly food of the eucharist and its method of provision, as the last of the series of christian 'Thanksgivings'. Justin, too, in *Ap.* I. 66, with his formula or ' "word" of *prayer* which comes from' Jesus Himself, suggests that something of the sort stood in the prayer as he knew it.

On the other hand, there are certain difficulties. In all the traditions the reference to the last supper is separated from the 'Thanksgiving' series by a sort of intervening clause or 'link' (Hippolytus *e*; Sarapion *c*; *Addai and Mari f*). And this link is not the same in any two of them, either in substance or expression. In each case the link itself does not seem at all closely related to the series of 'Thanksgivings'. Nor is the allusion to the last supper ever cast in the form of a 'Thanksgiving', but always of a statement. And in the one case where the original 'glorifying of the Name' closing the series of 'Thanksgivings' has survived in its primitive position (the Egyptian preface and sanctus) the allusion to the last supper comes *after* this.

This is of some significance. In later times, when the actual history is known to us of the process by which various supplementary items were appended from time to time to the body of the eucharistic prayer between this prayer and the communion, the order in which they are said represents as a rule the sequence in which they were adopted. This is true, *e.g.*, in the Roman rite. The *Agnus Dei* which was inserted *c.* A.D. 700 stands before the prayers for unity, etc., which are a still later insertion. We can never quite rule out the possibility of later rearrangement; *e.g.*, in the Roman rite S. Gregory *c.* A.D. 600 inserted the Lord's prayer *before* the *pax* which had been placed after the canon *c.* A.D. 400. But the presumption is generally that the earlier additions stand first and the later ones after them. The position of the institution narrative in the Egyptian tradition, both in Sarapion and S. *Mark*, is that it follows immediately upon the primitive conclusion (the sanctus) with a brief 'link' (Sarapion *c*) between them. This suggests that the institution narrative is originally an addition to the primitive prayer, though an early one, perhaps the very first[1] of all the various items which were appended in course of time to the primitive nucleus of the Egyptian prayer. From the mere position of the institution-

---

[1] I say 'perhaps' because the 'link' itself in Sarapion *c* has an interest of its own: 'Lord of powers, fill also this sacrifice with Thy power', coming immediately after the 'glorifying of the Name' in the sanctus. We must not forget that fragment of Theodotus (*c.* A.D. 160) cited by Clement of Alexandria: 'The bread is hallowed by the *power of the Name* of God . . . by this *power* it is transformed into *spiritual power*' (*Exc. ex Theod.* 82). The 'link' itself is thus apparently genuine second century material. It might represent the remains of an even earlier *stratum* of addition than the institution narrative which it now connects with the remains of the primitive Egyptian *eucharistia*.

reference in other traditions one might suspect that the same was true of them also.

But this can hardly be more than a suspicion, even in the case of the Egyptian prayers. One cannot exclude the possibility of a third century rearrangement of the Egyptian prayer when it had already received a certain number of items appended after the sanctus, a rearrangement by which an older reference to the last supper *before* the sanctus was transferred to a position after it (no doubt with some adaptation) in order to place it in a more central position.

For this much is certain. Whether the reference to the last supper belongs to the primitive nucleus or not, it is the centre or pivot of all the developed traditions of the prayer. It serves to cohere the *anamnesis* of the redemptive work of Christ in the opening series of 'Thanksgivings' with the more miscellaneous elements found in the 'second half' of the prayer. It is indeed from the reference to the last supper that the substance of this 'second half' grows in every case. In Hippolytus it contains that command to 'do this for the *anamnesis* of Me' which the 'second half' goes on to define: 'Doing therefore the *anamnesis* . . . we offer the bread and the cup', etc. In *Addai and Mari* it is the 'example', which in the Syrian gospel of Matthew contains the promise of that 'forgiveness of sins' for which the Syrian churches invariably prayed when they imitated that 'example' in their 'oblation' (*Addai and Mari i*). In Sarapion the church does what it does and its offering is what it is because of what our Lord did and said at the last supper: 'To Thee we have offered this bread, the likeness of the Body . . . This bread is the likeness of the holy Body *because* the Lord Jesus Christ . . . took bread . . . saying . . . "This is My Body" '.

As one reflects upon the great diversity in the 'second halves' of these three traditions there appears to be only one likeness of substance between them. Underneath their variety they are at bottom all of them independent attempts to do a single thing, to define the meaning of what the church does at the eucharist and relate it to what was done at the last supper. 'We *offer* to Thee the bread and the cup . . . and we pray Thee that Thou wouldest *grant to all who partake* to be made one, that they may be fulfilled with Holy Spirit for the confirmation of faith in truth' (Hippolytus). 'To Thee we have *offered* this bread. . . . We have *offered* also the cup . . . and *make all who partake* to receive a medicine of life, for the healing of every sickness and for strengthening of all advancement and virtue, not for condemnation . . .' (Sarapion). '. . . this *oblation* of Thy servants . . . *that it be to us* for the pardon of offences and the remission of sins and for the great hope of resurrection from the dead and for new life in the kingdom of heaven' (*Addai and Mari*). This is what the church does at the eucharist—*offers and communicates*; and it is this which the 'second half' of the prayer expresses and defines. It looks back to the offertory and expresses in words the meaning of that. It looks forward to the communion and prays for the effects of that. The descriptions of the effect of communion are quite differently defined in the three prayers, as can be seen at a glance. The descriptions of the offertory differ verbally more than could have been expected, considering that all three prayers are describing an identical action, of a great simplicity. But essentially they are doing one and the same thing, stating the meaning of the offertory and the communion. It is the function of the prayer to state the meaning of the whole rite.

At this point it may be objected, 'But what about stating the meaning of the prayer itself and of the fraction?' Why state the meaning of only the first and last items of the 'four-action shape'? The fraction was treated primitively as what it had been at the last supper and in the *chabûrah* ritual, a mere preliminary to distribution, without any of the symbolic meanings which were seen in it by later times. And as for the prayer, it was itself the statement of the meaning of the whole rite. A 'statement of the meaning of the statement of the meaning' is the sort of refinement which seems to be decisively marked as secondary by mere definition.

Nevertheless the step was taken in course of time, as the churches slowly lost sight of the original principles upon which their rites were framed. And always the statement of the meaning of the prayer is placed between the statements of the meanings of the offertory and the communion. Let us look at two fourth century prayers, from the East and from the West. This time let us take for a change two that we have not hitherto used, those of *Apostolic Constitutions, Bk. viii*, from Syria, and the Milanese canon cited in *de Sacramentis* by S. Ambrose, both from the last quarter of the fourth century.

The Eastern prayer runs thus:

a. 'Making therefore the *anamnesis* of His passion and death and resurrection and ascension into the heavens, and His second coming that shall be, wherein He shall come to judge the quick and the dead and reward every man according to his works,
*Meaning of the offertory*
b. 'We offer unto Thee, our King and God, according to His command this bread and this cup giving thanks unto Thee through Him for that Thou hast made us worthy to stand before Thee and minister as priests to Thee; `
*Meaning of the prayer*
c. 'And we beseech Thee that Thou wouldest favourably regard the gifts that lie before Thee, O God that lackest for nought, and be well pleased with them for the honour of Thy Christ, and send down Thy Holy Spirit upon this sacrifice, the witness of the sufferings of the Lord Jesus, that He (the Holy Ghost) may shew this bread to be the Body of Thy Christ and this cup to be the Blood of Thy Christ:
*Meaning of communion*
d. 'that they who partake of Him may be strengthened unto piety, may

receive the forgiveness of sins, may be delivered from the devil and his deceit, may be filled with Holy Spirit, may become worthy of Thy Christ, may receive eternal life, and that Thou mayest be reconciled unto them, O Lord Almighty.'

The Milanese prayer, which is either a 'first cousin' or more probably the direct ancestor of the present Roman canon, runs thus:

*a.* 'Therefore making the *anamnesis* of His most glorious passion and resurrection from the dead and ascension into heaven,
*Meaning of the offertory*
*b.* 'We offer to Thee this spotless offering, reasonable offering, unbloody offering, this holy bread and cup of eternal life:
*Meaning of the prayer*
*c.* 'And we ask and pray that Thou wouldest receive this oblation at Thine altar on high by the hands of Thine angels as Thou didst receive the offerings of Thy righteous servant Abel and the sacrifice of our patriarch Abraham, and that which the high-priest Melchizedek offered unto Thee:'
(At this point the quotation in *de Sacramentis* ends. But it is virtually certain that the prayer ended much as it ends in the present re-arranged Roman canon):
*Meaning of communion*
*d.* 'That as many of us as shall receive by this partaking of the altar the most holy Body and Blood of Thy Son may be filled with all heavenly benediction and grace.'

These two prayers each express what is felt as the fundamental meaning of the eucharistic prayer, at the obvious point, between the meanings of the offertory and the communion. The meaning they see in the prayer is different. The Eastern concentrates on 'consecration', the Western on 'oblation'. This is typical of a difference which since the fourth century has gradually hardened into a difference of ethos between the Eastern and Western rites and theologies. But it is a mistake to suppose that in the fourth century this distinction had yet acquired a rigidly geographical basis. Mr. W. H. Codrington has recently drawn attention[1] to a whole group of Syrian and Egyptian prayers which contain a reference to the 'Western' idea of the offering at the heavenly altar at this point of the prayer. A reference to this same idea is found elsewhere in the rite in *Ap. Const., viii.* itself, and in the liturgies of *S. Basil, S. John Chrysostom* and *S. Mark.*[2] And we must not forget that Sarapion's prayer is headed 'Prayer of Oblation', even though when it comes to formulate its meaning

[1] *Journal of Theol. Studies,* xxxix. (April 1934), *pp.* 141 *sq.*
[2] In *S. Mark* it is now at the offertory, but there is reason to think this is not its original position.

(in $e^1$) it does so in terms of 'consecration' closely allied in thought to those of *Ap. Const., viii. c.* Similarly it would be easy to find later prayers from Spain and Gaul in the West which state the meaning of the prayer in the 'Eastern' way. I am not sure that *Ap. Const., viii. c.* itself, with its reference to 'being well pleased with the gifts that *lie before Thee*', is not at least feeling after the 'Roman' idea of the oblation at the heavenly altar; while the Roman canon in its turn contains in the *Quam oblationem* before the institution narrative a petition for consecration expressing the same fundamental idea as the petition in *Ap. Const., viii. c.*, though it is put in quite different theological terms.

Nevertheless, these fourth century statements of the fundamental meaning of the prayer are different. Each concentrates on an aspect of the matter which was clearly recognised from an early date. One has only to remember the phrase of Theodotus in Egypt, *c.* A.D. 160, already quoted: 'The bread is hallowed by the power of the Name of God, remaining the same in appearance as it was when it was taken . . . it is transformed into spiritual power',[1] to see the antiquity of the notion of 'consecration' as the chief meaning and purpose of the prayer. On the other hand, one has only to recall the phrase of Irenaeus in the same generation, 'For there is an altar in heaven, and thither are our prayers and oblations directed',[2] to be sure of the equal antiquity of the idea of the heavenly altar at which the eucharist is offered.

But there is another and, it seems, a more penetrating way of regarding this difference of interpretation. In emphasising the meaning of the prayer as 'consecration', is not the one type simply stating in another way the meaning of the *communion*? And does not the other emphasis on 'oblation' only state in another way the meaning of the *offertory*? In the last analysis the prayer has no separate meaning of its own in the rite to be stated at all. It is not in origin either a 'consecration prayer' (in our familiar phrase) or a 'prayer of oblation' (as Sarapion called it) but what it was from the beginning—the *eucharistic* prayer. It is what is 'done' at the eucharist, the eucharistic action as a whole, the Shape of the Liturgy, which contains the meaning of the rite. It is the function of the prayer to put this meaning into words.

### A Critical Reconstruction of the Traditional Theory

It is time to draw the threads together. We can distinguish three main periods in the early history of the eucharistic prayer. Working backwards these are:

(1) A period in the later fourth and the early fifth centuries, when by a process of mutual borrowing and adaptation all the rites of the great sees

---

[1] *Ap.* Clement of Alexandria *Excerpta ex Theodoto*, 82.
[2] *Adv. Haer.*, iv. 18. 6.

are evolving in the direction of a general uniformity of structure and content, and even to some extent of phrasing, in their eucharistic prayers. This is the period which is set up as a norm by the exponents of the traditional theory, who assume that it represents faithfully tendencies which had operated uninterruptedly from the beginning. It is in fact the period which was decisive for the final form of the historic rites. It is represented by such documents as the Roman canon in the West, and *S. James*, *Apostolic Constitutions*, *viii.*, and *S. Basil* in the East (and to some extent by Sarapion, though this is in most respects a document of the preceding period).

(2) Behind this is a period covering (? the last quarter of the second century and) the third and earlier part of the fourth centuries. It is marked by the growth of considerable variety in both structure and contents of the unco-ordinated local traditions of the prayer. This is the period upon which the 'critical' school of liturgists have fixed their attention. It is represented by such documents as Hippolytus and *Addai and Mari* (in approximately their present form) and in its later stages by Sarapion and Cyril of Jerusalem. A great deal of work yet remains to be done on the details of the various traditions in this period. But enough is already known for it to be certain that those scholars are right who reject the traditional assumption that the post-Nicene tendency towards uniformity merely developed a pre-Nicene 'standard type'; or that the Syro-Byzantine outline of the prayer is anything more than one among several amalgams which emerged in the fourth-fifth century. The later fourth century tendency to uniformity was thus a reversal of a third century tendency towards great local diversity. But the critical school in its turn has assumed that the growth of variety in the third century goes back in principle to the very beginning in the apostolic age—so much so that we find Lietzmann and his followers postulating that the eucharistic liturgy never had any single origin at all, but two (or even more) original different sources in the apostolic age.

(3) What now of the period behind this again, before the solid evidence of the earliest liturgical *texts* begins, in the second century and the latter part of the first, which we have been investigating?

The evidence is delicate and scanty, but we seem to have found indications in this period of two distinct *strata* in the prayer. (*a*) There are traces of an original stage when the prayer consisted simply of a 'Naming' of God, followed by a series of 'Thanksgivings' and ending with a 'hallowing' or 'glorifying of the Name'. This can be connected with the outline of the jewish 'Thanksgiving' which formed an invariable part of that *chabûrah* ritual out of which the 'four-action shape' of the eucharist was derived in the latter part of the first century. (*b*) A second *stratum* appears to arise out of the reference to the last supper (which may or may not have formed the last member of the original series of Thanksgivings in the first *stratum*). This second *stratum* states the meaning of what is done in the celebration of the eucharist, and relates the present eucharistic action of the church to what was done at the last supper.

To me personally the most satisfying thing about the results at which we seem to have arrived is that at no stage of the argument does it require us to go beyond the known facts and the evidence as it stands. We require no silent revolutions accomplished by Antiochene gentile converts, no liturgical innovations by S. Paul, no pagan infiltrations from the mysteries, no inventions or misunderstandings of what happened at the last supper, to account for anything in eucharistic history. And there are no subsequent improbabilities or gaps in the evolution.

That the last supper was a *chabûrah* meeting seems to arise straight out of the New Testament evidence (and indeed from the facts of the case) when this is compared with the ordinary rabbinic regulations for the meetings of such *chabûrôth*. This appears to have been S. Paul's own understanding of it. The 'four-action shape' of the eucharist meets us as an universal fact in the second century. It arises quite naturally from the desire to mark off those particular elements in the *chabûrah* ritual to which our Lord had attached His new meaning, and to separate these from the remainder of the *chabûrah* rite, to which He had attached no special significance. S. Paul's difficulties at Corinth had foreshadowed the necessity of such a separation, at all events in the gentile churches, long before the end of the apostolic age. The 'four-action shape' does in fact detach just these elements from the *chabûrah* rite, leaving the remainder to continue as the *agape* or Lord's supper independently of the eucharist.

Among other constituents of the *chabûrah* ritual was the *berakah* or 'thanksgiving', preceded by a dialogue. Among the constituents of the eucharist was the *eucharistia* or 'thanksgiving', fulfilling the same function in the christian as in the jewish rite, and preceded by *the same* dialogue. Furthermore, there are traces of a very early stage at which the christian 'thanksgiving' in all traditions had the same outline as the jewish one, but with the contents rewritten in terms of that 'New Covenant' into whicn it was (according to the earliest tradition) the very purpose of our Lord to initiate His disciples by this rite. So far all is natural, almost inevitable.

Was a direct reference to the last supper included in this primitive *eucharistia*? It is impossible to decide. One can see very easily why and where it could be placed in the new christian rewriting of the *berakah*, and there are things in 1 Cor. xi. (*e.g., v.* 23: 'that which I also delivered unto you') which would make its inclusion from the beginning entirely natural.

On the other hand one must remember the immense difference which the circulation of written gospels must have made to the way in which christians regarded the historical origin of their faith, and to the store they set by detailed allusions to it. It is extraordinarily difficult for us to think ourselves back behind this change that the written gospels made in the possibility, and therefore the expectation, of such references. But I think I can understand how a gentile christian late in the first century, introduced to the eucharist for the first time after his baptism, would be content with a tradition that this rite as he found it had been instituted by Jesus, without expecting a detailed account of the institution to be incorporated into the prayer. More particularly would this be the case if his preparation for baptism had not included any biography of Jesus (before the gospels were written or circulating) and not much information about His life beyond the main facts of the. crucifixion and resurrection, and some stories of miracles with a number of parables and teachings. (It is, I think, now generally agreed that the primitive preparation for baptism laid emphasis on the Messiahship of Jesus and His atonement, and on moral instructions about conduct, rather than on the history or even the teachings of Jesus in His earthly life.) As for the relation of the eucharist to the *chabûrah*, what gentile convert would understand or care very much about that? It is one of the decisive reasons for placing the formation of the 'four-action shape' of the eucharist (which so carefully preserves that relation) right back in the period when even the gentile churches still looked to jewish leaders, that only jews could have made the changes involved in jewish custom with such discrimination. And for a jewish christian the mere fact that he was now keeping the familiar *chabûrah* ritual with a new meaning, and perhaps with a *berakah* rewritten in terms of the New Covenant, would be in itself a sufficient reminder of what Jesus was traditionally alleged to have said and done at the last supper, with no need for a specific rehearsing of it. At the most such an allusion as that in *Addai and Mari*—'we have received by tradition the example that is from Thee'—would suggest itself in such circles.

But once the written gospels came into general circulation (*c.* A.D. 100-150) even before they were canonised, they would suggest the incorporation into the rite of the sort of account of the institution they contained. The same would be true of the older account in 1 Cor. xi. But one notices that though in later times most rites incorporate other details of S. Paul's wording, no known rite has the words of institution over the chalice in quite his primitive form, 'This cup is the New Covenant in My Blood'. It looks as though all the institution narratives have been *suggested* by the gospels, even though they fuse them with matter from S. Paul, and treat them in other ways with great independence. I do not see why the incorporation of the institution narrative (or its development from the sort of allusion found in *Addai and Mari*) should be much later than the period of _he first general circulation of the gospels and their public reading in the church, quite early in the second century. This would account for Justin's description of the words of institution as a formula or 'word' of prayer (in *Ap.* I. 66) without difficulty, if it needs accounting for.

The process could hardly stop there, with the mere appending of the narrative to the old jewish model of the *eucharistia*. As the church became more and more a purely gentile society and lost contact with its jewish origins and jewish habits of thought and ways of piety, the sense of the importance and sufficiency of the jewish model of the *berakah* must inevitably fade, and even the understanding of the jewish basis of the traditional form of the christian prayer. The idea of the *berakah*, the series of 'thanksgivings' for the work and Person of Jesus the Messiah as in itself an adequate *anamnesis* of Him before God, had certainly been lost by the churches of the third century, or they would not have overlaid and displaced this jewish nucleus of the prayer with other elements as they did. Once the historical reference to the last supper had been elaborated or introduced, it provided another focus or centre in the prayer. By its mere presence it suggested the need to relate what the church is *now* doing in the eucharist to this original authority for doing it; and the institution narrative itself contained all the material necessary. 'Do this for the *anamnesis* of Me'—'We do the *anamnesis* of His death and resurrection.' 'Take, eat'— we take and eat, in offertory and communion. There is supplementary matter besides, but that is the framework of the prayer in Hippolytus, our earliest dated text.

The new *anamnesis* in a sense duplicates matter found in the old Thanksgivings, but with a different emphasis. The old matter concentrates on the Person of Christ—it is an *anamnesis* of '*Him*'—and on the effects of redemption. The new *anamnesis* derived from the historical narrative of the institution concentrates on the particular events in history by which redemption was wrought—'His death and resurrection.' We have already noted that Hippolytus *e* (the introduction to the institution narrative) regards the eucharist as the present means by which these 'effects' of redemption are actually achieved in the individual soul. Thus the institution narrative has drawn to itself before it the essence of the old 'Thanksgivings', just as it furnishes the basis for the whole second half of the prayer. It has become the focus or pivot of the whole, linking the old and the new material. And very rightly, for it contains in itself all that our Lord had said as to the new meaning to be attached by his followers to 'doing this', the very pith of that meaning of the rite which it was the function of the prayer to state.

The development in other churches was not quite the same; there is, *e.g.*, no *anamnesis* in Sarapion, nor, I think, originally in *Addai and Mari*. But everywhere there is the manifest intention that the second half of the prayer should state the meaning of offertory and communion in relation to the last supper. Everywhere the second half of the prayer has its roots in the allusion to the last supper, even though it was the eucharistic action, the Shape of the Liturgy from offertory to communion, that provided the substance of this part of the prayer.

The question arises as to the date when this development of the institution narrative into the 'second half' of the prayer may be called an accomplished fact. Where all opinions are bound to be tentative I can only put the matter as it seems to me. Hippolytus *c.* A.D. 215 is a *terminus ad quem.* More than one scholar has recently questioned whether the prayer as it now stands in the text of the *Apostolic Tradition* has not been interpolated since his day. On grounds of textual criticism I believe this suspicion to be true of one clause in Hippolytus *k*. But for the rest the textual tradition is astonishingly unanimous as to the substance in versions in Latin, Greek, Syriac and Ethiopic. And there is this further consideration: Hippolytus is a writer with a strongly marked personal style and vocabulary, who is much given to repeating little tags or catch-phrases of his own. Almost every clause in the prayer as it stands can be paralleled in style, vocabulary and even phrasing, some of them many times over, in other unquestioned works of his. And these parallels, some of which have been collected by Dom Connolly,[1] are found in all parts of the present text. The prayer as it stands may be taken as coming from his pen—more than that, as being of his composition. I mean by this, not that he is the inventor of this type of prayer, but that its phrasing and articulation bear unmistakable marks of his personal ideas.

In the circumstances in which the *Apostolic Tradition* was issued—as a conservative manifesto against contemporary innovations in the Roman church—we must attach a good deal of weight to Hippolytus' claim that he is setting down customs which had been traditional at Rome at least during his whole life-time, say from *c.* A.D. 175 or rather earlier. But this must not blind us to the fact that there are a number of phrases in the prayer which are distinctive of his own peculiar theology of the Trinity, and which the rest of the Roman church in his own lifetime might very well have refused to use. Yet the general form and structure of the prayer are very unlikely to have been unusual at Rome in his day. It would have stultified the whole purpose of his pamphlet in favour of the old ways if the first prayer he gave as an example was of a type unknown to the average Roman christian, or even one which his christian contemporaries would not recognise as like those in use there ever since they could remember. But that very 'tidyness' and closeness of articulation which distinguish his prayer from those of *Addai and Mari* and Sarapion are a sign that in the prayer of Hippolytus the material has been thoroughly fused and ordered by a single mind. It is the product, on strictly traditional lines, of a professional theologian. In *Addai and Mari* and Sarapion we have the much less orderly and coherent result of the gradual accumulations of tradition in local churches.

Nevertheless, Hippolytus supplies us with a lower limit which we can accept with some confidence. The eucharistic prayer at Rome had had some sort of 'second half' ever since he could remember—say since *c.* A.D. 175. If the evidence of Justin is to be taken at its face-value, the

[1] *Journal of Theological Studies,* xxxix. (Oct. 1938), *pp.* 350 *sq.*

Roman prayer had been expanded to include this only in the preceding quarter of a century. Development in some churches may have been less rapid, but it may well have been more so. Even in the second century the Roman church had deserved a reputation for conservatism.

The theory sketched here of the second century development of the prayer will probably seem to many impossibly radical. I can only plead against the traditionalists that the actual structure of the prayer in all traditions suggests that in its simplest form it contains two separate *strata*; that the 'Thanksgiving series' and the 'second half' spring from two different roots, serve two different purposes and are fused into a single prayer only by the allusion to the last supper. Even if I am wrong in supposing that the 'second half' is a later addition—and I have tried to shew that there is definite historical evidence to be discerned for thinking that it is—the construction of the prayer itself would still oblige us to believe that it was originally framed as two halves and not as a unity.

It is equally likely that liturgical experts who accept the theories of Lietzmann and his school will see here chiefly a return to the essential point of the traditional theory—*the single origin of the eucharistic rite*. This involves the rejection of that original 'duality' which scholars like Ceriani and E. Bishop avowed that they found in early liturgical history, and which their modern successors have traced to a fundamental division in eucharistic doctrine and practice between S. Paul and the judaic apostles headed by S. Peter. I must answer plainly that in its modern contemporary form this theory is only one more of those visitations by the ghost of F. C. Baur to which theological scholarship is still occasionally liable. The Tübingen romance of an apostolic schism is no more soundly based in the early history of the liturgy than it is in any other branch of church history. Its survival among liturgists after it had been discarded as untenable by historians (with the exception of Lietzmann himself in his *Beginnings of Christianity*, E.T., 1937) has been the principal hindrance to the progress of liturgical studies in the past twenty years.

S. Paul was a jew and a rabbinic student and a pharisee. Like the jewish church before him he used a thoroughly jewish rite at the eucharist, as did the Pauline churches after him. That was inevitable. The 'Pauline' eucharist arose at Jerusalem, from a new meaning given to something authentically, integrally, traditionally jewish, the *chabûrah* meal of the last supper. I have set out the evidence, and by that every theory in the end must stand or fall. But I claim that on the evidence it is right to assert that in the last analysis Frere and his predecessors were right, as against Lietzmann and his followers and predecessors, in attributing to the eucharist and the liturgy which performed it a single origin, and not a dual one. Their failure lay in a refusal to pursue the question to its roots, and to insist that if there was such a single aboriginal type of eucharistic prayer, it must in the nature of the case have been on a jewish model and not on a

Greek one. Developed in this direction the traditional theory of a single origin to the liturgy 'fits' the evidence at every point as the theory of a dual origin has never fitted it because it is not true.

Certainly there was a duality—it might be truer to say a plurality—about the interpretation of the eucharist from the beginning. One can trace it even in the New Testament.[1] But it is a multiplicity of meanings seen in a single action. That action was one and fixed from the evening of the last supper— 'do this'—and the rite that ensured its perpetuation was one and fixed in its form so far back as we can trace. What grew—as our Lord meant it to grow—and broadened and deepened and enriched itself in ever new ways as the christian generations passed was the meaning drawn from the words 'for the *anamnesis* of Me'.

[1] *Cf. p.4.*

# CHAPTER IX

## THE MEANING OF THE EUCHARIST

T HE eucharist is an action—'do this'—with a particular meaning given to it by our Lord Himself—'for the *anamnesis* of Me'. The action is performed by the rite as a whole, the meaning is stated by the eucharistic prayer. This is as true in that primitive period when the body of that prayer consisted only of a series of 'thanksgivings' which by their subject-matter formed an *anamnesis* of Jesus the Redeemer, as it is in later times when the developed 'second half' of the prayer enters with more or less detail into the meaning of the separate items of the rite. It is always the action as a whole which is fundamental, which moulds the prayer. In seeking, therefore, to determine the meaning of the eucharist, it is to the rite as a whole, to the Shape of the Liturgy, that we must look first of all, looking at it, however, always in the light of the interpretation given by the prayer.

In saying this and in asserting that the prayer is by original intention neither a 'prayer of consecration' nor a 'prayer of oblation' but a 'eucharistic prayer', there is no need to question the universally accepted notion that the prayer 'consecrates'. Nor, on a complete understanding of the matter, need there be any denial of the fact that 'consecration' is in and by itself the completion of a fully sacrificial action, by which something is offered to God—in adoration, thanksgiving, petition and propitiation—and is accepted by Him. 'Consecration' is in fact only the description of the offering and acceptance of sacrifice.

### Consecration and Sacrifice

It is the teaching of the Church of England, as exemplified in the rite of the Book of Common Prayer and emphasised in its rubrics governing a second consecration, that the recital of our Lord's 'words of institution' (as what is technically called the 'form' of the sacrament) over bread and wine (technically called the 'matter' of the sacrament) by the church's duly authorised minister effects 'consecration', without the addition of any further petition or statement of any kind. This is not necessarily to be interpreted as teaching 'consecration by formula', by the mere use of a magical phrase with a potency of its own, as is sometimes objected by those who wish us to regard consecration as the effect of the recitation of the whole 'prayer of consecration'. The latter view only substitutes consecration by a 'formula' of some hundreds of words for a 'formula' of some ten or twenty, and has nothing to recommend it. There is another and a better approach to the question.

Every external human action requires some determination of its 'significance'. In the case of the action of an individual this can be purely mental, his own consciousness of his own purpose. In the case of a corporate action of a number of people, it must be 'public' and recognisable, which is commonly achieved by the use of words. The eucharistic prayer is just such a public statement of the meaning or significance of the corporate eucharistic action of the church. If the question be asked, as it is inevitable at some stage of thought about the matter that it should be asked, merely because many eucharists are celebrated: Is there some *standard* statement of that meaning which will make it clear that any particular celebration means all that ought to be meant by the eucharist?—then the answer can only be that our Lord's own statement of that meaning, the seed from which all christian understanding of the eucharist has grown, furnishes an unquestionable standard. From the moment that statement has been made about a particular celebration by a person authorised to make it, that celebration *is* the eucharist, with all that the eucharist means.

It is quite possible to find in some of the fourth century fathers (notably Chrysostom,[1] Gregory of Nyssa[2] among the Asiatic fathers and Ambrose[3]) statements attributing a consecratory force to the words themselves as being the words of Christ acting in the eucharistic offering of the church. These statements seem to rest largely upon the fact that the particular rites used by these fathers did contain a full institution narrative. It now appears that some rites in the pre-Nicene period did not contain such a narrative; and it is possible that in absolutely primitive times no rite contained one at all. It seems probable, therefore, that it was along some such line as that outlined above that the use of our Lord's words of institution as 'consecratory' came to be accepted in the church, and that it is along these lines that it is now to be explained.[4] We need not call in question the 'validity' of those old Syrian rites which like *Addai and Mari* and that of

[1] E.g. *de Prod. Judae Hom.* 1. 6.   [2] *Oratio Catechetica*, 37.
[3] E.g. *de Benedictione Patriarch.*, 9. 38.
[4] I venture to draw attention to the awkward implications of the permission for re-consecration under one kind alone in the Anglican rite. It can be partly justified from the traditional teaching that since each species of the sacrament has its own 'form'—('This is My Body', and 'This is My Blood', or some variant of this)—the consecration of the Bread in the recitation of the prayer is effected before and without that of the Wine. But the completion of the sacrament by the consecration of the Wine is presupposed at the consecration of the Bread in the prayer. At a *re*-consecration under one kind alone the completion of the sacrament is not presupposed but ruled out. No doubt in the context of the whole rite a re-consecration cannot be thought of as a fresh celebration. But it is much harder for the non-theological mind to relate consecration to the rite as a whole, and to regard it as the authoritative pronouncement that 'this action is the Christian eucharist', when in fact it is an incomplete eucharist over which the pronouncement is made. It can hardly be denied that re-consecration under one kind alone encourages undesirable ideas about consecration among the less instructed, and that this particular application of the teaching that consecration is effected by the Dominical Words is open to the charge of 'consecration by formula' in a way that the teaching in itself is not. (There is, of course, the practical difficulty that when it is a deficiency of the consecrated Bread only which has to be remedied by a re-consecration, re-consecration under both kinds would involve the provision of another chalice.)

Cyril at Jerusalem contained no explicit assertion of adherence to the meaning given to the eucharist at the last supper in the form of an institution narrative. It is, as we have said, entirely possible that in this such rites are only survivals of the original practice of all christian churches. Yet even these rites, by their reference to the 'example' of the last supper, or by identification of the bread and wine with the Body and Blood spoken of by our Lord on that occasion, do indicate that their intention is to 'do this' with the meaning then attached to 'doing this'. That is the whole function of the prayer, to state the meaning of the action. That meaning can be drawn out and expounded; it cannot be added to.

Once the full institution narrative had made good its footing in any local tradition of the prayer it was bound sooner or later to become central in it, simply as the classical statement of this meaning, which the rest of the prayer only elaborates. Whether it was incorporated in a particular tradition early or late, it is hard for us to see how that church could henceforward suppose any other paragraph to be of comparable importance. But we have to remember that the question of the theory and composition of the prayer was never raised in the abstract or general form, 'Is there a "standard" statement of the meaning of the eucharist which ought to be found in every eucharistic prayer?' There was never any idea of the reconstruction of all the eucharistic prayers of all churches by a concerted action. What brought the theoretical question forward at all was the emergence in various churches of the idea of a 'moment of consecration'. Traces of this idea meet us, I think for the first time, in Eastern writers between A.D. 300 and 350 (Cyril, Sarapion, Athanasius), but they spread to the West in the next generation (Ambrose). Raised in this way, it was inevitable that individual churches and theologians should settle it in strict accordance with the contents of the particular tradition of the prayer with which they were familiar. They all placed the 'moment' and therefore the 'formula' of consecration at the most obvious point indicated by the actual language of their own prayer. Because prayers varied much in the contents of their 'second half' through independent development in the third century, fourth century ideas could vary a good deal as to the 'moment' of consecration. And because the fourth century was a period of continual liturgical revision in most churches, we find churches and even individual writers identifying the 'moment' of consecration, and therefore the 'formula' and the *theology* of consecration, now with one and now with another clause of the prayer, in a way which seems to us very confusing. The idea of such a 'moment'— and therefore of a crucial or essential section within the prayer—was a novelty; and in the still relatively fluid state of all eucharistic prayers it could not be fixed satisfactorily by local churches acting independently. What is interesting is to find that no church and no writer of the fourth century attempts to place the consecration 'moment' or 'formula' at the recitation of the series of 'Thanksgivings' which had formed the primitive nucleus of the prayer. The memory of the jewish origin and meaning of the *eucharistia* had completely faded from the mind of the hellenised churches of the fourth century, which everywhere sought for the formula of consecration in the 'second half' of their various prayers.

The echoes of this fourth century confusion lasted long. In the East one of them persists to this day in the Byzantine teaching (more or less accepted by the lesser Eastern churches) that consecration is not completed (or even not effected at all) until the institution narrative has been supplemented by a petition that the Holy Ghost will 'make' or 'shew' or 'transform' the bread and wine to be the Body and Blood of Christ. It does not seem unfair to suggest that such teaching really does amount to the idea of 'consecration by formula' in a way which the Anglican doctrine outlined above avoids. Yet it is not our business to criticise the Eastern teaching, but to understand it; and in this case the real explanation is not so much theological as historical. It is the result of the derivation of the Eastern (and particularly the Byzantine) liturgies from two separate liturgical types which have been fused but incompletely harmonised in the later eucharistic prayers. The incoherence in Byzantine eucharistic theology arises from the attempt to explain the composite Byzantine prayers on one consistent theory. The earlier stages of the liturgical history relating to this will occupy us briefly elsewhere in this chapter.

Turning now to the question of the eucharistic sacrifice, it is right for an Anglican to say bluntly that no theory of the eucharistic sacrifice can be supposed compatible with our own liturgical practice since 1549 except that which sees the properly sacrificial action not in any specific oblation or destruction of the Victim in the course of the rite, but in the fact of the consecration of the sacrament under two kinds separately, as a representative likeness of the death of Christ. This is the sense not only of our 'prayer of consecration', but of the statement in our Catechism that the eucharist was ordained for 'the continual remembrance ( = *anamnesis*) of the sacrifice of the death of Christ and of the benefits which we receive thereby'.

All theories of a fresh destruction or 'mactation', or even of a *status declivior*, of Christ in the eucharist are closed to Anglicans by the terms of our formularies, and we may be thankful that it is so. Though such theories are not altogether unknown in the early centuries, particularly in the East,[1] they seem to lie outside the broad line of the central tradition, and they have brought nothing but confusion into the doctrine of the eucharistic sacrifice whenever they have been adopted. It does not appear that the question as to *how* the eucharist is a sacrifice was ever treated of fully and scientifically by any author in the first five centuries, and their incidental statements about it vary to some extent.[2] But an enormous

---

[1] *Cf. p.* 283.
[2] Thus Augustine, exceptionally, associates the act of communion with the sacrificial action in a somewhat obscure passage (*de Civitate Dei*, x. 6), though he elsewhere makes it clear (*e.g. ibid.* xxii. 10) that it cannot strictly be a part of it.

preponderance of writers can be quoted both from the East and West, in all periods both before and after Nicaea down to about the year A.D. 1000, for the view accepted by most of them without discussion, that the eucharist is constituted both sacrament and sacrifice by the single fact of 'consecration'. On this view the offertory is not the vital sacrificial action but its basis and pledge; the communion is not that action but its necessary consequence.

The Anglican Catechism in the answer quoted above, 'the sacrifice of the *death* of Christ', betrays our own rather narrowly Western origin by its concentration on the 'death of Christ' as in itself the moment of His sacrifice. Many, perhaps most, primitive writers would have been unwilling so to limit the conception of His sacrifice, though Justin and certain early Roman and African writers do seem to take this view. It is true that the interpretation of Christ's death in particular as atoning and sacrificial was what in historical fact did more than anything else to reveal to the most primitive church the whole Messianic significance of our Lord's Person and office.[1] But it was quickly understood—before the end of the apostolic age itself—that His sacrifice was something which began with His Humanity and which has its eternal continuance in heaven. As the Epistle to the Hebrews, one of the later documents of the New Testament but still a first century document and 'apostolic', says: 'When He cometh into the world He saith, ... a Body hast Thou fitted for Me ... lo I come to do Thy will, O God.'[2] 'By His own Blood He entered in once into the holy place ... into heaven itself, now to appear in the presence of God for us'.[3] Calvary has here become only the final moment, the climax of the offering of a sacrifice whose opening is at Bethlehem, and whose *acceptance* is in the resurrection and ascension and in what follows beyond the veil in heaven. Even S. Paul, despite his insistence in I Cor. xi. that by the eucharist 'ye do shew forth the Lord's death', reveals by his next words 'till He come' that the first generation of christians saw more in the scope of the eucharistic *anamnesis* than simply 'the sacrifice of the *death* of Christ'. It included for them all that follows of His work both in this world and the world to come, something which is very inadequately represented by the lame addition in the Anglican Catechism of 'the benefits which we receive thereby'. Though the original illumination of the whole redeeming Person and work of Christ by His death continued to some extent to dominate the interpretation of the eucharist by theologians in the early church, the wider interpretation usually holds its place in the liturgies. (The chief exception is the prayer of Sarapion.) What the Body and Blood of Christ were on Calvary and *before and after*—'an offering and a sacrifice to God for us'[4]—that they are now in the eucharist, the *anamnesis* not of His death only, but 'of *Me*'—of the Redeemer in the fulness of His

[1] *Cf. pp.* 74 *sqq.*
[2] *Ibid.* ix. 12, 24.
[3] Heb. x. 5.
[4] Eph. v. 2.

offered Self, and work and life and death, perpetually accepted by the
Father in the world to come.

### The Eucharist as Anamnesis

The understanding of the eucharist as 'for the *anamnesis* of Me'—as the,
re-calling' before God of the one sacrifice of Christ in all its accomplished
and effectual fulness so that it is here and now operative by its effects in the
souls of the redeemed—is clearly brought out in all traditions of the
prayer: 'That it (*sc.* the eucharist now offered) may be to us for the pardon
of offences and for the remission of sins and for the great hope of resurrection from the dead and new life in the kingdom of heaven' (*Addai and Mari*);
'Wherefore we also making the likeness of the death have offered the bread,
and we beseech Thee through this sacrifice to be reconciled to all of us and
to be merciful' (Sarapion); the eucharist was instituted 'in order that He
might abolish death and rend the bonds of the devil and tread down hell
and enlighten the righteous and establish an ordinance and demonstrate
the resurrection' (Hippolytus). These are all so many ways of stating the
atonement and reconciliation achieved by the sacrifice of Christ. It is
important to observe that they are all here predicated not of the passion as
an event in the past but of the *present* offering of the eucharist. This is not
indeed regarded in the late mediaeval fashion as by way of a fresh sacrifice,
but as the perpetual 're-calling' and energising in the church of that one
sacrifice.

Chrysostom is typical of the early writers, Eastern and Western alike, in
his insistence both on the unity and the uniqueness of Christ's sacrifice
and on its relation to the eucharist. In a comment about the emphasis laid
by the Epistle to the Hebrews on this truth he says:

'What then? Do we not offer daily? Certainly we offer thus, making an
*anamnesis* of His death. How is it one and not many? Because it was offered
once, like that which was carried [in the O.T. on the day of Atonement]
into the holy of holies. . . . For we ever offer the same Person, not to-day
one sheep and next time a different one, but ever the same offering. Therefore the sacrifice is one. By this argument then, since the offering is made
in many places, does it follow that there are many Christs? Not at all, for
Christ is everywhere one, complete here and complete there, a single
Body. Thus, as when offered in many places He is one Body and not many
bodies, so also there is one sacrifice. One High-priest is He Who offered
the sacrifice which cleanses us. We offer even now that which was then
offered, which cannot be exhausted. This is done for an *anamnesis* of that
which was then done, for 'Do this' said He 'for the *anamnesis* of Me'. We
do not offer a different sacrifice like the high-priest of old, but we ever
offer the same. Or rather we offer the *anamnesis* of the sacrifice'.[1]

[1] S. John Chrysostom (Antioch, *c.* A.D. 390) *in Heb. Hom.* xvii. 3.

Chrysostom was a popular preacher who had felt the force of many of the new ideas in eucharistic theology which were coming to the front in Syria in his day. But here he is speaking as a theologian, and he is abiding by the older Syrian tradition much more firmly than either Cyril of Jerusalem a generation earlier or thàn his own younger contemporary Theodore of Mopsuestia. For him as for his predecessors in the pre-Nicene church, it is the absolute unity of the church's sacrifice in the eucharist with that of Christ—unity of the Offerer (for it is Christ 'our High-priest' Who offers through the church His Body), unity of the offering (for that which is offered is what He offered, His Body and Blood), unity of the effects ('which cleanses us')—it is the indissoluble *unity of the eucharist with the sacrifice of Christ Himself* which is the basis of the ancient eucharistic theology.

This unity of the sacrifice is effected by the 'consecration'. This appears clearly when we examine in detail the meaning given to the component parts of the eucharistic action. We have already considered sufficiently (*pp.* III *sqq.*) the general understanding of the offertory as 'oblation' (*prosphora*) in all the early traditions of the rite; and we have seen that the matter of this oblation is primarily 'the bread and the cup' (as representing 'ourselves, our souls and bodies')—'the gifts of Thy holy church', in the second century phrase. It was as obvious to the senses in the first or second century as it is to-day that from offertory to communion these gifts retain their physical qualities, all the experienced reality of bread and wine. Yet no language could be more uncompromising than that of the second century writers (and indeed that of the New Testament) about 'discerning the Lord's Body'—as to the fact that what is received in communion *is* the Body and Blood of Christ. There is no hesitation, no qualification. 'The eucharist *is* the Flesh of our Saviour Jesus Christ, which Flesh suffered for our sins and which God the Father raised up'.[1] 'The food which has been "eucharistised" *is* the Flesh and Blood of that Jesus Who was made Flesh'.[2] 'How can' the gnostics 'claim that the bread which has been "eucharistised" *is* the Body of their Lord and the Cup of His Blood, if they confess Him not to be the Son of the Creator of this world?'[3] It is as though the metaphysical questions about the correlation of bread and wine with Body and Blood which have so troubled the mind of the christian West since the ninth century simply did not exist for these writers.

They were not troubled by them, though they were perfectly well aware that they existed. It is 'the bread' that is 'the Body of the Lord' for Irenaeus, 'the food' that is 'the Flesh and Blood' for Justin. In this same paragraph Irenaeus is quite content to say that 'the bread from the earth receiving the invocation of God is no more common bread but eucharist, consisting

[1] Ignatius, *Smyrnaeans*, vi. 2.                    [2] Justin *Ap.* I. 66.
[3] Irenaeus, *adv. Haer.*, iv. 18. 4.

of two realities, an earthly and a heavenly.' It is the beginning of a formal eucharistic theology as opposed to sheer statements of belief. In Irenaeus' younger contemporaries, Clement of Alexandria, Tertullian and Hippolytus, we begin for the first time to meet with language which seeks to take explicit account of this persistence of the physical realities of bread and wine in the consecrated sacrament. This is described as the 'symbol' (*symbolon*), a 'figure' (*figura*) or 'likeness' (*homoiōma*) or 'antitype' (*antitypon*) of the Body and Blood of Christ. But the use of such language should not mislead us into supposing that it betokens any change of doctrine from the naïve 'realism' of the earlier period; it is only a first attempt at the formation of a technical terminology by the pioneers of scientific theology. So far as the extant evidence goes it is not for another hundred years, until well after the opening of the fourth century, that the use of such distinctions is traceable in the more popular and conservative language of the liturgical prayers. And even in the pre-Nicene theologians themselves its use has not, as we shall see, anything like the meaning which it would have in modern writers. The passages in which it is employed must be set beside others from the same writers in which they continue to use the unqualified language of the earlier second century writers and the liturgies, apparently without feeling any difficulty.

Yet the whole pre-Nicene church was obviously not just denying the evidence of its senses about the bread and wine in pursuit of a phrase when it spoke of the eucharist as being in very fact that Body and Blood of Christ which was born and crucified for us. The explanation of its almost crudely 'realistic' language lies, it seems to me, in two things. First, we have to take account of the clear understanding then general in a largely Greek-speaking church of the word *anamnesis* as meaning a 're-calling' or 're-presenting' of a thing in such a way that it is not so much regarded as being 'absent', as itself *presently operative* by its effects. This is a sense which the Latin *memoria* and its cognates do not adequately translate, and which the English words 'recall' and 'represent' will hardly bear without explanation, still less such words as 'memorial' or 'remembrance'. Secondly, and perhaps chiefly, the explanation lies in the universal concentration of pre-Nicene ideas about the eucharist upon the whole rite of the eucharist as a single action, rather than upon the matter of the sacrament in itself, as modern Westerns tend to do. In much Western teaching—certainly in much modern Anglican teaching—there is an exact reversal of the whole primitive approach to the question. We are inclined to say that because by consecration the bread and wine become in some sense the Body and Blood of Christ, therefore what the church does with them in the eucharist must be in some sense what He did with them, namely an offering. And our doctrine about the reality of the offering will be found to vary in its 'realism' or 'symbolism' precisely in accordance with the 'realism' or 'symbolism' of our doctrine of the Presence by consecration.

We make the sacrifice dependent on the sacrament. But the primitive church approached the matter from the opposite direction. They said that because the eucharist is essentially an action and the church in doing that action is simply Christ's Body performing His will, the eucharistic action is necessarily His action of sacrifice, and what is offered must be what He offered. The consequences of His action are what He declared they would be: 'This is My Body' and 'This is My Blood'. They made the sacrament depend upon the sacrifice.

It is obvious that such a view requires us to take the phrase 'the Body of Christ' as applied both to the church and to the sacrament not merely as a metaphor, however vivid, but as a reality, as the truth of things in God's sight. Both church and sacrament must *be* what they are called, if the church's act is to be truly Christ's act, her offering His offering, and the effects of His sacrifice are to be predicated of the present offering of the eucharist. And we find that the primitive church shewed nowhere the least hesitation about accepting the phrase 'Body of Christ' in both its senses as expressing an absolute truth and not merely a metaphor. In this the church went no further than the New Testament. Consider for a moment the implications, *e.g.*, of 1 Cor. vi. 15: 'Shall I take the members of Christ and make them members of an harlot?' Or again, 1 Cor. xi. 28 *sq.* '. . . eateth and drinketh judgement unto himself, not discerning the Lord's Body. For this cause many among you are sickly and ill'. This is pressing the *physical* truth of the phrase 'Body of Christ' in either sense about as far as it will go.

Origen, indeed, with his usual boldness of language, does not hesitate to speak of the church as 'the real (*alēthinon*) and more perfect (*teleiōteron*) Body of Christ' in direct comparison with that physical Body which was crucified and rose again.[1] And though other fathers do not seem to have imitated the second half of this phrase (which again goes no further than the description of the church as the 'fulfilment' (*plērōma*) of Christ in the Epistle to the Ephesians) yet they do use fairly commonly of the church the term the 'true' or 'genuine' (*alēthinon, verum*) 'Body of Christ'. The phrase for the church 'the Body of the whole Christ' (*tou pantos Christou sōma, totius Christi corpus*) which Origen uses elsewhere is found also in other writers, as is the description of the church as *totus Christus*, 'the whole Christ'. By contrast the term 'mystical Body' (*corpus mysticum, sōma mystikon*) which we are accustomed to apply only to the church, is applied in the first five centuries exclusively (so far as I have noticed) to the *sacrament*. By the thirteenth century the salutation *Ave verum Corpus natum* . . . could be taken without ambiguity to apply exclusively to the sacrament; while S. Thomas in discussing the sacrament could use the phrase *corpus mysticum* about the church in distinction from the sacrament, without fear of being misunderstood. But between the third and the thirteenth centuries these two terms, the 'true' and the 'mystical' Body, had exactly exchanged

[1] Origen (Alexandria, *c.* A.D. 235), *In Joannem,* x. 20.

their meanings. And it is to be feared that all over the West since then the refinements of theological language have greatly weakened the primitive force of the word 'Body' as applied both to the church and to the sacrament by contrast with the physical Body that was born of Mary.

### The Eucharist as Action

The unity (rather than 'union') of the church's eucharist with the sacrifice of Christ by Himself is one consequence of the general pre-Nicene insistence on the unity of Christ with the church, of the Head with the members, in one indivisible organism. We have noted Irenaeus' picturesque phrase that in her oblation 'that poor widow the church casts in all her *life* into the treasury of God'. The church corporately, through the individual offertory by each member for himself or herself personally, offers itself to God at the offertory under the forms of bread and wine, as Christ offered Himself, a pledged Victim, to the Father at the last supper. The Body of Christ, the church, offers itself to *become* the sacrificed Body of Christ, the sacrament, in order that thereby the church itself may become within time what in eternal reality it is before God—the 'fulness' or 'fulfilment' of Christ; and each of the redeemed may 'become' what he has been made by baptism and confirmation, a living member of Christ's Body. (This idea of 'becoming what you are' is the key to the whole eschatological teaching of the New Testament, of which we must shortly say something more.) As Augustine was never tired of repeating to his African parishioners in his sermons, 'So the Lord willed to impart His Body, and His Blood which He shed for the remission of sins. If you have received well, you *are* that which you have received'.[1] 'Your mystery is laid on the table of the Lord, your mystery you receive. To that which you are you answer "Amen", and in answering you assent. For you hear the words (of administration) "the Body of Christ" and you answer "Amen". Be a member of the Body of Christ that the Amen may be true.'[2]

Because the oblation of Himself to the Father by Christ is ever accepted, that of the church His Body is certain of being blessed, ratified and accepted too. The offertory passes into consecration and communion with the same inevitability that the last supper passed into Calvary and the 'coming again' to His own. But the unity of Christ and the church is not something achieved (though it is intensified) in communion; it underlies the whole action from start to finish.

It is the firm grasp of the whole early church upon this twofold meaning and twofold truth of the phrase 'Body of Christ' and their combination in the eucharist which accounts for those remarkable passages, commonest in S. Augustine but found also in other writers, which speak almost as though it was the church which was offered and consecrated in the eucharist rather

[1] Augustine, *Sermon* 227.          [2] *Sermon* 272.

than the sacrament. The best known is probably the magnificent paragraph of his *de Civitate Dei* in which he declares that 'The city of the redeemed itself, the congregation and society of the saints, is offered as an universal sacrifice to God by the High-priest, Who offered even Himself in suffering for us in the form of a servant, that we might be the Body of so great a Head ... This is the sacrifice of christians, "the many one Body in Christ". Which thing also the church celebrates in the sacrament of the altar, familiar to the faithful, wherein it is shewn to her that in this thing which she offers she herself also is offered to God.'[1]

There is a deep truth in this way of regarding the eucharist, which is slowly being recovered to-day by the clergy, though it is to be feared that the English lay communicant has as a rule little hold upon it. As the *anamnesis* of the passion, the eucharist is perpetually *creative* of the church, which is the fruit of that passion. This interpretation of the eucharist, which goes back to S. Paul and indeed in essentials to the first apostolic recognition of the 'atoning' character of Calvary, was not only the chief inspiration of the eucharistic devotion of the early centuries, but it was also a commonplace with the Western theologians of the early middle ages.[2]

It finds its mediaeval summary in the repeated assertion by S. Thomas Aquinas that the 'spiritual benefit' (*res*) received in the sacrament 'is the unity of the mystical Body.'[3]

I cannot forbear to quote in this connection the beautiful offertory prayer of the Roman missal for the feast of Corpus Christi, which is also by S. Thomas: 'O Lord, we beseech Thee, be pleased to grant unto Thy church the gifts of unity and peace, which by these offered gifts are mystically signified: through Jesus Christ our Lord ...' This is the very spirit of S. Paul still speaking through the mediaeval doctor. Doubtless Aquinas drew the conception from him by way of S. Augustine, who has a passage which is strikingly similar: 'The spiritual benefit (*virtus*) which is there (in the eucharist) understood is unity, that being joined to His Body and made His members we may be what we receive.'[4]

Unfortunately, after the time of S. Thomas this understanding of the eucharist passed more and more into the background of current teaching in the Western church, though it was still formally acknowledged by theologians.[5] The barren and decadent scholasticism of the fourteenth and

[1] *de Civ.*, x. 6.
[2] See the very interesting collection of texts from Baldwin of Canterbury (twelfth cent.), S. Peter Damian (eleventh cent.) and William of S. Thierry (twelfth cent.) and references to other writers by H. de Lubac, *Catholicisme*, Paris, 1938, *pp.* 64, 67, 307 *sq.*
[3] *Summa Theologica*, P. iii. Q. 73. A. 3; *cf. ibid.* AA. 1 and 6. (S. Thomas calls the 'spiritual benefit' the *res*, older theologians down to the end of the twelfth century called it the *virtus*, but this is a matter of terminology.)
[4] *Sermon* 57. 7.
[5] Cranmer devotes to it one paragraph out of his entire exposition of eucharistic doctrine (*Defence of the True and Catholic Doctrine, etc.*, I. xv.).

fifteenth centuries concentrated its attention in the field of eucharistic theology upon interminable debates around the question of the exact relation of the physical qualities persisting in the bread and wine to the presence of the Body and Blood of Christ. In point of fact these were primarily philosophical disputes between the philosophical schools of the Realists and the Nominalists, which were little concerned with eucharistic doctrine as such, but only with the eucharist as furnishing illustrations for purely philosophical theories. Though popular belief and devotion were not directly affected by these wire-drawn subtleties, yet the absorption of theological teachers in this particular aspect of eucharistic doctrine did in the end greatly encourage the characteristic bias of mediaeval eucharistic piety towards an individualistic and subjective devotion. The clergy trained under such influences were not likely to teach their people a balanced doctrine of the eucharist.

In the later fourteenth and fifteenth centuries popular eucharistic devotion becomes more and more one-sided, treating the sacrament less and less as the source of the unity and of the corporate life of the church (and through this of the spiritual life of the individual soul), and more and more only as a focus of purely personal adoration of our Lord therein present to the individual. The infrequency of lay communions which was still general in this period (though the position as regards this had improved somewhat in the thirteenth century upon what had been customary for lay folk ever since the fifth and sixth centuries) was no doubt partly responsible for this trend. Deprived of frequent communion and with a liturgy in Latin, private adoration was all that was left to the unlettered layfolk, even the most devout of them, with which to exercise their piety. But even where lay communion was commonly more frequent than it was in mediaeval England (e.g. in Western Germany and the Low Countries) we find the same purely individualistic piety exercising the same effect. In the Third Book of the *Imitation of Christ*, for instance, for all its moving and solid devotion to Christ in the sacrament, there is hardly a single sentence about the sacrament as the life and unity of the church. It is wholly preoccupied with the devout affections of the individual soul. The purity and intensity of the best mediaeval mystical piety must not blind us to the fact that it represents a complete reversal in eucharistic devotion of the primary emphasis laid by the no less ardent sanctity of the early church on the corporate aspect of the eucharist.

This one-sided mediaeval view of the sacrament as above all the focus of personal religion was maintained without much change by the protestant reformers and the catholic counter-reformation alike, save that both parties (with about equal energy) sought to replace personal adoration by personal reception of the sacrament, as the central point of lay eucharistic devotion. On the whole the Jesuits were more successful than Cranmer in promoting frequent, even weekly, lay communion among those who came under their spiritual direction. Our liturgy has one remarkable expression of the old doctrine that the *res* or *virtus* of the sacrament is 'that we are very members incorporate in the mystical Body of Thy Son which is the blessed company of all faithful people.' But it is one of the many marks of our derivation from the late mediaeval Western church that when the Catechism comes to state in a popular way the spiritual benefit received by the sacrament, it wholly ignores this, its ancient primary significance, to concentrate on the late mediaeval view that the *virtus* is 'the strengthening and refreshing of our souls by the Body and Blood of Christ as our bodies are by the bread and wine.' It would not be easy to estimate the impoverishment of lay eucharistic devotion, and the damage done to the ordinary Englishman's idea of the church of Christ, through the learning by rote of this mediaevally one-sided and defective answer by many millions of young candidates for confirmation during the last three centuries. The idea of holy communion as a purely personal affair, which concerns only those persons who happen to feel helped by such things, here receives formal and official encouragement. In the long run that is nothing less than the atomising of the Body of Christ.

The primitive church, on the contrary, was wholly aware of the necessity of keeping a firm hold on the truth of both meanings of the phrase 'Body of Christ', and of the certainty that neglect or misunderstanding of it in either sense must in the end be fatal to the understanding of the other. To see this one has only to note the way in which the ideas of church and sacrament as 'Body of Christ' cross and recross each other continually in S. Paul's thought in 1 Cor. x.-xi., so that it is their common communion in the 'one bread' which should prevent the Corinthians from making one another 'to stumble' over such things as the vexed question of eating meats offered to idols, and their factions and unbrotherly conduct generally which betrays itself in the poverty of their eucharistic worship. Or take again the warning of Ignatius: 'Mark ye those who hold strange doctrine touching the grace of Jesus Christ ... they have no care for charity, none for the widow, none for the orphan, none for the afflicted, none for the prisoner, none for the hungry or the thirsty. They abstain from the eucharist and (the common) prayer because they confess not that the eucharist is the Flesh of our Saviour Jesus Christ, which Flesh suffered for our sins and which God the Father of His goodness raised up'. It can hardly be doubted that Ignatius has in mind here 'the afflicted, the prisoner, the hungry and the thirsty' of Matt. xxv. 35 and the solemn declaration of Jesus, 'Inasmuch as ye have done it unto one of the least of these My brethren, ye have done it unto *Me*'—the very basis of the doctrine of the church as Body of Christ. Just as these heretics fail to discern Christ in His suffering members, so they fail 'to discern the Lord's Body'. And it will be found as a matter of observable historical fact in the English history of the last three centuries, from Andrewes and Laud through Wesley, F. D.

Maurice and the early Ritualists of the English slums down to Charles
Gore and Frank Weston, that a 'high' doctrine of the sacrament has always
been accompanied by an aroused conscience as to the condition of Christ's
poor. We must thankfully acknowledge that the converse has not always
proved true. There have been many who have devotedly served Christ in
His afflicted members who might not have been willing to 'confess that
the eucharist is the Flesh of Christ which suffered for our sins'. But it is
true, as protestant social historians like Troeltsch and Tawney and others
have repeatedly observed, that christian neglect or oppression of the poor
has generally been accompanied by a disesteem for the sacrament.

For the patristic like the apostolic church, however, the twin realities
of the church and the sacrament as Body of Christ were inseparably connected, and were regarded in a sense as cause and effect.[1] They were
integrated by the idea of the eucharist as our Lord's own action. We have
seen what a great variety of interpretations of the single eucharistic action
were already in circulation in the apostolic age, and these did not decrease in
later times. One can, however, trace the gradual elaboration of a synthesis
of all the main ideas about the eucharist into a single conception, whose
key-thought is that the 'action' of the earthly church in the eucharist only
manifests within time the eternal act of Christ as the heavenly High-priest
at the altar before the throne of God, perpetually pleading His accomplished
and effectual sacrifice.

The metaphors in which this conception was as a rule presented by the
Fathers are drawn from the striking imagery of the epistle to the Hebrews.
But this book does not stand alone in the New Testament; and though its
leading conception is not developed in the earlier epistles of S. Paul, it is
found in the epistle to the Ephesians and is implicit in all his thought. This
theme runs through all the later books of the New Testament. As Westcott
wrote on the words 'We have an advocate with the Father, Jesus Christ the
righteous, and He is the propitiation for our sins',—S. John here represents
the eternal pleading 'as the act of a Saviour still living and in a living relation with His people . . . He is still acting personally in their behalf and
not only by the unexhausted and prevailing power of what He has once
done. He Himself uses for His people the virtue of the work which He
accomplished on earth. . . . The "propitiation" itself is spoken of as something eternally valid and not as past'.[2]

It was this same conception which the whole early church understood
to be realised in the eucharist. Chrysostom in the fourth century may be

---

[1] There is a curious 'reversibility' about this idea as it appears in the fathers.
Sometimes (and perhaps this is on the whole commoner in pre-Nicene writers) the
sacrament becomes the Body of Christ *because* it is offered by the church which is
the Body of Christ. Sometimes, as in S. Augustine, the church is the Body of Christ
*because* it receives the sacrament which is His Body. Both ideas are true, and both
go back to S. Paul in 1 Cor. for their starting-point.

[2] Westcott, *Commentary on S. John's Epistles*, 1 John ii. 1 and 2.

cited out of a multitude of writers as presenting the concept in its maturity. Commenting on the words of Heb. x. 12 *sqq.*, 'After He had offered one sacrifice for sins for ever, He sat down at the right hand of God', he says: 'Do not because thou hearest that He "sitteth" suppose that His being called "High Priest" is mere words. For the former, His sitting, pertains to the dignity that He has as God, the latter [His priesthood] pertains to His love of men and His care for us. For this reason he [the author of the ep.] elaborates this point [of His priesthood] and dwells upon it (*vv.* 14 *sqq.*) for he was afraid lest the other truth [of His Godhead shewn by His sitting] should overthrow the latter [that of His priesthood]. So he brings back his discourse to this point, since some were questioning why He died, since He was a priest. Now there is no priest without a sacrifice. Therefore He also must still have a sacrifice. And in another way: having said that He is in heaven, he says and shews that He is still a priest from every consideration, from Melchizedek, from the oath ["Thou art a priest *for ever* after the order of Melchizedek"], from His offering sacrifice. . . . What are the heavenly sacrifices which he here speaks of? Spiritual things. For though they are celebrated on earth they are worthy of heaven. For when our Lord Jesus lies as a slain Victim, when the Spirit is present, when He Who sits at the right hand of the Father is here, when we have been made sons by baptism and are fellow-citizens with those in heaven, when we have our fatherland in heaven and our city and citizenship, when we are only foreigners among earthly things, how can all this fail to be heavenly? What? Are not our hymns heavenly? Is it not true that those very songs which God's choirs of angels sing in heaven are the songs which we on earth utter in harmony with them? Is not the altar heavenly? How? It has nothing carnal. All the oblations become spiritual. The sacrifice does not end in ashes and smoke and steaming fat. Instead it makes the oblations glorious and splendid'.[1] Or take again this brief statement: 'We have our Victim in heaven, our Priest in heaven, our sacrifice in heaven'.[2]

This was not a new application of the New Testament conception. From the days of Clement of Rome in the first century, for whom our Lord is 'the High-priest of our offerings' Who is 'in the heights of the heavens'[3] it can be said with truth that this doctrine of the offering of the earthly eucharist by the heavenly Priest at the heavenly altar is to all intents and purposes the only conception of the eucharistic sacrifice which is known anywhere in the church. It is the doctrine of Justin,[4] of Irenaeus[5] and Tertullian[6] in the West in the second century. Our Eastern sources on the eucharist are more scanty, but it is found in Clement of Alexandria in Egypt,[7] and perhaps in Polycarp's epistle to the Philippians from Asia Minor *c.* A.D. 115,[8] though the application to the eucharist in this case

---

[1] *In Heb. Hom.*, xiv. 1, 2.     [2] *Ibid.* xvii. 3.     [3] I Clem. 36, *cf.* 61.
[4] *Dialogue*, 117, 118.     [5] *Adv. Haer.* iv. 18.     [6] *Adv. Marc.*, iv. 9.
[7] *Strom.* iv. 25, *ed.* Potter, *p.* 637.     [8] *Ep.* 12.

is not brought out. In the third century it is universal, as central in the thought about the sacrament of Origen in the East[1] as of Cyprian in the West.[2] There is no need to multiply references. I believe that with the exception of three series of Origen's *Homilies* I have read every sentence of every christian author extant from the period before Nicaea, most of it probably eight or a dozen times or oftener. It is difficult to prove a negative from so vast and disparate a mass of material, but I have paid particular attention to this point for some years. I think I can state as a fact that (with two apparent exceptions which I will deal with in a footnote)[3] there is *no* pre-Nicene author Eastern or Western whose eucharistic doctrine is at all fully stated, who does not regard the offering and consecration of the eucharist as the present action of our Lord Himself, the Second Person of the Trinity. And in the overwhelming majority of writers it is made clear that their whole conception revolves around the figure of the High-priest at the altar in heaven.

This certainly is the conception of the early liturgical prayers. *Addai and Mari* is directly addressed to the Son throughout, and in what may be called its 'operative clause' appeals to Him to send His Spirit ( = 'Presence') upon the offering of the church, that it may become in truth the vehicle of the redemption He has achieved for the partakers. In Sarapion the 'operative clause' is no less clearly that the Word—the Second Person of the Trinity—may 'come' upon the bread and wine by an 'advent'—carefully made parallel so far as the use of the same word can do so with His advent upon the blessed Virgin at the incarnation. The prayer of Hippolytus, which is perhaps the earliest of them all in their extant forms, does not appear to have contained originally any such operative clause at all. (This is probably significant of the way ideas progressed during the third century to bring about the prevalence of such clauses as we now find in *Addai and Mari* and Sarapion later in the third and early in the fourth century. From the time of Cyril of Jerusalem onwards such 'petitions for consecration' are common in East and West alike in various forms. But

---

[1] *Hom.* in Lev. vi. 2; vii. 2; ix. 1, 3, 4, 5, 6, 9, 10; etc. etc.
[2] *Ep.* 63, etc.
[3] These exceptions are (1) The statement of Theodotus *ap.* Clem. Al. *Excerpta* 82 already quoted that 'the Bread is hallowed by the power of the Name'. At first sight this is an impersonal conception probably derived in substance, as it certainly is in form, from the jewish idea of the invocation of 'the name of God' as essential to the *berakah*. But elsewhere Theodotus makes it entirely clear that 'the Name of God' is for him a title of our Lord as the eternal Son of God. *Cf. Exc.* 21. 'The invisible part of Jesus is the Name, that is the only-begotten Son'; *Exc.* 33. 4. '. . . knowledge, which is a shadow of the Name, that is the Son'. Thus Theodotus, though a gnostic, is on this point in line with the general catholic tradition. The other (2) is the statement, unique in catholic pre-Nicene literature, of the Syrian *Didascalia*, c. A.D. 250. (*ed.* Connolly, *p.* 244): 'The eucharist through the Holy Spirit is accepted and sanctified'. I have discussed this statement elsewhere (*p.* 278), but I may note here that this author also knows the doctrine that christian offerings ought to be offered '*to* Christ the true High-priest' (*ed. cit. p.* 86) though this doctrine is not here applied to the eucharist.

consideration of such clauses is more conveniently deferred for the moment.) But the prayer of Hippolytus, though it is addressed to the Father, is entirely concerned with the *activity* of the Son, or Word, operating alike in creation, in His own incarnation,[1] in redemption and in the institution of the eucharist.

The important thing to notice from our immediate standpoint is that when the pre-Nicene church thought and spoke of the eucharist as an action, as something 'done', it conceived it primarily as an action of *Christ Himself*, perpetually offering through and in His Body the church His 'Flesh for the life of the world'. It is the perpetuation in time by way of *anamnesis* of His eternally accepted and complete redeeming act. As the Epistle to the Ephesians puts it: 'Christ loved the church and gave (*paredōken*) Himself for her' in His passion, 'that He might sanctify her by the washing of water' in baptism, 'that He might *present her* to Himself as the glorious church' in the eucharist. 'So ought men to love their wives as their own bodies' for they are 'one flesh' with them, with that indestructible unity with which Christ is one with the church, His spouse and bride. 'For no one ever yet hated his own flesh, but *nourisheth* and cherisheth it, just as the Lord does the church. For we are members of His Body'[2]. The sacrament of baptism is clearly in the writer's mind in *v.* 26; but the allusion to the eucharist as the perpetual 'presentation' to Himself of His bride the church by Christ[3] has been missed by most modern commentators, though the phrase '*nourisheth . . .* as the Lord the church' seems to make it obvious enough.

If we seek a summary of the conception of the eucharist as action we may well find it in the words of S. Paul at 2 Cor. iv. 10 *sq.* It is true that in S. Paul's thought these verses are applied to the christian life in general. But for him as for the whole of catholic tradition the eucharist is the *representative* act of the whole christian life, that in which it finds its continuance and its supreme manifestation. In the self-offering of the church and the christian in the liturgy 'We that live are always being handed over' —*paradidometha*, the word always used of our Lord's 'betrayal' or 'giving of Himself' to death for us (*cf.* Eph. v. 25 above)—'to death for Jesus' sake, that the life also of Jesus might be made manifest in our mortal flesh'. This interpretation of the eucharist as an entering into the self-

[1] 'Born of Holy Spirit and the Virgin' in Hippolytus' prayer (*c*) probably meant to him what we should express as 'Born of the *Word* and the Virgin': *cf.* his terminology in his *contra Noëtum* 16, where he asks 'For what was begotten of the Father but the Spirit, *that is to say the Word?*' This was the commonly used terminology of his day; *cf.* the expression he quotes from his rival, Pope Callistus, 'The Spirit which was made flesh in the Virgin' *ap. Philosoph* ix. 12. For other examples of this confusing 'Spirit = Word' terminology, *cf.* p. 276, *n.* 3.
[2] Eph. v. 25 *sqq.* (The words 'of His flesh and of His bones' after 'members of His Body' in the received text appear from the MS. evidence to be an early addition to the authentic text. They spoil the point.)
[3] *Cf* 2 Cor. xi. 2.

offering of Christ to death is echoed by Ignatius of Antioch as he foresees in terms of a eucharist his own impending martyrdom in the amphitheatre: 'I am God's wheat, and I am ground by the teeth of wild beasts that I may be found pure bread . . . supplicate the Lord for me that I may be found a sacrifice to God by means of these instruments'; and again, still speaking of his desire for the fulfilment of his martyrdom:'I desire the bread of God which is the Flesh of Christ, . . . and for drink I desire His Blood which is love incorruptible'.[1] In the proclaiming of the Lord's death until the end of time by the eating and drinking of the eucharist 'We bear about in the body the dying of the Lord Jesus, that the life also of Jesus might be made manifest in our body',[2] where the word 'body' may stand as well for the church corporately as for the individual christian.

## The Eucharist as Manifestation

There is a further idea which runs, often very subtly and allusively, through the liturgies and through much of what the early writers have to say about the eucharist. It pervades even the details of their language in a way which we can easily miss because their standpoint is in some things quite unfamiliar to our modern way of thinking. Thus, to take but a single instance, though a very revealing one, when Tertullian speaks of 'bread whereby Christ makes His very Body to be present'[3] he uses in the word *repraesentat* ('He makes present') a term which has for him and for other early Latin christian writers[4] a particular association or 'overtone' which is very significant.

*Repraesentatio* is the word by which Tertullian elsewhere describes that 'coming' of God's Kingdom for which we pray in the Lord's prayer.[5] He uses it more than once[6] of the second coming of our Lord to judgement, visibly and with power. The 'theophanies' or manifestations of God in the Old Testament, like those in the burning bush and at Sinai, are *repraesentationes*.[7] The Son is manifested by the voice of the Father at the Transfiguration *repraesentans eum*, 'declaring Him'—'This is My Son'.[8] The actual 'appearing' of men before the tribunal of God in body as well as in soul at the last judgement is a *repraesentatio*.[9] The secure fruition of God in the life to come by *repraesentatio et possessio* ('manifestation and possession') is contrasted with the obscure laying hold of Him by hope which is all that we can have in this world.[10] Tertullian declares that the *repraesentatio* (physical presence) of Christ in His earthly life is what the apostles saw

---

[1] Ignatius, *Rom.* iv. 1, 2; vii. 3.     [2] 2 Cor. iv. 11.
[3] *Adv. Marc.*, i. 14.     [4] *E.g.* S. Jerome, *Comm. in Matt.*, on xxvi. 26.
[5] *de Oratione*, 5.     [6] *E.g. adv. Marc.*, iii. 7.
[7] *Ibid.* iii. 10.     [8] *Ibid.* iv. 22.
[9] *Lib. de Res. Carnis*, 17 (twice). It is to be noted that in this chapter it is used as synonymous with *exhibitio*, the technical term for the 'production' of the actual person of a prisoner for trial before a court, which was the legal responsibility of the gaoler or the sureties.
[10] *Ibid.* 23.

and were blessed in seeing, which prophets and kings had desired to see
and had not seen.[1]

It is obvious, of course, that a word with such associations for Tertullian
cannot be adequately translated into English in connection with the
eucharist merely as 'bread by which He "represents" His Body.' A
similar caution is necessary in handling the use of such terms as 'symbol',
'antitype', 'figure', applied to the relation of the sacrament to the Body and
Blood of Christ. As Harnack long ago observed, 'What we nowadays
understand by "symbol" is a thing which is not that which it represents;
at that time "symbol" denoted a thing which in some kind of way really is
what it signifies'.[2] The 'symbol' *manifests* the secret reality.

But there is much more in this than a mere question of the meaning of
words. It brings us close to a whole habit of mind and thought about the
relation of this world and things in this world to the 'world to come' which
is almost entirely foreign to our ideas, but which is of the very substance
of early christian thinking and of the New Testament documents. We
must therefore try to gain at least an elementary grasp of it if we would
understand the apostolic conception of the eucharist and the primitive
rites at all. The primitive eucharist is above all else an 'eschatological' rite.
We have already referred more than once to this conception; this is the
most convenient point at which to investigate it a little more thoroughly.
Its explanation takes us afield, back behind the gospels into the Old Testament and the world of jewish thought from which our Lord and His
apostles and the gospel came.[3]

## Eschatology

One of the most striking differences between Greek and Hebrew modes
of thought lies in the different significance which these two races saw in
the process of history. From before *c.* 500 B.C. the Greek philosophical

---

[1] *Adv. Marc.*, iv. 25.

[2] Harnack, *Hist. of Dogma*, (ed. 2) 1888, I. *p.* 397. On Tertullian's use of *figura*
in general, see C. H. Turner, *Journal of Theological Studies*, vii. (July 1906), 595 *sq.*,
where he concludes that it means something nearer to 'actual and distinctive nature'
than to anything like 'symbol' or 'figure' in our sense. On 'antitype' I would note
that it was regarded as being so closely related to 'type' that the two words were
interchangeable in ancient usage. Some writers call the O.T. 'figures' the 'type' of
N.T. 'antitypes' (=realities); others reverse the terminology. Some call the sacrament the 'type' and the physical Body of Christ the 'antitype'; others call the sacrament the 'antitype' and presumably thought of the physical Body as the 'type'.
Hippolytus uses both 'type' and 'antitype' both for the 'figure' and the 'reality' in an
haphazard way, which indicates that the two terms conveyed to his mind not so
much an 'opposition' as a very close relation indeed.

[3] The clearest account of eschatological thought I know in English is the appendix on 'Eschatology and History' to Prof. C. H. Dodd's brilliant lectures on *The
Apostolic Preaching and its Developments* (1936). To this these paragraphs of summary are partly indebted, though I do not fully subscribe to his theory of 'realised
eschatology'. For a less 'platonised' account of the matter, see A. E. J. Rawlinson,
*The New Testament Doctrine of the Christ* (1926), *pp.* 32–41.

tradition had adopted a 'cyclic' view of history. Probably this was ultimately due to the influence of Babylonian astronomy and its theory of a
periodical revolution of the eight 'circles of the heavens' by which after
every ten thousand years all the stars had returned to the exact relative
position from which they had started, and the whole cosmic process began
again. Through the astrological doctrine of the control of earthly events by
the movements of the stars, this was interpreted to mean that each 'cycle'
(or according to Plato double-cycle) of the heavens caused an exact repetition on earth of the events of the previous cycle, inexorably, mechanically,
precisely. The Stoic school, who made much of this cyclic theory, often
illustrated it by the statement that every cycle would see Socrates; in every
cycle he would marry Xanthippe, drink the hemlock and die [1] Such a view
reduces history to a mere phantasm, without moral worth or purpose or
meaning. And though the Greeks were not as a rule so pessimistic as to
apply the full consequences of this iron doctrine to the significance of
individual human lives and actions, it stunted the development of Greek
thought in more than one direction.

The Jew had a very different philosophy of history. Where the Greek
saw only a closed circle endlessly repeating itself, the Jew saw a line—not,
perhaps, a straight line, for the sorrowful history of his nation made him
fain to confess that the unaided human mind could not follow all its
course—but still a line, with a definite beginning and end. The beginning
was the creation of the world out of nothingness by the sovereign Will of
God, which was the beginning of time and history. The end was what the
Old Testament calls the 'Day of the Lord', when time and history would
end with this world. Before the world and time, and always beyond the
world and time, there was God, 'the high and lofty One that inhabiteth
eternity'. At the close of time and the end of the world there is still God,
ruling in the 'age to come'.

The conception of the 'Day of the Lord' was probably taken over by the
Old Testament prophets from the Hebrew folklore, but if so they gave it
a wholly new meaning. It meant for them no sudden and irrational catas-
trophe which, as it were, would break history off short at a given moment.
History as a whole had in itself a direction, a purpose, a meaning. These
were given to it by the eternal purpose of God, Who ceaselessly over-rules
and guides all history towards an end which He has determined. Men who
dwell in the midst of the process of history, so to speak, cannot grasp its
purpose and meaning as a whole, because from the point of view of time it
is not yet completely worked out, though it is perfect in the mind of God.
To us the rule of God in this world is far from obvious; evil often seems to
triumph, chance seems to prevail, the holy purpose of God seems always
to be baffled. But secretly the kingly rule of God governs all history. When
the meaning of history is complete the ruling or 'Kingdom' of God in all its

[1] So *e.g.* Nemesius (a very interesting christian Stoic), *de Natura Hominum*, 38.

parts will be 'manifested', will be obvious and vindicated. In the later jewish theory it was the function of the mysterious being whom they called the 'Messiah' (the 'Anointed one')[1] to bring about this climax and completion of history which reveals its whole purpose, and so 'manifests' the kingship of God in all that has ever happened in time.

To take an illustration which is not altogether adequate[2] but which will serve, this conception of history is in a way rather like the mathematical process of a sum. The answer is a part of the calculation; it cannot be arrived at without the calculation; but without it the calculation itself is meaningless. When it is reached the answer 'manifests' something implicit throughout the whole process; the answer 'tests' the working and completes it; but it is also something which is separable from the process, which can be used as the basis of a new and different calculation. It is something 'beyond' the process, even though it is the result of it. And after the answer has been reached, there is no more to be done. That calculation *cannot* be continued; the only possibility is a fresh start on a new and different calculation.

The 'Day of the Lord', the *eschaton* ( = 'the End', hence 'eschatology', 'eschatological') is the answer to the agonising problem of history, with its apparent chaos of good and evil. This completion of history, 'the End' which manifests the 'kingdom' (*basileia* = 'kingship') of God throughout history in all its parts, does not interrupt history or destroy it; it fulfils it. All the divine values implicit and fragmentary in history are gathered up and revealed in the *eschaton*, which is 'the End' to which history moves. In this sense the 'Day of the Lord' involves a 'judgement' of history as a whole, and of all that goes to make up history. 'The End' is at once within history and beyond it, the consummation of time and its transmutation into what is beyond time, the 'Age to come'. Thus the prophets both foresee the *eschaton* as a definite event, and yet are forced to describe it in the fantastic language of myth, for no merely temporal conceptions framed from the events of time can describe it. The 'Age to come' is pictured as an age of supernatural blessings of all kinds; but whether the pictures are crudely drawn from earthly pleasures like a celestial banquet or are more spiritualised and poetic, they are all only symbols of a state in which all the partial values of time are perfectly fulfilled. To the religious mind of the jew this meant first and foremost the vindication of the validity of religion, more particularly of something which was the heart of his religion, the Covenant between God and Israel, to which Israel for all its striving always found itself being faithless. In 'the days of the Messiah' that Covenant would be transcended in a 'New Covenant', and in the fulness of His

---

[1] The actual word 'Messiah' is not attested until the first century B.C., but under other terms the conception goes back to the O.T. prophets.
[2] It is not adequate because it takes no account of the intervention of God in history.

Kingdom God Himself would have given to Israel the power to keep it. Through the Messiah God would thus 'redeem' Israel from its own sins and failures, as well as from the sorrows and catastrophes of temporal history.

The peculiar turn which primitive jewish christianity gave to this conception was the idea that in the life, death and resurrection of Jesus this 'purpose' of all history had *already been* manifested, and the Kingship of God conclusively vindicated. When the Messiah had in solid historical fact—'under Pontius Pilate'—offered Himself in sacrifice that the whole will of God might be done, the supreme crisis of history had occurred. When He passed through death to life and so by His ascension into the 'glory' (*shechinah*) of God,[1] in His Person the 'Age to come' has been inaugurated, in which the Kingship of God is unquestionable and unchallenged. In Him—in His human life and death—the rule of God in all human life had been proclaimed absolute and perfectly realised.

'In Christ!' The phrase is perpetually upon the pen of S. Paul. This is the meaning of the church, the Body of Christ. The redeemed, the New Israel of the New Covenant, are those who have been made 'members' of Him by baptism;[2] 'incorporated' (*symphytoi*) thus into Him, they have been transferred 'in Christ' into that Kingdom of God into which He entered at His ascension. 'God *has* resurrected us together with Christ and made us ascend along with Him and enthroned us along with Him in heavenly places in Christ Jesus.'[3]

### 'The Spirit' and Eschatology

The medium, as it were, by which Christians within time are already thus within the Kingdom of God in eternity is 'the Spirit'. We should beware of understanding the N.T. authors too rigidly in terms of developed Trinitarian theology, even though their writings laid down the lines upon which the fourth century theologians would one day rightly interpret the revelation of God to the apostolic church. In reality the thought of the jews who wrote most of the New Testament is often more akin to that of the Old Testament than it is to that, say, of S. Augustine's *de Trinitate*. As S. Peter explained the coming of 'the Spirit' at Pentecost: 'This is that which was spoken by the prophet Joel: "And it shall come to pass in the last days (*eschatais hēmerais*—this reference to the *eschaton* is a significant christian addition to Joel's actual words)—saith God, I will pour out of My Spirit upon all flesh" '.[4] It is the old semitic notion of 'the Spirit of God' as 'the Presence of God with power', of which we have already spoken.[5] Jesus, 'being by the right hand of God exalted has received of the Father the fulfilment of the promise about the Holy Spirit and has shed forth this which you now see and hear.'[6] This 'pouring forth' of 'the Spirit' is an indication

[1] This is, of course, the meaning of the 'cloud' at Acts i. 9.     [2] Rom. vi. 3–5.
[3] Eph. ii. 5 *sq.*     [4] Acts ii. 17, citing Joel ii. 28.
[5] *Cf. p.* 183.     [6] Acts ii. 33

of the *impersonal* view still taken of 'the Spirit'.[1] And in fact the idea of
the Spirit as it is developed in the earlier *strata* of the N.T. documents is
that of the 'power' or 'presence' of the Ascended Jesus in the eternal
Kingdom of God energising within time in His Body the church, so that
its members, or rather *His* members, 'walk no more after the flesh but after
the Spirit';[2] or as S. Paul puts it elsewhere, 'I have been crucified with
Christ yet I am alive; yet no longer I live but (the risen and ascended)
Christ liveth in me; and the life which I live in the flesh I live by the
faith of the Son of God'.[3] To 'walk after the Spirit' and for 'Christ to live
through me' mean for S. Paul the same thing. 'As many as are led by the
Spirit of God, these are sons of God'[4]—as Jesus, 'in' Whom they are by
'the Spirit', is the Son.

Baptism, which is a 'washing away of sins', is also the incorporation into
Christ by which we 'put on Christ', and are therefore transferred 'in Him'
into the Kingdom of God in eternity. The gift of the Spirit in confirmation,
as it were, validates this eternal fact about us *in time*. The unction of confirmation—'the seal' as the first five centuries called it (*sphragis, consignatio,
rûshma*) is God's act claiming full possession of goods which He has pur-
chased outright but which He has not yet removed to His own warehouse.[5]
For the christian, the gift of the Spirit is the 'earnest money', the sure
present 'guarantee', which is the pledge of an inviolable possession of the
Kingdom of God in eternity in Christ.[6] It is one of the most notable contrasts between pre-Nicene and modern Trinitarian thought that while we
are apt to regard the Holy Spirit as active in all men, far beyond the bounds
of the church and even the indirect influence of the christian religion, the
primitive church on the contrary confined the operation of the Holy Spirit
strictly to the 'redeemed' who had been incorporated into Christ by
baptism and received confirmation; while at the same time emphasising
that the eternal Christ, the *Logos* or Word, had an active relation to all men
as rational creatures.[7] 'The Spirit' is the power or presence of the Ascended
Christ which incarnates His glorified Body of heaven in the 'Body of
Christ', the church on earth. Baptism incorporates a man into that Body
from the eternal point of view, but the gift of 'the Spirit' in confirmation is
what makes him a living member of that Body *within time*.[8] Thus only the

---

[1] There is, of course, a 'personal' as well as an 'impersonal' doctrine of the Holy
Spirit to be found in the N.T. All that I am concerned to point out is that the
'impersonal' view is taken over from the O.T. and is therefore the more 'primitive'
in apostolic christianity.

[2] Rom. viii. 4.     [3] Gal. ii. 20.     [4] Rom. viii. 14.
[5] Eph. i. 13, 14.     [6] 2 Cor. i. 21 *sq.*
[7] See *e.g.* Origen *de Principiis* I. iii. 5, 6, 7, where this contrast is emphasised. *Cf.*
the text of the 'Apostles' Creed' in Hippolytus, *Ap. Trad.*, xxi. 17: 'I believe in the
Holy Spirit in the holy church' (and not outside it). *Cf.* also the doxology in Hippolytus' prayer, *p.*158.

[8] We must remember that the two sacraments were normally conferred within
five or ten minutes of each other. The idea of a baptised but unconfirmed christian
would have seemed to the pre-Nicene church a monstrosity: 'If any man have not

confirmed may take part in the eucharist, which is the vital act of the Body in time.

Thus the church, though 'in Christ' and one with Him in His eternal glory and kingdom, remained within time. 'The End' had come and yet history continued! Did not this fact suffice to discredit the whole conception? I venture to think that there has been a considerable modern misunderstanding of, at all events, the original jewish-christian eschatology on this point. For pre-christian jewish thought the *eschaton* had a double significance: (1) it manifested the purpose of history, and (2) it also concluded it. But even in jewish thought these two aspects were not regarded as necessarily coincident in time. To take but one example, Dan. vii., the classic eschatological passage of the Old Testament:—'One like unto the Son of Man (explained later as 'the people of the saints of the Most High') came with the clouds of heaven and came to the Ancient of Days . . . and there was given him . . . the kingdom'.[1] This is for Daniel the climax of history, but it is not simply its conclusion. In the immediately preceding verse he had written: 'As for the beasts (the earthly kingdoms) they had their dominion taken away, yet *a prolonging in life* was given them for time and time'.[2] What happened to them afterwards is never explained. It is irrelevant or trifling beside the unfolding of the ultimate purpose of history. But the continuance of some sort of earthly history for a while side by side with this overwhelming theme is at least hinted at.

In Jesus of Nazareth those jews who had accepted Him as Messiah understood that both aspects of the *eschaton* found their fulfilment. But it seems to be a mistake to suppose that for the original jewish christians the conception of the last judgment at the end of time represented an *adaptation* of eschatology to meet the disappointing postponement of those elements of finality and publicity which had failed to manifest themselves when they were first expected, immediately after the ascension. That was a later understanding of the matter by the gentile churches, to whom the whole eschatological conception was strange. Nothing is more certain than that the whole idea of 'the Spirit' and its activity in the church *postulates* a continuance of time as the sphere of its activity; and the idea of 'the Spirit' goes back into the very roots of jewish christianity.

The accident that so much of our New Testament material comes to us from Pauline sources, and thus represents a process of translation from

---

the Spirit of Christ, he is none of His' (Rom. viii. 9). It could only happen in the case of those baptised in grave emergency—sickness or some other danger of death—for normally baptism was only given in the presence of the bishop. If a man died, then baptism took its eternal effect. If he continued to live in this world he needed confirmation with the gift of the Spirit, the equipment of the christian *in time*; and he was expected to present himself to the bishop for it as soon as possible, *cf. e.g.*, Cornelius of Rome (*c.* A.D. 240), *ap.* Eusebius *Eccl. Hist.*, vi. 43, 14 *sq.* On the whole question of the relation of baptism to confirmation in the primitive church, see *Theology Occasional Papers*, No. v.

[1] Dan. vii. 13.                                    [2] Dan. vii. 12.

Hebrew to Greek modes of thought, makes it a delicate and hazardous matter to discern the exact bearing of christian ideas before that inevitably distorting process began.[1] But speaking tentatively and with a due sense of the difficulties of the matter, it looks as though for the *original* christian eschatology we have to get behind the teaching of S. Paul, for whom the *parousia* or 'coming' of our Lord is always in the future, at a 'last judgement' at the end of time. This is an adaptation for the benefit of gentiles.[2] There are traces of a non-Pauline usage of the term *parousia* = 'the coming', to describe what we should call the '*first* coming', of the incarnation only,[3] as something which *has already happened*. It is well known that the fourth gospel regards the last judgement as both a present fact and a future event. So, too, the 'coming of the Spirit' is for this evangelist both an historic event and a perpetual 'coming' of Jesus to His own. Such an attitude may well represent not so much a 'development' of Paulinism as the re-emergence of an older and more fully jewish eschatology. The original jewish church had preserved the tradition that our Lord Himself had said that in the sense of the conclusion of history, 'The *eschaton* is not yet'.[4] But it believed with all its heart that in Him the purpose of history had been revealed and the Kingdom of God had been completely manifested and demonstrated. Down to the time of Justin, who is the first to distinguish between the 'first coming' in humiliation and the 'second' to judgement, in our fashion,[5] the word *parousia* is never used in the plural.

There is but *one* 'coming', in the incarnation, in the Spirit, in the eucharist and in the judgement. And that is the 'coming' of 'One like unto the Son of Man' (who is 'the people of the saints of the Most High', *i.e.*, Christ and the church) *to the Father*. This is the end and meaning of human history, the bringing of man, the creature of time, to the Ancient of Days,

---

[1] I would like to draw attention to an essay by Dr. W. K. Lowther Clarke on *The Clouds of Heaven* (*Divine Humanity*, 1937, reprinted from *Theology*, xxxi. August and September, 1935, *pp.* 61 *sq.* and 125 *sq.*), of which insufficient notice seems to have been taken even in England. In his own words his thesis is that: 'When our Lord said: "Ye shall see the Son of Man sitting at the right hand of power and coming in the clouds of heaven", He referred to His Ascension, not to a Descent; to His vindication by the Father and only indirectly to a judgment of this world. The true meaning of His words was gradually lost until in the second century they were taken to mean a coming from heaven.' So far as I have any means of judging, the materials assembled by Dr. Clarke entirely bear out his contention, which seems to me in line with much in the jewish pre-history of christian eschatology. But such a view calls for a drastic revision of current theories about primitive christian messianism and eschatology generally, and in particular of the relation of the 'second coming' (*parousia*) to the paschal sacrifice of Christ in His death, resurrection and ascension together.

[2] Yet that S. Paul himself shared and understood the more jewish eschatology seems clear from 1 Cor. x. 11 where he speaks of christians 'upon whom the ends of the ages are come'. As Fr. L. S. Thornton, C.R. points out (*The Common Life in the Body of Christ*, London 1942, *p.* 334, *n.* 1.) 'a better translation would be: "For whom the ends of the ages overlap". "The present age" and "the coming age" meet in the Church'. And I would add, especially at the eucharist.

[3] So Ignatius, *Philad.*, ix. *Cf.* Acts vii. 52 (where the word is *eleusis*) and 2 Pet. i. 16.

[4] Mark xiii. 7.     [5] *Dialogue*, 121.

# THE MEANING OF THE EUCHARIST 263

in eternity. The same eternal fact can touch the process of history at more than one point, and if there is an apparent difference in the effects of such contacts, that difference is entirely on the side of the temporal process, for eternity knows no 'difference', and no 'before' or 'after'. This view of eschatology as manifesting the purpose of history already within time does not deny a 'last judgement'; rather it demands a total judgement of all history in the light of that purpose.

### Eschatology and the Eucharist

This brief and inadequate discussion will have served its purpose if it enables us to grasp more clearly the eschatological character of the primitive eucharistic rite. It is one of the strongest reasons for excluding any theory of influence from the pagan mysteries, or indeed from any hellenistic source whatever, on the primitive liturgical tradition, that not only is its form intrinsically jewish, but its content turns out upon examination to be deeply impregnated with a mode of thought altogether alien to the hellenistic mind. It is even true to say that though the increasingly gentile churches of the second, third and fourth centuries tried hard to retain the original eschatological emphasis in the eucharist, they did in the end find it something which in its original form the gentile mind proved unable to assimilate.

When we examine the early liturgical material, however, the evidence is plain. It is not merely that the language of the earliest prayers is full of eschatological reminiscences, so that Hippolytus opens by recalling that 'in the last times' (*ep' eschatois chronois*) God sent the Word 'to be the Redeemer and the Messenger of Thy plan' or purpose (*boule*), and *Addai and Mari* ends with communion 'for new life in the kingdom of heaven'. The whole conception of *anamnesis* is in itself eschatological. Dr. Dodd puts the matter clearly when he says: 'In the eucharist the church perpetually reconstitutes the crisis in which the kingdom of God came in history. It never gets beyond this. At each eucharist we are *there*—in the night in which He was betrayed, at Golgotha, before the empty tomb on Easter Day, and in the upper room where He appeared; and we are at the moment of His coming, with angels and archangels and all the company of heaven, in the twinkling of an eye at the last trump. Sacramental communion is not a purely mystical experience, to which history . . . would be in the last resort irrelevant; it is bound up with a corporate memory of real events'.[1]

The word 'memory'[2] here is, as always, not quite adequate to represent

[1] *Op. cit.*, p. 234.
[2] It is borrowed by Dr. Dodd from Prof. C. C. J. Webb's profound discussion of the idea of 'the memory of a society' in *The Historical Element in Religion* (1935), pp. 84 sq. I must admit that this idea as Prof. Webb treats it (whatever its validity in other directions) seems awkward to apply to the primitive eucharist in some ways. I do not think the primitive church would have agreed with Prof. Webb that

*anamnesis*. What the church 'remembers' in the eucharist is partly *beyond* history—the ascension, the sitting at the right hand of the Father and the second coming. What has helped to confuse the whole matter is the fact that the *anamnesis* paragraph of the eucharistic prayer in most of the present Eastern rites does now set these meta-historical facts of the resurrection and ascension, and the eternal facts of the enthronement and 'coming', side by side with the purely historical event of the crucifixion as being part of what the eucharist 're-calls'. We have already had one instance in *S. James* (h)[1] and another in the eucharistic prayer of *Ap. Const.*, viii.;[2] and it would be easy to cite others. But how far back does such an usage go in the Eastern rites, and where does it come from? Sarapion in Egypt has no *anamnesis* paragraph at all; nor apparently had Cyril at Jerusalem. If I am right against Mr. Ratcliff, *Addai and Mari* also had originally no such paragraph either; and in any case, to this day its *anamnesis* mentions only 'the passion, death, burial and resurrection'. Chrysostom at Antioch has no suggestion of the existence of such a paragraph in the Antiochene rite *c.* A.D. 390, nor has Theodore at Mopsuestia. Turning further afield the earliest and purest Gallican prayers have no *anamnesis* at all (*e.g.* the so-called *Masses of Mone*).

In fact the only early evidence for the existence of such a feature as the *anamnesis* paragraph comes from Hippolytus; the evidence as a whole suggests that it was a local peculiarity of the Roman rite down to the later fourth century. It first appears in the East in Syria *c.* A.D. 375, in the liturgy of *Ap. Const.*, viii. But it is universally admitted that the compiler of that rite (which as it stands is a 'made-up' liturgy, a literary production, not a service that was ever customarily used in any church) made use of the *Apostolic Tradition* of Hippolytus as one of his main sources. It seems that it was from Hippolytus' old Roman rite that he drew the idea of inserting an *anamnesis* paragraph into his own Syrian 'sketch of a model eucharistic prayer'. It was this enterprising Syrian author who first thought of elaborating 'the *anamnesis* of His death and resurrection' only, as he found it in Hippolytus, by the addition of 'His passion . . . and ascension into the heavens and His second coming that shall be', in a way which is typical of his treatment of his sources throughout his book. If one sets all the present *anamnesis* forms of the Eastern rites[3] side by side, it will be

'a memory, though always itself a fact of present experience, is essentially a present consciousness of something past as past, and not only of some present image or effect of what is past'. And there are other difficulties.

[1] *p.*1 70.

[2] *p.* 228. It will be convenient to have it set out again: 'Making, therefore, the *anamnesis* of His passion and death and resurrection and ascension into the heavens, and His second coming that shall be . . . (we offer unto Thee the bread and the cup . . .)'.

[3] *S. Mark*, Brightman, *p.* 133; *S. Basil* and *S. John Chrysostom*, *ibid. pp.* 328-29; *Armenian*, *p.* 438; *Ap. Const.*, viii, *p.* 20; *S. James*, *p.* 52; *S. James* (Syriac), *p.* 87; *S. Cyril* (Coptic), *p.* 178 (these two last are closely connected; probably the Coptic depends on the Syriac). *Addai and Mari*, *p.* 287, is independent of all the rest.

found that directly or indirectly they are all (except that of *Addai and Mari*) derived from the form in *Ap. Const.*, viii. It appears, therefore, that the custom of including the explicit mention of the ascension, the sitting at the right hand of God and the last judgement in the *anamnesis* only began in the East in the later fourth century. As so often, the present texts of the Eastern rites are a very unsafe guide to the conceptions of the primitive church. The present Roman *anamnesis* of the passion, resurrection and ascension only is nearer in form to the original usage as found in Hippolytus.

It is a little disconcerting at first sight to find that this, which has almost become the 'stock example' of the primitive eschatological interpretation of the eucharist, is not primitive at all, but a relatively late elaboration. But let us be quite clear as to the point at issue. It is not whether the eucharist was eschatologically interpreted by the primitive church; that is certain. What is in question is how that interpretation was expressed and how eschatology itself was originally understood. And I think that upon consideration it will be realised that this particular fourth-fifth century Eastern expression of it in the development of the *anamnesis* represents not the continuance but the *breakdown* of the primitive conception. By cataloguing, as it were, the meta-historical and eternal facts (of the resurrection, ascension, session and judgement) side by side with an historic event in time (the passion) the whole notion of the *eschaton* is brought in thought entirely *within time*, and split into two parts, the one in the historic past and the other in the historic future, instead of both in combination being regarded as a single fact of the eternal present. In the primitive conception there is but *one eschaton, one* 'coming', the 'coming *to* the Father' of redeemed mankind, which is the realisation of the Kingdom of God. That Kingdom is realised in its fulness in the sacrifice of Christ and its acceptance—'His death and resurrection'—of which the eucharist is the *anamnesis*. 'In Him' all the redeemed enter into that Kingdom. That is the purpose and meaning of all history, however long it may continue. The eucharist is the contact of time with the eternal fact of the Kingdom of God through Jesus. In it the church within time continually, as it were, enters into its own eternal being in that Kingdom, 'in Him', as Body of Christ, *through His act*.

That this is the original interpretation of the rite seems plain from the language of the early prayers themselves. In *Addai and Mari*, 'Thou *hast* restored our fall and raised our mortality . . . and condemned our enemies and granted victory . . . we *stand* before Thee at this time (for judgement)'; communion is 'for new life in the kingdom of heaven with all those who have been well-pleasing in Thy sight'. This is the language of achieved triumph, of the 'coming' of the 'Perfect Man', Head and members together, into the Kingdom of God by the gate of judgement. By a singular use of language which it is impossible to render adequately in English, but to which a Greek-speaking church could not be blind, Daniel had spoken of that 'coming of One like unto a Son of Man', who is in His own person 'the people of the saints of the Most High', 'to the Ancient of Days and He was brought near (*prosēnechthē*) unto Him'.[1] The word ordinarily translated 'was brought near' can just as well mean 'was offered in sacrifice'. It is no accident that for S. Paul the eucharist is at once the proclamation of the Lord's death and *the judgement of the world* as well as of the church[2]; or that S. John places in the midst of his account of the last supper the triumphant proclamation, '*Now* is the Son of Man glorified'.[3] The eucharist is nothing else but the eternal gesture of the Son of Man towards His Father as He passes into the Kingdom of God.

### '*The Spirit*' and the Eucharist

If this interpretation of the original meaning of the eucharist be correct, *viz.* that it is the contact of the church within time with the single *eschaton*, the coming of the Kingdom of God beyond time, it should follow that one consequence within time should be the gift to the church of that 'Spirit' by which, so to speak, the church maintains itself in time as the Body of Christ. And there is in fact a whole class of liturgical and patristic passages from the first four centuries or so, which have proved something of a puzzle to students, which do speak precisely as though what was received in holy communion was an accession of *pneuma* or 'Spirit'. In the East we may note a survival of this idea in the liturgy of S. James (*g*), 'He took the cup . . . and gave thanks and hallowed and blessed it and *filled it with Holy Spirit* and gave . . .'[4] The same idea is found in a number of Eastern writers, mostly Syrian, of whom the following quotation from S. Ephraem Syrus (fourth cent.) will give a sufficient idea: 'He called the bread His living Body and *He filled it with Himself and the Spirit.* . . . Take it, eat with faith, nothing doubting that it is My Body, and that *whoso eats it with faith eats in it fire and Spirit* . . . eat ye all of it, and *in it eat the Holy Spirit*; for it is in truth My Body'.[5] The same idea is found surviving in Theodore of Mopsuestia: At the communion 'the priest says loudly "the holy things for the holy people" because this food is holy and immortal, since it is the Body and Blood of our Lord, and is full of holiness *on account of the Holy Spirit Who dwells in it*'.[6] The same idea is found in Narsai and even later East Syrian writers.

In the West it is only necessary to cite the petition of Hippolytus' prayer (*k*) '. . . that Thou wouldest grant to all who partake to be made one, that they may be fulfilled with Holy Spirit'. This idea is found also in some Gallican prayers, *e.g.* this (in a similar position at the end of an

---

[1] Dan. vii. 13, in the version of Theodotion, which was used by the early church in preference to the LXX.
[2] 1 Cor. xi. 32, 33.       [3] John xiii. 31.       [4] *p.* 190.
[5] *Sermon in Holy Week*, iv. 4 (Ephraem, *Opera* ed. Lamy, I. 415 *sq.*).
[6] Theodore *Catecheses*, vi. ed. *cit.*, *p.* 108.

eucharistic prayer): 'beseeching Thee that Thou wouldest be pleased to pour Thy Holy Spirit into us who eat and drink those things that confer eternal life and the everlasting kingdom'.[1] Indeed, this most primitive notion is even now found in the Western rite. The post-communion thanksgiving of the Roman missal for Easter Day, which is also used at the administration of communion from the reserved sacrament throughout Eastertide, runs thus: 'Pour into us O Lord the Spirit of Thy charity, that we whom Thou hast satisfied with Thy paschal sacraments may by Thy love be made of one mind'. As S. Paul said, 'We have all been made to drink of one Spirit',[2] as Israel long before in the desert 'did all eat the same spiritual meat and did all drink the same spiritual drink'.[3]

The whole eschatological understanding of the eucharist is foreign to our way of thinking though it is of the essence of its primitive meaning. At the root of all primitive eschatology lies the paradox that by the christian life in this world you must strive 'to become what you are'. It is by the sacraments that you receive 'what you are', your true christian being; it is by your life that you must 'become' what they convey. By baptism a christian even in this world truly is 'a member of Christ, a child of God and an inheritor (not heir) of the Kingdom of heaven'. But because he is in the Body of Christ within time, the gift of the Spirit is given to him in confirmation that by His life in time he may become these things in eternal fact. The church is in the sight of God the Body of Christ; at the eucharist and by the eucharist for a moment it truly fulfils this, its eternal being; it becomes what it is. And the church goes out from the eucharist back to daily life in this world having 'received the Spirit of adoption, whereby we cry "Abba, Father" ',—the syllables always upon the lips of the Son when He dwelt in time. As S. Thomas said, the 'spiritual benefit' (res) received in this sacrament 'is the unity of the mystical body'—and in the New Testament this unity is above all 'the unity of the Spirit'.

[1] *Missale Gothicum*, Mass 79, *Post-secreta* (ed. Mabillon, Paris, 1729, *p. 298*).
[2] 1 Cor. xii. 13.          [3] *Ibid.*, x. 4.

# CHAPTER X

## THE THEOLOGY OF CONSECRATION

THE eucharist, then, manifests the true being of the church as the Body of Christ and of the christian as the member of Christ, because it manifests the being of Christ as the Redeemer—the Redeemer by the sacrifice of Himself. It is the act of Christ in His Body the church, transferring all who are 'in Him' into the eternal Kingdom of God beyond time. Of this interpretation the imagery of the eternal High-priest offering the earthly eucharist at the heavenly altar became the accepted expression from before the end of the first century, as the evidence of Clement shews. The heavenly Christ as the abiding 'propitiation for our sins' is the supernatural life of all who are His, who in the eucharist are at once 'offered' and 'brought to' the Father.[1] The individual effectively fulfils himself in this world as a living member of Christ above all by discharging personally his own proper function in the Body of Christ, his proper 'liturgy' (as bishop, cleric or layman) whose climax is his share in the 'doing' of the great corporate action of that Body prescribed by our Lord.

The eucharist, the characteristic vital act of the Body of Christ, is performed by the church as a whole (not merely by the clergy on behalf of the laity) in those two actions in which all have their part, offertory and communion. These are summarised by the twofold plural command, 'Take ye; eat ye . . .' (*labete, phagete*).[2] These words are no part of the authentic text of our oldest account of the institution, in 1 Cor. xi. 24, and the second, at all events, is very doubtfully original in Mark xiv. 22. Their real source in the liturgical tradition appears to be Matt. xxvi. 26, from which they have been interpolated into the other scriptural accounts of the last supper in many biblical MSS. But even if they are an addition to the absolutely primitive report of what our Lord actually said at that supper, they are in Matt. a first century addition—a sufficient indication that the apostolic church already understood by the command to 'do this' a *double* action, offertory and communion, and not one action only, to 'eat'.

### The 'Liturgy' of the Celebrant

Between these two corporate actions of offertory and communion is set the prayer—the prayer which consecrates and so sacrifices. This is performed not by the whole church but by one member of the Body only on behalf of the Body. It was so from the beginning, from the days when the bread-blessing and the *berakah* were said by the primitive president of the

[1] Dan. vii. 13.                    [2] Matt. xxvi. 26.

christian *chabûrah* in the name of the whole society at the beginning and
end of its corporate meal, following the invariable jewish custom which
had been observed at the last supper. It is for S. Paul the business of him
'who fulfils the place of a private person'[1] to say 'Amen' to the *eucharistia*
( == *berakah*, thanksgiving) said by someone else. So for Clement a generation later it is the 'proper liturgy', the especial function, of the *episcopē*,
'the bishop's office', to 'offer the gifts'.[2] This is what distinguishes the
christian 'high-priest' from the 'priestly' people of God.[3] Is there not here
some contradiction between this exclusive prerogative of an individual or
of one particular 'order' in the Body, and that *corporate* offering of the
eucharist which is insisted on in 1 Cor. xi. (as Dr. Moffat and others have
so carefully emphasised) and which reappears in Clement's own appeal,
'Let each of you, brethren, make eucharist to God according to his own
order'?[4]

Not at all. Because Christ is one with His church in its corporate unity
as His Body, the eucharist which is His act cannot be the act only of the
christian individuals present at it, whether considered singly or as a mere
aggregate, but of the church as an organism. But equally because Christ is
One in Himself, any particular eucharist is not the act of the local church
only, even in its organic unity; it must be the act of the whole catholic
Body of Christ, throughout the world and throughout the ages. The
eucharist is the 'coming' to the Father of redeemed humanity 'in Christ',
and can never be less than that, however many or however few may be
present at any particular celebration. The eucharistic prayer states the total
meaning of what is there done; and that meaning can only be authoritatively stated by one who is entitled to speak not only for the congregation
there present or even for the whole local church, but for the universal
church in all ages and all places.

There is only one member of a local church in pre-Nicene times who
bears a commission from outside itself, its bishop ordained by bishops
from other churches to a share in the universal apostolic commission. The
bishop can speak for his own church in virtue of his election by it as the
chosen centre of its unity, the chief organ of its corporate being, and
the guardian of its tradition. But he can speak also for the universal church,
because he has been accepted and consecrated into that apostolic college
to which our Lord committed not the charge of particular churches but a
special relation to or function in His Body, the whole church. As such the
bishop has authority to witness to and in the universal consent of the whole
catholic church.

The local *episcopē*, the 'bishop's office' in a local church, is already for
Clement in the first century the christian 'high-priesthood', the earthly
representative of that 'High-priest of our offerings' Who 'abideth in the
heaven of heavens', into Whose eternal offering of Himself the earthly

[1] 1 Cor. xiv. 16.     1 Clem., 44.     [3] *Ibid.*, 40.     [4] *Ibid.*, 41.

eucharist is taken up. As such the bishop is by office and 'liturgy' the proper minister of all sacraments to his own church, though he was soon forced by growth of numbers to exercise much of that ministry by delegating it to presbyters.

By contrast with the pre-Nicene bishop, who though president of a local church is also a successor of the apostles and a guardian of the universal church, the pre-Nicene presbyter is essentially the man of his own local church, the 'elder' chosen and ordained within itself for the day-to-day decision and administration of its own local concerns as a member of its 'executive committee', under the 'chairmanship' of its bishop. It is true that the steady practice of the church for some fifteen centuries past has now attached the exercise of the 'high-priestly' office of eucharistic celebrant to the second order of the ministry as well as to the bishop, as a regular and normal thing, so that this is now an inseparable duty and privilege of the presbyterate. It is, indeed, commonly regarded as the chief function of the presbyterate, with which in consequence the idea of eucharistic 'priesthood' has now become especially associated, to the practical exclusion of the old idea of the whole 'priestly' body of the church offering its priestly service to God in the eucharist. This is an unfortunate and unforeseen consequence of the hesitation felt in the fourth century (when the presbyterate for the first time found itself becoming chiefly employed in the administration of the sacraments) about applying to the second order the full title of 'high-priest', traditionally given to the bishop as minister of the sacraments. The compromise was then accepted of equating the presbyterate, not with the 'high-priesthood', but with the 'priesthood', of the Old Testament, while retaining 'high-priest' as a regular description of the episcopate. This usage described well enough the relation of a bishop and his presbyters as it had come to be in the fourth century. But it ignored the fact that the title of 'high-priest' had originally described the bishop simply as celebrant of the eucharist, and was intended to distinguish him not from the presbyters only but from the whole of the rest of the 'priestly' body, christians at large, laity as well as clergy. It was a great loss when the idea of this corporate priesthood of the whole church in the eucharist was obscured by attaching the title of the eucharistic 'priest' especially to the celebrant-presbyter. But it leads only to a further confusion of the whole idea when it is sought (as in much of the literature of the 'Liturgical Movement' in this country) to re-emphasise the 'priesthood of the laity' and the corporateness of the offering, without at the same time recognising that the celebrant-presbyter is in fact fulfilling the original '*high*-priestly' ministry of the bishop in the midst of the 'priestly' church, as the bishop's deputy.

We shall not get our ideas straight about the 'corporateness' of the eucharistic action or the 'priesthood of the laity' or the relation of the celebrant to the congregation or the function of the eucharistic prayer in the whole rite, unless we bear this fact in mind—that the celebrant, whether bishop or presbyter, is the '*high*-priest' in the midst of the 'priestly' people. But to complete the conception we need also to bear in mind the original distinction between the ministries of the universal church and the local churches, between apostles and elders, which meets us in Acts. The bishop is from one point of view only the chief minister of a *local* church, the president of the local council of presbyters. But he also came to exercise a ministry of the universal church as a successor of the apostles and a sharer in their universal commission. The ministry of all sacraments is exercised in the name of Christ and of His Body, that universal church which knows no local or temporal limitations. As such this ministry is properly only exercised by the episcopate as successors of the apostles. The ministry of the presbyter being by origin and in itself of local authority only, when he dispenses the sacraments he must be exercising the universal or 'apostolic' ministry of the bishop as the latter's delegate. Because every eucharist is the act of the whole church, the prayer which fixes its meaning as such an act is essentially a function of the universal ministry, the episcopate. And though the bishop in 'offering the gifts' by the prayer acts as the chosen 'high-priest' of his own local church, and frames it according to the local tradition of his church, he also imparts to that tradition all the authority of a recognised official 'witness' to the universal tradition of the catholic church. This function is exercised by presbyters, however normally and regularly, only by delegation.

### The Function of the Prayer in the Eucharistic Action

The eucharistic prayer thus vindicates for the present particular eucharistic action of a local church the whole accumulated depth of meaning attached to the eucharistic action by the universal church at every celebration since the crucifixion. The prayer said by the bishop or his authorised deputy takes up the corporate official act of his church into the corporate act of the whole Body of Christ, Head and members together, as 'the Son of Man' ( = 'the people of the saints of the Most High') 'comes' from time to the Father. Thus it becomes true that 'This is My Body', both of the local church self-offered at the offertory to become the Body, and of its offering. By the prayer of the Body of Christ the cup also of which that particular local church drinks is declared with the faith of the whole redeemed covenant-people and the authority of the Redeemer and Founder of the covenant Himself to be 'The New Covenant in My Blood'. It is the identity of the catholic church's action with the action of Christ Himself in His offering which constitutes 'the' eucharist. It is the identification of the action of a local church with that of the whole church which constitutes any particular celebration 'a' eucharist.

This is the meaning of being 'in *the communion* of the catholic church'—

that the whole Body of Christ accepts and makes its own and is, as it were, *contained in* the eucharistic action of a particular congregation. The eucharist of a group or society which repudiates or is repudiated by the catholic whole is thereby defective, however holy its members and however 'valid' the orders of its ministers. Its sacrament cannot have as its *res*, its 'spiritual benefit', the 'unity of the mystical body' in the full sense, just because the eucharistic action of that group or society cannot be fully identified with that of the whole church. We may willingly believe that our Lord will never turn away without grace any individual who comes to Him in good faith through devout participation in such eucharists. Yet it remains one effect of the hideous anomaly of schism within the Body of Christ, that though a schismatic church may have taken the greatest care to preserve a 'valid' succession; though like the Novatianists of the third century and the Donatists of the fourth it may make its boast of this and of the purity of its doctrine against the corruptions of the catholics; though it may truly consecrate and offer the Body and Blood of Christ in its eucharist; it is yet deprived of the full *res*, the 'spiritual benefit', of the eucharist—'the unity of the mystical body'—if its sacrament be done outside that unity. 'Leave there thy gift before the altar, and go thy way; first be reconciled to thy brother and then come and offer thy gift'[1]—holds true of churches as well as individuals.

So the prayer consecrates and sacrifices together—sacrifices by consecrating. For consecration in itself is nothing else but the acceptance by the Father of the sacrifice of Christ in His members—the sacrifice of 'the Body of Christ' in all its meanings.

From the beginning the prayer had this double function of stating a meaning which is at once an offering and a blessing, sacrifice and consecration. If we go back to the jewish pre-history of the rite, the bread-blessing and the *berakah* were more than a recognition of the fact that God provided the food and the drink. The blessing of His Name for them in some sense offered them back to God, and also 'released' them, as it were, for human consumption. The pagan, the Samaritan, the apostate, could not take part in the jewish *berakah* because it had this aspect of 'offering'. In jewish eyes 'it was sacrilege to partake of God's bounty without pronouncing the blessing of His Name for providing it. All belongs to God and we share in what is His when consecrating it by a blessing.'[2] This double action has been taken over into the christian prayer. We still offer to God 'of Thine own gifts and bounties', as the Roman canon has it. But it is no longer only God's natural bounty for which we thank Him, but His gift of 'the Bread of heaven in Christ Jesus', to quote again the words of administration in Hippolytus. The eucharistic prayer retains the character of the table-blessing of the New Covenant.

[1] Matt. v. 24.
[2] F. Gavin, *Jewish Antecedents of the Christian Sacraments*, p. 69.

And that Covenant is 'in My Blood'. From the day that our Lord's judicial execution by crucifixion was interpreted as 'atoning', and therefore as in some sense sacrificial, the vague sense of 'offering back to God' contained in the old jewish conception of the *berakah* was powerfully reinforced. Only a few hours before that sacrificial death He had Himself declared that 'This' bread 'is My Body' and 'This cup' is the Blood of the sacrificial Victim of the New Covenant. The inference that when His followers 'did this' as He had simultaneously commanded them to do it 'for the *anamnesis* of' Him, what is done with 'this bread' and 'this cup' is what He forthwith did with His Body and Blood—offered them in sacrifice— was irresistible. For the purely jewish church of the years immediately following the passion, sacrifice was necessarily of the essence of a covenant with God, not only for the inauguration of a covenant but as the centre of the covenanted life. For that jewish church the altar on Mt. Moriah and the daily sacrifice upon it still furnished an apparent proof that Israel was yet somehow the covenant-people of God.[1] Even S. Paul, for all his radicalism, still feels a strong sense of the continuing privilege of Israel in possessing the *latreia*, the divinely ordered worship of the Temple.[2] The fact that the Messiah by His sacrificial death had instituted a New Covenant did not destroy the inherited idea of the centrality of sacrifice in any divine covenant. On the contrary it enhanced it. And what our Lord had said and done at the last supper could not but concentrate the full force of this upon the eucharist. It was the common jewish expectation that the 'Thank-offering' alone of all sacrifices would continue in the days of the Messiah.[3]

It was the interpretation of the death of Jesus as sacrificial, reinforcing the vague idea already latent in the *berakah* of 'offering' the food of the *chabûrah* meal to God, which made the sacrificial interpretation of the eucharist inevitable from the outset. In the light of Calvary, Easter and Ascension together (understood in combination as the sacrifice and acceptance of the Messiah) no other interpretation of what Jesus had said and done at the last supper was possible for jews. In estimating the speed with which this interpretation of the eucharist was grasped we have to bear in mind that no belief whatever in Jesus as Messiah could make head against the ignominy of Calvary except upon the sacrificial interpretation of His death. Specifically christian Messianism *depended upon* that as its precondition. (It must, therefore, antedate S. Paul's conversion and come from the earliest days.) In its details the death of Christ might be equated with more than one kind of sacrifice, as S. Paul equates it with the Passover and the Epistle to the Hebrews with the Day of Atonement. This was only a matter of interpretation and illustration. In point of fact the Passover illustration was found to be more strikingly applicable to the christian feast

---

[1] Acts ii. 46; iii. 1; vi. 7; xxi. 26.  [2] Rom. ix. 4.
[3] *Pesachim* 79[a]. On the continuance of sacrifice in the Messianic Kingdom, see the very interesting rabbinic passages collected in Strack-Billerbeck, *Kommentar zum N.T.*, iv. 935–6.

of the *Pascha* as the annual commemoration of the actual historical *events* by which redemption was achieved;[1] while the Day of Atonement interpretation was felt to apply more naturally to the eucharist as the *anamnesis*, the 're-calling', of the *effects* of redemption. But when S. Paul in 1 Cor. v. 7 spoke of the death of Christ as a sacrifice and went on in turn to speak of the eucharist as the 'shewing forth' of that death in 1 Cor. xi., he was not launching upon the church two new ideas which would eventually lead to the interpretation of the eucharist as sacrifice by combination. He was merely repeating those interpretations of the eucharist and Christ's death, the combination of which from the outset had alone made the primitive jewish christianity of the Jerusalem church possible.[2] The proof that they had already been combined long before he wrote 1 Cor. is the existence of pre-Pauline christianity.

We have seen how the second century material which comes from the early christian re-writing of the *berakah* in terms of the New Covenant (*e.g.*, Hippolytus *a–d*, *cf. S. James b–f*) concentrates on the divine economy of redemption, on the plan of God for man from creation onwards, and on the Person and office of God the Son as Creator and Redeemer of mankind, rather than on the historical events by which Jesus of Nazareth wrought that redemption. Yet even this 'Thanksgiving for the New Covenant' necessarily finds its climax in the mention of the 'stretching forth of His hands' 'for His voluntary passion' (Hippolytus *d*). The eucharist is, as Justin said, above all 'the *anamnesis* of His passion which He suffered on behalf of the men whose souls are (thereby) cleansed from all iniquity'.[3] This is the foundation-sacrifice of the New Covenant.

But side by side with this element of 'Thanksgiving for the New Covenant' instead of the Old, the christian *eucharistia* inherited another element from the jewish *berakah*, another idea, the blessing of 'the Name' of God which released the food of the *chabûrah* for its consumption. This idea continued in an obscure way to operate in the christian understanding of the prayer. It does not seem fanciful to relate this aspect of the *berakah* more closely to the idea of 'consecration', while the 'covenant-thanksgiving' is related to the covenant-sacrifice. We have already several times referred to that passage of Theodotus which relates the 'transformation of the Bread into spiritual power' to the 'hallowing by the power of *the Name*'.[4] A similar notion lies behind the phrase of Irenaeus that 'the bread receiving the invocation (or 'naming', *epiklesis*) of God is no more common bread but eucharist'.[5] It seems, indeed, likely that the whole

[1] Hippolytus, *On the Pascha*, iii. (*c.* A.D. 210), seems to be the first christian document which equates the eating of the Passover with the reception of holy communion, but this is in a sermon for the paschal vigil, where such an identification would naturally suggest itself. Justin (*Dial.*, iii.) used the Passover symbolism of the historical events of the Passion, but never of the eucharist.
[2] *Cf. pp.* 76 *sq.*    [3] *Dial.* 41.    [4] *Exc.* 82, *cf. p.* 170.
[5] *Adv. Haer.*, iv. 18, 5.

primitive usage of the word *epiklesis* in connection with the eucharist is intimately connected with this jewish 'blessing of the Name' in all food benedictions, obligatory on jews and primitive christians alike in their table-blessings.[1] As we have seen, the formal traces of this idea lasted long in the church, especially in the rule that the prayer must begin with a 'Naming' of God and end with a 'glorifying of the Name', usually in the form of a somewhat elaborate Trinitarian doxology;[2] though it might be, as in *Addai and Mari* (and some other cases) a glorifying of 'the Name' of Christ. Similarly baptism 'in the Name of the Father and of the Son and of the Holy Ghost' eventually prevailed, though the at least equally primitive formula 'in the Name of Jesus' was accepted as valid by the especially conservative church of Rome, apparently right down to the Council of Trent.[3]

## Fourth Century Ideas of Consecration

By the fourth century, however, we meet with considerable changes everywhere in the ideas about consecration. Nowhere does the primitive nucleus of the prayer, the 'thanksgiving series', appear to have retained its original force as the prayer which 'eucharistised' the food. Its place as what may be called the 'operative' part of the prayer has been taken now by something presumed to have a more directly 'consecratory' intention, from the 'second half' of the prayer. In some churches it is the recital of our Lord's words—'This is My Body', etc.—which is now taken to identify the Bread and Wine with what He Himself had said that they are, His Body and Blood. This idea found in fourth century writers so representative of different traditions as Ambrose at Milan,[4] Chrysostom at Antioch,[5] Sarapion in Egypt,[6] and Gregory of Nyssa in Asia Minor,[7] must be presumed to go back in its origins at least to the third century. It might even be traced back to the second, since something like it is found in Justin;[8] while Hippolytus' prayer is clearly developed on the basis of the

[1] Dom Connolly has well brought out this aspect of *epiklesis* in an important article, *J.T.S.* xxv. (July, 1924), *pp.* 337 *sqq.* (*cf.* Armitage Robinson, *Theology,* viii. Feb. 1924, *pp.* 89 *sqq.*). But Dom Odo Casel (*Jahrbuch für Liturgiewissenschaft,* iv., *pp.* 169–178) is justified in his criticism that this idea of the 'potency of the Name' does not account for everything in ancient christian usage of the word. It seems, *e.g.*, impossible to bring the use of it by such a writer as Cyril of Jerusalem under this heading satisfactorily. What seems to be true is that it accounts satisfactorily for every single usage of *epiklesis* by the christian writers of the second century. In the later third and fourth century the word widens its meaning a good deal in some christian writers, another mark of the slow oblivion of jewish ideas in the increasingly hellenised churches of the period.
[2] *Cf.* Hippolytus, *Ap. Trad.,* vi. 4.
[3] Pope Nicholas I consulted by the Bulgarian bishops in the ninth century decided in favour of the validity of this form, as had Pope Stephen I in the third century and S. Ambrose in the fourth; in which they were followed (with reservations) by S. Thomas Aquinas (*S. Th.,* iii. 66, 6 *ad Imum*).
[4] *de Mysteriis,* ix. 52.          [6] *de Prod. Judae,* i. 6 (*cf. p.* 281).
[5] *Cf. p.* 163 (section *d*).          [7] *Oratio Catechetica,* 37.
[8] *Ap.* I. 66 (*cf. p.* 159).

central constructional position of the account of the institution in the prayer as a whole. But we have seen that Sarapion in the fourth century has already overlaid this idea (and the other, probably older still, of the importance of the 'Naming' of God) with the idea of a petition for the 'advent' of the Word upon the bread and wine parallel to His 'advent' at the incarnation in the womb of Mary. There need be no question—I do not see how there can be, in view of the language employed—that this petition would be understood by those who used and heard it as 'effecting consecration'. This idea of an 'invocation' of the Word found, as we have said, in other fourth century writers in Egypt, Syria and Cappadocia and in some later Gallican prayers in the West, in effect connects back the consecration of the eucharist with that initial 'thanksgiving' for the incarnation which formed one of the 'thanksgiving series' in the first half of the prayer.[1]

At this point it is important to note that the pre-Nicene theology of the incarnation as a rule regarded it, not as we do, as the effect of a conception 'by the *Holy Ghost* of the Virgin Mary', but as a conception 'by *the Logos* (the Word, the Second Person of the Trinity) of the Virgin Mary'. The eternal Word of God Himself, the creative *Logos* 'coming down to us' as Athanasius himself said, 'formed for Himself the Body from the Virgin'.[2] However perverse it may seem to us, 'the Spirit' which came upon Mary and 'the Power of the Most High' which overshadowed her (Luke i. 35) were unanimously interpreted by the second century christian writers as meaning the *Second* not the Third Person of the Holy Trinity.[3] And this interpretation, general in the pre-Nicene church, lasted on in many quarters during the fourth century. It is accepted and used by all the anti-Arian stalwarts, Athanasius, Hilary, Ambrose and Gregory Nazianzene, as a normal expression of orthodoxy. This 'Spirit = Word' terminology is obviously related to the 'Spirit = Presence-of-God' terminology, of which we have found traces in Syria.[4] It is also likely that both are originally connected in pre-christian jewish thought with the idea of the sanctity and 'power' of the Name of God, though this is not a matter which need concern us here.[5] The 'Spirit = Word' terminology is, like the 'Spirit =

[1] *Cf.* Hippolytus, *c.* (*p.* 157), *Addai and Mari d.* (*p.* 179) and the trace of it in Sarapion (*a*²); *cf. p.* 163.

[2] Athanasius, *de Incarnatione* 18 (*c.* A.D. 318).

[3] *E.g.* Justin *Ap.*, I. 13 (commenting on Luke i. 35): 'The "Spirit", then, and the "Power" from God it is correct to understand as none other than the *Word*'. Hippolytus, *contra Noëtum* 4: 'For He was Word, He was "Spirit", He was "Power" ' (*cf. ibid.* 16, cited *p.* 254, *n.* 1). Tertullian: (*adv. Praxean,* 26) 'This "Spirit" of God will be the "Word" Himself'; and again, 'The "Spirit" is the Word, and the Word the "Spirit" '. *Cf.* Irenaeus, *adv. Haer.*, v. 1, 3; S. Cyprian, *Q. Idola non.* 11; Lactantius, iv. 12, etc.

[4] *Cf. pp.* 183 *sq.*

[5] *Cf.* Exod. xxiii. 20 *sqq.*: 'Behold I send an Angel before thee . . . beware of him and provoke him not; for he will not pardon your transgressions: for *My Name* is in him. But if thou shalt indeed obey his voice and do all that I speak . . .', where the 'Angel' seems to combine all the notions of the 'Presence', the 'Name' and the 'Word' of God, together with the 'sanctity' and 'awfulness' of that Name.

Presence' idea in christian usage, a survival of the New Testament conception of the 'presence' of the heavenly Christ as the 'quickening Spirit'[1] in His members on earth, already spoken of.[2] What is important to our purpose here is that such language was still currently used of the eucharist in the fourth century, so that S. Ambrose does not hesitate to say to catechumens about the sacrament, 'The Body of Christ is the Body of "Divine Spirit", for the Spirit is Christ.'[3]

The parallel made by Sarapion and his contemporaries (which does not appear, I think, before the fourth century) between the consecration of the eucharist and the incarnation is important. It is obvious that as soon as the incarnation came to be understood generally as a ·conception by the Holy Ghost' and not a 'conception by the Word', the parallel would be likely to suggest that the eucharist also is an operation of the Holy Ghost. And the old terminology of 'Spirit = Presence' was as likely to lend itself to this transference of ideas about eucharistic consecration as the 'Spirit = Word' terminology. We do in fact find the argument that as Christ's Body was conceived in the womb of Mary by the Holy Ghost, so His Body is 'made' in the sacrament by the operation of the Holy Ghost, elaborated at some length in later Eastern writers, beginning with S. John of Damascus.[4] But I do not think it is found either in Syrian writers or elsewhere[5] before his time (c. A.D. 690–760).

But this parallel with the incarnation is not the basis of the theory of eucharistic consecration as an operation of the Holy Ghost when we first meet this idea, either as a theological doctrine in the *Didascalia* (Syria, c. A.D. 250)[6] or as practically expressed in the liturgy, in the Jerusalem rite described by Cyril in A.D. 347. Cyril's rite had no 'thanksgiving series' and therefore no memorial of the incarnation to which his petition for consecration could refer back. His invocation is based on no such parallel: 'We entreat God . . . to send forth the Holy Ghost . . . that He may make the bread the Body of Christ . . . *for whatsoever comes in contact with the Holy Ghost, this is hallowed and transformed.*'[7] No doubt such language is ultimately derived from the sort of 'Spirit = Presence' terminology found in *Addai and Mari* (rather than the 'Spirit = Word' terminology found in the pre-Nicene churches outside Syria). But there is no doubt whatever that by 'Spirit' here Cyril himself means the Holy Ghost, the Third Person of the Trinity. His petition for consecration is explicitly based not on a parallel with the incarnation, but on a theological theory about the office and mission of God the Holy Ghost in Himself. Cyril is here thinking in

---

[1] I Cor. xv. 45.  [2] Cf. pp. 259 sq.  [3] de Mysteriis, 58.
[4] de Fide Orthodoxa, iv. 13.
[5] S. Ambrose, de Mysteriis 53, has a comparison of the consecration with the Virginal conception by Mary, but there is no suggestion that both are operations of the Spirit; the emphasis is only on the supernatural character of both happenings. Ambrose (in 54) goes on at once to attribute consecration not to the Spirit but to our Lord Himself acting by the words of institution.
[6] Cf. p. 278.  [7] Cat., xxiii. 7.

terms of the doctrine of the Trinity, not like Sarapion in his invocation of the Word, in terms of the doctrine of the incarnation. Thus, though the invocations in Sarapion and Cyril are both 'consecratory' and so superficially parallel, they really rest upon rather different ideas about consecration.

There is a further point in which Cyril differs not only from Sarapion but from the whole pre-Nicene church. Sarapion follows the universal tradition in making the eucharist emphatically an action of Christ, the Word, the Second Person of the Trinity. But from end to end of Cyril's account of the liturgy and throughout his eucharistic teaching, Christ plays only a *passive* part in the eucharist. He is simply the divine Victim Whose Body and Blood are 'made' by the action of the Holy Ghost, that the earthly church may offer Him to the Father 'in propitiation for our sins'. The older tradition was that He is the *active* agent in the eucharist, who offers the church as found 'in Him'. Though Cyril is well acquainted with the conception of the heavenly High-priesthood of Christ as a general idea,[1] it is noticeable that he never applies this to the eucharist.

This is so considerable a change in eucharistic doctrine that it is desirable to be sure how far Cyril is an innovator in this respect. We have already seen that in the third century the Syrian *Didascalia* had remarked that 'the eucharist through the Spirit is accepted and sanctified'.[2] This occurs in the course of a polemic by the author against certain Syrian christians who are still observing the jewish ritual laws of 'uncleanness'. Some women among them are under the impression that at certain periods they ought to abstain 'from prayer and the scriptures and the eucharist'. The answer of this author is that they themselves do not imagine that in such periods they have ceased to possess the Holy Spirit given them in confirmation. 'Prayer is heard through the Holy Spirit, and the eucharist through the Spirit is accepted and sanctified, and the scriptures are the words of the Holy Spirit. If the Holy Spirit is in thee, why dost thou keep thyself from approaching the works of the Holy Spirit . . . Whether is greater, the bread or the Spirit that sanctifieth the bread?' So, later in the same chapter,[3] he inveighs against those who still regard the jewish rule that all contact with a corpse renders 'unclean'. 'Do you', he says, 'come together even in the cemeteries and read the holy scriptures and without demur perform your "liturgy" and your supplication to God; and offer an acceptable eucharist, the likeness of the royal Body of Christ, both in your congregations (*ecclesia*) and in your cemeteries and on the departures of them that sleep—pure bread that is made with fire and sanctified with invocations . . .' It would probably be unwise, as Dom Connolly says,[4] 'to put two and two together' and to conclude from a combination of these two passages that the author of the *Didascalia* necessarily used a liturgy

---

[1] *Cat.* i. 4; x. 4; x. 16; xi. 1.          [2] *Ed. cit.*, p. 244.
[3] *Ibid.*, p. 252.                          [4] *Ibid.*, p. lii.

resembling that of Cyril at Jerusalem a century later. So far as this latter passage goes, its evidence as regards practice would be entirely satisfied by the older notion of *epiklesis* as a hallowing by the invocation of the Name of God. But it is quite clear from the earlier passage that this author did share Cyril's theory that 'consecration' is effected by the action of the Holy Ghost, however the idea may have been expressed in his liturgy.

Cyril therefore had at least one predecessor in Syria as regards his theology, though so far as I know this statement of the author of the *Didascalia* is unique in all the third century christian writings, both in Syria and elsewhere. And so far as third century Syrian liturgical practice is concerned, if *Addai and Mari* is at all a representative rite with its eucharistic prayer addressed directly to the *Son*, then the Syrian churches were in line with the rest of the christian world in regarding the eucharistic consecration as effected by the Son, and not by the Spirit.

In the fourth century our Syrian evidence is considerably more extensive. From round about A.D. 330 comes the *Dialogue* of an otherwise unknown Syrian author called Adamantius. In this occurs the statement, put into the mouth of the heretical disputant, 'The Spirit comes upon the eucharist'. His orthodox opponent at once asks 'Why, then, did you say that the Spirit came down for the salvation of *all* men', since only christians receive the eucharist?[1] Evidently we have here another instance of the old confusing 'Spirit = Word' terminology, since this is a reference back to a previous discussion about the purpose of the incarnation. But it illustrates, I think, the sort of way in which this terminology could assist the spread of the new theory of consecration by the Holy Ghost.

An older contemporary of Cyril in Syria is Eusebius, bishop of Caesarea, the great church historian, in some ways the most learned christian of his time, though not a clear-headed or profound theologian. It is significant that in all his voluminous works which appeared throughout the first generation of the fourth century, this Syrian author never once refers eucharistic consecration to the action of the Third Person of the Trinity. True, he comes near it once in interpreting John vi. 63, 'It is the spirit that quickeneth; the flesh profiteth nothing', as referring to the eucharist. This he understands as meaning 'Let not the off-hand hearing of what I have said about (eating) flesh and blood disturb you; for these things "profit nothing" if they are understood sensually; but the Spirit is the lifegiver to those who are able to understand spiritually'.[2]

This is hardly Cyril's doctrine; and Eusebius' usual teaching is the doctrine of the eucharist as the act of the heavenly High-priest through His earthly Body, the church.[3] So firmly rooted in Syrian liturgical practice

[1] Adamantius, *Dial.* II (*ap.* Origen. *Opp. ed.* C. Delarue, Paris 1773, I. i., *p.* 824).
[2] *On the Theology of the Church*, iii. 12.
[3] *Cf. e.g.*, *Demonstratio Evangelica* V, iii. 18. 'Our Saviour Jesus, the Christ of God, after the manner of Melchizedek still even now accomplishes by means of His ministers the rites of His priestly work among men.'

was this doctrine of the eucharistic priesthood of Christ that the Syrian Arians (with whom Eusebius was suspected if not actually convicted of sympathy) were able to use it to emphasise in an heretical way the subordination of the Son to the Father.[1]

A writer who is roughly a contemporary of Eusebius, but a man of a very different calibre, is Aphraates, an East Syrian bishop and monk. His simplicity and earnestness represent the native genius and tradition of the Syriac-speaking semitic churches of the Syrian countryside at their best, as Eusebius with his Greek learning represents the hellenism of the Syrian cities. Aphraates again has no reference to consecration by the Holy Ghost; in his references to the eucharist he always takes it for granted that it is the act of the Son.[2] A rather later writer who is naturally taken together with Aphraates is S. Ephraem Syrus, the great poet of the Syrian churches. We have already seen that far from agreeing with Cyril that it is the Holy Ghost who makes the bread to be the Body of Christ, Ephraem on occasion exactly reverses Cyril's idea, and says that it is Christ Who 'called the bread His Body and filled it with Himself and the Spirit'.[3]

## S. Cyril's Doctrine of Consecration and the Rite of Jerusalem

It is important to realise that Cyril, though (as usual) he was not entirely an innovator in his doctrine of consecration, is still isolated among his own contemporaries even in Syria; because his doctrine was destined to have a swift and far-reaching effect. There can be little doubt, I think, that in framing it Cyril is chiefly influenced by the text of the Jerusalem liturgy as it was used by him in church. In that liturgy as he describes it, the whole weight of the eucharistic action rests on the single paragraph of the invocation, and the 'offering' which immediately follows. The 'thanksgiving series' has been replaced by the preface and sanctus borrowed from Egypt; then comes the invocation and offering; and the whole of the rest of the 'second half' of the prayer has been swallowed up in the unprecedentedly developed intercessions. Except for the single paragraph of the invocation all is either mere preliminaries or consequences. There is thus no option but to treat the invocation as 'consecratory', in and by itself. And in view of its actual phrasing there was no possibility but to treat the Holy Ghost as the active agent and Christ Himself as purely passive in the eucharist, as Cyril does. His theology is based upon his prayer.

[1] So the Arian compiler of the Liturgy of *Ap. Const.*, viii. '. . . Thee the whole bodiless and holy array of heaven worships; Thee the Paraclete worships (!) and before all Thy holy Servant Jesus the Christ, our Lord and God and the Messenger and High Captain of Thy power, the eternal and perpetual High-priest; Thee the well-ordered armies of the angels worship . . .' (This is what the compiler wrote; the text printed by Brightman, L. E. W., p. 18, is the ancient bowdlerised version of most MSS.)

[2] *Demonstratio*, xii. 6 (ed. Graffin. *Pat. Syr.*, i. 516–7); xxi. 9 (*ibid.*, 957); xxi. 10 (*ibid.*, 960).

[3] *Cf. p. 266.*

The influence of the Jerusalem rite on those of other churches in the formative period of the later fourth and early fifth century was very great indeed, and Cyril's form of invocation was adopted widely, especially in the East. But in other churches it was incorporated into eucharistic prayers of a more traditional construction, which still contained a 'thanksgiving series', and in some cases already possessed an institution narrative and an *anamnesis* section, none of which were to be found in Cyril's rite. The inclusion of such an invocation with its clear and novel doctrinal implications in prayers which had been framed upon other ideas raised obvious problems of interpretation.

## The Invocation of the Spirit

At Antioch, where an invocation of some kind had been adopted before A.D. 390, probably as a sort of supplement appended to the prayer proper, Chrysostom makes no real attempt to harmonise the old and the new. We have already seen how admirably he could expound the old conception of the eucharist as the action of the heavenly High-priest. Yet on occasion he, like Cyril, can speak as though Christ were purely passive in the eucharist: 'When the priest stands before the table holding up his hands to heaven and calling on the Holy Ghost to come and touch the elements, there is a great quiet, a great silence. When the Spirit gives His grace, when He descends, when you see the Lamb sacrificed and consummated, do you then cause tumult . . .?'[1] Here Christ is passive, and for the same reason that He is made to be so in Cyril's explanation; it is impossible to state the matter otherwise when the explanation is given in the terms of this type of consecratory invocation. Where Chrysostom transfers the 'operative' effect to another section of the prayer, we find him equally naturally taking a different view. 'It is not man who makes the gifts which are set forth to become the Body and Blood of Christ, but *Christ Himself* Who was crucified for us. The priest stands fulfilling a rôle (*schēma*) and saying those words, but the power and the grace are of God. "This is My Body", he says; these words transform ('re-order', *metarrhythmizei*) the elements. And just as that which was spoken "Increase and multiply and replenish the earth" was said once but is for all time operative in bestowing on our nature the power of procreation, so this which was spoken once *maketh complete* the sacrifice at every altar in the churches from then until now and until His coming again'.[2]

Chrysostom, *Hom. In Coemet.*, App. 3 (*Opp.* ed. Montfaucon, Paris, 1836, ii. 474 D). For similar teaching see *de Sacerdotio*, iii. 4 (i. 468 A); *de s. Pentecoste*, i. 4 (ii. 548 C.), etc.
[2] *de Prod. Judae*, i. 6 (*Opp.*, ii. 453 B). For similar teaching see *ibid.*, ii. 6 (*ibid.* 465 B); *in Mat. Hom.*, lxxxii. 4 (vii. 889 D), etc. For what seems to be a survival in Chrysostom of the old 'Spirit = Word' terminology in connection with the eucharist, see *in Heb. Hom.*, xiv. 1 (xii. 201 B).

Consecration by the Son and by the Spirit may be reconcilable doctrines, but they are two different ideas. Yet Chrysostom himself never attempts to reconcile these two ideas, which reflect the existence of different and unharmonised elements in the Antiochene prayer as he knew it. The same incoherence is not to be found in Cyril's theology, because the Jerusalem rite had eliminated everything from its prayer which might suggest another explanation than that plainly demanded by the language of its invocation. It seems clear that the difficulty of assimilating a consecratory invocation of the Holy Ghost on something like the Jerusalem model into a traditional prayer and theology which regarded the eucharist as the direct act of Christ Himself had not been satisfactorily met at Antioch in Chrysostom's time—nor, indeed, has it ever been met quite convincingly in all the fifteen centuries since.[1]

### The Invocation as Effecting the 'Resurrection'

It is, however, from the region of Antioch and not long after Chrysostom, in the *Catecheses* of Theodore of Mopsuestia, that we first meet with an exposition of the liturgical action which attempts to solve this difficulty. It was afterwards universally adopted by the devotional writers of the Byzantine church and is still generally accepted (with certain modifications) in the Eastern Orthodox churches to-day.

Theodore writes thus: 'We must think therefore that the deacons who (at the offertory) carry the eucharistic bread and bring it out for the sacrifice represent the invisible hosts of ministry (*i.e.* angels) with this difference, that through their ministry and these memorials (? *hypomnēmata*) they do not send forth Christ our Lord to His saving passion (like the angel in Gethsemane). When they bring up (the oblation at the offertory) they place it on the altar for the completed representation of the passion, so that we may think of Him on the altar as if He were placed in the sepulchre after having received His passion. This is why the deacons who spread linens on the altar[2] represent the figure of the linen cloths at the burial . . . (The deacons) stand up on both sides and agitate all the air above the holy Body with fans . . . they shew by this the greatness of the Body which is lying there; for it is the custom when the corpse of the great ones of this world is carried on a bier, that some men should fan the air above it . . . the same is done with the Body lying on the altar, which is holy, awe-inspiring and remote from all corruption, a Body which will very shortly rise to an immortal being.

[1] The best explanations I know are those of Nicolas Cabasilas in the fourteenth century (*Exposition*, 27–32. M.P.G. cl. 425 *sq.*), and Simeon of Thessalonica in the fifteenth (*Exposition* 86–88. M.P.G. clv. 733–730). That of Mark of Ephesus in the same period (M.P.G. clx. 1080–1089) is too inaccurate in its statements to be of much interest to-day. The modern orthodox manuals do no more than elaborate Cabasilas and Simeon, who in turn develop John Damascene.
[2] *Cf* p. 104.

'It is in remembrance of the angels who continually came to the passion and death of our Lord that the deacons stand in a circle and fan the air and offer honour and adoration to the sacred and awe-inspiring Body which is lying there. . . . This they do in order to shew that because the Body lying there is high, dreadful, holy and true Lord, through its union with the Divine nature, it is with great fear that it must be seen and kept.

'These things take place while all are silent, for before the liturgy begins all must watch the bringing up and spreading forth before God of such a great and wonderful object with a quiet and reverent fear and a silent and noiseless prayer. When our Lord had died the apostles went back and remained at home in great silence and immense fear. . . . When we see the oblation (placed) on the table—which denotes that it is being placed in a kind of sepulchre after its death—great silence falls on those present. . . . They must look at it with a quiet and reverential fear, since it is necessary that Christ our Lord should rise again in the awe-inspiring liturgy which is performed by the priestly ordinance, and announce our participation in unspeakable benefits'.

This is one of the passages in ancient christian writers in which we find something like a new immolation predicated of the Body of Christ in the eucharist. What is disconcerting is to find that this is connected with the *offertory*, not with the consecration. All this 'fear' and 'adoration' on which Theodore here lays such emphasis, and the fanning and other marks of reverence are addressed to what we should call the 'unconsecrated' elements, 'before the liturgy begins'. Yet so it certainly is. Theodore goes on from this point to describe the deacon's proclamations, the kiss of peace, the *lavabo* of the clergy, the reading of the diptychs (lists of names for intercession), certain preparatory prayers of the priest, the dialogue and finally the eucharistic prayer. This he calls 'the *anaphora*' (the earliest use, if I remember rightly, of this Byzantine technical term for the eucharistic prayer) and also 'the sacrifice' and 'the immolation of the sacrifice'. It is only when he has described the major part of the prayer that he reaches the main point of his interpretation, with his account of the consecratory invocation of the Holy Ghost. This in the rite of Mopsuestia was clearly of the same type as that in the North Syrian rite of *Ap. Const.*, viii., and as such a modification of that of the Jerusalem rite.

'It is necessary, therefore, that our Lord should now rise from the dead by the power of the things that are being done, and that He should spread His grace over us. This cannot happen otherwise than by the coming of the grace of the Holy Spirit[1]. . . . Therefore the priest offers prayer and supplications to God that the Holy Spirit may descend, and that grace may come therefrom upon the bread and wine so that they may be seen (? *hina phanōsin*) to be truly the Body and Blood of our Lord, which are the

[1] Rom. viii. 11.

memorials (? *hypomnēmata*) of immortality. Indeed the Body of our Lord, which is from our own nature, was previously mortal by nature. When the priest therefore declares them to be the Body and Blood of Christ, he clearly reveals that they have become so by the descent of the Holy Spirit, through Whom they have also become immortal, inasmuch as the Body of our Lord after it was anointed and had received the Holy Spirit was clearly seen so to become. In this same way, after the Holy Spirit has come here also we believe that the elements of bread and wine have received a sort of anointing from the grace that comes upon them and we hold them henceforth to be immortal, incorruptible, impassible and immutable by nature, as the Body of our Lord was after the resurrection.'[1]

This last sentence, teaching 'transaccidentation', is sufficiently remarkable; but what are we to make of the rest? It is quite clear that Theodore regards the bread and wine as being in some sense the Body and Blood of Christ from the moment the deacons bring them from the sacristy at the offertory. As such they are 'fearful', 'holy and true Lord' and to be treated with 'adoration', 'silent fear' and so forth, before the prayer or even the preparations for it have begun. But the sacrament at this stage is only the *dead* Body of Christ, entombed upon the altar.[2] It is the invocation of the Holy Ghost which Theodore declares brings about the 'resurrection' in the eucharist. The only comment we need make for the moment on this conception is to point out that the actual terms of his invocation as he reports them contain no trace whatever of this idea. The elements are there described as 'bread and wine' and not as the 'dead Body' of Christ. The Spirit is invoked upon them in order 'that they may be seen to be truly the Body and Blood of our Lord', not to bring about their resurrection. And Theodore himself is sufficiently conscious of the plain meaning of the prayer to add that 'when the priest declares them to be the Body and Blood of Christ, he clearly reveals that they have *become* so by the descent of the Holy Spirit', in the invocation and not at the offertory. There is evidently a disconnection between Theodore's explanation and the prayer of his rite.

But his statements give the clue to certain very peculiar features of the later Byzantine rite and the Byzantine devotional tradition. In this rite at the 'great entrance' (offertory procession) the deacons (and since the twelfth century the celebrant with them, an unprimitive feature which destroys the symbolism) bring the unconsecrated elements from the 'table of *prothesis*', where they have been elaborately prepared before the

---

[1] Theodore, *Catecheses* v. and vi. (*ed. cit. pp.* 86–104. I have curtailed the intolerable prolixity of some of the sentences, but everything above is from his text except the words in brackets).

[2] But Theodore does not share the horrible idea taught by certain High Anglicans of the seventeenth century that the *dead* Body of Christ is what we actually receive in holy communion. This is the very antithesis of the primitive notion of the risen Christ as the *life* of the church in the eucharist.

liturgy begins, in a solemn procession to the altar.[1] During this the people offer adoration to the elements borne by before their eyes, while the choir sings the *Cherubikon*, a hymn composed in the later sixth century:

> 'We who the Cherubim mystically figure forth
> and sing the thrice-holy hymn to the life-giving Trinity,
> lay we aside all worldly cares
> that we may receive the King of all things
> guarded invisibly by the armies of angels.
> Alleluia, Alleluia, Alleluia.'

Here are Theodore's deacons representing the angels, though they are no longer silent.

The profound reverence and actual worship rendered to the unconsecrated elements during this procession have been a source of embarrassment to Eastern theologians, and a standing puzzle to liturgists who have put forward various explanations—that anciently the reserved sacrament was carried in this procession (as in Gaul, but this custom was unknown in the East) or that it derives from the bringing of the *fermentum* from the bishop's liturgy to that of the parish churches (but this rite was always most elaborated at the bishop's own liturgy; and the *fermentum* was abandoned in the East by the fourth century). Theodore's explanation supplies the genuine origin. All the rest of his symbolism has passed into the Byzantine rite—the bearers of the elements representing the angels; the fanning deacons representing the angels hovering round the cross (the liturgical fans are in the form of metal seraphs to this day); the altar as the tomb of Christ—all these things are commonplaces of the Byzantine expositions of the liturgy.

What has not survived among them, however, with the explicitness found in Theodore is what gives coherence to this whole conception of the eucharist in his explanation of it—the idea that the elements, by the mere fact that they are the offering of the church, are already the Body and Blood of Christ from the moment of the offertory, apart from and before the uttering of the eucharistic prayer; and that the purpose of the prayer is to impart to them the *risen* life. Anyone who examines the prayers of the Byzantine *prothesis* (preparation of the elements at a table on the left of the altar before the liturgy begins) will observe that they with the accompany-

[1] In the palmy days of the Byzantine court in the eighth century the following was the order of this procession: first a sub-deacon with a lighted taper, then the archdeacon bearing on his head the veiled paten with the unconsecrated bread, behind him other deacons bearing empty patens. Behind them an arch-priest bearing the chalice with unconsecrated wine, followed by other priests with empty chalices. There followed another priest with the 'holy lance' (for cutting the bread at the preparation of the elements) and the spoon for administering communion. At the rear followed an escort of other deacons carrying the liturgical books, crucifixes, the sponge (for cleansing the vessels), the fans, relics, banners, etc. and finally, carried in solemn state, the *pallium* (scarf) of the episcopal celebrant, who himself awaited the procession at the altar.

ing rubrics are intended to reproduce vividly the treatment of our Lord's Body in His passion[1] (e.g. the 'stabbing' of the bread with the 'holy lance'). When this particular section of the *prothesis* was added to the liturgy (tenth–twelfth centuries) the idea that the *preparation* of the elements represents the passion itself and the offertory represents the entombment of His Body, 'after having received the passion' as Theodore says, was evidently still working among the Byzantines. It has since been allowed to 'fade' to its modern form, *i.e.* that from the preparation onwards the elements are the 'image' or 'likeness' (*eikōn*) of the Body and Blood, which become the 'reality' by the invocation of the Holy Ghost upon them.[2] The people still continue to pay reverence and worship to the elements at the offertory, though the original reason (that they were already the dead Body of Christ) has been somewhat modified. But this is only an instance of a rather mechanical adherence to liturgical tradition which particularly marks Byzantine church life after the ninth century.

The same ceremony of the 'great entrance' is now found through Byzantine influence in some of the other Eastern rites; and it is always accompanied by a chant connecting the procession with the angels. In the Greek version of the liturgy of S. *James* the chant is a hymn known from its first word *Sigēsato*, which has been attributed to S. John of Damascus (eighth century) and is in any case not likely to be much older than his time. It is well known to Anglicans in Moultrie's admirable translation, 'Let all mortal flesh keep silence' (English Hymnal No. 318). But it is an indication of the strangeness to our way of thinking of the whole conception of the eucharist which this hymn embodies, that though it was composed and is used in the East solely as an *offertory* chant, I do not think I have ever heard it used in an Anglican church except in connection with the *consecration*. Both the ceremony of the 'great entrance' and the *Sigēsato* are absent from the Syriac liturgy of S. *James*, a sufficient indication that this conception of the eucharist as the *anamnesis* of the resurrection in particular was no part of the original Syrian tradition. It must have entered the Byzantine rite from some other quarter, most probably from Asia Minor. The same idea of the offertory as in some sense 'pre-consecrating' the sacrament is now found among the Nestorians,[3] amongst whom it appears to have been introduced by Narsai of Edessa towards the end of the fifth century. But he avowedly borrowed the whole conception from Theodore of Mopsuestia.[4] The same notion is also found among the Armenians,[5] who seem to have borrowed the idea directly from Byzantium.

[1] Brightman, L. E. W., 356, 15–357, 20.
[2] This is not quite the New Testament and primitive usage of the word *eikōn*, but an adaptation of it evolved in Byzantine times as a result of the eighth century controversies in the East about the use of 'images' (*eikones*) in christian worship.
[3] Brightman, L. E. W., *p.* 267, *ll.* 30 *sqq.* (*col. a*).
[4] *Liturgical Homilies*, ed. Connolly, *p.* 3, *cf.* 14, 16.
[5] Brightman, L. E. W., *p.* 430, *ll.* 18 *sqq.* (*col a*).

We have already noted that the modern Eastern presentation of this theory, that the preparation and offertory of the elements makes them in some sense 'figures' of the Body and Blood of Christ, represents a certain 'toning down' of the idea as found in Theodore of Mopsuestia, that the offered bread is as such the dead Body of Christ and entitled to adoration. The reason for this weakening of the keystone of the whole conception in Byzantine eucharistic theology does not seem hard to divine. It is quite impossible to reconcile such an idea with the actual wording of the Byzantine liturgical prayers themselves. The authentic tradition that it is the prayer which establishes the meaning of the actions of offertory and communion, and therefore sacrifices and consecrates, is too plainly expressed in the Byzantine liturgies not to have imposed itself again to some extent in the course of time even on this aberrant explanation of the course of the eucharistic action. As in Theodore's rite, the alternative eucharistic prayers used in the Byzantine rite contain nothing whatever which can be twisted into supporting the idea that the invocation accomplishes a *resurrection* of a Body already present. (It is noteworthy that such an idea has no explanation whatever to give of the consecration of the chalice—either in Theodore or in later writers who adopt this theory.) The invocation formula of the liturgy of *S. John Chrysostom* (which appears to date in its present form from the sixth–seventh century) is closely akin to that of Cyril of Jerusalem: 'We entreat and beg and beseech Thee, send down Thy Holy Spirit upon us and upon these gifts that lie before Thee, and make this bread the precious Body of Thy Christ, and what is in this cup the precious Blood of Thy Christ, transforming them by Thy Holy Spirit'. Apart from the irrelevant interpolation of 'upon us and', not found in Cyril's form, and ignored in the rest of the invocation by the liturgy of *S. John Chrysostom* itself, this is purely a 'consecratory' invocation. As the text stands it can be interpreted in no other sense. The invocation in the liturgy of *S. Basil* (which is a later revision of a prayer at least as old as the fourth century, which seems to have come originally from Asia Minor, not Constantinople) is longer than that of the Constantinopolitan liturgy of *S. Chrysostom*, and substitutes the phrase '*shew* (*anadeixai*) this bread to be the very Body of Thy Christ', for the latter's word 'make'. This is more akin to the phrase of Theodore of Mopsuestia (as we might expect in a prayer originally from Asia Minor) and to the liturgy of *Ap. Const.*, viii.; and it is noteworthy that *anadeixis* is S. Basil's own word for the 'consecration'.[1] Here again, though the word 'shew' might suggest that the 'Body' as such is already present and requires only to be 'manifested', there is nothing whatever to suggest that the invocation effects a 'resurrection'. In the face of such explicit language as that of the prayers used in the Byzantine rites themselves, it would inevitably be difficult for the Byzantine clergy and the official tradition to press with any rigorousness

[1] *de Spiritu Sancto*, xxvii. 66.

the explanation of the eucharistic action given by Theodore, whatever might be the case among the laity, separated from the actual performance of the liturgy by the solid screen of the *ikonostasion*.

### The 'Eastern' and the 'Western' ethos

It is commonly said by liturgical theorists that while the Western rites find their centre and inspiration in the thought of Calvary, those of the East are chiefly concerned with the thought of the Resurrection. I am not disposed to deny that this is true so far as concerns the *devotional* approach to their own rites by Western and Eastern christians for the last thousand years. But it is exceedingly important to point out that this contrast of devotional approach has no basis whatever in the actual *prayers* of the Western and Eastern liturgies. The Western rite is specifically the *anamnesis* 'of the blessed passion of the same Christ Thy Son our Lord, *and also* of His resurrection from hell *and also* of His glorious ascension into the heavens', just as it is in those of the East (save that these latter rites have added the commemoration of His session and second coming). Apart from this there is no mention whatever of the passion in the whole Roman canon, save in the brief phrase 'Who on the day before He suffered took bread . . .' And there is equally no single trace of the so-called 'Eastern' conception to be found from end to end of the prayers of the Eastern rites, except only in the Byzantine preparation of the elements (which in this aspect is known to be an addition developed after the year A.D. 900), and in offertory chants and prayers (which again are known to date only from the sixth century and after). On the contrary, the plainest statement of what is supposed to be the 'Western' emphasis which I recollect in any liturgy is to be found at the beginning of the institution narrative in the Eastern rite of S. Basil (something as genuinely ancient as anything now in use in the East): 'And He left unto us these *memorials* (*hypomnēmata*) *of His saving passion*, which we have set forth according to His command. For being about to go forth to His voluntary and life-giving death, in the night in which . . .'[1] There could be no clearer evidence that East and West were originally at one upon the interpretation of the eucharist as being primarily what S. Paul called 'the shewing forth of the Lord's death', and S. Justin 'the *anamnēsis* of His passion';[2] even though that death and passion cannot be separated in the coming of the Kingdom of God from their consequences in the resurrection and ascension.

One can readily see how the Eastern 'ethos' could be developed from a one-sided insistence on certain elements of primitive tradition—*e.g.*, that the eucharist was instituted to 'demonstrate the resurrection' (Hippolytus *e*) and 'for new life in the kingdom of heaven' (*Addai and Mari i*). But the interpretation of the whole eucharistic action as essentially an '*anamnesis* of

---

[1] Brightman, *op. cit., p.* 327, *ll.* 19 *sq.*    [2] *Dial.* 41.

the resurrection' from a passion accomplished, as it were, in the sacristy 'before the liturgy begins' (for this is what the whole conception amounts to) is first found only in Theodore of Mopsuestia early in the fifth century; and it is fully developed in expression by the Byzantine *prothesis* only after another 500 years. It is hardly likely that the Byzantines derived the idea directly from Theodore, for he bore a bad reputation among them—which he fully deserved—as having been an out-and-out Nestorian before Nestorius himself. On the other hand, unlike most of the Byzantine liturgical tradition, this idea is not of Syrian origin. It was unknown in fourth century Syria, and it fits the 'Antiochene' type of liturgy such as *S. John Chrysostom* as awkwardly as it fits the rite of Mopsuestia described by Theodore. It is an interpretation artificially imposed on liturgies which were originally framed on a quite different interpretation of the eucharist. And since these liturgies are themselves of a form which had not been completely developed until the very end of the fourth century, the adoption of this interpretation of them is to be dated later still—in the fifth or sixth century; for no church would *form* a new liturgy to express a conception of the eucharistic action quite different from that which it actually believed at the time.[1]

### The Tradition of Asia Minor?

If one examines closely the fragmentary data to be gathered from the liturgy of *S. Basil*, from the writings of S. Basil himself, from Theodore's account of the actual text of the rite of Mopsuestia (not his explanation of it) and from *Ap. Const.*, viii., it is possible to gather a fairly clear idea of the original form of the conception which underlies all this group of rites from the southern fringe of Asia Minor. The bread and wine, by the very fact that they are *laid upon the altar* as the offering of the church, Christ's Body, according to His command at the last supper, become the 'memorials' (*hypommēmata*) of His redeeming passion. (Very much the same idea is to be found in Sarapion in Egypt in the fourth century—'to Thee we have offered (at the offertory) the bread, the likeness (*homoiōma*) of the Body of the Only-begotten. This bread is the likeness of the holy Body because' our Lord at the last supper said it was to be so.) And then in the invocation, 'the Spirit'—*i.e.* originally the '*Presence*'—of our Lord is asked 'upon the bread and the cup' (as Sarapion asks for the Advent of the Word) to 'demonstrate' or 'manifest' (by its effects in communion?) the reality *of the union* of the church's offering with His own—on Calvary and at the altar in heaven. So understood, the tradition of Asia Minor, though it has peculiar features, is at bottom only another way of expressing the classical

[1] It is at least possible that this view of the eucharist as an *anamnesis* primarily of the resurrection originated in the churches of Asia Minor, but the whole question of the liturgical tradition of Anatolia still awaits investigation. I will venture a prophecy that we shall eventually find it impossible to bring the core of that tradition under the general heading of 'Antiochene', as is now usual, though it has undergone considerable Antiochene influence at various periods.

tradition of the eucharist, as the *anamnesis*—the making present by effects—of the passion and resurrection. It 'shews' (*anadeixai*) the Lord's *death* as the Messianic sacrifice. This is fundamentally in line with S. Paul and the whole of the rest of primitive tradition.

### The 'Great Entrance' and the Preparation of the Elements

What has caused the obvious distortion in Theodore's explanation and in the later Byzantine conception is the necessity of accounting for two elements in the shape of their liturgies which are a foreign importation into the original scheme. These are (1) The offertory procession of the deacons from the sacristy, a Syrian custom which has replaced the original offering by the church corporately before the altar. Whatever its original intention of mere convenience, this had evidently become by Theodore's time an imposing ceremony, which had completely eclipsed that simple placing of the oblation on the altar—the altar, let us not forget, which was the symbol of Christ Himself—which primitively constituted or symbolised the conjunction of the church's offering of itself with that of Christ by Himself in the passion. It is now the *procession* which attracts attention, which impresses and evokes religious emotion; the actual offering has become merely the terminus of this. It is therefore the procession which Theodore has to account for, and since it can hardly be interpreted as in itself the central act of the eucharist (though it has already by the fifth century become the moment of the greatest ritual splendour in the whole rite and remains so still among the Byzantines) it must be regarded as the *consequence* of something. And since this is the opening of the eucharist proper, the whole centre of gravity of the rite has been shifted back to 'before the liturgy begins'—to something which has happened in the sacristy, in fact. The Byzantine *prothesis* only puts into action the underlying conception by its obvious symbolism of the enacting of the passion outside the eucharist altogether, and apart from the assembly of the church, 'before the liturgy begins'.

(2) But since the eucharist cannot thus have its primary significance transferred to a point before it begins without absurdity, a wholly fresh focus has to be found for it within the rite, and this is found in the 'resurrection' of the 'dead Body' of Christ entombed upon the altar. And since in the New Testament the resurrection takes place by the operation of the Spirit, this could provide a new explanation of the awkward and novel doctrine that the Holy Ghost and not God the Son is the active agent in the eucharist. The difficulty about the whole scheme is that it has nothing to do with the doctrine expressed and demanded by the Eastern liturgical *prayers* themselves. The pivot of the whole scheme, the invocation of the Holy Ghost, is capable only of one meaning—*viz.* that it effects the 'consecration', the making to be present in some way of a Body and Blood

which are *not* already upon the altar. This is its plain meaning in Cyril of Jerusalem, the first evidence we have of the use of such an invocation in the liturgy. It is also its plain meaning in the writings of Chrysostom at Antioch when the use of such an invocation was spreading rapidly at the end of the fourth century; it is the plain meaning of the words in the liturgies of S. *John Chrysostom, S. Mark, S. James* and the Armenian rite to-day. And though the actual wording of the invocations of S. *Basil,* of Theodore and of *Ap. Const.,* viii. seems to betray a derivation from what is ultimately a somewhat different idea—that of 'manifestation' rather than 'consecration'—yet this latter is the meaning to which they have all been assimilated. Nor was their original significance a 'resurrection' of the 'dead Body' of Christ, but a 'making real' or 'obvious' of the 'memorial of the passion' *at* the eucharist, not before the eucharist begins.

### The Invocation in the Modern Eastern Rites

This curious evolution is an illustration of the difficulty of interpretation caused by the importation into other rites of an invocation paragraph of the type made fashionable in the later fourth century by its use in the 'model' church of Jerusalem. At Jerusalem it caused no such difficulty, because the whole prayer was framed upon the theory which this paragraph so unequivocally expresses, that the Holy Ghost is the active agent in the eucharist and Christ Himself only the passive Victim. But appended to or inserted into other prayers already complete in themselves and framed on the doctrine that Christ Himself is the agent in the eucharist, the invocation demanded explanation. It must either reduce the remainder of the prayer to the level of a mere accompaniment to itself, or be ignored. This was inevitable. At its origin in Jerusalem this paragraph (with the sentence offering the sacrifice) *was* the whole of the 'eucharistic' prayer proper. Everything else consisted of preliminaries (the preface and sanctus) and of what in Cyril's opinion was dependent upon 'consecration'—the intercessions, whose special value was that they were offered 'over the sacrifice'. In the result, this type of invocation did come to take the same sort of central importance in the rites of other churches that it had in the Jerusalem rite. Whenever it was inserted, it reduced the remainder of the prayer to the level of a mere preparation for itself or dependence upon itself. The older interpretations of the eucharistic action to be found in local rites like those of S. *Mark* and S. *Basil* have been buried below the surface of their prayers by what is essentially the interpretation put upon the eucharist by Cyril of Jerusalem. And this interpretation, though it may go back obscurely to the 'blessing of the Name' of God in the original judaeo-ehristian *berakah,* and though Cyril had at least one fore-runner in the person of the third century Syrian bishop who wrote the *Didascalia,* was essentially something altogether new to the churches of the fourth century.

This interpretation of the eucharist and the liturgical practice which enshrines it are dear to the Eastern churches, and now venerable enough with age to pass unquestioned. It is in any case unsuitable for members of a church which accepted a complete upheaval of its own liturgical tradition by the authority of Parliament and the Privy Council less than four centuries ago to criticise on the ground of its unprimitive character a much smaller innovation freely accepted by the worshipping churches 1,400 years ago. No one has a right to require the East to abandon what has become its tradition. But the Easterns in their turn can hardly expect others to adopt it. It has the unfortunate effect of obscuring the universal understanding (which they themselves maintain with a happy illogicality) that the earthly eucharist is the act of Christ Himself, the High-priest of the heavenly altar, Who Himself offers, Himself prays, Himself consecrates, in the offering of His sacrifice. Upon this central conception the whole pre-Nicene church built its synthesis of all the wonderful variety of meanings seen in the single eucharistic action by the New Testament writers and the ancient authors. The Easterns have found their own ways of adhering to this truth, despite a doctrine of consecration by the Holy Ghost which can only be stated in terms which make of Christ a purely passive Victim in the eucharist. Viewed from the standpoint of liturgical history, it is an accidental result of the conflation of rites based upon two different conceptions of the eucharistic action. Historically the development of the present Eastern rites, and with them the present Eastern doctrine, is intelligible enough. Any doctrine which did not make the invocation clause the centre of the eucharistic action would be in plain contradiction with the language used by the liturgical prayers. But viewed in itself the Eastern doctrine brings not clarification but confusion, not gain but loss, in the understanding of the eucharist. We Westerns have enough confusions and losses of our own to deplore in the field of eucharistic teaching and devotion, without seeking to follow theirs.

### ADDITIONAL NOTE

### The Eastern Teaching on the Invocation

THE Eastern teaching as to the precise function of the *Epiklesis* or Invocation of the Holy Ghost in the eucharistic rite has varied a little at times, and is so often misrepresented, that it may be useful to state the facts plainly.

The teaching of Cyril of Jerusalem and Chrysostom in the fourth century has been sufficiently stated; that of S. John of Damascus (eighth century) goes a step further. In the course of the controversy about the use of images he was confronted by his opponents (who held that the eucharist is the only lawful 'representation' of Christ) with the fact that in the liturgy of *S. Basil* the elements are referred to as the 'antitypes' of the Body and Blood of Christ between the words of institution and the invocation. Damascene (who rightly replied that the eucharist is not a 'representation' of Christ, but His very Self) answered that this word referred to the still *unconsecrated* elements, since the consecration is not effected by the words of institution but by the subsequent invocation. This teaching he repeats more than once[1] in quite unequivocal terms.

He had, however, some difficulty in disposing of the passage of Chrysostom *de Prod. Judae*, I. vi, already cited (*p. 281*) in which the latter had said that the priest says ' "This is My Body"; this word transforms the elements'. Damascene rewrites what immediately follows in Chrysostom thus: 'In the beginning God said "Let the earth bring forth grass" and to this day *when the rain cometh*, urged on and strengthened by the command of God it bringeth forth its increase. God said "This is My Body" and "This is My Blood"; and "Do this for the *anamnesis* of Me". And this is done by His almighty command until He come. For thus He said, "until He come"; and the overshadowing power of the Holy Spirit comes as rain upon this new husbandry by the invocation'. But it is worthy of note that Chrysostom's illustration is not drawn from husbandry, with its useful possibility of the intervention of the rain, but from human generation. And Chrysostom's conclusion is the opposite of Damascene's: 'This word once spoken at every altar in the churches from that day until this and until He come, *maketh perfect* (*apartismenēn ergazetai*) the sacrifice'.

It was only in the fourteenth century that the question came to the fore again, this time in disputes between Greeks and Latins. Cabasilas and Simeon of Thessalonica already referred to (*p. 282 n. 1*) were the principal Greek apologists. Neither carries the matter any further than Damascene. Both deny the consecratory force of the words of institution in themselves, but only as fructified and applied by the invocation. Cabasilas is driven to misquote as well as misinterpret the passage of Chrysostom above. But both are careful to insist that though the invocation of the Holy Ghost is the consecration, Christ is the Priest Who consecrates thereby, though it is the Father Who is invoked to send down the Spirit.[2]

At the Council of Florence agreement was reached on this matter between the Eastern and Western churches somewhat along the lines of Chrysostom's teaching, but by a formula which insisted on the consecratory force of the words of institution in themselves which it was allowed that the invocation fructifies. But the Greeks accepted this only out of dire political necessity, and soon repudiated the settlement. Ever since then the general tendency of Orthodox theologians has been in the direction of

---

[1] *de Fide Orthodoxa*, iv. 13. M.P.G. xciv. 1141–1152 *passim*; *Hom. in Sabb. Sancto*, 35. M.P.G. xcvi. 637.

[2] Cabasilas, M.P.G., cl. 437. (I confess I do not fully understand this very embarrassed passage.)

stiffening opposition to the doctrine that the words of institution consecrate. There have been 'Westernising' reactions against this, especially in
Russia in the seventeenth century, where the first edition of the *Orthodox
Confession* of Peter Moghila, Patriarch of Kiev, stated that the words of
institution consecrate. A censored edition by the Greek Meletius Syrigo
restored the ordinary Greek teaching. Since the eighteenth century most
Russian theologians have adopted the modern Byzantine view that the
institution narrative is purely historical, and that the consecration is
effected solely by the invocation.[1] This is in effect a return to the doctrine of
Damascene behind Cabasilas, and ultimately to that of Cyril of Jerusalem.

Where the modern Orthodox doctrine differs from that of Cyril and of
the earlier writers in general is in making a consecratory invocation a *sine
qua non*. Cyril and his fellows had no idea of condemning other rites than
their own; they were speaking affirmatively only, of the rites they themselves knew and used. The modern Orthodox do condemn rites which do
not contain a consecratory invocation.[2] An example interesting to Anglicans
will be found in *Russian Observations on the American Prayer Book*, an
official document, edited by W. H. Frere.[3] The first observation made by
this committee of the Russian Holy Synod is that the American invocation
'cannot satisfy the Orthodox, since the phrase used is only "to bless and
sanctify with Thy Word and Holy Spirit these Thy gifts and creatures of
bread and wine" with no explicit mention of "making them" or "shewing
them to be" the Body and Blood of our Lord Jesus Christ' (*p.* 2). Before
the rite could be accepted as tolerable by the Orthodox this omission would
have to be remedied (*p.* 35). On this shewing it would appear that a great
deal of the discussion among ourselves about the 'oriental character' of
the second paragraph appended to the Prayer of Consecration in the proposed Prayer Book of 1928 was rather beside the point. It may or may not
have been desirable in itself. But it was not a satisfactory *epiklesis* as the
Easterns understand the term.

Historically, the invocation of the Holy Ghost in the eucharistic prayer
has been the cause of a good deal of unnecessary misunderstanding
between the Byzantine and Roman churches. This was comprehensible
when bitterness on political grounds had already arisen betwen them and
each side was therefore only seeking to accentuate its theological differences
from the other and treasuring every ground of condemnation which it could
invent—though it is hardly a frame of mind which will ever irradiate
eucharistic theology (of all subjects) with a very revealing light. But it was

[1] An exception among modern Greek theologians should be mentioned, K. I.
Dyovuniotis, *Ta Mysteria*, Athens, 1913, *p.* 115-16, who insists that the whole rite
from the *prothesis* onwards (including the lections) is necessary to the consecration,
though he adds that the invocation 'especially' (*kyriōs*) effects consecration.
[2] *Cf.* P. Bernadakis, *Catechesis* (Constantinople, 3rd ed. no date), *pp.* 169-170;
Anthimus VII., Patriarch of Constantinople, *Encyclical Letter*, 1896, § 10, and many
others.
[3] *Alcuin Club Tracts*, xii. (1917).

nothing less than fantastic that in 1927–28 we Anglicans should have permitted ourselves to discuss this subject chiefly by the method of hurling at one another some of the well-worn brickbats of the period of the fourth Crusade, without trying to investigate the subject afresh from a strictly scientific point of view.[1] History, and especially liturgical history, has a much clearer word to say on the matter than the theologians and ecclesiastical politicians then allowed to be heard. This is not the place to go into the scientific aspects of the question with any fulness, for it would furnish matter for a monograph. But I will try to suggest briefly the historical considerations within which it will one day have to be discussed.

1. It is quite easy to put together a long collection of Greek and Oriental pronouncements from the mediaeval and modern sources of which the following appears to be the most highly authorised in modern times. 'The one, holy, catholic and apostolic church of the Seven Oecumenical Councils was wont to teach (*paredecheto*) that the precious gifts (*i.e.* the eucharistic elements) are hallowed after the prayer of the invocation of the Holy Spirit by the blessing of the priest'.[2] After reading some twenty modern Greek Catechisms and Manuals, and between ten and twenty mediaeval Greek theologians on the matter, I think I can answer for it that this is entirely typical of the Greek tradition, which shews no wavering or inconsistency about this from at all events the eighth century onwards. The Russian tradition is much less clear-cut right down to the eighteenth century, though it has since come into line with that of the Greeks. The theological and liturgical tradition of the lesser Eastern churches so far as it is accessible, though rather less precise than the Greek, is in general agreement with it. Before the eighth century one can cite occasional Eastern authors, *e.g.* Chrysostom, *Hom. de Prod. Judae*, I. vi., and Severus of Antioch,[3] who—at least on occasion—take an entirely different view. But taking it by and large this is the unanimous Eastern view from the middle ages onwards: The petition that the Holy Ghost will 'make' or 'shew' or 'transform' the bread and wine to be the Body and Blood of Christ *effects*

---

[1] The chief exception to this stricture in the literature of the Prayer Book controversy is the article of Armitage Robinson already cited (*p.* 211 *n.* 2). Examples of the brickbat method of discussion will be found in the pamphlet *The Invocation of the Holy Spirit in the Prayer of Consecration,* by J. W. Hunkin (Cambridge, Heffer, 1927)—a fascinating illustration of all the known methods of misusing historical evidence—and the article *In Defence of the New Prayer Book,* by the present Bishop of Gloucester, *Church Quarterly Review,* civ., *pp.* 200 *sqq.,* esp. 208 *sqq.* (I cite these two because they appear then to have been on opposite sides, though Dr. Hunkin's conclusion—with which I personally happen to agree—is in complete contradiction with his preceding historical argument.)

[2] *Answer of the Great Church of Constantinople to the Papal Encyclical on Union,* 1896, *p.* 32.

[3] *VIth Book of Select Letters of Severus of Antioch,* ii. 2. ed. E. W. Brooks, p. 237: 'The priest . . . pronouncing his words in the person of Christ, says over the bread, This is My Body. . . . Accordingly it is Christ Who still even now offers, and the power of His divine words perfects the things provided so that they may become His Body and Blood.'

the consecration of the eucharist. Whether or not importance is to be attached to the previous recitation of the institution (they vary about this), without the invocation in an 'operative' form there is no consecration. It is not a desirable extra but a *sine qua non*, an essential or even *the* essential of the rite.

Those who have advocated its introduction among ourselves have often sought to obscure this feature of Eastern teaching. But it is to Easterns something really important, as the Orthodox rejection of the American form—'to bless and sanctify with Thy Word and Holy Spirit these Thy gifts and creatures of bread and wine'—as insufficient, indicates. And for my own part, looking at the matter purely historically, I cannot help thinking that the Greeks are, from their own point of view, entirely right, and ought to be allowed to know their own tradition better than their Western imitators. From the first formulation of the present Eastern tradition in Cyril of Jerusalem in A.D. 347 this has been the only reasonable interpretation of the words of the liturgical prayers themselves. It is not a matter of the gradual intensification of an idea originally reconcilable with a consecratory use of the institution. The unambiguous word '*make* this bread the Body', etc. is attested earlier in our sources than words like *apophēnē*, which might mean either 'make' or 'shew'; and the Jerusalem rite of the fourth century, in which—so far as the extant evidence goes—the whole practice and theory originated, had not, as we have seen, any institution narrative at all. It is true that the liturgies of S. Basil and S. Chrysostom as they now stand pray that God will send down the Holy Ghost '*upon us*' as well as upon the elements. But it is also noteworthy that no such addition to the petition is to be found in the fourth century sources. And the Greek theological tradition (rightly, as I think) makes nothing of this clause in its explanations of the invocation; indeed, I remember only one modern Greek manual which so much as mentions it.[1] The authentic 'Eastern' formulation of doctrine is that the invocation consecrates the eucharist. By the action of the Holy Spirit upon the elements the communicants receive the Body and Blood of Christ.

2. It is easy also to find Western prayers, and Western teaching, which are inspired by the same idea—but as regards the liturgies at all events, there is nothing which can be thought to antedate that great expansion of Byzantine ecclesiastical influence in the West which accompanied the Western expeditions of Justinian in the sixth century. When we turn to the oldest Western evidence available we find another idea which, I suggest, exactly reverses the conception of the Greek invocation. A fragment of the book of S. Fulgentius of Ruspe *contra Fabianum* appears to preserve reminiscences of the 'second half' of a sixth century African eucharistic prayer. The passage is as follows:

'Therefore since Christ died for us out of charity, when at the time of

---

[1] *Leitourgikē*, P. Rompotos, Athens, 1869, Bk. ii. 2, *pp.* 247–8.

sacrifice we make commemoration of His death, *we pray that charity may be bestowed upon us by the advent of the Holy Spirit:* humbly beseeching that by that self-same charity whereby Christ was moved to stoop to the death of the cross for us, *we also having received the grace of the Holy Spirit* may hold the world as crucified unto us and may endure to be crucified unto the world; and imitating the death of our Lord, as Christ in that He died, died once, but in that He liveth, liveth unto God, so we also should walk in newness of life and receiving the endowment of charity should die unto sin and live unto God. . . . For the very participation of the Body and Blood of the Lord when we eat His bread and drink His cup, doth admonish us of this that we should die unto the world and have our life hid with Christ in God . . . so it comes about that all the faithful who love God and their neighbour drink the cup of the Lord's charity, even though they drink not the cup of the Lord's bodily passion. . . . The cup of the Lord is drunk when holy charity is preserved . . . for by the gift of charity is bestowed upon us to be in truth that which in the sacrifice we mystically celebrate (*i.e.* the Body of Christ). . . . And so holy church when at the sacrifice of the Body and Blood of Christ she *prays that the Holy Ghost may be sent unto her*, asks for that gift of charity, whereby she may preserve the unity of the Spirit in the bond of peace: and since it is written that "love is as strong as death", she asks for that charity, which she remembers to have moved her Redeemer freely to die for her, for the mortification of His members that are upon earth. And so the Holy Spirit sanctifies the sacrifice of the catholic church: and therefore the christian people perseveres in faith and charity, while each of the faithful by the gift of the Holy Spirit worthily eats and drinks the Body and Blood of the Lord, because he both holds the right belief about his God and by living righteously is not separated from the unity of the Body (of Christ) the church'.[1]

This does not tell us a great deal about the actual wording of the prayer he is referring to. But to me it does not seem possible that Fulgentius could have written as he does here if the petition for the Holy Ghost had not been framed in quite different terms and with a quite different object from that of Cyril of Jerusalem and the Eastern 'invocation' tradition in general. This can hardly have been a petition for the consecration of the sacrament; from what he says of it, it must have been in the nature of a prayer *for the communicants.* It thus links up quite naturally on the one hand with that petition in Hippolytus (*k*) 'that Thou wouldest grant to all who partake to be made one, that they may be fulfilled with Holy Spirit'. On the other hand the same note is sometimes struck in the later Gallican and Mozarabic *post-pridie* prayers, which stand in the same position, of which this will serve for a specimen: (After the institution-narrative): 'This is the victim of love and salvation, O God the Father, whereby the world was reconciled unto Thee. This is that Body which hung upon the cross.

[1] Fulgentius, *contra Fabianum, Fragm.* 28

This also is the Blood which flowed from its holy side. Giving thanks therefore unto Thy love for that Thou didst redeem us by the death of Thy Son and save us by His resurrection, we beseech Thee, O God of love, to incline Thy mind unto us, that sprinkling these offerings with the benediction of Thy Holy Spirit, Thou wouldest impart holiness unto the inward man of them that receive (*sumentium uisceribus sanctificationem adcommodes*) that purified thereby from the stain of our sins we may rejoice abundantly in this day of our Lord's resurrection'.[1]

Clearly there is here no idea of 'consecration' in the petition for the Spirit. The elements are already the Body and Blood before it is reached. This is not the Eastern petition at all, which is concerned with the elements and consecration, but a quite different idea—a prayer concerned with the communicants and communion. It is closely related to that primitive teaching, of which we have seen ancient examples from East and West alike, that in receiving holy communion we receive an access of *pneuma* or 'spirit'. (*Cf. pp.* 266, *sq.*) Whereas the present Greek doctrine is that by the action of the Spirit on the elements we receive the Body and Blood of Christ, this reverses the idea and suggests that by receiving the Body and Blood of Christ we receive the action of the Spirit on our souls. There is not much doubt from the general lay-out of the evidence which is the older notion. But what I am concerned here to point out is that *both* views were certainly current from the fourth–eighth centuries. In discussing the evidence of particular writers in this period it is important to distinguish which way they are regarding the matter. This has not as a rule been done in such discussions of the matter as have come my way, with confusing results on the historical elucidation of the question.

3. In matters of controversy no doubt theology dictates the contents of liturgical prayers. Cranmer, for instance, framed a new liturgy to express what seemed to him a truer theology than that which underlay the old English rites. But in matters which are not controverted the *rôles* are reversed, and theology is apt to be a commentary on prayers, though not always a very faithful or illuminating one. There were no eucharistic controversies worth speaking of in the first eight centuries, and that 'the rule for prayer should determine the rule for belief' could anciently be taken as a maxim in such matters. The primary evidence, where it is available, on this question ought to be that of the liturgical prayers themselves. Where the explanations even of ancient commentators do not closely fit their terms (as *e.g.* in the case of Theodore and the rite of Mopsuestia, *p.* 287) it can be taken that the prayer represents the older evidence.

4. If the evidence of the fourth century prayers be analysed by itself it is obvious that no single or simple theological idea will suffice to explain the beginning of the present oriental liturgical *practice* in respect of the invo-

[1] Mozarabic *post-pridie* for fourth Sunday after Easter. *Lib. Moz. Sacr.*, ed. cit. *col.* 313.

cation or *epiklesis*. It is quite clear that the liturgical traditions embodied in the invocations of (*i*) *Addai and Mari*, (*ii*) Cyril of Jerusalem, (*iii*) Sarapion, (*iv*) *Ap. Const.*, viii, Mopsuestia, and *S. Basil*, do not represent one identical eucharistic theology. They need to be disentangled from one another, as well as from that other (and apparently older) theology of invocation represented by Hippolytus (*k*) and Fulgentius of which we have just spoken.

5. It was not only practice, represented by the phrasing of the invocations used in the different liturgies, which varied. There are considerable variations in the *teaching* about the invocation among the fourth and fifth century authors who used them. We need to bear in mind here two things: (i) The possibility that Greek writers of this period are 'translating' expressions from their liturgies, or from older writers, which in themselves represented the older and vaguer 'Spirit = Presence' or 'Spirit = Word' terminologies, into the ideas of developed fourth century Trinitarian theology, in which 'Spirit' means precisely and only the Third Person of the Trinity. Such 'translation' was done in all good faith, and is a typical example of the systematising and rationalising service rendered by Greek thought in general, and by Greek theology in the particular history of christian thought. But it is not necessarily true that the theological idea intended by the older expression was preserved in the process. (ii) The idea of a 'moment of consecration', and with it of an 'essential' or 'operative section' or clause of the prayer seems to come in somewhat suddenly in the fourth century. Dependent on this, but not necessarily identical with it, is the idea of a 'petition for consecration'. The Greek invocation is an example of a 'petition for consecration' which is regarded as the 'operative clause' and the 'moment of consecration'. But the *Quam oblationem* of the Roman canon is just as much a 'petition for consecration' though it has never been regarded as in itself 'consecratory' or marking the 'moment of consecration'. There are other examples of this latter type, which should be carefully distinguished from the other.

6. The *structural* importance of the institution narrative in the development of the 'second half' of those prayers which already embodied it in the second and third centuries has already been discussed (*cf. pp.* 227 *sqq.*). But this does not necessarily imply that it was then taken as strictly 'consecratory' in the later sense. Personally I see no evidence that it was so understood before the fourth century. What it does seem reasonable to say is that when the idea of a 'moment of consecration' did first arise—in the fourth century—the institution narrative would present itself as the obvious point at which to place that 'moment', by those whose rites already contained it. In those rites in which it was *not* then contained a different 'moment' would have to be found. The fact that no one tried to place the 'moment' in the christian *berakah* or 'thanksgiving series', which had formed the original nucleus of all prayers, indicates that the idea did not

arise until after the hellenised churches had a fairly lengthy development behind them, during which they had forgotten their origins.

A rough analysis of the contents of Hippolytus' prayer and *Addai and Mari*, representing Western and Eastern pre-Nicene types respectively, will help to make the matter clearer.

| Hippolytus | Addai and Mari |
|---|---|
| Thanksgiving Series (*a–d*) | Thanksgiving Series (*d–e*) |
| 'Link' (*e*) | 'Link' (*f–g*) |
| Institution Narrative (*f–g*) | Petition for Consecration ⎫ |
| Offering of Sacrifice (*h–j*) | Offering of Sacrifice ⎬ (*i*)[1] |
| Prayer for Communicants (*k*) | Prayer for communicants ⎭ |
| Doxology (*l*) | Doxology (*j*) |

These two rites are roughly parallel in their contents except that the one contains a fully developed institution narrative where the other has a 'petition for consecration'. But what is remarkable is that in the later development of the type of rite represented by Hippolytus, the 'link' actually turns into a 'petition for consecration'—the *Quam oblationem* of the canon, whose character is parallel to that of a good many Gallican and Mozarabic *post-sanctus* prayers. And the 'link' in the Eastern rites does turn into a full institution narrative coming before the offering of the sacrifice (*cf. S. James*); there are the obvious germs of this already in *Addai and Mari* (*g*). That is to say that the mere necessity of expressing the fulness of the eucharistic action led quite independently to the insertion of the *same* sort of things quite independently in these two very different traditions. Only the accidents of development caused the position of the petition and the institution to be reversed in the two types of rite. Why then did the two traditions come to attach such a different importance, the one to the petition and the other to the institution?

If we compare the rite of Cyril of Jerusalem as he himself describes it with *Addai and Mari*, we find that the preface has taken the place of the 'Thanksgivings' and the sanctus that of the 'link', while the old 'prayer for the communicants' has become the 'general intercessions', thus:

> Preface
> Sanctus
> Petition for Consecration
> Offering of Sacrifice (*cf. S. James l*)
> General Intercessions

As we have said, when the ideas of a 'moment of consecration' an and 'operative clause' came in, there is nothing in this prayer so constituted to

---

[1] It seems fair to say that *Addai and Mari* (*i*) does contain all three notions of petition for consecration, offering—'this *oblation* of Thy servants'—and prayer for the communicants, though they are not clearly distinguished. For the 'offering' at this point *cf.* also *S. James* (*l*) and also (*i*).

which these ideas could be attached *at all*, except the 'petition for conse-cration'. I would be prepared even to go a little further. Granted that there is a real complexity about the *theological* origins of the doctrine of conse-cration taught by Cyril, and that it has obscure but genuine relations with older ideas of some variety (concerning the 'power of the Name', 'Spirit = Presence', etc., as well as the theological doctrine concerning the operation of the Holy Ghost alluded to in the *Didascalia*), nevertheless a practical point of much greater simplicity arises in connection with the use of such a prayer. How soon would listening to it and worshipping by it actually *give rise* to the ideas of a 'moment of consecration' and an 'operative clause' among those who heard it—among the ordinary christian people? Cyril himself shews no sign of hesitation or apology over such ideas. They are already fully accepted in his *milieu*. Nor does he, like some of the later Easterns, try to allow some 'preparatory' force as regards the consecration to all that part of the prayer which precedes the invocation. For him it is the invocation alone which is 'operative'.

Cyril was certainly not the inventor of the idea of a 'petition for conse-cration'. But Cyril, or rather Cyril's rite, is the first extant evidence for the *identification* of the 'petition for consecration' with the 'moment of conse-cration', in the later Greek fashion.

7. Having regard to all these points, it might be advantageous in discus-sing the historical question of the invocation and the present oriental doc-trine concerning it, to distinguish clearly two separate questions: (*a*) The pre-Nicene origins and the post-Nicene variations of the particular ideas and practices described in the *Catecheses* of S. Cyril of Jerusalem. (*b*) The consequences upon Eastern eucharistic *theology* of the fusion of Cyril's type of *rite* with others which in the later second or third century had already developed a full institution narrative. (*S. James* gives us a fourth-fifth century example of the actual process of fusion.)

The full discussion of both these questions must necessarily pass beyond eucharistic and liturgical history proper into the field of eucharistic theology. But even the theological discussion will have to be conducted in the light of the very striking historical contrast already spoken of, *viz.* that while the pre-Nicene church with absolute unanimity (except for one sentence in the *Didascalia*) regards the eucharist as the action of the Second Person of the Trinity and speaks of Him always as *active* in it. Cyril and the whole theological tradition of which he is the earliest repre-sentative regards the Third Person of the Trinity as the agent of the eucharist, and speaks of Christ as *passive* in it. The two ideas may be held side by side, as in the later Greek tradition. What has yet to be demon-strated is that they can be stated in combination as parts of a single coherent idea. It is interesting to find that no author in the fourth century ever tried so to combine them. They state one *or* the other, or in the case of Chrysos-tom now one and now the other, without any attempt at a reconciliation.

Evidently the Antiochene church had not yet fully accepted the same doctrine as Cyril had taught at Jerusalem when it adapted his rite.

The present Eastern teaching is a combination of three things—that consecration is effected by the action of the Third Person of the Trinity; that consecration is effected by a 'petition for consecration'; and that the 'petition for consecration' marks the 'moment of consecration'. Those scholars who desire to shew that the orientals have preserved what was primitively universal in this matter will have some difficulty in finding that *combination* of ideas before the fourth century.

# CHAPTER XI

## THE SANCTIFICATION OF TIME

I T is one thing to have a knowledge of the course of liturgical history—of when this custom was introduced and where, of how such-and-such a prayer was given a new turn and by whom. It is quite another and a more difficult thing to understand the real motive forces which often underlie such changes. The hardest thing of all is to assess their effects upon the ideas and devotions of the vast unlearned and unliterary but *praying* masses of contemporary christian men and women, who have left no memorial of any kind in this world, but whose salvation is nevertheless of the very purpose of the church's existence. For those who seek not only to know but to understand the history of the liturgy the fourth century will always have a fascination quite as great as that of the obscure period of origins which precedes it.

To a large extent this is the formative age of historic christian worship, which brought changes the effects of which were never undone in the East or the catholic West at all, and some of which have survived even the up-heavals of the sixteenth century in the churches of the Reformation. It is true that the essential outline of the christian eucharist, the 'four-action shape', had been fixed for all time before the middle of the second century, and probably by the end of the first. It is true, too, that by the end of the second century that outline had been filled by forms that would undergo expansion and development, but never any radical reconstruction for the next 1,400 years. The fourth century did make quite considerable changes in these inherited forms, but they were essentially a matter of decoration and enrichment of the traditional pattern of worship received from the pre-Nicene past. What we can easily miss in studying the fourth century, just because it was on the whole so conservative of the pre-Nicene outline of the liturgy even when overlaying it with these devotional additions, is the extent of the very radical changes which then came over the *ethos* of christian worship. There is here a contrast between the fourth century and the sixteenth which is easily misunderstood, but which is striking as well as subtle. The fourth century was on the whole conservative in the matter of forms just where the protestant reformation was most deliber-ately revolutionary. Yet from one point of view it was certain fourth century changes which the sixteenth century reformers would have said they were seeking to undo. On the other hand the fourth century uncon-sciously carried through revolutionary changes in the *spirit* in which it interpreted the forms it preserved, a field in which the sixteenth century was wholly conservative, or rather never even understood that change might be possible. We shall return to this contrast later; here our concern is with the fourth century.

### From a Private to a Public Worship

The fourth century is an age of readjustment to a sudden change in the external situation of the church. Bitter persecution and the almost complete disorganisation of worship which it brought about were replaced by imperial patronage and state provision for worship in the space of much less than a decade. The next fifty years and more were a time of unparalleled liturgical revision all over christendom, when the churches everywhere were taking stock of their own local traditions, sifting their devotional value and borrowing freely from each other whatever seemed most expressive or attractive in the rites of other churches. At the beginning of this period the liturgical prayers themselves, not yet stereotyped by the predominant influence of a few great churches, were still free to exhibit the full riches of a great local variety. The eucharistic prayer everywhere was still fluid enough to incorporate new ideas or rather new expressions of old ideas; for the main themes of eucharistic devotion had by now clarified themselves along much the same lines everywhere in the general mind of the worshipping church, and had found the same point of synthesis in the doctrine of the eternal High-priest at the heavenly altar.

There was, too, an immense increase in the christian penetration and grasp of the content of the christian revelation during the century and a half that separates Novatian from Augustine, the *Didascalia* from Chrysostom, or (in a different way) Origen from Athanasius. It is not merely that the eucharistic prayer grows in scope, so that it increases in mere bulk to the extent that the prayers of the fourth century are more than twice as long as those of the third. A general progress in theological understanding of the faith and the marked rise in the level of christian culture from the secular point of view which occurs in the fourth century, enabled the church to express her eucharistic devotion with a new precision and an elegance of literary form which have never been surpassed. The rhythms, the diction, the theological expressions and many of the actual compositions of the fourth–fifth century are preserved and imitated by succeeding ages as those of the second and third centuries never directly influenced the phrasing of future generations. The compositions of the fourth century became classical, while those of the pre-Nicene period became liturgical curiosities, and eventually ceased to be copied or were revised out of existence. The fourth–fifth century is the golden age of liturgical writing, in which all the great historic rites begin to assume the main lines of their final form. And it happens that by a number of fortunate accidents we are much less incompletely furnished with strictly liturgical evidence from this brilliant period of transition than we are from either the three centuries which precede it or the three which follow.

Yet important as they were in themselves and enduring as were their effects, we have to see the liturgical developments with which all the churches were experimenting in the fourth century in their true perspective in the whole history of the liturgy. So far as form goes—the Shape of the Liturgy—they were all changes or additions of detail in a practice of worship whose main core and principles were still recognisably the same in the eighth century (our next comparatively well-documented period) as they had been at the end of the second. It was in the field of the *theory* of christian worship that the fourth century made its two revolutions.

i. During the sixty years or so between the accession of the emperor Constantine (A.D. 312) and that of the emperor Theodosius the Great (A.D. 379) it gradually became certain that henceforward the church would be living and worshipping no longer in a hostile but in a nominally christian world. As this grew yearly more obvious, and as that christian generation slowly died out which could remember being defiantly ranged against all external society in the long struggle of the Diocletian persecution (A.D. 303–313) the attitude of christians towards their own worship could not but insensibly change. They were no longer members of a semi-secret association organised against the law, towards which society at large and the state showed themselves resolutely hostile even when they were not militantly attacking it. On the contrary, christians were now the representatives of a faith shared by the emperors, which was rapidly becoming the directing conscience of civilisation. Their worship could not but be affected in spirit by such a change. From being the jealously secluded action of an exclusive association, it was little by little transformed—as large and influential sections of society received baptism in increasing numbers—into a public activity of the population at large.

ii. This transformation in the conception of christian worship in general brought with it another which particularly concerned the eucharist, still as previously the heart of christian worship. As the church came to feel at home in the world, so she became reconciled to *time*. The eschatological emphasis in the eucharist inevitably faded. It ceased to be regarded primarily as a rite which manifested and secured the *eternal consequences* of redemption, a rite which by manifesting their true being as eternally 'redeemed' momentarily transported those who took part in it beyond the alien and hostile world of time into the Kingdom of God and the World to come. Instead, the eucharist came to be thought of primarily as the representation, the enactment before God, of the *historical process* of redemption, of the historical events of the crucifixion and resurrection of Jesus by which redemption had been achieved. And the pliable idea of *anamnesis* was there to ease the transition.

The consequences of these two changes in tne general understanding of christian worship were in the end very far-reaching. They are with us yet, though our own times seem to be witnessing the rapid fading of at least the first of them, if not the second, almost without our being aware of it. But as these conceptions, then so new, are now disappearing from men's minds, so they first appeared in the fourth century, not consciously nor by a deliberate reversal of ideas, not altogether suddenly nor at once very obviously, but after long hidden preparation and with an aftermath of readjustments and the slow disappearance of survivals. It is impossible to name individuals who inaugurated the changes, though there are some who exemplify them; Cyril of Jerusalem, for instance, is as unmistakably a man of the new way of thinking as Lactantius is of the old. The new ideas arrived at different speeds in different churches. All one can say is that all christendom had accepted them in principle during the half-century between the Council of Nicaea in A.D. 325 and the Council of Constantinople in A.D. 381. Before that period we can watch the establishment of the pre-conditions of change, after it the working out of consequences.

Whether contemporaries realised it or not, these changes, from a private to a public worship and from an eschatological to an historical notion of the eucharist, had been maturing within the christian church for two generations before Constantine declared his faith in Christ. The edict of the Emperor Gallienus in A.D. 260, which permitted freedom of meeting to christians, though it did not prevent the martyrdom of individuals yet procured for the church forty years during which her corporate worship was for the first time legally protected from molestation. We have already noted the important consequence of this in the erection of christian 'churches', buildings specially designed for christian worship, which was a new feature of church life in most places in the last half or quarter of the third century. The new surroundings and setting could not fail to affect worship, chiefly in the direction of formalising and organising it in a new way. The rapid increase in christian numbers in the same period tended in the same direction. The informality of small—and above all, secret— gatherings, could not survive the transference. The old domestic character of eucharistic worship in the 'house-churches' inevitably took on much of the character of a public worship even in the first modest basilicas of the third century. And christian worship itself had now more than two centuries of organised existence behind it. Its traditions were acquiring more rigidity from immemorial custom and the prestige of antiquity— things which give a strictly ritual character to the repetition even of actions and practices of the most severely utilitarian origin.

This was not all. The new relation of the church to the law which the edict of Gallienus brought with it had its effect on the way in which christians regarded the world around them. Their old hostility to the whole secular organisation of life unconsciously diminished. In the later third century christians began to come forward before the world on something like an equal footing with their pagan neighbours, and to take an increasing share in the public and social life of the day. There is a significant influx of christians into the army and the civil service c. A.D. 275-300. Known christians began to be elected to local magistracies in the cities and to hold important administrative posts in the imperial household itself. No doubt they had to be discreet; but it was becoming possible for a man to hold christian beliefs and to frequent christian worship, and yet to take part in almost all the activities of social life.

The new freedom and the widening of christian interests brought their own dangers of compromise with pagan beliefs and morals and of lowering christian standards both in faith and conduct. Social life was permeated with traditional pagan customs and assumptions at every end and turn. 'Civilised living' was thoroughly pagan in its basis, and those christians who tried to enter into it were perpetually confronted with problems of casuistry as to how far a man might go in conforming to what was now often little more than an accepted convention or an expression of civil loyalty, and yet had in itself a pagan religious basis and meaning. Where was the line to be drawn which divided mere courtesy or social custom from actual disloyalty to Christ by the worship of heathen divinities? These, be it remembered, were regarded by christians not as mere false gods and non-existent, but as the cunning masks assumed by the very demons from whose fearful bondage Christ had died to ransom mankind. The christian magistrate might be called upon to offer the sacrifices of the civic cults on behalf of his city as part of the duties of his office. The christian soldier must as a matter of course take his oath of allegiance by the 'genius' of the deified emperor, whom the christian courtier must address with the ceremonies and language of 'adoration' prescribed by etiquette. The christian guest must overlook the fact that his host's hospitality was offered to him nominally in honour of some heathen festival. The christian bride must take part in the age-old pagan rites which wedded her to her pagan bridegroom. These things were part of the fabric of social life, and like a hundred other such occasions presented problems of conscience impossible for christians to solve satisfactorily in a non-christian world. They harass the church continually in the mission-field to-day. There is ample evidence that the line which separates christian courtesy from mere compliance and laxity was as often overstepped then as it is now in similar circumstances. Round about A.D. 300 we meet, for instance, with well-to-do christians in Spain who had accepted the social compliment of nomination to the local priesthood of the emperor-cult, refusal to comply with which was still the official test for christian martyrs. Some of them did not scruple to appear in public wearing the sacrificial fillet of their office, even if they had not actually fulfilled their duty of sacrifice in person. Similar scandals of various kinds were to be found all over christendom about A.D. 300.

The church reaped an unpleasant harvest of temporary apostasies from all this mingling with the pagan world when the tempest of the last and longest persecution broke upon her in A.D. 303. Yet if the world was ever to be christianised it is clear that the risk of the church being secularised in the process had to be faced. And the preparation for her mission to the world at large in the fourth century is precisely the breaking down of the old rigorism of her attitude towards pagan society during the last generation of the third. She was then beginning to regard herself as the salt of the world rather than an alien sojourner within it; she was preparing to try to christianise its life instead of ignoring or despairing of it. So the life of time as well as of eternity was becoming a proper sphere of christian interest. Here are the root causes of the great fourth century changes in the conception of christian worship, from a private to a public action, from an eschatological to an historical conception of the cultus. And these causes go back beyond the peace of the church under Constantine, beyond the great persecution under Diocletian, to changes which had been taking place within the church itself all through the last generation of the preceding century.

It may well be that these forty years of uneasy toleration between Gallienus a. Diocletian were more fruitful for the church in other directions than the text-books of church history would suggest. In the field of liturgy, at all events, their importance must have been considerable, though it was not immediately apparent. So far as one can see the real forces of the fourth century liturgical revolution were largely shaped then. The ambiguous legal position, by which christian worship was tolerated while christian allegiance was still in theory a capital crime, forced the church to be cautious in the development of her worship at just that stage in which it would be most likely to undergo a drastic revolution of form, the stage of its first transference from domestic meetings to a cultus regularly organised in special buildings. The ten-year-long interruption of all regular public worship which followed under Diocletian prevented the cramped forms of this transitional period from hardening prematurely into a permanent model, and at the same time lent to the new situation about worship under Constantine something of the aspect of a 'restoration' of the past, rather than the opening of a wholly new chapter. Just so at the Restoration of Church and State under Charles II in England, churchmen looked back to the good old days and desired to return to the old ways they had known before 'the late troubles'; and yet after a twelve-year interruption of their observance they found themselves making more changes than perhaps they realised. So under Constantine the church came to the restoration of her corporate worship with every intention of a reverent conservatism. But in fact the breach in continuity and the disorganisation caused by the great persecution had been too great for the new worship to be simply a restoration of the old. So many of the old bishops and clergy, those most familiar with the conduct of worship, had been martyred or had been deposed for apostasy in the persecution. The faithful laity, always effective guardians of liturgical tradition, had for so long been deprived of regular attendance at the familiar forms. The new situation and its opportunities were in essentials so different from the old, that liturgical prayer was in fact much freer to respond to new impulses than might have been expected in an age of deliberate return to the old ways. The core and outline of the old rites were faithfully preserved in most places, but upon this basis development was rapid.

It soon became clear that the new situation was not a mere respite but was likely to endure. Christianity was now a lawful religion in every respect, and also the personal religion of the emperor, though it was as yet by no means the religion of the state or of the majority of its citizens. The church could conduct her worship and her propaganda freely, though in theory the state did not directly assist in this. Yet there was the powerful indirect effect of the emperor's adherence, and of his personal encouragement of all who followed his example. And as the Roman state had always made provision for the conduct of public worship by all officially accepted forms of cult, so it now began to provide for the worship of the catholic church. This took the form chiefly of financial allowances and the grant of legal privileges and exemptions to the catholic clergy, and also of the rebuilding and erection of churches. There was nothing abnormal about this; the state had done as much for other cults for centuries past when they were officially recognised. But in this case Constantine saw to it that the provision made was unprecedentedly generous.

In Rome alone the emperor built nine new churches from the resources of his Privy Purse, including the exceptionally large and richly furnished basilicas of S. Saviour by the Lateran palace (the cathedral of Rome) and of S. Peter on the Vatican and S. Paul beside the road to Ostia over the tombs of the two Roman apostles. Pope Silvester built another, the *Titulus Silvestri*—the present San Martino ai Monti near the baths of Trajan—and private persons were not slow to follow such examples. Constantine built others at Ostia, Naples, Capua, Albano, Carthage, Jerusalem, Bethlehem, Mamre, Antioch, Thessalonica, and scores of other places in the provinces, besides a whole group in the new capital at Constantinople. And in all the cities round the Mediterranean local devotion began to multiply splendid new basilicas beside the old third century christian buildings which Diocletian had confiscated and Constantine had restored. By the last quarter of the century they were numerous in many places—so remote a place as the old christian centre in the frontier-town of Edessa boasted thirteen when Etheria visited it in 385—and in some provinces they were by then becoming numerous in the countrysides.[1] (We have noted one important

[1] The advance in the provision of rural churches varied greatly, even in neighbouring provinces. In Western Asia Minor, a christian stronghold since the first century, country churches were already common in the later third century, perhaps

consequence of this multiplication of churches in the effective breakdown everywhere of the old ideal of the single *ecclesia*, the single eucharistic assembly of the whole local church under its own bishop and presbytery. It brings about most important changes in the ideas held about the presbyterate and the eucharist, and also about the church.)

Yet it is perhaps not so much the provision of new churches or their size which are apt to strike a modern reader, as their furnishing. The gifts bestowed by Constantine on his Roman foundations[1] reveal how completely the church had accepted the liturgical consequences of the change from a private to a public worship within a few years of the peace of the church. At S. Peter's, to take an instance less exceptional than the Lateran which was especially closely connected with the court, the shrine of the apostle was of precious marbles and gold. The vaulting of the apse was plated with gold. There was a great cross of solid gold, and the altar was of silver-gilt set with 400 precious stones. There was a large golden dish for receiving the offertory of the people's breads, and a jewelled 'tower' with a dove of pure gold brooding upon it—probably a vessel for the reserved sacrament. There were five silver patens for administration, three gold and jewelled chalices and twenty of silver; two golden flagons and five silver ones for receiving the oblations of wine. There was a jewelled golden 'censer'—perhaps a standing burner for perfumed oil or spices rather than what we understand by the word. Before the apostle's tomb was a great golden corona of lights and four large standard candlesticks wrought with silver medallions depicting scenes from the Acts of the Apostles. The nave was lit by thirty-two hanging candelabra of silver and the aisles by thirty more.

S. Peter's was one of the great shrines of christendom, but its furnishings

even earlier. Yet they were still rare in the Eastern parts of the peninsula in the late fourth. Extant remains of country churches from the middle fourth century are fairly common in N.E. Syria. But in N.W. Syria we find Chrysostom in sermons preached at Antioch about 390 urging christian landowners to build churches and provide clergy for their country estates, in terms which suggest that little had yet been done in this region. In S. Egypt peasant congregations and rural churches were common in the third century; yet Theodoret tells us (*Eccl. Hist.*, iv. 21) that in A.D. 385 there were still whole districts in the Nile delta where no christian had ever been seen, and there is Egyptian evidence of a still later date suggesting that this is little if at all exaggerated. In the West, village-bishoprics multiplied in N. Africa during the third century, and christianity seems to have spread more widely in rural Spain than in most provinces, but we know very little about it. It was only in the fifth or even sixth century that country churches began to be provided in anything like adequate numbers in Gaul and Italy. In England, where the whole development of christianity was thrown back for two centuries by the Anglo-Saxon invasions (and which seems to have been exceptionally strongly attached to paganism in the fourth century) the beginnings of the rural parochial system date only from the time of Archbishop Theodore at Canterbury (A.D. 668–690).

[1] The list of these from a contemporary document is preserved in the *Liber Pontificalis*, ed. Duchesne, *pp.* 170–187. The fourth century origin of this list has been questioned, but see C. H. Turner, *Studies in Early Church History*, Oxford, 1912, *p.* 155, *n.* 2.

were not exceptional among churches of this class. At the Lateran there even appear items which were unrepresented at S. Peter's, such as silver bas-reliefs of our Lord among the angels and our Lord among the apostles. Nor was such furnishing confined to the churches of Rome. Constantine's smaller foundation of the *Martyrium* at Jerusalem, the cathedral of the Holy City (built before A.D. 333) testified to the same conception of worship, with its gilded and coffered ceiling and bronze screens, and its hemispherical sanctuary adorned with twelve tall marble columns standing free and bearing as many huge silver bowls (probably for perfumes).[1]

Lights and incense, golden chalices and jewelled altars—that was how the survivors of the Diocletian persecution worshipped at the eucharist! Yet this is not, as many will be inclined to think, a proof of the instant corruption wrought by imperial patronage, nor was it confined to churches built by the imperial treasury. Long before Constantine's first efforts in church furnishing, local churches were being built like that at Tyre (built about A.D. 314 at the first moment that it was possible after the persecution) whose cedar ceilings, delicately carved altar rails and mosaic pavements are enthusiastically described by Eusebius in the sermon he preached at its dedication. Such new churches obviously aimed at sumptuousness, even though they could not compete with the somewhat barbaric magnificence which satisfied the personal taste of Constantine. If the reader will cast his mind back to the impressive list of gold and silver plate and candlesticks possessed by the insignificant provincial church of Cirta before the Diocletian persecution began, he will recognise that this conception of worship is something which goes back into what we like to think of as the 'simple' worship of the church in 'the catacombs'. All that Constantine provided was the opportunity and in some cases the means for its free development. Quite apart from the directly imperial foundations, in the course of fifty years or so the generosity and labour of the christian people brought into being all over the Roman world thousands of churches ranging in size from little martyr's chapels in the cemeteries to the cathedral basilicas of the great cities. Wherever extant remains permit an examination of the question it is clear that christian art was called in at once to embellish them with all the available resources accumulated in this final century of the great antique civilisation. As a French writer has noted, whenever an author of this period sets out to describe a church, 'il use presque invariablement d'épithètes qui évoquent l'idée d'un décor éclatant. Point de basilique qui ne soit alors *splendens, rutilans, nitens, micans, radians, coruscans*'.[2] These are all adjectives of 'glitter'. With their tesselated pavements, the richly coloured marble facings of their lower walls, the glass mosaics of their clerestories and their gilded ceilings, these Constantinian

---

[1] The most up-to-date account in English of the Palestinian foundations of Constantine is that in the Schweich Lectures for 1937, *Early Churches in Palestine*, J. W. Crowfoot (London, 1941) *pp. 9 sqq.*
[2] J. Hubert, *L'art pré-roman*, *p.* 108.

basilicas must have been indeed a glowing and flashing sight when the brilliant southern sunshine streamed through the carved wooden traceries that filled their windows. To the contemporary church their gorgeousness was something of a token of the earnestness of her thanksgiving for the seemingly miraculous deliverance from annihilation in the ten grinding years of the great persecution.

The truth is that the English puritans' crusade against all forms of sensuous beauty in worship has had more effect than we realise upon our notion of the worship of the primitive church. It disconcerts us to find that that church did not share the puritan theory of worship so far as corporate worship was concerned. No small part of our liturgical difficulties in the Church of England come from confusing two things: protestantism—a purely doctrinal movement of the sixteenth century, confined to Western christianity and closely related to certain doctrinal aspects of fifteenth century Western catholicism, from which it derived directly by way both of development and reaction; and puritanism—which is a general theory about worship, not specifically protestant nor indeed confined to christians of any kind. It is the working theory upon which all mohammedan worship is based. It was put as well as by anybody by the Roman poet Persius or the pagan philosopher Seneca in the first century, and they are only elaborating a thesis from Greek philosophical authors going back to the seventh century B.C. Briefly, the puritan theory is that worship is a purely *mental* activity, to be exercised by a strictly psychological 'attention' to a subjective emotional or spiritual experience. For the puritan this is the essence of worship, and all external things which might impair this strictly mental attention have no rightful place in it. At the most they are to be admitted grudgingly and with suspicion, and only in so far as practice shows that they stimulate the 'felt' religious experience or emotion. Its principal defect is its tendency to 'verbalism', to suppose that *words* alone can express or stimulate the act of worship. Over against this puritan theory of worship stands another—the 'ceremonious' conception of worship, whose foundation principle is that worship as such is not a purely intellectual and affective exercise, but one in which the whole man—body as well as soul, his aesthetic and volitional as well as his intellectual powers—must take full part. It regards worship as an 'act' just as much as an 'experience'. The accidental alliance of protestant doctrine with the puritan theory of worship in the sixteenth century may have been natural, and was as close in England as anywhere. But it was not inevitable. The early Cistercians were profoundly puritan, but they were never protestant. The thorough protestantism of the Swedish Lutherans, with their vestments and lights and crucifixes, has never been puritan.

The puritan conception of worship may be right or wrong in itself—catholics must excuse a monk for finding it understandable and, in some respects at least, sympathetic. But from the point of view of history we have to grasp the fact that there was little in antiquity to suggest to the church that it was even desirable for christians. The elaborate ceremonial worship of the Jerusalem Temple had never been condemned on those grounds by our Lord. And though they came to regard it as in some sense superseded, it had never seemed *wrong* to the christians of the apostolic age, whose most revered leaders continued to frequent it until they were driven from Jerusalem. Images and metaphors drawn from the Old Testament accounts of it saturated the language of the new christian scriptures, and entered at once into the very fabric of eucharistic doctrine. Clement in the first century takes its practice as the most natural analogy of the christian eucharistic assembly. The independent traditions reported by the second century christian writers Hegesippus from Palestine and Polycrates of Ephesus from Asia Minor, that S. James at Jerusalem and S. John at Ephesus had worn the *petalon*, the golden mitre-plate of the jewish high-priest, in virtue of their christian apostolate, are not of value as historical statements. But they are good evidence of the way in which second century christians still found it natural to think of their own eucharistic worship in terms of the ceremonious worship of the Temple. Clement uses that parallel as an illustration. Both these early Easterns take it as a fact.

It is true that some christian apologists of the second century met the pagan charges of christian 'atheism' by adopting the essential puritan theory, and counter-attacking the ceremonies of pagan worship for being ceremonious. In Athenagoras and Tatian, for instance, there is a virtual repudiation of the legitimacy of such ceremonies in any 'pure' worship. But it is interesting to find that they draw their arguments on this topic not from anything in christian doctrine as such, but from pagan and especially from stoic ethical philosophy, in which such assaults on the irrationalities of pagan worship had been a commonplace for two centuries. The christian apologists could start, of course, from the undoubted fact that the cere-monies of the christian cult were comparatively simple and unadorned in their day. But in the course of their borrowed rationalistic argument they exaggerate this aspect of the life of the christian society as we know it from other contemporary documents. There were all the makings of a 'cere-monious' rather than a 'puritan' worship about the administration of the sacraments, even in the second century; and christian corporate worship centred in the sacraments. What is striking about the pre-Nicene liturgy is not so much its simplicity as what I have called its 'directness', its intense concentration and insistence upon the external sacramental *action* in itself as what really mattered, and its exclusion of all devotional accretions of a kind which stimulate or satisfy a subjective piety. This is a type of worship the very reverse of the puritan, for which the subjective experience, not the external action, is always the important thing.

What had produced and for a long while preserved the comparative sim-plicity of the christian ceremonies was no theory that external simplicity was desirable in itself, but the domestic origin of christian worship and the retention for so long of its character as the meeting of the 'household of God'. This involved no deliberate repudiation of beauty in worship where it was possible, nor any cult of plainness for its own sake. Music and painting, incised chalices of precious metal, and even sculpture, can all be proved to have been employed in the service of christian worship before A.D. 250 by literary evidence or by actually existing remains. These things were all modest enough in their development at this time, because the opportunities for their use and the means to acquire them were small. But in the furnishings of the christian cemeteries—as a rule the only christian corporate possessions of this date where we can look for specifically christian art—there is ample evidence that they were not thought unsuitable for christian use. The transference of christian worship from secret meetings in private houses to semi-public conditions at once produced things like the wall-paintings of the baptistery at Dura and the church plate of Cirta even in the third century. Already in the first century A.D. the Johannine Apocalypse had pictured the heavenly worship as a reality faintly reproduced in the earthly worship of the christian church. It is significant that the author found it natural and appropriate to describe worship 'in spirit and in truth' under the form of majestic ceremonial, with all the external accompaniments of lights and incense. He is in fact depicting christian worship as a *public* worship, under the only conditions in which it could then be imagined as a public worship—in heaven. It is not surprising that when the full liberty of public worship in this world was accorded her for the first time under Constantine, the church should have thought it right to realise heavenly ideals so far as might be on earth. It was part of the general translation of worship from the idiom of eschatology into that of time.

Of course such an elaboration of worship brings with it the danger of formalism, of a mere ecclesiastical ceremonial taking the place of a sincere surrender of the heart and will. The prophets of Israel had denounced the results of this, and many of the fourth century fathers did the same. But that danger no less besets puritan worship under the form of cant and hypocrisy, of pretending to a psychological religious experience which has not in reality been undergone, as the seventeenth century was to prove. Neither the puritan nor the ceremonious conception of worship is incompatible with christianity as a belief. Whichever theory is dominant in the worship of a particular age and place, some men can and will pretend to a reality of worship which is the accepted convention of their circumstances, while they in fact allow the natural man, left unconverted and unredeemed, to pursue his self-centred courses and not the Will of God. It is a danger inseparable from any system of *public* worship as such, christian or otherwise, and from the whole attempt to extend any form of religious experience from the naturally sensitive and devout to the unthinking and the average man throughout a whole population.

If such an ideal as 'a christian civilisation' be justifiable at all, the church was fully justified in accepting the mission, freely offered her by the world in the fourth century, of baptising not the human material only but the whole spirit and organisation of society. It was a formidable task, involving her own transformation from a spiritual *élite* into a world-embracing organisation. And the whole ancient world followed Aristotle in regarding 'magnificence' as a virtue of public life; right down to the definite triumph of the commercial spirit at the end of the seventeenth century, most European men did the same. The church of the fourth century did not hesitate to be magnificent, just because she did not refuse to be public. We ourselves still feel it right that the Town Council of a little borough should meet with more formality, with a greater dignity of surroundings and on occasion of official dress, than a group of company directors in an office. The latter may well be more important by the real standards of to-day, because they control more money. But we still feel that a certain dignity is due to the other gathering just because it is a 'public' and not a 'private' act. This is a fragment still surviving from the great fabric of 'public spirit' which vivified the city civilisation of the old mediterranean world.

· Outside the luxurious palaces and villas of the rich the domestic life of the ordinary man was still very simple by our standards. Apart from the huge slum tenements of some great cities, private houses were sometimes beautifully decorated; they were not usually very comfortable, though sufficiently well-adapted to their purpose in that climate; but they were seldom large or imposing. It was far otherwise with the public buildings which housed the corporate life of the little city-republics. Every city and *municipium*, even little country towns, vied with its neighbours in the size of these and the splendour of their furnishings—often to the point of embarrassing city finances. It was a point of honour, even with insignificant places like Silchester in Roman Berkshire, to have a town-hall which could accommodate the whole population at once; a theatre where the whole population could be amused at one time; a public bath-house where all could assemble together. And as the population grew, so these public buildings must grow with it, both in size and in impressiveness. The marks of the successive enlargements and redecorations brought about by the increase of population are still plain in many cases in the extant remains. There was no surer way known to the emperors to gain fame and the loyalty of their subjects than the erection of splendid public buildings in the cities of the empire. It was the ambition of every provincial of some substance to present to his native town some piece of architecture, useful or just beautiful—a public bath or a triumphal arch, a marble colonnade with frescoes or some striking piece of sculpture, by which its dignity might be increased. There was ostentation in this but there was also something better—'public spirit'—an instinct that all which concerned corporate and public life ought to be dignified and beautiful and, if possible, splendid.

More particularly did this feeling concern religion. What we should call 'piety' and personal devotion towards the deities of the civic cults was now languid in the extreme. The old guardian gods of the cities were little more than their religious embodiments; Athens worshipped Athena and Ephesus Diana of the Ephesians, and almost knew that they were worshipping their own best selves. Polytheism supplied other and more moving objects for the genuinely religious instincts of individuals, in the oriental cults and mysteries, and the immemorial local worships of heroes and the household gods, or the goblins and spirits of peasant superstition. But the civic cults of the 'great gods' were nevertheless the chief focus of the still vigorous corporate life of the cities. Their festivals and ceremonies marked the pattern of life, and rooted all human activities in the scheme of things, linking them with the whole natural order of existence. The ordinary man might feel little personal devotion towards Jupiter Capitolinus or Apollo, and address his own prayers to less imposing household gods or to a personal 'Saviour' like Mithras. But it meant much to him that the public sacrifices were duly offered in the city temples by the magistrates as the proper representatives of all the citizens, and that the traditional ceremonies which had brought luck to the city in his fathers' days were still exactly and beautifully performed by the hereditary custodians of the rites. And so the cities provided corporately with an astonishing lavishness for a perpetual round of public worship, in which no one, perhaps, felt any overwhelming religious interest, but which was the recognised centre of corporate and public life, and a chief opportunity to mark its proper dignity and splendour.

Into this atmosphere christian worship passed at once as it became a public worship, and the effects were notable. We shall speak of them in detail later, but here it is important to make clear the principle. For the result in principle was the catholic conception of public worship as it exists to-day in the East and West alike, a thing made suspect to Englishmen by the dominance among us for three centuries of an opposite tradition. Catholic worship is the result—by and large—of the blending of two things, of primitive christian doctrine with the sort of expression the whole ancient world considered suitable for any public act. And that union was fully effected for the first time in the fourth century, when catholic worship became for the first time not only a corporate but a fully public act.

Yet though the ceremonious tradition of catholic worship thus goes back uninterruptedly to the fourth century and can be shown to have a fair half or more of its roots in the third and second, and even in the New Testament itself, I do not know that it is fair to call it outright an older tradition of christian worship than its puritan rival. The monks and hermits of the fourth century were catholics in doctrine, but many of them had much of the puritan theory of worship. Augustine speaking fearfully

THE SANCTIFICATION OF TIME

of the enticements to ear and eye in the use of church music and beauty of adornment,[1] Jerome lamenting the substitution of a silver manger for one of sun-baked mud in the grotto at Bethlehem, the deliberate confinement of the recitation of psalms to a single voice while the rest of the company listened in silent meditative attention among the fathers of the desert, these things are clear evidence of the existence among the monks of the puritan theory, that worship is above all a matter of psychological attention, something purely mental which external things are likely to distract. And this puritan ideal of prayer undoubtedly is represented by certain aspects of christian life in the third and second centuries, things which are to be found substantially in the New Testament. Clear-cut antitheses are as a rule misleading in the study of history. But in this case it does seem more than arguable that while the ceremonious worship of the fourth century was a direct and legitimate development of the *corporate* worship of the pre-Nicene church in its new public setting, the strong puritan tradition in fourth century monasticism derives equally directly from the pre-Nicene tradition of strictly *private* prayer. This was largely unrepresented in the pre-Nicene corporate liturgy which, as we have seen, concentrated on actions rather than words.

The pre-Nicene church had held the two together without any difficulty, because corporate worship and private prayer were still practised under much the same conditions. In the fourth century they diverged more obviously because corporate worship had now become public. But the church was still able to combine the puritan and ceremonious theories of worship in a most fruitful alliance in the same church, because the exponents of both were alike catholic in doctrine. The monastic devotion of the divine office with its 'puritan' emphasis on edification was adopted by the secular churches as part of their corporate worship; just as the old pre-Nicene worship of the eucharistic *ecclesia* finally remained the centre of monastic devotion. The interactions of the two strains in catholic worship through the next twelve centuries are one of the most interesting studies in all liturgy. It was the accident that in the sixteenth century the adherents of the puritan theory of worship mostly adopted protestant doctrines which produced the present great differences between protestant and catholic worship (though as we have noted in the case of the Swedish Lutherans, the two lines of division still do not entirely coincide).

Those who are inclined to question this view must reflect that such differences as now exist between the public worship of the catholic church and those who left it at the Reformation were altogether unprecedented in the many bitter schisms of antiquity. The public worship of Nestorians and Monophysites (and even of allegedly puritan sects like the Donatists and Novatianists, so far as the evidence goes) developed upon the same principles as that of the catholics. No doubt the peculiar protestant

---

[1] *Confessions*, x. 33, 34.

doctrine of 'justification by faith alone', with its consequent antipathy to all external sacramental actions as '*effectual* signs of grace'[1], *i.e.* signs which cause what they signify, is one important reason for the protestant innovations upon the traditional forms of christian cultus. But another at least equally potent is the general acceptance by protestants as an ideal for public worship of a theory as to what constitutes the act of worship in itself which was originally considered by christians more suitable for private prayer.

In the fourth century, at all events, the puritan theory exercised no influence over the development of eucharistic worship. Yet though the liturgical consequences of the change to a fully public worship were accepted at once by the church without question, the outline or Shape of the Liturgy did not at once undergo any great adaptation. The conditions which had moulded it in pre-Nicene times still obtained. What was new was that the church was now free to work openly in them. Christians were still a minority of the population in most places, and the church was still a missionary body in an alien society, whose public tone and conventions were for many years still largely pagan. Her propaganda was now encouraged but only too often embarrassed by the actions of a nominally christian government. But her energy was much distracted from the urgent missionary task by the long misery of the internal struggle with the Arian heresy (c. A.D. 320–381), which was inordinately lengthened, complicated and embittered by the persistent interference of the emperors. The outline of the synaxis consisted still only of the proclamation of revelation by the reading of the scriptures, and the living witness of the church to its truth in the bishop's liturgical sermon, followed by the intercessions of the faithful. This outline retained all its old usefulness and justification. The eucharist still remained a mystery which might not even be described to the unconfirmed.

It is only as the second quarter of the century wears on from c. 325 towards 350, and society at large begins to be increasingly permeated by christian belief and not just affected administratively by the policy of emperors who happened personally to be christians, that the liturgy begins to respond to the new position of the church and the new character of her worship. The first effect of this is seen in the increased share in the conduct of corporate worship which falls to the clergy. We have seen that in the pre-Nicene eucharist the only part of the rite which belonged exclusively to the bishop, that which formed the 'special liturgy' of his office in the corporate worship of the whole church, was the recitation of the eucharistic prayer alone. Even the fraction and administration he shared with the presbyters and deacons; and he had no special part in the offertory performed by the people and the deacons. All but the single short prayer thus consisted of the corporate action of the church. When we look at the

---

[1] *XXVth Article of Religion.*

rite of Sarapion (*c.* 340) this has begun to alter. To the old eucharistic prayer, the only spoken text of the pre-Nicene rite, has been added a series of further prayers assigned to the celebrant alone—a prayer at the fraction, a prayer over the people between the communion of the clergy and that of the laity, a prayer of thanksgiving after the communion (a further prayer for the blessing of oil and water for the sick),[1] and a final prayer of benediction. And Sarapion is only representative of a tendency to surround 'the' prayer (as Sarapion himself still calls it) with secondary devotions, which is found increasingly in all rites in the fourth century. The increase in the mere quantity of the celebrant's 'liturgy' is not in itself important. The old rites were very brief, the bare bones of the liturgical action; this was the obvious way to expand them to fit their new dignity and formality. Even so, it was likely to alter the relative positions of the clergy and laity in what was meant to be a corporate action. But the really serious results came in with the disappearance of the people's offertory in the East during the fourth century, and the simultaneous rapid decline in the frequency of lay communions. The corporate action of the church disappeared, and what was left was a rite conducted chiefly by the prayers of the clergy, in which the people still made responses but had otherwise little part. Doubtless some increase in the share of the clergy in the conduct of worship was inevitable, as it necessarily became less spontaneous and more complicated in its public setting. But the increase in the number of prayers did have the undesigned effect of making these the outstanding thing in the rite, and so preparing the way for the change in its character, from a corporate action of the whole church to a service said by the clergy to which the laity listened.

In the third quarter of the century a new state of society is beginning to emerge, in which the dominant sections of the community are learning to make the christian assumptions about life and are adapting their practice of living to them. In the meanwhile forces had been building themselves up within the church itself which would make her able as well as willing to embrace with her worship the whole range of social existence in a new way, and to stamp upon ordinary human activities the imprint of christian doctrines and ideas.

### *The Coming of Monasticism and the Divine Office*

It may sound paradoxical to say that among the most important of these was the 'world-renouncing' movement of monasticism, yet such seems to be the fact. Between A.D. 325 and 375 the monastic movement was gaining

---

[1] In the old Roman rite this blessing when required was added as part of the eucharistic prayer itself, before the doxology. It is possible that this is the original meaning of an obscure direction by Hippolytus, *Ap. Trad.*, v. 1, for the use of a similar blessing of oil; or he may be directing the use of it separately from and after the eucharistic prayer, as in Sarapion.

impetus with every year that passed. The period of casual pioneering and tentative experiment was over before the middle of the century, and men moulded and deepened by the new intensification of the spiritual life were making their appearance on episcopal thrones, first in Egypt, then all over the East and finally in the West. Every year some hundreds or thousands of members of ordinary christian congregations were leaving the world to give themselves—their whole life and being—to nothing else but *worship*, so far as this might be possible for mortal man. The whole church could not but be familiarised thus with the idea that worship is not only the highest among man's activities (the pre-Nicene church had been well aware of that) but can become the supreme expression of his *whole* being, towards which every other activity can be directed.

This was precisely the idea needed to nerve the church to that great expansion of the scope of the liturgy which alone could enable it to sanctify and to express towards God the whole social activity of a new 'Christian world'. In the pre-Nicene church faith and worship could and did irradiate the whole life of the believer; but just because ordinary secular life was organised on a pagan basis, worship and daily life were two opposed things. Christian worship could not hope to express and consummate the daily life even of christians in all its aspects. It is true that by such means as the eucharists at christian marriages and funerals (which go back at least to the second century) the liturgy did very early begin to reach out towards the consecration of the mundane life of christians. But in a pagan world it was bound to remain essentially a world-renouncing and exclusive, not a world-embracing and inclusive act. The monk did make worship the end and aim of all his activities. The tension of worship was found to be too great to be borne without some relaxations, though he submitted to these only grudgingly, and in order that the tension might be borne the better. Bodily needs could not be altogether abolished even in the desert, but they could there be simplified to the point where they were altogether subordinate and directed to the primary end of worship. The church at large, just because she was in the world, could not renounce all secular life as the monk did, but she learned from him to sanctify it.

There are movements in the mind of a whole age which grow stealthily, as it were, so that all men's ideas have changed from those of their fathers' generation without conflict and almost unperceived. There are others which at their first onset strike the imagination and seem to challenge all possible opposition, without appearing in their triumphant progress to take much account of the disturbance they arouse. Of these last was the first rise of monasticism. It struck the imagination of all men when they heard of it, christian and pagan alike, on the whole rather painfully. The men of the fourth century lived in a declining world, the sunset of all antiquity. But it was a very splendid and attractive world nevertheless, and not ill-pleased with itself. And suddenly young men and women began

silently and resolutely to turn their backs upon it in large numbers, because
they had become intensely interested in something quite different. Of
course it set men talking; the movement carried with it enough extravagances to furnish any amount of gossip. It made sensible men furious; it
alarmed some emperors and bishops; it aroused bewilderment, denuncia-
tion and passionate admiration; but it could not be ignored. And it simply
went on. Vocations came to every rank in society from the highest to the
lowest. Arsenius, the confidant of the last great emperor, Theodosius, left
the imperial palace to go and live in a reed-thatched cell with an ex-
shepherd in Egypt, and looked back with unaffected and serene tranquillity
at the influence and luxury he had left. Moses, the captain of a band of
robbers, entered religion, and emerged again only to bring back his former
gang into the novitiate with him. Men and women, often the most attractive and gifted of their circle, rich or poor, seemed to leave their fellows
with a strange eager gladness at the first notes of that secret call. It was no
wonder that pagan intellectuals raged publicly at what they called 'the new
enchantment', half in fear and half in genuine heart-break for lost friends.
It was no wonder, too, that old-fashioned churchmen, headed as ever by
the clergy of Rome, grumbled loudly and said that the bishops ought to
take action to stop the whole new-fangled business. The bishops, as has
generally been the case with new christian movements, were not much
consulted at the outset, and had little effective opportunity for interference.
A few opposed it, but the majority stood aside to see how matters would
shape, and then put themselves at the head of the movement when it had
proved a success.

Augustine has told us in the exquisite cadences of his prose of a casual
conversation, typical of the period, which he had with a christian fellow-
countryman of his own, an officer at court, one afternoon at Milan while
he himself still hovered on the brink of christian belief. His friend laughed
and chaffed him when he found him reading S. Paul:

'Then the talk turned on what Pontitian told us of Antony the monk of
Egypt,[1] and a great name among Thy servants, though till that hour we
had not heard of him. . . . Thence he fell to talking of the numbers of the
monasteries, a sweet incense unto Thee, and of how the deserts and the
solitary places were now thus turned fruitful, all of which was new to us.
Even at Milan there was then a monastery by the city walls, full of good
brethren under the care of Ambrose the bishop, though we had not heard
of it. Pontitian went on talking and we listened spell-bound. He told us how
one afternoon at Trier, when the emperor had gone to the wild-beast shows
at the circus, he and three friends of his had gone for a walk in the orchards
beyond the city walls, and falling into pairs, one walked on with him, while
the other two strolled more slowly behind. And these two on their walk

[1] Hermit, the first great name in monastic history. He lived to be 105, having
been more than eighty years in the desert (d. A.D. 356).

THE SHAPE OF THE LITURGY

happened on a small cottage where lived some of Thy servants . . . and went in and picked up a copy of *The Life of Antony*. One of them began to read it [in the ancient fashion, aloud] and to wonder at it and be stirred. And as he read on, he thought to embrace that life himself and leave his career at court to serve Thee. Both of them were of those who are styled "Commissioners of State Affairs".[1] Then suddenly, filled with a holy love and a sober shame, and angry with himself, he looked at his friend and burst out, "Tell me, what is the good of all we are trying to do? What is the object of it? Is there anything more to be hoped for at court than to become the emperor's favourites? And is not everything about that unstable and dangerous? And through how many other dangers must we go to reach this greater danger? And how long before we reach it? But a friend of God I can become, if I want to, this very minute." He said this, and then in torment with the throes of a new life, he looked down again at the book. He read on, and his heart whereon Thou lookedst was changed, and his mind put off the world, as was soon seen. For while he read and struggled with the storm in his heart, he sighed a little while, and saw and chose his way. And now being already Thine, he said to his friend: "Now I have broken loose from all our hopes. I will serve God. From this hour in this place I begin. If you will not do the like, at least do not oppose me." The other said that he would stay with him and keep him company in so great a reward and so great a service. And to this day both of them are Thine. . . .

'But by this time Pontitian and the friend who was with him, having walked on through the orchards came back to look for them, and finding them said it was getting late and time to be going home. But they told them of their mind and purpose and how they had come to their determination, and begged them not to argue even if they would not join them. Then those two, who had gone through no such searchings of heart that afternoon, yet (as he told us) nevertheless envied them and wished them well and devoutly begged their prayers. And so they went back with heavy hearts to the palace, while the others stayed at the cottage with hearts set on high.'[2]

So it could take a man as swiftly as that!—An hour later when his friend had gone, Augustine in a passion of tears gave his own doubting sensual soul to God under the fig-tree in his little garden, and the most brilliant mind of the century was on a short road to the monastery.

That sort of conversation was going on all over the empire through those fifty years, often enough with the same results, and the consequences were prodigious. It is not only a matter of the scale of the monastic movement in itself, with its thousands of monks and nuns, and the effect of this on men's imaginations. We have to keep in mind its devotional repercussions on the church at large. The monk sought God for His own sake alone, and

[1] Confidential officers on the emperor's civil staff.
[2] Augustine, *Confessions*, viii. 6.

to tell the truth sometimes half-forgot the church when he forgot the world, in the ardour of pursuit. ('I too am a hunter', answered the hermit Macarius to the unsuccessful sportsman who stopped to ask him what he did in the desert, 'let us not both of us lose our quarry'; and turned back into his cell to pray.) But neither the church nor the world could forget the monk. For the hundreds who vanished each year to the supreme adventure of the soul in the desert and the hermitage, thousands who could not go to that heroic length only remained behind in the churches to emulate their example as best they could, either in their own homes or in little groups of ascetics like those of the cottage in the orchards outside Trêves. And quite apart from these professedly semi-monastic groups and individuals, there never was a time when so many of the *laity* gave themselves up with such ardour to the devout life while remaining in the world. We meet these un-organised domestic ascetics literally by the hundred in every great church in the fourth century. Despite all the christian disappointments of the times and the seeming mediocrity of the church's official action in face of the new opportunities, the world was steadily and surely flooding into her communion behind its nominally christian rulers. The new movement towards asceticism led by the monks was like some vast blind gathering together of the church's interior spiritual force, in self-immunisation from the torrent of worldliness which at times began to look like engulfing her as a result of the world's conversion. Of the bishops in the first half of the century it must be said that many were no more than imperial courtiers, venal, intriguing, unprincipled and worldly; while the great majority of their more respectable brethren—there are of course some great exceptions—seem to have been distinctly second-rate men, administrators rather than leaders. In such circumstances it was no longer so much the bishops as the monks and the devout laity who guided the devotion of the church.

The monk and his lay followers placed a quite new emphasis on an element in christian spirituality which had been present from the begin-ning, but which had hitherto found only restricted expression in christian corporate worship and none at all in the eucharistic rite—the element of deliberate personal 'edification'. At the beginning of the third century Hippolytus describes a *régime* of prayer which is recognisably semi-monastic in character.[1] The christian, married or single, is to rise for prayer at midnight, and again at cock-crow. There are prayers at rising for the day, at the Hours of the Passion at Terce, Sext and None, and again in the evening on going to bed—the equivalent of Compline; though there is as yet nothing quite equivalent to Vespers.[2] There is even the daily

[1] *Ap. Trad.*, xxxvi.
[2] I know of no evidence for any organised evening service corresponding to Vespers or Evensong, even on Sundays, from anywhere in Christendom before *c.* A.D. 360. The little ceremony of the *Lucernarium*, the blessing of the evening lamp with prayer and praise, was inherited by christianity directly from the jewish domestic piety of our Lord's time. It was transferred to the public evening service

reception of holy communion, received, however, not at a daily celebration of the eucharist but from the sacrament reserved by the faithful in their own homes.[1] There is, too, a prescription of daily 'spiritual reading', an anticipation of the *lectio divina* by which later monastic rules set so much store. This Hippolytus regards as a reasonable substitute for attendance at a daily 'instruction', held in an *ecclesia* at some sort of synaxis on week-day mornings.[2] This he prescribes daily for both clergy and laity, but it is plain from what he says that such frequency was not to be expected in practice. Perhaps in what he says of the duty of attending the 'instruction' and its daily session, he speaks in his private capacity as a professional 'lecturer' on christian doctrine, and the *ecclesia* to which he refers is the daily attendance of his disciples at the lecture-hall, rather than any sort of liturgical synaxis officially organised by the church.

This whole passage in the *Apostolic Tradition* suggests certain doubts. Hippolytus quite certainly intends to lay down this rule of prayer and meditation for all, clergy and laity, married or single, without exception. But how many of the humble slaves and freedmen and artisans who made up the great bulk of the third century church possessed books or could have read them if they had? I do not want to minimise the evidence for an average standard of devotion among the laity in the pre-Nicene church higher, perhaps, than it ever was again (though one may have doubts about that too—the laity of the fourth and fifth centuries were very devout indeed). The pre-Nicene evidence, especially for the observance of prayer at Terce, Sext and None, and for the ordinary practice by the laity of daily communion from the reserved sacrament at home, is widespread and ought not to be discounted. But the very energy with which Hippolytus recommends his rule of life suggests that what he is seeking to prescribe for all was in fact the practice of a comparatively leisured few among his own contemporaries. It is not on the whole likely that most christians, with their masters to serve or their living to earn, could attend daily instructions, or give themselves with such completeness to a life of prayer.

But what is more to our immediate point, all this represents the purely *personal* aspect of devotion, and stands quite apart, even as he presents it, from the corporate worship of the *ecclesia*. Even the daily communion from the reserved sacrament seems to emphasise a side of eucharistic piety —the longing for personal communion with our Lord—which was doubt-less always there in the hearts of the worshippers at the eucharist, but which received no liturgical expression whatever in the pre-Nicene rites,

in church when this came into being in the later fourth century, but previously to that it had remained a christian domestic rite, except when used as a preliminary to the paschal vigil.

[1] *Ap. Trad.*, xxxii. According to Hippolytus, the bishop's eucharist was celebrated on all Sundays, and it was not entirely confined to that day; though his language suggests that it was not yet common on other days (*ibid.*, xxiv).

[2] *Ap. Trad.*, xxxv. 2–xxxvi. 1.

where the whole emphasis is on the corporate aspect. It is true, of course, that the general aspect of devotion which may roughly be called 'subjective edification' was not altogether lost sight of in the corporate worship of the church. The ecclesiastical synaxis with its lections and sermon could serve this end, even though the liturgy of 'witness' rather than 'edification' was its real purpose. The longer week-day synaxes on the set fast-days or 'stations', when they came in, must have served it better. But how many could manage to attend them? And even these seem to have consisted almost entirely of lessons, interspersed with solo chants, and discourse, like the synaxis of Sunday but much lengthier. The elements of vocal praise by the congregation and of prayer were much smaller than one would expect.

There is said, too, to have been the 'vigil' service, at which the church, in hope of the second coming, regularly kept watch all through the Saturday night with lections and chants and prayers until the eucharist at cock-crow consoled her for the delay of the Lord's coming, by its proclamation of the Lord's death 'till He come'. Something of the sort seems to have formed the liturgy of the church at Troas[1] on the occasion of S. Paul's visit there. But how far was that exceptional and accidental, due to the special circumstances of the apostle's visit and his eloquence? How often, in any case, after the first joyful days were these vigils held? When one scrutinises the second century evidence there is room for suspecting that the pre-Nicene 'corporate vigils' of the church (except for that of the Pascha) are an invention of manuals of liturgical history. Hippolytus treats the baptismal vigil of the Pascha as something altogether peculiar, and has no mention of corporate vigils on other occasions but only of private nocturnal prayer at home. It has been thought that the Sunday synaxis originally developed out of the vigil. But when we first meet a description of it in Justin it has nothing whatever of the vigil about it, though it is held in the morning, before the work of the day—Sunday was not a public holiday—began. It is the nearest approach which christian worship then made to a public action, and from this point of view alone there was always good reason to hold it at a time when enquirers might be likely to attend. We may infer if we please from a phrase in the contemporary biography of S. Cyprian[2] that c. A.D. 250 it was already the custom in Africa to hold a vigil before the anniversaries of the great martyrs, as was certainly the case in later times. But such an inference is very uncertain. Looking at the pre-Nicene evidence as a whole it seems to me improbable that a vigil-service was at all a frequent devotion for the laity, and quite likely that it was confined to the baptismal vigil at Pascha (and also on occasions, one at Pentecost).

[1] Acts xx. 7.
[2] Pontius, *Vita Cypriani*, xiv.   The phrase seems to me an allusion to the paschal vigil.   It would be easier to decide, if we could be sure that the *Acta* of S. Saturninus of Toulouse, which record a similar custom, are in any sense a pre-Nicene document, but there is reason to doubt this.

The 'private meetings' (*syneleuseis*) and agape-suppers, of which we have spoken, did include a large element of 'edifying discourse', but these were gatherings of selected persons, not corporate assemblies which every christian had a duty or even a right to attend. As such they are outside the liturgy. When all proper allowance has been made for these and similar observances, it remains true that the corporate worship of the pre-Nicene christians in its official and organised forms, the synaxis and the eucharist, was overwhelmingly a 'world-renouncing' cultus, which deliberately and rigidly rejected the whole idea of sanctifying and expressing towards God the life of human society in general, in the way that catholic worship after Constantine set itself to do. On the other hand it also ignored, especially in its eucharistic rite, the expression of that subjective devotion and strictly mental attention which it is the paramount object of the puritan theory of worship to promote. The pre-Nicene church was able to contain the puritan and the ceremonious theories of worship together so easily, partly at least, because though the synaxis and sacramental liturgy with their emphasis on external acts formed almost the whole content of her corporate worship, yet in the circumstances of the time official corporate worship *could* only take a smaller part (quantitatively) in the living of the christian life than it did later, even though it was always its vital centre.

In the fourth century this was altered. The old worship of the *ecclesia*, the synaxis and eucharist (and the other sacramental rites) remained for a while the whole substance of corporate worship in the secular churches. But one cannot but be struck by the comparatively small place (which is not at all the same thing as a low place) occupied from the first in the *monastic* scheme of devotion by these ancient forms of worship. Monasticism was in no way anti-clerical or anti-sacramental in principle. In the heart of the deserts the congregations of hermits retained the weekly (sometimes more frequent) Sunday synaxis and the Sunday eucharist, which were duly celebrated under the presidency of monks who had received episcopal ordination to the presbyterate. The hermits retained, too, the practice of daily communion from the sacrament reserved in their own cells.[1] But it needs only a slight acquaintance with the literature of early monasticism to see what had happened. They had retained the traditional corporate worship of the pre-Nicene church not only in the forms but also in the *infrequency* which pre-Nicene conditions had made necessary for even devout christians living in the world. Yet virtually the monks' whole time was now free for worship; and so the staple of their devotional life became a great development of the pre-Nicene system of *private* prayer and the subjective aspects of personal edification in which the corporate worship of the *ecclesia* had been conspicuously lacking. It is only in the desert, for instance, that the regular recitation of the whole psalter 'in course' becomes a practice of christian devotion for the first time, and that

[1] S. Basil, *Ep.* xciii.

the psalter really begins to take in its own right the very large place it has always held since in the content of christian and corporate worship. Before this time it is used in the *ecclesia* only selectively, and as comment upon the other scriptures. But this element in worship, which in pre-Nicene times had been purely private, was from the first tending to become the larger part of what corresponded to public worship among the monks. Even before it became a corporate exercise in the common life of the monastic communities, first organised by S. Pachomius in Egypt *c*. A.D. 330, it had already become a matter of rule and organisation among the hermits.[1]

We are now chiefly concerned, not with the effects of this change of emphasis and proportion on the life of the monks themselves (which were not lasting, since the eucharist subsequently came to take a much larger place in the monastic routine), but with its repercussions on the church at large during the fourth century, and especially on the liturgy. It leads, of course, in the first place to the introduction of the divine office, an ordered course of services chiefly of 'praise' but with some reading of the scriptures, into the public worship of the secular churches. This amounts to the creation of what is virtually a fresh department of the liturgy, beside and around the old synaxis and eucharist.[2]

It was an obvious method of expanding the relatively meagre bulk of christian corporate worship to a length and frequency suitable to its new public setting. But while the old worship placed its emphasis chiefly on the corporate action of the church, the office, though it became a corporate devotion, is primarily intended to express and evoke the devout interior aspirations and feelings of each individual worshipper. It long retained the marks of its monastic and private origin, not only in its tendency not to follow closely the round of the liturgical cycle, but in the comparative

---

[1] The evidence is abundant that in this shift of emphasis in worship the monastic movement in general had no deliberate intention of cutting itself off from the hierarchy and the traditional devotional life of the church, whatever may have been the case with individuals. As late as the sixth century S. Benedict in his cave at Subiaco could be quite unaware that christendom was keeping Easter Day, and he might not have been as exceptional in this sort of isolation from the life of the church in the fourth century as he appears to have been in the sixth. But the deliberate adoption of such an attitude (as opposed to its accidental occurrence through solitude) was accounted by the desert fathers a sin of pride and a diabolical illusion. (*Cf*. *e.g.* the case in Cassian, *Collations*, i. 21.) And the Holy Rule of S. Benedict makes it abundantly clear that he had an adequate perception of the place which ought to be occupied by the eucharist and the 'ecclesiastical' organisation of worship generally in the christian life of all, whether monks or seculars, even though his Rule is naturally preoccupied with regulating ascesis and the specifically monastic devotion of the office. In this he is in line with all the best fourth century monastic tradition.

[2] It is significant that modern protestant public worship has retained the elements of the office in a form much nearer to that found in catholicism than are its eucharistic forms and devotion to those of catholics. It has made this monastic form of devotion (adopted by the church at large only in the later fourth century) into the almost exclusive substance of its public worship, relegating the sacramental liturgy the pre-Nicene *ecclesia* to the position of an optional appendage.

absence from its public performance of the sort of external ceremony with which the early church had gradually surrounded the public offering of the eucharist. But as the two departments of the liturgy, the new and the old, became co-ordinated, the mere existence of the office was bound to some extent to affect the way in which the old liturgy of synaxis and eucharist was regarded, and also its content.

We need not here go deeply into the obscure history of the first organisation of the divine office in secular churches. It appears there as a direct result of the monastic-ascetic movement, one of whose chief effects from the outset had been a great increase in the regular practice of private nocturnal prayer by the devout laity in their own homes. In A.D. 347–8 at Antioch a confraternity of ascetic laymen under the direction of the orthodox monks Flavian and Diodore adopted the custom of meeting together for this exercise in private houses. They were soon induced to remove their meetings to a basilica by the arianising bishop, who was anxious to keep the activities of this influential orthodox group under his own eye.[1]

Thus accidentally was first established the custom of a daily *public* vigil service, whose contents were the ordinary monastic devotion of reciting psalms and canticles and listening to reading.

The custom spread rapidly, but there can be little question that the real centre and example for its diffusion through the church at large was not so much Antioch as Jerusalem, where it must have been adopted very soon after its first invention in the Syrian capital. As far back as the second century christians in other lands had felt the attraction of the sacred sites in Jerusalem,[2] and as soon as the peace of the church made such devotion easier to fulfil, the practice of christian pilgrimage thither increased. It was made fashionable by the example of Constantine's mother, the British princess S. Helen, *c.* A.D. 325, which attracted the interest of her son, and was probably the cause of his foundation of the splendid churches at Calvary and on the Mount of Olives. The flutter caused by the prolonged visit of this devout *grande dame* among the members of what was then a small and unimportant provincial church, glorious only in its site, is still reflected in the legend of the Invention of the Holy Cross. The narrative of a humbler pilgrim from Bordeaux in A.D. 333 is still extant; and from this time onwards Jerusalem was becoming more and more a 'holy city', whose principal activity, and indeed industry, towards the end of the century had become the practice of the Christian religion. A considerable proportion of the population after *c.* A.D. 350 came to consist of monks and domestic ascetics from other lands who had settled in and around the city out of devotion. When one adds to these the throngs of transient pilgrims and those who lived by ministering to their wants, one has a picture of a somewhat specialised christian population, for whose desires and needs the

---

[1] Theodoret, *Hist. Eccl.*, II., xxiv.
[2] *E.g.* Melito of Sardis, *ap.* Eusebius, *H.E.*, *IV*. xxvi. 9.

old provision of a Sunday synaxis and eucharist with two or three lesser synaxes on week-days would rapidly reveal its inadequacy.

The organisation of the divine office at Jerusalem must be one of the personal achievements of S. Cyril. He became bishop there *c.* A.D. 350, just when the first germs of the public office were making their appearance at Antioch. In his *Catecheses* delivered as a presbyter in the spring of 347–8 there is a complete absence of reference to any services of the sort, which would be inexplicable, if they already existed. But by the time of the pilgrimage of Etheria-Silvia in A.D. 385—the year before S. Cyril's death—there is a whole daily round of offices at Jerusalem, from the Night Office an hour or two after midnight lasting till Lauds at cock-crow, on through Sext and None daily (public Terce is still specially reserved for Lent) and ending with Vespers, which lasted until after sunset. The whole series is under the direction of the bishop and his clergy, some of whom preside over the performance of every office, as the bishop himself does at Lauds and Vespers accompanied by them all. It is nothing less than the reception for the first time into the public worship of a secular church of the monastic ideal of sanctifying human life as a whole and the passage of time by corporate worship. It marks the end of the pre-Nicene tradition that corporate worship should express only the separateness of 'the holy church' from the world out of which it had been redeemed.

Conditions at Jerusalem were exceptional in the degree to which properly monastic circumstances were reproduced in the life of a whole local church; but something of the same kind was growing up in other churches. Not only was a growing proportion of the leisured class everywhere becoming christian, but the second half of the century saw a considerable increase in the number of domestic ascetics among the labouring classes, who while continuing to earn their own living were prepared in pursuit of the ascetic ideal to reduce their needs to a minimum and to devote the time thus gained to religious exercises. For the first time there appears a considerable christian public which has the leisure to attend frequent public services; and the monastic-ascetic movement brought with the opportunity the desire. The example of Jerusalem, everywhere reported by returning pilgrims, was there to stimulate the demand of the laity for the holding of such services in their own churches. The secular clergy, not always very enthusiastically, were obliged to undertake the supervision and public recitation of some offices in the churches. Daily services of this kind became general in the last quarter of the fourth century. In the West Rome appears to have adopted them at this time, almost certainly about A.D. 382 under Pope S. Damasus; and the tradition is constant that that great organiser of the Roman liturgy deliberately modelled the Roman office in its main lines on that of Jerusalem. At Milan the beginnings of the office appear to go back to A.D. 386, when the troubles provoked by the Arian empress Justina caused the faithful to assemble and keep watch at night in the basilicas, during which time S. Ambrose occupied their minds with a vigil service on the new Eastern model. The observance was then continued permanently after the immediate occasion for it had passed.

But for a century or two the full round of offices, and above all the long Night Office, were in much greater favour as a public devotion with the monks and the devout laity than with the secular clergy, who only slowly and reluctantly accepted the obligation of reciting them daily as an inherent part of clerical duties. It was otherwise with Lauds and Vespers, the daily offices of praise at dawn and sunset, which had been established in almost all secular churches before the end of the fourth century. These had been specially favoured by the secular clergy from the outset (as they were at Jerusalem in Etheria's time) and they retained traces of the fact, as Nocturns and the Little Hours retained special traces of monastic practice. The secular clergy still did their bible-reading as the pre-Nicene church had done it, as part of the public worship of the church at the synaxis; the monks did theirs as an inheritance from the *lectio divina* as part of the Night Office.[1] The offices of Lauds and Vespers therefore, as a devotion for which the secular clergy felt themselves primarily responsible, never contained any but the smallest element of bible reading. And at Lauds, at all events, there was never any continuous recitation of the psalter, but instead certain selected psalms were used, some of them every day. (The same was probably true originally of Vespers, but the evidence is much less clear.) The selection of psalms for Lauds is much the same all over christendom, and must be of considerable antiquity. It probably spread from the Jerusalem church of the fourth century. Particularly interesting is the general daily use of Pss. 148, 149 and 150 together as a sort of climax to end the dawn psalmody. The private recitation of these three psalms at

[1] It was done, too, on a different principle. The old purpose of the lections at the synaxis had been the proclamation of revelation. There was therefore a strong tendency at the synaxis to select lections from *different* books, in order to manifest the coherence of revelation in the different parts of the bible and make them illustrate one another. (*Cf.* our epistle and gospel at the eucharist.) The purpose of the *lectio divina* was the orderly and continuous study of the bible. There was therefore an almost universal tendency for the lessons at the Night Office to be not selected from different books but continuous from the same book, and for some of them to be taken not from the bible but from commentaries upon it, explaining the passage of scripture already read. There are few historical statements more in need of revision than those of the preface 'Concerning the Service of the Church' in the Book of Common Prayer, that 'the ancient fathers . . . so ordained the matter that all the whole Bible should be read over once every year . . .' in public worship, and that 'this godly and decent order hath been . . . broken and neglected . . . with multitude of Responds, Verses. . . .' Nothing is more certain than that the *selection* of lections in public worship were a point of distinction between the pre-Nicene public worship (continued for a while in the post-Nicene secular churches) and the continuous reading introduced by the monks. The unbroken recitation of the whole psalter straight through, instead of the daily recitation of certain fixed and selected psalms as had been the jewish and pre-Nicene custom of private prayer, was likewise a monastic innovation of the fourth century, which Cranmer in the same document supposes primitive. (I am not here concerned with which is the better system, but with the historical truth of the matter.)

dawn was a custom general with pious jews in the first century. Like the blessing of the evening lamp at public Vespers it must have been transmitted to the infant church by its jewish nucleus in the apostolic age, and then handed down as a piece of christian domestic piety until in the fourth century it was transferred to the new public service in the church at dawn. Thus Lauds, like Vespers (with its jewish blessing of the evening lamp) and the eucharist, each centred around a devotional practice which must have been entirely familiar to our Lord and His disciples before the crucifixion.

The office as a public function in secular churches was not only a considerable extension of the field of corporate worship. It was, by contrast with the eucharist, from its first introduction a really public devotion, open to all comers. There was for a while a practice of expelling the unconfirmed before the concluding prayers at the office as at the synaxis: but the element of prayer in the secular office was never a large one, and the bulk of the office and its most important part, the 'worship' of the psalms, was always open to all. There was no strong tradition of exclusiveness attaching to it from the past, as in the case of the eucharist. This openness of the office did something to prepare the way for the open celebration of the eucharist; but even the old christian exclusiveness about that was bound to break down as the world became nominally christian.

When one considers the rigidity with which this old 'exclusive' notion of christian corporate worship was held—so that e.g., all the sets of catechetical instructions extant from the later fourth and fifth centuries still give the new christian laity their first instructions about baptism, confirmation and the eucharist only *after* they have received those sacraments—one sees something of the change the monastic movement thus made indirectly in the theory of christian worship. When one considers, too, the immense problem which the conversion of the empire put before the church in the mere provision of a corporate worship responsive to the new needs— given her previous 'world-renouncing' tradition on the matter—one appreciates better the service rendered to the liturgy by the fourth century monastic movement. Nothing less striking to the imagination or less impressive in its scale could have sufficed to change the christian conception of worship with the necessary speed. Nothing less whole-heartedly spiritual in its fundamental purpose could have carried through such a revolution safely. Without the salt of monasticism the church could only have received the world into itself by itself becoming secularised. And the result could only have been the secularising of the eucharist, the heart and life of christian worship. Or else, if the church had succeeded in retaining her integrity, she must have been content to remain an *élite*, excluding from her fold and her worship the common man, whom God made and loves, and the daily life for which God made him. Once the world had freely opened itself to her under Constantine, she must choose either to try to absorb it and christianise it or to withdraw for ever from all deliberate contact with it. The existence of the monks with their passionate 'other-worldliness' in such numbers and authority was an effective standing protest against worldliness in the church. It is not too much to say that this was the principal safeguard in that mingling of the church with the world which marks the fourth century. And by adding to corporate worship a whole new sphere in which the subjective elements of piety and edification could find the scope which they had lacked in the corporate worship of the pre-Nicene church, the monks made it possible to preserve the pre-Nicene tradition of worship itself unchanged as the centre of the new approach to life in a christian world.

In the end the gain was not all on one side. The monk and his imitators gave the church the divine office and the conception of the *whole* life of man as consummated in worship, instead of regarding worship as a department of life, like paganism, or the contradiction of daily life, like the pre-Nicene church. The church at large after a while gave back to the monk that centring of all specifically christian life on the eucharist as the extension of the incarnation—a thing which in his own first enthusiasm he had sometimes been in danger of forgetting. This the secular churches never lost sight of by reason of their firm maintenance of the pre-Nicene tradition of worship, with the synaxis and eucharist as its central act. From the fourth century onwards this fruitful interplay between the secular and monastic elements in the church never wholly ceases to enrich and fortify christian devotion in different ways at different times. Perhaps it is not fanciful to ascribe that gradual 'secularisation' of the spirit and content of their public worship which the most spiritual minds in the churches of the Reformation now openly deplore, in part to their destruction along with monasticism of its insistence on intellectual worship for its own sake, or rather for the sake of the goodness and beauty and majesty of God alone, which evoke worship as the chief end of human life as a whole. This was the great balancing element that the monk brought to christian public worship in the days when the church first faced the novel dangers of a christian world. Without monasticism and its witness, despite all the noble efforts of protestant puritans to achieve a christianity that shall be in the world but not of it, the protestant churches to-day seem to be facing exactly the same alternatives as the catholic church in the reign of Constantine—the impossible choice between inner secularisation of themselves and their worship, or renunciation of the mission to christianise the daily life of society at large.[1]

---

[1] In these circumstances one must watch with hope and sympathy the progress of such groups as the Iona community among the Scottish Presbyterians, and *Les Veilleurs*, a somewhat similar group founded by Wilfrid Monod among the French Huguenots. Their connection with the 'liturgical movement' among their co-religionists is obvious and important.

## The Development of the Christian Calendar

The acceptance of the divine office in various forms as part of the public worship of the church was not the only enrichment in the scope of the liturgy which was taking place during the second half of the fourth century. A different sort of development is represented by the rapid expansion of the christian liturgical calendar during the same period. No less than the organisation of the office this helped to equip the liturgy to fulfil a social as well as a strictly devotional function. The office, when it had been fully organised, enabled the church to set about sanctifying human life within time by consecrating the chief natural points of every day—the quiet of the night, dawn, the beginning of work, the approach of the day's heat, noon, the return to the afternoon's work, sunset, rest—with appropriate christian prayers, publicly offered on behalf of the whole community. So in the same way the liturgical cycle, when its main outline had been completed, sanctified the annual round of the seasons, and set out to imprint on the rhythm of nature and its reflection in social life the stamp of distinctively christian ideas. There is no more effective method of keeping the plain christian man and woman in mind of the elementary facts of christian doctrine than the perpetual round of the Hours of the Passion set in the ordered sequence of the liturgical seasons. The centrality of Jesus of Nazareth as the only Redeemer of mankind is the incessant lesson of them both, when they are properly understood. Even the great increase in the importance of saints' days which is noticeable in the fourth century told in the same direction. The new cultus of the local martyrs of the past as the patrons of their own cities and provinces enabled the church to give a christian turn to the local patriotism and civic spirit which were still the healthiest elements in the decaying political life of the empire. And since these local heroes owed their celebrity to the fact that they had ' witnessed' outstandingly for the Lordship of Jesus against the world in the places where they were venerated, their cultus enabled the church to set forth Jesus as the Lord not only of universal history but of homely local history as well, which to the average man was a much less vague conception.

Neither office nor calendar was altogether a new thing in the fourth century, but a new development of things which in the second and third centuries had been growing up in connection with semi-private devotions rather than the corporate worship of christians. The fourth century saw the church officially adopt both, and adapt them to her new needs; and it was soon found that the mere fact that they were well-known to be going on in church was a teaching instrument of no small value in a half-christian society, even for those outside the church and for christians who had little leisure or inclination for frequent attendance at public worship. But the development of the two, though it went on side by side, was for a while carried on to some extent independently and under rather different influences. The office originated with the monks and the devout laity; the annual calendar was developed chiefly by the bishops and the secular clergy. The cycle of the office was based upon the day and the week; that of the synaxis and eucharist (which lies behind the later 'ecclesiastical calendar') was based upon the year.

In the year A.D. 350 both office and calendar were just beginning to be more or less officially organised; by the year A.D. 400 both were complete in all essentials, and had begun to be accepted everywhere in their new forms. But there was a period of confusion between these two dates during which they had not yet been brought into close correspondence in many churches. Thus the Spanish nun Etheria in A.D. 385 notes as something quite new to her and quite different from the practice of her convent at home, that at Jerusalem on feast-days, both of our Lord and of the saints, the psalms and hymns and lections were not those for the current day of the ordinary weekly cycle of the office, but were specially chosen to be appropriate to the feast. And it is in fact highly probable that it is to the fourth century Jerusalem church and its liturgically-minded bishop S. Cyril that we owe not only the first organisation of the daily office in a secular church, but also the invention of the 'proper' of saints and in great part of the 'proper' of seasons as well. Other churches, especially in the West, were rather slow to adopt this new idea of varying the ordinary daily and weekly round of psalmody on feast days. The unvarying collects at the offices of Prime and Compline[1] in Western breviaries, and the Little Hours with their hymns and psalmody unchanged throughout the year, even on the greatest feasts,[2] witness to the original monastic preference for an unchanging round of offices based upon the hours of the day and the days of the week, not upon the year and the ecclesiastical calendar. At Milan even the collects of the Little Hours (on ferias) are still unvarying, while those at Lauds and Vespers form a weekly cycle unconnected with the collects used at mass; and there is good evidence that this was also the Roman practice in the fifth century.

In elaborating the calendar as in adopting the public celebration of the office, the church was not deliberately seeking to enlarge the scope of her worship or to alter its theory, though in both cases this was the result. We think of the liturgical calendar as regulating the occasions and the content of the liturgy, and after its official organisation it usually had this effect. But this was hardly its original character. In the fourth century it reflects

[1] Still preserved in the Book of Common Prayer as the unvarying third collects at Morning and Evening Prayer.
[2] Since 1913 this psalmody in the Roman Breviary has varied. In Carolingian Gaul a custom grew up of varying the hymns on occasion at the Little Hours and by an exception the ordinary hymn at Terce is changed to *Veni Creator* during the Whitsun Octave in the Roman and Monastic Breviaries. But like the variable hymns at Compline in some of the mediaeval 'derived' Breviaries (Sarum, Paris, Dominican, etc.) this is an infiltration into the older traditions of the office from this early mediaeval French peculiarity.

rather than regulates current liturgical practice. There was then little of the authoritarian theory of liturgy which has prevailed in the West since the sixteenth century. A feast or observance is nowadays supposed to be inserted in the calendar only by 'lawful authority'. Once inserted it is supposed to be kept by all because authority has placed it there; and what is not in the official calendar has no business to be kept by anyone. (That at least is the official theory not only in the Roman church but in the Anglican and in the established Lutheran churches of Scandinavia. But in fact both the Roman and Anglican churches tend in practice to be rather more primitive in their way of going about things. A long list of modern additions to the calendars of both churches might be quoted which were in fact rather official recognitions of an observance already existing in some quarters than the imposition of something wholly new.) In the fourth century, when the calendar was in the making, churches adopted from each other or evolved for themselves observances and commemorations for all sorts of reasons, devotional, scriptural, local or theological, or because they were the newest ecclesiastical fashion. In time their calendars recorded what had become established practice, but often there was a long gap between the establishment of the practice and its official embodiment in a calendar. (Enforcement is a later conception altogether.)

In this as in so many other ways the fourth century was a time of expansion and experiment, which led to great and undesigned changes, even though the roots of the fourth century innovations are planted firmly in the pre-Nicene past. Before the end of the fourth century the calendar shewed the full effects of the new liturgical transposition from eschatology to history, and had taken the main outline of its permanent form. But in order to understand this fully it is necessary first to consider the pre-Nicene calendar from which the fourth century changes began.

## (A) The Pre-Nicene Calendar

The primitive liturgical cycle was of extreme simplicity, not from poverty of possible material but because it reflected the primitive eschatological understanding of the liturgy, which had virtually no place for historical commemorations. It consisted originally everywhere of the same two elements, the observance (by the holding of an *ecclesia* for the synaxis and eucharist) of (1) two annual feasts, the Pascha and Pentecost, and (2) of the weekly 'Lord's Day' on Sunday. This is still the content of the calendar for Hippolytus at Rome and for Tertullian in Africa, *c.* A.D. 215, as it is for Origen in Egypt twenty years later.[1] Let us examine the significance of this original liturgical cycle.

[1] *contra Celsum*, viii. 21. Set fast days and martyrs' anniversaries are beginning to be added by Tertullian and Origen, but fasts are still matters of purely private devotion for Hippolytus, who in this represents Roman conservatism; and he seems to know nothing of an *ecclesia* on martyrs' anniversaries.

*Sunday.* It is still too often assumed that the observance of the christian Sunday is a continuation on a different day of the jewish sabbath. It is more than likely that the idea of such a weekly observance was suggested to the first jewish christians by familiarity with the sabbath; hellenism furnishes no close analogies. But the main ideas underlying the two observances were from the first quite different. The rabbis made of the sabbath a minutely regulated day of *rest*, the leisure of which was partly filled in by attendance at the synagogue services which were somewhat longer on sabbath than on other days. But though the sabbath rest was emphatically a religious observance, based on the fourth commandment, it was the abstinence from work, not the attendance at public worship, which pharisaism insisted on; and indeed this was the only thing the commandment in its original meaning prescribed.

By contrast Sunday was in the primitive christian view *only* the prescribed day for corporate worship, by the proclamation of the Lord's revelation and the Lord's death till He come. Sunday marked the periodical manifestation in time of the reality of eternal redemption in Christ. As such it was an *anamnesis* of the resurrection which had manifested to His first disciples the Lord's conquest of sin and death and time and all this world-order. But there was no attempt whatever in the first three centuries to base the observance of Sunday on the fourth commandment. On the contrary, christians maintained that like all the rest of the ceremonial law this commandment had been abrogated; and second century christian literature is full of a lively polemic against the 'idling' of the jewish sabbath rest. Christians shewed no hesitation at all about treating Sunday as an ordinary working day like their neighbours, once they had attended the synaxis and eucharist at the *ecclesia*. This was the christian obligation, the weekly gathering of the whole Body of Christ to its Head, to become what it really is, His Body. It was only the secular edict of Constantine in the fourth century making Sunday a weekly public holiday which first made the mistake of basing the christian observance of Sunday on the fourth commandment, and so inaugurated christian 'sabbatarianism'.

Early christian documents on the contrary go out of their way to oppose the two observances. So *e.g.* the so-called *Epistle of Barnabas* (c. A.D. 100–130) introduces God as rebuking the whole jewish observance of the sabbath, thus: ' "It is not your present sabbaths that are acceptable unto Me, but the sabbath which I have made, in the which when I have set all things at rest, I will make the beginning with the eighth day, *which is the beginning of another world.*" Wherefore we (christians) also keep the eighth day for rejoicing, in the which also Jesus rose from the dead, and having been manifested ascended into the heavens'.[1] Here Sunday is a festival, but not a day of rest. It is eschatological in its significance, as representing the inauguration of the 'world to come', supervening upon this world and

---

[1] *Ep. Barn.*, xv. 9.

time. It is only secondarily a memorial of the historical fact of the resurrection of Jesus, and it is observed as such only because in His resurrection and ascension christians have been really but spiritually transferred into 'the heavens' 'in Christ', Who is 'manifested' to His own in the *ecclesia*.

It seems likely, therefore, that Sunday was from its first beginnings a christian observance independent of the sabbath, though its weekly observance was probably suggested by the existence of the sabbath. It had a purpose of its own, the 'shewing forth' of redemption as already an achieved thing 'in Christ'. The change of day, if change there was, from Saturday to Sunday, must have been made very early indeed, for it was already an accomplished fact when S. Paul wrote 1 Cor. xvi. 2, c. A.D. 57. No echoes of a sabbatarian controversy reach us from the New Testament, though the judaisers are 'judging' Pauline converts in Asia Minor in respect of feast days and new moons and sabbaths in the Epistle to the Colossians.[1] But presumably, since the date of this is not earlier than 1 Cor., they were endeavouring to persuade the Colossians to keep the sabbath in addition to Sunday, not instead of it. Yet the invention of Sunday with its eschatological meaning must go back to an origin in strictly jewish circles, for eschatology in general was always a jewish mode of thought, assimilated only with difficulty by gentile christians. Pauline converts, and the gentile christians generally, naturally adopted the specifically christian observance of Sunday as a matter of course when they became christians. The additional observance of the jewish sabbath as well as the christian Sunday was in later times a badge of the dwindling jewish-christian churches, and it is likely that this state of affairs goes back to apostolic times.

*The Two Christian Feasts* of the primitive cycle, Pascha and Pentecost, seem to have come down in the church from apostolic times like the observance of Sunday. They are both obviously derived from jewish feasts, Passover and Pentecost, to which they are related rather more closely in meaning than Sunday is to the Sabbath. Here again, however, it is interesting to note that the christians at a very early period changed the jewish method of fixing the date of these movable feasts (which by jewish usage were not confined to any one day of the week) so that they were always observed by christians on a Sunday. Except in Asia Minor, where the churches in the second century followed the jewish reckoning for fixing the Pascha, the christian Sunday reckoning of this feast was already of immemorial antiquity everywhere c. A.D. 195. At that time a world-wide series of councils held from Osrhoene on the Euphrates to Gaul discussed the matter at the invitation of Pope Victor I; and the orthodox churches of Asia came into line with the rest of the catholic church early in the third century. The churches of Asia and their opponents in Victor's time alike claimed that their reckoning was the authentic 'apostolic tradition'. But the fact that outside Asia all christians, not excepting those of Palestine, had

[1] Col. ii. 16.

always held to the Sunday reckoning longer than anyone could remember, suggests that the change from the jewish reckoning had been made within the first century, if not in the apostolic age itself. It is quite possible that the Asiatic custom was an early reaction to jewish usage under the influence of some judaising movement in the latter part of the first century, similar to those combated earlier by S. Paul in his epistles to the Galatians and Colossians.

*The Pascha*, or christian Passover (Pascha is the Greek form of the Hebrew *Pesach* = Passover) was, like its jewish prototype, a nocturnal festival. A vigil was held from the evening of Saturday to dawn on Sunday. After the preliminary blessing of a lamp or lamps by the deacon, there followed a series of lections interspersed with chants, in the usual fashion of the synaxis. It appears that in the Roman rite *c.* A.D. 200 the lessons included Hosea vi. and the account of the Israelite passover in Exod. xii. (which are still read in the Roman missal at the Liturgy of the Presanctified on Good Friday). It is also clear from the recently discovered homily *On the Passion* of Melito, bishop of Sardis, *c.* A.D. 190, that the paschal liturgy of Asia Minor agreed with that of Rome at least in including the lesson from Exodus. Since these two great churches differed vigorously all through the second century on the fixing of the date of the Pascha, it is probable that the points on which their paschal liturgies agreed in that period are independent survivals of a rite drawn up at a very early date indeed, and not due to second century borrowings. Nothing could more clearly indicate the close original connection of the christian with the jewish 'passover' than the choice of this lesson. There followed a lection from the gospel of S. John, the account of the death and resurrection of our Lord, extending from the trial before Pilate to the end of S. John's account of the resurrection, with its hint of an ascension on Easter Day itself.[1] This choice of lessons is in the exact spirit of S. Paul's phrase 'Christ our passover was sacrificed for us; therefore let us keep the feast with joy.'

After the lessons came a sermon by the bishop, followed by the solemn baptism and confirmation of the neophytes, who proceeded to take their part for the first time as new members of Christ in His prayer and offering, by joining with the rest of the faithful in the intercessory prayers and then as offerers in the paschal eucharist.

The primitive Pascha has therefore the character of a liturgy of 'Redemption' rather than a commemoration of the historical fact of the resurrection of Jesus, such as Easter has with us. Like the jewish passover it commemorated a deliverance from bondage, in the case of christians not from Egypt but from the bondage of sin and time and mortality into 'the glorious liberty of the children of God'[2] and 'the everlasting kingdom of our Lord and Saviour Jesus Christ'.[3] The life, death, resurrection and

---

[1] *Cf. Ep. Barn.*, cited on *p.* 336.     [2] Rom. viii. 21.     [3] 2 Pet. i. 11.

ascension—the paschal sacrifice—of Jesus was, of course, the means by which this redemption was achieved. 'In Him' every christian had gone free from slavery to time and sin and death. But these events of the passion, resurrection and ascension did not stand isolated in primitive christian thought. When the paschal liturgy was thoroughly revised at Jerusalem in the fourth century, the old lections from Hosea and Exodus were replaced by a new and much longer series, beginning with creation and the fall, and continuing with the deliverance of Noah, the call of Abraham, the deliverance from Egypt and a series of prophetic lessons from Isaiah and other prophets (including the old lesson from Exod. xii). This Jerusalem series, or selections from it, appear in almost every liturgy for the paschal vigil in christendom down to the sixteenth century. Though the use of this extended Jerusalem series of lessons in the liturgy cannot be traced further back than the fourth century, it is remarkable that the themes of many of them occur in the two earliest patristic paschal sermons extant, those of Melito and Hippolytus. Some of them are clearly to be found in the first three chapters of 1 Pet., a section of the epistle which has been reasonably supposed to have been originally composed as a sermon to the newly baptised at a paschal eucharist in the first century.

Certainly from very early days the Pascha as the feast of redemption was regarded as the most suitable occasion for the conferring of the sacraments by which redemption is appropriated to the individual—baptism into Christ's death and resurrection,[1] and confirmation by which 'the Spirit of Him that raised up Jesus from the dead' is imparted to 'dwell'[2] in the members of His Body. The general idea of redemption celebrated by the paschal feast thus lies close behind the whole pre-Nicene liturgy and theory of the other sacraments as well as the eucharist. The identification of Christ with His church was accepted without reserve by the christian thought of the pre-Nicene period. Redemption is by the entering of a man 'into Christ', and we must beware of treating phrases like 'putting on' Christ in baptism[3] and the 'anointing' (literally 'Christing') with His Spirit in confirmation[4] as mere metaphors. However much we may be disposed to soften the literalness with which the New Testament authors intended these and similar expressions, there are too many of them and they express too clearly a change of spiritual status at a definite point of time connected too precisely with a sacramental act, to be disregarded. Whatever the difficulties it may cause to our way of thinking, it must be accepted that the first century did not share the anxious 'spirituality' of the nineteenth. Above all, we must not minimise the literalness with which they were universally understood by the early church, which taught without hesitation that a man received the redemption of Christ *by means* of the sacramental acts which made him a 'member of Christ' and a 'member of the

---

[1] Rom. vi. 3, 4.                          [2] *Ibid.*, viii. 11.
[3] Gal. iii. 7, i.                          [4] 1 John ii. 27.

*ecclesia'*. These were not two different or even two simultaneous incorporations; they were the same thing. The church as the Body of Christ is one with Him. (One sees the shortness of the argument to Cyprian's conclusion: 'Outside the church no salvation'. The marvel is that the Roman church resisted it, and that the church as a whole rejected it.)

Therefore a man received the sacraments of redemption at the Pascha, the feast of redemption; in the midst of the Body of the redeemed, into which he was being incorporated; and at the hands of the bishop, the representative of the Father Who is the husbandman Who tends the vine and all its branches.[1] And only having thus entered 'into Christ' *could* a man for the first time enter into His prayer and His sacrifice at the paschal eucharist. The whole of early sacramental thought is thus closely knit together with the doctrine of the church as the Body of Christ, and redemption as 'incorporation' into Him in His Body.

The catechumens who were to receive baptism at the Pascha had to undergo preparatory fasts[2] and daily exorcisms for a fortnight or more before the feast,[3] to purify them for their initiation. But the laity who had already received these sacraments were not yet required to do anything so rigorous. As the culminating point in the christian year, the Pascha was recognised to require some personal preparation from all, but there was as yet nothing corresponding to Lent and Holy Week. At the end of the second century all christians fasted before the Pascha, some for a day, some for forty hours continuously, some for a week, according to their devotion.[4] After the Pascha the 'great 50 days' which intervened between Pascha and Pentecost were already recognised in the same period as a continuous festival, during which all penitential observances such as fasting and kneeling at corporate prayer were forbidden, as they were on ordinary Sundays also.[5] The reason was not yet that which made this season a festival in later times, the presence of our Lord with His disciples from Easter to Ascension. There was no such idea of any historical commemoration about it; the Ascension was still included in the celebration of the Pascha, not kept as a separate feast forty days later.[6] But just as for the jews the fifty days of harvest between Passover and Pentecost symbolised the joyful fact of their possession of the Promised Land, so these fifty days symbolised for the christian the fact that 'in Christ' he had already entered into the Kingdom of God. Like the weekly Sunday with which this period was associated both in thought and in the manner of its observance, the 'fifty days' manifested the 'world to come'.

[1] John xv. 1.   [2] Justin, *Ap.* I, 61.
[3] Hippolytus, *Ap. Trad.*, xx. 3.
[4] Irenaeus, *Ep. to Victor* (c. A.D. 195), *ap.* Eusebius. *Eccl. Hist.*, v. 24. It is likely that this second century christian fast before the Pascha was developed from a jewish custom of fasting before the Passover. *Cf. Pesachim* x. 1.
[5] Irenaeus, *On the Pascha*, cited in ps.-Justin, *Quaest. et Resp. ad Orthodoxum*, 115.
[6] *Cf.* Hippolytus, *On the Pascha*, vi. 5, *ad fin.*

The only other feast of the primitive christian cycle was Pentecost, which closed these 'fifty days' after Pascha. In the Old Testament Pentecost appears as an agricultural festival at the close of the grain harvest which began at Passover; but in the later jewish idea Pentecost commemorated the giving of the Law on Sinai and the constitution of the mixed multitude of Egyptian refugees into the People of God. The church retained it to celebrate not only the events recorded in the second chapter of Acts but her own character as the 'People' of the New Covenant, and the fact that 'the law of the Spirit of life in Christ Jesus hath made' her members 'free from the law of sin and death'.[1] There was a real appropriateness in thus returning, as it were, into time from the long celebration of the eternal Kingdom of God and the heavenly reign of Christ during Paschaltide, with a final celebration of the gift of that Spirit by Whom the presence of the heavenly Christ is perpetually mediated to His members in time. As the Pascha dramatised the fact of eternal redemption, so Pentecost dramatised the fact of the christian's possession of (or by) the Spirit, which made that redemption an effective reality in his life in time. Those catechumens who had for some reason missed receiving baptism and confirmation at the paschal vigil were allowed to do so at Pentecost. But apart from these two feasts baptism was conferred at other times only in case of the grave illness of a catechumen or of some other danger of death, e.g. persecution; and was followed if possible by confirmation by the bishop privately as soon as might be. But there was a distinct feeling that there was something irregular about such private reception of these sacraments; e.g. it disqualified a man for ordination in later life.[2] They were properly only to be received at the Pascha or Pentecost in the midst of the ecclesia, because only in and through the church does a christian receive either incorporation into Christ or the gift of His Spirit.

Such was the original christian liturgical cycle, a weekly proclamation and manifestation of redemption on Sunday, and two annual Sunday festivals which emphasised the ordinary Sunday message quite as much as they commemorated particular historical events. It is obvious that the whole system arose in a jewish milieu and not a hellenistic one; but the jewish meaning of the whole has been transformed by a christian eschatological interpretation. The universality of this cycle in the later second century, its immemorial antiquity even then, its jewish character and its eschatological emphasis, all force us to look in the first century and probably in the apostolic age itself for its elaboration.

The Additions made to it in various places in the course of the second and third centuries have a recognisably different character. They took the form of set fast-days and of christian historical commemorations. But these never rivalled the Sunday cycle and its two great feasts in importance

[1] Rom. viii. 2.
[2] Cf. the case ap. Eusebius, Eccl. Hist., VI. xliii, c. A.D. 240.

during pre-Nicene times. It is uncertain which class of additions is the earlier.

At some point in the second century the custom arose in the East of keeping all Wednesdays and Fridays outside the 'great fifty days' as fasts, observed with a synaxis and in some churches with a eucharist also. These two weekly fasts, which were later known in the West as 'stations',[1] are referred to in the document known as the *Didache*, which scholars of the last generation considered to date from the earlier part of the second century. This carried with it the implication that the stations were an innovation of the late first or very early second century, or perhaps even a part of the original cycle. But the apparently increasing tendency now to date the *Didache* somewhat late in the second half of the second century raises difficulties. It leaves us in fact with no dateable evidence for the existence of the regular Wednesday and Friday stations before Tertullian's work *On Fasting*, written somewhere about A.D. 215. Justin does not mention them. The *Shepherd* of Hermas, a Roman document written between *c*. A.D. 100 and 160 (more probably towards the end of that period) knows the term 'station' as a name for a private fast undertaken by an individual,[2] but says nothing whatever of a corporate fast or an observance with synaxis or eucharist. The same is the case with Hippolytus in his *Apostolic Tradition*. Tertullian's observations on the way in which the matter was regarded by the orthodox in his day—he writes as a member of the rigorist sect of the Montanists—are interesting. They maintain, he says, that a fast before the Pascha is the only fast of apostolic institution, and the only one of obligation on all christians. All others are a matter of private devotion and choice, even the stations on Wednesdays and Fridays.[3] The orthodox despise the compulsory stations of the Montanists, and call their method of observing them new-fangled.[4] The evidence taken as a whole suggests that Tertullian is reporting the matter correctly, and that in fact the station days were really an Eastern development of the later second century, an accompaniment of that wave of rigorism which in this period produced the austere sects of Encratites and Montanists.

However reluctant the orthodox at Rome (whom Tertullian has particularly in mind) may have been to accept the Eastern innovation of the two weekly stations, it was about this time that the Roman church elaborated its own system of corporate fasts. These were the seasonal fasts of the Ember Days, on the Wednesday, Friday and Saturday of the weeks which marked the chief agricultural operations of the year in Italy. The *Liber Pontificalis*,[5] a late authority, attributes their institution to Pope Callistus (A.D. 217–223) and however this may be, there is no doubt that this represents about the date of their origin. They seem to have been instituted as a

---

[1] From the Latin military term *statio*, a watch, a turn of guard duty, or a parade.
[2] *Similitude*, v. 1.      [3] *de Jejunio*, 2.      [4] *Ibid.*, 10.
[5] ed. Duchesne, *p.* 141.

deliberate counter-observance to the licence of the pagan harvest festivals,[1] a motive which inspired more than one addition to the calendar in later times. (In the same sort of spirit the *Didache* opposes the stations to the customary jewish fasts on Mondays and Thursdays.) Down to the end of the sixth century the Ember fasts were observed only at Rome. It was Anglo-Saxon missionaries and monks, who had received this purely Roman custom from the Roman S. Augustine at Canterbury, who first secured their adoption in Germany and Gaul in the eighth and ninth century; and they spread to Spain only in the tenth-eleventh. These Western fasts were never adopted at all in the East, though the Eastern station days were at one time widely adopted in the West.

The gradual development of the great fast which is common to all christendom, that of Lent and Holy Week, is most conveniently treated later under the fourth century, the period of its final organisation, though it has its roots in the second century.

*Saints' Days.* An innovation of the second century with far-reaching liturgical consequences was the introduction of the festivals of the saints, at this period confined to those of the martyrs. It is likely that in this, as in the introduction of fixed fast days, the East led the way and the West followed, with Rome somewhat behind all other churches in the adoption of new customs.

The earliest clear record comes from Asia Minor, in a letter written in A.D. 156 by the church of Smyrna to the neighbouring church of Philomelium, recounting the recent martyrdom of its bishop Polycarp. After an attempt to burn him at the stake which was frustrated by the wind, the eighty-six-year-old bishop was despatched with a dagger. Then 'the jealous and envious Evil One, the adversary of the family of the righteous, having seen the greatness of his witness and his blameless life from the beginning, and how he was crowned with the crown of immortality and had won a reward none could gainsay, managed that not even his poor body should be taken away by us, although many desired to do this and to touch his holy flesh. So the devil put forward Nicetes . . . to plead with the magistrate not to give up the body, "lest", so it was said, "they should abandon the Crucified and begin to worship this man" . . . not knowing that it will be impossible for us either ever to forsake the Christ Who suffered for the salvation of the whole world of the redeemed—suffered for sinners though He was faultless—or to worship any other. For Him, being the Son of God, we adore, but the martyrs as disciples and imitators of the Lord we cherish as they deserve for their matchless affection towards their own King and Master. May it be our lot also to be found partakers and fellow-disciples with them.

'The centurion, therefore, seeing the opposition raised . . . set him in the midst of the pyre and burned him after their fashion. And so we

---

[1] Dom G. Morin, *Revue Bénédictine*, xiv., p. 337 *sq.*

afterwards took up his bones, which are more valuable than precious stones and finer than refined gold, and laid them in a suitable place; where the Lord will permit us to assemble together, as we are able, in gladness and joy, to celebrate the birthday of his martyrdom for the commemoration of those that have already fought in the contest and for the training and preparation of those that shall do so hereafter. . . . Having by his endurance overcome the unrighteous ruler and so received the crown of immortality, he rejoiceth in company with the apostles and all righteous men, and glorifieth the Almighty God and Father, and blesseth our Lord Jesus Christ, the Saviour of our souls and pilot of our bodies and the shepherd of the catholic church which is throughout all the world.'[1]

This passage is interesting for more than one reason. It expresses very touchingly the reverence of the persecuted church for the relics of the martyrs whom she reckoned her chief glory. But it also expresses with a curious precision by the mouth of the pagan 'devil's advocate' Nicetes (who was egged on by the jews) the sort of argument against such reverence with which later ages were to become familiar in the mouths of protestants, and also the sort of reply which catholics have always made. (Nothing could better illustrate the unprimitive character of much in protestant polemic against the cultus of the saints and their relics which was sincerely put forward in the sixteenth century as a return to genuine 'apostolic' christianity, than the unaffected religious reverence with which his disciples forthwith treated the body and the memory of this last survivor of the apostolic age.) What is above all of interest for our present purpose is that it enables us to estimate how closely and how naturally the cultus of the saints is to be connected with the ordinary funeral rites of christians.

In the first glad days when the 'good news' of the gospel of redemption brought such overwhelming exultation to those who received it that the world, the flesh and the devil seemed to lose their whole power over the redeemed, 'the saints' had meant the whole body of the faithful. The death of every christian seemed to mean only the immediate realisation of his true being as a member of Christ in the kingdom of heaven. Later, in the second century, the beginnings of the decline in the vividness of the eschatological understanding of the faith, and a saddening acquaintance with the frequency of post-baptismal sin even among sincere and persevering christians, between them brought the church to a more sober mind. It was better appreciated that the blinding holiness of the open vision of God might exact some further purification after death for even devout and good men, let alone for the generality of christians. A fully developed doctrine of purgatory is already accepted in the Acts of the African martyrs Perpetua and Felicity[2] (c. A.D. 200) of which hints are to be found

---

[1] *Martyrium Polycarpi*, 17-19.
[2] *Passio*, 7 and 8.

in previous christian literature.[1] Tertullian and other writers speak of the 'annual oblation' of the eucharist on the anniversary of the death of departed christians,[2] which Cyprian calls a 'sacrifice for their repose'.[3]

Only in the case of those who had actually died as martyrs could there be no possible hesitation as to their fitness in the moment of death for the presence of God.[4] They were already like Polycarp 'rejoicing with the apostles and all righteous men'. For them there could be no possibility of need for the church's intercessions at the anniversary eucharist, and the church of Smyrna accordingly speaks of it in his case as a 'commemoration of those who have already fought' victoriously, to be kept 'with gladness and joy', 'for the training and preparation of those that shall come after'. To this second century cultus there was needed only the addition of the idea of seeking the martyr's prayers for his brethren still on earth, for the final form of the eucharistic cultus of the saints to be complete. This development the third century brought in full measure, along with the practice of direct invocation of the saints.

How far this last development was entirely an innovation in the third century it is not easy to say, since the available evidence of literature and *graffiti* is very fragmentary and casual. The idea of the great saints and heroes of the past interceding before the throne of God for His people militant here in earth was sufficiently familiar to the jews of the second century B.C. to be taken for granted in 2 Maccabees xv. 12-16; and there was nothing in the New Testament or in early christian teaching to reprobate such an idea. The eschatological notion that *all* christians even in this world had been transferred to 'the heavenlies' in Christ would of itself tend to make the idea of such a communion of saints seem more natural, by diminishing the sense of the barrier interposed by death.

Be that as it may, there is no direct application for the prayers of the aints in the second century references to the veneration of martyrs and their relics. The great majority of these seem to be traceable directly or indirectly to the churches of Asia Minor. This may be due merely to the fact that we are not well provided with information from other churches in this period, but it is also possible that certain phrases in the Revelation of S. John had greater influence there than elsewhere, even if they do not witness to a special development in this direction among the churches of Asia Minor before the end of the first century. But the whole circle of ideas which resulted in the development of the cultus of the martyrs was being adopted in some parts of the West in the time of Tertullian c. A.D. 200

[1] The idea of 'baptism for the dead', which is not reprobated by S. Paul in 1 Cor. xv. 29, with that of our Lord preaching to the dead (1 Pet. iii. 19)—they are curiously combined and developed by Hermas, *Shepherd, Sim.*, ix. 15, 16—are perhaps at the basis of the whole development of the doctrine of a possibility of purification after death during the second century.
[2] *de Corona*, 3.     [3] *Ep.* I, 2.
[4] Hermas, *Vis.* III, i. 9–II, 2. *Cf. Mart. Polycarpi* above.

—witness the opening and closing paragraphs of his edition of the Passion of S. Perpetua and her companions, and especially the address in the latter—'O most brave and blessed martyrs! O truly called and chosen unto the glory of our Lord Jesus Christ! etc.' This may be no more than rhetorical in intention, but it is the first direct address to christian saints in the extant christian literature. The first known request for prayers to the saints in the technical sense is addressed to the jewish martyrs of the Old Testament, the three holy children Shadrach, Meshach and Abednego, in Hippolytus' *Commentary on Daniel*, ii. 30. This again has been treated as rhetorical by some modern scholars, but invocations of christian saints who had been Hippolytus' contemporaries in life have been found on the walls of the catacomb of S. Callistus, which there is good reason to think were scratched there very soon after their burial. When Origen in Egypt came to write the first christian technical treatise *On Prayer c.* A.D. 231, he could take it for granted, rather than argue, that the angels and saints pray for us in heaven, and that it is lawful and usual for christians to pray to the saints and to thank them for benefits received through their intercession.[1] Evidently invocation as a practice was becoming usual more or less every-where during the period *c.* A.D. 200-230 even if it had not been known before.[2] The cultus of the martyrs and their relics flourished everywhere during the third century, to such an extent that by the time of the peace of the church it was sometimes taking superstitious forms to which the ecclesiastical authorities felt bound to object.[3]

The church of Rome seems once more to have been somewhat slow in adopting this liturgical innovation. It is a remarkable fact that except for the apostles Peter and Paul, whose tombs were already objects of pride and veneration to the Roman christians in the second century,[4] no Roman saint of the first or second century is named in the earliest Roman calendar which has reached us, the 'Philocalian calendar' or *Depositiones Martyrum*, compiled in its present form in A.D. 354. Though it is easy to detect under-lying the present text several older recensions, of which the earliest was certainly compiled about a century before the present form, the earliest Roman name (apart from SS. Peter and Paul) which appears in this first *stratum* is that of Pope S. Callistus, who was martyred in A.D. 223. The Roman church had of course numbered multitudes of martyrs before him, but the absence of their names from the liturgical calendar is probably due to the close association of the martyr-cult with the actual tombs of the martyrs. The first acquisition of a burial-ground which was the corporate

[1] *de Oratione*, xi. and xiv.
[2] There appears to be a casual reference to this practice in *Acta Pauli*, x. 5 b. (M. R. James *Apocryphal N.T.*, p. 296), a document dated *c.* 160-170 A.D. But it is difficult to be certain that this formed part of the original text.
[3] *E.g.*, the incident described as taking place at Carthage, *c.* A.D. 315, by Optatus, *adv. Schism. Donat.*, i. 16.
[4] Eusebius, *E. H.*, II. xxv. 7.

possession of the Roman church, where all the christian dead might lie together, dates only from the early years of the third century; and Callistus was the first prominent martyr connected with it, though he was not actually buried there. Earlier christian burials at Rome, including those of the martyrs, had taken place in various private properties, which were not necessarily reserved for christian burial. It may thus be that the Roman church had no exact record of where the earlier martyrs lay, or that she had not access to their graves for liturgical celebrations. However that may be, it seems clear that the first Roman compilation of a record of the 'depositions' of the martyrs was suggested by, or is somehow connected with, the acquisition of the first christian cemetery at Rome under the direct control of the church authorities, in the early third century. The complete absence of second century names, including that of an eminent bishop the memory of whose martyrdom had not perished (Pope S. Telesphorus, martyred c. A.D. 132)[1] suggests strongly that no such record had been kept before; and that when it was first compiled there were no second century traditions available—a sufficient indication that martyrs' anniversaries had not been kept at Rome in the second century. At all events the custom seems to have been accepted there by about A.D. 244 (almost a century after it was normal at Smyrna) when Pope Fabian made a special journey with some of his clergy to Sardinia to fetch back the relics of his martyred predecessor Pontianus, who had died there in penal servitude for the faith some fifteen years before.

### (B) The Post-Nicene Calendar

Even in the third century the long series of persecutions was importing a certain connection with local history into the christian year in all churches, by adding a number of local martyrs' anniversaries to the old non-historical cycle of the Sundays and the two great feasts and the (newer) set fast-days. This new quasi-historical cycle of the martyrs and the old eschatological one of the Sundays continued in use side-by-side down to the end of the third century and even well into the fourth, without affecting one another's character greatly or becoming fused, largely because they were serving somewhat different needs. The eschatological ecclesia in the new church buildings of the later third century was now becoming, as we have seen, a properly 'public' act as regards the synaxis. To some extent it had acquired characteristics of a public cultus even at the eucharist. Attendance at this Sunday ecclesia remained the only christian obligation. The eucharists on other days at the actual tombs of the martyrs were celebrated by the bishop and the clergy, and were attended no doubt by the leisured and the specially devout among the laity. But the bulk of the

---

[1] The only martyr among the early Roman bishops in the list given by Irenaeus, adv. Haer., III, iii. 3.

church could not often be present on such occasions, nor could they have been accommodated in the little cemetery chapels if they had come. As a result, the eucharists at the martyrs' tombs, thus frequented chiefly by an inner circle, retained much more of the 'domestic' character of primitive christian worship—a gathering of the 'household of God' to do honour to and rejoice with a member of the family who had added signal glory to the annals of the christian *gens*.

But in the fourth century the whole current of the times was with the new *historical* understanding of the liturgy, and little by little this began to affect the older cycle. The key-point of the old conception lay in the eschatological conception of the Pascha. Once this had begun to be interpreted as a primarily historical commemoration of the event of our Lord's resurrection (in the fashion of our Easter) the way was clear to the combination and fusion of the two cycles, historical and eschatological.

*The Transformation of the Pascha.* It is not Rome but Jerusalem which is the centre of innovation. The special circumstances there easily suggested the idea of a local commemoration of the events in the last days of our Lord's life on the actual or supposed sites on which they had occurred. Thus Etheria in A.D. 385 describes a fully developed and designedly historical series of such celebrations in which the whole Jerusalem church takes part. It begins on Passion Sunday with a procession to Bethany where the gospel of the raising of Lazarus is read. On the afternoon of Palm Sunday the whole church goes out to the Mount of Olives and returns in solemn procession to the city bearing branches of palm. There are evening visits to the Mount of Olives on each of the first three days of Holy Week, in commemoration of our Lord's nightly withdrawal from the city during that week. On Maundy Thursday morning the eucharist is celebrated (for the only time in the year) in the chapel of the Cross, and not in the *Martyrium;* and all make their communion. In the evening after another eucharist the whole church keeps vigil at Constantine's church of Eleona on the Mount of Olives, visiting Gethsemane after midnight and returning to the city in the morning for the reading of the gospel of the trial of Jesus. In the course of the morning of Good Friday all venerate the relics of the Cross, and then from noon to three p.m. all keep watch on the actual site of Golgotha (still left by Constantine's architects open to the sky in the midst of a great colonnaded courtyard behind the *Martyrium*) with lections and prayers amid deep emotion. In the evening there is a final visit by the whole church to the Holy Sepulchre, where the gospel of the entombment is read. On Holy Saturday evening the paschal vigil still takes place much as in other churches, with its lections and prayers and baptisms, though there is not much doubt that the actual contents of the Jerusalem liturgy for this vigil had been considerably recast by this time. The only special observance is that when they had all received confirmation the new christians in their white robes headed by the bishop visit the Holy Sepulchre itself to listen to the gospel account of the resurrection, in which they have themselves just mystically taken part. Then comes the great midnight mass of Easter, at which they make their first communion in the midst of the rejoicing church. In the afternoon of Easter Sunday there is a visit to the pre-Constantinian church of Sion, on the site of the upper room in which Jesus had appeared to His disciples on the first Easter evening. One notes the absence of the eucharist on Good Friday and Holy Saturday, which has passed into the tradition of all christendom. And all through, interwoven with these special observances, the perpetual round of the daily divine office with its special psalms and lessons continues with as little abbreviation and interruption as possible, like an unending comment of praise and grief uttered by the church upon the particular event being celebrated.

The intention of all this is obvious enough. The dramatic exploitation of the *genius loci* in the interests of devotional feeling is quite legitimate, and would be suggested by the existence of the sacred sites themselves, even if the munificence of Constantine had not supplied the convenience of a number of churches on those sites. After all, no one can fail to be affected by the strictly historical appeal to piety in connection with the events of the passion, least of all at Jerusalem; and there is ample evidence that all christendom had already begun to feel the thrill of it before the middle of the fourth century. But a recognition of the naturalness of such a cycle of historical commemorations at Jerusalem must not blind us to its disintegrating effects on the original eschatological conception of the paschal feast when this cycle came to be imitated elsewhere. In particular the solemn commemoration of the passion on Good Friday *apart from* that of the resurrection at the paschal vigil, at once transformed the Pascha from a 'feast of redemption' into an historical commemoration of a particular event, the resurrection of Jesus of Nazareth from the tomb in the garden of Joseph of Arimathea. In consequence the old idea of the 'paschal sacrifice' of Christ (of which the eucharist is the *anamnesis*) as constituted by its offering in the passion *in combination with* its acceptance by the Father in the resurrection and ascension, was seriously weakened. This in the end had consequences on eucharistic doctrine the results of which are with us yet;—they are, for instance, written plainly in the liturgy and catechism of the Book of Common Prayer, with their entire concentration on 'the death of Christ' to the exclusion of the resurrection and ascension in connection with the eucharist.

When we enquire as to the date and circumstances of this liturgical revolution, we are forced, I think, to see its original motive and impulse in the personal ideas and liturgical initiative of that interesting person, S. Cyril of Jerusalem. At the time of Etheria's pilgrimage (A.D. 385) a year before the end of his long episcopate, she found the whole cycle of historical commemorations there fully developed; it was evidently spoken of to her by members of the local church as something customary there, not as an absolutely recent innovation. But in his *Catecheses* delivered in Lent and Easter Week in A.D. 348, a few years before he became bishop, Cyril has not a word of reference to any such observances. In Etheria's time the catechumens attended the whole round of these special observances; indeed even the pagans could not have been excluded from such ceremonies held in the open air and in the city streets. It seems quite inconceivable, if one studies the contents of the *Catecheses*, that so many and such moving commemorations should have left no trace whatever on discourses about the very events this cycle dramatically re-enacted, delivered in the very season in which his hearers were attending them, if the cycle had already been in existence. Cyril is by no means unaware of the inspiration of the sacred sites, and the privilege of his own church in possessing them. Again and again he pointedly refers his hearers to this unique circumstance of church life at Jerusalem, speaking of 'this Golgotha', which he says they can see through the open doors of the basilica; or of the descent of the Holy Ghost at Pentecost 'here in Jerusalem, in the church of the apostles up on the hill . . . and it would truly be a very fitting thing if, just as we teach of the things concerning Christ and Golgotha here at Golgotha, so we should give the instructions on the Holy Ghost in the church up the hill'.[1] And he goes on to give a rather lame mystical reason why this 'very fitting thing' is not done. In this passage, I think, speaks plainly the mind which delighted to elaborate the topographical and historical cycle of Passiontide when Cyril had himself succeeded to the episcopal throne, and could order the liturgy of his church after his own heart.

*The Work of S. Cyril.* There is a personal factor here which has been unaccountably neglected by students of the liturgy. Cyril's Holy Week and Easter cycle is at the basis of the whole of the future Eastern and Western observances of this culminating point of the christian year. He gave to christendom the first outline of the public organisation of the divine office; and the first development of the proper of the seasons as well as of the saints. He was certainly the great propagator, if not the originator, of the later theory of eucharistic consecration by the invocation of the Holy Ghost, with its important effects in the subsequent liturgical divergence of East and West. In the Jerusalem church in his time we first find mention of liturgical vestments, of the carrying of lights and the use of incense at the gospel, and a number of other minor elements in liturgy and ceremonial, like the *lavabo* and the Lord's prayer after the eucharistic prayer, which have all passed into the tradition of catholic christendom. Above all, to him more than to any other single man is due the successful carrying through of that universal transposition of the liturgy from an eschatological to an historical interpretation of redemption, which is the outstanding mark left by the fourth century on the history of christian wor-

---

[1] *Catechesis*, xvi. 4.

ship. Such a change might have expressed itself in more than one way. The particular form it did take everywhere for the next 1,100 years, and which it still retains among all christians outside the inheritors of the protestant Reformation, was shaped in the exceptionally 'advanced' ritualistic church of Jerusalem in the fourth century. More particularly it bears the impress of the individual mind and temperament of its very interesting and lively and (in the best sense of the word) 'ceremonious' bishop, S. Cyril. On these grounds alone he is deserving of a personal study from this particular point of view, which he has not to my knowledge yet received, but which cannot be more than sketched here.

Despite the immense effect of his virtual invention of Passiontide and Easter (in our modern understanding of those seasons) with its disintegration of the old eschatological understanding of the Pascha and the eucharist, there is no need to give him anything of the air of a deliberate revolutionary. His innovations in this, as in all other respects, were inspired by purely local circumstances and opportunities. It is most improbable that in any of his liturgical schemes he ever looked beyond the devotional needs and the immediate setting of his own church. When, for instance, we find him including 'the patriarchs, prophets and apostles' alongside 'the martyrs' in his enumeration of the saints in the eucharistic prayer, we are struck by the difference from the lists confined to *local* martyrs only, which meet us in all other churches in the fourth century. This is the germ of an universal calendar, transcending the interest of merely local history, and including the heroes of all christendom, scriptural and post-scriptural alike, in its catholic pride. But we must not forget that at Jerusalem the Old Testament worthies and New Testament apostles alike could legitimately be numbered among the glories of the *local* church, and admitted to a place in its local calendar on just the same ground that Peter and Paul alone could find a place in the contemporary local Roman list of the *Depositiones Martyrum*.[1]

---

[1] It is to Byzantium after it had become Constantinople that we must look for the real origin of an 'universal' calendar. The new capital on the Bosphorus had inherited from its predecessor a christian past as undistinguished as the secular history of the little provincial port in the ecclesiastical province of the archbishop of Heraclea, out of which Constantine made his 'New Rome'. It was forced to borrow the saints of other cities and to transport their relics to new shrines within its own walls in order to eke out its own scanty and obscure local calendar, to uphold its new secular dignity and ecclesiastical pretensions. This is the origin of the 'translations' and dismemberments of the bodies of the saints, which other cities soon copied. The further step from celebrating the feast of a saint over a portion only of his remains to celebrating it over none of them, but simply in his honour, was soon taken, especially in Gaul (another church with comparatively few local martyrs of its own) and this is the real beginning of a non-local calendar. At Rome the close connection of the saint's feast with his actual tomb was kept up better than elsewhere down to the sixth century, and did not wholly die for centuries after that. The real transformation of the Roman calendar from a local to an 'universal' list only begins in the thirteenth century, under the influence of Franciscan curial officials and other perplexing phenomena.

Cyril shared to the full that rather parochial pride in and sense of the historic tradition of his own local church, which in most christians of the fourth century takes the place which devotion to the city-republic had taken with the Greeks, and which civic pride had replaced under the empire. (Its equivalent with us is national patriotism; but the universal state of the empire was too big to evoke the emotion of love; it aroused only awe.) I do not think there is any element in S. Cyril's liturgical work which is not quite simply and fully accounted for by this, and by his personal temperament as his *Catecheses* reveal it. After all, his was no ordinary church, but the very theatre of salvation. Once the actual history of redemption had aroused the special interest of christians, as it was doing everywhere in the fourth century, no one at Jerusalem of all places could fail to answer to its appeal. And the bishop of a great pilgrim centre has a special duty in connection with the local 'attraction', the fulfilment of which need not necessarily be commercial or self-important or anything but sincerely religious in its motive.

To say this is not to discredit the individuality of his work. We have already noted the rather special semi-monastic conditions which prevailed in the secular church of Jerusalem, and the advantages offered by Constantine's splendid foundations. All this and all the wider prevailing tendencies of the time told in favour of his innovations. But he was the very man to make the fullest use of such exceptional opportunities, able, devout, gifted with imagination and an admirable turn for popular preaching; his *Catecheses* are quite first-class as instructions for beginners in christian knowledge, simple, lively and complete. He had just those qualities of earnest sympathy with the religion of unlearned people, combined with a real if not very profound theological understanding of doctrine, which were needed to bring the archaic conceptions of the liturgy into living contact with the new needs of the fourth century.

He was one of those men who, though without the exceptional religious power of an Athanasius, yet succeed in crystallising into definite and clear expression the religious ideas and aspirations of the better sort of average christian in their own time. Under the appearance of pioneering, such men are often most truly and representatively 'contemporary', the more so because they are more closely in contact with the mind of the coming generation than of that which is strictly their own. There are half-a-dozen topics ranging in importance from the Godhead of the Holy Ghost down to the use of 'numinous' language like 'terrifying' or 'awe-inspiring' concerning the consecrated eucharist, on which Cyril spoke to his confirmation candidates in A.D. 348 with a plainness and simplicity which are almost unique in the extant christian literature of the next twenty years, but which can then be paralleled a dozen times over in the writers of the following generation. The fact that the majority of the subjects in which he thus seems in advance of his time are concerned with the liturgy rather than with pure theology, is more an indication of the direction in which his personal interests lay than of any remoteness from the technical theological movements of the day. At least one major subject about which he reveals no shadow of hesitation in A.D. 348, the deity of the Holy Ghost, was to cause a good deal of heart-burning to a professed theologian of the calibre of S. Basil the Great before many years were over.

It seems typical of his relation to his times that though he must have been elaborating and putting into practice his new conception of the liturgy at Jerusalem in the 50's and 60's of the century, it is not during this period that we hear of widespread imitation elsewhere, though returning pilgrims must have been carrying the tale of what was being done in Jerusalem all over christendom every year. In the 80's and 90's of the century the new Jerusalem observances begin to come in like a flood all over christendom. They even affect Rome before the end of the century, which in matters liturgical usually required two or three generations (if not two or three centuries) of consideration before adopting new ideas. I hope it is not reading too much into the evidence to suggest that the men of Cyril's own generation, anti-arian stalwarts who were bishops much about his own age, and had been brought up in the old ways—'on the prayer book', so to speak—were not altogether free from misgivings about his innovations.[1] Perhaps, too, they remembered the old scandal about Cyril's consecration as the candidate of the Arians against the catholics. It was when the men whom he really represented, the men of the next generation, began in their turn to succeed to episcopal thrones, that his ideas began to be put into practice in other churches. The eager curiosity with which Etheria notes the Jerusalem ceremonies and the enthusiasm with which she writes them down for the sisters in her convent at home in the West of Spain, are vivid evidence of the extent to which 'the way they do it in Jerusalem' was exciting the interest of the remotest churches towards the end of the century. During his long episcopate of thirty-five or thirty-six years a whole new generation of christians had grown up in a new christian world, to whom the Jerusalem rite had always represented the 'correct' ecclesiastical fashion. To such men the church of the Holy City, now the goal of pilgrims and the chosen home of famous monks and writers and ascetics from all lands, naturally seemed the ideal of a christian church, to be imitated so far as one had the chance.[2]

*The Organisation of Lent.* The institution of Lent, unlike that of Holy Week and Easter, is not directly due to the initiative of the Jerusalem church, though it was early adopted there and formed part of that 'Jerusalem model' of liturgy which began to spread in the later fourth century.

A fast of a day before the Pascha was, as we have seen, a primaeval

[1] *Cf. p.* 441, *n.* 1.
[2] We are not altogether unacquainted with such a situation ourselves, and the changes it can insensibly bring about in public worship after a generation. How many Anglican bishops now discreetly 'follow Fortescue' in certain things?

christian observance probably inherited from judaism. Before the end of the second century this was being voluntarily extended by the devout to two days (as is prescribed by Hippolytus)[1] or even a week, and to two weeks by the enthusiasts of the Montanist sect. This, however, is not so much the direct origin of Lent, either as a season or as a fast, but rather a foreshadowing of the specially strict fast of Holy Week. Lent, properly speaking, derives from the strict special discipline of the catechumens during the final stage of their preparation for baptism at the Pascha. In later times this seems to have lasted for some two and a half weeks at Rome,[2] and there seem to be clear traces of the same discipline in Hippolytus, *Ap. Trad.*, xx, at the beginning of the third century. It was during these three weeks that they attended the special classes on christian doctrine called *Catecheses* (*cf.* 'Catechism'). The pre-baptismal fasts of the catechumens are mentioned by Justin *c.* A.D. 155 as traditional in his day. But it is likely that the introduction of the daily exorcisms which accompanied them by the time of Hippolytus, and the regular organisation of this final stage of the catechumenate generally, date from the latter half of the second century, between Justin and Hippolytus.

In the fourth century through the influence of the monastic-ascetic movement it became customary for the faithful at large to join the catechumens in their special pre-baptismal fast; and the clergy also encouraged them to attend the instructions on christian doctrine by way of a 'refresher course'. (The same thing has been tried in connection with confirmation classes in our own day with excellent results.) The extension of the whole observance to a period of six weeks took place during the second quarter of the fourth century. It seems to have been due to a reorganisation of the instructions to secure better attendance, by spacing them over a longer period, but it brought with it an extension of the fast. Sundays, and in some places Saturdays, were not fast days, and Lent therefore began with the eighth, seventh or sixth Sunday before Easter in different churches. The step of identifying the six weeks' fast with the 40 days' fast of our Lord in the wilderness was obviously in keeping with the new historical interest of the liturgy. The actual number of '40 days' of fasting was made up by extending Lent behind the sixth Sunday before Easter in various ways. But the association with our Lord's fast in the wilderness was an idea attached to the season of Lent only *after* it had come into existence in connection with the preparation of candidates for baptism. (An historical commemoration would strictly have required that Lent should follow

---

[1] *Ap. Trad.*, xxix. 2.

[2] The mass for Wednesday in the fourth week of Lent in the Roman missal still preserves the clearest traces of the *apertio aurium,* the final 'scrutiny' at which the 'candidate' for baptism was 'elected'—the whole terminology of the catechumenate of the Roman church has passed into our political vocabulary !—after which they underwent their final preparation. The scriptural texts of the chants and lessons of this mass form a beautiful instruction on the meaning of baptism as understood by the early church.

immediately upon Epiphany, after this had been accepted as the commemoration of our Lord's baptism.)

Various methods of calculating the length of the fast are found in the fourth century. At Jerusalem in A.D. 348 the 'forty days' are already spread over eight weeks, neither Saturday nor Sunday being fasted, and the special fast of Holy Week forming a ninth week of separate observance at the end. (This arrangement has permanently influenced the Eastern method of keeping Lent.) At Alexandria S. Athanasius in his Paschal Letter to his people for A.D. 329 still exhorts them to keep a fast only of one week before the Pascha, in the old fashion. But in the year A.D. 336 he asks them to keep a fast of forty days, and henceforward this is his rule. But he evidently found some difficulty in getting it generally observed. His exhortations grow more urgent as the years pass, and in A.D. 339, writing from Rome, he begs them to observe the full Lent of forty days, 'lest while all the world is fasting we in Egypt be mocked because we alone do not fast'.

This would seem to imply that Rome already observed a six weeks' Lent in A.D. 339, and this is also the plain indication of S. Leo's Lenten sermons preached in the years round about A.D. 450. Yet the Byzantine historian Socrates, writing rather before S. Leo's time, says categorically that Rome in his day still kept only the old three weeks' fast of Lent, originally prescribed for the special preparation of the catechumens. The curious thing is that the lections of the Roman missal still preserve plain traces of a three weeks' Lent to this day. It is conceivable, though perhaps not likely, that the Lenten synaxes, at which the catechetical classes were given, were at Rome still crowded into the last three weeks of Lent down to the sixth century, while the fast began three weeks before the classes. More probably Socrates is mistaken; in which case the present traces of a three weeks' cycle of lessons for the catechumens before Easter in the missal must have come down almost unchanged from before A.D. 340, though the discipline of the catechumens has been revised many times since then—another example of the obstinacy of Roman liturgical tradition.[1] It was not until the later seventh century that the full total of forty days of actual fasting (Sundays not being included) began to be observed at Rome by the addition of Ash Wednesday and the three following days before the old beginning of Lent on the Sunday.[2] The moving ceremony of the imposition of ashes on the brows of the faithful beginning their Lenten fast, accompanied by the

---

[1] The present arrangement of the Lenten masses in the missal dates in the main from the time of Pope Hilary (A.D. 461–467) with some important rearrangements by S. Gregory the Great, c. A.D. 595, and a few additions and retouchings during the seventh century. Cf. G. Callewaert, La Durée et le Caractère du Carême ancien, Bruges, 1920 (esp. pp. 86–96), and S. Grégoire, Les Scrutins et quelques Messes Quadragésimales; Ephemerides Liturgicae, liii. (1939), pp. 191 sqq.
[2] The collect in the Book of Common Prayer for Sunday Lent I has echoes of the old collect in caput jejunii in the Roman missal which presupposes that Lent begins that day. The Lenten office of the Roman Breviary still begins on the Sunday, not on Ash Wednesday.

words 'Remember, man, that dust thou art and unto dust shalt thou return', from which Ash Wednesday gets its name, is not a 'Roman' ceremony at all. It seems to have originated in Gaul in the sixth century, and was at first confined to public penitents doing penance for grave and notorious sin, whom the clergy tried to comfort and encourage by submitting themselves to the same public humiliation. It spread to England and to Rome in the ninth or tenth century, and thence to Germany, Southern Italy and Spain.

Thus Lent in the form we know does not originate as an historical commemoration of our Lord's fast in the wilderness or even as a preparation for Holy Week and Easter, but as a private initiative of the devout laity in taking it upon themselves to share the solemn preparation of the catechumens for the sacraments of baptism and confirmation. It was the fact that these were normally conferred at the paschal vigil which in the end made of Lent a preparation for Easter. It was officially organised and adopted by the church as a season of special penitence and prayer, not as especially related to our Lord's sufferings, but because it was a practical answer to a new need which was becoming increasingly pressing from about A.D. 320–350. Except for the days before the Pascha, fasts and ascetic exercises in the third century had been still largely a matter of voluntary choice and private devotion. The pressure of a hostile world then sufficed to keep the standard of christian self-discipline high. With the relaxation of this pressure after the peace of the church, there was a greatly increased danger of a lowering of the standard for the majority of christians, despite the ascetic ardour of the devout. And in spite of the care taken about the instruction of the catechumens and the insistence on their attendance at the *catecheses*, the great mass of conventional converts which was now flooding into the church was very apt to remain not more than half-christian in its unconscious assumptions.[1] The clergy welcomed the opportunity of driving home fundamental christian doctrine and ethics on the mass of the faithful which their attendance at the catechumens' classes presented. And a fast of forty days imposed on all alike was at least a salutary assertion of the claims of christian self-renunciation upon the life of even the lax and worldly.

---

[1] Too much has been made of the church's readiness to accept easy conversions from heathenism in the fourth century. She did do all she could to impress on them the need for sincerity. The catechumenate was a probation of at least two years, and no one was admitted to baptism without sponsors who witnessed to their good behaviour during this period, and without the church at large having a right to give testimony against their sincerity. And the penitential system, which visited post-baptismal sin with excommunication and prolonged physical penance, was still severe to the point of being unworkable. The custom, which grew up in the fourth century, of deferring baptism till late in life, or even, like Constantine, till the deathbed, was most unsatisfactory. But at least it witnesses to the fact that the church *did* make it clear that baptism was a grave step, and that a very high standard was in practice required of the baptised, which the worldly and the conventional were not prepared to try to reach. And it was only to those who received baptism that the church offered either remission of sins or eternal salvation.

The importance of Lent lay precisely in this, that it was not just one more ascetic exercise for the devout, but that it was recognised as being of *universal* obligation. Those who wished might continue to pray and to fast with fervour at other seasons; the sanctity of the church as a whole might help to carry a considerable number of slack christians. But Lent was intended to be a strictly *corporate* effort of the whole church, from the bishop down to the humblest catechumen, to live at least for a season as befitted the Body of Christ—in fervent and frequent prayer and in a serious and mortified spirit, in order that at their corporate Easter communion all might be found truly members of the Body. The fast was not a merely mechanical discipline, though it was a severe one. The old Lenten sermons, *e.g.* those of S. Leo, insist strongly on mutual forgiveness and forbearance, on the intensification of private prayer and generosity in almsgiving, and on regular and devout attendances at biblical and doctrinal instruction, as Lenten observances just as strictly required of the christian as the physical abstinence from food. When the whole world was becoming nominally christian there was a great wholesomeness about this annual requirement of a season of serious self-discipline for christian reasons, which should cover every aspect of social life—as it soon came to do. It reminded the careless and the sinful christian, as insistently as it did the devout, of the claims of the christian standard: 'Be not conformed to this world, but be ye transformed by the renewing of your mind'.[1]

*Other Feasts of our Lord.* The application of a strictly historical meaning to the ancient feast of the Pascha was not the only development of this kind which the fourth century witnessed. Other events of our Lord's earthly life began to receive similar commemoration in the liturgy. Christmas as the feast of our Lord's birth at Bethlehem was already being kept at Rome in A.D. 354. It is not probable that it is a feast of Roman origin, for it is clear that it had already been observed fairly widely in the West before this date, perhaps in some places before the end of the third century. It had not yet been accepted at Jerusalem when Etheria visited the Holy City in 385; but it was just beginning to be observed at Constantinople and Antioch at about that time. Alexandria adopted it somewhere about A.D. 430, and Jerusalem followed suit soon after. The Eastern churches, from the third century in some cases, had already begun to observe a feast of our Lord's birthday on January 6th as 'Epiphany', the feast of His 'manifestation', the origins of which may well go back to the late second century in some places. In the later fourth century East and West began, as it were, to exchange feasts, and to keep Christmas and Epiphany side by side. There was a rough readjustment of their meanings, Christmas remaining a birthday-feast while Epiphany became the commemoration of the other 'manifestations' of Christ—to the Magi, at His Baptism and at Cana of Galilee. Rome, followed by Africa, was somewhat slow to accept this duplication

[1] Rom. xii. 2.

of feasts, but Epiphany had been adopted there before A.D. 450, just as Alexandria had rather tardily adopted the Western feast of Christmas.[1] Local interests at Jerusalem had already by A.D. 385 rounded off the Birthday feast with a celebration of our Lord's Presentation in the Temple on February 15th (forty days after His birth, calculated from January 6th, the old Jerusalem feast of the Nativity; this was later put back to February 2nd —our feast of the Purification—to accord with December 25th).[2] Jerusalem, too, seems to have been the centre from which the observance of a special feast of the Ascension spread over the rest of the church. Etheria mentions there a special feast forty days after Easter, without, however, directly connecting it with the Ascension. The ancient conception of the Paschal feast had included in its scope the Ascension along with the Resurrection and the Passion. It is possible that some hesitation was felt about detaching the commemoration of the Ascension from the Resurrection when the Pascha was transformed into Easter, in view of the suggestions in the gospels of Luke and John about an Ascension on Easter Day. The other Jerusalem festival of the fourth century which Etheria mentions is the feast of the Dedication of Constantine's basilicas at Jerusalem on September 14th, which under the title of the Exaltation of the Holy Cross has since been accepted all over the christian world; though Rome seems—once more— to have received it only in the eighth century.

Such were the historical feasts commemorating events of our Lord's life which were beginning to be universally observed by the end of the fourth century. All others, the Circumcision, Annunciation, Transfiguration and so forth are later—some of them much later—in origin, as are also that whole class of feasts which commemorate theological doctrines and ideas rather than events, e.g. 'Orthodoxy Sunday' in the East (ninth-tenth century) or those of Trinity Sunday (tenth century at Liége, adopted at Rome A.D. 1334) and Corpus Christi (A.D. 1247 at Liége, A.D. 1264 at Rome) in the West.

Yet comparatively few as they are, this fourth century group of historical feasts sufficed to establish the whole principle of the christian liturgical cycle for the future; nothing has been changed or added since but details and decorations. Ever since c. A.D. 400 the main substance of the annual

---

[1] In the East the Armenians alone, isolated in their mountains, have never accepted the Western feast of December 25th, and still keep Epiphany as our Lord's birthday. On the origins of Christmas and Epiphany see the interesting essay Les Origines de la Noël et de l'Épiphanie, by Dom B. Botte, Louvain, 1932.

[2] Rome only accepted this feast about A.D. 700 when it was introduced by the Syrian Pope, Sergius I. It was first observed at Constantinople in A.D. 542 under Justinian. It seems to have spread in the West chiefly from Rome, but it was first called 'the Purification' and kept as a feast of our Lady in eighth century Gaul. At Rome it was kept as a feast of our Lord, in the Eastern fashion (cf. the invitatory of Mattins in the Roman Breviary: 'Rejoice and be glad, O Jerusalem, to meet thy God'). It has now been proved that the Roman procession with candles before mass on this day has no connection with the pagan ceremonies of the Lupercalia, as used to be supposed.

cycle everywhere has consisted of two groups of historical commemorations of events, the one referring to our Lord's birth and the other to His death, to the virtual exclusion of all that happened between them. The cycle concludes with the two pre-Nicene feasts of the Pascha (resolved into Easter and Ascension) and Pentecost, both transformed by a new and more strictly historical interpretation. By the accident that both the old Nativity feasts happened independently to have been fixed at mid-winter[1] while the Pascha was derived from a jewish spring festival, the whole series is awkwardly compressed into less than half the year, while the other half stands vacant. Yet notwithstanding this drawback, later ages have never attempted to tamper with the results of the haphazard development of the fourth century; though they have supplemented them with a variety of miscellaneous observances only loosely related to the main cycle, e.g. Nativity of S. John Baptist and Transfiguration. Together with the season of Lent, itself of fourth century organisation, and the (purely Western) season of Advent as a preparation for Christmas, developed in the fifth century and after,[2] the fourth century historical cycle still governs our own christian year.

*Sunday*. We have seen the part played by Sunday in the old eschatological conception of the liturgical cycle—that of a sort of weekly Pascha. When the elaboration of Holy Week brought the Pascha definitely within the historical conception it was inevitable that Sunday also should somewhat change its character. The aspect of a weekly memorial of the resurrection, which had not been wholly wanting in pre-Nicene times, though it had always hitherto remained secondary to the idea of manifesting the 'world to come', becomes more prominent in the fourth century attitude towards Sunday, in keeping with the new general emphasis on history. In theory this idea of Sunday as a little weekly Easter has been retained ever since. Yet in practice there is no evidence that it has ever made very much appeal to popular piety in any part of christendom.

It did not prove altogether easy to fit in the weekly Sunday with the new notion of an annual round of historical commemorations, and Sunday has never played quite the same main part in the structure of the liturgical cycle after the fourth century as it did in that of the pre-Nicene church. For centuries, as we shall see, the Sunday cycle was rather strangely

---

[1] There is no authentic historical tradition behind either Christmas or Epiphany. Both seem to have originated as counter-festivals to birthday feasts of pagan gods. Such early palestinian tradition as there is seems to be in favour of a date for our Lord's birth in the summer, but it amounts to very little in the nature of real evidence.

[2] It seems originally to have been of Spanish or Gallican invention. The Eastern church has no liturgical Advent, though the Sunday before Christmas has a somewhat distinct liturgical character of its own. The Easterns also keep an 'Advent' fast of six weeks from November 14th in imitation of Lent, but in practice it is not much observed outside the monasteries. The Gallican churches also fasted—from November 11th—but Rome never accepted the Advent fast, and cut down the six Advent Sundays of the Gallican cycle, first to five and then to four.

neglected in the development of the liturgy; and it still has in all rites a little of the character of a stop-gap, something upon which the liturgy falls back when the historical cycle has nothing more interesting to offer.

Yet it could not be allowed to fall into disuse. A regular meeting for the eucharist was in itself too valuable to devotion; the apostolic tradition that this was *the* day for corporate christian worship was too firmly rooted; and the new historical cycle was in any case too scrappy and too ill-arranged to provide a substitute. A new basis was therefore found for Sunday by making it what it had never been before, a weekly holiday from work. In A.D. 321 Constantine issued an edict forbidding the law-courts to sit upon that day, and the enforcement of an official holiday brought daily life to something of a standstill (as in the case of a modern Bank Holiday). The result was in large part to carry out Constantine's design of rendering attendance at christian worship possible for all his subjects, christian or otherwise—it was largely a propaganda measure; though the church had difficulty in some places in securing that its provisions were extended to that large proportion of the population who were slaves.

### The Organisation of the Propers

*The Organisation of the Lectionary for the Synaxis.* We are accustomed to the idea that every Sunday and Holy Day shall have its own 'proper' at the eucharist, a collect, epistle and gospel of its own, more or less appropriate to itself, and recurring on that day each year in a fixed sequence in accordance with the calendar. In all older Western rites than our own this 'proper' is more extensive than with us, comprising at least two other variable prayers besides the collect (an offertory prayer and a thanksgiving) and also a number of chants.[1] The Eastern rites have a system of their own for varying the prayers, but in all Eastern rites the 'proper' of each day includes at least one variable chant, the psalm-chant corresponding to the Western 'gradual' between the epistle and gospel, (and usually others) as well as the lessons. Such a system of 'propers' was to be found in the synagogue liturgy of our Lord's time, the lessons for the sabbaths being arranged on a three years' cycle, though certain greater festivals stood out from the system and had the same lessons every year. The psalm-chants between the synagogue lessons seem also to have been 'proper' to the day like the lessons, not selected at discretion.

It is clear that the two great christian feasts of the Pascha and Pentecost had their own 'proper' lections and chants, even in the second century; and there are indications that these were more or less the same selection every-where at that time. What is by no means clear is that the christian Sunday worship inherited from the synagogue anything like the regular cycle of

---

[1] This is the ordinary Roman arrangement; in the Milanese rite there are four variable prayers; in the Gallican rites every single prayer in the rite except the institution narrative in the *eucharistia* varies in every mass.

sabbath lections, either on a one- or a three-year system. It may have done so; but the desire to include the new christian scriptures and then to give them the place of honour in the lectionary system must in any case have sufficed to break up all trace of any such survival from the jewish lection-aries during the first half of the second century. And the lack of agreement as to which documents of the new christian literature were suitable for public reading at the synaxis, which is still noticeable in the later second century[1] and in some places even after that, would prevent the compiling of lectionaries of more than local authority down to the fourth century. Indeed, I know of no serious evidence for the existence of any organised cycle of lessons for the ordinary Sunday synaxis anywhere in pre-Nicene times.

The organisation of Lent in the fourth century led quite naturally to the adoption in different churches of a fixed series of specially selected lessons for the synaxis in this season, on which the instruction of the catechumens could be based. But it is evident from what remains of the fourth century catecheses that this series varied from church to church. The general adop-tion of the new cycle of historical commemorations (Christmas, etc.) in the later fourth century further increased the content of the fixed lectionary in every church. But though the subject of these feasts naturally limited the choice of New Testament lessons to certain passages, there is enough fourth century evidence of variation in them from church to church to suggest that in adopting the observance of these festivals each church still felt free to interpret them in its own way (e.g. in the case of the Epiphany). The rise in the importance of martyrs' feasts during the fourth century, of which we shall treat in a moment, further increased the fixed contents of the lectionaries. But since each church at first celebrated only its own local martyrdoms, and the lessons were chosen—often with a good deal of ingenuity—to allude to some particular circumstance of the way in which particular martyrs had won their crown, there was a wide variety in differ-ent churches here also. The borrowing of festivals of particularly well-known martyrs by 'foreign' churches, however, tended to carry with it the borrowing of the 'proper' lections with which their festival was celebrated in their native city; and certain passages of scripture were naturally indi-cated as appropriate everywhere to the general topic of martyrdom, where there were no such particular circumstances to be commemorated beyond the fact of death in witness for Christ. The 'proper' of the martyrs is thus (apart from the ancient lections of the Pascha) the first element of the fixed eucharistic lectionary to take a form roughly the same in all churches; and from this 'proper' develops the 'common' of martyrs, which was largely formed from it about the ninth century.

None of this solved the problem of the ordinary Sunday lections, which

---

[1] See e.g. the dispute about the public reading of the 'Gospel of Peter' in the church of Rhossos in N. Syria ap. Eusebius, E.H., iv. 24 (c. A.D. 190).

seems to have been fumbled with for centuries. The fifth century lectionary of Edessa[1] makes no provision whatever for the 'green' Sundays. We know the contents of the Jerusalem lectionary of the sixth century from a much later Armenian version and various other materials,[2] but it is doubtful if the lessons for the ordinary Sundays which some of these now contain formed any part of the original nucleus. The present Eastern Orthodox system of 'Sundays of Matthew' and 'Sundays of Luke' from Pentecost to Septuagesima (interrupted only by the feasts of the Christmas cycle, since the Easterns have no Advent) is a Byzantine invention which cannot at present be traced back beyond the eighth century, and is probably not much older in its origin. We know roughly the contents of the Roman lectionary of the seventh century[3] and here for the first time we begin to find definite traces of a fixed system of lections for what we should call the 'green' Sundays. But even here these are somewhat awkwardly handled, ten sets of lessons being provided for the Sundays after Epiphany though more than six are never required, while the season after Pentecost (Trinity being a purely mediaeval invention) which never requires less than twenty-four and may require twenty-seven receives only twenty. We have here, however, the first clumsy beginnings of the present universal Western arrangement (inherited by the Book of Common Prayer) by which the whole service—proper chants, lections and prayers—for Sundays unwanted after Epiphany is transferred to fill up deficiencies after Pentecost. The fixed service for the last Sunday after Pentecost (or Trinity), which is always reserved for the Sunday next before Advent, is a relic of the old five-Sunday Advent, as its contents make plain both in the Roman missal and the Book of Common Prayer.

The early Western arrangements elsewhere are even more sketchy than those of the Roman capitulary. The sixth century epistle-lectionary of Capua[4] gives simply a list of eleven 'quotidian' epistles to be used on any day between Epiphany and Sexagesima, another for any week-day between Sexagesima and Quinquagesima, and none at all for the 'green' season after Pentecost. The capitulary is not complete. But since provision is made for the chief saints' days after Pentecost, presumably the eleven 'quotidian' epistles given after Epiphany are to serve also for the Sundays of this period. The seventh century Neapolitan gospel lectionary[5] gives gospels for four Sundays after Epiphany, and thirty-nine 'quotidian' gospels to serve for after Pentecost. The eleventh century Toledo lectionary, which, however, may well represent the arrangements of the sixth or

[1] Published by F. C. Burkitt, *Proceedings of the British Academy*, Vol. xi.
[2] Published by F. C. Conybeare, *Rituale Armenorum*; and A. Baumstark, *Nicht-evangelische syrische Perikopenordnungen des ersten Jahrtausends*, Munster, 1921.
[3] From the 'Wurzburg Capitulary' published by Dom G. Morin, *Rév. Ben.*, xxvii (1910) 41–74.
[4] Published by Dom G. Morin, *Anecdota Maredsolana*, Vol. I (1893), p. 436 *sqq.*
[5] *Ibid.*, pp. 426 *sq.*

seventh century Spanish church[1] has no provision for Sundays after Epiphany at all, but ends with a set of twenty-four 'quotidian' Sundays to be used when nothing else is provided. The sixth century Gallican lectionary of Luxeuil[2] allows for five Sundays after Epiphany and has now two sets of 'quotidian' lections at the end; when the MS. was complete there were perhaps six of these.

It is the same story when we examine the provision of proper collects for 'green' Sundays, after the invention of variable prayers at the eucharist had made these seem necessary. The *Gelasian Sacramentary*, the oldest Western mass-book of which we can speak with any certainty, represents in substance the Roman rite of the sixth century. This makes no arrangements whatever for the Sundays after Epiphany, or after the octave of Pentecost. But in the third of the three 'books' into which its contents are divided it has a collection of sixteen different masses 'for Sundays', six others for 'quotidian days' and ninety for various occasions. Of the Gallican and 'mixed' books all that need be said is that the oldest of them, the *Masses of Mone* (sixth-seventh century) contains six masses for Sundays; so does the *Missale Gothicum*, though they are different ones. The *Missale Francorum* has four; the *Bobb'o Missal* ten, apparently drawn from two separate older Gallican collections of five each. The Spanish Mozarabic rite of the eleventh century had still no more than seven in its authentic form,[3] though sixteen others, probably of later composition, can be gathered from other sources.[4] In the Milanese rite to this day complete provision is made for only six 'green' Sundays, though they are repeated with the various parts shuffled in different arrangements, so that no two Sundays have exactly the same service.

From all this and a good deal of further evidence of the same kind, it is possible to reconstruct the Western history of the formation of the eucharistic 'propers' thus: The only certainly pre-Nicene elements in the modern proper are the ancient paschal lections now read in the Roman rite on Good Friday. The next oldest are probably the long series of Old Testament lections on Holy Saturday. Among the next oldest are some of the propers of the Seasons, which everywhere consisted by the end of the fifth century of the feasts of the Christmas cycle[5] together with Lent and the historical commemorations of the Easter cycle (Palm Sunday, Ascension, etc.). The propers of some of the lesser martyrs (not of apostles, except SS. Peter and Paul on June 29th) are certainly as old

[1] *Ibid., pp.* 1 *sq.*
[2] Published by Dom J. Mabillon, *de Liturgia Gallicana*, 1729, *pp.* 106 *sq.*
[3] *Liber Mozarabicus Sacramentorum*, ed. Dom M. Férotin, 1912, *pp.* 507 *sq.*
[4] *Ibid.,* p. 614.
[5] It is a singular instance of liturgical tradition that the saints' days after Christmas (Stephen, etc.) which originated in the *Temporale* (proper of seasons) and not the *Sanctorale* (of saints) are still printed in the proper of seasons and not in that of the saints (collected after the last Sunday after Trinity) in the Book of Common Prayer. We inherit this arrangement from the Roman missal.

and in some cases probably older than those of this group of masses of the Seasons.

The earliest addition to this nucleus appears to have been the masses for the five Sundays of Easter-tide, followed by the six (later five, then four) Sundays of Advent and the three Sundays before Lent, all of which had been fixed before the end of the sixth century. The Eastern propers had reached about the same state of development by the fifth century and probably rather earlier (except for the absence of Advent).

The development of the Sunday propers for the rest of the year was much slower both in the East and West, and was never more than roughly completed. At first the ordinary Sundays had no proper at all, but were drawn from a sort of pool, a 'common' of Sundays, containing a number of alternatives, at first comparatively few and later slowly enlarged, to be used at the discretion of the celebrant. It appears to have been the Roman sense of order and convenience which first prompted the assignment of a proper to each 'green' Sunday. At all events we know that by c. A.D. 700 there were missals of the pure Roman rite circulating in Italy which had a complete and separate proper assigned to each of the Sundays after Pentecost.[1] Yet this arrangement was reckoned so little a part of the official Roman rite nearly a century later c. A.D. 790, when Charlemagne obtained from Pope Hadrian I a copy of the authentic Roman sacramentary for the correction of the liturgical confusion in Gaul, that the official book sent for this important purpose contained no arrangements whatever for 'green' Sundays, not even a set of 'quotidian' masses. The development of the propers in the Roman rite had evidently remained officially at about the stage it had reached in the sixth century (Advent to Epiphany, Septuagesima to Pentecost, and scattered saints' days and fast-days throughout the year). Alcuin of York, Charlemagne's chief adviser in issuing this new official French edition of the *Gregorian Sacramentary c.* A.D. 790, was obliged to draw on older 'unofficially supplemented' Roman books already in circulation in Gaul for the materials necessary for the 'green' Sundays.

Provision is made in Alcuin's edition for four Sundays in Advent, two after Christmas, six after Epiphany, three before and six during Lent, five after Easter and twenty-four after Pentecost,[2] the arrangement which has since slowly won its way everywhere in the West.

---

[1] *Cf.* the palimpsest fragments of a Gregorian Sacramentary at Monte Cassino, published by Dom A. Wilmart, *Rév. Ben.*, xxvi. (1909), *pp* 281 *sq.*

[2] The Low German invention of Trinity Sunday, displacing the first Sunday after Pentecost, was not allowed at first to disturb the hard-won uniformity of arrangements for the post-Pentecost season. The old proper of the first Sunday after Pentecost was retained, even in those churches which accepted the new feast, to be used on the weekdays following Trinity Sunday. The further invention of an octave for Trinity Sunday (a typical piece of mediaeval elaboration) did upset the series. A few churches which accepted the octave dropped the proper of the first Sunday after Pentecost, but others dropped one or another of the later members of the series, in order to keep to the provision of twenty-four Sundays. Sarum made certain changes of its own and followed the German reckoning 'after Trinity', not

The older books from which Alcuin compiled his edition were not complete copies of the service for anyone to use, but were constructed to serve the purpose of one particular 'order' alone, and contained only what was necessary to the 'liturgy' of that 'order'. Thus the celebrant used a 'sacramentary', a book containing all the prayers used by the celebrant at the administration of any of the sacraments (not the eucharist only on any occasion in the year. But the sacramentary contained no lections or chants, because the saying of the prayers was the 'liturgy' of the celebrant in the corporate worship of the church, but the reading and singing were the 'liturgies' of other orders. So the deacon had a 'gospel book' containing no prayers, but all the gospel lessons publicly read in the course of the year. The sub-deacon had a 'lectionary' containing the other lessons; and the choir, so far as they used books—nearly all the singing was done from memory—had an *antiphonarium missae* containing all the words and a sort of outline or sketch-map of the musical settings in the difficult neumatic notation of the day. (These last were rare books—the archcantor or *paraphonista* of great churches might have one, but probably no one else. The members of the choir sang both words and music by heart.)

This arrangement of liturgical books continued for some while after Alcuin's arrangement of Sunday propers, and the various books employed for making the basic collection of these propers in the West were never more than roughly co-ordinated. The epistle-lectionary represented a selection older by a century or more than the gospel-lectionary and was planned on a different principle. The two sets of lections are consequently frequently out of step. The chant-books provided for three Sundays after Epiphany (*cf.* the seventh century gospel book of Naples, which probably represents an earlier stage in the development of the Roman rite) and for only twenty complete Sunday services after Pentecost (like the *Gelasian Sacramentary* of the sixth century) and some odd extra pieces. This meant that the introit, gradual, offertory and communion—just as integral a part of the Sunday proper as the collect or the gospel—on some Sundays had to be borrowed or repeated from the proper of others. Choirs are still apt to be rather truculently conservative in the music they will or will not sing in worship, and the Papal *schola* of the seventh century were evidently whole-hearted in their adherence to this tradition. After the extensive reorganisation of the Roman chant by Pope Gregory the Great *c.* A.D. 600

the old English 'after Pentecost'. Cranmer partly followed Sarum, and partly shuffled the gospel series according to his own taste, but followed slightly different principles in his selection of epistles, with confusing results. Our eucharistic lectionary therefore consists of the *débris* of a system which originated at Rome in the sixth century, and was revised piecemeal at least three times before the Reformation, revised again by Cranmer and again in details since. The present Roman missal follows for the green Sundays a slightly different selection made at Rome in the seventh-eighth centuries, but this also has been so tinkered with since as to be little more coherent than our own.

they virtually refused to learn any new music at all for a century or more, and simply adapted or transferred the old music to new occasions when it was required. The matter was made all the more difficult by the fact that the words were treated by the singers chiefly as a *memoria technica* for the complicated neums of the music. To change the words might easily affect the accurate tradition of the chant.[1] This introduced a few pieces of a quite striking inappropriateness into the Sunday propers—*e.g.*, the offertory for the twenty-first Sunday after Pentecost, a lamentation over Job's boils which has no reference to anything else in the proper of the day. There was a shortage of music for the Sundays of this season; this piece happened to be in the repertory of the *schola*, and the singers liked the tune—it is indeed an effective and rather showy piece of music. And since the words were inseparably wedded to the setting in their minds, words and music had to go together into the cycle of the propers, as a little memorial to the musical obsessions and liturgical tiresomeness of some choirmen throughout all ages. But such things are rare. The texts are scriptural or based on scripture (with less than a dozen exceptions in the whole annual cycle) and are seldom unfitting to their purpose, though the graduals and introits are as a rule more closely connected together in ideas than the offertories or the communions.

Besides the proper lessons and chants, the third element which in the West goes to make up the proper of any particular day is the proper prayers. We shall discuss later the first origin of these variable prayers in the liturgy. Here it is sufficient to say that by the time the 'green' Sundays came to be provided with propers these variable prayers were expected to

---

[1] At Rome every item of the proper for each liturgical day throughout the year was supposed to have its own individual setting, and though there were some repetitions the whole *corpus* formed a treasure of church music of the highest order without parallel in any other church, even at Byzantium. Those Anglicans who judge 'plainsong' from the psalm-tones and a few hymn tunes alone, without hearing the propers, and therefore suppose it to be 'monotonous', are like those who should judge the pictures in the National Gallery solely by the brown and grey pasteboard surrounds in which some of them are framed, and declare painting to be dull. The propers are the very essence of the chant. To have worshipped with them to their own ever-varying settings through the whole annual cycle is an unforgettable musical experience. Nothing else can so teach the capacity of music to express all the possible range of human thought and emotion by pure melody alone. Unfortunately like all such 'art-music', the propers are not quite easy; and they are in most cases inseparably wedded to the Latin text, and therefore closed to Anglicans. Even among Roman Catholics in England they are nearly always sung to psalm-tones, except at Westminster Cathedral and in a few great monasteries. Yet there was a time when they seemed specially adapted to the English taste and genius. The Anglo-Saxon church learned the authentic tradition in the golden age of the chant, the seventh century, from a series of Roman experts specially sent out to this foremost centre of the Roman rite outside Rome, so that Bede can talk proudly of 'the chant of the Romans, that is of the Cantuarians' (*Eccl. Hist.*, II. xx). England remained one of the purest sources of the authentic tradition down to the Frenchifying of our ways of worship which began at the Norman Conquest, and culminated in the thirteenth century with the compilation of the 'Use of Sarum' from Norman and French custumals.

be a group of at least three[1]—collect, secret (offertory prayer) and post-communion or thanksgiving. To these all churches outside Rome itself usually added a proper preface,[2] varying with the day just as the collect did. The original principle of the collect seems to have been that it should have some connection with the immediately following scriptures for the day. But in the case of the Sunday collects of Alcuin's edition this was impossible, since they had originally been drawn—each along with its secret and post-communion—from the general 'pool' of prayers to be used on 'quotidian' Sundays at the celebrant's discretion, found in the Roman sacramentaries of the fifth and sixth centuries. Prayers originally framed in general terms to fit any Sunday were thus assigned to be used always on one particular Sunday, and always in conjunction with a particular set of lections and chants, most of which had originally been selected without reference to the rest.[3] (This applies only to the 'green' Sunday propers, not to the older propers of the season and the martyrs.)

Alcuin's own selection of prayers for the Sundays is textually identical with that in 'unofficial' use in the neighbourhood of Rome and probably at Rome itself a century before. But various tenth and eleventh century MSS. shuffle the collects for the 'green' Sundays in the most aimless manner, and break up the sets of three (collect, secret and post-communion) in the Sunday propers and redistribute their members. It can hardly be said that this vitally affected the coherence of these propers, since they really have none to affect. Liturgical commentators for the past century have delighted in finding consistent trains of thought and mystical explanations running through the whole service for each Sunday. But the truth is that anything of this kind which they have found is a product of their own piety or ingenuity. The propers for the 'green' Sundays are collections of fragments arbitrarily distributed.

This is not to say that many of the separate fragments are not in themselves both ancient and beautiful. The prayers in particular are lovely things, grave, melodious and thoughtful, and compact with evangelical doctrine—characteristic products of the liturgical genius of Rome in the fifth and sixth centuries. Cranmer's reputation as a writer of English prose largely rests on his translations of some seventy of these prayers (out of a *corpus* of many hundreds) in the Book of Common Prayer. And rightly so, for his are among the very best translations ever made, and his products when he is not working on a Latin original are not always so happy. But a careful analysis shows that though using on an average fifty-sixty per cent. more words he rarely makes more than between two-thirds and three-quarters of the points in his originals. (One might usefully draw the attention of the modern compilers of prayers to the fact that the vein he worked

---

[1] *Cf. p.* 360, *n.* I.    [2] *Cf. p.* 542.

[3] The chant of the gradual is sometimes connected with that of the introit even on the 'green' Sundays, and sometimes has an evident connection with the gospel on the *earlier* Sundays after Pentecost.

so carefully is by no means exhausted, though the compilers of various 'Anglo-catholic' missals do not seem to have found translation an easy art, probably through trying to be too literal.)

So the organisation of the propers was completed, after a delay of some three or four centuries, by the organisation of the propers of the Sundays, which one might have supposed would be one of its primary elements.

The fact is that it was the idea of historical commemoration, virtually an invention of the fourth century, which first brought about the organisation of the proper at all. Once the immediate demands of that new idea had been met, the propers remained in a state which exactly reflected the development of this historical cycle of commemorations. The Sunday *ecclesia* came down from the quite different eschatological conception of worship in pre-Nicene days. It was never fitted into the historical cycle, and thus played no part in the development of the propers which this brought about. It was a curious consequence of this divorce of the Sunday cycle from the later 'christian year' that the two were so tardily brought into line in the provision of texts for their liturgical observance. Yet throughout the period from c. A.D. 400 to c. A.D. 700-800 during which the two cycles continued in use side by side in such different states of elaboration, Sunday remained what it had been in apostolic and pre-Nicene times, *the* day for corporate christian worship at the eucharist, when attendance was recognised as of obligation upon every christian. The greatest honour which could be paid to a feast of our Lord or a local patron saint was to extend to it the obligations of worship which every Sunday retained by immemorial right, and the holiday observance which Constantine had decreed for Sundays and the feasts of the martyrs. It was, indeed, only slowly that even the greatest historical feasts obtained this privilege. Sunday had been a recognised public holiday since A.D. 321, but Epiphany, for instance, was only recognised officially in the same way in the reign of Justinian c. A.D. 540 (though the celebration of games in the arena on that day was forbidden for a while c. A.D. 400).

There could, I think, be no more instructive example of the tenacity of the unconscious tradition which has everywhere governed the development of the liturgy than the history of the slow elaboration of the propers and the (to us) surprising order in which its various sections were completed. I am free to confess that in my own studies I have found in it a needed warning against the foolishness of *a priori* judgements as to the actual process of liturgical history. How many of us modern Anglicans would have supposed that the church would have felt the need for a complete service for S. Lawrence' day (August 10th), or S. Peter's Chair (February 22nd) three or four centuries before making provision for the ordinary Sundays of the year or the feast of the Annunciation? Yet so it was. And until we have recognised the fact we have not even begun to know the history of the liturgy; and until we can explain it we have not begun to understand that history or the christian mind which made it. Yet it is only by entering into that universal christian mind and thinking with it that we modern christians enter into the fulness of our christian inheritance.

### Saints' Days in the Post-Nicene Calendar

As we have seen, this was an element in the calendar which in some churches, at all events, was already in existence *c.* A.D. 150 at the latest, and which the fourth century changes did little more than systematise. Yet even here there is a very significant change in terminology, which illustrates once more the far-reaching effects of the change from an eschatological to an historical interpretation of the liturgy.

The second century word for a martyr's feast was always, as in the *Martyrdom of Polycarp*, his 'birthday' (*genethlion, natale, natalitia*). Tertullian still uses the same term for the annual intercessory 'requiem' on the 'birthdays' of less venerated christians[1] *c.* A.D. 215. The frame of mind which lies behind the term is eloquently expressed by Ignatius of Antioch a century earlier, when he feared that the Roman church might use secret influence with his judges to procure him a respite from martyrdom: 'It is good for me to die for Jesus Christ rather than to reign over the bounds of the earth. . . . The pangs of *a new birth* are upon me. . . . Do not hinder me from *living*; do not desire my death. Bestow not on the world one who desires to be God's. . . . Suffer me to receive the pure light. When I am come thither, then shall I be a man'.[2] The true life of the christian is in eternity, into which he is born by death, above all by martyrdom in which he is, as Ignatius says, 'an imitator of the passion of my God'. 'Him I seek, Who died on our behalf; Him I desire, Who rose again'.[3] As S. Paul had said before him, 'I count all things but loss for the excellency of the knowledge of Christ Jesus my Lord . . . that I may win Christ and be found in Him . . . that I may know Him and the power of His resurrection and the fellowship of His sufferings, being made conformable unto His death, if by any means I might attain unto the resurrection of the dead'.[4] The martyr did in literal fact 'count all things but loss' for Christ, and 'become conformable unto His death'. His was therefore the certainty of 'attaining unto the resurrection of the dead'. For him 'to depart and be with Christ is far better'. He had in Ignatius' words 'come thither and was now a man'. Eschatology reversed all human standards for the christian.

But by the fourth century we find a change. In the Roman calendar of A.D. 354 the entries of the martyrs' feasts are no longer designated their 'birthdays' but their 'burials' (*depositiones*). The earthly, not the heavenly, event is now the object of the liturgical celebration; time and earthly history, not eternity, have become the primary interest of the calendar. More

---

[1] *de Corona*, iii., iv.       [2] Ignatius, *Rom.*, vi. 1 and 2.
[3] *Ibid.*, 2 and 3.       [4] Phil. iii. 8 *sq.*

striking still, the old term *natale* is still used once in this fourth century calendar, on February 22nd, *Natale Petri de Cathedra*, 'The birthday' (or 'inauguration') 'of Peter's Chair'—the annual commemoration of our Lord's charge to S. Peter—'Upon this rock I will found My church'. In this passage of S. Matthew's gospel the ancient church then saw, not so much the inauguration of the Petrine primacy of the bishops of Rome (though something of this kind was understood by it in the African church from the third century onwards)[1] but the inauguration in his single person of the episcopal office, to which the other apostles were also admitted after the resurrection.[2] Here the word *natale* itself is used to designate an event which, whatever the perpetuity of its consequences, is emphatically regarded as a temporal and historical inauguration and not an eternal one. In the same way in the entry in this calendar for December 25th, 'Christ was born (*natus*) in Bethlehem of Judaea'; it is a birthday *into time*, not into eternity, which is celebrated. Through the calendar history is taking the whole place of eschatology in the understanding of the liturgy.

This fourth century Roman calendar of the *Depositiones* is interesting not only as the earliest liturgical calendar which has survived, but because in several ways it shows the first beginnings of the new ideas at work which would altogether reshape the liturgical calendar in the future. Without attempting a detailed commentary let us look at some of these.[3]

The calendar is in itself obviously a retouched edition of the official arrangements made at Rome about the calendar soon after the peace of the church, about A.D. 312.[4] But under this it is not hard to discern an earlier Roman calendar of the period before the great persecution of 303-313, whose first recension appears to be connected with the organisation of 'the cemetery' of S. Callistus, and may well date from about A.D. 240. To this nucleus additions seem to have been made during the latter part of the third century.

The first thing which strikes us is that there is no reference whatever to the original christian cycle of the Sundays and Pascha and Pentecost, or even to the relatively fixed Roman fasts of the Ember Days. The whole

---

[1] *Cf*. Cyprian, *Ep*. lix. 14; *de Unitate*, iv. (in the original text rediscovered by Rev. M. Bévenot, S.J., in his brilliant essay, *ap. Analecta Gregoriana*, xi, Rome 1938; also published as No. 4 of *The Bellarmine Series*, London 1939); Optatus, *adv. Donat*. II, ii; Augustine, *Ep*. liii.

[2] *Cf*. the non-Roman evidence cited by Batiffol, *Cathedra Petri*, Paris, 1938, *pp.* 125 *sqq*.

[3] It may be studied in various editions. Those of Mommsen, *Ueber den Chronographen von* 354 (1850), *pp.* 580 *sq*., and L. Duchesne *ap. Liber Pontificalis*, t. I, Paris, 1885, *pp.* 10 *sq*. are standard. There is a useful discussion by W. Frere, *Studies in the Early Roman Liturgy* I: *The Kalendar* (Alcuin Club Coll. XXVIII, Oxford 1930). But the above remarks follow none of the editions.

[4] Duchesne regards it as a *selection* from a Roman calendar whose full form can be reconstructed from the *Hieronymian Martyrology*. It seems to me that this fuller Roman calendar is on the contrary an *expansion* of the calendar of 354, a new edition put out *c*. A.D. 380.

movement from which the calendar and the propers are beginning to
develop is still quite outside this original christian eschatological scheme
of worship. The beginnings of the later historical cycle are there, in the
entries of Christmas (a feast which at Rome is almost certainly a fourth
century innovation) and our Lord's charge to S. Peter or 'S. Peter's Chair',
which is probably a Roman development of the later third century. But
this cycle of historical feasts of our Lord is only in its first beginnings; the
great bulk of the entries are 'burial'-days—*depositiones*—of Roman martyrs
and bishops.

What strikes us about these is first their restricted number and secondly
their local interest. Out of all the hundreds of men and women who had
shed their blood for Christ on the soil of Rome in the preceding centuries
some fifty names grouped in twenty-four feasts comprise the whole
'proper' of the Roman church. Apart from the two Roman apostles Peter
and Paul on June 29th there are no names from the first century,[1] none at
all from the second—not even Pope Telesphorus or the famous Justin and
his companions or Ptolomaeus and Lucius or the senator Apollonius,
whose *Defence of Christianity* at his trial before the senate was a piece of
christian apologetics well known even in the East.[2] Two feasts, those of Par-
thenus and Calocerus on the 19th May and of Basilla on the 22nd September,
are singled out as the result of the ten years of the Diocletian persecution,
though in fact Roman martyrdoms were then numerous. Though some
other names in the list really come from this period, the majority are
from between A.D. 220 and 260. What is also noticeable is that in every
case the location of the martyr's burial-place, and therefore of the anniversary eucharist on his festival in the chapel at his tomb, is named in the
calendar. The liturgy of saints' days is still strictly tied down to the actual
burial place of the saint commemorated. Only in the sixth century, when
the devastations of the Goths and the raids of the Lombards had made it
impossible to celebrate their festivals in the cemetery-chapels outside the
city, were the relics of the martyrs translated to new shrines in churches
within the protection of the city walls, and even then their feasts were
kept for a while only in the particular basilica in which their remains had
been re-buried. In the fourth century the liturgy in the *tituli*, the parish
churches, still kept strictly to the old eschatological cycle of pre-Nicene
times, slowly growing now by the addition of feasts of our Lord.[3] A
single eucharist, celebrated by the Pope in person or by a presbyter
specially delegated for the purpose at the martyr's tomb, formed the whole

[1] Unless the 'Clement' commemorated on November 9th with Sempronianus,
Claudius and Nicostratus, be the third bishop of Rome, c. A.D. 90–100, who wrote
the epistle to the Corinthians which we have quoted. This seems to me not very
probable.
[2] Eusebius, *E.H.*, v. xxi.
[3] The Lenten synaxes were held in the parish churches; but on week-days there
seems to have been only one such gathering, presided over by the Pope, and held at
the different churches in turn.

celebration of a saint's day, of which the parish churches took no official notice. The clergy were all there at the cemetery chapel around their bishop, along wi h the Papal choir and such of the laity as felt disposed to attend. In a curious way the liturgy of the martyrs' feasts thus retained the original character of a 'domestic' celebration of the honour of one of its members by the household of God, long after the growth of numbers had made this impossible in more than symbol in the case of the Sunday *ecclesia* in the parish churches.

The same thing holds true of the anniversary celebrations at the tombs of Popes who had not been martyrs, the day and place of which are also noted in this calendar. The list of these Papal *obits* of Popes who died in peace is complete from Pope Denys who died in 269 to Julius I who died in 352, excepting apparently Pope Marcellinus (d. A.D. 304).[1]

In the case even of great bishops like S. Silvester who had died in peace, the Roman church still hesitated, as she had in the second century, to place them quite on a level with the martyrs. There was still an element of intercession *for* them and not of complete assurance of triumph in these celebrations at their tombs. A collect for the anniversary of Pope Silvester which happens to have been preserved, illustrates well the deprecatory tone she still assumed on these occasions:

'O God, the portion in death of them that confess Thee, be graciously pleased to accept our supplications which we make on the anniversary (*in depositione*) of Thy servant Silvester the bishop; that he who laboured faithfully in the service of Thy Name, may rejoice in the everlasting company of Thy saints'.

Another prayer, the *Hanc igitur* of the same mass, shows how easily and naturally such sentiments could pass into the same sort of veneration as was felt for the martyrs: 'We beseech Thee, therefore, O Lord, graciously to look upon this oblation we humbly offer in commemoration of Saint Silvester Thy confessor and bishop; that both we may be profited by this act of devotion and he may be glorified in bliss everlasting'.

We have no means of judging when either of these prayers was composed or whether they represent successive stages in the reverence with which the memory of 'the Pope of the long peace' was regarded by future generations in the Roman church. But neither of them is likely to be older than the fifth century. The following, however, apparently composed for the funeral of Pope Sixtus III, who died in the octave of S. Lawrence and was buried near his tomb in A.D. 440, are more likely to be the work of actual

[1] He is actually entered by the scribe in the place of Pope Marcellus (A.D. 309). There is a good deal of natural confusion in records between these two names. Marcellinus was probably omitted on account of his equivocal conduct in the Diocletian persecution, though the evidence as to what the scandal actually was is late and untrustworthy. Mommsen, however, thinks he was originally included in the list, and that the muddle over the name of Marcellus is due to the accidental omission of the entry for Marcellinus. It may be so, but Duchesne is probably right in arguing for deliberate omission.

contemporaries of the dead bishop: 'O Lord our God we beseech Thee hearken to the prayers of Thy blessed martyr Lawrence and aid us; and establish the soul of Thy servant N. the bishop in the light of everlasting bliss'. 'We beseech Thee, therefore', etc. (as above) . . . 'that he who followed in the office of Thy Vicar upon the throne of blessed Peter the apostle, may by the abundance of Thy grace receive the eternal portion of the apostolic office'. Another for the funeral of Pope Simplicius (A.D. 483) seems also to be contemporary: 'We humbly entreat Thy majesty, O Lord, that the soul of Thy servant bishop Simplicius, freed from all ⟨stains⟩ which it had gathered in the flesh (humanitus) may be found worthy of the lot of all holy pastors'.[1]

We have already found in Cyril's Catecheses[2] the same distinction made in the liturgy of Jerusalem in A.D. 348 as is found in these Roman liturgical documents, between the commemoration of ' . . . the apostles and martyrs, that God by the intercession of their prayers may receive our petitions', and the intercessions of the earthly church in her turn 'on behalf of the holy fathers and bishops and generally of all who have fallen asleep among us, believing that this will be of the greatest possible assistance to their souls'. The venerated bishops of the past who happened not to have been called upon to face martyrdom are obviously tending both in East and West c. A.D. 350 to form a third group midway between the martyrs who are assuredly in heaven and the faithful departed who may still need the prayers of the church. But they are still just on the latter side of the line. And it happened that the fourth century had inherited from the third the term 'Confessor', which by an extension of meaning could be made to include these bishops.

The Confessors. It frequently happened during the third century persecutions that a christian called upon to confess his faith before the heathen authorities was not put to death, but was punished instead with torture or scourging or penal servitude, if the policy of the government for the time being happened to be one of comparative leniency. Such men and women who had not flinched before the supreme penalty but had not actually been called upon to pay it, were treated with extreme reverence by their fellow-christians if they were subsequently set at liberty, as a sort of 'living martyrs'.[3] Third century literature contains a good deal about the difficul-

[1] All these specifically Papal prayers have been accidentally preserved among the ordinary funeral prayers of the seventh century Veronese collection of older Roman and other material which goes by the misleading name of the Leonine Sacramentary. It would not be surprising, however, if in this case the prayers for the 'deposition' of Sixtus III were really from the pen of S. Leo, who was his successor in the Roman see. Both the latinity and the sentiments have a very Leonine ring.
[2] Cf. p. 194.
[3] Hippolytus, Ap. Trad., x. 1 and 2, says that such confessors (provided they have actually suffered at the hands of the authorities, and not merely undergone social inconvenience) are ipso facto to be reckoned presbyters, without ordination) though for the episcopate (still the only specifically 'priestly' order in the hierarchy, they do require the laying on of episcopal hands.

ties some of them caused by their pretensions. Terminology varied a little but by degrees 'martyr' came to be reserved strictly for those who had been killed 'out of hatred of the faith', while 'confessor' remained the title of honour for those who had witnessed for the faith without flinching, but through no fault of their own had not received the assured crown of martyrdom. There were many such among the survivors of the Diocletian persecution in the fourth century, and from their ranks were drawn many of the most revered bishops of the first generation of christian freedom. When such men came to die in the course of nature, there could be little hesitation about setting them freely alongside their brethren who had suffered death at the hands of the persecutors. And it happened that many of these men after the peace of the church had to endure fresh persecutions at the hands of the Arian government under the emperors of his house who succeeded Constantine. The assimilation to the 'confessors' of the Diocletian persecution of all who suffered with them in these fresh troubles was inevitable. And so we find in an invocation (wrongly) ascribed to S. Ambrose, the distinction already accepted, 'I ask for the prayers of the martyrs, who did not hesitate to shed their blood for the truth ... I entreat the intercessions of the confessors, who endured the battle with our enemy the tempter, while they lived a holy life in the catholic peace, or also the gainsaying of the heretics in the lengthy conflict, and to say truth, won the palms of a longer-drawn-out and secret martyrdom'.[1] The 'confessors' are here becoming any men of holy life who have rendered great service to the church without martyrdom.

The step of adding such names to the official calendar was probably taken first, and with a certain hesitation, in the East. It was indeed difficult to draw any clear lines of distinction. S. Gregory Nazianzene's funeral oration for S. Athanasius clearly regards its subject as a saint already in glory. But having regard to the innumerable troubles inflicted on Athanasius by the allied Arians, jews and pagans, such a man could well be numbered with the 'confessors' in the old sense, quite apart from the unique services he had rendered to the church both as bishop and as theologian. The decisive step was taken in Gaul, where the uniquely beloved apostle of rural France, S. Martin of Tours, whose gentle sweetness and supernatural holiness of life had been the joy and awe of his flock during his own lifetime, was treated as a saint in heaven from the moment of his death. Yet a note scribbled by his biographer and devoted friend Sulpicius Severus on the day the sad news reached him, shews how strong the old tradition still was, and how much the innovation was felt to need excuse: 'He is with the apostles and prophets ... second to none in the company of the righteous as I hope, I believe, I am certain. ... For though the state of the times afforded him no chance of martyrdom, yet he will not lack the glory of a martyr, for in desire and in courage he could have

---

[1] Pseudo-Ambrose, *Precatio*, ii. 19. P.L., xvii. 842.

faced martyrdom and gladly (if he had been born in the days of Hadrian or Diocletian) . . . but though he did not bear these pains, he fulfilled his martyrdom without shedding his blood' by his sufferings in the cares of his office, his unwearied asceticism and his missionary labours.[1] A few days latel all hesitations are gone. In a note to his wife's mother Sulpicius writes, in words which the Gallican church afterwards set to music as part of S. Martin's office, 'Martin with joy is received into Abraham's bosom; Martin, here poor and humble, enters heaven rich; thence, as I hope, our protector, he looks down on me as I write this and on you as you read it'.[2]

Sulpicius is already a Frenchman with his wit and his exquisite style and his *idées claires*. There is the silver clarity of the landscapes of his own Touraine in his singing gallic Latin. But Rome had not the quickness of Gaul in accepting new ideas. The *Gelasian Sacramentary*, the Roman rite of the sixth century, still contains no Roman bishops who were not martyrs (or who were not supposed to have been). Even the *Gregorian Sacramentary c.* A.D. 600 contains only two, SS. Silvester and Leo. To these the seventh century soon added the name of S. Gregory himself, and it was with these three episcopal 'confessors' (in this new sense) alone in its calendar that the book was adopted by Alcuin *c.* A.D. 790–800.

But the Gallican churches for centuries had been accustomed to include the *depositiones* of their own past bishops who had not been martyrs among their feasts, and not merely among the anniversaries of the other christian dead. They naturally soon adapted the Roman book to their own custom and calendar. In the same way we find that the Carthaginian calendar of the early sixth century[3] already commemorates the *depositiones* of the Carthaginian bishops, and the great names of other African sees like S. Augustine of Hippo, apparently on a level with the martyrs. The inclusion of the names of great ascetics and monks had already begun in Egypt in the late fourth century, and was justified on the same lines as had been the innovation in the case of S. Martin at Tours. So the way was opened to the expansion of the calendar to include all classes of saintly christians and not the martyrs only. But there can be no doubt that it was from the fusion of the two lists of the anniversaries of the martyrs and the anniversaries of bishops who had not been martyrs that this expansion first began.

*The feasts of our Lady, Apostles, S. Michael, etc.* The process by which the great names of the New Testament came to be included in the calendar is similarly a slow one, and for the first 800 years of christian history was clearly dominated by the same sort of considerations of local interest which governed the calendar of the martyrs. We have seen that at Jerusalem in A.D. 348 the prophets and apostles of biblical history were already included in the eucharistic prayer along with the local martyrs, because at Jerusalem they could be considered as being among the glories of the *local*

---

[1] Sulpicius Severus, *Ep.* I.      [2] *Ibid., Ep.* III.
[3] First published by Dom J. Mabillon, *Analecta Vetera*, vol. iii., p. 398.

church. At Rome in the same period they kept only the feast of SS. Peter and Paul, who had been martyred on the soil of Rome. And even so, the date chosen for their joint festival, June 29th, commemorates not the day of their deaths, but a temporary removal of their relics from their separate tombs (on the Vatican and by the road to Ostia) to a safer hiding-place in the catacombs of S. Sebastian during the Decian persecution of the third century. This feast is therefore a monument of local church history and not a repercussion of the New Testament on the calendar, and is as closely connected with the cultus of relics and the burial places of the saints as any other martyr's feast.

The real beginnings of the deliberate association of the New Testament with the calendar of the saints are obscure, but they must probably be sought in the East in connection with the spread to other churches of the 'Jerusalem model', which would not have the same *local* justification elsewhere than in the city of its origin. From our modern point of view the process by which this association of the N.T. with the calendar came about is surprising, because it is not governed by doctrinaire considerations of what would best complete the calendar, but primarily by the availability of relics, or supposed relics, around which the liturgical commemorations of N.T. saints could take form.

It is for this reason that—to take an instance surprising enough to the modern way of thinking—the feasts of our Lady are as a class so slow in their development. There were no relics available. Of her five great feasts in the modern Western church, two—the Purification and the Annunciation—begin really as feasts of our Lord. The Assumption is added to the historical cycle concerning the events of our Lord's life as a sort of afterthought, before the seventh century and apparently first in Syria.[1] The feasts of the Nativity and Conception of our Lady appear to have been added to the Eastern calendars sporadically in the seventh-eighth centuries to complete, as it were, a lesser historical cycle of events in our Lady's life. But it is significant that the oldest Eastern feast of our Lady, historically speaking, is that which we call 'the Visitation' (officially accepted at Rome only in 1389), which is really the feast of the deposition in the church of Blachernae at Constantinople of a relic of our Lady's veil in the year A.D. 469. Even in the case of our Lady the cultus of 'secondary' relics is thus at the basis of the idea of liturgical commemoration.

At Rome none of the five great feasts of our Lady is older than *c*. A.D. 700, when the Purification, Annunciation, Assumption and Nativity were

---

[1] The first definite reference to a liturgical celebration of her *koimēsis* (Falling Asleep) seems to be in a sermon by Modestus, Patriarch of Jerusalem, who died in A.D. 634 (M.P.G., lxxxvi. 3301 *sqq.*), but it was not then a new institution. This seems to be the feast on August 15th, the date eventually adopted by East and West. But there are obscure traces of an Egyptian feast in January which is probably older than Modestus' time, and the Gallican churches for a while adopted this January feast.

taken over from Byzantium by the Syrian Pope Sergius I. The Immaculate Conception was a feast (and a doctrine) first developed in the West in the Anglo-Saxon England of the early eleventh century on an older and rather different Byzantine basis.[1] In the twelfth century it began to spread on the continent under English auspices, though in the face of a good deal of opposition. It was officially accepted at Rome only by Pope Sixtus IV in 1477, though it had been observed in some churches there for at least half a century before. (The doctrine on which the Anglo-Saxons had based their observance was not officially promulgated by Rome for nearly another five centuries after this, when Pius IX did so in 1854.) The only older Roman commemoration of our Lady is the special character given to the mass of the Octave Day of Christmas in the *Gregorian Sacramentary* (*c.* A.D. 600) as the commemoration of the reality of Mary's motherhood of Jesus. The Gregorian texts of this are very beautiful and evangelical in themselves, and very exactly in keeping with the teaching of the Council of Chalcedon in A.D. 451 as to the complete reality of His Manhood as Son of Mary. But comparison with the *Gelasian Sacramentary* of the previous century shows that this special character of the Octave Day at Rome did not go back far behind A.D. 600, and it afterwards disappeared in face of the Byzantine and Gallican custom of keeping that day as the feast of the Circumcision of our Lord.[2]

The feasts of apostles and evangelists, etc., which are found in the Western calendars, and many of which have been inherited from them by the Book of Common Prayer, are mostly not very ancient and have curiously mixed origins. The feast of S. Andrew on November 30th is among the oldest and goes back to the fifth century. It appears to be connected in some way with a famous relic of the saint which eventually found a resting place in S. Peter's. The feast of S. John on December 27th is likewise of the fifth or even perhaps the later fourth century, and seems to have originated at Jerusalem, though the evidence is rather confused. That of SS. Philip and James on May 1st is really the dedication or rededication feast of a Roman church containing relics of these apostles in A.D. 561. Similarly the feast of S. John before the Latin Gate (May 6th) is the dedication feast of a Roman basilica near the *Porta Latina* in the time of Pope Hadrian I *c.* A.D. 790, though the event the liturgy commemorates (an attempt to martyr S. John the apostle during an alleged visit to Rome in the reign of Nero) was already traditional at Rome when Tertullian reported it *c.* A.D. 200.[3] But it is likely that the Roman date was chosen to agree with an older Eastern feast commemorating a miracle wrought by the relics of the apostle at his tomb in Ephesus. Of the feasts of S. John the

[1] Naples had for a while kept the Byzantine feast in the tenth century, but it was afterwards discontinued there under Roman influence.

[2] But the 'Gregorian' character of January 1st as a celebration of Mary's motherhood still dominates the office for the day in the Roman Breviary.

[3] *Lib. de Praescr.*, 36.

D.S.L.

Baptist, the Nativity on June 24th depends for its date on the Western celebration of our Lord's birthday on December 25th, and S. John's feast is as we should expect, like Christmas, of Western origin. S. Augustine remarks that it was celebrated in Africa 'by the tradition of our forefathers', which carries us back at all events to *c*. A.D. 375, perhaps rather earlier. The feast appears to have been accepted at Rome during the fifth century. The other feast of the Baptist on August 29th, kept in the West as the anniversary of his martyrdom, seems to be the original Eastern feast of the Baptist, and commemorates the supposed finding of his relics. It is probably not older than the fifth century and was not accepted at Rome before the middle ages. The feast of S. Michael on September 29th commemorates the dedication of a chapel in honour of the archangel in the suburbs of Rome (destroyed many centuries ago) at some date during the sixth century. The feast of S. Stephen, December 26th, seems to have originated at Jerusalem in the fourth century (before December 25th had been accepted there as the date of our Lord's birth). The supposed discovery of his relics in Palestine A.D. 415 caused great excitement in christendom, and after this his feast was rapidly propagated everywhere by the bringing home of numerous portions of these by returning pilgrims.[1] The feast seems to have been adopted at Rome with less delay than usual, soon after the middle of the fifth century, and the same holds true of the feast of the Holy Innocents on December 28th, which was observed in Africa in Augustine's time.[2] The feast of S. Peter's Chains on August 1st commemorates the dedication of a Roman basilica in A.D. 461, in which the relic of the apostle's chains was preserved.

These are the only festivals of New Testament personages found in the *Gregorian Sacramentary* sent to France in A.D. 790 for Alcuin's liturgical reform. It is obvious how closely connected most of them are with the cultus of relics. But none of them have anything like the antiquity or the interest of the third century feast of S. Peter's Chair on February 22nd.[3] Most of the other feasts of apostles, etc., in the Prayer Book Calendar are of later date. That of the Conversion of S. Paul on January 25th, which is a feast of Gallican origin, commemorates a translation of some portion of

[1] For the interest excited in Africa and the spread of the cultus of S. Stephen there in the years after 415, *cf.* S. Augustine, *Serm.* 316, 320, 321, 322, 323, 324; *Ep.* 212; *de Civitate*, xxii. 8, etc.
[2] The name 'Innocents' appears to have been a Roman peculiarity. The African name was *Infantes*, a name also found in Spain, where the feast was observed (more logically) after Epiphany.
[3] The alternative date for this on January 18th is a later Gallican device for removing the feast out of the possible orbit of Lent, when no feasts were kept in Gaul. (The duplication of the feast in the Roman calendar dates only from the sixteenth century.) The supposed connection of the feast with the ancient curule chair said to have been used by S. Peter as his *cathedra*, and now preserved under the bronze Papal throne in S. Peter's, only goes back to the sixth century (Duchesne, *Origines du culte chrétien, p.* 269) though the chair itself is a genuine relic of imperial pagan antiquity, and might be authentic.

his relics to an unknown basilica in the South of France somewhere in the fifth or sixth century. All Saints' Day begins as the dedication feast of the Roman church of S. Mary and All Martyrs (constructed out of the old first century Baths of Agrippa) on May 13th in A.D. 609 or 610. The date was arbitrarily transferred to November 1st during the first half of the ninth century to make it easier to supply the numerous pilgrims with provisions, which were apt to be scarce at Rome in May.[1]

The amplification of this haphazard collection of feasts into a series which should contain all the chief names in the New Testament only begins in the tenth century and was not really completed before the fifteenth, and then only in the roughest fashion. In the Book of Common Prayer it has not been completed yet, since the name of S. Joseph is still missing from the calendar of Red Letter Days, though some Anglo-Saxon churches had observed a feast in his honour on March 19th before the Norman Conquest. It was grudgingly accepted as a commemoration of the lowest rank in the Roman calendar by Pope Sixtus IV in 1474 along with another festival (also of old English origin in the West), that of S. Anne. The East has completed the commemorations of the New Testament saints on quite different dates and with an equal lack of consistent plan, though with greater thoroughness and at a rather earlier period (in the seventh-eighth centuries for the most part). The propers for these Western feasts are mostly of mediaeval arrangement.

Thus this last mediaeval stage of the rounding off of the calendar is only the end of a long process which begins in the fourth century with the exchange of feasts between churches, as East and West exchanged Epiphany and Christmas, or as Rome and Constantinople later exchanged SS. Peter and Paul and the Annunciation. There are the first signs of the beginning of this process in the Roman calendar of the *depositiones* in 354. In this list two entries, those of the famous second century African martyrs SS. Perpetua and Felicity in March and the third century S. Cyprian of Carthage in September, stand out as the only non-Roman names in the list. But in each case the entries are marked 'in Africa', and no Roman locality for the celebration of the eucharist in their honour is attached to the anniversary,[2] which suggests that there was as yet no *liturgical* cultus of these foreigners at Rome. But other churches soon adopted some of the most famous Roman saints, *e.g.* S. Lawrence. At first they translated some small portion of the saint's relics or even napkins which had been in contact with them, to serve as an excuse for the festival—so inseparable was

---

[1] Beleth, *Rationale*, 127. M.P.L., ccii. But Frere (*op. cit., pp.* 136 *sqq.*) gives reasons for suspecting that the feast of Nov. 1 originated as the dedication feast of a chapel dedicated to All Saints in S. Peter's at Rome by Pope Gregory III (A.D. 731–741).

[2] The word *celebratur* in the notice of S. Cyprian is probably a corruption for 'Cornelius', the Roman martyr honoured on that day, as Mommsen and Duchesne are agreed.

the connection of the cultus with the actual relics of the saints down to the end of the fourth century. It was only when the idea of historical commemorations as such had grown familiar from the cycle of feasts of our Lord that martyrs' feasts could begin to be borrowed freely between different churches without this pretext. Such interchange of saints was one little aspect of the slow post-Nicene breaking down of the old self-centredness of the city-bishoprics. This was never undertaken as a policy by the church, as Diocletian and Constantine undertook to centralise the old self-government of the city-republics. It came about voluntarily and gradually in answer to the new needs of the times for corporate rather than parallel action between the churches, and the process was by no means complete for centuries after the Roman empire fell.

But this borrowing of martyrs' feasts began to enrich the local calendars with something more than their old parochial interest during the later fourth century. Yet it was centuries before the ordinary lay-people felt the same interest in 'imported' saints, however illustrious, as they had always felt towards their own local martyrs, however obscure, fellow-citizens of their own as they felt these to be and a credit to the town. S. Augustine has a charming little sermon for the feast of the Roman S. Lawrence which begins: 'The martyrdom of the blessed Lawrence is famous—but at Rome, not here, so few of you do I see before me this morning! Exactly as the glory of the city of Rome cannot be hid, so the glory of its martyr Lawrence cannot be hidden either. I do not understand how the glory of so great a city came to be overlooked by you. So your little gathering shall hear only a little sermon, for I myself am feeling too tired and hot to manage a long one'.[1]

Perhaps the heat of a Tunisian August had something to do with the small attendance that day, but it is another story when we look at the texts with which the churches celebrated their own native saints. 'Though the unity of the faith makes us all venerate with one and the same honour the glorious sufferings of all the martyrs which various places in different provinces have deserved to nurture, and they should have no difference in the reverence paid them who all died in the same good cause: yet love of one's own city (civilis amor) claims something for itself in the rendering of homage, and his native province adds a natural affection to the honouring of God's grace in the martyr. For all the greater is that joy whereto assists the love of one's own town (patriae affectus). And this we owe to the holy and most blessed Vincent, whose we are as he is ours. He has exalted the people of his native soil as their patron and their glory'. That is the opening of the mass of S. Vincent in the Mozarabic rite that spread from Toledo all over Spain. But one cannot doubt that the text is originally the product of civilis amor, that the words were first composed in his own church of Saragossa—'Whose we are as he is ours'.[2] Or take again the Gallican proper

[1] Serm. 303.    [2] Liber Mozarabicus Sacramentorum, ed. cit. col. 112.

preface for the feast of S. Saturninus of Toulouse, the pre-Nicene martyr-bishop whom legend declared to have been consecrated by the hands of S. Peter himself: 'It is very meet and right. . . . And most chiefly should we praise Thine almighty power, O God in Trinity, with special devotion and the service of our words of supplication for the triumphant sufferings of all Thy saints: But especially are we bound at this time to exalt with due honour the blessed Saturninus, the most loud-thundering (*conclamantis-simum*) witness of Thine awful Name: whom the mob of the heathen when they thrust him from the temple thrust also into heaven. Nevertheless thine high-priest sent forth frcm Eastern regions to the city of the Tolo-satians, in this Rome of the Garonne as Vicar of Thy Peter fulfilled both his episcopate and martyrdom. Therefore . . .'.[1] 'This Rome of the Garonne'! There is all the Frenchman's deep and tender feeling for his *pays natal* behind the deliciously absurd phrase. And how little French provincial catholicism has changed in its spirit and taste in all the fourteen centuries or so since this was written! The pretentious language in such homely Latin of many of these Gallican prayers is the equivalent of the heavy white marble statues, the gilt wire stands of ferns and the innumer-able overwrought candlesticks and devotional bric-a-brac that express the real pride and affection of *les paroissiens* for the parish churches of the smaller country towns of France to this day.

This special pride and trust in the local martyrs was not a new thing in the fourth century. In the third century Origen records that he had learned from his own teachers in the faith that the martyrs prayed especially for their own beloved children, and that the blood of its martyrs was especially potent to increase their own church.[2] They were not only its greatest glory and fulfilment before God, but a sort of permanent deputation from it in the presence of God Himself to plead its needs.[3] (There is assimilation here between christian and civic life. Deputations to the emperor to plead the needs or excuse the faults of the cities were of frequent occurrence. To be chosen to take part in such an embassy by one's fellow-citizens was a signal recognition of merit.) It was but natural that in the fourth century as the whole population of a town was by degrees converted, those who had for so long been regarded as the special patrons of the church there should come to be regarded as the heavenly patrons of the town itself, of all their own fellow-citizens now identical with the membership of the local church. The guardian gods of the cities had always been regarded by pagans as in some sense their fellow-citizens, a sort of heavenly senators, with an interest in the city similar to that of its earthly inhabitants. In the popular mind the local martyrs inevitably succeeded to the same position when faith in the power of the old guardians died. It was after all only through

---

[1] *Missale Gothicum*, No. xvi. ed. Dom J. Mabillon, *de Liturgia Gallicana* (1729), p. 220.

[2] *Exhortation to Martyrdom*, xxx. lviii., *cf. in Jesu Nave Hom.*, xvi. 5.

[3] Eusebius, *de Mart. Pal.*, 7, *cf. Acta* of S. Fructuosus, 5 (*c.* A.D . 250).

their heroism in the past that the local church had survived. Now that city and bishopric were two sides of the same thing, services to the one had become services to the other. The fortitude of the martyr, the splendour of his shrine and the multitude of his miracles became objects of civic pride, like the great deeds of other bygone sons of the city and the handsomeness of other public buildings. The fantastic exaggerations and downright inventions introduced into the edifying histories told to visitors at the shrine were the product not so much of superstition as of local patriotism.

That there were many deplorable excesses and abuses in all this ought not to be denied. The old feast-days of the city gods had had a social side to them as detestable to the pre-Nicene church as their religious aspect. (They were indeed often occasions of special danger to christians from the mob.) They had been public holidays, given over by pagans to merry-making much more than to prayer, which often degenerated into wild licence. As early as A.D. 321 Constantine had ordered that the feasts of the martyrs should be public holidays like Sundays, but this does not seem to have been carried out until, with the decline of pagan numbers and the decay and suppression of pagan public worship, the feasts of the new christian patrons succeeded gradually to the public honours of the old pagan ones. Unfortunately, though the church insisted as paganism had never done on the strictly religious object of such festivals, the old way of celebrating them was too often transferred by the people to the new celebration. Such popular holidays always carry with them the same tendencies whatever their occasion (*cf.* Good Friday as a Bank Holiday in England). The remaining pagans and other enemies of the church were quick to take scandal, and to accuse the church of 'turning the idols into martyrs and their banquets into *agapae*', as Faustus the Manichee declared in controversy with Augustine.[1] That this was in effect what often happened is true, but it is only fair to the church to say that we know of it chiefly from the energetic measures she took to counter the danger, and the passionate remonstrances of the clergy. And it had its good side. If the church was to christianise daily life, the civic pride of the towns and their local patriotism were the healthiest forces left in public life. In the collapse of civilisation that was coming they were going to be of incalculable value in maintaining such public order and cohesion as survived. In strengthening these things by giving them a christian focus and consecration the church was fulfilling the new social function which had fallen to her for the future better than she understood. But this does not lessen the force of Augustine's shamed admission to Faustus that in this matter the teaching of the church about the martyrs was one thing, and what she had to put up with from the practice of christians was too often another.[2]

[1] Augustine, *contra Faustum*, xx. 21.
[2] The accusation that the christian martyrs themselves were often unhistorical and only the old gods under a thin disguise, deliberately left by the church to satisfy the incurably polytheistic population, is unfair and has repeatedly been dis-

Despite the devotion of particular churches to their own martyrs, the importing of foreign saints into local calendars, for which the ecclesiastical authorities rather than the people were usually responsible, did as a rule do something to maintain a sense of proportion. Thus we find from the sermons of S. Augustine that the church of Hippo in his day kept not only the feasts of African martyrs with uncouth Punic names like Guddens, and the *depositiones* of its own past bishops, like that Leontius whose anniversary fell one year upon Ascension Day, but foreigners like the Roman Lawrence and the Spaniards Fructuosus of Tarragona and Vincent of Saragossa.

Two interesting fragments of calendars from the later fifth century illustrate very well the stage which had by then been reached in this blending of the old local and the newer universal characteristics. The one, probably rather the later in date, is from Spain, found in an inscription in the 'Court of the Orange Trees' which still surrounds the old church of Santa Maria la Mayor—'Great S. Mary's'—at Carmona, not far from Seville. It is incomplete, but apparently lists all the feasts observed there in the first six months of the year *c.* A.D. 480.

'Dec. 25. Nativity of our Lord Jesus Christ according to the flesh.

Dec. 26. S. Stephen.

Dec. 27. S. John the apostle. [Most Spanish churches kept the Spanish S. Eugenia on this day and postponed S. John to the 29th.]

Jan. 21. SS. Fructuosus, bishop and Augurius and Eulogius, deacons [Spanish MM. *c.* A.D. 250 at Tarragona].

Jan. 22. S. Vincent, deacon [M. at Saragossa, Spain].

May 2. S. Felix, deacon [M. at Seville, Spain].

May 4. S. Threpta, virgin [An early South Spanish saint of whom little is known].

May 13. SS. Crispin [bishop?, Martyred at Ecija, near Seville] and Mucius [*i.e.* Mōkios, a M. of Constantinople, whose relics—and consequently cultus —were widely distributed over the West in the early fifth century].

June 19. SS. Gervase and Protase [MM. at Milan, the discovery of whose relics by S. Ambrose (A.D. 386) attracted great interest all over the West].

June 20. S. John the Baptist.'[1]

Here the calendar breaks off. The long gap between January and May

proved (*cf. e.g.*, H. Delehaye, *Les Origines du culte des martyrs*, 1933). The martyrs were (as a rule) genuine enough; their names and the dates of their *depositiones* were handed down by unbroken liturgical tradition at their tombs. But they *did* succeed in the popular mind to the position of the old city-gods, and there *was* assimilation in the manner of popular cultus. Popular fancy later produced legends on a conventional pattern which are often wildly remote from the true circumstances of the saint as revealed by contemporary sources. 'What the Virger said' to the pilgrims is rarely in the nature of historical evidence.

[1] The inscription was discovered and published by Padre Fita y Colomé in 1909, but can be conveniently studied in Dom Férotin's ed. of the Mozarabic *Liber Sacramentorum*, 1912, *pp.* xliii. *sq.*

is due to the possible range of Lent, during which no feasts were observed in Spain. What is more surprising is the absence of the (originally Eastern) feast of the Epiphany and 'The Murder of the Infants' (Holy Innocents) missing in January, since both were kept in most Spanish churches by this time. Perhaps it is due to the carelessness of the stone-cutter; more probably Carmona was a rather old-fashioned country church. Half the entries are still those of the old Spanish martyrs, though the 'international' saints of the New Testament are making their appearance. But the lesser apostles like Matthias are still some centuries from inclusion; and the Eastern feast of the Purification, already in use at Jerusalem for a century, is like the (later) Annunciation still not mentioned. There is a hint of Roman influence in the dating of S. John the apostle, and it is probably by way of Rome that the Jerusalem feast of S. Stephen has reached Carmona. The translation of relics has introduced the foreigners Gervase and Protase from Milan and the Byzantine Mucius.

The other calendar comes from a very different church. Spanish christianity was urban in organisation, with deep roots in pre-Nicene traditions, and was even then fanatically orthodox. The Goths were nomad barbarians preying upon the collapsing imperial provinces in the inner Balkans, whose wandering churches were tents, like the dwellings of their loosely organised tribes. They had received baptism only in the later fourth century, at the hands of missionaries from the Eastern church during the long Arian domination of Constantinople, and were consequently firmly imbued with the Arian heresy. A fragment of a Gothic calendar which has survived—a tiny relic of the Ostrogothic kingdom of Italy in the fifth century—reveals a glimpse of their church life in the Balkans before their migration to the West and the sack of Rome. All that survives is the list of feasts from October 23–November 30.[1]

'Oct. 23. Numerous martyrs for the folk of the Goths, and Frithigern (?) [Probably refers to the first christian Gothic chief. A number of his followers were martyred by his pagan overlord, Athanaric, though Frithigern escaped to Constantinople A.D. 369].

Oct. 29. Memorial of the martyrs who with the priest Wereka and the clerk Batwins were burnt in their church for the folk of the Goths. [The Greek historian Sozomen (*E.H.* vi. 37) records this burning alive of a whole Gothic congregation in their church-tent in the same persecution of Athanaric *c*. A.D. 370.]

Nov. 3. Constantius the emperor [of Constantinople, *d.* A.D. 361. A fierce Arian, patron of the first Arian Gothic missionary Ulphilas].

Nov. 4. Dorotheus the bishop [Arian bp. of Constantinople, and a sort of pope of Eastern Arianism, *d.* A.D. 407].

---

[1] This calendar was found at Milan, and published by H. Achelis, *Zeitschrift für N.T. Wissenschaft*, I (1900), *pp.* 309 *sq.* I follow the corrections and comments of H. Delehaye, *Analecta Bollandiana*, xxi., *pp.* 275 *sq.*

Nov. 14. Philip the apostle at Jerusalem.

Nov. 19. Memorial of the Old Women martyrs at Beroea, to the number of 40 [A group of Greek pre-Nicene martyrs in Thrace, honoured also in Greek calendars].

Nov. 30. Andrew the apostle'.

Here again the local—in this case tribal—martyrs are a prominent element in the calendar, reinforced by a sectarian interest in Arianism. The confessors (in the persons of Frithigern, Constantius and Dorotheus) who had not suffered martyrdom have found a place beside them in this Eastern calendar, though it is probably rather older than the Spanish one, which still admits none but martyrs and New Testament commemorations. The pre-Nicene Beroean martyrs are a mark of the Thracian origin of the first mission to the Goths. The influence of Constantinople, headquarters of Arianism in the second half of the fourth century, during which the Goths were converted, is strong; and that of the local Jerusalem calendar is seen in the entry of Philip, as it is in that of Stephen in the Spanish list. The feast of S. Andrew is Constantinopolitan and Thracian (he was said to have evangelised Thrace, and his relics were translated thence to Constantinople in A.D. 363) but it was becoming universal in the later fifth century, as we have said.

The fascinating thing is to see precisely the same sorts of influence at work (with local variations) in the same period upon the liturgy of the Arian nomads of the Balkans and that of the urban catholics of Spain in the old civilised imperial world—two churches as far apart in ecclesiastical tendency as they were geographically, socially and racially.

### The Fourth Century and the Liturgy

It is time to sum up, to see the trees of this long chapter as a wood.

The pagan Roman empire was like some great crucible, into which were poured all the streams of culture welling up out of the dimness of pre-history; from Egypt and Mesopotamia, even in lesser degree from Persia and in thin trickles from the alien worlds of India and China; in Anatolia from the long-dead Hittite empire and old Phrygia; as well as from Minoan Crete and Achaean Greece and Ionia, and from semitic Tyre and Carthage. All these, with the raw cultures of the North and West, were formed by the dying flame of Hellas and the hardness of Rome into the unified mediterranean world of the first and second centuries—the *Civitas Romana*.[1] Into that had flowed all the forces of antiquity. Out of it must come anything that could create a future different from itself.

But in the third century the mixture curdled and crusted. The empire

[1] *Universum regnum in tot civitatibus constitutum dicitur Romana Civitas.* Augustine, *de Consensu Evang.*, ii. 58. For the awe which the universality and duration of Roman rule already excited in the first century A.D. see Dionysius of Halicarnassus, *Rom. Ant.* I. iii. 3.

was an awe-inspiring achievement, the apotheosis of human power. In the last analysis it represented nothing else but the lust of the flesh and the pride of life triumphant and organised to the point of stability. After the accession of the emperor Aurelian in A.D. 275, despite economic difficulties and military disasters, the third century empire looked as though it might perpetuate itself indefinitely, simply because it had absorbed into its own system or crushed to impotence every earthly force which might have transformed it into something new. The alternative to it was sheer blind chaos. And the extremely able political and military reorganisation of Diocletian *c.* A.D. 300 gave promise of further strengthening its basis. The very universality and success of the empire, as Augustine saw, were deadly to the future.[1] In such a case history for centuries to come would have consisted of a long record of pointless civil wars and palace politics, varied only by natural disasters and the measures taken for their remedy. Something of what that would have meant for the human spirit may be guessed from the fascinating but in the last resort stagnant and suffocating history of Byzantium and its strange frozen civilisation, where Diocletian's empire dressed in christian vestments continued immobile for another thousand years.

The catalytic came from Judaea. The death and resurrection of Jesus of Nazareth in themselves caused no tremor or sound in the wider Roman world. But from them sprang the christian church—the one element in that world which refused to be included in the imperial synthesis. The empire made one convulsive effort after another to annihilate this alien force within itself, or at least to disperse its power of effectual challenge as it had done with judaism. That is the inner meaning of the long agony of the persecutions, and the obstinacy of the christian refusal to conform to emperor-worship. That worship seems to us now a mere convention and so it was then, in the sense that no thoughtful pagan took it with any seriousness in the theological sense. But it was a convention which summed up profoundly the whole theory upon which the empire was built and all human life was lived—the apotheosis of human power. We who have lived to see the terrible force of such conventions in similar totalitarian states can better understand the third century than the historians of the last generation.

Diocletian undertook the final life-and-death struggle to annihilate the church reluctantly, as the *sine qua non*, the necessary completion, of his drastic reorganisation and renewal of the empire. The reign of Constantine was the open acknowledgment of the empire's final impotence to rid itself of the church. But the end is not quite yet. The church's struggle against Arianism and its imperial patrons in the fourth century is only the defeat of the last attempt of the empire, and of imperial pagan thought in a new

---

[1] *Tantummodo mortalis est ista victoria (terrenae civitatis),* Augustine, *de Civ. Dei,* xv. 4. See the whole passage, one of the most penetrating in this brilliant but uneven book.

christian disguise, to have its own way with the christian church from within. It is virtually ended with the dying cry of the sentimental reactionary Julian, the last emperor of the old tradition, 'Thou hast conquered, Galilaean!'—whether in fact Julian ever uttered the words or no.

For three and a half centuries—or for ten times as long as Augustine saw it, ever since the Tower of Babel—'Two loves had built two cities',— and now at last came the final creative synthesis of the whole of antiquity. In one swift generation c. A.D. 375–410 the *Civitas Romana* bowed itself at last to enter the City of God, and was baptised upon its deathbed like so many of its sons. But it died christian in the end, which was all that mattered after it was dead.

It is not merely that in this period the effective majority of the governing classes and even of the masses accepted christian beliefs and began to receive christian sacraments, though that is the external fact. But now life as a whole, social and political life as well as the personal conduct of individuals, begins for the first time to feel the impact of the gospel and to be framed on christian assumptions. A gentler spirit invades the laws regarding women and slaves. Christian piety begins to cover the world with orphanages and hospitals for the sick and refuges for the aged. They were too few for the miseries of the times, but they were the product of a charity which paganism had never known at all. The worst atrocities of the amphitheatre, the gladiatorial butcheries, were ended just after A.D. 400 in response to christian protests. Political power was first made to acknowledge that it, too, as well as private actions, is subject to the law of God, when the emperor Theodosius was obliged to do public penance as a christian communicant for ordering a massacre at Thessalonica, for which no one would have thought of calling his predecessors to account.

It is easy enough to exaggerate the practical achievements of the christian church in these directions during this last generation of the real Roman empire. Social life was only beginning to be christianised. But what was done is not to be discounted. When one understands the sort of things which passed unquestioned in the world of the first three centuries[1] one appreciates better the significance of the christian empire. When all due allowance has been made for the malice of the pagan writers and their desire for literary effect, the lurid picture which S. Paul draws of gentile life in Romans i. can be substantiated point by point from Suetonius and Tacitus, the accepted self-portraits of paganism. It is not that there was nothing noble in pagan manhood; there was much, for man is not by nature ignoble. But it is when one considers, for instance in Plutarch's *Life of Brutus,* the sort of flaws in character and conduct which the thoughtful ethical philosopher was then prepared to tolerate in a man whom he sincerely regarded as decently virtuous and held up for admiration, that one sees the vastness of the change the gospel brought to the *theory* of

[1] *Cf. e.g.* Tacitus, *Annals* VI, v. 9.

human life. The unlimited right of power, deliberate cruelty, lust, the calculated oppression of the helpless, these things were accepted motives in pagan life. They did not disappear at the end of the fourth century with the christian triumph; they were not even more than checked in practice. But at least they were now publicly reprobated and challenged in the name of justice, pity, purity and mercy. They were beginning to be generally regarded in practice as sins, and not as the inevitable and natural way in which men may behave when they can.

This was the achievement of the church in the fourth century, and it is to my mind a great one, though it is not always appreciated either by christian moralists or secular historians. Our own age has been shocked by the cynical horrors of which its own neo-paganism has proved capable, to the point of determination that *the symptoms* must be eradicated by force, cost what it may. But I do not see why such things should greatly surprise students of classical antiquity. They are among the familiar fruits of the pagan ideal, the apotheosis of human power. Perhaps modern christians and post-christians alike, weary of the tension of christian belief in a deeply secularised order of society, have been over-anxious to hurry the church back to the catacombs, from which she emerged to put an end to this pagan theory of human life. If she should ever return to them she would survive, as Russia shews; but it would be the worse for the world. That theory in some form is Europe's only alternative religion, whether men try to set in the place of the Faith 'our Saviour Adolf Hitler'[1] or the ikon of Lenin or the inscrutable wisdom and providence of an impersonal L.C.C. The men and women who refuted and smashed that theory of the sufficiency of power were the noble army of martyrs. If popular devotion at once lost its sense of proportion between the honour due to the martyrs and the worship of the martyrs' Lord, it is at least evidence of the immensity of the general gratitude for the martyrs' achievement and the reality of the ordinary man's sense of release.

The extent to which the church gained or lost in her inner spirituality by her entrance into the world may be argued endlessly, but the conventional contrast between a comparatively spotless pre-Nicene church and a corrupt fourth century establishment is not borne out by the evidence. One has only to read attentively the pre-Nicene fathers or even the epistles of the New Testament to find glaring examples of all the faults save one which can fairly be charged against the church of the fourth century. As Augustine said 'These two cities (of God and the world) are confounded together in this world and are utterly mingled with each other, until they be wrenched apart by the final judgement',[2] and they always were. The one later fault of which the pre-Nicene church was innocent was an undue

[1] He is after all no more ridiculous than the 'Divine Heliogabalus' or sinister than 'our Lord and God Domitian', titles which the Roman Senate was prepared to hear without protest while those emperors lived.
[2] *de Civ. Dei*, I, 35.

deference to the secular ruler in the things of religion. This was largely a
matter of opportunity. But it was a serious weakness in the fourth century,
which more than once endangered all that the fortitude of the martyrs had
preserved. Yet it was chiefly an episcopal vice—though it is fair to say that
only the bishops were much exposed to the temptation—and it turned out
to be only a passing phase in the fourth century, at least so far as the West
was concerned.[1] Contact with the court proved so unsettling to bishops
that councils in the West forbade them to visit it save with the leave publicly obtained of the provincial synod.

But it is clear that before the end of the century the calibre of the episcopate had in the average greatly improved. Augustine, the ornament of three
universities before he was thirty-two; his friend Alypius, 'Baron of the
Exchequer' (as we should say) for Italy before he was thirty; Paulinus of
Nola, sometime governor of Spain; Ambrose, Consular of Italy—one of
the key-posts in high politics—when he was forty-two: such men were now
content to give their maturity to the church as bishops not only of great
cities but of little country towns. In the East, where the general improvement was perhaps less marked, Basil in Cappadocia did not hesitate to
refuse the emperor's offerings because he was an Arian; even at Constantinople John Chrysostom was no more a flatterer of the court than Ambrose
himself. Such men had a proven greatness of their own apart from
their office, which even ecclesiastical leaders in the preceding generation (like Eusebius of Vercelli on the one side or Acacius on the other) had
not manifested, much less the hack voters of the imperial majority at
the incessant episcopal councils of the Arian *régime*. (Athanasius is a figure
apart.)

The Englishman with his memories of great clerical civil servants in
English history, Cardinals Beaufort and Morton and Wolsey, Archbishops
Cranmer and Laud and their fellows in Tudor and Stuart times, is much
inclined to see in the fourth century the entrance of the church into 'politics'. In the sense that the church through individual bishops now had
access to the source of policy and could directly influence administration
this is true, as it could not in the nature of the case be true in pre-Nicene
times. But the bishops acquired no legal or constitutional rights against the
imperial autocrat. They did, however, acquire judicial functions in their
own cities, though their jurisdiction was in reality only a continuation of the
old consensual reference of christian quarrels to the bishop in pre-Nicene
times. Constantine recognised these voluntary christian courts and undertook to enforce their awards by the power of the state, forbidding the civil
courts to hear cases a second time on appeal from the bishop's decision by
disappointed litigants. But the bishop's court heard only such cases as the

[1] Except for the Council of Ephesus in A.D. 432 no Eastern Council cf bishops
ever voted even on dogmatic questions contrary to the known opinion or wishes of
the reigning emperor.

parties agreed to bring before him; the courts of the cities and the empire were still open to all who preferred to bring their cases there. The bishops, too, towards the end of the century acquired many of the functions of executive magistrates in their own see cities. No doubt this brought with it new dangers and new temptations. When the barbarian invasions turned all local authority into a 'Lordship' of some kind, it brought about a disastrous feudalisation of the episcopate, which has obscured its character in men's minds to this day. But the bishops were, when these powers were thrust upon them in the fourth century, virtually the only *elected* representatives of their fellow-citizens of any kind. If their voluntary tribunals were crowded it was because men found there a justice more impartial and less expensive than in the notoriously corrupt secular courts. If the emperors and the citizens entrusted to the bishop the functions of 'defender of the city', it was because all men saw in his office the best security against the rapacious and ubiquitous bureaucracy which was rapidly strangling both the imperial initiative and the city republics.[1]

And in another sense the church certainly did not become political in the fourth century. When Athanasius or Ambrose successfully opposed the declared policy of the emperors of their day, they made no claim whatever to a share in the authority or work of government. What they claimed was the right of conscience to disobey imperial orders which were in their judgement wrongful and *ultra vires*, because they clashed with the Law of God. It was the first successful political opposition to the central government other than by force of arms in the history of the empire. But it was only the claim of the martyrs voiced in different circumstances. In this fashion the church had never been and never ought to be 'outside politics'. It was as much a political act for Cyprian to refuse to obey the order of the 'Great Leviathan' to sacrifice to itself under Decius in A.D. 250 and to incite others to refuse, as it was for Athanasius to refuse to admit Arius to communion at the emperor's orders, or for Ambrose to refuse to hand over a christian basilica to Arian courtiers and to rouse the faithful to a 'stay-in strike'. It is the teaching of the New Testament that the Kingdom of God among men comes in and through the events of history, through what men make of real life as it has to be lived 'here and now'. Jesus of Nazareth was not a remote and academic sage teaching a serene philosophy of the good life. A man who would be Messiah handled the most explosive thing in Near Eastern politics. The world misunderstood Messiahship; but He died on a 'political' charge and so did every christian martyr in the next three centuries. There is indeed a 'political' border-land which the church cannot cross without leaving her mission. But all the same the church cannot leave real life and retire to some 'purely spiritual mission' of pietism without ceasing to be christian. And in the fourth century, as always before

[1] On the development of municipal functions in the episcopate see A. H. M. Jones *The Greek City from Alexander to Justinian*, Oxford, 1939, *pp.* 192 *sqq.*

and very often after, it was the state and not the church which provoked their clashes by aggression beyond its own proper functions.

If the actual course of events in the first twenty years of the century be studied attentively from year to year (and in A.D. 310–15 so far as possible from month to month) as it presented itself to contemporaries without foreknowledge of the future, the strange turn of christian fortunes in the fourth century appears not as the reversal but as the fulfilment of all that had gone before. It was the empire, not the church, which acknowledged defeat at the end of the great persecution, and abruptly reversed its policy. To say this is not to question the sincerity of Constantine's rather vague adherence to the God of the christians, which all recent secular historians have vindicated.[1] But the question is really not whether the church ought to have accepted his proffered alliance but whether in fact it could possibly have been avoided if the church had wanted to do so. The new emperor of his own accord publicly acknowledged himself in some sort a believer in christianity, and proceeded as such to take his own political and administrative measures, without any organised consultations with the church. Short of refusing to accept him even as a catechumen on the sole ground that he was an emperor,[2] there was nothing that the church could do in the matter but acquiesce. That christian and especially episcopal shortsightedness soon brought to a head the dangers latent from the first in such a position does not alter the fact that the church had no active part whatever in bringing it about. And once it had come about the fourth century church, after a generation of bewilderment at the suddenness of the change from pre-Nicene conditions, on the whole rose as boldly to the greatness of the opportunity now set before her as the pre-Nicene generations had risen to their own.

The christian intensity of the pre-Nicene church may at times have been greater, just because it was by the action of the world a more strictly selected body; but the process of selection and training *on the church's side* did not vary in the fourth century from what it had been in the third. The pre-Nicene church had steadily resisted the temptation to make of christianity a thing open only to a specialised aristocracy, whether its standard was to be intellectual, às the gnostics desired, or that of spiritual perceptiveness, as the Montanists insisted, or that of an unnaturally austere morality, such as was taught by the Encratites and to some extent by later bodies like the Novatianists. On the contrary the church always insisted that christianity was intended by God for every man. Her measure of a christian was simply 'communion', *partaking in* the corporate act of *worship*,

---

[1] Cf. e.g., F. Lot, *The End of the Ancient World*, pp. 29 sq.
[2] Tertullian would apparently have done so (*Apol.* xxi). It was easy enough to say this c. A.D. 200 when there was not the remotest prospect of Caesar becoming a christian. It was a different matter at the end of the Diocletian persecution, when the church was greatly disorganised and in many places at the last gasp of exhaustion. In any case, with whom did it rest to make such a decision?

with the belief which qualified a man for this and the conduct which befitted it in daily life. The attitude of the world, not of the church, brought
it about that exceptional gifts of character were required to be a good
communicant under pre-Nicene conditions. The hunger of the world then
was for martyrs, and from her communicants the church furnished them
sufficiently for the world's need.

When the work of the martyrs had been done the world's need changed.
It was no longer only the exceptionally resolute but *l'homme moyen sensuel*,
the average pagan man, whom the world itself now presented to the church.
And strenuously she tried to train him for God. To pagan materialism she
opposed the whole-hearted other-worldliness of her monks. To the pagan
tolerance of sin she opposed the example of innumerable domestic ascetics
and virgins living the life of devotion in their own homes. To pagan exploitation of the helpless and the denial of full human rights to the slave she
opposed the prodigality of christian almsgiving (it was in fact enormous)
and a rigid insistence that at her altar all christians free or servile were
equal. Not even the christian emperor, as Valens and Theodosius found,
was to have the privilege of giving scandal by his misbelief or misconduct
any more than other communicants. Right faith and right conduct were
still the only requirements of the christian worshipper, and the act of
*christian worship* was still the only measure of a christian in the eyes of the
church. But the range of christian belief and conduct now covered the
whole of human life, as it could not do in pre-Nicene days. The century
ends with a great constellation of christian doctors and theologians who
presented the faith both to the church and to the human mind at large, no
longer only as a theological system with an inner coherence superior to the
pagan myths, as the old Apologists had done, but as the key to the riddle
of all human existence, with its sorrows and littleness, yet shot through with
an almost divine beauty and terror and hope. Christian philosophy (which
except at Alexandria is virtually the creation of the fourth century) not
only out-thought the exhausted tradition of pagan speculation, as the monk
out-lived the instinctive assumptions of the pagan materialist and the
martyr had out-fought the resolution of the persecutors, but it proved
easily capable of absorbing all that was best in the classical tradition of
metaphysics and literature. On the pagans' ground, Augustine is a more
penetrating philosopher of history than Ammianus Marcellinus, Basil is a
better Greek philosopher and rhetorician than Libanius, Jerome is the
most accomplished Latinist since Cicero.

The missionary triumph of the fourth century was not less christian than
the dogged faithfulness of those before it, though it reaped with joy
where they had sown with tears. And in its effect upon the world and upon
the church it was incomparably more many-sided. It is no wonder if the
liturgy—the supreme expression of the church's life—has ever since
borne the marks of that immense expansion of its grasp on human living,

to the partial obscuring of its earlier character. Yet the liturgy remained then and has remained since what it always had been, the worshipping act of the Body of Christ towards God, by which His eternal kingdom 'comes' in time.

That kingdom had come in Jesus of Nazareth, in and through His life and death and resurrection, as real events humanly lived. He proclaimed the gospel, the divine truth about God and man, in and to the whole complex of circumstances in which history had placed Him. And He bore deliberately all the consequences to His own being and living as an individual of the resulting clash between that truth and those circumstances. At the last moment possible before those consequences reached their final climax, in the course of the last supper, He *did* something which expressed the whole meaning of His acceptance of them. Thereby He *imposed upon* the event which He accepted—which was in itself no more than a judicial murder of a not uncommon kind—the character of a voluntary sacrifice to God, redeeming His circumstances by bringing them along with Himself under the Kingship of God. And because He was not merely a man, but God incarnate and representative Man, that complete sacrifice of Himself to God is the potential redemption of all human circumstances, of the whole of time and human history.

But His proclamation of the gospel in His circumstances, and His offering of Himself to bear the outcome of it in the circumstances, are a 'liturgy', a voluntary service which is yet officially exacted from Him, addressed to God. The one is the liturgy of His Spirit, the other in the last resort was exacted from His Body and Blood. And the church which is His Body did nothing else in her liturgy but enter into His. In the synaxis, the 'meeting', she proclaimed the gospel and witnessed to its truth both to herself and, so far as it would listen, to the world. She did this simply by the lections, the announcement of the Word of God, and by the explanatory sermon of her prophetic and accredited teacher, the bishop. She spoke not as one arguing or speculating, but as a witness or a messenger delivering a message which it is not his to change or invent, but only to deliver faithfully in the very Spirit of the sender. And having told her message by the power of the Spirit, she prayed within herself in the same Spirit that it might be accepted by all to whom it was addressed.

And having delivered her message she too had to accept the consequences into her own being, to enter as His Body into the liturgy of His Body, in the eucharist which was the *anamnesis* of Him, the Sacrificed. She too brought her body in all its members to accept the full consequences of the clash between that true message and the 'here and now' of life. She, too, took bread and a cup and gave thanks and brake and distributed, entering into, not merely repeating, His own act. And she, too, thereby brought herself and all her members into the 'coming' of the kingdom of God, which comes fully and perfectly in Jesus. 'The Bread of Heaven in Christ

Jesus'; 'In God the Father Almighty, and in the Lord Jesus Christ and in the Holy Spirit in holy church'—the primitive words of administration! That and no other *is* the eucharist of the first four centuries.

We, with the more apocalyptic mood of the moment, may regret that the fourth century church lost her hold so completely on the older eschatological understanding of the liturgy, and substituted for it an historical interpretation. Yet we must ask ourselves, *Could* the barbarian Europe that was coming in the fifth and sixth centuries possibly have understood anything but the historical interpretation of the eucharist? What would the Merovingians have made of eschatology? In any case, I do not think it is hard to see why this change happened in the fourth century. While the world hungered for martyrs the church had trained men and women for christian dying, since that was what the clash of the circumstances of history with the truth of the gospel then demanded. The emphasis then had to be on the translation of the temporal into the eternal, already accomplished 'here and now' for the christian 'in Christ'. When the need of the new christian world was for daily holiness, she trained men and women no longer for christian dying but for christian living; for that was what the clash of earthly circumstances with the truth of the gospel now exacted. The emphasis was now all on the translation of the eternal into history and time, accomplished once for all in Jesus Christ, and by us successively in Him. But she trained the confessors as she had trained the martyrs—by the liturgy; for that is her act, her life—because it is her Lord's act and His life.

The century which had opened with the fury of Diocletian reaffirming the strength of the empire closes with the hymns of Prudentius, the last authentic poet of classical literature—at once 'the Virgil and the Horace of the christians', as so fastidious a scholar and critic as Bentley called him. He had been a pagan, a loose-living Spanish officer at the imperial court, who settled to write poetry at the approach of old age:

> *Ex quo prima dies mihi*
> *quam multas hiemes volverit et rosas*
> *pratis post glaciem reddiderit, nix capitis probat.*[1]

The lyrical preface the old penitent set at the head of his *Cathemerinon* says perfectly for his whole generation all it felt of sadness and of hope:

> *Dicendum mihi: quisquis es*
> *mundum quem coluit mens tua perdidit:*
> *non sunt illa Dei, quae studuit, cuius habeberis.*
> *Atqui fine sub ultimo*

[1] No translation can catch the melody of the Latin. Here is a bare rendering:
> *Since I first saw the light*
> *How many winters fled have given back*
> *The roses to the frost-bound earth, this snowy head declares.*

*peccatrix anima stultitiam exuat:*
*saltem voce Deum concelebret, si meritis nequit:*
    *hymnis continuet dies,*
*nec nox ulla vacet, quin Dominum canat:*
*pugnet contra hereses, catholicam discutiat fidem,*
    *conculcet sacra gentium,*
*labem, Roma, tuis inferet idolis,*
*carmen martyribus devoveat, laudet apostolos.*
    *Haec dum scribo vel eloquor,*
*vinclis o utinam corporis emicem*
*liber, quo tulerit lingua sono mobilis ultimo!*[1]

So the last christian generation of the old Roman world looked wistfully
into the future knowing the end had come, and turned to God. In all its
unhappiness and its carnality that world had always loved beauty; and now
at the end there was given it a glimpse of the eternal Beauty. And it cried
out in breathless wonder with Augustine, 'Too late have I loved Thee,
Beauty so ancient and so new!'[2]

There is a sort of pause in events round about the turn of the century
while that whole ancient world—still so magnificent—waits for the stroke
of God, and trusts Him though it knows He will slay. It is like some wind-
less afternoon of misty sunshine on the crimson and bronze of late October,
when time for an hour seems to stand still and the earth dreams, fulfilled
and weary, content that winter is at hand. The whole hard structure of the
*civitas terrena,* the earthly city that had once thought itself eternal, was now
ready to dissolve into a different future. Gibbon was right. The foundation
of the empire was loosened by the waters of baptism, for the empire's real
foundation was the terrible pagan dream of human power. Its brief christian dream of the City of God which alone is eternal was broken by the

---

[1] *This must I hear:* '*Everyman,*
*thy mind hath lost the world it loved. The things*
*that are not God's thou soughtest, yet thou shalt be His at last'.*
    *At least ere I go hence*
*my sinful soul shall put off folly, and*
*my voice shall praise God, as my deeds have never done.*
    *The whole day shall be linked*
*with hymns, nor any night be silent in His praise.*
*I will taunt heresies and expound the catholic faith,*
    *trample on heathen rites*
*bring shame upon the Roman idols, pay*
*my song's homage to the martyrs, and the apostles praise.*
    *With pen and tongue thus busy,*
*Death, you shall free me from the body's fetters*
*and bear me to Him Whom my lips' last motion still shall name.*'
                        (*Cathemerinon, Praef.,* 31 *sq.*)
The poems were published *c.* A.D. 405, but appear to have been written in the
preceding years.
                 [2] *Confessions,* x. 27.

roaring crash of the sack of Rome by the Goths in A.D. 410. The world went hurrying into the darkness of seven long barbarian centuries, but pregnant now with all the mediaeval and modern future. It was the achievement of the church in the single century that had passed since Diocletian that, though all else changed in human life, it was certain to be a christian world, that centred all its life upon the eucharist.

# CHAPTER XII

## THE DEVELOPMENT OF CEREMONIAL

ONE result of the fourth century transformation of the eucharist into a fully public act is a certain elaboration of ceremony in its performance. This does not directly concern the subject of this book, since the Shape of the Liturgy by which the eucharistic action is performed is hardly affected by this. The introit-chant, which covered the processional entrance of the clergy, seems to be the only item in the outline of the rite which was introduced for purely ceremonial reasons. The eucharistic action and its meaning remained in themselves what they had always been. But the actual performance of the action is to a certain extent formalised in a new way in the fourth century. There is a new emphasis on its earthly and human aspect, consistent indeed with the acceptance of a mission to human society as such and that sanctification of social living in time which the church first undertook in the fourth century, but also a symptom of the decline of the old eschatological understanding of the rite.

Yet here also the Constantinian and post-Nicene church made no deliberate breach with the past and was quite unconscious of any new beginning. As we have seen, from the very fact that it was a corporate action the pre-Nicene eucharist had had an aspect of ceremony ever since the first formation of the liturgical eucharist apart from the supper, in that it required a good deal of concerted movement by all the various 'orders' of participants for its performance. This core of the action, which was everywhere the same, is in its origin wholly utilitarian—it is the simplest and most natural way of getting the corporate eucharistic action 'done'. But by the fourth century it had already hardened into something very like a traditional ritual by the mere passage of centuries. The post-Nicene church had obviously every intention of conserving this pre-Nicene body of customs intact, and it does in fact form the whole basis of the later eucharistic rites. But it soon began to be overlaid and accompanied by a variety of new customs. Some of these, like the solemn processional entry of the clergy at the beginning of the rite, were suggested quite naturally by the new public conditions of worship and its more formal setting. Others, like the *lavabo*, were deliberately symbolical, and intended to remind the worshippers in various ways of the solemnity of what they were about. These may be innovations, but they seem natural products of the new situation. Now that not only the spiritually sensitive but the average man and woman were increasingly becoming regular attendants at christian worship, the introduction of such reminders of its solemnity was a necessary part of the church's care for her members. The Reformers of the sixteenth century, who regarded the eucharist primarily as something 'said' by the clergy, set themselves to achieve exactly the same object by prescribing solemn and lengthy 'exhortations' to be said by the minister to the worshippers (of which specimens still remain to us in the 'Long' and 'Short Exhortations' of the Prayer Book rite). The fourth century church took more literally the command '*Do* this in remembrance of Me', and therefore addressed such reminders to the people by symbolical gestures and actions rather than by words. But the purpose in both cases is exactly the same. It is the change made by regarding the rite as something 'said' and not something 'done' (which is essentially the work of the Latin middle ages and not of the Reformers) that makes it difficult for modern Western christians, protestant and catholic alike, to enter immediately into the mind of the early church.

Mr. A. D. Nock in his brilliant study of the psychological process behind the conversion of the pagan world to christianity has remarked that 'Even in the fourth century, when the Eucharist acquired a dignity of ceremonial appropriate to the solemn worship of the now dominant church, it is not to me clear either that there was a deliberate copying of the ceremonial of the mystery dramas or that any special appeal was made by the ritual to the mass of new converts'.[1] I venture to hope that what has been already written is sufficient comment on the question of possible copying of the mysteries in pre-Nicene times. We have seen that there is in fact no element in the eucharistic ceremonial, such as it was, of the first three centuries which is not completely explained by a directly christian or pre-christian jewish origin. As for any appeal of ceremonial to the fourth century converts, there is nothing in the evidence which suggests that this was its intention. The eucharist was now being performed in a world where every public act secular or religious had always been invested with a certain amount of ceremony as a matter of course. Christian worship was now a public act, and any different treatment of it was simply not thought of. A few notes on the chief adjuncts of ceremonial and their introduction and development will make clear, I think, how spontaneous the whole process of the post-Nicene development of ceremonial really was.

### Vestments

What one may call 'official costume for public acts' both in the case of magistrates and priests had been common in classical Greece and usual all over the Near East for many centuries before the christian era. In Italy and the West, particularly at Rome, the wearing of such 'official' robes, either

---

[1] A. D. Nock, *Conversion: The Old and the New in Religion from Alexander the Great to Augustine of Hippo*, Oxford, 1933, *p.* 204. Mr. Nock's conclusions are reached chiefly from the pagan evidence, on which his judgement is authoritative. But they coincide with my own, reached mainly on the basis of the christian evidence.

secular or religious, had always been much less developed; though the elements of the idea are to be discerned, e.g. in the *toga praetexta* of the magistrates (the ordinary dress of a gentleman, with a broad purple stripe) and the *apex*—the special skin cap worn on some occasions by the Roman pontiffs and flamens. But speaking broadly, the elaborately vested Maccabean high-priest performing the rites of the Day of Atonement on the one hand, and on the other the pagan Roman *rex sacrorum* performing the not very dissimilar rites of the *poplifugium* in the toga which every Roman gentleman wore about the city every day, represent from one point of view a contrast of types whose basis is geographical much more than dependent on different ideas of worship.

It is therefore not surprising to find that the earliest mention of a special liturgical garment for use at christian worship comes from the Near East, and specifically from Jerusalem. We learn incidentally from Theodoret that *c.* A.D. 330 Constantine had presented to his new cathedral church at Jerusalem as part of its furnishing a 'sacred robe' (*hieran stolēn*) of gold tissue to be worn by the bishop when presiding at the solemn baptisms of the paschal vigil.[1] From the words employed this looks like some sort of special liturgical vestment. But this very characteristic initiative of the ritualistic Jerusalem church was not followed up. The next mention of such things comes likewise from Syria, in a rubric of the rite in *Ap. Const.*, viii. (*c.* A.D. 375) directing that the bishop is to celebrate the eucharist 'clad in splendid raiment'.[2] But the word *esthēta* in this case makes it clear that all the author has in mind is a sumptuous specimen of the ordinary lay costume of the upper classes at this period, not a special hieratic vestment (*stolē*) like those of the Old Testament high-priests. And in fact the Roman type of sacerdotal functioning in ordinary dress did prevail in christian usage everywhere over the graeco-oriental type of a special liturgical dress. All over christendom ecclesiastical vestments derive from the lay dress of the upper classes in the imperial period, and not from any return to Old Testament precedents such as the mediaeval ritualists imagined.

*The Chasuble, Tunicle and Alb.* Since the second century the old Roman *toga virilis* had been more and more disused as an everyday garment, and was no longer worn even at ordinary meetings of the senate.[3] In place of

---

[1] Theodoret, *Eccl. Hist.*, ii. 27.

[2] *ap.* Brightman, *op. cit.*, p. 14, *l.* 8. For further incidental references to the 'splendour' of episcopal clothes *cf.* S. Gregory Naz. *Orat.* 20 and 32; Ammianus Marcellinus, xxvii. 3, etc. Both christian and pagan authors refer to episcopal dress outside church as well as in, and make it clear (*a*) that there was no difference between the two, and (*b*) that there was no difference between clerical and lay dress in this period *c.* A.D. 375-400.

[3] Its history is exactly that of the English peer's dress of parliament robes. From being a customary dress it becomes a sort of full-dress uniform. Ultimately it is worn only at specially convened meetings presided over by the emperor (*cf.* opening of Parliament) and by certain magistrates on particular occasions, *e.g.* the consuls and the *praefectus urbis* (*cf.* Royal Commissioners in the House of Lords) and at the trial of a senator (*cf.* the trial of a peer).

the toga the upper classes adopted a costume, apparently Ionian in origin, consisting of a linen robe with close sleeves, covering the whole body from neck to feet, the *linea*, above which was worn a sort of tunic with short close sleeves (*colobium* or *tunica*) extending to the knees. On formal occasions and out of doors both men and women wore over this the *paenula* (also called *planeta*, *casula* and occasionally *lacerna*[1])—a large round piece of stuff with a hole in the centre for the head to pass through, which fell in folds over the shoulders and arms and draped the whole body down to the knees.

The contemporary account of the martyrdom of S. Cyprian in A.D. 258 reveals him as wearing this dress. When he reached the place of execution 'he took off the red *lacerna* that he was wearing and folded it and knelt down upon it and prostrated himself in prayer to the Lord. And when he had taken off his *tunica* and handed it to the deacons, he stood up in his *linea* and awaited the executioners'.[2] These are in essentials the pontificals of a mediaeval bishop. But Cyprian is wearing them simply as the ordinary lay gentleman's dress of the day.

By the end of the fourth century this peaceful costume in turn was beginning to go out of fashion in favour of a more military style[3] brought in by the barbarian mercenaries whose commanders were becoming the most influential people in the state. By a law of A.D. 397, however, senators were ordered to resume the old civilian style of the *paenula* worn over the *colobium* or *tunica* and the ungirded *linea*; while civil servants were ordered to wear the *paenula* over the girdled *linea* as part of their full dress.[4] (The *cingulum* (belt) was a distinguishing badge of military as opposed to civil office. Hence the *officiales*, whose service ranked as a *militia* and was subject to military not civil law, are to wear the girdle visibly, but the senator, as a civilian, does not.) In the rigidly organised late empire this law sufficed to fix the costume of the great nobles and the higher officials. Two centuries later, in the apparently contemporary portrait of Pope S. Gregory I standing between his father the senator Gordianus and his mother, the costume of all three is still exactly the same—chasuble worn over the tunic with the ungirded linen alb. The mother wears a sort of linen turban, and the Pope is distinguished from the layman his father by the *pallium*—a sort of scarf of office which was the only strictly liturgical vestment which the Popes as yet tolerated. But otherwise the costumes of the bishop, the layman and laywoman are exactly the same.

*The Pallium and Stole.* Even the use of the pallium was not very ancient in the Roman church, dating perhaps from the end of the fifth century.

---

[1] There is some doubt about the meaning of this word, which sometimes means an open cloak. But there are certain passages where it clearly means the same garment as the *paenula*.
[2] *Acta Proconsularia S. Cypriani*, 5.
[3] The *tunica lanicata* (the origin of the modern shirt) and *chlamys* or cloak.
[4] *Codex Theodosianus*, xiv. 10, 1.

Before that time the whole idea of any such mark of distinction had been entirely contrary to the local Roman tradition. Pope Celestine I *c.* A.D. 425 had gone so far as to rebuke the bishops of the South of France, among whom the use of the *pallium* and girdle at the eucharist was already customary, with what seems unnecessary vigour: 'It is small wonder that the church's custom should be violated by those who have not grown old in the church, but entering in by some other way have introduced into the church along with themselves things which they used to wear in another walk of life (*i.e.*, the magistracy, from which so many bishops were then recruited). . . . Perhaps men who dwell in distant parts far from the rest of the world wear that dress from following local custom rather than reason. Whence came this custom in the churches of Gaul, so contrary to antiquity? We bishops must be distinguished from the people and others by our learning not by our dress, by our life not by our robes, by purity of heart not by elegance . . .'[1] To the plea that this is only a literal following of the evangelical injunction to have 'the loins girded', etc., he answers drily that they will need to stand at the altar with a burning lamp in one hand and a staff in the other to fulfil what follows, and roundly bids them to have done with such 'worthless superstitions'.

Yet there is evidence from the East as well as from Gaul that in other churches less sturdily old-fashioned than that of Rome some equivalent of the *pallium* had already been accepted as a special badge of the liturgical ministry almost everywhere during the later fourth century.[2] It is in fact *the* liturgical 'vestment' (*stolē*) of all orders at this time. In its episcopal form the *pallium* is simply the old 'scarf of office' worn by the emperor and consuls, a badge granted to numerous other officials during the fourth century. It was adopted by the clergy in various forms, becoming the *pallium* of the Pope and (later) of archbishops and certain privileged bishops in the West, but worn by all bishops since the fifth century in the East. For the lower clergy it becomes the 'stole' worn in different ways by bishops, priests and deacons as a badge of distinction.[3] Most *pallia*, lay and clerical alike, were of coloured silk. But the Popes when they adopted this little piece of vanity wore it in the form of a simple white woollen scarf

[1] Celestine I, *Ep.* iv. The same idea that it is not vestments like those of the O.T. priesthood but holiness which distinguish the christian priesthood is drawn out with an almost puritanical insistence in the Roman prayer for the consecration of a bishop in the present Roman pontifical, found already in the *Gelasian Sacramentary c.* A.D. 500. It probably goes back to the time of Leo I *c.* A.D. 450, if not to that of Celestine himself twenty-five years before.

[2] The last exception that I know is at Ruspe in Africa, where S. Fulgentius (sixth century) according to the contemporary *Vita* refused out of humility to wear the *orarium* like other bishops. But this is noted as something peculiar. Fulgentius wore a chasuble (of common and coarse stuff) out of doors, as the ordinary dress of the day, but celebrated in his working clothes (*i.e. without* it).

[3] The fashion of deacons wearing the stole on the left shoulder seems to have spread from the region of Antioch. At least it is first attested there by pseudo-Chrysostom (*de Fil. Prod.* 3; perhaps by Severian of Gabala) and Theodore of Mopsuestia (*Catecheses,* ed. *cit., p.* 84).

embroidered with black crosses.[1] And apart from the Pope's *pallium* Rome so far remained faithful to Celestine's principles as not to adopt the stole in any form, for bishops, priests or deacons, right down to the twelfth century, when it was introduced from beyond the Alps.

*The Maniple.* Just as the *pallium* and stole derive from the secular 'scarf of office', so the vestment known as the maniple (*fanon, sudarium*) derives directly from the *mappula,* a sort of large handkerchief which formed part of the ceremonial dress of consuls and other magistrates, carried in the hand or laid across the arm. The carrying of the maniple in the left hand at the liturgy did not die out at Rome or in England before the twelfth century,[2] though by then the present custom of fixing it to the left arm throughout the rite was firmly established in France. The use of the *mappula* by the clergy is attested at Rome in the sixth century,[3] but it is found as a special badge of the deacon in Egypt a century before this.[4]

*The Dalmatic.* This was a form of *tunica* with large sleeves, which came into use in the second century as a tunic which could be worn in public without the chasuble (though it was noted as a breach of decorum in the emperor Commodus that he appeared sometimes at the circus clad only in the dalmatic without the chasuble). In the fourth century it seems to have become a sort of undress uniform for high officials, and as such it began to be worn by important bishops, though always under the chasuble. It was adopted by itself, however, as a normal dress by the seven regionary deacons of Rome, whose duties, as superintendents of what was now virtually the whole poor relief system of the city (pauperised for centuries by the system of *panis et circenses*) and the estates which formed its endowment, were becoming administrative and financial rather than religious. For a while this remained a peculiarity of the Roman deacons, but it spread gradually to other Western churches,[5] where it eventually became the distinctive vestment of deacons. It is symbolic of a good deal in church history that the adoption of this dress, which was virtually a badge of preoccupation with secular affairs, was at Rome confined to the deacons, while in the Byzantine church it became the special vestment of archbishops.[6] Even the Roman deacons, arrogant and worldly as a long series

[1] It is this Papal *pallium* which still appears on the armorial bearings of the sees of Canterbury and York.

[2] *Cf. e.g.* the English miniatures reproduced as Plates i and ii in the *Lanalet Pontifical* (ed. G. H. Doble, H.B.S., 1937). The Eastern bishop's *epigonation,* now attached to his girdle, was similarly carried in the hand down to the ninth century.

[3] Duchesne, *Origins etc.,* E. T. 1931, *p.* 383.

[4] S. Isidore of Pelusium (c. A.D. 410), *Ep.* I. cxxxvi.

[5] When Pope Symmachus granted the use of the *pallium* and dalmatic to S. Caesarius of Arles c. A.D. 510, he also granted his deacons the right to wear the dalmatic 'as in the Roman church'. (*Vita S. Caesarii,* I, iv. *ap. Acta SS. Boll.,* v. 71). These are apparently not intended as purely liturgical ornaments but as civil distinctions.

[6] In Russia, of all bishops. The dalmatic has never been adopted by the dissident Eastern churches for their bishops, or by the deacons of any Eastern rite, whose garment, the *sticharion,* is derived from the ungirded linen alb, a form it still retains in Egypt.

of critics from the fourth to the sixth century declared them to be, hesitated to perform their liturgical functions in this uniform of a secular official. The Pope, who as the chief citizen of Rome sometimes wore a dalmatic, always covered it in church with the chasuble of the private gentleman. The deacons at least began their ministry at the altar dressed in the same way. But before performing his special 'liturgy' of singing the gospel (and down to A.D. 595 the preceding solo of the gradual) the Roman deacon put off his chasuble, which he only resumed after assisting to administer communion. There was no mystical or symbolic meaning in this; it was simply for convenience of movement. In Lent the Roman deacons acknowledged the special seriousness of the season by leaving off their dalmatics in church and wearing their chasubles throughout the rite. But even so they wore them from the gospel to the communion rolled up bandolier-wise around the body over the left shoulder and tied under the right arm—something like a British soldier's greatcoat in the period of the Boer War. (This curiously informal behaviour is still perpetuated in the ceremonial of the Roman rite in Advent, Lent and Ember-tides.)

*The Camelaucum or Tiara.* It is the same story with the other vestments that originated before the middle ages. The Papal tiara, for instance, is derived from the *camelaucum* or *phrygia*, a 'cap of state' worn by the emperors and very high officials in the fourth century. (The statue of Constantine on his triumphal arch at Rome is wearing one. A version of the same headgear was worn by the doge of Venice and other Italo-Greek potentates.) Its use seems to have been allowed to the clergy by the emperors everywhere in the fifth century. In the East, in the form of the 'brimless top-hat' doubtless familiar to most readers, it became the normal headgear of all clergy (white for patriarchs like that of the Pope, purple for bishops and black for others). Like the Western biretta, it began to be worn by Easterns in church as well as out of it during the later middle ages. Down to the tenth century the Popes kept it as a strictly non-liturgical vestment, to be worn to and from church and on other public occasions, but not in service time like the later mitre, though the latter seems to have evolved from it by a process of variation. When the Popes became secular rulers in their own right (from the ninth century onwards) they successively added the three crowns (the last was added in the fourteenth century) to the *camelaucum* as a secular headgear, but they have never worn this crowned *camelaucum,* the ornament of a secular ruler, whi' : celebrating the eucharist.

*The Campagi or Shoes.* The special liturgical shoes and stockings of Western bishops also originated as a secular ornament, worn outside church as well as at the liturgy. As far back as the early days of the Roman republic consuls and triumphing generals were distinguished by high-laced shoes of a particular form and a bright red colour; and patricians were distinguished from plebeians by a particular form of black shoe. In the fourth century A.D. when all dress was formalised and regulated with a sort of childish care into nicely distinguished badges of rank, the wearing of different forms of shoes by different orders of officials was a matter for imperial edicts. The purple boots of the Byzantine emperors became, like the purple chasuble embroidered with golden bees, the most jealously guarded symbol of imperial power, even more so than the diadem. To assume them was to claim the throne. In adopting the *campagi* as part of their liturgical dress, probably in the fifth century, the Popes were only carrying out their customary policy of celebrating the liturgy in the normal dress of important laymen of the time. But by the sixth century the *campagi* like the *pallium* must have come to be reckoned a distinctive sign of their episcopal office.[1]

These are the only ecclesiastical vestments worn in christendom before c. A.D. 800.[2] In their adoption there is evidence of a definite policy pursued everywhere during the fourth and fifth centuries, *viz.*, that the liturgy should be celebrated always in the garments of everyday life. The use of symbolical liturgical vestments like those of the Old Testament priests or the white dress of the neophytes after baptism in the pre-Nicene church was deliberately avoided. The only exception, if it can be called such, was the introduction of the stole; but scarves of office of all kinds were so commonly used in social and civic life in the later fourth century that this, too, can be brought under the same heading, even though Rome thought otherwise and refused to adopt it for seven centuries or so, except for the bishop.

What turned this clothing into a special liturgical vesture was mere conservatism. When the dress of the layman finally changed in the sixth and seventh centuries to the new barbarian fashions, the clergy as the last representatives of the old civilised tradition retained the old civilised costume. From being old-fashioned it became archaic (like the court-dress of the Moderator of the Scottish Kirk) and finally hieratic (like the chimere of the Anglican bishop, which begins prosaically in the twelfth century as a form of overcoat).

But this last stage was only reached by degrees, and was not complete before the seventh-eighth century. Where the old tradition lingered amongst the laity, there the old dress lingered for laymen too, as we see from the picture of S. Gregory and his father Gordian, c. A.D. 600. But though the old-fashioned patrician families of Rome might preserve the traditional dress in everyday life, elsewhere it had already vanished. The fourth Council of Toledo in A.D. 633 orders the public restoration before the altar of the chasuble, stole and alb to an unfrocked priest who is being restored to the use of his orders—a provision which tells its own story; the old costume has become a strictly clerical vestment, a liturgical symbol. The

[1] See the evidence cited by Duchesne, *Origins, ed. cit., p.* 395.
[2] The amice or *anagolaium* appears for the first time in the *Ordo Romanus Primus,* and therefore may go back before A.D. 800. It is originally a convenience rather than a vestment—the equivalent of the British workman's 'sweat-rag'.

Byzantine emperors continued to wear it in proud assertion of their claim to continue in unbroken succession the office of the Roman Caesars. In 1453 the last emperor of Constantinople fell in the breach fighting to the end, still clothed in the purple chasuble embroidered with golden bees. Charlemagne adopted this with the purple buskins when he laid claim to the imperial dignity in A.D. 800; and from him it passed to the kings of France as their coronation robe. The last public use of it by a layman was at the coronation of Charles X of France at Rheims in 1825.

We can better understand the process if we compare it with the history of a garment with which we are more familiar. A century ago the black frock-coat was still the dress of every Englishman above the condition of a labourer. Even forty years ago a large proportion of the upper classes wore it on Sundays and on any occasion of formality. Now it is gradually becoming an undress uniform for royalty, diplomats and statesmen, and for people in certain formal positions, shopwalkers, undertakers, important station-masters—and Anglican dignitaries. Even bridegrooms had abandoned it for the morning coat before the war. It was adopted for use in conducting divine worship by many non-conformist divines in the last century, precisely because it was the normal lay dress of the time. But many of them retain it to-day when it has ceased to be so, and their people would be mildly shocked by a change. One delightful old Baptist lay-preacher whom I knew in Pembrokeshire nearly thirty years ago always referred to it as his 'preaching coat', and would never have used it for any other purpose. It is on its way—just like the chasuble—to becoming a vestment, a special royal and liturgical garment.

The case is, however, quite different with the vestments which developed later, the Mitre, Cope and Gloves, and the choir dress of Surplice, etc. These mediaeval vestments were of deliberate clerical invention, and were meant in their ecclesiastical form to be worn only at the liturgy, and as clerical marks of distinction from the remainder of the worshippers.

*The Mitre.* The advocates of an inner connection of the catholic eucharist with the pagan mysteries have had interesting things to say in the past about the episcopal mitre, the headgear whose very name recalls the hierophant of Mithras. It is unfortunate for such theories that the mitre (*mitra, mitella*) first appears in christian use as the distinctive headgear of the only person who had no particular function in the liturgy—the deaconess. References to its use by deaconesses in Africa are found in the later fourth century.[1] It passed thence to Spain where a seventh–eighth century mention of the *mitra religiosa* in the form for the installation of an abbess (reckoned *ex officio* a deaconess) is preserved in the Mozarabic *Liber Ordinum*.[2]

[1] *E.g.* S. Optatus, *adv. Donatistas*, ii. 19; vi. 4 (*ed.* Ziwsa, *pp.* 54, 149).
[2] *Ed.* Férotin, 1904, *pp.* 66–7. The mitre of the Abbess of Las Huelvas which caused such alarm and despondency to canonists in the fourteenth century was evidently a survival of this old Spanish custom. It should perhaps be mentioned

The German scholar Pater Braun in his exhaustive discussion of every piece of evidence which has ever been alleged for the antiquity of the episcopal mitre appears to have proved decisively that no liturgical headgear whatever was ever worn by the clergy at the liturgy anywhere before c. A.D. 1000.[1] The change in this comes during the eleventh century in the West. The first mention of an episcopal mitre in literature is the grant on Passion Sunday A.D. 1049 by Pope S. Leo IX to his own former archbishop Eberhard of Trier of the right to wear 'at the liturgy' (*in ecclesiasticis officiis*) 'the Roman mitre', 'after the Roman fashion'. In 1051 the Pope grants the same privilege to the seven 'cardinals' (*i.e.* principal chaplains) of the cathedral of Besançon when acting as celebrant, deacon or subdeacon at the high altar on certain great feasts. This privilege of wearing mitres at the liturgy was granted to a number of other chapters of canons (even for their subdeacons) during the next half century or so, sometimes on the occasion of the grant of a mitre to their bishop, sometimes actually before this. In 1063 the mitre was granted to Abbot Elsin of S. Augustine's, Canterbury (the first of many such grants to abbots); and though Braun takes it for granted that this proves that the mitre had already been granted to his archbishop, Stigand's pontificals in the Bayeux Tapestry (which are very carefully portrayed) do not include the mitre at Harold's coronation.

Great churches like Milan only obtained the privilege of the mitre at the beginning of the twelfth century,[2] and it was not until the middle or third quarter of that century that it came about that so many bishops had acquired the right to use it by specific Papal grant that it began to be regarded as an inevitable part of a bishop's costume, and the remaining non-mitred bishops simply usurped it without obtaining a Papal grant. Abbots, conventual priors and other dignitaries continued to obtain it individually by a privilege from the Pope in the old way until the seventeenth century, when the few remaining non-mitred abbots were granted the use of it *ex officio*.

The real origin of the liturgical mitre would therefore seem to be as follows: We know that in the tenth century the Popes still did not wear their *camelaucum* at the liturgy. But somewhere soon after A.D. 1000 they must have begun to do so, differentiating however between this use of it and that outside church by reserving the 'crowned' *camelaucum* (for the first of the three crowns had by now been added to the papal cap) for secular occasions. It is this new use of the *camelaucum* in church which is allowed to Eberhard of Trier; and the grant to the cardinals of Besançon in 1051 suggests that it was already used in church by the Roman cardinals

that the other modern derivative of the same headgear is the *bonnet rouge*, the 'Phrygian Cap of Liberty' of the French Revolution. It is a bewildering reflection that this traditional headgear of 'Marianne', the Anglican deaconess' bonnet and the Papal tiara are all by origin one and the same article—the *phrygia*.

[1] J. Braun, S.J., *Die liturgische Gewandung*, Freiburg-i-B., 1907, pp. 431–462.
[2] M. Magistretti, *Delle vesti ecclesiastiche in Milano*, Milan, 1897, p. 69.

before this. The mitre is thus the one and only liturgical ornament of purely Papal origin; and the right of others to use it, whether bishops or priests or deacons or subdeacons or even laymen (some mediaeval princes, e.g. the kings of Hungary and some dukes of Bohemia, were granted this as a compliment), depended originally on a Papal privilege even more strictly than did the use of the *pallium*. It is in no sense a symbol in itself of episcopal orders, even though it is now worn by all Western bishops, including Swedish Lutherans and others who are not in communion with the Pope. Apart from Papal initiative it would have remained an ornament not of the bishop at all, but of the deaconess.

The Eastern mitre, in the form of a crown, has a wholly different origin. It seems to derive from the *touphan*, a sort of jewelled turban borrowed by the Byzantines from the Persians.[1] But its use by ecclesiastics in church is not older than the sixteenth century. The great Byzantine canonist Balsamon states categorically c. A.D. 1200 that all Eastern ecclesiastics are bare-headed at the liturgy with the sole exception of the Patriarch of Alexandria and his twelve 'cardinary' priests, who wear a *loron* (diadem), a right which he says was acquired by S. Cyril as the Papal legate at the Council of Ephesus in A.D. 432.[2] The same statement is twice repeated by Simeon of Thessalonica in the fifteenth century.[3]

*The Cope*, of silk or velvet and embroidery, is an elaboration for the deliberate purpose of ecclesiastical display in church of the homely cape for keeping warm. It was invented in the great French capitular and conventual churches during the ninth century, and was in occasional use for semi-liturgical functions (*e.g.* the dialogue at the Easter Sepulchre) in England in the later tenth century. It was still not in use at Rome in the twelfth century.[4]

[1] See John Tsetses, *Chiliades*, viii. 184 *sq.*
[2] Balsamon, *Meditata*. ii. M.P.G., cxxxviii. 1048. B. (I take it that *Papa* in this passage refers to the 'Pope' of Alexandria, not of Rome, though Migne's note *ad loc.* assumes the opposite.) The story of the quasi-grant to S. Cyril in the form Balsamon gives it is clearly apocryphal, but the alleged Roman origin is interesting. The Armenians adopted the Western mitre when they were in communion with the Pope in the fifteenth century; but the Syrians and Copts have never adopted any form of mitre for their bishops, though the Coptic patriarch still wears a sort of golden helmet (of a quite different pattern from the Byzantine mitre), the *loron* of the patriarchs of Alexandria. The Abyssinians appear to have adopted the Byzantine mitre for use by *all* clergy at the liturgy in the course of the last two centuries, probably through contact with the Greek rite at Jerusalem.
[3] *Expositio.* 45. M.P.G., clv. 716; *Responsa*, etc. 20. *Ibid.* 871. *Cf.* Goar, *Euchologion*, p. 314.
[4] The various Eastern semi-liturgical robes like the Greek *mandyas* and the Syrian *burnus* which correspond vaguely to the Western cope have an independent origin, as adaptations of the traditional oriental 'robe of honour'. None of them seem to go back as ecclesiastical vestments beyond the thirteenth century, before which date the *phelonion* (chasuble) seems to have been the only church-dress of priests and bishops. It is perhaps worth remarking that this Eastern chasuble itself only assumed its present stiff and rather ungainly cope-like form after the thirteenth century. Earlier Greek and Syrian miniatures shew it as closely resembling the mediaeval Roman chasuble.

*The Episcopal Gloves.* The use of gloves does not seem to have been known in antiquity at all. They first appear as episcopal ornaments in Gaul during·the ninth century and were adopted at Rome during the tenth or eleventh century. A trace of their late origin in episcopal costume is to be found in the fact that in the Western *Pontificale* they are assumed by a new bishop not when he puts on the old pontifical vestments at the moment of his consecration, but only after the communion (like that other afterthought the mitre, which is placed upon his head at the same point of the rite, after all that relates to his episcopal consecration has been concluded). Their liturgical name *chirothecae* suggests that they came into the Latin churches from the Greek countries; but the liturgical use of gloves (properly so called) is unknown in the East. Byzantine court-dress, however, included a pair of embroidered cuffs (*epimanikia, manualia*), which appear among the vestments of most Eastern rites. These were borrowed from Byzantium by some Spanish and French churches in the eighth century. They may be regarded as embryonic gloves. At all events, their use in the West as episcopal ornaments went out when that of gloves came in.

*Choir-Dress. The Surplice.* At the eucharist all the clergy down to and including the acolytes (with the partial exception of the deacons) wore the chasuble in the fifth century; and traces of this practice continued at Rome down to at least the ninth century.[1] But clerical dress at the divine office, at all events in the case of the lower clergy, seems to have been always the girdled *linea*, or alb, the 'undress' of the middle classes at home.[2] It was not a very warm costume, and the difficulty of heating the church, especially for the long night office, was solved by heating the man instead. Thick fur coats (*pelliceum*) worn under or over the alb were a necessity. The awkwardness of such bundlesome garments under the girdled alb led to the disuse of the girdle, and the surplice (*superpelliceum*) is simply the alb adapted for use 'over the fur coat'. The graceful flowing sleeves of the mediaeval surplice seem to have been added early in the thirteenth century, as part of the deliberate beautifying of all church vestments which is a noticeable feature of that period. Before that time the comparatively close sleeves of the *cotta* (then still a garment which came below the knees) preserved more nearly the original resemblance to the ungirded alb.

*The Rochet* is simply the alb or *linea* retained as a secular dress by the clergy for use *outside* church. It is an unliturgical garment, over which both priests and bishops were perpetually being reminded by mediaeval synods that they ought to assume the surplice whenever they had to perform any

[1] The rubrics of the Greek rite still expect the lector ( = Western subdeacon) to wear the chasuble like the celebrant (but not the stole) though I do not think this ever happens in practice now. *Cf.* Goar, *Euchologion, p.* 236. It was also used on occasion by the archdeacon of the palace at Constantinople.
[2] The monks from motives of asceticism never wore linen, and recited their office in their working clothes. Hence the older monastic orders never adopted the surplice for the office, but still say it in their habits.

properly ecclesiastical duty whatever. It retains its character as a secular dress for the clergy in the Church of England, as the distinctive robe of bishops at sittings of the House of Lords. As a semi-clerical but obviously non-priestly dress it was recommended by many councils as a suitable garb for sacristans and sextons, and for laymen who had not received even the first clerical tonsure when serving mass. Its origin as a properly liturgical vestment appears to lie in its tolerated use after the middle of the thirteenth century by parish priests for administering baptism, when the new long sleeves of the surplice were liable to trail in the font.

Apart from this, its use *in church* as a distinctive garment for prelates and dignitaries has a slightly unedifying origin. It appears that in the late twelfth century the canons of S. Peter's at Rome got into the way of not troubling to put on the surplice over the rochet (which they still wore as part of their out-door dress) for the daily recitation of the office in church. Ignorant copying of this slackness by foreign prelates visiting Rome set a new fashion, which by the fifteenth century had hardened into a general custom; though the rubrics of the liturgical books have never yet ceased to require the use of the surplice over the rochet by dignitaries for even the most trivial liturgical duties. The fastening of this little piece of mediaeval Italian slovenliness upon all Anglican bishops by the rubrics of the Prayer Book of 1552 is one of those curiosities of liturgical history which add at once to its interest and to its complications.

The various forms of *almuce, mozzetta, hood, tippet, scarf*, etc. are all mediaeval or later. They are all derived ultimately from the fur coat or cloth cape worn *over* the *linea* (instead of under it) for warmth. They are formalised in various ways (shape, colour, material) partly as badges of rank and distinction amongst the clergy themselves, partly in order to distinguish the ordained from the unordained cleric when all alike are wearing the surplice.

The Eastern church has never developed a choir-dress for the secular clergy, chiefly because since the seventh or eighth century the Eastern secular clergy has abandoned the regular recitation of the office to the monks, who like all monks recite it in their habits. When the oriental clergy do conduct parts of the office in public they wear their eucharistic vestments, as at the administration of all sacraments. This would seem to have been the practice of Western clergy, too, before the invention of the cope and surplice.

This review of the history of vestments, though sketchy, is sufficient to establish two main points:

1. That in the fourth century, as before, the 'domestic' character of early christian worship asserted itself even after the transference of the eucharist to the basilicas sufficiently to prevent the adoption anywhere of special ceremonial robes, such as were a usual part of the apparatus of the pagan mysteries. There was indeed no intention whatever of setting up any

distinction of dress between clergy and laity at the liturgy. (The adoption of the stole would find its modern equivalent, I suppose, in something like a clerical collar, or a steward's rosette at a secular meeting.) 2. That by the beginning of the middle ages such a distinction had grown up accidentally by the mere fact that the clergy in church retained the old universal costume after the laity had discarded it. The idea of a special liturgical dress for the clergy came then to be accepted as something right and desirable in itself—an idea which has persisted. For it is to be noted that the adoption by the minister of a Geneva gown and preaching bands, or of a surplice and academic hood, is as much the adoption of a special liturgical costume as the use of eucharistic vestments. For that matter in these days the Salvation Army's poke bonnet and the black frock coat with a white bow tie follow the precedent of the mitre and *pallium*, not that of the chasuble and dalmatic, in that the use of these things is deliberately intended to *distinguish* the wearer from his or her fellow christians at the liturgy; whereas the older vestments were originally intended to do exactly the opposite.

## *Insignia*

Ancient Rome might look a little askance at official costume, but it had no such tradition against the display of other insignia of office. The consul had his *fasces* borne by lictors and magistrates their curule chairs; the augur carried his curved wand, the *lituus*; the senator had his ivory rod, and so on. Such symbols are the Western equivalent for the official robes of Greece and the Near East, where insignia were less common (*e.g.*, the O.T. high-priest had vestments, but no equivalent to the pastoral staff). The general christian acceptance in the fourth century of the Western principle of *not* using special liturgical robes makes it a little surprising that the other Western practice of the display of symbols of office instead was not accepted. But that the church was very slow in adopting such things is clear from the evidence.

*Crosses.* Constantine set the example of using the cross in insignia, both by mounting it upon the imperial diadem (and on the shields of his troops), and especially by his use of it on the *labarum*, the most important of the standards borne before the emperors. This he now made to consist of a gilded cross surmounted by the monogram of Christ, from the arms of which hung a banner of purple silk. He also set a gilt cross above the figure of a dragon on a pole which had formed the cavalry standard of Diocletian's army.

The church, however, did not quickly adopt this carrying of a cross from the ceremonial of the court into that of the liturgy. The first we hear of crosses in a christian procession is some seventy years later. Chrysostom at Constantinople organised torch-light processions to counter the street-propaganda of the Arians, and these carried silver crosses, to the arms of which were affixed burning candles. But it is clear that this was not a transference to the streets of something already practised in the liturgy, but a novelty devised to attract attention, for the crosses were specially presented by the empress for the occasion.[1] The carrying of 'handcrosses' (perhaps originally reliquaries) by dignitaries in church came in during the sixth century, and we hear of crosses carried in procession in Gaul during the fifth and sixth century. One was carried at the landing of Augustine of Canterbury in Thanet in A.D. 596, but here again it is possible to suspect an *ad hoc* device to attract attention rather than a piece of customary ceremonial.

In the *Ordo Romanus Primus*, which though it was compiled *c.* A.D. 800 seems to reflect the Papal ceremonial of the seventh-eighth century with considerable exactness, there is twice mention of a number of crosses carried *behind* the Pope, apparently not by clerics but by lay servants. It reminds one of the eagles and other standards carried by slaves behind the consul and other Roman magistrates. It is a piece of secular rather than religious pomp. But there is nothing in the Papal procession at this date corresponding to the later Western processional cross at the head of the procession, or to the special Papal cross. These both seem to owe their origin at Rome to a suggestion which that lover of ceremony for its own sake, the Frankish emperor Charlemagne, made to Pope Leo III in A.D. 800. When the Pope tactfully agreed with the happy idea of his distinguished visitor, he was at once presented with a magnificent jewelled cross for the purpose. This he ordered to be carried before him annually at the head of the procession of the 'Greater Litanies' on April 25th (not yet kept at Rome as S. Mark's day).[2] From the Papal procession the idea spread to the parish churches of Rome, which all acquired 'stational crosses' for use in procession during the ninth century. But the practice must have been well established at France long before Charlemagne brought about its adoption at Rome. Not only have we the occasional mentions of processional crosses by Gregory of Tours and other authors of the fifth and following centuries; but every parish church has already its own 'stational cross' for use in the Gallican 'Litanies' on the Rogation Days, in Angilbert's *Ordo* at S. Riquier in Picardy *c.* A.D. 805.

The bearing of a special cross before archbishops everywhere within their own province appears to be a copying of this special Papal custom inaugurated by Leo III *c.* A.D. 800. It had already come into general use before the eleventh-twelfth century, when it caused continual troubles in England between the sees of Canterbury and York.

*Altar Crosses.* The placing of a cross actually upon the altar during the liturgy is often said to be derived from the use of the processional cross, the head being detached from the staff after the procession and stood before

[1] Sozomen, *Eccl. Hist.*, viii. 8; Palladius, *Dial. de Vita Chrysost.* 15.
[2] *Liber Pontificalis, Vita Leonis* iii.

the celebrant during the eucharist. It does not seem that this was the origin of the altar cross, though it was the custom in some thirteenth–fourteenth century churches. The placing of anything whatever upon the altar except the bread and cup for the eucharist was entirely contrary to normal christian feeling down to *c.* A.D. 800.[1] In the ninth century, however, this was so far modified that out of service time the gospel book, the pyx with the reserved sacrament and reliquaries began to be admitted as ornaments placed upon the altar itself. But we still hear nothing of altar crosses. For centuries precious crosses had sometimes been hung above the altar, as had crowns, lamps and other ornaments; and standing crosses now began to be set up near it.[2] But the first definite reference to an altar-cross of the modern type appears to be by Pope Innocent III (then still a cardinal) *c.* A.D. 1195, who tells us that at the solemn Papal liturgy a cross between two candlesticks is placed actually upon the altar. The custom spread gradually through the West during the thirteenth and fourteenth centuries, though it hardly became universal before the sixteenth. The Roman custom, however, during most of the middle ages was to remove these novel ornaments as soon as the liturgy was over, leaving the altar outside service-time as bare as it had always been in the past. This removal was still practised in many French churches down to the eighteenth century, and survives in a few Spanish churches to this day.

*The Pastoral Staff.* We have seen that Pope Celestine *c.* A.D. 425 regarded the use of a special staff by a bishop in the light of a *reductio ad absurdum* of superstition. Rome has so far proved faithful to his ideas that the Popes have never yet adopted the use of a pastoral staff.[3] Pastoral staffs, however, did come into use elsewhere. They seem to be mentioned first in Spain in the early seventh century.[4] They were then borne by Spanish abbots and abbesses as well as bishops, as symbols of office.[5] From Spain they appear to have been adopted first by the Celtic and then by the Anglo-Saxon churches,[6] and to have spread over the West outside Rome in the eighth-ninth centuries.

---

[1] There seems, however, to be a cross ('the adorable wood') *upon* the altar, along with the gospel book in Narsai, *Hom.* xvii. *ed.* R. H. Connolly, *p.* 12 (Edessa *c.* A.D. 450). This is, I think, the earliest instance.

[2] *E.g.,* one in S. Peter's 'of silver gilt which stands beside the high altar', *Lib. Pont., Vita Leonis* iii.

[3] This has been denied *e.g.* by Kraus, *Geschichte der christlichen Kunst,* ii., *p.* 500, and by other authors. But all the *locally* Roman evidence of an early mediaeval use of a staff by the Pope seems to relate to the *ferula,* a sort of secular sceptre not used in church. Pope Innocent III specifically denies that the Popes had ever used the *baculum,* the pastoral staff proper; and he seems to be correctly reporting the tradition.

[4] S. Isidore of Seville, *de Officiis Eccles.* 5; ivth Council of Toledo, *can.* 28 A.D. 633).

[5] *Liber Ordinum, ed. cit., coll.* 60, 68.

[6] *Penitential* of Archbp. Theodore of Canterbury, *c.* A.D. 690, P.L., xcix. 928–9. It is noticeable that the Anglo-Saxon abbot is here invested with staff, *pedules* (*i.e.* liturgical shoes) and *staminia* (? = dalmatic). I do not know when these English

The Greek episcopal staff has a separate origin. It is derived, as its form indicates, from the crutch or leaning-stick employed by the Eastern monks as a support when standing through the long offices. Eastern bishops being recruited almost entirely from the monastic orders, they retained as bishops the staff to which they were already accustomed, merely giving it a more expensive and dignified form.

*The Episcopal Ring.* Signet rings were, of course, worn by bishops as by other christians from early times. The first mention of a ring as being, like the *pallium* and staff, a special symbol of the episcopal office is in the twenty-eighth canon of the Spanish Council of Toledo in A.D. 633.

None of these symbols of office, however, appear to go back to the period of transition from a pagan to a christian world in the fourth century. They developed only by degrees, in the seventh–ninth centuries, when deliberate imitation of the pagan rites of antiquity is, to say the least of it, very improbable. It remains, however, to notice one set of christian insignia which do go back certainly to the later fourth century, and to point out their significance.

*Fourth Century Insignia.* A document called the *Notitia Dignitatum Imperii Romani*, a sort of combination of Burke's Peerage, Imperial Gazetteer and Directory of the Civil Service, reveals that *c.* A.D. 400 certain high officials had the privilege of being preceded on occasion like members of the imperial family, by attendants bearing lighted torches and incense. When entering their courts to dispense justice these officials added to these *insignia* their *Liber Mandatorum* or 'Instrument of Instructions', a document which they received on taking up their office, setting forth the general line of policy which the reigning emperor intended them to follow. The particular copy of the *Notitia* which happens to have survived seems to have been drawn up at two different times. The portions dealing with the Western part of the empire reflect conditions *c.* A.D. 405; those dealing with the East seem to refer to a rather later period. But a number of scattered references in much earlier writers make it certain that the distinction of being preceded by incense and torches is something which goes back for some centuries before this in the case of Roman magistrates.[1]

This custom seems to have been adopted by christian bishops in some places towards the end of the fourth century, at which time the state was placing upon them some of the duties of civic magistrates in their see-towns. But though these distinctions would thus seem to have originated much more from the secular than the strictly religious aspect of their position, a religious turn was given to it by the substitution of the gospel book as the 'Law of Christ' for the *Liber Mandatorum* of the secular official.

The first fairly certain reference to the episcopal use of these insignia

abbatial ornaments became so confused with properly episcopal privileges as to be supposed to require a special Papal grant for their use; but presumably it came about after the Norman Conquest by false analogy with the mitre.

[1] Horace, *Satires* I, v. 36; Tertullian, *Apologeticus*, 35; etc.

appears to be in a poem by the Italian S. Paulinus of Nola just after A.D. 400;[1] and there can be little doubt that its adoption, in some churches at least, both in the East and West, dates from about or rather before this time. It may be connected with the introduction of a solemn processional entry of the bishop and clergy at the beginning of the liturgy, which replaced the old greeting of the assembled church after an informal arrival, as the opening of the synaxis. We are rather in the dark as to when this procession was first introduced, except that at Rome the chant which accompanied it, the introit-psalm, is said to have been an innovation of Pope Celestine I (A.D. 422–432). The procession itself may be rather older than the practice of accompanying it by a chant; and taking into account the normal delay at Rome in the adoption of new liturgical practices, we might well suppose that the procession was at least twenty or thirty years older in some Western churches.

At all events, c. A.D. 400 and perhaps rather earlier, the bishop on entering and leaving the church began to be preceded by the torches, incense and book of a magistrate, a practice which had originally no particular christian symbolism at all. An exact modern parallel is the preceding of Anglican dignitaries in procession by a beadle or verger carrying just such a 'mace' as precedes the Speaker of the House of Commons or a Mayor. At its beginning the use of these episcopal insignia had no more significance than that of the cathedral verger 'pokering' the canon in residence to read the second lesson. But when we first meet these processional lights before the bishop in the Roman rite they have already become seven in number (instead of the Praetorian Prefect's four and the lesser magistrate's two). It may be that here the seven golden candlesticks of the Apocalypse have come in to give a christian turn to the old secular emblem. The bishop is the earthly representative of Christ, as the eucharist is the earthly manifestation of the heavenly worship, and the adaptation would easily suggest itself.

The use of the seven processional torches at the bishop's liturgy spread widely through the West from the ninth century onwards, chiefly through an adaptation of the *Ordo Romanus Primus*[2] made c. A.D. 800 which formed the basis of episcopal ceremonial·in France for some centuries to come, and which was more or less widely adopted from there in England and Germany. Its only survival to-day other than in the Papal mass is in the special pontifical ceremonial of the archbishop of Lyons (which is not 'Gallican' in origin as has been too often supposed, but represents the ceremonial of the Papal rite as modified for adoption in the palace chapel of Charlemagne, which was introduced at Lyons by Bishop Leidrad, c. A.D. 810).[3]

---

[1] *Carmina*, xxii. 203 *sq.*
[2] The so-called *Ordo Romanus Secundus.*
[3] See Dom D. Bruenner, *L'Ancienne liturgie romaine: le rite lyonnais* (Lyons and Paris, 1935).

Whether the use of seven candles upon the altar by Western bishops when pontificating has any direct connection with the Pope's seven processional torches (as has often been suggested) seems more than doubtful. When candles first appear upon the altar at the Pope's eucharist they are not seven but two; and the seven altar candles when they do appear in the Papal mass do not replace the seven torches, but are an addition to them.

The use of two torches carried before the presbyter as celebrant of the eucharist seems to perpetuate the original form in which this honour was paid to bishops. It was probably an unreflecting continuance of custom when bishops finally ceased to be the normal celebrants of the eucharist for all their people at a single stational eucharist, and parish priests became their regular substitutes for particular districts. As the bishop's delegate, no doubt, any celebrant seemed entitled to the same marks of honour, even though originally these particular insignia denoted rather the bishop's personal importance as a civic leader than his sacerdotal character as celebrant of the eucharist.

Another symbol of the same kind which *may* have come into use in the late fourth or early fifth century is the *umbella*, a sort of flat 'state umbrella' carried over the heads of Byzantine magistrates and officials.[1] It was also carried in front of the Byzantine emperor as a symbol of authority. In this fashion it seems to have been used by some of the Popes as a symbol of quasi-ducal authority in Rome after the ninth century, as it was by the doges of Venice and certain other Italian potentates in the early middle ages. It is doubtless from this that its use above the arms of the Cardinal Camerlengo of the Roman church during vacancies in the Holy See is derived, since the Chamberlain acts as emergency *locum tenens* of the temporalities of the see during the *interregnum*. But it never became a part of the Papal liturgical insignia[2] nor a general symbol of the episcopal office. It had in fact no more religious significance than the state umbrella and fan

---

[1] See the curious Byzantine regulations about colour and materials, etc. for different offices in Codinus Curopalata, *de Officiis*, iv. (*ed.* Paris, 1648, *pp.* 50 *sq.*).

[2] It does not appear in the Papal procession at mass. Its use as a sort of canopy over the reserved sacrament appears to derive from the carrying of the sacrament before the Pope on journeys, first *along with* the *umbella*, and then beneath it. The perpetual preceding of the Pope by the sacrament in the middle ages is itself a relic of primitive times. In the fourth century bishops usually carried the sacrament about with them in *enkolpia* or pyxes, for the purpose of giving communion at need; the Popes did not abandon this custom in some form right down to the sixteenth century. See the interesting evidence collected by W. H. Freestone, *The Sacrament Reserved*, London, 1917, *p.* 65. It is perhaps worth remarking that though fans figured among the insignia of the imperial procession, the two carried behind the Pope appear to be derived rather from the liturgical fans of the fourth-fifth century (*cf.* Theodore of Mopsuestia, cited *p.* 282), whose use did not altogether die out in the West till the fifteenth century. Like the *sedia gestatoria*, or portable throne, on which the Pope is now carried into S. Peter's, the fans only appear in the Papal procession in Renaissance times. The earlier rule was that the Pope always rode in procession to mass, except on penitential days when he walked. The *sedia* has no direct connection with the litter or sedan chair of the classical period.

now carried behind the Viceroy of India in public. But in a small number of ancient parish churches round about Arles in Provence—that stronghold of the old usages of *Romania*—the *umbella* is still carried over the head of the parish priest (but not, it is said, of anyone else) when he goes to the altar to sing mass on great feasts. I should be prepared to believe that this custom has come down by unbroken tradition from the last days of the empire in these cases, though I know of no evidence to prove it.

Here again, then, in the use of symbols and insignia, it seems quite impossible to bring home to the fourth century church any imitation of the pagan mysteries. The carrying and exhibition of symbolic objects in processions and liturgical rites was a notable feature of the mysteries in so far as they were public cults—and indeed of classical pagan worship generally. But what emerges from the evidence is that the christian church made *no* ceremonial use of such things in the fourth century at all. The only possible exception is the Eastern offertory procession of the Great Entrance, first attested in its developed form by Theodore of Mopsuestia[1] early in the fifth century. Those who wish to may lay emphasis on the general resemblance of this to a mystery rite, though I have failed to find any particular pagan rite to which it can be compared at all closely in detail. For my own part, given the Syrian custom attested by the *Didascalia* in the third century, of the deacons bringing the people's offerings of bread and wine from the sacristy at this particular point of the rite, I think the 'Great Entrance' much more likely to be simply a ceremonialised form of this purely utilitarian bringing of the bread and wine to the table when they were required for the eucharist, than anything derived from the procession of the 'dead Attis' or such-like mystery cult functions.

Apart from this, the only portable symbols which were adopted anywhere before the end of the fourth century were the gospel book and the torches and incense carried before the bishop; and these were taken over from the civil ceremonial of the magistrate, not from the pagan cults, and had no religious significance. It is only centuries afterwards, when the pagan mysteries had long been forgotten, that the natural symbolic instinct produced the carrying of such objects as crosses and pastoral staffs in the christian liturgy.

### Lights

The episcopal insignia first introduced two things into christian eucharistic worship, portable lights and censers, which play a considerable part in later ceremonial both in the East and West. But torches and candles have also been used in catholic worship in other ways which have not all this origin.

*At Funerals.* The lighting of torches at funerals was a mourning custom common to all mediterranean religions, to which pre-christian judaism

[1] *Cf. p.* 282.

had been no exception. The contemporary *Acta* of S. Cyprian's martyr-dom (A.D. 258) reveal that the pre-Nicene christian church also made no difficulty about accepting this universal token of mourning. It describes how after a hasty temporary burial Cyprian's body was subsequently removed by the christians 'with candles and torches'.[1] There was no change made about this after the peace of the church. Eusebius describes the candles burning on golden stands around the bier at the funeral of Con-stantine in A.D. 337[2] and S. Gregory of Nyssa describing his own sister's funeral in A.D. 370 tells how deacons and subdeacons two abreast bearing lighted candles escorted the body in procession from the house.[3] The custom was universal both in the East and the West, and continues so to this day.

Here (at last) is something in catholic custom which is certainly of pagan origin. Both the bier-lights (which have never died out at state funerals in post-Reformation England) and the Western *chapelle ardente*, and the candles held by the mourners at the Western requiem and the Eastern *panikhida* have all a common origin in very ancient pre-christian pagan observance. Mourning customs are always one of the most persistent elements of older practice through all changes of religion, chiefly because they depend on private observance by grief-stricken individuals much more than on official religious regulation; and no ecclesiastic is going to go out of his way to rebuke harmless conventions which may do a little to assuage sorrow at such a time. (So *e.g.* the modern West African christians, both catholic and protestant, wear white at funerals in Ashanti, simply because a plain white 'cloth' in place of the normal brightly coloured native dress is the traditional mourning of Ashanti pagan custom.)

*At the Gospel.* S. Jerome writing in A.D. 378 from Bethlehem says that 'throughout all the churches of the East when the gospel is to be read lights are kindled . . . not to dispel the darkness but to exhibit a token of joy . . . and that under the symbol of corporeal light that light may be set forth of which we read in the psalter, "Thy word is a lantern unto my feet and a light unto my paths".'[4] This is one of those little symbolical actions like the *lavabo* with which, as we have said, the fourth century churches soon began to overlay the bare outline of the pre-Nicene rite, a process in which the Jerusalem church was the pioneer. In this case the context suggests that these lights were not so much part of the official ceremonial as kindled and held by the people. It is therefore probably more closely connected with that popular pagan custom of lighting lamps and candles both at home and in the sanctuary as a general sign of religious festivity, than with the later christian ceremonial carrying of two candles by acolytes at the reading of the gospel. It had from time immemorial been a pagan usage to hang lighted lamps about the doorways of the house on days of religious festivity,

---

[1] *Acta Proconsularia S. Cypriani*, 5.
[2] *Vita S. Macrinae, ad fin.*
[3] *Vita Constantini*, iv. 66.
[4] *contra Vigilantium*, 3.

about which more than one of the pre-Nicene fathers make scornful observations.[1] Popular piety carried on the practice to celebrate christian festivals, though it was discouraged by the church.[2] But this popular use of
lighted candles with their natural symbolism of cheerfulness and joy was
too harmless to be rigidly excluded (cf., e.g. the use of candles on christmas
trees in Wesleyan chapels) and they make their way into various minor
ceremonies of the liturgy towards the end of the fourth century. It is e.g.
at this time that the presentation of a lighted candle to the neophyte after
baptism (as well as the pre-Nicene white robe) begins to be introduced;
and it is likely that this kindling of lights at the gospel in the East of which
S. Jerome speaks is another quasi-liturgical observance of the same kind,
introduced about the same time.

The more strictly official carrying of two lights at the gospel is first
mentioned by S. Isidore of Seville early in the seventh century,[3] but since
he mentions that they were extinguished as soon as the gospel had been
read, this may have a purely utilitarian origin, like the use of the prelate's
'hand-candle' (scotula), the origin of which seems to be lost in antiquity.
Anyone who has inspected ancient liturgical books, with their close writing
and frequent contractions of spelling, will understand the need of a light
near the book even in daylight for the public reading of the text. It is possible that once more Rome was somewhat behind other churches in the
adoption of the lights at the gospel. The absence of them at the paschal
vigil mass (on Holy Saturday) is probably a little piece of conservatism at
this most archaic service in the whole year,[4] reproducing the customary
absence of ritual pomp at the singing of the gospel at Rome perhaps as late
as the fifth or sixth century. It is only in the Ordo Romanus Primus that we
first hear of two candles carried at the singing of the gospel in the Roman
rite. Here it is clear from the whole setting and from what is done with
them that they have a ceremonial, not an utilitarian, purpose. They precede the subdeacons with the censer (the book is not censed as yet), but the
gospel is sung from the top of the ambo (pulpit) steps while the lights remain below. The gospel book preceded by lights and incense has in fact
come to be treated as symbolic of the Person of Christ proclaiming the
gospel. Probably the lights which had been carried before the bishop for
two or three centuries by now had introduced this new idea in connection
with the book of the gospels.

*Illumination.* We have already seen (p. 87) that the ceremonial bringing
in and blessing of a lamp was a customary part of the ritual at a *chabûrah*

[1] Tertullian, *de Idololatria*, 15. Lactantius, *Instit.*, vi. 2; etc.
[2] *E.g.*, S. Gregory Nazianzene, *Oratio* v. 35. S. Jerome, *loc. cit.*, though he half
defends such practices against the puritan Vigilantius, declares it is due to 'the
ignorance and simplicity of laymen or at least of over-devout women'.
[3] *Etymol.* VII. xii. 29.
[4] Their absence at the Passion gospels in Holy Week has a symbolic reason, and
is almost certainly a later touch in the ceremonies.

meal such as the last supper.[1] But this continued in christian liturgical use
only at the agape, not at the eucharist. It survived at the vigil also, and was
introduced into the public service of the *lucernarium* from the practice of
christian domestic piety when public evening services began to be held in
the later fourth century.

Nevertheless, illumination was, of course, sometimes needed for practical purposes at the early morning eucharists of the pre-Nicene church,
and was provided in the ordinary way, as the candlesticks and lamps of the
church of Cirta show.[2] But there was no ceremonial or symbolical use of
lights whatever at the eucharist in the pre-Nicene church. After the peace
of the church a number of fourth century authors speak incidentally of
the great quantity of lights, both candles and lamps, sometimes employed
in the churches at Vespers and the Night Office.[3] We have already noticed
the lavish scale on which Constantine provided for the lighting of S.
Peter's.[4] But though there is an advance here from mere utility to decoration, there is nothing corresponding to the later symbolic use of altar lights;
though perpetually burning lamps at the martyrs' tombs are found before
the end of the fourth century. Curiously enough neither the precedent of
the seven-branched lampstand of the O.T. Tabernacle nor that of the
seven lamps burning before the throne of God in the Apocalypse seems
to have exercised any marked influence before the beginning of the middle
ages.

*Candles on the Altar.* For reasons already stated the standing of any
object whatever on the altar was entirely contrary to the devotional conventions of the early church. Lamps and candelabra were hung above it,
and standard candlesticks were stood around—sometimes six or eight of
them. But the altar itself remained bare of such ornaments for almost
the first thousand years of christian history in the West, and perhaps to an
even later date in the East.[5] This feeling of the special sanctity of the altar
began to break down in Gaul in the eighth century in certain respects, but
it is not until the ninth century that we find candlesticks being stood upon
it, and for some while they were not common even in great churches.
There was one which was placed upon the altar in Winchester cathedral
c. A.D. 1180, but apparently as a special little ceremony on Christmas day
only, and this is the earliest English reference to such a practice that I

---

[1] For the rabbinic rules see *Berakoth*, M. viii. 5, 6, 7; T. vi. 7, 8.
[2] *Cf. p.* 24.
[3] *E.g.* Etheria, *Peregrinatio*, ed. Geyer (C.S.E.L. 38), *p.* 72; Paulinus of Nola,
*Carmina*, xxxvii. 389 *sq.*
[4] *Cf. p.* 310.
[5] The date when the Easterns first set candlesticks actually upon the altar seems
impossible to determine. J. Braun, *Das christliche Altargerät* (Munich, 1932), *p.*
498 even suggests 'the end of the middle ages'. Narsai, *Hom.*, xvii., *p.* 12 knows the
cross upon the altar, but has no mention of candles, only 'lamps'. What I think is
certain is that, in the East as in the West, 'standard' candlesticks around the altar
and processional lights are at least five or six centuries older than the altar-candle-
sticks themselves.

know.[1] This custom of one altar candle (moved around with the book at low mass) became fairly common in France in the thirteenth century, and was still not unknown in England as late as the fifteenth century. It is said to survive to this day at low mass in Carthusian monasteries.

It is not, however, until the very end of the twelfth century (c. A.D. 1195) that we first find candles upon the altar at Rome; and then they are two in number at the Pope's 'stational' mass on the most solemn feasts.[2] By A.D. 1254 the number on such occasions had risen to seven.[3] Further than that it never went. The Papal custom of two candles on the altar was widely adopted in the early thirteenth century, and lasted without change in some of the great French and Spanish collegiate churches down to the eighteenth century.

It is by no means clear how the current notion that two candles was the specifically 'English Use' originated. The multiplication of altar candles was in fact rather characteristic of England and the North generally, once the custom of having them at all had come in. Thus e.g., at Chichester before the end of the thirteenth century the custom on feasts was to burn seven tall lights each of two pounds' weight of wax upon the altar and eight more in trabe (on a shelf above the altar-screen—the fore-runner of the Renaissance 'gradine').[4] At S. Augustine's Canterbury there were two such trabes with a row of six candles on each, and apparently a third row of six actually upon the altar.[5] At Exeter early in the fourteenth century there were still no candles on the altar itself, but a row of ten behind it.[6] At Lincoln there were five;[7] at S. David's cathedral there were fourteen;[8] and so on. There appear in fact to be instances from mediaeval England of every number of altar candles from one to twenty, except seventeen and nineteen.[9]

If we enquire the reason for the widespread increase in the number of altar candles during the thirteenth century, it is to be found, I think, in the change in the shape of the Western altar from the antique fashion of a cube

[1] See the list of church ornaments presented by Bp. Henry of Blois to the cathedral. E. Bishop, Liturgica Historica, p. 400.
[2] Innocent III, de Sacro Altaris Mysterio, ii. 21.
[3] E. Bishop, op. cit., p. 311.    [4] Archaeological Journal, xxxv., p. 386.
[5] Customary of S. Augustine's Canterbury, etc., ed. Sir E. M. Thompson (H.B.S. 1904) ii., p. 271.
[6] Ordinale Exon., ed. J. N. Dalton (H.B.S. 1909), ii., p. 540.
[7] H. Bradshaw and C. Wordworth, Statutes of Lincoln Cathedral, 1892, i., p. 288.
[8] Brit. Mus. Harl. Ms., 1249, f. 5, cited E. G. C. F. Atchley, History of the Use of Incense, London, 1909, p. 325.
[9] Perhaps the origin of the 'English two candles' myth lies in the Royal Injunction of 1547 to the clergy 'to suffer to remain still' (i.e. when the rest have been taken away) 'only two candles upon the High Altar'. The explanation lies, not in any care for old customs, but in the further order issued later to collect all superfluous church plate for the benefit of the Privy Council. Part of the wording of this Order in Council, then still in force, was embodied by Cranmer in the rubrics of the book of 1549. This may or may not constitute an authoritative Anglican ruling on altar lights, but it had nothing to do with 'old English customs', which varied indefinitely.

some 3 ft. square to that of oblong altars 10, 12, or more feet long, in the new gothic churches. The increase in the number of candles comes in first in the great churches, which were mostly being rebuilt about then in the new style, only because the new shape of altar came in first in the great churches, which always tend to set fashions.

Such things have nothing to do with religion or its practice (or even with what is called 'loyalty'), as the mediaeval churchmen were sensible enough to perceive. But the portentous behaviour of nineteenth century English bishops and lawyers, and the 'fond things vainly invented' by some ritualists, have succeeded in impressing it upon the mind of most modern Englishmen that they somehow closely concern the genius of christianity. Such questions were formerly decided by custom, by aesthetics or by mere convenience, not by courts of law. To the mediaeval taste a row of candlesticks looked better than two on a long altar, and so they had a row—of three, four, five, six, seven, eight, nine, ten or whatever number their finances or fancy or just the fashion of the moment suggested; or they varied the number on different days according to the rank of the feast or the dignity of the celebrant. In Germany and Holland in the fifteenth century some churches took to having hundreds; in the same period in Sicily and Sardinia some churches preferred to retain only two; and nobody questioned their right to do as they liked in either case. The modern Anglican celebrant can have six candles upon his altar like some of the Avignon Popes in the fourteenth century, or seven like the Popes at the end of the thirteenth century, or two like the Popes at the end of the twelfth century, or even none at all like the Popes at the end of the eleventh century—and be happily conscious that historically he is being just as 'Roman' whichever he does. If he really wants to be 'primitive' in such matters, he must celebrate facing the people across the altar—like all the Popes in every century—and with no candles and no cross (and no vases of flowers or book-stand)—like all the Popes for the first thousand years. What preposterous nonsense it is to try to erect sacristy orthodoxies and even tests of theological allegiance out of these minute details of pious furnishing, that have varied endlessly throughout christian history and have never meant anything in particular by all their changes!

*Lights as Votive Offerings.* The burning of votive candles as well as other lights (and incense) at the tombs of 'heroes' and before the statues of the gods was a general practice in mediterranean paganism, and was not unknown in pre-christian judaism at 'the tombs of the prophets'. The introduction of this form of popular devotion at the tombs of christian martyrs even before the end of the pre-Nicene period seems to be witnessed to by a canon (34) of the Spanish Council of Elvira c. A.D. 300 forbidding it (though this interpretation of the canon is not quite certain). The Council's prohibition certainly did not end the practice, even in Spain. A century later the Spaniard Vigilantius of Barcelona, exhibiting that impatience of folk-religion which is at once the strength and the limitation of puritans in every age, made a violent attack on the general use of this practice in his own day by christians at the tombs of the martyrs. To this S. Jerome made an equally intemperate reply, comparing those who observed it to the woman who poured ointment upon the Lord, and their critic to Judas Iscariot.[1] More than one bishop made attempts to restrain the practice, but as such expressions of popular piety are usually wont to do, it proved stronger in the end than all ecclesiastical regulations. The lighting of lamps and candles at the tombs of the saints became a normal feature of all such christian sanctuaries and places of pilgrimage from the fifth century onwards, if not from the end of the fourth.[2]

*Candles offered to Images.* The cultus of relics of the saints concerned the honouring of the actual bodies of the martyrs or portions of them, something which has been and will be again at the last day an integral element in their personalities. A further step was taken when the same honours were paid to statues and pictures of the saints and of our Lord Himself. The fourth century church accepted the cultus of relics without much question, but it was much more reluctant to allow this second step to be taken, being still very sensitive on that question of 'idolatry' upon which the conflict of the martyrs had turned. Pictures of our Lord and of the saints had been known as decorations (in the catacombs and elsewhere) and means of instruction (*e.g.* the baptistery at Dura) since the late second or early third century at the latest. As such, pictures and statues continued in use during the fourth century, though there were protests about this,[3] and the Spanish Council of Elvira had forbidden such decorations in churches.[4] But there is no single case, I think, of that ecclesiastical toler-

---

[1] *adv. Vigilantium*, 7.

[2] How inveterate and—presumably—how harmless the instinct to do this can be, is shewn by the lighting of candles on occasion around the 'shrine' of the Unknown Warrior by the Anglican authorities of Westminster Abbey. This has become in our days a place of pilgrimage fulfilling in popular devotion very much the same *rôle* as the martyrs' tombs in the fourth century—witness the scenes enacted there in September 1938 and 1939.

[3] *E.g.* Eusebius, *Ep. to Constantia.*

[4] *Can.* 36, 'Pictures ought not to be in a church, lest that which is worshipped and adored be drawn on the walls'. The exact turn of thought here is worth noting. The motive of the prohibition is not so much the fear of idolatry, of their being worshipped, as the idea that there is irreverence in the very attempt to portray the infinite Divine. This seems to be the general pre-Nicene, and for that matter post-Nicene, attitude towards pictures of the Godhead, down to the eighth century. (*Cf.* S. John Damascene, *Orat. de Sacris Imaginibus*, ii. 5, where arguing for the cultus of images he still insists: 'We should indeed be in error if we made an image of the invisible God'.) Representations of our Lord's Humanity and of the saints could not be subject to this objection, unless, like Tertullian, christians were to adopt the semitic dogma (found both in Judaism and Islam, but it is a racial—Bedouin—feeling rather than an intellectual belief) that *all* representational art is as such morally wrong. (How far was Tertullian's Carthaginian—ultimately Phoenician?—temperament the cause of his rigidity?) There is ample evidence that the pre-Nicene church did not adopt this line about art. (*E.g.*, the professional painter is to be admitted to baptism provided he is not employed in the manufacture of idols,

ance and even encouragement then given to the popular cultus of relics being extended to the cultus of pictures or statues of Christ or the saints during the fourth or the first half of the fifth century. There is, too, a noticeably academic tone about christian homilies on 'the peril of idolatry' in this period,[1] which contrasts with the urgency of clerical denunciations of abuses in connection with the relic cult, and suggests that any tendency towards an undue veneration of pictures and images was not a very widespread problem in the church, before the fifth century at all events. The distinction of christian ideas and practice from those of a still living and observable paganism was as yet too obvious to need much emphasis. It was only *after* the disappearance of paganism that disputes began about the christian use of images—a point which needs more consideration than it has received in most histories of the controversy.

There remained, however, in the new christian world one particular survival from the past which was outside the control of the church, and which was bound sooner or later to raise in some form the whole question of the cultus of images. The emperor-cult had always been the centre of the practical problem of 'idolatry' for christians. The usual test for martyrs had been whether they would or would not 'adore' the emperor's image with the customary offering of incense. But the *Notitia Dignitatum* (c. A.D. 405–425) reveals that this particular method of demonstrating loyalty had survived in full working right through the period of the conversion of the empire.[2] In the fifth century the portrait of the reigning emperor was still set up in the courts of justice and in the municipal buildings of the cities surrounded by lighted candles, and incense was still burned before it. The Arian historian Philostorgius brings a charge of idolatry against the orthodox of Constantinople in his day (c. A.D. 425) in that they burn incense and candles before the statue of the emperor Constantine, the founder of the city.[3] (It is worth remarking that this seems to be more than a century before we have any definite evidence of a similar cultus paid to specifically *religious* pictures and images.) One can see how this had come about. When Constantine and his successors became personally christians, they still as emperors remained 'divine' (or at all events the working centre of the old state religion)[4] for that large majority of their subjects who still remained pagan. For these the old forms of reverence simply remained in use. To change them might have been politically dangerous; it would certainly have been unsettling to pagan public opinion. And now that the emperor

*Ap. Trad.*, xvi. 11.) And though it was not unknown for individuals to adopt it in the fourth century, it was not the common or normal attitude either of laymen or ecclesiastics about either art in general or specifically 'sacred' art.

[1] *E.g.*, Augustine, *Enarr. in Ps. cxiii*, ii. 5; *Ep. cii*, iii. 18.
[2] *Not. Dign.*, ed. Boecking, *P. Orient.*, iii., *p.* 12; *P. Occid.*, ii., *p.* 8.
[3] Philostorgius, *Eccl. Hist.*, ii. 17.
[4] They retained the pagan title and office of *Pontifex Maximus* and the political control of pagan worship which that gave them down to the time of Gratian (A.D. 375), though they did not personally fulfil its ritual functions.

publicly disbelieved in his own divinity, many christians found it more possible to pay the conventional 'adoration'[1] to the imperial portrait as a matter of etiquette.

Yet this cultus of the emperor's ikon was by tradition a religious veneration and was well understood to be so. It was bound to suggest the lawfulness of a similar cultus to the ikons of the King of heaven and the saints, and we do in fact find it brought forward as an argument in favour of the cultus of christian images, once that began to be debated.[2] This is not the place to consider the immense disturbance which the facing of that question occasioned all over christendom in the eighth and ninth centuries, or the rather different lines on which it was settled in the East and West respectively.[3] All that concerns us now is the extent of the connection of such cultus of images with the official liturgy of the church and the date when it began.

In the West there is virtually never any such connection at all. The Western church has officially practised and encouraged the cultus of images by the clergy and laity in a variety of ways; but it has always kept it dissociated from the eucharist and the office. At the most all that could be cited is the setting of a crucifix upon the altar during the celebration of the eucharist, and its incidental censing during the censing of the altar.[4]

---

[1] *Proskynesis*, a word of elastic meaning. It could mean religious adoration in the strict sense; it could also imply that lesser reverence formerly demonstrated, *e.g.*, by serving kings on bended knees.

[2] Mansi, *Concilia*, t. xii. 1014, 1068.

[3] Briefly, the West took in the end what seems the commonsense view, that it is hardly possible for an educated Western man to commit what the O.T. means by 'idolatry', *viz.* the paying of divine honour literally *to* an image. There is always a mental reference to that which it represents. (*Cf.* S. Thomas, *Summa Theol.*, III., xxv. a. 3.) Whether this solution holds equally good for all parts of the mission field, or even in all parts of Europe, is perhaps another question; though I found in West Africa that the ju-ju priests, and perhaps the worshippers, look on their fetiches in much the same way. (That great field-anthropologist, the late R. L. Rattray, once told me that he fully agreed with this estimate.) The Eastern view, as stated by S. John of Damascus and S. Theodore of the Studium, is more alarming to the protestant mind. There is, however, a most interesting exposition and defence of it, against the Western Thomistic view, by the (R.C.) V. Grummel in Vacandard, *Dict. de Theol. Cath.*, *s.v. Images (Culte des)*. The whole question has recently been treated with his usual sympathy and learning by Prof. E. Bevan in *Holy Images* (1940), (part of his Gifford Lectures, but published separately) but without coming to any very clear conclusions. If I may be allowed a personal word, I think a great deal of christian iconoclast violence on the subject has been due to the inveterate tendency of all puritans to 'verbalism', to restricting worship and prayer to what can be expressed *in words*, with direct mental attention. I have never personally been assisted to vocal prayer in any sort of way by an image or crucifix; but I have frequently been assisted to 'recollection' for mental prayer by the sight of them, or by holding a crucifix. If words formed or thought with attention be the only thing conceived of as 'prayer', then images are certainly either distractions or idols. But if prayer be something which can be both wider and deeper than that, then it would seem that they can be, as the orthodox have always contended, both an assistance and a medium of true worship.

[4] In the office, statues (or side-altars) of saints are sometimes censed during *Magnificat* at Vespers on their feasts, but this is a permitted, not a prescribed ceremony of the rite.

But even this slight connection does not begin until the thirteenth century.

In the East the connection is stronger. Not only does the veneration of ikons play a much greater and more intimate part in the personal devotion of the Orthodox East[1] among clergy and laity alike than is common in the West, but their censing and veneration in a carefully prescribed order is laid down as an official part of the orthodox liturgy, both at the eucharist and at the office, as well as at other services. They are regarded not as mere reminders of what they portray, but as actually *mediating* the participation of their originals in the earthly worship of the church. Accordingly their veneration is an integral part of divine worship, just as rejoicing in the fellowship of our Lady and all saints and angels will be a real part of the joy and worship of the redeemed in heaven, which the earthly worship of the church 'manifests' in time. But here again it is doubtful if this conjoining of the veneration of images with the official liturgy is really ancient in the Byzantine church. It probably began in the ninth century, as part of the great renewal of emphasis on the cultus of images which accompanied the final overthrow of the iconoclast emperors. In any case it can hardly be older than the introduction of the custom of a preliminary censing of the altar and sanctuary, which is first mentioned in Syria only in the late fifth century[2] but probably was not adopted at Constantinople till the sixth-seventh century.

### Incense

The use of incense both for domestic purposes and in the cultus goes back for some centuries before the christian era all round the mediterranean basin. In the Near East it is much older than in the West, doubtless because the materials—gums and spices—are indigenous to those countries and not to the West. Its religious use in the Old Testament need not detain us, since it has no early connection with its use in christian worship other than through the use of Old Testament symbols in various ways by the writers of the New.[3]

*At the chabûrah meal.* There is, however, a domestic use of incense in judaism which is worth recording because of its possible connection with the last supper. The burning of spices in the room after the evening meal was a common custom in all the mediterranean countries, but among the jews it was—like everything else—given a religious colouring, especially at the domestic rite of supper on formal occasions, of the type under which the *chabûrah* meeting was included. The ceremonial introduction and blessing

---

[1] The dissidents are much less demonstrative in this respect. The Nestorians have no ikons. The Monophysites use them as decorations, and are said to have begun to copy Orthodox customs in their veneration to a certain extent in quite modern times.

[2] Pseudo-Dionysius Areop., *de Hier. Eccl.*, iii. 2.

[3] Phil. iv. 18; Rev. v. 8, etc.

of a lamp has already been spoken of. It was at this moment that the spices also were introduced and blessed and burned. In the first century A.D. the question was disputed between the rabbis as to the order in which the lamp and the spices (or the chafing dish in which they were burned) were to be blessed. The school of Shammai held that first the lamp was to be blessed, then the 'Thanksgiving' was to be said, then the spices were to be blessed and burned. The school of Hillel held that both lamp and spices were to be blessed and used before the 'Thanksgiving' was said.[1] This was not an exceptional rite but one of such normal occurrence that the omission of the bringing in of spices (to save unnecessary labour on the Sabbath) at the Friday evening meal with which the Sabbath began, became a special sign of the Sabbath; as their reappearance at the Saturday evening meal was a sign that it was over. The reappearance of the burning spices on Saturday evening was especially associated with the *habdalah*, the prayer with which the domestic keeping of the Sabbath ended.[2] In the form of the 'habdalah spice-box' this domestic use of incense has descended into the practice of the modern orthodox jewish home, though it is not now burned, but only smelled at.[3] The last supper was a formal *chabûrah* meal, at which the ordinary rules for such occasions were observed, and it was not held on the eve of sabbath, which was specially marked by the omission of the burning of spices. It is true that the N.T. accounts do not mention this; but then neither do they mention the bringing in and blessing of the lamp, with which the spices were closely associated, though we may infer that there must have been one.[4] They are not meant to be full reports of every detail of the meal.

*In Christian Worship.* It is probably due to familiarity with the hallowed usage of incense in the Temple worship and also in this domestic way at the *chabûrah* meetings of the primitive church at Jerusalem, that there is no trace in the New Testament of hostility to the use of incense in worship. It is even taken for granted as playing a prominent part in the ideal christian public worship of heaven.[5] Such hostility developed later in the gentile churches during the persecutions.[6] The mere fact that the ordinary test for a christian was the command to burn incense to a heathen divinity was sufficient to cause it to be regarded with something like horror, despite the precedents of the Old and New Testament. These were allegorised away as referring only to 'prayer',[7] and the rationalistic arguments of pagan philosophers against the employment of incense in pagan worship were rather curiously seized upon as part of the christian apologetic for its dis-

[1] *Berakoth, Mishna*, viii. 5. *Cf. Tosefta*, vi. 6 (*pp.* 68–9).
[2] *Cf.* I. Abrahams, Notes on the *Jewish Authorised Prayer Book, p.* clxxxii.
[3] That it was anciently burned *cf. Berakoth, M.*, vi. 6 (*p.* 48).
[4] John xiii. 30.      [5] Rev. v. 8; viii. 3, 4, etc.
[6] Tertullian, *de Idololatria*, ii.; Arnobius, *adv. Gentes*, vi. 1; Lactantius, *Instit.*, vi. 25, etc.
[7] Irenaeus, *adv. Haer.*, IV. xv. 11; Origen, *contra Celsum*, viii. 17, etc.

use.[1] *Turificati*, 'incense-burners', without further description, became a technical name for the apostates who by obedience to the magistrate's command had forfeited not only the heavenly crown of martyrdom but all participation in the earthly worship of the church. Nothing can be more certain regarding the worship of the pre-Nicene church than that incense was not used at it in any way during the second and third centuries.

It was only after the peace of the church that the burning of perfumes in christian churches began.[2] It must have become fairly widespread before the end of the fourth century for we hear of it almost simultaneously at Jerusalem and at Antioch in the East[3] and at Milan and Nola in Italy.[4] But there is nothing in most of these fourth century references to suggest more than a 'fumigatory' use of incense to perfume the churches. We do not even know that it was burned during service time, and not simply as a preparation for the assembly of a large and somewhat mixed gathering of people in a not too-well ventilated building. This is much more analogous to the domestic than the liturgical use of incense. The use of it borne before the bishop as a mark of honour, which comes in at about the same period, is nearer to a ritual usage, but even this is a borrowing from secular customs and not religious in its origin.[5]

By the end of the fifth century some use of incense in christian churches appears to have been more or less universal. But it is clear that in the large majority of cases this had still no more directly religious significance than, *e.g.*, the use of music. It was now an accepted part of the general setting in which the eucharist was held; but the Old Testament notion of incense as in itself an *offering* to God (whether in combination with other sacrifices or alone) had hardly made its appearance. The text of Malachi i. 11 'in every

[1] Eusebius, *Praep. Evangelica.*, iv. 10 (citing Porphyry); iv. 13 (citing Apollonius)
[2] *Cf. p.* 310.
[3] Etheria, *Peregrinatio*, ed. cit., *p.* 73; Chrysostom, *in Mat. Hom.*, lxxxix. 4; *cf. Apostolic Canons*, 3.
[4] Ambrose, *de Cain et Abel*, I, v. 19; Paulinus of Nola, *Carmina*, xiv. 100; xxvi. 410.
[5] Etheria (*loc. cit.*) refers to the use of incense at Jerusalem while the gospel is read by the bishop (at Lauds, not at the synaxis, but she never describes the synaxis rite). This may well be a ceremonial use, but is probably more closely connected with veneration for the bishop than for the gospel. There is mention of burning incense in the funeral procession of Peter, bishop of Alexandria in A.D. 311 (*Acta*, M.P.G., xviii. 465). But since these were compiled in their present form only in the seventh century they are quite unreliable for a detail of this kind, even though they appear to rest on good older sources. The earliest contemporary reference to incense in a christian funeral procession appears to be at the death of S. Honoratus in Gaul A.D. 430 (Hilary of Arles, *Sermo de Vita Scti. Honorati.*, vii., M.P.L., l. 1269). Both jews (*cf. Berakoth*, M., viii. 7) and pagans had burned incense at funerals, perhaps originally only as a deodorant, though it came to have a religious significance. But there is no pre-Nicene evidence that the christians accepted this custom as they accepted the funeral torches. The use of spices and unguents poured on the corpse as a preservative (*cf.* the burial of our Lord) was also common to jews and pagans—see Prof. A. O'Rahilly, *The Burial of Christ*, Cork, 1942, *pp.* 6–11—a most interesting collection of evidence—and this was continued without question by christians. *Cf.* Tertullian, *Apol.* 42.

place *incense shall be offered* unto My Name and a pure offering' had, as we have seen, done yeoman service ever since the second century in expounding the sacrificial nature of the eucharist as the 'pure offering'; but the reference to incense had invariably been ignored or allegorised away.

There is, however, one exception to this way of regarding the use of incense. Lietzmann has rightly drawn attention[1] to a passage in the *Carmina Nisibena* of the East Syrian S. Ephraem composed in A.D. 363, which reveals that this thoroughly jewish idea of the smoke of incense as in some sense an atonement or 'covering' for sin[2] was already fully accepted in these predominantly semitic churches. Addressing Abraham, the contemporary bishop of Nisibis, Ephraem says:

> 'Thy fasts are a defence unto our land,
> Thy prayer a shield unto our city;
> Thy burning of incense is our propitiation;
> Praised be God, Who has hallowed thine offering.'[3]

Clearly this propitiatory 'censing' here is a liturgical function which the bishop performs on behalf of his flock, like prayer or the consecration of the eucharist. A large number of other Syrian texts of the same character can be cited from the late fifth to the eighth century, all indicating the acceptance of the same idea of incense as a 'sin offering'. In this period the notion passed into the christian liturgies. A 'prayer of incense' found in the oldest MS. (ninth century) of the Jerusalem *Liturgy of S. James* runs thus: 'Thou that art made High-priest after the order of Melchizedek, O Lord our God, Who offerest and art offered and receivest the offerings; receive even from our hands this incense for a savour of sweetness and the remission of our sins and those of all Thy people'.[4] A variant of this idea is to be found in the Alexandrian *Liturgy of S. Mark*: 'We offer incense before the face of Thy holy glory, O God; and do Thou accepting it upon Thy holy and heavenly and spiritual altar send down upon us in return the grace of Thy Holy Spirit'.[5] Other examples could be cited from all the Eastern rites.

[1] *Messe und Herrenmahl*, p. 86. Having criticised certain parts of his book, it is only just that I should draw attention to the soundness of this section of it—an improvement on E. G. C. F. Atchley's *History of the Use of Incense* (1909) which is not much more than a valuable collection of materials.

[2] When the jewish high-priest on the Day of Atonement went into the Holy of Holies to sprinkle the blood of the sin-offering before the mercy-seat, he carried a censer in his hand. The idea was apparently that only through the cloud of the incense smoke could a sinful man even in so representative an office come *safely* face to face with the presence of an infinitely holy God. It is probably this conception which leads the author of Hebrews to ignore the censer in his detailed application of the rites of the Day of Atonement to our Lord's high-priestly entry 'into the holy place' (ix. 11 *sq.*) though he had mentioned the 'golden censer' in ix. 4.

[3] Ephraem Syrus, *Carmina Nisibena*, xvii. 37 *sq.*

[4] *Lit. of S. James*, ed. J. Cozza-Luzi, *ap.* Mai, *Nova Patrum Bibliotheca*, t. x., p. 46 (not in Brightman's text).

[5] Brightman, L. E. W., p. 118, *l.* 26*sq.*

Similar ideas reached the Gallican churches about the tenth century, probably from Eastern sources, and began to penetrate into the liturgies in the same sort of phrases. I cite the two following because these alone eventually passed from Gaul into the official Roman rite of the Pian missal in the sixteenth century, and so became more or less universal in the West. (a) A blessing of incense at the offertory: 'By the intercession of blessed Michael[1] the archangel standing at the right hand of the altar of incense and of all His elect, may the Lord graciously bless this incense and accept it for an odour of sweet savour. Through Christ our Lord.' (b) During the censing of the oblations which follows: 'May this incense which Thou hast blessed ascend up unto Thee, O Lord, and may Thy mercy descend upon us'; where the Egyptian idea of an 'exchange' of incense for grace seems to be latent though somewhat vaguely expressed.

In the development of the christian use of incense we seem therefore to be able to trace the influence of three different factors: (1) The domestic or 'fumigatory' use. (2) The 'honorific' use of it before the bishop, which no doubt made it easier to transfer the idea of burning incense before the altar as a mark of reverence and so of an offering to God. There can be little doubt that this is the genesis of the Western censing of the altar. It is probable, too, that the contact with the instincts of folk-religion in the popular martyr-cult assisted in this. The custom of burning incense at a martyr's tomb in his honour, which is attested in some places in the fifth century, shades off easily into the idea of an 'offering' to the saint to procure his intercession. (3) The purely Old Testament idea of incense as a sin-offering, which begins to infiltrate into christian worship in Syria in the fourth century, and spreads gradually over the East and then penetrates into the West. Though this idea is accepted in isolated phrases in the liturgical texts, and has certainly—combined with (2)—operated to affect ceremonial in obvious ways both in the East and the West, it has never been formally accepted as a doctrine anywhere. It is noteworthy that in the conservative Roman rite all blessings of incense and censings of persons and objects were still unknown as late as the twelfth century,[2] though by then they were more or less universal everywhere else. In the Papal mass of the twelfth century incense was still used as it had been everywhere (except in Syria) in the fifth century, only to scent the air and as a mark of honour carried before the bishop and the gospel book.[3]

[1] In Gaul 'Gabriel', in allusion to Luke i. 11. The substitution of Michael transfers the ref. to Rev. viii. 3.
[2] At the same time, S. Gregory·I, Ep. 52, 'We send you by the bearer . . . incense to be offered to the bodies of the holy martyrs' shows that the idea had been accepted at Rome in the highest quarters by A.D. 599 in connection with the cultus of relics, though still excluded from the rigid tradition of the liturgy there.
[3] The only place where the Roman use of incense can still be seen in its original fashion seems to be Chichester Cathedral (where however, they add an extra use of it in a Gallican procession of the elements). But this is a modern piece of Romanising, not a restoration of the mediaeval Chichester use, which was more elaborate.

Such post-Reformation Anglican use of incense as there was before the later nineteenth century did not develop so exclusively as one might expect along the lines of the early 'fumigatory' use, though this was commonest. But the puritans under the Laudian *régime* were loud in their denunciations of censings 'to' altars, which suggests that the Carolines were influenced chiefly by Eastern precedents. It is a pity that we have no detailed description of the use of censing at Ely Cathedral, where it continued at least down to A.D. 1747. It ended because 'Dr. Thos. Green, one of the Prebendaries and now (1779) Dean of Salisbury, a finical man, tho' a very worthy one, and who is always taking snuff up his Nose, objected to it under Pretence that it made his Head ache.'[1]

### *Summary*

This brief and inadequate survey of the development of the accessories of ceremonial will have served its purpose if it makes clear how far it was from the intention of the fourth century church to convert men from heathenism by any imitation of the pagan ceremonies to which they were accustomed. The whole core and substance of the ceremonies as well as the rites of the eucharist in the fourth century were continued unchanged from pre-Nicene times; they can be traced back uninterruptedly through the formation of the 'four-action shape' of the eucharist to the *chabûrah* rite of the last supper. Even such things as vestments, lights and incense in their use at the eucharist only begin to take on a properly ceremonial or symbolic character after the fifth century (at the very earliest), by the lapse of time through several generations. They have all either a utilitarian or secular origin in their liturgical use, and are given a particular christian meaning only through the inveterate instinct of men to attach symbolic interpretations or at least a ceremonious performance to all public acts which are regularly repeated.[2]

Yet there undoubtedly was a measure of assimilation both in practices and beliefs to the old pagan folk-religion during the fourth century. But it is in the practices of the martyr-cult, not in the eucharistic liturgy, that this is to be found. It is certain that in this field pagan practices and ideas did in the end succeed in naturalising themselves within catholic christianity, and came to be not only tolerated but encouraged by the clergy after the fifth

---

[1] Brit. Mus. Add. MS. 5873, *f.* 82 *b*, cited in *Hierurgia Anglicana, ed.*[2] Vernon Staley, London, 1902, ii., *pp.* 183 *sq.* The devastating effects of incense on the physical system of many modern English protestants are well known. Curiously enough there are no complaints of them from the seventeenth century English puritans and they were totally unknown to the jews and pagans of antiquity, or to the christians of the first 1,500 years. Dr. Thomas Green appears to be the first recorded sufferer, and deserves to be sympathetically commemorated as such.

[2] *Cp. e.g.* the ceremonies which have come to surround the taking and presentation of the collection in Anglican churches (especially in some cathedrals). And now in some dioceses in the mission field the people have come to add a sign of the cross and a bow by each contributor as he puts in his money, in token of 'giving to God'.

century. The whole apparatus of the cultus of images, relics, holy wells, etc. in the forms which it was allowed to assume during the dark ages has a recognisable relationship to the same things in pre-christian paganism. But it is relevant to remark that just those elements in paganism which were taken over into christian popular devotion were many thousands of years *older* than that 'official' paganism of the emperor-worship and the Olympian gods and the Eastern mysteries which the church over-threw. These popular practices had been assimilated by pagan 'theology', as it were, and underlay it and survived it, just as they have survived con-version to christianity, and also conversion to judaism and Islam. Similar practices of offerings of lights and incense at the reputed tombs of *welis* and saints and prophets and marabouts are to be found in the popular mohammedanism and judaism of the Near East and North Africa to this day.

It is not a sufficient defence of such practices in themselves to say that they are an instinctive popular way of practising any religion, which has come down unchanged from the morning of the mediterranean world. Yet this does make clear the process by which they passed over into christian usage. It was not by way of the liturgy, which was under the control of the clergy, but through the individual expressions of piety of a multitude of half-instructed converts in the latter half of the fourth and especially the fifth century. The church allowed personal piety free play—how could she do other?—outside the liturgy; and in various ways it took the old instinc-tive lines. But these found their only point of contact with christian public worship at the shrines of the martyrs. This is a rather different thing from the old charge of the deliberate paganising of christian worship. It should always have been obvious to intelligent students of the period that when the clergy were preoccupied (as they were in the fourth and fifth centuries) with deeply philosophical problems of the nature and being of God and their relation to the incarnation, Plato and Aristotle were likely to present a much greater temptation to the fundamental paganising of christian thought by the clergy than the lower strata of the old peasant superstitions which haunted the countrysides, but which had been despised by all educated pagans for centuries.

It would certainly have been more satisfactory to the modern mind if the church had taken a firmer line with these things in the fourth and fifth centuries, and prevented their recrudescence within christianity; though to one who considers the actual field of their infiltration in the contemporary setting the practical difficulty of preventing it seems very great. The academic critic must make his reckoning with the fact that the actual compromise with them achieved in the fifth and following centuries is in itself no more, but also no less, defensible than the failure to deal firmly with the similar superstition that 'An angel went down at a certain season into the pool of Bethesda and troubled the water: whosoever then first stepped in was made whole of whatsoever disease he had'.[1] In the dark ages when 'not many wise men after the flesh' were available, the church was content to believe with the apostle that 'God has chosen the foolish things of the world to confound the wise, and base things of the world and things which are despised hath God chosen, yea and things which are not'.[2] It may be a pity, but it is a fact, that it is impossible to reduce christianity either to a spiritual philosophy or even to a pure theology. It is always a *religion*, which means partly a practice, for—amongst others—the immense numerical majority of uneducated people, who have their own place and office in the Body of Christ. What the church of the dark ages did not do, at all events in the West, was to allow such practices any foothold in the liturgy of the eucharist. Even in the East they remained on the margin of the liturgy.

The deliberate invention of symbolical gestures and actions and cere-monies in the liturgy to express and evoke adoration, purity of intention and so forth, is something which begins, as we have seen, in the fourth century with the transformation of the eucharist into a public worship. It is a subject with immense ramifications and fascinating bye-ways into which this is not the place to enter. But I think it can be laid down as an almost invariable rule that when each separate instance (*e.g.*, genuflection, the *lavabo*, censing of the altar, etc.) is traced up to its beginnings, they have always the same history. They begin in Syria, usually in the fourth-sixth century, and radiate outwards, south to Egypt and north to Byzantium. In the West (to which they came sometimes by way of Byzantium, sometimes from Syria, and often first to Spain) the great Western centre of interest in such devotional side-issues is always France, the first home or at least the chief propagator of so many modern popular devotions—the Rosary, the Sacred Heart, 'Reparation', and so forth. From France they spread out-wards to England, to Germany, to North Italy—and ultimately to Rome.

We shall not get very far in understanding the inner process of the history of the liturgy unless and until we understand that it expresses and must express something of the *life* of the christian peoples; and that their natural characteristics do to a large extent enter into their religious life to be supernaturalised by grace. The perfervid devotionalism of the Syrian, which comes out so strongly, *e.g.*, in Ignatius of Antioch c. A.D. 115 (and for that matter in Saul of Tarsus and some of the O.T. prophets)—the cere-moniousness of the Byzantine, with his love of etiquette—the *naïveté* of the Copt and his love of repetitions—the French mutability and love of some new thing—that special 'tenderness' of English devotion, which manifests itself in a love of rather sentimental hymns and vocal prayers in the first Anglo-Saxon private prayer books that we have—the prosaic practicality and the almost stuffy conservatism of the local church of Rome—these things do not change from century to century, and they are not annihilated when men come to pray. It is no accident that the deacon still leads the

<hr/>

[1] John v. 4.                      [2] 1 Cor. i. 26 *sq.*

intercessions of the people in the Byzantine litanies with the very gestures and phrases prescribed by etiquette for the spokesman of a deputation to the Eastern emperor—that the Gallican ceremonial and rites are florid and have a greater number of variable prayers than any other—that the chivalrous doctrine that the Mother of God was never under the guilt of original sin appeared first in Anglo-Saxon England, where the treatment of women was much in advance of that common in Europe in the eleventh century—that Irish devotion has enthusiasm but practically no 'liturgical sense' whatever right through the centuries—that the Roman rite has about it still an archaic angularity and abruptness, a concentration on the performance of the eucharistic action rather than talking about it, which is no longer found in any other rite.

These matters of temperament are not only relevant to—they are the actual *cause* of—the course which the history of liturgical details has taken in christendom. To ignore them is to make that history incomprehensible. But having understood their importance, we shall not be misled into making them a justification for misunderstanding the unity of the eucharist. They affect the details only of its performance. The main structure of the liturgy is always and everywhere the same, however much it be overlaid with local ways and decorations, because the eucharist is always identically the same action—'Do this'—with the same meaning—'For the *anamnesis* of Me.' In so far as the christian Syrian and Byzantine and Copt and Englishman and Frenchman and Roman are all christians and so partakers in the one eucharistic action and experience of the one Body of Christ, the Shape of the Liturgy by which that action is performed is bound to be the same in all essentials for them all.

# CHAPTER XIII

## THE COMPLETION OF THE SHAPE OF THE LITURGY

WE have seen that the two halves of what we call the eucharistic rite were originally two distinct rites, the synaxis and the eucharist, either of which could be and frequently was celebrated without the other. They had different origins, served different purposes and were to some extent attended by different people. The eucharist, the Liturgy of the Body of Christ, was for the members of the Body alone. They had an absolute obligation to be present at it every Lord's day, since the 'vital act' of the Body would be incomplete unless each member actively fulfilled in it what S. Paul calls 'its own office', the 'liturgy' of its order. Those outside the Body, whether casual enquirers or enrolled catechumens, could attend only the synaxis and not all of that, since they were dismissed before the prayers with which it ended. Yet the synaxis is not rightly regarded either as a mere propaganda meeting for outsiders or even primarily an instruction service for the faithful, though the lections and sermons enabled it to serve both purposes. By intention though not in form it was an act of worship, the Liturgy of the Spirit, in which the church indwelt by the Spirit adored as well as proclaimed the divine redemption wrought through Jesus. The intercessory 'prayers of the faithful' which followed demonstrated, so to speak, the efficacy of that redemption by exercising His priestly power of intercession for all men bestowed upon the church, and on the church alone, 'in Christ'. Though the individual's obligation to attend the Sunday synaxis may have been less strict than in the case of the eucharist, the faithful were expected to take part in this corporate witness to the fact of the christian redemption. They were the only people qualified to exercise its consequence in the concluding intercessions, by appearing corporately before God, 'accepted in the Beloved', to plead for the world.

We have traced out the exceedingly simple primitive structure of these two rites, which it may be convenient to set out again.

| Synaxis. | Eucharist. |
|---|---|
| A. Greeting and Response. | A. Greeting and Response. |
| B. Lections interspersed with | B. Kiss of Peace. |
| C. Psalmody. | C. Offertory. |
| D. The Bishop's Sermon. | D. Eucharistic Prayer. |
| E. Dismissal of the Catechumens. | E. Fraction. |
| F. The Intercessory Prayers of the Faithful. | F. Communion. |
| (G. Dismissal of the Faithful.) | G. Dismissal. |

(When it was held separately the synaxis seems to have concluded with some sort of dismissal of the faithful.)

We have now to trace the addition to this primitive nucleus of a 'second *stratum*', as it were, of additional devotions, filling in, supplementing and in certain cases obscuring this bare primitive outline which concentrates so directly upon the essential action of the rite. In dealing with this 'second *stratum*' it is unfortunately much more difficult to avoid being technical. We have to take account of more facts, and the facts themselves are more complicated. The need of the period in which the 'second *stratum*' was added (from the fourth century to the eighth) was to adapt the old pre-Nicene tradition of christian worship to its new 'public' conditions and function. But this need was felt by different churches with a different intensity and at different times. And the practical break-up of the christian empire in the fifth century—it still continued as a theory, so mightily had the universal dominion of Rome impressed the imagination of the world—forced the local churches to meet the new needs to some extent in isolation, so that different schemes of additions appeared in different regions.

Before the fifth century her existence within or alliance with an effective universal state had enabled the church readily to put into practice her catholic ideal by the intercommunication of distant churches. When the old Roman world began to break up, the christian world even in the practical breakdown of communications was still quite aware of its own unity; local churches were still quite willing and eager in most cases to borrow from elsewhere improvements and novelties in things liturgical. The result is that though the regional churches were in practice becoming sufficiently isolated to develop a considerable amount of variety in the new prayers of this 'second *stratum*', there was also a good deal of borrowing and cross-borrowing in various directions, due to occasional contacts, which complicates the individual history of the local rites a good deal. A new observance in the liturgy, *e.g.* of Milan in the fifth century, may be something evolved locally to meet a local need. Or it may equally well be something borrowed from Rome to the south, because of Rome's prestige as the Apostolic See; or from Gaul to the north-west, because it is new and interesting; or something brought back from Jerusalem by returning pilgrims, full of 'the way they do it' in the Holy City of men's holiest dreams and emotions in that age. All this needs careful disentangling if we are to make out the true history of rites, and above all the true reasons for changes, and their effects. And often enough the fragmentary evidence enables us to give only an approximate answer to questions we should like to ask about when and where such and such an observance, destined it may be to affect the development of eucharistic rites for centuries to come, first took shape and why.

It is impossible, therefore, to avoid a certain measure of complication in dealing with this 'second *stratum*' of prayers in the liturgy, though I have done my best to make it intelligible to the non-technical reader, because it is an essential part of the history of the eucharistic rites which christians use to-day. But first it is necessary to say something of the process by which the two halves of the rite, originally distinct, came to be fused into a single continuous whole, for this process is the background of the addition of the prayers of the 'second *stratum*' to the old universal Shape of the Liturgy which had come down from pre-Nicene times to all churches alike.

## A. The Fusion of Synaxis and Eucharist

Strictly speaking there was no conscious or deliberate process of fusion. As whole populations became nominally christian, there ceased to be anybody not entitled and indeed obliged as a member of the faithful to be present at both rites. Confirmation was now received in infancy along with baptism as a matter of course by the children of christian parents. In a christian population the only people whose attendance at the eucharist could be prevented were the excommunicated—those who for conduct or belief incompatible with membership of Christ's Body had been deprived of their rights and functions in the liturgical act of the Body. In Cyprian's phrase, they had been 'forbidden to offer', and by consequence to make their communion, for we must not forget that in primitive terminology those whom we call 'the communicants' are always called 'the *offerers*' —*offerentes, hoi prospherontes*, not *communicantes, koinōnoi*. The change of term to 'communicants' reflects an immense shift of emphasis in devotion. It goes along with a change in the status of the laity from participants in a corporate act with the celebrant to passive beneficiaries of and assistants at his act. These changes were not completed before the mediaeval period, and indeed constituted between them the essence of that mediaeval way of regarding the eucharist which has proved so unfortunate in different ways all over christendom.

The roots of these changes go deep, right into the subsoil of the modern church. As far back as the fourth-fifth century the laity in general, especially in the East, were becoming infrequent communicants, out of a new devotional sentiment of fear and awe of the consecrated sacrament, of which we shall say a little more later. Thus, though they remained in name the *offerentes* or *prospherontes*, the faithful did in fact largely cease to offer their *prosphorai* of bread and wine, at all events with the old significance and as a normal weekly rule. The introduction of the devotional novelty of a special 'holy loaf' made by clerical hands as alone sufficiently holy for sacramental consecration further robbed the survival of the lay oblation of bread and wine (in so far as it did survive) of significance. From being the matter of sacrifice and the substance of self-oblation, the layman's *prosphora* sinks to the sphere of the Eastern *eulogia* and the Western *pain bénit*, mere tokens of a holy thing which the unhallowed layman *ought* not to receive. It is not surprising that the distinction between the faithful and the excommunicate became too difficult to enforce so far as mere presence at the eucharist was concerned (and nothing else but presence was now in question). The dismissal of penitents (*i.e.* those under discipline) vanished from most rites in the fifth-sixth century even in form, and was no more than an empty survival where it remained.

The deacons continued to proclaim the dismissal of the catechumens before the intercessory prayers as in the pre-Nicene church, but there were ceasing to be any catechumens to depart. By the seventh century this, too, had become a mere form. But where the prayers were kept up in some way at their primitive position after the sermon, the deacon's dismissal of the catechumens was generally maintained as a sort of prologue to them, though the bishop's departure-blessing of the catechumens which preceded it usually fell into disuse. Where the precedent—set at Jerusalem as early as *c.* A.D. 335—of transferring the intercessions from the synaxis to the second half of the eucharistic prayer had been followed, the deacon's dismissal of the catechumens was apt to disappear altogether from the rite, as *e.g.* in the Syriac *S. James.*[1]

With the disappearance or toning down of the dismissals the most emphatic mark of division between fully 'public' and specifically 'christian' worship was weakened, and the two services held one after the other on Sunday mornings soon came to be thought of as a single whole, because the same congregation now attended the whole of both rites as a matter of course. This stage had been reached in many places by the end of the fifth century. By the end of the sixth the holding of either rite without the other had come to be regarded as an anomaly.

But in the fourth century this fusion was hardly begun. The distinction is fully recognised, for instance, by Etheria in her account of Sunday morning worship at Jerusalem in A.D. 385: 'At daybreak, because it is the Lord's day, all proceed to the great church which Constantine built at Golgotha behind (the site of) the Crucifixion, and all things are done according to the custom everywhere (at the synaxis) on Sunday; except that (here) the custom is that of all the presbyters who sit (in the stalls round the apse) as many preach as wish, and after them all the bishop preaches. They always have these (many) sermons on Sundays, that the people may always be well taught in the scriptures and the love of God. And the preaching causes a long delay in the dismissal of the *ecclesia*, whereby it is not given before ten o'clock or sometimes eleven. But when the dismissal has been done, in the way it is done everywhere, the monks escort the bishop to (the church of) the Resurrection (on the other side of the great paved court enclosing Golgotha) and when the bishop arrives to

[1] In the West the dismissals were lost in the Roman rite probably in the sixth century, though they survived in S. Italy to a later date (*cf.* S. Gregory, *Dialogues,* ii. 23). In Gaul they survived till at least the eighth century in some places. They are still found in the Mozarabic books and traces of them remain in most Eastern rites.

the singing of hymns, all the doors of the basilica of the Resurrection are
thrown open. All the people go in, but only the faithful not the catechumens. And when the people are in, the bishop enters and goes at once inside the screens of the *martyrium*[1] in the cave (of the Holy Sepulchre, where
the altar stands). First thanks are given to God (*i.e.* the eucharistic prayer is
said)[2] and then prayer is made for all (*i.e.* the intercessions). Afterwards
the deacon proclaims aloud. And then the bishop blesses them standing
within the screens and afterwards goes out. And as the bishop proceeds
out all come forward to kiss his hand. And so it is that the dismissal from
the eucharist is delayed nearly to eleven or twelve o'clock.'[3]

Here the two rites are not only distinct, but held in different churches.
The synaxis is public, and at Jerusalem exceptionally lengthy. The
eucharist is still exclusively for the faithful and comparatively short—less
than an hour. Etheria is trying to be discreet in describing its details, in
deference to the old discipline of not publicly revealing the content of the
rite. But she manages to let her sisters in Spain know how 'the way they do
it in Jerusalem' differs from things at home in Galicia—by the (rather
overwhelming?) number of sermons, and the bishop's processional
exit from the synaxis and entrance at the eucharist, and by the postponement of the intercessions from the synaxis to the eucharist, the hidden
consecration, and the final blessing.

The postponement of the intercessions to the eucharist had a practical
advantage at Jerusalem, arising out of the local custom of transferring the
congregation from one church to the other between the two rites. The
catechumens could be left outside in the courtyard without the delay of
getting them out of the midst of the synaxis-congregation before beginning
the intercessions. Perhaps the transference of the intercessory prayers to
the eucharist began at Jerusalem out of this utilitarian motive. Shorn of
the prayers the synaxis became a wholly 'public' service, and all the
strictly christian worship was concentrated in the eucharist.

[1] This word shows how the martyr-cult had taken possession of the imagination
of the age. It means strictly speaking the tomb, the actual resting place, of a martyr's
bones. Here it already means simply the most important and sacred spot in a
church. There was no *martyrium* in the church of the Resurrection, but only the
cave-tomb from which our Lord had risen, in which the altar stood. (The eucharist
was only celebrated once a year, on Maundy Thursday, in the other church, which
may not have had a permanent altar at all.)
[2] It is noticeable that Etheria says nothing about the offertory, either by way of the
people's oblation for themselves or of a procession of deacons, as in Theodore of
Mopsuestia and the Byzantine rite. Cyril of Jerusalem also never mentions an
offertory, and the present Syriac *S. James* has not got one. Is it possible that the
liturgical 'new model' at Jerusalem had done away with the pre-Nicene offertory
altogether, and that the bread and wine were simply 'discovered' on the altar when
the congregation came in from the other church? It would force us to look elsewhere than Jerusalem for the origins of the 'Great Entrance' and the whole complex
of ideas surrounding it in Theodore and the Byzantine rite—but not, I think, outside the limits of Syria and those regions of Southern Asia Minor which were
vaguely dependent on the church of Antioch.
[3] *Peregrinatio Etheriae*, ed. *cit.*, p. 74.

But when this local Jerusalem custom began to be imitated in other places where there was no second church, and both services were held one after the other in the same building,[1] the transference of part of the synaxis into the second half of the eucharistic prayer must have gone some way of itself towards fusing the synaxis and eucharist, by eliminating precisely that point of the rite at which the distinction between the 'public' and christian worship had hitherto been made.

Yet whatever other factors may have helped to break down the distinction between synaxis and eucharist, it was undoubtedly the disappearance of adult catechumens which finally ended the need for any such distinction. The moment at which the whole population (to all intents)[2] could be said to be nominally christian naturally varied a good deal in different places. A fair test is the lapse into disuse of the 'discipline of the secret'— the old rule of never describing the eucharist openly in the presence of the unconfirmed or in writings they might see. At Rome this stage had been reached c. A.D. 450. The sermons of Pope S. Leo preached in the presence of any catechumens there might be, and also his official correspondence, speak of the details and doctrine of the eucharist with a complete absence of that mystification still indulged in by S. Augustine in his sermons and by Pope Innocent I in his letter to Decentius only a generation before.[3] Yet at the opposite end of christendom a few years later Narsai makes it clear that at Edessa there were still adult catechumens, and their expulsion from the liturgy was still a living reality.[4] And the eucharist could still be celebrated there without being preceded by the synaxis, at all events at the paschal vigil, just as we find it at Rome in the second and third century.[5] But even at Edessa after another 200 years there are no longer any catechumens, and the deacons are ceasing in practice to command their withdrawal from the liturgy, though it still remains in the text of the Edessene rite.[6]

The fusion of synaxis and eucharist was thus taking place gradually c. A.D. 400–500 in most places. But during this period each continued to be celebrated without the other on occasion. Thus the Byzantine historian Socrates (c. A.D. 440) says that the synaxis 'without the mysteries' is still held every Wednesday and Friday (the old 'station days') at Alexandria in

---

[1] The removal of the congregation to another building for the eucharist was perhaps commoner than is supposed. S. Augustine mentions it in Africa, *Serm.* 325.

[2] There were still cliques of educated people professing classical paganism in the sixth century, chiefly in Byzantine academic circles, where it was a cherished pose. There was also a great deal of more sincere rustic immobility in ancestral peasant cults down to the seventh–eighth centuries in some provinces of the old empire— quite apart from the unevangelised heathenism outside the old imperial frontiers.

[3] *E.g.*, Leo, *Serm.* lxiii. 7; xci. (*al.* lxxxix.) 3; *Ep.* lix. (*al.* xlvi.) 3. One may wonder how far Augustine and Innocent speak as they do in formal deference to a convention, not because the rule still had much practical value.

[4] *Hom.*, xvii., *ed. cit.*, *p.* 2.           [5] *Ibid.*, xxi., *p.* 55.

[6] James of Edessa (seventh century), *Ep. to Thomas the presbyter; ap.* Brightman, L. E. W., *p.* 490, *ll.* 35–7.

his time.[1] But he looks on this as an old local peculiarity and seems to have no idea of its former universality. Perhaps he was confused because in the contemporary Byzantine rite such a synaxis without the eucharist already always took the form of the 'Liturgy of the Pre-sanctified', *i.e.* of a synaxis followed by communion from the reserved sacrament, as the close of a fast day—which rather disguises the nature of the rite.[2]

In the West the synaxis apart from the eucharist persisted chiefly in Lent, as a relic of the old instruction-classes for the catechumens. It was ultimately restricted first to Holy Week and finally to Good Friday only. When the Roman church first began to observe Good Friday as a commemoration of the Passion separate from that of the Resurrection on Easter Day (instead of both together at the paschal vigil)—in S. Leo's time *c.* A.D. 450 this change had *not* yet been made—the old Roman texts of the paschal vigil were transferred bodily with a minimum of adaptation to a synaxis without the eucharist on the Friday, to make way for the new series of lections at the Saturday vigil drawn up in the church of Jerusalem in S. Cyril's time.[3] In the sixth century this synaxis composed of the old Roman texts of the second century for the Saturday vigil continued to be the only strictly official observance on Good Friday at Rome.[4] This synaxis ended with the intercessory 'prayers of the faithful' in the Papal rite.[5] But the communion of the Pre-sanctified had attached itself to the synaxis in

[1] Socrates, *Eccles. Hist.*, v. 22 (21).

[2] In the Byzantine rite this is made up of elements drawn from vespers as well as the synaxis, followed by communion from the reserved sacrament, and is the only form of liturgy allowed in Lent except on Saturdays, Sundays and the Annunciation. It is first attested at Byzantium as the Lenten substitute for the liturgy by can. 52 of the Council *in Trullo* (A.D. 692), which takes it for granted that this is the only conceivable thing in Lent (which was not universally the case). But S. Sophronius at Jerusalem in A.D. 646 already calls it an 'apostolic' institution (*i.e.* it was in general use so far as he knew and not instituted within living memory). Though it is not always safe to assume that what was taken for granted in the East in one century had so much as been thought of two centuries before, something in the nature of the Liturgy of the Pre-sanctified can be traced back to pre-Nicene times on fast-days in the West, so that we may believe it was in use at Byzantium *c.* A.D. 440. At all events I see no other explanation of Socrates' remarks about the synaxis at Alexandria 'without the mysteries' in his day.

[3] *Cf. p.* 339.

[4] See the (local) Roman *Ordo* for Holy Week in the Einsiedeln MS. *ap.* Duchesne, *Origins, ed. cit., p.* 482. The text of the prayers is in the *Gregorian Sacramentary, ed.* Wilson (H.B.S., 1915), *pp.* 51 *sqq.*

[5] So also did a similar synaxis on Wednesday in Holy Week at one time. The Roman Holy Week observance apparently consisted of a strict fast every day, synaxis without the eucharist on Wednesday and Friday, and the paschal vigil on Saturday night with its baptisms and confirmations followed by the midnight mass of Easter. The consecration of chrism at a mass on Maundy Thursday was apparently added in the fifth century. It seems meagre, but it is entirely characteristic of the Roman liturgical spirit in the fifth–sixth century. All else in the modern Roman rite—the procession of palms, the dramatic rendering of the passion gospels, the reproaches and veneration of the Cross on Good Friday, the prophecies of Holy Saturday—all these things so vivid and dramatic in their symbolism are demonstrably foreign accretions from Syrian, Spanish and French sources, only slowly and reluctantly accepted into the Papal rite between the seventh and fourteenth centuries.

the parish churches of Rome on Good Friday long before it was accepted in the official rite of the Pope. It was probably a survival, unchanged in the popular tradition of devotion since pre-Nicene times, of communion *at home* from the reserved sacrament on those fast days on which there was no celebration of the eucharist, which had transferred itself to the parish churches when domestic reservation began to be given up (? in the fifth century).

So much for the synaxis without the eucharist. The eucharist without the synaxis seems to have disappeared everywhere in the East after *c.* A.D. 500. It lasted longer in some places in the West, but only as a special survival on Maundy Thursday. On that day in some Western churches there were three eucharists[1]—one for the reconciliation of penitents in the morning, one for the consecration of the chrism at mid-day, and one in commemoration of the last supper in the evening.[2] At the first eucharist there was no synaxis, the long rite for the reconciliation of penitents taking its place. At the second the synaxis precedes the eucharist in the normal way. At the third the eucharist is celebrated without the synaxis, beginning, as we should say, at the offertory. This is, of course, the 'typical' eucharist of the year, and its holding in this primitive fashion may have been due to a lingering tradition of what constituted the rite of the eucharist proper. Since the synaxis had already been held that day, there seemed to be no need to impose it again on the congregation and celebrant already weary with the long fast.[3] But we hear no more of this evening eucharist on

---

[1] The multiplication of eucharists on that day seems to have begun at Jerusalem, where there were two in Etheria's time. S. Augustine *c.* A.D. 400, *Ep.* liv. 5 (*al.* cxviii. or *ad Januarium* I, iv.) refers with some irritation to the idea that this is the only 'correct' thing to do on that day: 'If some one on pilgrimage in another country where the people of God are more numerous and more given to attending services and more devout, sees for instance that the eucharist is offered twice on Thursday in the last week of Lent, both in the morning and evening; and on returning home where the custom is to offer it only in the evening—if he then makes a fuss that this is wrong and not the correct thing to do, that is a childish way to behave. We should not imitate it ourselves, though we may put up with it from others; but we should correct it among our flock'. One suspects that there must have been a good deal of this sort of feeling among bishops at the way lay ceremonialists on returning from Jerusalem treated the Cyrilline rite as the only 'correct' thing. One would like to have, *e.g.*, the entirely candid comments of Etheria's Warden about the repercussions of her jaunt to the holy places on the convent services after she got home to Spain. Christian human nature is endearingly the same after nearly 1,600 years!

[2] Rome may have had these three eucharists in the sixth century, but the texts of the prayers for them in the *Gelasian Sacramentary* (*ed.* Wilson, *pp.* 63–73) do not appear to be Roman, but Italian or French, except for the formulae for blessing the holy oils. The Roman prayers (for a single eucharist) are in the *Gregorian Sacramentary* (*ed.* Wilson, *pp.* 48 *sqq.*). Martène, *de Ant. Eccl. Rit.* iv., xxii., vi. 5, mentions a 'most ancient Roman *Ordo*' which agrees with the Gelasian practice. But this is now supposed to be a German monastic adaptation of a Roman *Ordo*, made in the (?) eighth century (No. xvii. in Andrieu's enumeration). Whatever its origin, this document is the latest piece of evidence I have found for the celebration in the West of the eucharist without a synaxis.

[3] Some modern Anglicans are said to celebrate the eucharist in the evening, beginning with the offertory and the invitation 'Ye that do truly'. There can, of

Maundy Thursday after the ninth century. Apart from the single exception of the Liturgy of the Pre-sanctified (really a synaxis without the eucharist, though the appended communion from the reserved sacrament partly disguises the fact) the two rites had finally become a single indivisible whole all over christendom well before A.D. 800.

There is one further aspect of this fusion of the synaxis and eucharist which should be mentioned, though I am not in a position to answer the further questions which it raises. The period during which this fusion came about is precisely that in which mere *presence* at the eucharist, instead of the old liturgical and communicating participation in the eucharistic action, definitely established itself in most places as the substance of the ordinary layman's eucharistic devotion. Was there some connection between the two movements? At the pre-Nicene synaxis a passive part was all that was possible for the congregation; the reader, the singer of the gradual, the preacher, necessarily acted while the rest listened. It was only when the intercessions were reached that even the pre-Nicene synaxis became an effectively corporate act.

The transference of these intercessions into the second half of the eucharistic prayer, which was essentially the celebrant's own individual contribution to the corporate act, certainly went far to destroy their corporate nature. In the liturgy of S. *James* and even in S. Cyril's account of the matter they have become simply a monologue by the celebrant, in which the people have nothing to do but listen. I cannot think it is entirely accidental that this impulse towards 'non-communicating attendance' should apparently have begun in Syria, and that in the same period the Jerusalem rite, soon to be so widely imitated in the East, should have undergone this particular change. For it cannot have been without some effect that this most influential liturgy sho··ld have substituted at the very point at which the older rites prayed for the communicants and the effects of a good communion a very lengthy intercession for all sorts of other concerns, based on the novel doctrine of the special efficacy of prayer in the presence of the consecrated sacrament. This idea was taken up by the preachers, *e.g.* Chrysostom; and it has received 'extra-liturgical' developments in the mediaeval and modern Latin churches. It is not possible to deny its devotional effectiveness, though it may not be so easy to justify on theological

course, be no possible objection to the omission of the synaxis on grounds of primitive precedent, and if the fast is kept, it would even seem humane to do so. Indeed, if one wanted to Romanise in an old-fashioned way, this would be an excellent method of doing it. Back to Hippolytus! Most of the sixteenth century reformers, however, were insistent that 'the proclamation of the Word of God' was necessary to the *validity* of the eucharist, a position stoutly maintained by modern protestant theologians. I do not clearly understand what is meant by this doctrine, but it seems excessive that it should be thought necessary for those among us who have been suspected of protestantism to disavow it by the elimination of even one minute's Bible reading from the eucharistic rite. The liturgy of the Spirit ought not to be entirely neglected for the liturgy of the Body; and it is not adequately replaced by Evensong, the monastic origin of which gives it a different basis and direction.

as on psychological grounds. That is not here our concern. The point is that in the fourth century it was new, and the expression of it by *substituting another idea for that of communion* just before the communion act itself was new too. Coming at that particular point it can hardly have been without some effect on eucharistic devotion among those who paid attention to the prayers. Doubtless there were all sorts of psychological influences at work in producing the new idea of the laity's wholly passive function at the eucharist—the instinctive feeling that communion was not for everybody, the new language of 'fear' of the sacrament, and so on—as well as a certain inevitable lowering of the temperature of devotion in an 'established' church which was coming to include the average man as well as the naturally devout. But it may very well be that amongst those influences we have to reckon with some unforeseen effects of the liturgical changes made in the structure of the Jerusalem rite. And it remains a fact, explain it how we may, that the passive receptiveness—the being reduced to mere listening—which was always necessarily the layman's rôle in the first part of the synaxis, became his rôle also at the eucharist proper (which it had never been before) just in the period in which synaxis and eucharist began to be regarded as parts of a single rite.

## B. The Completion of the Shape of the Synaxis

The tradition of the liturgy was as tenacious of its inherited forms in the fifth century as it had always been, and so the process of adaptation to new needs took the form of additions to the old nucleus much more often than of substitutions for it. This is noticeable in the synaxis. As the pre-Nicene church had transmitted it from the synagogues of the apostolic age, this rite might well seem unnecessarily abrupt in its opening. And however faithful to its origins and well adapted to its pre-Nicene purpose, it was everywhere defective in the elements of vocal praise and prayer, especially where the intercessions with which it should have concluded had been transferred to the second half of the eucharistic prayer. Once the decline of the catechumenate began to make it unnecessary to continue the old restrictions on these aspects of worship at the synaxis, it was right that attempts should be made to remedy these deficiencies. This was done by adding an 'Introduction' to the old nucleus, of a more directly worshipful character than the old conditions had allowed.

### The Introduction

The uniformity of the ancient material in all churches will not have prepared the reader for the apparent complexity and diversity of the material added by the 'second *stratum*' in the various churches, as shewn in the table on the endpapers (which has been simplified in some columns by the omission of what are known to be mediaeval insertions).

The items A, B, C, D, E, are found in all.[1] These are the ancient nucleus. But of the other items prefixed to this, though each appears in several rites, none but the 'hymn' appears in all, and this in two different forms ($\beta$ and 3) while some are in different positions in the rites in which they are found, *e.g.* the 'prayer' (§) in the Egyptian and Western groups.

Yet a few minutes' study of this table with due regard to the approximate date of the appearance of the items in the various rites reveals that all this complexity has a comparatively simple explanation. It arises from the fusion in various ways of three different forms of Introduction. These three forms I have called I, II and III, distinguishing their contents by three different prefixed symbols to assist their identification. Those of I are $\alpha$ and $\beta$; the single item of II is marked §; and the components of III are 1, 2, 3. All three forms (I, II, III) arose in the East during the fourth-fifth century, and have originally a geographical basis. We shall discuss them individually, and then ascertain the uses made of them in the Western rites, which form a fourth group (IV).

### The 'Far Eastern' Introduction (I)

The first scheme consists of ($\alpha$) a preliminary censing by the bishop or celebrant, followed by ($\beta$) the singing of a group of psalms, prefixed to the lections. Geographically it begins in what is for us the 'far east' of classical christendom, though ($\alpha$) the censing was afterwards adopted by the central group of Greek churches. We think and speak of these Greek churches as 'the Eastern churches', but the Mesopotamians and other 'far Easterns' habitually called them 'the Western churches', and the Greek theologians 'the Western doctors'. The Greeks always stood for Western and European ideas in the mind of these semitic christianities, for whom the Latin West was generally too remote to be taken into account.

We have already noted the special importance attributed to the bishop's 'censing' by S. Ephraem in East Syria before A.D. 360.[2] The same notion of censing as a propitiation and a preliminary even to private prayer is found in Syria in the fifth and sixth centuries. Thus in A.D. 521 the hermit Zosimas in Phoenicia 'At the very moment of the earthquake at Antioch suddenly became troubled . . . called for a censer and having censed the whole place where they stood, throws himself on the ground propitiating God with supplications' and afterwards told his companions of what was then happening at Antioch—an instance of his well-authenticated 'second sight'.[3]

But the first description of censing as a preliminary to the liturgy, and of the Oriental introduction to the synaxis as a whole, is found in those remarkable writings which succeeded in imposing a system of neoplatonic

---

[1] With the possible exception of the first two columns (which represent Mesopotamia) where A, the preliminary greeting, may always have been absent.
[2] *Cf. p.* 428.                    [3] Evagrius, *Eccl. Hist.*, iv. 7.

pagan mysticism upon all christendom under cover of the name of Dionysius the Areopagite, the convert of S. Paul.[1] The date and country, though not the identity, of this enterprising forger have been determined within narrow limits.[2] He wrote c. A.D. 485 in that interesting strip of country behind and to the north of Antioch, which forms a borderland between N. Syria and Mesopotamia on the one hand and Asia Minor proper on the other, a region which has given to mankind not only such minds as Poseidonius and S. Paul and Nestorius, but a multitude of ideas and inventions. In his high-flown way Pseudo-Denys describes the opening of the synaxis thus: 'The hierarch having ended a sacred prayer [? privately] before the divine altar, begins by censing there and goes throughout the whole enclosure of the sacred edifice. And returned once more to the holy altar, he begins the sacred melody of the psalms, the whole well-ordered ecclesiastical array chanting along with him the holy psalmic song'.[3]

These psalms ($\beta$) survive in the *marmitha* psalms of the present E. Syrian rite,[4] and also, apparently, in the 'psalm of the day' and *saghmos jashou* ('dinner-time psalms') of the Armenian rite.[5] This rite, however, has at some time incorporated into itself the whole Greek scheme of the introduction (III), part of it being interpolated into the middle of the ($\beta$) psalmody of the original Armenian Oriental scheme (I).[6] This ($\beta$) psalmody failed to establish itself in the Greek rites when ($\alpha$) the censing was taken over by them, because the purpose of the psalmody was already served in the Greek liturgies by the 'hymn' (3) introduced at the same point in the Greek scheme c. A.D. 440. We find a preliminary censing before the liturgy mentioned at Constantinople c. A.D. 565,[7] and it is likely to have been used in the Greek Syrian rites before then, since the idea of censing as a preliminary to prayer was well known there before that date. But at Constanti-

[1] Acts xvii. 34.
[2] J. Stiglmayr, *Das Aufkommen der Ps.-Dionysischen Schriften usw.*, Feldkirch, 1895, makes out his case for the place and date of these writings as completely as his later essay, *Der sog. Dionysius Areopagitica und Severus v. Antiochen*, published in *Scholastik*, 1928, pp. 1–27, 161–189 (cf. ibid., 1932, pp. 52 sqq.) fails to do for his proposed identification of Ps.-Denys with Severus of Antioch. (As the latter has won a certain following in this country I may call attention to the devastating criticisms by J. Lebon, *Rev. d'histoire ecclésiastique*, 1930, pp. 880 sqq., and 1932 pp. 296 sqq.)
[3] Ps.-Denys, *de Eccl. Hierarch.*, iii. 2.
[4] Brightman, L. E. W., p. 253.          [5] *Ibid.*, p. 425.
[6] The history of the Armenian rite is obscure. It seems to have begun as a rite of the Cappadocian type (of which S. Basil is the main relic), to have undergone influence from Jerusalem, and finally to have been heavily Byzantinised, while certain details of the Western Roman and Dominican rites were taken over by it during the period of union with the West in the fifteenth century. It is difficult in its present form to know whether to treat it as a fundamentally Byzantine rite incorporating certain old local features (in which case ($\alpha$) and ($\beta$) in col. 3 should be bracketed and 1, 2, 3 left clear) or as an Anatolian rite heavily overlaid with Byzantine details, as I have done. What is certain is that it combines the whole of Introductions I and III.
[7] *Vita Eustathii Patriarchae* (A.D. 552–582), M.P.G., lxxxvi., 2377.

nople the preliminary censing was performed by the deacon and not by the bishop as in the East, because the Greek bishop continued to enter the church only during the 'entrance chant' (1) of the original Greek introduction scheme (III), to which the censing ($\alpha$) drawn from the Eastern scheme (I) had been prefixed. In Egypt we have a mention of the same sort of preliminary censing ($\alpha$) before the synaxis in a document which in its present form can hardly be as old as the fifth century and seems more likely to be of the later than the earlier part of the sixth.[1] Roughly speaking, the preliminary censing ($\alpha$) of the 'Far Eastern' Introduction (I) had been incorporated into all Eastern rites but one before A.D. 600. Curiously enough the E. Syrian rite of Edessa has no censing ($\alpha$), though it has the psalmody ($\beta$). It may be that it once existed in this rite, but the prefixing of a long formal preparation of the elements and the celebrant on the Byzantine model in later times has eliminated it. Or it may be that the ($\beta$) psalmody before the lections was introduced in the earlier fourth century before there was any use of incense in church; and that *Addai and Mari* thus preserves the first stage ($\beta$ psalmody alone) of the type of Introduction of which Ps.-Denys in the next century gives us the developed form ($\alpha$ censing followed by $\beta$ psalmody).

The first censing of the altar in the Western rites does not appear before about the tenth century in Gaul, and was not adopted at Rome until the twelfth; it spread not very rapidly in the derived Western rites during the middle ages. In view of the fact that some early Western ceremonials, *e.g.* at Milan, give this initial censing to deacons or minor ministers and not to the celebrant, it is conceivable that it began in the West as an imitation of Byzantine ways. But the Gallican ceremonialists were quite capable of developing this rite for themselves out of the old fourth century Western custom of merely carrying a smoking censer before the bishop in the entrance-procession as a mark of honour. And it is to be noted that the Western rites, unlike the Easterns, all kept the entrance-chant as the effective opening of the rite, and did not prefix the censing to it, as at Byzantium. The Western initial censing, late in making its appearance, never became more than an accompaniment to something else in the rite, a piece of ceremonial performed while something else was going on, and did not develop, as in the Eastern rites, into an item in the structure of the rite on its own account.

### The Egyptian Introduction (II)

The second scheme seems to be locally Egyptian in origin. It consisted simply of the old pre-Nicene greeting (A), followed by a prayer (§), prefixed to the lections. In the earliest document of the Egyptian rite available (Sarapion, c. A.D. 340), we find that the synaxis begins with a prayer headed 'First Prayer of the Lord's (day).' It runs thus:

[1] *Canons of Athanasius*, 7, ed. W. Riedel and W. E. Crum, 1904, p. 16.

'We beseech Thee, Father of the Only-begotten, Lord of the universe, Artificer of creation, Maker of the things that have been made; we stretch forth clean hands and unfold our thoughts unto Thee, O Lord. We pray Thee, have compassion, spare, benefit, improve, increase us in virtue and faith and knowledge. Visit us, O Lord: to Thee we display our own weaknesses. Be propitious and pity us all together. Have pity, benefit this people. Make it gentle and sober-minded and clean; and send angelic powers that all this Thy people may be holy and reverend.[1] I beseech Thee send "holy Spirit" into our mind and give us grace to learn the divine scriptures from ⟨the⟩ Holy Spirit, and to interpret cleanly and worthily, that all the laity here present may be helped; through Thy Only-begotten Jesus Christ in ⟨the⟩ Holy Spirit, through Whom to Thee be glory and might both now and to all the ages of the ages. Amen.'

This prayer immediately preceded the lections. It is, by its position, the earliest 'collect' we possess, and a surprisingly early case of disregard for the rule that prayer might not be offered in the presence of the catechumens. Perhaps Sarapion would have argued that this was not so much a prayer 'with' them as 'for' them, which was allowed. This Egyptian collect is not, as with our eucharistic collects, a variable prayer connected with the day in the ecclesiastical calendar, but one always the same, closely connected by contents and position with the reading of the lections which it introduces. The bishop prays not only in the name of his church—'we beseech Thee'—but in his own name—'I beseech Thee'—when he prays for himself, for the special gift of the Holy Spirit to interpret the message of the scriptures for the laity. The whole construction suggests an originally private devotion of the bishop which has been turned into a public and audible preliminary to the lections.

Sarapion gives us only the prayers said by the bishop-celebrant, not their setting in his 'dialogues' with the people and the responses and other parts of the corporate worship offered by the deacon and others. For this we must turn to the Greek *Liturgy of S. Mark*, the mediaeval descendant of the fourth century rite of Alexandria. In this late form the Introduction has been Byzantinised. The Byzantine formal entrance of the bishop has been introduced, accompanied by the sixth century Byzantine processional chant, the *Monogenes*. After this follows at once the original Alexandrian opening of the synaxis. The deacon cries 'Stand up for prayer'—calling the church to order, as it were; and the celebrant greets the church, 'Peace be to all', and is answered, 'And with thy spirit'. The deacon repeats 'Stand up for prayer', to which the people answer 'Lord have mercy'. Then the celebrant chants his collect:

'Master, Lord Jesus Christ, the co-eternal Word of the everlasting Father, Who didst become like unto us in all things, sin excepted, for the salvation of our race; Who didst send forth Thy holy disciples and apostles

---
[1] Almost the meaning is 'respectable'.

to proclaim and teach the gospel of Thy kingdom, and to heal every disease and sickness among Thy people: Do Thou now also, Master, send forth Thy light and Thy truth, and illuminate the eyes of our understanding for the comprehending of Thy holy oracles, and enable us to hear them so that we be not hearers only but doers also of the word, that we may be fruitful and bring forth good fruit thirty and sixty and an hundredfold, and so be worthy of the heavenly kingdom . . .'[1]

This is addressed to the Son, and contains a number of technical anti-Arian terms (e.g. *synaïdios*) which were specially emphasised at Alexandria in the time of the teacher Didymus the Blind, in a particular phase of the Arian controversy c. A.D. 370.[2] They suggest that this also is a fourth century composition, though somewhat later than Sarapion's. Here again the Egyptian collect is directly connected with the lections, and asks for the fruitful hearing of the apostolic proclamation of redemption by the lessons and the sermon. This preliminary prayer (§) forms the whole of the Egyptian Introduction to the synaxis (II).

We shall deal later with its borrowing by the Western rites. It was never incorporated into the other Eastern Introductions. Instead the Egyptian rites themselves later incorporated the censing (α) from the Far Eastern scheme (I) and the entrance chant (1) and hymn (3) of the Greek scheme (III).

### The Greek Introduction (III)

This is rather less homogeneous than the other two—or rather, perhaps, its full development was reached somewhat later. It consists of (1) a solemn processional entry of the bishop and clergy to the singing of a chant of some kind (*Eisodikon*), followed at once by the old opening greeting (A). There follow (2) a litany and (3) a hymn before the lections (B).

1. *The Entrance Procession and Chant.* We have seen that at Jerusalem in Etheria's time the bishop's entrance into the church of the Resurrection for the eucharist was specially delayed until all the people had taken their places, in order that he might enter in procession through their midst; and this though they had all been gathered together just before at the synaxis in the other church across the courtyard. Etheria does not describe the entrance of the bishop for the synaxis. But since she tells of a similar formal entrance of the bishop for two of the daily offices, and a processional departure of the bishop from both synaxis and eucharist it seems a fair inference that the synaxis also began with a processional entrance of the clergy—a typically Cyrilline touch of ceremony.

---

[1] Brightman, p. 117.
[2] Had this prayer been composed in the fifth or sixth century, the interest would have shifted to the Nestorian or Monophysite questions. The Coptic rite substitutes a much later prayer (Brightman, p. 147) but retains a heading reminiscent of Sarapion's—'The first prayer of the morning'.

THE COMPLETION OF THE SHAPE 449

There is no procession or opening greeting in the liturgy of *Ap. Const.*
(Bk. ii. or Bk. viii.), which begins straight away with the first lection, like
the Roman synaxis on Good Friday. But S. John Chrysostom in homilies
preached at Antioch *c.* A.D. 390 and at Constantinople soon after A.D. 400
refers to some sort of formal entrance and the immediately following
greeting: 'When the father enters he does not mount up to this throne
before beseeching for you all this peace.'[1]

The fifty-sixth canon of the Council of Laodicea in Asia Minor (*c.*
A.D. 363) lays it down that 'Presbyters ought not to enter and sit down on
the *bema* (in their stalls round the apse) before the entrance of the bishop,
but to enter with the bishop'—an indication that the old informality was
beginning to give way to the more dignified arrangements of a fully public
worship in this region during the latter half of the fourth century. I can
find no mention of any sort of formal entrance of the clergy for the liturgy
in the writings of the Cappadocian fathers from the Eastern part of Asia
Minor in this period. But S. Basil specifically tells us that much in the performance of the liturgy in his church of Neo-Caesarea—the chief church
of this region—was rather 'slovenly, owing to its old-fashioned arrangement', and this may be a point he has in mind.[2] (This equation of 'slovenliness' with 'old-fashioned' is a permanent feature of the history of liturgy
and is worth pondering by the 'up-to-date' of all periods—perhaps with
some searchings of heart.)

In all this fourth century Eastern evidence, however, though the entrance
procession of the bishop and clergy seems to be taking shape, there is no
direct mention of a chant. The first talk of this seems to come from Rome
in the time of Celestine I (A.D. 422–432). It may be that Rome for once set
a new fashion in the liturgy.[3] Yet we must remember that the processional
entrance itself is attested in the East, *e.g.* at Laodicea, some sixty years
before this, and that Etheria's 'hymns' during the bishop of Jerusalem's
procession between the two churches may have continued while he passed
between the ranks of people in the basilica of the Resurrection, though she
does not say so. On the other hand the 'silence' of the offertory procession
is emphasised by Theodore of Mopsuestia[4] in a way which suggests that
silent processions may have been found particularly impressive by Easterns
at this time, though to modern Western eyes they usually seem slightly
depressing.[5]

[1] S. Chrysostom: *adv. Judaeos*, iii. 6; *in Mat.* xxii, 6; (preached at Antioch), *cf.*
*in Col.* iii. 3 (at Constantinople).
[2] S. Basil, *de Spiritu Scto*, xxix. 74.
[3] There is no mention of singing in the description of a bishop's processional
entrance by Paulinus of Nola, *Carmina*, xiv (*c.* A.D. 400). There was no introit,
apparently, in the African rite.
[4] *Cf. p. 283.*
[5] The *Acta* of a Council at Constantinople in A.D. 536 (Labbe-Cossart, *Concilia*,
v. 1156 D) speak of the singing of the *Benedictus* after the entrance of the bishop but
before the *Trisagion*, which has given occasion to a number of authors to suggest or

We reach firmer ground as to the Greek entrance-chant in A.D. 535-6. The emperor Justinian at the close of his pro-Monophysite period, at a time when the monophysite patriarch Severus of Antioch was actually staying as his guest in the palace, composed a 'prose hymn' generally known from its first word, *Monogenes*.[1] This class of composition is known to us in the West chiefly by specimens of Eastern origin (*e.g. Gloria in excelsis* at the eucharist).

Justinian's hymn forthwith became the entrance-chant at Constantinople and Antioch. But shortly after this he changed sides, and proceeded to persecute the Monophysites with his usual cold-blooded efficiency. The Syrians and Egyptians soon came to execrate him as the incarnation of Byzantinism, and accordingly the monophysite rites of Syria and Egypt do not contain his hymn. To the 'royalist' Greek churches of Antioch and Alexandria his authorship was on the contrary a recommendation, and the *Monogenes* remained the first item of the Greek Introduction in the Greek rites. The Armenians (who had largely escaped Justinian's missionary methods and therefore felt less strongly about his authorship) adopted it when they incorporated the Greek Introduction (III) into their own rite, though they have spasmodically patronised a monophysite or anti-Byzantine interpretation of the Creed.

2. *The Litany*. The origin of litanies and their first position in the rite, at the 'prayers of the faithful' after the sermon, are more conveniently dealt with later. Here we are concerned with the insertion of a litany in the Introduction to the synaxis between the entrance-chant and the hymn.

It will be noted that the Byzantine rite contains no litany at this point, and I know of no evidence that it ever did so. The Greek *S. James*, the rite of Antioch-Jerusalem, does contain one. There seems to be no evidence as to when it appeared in the local rite of Antioch, but it cannot be traced before the ninth century. Yet besides the fact that *S. James* now contains a litany at this point, which despite its Byzantinised text was not taken over in this position from Byzantium, there is the fact that when the Roman and Milanese rites came to take over the Greek scheme of Introduction in the

repeat that this was the original entrance-chant in the rite of that city. I cannot think that anyone reading the context carefully could doubt (*a*) that on this occasion *Benedictus* was not sung during the bishop's entrance, but some while after it; (*b*) that it was not part of the rite at all, but the climax of the disorder and 'brawling' which disturbed this particular celebration of the eucharist. It was not sung by the choir but by the rioters.

[1] Theophanes, *Chronographia*, 6029. This has been questioned, but see V. Grumel's brilliant vindication, *Echos d'Orient*, xxvi. (1923), *pp. 398 sqq. Monogenes* is no longer the Byzantine entrance-chant, having been transferred to the *Enarxis*, a preparatory rite borrowed from the *Typica* (part of the divine office) about the ninth century. In the Antiochene, Alexandrian and Armenian rites, which all borrowed this piece from Byzantium, it is an entrance-chant, which sufficiently indicates its original function in their common source. The present Byzantine *Eisodika* (variable entrance-chants) are also taken from the office for the day, but I have failed to find evidence as to when they replaced the *Monogenes* in this function. (Was it when the *Enarxis* was inserted?)

fifth-sixth century they both inserted at this point a litany, whose text in each case is based on a Greek original. The 'Three Great Prayers', the Egyptian equivalent of a litany, occur at this point in the Coptic *S. Mark*.[1] All these facts would be adequately explained by the supposition that the litany here originated in the local use of Jerusalem (as to which unfortunately we have very little evidence in the fifth-eighth century) and that it spread north to Antioch and (after a fashion) south to Egypt and West to Rome, as local Jerusalem customs were so apt to do. And as for its peculiar position, before the hymn instead of after the sermon, there is a possible explanation in the fact that when litanies were becoming fashionable in the East as a substitute for the old prayers of the faithful—in the fifth century —the Jerusalem church was precluded from making use of this, the latest liturgical novelty, at the position normal in other rites, by the fact that it had long ago transferred these particular prayers to a point after the consecration. Whether this be the right explanation of affairs at Jerusalem or no, we shall find that when Pope Gelasius at Rome (A.D. 492-6) wanted to get rid of these same antique 'prayers of the faithful', and at the same time wanted to take over the new fashion of litanies, he did adopt precisely this expedient of inserting it after the entrance-chant, just where it stands in the liturgy of *S. James*.

3. *The Hymn.* The equivalent of the group of psalms (β) before the lections in the Oriental scheme (I) is found in the Greek scheme (III) as another 'prose hymn' (3). In the Greek rites this is the *Trisagion*, the words 'Holy God, Holy Mighty, Holy Immortal, have mercy upon us', repeated three times to a particularly noble melody. This hymn is said to have been divinely revealed (variously to a boy, or a presbyter or the patriarch himself) at Constantinople in the time of the patriarch S. Proclus (A.D. 434-446) as the authentic text of the hymn sung by the angels in heaven. Whatever we may think about this, we have the contemporary testimony of Proclus' banished predecessor, the heretical ex-patriarch Nestorius, that it was inserted into the liturgy at Constantinople between A.D. 430 and 450.[2] It had been adopted at Antioch before A.D. 471 when the monophysite patriarch Peter 'the Fuller' caused a great commotion by adding the clause '. . . immortal, *Who wast crucified for us*, have mercy . . .' and thus turned this Trinitarian hymn into a proclamation of the monophysite doctrine of Christ's single Divine Nature. In this interpolated form it was adopted by all the Syrian and Coptic Monophysites, who at some time have transferred it from before the lections to a place among the chants between the epistle

---

[1] The Greek now places them among the preparatory devotions later prefixed to the censing and *Monogenes*. But the opening part of both versions of *S. Mark* has been perturbed by 'Syriacisation' in the case of the Coptic (sixth-eighth century) and 'Byzantinisation' in the case of the Greek (eighth-eleventh century) so that the dating of each item has to be considered independently, and the original order cannot always be discerned.

[2] Nestorius, *Bazaar of Heraclides*, ed. Bedjan, p. 499.

and gospel. The East Syrians (Nestorians) had adopted it in the Greek position before the eighth century, when it is mentioned by the Nestorian Abraham bar Lipheh. I cannot trace the date of its adoption by the Armenians.

The Greek Introduction is thus made up of elements from two centres, Jerusalem and Constantinople. But it is a scheme as clearly marked as the Oriental and Egyptian schemes, and has spread even more widely than its two rivals. The general trend of influence in liturgical history is always from East to West. The Egyptian Introduction has spread to the Latin churches but not eastwards; one item of the Oriental scheme has spread westwards into the adjacent Greek churches; the Greek Introduction has been copied among the Latins. Only the influence of Jerusalem has been strong enough to work against this current, and spread some marks of the Greek Introduction into the Oriental area.

### The Western Introductions (IV)

*a. At Rome.* The history of the Roman rite is better documented in the fifth–sixth centuries than that of other Western rites, and since Rome exercised an influence of its own in the West, it is convenient to begin with that. When we look at the developed Roman Introduction: (1) Introit or Entrance Chant, (2) Litany, later replaced by the *Kyries*, (3) Hymn (*Gloria*), followed by the Greeting and Prayer or Collect, it is clear that it consists structurally of the Greek Introduction (III) followed by the Egyptian one (II) as a sort of double prelude to the lections. It might even be made to appear that the Egyptian (II) scheme was added in the later fourth century and the Greek Introduction (III) prefixed to that during the fifth. This is a neat solution, and may even be true, though it depends on the date of the institution of the collect at Rome. Probst and others have attributed this to Pope S. Damasus (A.D. 366-384) But the documents hardly bear out this tidy idea of the development of the Roman Introduction when the evidence for each item in it is examined separately.

1. *The Introit.* That erratic document the *Liber Pontificalis* says of Pope Celestine I (A.D. 422–432) that 'He ordained that the 150 psalms of David should be sung antiphonally by all before the sacrifice, which used not to be done, but only the epistle of blessed Paul used to be read and the holy gospel'.[1] The singing of the entire psalter by the congregation at one session before the eucharist can hardly be what is meant; and Duchesne interprets this as referring to the first beginnings of the public recitation of the divine office in the Roman basilicas (as distinct from semi-private services in the oratories of the Roman monasteries). It seems to me that the psalm-chant here described is something much more closely connected with the eucharist than that; certainly it is 'before the sacrifice', but no more so than

---

[1] *Liber Pontificalis, ed.* Duchesne I, *p.* 230.

the epistle and gospel in the compiler's eyes, *i.e.* it refers to the institution of a chanting of psalms in the synaxis. The tract and gradual between the lections are certainly older than this, and there remains only the introit, the psalm which by the sixth century was certainly customarily sung at Rome to cover the Pope's processional entry.[1] The entrance procession had been adopted in the East in some churches at least sixty years before. The chanting of psalms at the eucharist was being extended from the old chants between the lections to other parts of the rite in Africa (though we hear nothing of an introit there) some years before this.[2] The adoption of the procession would appeal to the Roman sense of dignity; and some sort of accompanying chant would hardly be long in making its appearance, just because of the slightly depressing effect of silent processions.

2. *The Litany.* Alcuin has preserved for us the text of a Latin litany which he styles *Deprecatio Gelasii* (*The Intercession of Gelasius*).[3] It is manifestly based on an Eastern model, but Edmund Bishop has shewn that it is undoubtedly of local Roman manufacture in the details of its phrasing, and that there is reason to accept the attribution to Gelasius.[4] Quite recently Dom B. Capelle has pointed out that down to the time of that reputed reformer of the Roman rite Pope Gelasius (A.D. 492-6), the intercessions are frequently referred to at Rome as coming at the end of the synaxis in the old form. After his time they completely disappear at that point except in Holy Week[5] (when they might very well keep their old place as a climax to the synaxis celebrated without the eucharist, to avoid ending abruptly with the sermon). In the sixth century a litany was certainly employed in the Introduction at Rome. These coincidences are too numerous to be accidental. Though the *Liber Pontificalis* says nothing about it in its vague notice of Gelasius' liturgical innovations—but then it says nothing of his work upon the Roman eucharistic prayer either—it seems that Gelasius inserted the litany into the Roman Introduction.

It still retained the form of an Eastern litany, with responses said by the people to petitions by the deacon (or by the choir), at least on occasions, down to the time of Pope S. Gregory the Great (*c.* A.D. 600). But changes were made by him, or more probably had already begun before his time. Writing to the bishop of Syracuse in self-defence against the charge of

---

[1] The phrase *Constituit ut psalmi David CL . . . psalli* is odd. Could *CL* possibly be a corruption for *ctm*? *ct* or *cts* is found as an abbreviation for *cantus* ('chant') in some later MSS. of the *Antiphonarium Missae.*

[2] *Cf. p.* 492.

[3] M.P.L., ci. 560 *sq.* The full title is 'The Intercession which Pope Gelasius ordained to be sung for the universal church'.

[4] E. Bishop, *Journal of Theological Studies*, xii. (1911), *pp.* 407 *sq. Cf.* W. Meyer, *Nachrichten der k.G.d. Wissensch. zu Göttingen, philol.-hist. Klasse*, 1912, *pp.* 84 *sqq.*, who reaches the same conclusion on purely philological not liturgical grounds.

[5] Dom B. Capelle, *Rév. d'hist. ecclés.*, xxxv. (1939), *pp.* 22 *sq.* The last previous reference to the old intercessions is in the time of Gelasius' immediate predecessor, Felix III, in A.D. 487-8 *cf.* A. Thiel, *Epistulae Rom. Pont. genuinae*, Braunsberg, 1868, I, 263.

Western purists that he had followed the customs of Constantinople in the changes he had recently made in the Roman rite, S. Gregory says: 'We neither used to say nor do we say *Kyrie eleison* as it is said among the Greeks. For among them all (the congregation) sing it together (as a response to the deacon). But with us (something) is sung by the choir and the people answer it (*a populo respondetur*). And *Christe eleison* which is never sung by the Greeks is (at Rome) sung as many times (as *Kyrie eleison*). But on non-festal days we omit certain things usually sung (*i.e.* the petitions) and sing only *Kyrie eleison* and *Christe eleison*, so that we may spend somewhat longer on these words of supplication.'[1]

Whether the omission of the litany on ordinary days had begun before S. Gregory's time we cannot say for certain, because the *Gelasian Sacramentary*, our chief clue to the Roman rite in the century before S. Gregory's reform, does not contain an *Ordinary* or outline of all the invariable parts of the rite, but only the text of the prayers said by the celebrant. But it is probably significant that in its rubric directing the omission of the synaxis at the reconciliation of penitents on Maundy Thursday (a 'non-festal' mass which would in any case not include the *Gloria*) the *Gelasian Sacramentary* simply directs 'On this day there is no psalm (introit) nor greeting, that is he does not say "The Lord be with you"' (but begins straight away with the prayers for the penitents).[2] But at the baptismal eucharist at the end of the paschal vigil (the festal mass of Easter) we find 'Then while the litany is sung (the bishop) goes to his throne, and intones Glory be to God on high'.[3] Here the litany seems plainly to be as much a feature of the rite reserved for festivals as is the *Gloria*. And there are no *Kyries* between Introit and Greeting-Collect at non-festal masses like that of the penitents on Maundy Thursday because S. Gregory had not yet invented them.

What S. Gregory's work on this part of the Roman rite seems to amount to is this: he left the litany on festal days perhaps more or less as it had been before (though it is as well to note that we have no evidence either way whether or not the text of the *Deprecatio Gelasii* as preserved by Alcuin still represented the current usage at Rome at the end of the sixth century). On non-festal occasions S. Gregory instituted repetitions of *Kyrie eleison* and *Christe eleison* between the introit and the greeting and collect, where previously nothing had intervened on non-festal days when the litany was not said. Though there is no direct evidence on the point I see no reason to doubt that these as S. Gregory fixed them numbered nine

---

[1] *Ep.* ix. 12 (*ed. Ben.*) written A.D. 598. All is not quite plain here. Did the choir (not the deacon) sing the petition at Rome in the old usage? Or does he mean that the text sung by the choir is the first *Kyrie*, to which the people 'respond' the second, and the choir the third and so on, as between priest and server at a modern low mass? I think the second sentence ('But on non-festal days' etc.) refers to S Gregory's own new usage, not to the old 'litany' in the strict sense.
[2] *Gelasian Sacramentary*, ed. Wilson, p. 63.
[3] *Ibid.*, p. 87. There is no introit psalm because the Pope has already been in the church for some hours, officiating at the vigil and baptisms and confirmations.

(with *Christe eleison* for the middle three) sung alternately by the choir and people.[1]

But S. Gregory's innovation of the *Kyries* used as a chant *instead of* the litany on non-festal days soon ousted the use of the litany on festivals also. The text of the litany as used on festivals has left no trace in any extant MS. of the *Gregorian Sacramentary*. The litany, greatly developed and in some things transformed, continued to hold a place in Roman usage, but as an almost separate rite[2] conducted in procession through the streets outside the church as a preliminary to the eucharist on days of solemn supplication. It was thereby enabled to survive as an actual part of the Roman eucharistic rite at the Easter and Whitsun baptismal masses and (transferred to a later point in the rite) at ordinations and monastic professions. In this form, as a solemn supplication, it was adopted in France for occasions like the processions of the Rogation Days, at first as an addition to and then instead of the old French 'procession' of penitential psalms, certainly before the end of the eighth and perhaps before the end of the seventh century.[3]

3. *The Hymn.* We have seen that before the time of Pope Celestine I nothing whatever preceded the lections; and even after he had introduced the introit it formed the whole of the Roman introduction, according to the

[1] The statement of *Ordo Romanus I* that the number of *Kyries* depends on the caprice of the Pope, who nods to the choir master when he has had enough, takes no account of the Roman peculiarity of singing *Christe eleison* 'as many times' (*totidem vicibus*). I cannot help thinking the *Ordo* has here suffered some Frankish alteration. The first document which attests the present usage is *Ordo Romanus II* (*IV*. in Andrieu's enumeration, Duchesne's *Ordo of S. Amand*). The leaving of the number unfixed would be very unlike that sort of orderly precision which distinguishes the rest of S. Gregory's liturgical work, and which is indeed a most obvious trait in his whole personal mind and character.

[2] Nevertheless its original function as part of the Introduction to the eucharist was never forgotten, *cf.* the rubric in the *Gregorian Sacramentary*, ed. Wilson, *p.* 1.

[3] A word should be said here as to the transformation wrought in the form of the Roman litany by the prefixing to it of a long series of invocations of saints with the response 'Pray for us'. This has been treated excellently by E. Bishop, *Journal of Theological Studies*, vii. (1905), *p.* 122, and his conclusions carried further by F. J. Badcock, *ibid.*, xxxiii. (1932), *p.* 167. The results of their enquiries appear to be that Anglo-Saxon England was the first chief focus of this new devotional addition to the litany in the West, *c.* A.D. 700, and that it was propagated in Gaul and on the continent generally chiefly by Anglo-Saxon and Irish influence. But here, as is so often the case with what appear to be 'insular' innovations in Western practice, the real roots lie in the East. What lies behind the Anglo-Saxon devotions is a *Greek* document, perhaps introduced into England during the pontificate of the Greek-Syrian Pope Sergius I, A.D. 687–701, but coming ultimately from Asia Minor in the fourth-fifth centuries. This Greek document seems to have had no immediate effects on local Roman usage in respect of invocations in the litany. These invocations came to Rome as it were 'on the rebound', by Anglo-Saxon influence *via* Gaul. The original Roman litany, the *Deprecatio Gelasii*, knows nothing of them. It is interesting to reflect that Cranmer in 1552, by removing such invocations as remained in his 1544 litany, actually removed the one substantial-English contribution to the Western litany form, and made the Prayer Book litany much more 'Old Roman' in structure, as well as in the occasions prescribed for its use. On the early history of litanies in the West *cf.* also E. Bishop, *Journ. of Theol. Studies*, xii. (1911), *pp.* 405 *sqq.* (and *Appendix* to Dom Connolly's *Homilies of Narsai*, *pp.* 117–121) and a characteristic letter posthumously published, *Downside Review*, xl. (1921), *pp.* 91 *sq.*

*Liber Pontificalis.* This was probably the Constantinople and Jerusalem usage of the time, and lasted at Rome from *c.* A.D. 430 till the introduction of the collect, of which we shall say more in a moment. Jerusalem may have introduced the litany after the entrance chant quite early in the fifth century; Rome certainly followed suit at the very end of the century. Meanwhile Constantinople had introduced the hymn of the *Trisagion* between the entrance chant and the lections (before A.D. 450), and Antioch (and probably Jerusalem) had done the same before *c.* A.D. 470. Once more Rome followed the Eastern custom, but after a generation or two. Pope Symmachus (A.D. 498–514) 'Ordained that on every Sunday and martyr's feast the hymn "Glory be to God on high" should be said.'[1] Both the position of this hymn and the frequent Roman description of it as 'the Angels' hymn' witness to its relation to 'the Angels' hymn' of the *Trisagion* at Constantinople. The Eastern structure of *S. James*—(1) *Eisodikon* ( =entrance chant, *Monogenes*), (2) litany, (3) *Trisagion* ('hymn of the Angels') is exactly reproduced by the Roman (1) *Introitus* ( =entrance chant', a psalm), (2) litany, (3) *Gloria* ('hymn of the Angels'). The Roman church refused to change its old scriptural entrance-chant of a psalm for the new Greek *Monogenes*, composed by an emperor of dubious orthodoxy; and likewise substituted *Gloria in excelsis* as the scriptural 'hymn of the Angels', to avoid being committed to the apocryphal legend of the divine revelation of the *Trisagion*. But it adopted the whole (III) Greek structure of the Introduction—entrance chant, litany, hymn—nevertheless, though it did so only item by item.

The *Gloria* was no new composition when it was put to this new use at Rome *c.* A.D. 500. It is found in Egypt, Syria and Asia Minor in the fourth-fifth century, and is said to have been introduced into the West by S. Hilary of Poitiers *c.* A.D. 363, who had come upon it during his banishment in the East. The number of local variants in the text of the hymn already found in the fourth century indicate an origin in the third, or even perhaps the second century. It had been a pre-Nicene Eastern 'hymn at dawn', and thus found its way into the new public morning office of Lauds in the East, where it formed a sort of 'greater doxology' at the end of the psalmody. In this position the Roman church seems always to have employed the *Benedictus* or Song of Zachariah. The *Gloria*, the old hymn which began with the song of the angels at Bethlehem, was therefore available at Rome for use at the eucharist, when current fashion suggested the need of an 'Angels' hymn' before the lections of the synaxis. There could indeed be

[1] *Lib. Pont., ed.* Duchesne, I, *p.* 263. It seems hardly necessary to refute the assertion of the same authority that Pope Telesphorus (martyred *c.* A.D. 130) 'ordained that before the sacrifice the Angels' hymn . . . should be said but only on Christmas at night' (*Ibid.,* I, *p.* 129). The festival of Christmas did not exist until, at the earliest, a century and a half after Telesphorus. At the most the statement may attest a vague tradition that the *Gloria* was occasionally used at Rome before Symmachus systematised and made official a growing practice. The *Gloria* was in fact more closely connected with Easter than Christmas at Rome.

no more suitable text than this to celebrate the redemption which the scriptures announce.

But it is perhaps a symptom of the reluctance with which the Roman church accepted innovations which had not an obvious practical purpose (like the introit), that both the litany and the hymn, which in the East became at once fixed and unvarying parts of the rite whenever it was celebrated, were adopted at Rome only as 'decorations' suitable to elaborate it for festivals, but not, integral to the real purpose of the liturgy. This 'occasional' use may, too, reflect the growing influence of the calendar on the Western rites, which gives rise to the use of variable prayers in the West during the fifth century, an innovation which the East did not adopt in that form.[1] But there is also something of the Roman concentration on the main purpose and end of the liturgy and the sense of its form (which comes out again in the directness and brevity of the Roman prayers) about this reluctance to amplify the rite on all occasions with purely decorative additions. It seems indeed to have been felt at Rome that a hymn at this point was suitable even on feast-days only at the specially solemn 'stational' eucharist of the bishop. It is mentioned only once in the *Gelasian Sacramentary*, at the Easter vigil (when any celebrant might use it). But the *Gregorian Sacramentary*, though it follows Pope Symmachus' ruling that the *Gloria* was to be used on Sundays and feasts, restricts this to the stational eucharist celebrated by a bishop for his whole church. Presbyters are permitted to use it only on Easter Day (to which later custom added the anniversary of a priest's own ordination). It was only in the eleventh or twelfth century that priests began to use it on all Sundays and festivals like bishops.[2] The omission of the *Gloria* on Sundays in Advent and from Septuagesima to Easter is not indicated in the *Gregorian Sacramentary*, but is suggested by the *Ordo Romanus Primus*, where it is used *si tempus fuerit* 'if it is the season for it'. This further restriction in the use of the hymn (which is not found in the Eastern use of the *Trisagion*) may not have suggested itself until the seventh century.

4. *The Greeting and Prayer.* The synaxis on Good Friday in the Roman missal—the only really ancient specimen surviving of the old form of the Roman synaxis—opens abruptly, without introit (or of course *Kyries* and *Gloria*) and also without a collect. This seems to bear out the statement of the *Liber Pontificalis* that when Celestine first prefixed the introit no other text intervened between it and the lections. It is true that modern liturgical scholars have almost unanimously attributed the origin of the Roman collect to S. Damasus fifty years before Celestine. But this question is so closely bound up with the whole problem of the origin of prayers varying with the calendar, in the Western rites as a group and not the Roman rite

[1] *Cf. pp.* 529 *sq.*
[2] Berno of Reichenau, *de Quibusdam, etc.,* ii. (eleventh century) M.P.L., cxlii., 1059, still complains of the restriction.
2 H                                                                 D.S.L

alone, that it seems better to leave it for discussion in this larger setting in the next chapter, and to rest the case for the moment upon the evidence of the *Liber Pontificalis* that there was still no collect in Celestine's time *c.* A.D. 430. But if its insertion is later than this, there is reason to think it appeared not very much later, say within the next twenty or thirty years.

From the fact that the greeting at Rome is placed before this prayer, as in the Egyptian rite (and not immediately after the entrance chant as at Constantinople, or in its original place immediately before the lections as in Spain), we may be justified in supposing that the custom of a prayer before the lections was borrowed at Rome from Alexandria; and we do in fact find that from *c.* A.D. 430-445 relations between the Roman and Alexandrian churches were closer than at any other time between the visit of Athanasius to Rome in A.D. 339 and the last *rapprochement* of these two sees in the time of S. Gregory the Great *c.* A.D. 595. But it must be noted that while the Alexandrian collect of the fourth century is an unchanging prayer, the same on all occasions, the Roman collect when we first meet it is already one which varies with the occasion. There may have been a period when the Roman collect also was unvarying and referred simply to the hearing of the scriptures, like the Egyptian ones. But if so, this period must have been short, for it has left no trace whatever in the Roman evidence.

The following seems, then, to be the approximate history of the Roman Introduction to the synaxis. Celestine I prefixed the introit, the chanting of a psalm during the entrance procession, *c.* A.D. 430. Before that time there had been no Introduction whatever at Rome before the lections. In the next twenty years or so the Egyptian Introduction (II) of a Greeting and Prayer was set between the introit and the lections. There must after that have been a period when the Roman Introduction consisted simply of introit, greeting and collect, followed by lections. This is precisely the arrangement still implied for non-feast days in the first rubric of the sixth century *Gelasian Sacramentary* cited on *p.* 453. At the very end of the fifth century Gelasius added the litany, probably from the rite of Jerusalem, between the introit and the greeting. A few years later Symmachus again added the hymn between the new litany and the greeting. Perhaps the litany, and certainly the hymn, were from the first special to Sundays and feasts. They were placed where they were to avoid disturbing the Egyptian 'group' of greeting and prayer; which suggests that the Egyptian idea of the prayer as specially connected with the lections immediately after it had at one time obtained a foothold at Rome. The whole Roman Introduction is therefore a product of the period between *c.* A.D. 430 and *c.* A.D. 500, precisely the period when we have seen that the adult catechumenate was ceasing to be of any practical importance at Rome. The Introduction at Rome represents, therefore, the adaptation of the old pre-Nicene synaxis, which had had to serve the purposes of propaganda outside the ranks of the faithful, to the needs of a 'public' worship in the new christian world.

*b. The Western Introduction outside Rome.* We are on much less secure ground in dealing with the Western rites other than that of Rome right down to the seventh, and in many matters the ninth, century. Before then the evidence available is both less in quantity and more ambiguous in quality than in the case of the Roman rite; and the subject is encumbered with modern theories, no one of which seems to account for all the facts. We shall not enter upon them, but merely note what evidence is available, and what it indicates.

It is necessary at the outset, however, for the sake of those who have read the usual manuals, to take account of two modern discoveries which seriously alter the bearing of this evidence. Dom Wilmart's demonstration —the word is not too strong—that the so-called *Epistles of Germanus of Paris (d. A.D. 576)* have nothing to do with Germanus or Paris, but were composed in the South of France (or perhaps in Spain) *c.* A.D. 700, will necessitate a considerable reconstruction of what one might call the 'usual' theory—though in fact it is mainly of French construction—of the history of the 'Gallican' rite.[1] The term 'Gallican' was first used to cover only the old local rites used in some parts of what is now geographically France before the end of the eighth century.[2] These rites have some clear resemblances to the Spanish Mozarabic rite. Successive French authors—Martène, Le Brun and above all Duchesne—grounding themselves on these resemblances, and noting parallels real or supposed in other Western rites, and assuming always that the 'French' rites were the parent, or at all events the purest representative, of the whole group, have extended the term 'Gallican' to mean in practice 'all Western European rites other than that of the city of Rome'. Not content with thus stretching the meaning of the term, some disciples of this school speak of '*the* Gallican rite' as originally observed throughout the whole West including Africa, leaving the Roman rite as an isolated enigma confined to the city and suburbs of Rome. Upon analysis, it will be found that the key-point of the theory is

[1] See Dom A. Wilmart, art. *Germain de Paris (Lettres attribuées à Saint)* in the *Dict. d'arch. chrét. et de lit.*, vi., 1049 *sqq.* (1924). The headlong onslaught, on the contributor almost as much as his contribution, by the editor in a later art. of the same work, *s.v. Messe*, § xxxiii., *ibid.*, x. 648 *sqq.*, does not restore the credit of the *Letters*. For Duchesne's misuse of them see *Origins (ed. cit.)*, p. 189 *sq.* Doubts were first hinted as to the authenticity of the document by the patristic scholar H. Koch, and later by O. Bardenhewer; they were first plainly stated on liturgical grounds by E. Bishop, *App. to Narsai*, p. 89, *cf. Liturgica Historica*, pp. 130 *sa.* Duchesne never defended his dating of 'Germanus', and the note (incomprehensible from so great a scholar) appended to the later French edd. of his *Origines* (E. T. 1931, p. 574, *n.* 2) seems to shew that he failed to recognise the disastrous effects of the new view on his whole theory of the history of Western liturgy in general. Batiffol attempted to rescue the impugned authorship of Germanus, *Etudes de liturgie, etc.*, 1919, pp. 245 *sqq.*, but was refuted by Dom Wilmart, *art. cit.*
[2] This is *e.g.* its sense in Dom Mabillon's *de Liturgia Gallicana*, the pioneer work on the subject in 1685.

always the *Letters of Germanus*. Now that these turn out to be at least as
much Spanish as French,[1] and to represent 'Gallicanism' not in its early
purity but in the period of its admitted decadence after it had been transformed by a number of foreign elements, the term needs to be handled with
more caution. We are thrown back on the older genuinely French evidence
for the French rites, which is less abundant than one could wish. To avoid
begging any questions the word 'Gallican' ought to be used only in its
original sense of rites which existed within the geographical boundaries of
what is now called France, which was then neither a racial nor a political
nor an ecclesiastical unity. (When it is used in the wider modern sense of
'Western but not Roman' it will henceforward be placed in inverted
commas.)

The second fact of which account must be taken is Dom Connolly's
vindication of the authorship of the treatise *de Sacramentis* for S. Ambrose
of Milan *c.* A.D. 400.[2] Here at the end of the fourth century Milan is already
using what is recognisably an early form of the Roman canon. It means
that the Milanese rite is fundamentally a Roman—or as I should prefer to
put it, an Italian—rite, which in the course of later history has received
some 'Gallican' decorations,[3] and not an originally 'Gallican' rite which
has been subsequently Romanised. With the recognition of this we must
abandon forthwith Duchesne's theory that Milan was the centre of diffusion for the 'Gallican' rite in the West, whither he supposed it had been
imported from the East by Ambrose' oriental predecessor, Auxentius, *c.*
A.D. 360. With the elimination of the theory of an oriental origin for all
non-Roman Western rites the greatest single unnecessary obstacle to a
clear understanding of the development of the eucharistic liturgy in the
West is removed.

So much by way of general preface to the special question of the Introduction to the synaxis in the West outside Rome. We shall return to the
larger issues later; here the facts are these:

*At Milan.* We know virtually nothing of the development of the Milanese
rite between the late fourth century (in *de Sacramentis*) and the ninth, when
its text comes into view in the *Sacramentary of Biasca*.[4] The Introduction

---

[1] The region of Narbonne, to which Wilmart attributed them, belonged to the
Visigothic kingdom of Spain, and its inhabitants were at this time more Spanish
than French, both in race and feeling, and by ecclesiastical attachments, *e.g.* its
bishops usually attended Spanish councils. Some scholars would probably prefer
to say outright that 'Germanus' is a Spanish document both geographically and
liturgically; though there seem to me to be some French elements in the rite it describes. But was this rite ever in practice used as it stands in any church?
[2] *Art. cit. Downside Review* LXIX (1941), *pp.* 1 *sq. Cf.* also Dr. J. H. Srawley in
*J.T.S., XLIV* (July 1943), *pp.* 199 *sqq.*
[3] This has always been the view of the best Milanese experts, *cf. e.g.,* A. Ceriani,
*Notitia Liturgiae Ambrosianae, etc.,* Milan 1895. For a characteristic and charming
*boutade* of Duchesne's in reply, *cf. Origins, ed. cit., p.* 89, *n.* 1.
[4] Collated by A. Ratti and G. Mercati in *Missale Ambrosianum Duplex:* Milan
1913, under the symbol A.

is arranged thus: 1. The *Ingressa*, a psalm chant analogous to but not identical with the Roman introit. 2 (*a*). A diaconal litany, which like the Roman *Deprecatio Gelasii* is based on an Eastern text, but not identical with the Roman version. There are two forms of this litany at Milan, one used on the first, third and fifth Sundays in Lent, and the other on the second and fourth. It is not used at other times. *Or* 2 (*b*). When the litany is *not* used at Milan there is a hymn, consisting of *Gloria in excelsis* (in somewhat expanded form). 3. After the litany or the *Gloria*, there always follows *Kyrie eleison* repeated thrice. 4. After the *Kyrie* follows the greeting and the collect as at Rome[1] (and then the lections).

This differs from the Roman Introduction, *a*. in making the litany and hymn alternatives; *b*. in the insertion of the threefold *Kyrie* after the hymn, or after the litany in Lent.

*a*. The atrophy of the litany seems to have taken rather different forms at Milan and Rome. At Rome it disappeared altogether, replaced by the ninefold *Kyrie*, first inserted as an alternative to it by S. Gregory *c*. A.D. 595. At Milan it survived in Lent, as a special observance.

*b*. The Milanese threefold *Kyrie* does not seem to be any sort of survival of a litany, despite all that has been said to that effect by French scholars.[2] There are no petitions by the deacon, and no trace that there ever were any. On the contrary, the threefold *Kyrie* is *appended to* the Milanese litany when it is said, just as it is to the *Gloria* at other seasons. Musically, it is treated as a hymn. A similar threefold *Kyrie* as a hymn is found in some of the French rites, where it goes back to the Council of Vaison in 529, which instituted it in France, in imitation of 'a custom which has been introduced both in the Apostolic See and in all the Eastern and Italian provinces.'[3] 'Italy' means at this time what we call 'North Italy'—the region of Milan. The Milanese *Kyrie* is therefore not a 'Gallican' feature imported into the Milanese rite, but something which existed at Milan before the French rites borrowed it. It seems in fact to be the original Milanese form of 'the hymn' before the collect. We do not know when it first came into use there for this purpose, but it seems (from the phrase *intromissa est* used at Vaison) to have been supposed to be fairly new everywhere in A.D. 529, *i.e.* the *Kyries* were adopted at Milan about the same time as the *Gloria* at Rome.

[1] At Milan the collect is called *oratio super populum*, which at Rome meant a sort of blessing (*cf. p.* 518). But the Milanese *orationes s. p.* are the exact equivalents of the Roman collects, and in some cases the same prayers are used.
[2] Doubtless some confusion has been caused by the inveterate habit of associating the Roman ninefold *Kyrie* with the litany it replaced. But the *Kyrie* is not a 'litany' in the Eastern or Milanese or Gelasian sense, since there are no petitions, the essence of the Eastern litany form. S. Gregory more or less admits to having made a new departure in this, and it is much better to keep the word 'litany' for a single type of prayer.
[3] This canon does not necessarily mean that the *Kyries* (without petitions) ante-date S. Gregory at Rome. It does not state at what services the *Kyrie* had been introduced in other churches, probably because customs varied; but sets out the use it intends to be followed in France 'at mattins, mass and vespers'.

Both met a need instinctively felt for a 'hymn' before the lections, to adapt the old synaxis form to the new conditions. When, later on, the Roman hymn spread northwards, the native Milanese equivalent, the threefold *Kyrie*, was short enough to be added to it instead of being displaced.[1]

So far as its Introduction goes, therefore, the Milanese rite developed under much the same conditions as the Roman rite, and in the same period. It shews later signs of the influence of the Roman rite to the south of it during the sixth–ninth centuries, just as naturally as it shews other signs of the influence of its other neighbours, the Gallican rites to the north-west of it, during the same period. Eucharistic rites never have existed in water-tight compartments or rigidly excluded each other's influence. On the contrary they have borrowed freely from one another in all ages down to the sixteenth century, and this even across the barriers erected by open breaches of ecclesiastical communion. The Milanese rite in its basis is neither French nor Oriental but Italian, like the Roman. And like the Roman rite it has had its own local history within the general Italian setting, which has left its marks upon its modern form. All things considered, this account of the matter is only what might have been expected.[2]

*In Spain.* The exact history of the Spanish Introduction is not very easy

---

[1] This threefold *Kyrie* is repeated at Milan at the offertory and again after the communion. This is a convenient point at which to kill a hare assiduously pursued by various amateur liturgists in England. Starting from the assumption that the Milanese *Kyries* represented a litany and forgetting for the moment that the litany at Milan is alternative with the *Gloria*, they enunciate a theory that the *Gloria* at Milan is in its 'correct' place before the litany, whereas in the Roman rite it forms an 'interruption' between the litany (represented by the *Kyries*) and its concluding collect. There appear to be six separate errors combined in this theory. (*a*) The *Kyries* at Rome and at Milan are not a litany but a hymn. (*b*) The collect at Rome and at Milan is connected both by origin and contents with the lections not the litany. (*c*) The collect entered the Western rites some fifty years before the deacon's litany and from quite different sources. (*d*) If the collect *had* any connection with the litany, the interposition of a piece of music between a litany and a prayer by the celebrant is not unusual (*cf. e.g.*, the three consecutive examples in the Byzantine rite, Brightman, L. E. W., *pp.* 362–7; there are others). (*e*) At Milan itself the original arrangement seems to have been litany, *Kyrie*-hymn, collect—*i.e.*, precisely the Roman arrangement, but with a different hymn. (*f*) The notion that the Eastern litanies are concluded by a prayer seems itself to be mistaken (*cf.* p. 479).

[2] P. Lejay (*Dict. d'arch. chrét. et de lit.*, s.v. *Ambrosien* (rit.) I, 1402) suggested that the *Benedictus* was at one time used in the Milanese Introduction as in France, on the ground that an occasional collect in Milanese MSS. is headed *collectio super prophetiam*. He gives no references and I have wasted a good deal of time in verifying the fact that no collect in either of the two earliest MSS. is headed anything but *oratio* or *oratio super populum*. I am at a loss to account for his statement unless (like Mr. E. C. G. F. Atchley, *The Ambrosian Liturgy*, 1909, *p.* xi.), he mistook the *Bobbio Missal* for an Ambrosian book. This miscellany might be classified as Irish or Gallican or Roman or, at a pinch, Mozarabic, but certainly not Ambrosian, though it has borrowed three collects which now appear only in Ambrosian books. Nevertheless, three English writers have since repeated without investigation the statement that the *Benedictus* once followed the *Kyrie* hymn at Milan but has now 'entirely disappeared'. There is no evidence whatever for this statement.

to make out, but the following are the main facts. The Mozarabic Introduction is as follows: 1. The *Antiphona ad praelegendum*, (usually) a psalmchant, corresponding to the introit. (2. On great feasts, an interpolated version of the *Trisagion*, the interpolations varying according to the day.) 3. On Sundays and all feasts *Gloria in Excelsis*. 4. The collect. 5. The greeting. 6. The lections. We are handicapped as to the history of the different items by the fact that neither of the two earliest known Spanish MSS.—the *Antiphoner of Léon* (ninth-tenth century)[1] which contains the chants and the music of the rite, and the *Sacramentary of Toledo* (ninth century)[2] which contains the prayers—is equipped with an 'Ordinary' of the rite as a whole. Furthermore, it is uncertain just how old the arrangements are to which either of these MSS. witnesses. Both of them are substantially copies of older MSS. going back to the later seventh or eighth centuries. But it is possible (*a*) that one or both of the extant MSS. have to some extent been brought up to date, to conform to current custom when they were written, (*b*) that in some things this was not done, and that they witness to a state of affairs which was obsolete or obsolescent in the ninth century. The following facts are to be noted:

1. On all fast days the modern Mozarabic mass begins without any introduction at all, but simply with the greeting and lections, like the primitive rites. In the *Antiphoner of Léon*, however, the *Antiphona* is always said, even on fast days, unless the office of None has just been said in choir (when there would naturally be no entrance-procession, since the clergy would be already in church). This appears to witness to two stages: *a*. A period when there was no Introduction at all beyond the preliminary greeting, as at Rome before Celestine, *c*. A.D. 430.[3] (It is noteworthy that the African rite, which has been supposed to have some affinities with that of Spain, seems never to have developed an Introduction at all.) *b*. A period when the Introduction consisted only of entrance chant (*Antiphona*) followed at once by greeting and lections, as at Rome in the period immediately after Celestine's innovation.[4]

2. The variable *Trisagion* on great feasts is evidently an instance of that growth of Byzantine influence which followed Justinian's reconquest of part of Spain in the sixth century. How soon it was interpolated into the rite after that date it is impossible to say. The first evidence of its use (on four days in the year) is in the ninth century *Antiphoner*,[5] to which some eleventh century MSS. add three other days. In the earliest MS. which gives any sort of 'Ordinary' (*Toleten*. 35, 4)[6] of the tenth century, it is

---

[1] *Ed.* by the Benedictines of Silos under the title of *Antiphonarium Mozarabicum*, Léon, 1928. I am indebted to the Rev. W. S. Porter for drawing my attention to the importance of this MS., and for other information about the Mozarabic rite.
[2] *Ed.* by Dom M. Férotin under the title of *Liber Mozarabicus Sacramentorum* Paris, 1912.
[3] *Cf. p.* 453.
[4] *Cf. p.* 458.
[5] *Ed. cit. pp.* 29, 38, 45, 160.
[6] *Lib. Moz. Sac., col.* 697.

ignored altogether, but this is not unnatural in the case of an exceptional festal feature of the rite. All things considered, it may well have formed part of the late seventh century arrangements which were copied into the ninth century *Antiphoner*, but it is hardly likely to be much older than that. It is noticeable that S. Isidore in his description of the Toledan rite in the early years of the seventh century does not mention it.[1]

3. The first reference to the use of *Gloria in excelsis* in the Spanish mass 'on Sundays and all feasts' appears to be in the late eighth-century writing of Beatus of Liebana and Etherius of Osma *adv. Elipandum*.[2] It is found (apparently with three different musical settings) in the ninth century *Antiphoner*,[3] in one of which the wording contains variants somewhat akin to those of the Milanese version. Its use is evidently borrowed from Italy as the use of the *Trisagion* is borrowed from the East, perhaps at about the same time, though it became the normal hymn of the Introduction, while the *Trisagion* was an occasional extra for special feasts. The Roman rite as a whole was in use in some parts of Spain, *e.g.* Galicia, in the later sixth century, which may have led to the adoption of the Roman hymn in other places which were properly Mozarabic in rite. But such early seventh century references to the *Gloria* as I have found in Spain all seem to refer to its use at Lauds (*e.g.* can. 12 of the fourth Council of Toledo A.D. 633).

4. The Collect. There is some contradiction in the evidence about this. S. Isidore in the early seventh century says nothing of a collect before the lections, but specifically calls the *Missa* after the sermon the '*first* prayer' of the rite. The ninth century *Lib. Moz. Sac.* likewise makes no provision for what we should call a 'collect' at all, and though some of the masses in the eleventh century *Liber Ordinum* have a variable collect, others, like those of the ninth century *Sacramentary*, are still without any prayer in this position. It would appear from all this that the variable collect made its first appearance in the Spanish rite surprisingly late—in the tenth–eleventh century.

The only difficulty in accepting this account of the Spanish Introduction is a little rubric in the *Antiphoner*, which orders that on Palm Sunday after the *Antiphona ad praelegendum*,[4] '*Kyrie eleison* is not said' (as though it *were* said

---

[1] Dom Séjourné, the chief authority on this period of Spanish history, also concludes that the *Trisagion* is a seventh century interpolation (*S. Isidore de Séville*, Paris, 1929, p. 168). It should also be noted that in the modern rite *Benedictus* (the Song of Zachariah) is sung in place of this *Trisagion* on the Sunday before the Nativity of S. John the Baptist. In the ninth century *Antiphoner* it is sung instead of the *Gloria* on the feast itself (*ed. cit.*, p. 164). This appears to be only indirectly connected with the Gallican custom of using *Benedictus* as the normal 'hymn' of the Introduction, and to be suggested by its suitability to the day. *Benedictus es* (the Song of the Three Children, *vv.* 29–63, selections) is found in two MSS. between the collect and the lections; but the fourth Council of Toledo in A.D. 633 had ordered it to be sung between the O.T. and epistle lections, and this is its normal place in eleventh century MSS. (*cf. Antiphoner, ed. cit.,* p. 235).

[2] P.L., xcvi. 935.        [3] *Ed. cit., pp.* 234–5.

[4] *Antiphoner of Léon, ed. cit.,* p. 110. The Latin is *Quumque ipsius antifone caput repetierint et explicaberint, non dicitur kirieleison sed statim colligit episcopus orationem, et post collecta oratione, etc.*

on other occasions) 'but the bishop forthwith says the collect, and after the collect there follow the lections.' This looks as though the Roman Introduction (of penitential seasons), introit, *Kyries*, collect, lections, were the normal thing in some Spanish churches when the *Antiphoner* was compiled. Whether this was the case or not, I am unable to say; but I know of no other evidence for it, or for the use of the *Kyries* at all in the Spanish Introduction.[1]

If we may ignore this tantalising statement, the history of the Spanish Introduction appears to be approximately as follows: It begins, like the Roman, as an entrance-chant followed by the greeting and lections. Perhaps in the late sixth century, more probably in the seventh, the Roman 'hymn' was inserted on Sundays and festivals, supplemented on great feasts by the Byzantine one. This formed the whole Introduction down to the tenth century. Then the use of the variable collect before the lections was taken over from the other Western rites; but it was attached in thought to the Introduction which preceded it[2] rather than to the lections which followed it, as in the Roman idea. The greeting therefore was left preceding the lections in the primitive position, to mark the break between them and the Introduction, and not placed before the prayer as in the Egyptian and Roman rites.

*The Gallican Rites.* We are now in a better position to approach the real difficulty in discerning the development of the Western Introductions—the French evidence. Deprived of the delusive certainties of 'Germanus', our information has to be pieced together from various sources, always a process which offers plentiful opportunities of error.

'Germanus' presents us with the following elaborate opening: 1. The *Antiphona*, an entrance-chant (a psalm?). 2. Greeting. 3. *Trisagion* (which he calls by its Greek name, *Aius*). 4. A *Kyrie*-hymn, like that at Milan. 5. The *Benedictus* (Song of Zachariah). 6. The O.T. lection and Epistle. 7. *Benedictus es* (Song of the Three Children). How much of all this can we verify from other sources?

1. No other early Gallican document offers any evidence of such an entrance-chant, and since 'Germanus' calls it by its Spanish name *Antiphona*, we may perhaps dismiss it from the original Gallican rite as a later Spanish importation. 2. The Greeting. What is noticeable is that this is placed in the Antiochene position immediately after the entrance, and not as in Italy before the collect; or as in Spain, before the lections. 'Germanus' has no reference to a collect in the Introduction at all, though the Gallican

[1] There may be some confusion in the *Antiphoner* between the Introduction of the mass and a point in the blessing of palms (before the procession) on the same day where there is a threefold *Kyrie* after which *colligitur ab episcopo haec oratio . . .* (*Lib. Ord., ed. cit., col.* 182). But if so, I do not see how it has come about.
[2] Some of the variable collects take up the words of the *Antiphona ad praelegendum, cf. Lib. Moz. Sac., col.* 905 (MS. *Emilianensis* iv., eleventh cent. Collect for Lent iv.) *Lib. Ord., col.* 231, 366. Just so some of the Gallican collects take up the words of the *Benedictus* preceding them, *cf.* p. 467.

evidence of the seventh-eighth century places one after the *Benedictus*. Taken in conjunction with the absence of a collect from the Spanish rite down to the ninth-tenth century, this omission in 'Germanus' is significant of its 'Hispanising' tendency.

One notes next the collocation of the opening *Antiphona* with a version of the *Trisagion*, as in Spain. The group of three successive chants *Trisagion*, *Kyrie* and *Benedictus*, seems elaborate, but here 'Germanus' begins to make contact with other Gallican evidence. The *Bobbio Missal* (seventh-eighth century) which, though probably compiled originally by an Irishman and written in Italy, contains a great deal of French material, makes provision in the Introduction for the *Trisagion* (which it calls *Aios*), the *Gloria in excelsis*, the *Benedictus* (which it calls *Prophetia*) and a deacon's Litany (which it calls *Prex* or *Preces*). It places them in that order, but does not specify the way in which they are to be fitted into the rite. The *Gloria* and the Litany come, however, from a Celtic Ordinary, as we shall see; so that we are left with *Trisagion* and *Benedictus* in that order, as the compiler's idea of the Gallican Introduction, as in 'Germanus'. (Probably in arranging for all four chants the compiler of *Bobbio* is trying to make his book do for churches which used either system, though he does not say that they are alternatives.)

We have, however, an earlier reference to the *Trisagion* in Gaul, in the almost contemporary life of S. Gaugericus, bishop of Cambrai c. A.D. 600.[1] It is to be noted that while the Spanish books have their *Trisagion* in the orthodox form, the *Bobbio Missal* plainly implies that it expects it to be sung in the Gallican use with the Syrian monophysite interpolation 'Who wast crucified for us'. Furthermore, there is a threefold *Kyrie eleison* after the *Trisagion* in the Syriac *S. James*, as in 'Germanus'.[2] Taking this in conjunction with the Antiochene greeting immediately before the *Trisagion* in 'Germanus', it seems fairly easy to see whence the model for all this part of the 'Germanus' rite in its present form was derived—from Syria.[3]

The *Kyrie*-hymn is appended to the *Trisagion* in Gaul as it is appended to the *Gloria* at Milan, and probably for the same reason—that it is the original opening chant, dating from can. 3 of the Council of Vaison in

---

[1] *Analecta Bollandiana*, vii. (1888), p. 393. But the occasion on which he is said to have used it is not at the eucharist, as Duchesne implies, *Origins*, p. 192, n. 1.

[2] The text of 'Germanus' at this point is corrupt. It is possible that he means *Kyrie eleison* was sung once only by three singers.

[3] At the same time this does not demonstrate its late date. Syrian ecclesiastics occupied some important positions in sixth century Gaul. (*Cf.* L. Bréhier, *Byzantinische Zeitschrift*, xii (1903), pp. 1 sq., and especially 27-8.) There was too (which Bréhier does not note) a Syrian merchant, Eusebius, who became bishop of Paris c. A.D. 592 and upset people by filling the place with Syrian clergy. (Gregory of Tours, *Hist. Franc.*, x. 26.) For a Syrian bishop in Spain see can. 12 of the Council of Seville in A.D. 618. In such circumstances it is not surprising to find foreign Syrian elements imported into the Western rites. Unless and until liturgists will pay some attention to this sort of historical influence at work, and allow for it, the history of the liturgy will remain incomprehensible.

A.D. 529. The *Trisagion* was imported into Gaul from Syria later in the century, but the native hymn was brief enough to survive as an appendage to the new importation.[1] We do not hear of the *Trisagion* in Gaul until the very end of the sixth century, which is the period when evidences of the importance of Syrians in Gaul are most numerous.

The evidence for the use of the *Benedictus* in the Gallican rite is solid and satisfactory. Two collects in the Burgundian *Missale Gothicum* (eighth century), seven in the *Bobbio Missal* (seventh–eighth century) and two in the oldest extant Gallican missal, the *Masses of Mone* (seventh century) are all plainly intended for use after the *Benedictus*. Gregory of Tours in the sixth century speaks of the bishop intoning the *Benedictus* at an early point in the liturgy at Tours.[2] It evidently held the place in the sixth century French rites that *Gloria in excelsis* held in the sixth century Italian rites, as the 'hymn' before the collect. Its use in place of the *Gloria* is probably due to the fact that in the sixth century the *Gloria* in France was used at Lauds in the place where the Italian office-books used the *Benedictus*.[3]

Little can be inferred from the use of the 'Song of the Three Children' after the epistle in 'Germanus'. The true Spanish place for it was before the epistle, between that and the preceding O.T. lesson, but this was not always adhered to.[4] The Gallican lectionary of Luxeuil mentions it twice— once after the O.T. lesson and once after the epistle—which does not help. It is found in the Roman rite after the last O.T. lesson on Ember Saturdays, so that its use is common to all the Western rites. Gregory of Tours mentions it only at Mattins in Gaul.[5]

We find in Gaul, therefore, c. A.D. 600 an Introduction consisting of (1) the *Trisagion*, (2) the threefold *Kyrie*, (3) *Benedictus*, (4) greeting and collect. It is obvious that the developed Gallican structure is precisely the same as the developed Roman one—(1) entrance-chant, (2) *Kyries*, (3) hymn, (4) greeting and collect, though the texts used are not the same and the *Kyries* in Gaul are older by three-quarters of a century than at Rome. It is further noticeable that the Gallican rites of the seventh (and presumably the sixth) century, have the greeting and a variable collect immediately before the lections—a feature which did not

---

[1] Duchesne supposes that the same canon of Vaison instituted the *Trisagion*, since it orders that *Sanctus, sanctus, sanctus* shall be sung at all masses, including those of Lent and requiems, 'in the way it is now sung' at public masses. But this seems to refer to what we call the sanctus, not the *Trisagion*, which in Gaul was always sung in Greek, and went by the name of the *Aius*. If the fathers of Vaison had meant a Greek chant, they would not have translated the name, as is demonstrated by what they say of the *Kyrie eleison* in the same canon. That the sanctus proper should first have entered the Western rites about this time, and as a festal chant like the Greek *Gloria in excelsis*, is not surprising (*cf.* pp. 538 *sqq.*).

[2] Gregory of Tours, *Hist. Franc.*, viii. 7.

[3] S. Caesarius of Arles, *Regula SS. Virginum* (*Recapitulatio*), 69, *ed.* Dom Morin (Bonn, 1933), *p.* 24.

[4] *Cf. p.* 464, *n.* 1.          [5] Gregory of Tours, *Vitae Patrum*, vi., *ad fin.*

yet exist in the Spanish or African rites, or indeed in any but the Italian ones. The coincidence can hardly be accidental. The Roman Introduction, completed by the end of the fifth century, was known and deliberately imitated by the French churches of the sixth century, even though the imitation was by no means servile.

The question now seems legitimate—was S. Gregory in instituting the ninefold *Kyrie* at Rome influenced rather by the use of the threefold *Kyrie*-hymn at Milan and in Gaul than by any reminiscences of the Roman litany already obsolescent as a normal feature of the Roman rite? For what its evidence is worth for Roman practice in the sixth century, the *Deprecatio Gelasii* witnesses that *Kyrie eleison* was *not* the old Roman litany-response, but the Latin phrase *Domine exaudi et miserere*.

*The Celtic Introduction.* The *Bobbio Missal*, as we have said, has a 'mixed' Introduction which sets Irish and Gallican elements side by side. The subtraction of the latter leaves an 'Ordinary' or outline of the rite almost identical with that found in the pure Irish *Stowe Missal*. This latter was copied *c.* A.D. 800 from an older Irish MS. written not later than *c.* A.D. 650 and probably somewhat earlier. The common elements of the *Bobbio* and *Stowe* books present us, therefore, with the Irish rite of the first half of the seventh century.

This earliest known Irish rite is recognisably the Roman rite both in structure and contents. It is, of course, 'Roman' in the usual Irish way, both old-fashioned and curiously embellished, for Ireland was a long way off and Irish scribes were inveterate and often wayward 'improvers' of the texts they copied, whose taste in things liturgical was always for the unusual. But apart from such 'tinkerings' (as Edmund Bishop was wont to call the Irish way with liturgical documents) the Irish rite is Roman not only in substance but in eighty per cent of its details.

The Introduction in *Stowe* is as follows: 1. A collect (drawn from the *Gregorian Sacramentary*) is sung: 'O God Who having confided unto blessed Peter Thine apostle the keys of the kingdom of heaven didst bestow on him the pontifical office of loosing and binding souls: mercifully receive our prayers; and by his intercession we entreat Thee, O Lord, for help that we may be loosed from the bondage of our sins; through...' There follows 2. *Gloria in excelsis*, 3. the greeting and collect, 4. the epistle, followed by 5. a gradual chant and a deacon's litany, which is related to the *Deprecatio Gelasii* (*i.e.* it seems to be an independent translation and re-working of the same Greek original).[1] The Celtic Introduction when we first meet it thus consists of 1. a Roman prayer, 2. the Roman hymn, 3. the Roman variable collect—with a litany similar to the Roman

---

[1] *Bobbio* reproduces the scheme thus: 1. The same fixed collect, 'O God', etc. (2. The Gallican *Trisagion*.) 3. *Gloria in excelsis*. (4. The Gallican *Benedictus*.) 5. The greeting and collect. 6. Old Testament lection and epistle. 7. The *Prex* (apparently a deacon's litany after the epistle, but it does not give the text).

one, but after the epistle instead of before the hymn.[1] There is not much doubt of where the materials of the Irish rite were drawn from, even if *Stowe* did not professedly give them as the 'collects and prayers of the mass of the Roman church'. Though evident traces of S. Gregory's reforms of the Roman rite are to be found in both *Stowe* and *Bobbio,* both books preserve details of the pre-Gregorian Roman rite, notably in some readings in the canon.[2] It is conceivable that what we have is a revision of an older Irish version of the Roman rite, brought into line *c.* A.D. 620–650 with the recent Gregorian reforms.

*Conclusion.* This has had to be a lengthy and somewhat technical consideration, but it has enabled us to clear up a series of problems which have evidently given rise to much perplexity in the minds of all the compilers of liturgical histories and text-books. The facts appear to be as follows: The original nucleus of the synaxis sufficed the church as long as she existed in a heathen world and for a generation or two afterwards. When the world at large began to turn towards christianity and the synaxis began to need adaptation to a *public* worship, three different schemes of Introduction arose in the East, which had all found their final form before the end of the fifth century. The same needs were felt in the West, but development there was rather slower. The Roman Introduction which combined the Greek and Egyptian schemes was built up piece by piece between *c.* A.D. 425 and 500, and the Roman scheme thus formed was the basis of the other Western schemes. The frequency with which we find that it was borrowed *without* the Gelasian litany suggests that it spread chiefly in the later sixth century, when it appears that the litany was dropping out of regular use at Rome itself. It can be suggested that, in return for the Roman outline of the Introduction, the other Western churches contributed to the Roman rite the *Kyrie*-hymn with which S. Gregory replaced the Roman litany; though S. Gregory gave it a local Roman adaptation in making it ninefold instead of threefold, and inserting *Christe eleison.* Just so the other Western rites adapted the Roman Introduction to some extent when they took it over. So in the same way we find that in adopting elements of the Eastern Introductions the Roman and other Western churches freely exercised their own taste and judgement.

All over christendom the addition of the Introduction was intended to serve the same purpose—to strengthen the element of *worship* in the synaxis, once the decline of the catechumenate had removed the restriction on this caused by the presence of non-christians. It is thus natural that the

---

[1] *Stowe* calls this litany the '*Deprecatio* of S. Martin' (of Tours). The text is found in other Irish MSS. without this ascription, but it might indicate the region where the compiler of *Stowe* supposed it to have come from, though little reliance can be placed on his ascriptions of prayers to 'S. Augustine', 'S. Gregory' and so forth, in other cases. It is noteworthy that the French rites, so far as they give evidence of a litany, place it after the sermon, but the Spanish rites have a sort of litany after the epistle in Lent.

[2] *Cf.* E. Bishop, *Liturgica Historica, pp.* 90–94.

only item of the Introduction which is found in all rites in some form is the 'hymn' before the lections,[1] whether it be drawn from the Psalter as in the 'Far Eastern' rites, or is in the form of a 'prose hymn' as in the Greek and Western rites.

### The Lections and Chants

Though the order in which lections from the various parts of the Bible were read was already fixed in pre-Nicene times,[2] there appears to have been no such general agreement then as to the number of lections which should normally be read at the synaxis. The absence of other elements than lections (with the accompanying chants and sermon) gave time for a relatively large number of passages to be read without unduly prolonging the service. This multiplicity of the pre-Nicene lections continued in some churches in post-Nicene times, especially in Syria.[3] But towards the end of the fourth century the growth of other elements in the synaxis brought about the limitation of the lections in most churches to three, (1) from the O.T., (2) the apostolic writings and (3) the gospel, as a normal rule. In Africa, Spain and Gaul, and perhaps in some other churches, it was then customary on martyrs' feasts to substitute for the O.T. lection an account of the martyr commemorated on that day; and in some churches lections from apocryphal 'apostolic' writings were even substituted on occasions for the second lection from the canonical epistles.[4] The use of uncanonical gospels for the liturgical lessons is attested in the second century,[5] and that of 'harmonies' or conflations of the four gospels like Tatian's *Diatessaron* (second century) lasted on, especially in Holy Week, to as late as the seventh or eighth century in many churches from E. Syria to Spain. At Rome, however, a rigidly scriptural tradition always prevailed in the matter of the lections, which excluded not only apocryphal writings and 'harmonies' but also the historical 'acts' of the martyrs from the eucharistic liturgy; though the latter were accepted into the lessons of the Roman office, apparently in the seventh century. One main result of the general spread of Roman influence through the Western churches was the elimination of all non-scriptural lections at the eucharist in the West.

[1] Except, as stated on p. 451, among some Monophysites who have transferred it to after the epistle, and among Anglicans who have transferred it to after the communion and thanksgiving. In other post-reformation rites, *e.g.* the Swedish Lutheran, the 'hymn' remains in its oecumenical position, as it did in the first Anglican Prayer Book of 1549.

[2] *Cf.* p. 39.

[3] So *e.g. Ap. Const.*, viii., whose relatively undeveloped synaxis, without any Introduction, has five lections from the Law, Prophets, Epistles, Acts and Gospel. Four or five or even more lections are still found in the E. Syrian (Nestorian) and Monophysite rites on occasion, and also at Rome on Ember Saturdays.

[4] Two such have survived in the *Bobbio Missal*, ed. E. A. Lowe, (H.B.S.) I., *pp.* 106, 129.

[5] Eusebius, *Eccl. Hist.*, vi. 12.

In the fifth century the church of Constantinople began to reduce the normal three lections to two by the abolition of the first (from the O.T.). Rome followed suit in the late fifth or early sixth century, though the process was slower at Rome; the full three lections are still found provided for a few days in the year in the seventh century Roman lectionary list known as the 'Wurzburg Capitulary'. Indeed it may be said that the process of 'dropping' the O.T. lesson was never completed at all in the Roman rite, since the Wednesday and Saturday Ember Days still retain two and five O.T. lections each in the Roman missal; and on the weekdays of Lent and certain other days it is not the O.T. lesson but the epistle which has vanished. It does in fact not infrequently happen that the aptest comment on a passage of the gospels is furnished not by the New Testament but by the Old. In retaining the liberty of using passages from any part of the Bible in combination with the gospel the sixth century Roman church shewed good judgement, though the subsequent dislocation of the Roman lectionary[1] prevents this wisdom from being always apparent in the modern missal.[2] The omission of the third lection from other rites than the Byzantine and Roman was both later and less usual, though it had begun in many churches by the seventh-eighth centuries, at least on ordinary days.[3] It is sometimes suggested that the possession of three lections is a characteristic of the 'Gallican' rite while two is 'Roman'. But all rites, or at all events all Western rites, were three lection rites in the early fifth century. The retention of three lections therefore gives no real clue to the *origin* of a particular rite; it is at the best one indication of its later history.

The chants which came between the lections have their own history, which is still obscure in certain points, but which need not detain us here. The psalm-chant with Alleluias (gradual), which came down from the synagogues of our Lord's time was always reserved for the place of honour immediately before the gospel.[4] The invention of Lent in the fourth century led to the suppression of the Alleluias during this penitential season (and of the verse which had been added after them in the Roman rite, apparently from Byzantium, during the seventh century). In their place was substituted the Tract, a psalm-chant which had formerly intervened between the Old Testament lesson and the epistle, the retention of the O.T. lesson during this season apparently leading to the retention of the chant which was regarded as a comment upon it. The Gallican rite made various innovations in the way of elaborating and adding to

[1] *Cf. p.* 364, *n.* I.
[2] For examples see Dom B. Capelle, *Note sur le lectionnaire romain de la messe avant S. Gregoire, Rév. d'histoire ecclésiastique,* xxxiv. (1938), *pp.* 556 sq.
[3] The majority of masses in *e.g.,* the *Bobbio Missal* (which in respect of its lectionary is a Gallican book, with a lectionary similar in contents to the Gallican lectionary of Luxeuil) have already lost the first lection.
[4] Except in the Mozarabic rite, where it was transferred to immediately after the gospel by can. 12 of the fourth Council of Toledo in A.D. 633, for reasons which cannot now be discovered.

the chants between the epistle and gospel, of which the latest were the mediaeval Sequences, metrical compositions (not always of a very edifying character) of which five of the best are still to be found in the modern Western rite.[1] But all these changes are characteristically French mediaeval elaborations upon the simple psalm chants, with Alleluias added before the gospel, which had always been interposed between the lections of the synaxis since the time of the apostles. These are still found in every rite of catholic christendom with one exception. Archbishop Cranmer directly forbade the use of any chant whatever between the epistle and gospel in 1549.

The business of the preacher of the sermon which followed was to expound and interpret the salvation declared in the scriptures which had just been read, as is clear e.g. from the Egyptian prayers before the lections already quoted.[2] The same note is echoed in the prayer after the sermon in Sarapion's collection, a feature of the Egyptian rites which appears to be unique as a developed formal constituent of the rite.

### The Prayer after the Sermon

In the synaxis rite of Sarapion it runs thus:

'After the rising up from the sermon—a prayer:

'O God the Saviour, God of the universe, Lord and Fashioner of all things, Begetter of the Only-begotten, Who hast begotten the living and true Expression (of Thyself, charactēra, cf. Heb. i. 3), Who didst send Him for the rescue of the human race, Who through Him didst call mankind and make them Thine own possession; we pray Thee on behalf of this people. Send forth "holy spirit" and let the Lord Jesus visit them; let Him speak in their understandings and dispose their hearts to faith; let Him Himself draw their souls to Thee, O God of mercies. Possess Thyself of a people in this city also, possess Thyself of a true flock: Through . . .'

Apart from the renewed insistence on the theme of the 'rescue' of humanity in Jesus, we may note here the survival of the notion—becoming a little old-fashioned in Sarapion's day—of impersonal 'holy spirit' (without the definite article) as the medium whereby the Lord Jesus 'visits' His members on earth and Himself speaks in their understandings and disposes them to believe. Theology in the fourth century was beginning to attribute such operations to the Personal action of the Holy Spirit, but a brief comparison of Sarapion's expressions with e.g. another Egyptian work, S. Athanasius' de Incarnatione, will shew that he was by no means alone in still retaining the older attribution to the Logos, the Second Person. His 'invocation' of the Logos to supervene in the consecration of the eucharist is quite of a piece with the rest of his theology.

---

[1] Victimae paschali laudes (tenth cent.) for Easter Day is the oldest.
[2] Cf. p. 447.

The prayer after the sermon has disappeared from the text of the Alexandrian liturgy of *S. Mark* (no doubt through the infrequency of preaching in Byzantine times). But it is referred to several times by Origen in his homilies at Alexandria during the third century,[1] and once by S. Athanasius in the fourth.[2] Evidently the rule against praying in the presence of catechumens was differently interpreted in Egypt from the way in which it was understood elsewhere.

In the later fourth century in Africa, and perhaps elsewhere, the place of this prayer was to some extent supplied by a long fixed 'ascription' at the end of the sermon. Three of Augustine's sermons have preserved the full text of this as their concluding paragraph,[3] and the cue for it ends quite a number of others: 'Turning unto the Lord God the Father Almighty with a pure heart let us render unto Him, so far as our littleness may, most hearty and abundant thanks: beseeching His singular goodness with our whole intent that of His gracious favour He would vouchsafe to hear our prayers; and by His might drive far the enemy from all our doings and thoughts; increase in us our faith, govern our minds, grant unto us spiritual desires and bring us to His everlasting bliss; through Jesus Christ His Son our Lord, Who with Him liveth and reigneth in the unity of the Holy Ghost, God for ever and ever. Amen.'

The way in which this prayer takes the ostensible form of an address or exhortation to the people (known as a *praefatio* by contrast with an *oratio* addressed directly to God) is a characteristic of Western rites which we shall meet again. But the sermons of S. Fulgentius of Ruspe, an African bishop a century later than Augustine, end not with an invariable ascription but with a variety of formulae, frequently containing a reference to the feast or saint of the day. It is a little indication of the way in which during the fifth century the ecclesiastical calendar came to exercise an influence over the old fixed prayers of the liturgy in the West, a tendency which had hardly begun in Augustine's day. S. Leo's sermons at Rome *c.* A.D. 450 end with the simple ascription 'through Jesus Christ our Lord. Amen', occasionally elaborated into a Trinitarian form with the usual Roman collect ending 'Who liveth and reigneth ...'—an instance of the Roman temper of simplicity in such things.

## C. The Junction of Synaxis and Eucharist

After the sermon followed the dismissals of the catechumens and penitents and the intercessory 'prayers of the faithful'. These latter, a part of the synaxis but attended only by those about to attend the eucharist, had always formed a sort of intermediate section between the two rites when they were celebrated in sequence. The fusion of the two separate services

[1] Origen, *in Gen.* ii. 6; *in Num.* xvi. 9; xx. 5; etc.
[2] Athanasius, *Hom. de Semente*, 17.
[3] Augustine, *Sermons* xxxiv; lxvii; cclxxii.

in the fifth century did not destroy this special character of this part of the liturgy, though it brought changes of various kinds, due to the need for adapting the pre-Nicene tradition to the new purposes of a public worship. It was natural, too, that new items which it was desired to include somehow in the Shape of the Liturgy, but which had no obviously indicated place in the structure of the rite—*e.g.* the creed—should tend to be inserted at this point.

In the fifth century christendom was markedly beginning to fall apart. The question of Byzantine centralisation was dividing Syria and Egypt from the Balkan and Anatolian churches. The West was being parcelled up between a number of barbarian tribal kingdoms, though the old Romanised populations carried on a good deal of the tradition of the fourth century underneath the political overlordship of the new masters, and the Western churches were now the mainstay of what remained of the civilised tradition. But the growing political divisions meant that the fifth century changes in the liturgy were carried out by churches no longer in the close contact with each other that alliance with the universal empire of the fourth century had ensured. The result is a growing diversity again (after the period of convergence in the fourth century) among the various liturgies, which probably reached its height in the seventh–eighth century. After that the restoration of the Western empire by Charlemagne in A.D. 800 results in a general tendency towards uniformity in the West on the basis of the Roman rite, in the particular form in which the emperor had adopted this in his palace chapel. Despite a certain reaction against this 'Romanism' during the political confusion which followed Charlemagne's death, most of the effects of his work were never undone in Western liturgy until the sixteenth century. In the East, the submersion of the christian churches of Egypt and Syria under successive waves of mohammedan conquest in the seventh–eighth centuries, eventually caused the christians living as serfs under Islam to look towards Byzantium as in some sort the christian stronghold of the East. Though their experience of Byzantine bureaucracy and Byzantine ecclesiastical politics had been so disastrous that they never forgot their bitterness against her sufficiently to enter again into communion with the Byzantine 'orthodox' patriarchs, yet Byzantium had at least the prestige of being the one free church of the East, and Byzantine ecclesiastical ways tended to spread among the dissidents in consequence.

The result of all this is a good deal of diversity in the arrangement of the items which belong to this 'second *stratum*' in the Shape of the Liturgy, and in the way in which various churches fitted them into the traditional outline which had come down everywhere unchanged from pre-Nicene times. Nevertheless one can distinguish certain groups in the table opposite (*p.* 475). I do not propose to go into all the diversities, some of which are unimportant. Others, however, have had a considerable effect upon the devotional ethos of the rites in which they are found.

The dismissals and prayers belong to the old synaxis. The latter were

| East Syrian | Byzantine | Jerusalem | Egyptian | Roman | Franco-Spanish |
|---|---|---|---|---|---|
| — | — | — | Prayer after Sermon | | — |
| Dismissals | Dismissals | Dismissals lost in ? 5th cent. | Dismissals attested in 5th cent. | Dismissals lost in 6th cent. | Dismissals |
| Prayers lost in 5th cent. | Prayers now replaced by a Litany | Prayers moved in 4th cent. | Prayers | Prayers lost c. A.D. 495 | Prayers lost before A.D. 600 |
| *End of the Synaxis* | | | | | |
| | | | | Prayer 'of the day' lost in 6th cent. | Prayer 'of the day' |
| Offertory Procession | Offertory Procession | [ Offertory Procession placed here in ? cent. | — | — | [ Offertory Procession introduced ? 6th cent.[1] ] |
| — | Offertory Prayer | Byzant. Off. Prayer placed here in ? cent. / Creed ] | | | |
| Creed | Creed | | Creed (Here in Coptic; during Offertory in Greek) | [ Creed introduced 11th cent. ] | [ Creed introduced 8th–9th cent.[2] ] |
| Pax | Pax | Pax | Pax | Pax moved c. A.D. 400 to after Fraction | Pax moved ? cent. to after Offertory |
| — | — | Original Offertory Procession ? | Oblation | Oblation | Oblation |
| Names | | | | | Names |
| — | | Offertory Prayer | Offertory Prayer | Offertory Prayer | Offertory Prayer |
| | | | | | Pax |
| Beginning of Euch. Prayer | Beginning of Euch. Prayer | Beginning of Euch. Prayer | Beginning of Euch. Prayer containing Names | Beginning of Euch. Prayer containing Names | Beginning of Euch. Prayer |

[1] The Offertory Procession is now placed *before* the *Missa* and *Alia* or Prayer of the Day, but this is probably its position when first introduced.

[2] Creed after Fraction in Spain, introduced in 6th cent.

declining in popularity during the fifth century, and being replaced either by newer forms of intercession like the litany, or by various ways of commemorating the living and the dead in the eucharist proper—a practice which I have called 'the Names', to avoid begging certain questions connected with the particular custom known as the 'recitation of the diptychs'. Only in the Egyptian rites did the old 'prayers of the faithful' persist in something like their original form as well as position.

For the rest, the columns fall easily into two groups—those which have the 'oblation' by the people for themselves before the altar, comprising the Egyptian and Western rites; and those which have instead the 'offertory procession' of the deacons from the sacristy, in the form first fully described by Theodore of Mopsuestia. The primary example of these is the Byzantine rite; but the position of the offertory in the East Syrian and Jerusalem rites is somewhat obscure,[1] though it is probable that they were

---

[1] The order in the present E. Syrian rite is, 1. The *Caruzutha* (now a form of litany, originally a long 'bidding' by the deacon) followed by a blessing, apparently a trace of the old dismissals. 2. The Dismissals (in a later abbreviated form). 3. The Offertory (placing of the elements upon the altar by the priest; but though the deacons enter the sanctuary in procession at this moment, they do not *bring with them* the elements, which have been on a sort of credence since their preparation before the synaxis). 4. The Creed. 5. The 'Names'. The order in Narsai is, 1. Dismissals. 2. Offertory procession *actually bearing* the elements from the sacristy. 3. The Creed (*ed. cit., p.* 3). 4. The deacon announces 'the Names'. 5. A prayer ('of the veil'?) by the celebrant. 6. The deacon announces the Pax. 7. During the giving of the Pax the deacon reads out 'the Names'. The order in Ps.-Denys is as in Narsai, except that the creed seems to precede, not follow, the offertory procession. There has evidently been a good deal of variation in the order of the items in this part of the E. Syrian rite at different times. The case of the Jerusalem rite is even more obscure: S. Cyril says nothing about an offertory; and S. James in its Syriac form has no offertory procession, the elements being upon the altar before the service begins. The Greek S. James has the procession in the Byzantine place and in so heavily Byzantinised a form that I am disposed to take the whole item *at this point* for a fairly late Byzantine interpolation. But the Greek S. James also has two 'offertory prayers' proper after the kiss of peace, which suggests that this is the original point of the offertory in all the Syrian rites, since it is found there in *Ap. Const.*, viii. The Egyptian rites have adopted the Byzantine preparation of the elements before the synaxis (but on the altar, not at a separate table) immediately after which there is a sort of procession in which they are carried three times round the altar and replaced upon it. There is no procession at the offertory in the Coptic rite (though the Greek S. Mark has adopted it from Byzantium in one late MS.) and the deacon's command to the people to bring up their offerings still remains in its ancient position, before the offertory prayer. Some French rites had adopted the offertory procession in the sixth cent. (Gregory of Tours, *de Gloria Mart.* I, 96) and there is one in 'Germanus'. The Spanish rite also has one in the modern text. But the Council of Mâcon can. 4 (A.D. 485) and the Council of Elvira can. 29 (c. A.D. 305) guarantee that both these rites were originally 'oblation' not 'procession' rites. At Milan there is now a 'procession' with the *empty* vessels at the Byzantine position, but the 'oblation' of the people still takes place at the original Western position, in the ritual form of an offering of bread and wine by a college of almsmen and almswomen, the *vecchioni*. The Anglo-Saxons had the 'oblation' before the Norman Conquest, but the Frenchified rite of Sarum in the thirteenth century destroyed the native English tradition by an imitation of the Gallican 'procession'. The first spread of the 'procession' rite in the West appears to coincide with Justinian's partial restoration of Byzantine rule in the Western Mediterranean during the sixth century.

both 'procession' rites, not 'oblation' rites, from at all events the fifth century.[1]

A further interesting subdivision arises from the fact that all the Western rites seem to have stood together in the fifth century in placing a variable prayer before the Pax and the offertory, which I have called the 'Prayer of the Day', of which all the Eastern rites (including the Egyptian) know nothing. The Western rites might in fact be placed in a single column in this table but for the awkwardness of shewing two facts. One is the curious position of the Pax (after the offertory prayer) in the Spanish and Gallican rites. This can hardly be its original position, but it was already placed there traditionally in Spain in the time of S. Isidore of Seville (c. A.D. 600), and there seems to be no evidence as to when or why it was moved from its (presumable) original position *before* the offertory, where it stood in all the pre-Nicene rites. The other point in which the Western rites vary among themselves is that in Spain and Gaul the recital of the 'Names' of the offerers is attached to the offertory, as early as can. 28 of Elvira (c. A.D. 305) in Spain; while at Rome and Milan, as in Egypt, it was inserted at an early point in the eucharistic prayer, and this apparently before c. A.D. 390.

In the Eastern rites, as in the Western, the offertory prayer naturally follows immediately upon the placing of the elements on the altar. This later insertion of an explicit offertory prayer links the offertory closely to the eucharistic prayer, but the Eastern rites have spoilt the connection by the insertion at this point of the creed, a late sixth century innovation, and the transference to this point of the Pax, originally the prelude to the offertory.[2] The East Syrians seem never to have adopted the offertory prayer in the strict sense, retaining, I suppose, the primitive notion that the solemn placing of the elements upon the altar *is* an offering of them, needing no explicit verbal expression.[3] It remains to discuss certain particular changes and insertions in the various rites, the reasons for them (where these can be discerned) and their consequences for the particular ethos and devotional convention of the rites in which they were made.

### The Invention of Litanies

The litany form of prayer appears for the first time fully developed in the North Syrian rite of *Ap. Const.*, viii. c. A.D. 370. It is interesting to note the

---

[1] *Cf. pp.* 122 *sq.* But *cf.* also *n.* 2 on *p.* 438.

[2] *Cf.* Matt. v. 23, 24. Was the Pax transferred to this point when all the deacons came to be occupied with the elaborated 'procession' and so could not proclaim the Pax at the old place? It is still *before* the offertory in *Ap. Const.*, viii. and in the homilies of Chrysostom c. A.D. 400.

[3] So in the modern rite (*cf.* Brightman, L. E. W., *pp.* 267 *sq.*). The prayer which Narsai outlines after the creed (*ed. cit., p.* 8 top) is nearer in substance to the usual Eastern 'prayer of the veil' than to an 'offertory' prayer proper, as found in other Eastern rites.

exact forms in which it is found there. The dismissal of the catechumens begins by their being commanded by the deacon to kneel; he then proceeds to proclaim a series of petitions on behalf of them, to each of which the laity answer *Kyrie eleison*: 'that He Who is good and loveth mankind will pitifully receive their prayers and entreaties' (*Kyrie eleison*); 'that He will reveal unto them the gospel of His Christ' (*Kyrie eleison*); 'that He will enlighten them and establish them with us' (*Kyrie eleison*)—and so forth. These are prayers *for* the catechumens, in which they themselves take no part. After eighteen of these petitions, the catechumens are bidden to rise and then to pray for themselves: 'Entreat for the peace of God through His Christ'; 'Entreat that this day and all the days of your life be peaceful and sinless'; 'that you make christian ends', and so forth. Then they are bidden to bow for the bishop's blessing, which he gives in the form of a longish prayer, and the deacon proclaims 'Depart in peace, ye catechumens'.

There follow three more sets of dismissals on the same plan; for those possessed by evil spirits, those in the last stages of preparation for baptism and the penitents respectively. Each class is prayed over by the deacon and people in a series of petitions with the response *Kyrie eleison*, and dismissed with the bishop's blessing in the form of a prayer. The whole business seems very elaborate and can hardly have taken less than twenty minutes or so to perform. But the evidence of Chrysostom's homilies preached at Antioch[1] guarantees that the compiler has not imagined this system, but has on the whole kept faithfully to the Antiochene practice, though he has probably expanded it in some respects.

There follow the real 'prayers of the faithful', intercessory petitions for the world at large proclaimed by the deacon, answered by the prostrate people with *Kyrie eleison*. But these petitions are slightly different from those said over the catechumens etc. in their construction: 'For the peace and good order of the world and the holy churches let us pray; that the God of the universe may grant us His own everlasting peace that cannot be taken away and preserve us to pass all the days of our life in unmoved righteousness according to godliness.'[2] If we look back to the old intercessions (*p.* 42) we shall find that they consisted of 1. a subject given out by the deacon or celebrant, 2. the people's prayer in silence, 3. a brief collect or prayer by the celebrant, summing up the people's prayers. What seems to have happened here is that the celebrant's collect after each pause for silent prayer has been slightly adapted and *appended to the deacon's bidding.* 'For the peace . . . let us pray' is the old deacon's bidding; 'that etc.' (which has no parallel in the biddings over the catechumens) is the celebrant's collect.

In form the change may not appear very great, but the effect is considerable. Under the old system the whole church did the substance of the *praying*, individually and in silence. The 'liturgies' of the deacon and celebrant only acted as a sort of 'framework' in what was a really corporate intercessory act. In the litany this has been altered. It has become a dialogue, between the deacon and the people, with the former very much predominant; and the celebrant has been eliminated. It is true that the people now have a vocal part, the *Kyrie*, but they are no longer the obvious active interceders; they have become a sort of chorus. And the celebrant has been excluded altogether from the intercessions.[1] It is true that in *Ap. Const.*, viii. the litany is followed by a prayer by the bishop. But if it be compared with the prayers over the catechumens and penitents which have just preceded the litany of intercession, it will be found that this prayer is not any summary or conclusion of the prayers 'for all sorts and conditions of men' which have been offered in the litany. It is a departure-blessing or dismissal of the faithful there present, a prayer *for* not *with* those who have been interceding, exactly comparable to the blessings of the catechumens, etc. before they leave the assembly. It marks the end of the synaxis, still an independent rite. Even if the eucharist is to follow, it may do so in another building or after an interval. But there is no justification in this case—or I would add in any other—for supposing that a prayer by the celebrant necessarily *summed up* or *concluded* the intercessory litany in the East. That consisted simply of the people's response to the deacon's petitions, which had absorbed the old celebrant's part in the intercessions.[2]

This curious evolution asks for some explanation beyond mere caprice,

[1] I suggest that anyone interested in the development of litanies should study in this order, 1. The 'Prayer for the People' (No. 27) in Sarapion, which is a sort of incipient litany. 2. The Coptic Intercessions (Brightman, *pp.* 172–3, then *pp.* 165–171, 160–1, 114–15). 3. The Nestorian *Caruzutha* (which was not originally a litany, but a long proclamation by the deacon; but that does not affect the interest of its evidence on the development of the litany form)—first the form in Brightman, *pp.* 263 *ll.* 22 *sqq.*, and then the alternative form *ibid.*, *p.* 262. This will shew every stage of the elimination of the celebrant from the Eastern intercessions. I should add that the litany in *Ap. Const.*, viii. has 29 petitions, of which 8 have no 'that' clause added to the deacon's bidding. Some of these certainly, and all of them probably, were invented by the compiler; and so his source contained no celebrant's collect to append to these biddings, and for some reason he did not trouble to invent one.

[2] It may be asked, what of the prayers now recited silently by the celebrant in the Eastern rites during the litany-dialogue of the deacon and people? It is commonly said that these were formerly recited aloud after the litany, but this seems to be a mere guess, unsupported by evidence. And if one reads the prayers it is very difficult to see how it could ever have been supposed that they had any real connection with the litanies, *e.g.*, the two 'prayers of the faithful' in the ninth cent. rite of *S. Basil* (Brightman, *pp.* 316 *sq.*) or the two alternative forms in *S. Chrysostom* (*ibid.*) are obviously private devotions of the priest, protesting his personal unworthiness to offer the eucharist. They seem from their contents to have a connection with the prayer mentioned by Theodore of Mopsuestia, *Catecheses, ed. cit.*, *p.* 89 (who has no litany), but prayers of this tenor are common in all the Eastern (non-Egyptian) rites. There is ground for thinking that in some cases the people's litany is secondary, put in to occupy their attention while the priest proceeds with the liturgical action at the altar, and in other cases the private prayer is provided to fill up the priest's time while the litany is proceeding.

and it seems to have had an entirely practical origin. In Syria in the later fourth century there had been introduced the 'sanctuary veil', a silk curtain cutting off the celebrant and the altar altogether from the sight of the congregation during the celebration of the eucharist.

### The Veil and the Screen

To understand the real meaning and purpose of this innovation we must go back a little. We have already noted in S. Cyril's *Catecheses*[1] the first beginnings of the use of words like 'awful' or 'terrifying', and the 'language of fear' generally, in reference to the consecrated sacrament. By the last quarter of the century this novel idea had taken a firm hold in Syrian devotion—it is notable, for instance, in Chrysostom's sermons. Perhaps it found a specially congenial soil in Syria, where since time immemorial 'the holy' had also meant in some way 'the dangerous'.[2] It spread outside Syria northwards very soon. We find it, for instance, in Theodore (an Antiochene by training) at Mopsuestia,[3] who does not hesitate to say that the faithful *should be afraid* to draw nigh unto the sacrament without a mediator and this is the priest who with his hand gives you the sacrament.'[4] We are evidently far in thought (but only a few years in time) from the days when the laity communicated themselves daily at dawn from the sacrament reserved in their own homes. It is a symptom of that decline—swift and sudden in the East, slower but steady in the West—in the understanding of the position of the laity as an 'order' in the church, a decline which begins in the fourth century. The word *laïkos* 'a layman' in the East *c.* A.D. 300 still meant 'one of the People (*laos*) of God', with all the rights and high duties and destinies that implied. By *c.* A.D. 450 it had almost come to mean 'profane' as opposed to 'sacred'. (There is required only one more step to reach the modern French meaning, *e.g.* in the phrase *lois laïques*, where it means 'anti-christian'.)

The veil which hid the sanctuary during the eucharist in the Syrian churches is the natural product of this frame of mind. 'Liturgy' is becoming the special function of the clergy alone, for their sacred character protects them in the 'numinous' presence of the sacrament, charged as it is with 'terrifying' power. The 'profane' laity have no such safeguard, and therefore the veil was introduced, to hide them from it rather than it from them. Perhaps the Old Testament precedent of the tabernacle veil had something to do with the innovation, but an origin in the same frame of mind rather than in deliberate imitation seems the truer explanation. And the earliest reference to the veil that I can find is in a homily of S. John Chrysostom preached at Antioch soon after A.D. 390: 'When the sacrifice is borne forth (for the communion) and Christ the Victim and the Lord the

---

[1] *Cf. p.* 200.
[2] *Cf. p.* 283.
[3] *Cf.* 2 Sam. vi. 7.
[4] Theodore, *Catecheses*, vi., *ed. cit.,p.* 119.

Lamb, when thou hearest (the deacon proclaim) "Let us all entreat together . . .", when you see the veil drawn aside—then bethink you that heaven is rent asunder from above and the angels are descending.'[1] There is no veil in *Ap. Const.* and it may not yet have been common outside Antioch. But if we are thinking of origins, I should be inclined to look behind Antioch to the church of the *Anastasis* at Jerusalem, where, as Etheria has told us,[2] the sacrament was consecrated, not exactly behind a veil, but still out of sight of the congregation, inside the cave of the Holy Sepulchre behind its great bronze screens. So far as the evidence goes, it was at Jerusalem that 'the language of fear'—which is at the very roots of this whole conception—first began to be used about the sacrament.

The atmosphere of 'mystery' and 'awe' which is the special ethos of the Byzantine rites seems to be very largely a product of the local churches of Syria in the fourth century. It is true that the veil in modern orthodox churches is only a relic of its former self, a mere door-curtain inside the central gates of a solid masonry screen, whose outer face is covered with the sacred ikons. The first occurrence of this further barrier between the laity and the consecrated sacrament seems to be in Justinian's glorious rebuilding of the cathedral of the Holy Wisdom at Constantinople c. A.D. 570.[3] It would appear, too, that in its main features (apart from the decoration with ikons, which may be a later development) this screen was originally nothing but a straightforward copy of the traditional backscene of the Byzantine theatre with its three double doors. The idea was perhaps not so inappropriate as it may seem. The Byzantine rite had by this time taken on some of the characteristics of a drama.

What I am concerned to emphasise here is that the sixth century introduction of the solid screen at Constantinople did no more than confirm the great consequence of the introduction of the veil in Syria in the fourth century. This was the *exclusion* of the laity from the process of the liturgical action. When all has been said that is true—and very much is true—of the real spiritual participation of the orthodox laity at all periods in the liturgical worship, it also remains true that the screen to a large extent forces upon the Eastern liturgies the character of two simultaneous services, the one proceeding outside the screen for the people, conducted chiefly by the deacon; the other—the real liturgical action—proceeding inside the screen conducted by the celebrant. Despite the general connection of the two and their spasmodic unification, and the function of the deacon who acts all the time as a connecting link, this duality is unmistakable at the actual performance of the liturgy in an orthodox church. And that character was originally given to it by the adoption of the veil and the hidden consecration in Syria during the fourth century. It is a quite different tradition of

---

[1] Chrysostom, *in Ephes.*, iii. 5.  [2] *Cf. p.* 438.
[3] K. Holl's article on this in *Archiv. f. Religionswissenschaft*, ix. (1906), pp. 365 sqq., appears to be still trustworthy on the architectural side, though its liturgical conclusions need revision in the light of the discovery of Theodore's *Catecheses*.

worship from our own, though we need not therefore condemn it or even criticise it. But we must grasp the essential difference between Eastern and Western eucharistic devotion, which begins in the fourth century—that while in the East the whole assumption and convention of the devotional tradition is that the people ought *not* to see the consecration, or indeed the progress of the liturgical action, in the West the devotional tradition assumes that they *should* see it. And when the new liturgical fashion for the 'eastward position' of the celebrant had for the first time made this difficult in the West, the new ceremony of the Elevation was deliberately introduced to shew them the sacrament.[1]

The litany in the Eastern rite is more comprehensible in the light of all this. After the catechumens, etc. had retired the celebrant blessed the faithful at the end of their prayers as he had blessed the others, and so dismissed them in their turn. But if—as normally on Sundays—the eucharist was to follow, this final blessing of the faithful was not given. Instead the celebrant retired at once within the veil to prepare to celebrate, murmuring private prayers of deprecation for his own unworthiness (of the kind which now figure as the 'prayers of the faithful' in the Byzantine rites)[2] leaving the intercessions to be conducted by the deacon outside the veil. It would be difficult, and in any case unedifying, to conduct the old 'trialogue' of deacon, people and celebrant through the curtain; it was much easier to allow the deacon to add the celebrant's part in the intercessions to his own. Hence the litany.

Silent recitation—at least in great part—of the prayers at the eucharist would in any case have been likely to follow from this new separation of the celebrant and people, even if the psychological question of 'reverence' had never occurred to anyone. But it seems that in fact the latter was the determining cause of the introduction of the silent recitation of the eucharistic prayer, in the far East and the West at all events.[3]

[1] The assertion is sometimes made that at Rome or in France in the sixth or seventh century the altar was hidden at the consecration by curtains, but the evidence appears very uncertain. The Western solid choir-screen began in the great conventual and collegiate churches of the North as a protection for the chapter and singers—the only usual congregation in such buildings—against draughts. In other words the Eastern screen was meant to shut the congregation *out*, the Western one was meant to shut them *in*. The pierced screens of our parish churches are an imitation of the greater churches, but adapted to let the congregation see. The mediaeval Lent veil which did hide the Western altar, has an obscure origin, but I suspect that it was imported from Syria, first in Sicily.
[2] Brightman, L. E. W., *pp.* 316 *sq.*
[3] The historical facts about this practice, which many people find so irritating, seem to be, 1. That the whole prayer was originally chanted aloud on a sort of *recitative*, like the ancient jewish prayers. 2. That the whole prayer except certain cues (before the sanctus and the concluding Amen) was already said inaudibly in E. Syria in the time of Narsai in the fifth century (where there was still *no* veil). 3. That in the sixth century the same custom was being introduced in some Greek churches, and by the seventh–eighth the silent recitation of most of the prayer (including the invocation but not the words of institution) had been adopted at Constantinople. 4. That except for the preface and certain cues, silent recitation

The main action of the eucharist was thus removed from the sight of the Eastern people. Except for the Great Entrance and the Communion all took place behind the veil or screen. It is not surprising that the 'Great Entrance' procession, when the sacrament was 'carried to burial' with solemn pomp, and its reappearance after an interval dramatically brought forth 'resurrected' at the moment of communion, became the twin focus of popular eucharistic devotion in the Greek churches.

Those who will may emphasise the 'Eleusinian' parallel thus produced in the Greek rite. For my own part I am clear that this interpretation of the eucharist was only built up by very gradual stages in the Greek churches and by successive independent changes in the presentation, not the contents, of the Greek liturgies, the prayers of which do not lend themselves very patiently to this interpretation. Some of the changes which ultimately had the most 'Eleusinian' effects began not in Greece at all but in Syria. Taking into account the late date at which the parallel—which can I, admit, be made to appear very striking—was finally developed, there can be little question of any direct imitation of hellenistic mysteries in the Byzantine rites. At the most all that could be suggested is a similar temper of thought underlying the Eleusinian mysteries and Greek eucharistic devotion. But we know too little about the former for any such parallel to be much more than an exercise of the imagination.

The Eastern people retained as their part in the liturgy listening to the lections (which the orthodox populations have always done with assiduity) and participation in some of the chants (though the admirable melodies of most of these were too difficult for the people and had to be left to the choir)—and the litany! It was natural this should be popular; it was the only devotion in the whole rite in which the laity as such now had any active part. From being used only at the intercessions which closed the synaxis it began to be repeated at other points in the rite, as an act of corporate prayer *accompanying* the liturgical action proceeding in mystery beyond the veil. It is now repeated no less than nine times in various forms, in whole or in part, during the Byzantine eucharist. With so many of the liturgical prayers said in silence, the litany forms the main substance of the people's prayer.

There may be a certain evidence of liturgical decadence in this acceptance of the need to occupy the attention of the congregation with irrelevant devotions while the liturgical action—the eucharist proper—proceeds apart from them behind the screen. But even so, Westerns are hardly in a position to remark upon it. The Eastern litany is at least a corporate

was the rule at Rome before *c.* A.D. 700 (where also there was *no* veil). 5. That in Gaul all the prayer was sung aloud except for the paragraph containing the words of institution, which in the seventh century was already called *secreta* or *mysterium*. The use of the normal speaking voice for the eucharistic prayer appears to be an innovation of the Lutherans in the sixteenth century. Anciently it was either sung or whispered.

devotion provided by the church for the faithful, magnificently phrased and noble in its all-embracing charity. The Western 'low mass', dialogued in an undertone between priest and server, is in a different way just as degenerate a representative of the old corporate worship of the eucharist. The faithful, it is true, can see the action and associate themselves continually with it in mind in a way that the Eastern layman cannot quite do. But the Western laity, unprovided with any corporate devotions whatever, are left with no active part in the rite at all. They listen and pray as individuals, adoring in their own hearts the Host elevated in silence, and then passively receive communion. All this throws the whole emphasis in Western lay devotion upon *seeing*, and on individual silent prayer. This question of 'seeing' is really at the basis not only of the difference of Eastern from Western eucharistic devotion, but of Western catholic and Western protestant doctrinal disputes. Is what one *sees* elevated or 'exposed'—a significant word!—to be *adored* as such? Posed thus, apart from its context in the corporate offering, the question is distorted. But what caused it to be posed in this way in the sixteenth century, and made the reality of the Body and Blood of Christ a centre of controversy in the West as it never had been in the East, was precisely the growth of low mass as the normal *presentation* of the eucharist to the laity during the mediaeval period.[1]

We see, too, now why the litany never proved nearly so popular in the West as in the East. Though it was introduced at some time or another

---

[1] I am not attacking the practice of the 'simple said service' or even of private masses. They are a necessity under modern conditions. But it is important to take account of this Latin invention of the 'simple said service' as the *normal* presentation of the eucharist in explaining the history of eucharistic devotion and doctrine in the West. There are two sides to the matter. In extending to the presbyter the liturgical 'priesthood' of the bishop and making him the usual celebrant of the eucharist, the church has laid upon him the necessity of fulfilling his 'liturgy' regularly and frequently. His 'liturgy' is not merely his 'possibility', it is the ground of his 'being' in the Body of Christ. And he does not fulfil this by simply attending the eucharist celebrated by another priest. On the contrary in so doing he abdicates his function and usurps that of a layman, which is a double violation of the principle of 'order'. On the other hand, 'concelebration' has died out of our tradition. It is not found entirely satisfactory even in the East, where the alternative custom of quasi-private sung celebrations in *parecclesiai* (little 'churches' adjoining the main church, in effect side-chapels, though they are treated as separate churches to conform nominally to the rule of only one eucharist in a church on one day) has long been practised in monasteries and other churches where there are many priests. On the other hand, if every priest *ought* to celebrate regularly and frequently, he cannot be provided every time with all the assistance for a high mass. The 'simple said service' is the only way out, and the lay devotional tradition of the West, not least in England, has in the course of centuries not only conformed to it but come on the whole to prefer it. The modern problem is how to get the laity to participate *actively* in the liturgy, and we shall not solve it merely by diminishing opportunities of celebrating for the clergy. The *messe dialoguée* of the French 'liturgical movement' is one way of doing this. But here again, the emphasis is laid on their participation in certain devotions like the 'preparation' which are by origin and nature *private* devotions of the priest. Their real participation, which was originally not only in the chants but in the *action* of the liturgy, is a thing much more difficult to restore.

into most Western rites—I see no evidence that it was ever used in Africa—it disappeared from them again often without trace, because the people felt no need of it. It was the Eastern laity's substitute for *seeing* the action of the liturgy, their way of associating themselves with it beyond the screen. The particular conditions which made it so popular in the East simply did not exist in the West, where the people found other substitutes in sight and private prayer for their old active participation in the rite.

### The Creed

The introduction of the creed into the liturgy has a curious history. Its original usage was at baptism. From the earliest days repentance and the acceptance of the belief of the church was the condition *sine qua non* of baptism into the Body of Christ,[1] and formal interrogation as to both was made of converts before they received the sacraments. A statement of belief that 'Jesus is Messiah' with all that this implied might be accounted sufficient in jewish circles, with their background of unwavering mono-theism. But more was rapidly found necessary among the gentiles, to furnish security that the convert was not simply accepting 'the *Kyrios* Jesus' as one more 'Saviour' among his 'gods many and lords many'. The baptismal creed was elaborated as a series of three questions dealing respectively with the three Persons of the Holy Trinity, and clear traces of it in this short form are to be found in the first half of the second century. The prevalence of gnosticism with its denials of the goodness of creation and the reality of our Lord's Manhood brought further elaboration in the later second century—the affirmations that 'God the Father' is 'Maker of heaven and earth' (and therefore that creation is essentially good as the act of a good God); that Jesus Christ is not only 'His only Son' and 'our Lord', but was truly conceived and born of a human mother, the Virgin Mary, and truly 'suffered' at a particular point in history 'under (*i.e.* in the governor-ship of) Pontius Pilate' and 'died' as all men die, and was 'buried' as a dead body (and was not spirited away into heaven from the Cross or before the crucifixion, as the gnostics taught); and further that 'the Holy Spirit' is 'in the Holy Church' (alone, not in self-constituted gnostic cliques). We find it in this form in Hippolytus' account of baptism,[2] as a threefold question and answer, in a text which is the obvious parent of our 'Apostles' Creed'.

The Council of Nicaea in A.D. 325 carried the use of the creed a stage further. It was no longer to be only a test of belief for those entering the church from outside. Since misbelief had shewn itself to be prevalent in the East not only among those who had been baptised but amongst bishops and clergy, the creed was to be made a test for those already within the church, by solemn affirmation of which they might prove that they believed what the church had always believed and not some new private invention

---

[1] Acts ii. 38; viii. 37; etc.   [2] *Ap. Trad.*, xxi. 12 *sqq.*

of their own. And since the old formulae, however well they might serve to distinguish a pagan or a jew from a christian, were too imprecise to distinguish an Arian from an orthodox christian, the Council drew up a new creed, that which in an elaborated form we know as the 'Nicene Creed'. The basis appears to have been the old baptismal creed of Jerusalem, but the council added to the second section dealing with our Lord Jesus Christ a carefully worded formula—'God of God, Light of Light, very God of very God begotten not made, of the being of the Father, of one substance with the Father', which no Arian could conscientiously recite. In acting thus the Council was acting in precisely the same way as the church of the second century in adding the anti-gnostic clauses, and indeed as the apostles had acted in requiring the original affirmation that 'Jesus is Messiah', which no unconverted member of the old Israel would make.

The precise stages by which the Nicene Creed as drawn up by the Council became our present 'oecumenical' or 'Niceno-Constantinopolitan' Creed are obscure. What is certain is that the Council did not draw it up with any intention of inserting it into the liturgy in any connection, and that it did not replace the older local creeds at baptisms, even in the East, for a considerable time. In the West the old Roman creed which we call the Apostles' has everywhere persisted to this day as the test of a catechumen's faith at baptism. The Nicene Creed was a theological statement of the church's faith for christians, not a test for converts from paganism.

In the monophysite troubles of the fifth century which followed upon the Council of Chalcedon (A.D. 451) it became the policy of the monophysite or federalist party to cry up the Council of Nicaea in order to slight 'the emperor's Council' of Chalcedon, which they rejected. With this end in view the monophysite patriarch of Antioch, Peter 'the Fuller' in A.D. 473 instituted the custom of publicly reciting the Nicene Creed at every offering of the liturgy, as an ostentatious act of deference towards the venerable Council of Nicaea, whose teachings he declared that the Chalcedonians had abandoned. In A.D. 511, the patriarch Macedonius II of Constantinople—a pious but not very wise eunuch—was banished and deposed by the monophysite emperor Anastasius, after a series of diplomatic manoeuvres which has few equals for unsavouriness even in the annals of Levantine christianity. Macedonius' intruded successor, Timothy—a man who appears to have had as little real concern for Nicene theology as for the Ten Commandments—at once introduced the monophysite practice of reciting the Nicene Creed into the liturgy of Constantinople, in order to secure the political support of the monophysite emperor and the federalist party generally. When by the vicissitudes of political fortune the orthodox once more secured control of the see of Constantinople, they dared not incur the odium of seeming to attack the memory of Nicaea by discontinuing this use of the creed; and so this originally heretical practice became a permanent feature of the Byzantine liturgy.

The West held aloof for a while, but the third Council of Toledo (can. 2) in A.D. 589 directed that 'For the fortifying of our people's recent conversion' from Arianism the creed should be recited 'after the fashion of the Eastern fathers' by all in a loud voice. But this Spanish Council placed this recitation after the fraction[1] 'that first the people may confess the belief they hold, and then with their hearts purified by faith' proceed to their communion. Its adoption among the Goths in Spain thus put it to its original purpose as a test for Arians, but in a new way, by making its recitation a preliminary to communion. In this unusual position it remains in the Mozarabic rite. Spanish catholicism was always apt to make use of its belief as a weapon, witness the 'damnatory clauses' of another Spanish document, the so-called 'Athanasian Creed'. It was in Spain also that the *Filioque* clause was first added to the Nicene Creed as an anti-Arian declaration, which subsequently caused so much unnecessary trouble between the West and the East.

In Gaul the emperor Charlemagne seems to have been the first to introduce the singing of the creed, in the liturgy of his palace chapel at Aix in A.D. 798. Some other churches of his dominions did not adopt it until almost a century later, but it spread generally in Frankish churches fairly quickly. Some Frankish monks at Jerusalem got into trouble for singing it with the *Filioque* as early as A.D. 806, and defended themselves with the plea that they had heard it 'sung thus in the West in the emperor's chapel.'[2]

Charlemagne thus used the Spanish text of the creed, but he did not place it at the Spanish position after the fraction, but where we now recite it, immediately after the gospel. There seems to be no doubt that this was a usage which had been growing up in the Italian churches outside Rome. It stood in this position in the rite of Benevento in the eighth century,[3] and there is some evidence that the same custom had been introduced at Aquileia in N. Italy by its bishop Paulinus (A.D. 786–802).[4] Rome, perhaps from mere conservatism, or perhaps misliking the heretical origin of the custom, long held out against the innovation. The recitation of the creed at the eucharist was first adopted by Pope Benedict VIII in the year A.D. 1014, under strong pressure from the Emperor Henry II, who was shocked when visiting Rome to find that it had no place in the Roman rite as it had in that of his own chapel.[5] Even then Rome adopted it somewhat

[1] The order in Spain was fraction, creed, *praefatio* and Lord's prayer. The *praefatio* and Lord's prayer (without the creed) followed the fraction in Gaul also, instead of preceding it as at Rome and in the East.
[2] Diplomatic complications ensued, involving Pope Leo III, who still did not use the Spanish *Filioque* at all, and wished that the emperor should not do so either.
[3] Dom R. J. Hesbert, *L'Antiphonale Missarum de l'ancien rit Bénéventain* in *Ephemerides Liturgicae*, lii. (*N.S.* 12), 1938, p. 36.
[4] Dom B. Capelle, *L'Origine antiadoptianiste de notre texte du Symbole* in *Recherches de théologie ancienne et médiévale*, I (1929), pp. 19–20.
[5] Berno of Reichenau, de *Off. Missae*, ii. (M.P.L., cxlii. 1060). The attempts to show that the creed was recited in the Roman rite before this all break down upon examination.

half-heartedly. It never became there, as in the East, an invariable element of the rite, but was reserved for Sundays and the greater feasts, as an appropriate expansion offering opportunities for singing. In later times there has been added the recitation of the creed at the eucharist on the minor feasts of those saints who are venerated as 'Doctors of the Church', who by their writings have expounded and defended the faith which the creed sets out. Once more we can trace the repugnance to the Roman liturgical instinct of all additions to the rite which play no clear logical part in the performance of the eucharistic action, and so may confuse the bare simplicity of its outline, even while adorning it.

### The Prayer 'of the Day'

This prayer is peculiar to the Western rites. It seems to have stood at the same point in all of them in the fifth century, *viz.* after the dismissals which closed the synaxis and before the kiss of peace which formed the ancient opening of the eucharist. It thus formed a new opening prayer to the eucharist proper. It varied with the day, and its introduction is probably one of the earliest examples of that special influence of the calendar on the prayers of the eucharistic rite which is a peculiar feature of the Western liturgies as a group. The simplest thing is to give some examples of this prayer in the various rites, beginning with that in which it is most fully developed and has most completely maintained its function, the Spanish Mozarabic rite.

In the Spanish books this prayer is always constructed in two parts, the one addressed to the congregation, the other directly addressed to God, known respectively as the *missa* and *alia*—'the mass' and 'the other' (prayer). Here is the ninth century Mozarabic prayer 'of the day' for Tuesday in Holy Week:

*Missa:* 'Offering the living sacrifice to our most loving God and Redeemer, we are bound, dearly beloved brethren, both to entreat Him by our prayers and do penance by our tears: for His holy Pascha draws near and the celebration of His passion is at hand, when by the penalty of the torment laid upon Him He burst the gates of hell. Let us serve Him by fasting and worship Him by contrition of heart, seeking of Him that He will through abstinence cleanse our flesh burdened with sins and rouse our dull mind to love Him by the approaching celebration of His death.

*Alia:* 'O Christ our Saviour, God, at the approach of Whose passion we rejoice, and by the yearly return of the celebration of Whose resurrection we are raised up: do Thou cleanse our flesh brought low with fasting from the weight of our sins. Do Thou sanctify the soul that has earnestly desired Thee: grant light unto the eyes: give cleanness to body and soul: that worthily adorned (*vestiti*) with all virtues we may be found meet to behold the glory of Thy passion.'[1]

[1] *Lib. Moz. Sacr., ed. cit., coll.* 228 *sq.*

Though the Mozarabic terms are *missa* and *alia*, this is an example of the old Western *praefatio* and *oratio* structure of which we have already spoken, the two parts forming a single prayer. After the *praefatio* there was originally a pause for silent prayer, followed by the celebrant's *oratio*. We have had an example of the same structure in the Roman intercessory prayers, with the celebrant's bidding 'Let us pray, beloved brethren, for ...' (followed by the deacon's command to kneel at the great intercessions, and perhaps on other occasions in penitential seasons) and then after the people's silent prayer, the collect.[1] Another survival of the same thing in the Roman rite is the celebrant's address before the Lord's prayer after the canon, 'Let us pray: Instructed by saving precepts and taught by divine example we make bold to say: Our Father ...'. In this case the Lord's prayer itself takes the place of the pause for silent prayer, and the celebrant concludes with a collect which is now said inaudibly in the Roman rite (except on Good Friday at the communion of the Pre-sanctified) but is still always recited aloud at Milan. Other Roman survivals of the full *praefatio* are to be found before the collects in ordination masses. Indeed, it has not entirely disappeared before any Roman collect, for the celebrant always 'prefaces' his 'prayer' (*oratio*), addressed to God, with *Oremus*, 'Let us pray', addressed to the people. The Eastern rites have no such address before their prayers. It is very typical of the different genius of the two Western liturgical types, Italian and Franco-Spanish, that starting from the same sort of formula of a single sentence or so, the one should tend to cut it down always to the same single word, and the other should expand it to a paragraph or more (some Mozarabic *praefationes* are fifty or sixty lines long) and vary it on every occasion that it is used.

There are sufficient indications that throughout the West *all* the prayers of the liturgy except the eucharistic prayer were at one time constructed in this way, with an address to the people followed by the prayer proper. But by the time our oldest extant liturgical MSS. were written the system was in full decay, the address being often reduced to a few words, or more usually omitted altogether. The cumbersomeness, and also the somewhat offensive clericalism, of prefixing an exhortation to the people by the priest every time prayer was to be offered was too much for the tradition. And even Spanish fecundity of liturgical expression boggled at the task of finding a sufficient number of different 'prefaces' for all the variable prayers of this most mutable rite. The *missa* and *alia*, however, in the Mozarabic rite retained the full form and even expanded it considerably,[2] for a particular reason. There was no collect or other prayer in the Mozarabic rite before the lections until the tenth century or so. Thus the *missa* and *alia* together formed the *first* prayer of the day, and had the function of 'striking the keynote' as it were of the special liturgical character of the

---

[1] *Cf. p. 42.*

[2] The example above was chosen chiefly as being one of the shortest in the year.

mass. When the variable 'collect' before the lections was introduced into the Spanish rite, it more or less duplicated this function; but by then the *missa* and *alia* were too strongly entrenched in Mozarabic tradition to be attenuated. At Rome the 'prayer of the day' disappeared, but it was the 'collect' not the 'prayer of the day' which tended to be eliminated in Spain, being altogether omitted on all fast days. Mozarabic masses were cited by the first words of this prayer (whence the name *missa*?) just as Roman masses were and are cited by the first words of the introit, as a convenient way of referring to the mass of different occasions and days (*e.g. Requiem, Laetare, Quasimodo*, etc.).

In Gaul we find the same arrangement of *praefatio* and *oratio* at the same point of the rite. But here the Roman 'collect' before the lections was introduced much earlier than in Spain (sixth–seventh century?) and in the later Gallican books is already tending to oust the *praefatio* and *oratio* from their original function of emphasising the particular point of the liturgy of the day. Originally the Gallican 'collect' before the lections appears to have had the character of a mere preparatory prayer, leaving the reference to the saint or the day to the prayer 'of the day' after the gospel. The following, from the mass of S. Germanus of Autun in the oldest Gallican collection extant, the *Masses of Mone*, will make the difference plain:[1]

*Collect (before the lections)*: 'O pitiful and pitying Lord, Who if Thou didst repay us according to our deserts, wouldst find nothing worthy of Thy forgiveness; multiply upon us Thy mercy that where sin hath abounded, the grace of forgiveness may yet more abound. Through . . .

*Praefatio (after the gospel)*:[2] 'With one accord, my dear brethren,[3] let us entreat the Lord that this our festival begun by the merits of our blessed father the bishop Germanus may by his intercession bring peace to his people, increase their faith, give purity of heart, gird their loins and open unto them the portal of salvation. Through . . .

*Oratio ante nomina*. 'Hear us, O Lord holy, Father Almighty, everlasting God, and by the merits and prayers of Thy holy pontiff Bishop Germanus, keep this Thy people in Thy pity, preserve them by Thy favour, and save them by Thy love. Through . . .'.

At Milan the prayer 'of the day' is known as the 'prayer over the corporal' (*oratio super sindonem*) i.e., the first prayer said after the cloth has

---

[1] These prayers appear as the second of Mass x. and the first and second of Mass xi. in the editions of Mone (*p.* 37) and Neale and Forbes (*pp.* 28 *sq.*). But Dom Wilmart's article in the *Révue Bénédictine* (1911), *p.* 377, based on a fresh examination of the MS., rearranges its leaves, so that these form items 2 and 3 of Mass vii. (item 1 being an *apologia* or private prayer for the celebrant). There is need of an entirely new edition of this, the key-document for the history of the Gallican rites.

[2] Mis-headed in MS. as *Collectio*.

[3] *Fratres carissimi*, the normal Gallican substitute for the Roman *fratres dilectissimi*. Anyone who has heard a modern French *curé's* frequent apostrophes to *mes chers frères* will recognise the survival.

been spread by the deacon upon the altar, which as we have seen[1] was the first preparation made for the celebration of the eucharist proper. It is preceded by 'The Lord be with you', 'And with thy spirit', and 'Let us pray' —precisely like the collect before the lections, from which in the Milanese rite it is indistinguishable in function by its contents. Indeed a few prayers which are employed in one Milanese MS. as collects proper are exchanged by others with the corresponding *super sindonem* prayers, without the mistake being detectable from the contents of the prayers.

In the Roman rite there is no longer a prayer 'of the day'. But before the offertory the celebrant still turns to the people for 'The Lord be with you', 'And with thy spirit', and turns back saying 'Let us pray'—but no prayer follows. Something has dropped out of the rite, and the close analogy of Milan suggests that it is a *super sindonem* prayer.[2] Nor perhaps are we altogether without information as to the actual 'prayers of the day' used on some of the days of the liturgical year at Rome in the fifth–sixth century. Liturgists have long been puzzled to account for the fact that while the masses of the Roman *Gregorian Sacramentary* have only a single collect before the lections, the pre-Gregorian *Gelasian Sacramentary* usually gives two. A certain number of these supplementary Gelasian collects reappear in the Milanese rite as *orationes super sindonem*. I suggest that when the prayer 'of the day' was abolished at Rome (was it by S. Gregory?) some Italian church south of Rome did not at once follow suit, and retained the *super sindonem* prayers. Our unique copy of the *Gelasian Sacramentary*, though it reproduces the substance of a pre-Gregorian Italian book, was made in France *c.* A.D. 700. It was thus written a century or more after the Gregorian reform (*c.* A.D. 595) and with full knowledge of the changes introduced by S. Gregory, to which in many important details it has been accommodated (*e.g.* it incorporates all the changes he had made in the text of the canon). But it descends, so far as its 'propers' are concerned, not from a sacramentary used in the city of Rome itself, but from an Italian book from the country south of Rome (? Capua), as is proved by its calendar. I suggest that this South Italian book retained the *super sindonem* prayers, which the scribe of our *Gelasianum* MS. has preserved, merely omitting their headings to bring the copy he was making into line with the current Roman and Frankish use.

We can, I think, understand the disuse of the prayer 'of the day' in the Roman rite. Once the variable 'collect' before the lections had made good its footing in the rite, it anticipated the function of the prayer 'of the day' after the lections. The first prayer thus 'struck the key-note' of the day at a

---

[1] *Cf. p.* 104.

[2] Duchesne (*Origins, ed. cit., p.* 172), suggests that this abortive 'Let us pray' is a trace of the old Roman intercessory prayers of the faithful. The difficulty is that these prayers, as they have survived on Good Friday, do *not* begin with 'The Lord be with you', but in the still older fashion with *Oremus, dilectissimi fratres*—a *praefatio*.

more appropriate point in the rite than did the second, once the lections of the synaxis had come to be thoroughly fused with the eucharist proper as parts of a single whole. And so, finding itself with what were virtually two 'collects', one before and one after the lections, both fulfilling the same function, the Roman church dropped the 'prayer of the day' at some time in the sixth century in favour of the 'collect' before the lections; though the latter was a custom imported from Egypt in the course of the fifth century, while the prayer 'of the day' was an element in the Roman rite which it shared with the other Western churches.

We have insufficient evidence about the African rite to be sure whether it contained a prayer 'of the day', though there are texts which might reasonably be conjectured to refer to it.[1]

The interest of this prayer 'of the day' is twofold. First, it is a feature which is common to all the Western rites and missing from all the Eastern ones. It thus gives an indication that the Western rites under their later divergence originally form a real group, going back to a common type. Secondly, from its character and position its introduction must go back to the period before the synaxis and eucharist were properly fused, but after the formation of the liturgical year—say round about A.D. 420–30. Only at that time could it have been felt necessary to insert a prayer specially intended to bring the fixed prayers of the eucharist proper into direct relation to the lections that had just been read, and to the day in the liturgical calendar. Its institution is thus probably the earliest effect of the calendar on the prayers of the eucharist, which became so marked a feature of all Western rites in the fifth century and after.

### Offertory Chants

We have seen that the offertory procession at Mopsuestia in Theodore's time advanced from the sacristy to the altar in dead silence, a point on which Theodore lays special emphasis;[2] and there is no mention of music or singing at this point of the rite in Narsai.[3] It is interesting to find that the Western oblation by the people before the altar appears also to have been originally performed in silence. The interest of the pre-Nicene church both East and West is concentrated on the *action* of offering. No need was felt to 'cover' this, as it were, with music. The first we hear of an offertory chant is from S. Augustine in Africa, who notes in his *Retractations* the introduction in his own days at Carthage of 'the custom of reciting (*dicerentur*) at the altar hymns taken from the book of psalms both before the oblation and while that which had been offered was being distributed to the people', and how he himself had been oblig.d to write a pamphlet in defence of the innovation.[4]

---

[1] *Cf. p.* 498, *n.* 1.    [2] *Cf.* p. 283.    [3] *Hom.*, xvii., *ed. cit., pp.* 3–4.
[4] S. Augustine, *Retractations*, II, 11 and 17.

So far as can be made out from the obscure and scanty evidence the original form of this psalmody was what the ancients called 'responsorial', *i.e.*, a solo singer sang the verses of a psalm to an elaborate setting, the people and choir joining in with a chorus or refrain between each verse—the 'antiphon'. At Rome, when the offertory and communion psalms were adopted, a plain psalm chant sung by the people seems to have been adopted for the verses, the 'antiphonal' melody being more elaborated and left to the choir. When the people's oblation gradually fell into disuse on normal occasions (as lay communions grew more infrequent) less music was required to 'cover' the offertory ceremony; and so the psalm verses were cut down until by degrees they vanished altogether (except at requiems), leaving only the elaborate melody of the antiphon to be rendered once by the choir as a sort of 'anthem' at the offertory. The same thing happened with the communion psalm. But two or three psalm 'verses' are still found on occasion attached to the antiphon in Roman choir books of the eleventh century. We do not know when the Roman church adopted the African custom of singing psalms at the offertory and communion, in addition to the pre-Nicene chants between the lections and its own early fifth century innovation of a psalm-chant during the processional entry. But a careful study of the texts of the offertories and communions in the Gregorian antiphonary suggests that they are a later development than the introit psalms. Not only are there few (if any) survivals of the pre-Vulgate text of the scriptures in these chants, of a kind which are not infrequent in the graduals and tracts and found occasionally in the introits; but they are usually chosen without close connection with the introit (which often has a connection of thought with the gradual). On the other hand, offertory and communion often seem to have a connection of thought between themselves. Perhaps a simultaneous adoption at Rome later in the fifth century than the introit would satisfy all the known facts.[1]

The Western rites thus equipped themselves with offertory chants independently of and before those of the East. There does in fact seem to have been much more general interest taken in church music in the West than in the East from the fourth century onwards. There was singing in the Eastern liturgies, at all events in the synaxis and (after its adoption) at the sanctus of the eucharist. The Eastern rites would have been untrue to the primordial origins of the eucharist in the *chabûrah* supper with its psalm-singing if they had excluded singing altogether. But if one looks at an Eastern exposition of the liturgy earlier than the seventh or eighth century, whether it be Cyril of Jerusalem or Theodore or Narsai, one finds that when music is mentioned it is passed over as something incidental, which excites no interest. In the West there is a series of writers beginning with Augustine who discuss with evident appreciation the part of church music

[1] There are no *offertorium* and *communio* chants in the very archaic mass for the Easter vigil on Holy Saturday

in worship, its legitimacy, its appropriateness and emotional effects, in a way which so far as I know is unparalleled in the East at this date. And whereas when the Eastern writers wish to dilate on the impressiveness of the eucharistic rite their emphasis is regularly on what strikes the eye—on the ceremonial and the vestments[1]—comparable Western writings like S. Isidore *de Officiis* and pseudo-Germanus lay their emphasis rather on the splendour of what is *heard*—the church music; and they evidently ascribe the same sort of emotional effect to this as is made on the Easterns by the ceremonial.

There is here not much more than a difference of psychology, so far as the early centuries are concerned. The Easterns developed a church music of a very high order. The researches of Herr Egon Wellescz and Professor Tillyard are teaching us that Byzantine church music of the golden age (much of which has a Syrian origin) was equal to the best that the West could produce. And the Westerns developed a ceremonial, stately enough in its own way though it never attained to anything like the dramatic quality found in the Eastern rites; and in Gaul (and perhaps during the middle ages generally) Western ceremonialists were apt to mistake mere fussiness and elaboration for dignity. But that the popular emotional interest in the East and West varied between ceremonial and music in the way described seems clear. This had some effect on the later liturgical history of the two halves of christendom. It was the special perfection and completeness of the Roman chant which as much as anything else spread the Roman rite in the West from the eighth century onwards, for the chant fitted the rite and it was difficult to adopt one without the other. But it is the spread of Byzantine ceremonies (*e.g.* the 'prothesis' or ceremonial preparation of the elements before the synaxis, and the 'great entrance') which has so largely Byzantinised the rites even of the dissidents in the East.

The Western appreciation of and interest in the music of worship has survived even the triumph of the puritan ideal among the churches of the Reformation, except among the most austerely consistent of the sects. This is true not only *e.g.* of the Anglican 'cathedral tradition', but among Prussian Calvinists whose grim worship still admits their lovely *chorales*. The point is that oriental puritans admit no such illogicality. Islam has neither instrumental nor choral music in its corporate worship. As a mohammedan *mallaum* once shrewdly remarked to me of a Wesleyan mission—'They will have beautiful sounds but not beautiful sights or odours like you in their worship. Yet the sounds are more distracting from true prayer than the sights or odours would be, which is why we true believers

---

[1] *E.g.* Narsai: 'The priests now come in procession into the midst of the sanctuary and stand there in great splendour and in beauteous adornment' (*p.* 4). 'The sacrament goes forth on the paten and in the cup (for the communion) with splendour and glory, with an escort of priests and a great procession of deacons' (*ibid., p.* 27).

*admit only words'*. That is the puritan theory of worship in a nutshell—to 'admit only words'. The Western interest in 'church song' which begins in the fourth century with Ambrose and Augustine has certainly shewn itself very strong to overcome this instinct of puritanism in any department of worship. It is curious that it has nowhere (I think) been strong enough to retain among protestants the old *recitative* or intonation of lections and prayers to a very simple chant as in the synagogue and the primitive christian church—the one and only sphere in which Islamic custom has preserved music in its liturgy.[1]

### Offertory Prayers

We have seen that none of the pre-Nicene rites contain any offertory prayer at all. The interest is concentrated upon the action, and the setting of the bread and wine upon the altar in and by itself constitutes the offering of them to God. The addition of an explicit commendation of them to God is an innovation of what I have called the period of the 'second *stratum*', the fifth–eighth centuries. It is an indication that the period when the eucharist is recognised as primarily an action, in which every member of the church has an active part, is passing into the later idea of the eucharist as primarily something 'said' by the clergy on behalf of the church, though it was centuries before this idea took complete control of the presentation of the liturgy.

There is still no offertory prayer in Sarapion; nor is there any such prayer in *Ap. Const.*, viii, thirty or forty years later in Syria. There is no means of telling how old the offertory prayer found in the ninth century text of the liturgy of *S. Basil* may be, but it is likely to be as ancient as any used in the East and is in itself so fine a prayer as to be worth citing as a representative of the later Eastern prayers:

'O Lord our God Who didst make us and bring us into this life, and show us the ways unto salvation, and grant us the grace of the revelation of heavenly mysteries: Thou art He Who did set us in this ministry in the power of Thy Holy Spirit. Be graciously pleased, O Lord, that we should be ministers (*diakonous*) of Thy New Covenant, officiants (liturgisers, *leitourgous*) of Thy holy mysteries. Receive us as we draw near unto Thy holy altar in the multitude of Thy mercy that we may be made worthy to offer unto Thee this reasonable and unbloody sacrifice on behalf of our own sins and the ignorance of the people. Receive it upon Thy holy and heavenly and spiritual altar for a savour of sweetness, and send down in return upon

---

[1] I hope it will not seem shocking to compare moslem and christian methods of worship. But as I have said (*p.* 312), the puritan and ceremonious conceptions of worship are a cross-division which cuts right athwart creeds. And from the standpoint of comparative religion it is more scientific to treat Islam as an erratic deformation of the judaeo-christian development than as an independent faith. It did not arise independently of the latter.

us the grace of Thy Holy Spirit. Look upon us, O God, and behold this our worship, and accept it as Thou didst accept the gifts of Abel, the sacrifices of Noah, the whole-burnt-offerings of Abraham, the priestly offerings of Moses and Aaron, the peace-offerings of Samuel; as Thou didst accept from Thy holy apostles this true worship, so accept also from the hands of us sinners these gifts in Thy goodness, O Lord, that being found worthy to liturgise blamelessly at Thy holy altar we may receive the reward of faithful and wise stewards in the day of Thy righteous repayment, through the mercies of Thy only-begotten Son with Whom Thou art blessed with Thine all-holy and good and life-giving Spirit, now and for ever and for ages of ages. Amen.'[1]

The earliest suggestion of such a prayer in christian literature is, as we have said, in the letter of Pope Innocent I to Decentius (c. A.D. 415), but we have no evidence when the Roman prayers first assumed their present form,[2] of which the following are specimens taken almost at random:

For the Epiphany: 'We beseech Thee, O Lord, graciously to behold the gifts of Thy church: wherein is set forth no longer gold and frankincense and myrrh, but what by those gifts is declared and sacrificed and received, even Jesus Christ Thy Son our Lord . . .' For the second Sunday after Epiphany: 'Sanctify, O Lord, our offered gifts: and cleanse us from the stains of our sins; Through . . .' For Low Sunday: 'Receive, we pray, O Lord, the gifts of Thy jubilant church, and since Thou hast given her reason for such mighty joy, grant her also the fruit of endless bliss. Through . . .' For the fifth Sunday after Pentecost (fourth after Trinity): 'Be gracious, O Lord, unto our supplications and mercifully receive these oblations of Thy servants and handmaids; that what each has offered to the honour of Thy Name, may avail for the salvation of all; Through . . .'

These set forth with simplicity the spirit of the people's oblation, brought into contact now with the offerings of the wise kings, now with the thrill of the Easter joy, and in the 'green' seasons with the endless desire of the soul for purity and salvation.

The offertory prayers of the other Western rites are rather less directly expressed. Here for instance is the Mozarabic *post nomina* or offertory prayer for Easter Day: 'Having listened to the names of those who offer, we pray Thee, Lord of love, to deign to be present to us at our prayer, to be found when Thou art sought, to open at our knocking. Write the names of the offerers in the heavenly book, shew forth Thy promise in the holy, Thy mercy in the lost. And because the prayer of our infirmity is weak, and we know not what to ask, we call to the aid of our own prayers the patriarchs taken into the heavenly company, the prophets filled with the divine

---

[1] Brightman, L. E. W., *pp.* 319 *sq.*
[2] I cannot help doubting whether Innocent I is referring to a *separate* 'offertory prayer'. I suggest that he has in mind the prayer which now forms the first paragraph of the Roman canon (*cf. pp.* 500 *sqq.*).

Spirit, the martyrs crowned with the flowers of their confession, the apostles chosen for the office of preaching. Through whom we pray to Thee, our Lord, that all who are terrified by fear, afflicted by want, vexed by trials, laid low by sickness, bound captive by sufferings, may be released by the presence of Thy resurrection. Be graciously mindful also of the spirits of them that sleep (*pausantium*), that the outstretched pardon of their offences may allow them to attain to the bosom of the patriarchs, by the help of Thy mercy Who livest . . .'[1]

The custom of reading out 'the Names' between the oblation and the offertory prayer in the Spanish church, and also the adoption of the oriental fashion of the diptychs have done a good deal to confuse the tenor of most of the Spanish offertory prayers. But even making allowance for this, there is usually a lack of simplicity about them and a striving after effect which results in turgid language; here, for instance, the allusion to Easter as 'the presence of Thy resurrection' releasing sufferers is clumsily made.[2] One reason at least why the Roman rite was so largely adopted in the West without compulsion and by the gradual acceptance of so many local churches in the seventh–tenth centuries[3] lies precisely in this, that on the whole it was a simpler and more expressive rite. The old local rites were redolent of the soil on which they arose, and rightly dear to those who used them from ancestral tradition. But rite for rite and prayer for prayer the Roman was apt to be both more practical and better thought out; and those who compared them carefully could hardly fail to notice it. Hence the growing voluntary adoption of Roman prayers and pieces and chants, and ultimately of the Roman Shape of the Liturgy as a whole, which is so marked a feature of liturgical history in the territories of the Gallican and Mozarabic rites during the seventh and eighth centuries, when the Popes were in no position to bring pressure to bear on anyone to adopt their rite.

To complete our survey: the Milanese offertory prayers, though by no means identical with the Roman series, are cast in the same mould, and need not be illustrated. The Gallican ones are usually similar to the Mozarabic. The following from the *Missale Gothicum* for Easter Day will serve for comparison: 'Receive, we beseech Thee, O Lord, the Victim (*hostia*) of propitiation and praise and be pleased to accept these oblations of Thy servants and handmaids which we offer at the Resurrection of our Lord Jesus Christ according to the flesh. And grant also by the intercessions of Thy saints unto our dear ones who sleep in Christ refreshment in

---

[1] *Lib. Moz. Sacr.*, ed. Férotin, coll. 255 sq.

[2] For purposes of comparison here is the Roman offertory prayer for Easter: 'Receive we pray Thee, O Lord, the prayers of Thy people together with the offering of their hosts, that by Thy operation they may suffice us for the receiving of that heavenly remedy which had its beginning in the Easter mysteries:' . . . where the *paschalia mysteria* is a double allusion to the first Easter Day and the paschal baptism and first communion of each communicant.

[3] This was not universally the process by which it was adopted (*cf. pp.* 561 *sqq.*) but it does account for a great deal of its progress.

the land of the living: Through . . .' Here again the reading of 'the Names' of the departed and the saints immediately before has produced the incongruous addition of the last clause; though the undying French devotion to the memory of their dead, their *cari nostri*, which on the 2nd of November can still always bridge the great gulf between the French clerical and anticlerical, is something very near the heart of French religion in every age.[1]

### The 'Names' and the 'Diptychs'

The intercessory 'prayers of the faithful' at the synaxis, like the petitions of the later litany which replaced them in the East, were general prayers— *i.e.*, they spoke of classes of people, catechumens, penitents, travellers, pagans and so forth, without specifying individuals. The congregation were no doubt expected to particularise silently those in whom each was personally interested during the pause between the bidding and the collect. The only names publicly mentioned seem to have been those of the Roman emperor and the local bishop. But while this public intercession 'by categories' sufficed at the synaxis, the eucharist even in pre-Nicene times was felt to require something more personal, as the domestic gathering of the household of God.

It may be that the need for particularisation was first felt at that peculiarly personal occasion, the eucharist offered for a departed christian, when S. Paul's teaching that the eucharist is always an anticipation of the judgement of God[2] takes on a special poignancy. At all events, the earliest mention of the naming of an individual in the prayers of the eucharist proper, in the first epistle of S. Cyprian of Carthage, occurs in this connection. It deals with the awkward case of a bishop lately dead, who had deliberately violated a rule made by a recent African Council against the inconvenient practice of appointing clergymen as executors. Cyprian decides in accordance with the Council's ruling that 'there shall be no oblation on his behalf (at the offertory) nor shall the sacrifice be offered for his repose, for he does not deserve to be *named in the prayer* of bishops who has sought to distract the bishops and ministers from (the service of) the altar.'[3] Thus in Africa *c.* A.D. 240 it was already customary to name individual dead persons in the course of the *prex*, the eucharistic prayer, at all events at funerals and requiems. (Cyprian is not legislating for the deceased's own church, where the actual funeral would take place, but for Carthage and other churches where a eucharist would customarily have been 'offered for his repose'). It may be an accident, but Cyprian appears never to mention any 'naming' of living individuals at any point of the rite.[4] S. Augustine a

---

[1] There was an *oratio* at the African eucharist before the eucharistic prayer (*cf.* Augustine *Ep.* cxlix. (*al.* lix.) 16). But whether it was a 'prayer of the day' or an offertory prayer I am unable to say from the evidence

[2] 1 Cor. xi. 29, 32.                    [3] Cyprian, *Ep.* I ,2.

[4] *Ep.*, xvi. 2, might just possibly be pressed to mean this.

century and a half later has likewise no mention of the 'naming' of living individuals in the African rite, but his evidence as to the 'naming' of the dead is difficult to interpret.[1] What he does make clear is that by his time the Jerusalem practice of 'naming' certain martyrs in the course of the eucharistic prayer had been adopted in Africa.[2]

We have already noted[3] that in Sarapion's eucharistic prayer there is to be a pause for 'the reading out (*hypobole*) of the names' of the departed only. Likewise in Cyril's account of the Jerusalem rite particular dead persons are named in the intercessions which follow the consecration, because of 'the special assistance of their souls for whom prayer is made in the presence of the holy and most awful sacrifice'.[4] From the defence of the practice which Cyril thinks it right to make, one would suppose that this naming of individual souls in the eucharistic prayer was a fairly recent innovation at Jerusalem, and had been causing some discussion there. In Sarapion's rite likewise, the 'naming' of the dead appears to be a fairly recent interpolation, with no connection with what precedes and follows.

So much for the early evidence for the naming of the dead at the eucharist. Now as concerns the naming of the living. The earliest evidence of this comes from Spain. The Council of Elvira (*c.* A.D. 305) in its 29th canon forbids the names of those possessed by evil spirits 'to be recited at the altar with the oblation'.[5] Canon 28 prohibits an abuse which had grown up by which persons under excommunication—probably those who for social reasons had made some excessive compromise with pagan conventions— were allowed to offer their *prosphora* and have their names read out with the rest, provided they did not actually make their communion. All this would suggest that this 'naming' of the living in the Spanish rite was practically a roll-call of the faithful, and took place as each made their oblation or perhaps all together immediately afterwards. We can see now why the Spanish offertory prayers are called 'the prayer *ad nomina*' ('at the names') and why they take the form they do. In a small church where the members were well known to one another the omission of a name week by week would leave a stigma, and perhaps that is the origin and purpose of the custom. The 'Names' are those of the communicants (or 'offerers' as the ancient church thought of them) of that particular eucharist. Some of the later Mozarabic prayers are explicit that they are the names *offerentium et pausantium* 'of the (living) offerers and the departed'. It is possible that this was already so in pre-Nicene times, the relatives or representatives of

---

[1] E. Bishop, *Appendix to Narsai*, p. 112, comes to the conclusion that there was no 'naming' of the dead, but only a 'general commemoration' in Augustine's rite. I cannot help thinking he is somewhat arbitrary in his interpretation of Augustine *de Cura Gerenda pro Mortuis* 6, which seems to me to imply that there *was* a 'naming', as well as a general commemoration. *Cf.* also *Serm.*, clix. 1.
[2] *de Civ. Dei*, xxii. 10; *Serm.*, clix. i. *de Sancta Virginitate* 45, etc.
[3] *Cf. p.* 164.     [4] Cyril, *Cat.*, xxiii. 9 (*p.* 195).
[5] Can. 37 forbids them to be baptised, or if already christians, to receive holy communion except on their deathbeds.

the dead offering in 'the name of' those departed from that church in its peace and communion, a touching illustration of the vividness of belief in the communion of saints and the unity in Christ of all christians living and dead. But though the early Spanish evidence does not contradict such an idea, it does not explicitly support it. Early practice in Africa and Spain was evidently not the same. Cyprian's 'naming' of the *dead* is in the course of the eucharistic prayer. The Spanish 'naming' of the (living) *'offerers'* is before it begins.

Before turning our attention to the East it will be as well to take here the earliest Italian evidence on the subject, though it is only at the end of the fourth and early in the fifth century that any is available. S. Ambrose at Milan tells us that 'prayers are asked for kings, for the people and the others'[1] at an early point in the eucharistic prayer itself. We shall find that another N. Italian prayer of about the same date seems to have had the same arrangement. It is also the point which seems to be implied in Innocent I's description of the Roman rite c. A.D. 415: 'Your own wisdom will shew how superfluous it is to pronounce the name of a man whose oblation you have not yet offered to God (?by the offertory prayer). . . . So, one should first commend the offerings and afterwards name those who have made them. One should *name them during the divine mysteries and not in the part of the rite which precedes*, so that the mysteries themselves lead up to the prayers to be offered'. Whether the offerings are here 'commended' to God by a detached offertory prayer proper, or whether Innocent simply has in mind the first paragraph (*Te igitur*) of the present Roman canon (which also 'commends' the offerings) there can be no doubt that c. A.D. 400 the 'Naming' of the offerers at Rome comes in approximately the same place as at Milan, in the eucharistic prayer itself.

As now arranged the canon runs as follows: After the whispered offertory prayer by the celebrant (and the preface and sanctus, which in their present form are a later interpolation not contemplated by Innocent I),[2] the prayer opens abruptly:

'We therefore humbly pray Thee, most merciful Father, through Jesus Christ Thy Son our Lord and beseech Thee that Thou wouldest hold accepted and bless these gifts (*dona*), these 'liturgies' (*munera*)[3], these holy and unspotted sacrifices: which first we offer for Thy holy catholic church, that throughout all the world Thou wouldst be pleased to give her peace, safety, unity and Thy governance:

[1] S. Ambrose, *de Sacramentis*, iv. 4, c. A.D. 395.
[2] *Cf. p.* 539.
[3] *Dona* are 'free gifts', *munera* are payments which fall on a man by virtue of the office he holds, *i.e.* exactly 'liturgies' in the old sense. This sense persisted in the local Roman liturgical terminology down to at least the sixth century, *cf.* the examples collected by Dom O. Casel, *Oriens Christianus* (series III), vii. (1932), *pp.* 289 *sqq.* Note that in the Roman conception the people's oblation is still their *munus*, or 'liturgy' in the Pauline sense. The *people* are still in the old phrase the 'offerers', along with the priest.

'Together with Thy servant N. our Pope [and N. our bishop and all the orthodox and the worshippers ⟨who are⟩ of catholic and apostolic faith] remember Thy servants and handmaids N. and N. and all who stand around, whose faith is accepted of Thee and whose devotion known [for whom we offer unto Thee, or][1] who offer unto Thee this sacrifice of praise, for themselves and all who are theirs . . .'[2]

Just as the Mozarabic rite with its *ad nomina* offertory prayer still preserves the 'naming' of the offerers at the same point of the rite as in the days of the Council of Elvira *c.* A.D. 305, *viz.* at the offertory; so the Roman rite equally seems to preserve the position of the 'naming' customary in Italy *c.* A.D. 395, *viz.* soon *after* the offertory, in an early passage of the eucharistic prayer itself. Which of these represents the older tradition in the West is a point on which opinions will probably differ.[3]

We may note here two points: 1. That whereas in Sarapion and at Jerusalem and probably in Africa, the only names read out appear to be those of the dead; at Rome and in Spain, so far as the evidence goes, the only names anciently read out were those of the living. And in fact it has been demonstrated[4] that the commemoration of the dead which now appears as an invariable paragraph of the Roman canon, though it is genuinely ancient and of Roman composition, was originally only inserted in that prayer at funerals (and requiems generally), and formed no part of the Roman rite on other occasions. Its transformation from an occasional to an invariable part of the canon began in France in the eighth-ninth century, and was not accepted at Rome until the ninth-tenth, and in some Italian churches not

[1] This, like the other clause bracketed earlier in the paragraph, is a later Frankish interpolation into the authentic Roman text, *cf.* E. Bishop, *Liturgica Historica*, p. 95. In the Roman idea it is *the people themselves* who are the offerers; in the Gallican interpolation it is the priest who offers *for* them.

[2] For a special example of the 'Naming' at this point in the Roman canon see the *Gelasian Sacramentary*, *ed.* Wilson, *p.* 34 (the Lenten 'Scrutiny' masses). I am unable to be sure of the date and provenance of this particular example (whether Roman, Italian or French, and of the fifth or sixth century).

[3] My own guess is that the Mozarabic position is likely to be the original one. Innocent is objecting in his letter to Decentius to the practice in Italian country churches in 1. giving the Pax and 2. reading the 'Names', both before the 'offertory prayer'. They were therefore *not* copying 'Gallican' customs (whatever modern scholars may have supposed) since the distinctive Mozarabic-Gallican custom was, 1. Names, followed by 2. Pax. On the contrary, we know that since the time of Justin the Pax had been the first item in the Western rite. Rome in Innocent's day had transferred it to immediately before the communion, but these country churches kept it in the original position. It is likely that their other difference from the current Roman rite (in which they agree with the practice of Spain and Gaul) was also due to conservatism. I suggest that it is the *introduction* of an offertory prayer towards the end of the fourth century which brought about the rearrangement of this part of the Western rites. It was inserted *before* the old 'Naming' in some rites (*e.g.* Rome and Milan), *after* it in others (*e.g.* Spain and Gubbio). Perhaps it was likewise the introduction of the 'Prayer of the Day' about the same time which was responsible for the transference of the Pax (to different positions) in both the Italian and Spanish-Gallican rites.

[4] E. Bishop, *Liturgica Historica*, *pp.* 96 *sqq.*

till the eleventh century. 2. It is also plain that all this early evidence contemplates only the reading out of names of strictly local interest, whether they are those of living communicants or of deceased members of the local or neighbouring churches. The 'Names' are in fact the 'parochial intercessions'.

In all this, however, we have met nothing which quite corresponds to the Eastern 'Diptychs'. These were two conjoined tablets, the one containing the names of living persons to be prayed for, the other containing a list of saints commemorated and of the dead persons recommended officially to the prayers of the church.[1] It is first and foremost this *combination* of lists of the living and dead which distinguishes the 'diptychs' proper from the various customs of 'naming' which we have just been studying.

The diptychs come into sudden prominence at Constantinople c. A.D. 420 in the course of the disputes which took place there over the insertion or omission of the name of S. John Chrysostom, the 'deposed' bishop of that city who had died in exile in 407. From the official correspondence with other churches which arose about this[2] we learn that at that time at Constantinople the diptychs (1) comprised separate lists of names, of the living and dead; (2) that each list was arranged in 'ecclesiastical' precedence, bishops first, then other clergy and finally laity; (3) that the whole succession-list of past bishops of Constantinople was included in the diptych of the dead, while the list of dead emperors headed the departed laity. It is clear also that at Antioch and Alexandria there were then diptychs of some kind, or at least lists of the dead. From the fact that these two churches were urged (and in the one case agreed and in the other indignantly refused) to follow Chrysostom's own church of Constantinople in inserting his name among the dead, it is clear that some non-local names (besides departed emperors) must have been included in the case of the two southern churches; one would expect it to have been the same at Constantinople, though the evidence does not actually make this clear. But of the principle upon which such foreign names were selected—and some selection was necessary if the lists were not to grow intolerably long—we learn nothing.

From this time onwards, and especially down to c. A.D. 600, the diptychs are constantly in question in the East in connection with ecclesiastical politics, and accusations and counter-accusations of heresy. From the fifth century onwards the four great Eastern sees[3] were supposed each to name

[1] Two texts of the Jerusalem diptychs (eleventh and nineteenth centuries), and one of the Constantinopolitan diptychs (fifteenth century) will be found in Brightman, L. E. W., *pp.* 501-3 and 551 *sq.*

[2] *ap.* Nicephorus Callistus, *Eccl. Hist.*, xiv., 26 *sq.* The information it contains about the diptychs is anatomised by E. Bishop in the *Appendix* to Dom Connolly's *Hom. of Narsai, pp.* 102 *sqq.*, which is summarised above. Though I have carefully examined the texts for myself, there is—as so often—no gleaning behind that great scholar.

[3] Alexandria, Antioch, Constantinople and Jerusalem. When in communion with Rome they named the Pope also, but Rome never adopted diptychs, and so was unable to return the compliment.

the reigning patriarchs of the others in their diptych of the living. But in the interminable disputes and alliances and counter-alliances of patriarchates which went on under theological pretexts in this period (in all of which the question of the centralisation of the political control of the East at Byzantium was seldom far from anyone's mind), the solemn insertion or erasure of names and sees in the diptych of the living was little more than a public register of how the political position stood at the moment. The confusion was just as great in the diptych of the dead. As the political balance between Melchites ('King's Men', as the orthodox were called) and Monophysites (or federalists) swayed to and fro, royalists and heretics succeeded one another in the same bishopric, and solemnly inserted or re-inserted, or ejected with anathemas the names of their predecessors in the local diptychs. The name of Dioscorus, the monophysite patriarch of Alexandria condemned by 'the emperor's Council' (as both heretics and orthodox termed the Council of Chalcedon in the East) was removed from the Alexandrian diptychs by his orthodox successor Proterius, the nominee of the Byzantine government. When Proterius in turn was murdered by *his* monophysite successor, Timothy 'the Weasel', the name of Dioscorus was restored, and that of Proterius removed with execration at the very moment when Constantinople was loudly numbering him among the martyrs. Names were removed or reinserted wholesale in some churches, according as the dead bishops had or had not agreed with the living one. Bishop Peter of Apameia in Syria removed the names of all his predecessors for some fifty years back at one stroke. Nothing much less like an 'intercession list' than the diptychs in actual Eastern practice can be imagined.

Yet it seems certain that it was in this that they had originated. In the liturgy of *S. James* the diptychs have always stood at just that point of the rite at which Cyril of Jerusalem (A.D. 347) mentions the 'naming' (of the dead only)—in the intercessions after the consecration; and they stood at the same point in the Antiochene and Constantinopolitan rites *c.* A.D. 390–400.[1] But it is noteworthy that as at Jerusalem in Cyril's time, so at Antioch and Constantinople fifty years later, *only* the dead are spoken of as being actually 'named' individually; and those named are very clearly, from what both Cyril and Chrysostom say, the 'parochial' dead, those personally known and loved and mourned by members of the congregation, together with a list of the past bishops of the see. But it is entirely clear from the course of the disputes about the insertion of the name of Chrysostom *c.* A.D. 420 that the lists by then had assumed a somewhat different character. They were now *officially* compiled, and admittance to them implied something more than just being dead. It was a judgement of the orthodoxy and of

---

[1] E. Bishop, *Appendix* to *Narsai*, *pp.* 109–11 (*cf. Journal of Theol. Studies*, xii. (1911), *pp.* 319–28; and *ibid.*, *pp.* 400 *sqq.*) has shewn that Brightman, L. E. W., *pp.* 535–6, must be corrected on this point in the light of S. John Chrysostom, *Hom. xli. in* 1 *Cor.*; *Hom. xxi. in Act.*

the eminence of the departed. It would appear, therefore, that the diptychs, in the form they finally took in the East—*i.e.* a combination of lists of both living and dead persons—and for the purpose they came to serve in the Greek churches—*i.e.* an index of ecclesiastical politics—are a development of the church of Byzantium in the years between *c.* A.D. 405 and 420. When one considers the peculiar state of that particular church at that time, as it is described in the lively but disillusioning pages of the Byzantine layman Socrates, I for one am not entirely surprised.

Whether in the properly Greek churches amid all this clash of great names and high policy the ordinary parochial dead—the communicants or the presbyters and deacons who did the pastoral work that must have gone on—ever got remembered in the diptych of the dead by name, we have not sufficient evidence to decide. So far as the great churches are concerned it is very unlikely; in the countrysides it may have been different. Nor do I see anything to suggest that the names of the living *communicants* (as in the West) or subjects for parochial intercession like the names of the sick, were ever entered on the Greek diptych of the living. That was reserved for the emperor and his family, the patriarchs of the great sees and the local bishop. First and last, the Greek diptychs properly so called have always been what they already are when we first hear of them at Constantinople *c.* A.D. 420—instruments of strife in high places and not much more.[1]

The entry of the four oecumenical councils, inserted (rather oddly) into the diptych of the dead by the church of Constantinople in A.D. 518, removed the diptychs further than ever from the notion of an intercession list. But this too was a political move. The Byzantine (or 'centralising') party had just recovered control of this see from the Monophysites who rejected the Council of Chalcedon. It was at first proposed to insert in the diptych only a commemoration of the first two general councils, which everyone accepted. The Byzantines changed their minds and inserted the fourth (Chalcedon) and with it the third, not so much because it was orthodox (they had themselves originally proposed the commemoration of the first two councils only) as because they realised that this would affirm the renewed opposition of the church of Constantinople to the federal claims of Syria and Egypt, which rejected the fourth Council.

The case is rather different with the history of the diptychs in the Egyptian and East Syrian rites.

In Egypt in the liturgy of *S. Mark* there is in fact only one diptych in which individuals are named—that of the dead. It consists, as in Sarapion, simply of a list of names read out in the course of the eucharistic prayer, which cannot be set down in the liturgical MSS. because it is not an

---

[1] The riots, accompanied in some cases by murder, which took place in Greece about A.D. 1920 over the entry or extrusion of the names of King Constantine and the patriarch Meletios Metaxakis of Constantinople adequately maintained ancient practice.

'official' list at all, as in the Greek diptych. It varied from church to church and from month to month, the names entered being those of the 'parochial' dead.[1] But though the Alexandrian rite has thus retained exactly the form of the 'naming' of the dead found in Sarapion's rite c. A.D. 340, it has shifted its place, and appended it to the lengthy intercessions 'by categories' for the church and the world—*for the living*—which it places after the first paragraph of the eucharistic prayer. This is precisely the point at which the Roman and Italian evidence of the late fourth and fifth centuries places its (much less developed) intercession for the church followed by the 'naming' of the *living*. (This is one of several coincidences of structure between the Alexandrian and Roman rites c. A.D. 400 which deserve more attention than they have received in modern study.)

The coincidence may well have been even more striking in some Egyptian country churches than at Alexandria itself. The chance discovery of a seventh century Egyptian diptych from the region of Thebes in Upper Egypt[2] reveals that there, besides the patriarch of Alexandria and the local bishop, it was precisely the *living* communicants, the 'offerers', who were named, as in the West: 'And for the salvation of the most pure clergy standing around and the Christ-loving laity; and for the salvation and bodily health of the offerers so-and-so (*masc.*) and so-and-so (*fem.*) who have offered their oblations this day, and of all offerers' (*i.e.* of all who are regular communicants, but are not 'offering' at this particular celebration).

In the East Syrian rite what Brightman calls 'The Diptychs' are read out at the offertory[3]—as in the Mozarabic rite. There are two 'books', of the living and dead, not quite the same in character. That of the living is brief and general in its contents, a summary of categories of people, in which the only individuals mentioned by name are the Nestorian patriarch and the local Nestorian bishop. The 'book of the dead', on the other hand (with various alternative forms) takes up approximately eleven times as much space as its fellow in Brightman's print. It consists of long lists of proper names, which include not only the great saints of the Old and New Testament and the succession-list of the Nestorian patriarchs of Mesopotamia, but all sorts of local worthies like 'Rabban Sabha and the sons of Shemuni who are laid in this blessed village' and 'the illustrious among athletes and providers of churches and monasteries, generous in alms, guardians of orphans and widows, the Emir Matthew and the Emir Hassan and Emir Nijmaldin who departed in this village.' And these loving and intimate local details vary from one MS. to another in a way that the stereotyped form of the Greek diptychs has never varied. It is clear, I think, that while the East Syrian diptych of the dead represents a genuine

[1] Brightman, L. E. W., *pp.* 126 and 165.
[2] Publ. by W. E. Crum, *Proceedings of the Soc. for Biblical Archaeology*, xxx. (1908), *pp.* 255 *sqq.*
[3] Brightman, L. E. W., *pp.* 275 *sqq.*

2L                                                                          D.S.L.

survival of the 'naming' of the 'parochial' dead, known and mourned by the congregation, the diptych of the living on the contrary represents an imitation of the formal Greek practice, inserted in the period when it had come to be taken for granted that there ought to be two diptychs.

It is clear from Narsai[1] that in the later fifth century the East Syrian rite already contained both diptychs in much their present form. But the little prayer which according to him the people add after them runs thus: 'On behalf of all the *catholici* (Nestorian patriarchs), on behalf of all orders deceased from holy church; and for those who are deemed worthy of the reception of this oblation, on behalf of these and of Thy servants in every place, receive, Lord, this oblation.' In most rites the people's prayers have a way of being more archaic than the clerical formulae they accompany. This prayer would suggest that it originally followed a 'naming' of the dead (headed by a succession-list of the Nestorian patriarchs) which was *not preceded* by a diptych of the living; and that if any living persons were subsequently 'named', they were *the communicants*, as in the West.

It may be said, What then of the Western diptychs? What of those famous Roman diptychs, which as a number of modern scholars (beginning with Bunsen a century ago) have pointed out, resulted in the 'dislocation' of the Roman canon? What of the old Irish diptychs in the *Stowe Missal*, which once proved (somewhat inadequately) the 'non-Roman' character of the Celtic rites? What of the Mozarabic rite, which it has been said 'has retained the diptychs in the position they originally occupied in all the primitive rites'?[2] What of actual surviving ivory tablets which served this purpose, like that containing the list of the early bishops of Novara now at Bologna, or the Barberini diptych in the Louvre? In order to ascribe one of the institutions most venerated by generations of liturgists to a comparatively late initiative of the Byzantine church, are we not overlooking the multitudinous evidence that the West also, Rome included, once had diptychs?

I think we must distinguish carefully what we mean by 'diptychs'. If we mean simply lists of 'names' read out at the eucharist, whether of the communicants or (alternatively) of the dead, then the West had these customs before ever Constantine came to Constantinople. But if we mean that *combination* of lists of the eminent living and dead, officially drawn up and regulated from time to time by the higher ecclesiastical authorities, which is what 'the diptychs' were understood to mean by the church of Constantinople when it first instituted them, then the West never had any 'diptychs' properly so called at all. In the fifth and sixth centuries there was a tendency to copy *some* of the new Eastern fashions in this matter in many Western churches, including Rome. But it will be found upon examin-

---

[1] *Homilies, ed. cit., p.* 10.
[2] W. C. Bishop, *The Mozarabic and Ambrosian Rites (Alcuin Club Tracts,* xv., 1924, p. 33).

ation that it was Syrian rather than Byzantine customs which chiefly proved attractive.

The Roman 'diptychs' are a myth. The most prominent feature of the Byzantine diptych of the living was the commemoration by each great church of the reigning patriarchs of all the other patriarchal churches. The local Roman 'naming' of the living at the beginning of the canon never mentioned any prelate whatever except the local bishop, the Pope. In the occasional pothers about the insertion of the Pope's name in the Eastern diptychs, when communion was restored after a schism at various times from the fifth to the eighth centuries, there was never a suggestion by either side that Rome should return the compliment. Both parties knew that the Roman rite contained no opportunity of doing so, having retained the old purely local or parochial character of its 'naming' of the living.

As for the diptych of the dead, it did not exist at Rome. Edmund Bishop has shewn by the irrefutable evidence of the earliest extant MSS. of the Roman canon that the commemoration of the dead now found in the second half of that prayer has had a somewhat involved history.[1] It is ancient and of genuinely Roman composition, but at Rome itself down to the ninth century it formed no part of the Roman canon as recited in the public masses of Sundays and festivals. It was a peculiarity of funeral and requiem masses, like a 'proper' preface for a festival, only inserted on specifically funerary occasions. Its use as an invariable part of the canon on all occasions begins in Frankish Gaul in the seventh-eighth century. The particular recension of the text which was eventually adopted betrays the hand of those Irish monks who in so many matters are at the bottom of Western innovations in liturgy during the dark ages. The Roman church only began to adopt this French novelty of commemorating the dead in *all* masses during the ninth century, and Italian MSS. of the Roman rite which did not allow for the new fashion were still being copied in the eleventh century. The absence of any 'naming' of the *dead* whatever in the authentic Roman rite on ordinary occasions[2] is one contrast with the Eastern diptychs, which as we have noted owe their origin to the 'naming' of the dead in the fourth century Jerusalem liturgy. The purely local and parochial character of the 'naming' of the *living* in the Roman rite, by contrast with the international and diplomatic emphasis of the 'naming' of the living in the Byzantine diptychs, is another. Between them they make any application of the Byzantine term 'diptych' to the Roman 'commemorations' wholly misleading.

In so far as the alleged 'dislocation' of the Roman canon does not arise from mere modern misunderstandings of the tenor of its exceptionally archaic prayers, its cause must be looked for chiefly in things like the

[1] E. Bishop, *Liturgica Historica*, pp. 96 sqq.
[2] Note that there is no prayer for the dead in the old Roman synaxis intercessions (as these are preserved in the *Orationes Solemnes* of Good Friday).

clumsy insertion of the sanctus in the fifth century. But there is one element connected with the *origins* of the diptychs at Jerusalem, which has had some effect. Cyril's account of the 'naming' of the dead there *c.* A.D. 348 mentions the saints and a catalogue of the dead bishops of Jerusalem, as well as the more ordinary 'faithful departed'.

We have seen that a 'naming' of martyrs in the eucharistic prayer had been adopted in S. Augustine's rite (from Jerusalem) *c.* A.D. 410, though we hear nothing of a catalogue of the dead bishops of Hippo. The 'naming' of the saints in the eucharistic prayer was adopted at Rome, somewhat awkwardly and in a rudimentary fashion, apparently in the time of that innovating pontiff, Pope Gelasius (A.D. 492-6).[1] The lists were elaborated by haphazard additions during the sixth century, but their present arrangement appears to date only from the reforms of Pope S. Gregory I, *c.* A.D. 595. By contrast with the deliberately 'international' character of the lists of saints in the later Jerusalem diptychs, the Roman lists never quite lost their old-fashioned parochial character. The list of men martyrs still includes only four non-Roman names out of sixteen; and one of these, Ignatius of Antioch, had been martyred at Rome. The women martyrs contain four foreigners out of seven, but two of them, the Sicilians Agatha and Lucy, were introduced (almost certainly) by S. Gregory himself in his final revision; and the Balkan Anastasia, though her popularity was chiefly due to Greek settlers at Rome, seems to have got into the canon by confusion with the 'Anastasia' who had built an old Roman parish church, the *titulus Anastasiae.*[2] The Roman canon never adopted the other Jerusalem innovation of a catalogue of the past bishops of Rome, despite the occurrence of the names 'Linus, Cletus, Clement, Sixtus', which has been supposed to be the relics of one. It appears probable that Pope Sixtus II (martyred A.D. 258) had been commemorated in the canon for about a century before the name of Clement was added, and that Linus and Cletus were only inserted later still by S. Gregory I, in the final revision.

In the Irish *Stowe Missal,* however, there is a 'diptych of the dead' (though not one of the living) fitted into the text of the Roman canon. It contains a long list of Irish names, the owners of which with one doubtful exception—Maelruen—had all died before A.D. 739. (It may be remarked that the diptych had thus received at the most one addition in the century before the present MS. was copied, which suggests that the diptych of the dead was not a very living institution in the Irish rite.) But a comparison

---

[1] P. B. Whitehead, *The Acts of the Council of 499 and the date of the prayers Communicantes and Nobis Quoque, etc.,* in *Speculum,* iii. (1928), pp. 152 sqq.

[2] On all this question see V. L. Kennedy, *The Saints of the Canon of the Mass* (*Studi di antichita cristiana* XIV), 1938. To complete, *cf.* V. Maurice, *Les Saints du canon de la messe au moyen âge* in *Ephemerides Liturgicae,* lii (1938), pp. 353 sq. (The older literature is summarised in Kennedy.) I take it, despite Edmund Bishop's argument to the contrary, that Felicity in the canon is the Roman widow, not the African slave-girl.

of the *Stowe* diptych[1] with that found in the Mozarabic rite[2] will, I think, convince anyone of the origin of this supposed Irish practice. The Spanish diptych has been 'localised' and adapted in the usual Irish way; but the Irish document is not a native product, but a direct copying of Spanish custom.

And if one wishes to pursue this 'key' Western diptych of the dead in the Mozarabic rite to its source, a comparison of it with the diptychs of the dead in the Syrian rites[3] will at once supply the solution. The Mozarabic document is simply an adaptation of the Syrian custom.[4] Some Western churches adopted the Jerusalem custom of reciting a complete succession-list of their bishops in the eucharistic prayer, which in some cases lasted as late as the fifteenth century. What does not exist is any Western example of the specifically Byzantine custom of naming the chief foreign bishops with whom the local bishop was in communion in the diptych of the living.[5]

It may be well to sum up here what is known about the practice concerning public intercessions in the course of the liturgy in various churches, since nothing has caused more confusion in the various manuals of liturgical history, and far-reaching (and quite erroneous) theories have been based upon those confusions.

We have to distinguish clearly as regards origins between the intercessions at the synaxis and those at the eucharist. Those at the synaxis were offered for *categories* of persons, the only individuals mentioned by name being the local christian bishop and the Roman emperor. They took the form of a bidding, a pause for silent prayer and a collect. In the fourth century at Jerusalem these 'prayers of the faithful' were transferred bodily from the end of the synaxis to after the consecration, and made a part of the celebrant's eucharistic prayer. This innovation was afterwards widely

---

[1] *The Stowe Missal*, ed. Warren, (H.B.S.) II, 1915, *pp.* 14–16.
[2] *Missale Mixtum*, ed. Lesley, M. P. L., lxxxv., *coll.* 114 sq.
[3] Brightman, L. E. W., *pp.* 92 sqq., 276–277, and 501 sq.
[4] The same is less obviously true of the diptych of the dead from the monastery of S. Cross at Arles, found attached to the 'Rule' of S. Aurelian of Arles (*d.* A.D. 546) printed in Migne, P. L., lxviii., *coll.* 395 sqq. All the Western documents have the tell-tale Syrian peculiarity of arranging the saints in a rough chronological order of death, 'John Baptist, *Stephen*, Peter, Paul'. From the number of dead abbots it contains this particular Arlesian diptych can hardly be older than the seventh century, and the peculiarities of its list of saints are obviously connected with the relics which the monastic church enshrined.
[5] With the exception, of course, of the Pope. But even this comes in rather late. The diptychs of every *Eastern* church in the fifth century named the local patriarch as well as the local bishop, and the·custom spread to the West, though the Popes as a rule shewed little interest in enforcing it. The Council of Vaison in Gaul ordered it in A.D. 529, but I do not think any evidence that this was carried out is to be found in Gaul before the ninth century. Ennodius (*Libellus de Synodis*, 77) informs us that the Pope was already 'named' at the eucharist in Italy in the sixth century, and a *Greek* Sicilian diptych of the eighth century inserts Pope Hadrian I as 'Hadrian, patriarch of the City' (*Dict. d'arch. chrét. et de lit.*, iv. 1089). The Pope is 'named' in the Mozarabic diptych in the eleventh century *Liber Ordinum* (*ed.* Férotin, *col.* 235) and the custom was becoming general in the West by this time.

imitated in the East. In christendom as a whole these prayers at the end of the synaxis suffered an eclipse during the fifth century. In the West they disappeared altogether (except for special survivals in Holy Week). In the Byzantine church they were replaced by the new Antiochene fashion of litanies. Later imitations of this Byzantine novelty in some sort re-intro-duced traces of them into some Western rites (*e.g.* the Mozarabic) in the form of litanies. But a comparison proves in every case, I think, the depen-dence of these later Western litanies on the Constantinopolitan text, and forbids us to treat them as any sort of authentic survival of the ancient Western pre-Nicene 'prayers of the faithful'. These had been dropped from the Western rites perhaps a century before the first Western imita-tions of the Byzantine litany made their appearance. Only in the Roman rite on Good Friday, and in the Egyptian liturgy of *S. Mark*, do the pre-Nicene 'prayers of the faithful' still survive in something like their original form.

The pre-Nicene intercessions at the eucharist proper were much more personal than those at the synaxis, and 'named' specific individuals. In Spain and Italy these were names of *living* persons, chiefly the communi-cants, and the same may have been the case originally in Syria and in some Egyptian churches. But in the oldest known Egyptian rite (Sarapion), and at Jerusalem, Antioch and Constantinople, the first evidence we have is of the 'naming' of the *dead* only, and the same appears to be true of pre-Nicene Africa. There is good ground for thinking that the original position of these lists of 'names' of the living was at the offertory, at all events in the West. The 'naming' of the dead after the consecration at Jerusalem may conceivably have been transferred to that point from the offertory at the same time as the intercessions from the synaxis, but there is no evidence on this. And in Africa in pre-Nicene times the dead were 'named' in the course of the eucharistic prayer.

The first *combination* of lists of names of living and dead, 'the diptychs' properly so-called, was made at Constantinople in the early fifth century, but these did not so much replace the old intercessions (now attached to the eucharistic prayer) as fulfil a new official and diplomatic purpose. Out-side the properly Greek churches, in East Syria, Egypt and the West, the older custom of 'the Names' continued in force at the old position, at the offertory. Imitation of Byzantium brought about the partial adoption of the *form* of diptychs in Syria, whence it spread to some Western churches in the sixth-seventh century. But in the non-Greek churches these imitations of the Greek diptychs always retained a 'parochial' and local interest, by contrast with the purely official character of the Byzantine custom. In the non-Greek rites, after the fusion of synaxis and eucharist these very ancient lists of 'Names' coming after the offertory in some sort supplied for the loss of the old 'prayers of the faithful' before the offertory, though they have no original connection with them. The 'prayers of the faithful' were the intercessions of the synaxis, the 'Names' were the intercessions of the eucharist, in the days when these were still two separate rites.

## D. The Completion of the Shape of the Eucharist

Just as the period of the 'second *stratum*' equipped the rite of the synaxis with a wholly new Introduction, so it equipped the rite of the eucharits with a wholly new Conclusion. Just as the tendency of the synaxis was to prefix new items before the old nucleus, so the tendency at the eucharist was to append them, leaving the old core of the rite relatively unchanged in both cases. The 'second half' of the eucharistic prayer had begun to be added to the original 'thanksgiving series' in the second century, and various additional items and paragraphs had been appended and then fused into the prayer in the course of the third and early ·fourth century. Then at Jerusalem, by the time of Cyril, the Lord's prayer had been appended to the whole. Its independent existence as a prayer outside the eucharist had secured for this last addition that it should be allowed to remain as a separate item, and not be fused into the eucharistic prayer itself, as had happened to previous additions to that prayer. But even in this case we have seen that at Milan the Lord's prayer was for a while placed between the body of the eucharistic prayer and its concluding doxology.

In the fourth century the tradition that in the rite of the eucharist proper there could be only a single prayer—'*the*' prayer, the *eucharistia*—was beginning to break down. Supplements come to be made in this period which are no longer incorporated perforce into 'the' prayer itself, but are separate items. One such is the separate offertory prayer (of the ?5th century). This puts into words the meaning of the offertory, which the pre-Nicene church had been content to express by the bare action. Other such separate prayers were added even earlier to put into words the meaning of the fraction and the communion, which formerly the church had also been content to leave to speak for themselves.

There appears, too, for the first time something which would one day become the keynote of mediaeval and modern eucharistic devotion, the idea of special prayers in preparation for the individual act of receiving communion. However strange it may seem to us, this is an innovation in the fourth century. The old rite of offertory, prayer, fraction and communion had been unable to express this 'communion devotion', except in the course of the eucharistic prayer. We can see the beginnings of this in Hippolytus (*k*), but here the emphasis is still on the *corporate* effects of communion—that all the communicants 'may be made one'. Sarapion (*e²*) strikes a new note: 'Make all who partake to receive a medicine of life . . . *not for condemnation*, O God of truth . . .' It remains to be seen how this is amplified outside the eucharistic prayer itself.

### In Egypt

Sarapion has no trace of the Lord's prayer after the eucharistic prayer, but continues at once from its closing doxology and Amen with the rubric:

'*After "the" prayer the fraction and in the fraction a prayer*:

'Account us worthy even of this communion, O God of truth, and make our bodies to compass purity and our souls prudence and knowledge. And make us wise, O God of compassions, by the partaking of the Body and the Blood, for unto Thee through Thy Only-begotten ⟨is⟩ glory and might in holy Spirit . . .

'*After giving the fraction to the clerics, laying on of hands [i.e. a blessing] on the people*:

'I stretch out the hand upon this people and pray that the hand of the truth may be outstretched and a blessing be given unto this people through Thy love of men, O God of compassions, and through the present mysteries. May a hand of piety and power and discipline and cleanness and holiness bless this people, and continually preserve it to advancement and progress: through . . .

'*After the distribution to the people a prayer*:

'We thank Thee, Master, that Thou hast called those who have strayed, and hast taken to Thyself those who have sinned, and set aside the threat that was against us, granting mercy by Thy loving-kindness and wiping ⟨that threat⟩ away by repentance and casting it off by the knowledge ⟨that leads⟩ to Thee. We give thanks to Thee that Thou hast granted us communion of ⟨the⟩ Body and Blood. Bless us, bless this people, make us to have a share in the Body and Blood: through Thy Only-begotten Son, through Whom . . .'

[*There follows a blessing of oil and water offered for the sick,*[1] *followed by the final blessing of the eucharistic rite.*]

'*Laying on of hands after the blessing of the water and oil*:

'O God of truth that lovest mankind, let the communion of the Body and the Blood go forth along with (*symparabaineto*) this people. Let their bodies be living bodies and their souls be clean souls. Grant this blessing to be a safeguard of their communion and a security to the eucharist that has been held. And beatify them all together and make them elect: through Thy Only-begotten Jesus Christ in 'holy Spirit', both now and for ever and world without end. Amen.'

The old eschatological note is almost entirely missing from all this, only appearing in the last sentence of the final blessing. For the rest it is recog-

---

[1] The opening of this blessing is an interesting example of survival of the old idea of the power of 'the Name of God' of which we have found traces in Sarapion's eucharistic prayer (*cf. p.* 170): 'We bless these creatures through the Name of Thy Only-begotten Jesus Christ; we name the Name of Him Who suffered, Who was crucified and rose again, and Who sitteth on the right hand of the Uncreated, upon this water and upon this (oil) . . .'

nisably the 'modern' feeling of sacramental devotion that it expresses, concentrated on *reception*. The prayer at the fraction (carefully distinguished from 'the' prayer) shews that the fraction is still looked upon as a mere utilitarian preparation for communion, not a dramatic or symbolical act. Particular attention may be called to the blessing of the people *before* communion, which is found in all rites by the end of the fourth century. Its pointed bestowal upon the people after the clergy have made their communion suggests that it is a symptom of that increasing feeling that the 'profane' laity ought not to communicate, which soon led to their general abstention. It is designed to encourage and fit them to receive. The discerning reader who compares *the things asked* for the communicants in Hippolytus *k* (*p.* 151) or *Addai and Mari i* (*p.* 179) with those in Sarapion (*e²* *p.* 164) and the prayers on *p.* 512, may detect the beginnings of a new psychological attitude towards the act of communion in the fourth century.

### In Syria

Cyril of Jerusalem has a different system, though its emphasis is the same. He does not mention the fraction and there is no blessing of the people, so that Sarapion's first two prayers have no equivalent in the contemporary Jerusalem rite. Instead, the Lord's prayer, with its petitions for daily bread and the forgiveness of trespasses 'as we forgive' (both of which Cyril explicitly interprets as a preparation for communion),[1] acts as the people's preparation. Then comes the bishop's invitation 'Holy things for the holy' and the people's reply 'One only is holy'. The people receive communion with bowed heads 'as adoring and worshipping', and answer 'Amen' to the words of administration. Meanwhile a solo singer chants Psalm xxxiv, with its refrain or chorus 'O taste and see how gracious the Lord is'. Finally they are bidden, 'While you wait for the prayer give thanks to God Who has accounted you worthy of such great mysteries'.[1] Evidently there was now a post-communion prayer at Jerusalem, but whether it corresponded more closely to a 'thanksgiving' or a 'blessing' is doubtful in view of the other Syrian evidence.

The North Syrian 'communion developments', as represented by *Ap. Const.*, viii. (supported in some points by the Antiochene writings of Chrysostom) are different again. There is no Lord's prayer, but immediately after the doxology which concludes the intercessions attached to the eucharistic prayer the bishop greets the church 'The peace of God be with you all'[2] to which the people answer 'And with thy spirit'. There follows a series of 'proclamations' by the deacon, 'bidding' the people to pray for various objects, some connected with their communion, others being brief intercessions. There is no direction that the people shall answer *Kyrie*

---

[1] S. Cyril of Jerusalem, *Cat.*, xxiii. 22.
[2] *Cf.* the Roman formula at the same point, 'The peace of the Lord be always with you', to which the kiss of peace is attached.

*eleison*, but the whole has the appearance of a litany. It was apparently during this bidding that the fraction took place. There follows a solemn blessing of the people by the bishop: 'O God the mighty and mighty-named, mighty in counsel and powerful in deeds, God and Father of Thy Holy Servant (*pais*) Jesus our Saviour: Look upon us and upon this Thy flock which Thou hast chosen through Him unto the glory of Thy Name. And hallow our bodies and soul (*sic*); make us worthy, being purified from all defilement of flesh and spirit, to receive of these good things here lying before Thee; judge none of us unworthy, but be Thou our helper, our succour and defender, through Thy Christ with Whom unto Thee be glory, honour, praise and laud and thanksgiving with the Holy Ghost for ever. Amen'. (Even more clearly than in Sarapion this blessing is an encouragement and preparation of the communicants.)

The deacon then cries 'Let us attend' and the bishop gives the invitation —'Holy things unto the holy' to which the people reply with a sort of prose hymn, 'There is one holy, one Lord Jesus Christ to the glory of God the Father, blessed for ever. Amen. Glory be to God on high, and in earth peace, goodwill towards men. Hosanna to the Son of David. Blessed is He that cometh in the Name of the Lord. God is the Lord Who hath shewed us light. Hosanna in the highest.'

The communicants answer 'Amen' to the words of administration—'The Body of Christ', and 'The Blood of Christ, the cup of life'. Meanwhile Psalm xxxiv is chanted, as at Jerusalem. There follow (1) a thanksgiving prayer (which rather wanders from the point into a repetition of the intercessions) and (2) a lengthy blessing, *after* which the deacon's 'Depart in peace' dismisses the people.

The Antiochene rite as described by Chrysostom does not altogether support *Ap. Const.* in its details. The Lord's prayer is said at Antioch as at Jerusalem. The psalm sung during the communion is cxlv (in the English numbering, cxliv in that adopted by the primitive church) which is certainly no less appropriate. After the communion there is a thanksgiving prayer, but it appears to have been of recent introduction, since Chrysostom has some difficulty in persuading the people to remain for it. He compares those who hurry out at the communion (the ancient completion of the rite) to Judas bursting out of the upper room on his mission of betrayal, and those who remain to his fellow-disciples awaiting the psalm at the end of supper and going out with the Lord.[1] We shall meet again this inclination of the laity, based on traditional practice, to treat the post-communion as an optional 'extra'. He has nothing about a final blessing after the thanksgiving. The conclusion is still the deacon's 'Depart in peace'.

Theodore's rite at Mopsuestia, however, omits the Lord's prayer like *Ap. Const.*, viii. Evidently this Jerusalem innovation had not yet reached his church. The fraction follows immediately upon the intercessions that

[1] *de Bapt. Christi*, 4 (*opp., ed. cit.*, ii. 374 C. *sq.*).

conclude the eucharist prayer and is done 'so that all of us who are present may receive (communion)'.[1] This is accompanied, as in Sarapion, by a prayer of 'thanksgiving for these great gifts',[2] and a blessing of the people. Then comes the 'signing of the Body with the Blood', and the placing of a portion of the Host in the chalice. Then the deacon says 'We ought to pray for those who presented this holy offering'. 'The priest finishes the prayer by praying that this sacrifice may be acceptable to God and that the grace of the Holy Spirit may come upon all, so that we may be able to be worthy of its communion, and not receive it to punishment', and again blesses the people.[3] Then follows the invitation 'Holy things . . .' and its answer. Then follows the communion received with 'adoration' and 'fear'—the actual phrasing of Cyril's *Catecheses* obviously inspires Theodore's instructions at this point—but there is no mention of an accompanying psalm. 'After you have received . . . you rightly and spontaneously offer praise and thanksgiving to God. . . . And you remain, so that you may also offer thanksgiving and praise with all, according to the rules of the church, because it is fitting for all those who received this spiritual food to offer thanksgiving to God publicly . . .'[4] There is nothing about a final blessing or the deacon's dismissal in Theodore.

### In the Byzantine Rite

It is clearly the North Syrian rite of Chrysostom's time which has governed the 'communion devotions' and post-communion of the present Byzantine rite, but the exact form does not appear in any of our extant North Syrian sources. There is the double blessing (as in Theodore) with the Lord's prayer between them (as in Chrysostom). The deacon's proclamation 'Let us entreat on behalf of the holy gifts that have been offered and hallowed' is followed by other intercessions, and the priest's prayer for worthiness of reception 'and not unto judgement' and the gift of the Holy Ghost, are as in Theodore.

The manual acts (fraction, etc.) have been complicated by the peculiar and mysterious addition of the pouring of a few drops of hot water into the chalice by the deacon (known as the *zeon* or 'living water'). This ceremony is found only in the Byzantine rite, but it appears to be ancient there. In the sixth century the refractory Armenian patriarch Moses when summoned to Constantinople to appear before the emperor Maurice is reported to have answered, 'God forbid that I should cross the River Azat or eat leavened bread or drink hot water.'[5] Since the second of his disinclinations reflects on the Byzantine eucharist, the third may very well refer to the *zeon*

---

[1] Theodore, *Catecheses*, vi., *ed. cit., p.* 107.   [2] *Ibid., p.* 105.
[3] *Ibid., p.* 108.   [4] *Ibid., p.* 114.
[5] Cited by P. Le Brun, *Explication de la Messe* (1726), ii., *p.* 413, *n.* 29. I have not been able to ascertain what oriental authority underlies P. Combefis, *Narration touchant les Arméniens, Auctarium Bib. PP.* iii., *p.* 282, which is all that Le Brun cites by way of authority, nor how far it is reliable.

as an already established Byzantine peculiarity. The Greek devotional tradition explains it variously as symbolising 'the fervour of faith' or 'the descent of the Holy Ghost'. But these are explanations devised for an existing traditional practice, not its originating cause—as to which, however, I am unable to make any suggestion.

The communion in the Byzantine rite is now accompanied by two chants, the one 'Blessed is He that cometh in the Name of the Lord, God is the Lord who hath shewed us light' (*cf. Ap. Const.*, viii.), the other a Byzantine 'prose hymn' with a peculiarly striking melody:

> O Son of God, take me this day for a partaker
> Of Thy mystic supper,
> For I will not tell Thy secret to Thine enemies,
> I will not betray Thee with a kiss like Judas
> But like the thief confess Thee;
> Remember me, Lord, in Thy kingdom.

Immediately after the communion there is a further blessing of the people with the consecrated sacrament, of which a good deal is made in the Byzantine liturgical commentaries, in which it is said to symbolise our Lord's blessing of His disciples at the Ascension.[1] It is in fact a sort of *substitute* for communion devised to satisfy Byzantine non-communicant eucharistic piety.

The choir then sings the 'departure chant' of the day, a variable chant corresponding to the Western communion chant.[2] The 'thanksgiving' proper has disappeared from the modern rite, though a short thanksgiving prayer was still found here in the ninth century, in the liturgies both of *S. Basil* and *S. Chrysostom*.[3] All that is now left is a truncated version of a diaconal litany which formerly preceded the thanksgiving, followed by the dismissal 'Let us depart in peace', said by the deacon. The 'prayer behind the pulpit' (*opisthambōnos*), for which the priest comes out of the sanctuary, represents a sort of 'conducted devotion' after the service rather than an integral part of the rite, though its opening sentence fulfils also the purpose of a departure-blessing.

The Eastern communion devotions and thanksgiving are thus a product of the fourth century, and their development may be said to have been completed in principle by A.D. 400. In the West, development was less rapid.

---

[1] Some of the comments made upon it by Byzantine devotional authors are curiously anticipatory of devotional writings about the rite of Benediction in nineteenth century France, though I do not think there is any direct dependence of the Western authors on their Eastern predecessors.

[2] An old fixed chant known as the *Plērothēto*, introduced by the patriarch Sergius in A.D. 624, has disappeared at this point since the fourteenth century.

[3] Brightman, L. E. W., *p.* 342.

## In Africa

We have seen that the singing of a psalm during the communion
was a novelty in Africa[1] (adopted from Jerusalem?) early in the fifth century, and does not appear to have been taken up elsewhere in the West for
some time after that. A letter of Augustine's written *c.* A.D. 410 rather
before the adoption of this novelty gives us the order of the prayers of the
eucharist 'which' he says 'every church or almost every church customarily observes'. There is a prayer 'before that which is upon the Lord's
table begins to be blessed'; (the 'prayer of the day', or an 'offertory'
prayer?). There follows the eucharistic prayer 'when it is blessed and
hallowed and broken for distribution, which whole prayer almost every
church ends with the Lord's prayer'. (It is interesting to find the prayer at
the fraction and Lord's prayer included within the eucharistic prayer; it
shows how the appending of items to 'the' prayer was understood not to
violate the old rule that the eucharistic prayer proper must be a single
whole.) The kiss of peace followed at this point. Then 'the people are
blessed. For then the bishops like advocates present those whose cause
they have undertaken before the most merciful judgement seat of God by
the laying on of hands. When all this has been done and the great sacrament partaken, the thanksgiving ends all'.[2]

It seems certain that there was less uniformity even among the Western
churches at this time than Augustine supposes; but this outline probably
holds good in the main for all the African churches at least. What is particularly interesting is to find the blessing of the people before communicating
in the African rite at this early date. During the Pelagian controversy
Augustine was accustomed to quote the custom of blessing the people, and
also the contents of some of these blessings, as an argument against Pelagius.[3] It seems to be assumed by those liturgical authors who have treated
of the matter that it is always to this pre-communion blessing that Augustine is referring. I see no grounds for this assumption in the evidence, since
this was not the only occasion when a blessing was given in public worship.
It is unlikely—given his usual reserve about the contents of the eucharistic
prayers—that Augustine would cite a eucharistic blessing, when others
given at the more 'public' worship of the synaxis and the office were available to prove his point. But if the assumption is justified, it is important to
note that Augustine cites more than one formula, adding on one occasion
'and others like these' (*et caetera talia*). If these are pre-communion blessings, then in Africa this had already become a variable formula, not a
fixed one, as it remained in the East. (This would be one of the earliest
suggestions we have of the introduction of variable prayers at the eucharist,
which afterwards became a notable feature of all Western rites.)

---

[1] *Cf. p.* 492.    [2] Augustine, *Ep.*, cxlix. (*al.* lix.), *ad Paulinum* (of Nola), 16.
[3] *Epp.*, clxxv. 5; clxxix. 4; *Serm. Fragm.*, i (*al.* iii.), 3; etc.

*The Roman Communion Blessing*

At Rome also there appears to have been a blessing of the people before communion in the late fourth century. The mysterious Roman author who goes under the name of 'Ambrosiaster' (*c*. A.D. 385) tells us: 'The priests, whom we call bishops, have a form drawn up and handed down to them in solemn words, and they bless men by applying this to them . . . and though a man be holy, yet he bends his head to receive the blessing.'[1] This looks like a fixed form, as in the East, not a variable one as later in the West.

The custom had fallen out of the Roman rite by *c*. A.D. 500, but Dom Morin has suggested[2] that some of the formulae have survived in the special *oratio super populum* (prayer 'over the people') now appended to the post-communion thanksgiving prayers in the Roman rite during Lent. These prayers (of which there is one for each week-day in Lent) are now not always distinguishable from ordinary collects in structure. But in a number of them the celebrant instead of praying *with* the people (in the first person plural) prays *for* them (in the third person plural), making a sort of 'prayer-blessing' (like the final blessing in Sarapion, *p*. 512.), and this appears to be the original type.[3] And they are preceded by a 'proclamation' by the deacon, 'Bow down your heads unto the Lord', which is verbally identical with the deacon's 'proclamation' before the pre-communion blessing in some of the Eastern rites.

Whether it be true that the Lenten *oratio super populum* at Rome is a survival (transferred to after the thanksgiving) of the blessing before communion, or whether this Lenten peculiarity has some other origin, the fact that the Roman rite in the fifth century always had a blessing before the communion appears to be certain.[4] And it has this much importance, that it is one more little piece of evidence going to shew that in the fifth century all the Western rites formed a group and were similar in structure. For this pre-communion blessing perpetuated itself in some of the non-Roman Western rites, and persisted as a special local custom in many Western churches even after the adoption of the Roman rite.

*In Spain*

Before discussing the Roman thanksgiving prayer it will make for clarity to turn to the early Spanish and French rites. The ninth century Spanish *Liber Mozarabicus Sacramentorum* presents us with the following preparation for communion. After the (variable) eucharistic prayer comes the

[1] Ambrosiaster, *Quaest.* 109.

[2] *Revue Bénédictine*, xxix. (1912), *p*. 170 *sq.* (The arguments are suggestive rather than conclusive.)

[3] *Cf.* this (for the Ember Saturday in Lent): 'O God, may the blessing they have desired strengthen Thy faithful people: may it cause them never to depart from Thy will, and ever to rejoice in the gifts of Thy loving-kindness: through . . .'

[4] *Cf.* Dom Ménard's note on the *Gregorian Sacramentary*, M.P.L., lxxviii. 286–8.

fraction, then the creed, followed by the *praefatio* to the Lord's prayer (varying in every mass), then the Lord's prayer itself; after this, a threefold blessing and the communion. The following, for New Year's Day, is likely to be one of the older compositions in the book and will serve for an example:

*Praefatio*: 'O Lord Who art the great day of the angels and little in the day of men, the Word Who art God before all times, the Word made flesh in the fulness of time, created beneath the sun Who art the sun's creator: Grant unto us the solemn assembly of the church's dignity in Thy praise on this day (*sic*), that we who have consecrated the beginning of the year to Thee with these firstfruits, may by Thy grace sacrifice to Thee the whole time of its course by such ways and works as shall please Thee (*totius temporis spatium tibi placitis excursibus atque operibus facias inmolari*). For at Thy command we pray to Thee from earth, Our Father . . .' There follows this threefold blessing, preceded by the deacon's proclamation, 'Bow yourselves for the blessing.' 'May all of you who welcome the beginning of this year with His praises be brought without sin to its ending by the abiding protection of our Saviour. Amen. And may the same our Redeemer so grant unto you that this year be peaceful and happy that your heart may ever be waiting upon Him. Amen. That blessed of Him Who made heaven and earth that which you now begin in tears you may afterwards fulfil with spiritual songs. Amen.'[1]

What is interesting is to find that in the ninth century this threefold blessing is still the concluding text of the rite so far as the celebrant is concerned. Just as the Spanish rite at that date had developed no collect in the introduction before the old nucleus of the synaxis, so it had developed no thanksgiving-prayer after the old nucleus of the eucharist, but virtually ended with the communion. The fourth Council of Toledo in A.D. 633 (can. 18) had sternly reprimanded those who attempted to transfer the blessing from before the communion to after it, and had ordered that communion should end the rite as heretofore; and the Council's legislation had evidently maintained the old ways for another 200 years in Spain. But when the *Liber Sacramentorum* was written the custom of saying a short public thanksgiving prayer (*completuria*) after the communion was just beginning to spread, doubtless through imitation of the Roman rite. Four days in the year are provided with a *completuria* in this MS.; more are found in those of the next century, and in the eleventh century *Liber Ordinum*, the majority of the masses are so equipped. But by that time the episcopal blessing before the communion was so unalterably fixed in Spanish tradition that it was never transferred to the end of the rite, even after the thanksgiving prayer had been added in the ninth–tenth century. It still remains where the fourth Council of Toledo fixed it, before the communion.

[1] *Liber Mozarabicus Sacramentorum, ed. cit.*, col. 85 *sq.*

The developed Mozarabic post-communion of the middle ages runs thus: after the communion the choir sing an anthem (corresponding to the Roman *communio*) followed at once by a brief (variable) thanksgiving collect. Then the celebrant greets the church with 'The Lord be always with you'; R̦. 'And with thy spirit.' The Spanish deacon's ancient dismissal, 'Mass is over', is amplified to 'Our solemnities are completed in the Name of our Lord Jesus Christ. May our devotion be accepted in peace.' R̦. 'Thanks be to God.' This presents in its structure a close parallel with the early mediaeval Roman conclusion.

### In Gaul

In Gaul the arrangement was slightly different. The fraction came immediately after the end of the eucharistic prayer; then followed the Lord's prayer with its *praefatio*. Then the deacon sang 'Bow down for the blessing' and the bishop pronounced the threefold blessing divided by the people's 'Amens' as in Spain.[1] But in France the blessing in its full form became a special episcopal prerogative, and priests used a shorter and less elaborate form. The 'episcopal benedictions' became a special feature of the eucharist in France. Pope Zacharias already viewed them somewhat severely in A.D. 751 as 'not according to apostolic tradition but done out of vainglory, bringing damnation on themselves, as it is written "If any one preach unto you another gospel than that which was first preached unto you, let him be anathema".'[2] Nevertheless, they survived the adoption of the Roman rite under Charlemagne, and lasted in many French churches into the eighteenth century, and at Autun into the twentieth.

A different set of these benedictions was provided for every liturgical day in the year, some of them with five, seven, eight or nine clauses, all divided by 'Amens'. From Gaul the custom spread to England, Germany, and even one or two Italian and Hungarian churches.[3] In England they lasted down to the Reformation at the mass of a bishop or abbot.

The interesting thing is that the early French evidence reveals the same absence of a thanksgiving prayer as in the early Spanish rite. Not only does the Council of Orleans in A.D. 512 (can. 1) insist that the bishop's blessing before the communion is the end of the rite, before which no one must presume to depart; but S. Caesarius of Arles in sermons preached about the same time reveals the difficulty of inducing the laity, now that they no longer communicated, to remain even as long as that. He repeatedly

[1] *Cf.* the Gallican *Ordo* printed as *Ordo Rom.*, vi. (M.P.L., lxxviii., 993).
[2] *Ep.* to Boniface of Mainz, M.G.H.; *Epist. Merov. et Karol, I, p.* 371.
[3] The full Gallican collection of the seventh century can be reconstructed from a Freising MS. of the eighth century to which Dom Morin drew attention in *Rev. Ben. (art. cit.)* in 1912, which appears to be still unpublished. This is a pity, since this collection apparently underlies all those of other countries, except perhaps the Spanish ones. And comparison with these latter might help to clear up the difficult question of the relation of the seventh century Gallican rite to the Mozarabic.

exhorts them to stay until 'the whole mass' (*missas ad integrum*) has been completed, which, he says, is not until the bishop's blessing after the Lord's prayer has been given.[1] The earliest Gallican liturgical MS., the *Masses of Mone*, has added a short thanksgiving collect after the communion at all masses, varying with the day. But this is evidently a seventh century addition to the true Gallican rite, based on the Roman model. 'Germanus', for what its evidence is worth, has still no prayer of any kind after the benediction before communion. But since it also prescribes the saying of the creed as a preparation for communion, which is a Spanish not a French custom, it is perhaps no longer representative of what had come to be the general contemporary French practice *c.* A.D. 700.

### The Roman Post-Communion

When the episcopal blessing before communion formed the final prayer of the rite, followed only by the communion (in which the majority of the laity no longer took part), it naturally came to be regarded as a sort of climax. What appears to have caused its removal at Rome is the introduction of a brief thanksgiving or post-communion prayer after the communion, parallel to the collect before the lections. When this was first adopted at Rome is obscure, but it must have been some time during the fifth century. Post-communions are provided as systematically as collects for all masses in the *Gelasian Sacramentary*, whose groundwork seems to date from *c.* A.D. 500. But I have been unable to discover any earlier reference to any thanksgiving prayer at Rome, and the analogy of the Spanish and French rites suggests the possibility that its adoption took place after that of the collect, perhaps only towards the end of the fifth century. Many of the postcommunions themselves are hardly comparable with the collects in their workmanship, either for range of ideas or expression, which suggests that they may date from a rather different period, though both sets of prayers have the same structure.

### The Western Conclusion

The introduction of a concluding prayer after the communion may well have suggested to the Roman sense of form the idea of removing the solemn blessing, which had previously come before the communion, to after the thanksgiving (the position of the *super populum* in Lent). But the old tradition that the deacon's dismissal ought to end the rite died hard at Rome. The blessing after the thanksgiving was in form hardly distinguishable from a second postcommunion collect and served no particular purpose, since it was still followed by the deacon's *Ite missa est*. And so it was dropped altogether (except in Lent, a season when archaisms are apt to survive in all rites).

[1] *E.g., Serm.* 281, 2; 282, 2; in the *App.* to the *Sermons* of S. Augustine (which are by Caesarius).

The brief blessing 'May God Almighty, the Father, Son and Holy Ghost, bless you' which now follows the *Ite missa est* in the Roman rite begins as a sort of informal piece of politeness. In the *Ordo Romanus Primus*, as the Pope goes out to the sacristy after mass other bishops step forward to ask his blessing, and he replies 'May God bless *us*'—a courtesy. The people bow to him as he passes through the congregation in procession to the sacristy, and he replies by signing them with the cross. Only in the eleventh century did priests as well as bishops begin to bless the people as they went from the altar. The custom spread, apparently from France, but not very quickly, during the middle ages. In England the mediaeval derived uses (*e.g.* Sarum, Westminster and Hereford) did not adopt it. The present forms (differing for priests and bishops) were not finally fixed in the Roman missal until the pontificate of Clement VIII in the seventeenth century.

The blessing is always *said* by priests in the Roman rite, even at a sung eucharist, an indication that it is no inherent part of the public rite,[1] but rather to be classed with those semi-private devotions like the 'last gospel' (John i. 1-14) and the 'preparation', which grew up as a sort of 'third *stratum*' during the middle ages, around the completed Shape of the Liturgy, rather than as part of it. The real end of the rite is communion and the deacon's proclamation that it is complete. To this the 'second *stratum*' added a brief and formal thanksgiving—for how can *public* thanksgiving for such an intimate thing as the union of the soul with God be anything but formal? Even though it is right that we should all give thanks together for the same gift, it was also a right instinct which made it brief—a gesture only—and left the soul to its Lord, sending it back with Him to daily life with 'Depart in peace' or some such phrase. There is a certain 'clericalism' about reinforcing *communion* with a priestly blessing, however true it be that 'the blessing of a good man availeth much'. The primitive church rejoiced in such blessings and multiplied them, but she did not choose this particular moment for imparting them.

### E. The 'Third Stratum'

The Shape of the Liturgy as it stood *c.* A.D. 800 all over christendom remains substantially intact henceforward, because it is an organically completed thing, logically adapted to express the eucharistic action it performs in a society which is nominally christian in its assumptions about human life as a whole. It consists roughly of four parts: the introduction (added by the 'second *stratum*'); the old nucleus of the synaxis (minus the concluding intercessory prayers which had atrophied in different ways in all rites); the old nucleus of the eucharist; and a brief appended thanksgiving (the other addition of the 'second *stratum*'). Henceforward the

---

[1] The bishop seems always to have sung his final blessing. Perhaps this is a trace of its indirect derivation from the old solemn blessing before the communion.

additions and changes made have about them the character of mere decorations, rather than of structural changes, though they are numerous and various and continual enough in all rites.

A sufficient illustration is the history of the *Agnus Dei* in the Roman rite. This little prose hymn 'O Lamb of God that takest away the sins of the world, have mercy upon us' was first introduced into the Roman rite during the fraction immediately before the communion by Pope Sergius I (A.D. 687–701). This act of adoration of our Lord present in the sacrament (for it is intended as such) is a somewhat 'un-Roman' form of eucharistic devotion. But its origin is explained by the fact that Sergius was himself a Greek, born in Syria; the idea of 'the Lamb of God' had for centuries attracted a special devotion in the Syrian church. The *Agnus Dei* is in fact only one more of those 'Syrian importations' of which we have had other instances, which were constantly enriching Western forms from the fourth century to the eighth. As Sergius introduced it the hymn seems to have been sung twice, once by the choir, and then repeated by the people. This continued down to the eleventh century. In the twelfth century the liturgist Beleth describes it as being sung three times in French churches, with 'grant us peace' substituted for 'have mercy upon us' at the third repetition. At the end of the thirteenth century, however, it was still being sung at Rome without this new variation, a custom maintained to this day in the Pope's cathedral, the Lateran basilica. Yet another little variation for use at funerals had made its appearance in France during the eleventh-twelfth century—the substitution of 'grant them rest' for 'have mercy upon us'. This in turn led to the further change of adding '. . . rest *everlasting*' at the third repetition at funerals, in those churches which substituted 'grant us peace' at the third repetition on ordinary days.

When a single small item of late introduction can go through so many variations in a few centuries it is obvious that the following of all the innumerable changes in the details of rites ceaselessly made and remade all through the middle ages would be a wearisome and lengthy business. Especially is this the case with the additions made by what I have called the 'third *stratum*'—c. A.D. 800–1100. These additions were not protected from change either by their structural usefulness, like those of the 'second *stratum*', or by immemorial tradition like the primitive nucleus; and in consequence the persistent innovating tendency of the clergy in all ages with regard to details of the liturgy had comparatively free play with these, and also with minor matters of ceremonial whose development or alteration goes on persistently in all rites down to the sixteenth-seventeenth century. But these little matters of fashion and fancy change nothing in the main outline of the Shape of the Liturgy, which remains everywhere much as it was *c*. A.D. 800.

After this the persistent desire to improve upon the traditional liturgy, restrained by its 'completeness' as a whole, finds expression chiefly in the composition of 'devotions' preparatory to and looking back upon the liturgical action itself—'preparations' and 'thanksgivings'—which are of the greatest interest from the point of view of the history of religious psychology, but are less closely connected with the history of the liturgy itself.

A few words must be said, however, of the instances of this tendency which have managed to attach themselves as official and prescribed parts of the rite in the liturgies of the East and West alike—the 'preparation' and various post-liturgical devotions.

In both the Byzantine and Roman rites there is now an officially prescribed 'preparation', a series of devotions for the priest and his assistants, before the service begins. The forms now in use in both cases begin to take shape about the eleventh-twelfth century,[1] and reach their present text in the sixteenth century. In both cases the process begins with the prefixing of a single private prayer to be said by the celebrant in the sacristy, which is found in both East and West as far back as the seventh century. Certainly private devotion had always exacted devout preparation from clergy and laity. But it is a different thing when official regulation begins to prescribe the form of private devotion, and to draw its exercise into the sphere of the fixed liturgical action instead of leaving it to its own natural field—the individual's personal preferences under the action of grace. It presages a good deal that has subsequently taken place in the way of 'psychologising' the eucharist, and removing the emphasis from the corporate action to the individual's subjective feelings and thoughts about that action.

It is further noticeable that whereas this earliest Eastern 'prayer of preparation' in the seventh century is concerned with the preparation of *the elements*, the earliest Western prayers (*apologiae* as they are called) are true to the inherent Western bent for 'psychologising', and are wholly concerned with the preparation of *the priest*. This original difference of bias in the devotion of the two churches is something which has persisted, not only in their preparatory devotions but in their eucharistic devotion as a whole. Thus while the Eastern veneration for even the unconsecrated elements has made the great entrance one of the moments of supreme worship in the rite, the Western tendency has been to make of these psychological reactions of the individual not merely a preparation for the rite, but something which is of its very structure. We find these *apologiae* prefixed to the Western rites in the seventh century; but from the thirteenth onwards the missals prescribe them for the celebrant to say while the choir are singing the introit, *Gloria*, gradual and creed, in fact at every moment the liturgical

---

[1] The history of the Byzantine forms can most usefully be studied in Dom P. de Meester's valuable essay, *Les origines et les développements du texte grec de la liturgie de S. Jean Chrysostome* (Chrysostomika II, Rome, 1908, pp. 245 sqq.), supplemented by Brightman, L. E. W., pp. 539–551. The best general account of the Western forms is still that in Bona, *Rerum Liturgicarum Lib.*, II, ii (Paris 1672), caps. 1 and 2, though it needs supplementing from texts discovered since.

action leaves him free.[1] It is in this period too that we begin to find private prayers of the same kind inserted between the old public *Agnus Dei* and the priest's communion. Let us be quite clear as to the point. Piety and edification may take many forms, and modern eucharistic piety still feels this particular mediaeval form to be entirely good and natural. But it is legitimate to point out the difference between this and the piety of the primitive church, for which the *corporate liturgy itself* formed the substance of devotion, and the *corporate action* its expression. In the middle ages it begins to be the *supplementary prayers* and the *private emotions* which take their place in this respect.

It is true that in the middle ages these 'devotions' are still only something which *accompanies* the liturgy, which continues uninterrupted by them, as it were, in the centre of the field. In the sixteenth century a further stage is reached in practice. Either, as in a good deal of Latin devotion, the text of the liturgy is ignored altogether for purposes of devotion, and 'methods of hearing mass' entirely composed of these supplementary prayers are put together for the benefit of all but the celebrant. Or else, as in the sixteenth century Anglican rites, the supplementary devotions invade the liturgical action and become formal parts of it—even main parts of it, which break up the old apostolic and primitive action by an elaborate commentary of prescribed subjective repercussions which it is thought desirable that it should have on those present. The Anglican exhortations, the confession with its highly emotional language, the comfortable words and prayer of access—all of these are thoroughly in line with the piety of the mediaeval *apologiae*, and echo their language. The only change is that they are no longer private and supplementary prayers, but public and prescribed, and have been made a part of the liturgical action itself. Coming where they do, as a lengthy interpolation between the offertory and the consecration (which primitive christian thought had seen as two parts of a single action so closely united that a single word *prospherein* would cover them both) these devotions would have been incomprehensible to the pre-Nicene church. That church never developed anything comparable because it understood the eucharist as being for all who took part in it an *action*—'Do this'—not the *experience* of an action. Even when the post-Nicene church began to develop something of this kind, it placed them at the obvious point for such a development—before the communion. The mediaeval church on the contrary would have understood easily enough what Cranmer intended, even though it was itself still too loyal to primitive

---

[1] There are *e.g.*, six *apologiae* prescribed to be said by the celebrant during the *Gloria* in the Westminster Lyttlington Missal (fourteenth century). The practice had certainly begun in the twelfth century or even earlier; *e.g.*, S. Thomas of Canterbury was accustomed to use the devotions compiled by S. Anselm while the choir was singing, because he found them particularly moving (*Vita S. Thomae*, by Herbert of Bosham, iii. 13, *ed.* J. C. Robertson, *Materials for the History of Thomas Becket*, London, 1873, III, *p.* 209 *sq.*). But I do not recollect noticing such prayers provided in the *altar-books* before the thirteenth century.

forms to bring about such an upheaval of the Shape of the Liturgy as this long interpolation involves.[1]

The additional devotions after the liturgy which correspond to the 'preparation' before it—the 'last gospel' (John i. 1-14) and thanksgiving office (*Benedicite*, Ps. 150, etc.)—have much the same history. They begin as private devotions in the eleventh-twelfth century and have become a prescribed appendage to the rite by the sixteenth. They are part of that ceaseless process of accumulating 'devotional extras' around the essential liturgical action, which is the special mark of the piety of the 'third *stratum*'. In these cases its result is obviously edifying and good; in some others (*e.g.* the interlarding of the rite with private *apologiae* of the priest) it is difficult not to see in its manifestations only a false emphasis on inessentials.

[1] How incurably mediaeval our Anglican eucharistic devotion remains is illustrated by some regulations issued by an English bishop to his diocese in December 1941. Urging the retention of these devotions even when no communicants other than the celebrant are expected, he writes: 'Without this section the element of confession and humility, which is as essential for a corporate approach to the Prayer of Consecration as it is for the individual human approach to it, is absent from the service'. It is regrettable that the whole primitive and patristic church should thus have been without the 'essential' corporate approach to the consecration; and it must be said that the idea that one cannot worthily be present at the consecration without first expressing confession and humility—but can profitably hear the Word of God in the scriptures at the synaxis without doing so?—was the heart of mediaeval eucharistic piety. One had supposed that it was the primary purpose of our Reformers to destroy it. These devotions were not placed where they are by Cranmer as a preparation for the consecration—he repeatedly said he did not believe there was any 'consecration' in this sense—but as a substitute for the offertory (*cf. pp.* 662 *sq.*). The confusion in our ideas had been caused by the revisers of 1662 who re-established the idea of a 'Prayer of Consecration' which Cranmer had deliberately eliminated, and restored the offertory of bread and wine, and yet left these devotions in the position at which he had placed them with a wholly different understanding of the eucharist in view. They must now be treated either as 'communion' devotions in the strict sense (in which case they should now come before the communion), or else as meaningless survivals which now unnecessarily destroy the structural logic of our rite (and foster the sort of unhealthy mediaevalism illustrated by the well-meaning regulation above, by over-emphasising the consecration at the expense of the action as one whole).

# CHAPTER XIV

## VARIABLE PRAYERS AT THE EUCHARIST

WE turn now to consider an innovation of the post-Nicene period whose effects have been considerable—the introduction of variable prayers at the liturgy. We Anglicans are so accustomed to the fact that in our rite at least one of the prayers, the collect for the day—and on occasions part of the preface also—varies according to the day in the ecclesiastical calendar, that probably few communicants or even celebrants ask themselves why this should be. Yet it is a peculiarity of the eucharist, distinguishing it from the administration of the other sacraments. On whatever day in the year baptism, say, or confirmation is administered, not only the outline of the rite but the actual wording of all the prayers is identically the same.

It is true that the varying of these prayers under the influence of the calendar does not affect the Shape of the Liturgy. Granted that there is to be a prayer before the lections or some sort of introduction to the sanctus, it makes no difference whether these are always the same, or are chosen at will from two or three variants, or whether different ones are provided for each day in the year. The structure of the rite would remain in each case the same. But an essay such as this would be notably incomplete without some discussion of the origins of this practice, even though we cannot do more than touch upon some of the problems it presents.

The influence of the calendar upon the prayers of the rite is only one of the repercussions of that construing of the eucharist in terms of time and history which begins in the fourth century, though it is an important index of the progress of this new idea. Our variable collect and preface are only fragmentary survivals of what in all other catholic rites is a much more extensive system of variation. The elaboration of different variable elements of this kind, and (in the West especially) the mutual interchange of such texts between different churches and regions, make up between them the most important part of the history of the liturgy for more than a thousand years—from the fifth century to the sixteenth. This intricate process must be left to another chapter. Here we are concerned with origins.

It is necessary to be clear as to what we mean by 'variable elements'. The synaxis had from apostolic times contained 'variable elements' in the lections and chants. From an early date certain texts of this kind were appropriated to particular occasions like the Pascha. But the liturgical cycle was still so simple that this recurring element covered only a small part of the year, and we have no evidence of a cycle of lections and chants for the ordinary Sundays in pre-Nicene times, despite the precedent of the three-year cycle of lections and chants in the synagogue. It is not, however, with lections and chants that we are now concerned, but with the prayers said by the celebrant.

The intercessory prayers at the end of the synaxis appear to have been fixed in their order and content, if not their phrasing, from a very early period; though this doubtless did not exclude the possibility of the offering of special ones on occasion. At the eucharist proper the only possible variable element was 'the' prayer, the only verbal text in the rite; even the dialogue preceding it was 'fixed' because of the need of co-ordinating the celebrant's versicles with the people's responses. The episcopal celebrant was allowed, and even perhaps expected, to extemporise some of the phrasing of this prayer within the traditional outline, in virtue of his prophetic *charisma*. But it is a permanent feature of liturgical history from the second century to the sixteenth that liturgical changes are more usually made by addition to what is already customary than by substitution for it, and it is still a fact that they are much more easily accepted by the laity in this way. The pre-Nicene history of the eucharistic prayer is the history of local additions made to its primitive universal nucleus in different ways by different churches. And (to my mind) pre-Nicene texts like those of the prayers of Hippolytus and *Addai and Mari*, with their perpetuation of archaisms not only of language but of doctrine, suggest that the 'liberty of prophesying' enjoyed by bishops in reciting the eucharistic prayer was in practice a good deal curbed by tradition.

In the fourth century fixity of texts of the prayer definitely begins to set in. As a matter of convenience, the longer prayers produced by successive additions over two centuries now required the use of a MS. by the celebrant. The unique extant MS. of Sarapion's Sacramentary is a later (eleventh century) copy of such a MS. first put together by a bishop for his own practical use *c.* A.D. 340. The use of such MSS. in itself made for still greater fixity. And the prayers themselves had now been expanded to include most of the ideas in circulation about the meaning of the eucharist, and fully expressed the eucharistic action in words, so that there was less need for new additions. The fourth century rise in the level of christian culture had clothed them with an adequate literary form, so that the average bishop at the end of the century was no longer much tempted to think that he could improve on the traditional phrasing. In the second century Irenaeus had appealed to the general sense of the eucharistic prayer in support of his arguments against the Gnostics.[1] In the fourth century christian writers and speakers everywhere appeal incidentally not only to the general sense but to phrases and even isolated words of the prayer used in their own church as something fixed and known, by which they can support their arguments.[2] No doubt it was still easy for an inno-

---

[1] Irenaeus, *adv. Haer.*, iv. 18. 4.

[2] So Cyril at Jerusalem and Theodore at Mopsuestia in their *Catecheses*, Chrysostom at Antioch and Constantinople in his sermons, Ambrose at Milan in *de Sacramentis* and Victorinus Afer at Rome (*adv. arium*, ii. 8). It is a universal tendency.

vating bishop to make changes, and especially to add to the traditional prayer clauses embodying new liturgical fashions, when someone came home from abroad and impressed him with the novel idea of commemorating the saints by name in the canon or of invoking the Holy Ghost to effect consecration. But when the people went to the eucharist on a Sunday morning in the later fourth century they no longer expected to hear the bishop chant a prayer which was even verbally different from that which they had heard last Sunday. At the end of the fourth century it looked as though the prayers at the eucharist would remain as fixed and invariable as those for baptism or ordination.

What changed the course of liturgical history was the immense development of the liturgical calendar towards the end of the fourth century, though it took a little while to have its effect on the liturgy. Just because the eucharistic action is *the* act of the church's life towards God, it could not fail to be affected by this new rhythm and colour given to that life, in a way that baptism and confirmation[1] or other rites like penance would not be affected. The introduction of variable prayers is the result of the impact of the calendar on the liturgy.

### Variable Prayers in the Eastern Rites

It is often said that the effect of the calendar on the prayers is confined to the West and unknown in the East.[2] Yet it would seem truer to say that Eastern and Western rites express the same impulse in rather different ways. To take a simple instance: the Byzantine rite has two different liturgies, those of *S. Basil* and *S. John Chrysostom* (besides the Lenten *Liturgy of the Presanctified*). But when we ask the occasions of their use, we find that it is not at all a matter of free choice by the celebrant (as *e.g.* between the alternative rites of the Scottish Episcopal church) but is governed strictly by the calendar. The liturgy of *S. Basil* is always used on the Saturdays and Sundays of Lent, certain vigils and the feast of *S. Basil* (January 1st). Any celebration in an orthodox church on those days is done according to *S. Basil*, not according to *S. John Chrysostom*. On other days *S. Basil* is never used and *S. John Chrysostom* always is. And if we ask how these two liturgies differ, we find that in both the structure and outline are the same; the deacon's part is the same; the people's responses are exactly the same; even the hymns are always the same except for certain chants (*e.g.* the chant between the lections) which always vary with the day. What is different in one from the other is only the text of the prayers said by the celebrant.[3] The

---

[1] Still administered together normally only on fixed occasions—Pascha and Pentecost, to which Epiphany and even certain martyrs' feasts were beginning to be added in some churches.

[2] The classic statement of this view is by Dom Cagin, *Paléographie Musicale* V (1896), pp. 14 *sqq.*

[3] It is hardly necessary to say that the theory which goes back to pseudo-Proclus (eighth–ninth century) that *S. John Chrysostom* is an abbreviation of *S. Basil* and

Byzantine rite thus has variable prayers, and what governs their use is the liturgical calendar, just as in the West. In one respect the variability of the Byzantine rite is much greater than that of some Western rites, *e.g.* the Roman, in which the eucharistic prayer (apart from the preface and two other clauses) never varies on any day in the year. In the Byzantine rite even the whole eucharistic prayer itself is variable according to the calendar, along with all the other prayers of the celebrant, though the choice is always limited to one of two complete sets of prayers.

The same principle somewhat more developed is found in the other Eastern rites. The Abyssinian rite has fourteen different eucharistic prayers for use on different liturgical days; the Coptic rite has three, one of which is used only once a year; the Nestorians have a different three. The Syrian Jacobites have more than seventy different eucharistic prayers, and though not all are assigned to particular days, the great feasts have their assigned prayers; it is only on lesser days that a choice is left to the celebrant (as it was left *e.g.* to the Gallican celebrant to choose which of three or four sets of prayers he would use on an ordinary Sunday). Only, I think, in the Armenian rite is a single set of celebrant's prayers now made to do duty for all occasions; and this is a fairly modern development, for at least four old Armenian alternative eucharistic prayers are known, besides Armenian translations of eucharistic prayers from other churches.

The real points of distinction between East and West in this matter appear to be two: 1. that the Eastern choice of variable prayers is limited to a much smaller number of *sets* of prayers than are found in the Western rites, though variation goes further in that when the prayers do vary, they *all* vary (in this being more like the Gallican than the Roman); 2. that there is as a rule no reference in the text of the prayers to the day in the liturgical calendar, though this is the cause of their varying.[1] Each set of Eastern prayers might be used on any day in the year with equal appropriateness; it is only by an arbitrary traditional assignment that they are associated with particular days in the calendar. But a Western set of variable prayers, *e.g.* for Easter, could hardly be used for Christmas.

The Eastern sets were in fact each of them composed to be a fixed un-

the latter of S. *James* will not survive a comparison of the contents of their prayers. S. *John Chrysostom* is not a shortening of S. *Basil* but a different set of prayers, most of which are shorter and simpler than the corresponding prayers in S. *Basil*, but some of which are rather longer. The relation of the two sets is best described as that of independent compositions on the same themes. S. *Basil* is appreciably the older, probably by some two centuries or more.

[1] This is true of the Byzantine rite and of most Eastern rites, but not of all: *e.g.* the Abyssinian 'Anaphora of our Lady Mary' used on feasts of our Lady would hardly be appropriate on other days (being partly addressed directly to her); and that for use on ordinary Sundays contains a good deal about 'the holy christian Sabbath' (including the appeal to it to 'intercede for us'). Other examples of reference to the day in the text of the eucharistic prayer might be cited from the East. But the above rule is generally true, and represents the old universal practice of the East.

varying liturgy used throughout the year, in the fourth century fashion. Some Eastern churches already had several such sets in the fifth century, which they preserved as genuine alternatives with no connection with the calendar. One set was the traditional rite of that church, and its basis went back to pre-Nicene times; the others were new compositions by fourth or fifth century bishops or scholars. These new products usually embody the old ideas and some of the old phraseology, but recast and made more coherent than was usually the case with the older prayer, formed as this had been by the gradual accumulation of several strata of additions. These later re-workings of the old tradition did not invariably oust the old text altogether. Either the old text or the new was relegated to special seasons or occasions, such as Lent or the feast of the supposed author of the text, to make sure that it was kept in occasional use. Thus the alternative sets of prayers arose in the East quite independently of the calendar; but after the fifth century the calendar comes to regulate their use, even though it does not as a rule affect their contents.

### Variable Prayers in the Western Rites

There is evidence that in the first half of the fifth century the system now found in the East, of *alternative* eucharistic prayers containing no special reference whatever to the day in the liturgical calendar, was coming into force in some places in the West also.[1] But a different system prevailed in the end all over the West, perhaps because the Western churches did not at first so readily adopt alternative versions of their old fourth century fixed prayers as the Eastern churches had done, and so when changes did come to be made in the end the influence of the calendar had become sufficiently strong to dominate the whole process.

The special characteristic of the Western variable prayers is that they not only refer to but are actually based upon the liturgical commemoration of the day in the calendar. The question of the date when the Western rites first began to adopt this kind of variation is one of the most obscure in the whole subject of the liturgy; but since a right estimate of this, and the related questions of where and how it came about, seems the best basis for a clear understanding of the influences which have made all the later history of the Western rites for the next 1,000 years and have been potent in the formation of our own, I propose to discuss it a little more closely.

We can say with certainty that this special Western principle of variation had been fully developed by c. A.D. 500 all over the West, except perhaps in Africa where we have no evidence at all as to whether it ever developed or not. (In what follows Africa is therefore intended to be excluded from all generalisations about 'the West', except where it is specifically included.) There is some evidence that it was being developed in Gaul by c. A.D. 450.[2]

---

[1] *Cf. pp.* 536, 540 *sqq.*          [2] *Cf. p.* 558.

In Spain we have good evidence that it was already fully operative by *c.*
A.D. 500.[1] We have positive evidence of its acceptance in Italy also by *c.*
A.D. 500 in the shape of the *Gelasian Sacramentary,* a book the first compilation of which can be placed with some confidence at about that date,[2]
and in which the Western system of variation according to the calendar is
already fully operative. If we could be more certain of the origins of the
document known as the *Leonine Sacramentary* we might be able to push
the question further back at Rome. But for reasons given later[3] the *Leonine*
book does not with any certainty enable us to get behind the *Gelasian* one.
One may hope and suspect that certain texts in it go back into the fifth
century, perhaps even to the time of Pope S. Leo himself (*c.* A.D. 450); but
I am not aware that this could be actually proved in the case of any individual item in it.

Taking *c.* A.D. 500 as the lower limit for the Western development of the
principle of variation by the calendar, can we find an upper limit for its
origin? The scholar who has most patiently sought to do this is the German
F. Probst, who came to the conclusion that this kind of Western prayer
began in the time of Pope S. Damasus (A.D. 366–384), whom he credits
personally with the invention of the noble Roman collect style.[4] Probst's
thesis seems to have been accepted without further investigation by later
scholars. It may be true. One would like to think it was. Damasus is a not
unsuitable figure for such a part, with his love for the martyrs and the
history of his own great church. Yet the case when it is examined seems far
from secure. It rests on no single item of solid evidence, but only on
inferences and probabilities, and on assigning an earlier date to some of the
material in the *Leonine Sacramentary* than now seems possible.[5] I must
confess to doubts not only as to whether Damasus himself is the inventor
of the Roman collect style or the Western variable prayers in general, but
whether his period is the right period or Rome is the right church in which
to look for their origins.

First, the older portions of the Roman canon, which unquestionably
come from the fourth century and are therefore our only measure of Roman
liturgical style about the time of Damasus, are much less terse and more
flowing in their Latinity than the lapidary collect style. If one must associ-

[1] *Cf. p.* 558.
[2] See the very useful art. by Mr. J. S. Sinclair, *The Development of the Roman
Rite during the Dark Ages* in *Theology,* xxxii. (1936), *pp.* 142 *sqq,* which argues
convincingly for a date between *c.* A.D. 475 and 510, with 525 as an extreme lower
limit. I accept *c.* A.D. 500 as a useful middle date, without prejudice to the further
question of any connection of the book with Pope S. Gelasius (A.D. 492–496) or any
other individual Pope.
[3] *Cf. p.* 568.
[4] *Liturgie des vierten Jahrhunderts, usw.* (Münster, 1893), *pp.* 455 *sqq.,* summarising
arguments at greater length in *Die ältesten römischen Sacramentarien, usw.* (Münster,
1892), *passim.* R. Buchwald, *Das sog. Sacr. leonianum* (Vienna, 1908), *pp.* 23–4 finds
further arguments to the same effect (some of which are very erratic).
[5] *Cf. p.* 568.

ate the name of a particular Pope with the latter, that of Leo would present itself to anyone with a feeling for style much more readily than that of Damasus. The products of Damasus' pen which we can with certainty identify as the work of his own mind without the assistance of the Papal chancery—the metrical epitaphs he composed for the tombs of the Roman martyrs—do not by any means suggest the possession of such literary gifts as could create the Roman collects. They are frequently execrable and never better than second-rate. It is true that Damasus would not be the last liturgical author whose attempts at poetry were less happy than his prose; Cranmer would furnish a case in point. But the taste which enabled Cranmer to write liturgical prose of the first order was quite sufficient to warn him of the unwisdom of publishing his verses; whereas Damasus inscribed his in the exquisite lettering of Philocalus on every famous pilgrimshrine in Rome for all the christian world to read. His authorship of these *Epigrammata* may not be a decisive argument against his capacity to invent the austere and delicate collect style; but I am inclined to think his perpetuation of them tells against it, nevertheless.

Secondly, one would not *a priori* look for the beginnings of so great an innovation first of all in the somewhat rigid conservatism of the Roman church. The basing of the prayers of the eucharist on the liturgical commemoration of the day is an idea which is a response, I should say, to sheer poetic feeling—of a kind which the more prosaic genius of that church rarely compassed for itself, though it could on occasion give magnificent expression to such ideas when they were presented to it from outside.[1] It is true that this is a specifically Western idea, and that Rome is still in the fourth-fifth centuries the heart of the West. But it was hardly the brain. Again and again during the remaking of Europe—from say, the fifth century to the twelfth and even later—we are confronted by the fact that the *creative* centre of new 'specifically Western ideas'—in theology, in poetry and architecture, in liturgy (which is related to all these arts), in law and political theory, in military tactics—in the things of the mind generally—is never at Rome and always in Gaul. This is true of the origins of ideas in all departments, even though the final application of them is often Italian rather than French.[2] I pass over the fact that the composition of variable prayers seems to be actually attested in France some forty or fifty years before it is attested at Rome;[3] that may perfectly well be a mere chance of the survival of evidence. But the Roman rite adopted the idea of variable prayers with a good deal of reserve. Except for the preface and two (originally three) of its clauses, the eucharistic prayer—the most

[1] *Cf. e.g.* the Roman office for the last three days of Holy Week, which embodies in a wholly Roman form ideas originally derived from the Jerusalem church of the fourth century.
[2] *E.g.* the Lorraine canonists and Pope Gregory VII; the troubadours and Dante; Abelard and S. Thomas Aquinas.
[3] *Cf. pp.* 558 *sqq.,* 535.

important prayer of the rite—was always verbally the same on every single day in the year at Rome, as all eucharistic prayers everywhere seem to have been in the fourth century. But there is another type of Western rite found in South France and also in Spain, which shewed no such hesitation about applying the new Western idea. These Gallican and Mozarabic rites are the most mutable in christendom, varying every word of every prayer said by the celebrant, including the whole eucharistic prayer (except the single paragraph containing the account of the institution) on every liturgical day in the year. If thoroughness of application be any criterion, the varying of the prayers of the eucharist according to the calendar is a principle more fundamental to the Spanish and French liturgies than to the Roman. Accordingly it is not at Rome that I should look for its origin but in the more supple and nimble genius of the French churches and peoples.

Thirdly, the period of Damasus (A.D. 366–384) seems too early for the elaboration of variable prayers *based on* the liturgical year. It is the conception of the christian year as an already accepted and completed notion regulating the liturgy which is the actual inspiration of the Western variable prayers. They presuppose it and embody it, which suggests (to my mind) a later period than that of Damasus, in whose time the christian year was still only in course of formation. Rather one would look to a period after the calendar which he helped to develop had become an entirely familiar conception to the worshipping church. One would expect, too, that the collect—closely associated with the ever-varying lections—would be among the earliest prayers to vary with the day. But we have seen[1] that there is evidence that a generation after Damasus' death there was still no collect at all, fixed or variable, before the lections at Rome. It is—in the Roman rite at least—the prayers of the 'second *stratum*' in the liturgy—collect, prayer 'of the day', offertory prayer, thanksgiving, which, besides the preface, exhibit the impact of the calendar. But with the doubtful exception of the offertory prayer, all these make their first appearance in the Roman rite in the fifth century, not the fourth. And even after their acceptance, we may have to allow for a period during which they were still fixed and unchanging like the corresponding Eastern prayers, before the Western principle of variation was allowed to affect them.

No one can be better aware than I am of the fact that this argument rests only on inferences and probabilities, like that of Probst to which it is opposed. But on a question about which solid evidence is wholly lacking we can none of us do more than weigh inferences and probabilities and make our guess according to our lights (stating plainly that it is a guess and why we have come to our particular opinion).

On the whole, taking the usual Roman slowness to adopt liturgical novelties into account, I should not expect to find prayers varying with the calendar in the Roman rite much before A.D. 450, and I should not be greatly

[1] *Cf. pp.* 452, 457 *sq.*

surprised if it were one day shewn that they made their first appearance there only in the latter half of that century. For what its evidence is worth, the first Pope to whom the *Liber Pontificalis* assigns the composition of what look like such prayers is Gelasius (A.D. 492–496), who, it is said, wrote *praefationes* and *orationes* of the sacraments *cauto sermone* (? 'in a sober style').[1] Since we must guess on this matter, all things considered, the fifty years from *c.* A.D. 430–480 seem to me a much more likely period than that from *c.* A.D. 380–430 for the beginnings of the Roman variable prayers.

Some other Western churches may well have been beforehand with Rome in this matter. But there is another stage in the West of which we have evidence to be taken into account. This is the stage now represented by the Eastern rites, of *alternative* sets of prayers which contain no reference to the day in the calendar, but are simply alternatives to be used at choice, suitable in themselves for any day in the year.

We have noted the possibility that in Africa the bishop's blessing before communion was already a variable formula in Augustine's time.[2] Though the evidence in this particular case is weak, we can trace considerable activity in the field of new liturgical composition in Africa round about A.D. 400. In A.D. 397 the Council of Carthage had felt obliged to lay down in its twenty-fourth canon '(a) That no one in prayers should address the Father instead of the Son or the Son instead of the Father. (b) And when standing at the altar, the prayer shall always be addressed to the Father. (c) And if any one copies out prayers for himself from some source, he shall not use them unless he have first shewn them to his more instructed brethren.'

(a) here seems to refer to the appending of doxologies to any prayers; it is still easy enough forgetfully to end a collect addressed to the Father with the words 'Who livest and reignest with the Father . . .', and so on. (b) refers to the eucharistic prayer, and is a new restriction on an older liberty.[3] (c) may refer to private prayers, but from the context is probably to be taken as referring to bishops borrowing prayers from all sorts of sources to use in the public liturgy of their churches. In those days not all bishops were reckoned to be *ex officio* liturgical experts or even wary theologians. With the amount of Arian and other heretical literature then in circulation the council might reasonably feel nervous about the indiscriminate adoption into the official rites of their churches of everything which might happen to catch some bishops' fancy.

---

[1] Even this is ambiguous. I take it to mean liturgical compositions arranged in the form of 'address, pause and collect' of the old Western type (*cf. p.* 489). *Praefatio* never means 'preface' in our sense (of an introduction to the sanctus) but an 'address' to the people, in the *Gelasian Sacramentary* (*ed.* Wilson, *pp.* 53, 57). This statement of the *Lib. Pont.* could mean that Gelasius composed only 'homilies and discourses about the Sacraments', and not liturgical pieces at all, though I do not think that is what is intended.

[2] *Cf. p.* 517.   [3] *Cf. p.* 180.

THE SHAPE OF THE LITURGY

Five years later the African Council of Milevis had to return to the charge, and this time there is no beating about the bush. 'It was resolved ... that the prayers and collects or masses (*preces vel orationes seu missae*) which have been approved of in council, both "prefaces" and "commendations" or blessings (*sive praefationes sive commendationes seu manus impositiones*) shall be used (*celebrentur*) by all. Nor shall any others at all be said in the *ecclesia*, save such as shall have been drawn up or approved by the more prudent in synod, lest by chance anything should have been composed contrary to the faith, through either the ignorance or the deliberate purpose of any individual.' It is difficult to be sure of the exact distinction of meaning between some of the technical terms used here, or of the force of the conjunctions. But the canon is clearly provoked by the incapacity of some bishops as guardians of the liturgy in their churches. The position is sufficiently serious for the council to set about restricting the ancient liberty of every church to order its own rite, by issuing an official collection of prayers for use throughout the province. Evidently new prayers are making their appearance in some numbers; and this is expected to continue, since provision is made for the censorship of future episcopal compositions. The new official collection (from the fact that all the terms are in the plural) seems to have provided more than one formula for the same purpose, at least in certain cases. But there is nothing to suggest that the use of these alternative forms is to be regulated by the calendar.

This African book *c.* A.D. 400 seems to be a class of compilation midway between the Egyptian *Sacramentary of Sarapion c.* A.D. 340 and the Italian *Gelasian Sacramentary c.* A.D. 500. Sarapion gives the celebrant's prayers (and only the celebrant's) at all the rites of the church. It is a manual for fulfilling the bishop's 'liturgy', and nobody else's, at those rites. It represents the tradition of a single local church, enriched to some extent by borrowings from elsewhere (*e.g.* Alexandria),[1] but given the form in which it is set down by the single church of Thmuis. And it gives one formula for each purpose.[2] The prayers are fixed and invariable; there are no variations for feasts and fasts, no special forms for special occasions.

This African book of the Council of Milevis *c.* A.D. 400 seems to be still a collection of celebrant's prayers; but it represents a comparison and sifting of the local traditions of *a number* of individual churches There may have been a certain amount of re-writing and editing before publication. The very fact that it draws on the liturgical tradition of more than one church may be one reason why, unlike Sarapion's book, it contains more than one formula for some purposes, none of which are necessarily to be used on any particular day.

The *Gelasian Sacramentary c.* A.D. 500 is still chiefly a collection of cele-

---

[1] *Cf. p.* 165.
[2] Some of the intercessory prayers at the end of the synaxis in Sarapion may be intended as alternatives; at least they duplicate each other's contents to some extent. But I see no way of being certain of this.

brant's prayers for all sacramental rites; and for some of these (*e.g.* confirmation, ordination) it still gives only a single set of prayers to be used whenever needed, just like Sarapion. But at the eucharist all is now different. Certain prayers of the rite (collect etc.) have a large variety of alternatives; but each one is assigned to a particular day in the calendar or a particular 'intention', and is chiefly about the commemoration kept on that day, or concerned with that intention. (There is the 'pool' of prayers for 'green' Sundays, and a small amount of repetition, but that is the principle.) The calendar has taken almost complete control of the variable prayers. Only for days when the calendar contains no special commemoration does the Gelasian book provide a number of variable prayers for different 'intentions', for the sick, for a barren wife desiring children, and so on. This domination by the calendar is the special characteristic of all extant Western books from *c.* A.D. 500 onwards. And its development is (to my mind) the special mark left by the fifth century on the history of all the Western rites.

### The Preface and Sanctus in the West

I am encouraged to believe that this is a true account and dating of the Western 'variability according to the calendar' by what little can be made out of the development of a Western 'variable' of which we have hitherto said nothing—the 'preface' in the modern sense of an introduction to the sanctus. In all Western rites alike, whatever their treatment of the body of the eucharistic prayer, the first paragraph of that prayer leading up to the sanctus is variable to some extent, and I happen to have come upon some hitherto unused evidence as to how and when this came to be so.

Hippolytus' prayer *c.* A.D. 200 has no sanctus and strictly speaking no 'preface' in the later sense, *i.e.* no description of the angelic worship leading up to the words of the angelic hymn. Instead it opens with a 'thanksgiving series' like all such pre-Nicene prayers. The present Roman canon and all Gallican eucharistic prayers have no such 'thanksgiving *series*', but instead open with a 'thanksgiving' in quite general terms, leading up (on festivals or other special days) to a commemoration of the day. This is followed by a description of the worship of heaven with a climax in the earthly church's participation in the song of the angels, 'Holy, holy, holy'. The prayer then proceeds somewhat abruptly to what corresponds to the 'second half' of the pre-Nicene prayers. The preface and sanctus have thus replaced the pre-Nicene 'thanksgiving series' in all the Western rites, somewhere between Hippolytus (*c.* A.D. 200) and—at the latest—S. Gregory I (*c.* A.D. 600). How has this happened?

We have seen that the sanctus, preceded by an account of the angels' worship, is to be traced at Alexandria in the works of Origen *c.* A.D. 230 and probably goes back in the Alexandrian use to a period well before that date.[1] But we have also seen that at Alexandria it originally formed not the introduction before but the conclusion after the 'thanksgiving series'; *i.e.* it was the climax of the doxology after the most ancient part of the Alexandrian prayer.[2] The description of the heavenly worship and the sanctus make their appearance for the first time in Syria in Cyril of Jerusalem in A.D. 347, in a form clearly borrowed from Egypt. But in Syria they are no longer in the Egyptian position *after* the 'thanksgiving series'. Where the 'thanksgiving series' has been retained (as at Antioch) the preface and sanctus have been placed before them; where the 'thanksgiving series' has been lost (as at Jerusalem) the preface and sanctus have been substituted for them. In Syria in the fourth century the preface and sanctus thus appear for the first time as an 'introduction' to the eucharistic prayer, as they appear in the Western rites during the fifth-sixth centuries.

The suggestion that the preface and sanctus in the Western rites are one more importation from Syria is borne out by a curious piece of evidence. In Origen and the Egyptian rites, in all the Greek rites and in Greek authors generally, the text of the liturgical sanctus runs, 'Holy, holy, holy, Lord of Sabaoth', following the text of Is. vi. In the Syriac liturgies alone of the Eastern rites, it runs 'Lord *God* of Sabaoth'. And all the Western rites have this Syrian interpolation, 'God'. Nor do I think that anyone who compares the ordinary non-festal form of the preface in the Roman rite with that found in *Ap. Const.*, viii.[3] will have any doubt as to where this particular Western preface comes from; it is a simplified form of the ordinary 'lead up to' the sanctus in the Syrian rite.

We can most conveniently begin the consideration of the history of the adoption of this Syrian custom of prefixing the preface and sanctus to the eucharistic prayers of the West with the third canon of the South French Council of Vaison in A.D. 529: 'At all masses, whether early masses (*matutinis*) or in Lent or in those which are offered for the commemoration of the dead, *Sanctus, sanctus, sanctus* should be said in that arrangement (*eo ordine*) in which it is now said at public masses'. Here the sanctus is already a part of the South French rite, but it is customary to omit it at requiems and in penitential seasons, and also apparently at what we should call 'low' or 'private' masses, *i.e.* supplementary masses said in the early morning before the bishop's 'stational' mass (or at all events before the 'public' or 'high' mass, to use the later term). The sanctus is in fact a special feature of the stational liturgy on Sundays and saints' days, precisely as the *Gloria* in the contemporary Roman rite was restricted to the bishop's 'stational' liturgy on such days, and was omitted in penitential and other non-festal masses and also in the supplementary masses said by presbyters. And since the main tenor of this third canon of Vaison in other matters is the bringing of South French custom into conformity with what it has become customary to do elsewhere and especially in what it calls 'the Apostolic see',

[1] *Cf. p.* 165.    [2] *Cf. p.* 221.    [3] Brightman, L.E.W., *p.* 118, *ll.* 24 *sq.*

it would not be surprising if the use of the sanctus indiscriminately at all masses was then a fairly recent modification at Rome of a previous practice of using the sanctus only at the 'stational' liturgy on Sundays and saints' days. But on this we have no Roman evidence.

When did the use of the sanctus at all in the Western rites first begin? S. Ambrose at Milan just before A.D. 400 in describing the opening of the eucharistic prayer to the catechumens in *de Sacramentis* uses the following phrase: 'All the other things which are said in the earlier part (of the prayer) are said by the priest—praises are offered to God (*laudes Deo deferuntur*), prayer is asked for kings, for the people and the rest; when it comes to the consecration of the venerable sacrament, the priest no longer speaks in his own name, but he uses the words of Christ'.[1] Were it not that these 'praises' are said specifically to be 'said by the priest' it would be natural to take them as referring to the people's hymn of the sanctus. As it stands, and taken in conjunction with other evidence about to be produced, we must, I think, take it as referring to the initial 'thanksgiving series', still standing intact at the opening of the Western eucharistic prayer *c.* A.D. 400. After all, this is precisely the way in which Justin had spoken of that 'thanksgiving series' standing at the opening of the Roman prayer *c.* A.D. 150: the bishop 'sends up praise and glory to the Father'.[2] The sanctus does not appear to be mentioned by Ambrose.

The same seems to be the case with the African rite as described by Ambrose' convert, S. Augustine (d. A.D. 430). Again and again he reminds his people in his sermons of the preliminary dialogue and cites its exact words. Never once does he hint that it leads up to a hymn sung by themselves, though one would have thought that he had left himself no option but to allude to it, if it then stood in the African rite.[3] Nor is there any allusion to the sanctus in the rite of Rome or Gubbio in the letter of Pope Innocent I to Decentius *c.* A.D. 415, though it deals specifically with just this part of the service.

Chance has, as a matter of fact, preserved for us the opening paragraphs of two Latin eucharistic prayers of this period which explain the whole situation (and incidentally, I think, shed light on the meaning of Innocent I). They have been unaccountably neglected by all the liturgists of the nineteenth and twentieth centuries, but they shew us what the opening of the Latin eucharistic prayers was like before the adoption of the Syrian preface and sanctus. They thus enable us on this particular matter to get behind the later divergence of the Franco-Spanish and Italian groups of liturgies, to the basic 'Western' type. In 1827 Cardinal Mai published from a Milanese MS. some fragments of a controversial work which has the almost unique distinction of being written by a Western Arian. This author's argument is that the catholics do in practice subordinate the Son

---

[1] S. Ambrose, *de Sacramentis*, iv. 4. 14.    [2] Justin, *Ap.*, I. 65, cited on *p.* 222.
[3] *E.g. Serm.*, liii. 14.

to the Father just as much as do the Arians themselves; witness the texts of
their own official catholic prayers. After quoting from the exorcism of the
catechumens, the baptismal creed and the formula of confirmation, he
continues: they do the same 'in their oblations saying:

*A*1. "It is meet and right that we should here and in all places give
thanks unto Thee, O Lord holy, almighty God; nor is there any other
through whom we can have access unto Thee, make prayer unto Thee,
offer sacrifice unto Thee, save by Him Whom Thou hast sent unto us etc."
'And again:

*B*1. "It is meet and right, it is just and right, that we should above all
things give thanks unto Thee, O Lord holy, Father almighty, everlasting
God, Who hast deigned to shine on our darkness by the incomparable light
of Thy goodness, sending unto us Jesus Christ the Saviour of our souls:

2. "Who humbling Himself for the sake of our salvation subjected Himself even unto death, that He might restore us to that immortality which
Adam had forfeited (and) make us heirs and sons to Him.

3. "We cannot worthily give thanks to Thy great mercy for such loving
kindness nor praise Thee; but we pray Thee of Thy great and merciful
love to hold accepted this sacrifice which we offer unto Thee, standing
before the face of Thy divine love, through Jesus Christ our Lord and God:
through Whom we pray and beseech . . ." ' (here the quotation breaks off).[1]

The date of this document can unfortunately only be fixed vaguely,
between *c.* A.D. 380 and 450 (or even a little later). It probably comes from
N. Italy as Mai suggested.[2] The Arian has evidently got hold of the sacramentary of the local church. This contains only one set of formulae for
baptism and confirmation (like Sarapion and the *Gelasian Sacramentary*)
but *alternative* eucharistic prayers (like the Eastern rites and (?) the African
collection of Milevis). Both of these N. Italian prayers are related to the
Roman canon, but probably as 'brothers' rather than as ancestors. They
are specimens of Italian local rites, much as Sarapion is a specimen of an

---

[1] A. Mai. *Scriptorum Veterum Nova Collectio.* t. iii. (1827) pt. ii., *p.* 208 *sq.* (As
these texts are difficult of access I give them for the convenience of students.)
'. . . *in oblationibus suis dicentes:* (A)(1) *Dignum et iustum est nos tibi hic et ubique
gratias agere, Domine sancte, omnipotens Deus; neque est alius per quem ad te aditum
habere, praecem facere, sacrificationem tibi offerre possimus nisi per quem tu nobis
misisti etc.* Item (B) (1) *Dignum et iustum est, aequum et iustum est nos tibi super omnia
gratias agere, Domine sancte, Pater omnipotens, aeterne Deus, qui incomparabili tuae
bonitatis ⟨luce⟩ in tenebris fulgere dignatus es, mittens nobis J. X̄tm̄ suspitatorem ani-
marum nostrarum* (2) *qui nostra⟨e⟩ salutis causa humiliando se ad mortem usque
subiecit ut nos ea quae Adam amiserat immortalitate restitutos efficeret sibi heredes et
filios.* (3) *Cuius benignitatis agere gratias tuae tantae magnanimitati quibusque laudibus
nec sufficere possumus petentes de tua magna et flexibili pietate accepto (l. acceptum)
ferre sacrificium istud, quod tibi offerimus stantes ante conspectum tuae divinae pietatis
per J. X̄tm̄. Dn̄m̄. et D̄m̄. nostrum: per quem, petimus et rogamus . . .*'
[2] G. Mercati (*Studi e Testi,* vii., 1902, *p.* 55) suggested the Danubian provinces
as an alternative.  But comparison of the baptismal texts it cites with those later
published in Dom Wilmart's *North Italian Services of the 11th Cent.* (H.B.S., 1931)
leaves no doubt that these are from the same region, though much earlier.

Egyptian local rite, from the period before the influence of the great sees had overwhelmed the local traditions. Of the first fragment nothing need be said save that it still represents the eucharist as the *parousia* of the church 'in Christ' before the Father in the old eschatological style, and that one or two other small points suggest that it may be rather older than the second. In the latter the remains of the old 'thanksgiving series' are plain in (1) and (2). And it is continued far enough for us to be sure by a comparison with the Roman prayer that it has reached the equivalent of the *Te igitur* paragraph without any 'preface' (in the later sense) or sanctus at all.

It is possible that we are not wholly without information about the transformation of this kind of opening into the preface and sanctus in the Western rites. It has always been the tradition of the church of Milan that its bishop, Eusebius (A.D. 451–465 or 6) was responsible for a wholesale rebuilding of the churches of his diocese devastated by the Gothic invasion, in the course of which he renewed their burned service books; he is also traditionally credited with the authorship of the Milanese 'proper' prefaces for the greatest feasts of the year. A recent examination of these has revealed an agreement in a rather unusual use of the *cursus* (prose rhythm of the *clausulae* of Latin sentences) between these texts and the only extant epistle of Eusebius, and also the use in one of them of a life of S. Nazarius traditionally ascribed to his authorship.[1] The arguments are not absolutely decisive; in the circumstances that is hardly to be expected. But so far as they go, they definitely support the tradition of his authorship of these, the oldest of the Milanese prefaces. And Ennodius, who knew him, tells us that he was a Greek from Syria.[2] Once more we are pointed towards Syria as the source of the Western preface and sanctus, and about the middle of the fifth century as the date of its introduction. And the preface is one of the Western variable prayers.

Milan in S. Ambrose' day had followed 'the customs of the Roman church in all things', even though he felt that this need not exclude the addition of local Milanese customs.[3] Eusebius may have been imitating a recent Roman innovation, or he may equally well have been showing the Roman church the way. The Syrian hymn could not be inserted into the old Latin prayers without some readjustment, and a clause leading up to it. If its use was at first restricted to festal occasions, the simplest way was to substitute some commemoration of the particular feast which was the occasion for the use of the sanctus that day, for the old 'thanksgiving series' as it now stood, telescoped to some extent, as in the Italian prayers on *p.* 540. And this is precisely what all the oldest Italian proper prefaces,

[1] A. Paredi, *I Prefazi ambrosiani*, Milan, 1937. (On the date and origin of the later Milanese prefaces see Dom Wilmart, *Ephemerides Liturgicae*, L (1936), *pp.* 169 sqq.)
[2] Ennodius, *Carmina*, II. 86.
[3] S. Ambrose, *de Sacramentis*, iii. 1. 5.

Roman or Milanese, do—leaving the equivalent of paragraphs (1) and (3) in that Italian prayer (B) intact. All this suggests that the 'proper' prefaces are older than the 'common' form, since it was only on special days that the sanctus, and therefore an introduction to it, were needed.

The extension of the use of the sanctus from festivals to all celebrations without exception (contemplated by the Council of Vaison only in A.D. 529) raised the question how it was to be introduced on non-festal occasions, when there was no special commemoration obviously suggesting itself to replace the general 'thanksgiving' for the saving work of Christ. The Gallican and Mozarabic rites, followed in this respect by the Milanese, solved the problem by providing a 'proper' introduction to the sanctus for every occasion for which they provided other 'proper' prayers—*i.e.* for every liturgical day or occasion in the year. The Roman rite, equally characteristically, solved it by providing a single form of preface for all occasions except those great feasts, on which alone the sanctus had at first been used in the West, and which therefore already had their own 'proper' forms. And it found this common form in a simplified and abbreviated version of the single invariable introduction to the sanctus in the Syrian rite from which the use of the sanctus had originally been borrowed in the West.[1]

### The East and the West

We have here, in this little matter of the preface and sanctus, something which is singularly representative of the relations and contrasts of the various types of rite which are growing up in the fifth century. The Syrian rite of the fourth century had borrowed the preface and sanctus from the old pre-Nicene Egyptian tradition, but it had put it to a new use. And it is the new Syrian usage, not the original Egyptian one, which spreads all over christendom in the fifth century, so that it soon presents the appearance of a custom so universal as to be taken for something very ancient if not apostolic. But though they accept the new custom from Syria the Western churches at once transform it to their own mind and spirit, whereas the other Eastern rites preserve it, not in its original Egyptian form or position, but very much in the form in which they have borrowed it from Syria.

The variable preface is something more than an expression of the peculiarly Western influence of the calendar on the prayers of the rite. Over against the single invariable lengthy Eastern preface, the shorter mutable Western ones are the product of something different in Western *history* from that of the East. The Eastern pattern of religion is something

[1] Of the Roman books the *Leonine Sacr.* has 267 'proper' prefaces, the *Gelasian* 54 and the *Gregorian* 13. This looks like a steady diminution of the Roman use of 'proper' prefaces. But Dom P. Alfonzo, *L'Uso dei prefazi nei Sacramentari Romani, Eph. Lit.*, liii. (1939), *pp.* 245 *sqq.*, has shewn from other evidence that the large number of prefaces in *Le.* and *Gel.* represents Italian provincial not local Roman usage, and that the restraint of *Greg.* continued traditional Roman custom. (I am not sure *Greg.* did not increase the Roman proper prefaces by one.)

immutable, hieratic, timeless, seeking always to transcend temporal life. The Western idea of religion on the contrary is something more supple and practical, which seeks always to pervade the temporal with the spiritual, and clings closer to the things of time in the certainty that time has been and is being redeemed. It is inevitable that such differences of approach should express themselves in the different fashion of their prayers.

And in the slighter differences between the various Western expressions of the common Western principle, too, we can discern something which is the product of difference of history. Despite certain superficial approximations to the Eastern rites due to deliberate later borrowings, the French and Spanish rites in their perpetual mutability are at the opposite extreme of spirit from the unvarying Eastern rites. And the Roman rite which geographically stands between them, is between them, too, in the fashion of its prayers, with its relatively fixed and unchanging canon like the Eastern rites, and its ever changing lesser prayers like those of the other Western churches. Right down to the eighth century, even in some measure down to the eleventh, Rome is not, properly speaking, a truly 'Western' church. The Greek emperor at Constantinople is still its temporal ruler, and though an absentee, by no means always a mere distant figure-head—as several Popes, dragged to Constantinople as prisoners and there bullied or murdered, were to find. In the city itself a large Greek-speaking population served by Greek clergy followed Eastern rites with a wholly Eastern way of devotion; and there were Greek and Syrian and Egyptian monasteries in Rome. Some of these orientals were from time to time elected to the throne of S. Peter (*e.g.* Zosimus, Hormisdas, Sergius I) just as the Spaniard Damasus and the Sardinian Hilary or the Tuscan Leo I could be chosen by the Roman clergy and people as the most suitable cleric of that church available, no less than the Romans Gregory or Hadrian. Despite the breakdown of easy communications in the fifth century, the subsequent Popes are as unavoidably involved in the interminable theologico-political wranglings of Eastern patriarchs and the successive attempts of Byzantine emperors to enforce new heresies upon their subjects, on the one hand, as they are concerned on the other with the evangelisation of Kent or Frisia, or the establishment of the new national kingdom of the Franks with its promise of a more stable and peaceful government in France. Rome is still not only the heart of Western christendom, but the meeting point of East and West. And its liturgy reflects the fact.

Yet we should be mistaken if we took this to mean that it was merely a passive centre where foreign traditions converged and fused of their own native force without assimilation. The action upon all these foreign ideas of the local Roman liturgical tradition, with its special gifts of terseness and sobriety and the old Roman *gravitas*, is unmistakable and potent. What Rome took over from Syria or Gaul it took in its own way and re-moulded to its own mind, just as (in the case of the preface and sanctus)

Syria had made a new use of a custom borrowed from Egypt, and the West in turn gave a new twist to the borrowed Syrian introduction to the sanctus by subjecting it to the influence of the calendar. But it was of incalculable importance that throughout the dark ages Rome kept a foot in either world, and was concerned with both, as neither East nor West was then concerned with the other. East and West had been drifting apart since the third century, though the universal empire and the oecumenical catholicism of the fourth century had done much to draw them together again. The break-down of communications in the fifth century which accompanied the collapse of the Western empire, and the break-down of ecclesiastical intercommunion in the fifth and sixth centuries through the repeated breaches between Constantinople and Egypt, and Constantinople and Syria, and Constantinople and the West, are twin signs and causes of the break-up of the old oecumenical catholicism. Behind them all is the steady endeavour of 'the royal church' (as Constantinople proudly called itself) to assert the theocratic power of the Byzantine emperor—the baptised Diocletian—over the faith of the universal church. Perhaps the most fatal of all these breaches in its final consequences, though not the most remarked, was that which involved the virtual exclusion of Alexandria from christendom after the Council of Chalcedon (A.D. 451). Ever since the days of Athanasius his church had been the link between Rome and the real East. It was a tragedy for christendom that Rome was forced to side with Constantinople on the point of orthodoxy at Chalcedon by the heresies of the Alexandrian patriarch Dioscorus. The dropping out of Alexandria—excommunicated by both churches—left Rome and Constantinople face to face. The sundering of christendom into Eastern and Western fragments behind these two centres was inevitable after that; and the later development of each half suffers badly from one-sidedness.

Yet for centuries the old understanding of christendom as a single body persists even across the barriers of excommunication, and men feel the unity of worship and an interest in each other's liturgy, even while quarrelling most violently about dogma. Just as there are for many centuries Syrian monks in Rome, so there are Frankish monks at Jerusalem; and it is typical of the difference in receptivity of the two churches that while the Papal rite adopted the Syrian *Agnus Dei* from the former, the Greeks made a riot and ultimately a schism about the use of the *Filioque* by the latter. Despite the break-down of communications (which affects the West much more than the East) and the rending of christendom (which, through the Monophysite and Nestorian schisms, affects the East much more than the West) liturgical documents and customs continue to travel unpredictably like thistledown throughout the dark ages, carried by scores of anonymous pilgrims and monks and traders and refugees. The purest extant MSS. of the Alexandrian liturgy of *S. Mark* were copied in Sicily and Calabria; the Roman mass turns up in Georgian and Armenian translations (with the addition of an Egyptian invocation) in the Caucasus in the eleventh century, having travelled by way of Albania and Mt. Athos and Thessalonica, and been put into Greek on the way; the first appearance in the West of Greek litanies of the saints from Asia Minor is in the monasteries of Anglo-Saxon England.

The break-up of the old imperial world in the fifth century, and the break-up of christian unity in the sixth, do result in real liturgical divergences between East and West, and between regions within the larger fragments. But this curious impalpable web of liturgical transmissions does something to keep the lines of demarcation from growing hard and rigid. And the peg upon which this was hung was the surviving oecumenical position and interests of Rome, which all men still recognised in East and West alike as part of their own inherited tradition. The re-establishment of a Western emperor in the person of Charlemagne in A.D. 80ͻ was a blow to the tenderest point of Byzantine pride. The Pope's shaιe in this weakened many of Rome's Eastern contacts, and henceforward Rome becomes increasingly a Western church. Thereafter these 'underground' liturgical transmissions grow fewer, and Eastern and Western worship develops in isolation for more than two centuries. Yet it is no accident that when the East and West met again face to face in the Crusades, after a virtual separation of 300 years, they thought and spoke of ιach other respectively as 'Franks' and 'Byzantines', but each still thought and spoke of themselves (and still do to this day) as 'Romans'.[1]

The admission of the new influence of the calendar on the prayers is perhaps the greatest single innovation in the liturgy which the West ever made for itself. As a rule it had hitherto been the East which had innovated and the West which had followed. But a new state of affairs is beginning, in which East and West go their separate ways. The rise of this new and Western peculiarity in the fifth century is only a sign that divergence has begun. It is upon this background that we must set the later developments.

[1] *Ekklesia roumike* still means in the Near East a Byzantine or Orthodox church, not a Latin one.

# CHAPTER XV

## THE MEDIAEVAL DEVELOPMENT

### A. The Development of the Eastern Rites

THE main lines of all the Eastern traditions had been reached before the end of the fourth century, and after this the process in all of them is no more than one of adjustment and development of detail. No new principle arose in the fifth century, as it did in the West, to give a new turn to liturgical development. After the sixth century the process resembles to this extent that which we shall find in the West, in that it is one of approximation between all the Eastern rites, as there is after this date an approximation between all the Western rites. And in both cases the basis chosen is the rite of the 'holy city', Jerusalem in the East, Rome in the West. But in each case it is the rite of the holy city as modified in the dominant political centre, Byzantium in the East, the Frankish homelands of Gaul and the Rhineland in the West.

But there the resemblance between the Eastern and Western process of development ends, for the methods pursued in the two halves of christendom were different. The comparative freedom in which the churches were left to achieve the process in the West results in a real synthesis, in which the old local rites each contribute a good deal to the final result, and lose themselves in it. The methods employed in the East were different, consisting in political pressure and compulsory Byzantinisation. Not only did the Byzantine rite itself assimilate little or nothing from other sources after the sixth century, but the attempt was made to enforce its local development verbally and identically on all the churches which the emperor could reach.[1] The legacy of Byzantine bureaucracy was too bitter for such

---

[1] A characteristic example of the Byzantine mind is to be found in the great canonist Theodore Balsamon. In A.D. 1194 the Greek patriarch of Alexandria then visiting Constantinople caused a scandal in the capital by celebrating according to the rite of his own church, S. Mark, and alarmed at the outcry, consulted Balsamon as to the lawfulness of the use of S. Mark and S. James. Balsamon replies that 'the catholic church of the most holy and oecumenical throne of Constantinople in no way recognises these liturgies. We declare therefore that they ought not to be received. And even if they were written by these saints they ought to be condemned to entire disuse . . . all the churches of God ought to follow the custom of New Rome, that is Constantinople' (and use S. Basil and S. John Chrysostom); for the emperor Justinian had ordered 'On all points on which there is no written law, the custom obtaining at Constantinople shall be followed' (Balsamon, Responsa, I, M.P.G., cxxxviii, 953). The interesting thing is that Balsamon was at this time Greek patriarch of Antioch, and yet had never even troubled to discover whether there did or did not exist a liturgy of S. James, the traditional rite of his own see! He knew of it only by hearsay from the Trullan canons. Along with S. Mark (centuries older than the Byzantine rite) it is swept into limbo on the strength of a misapplied sentence from Justinian. Literally dozens of examples of this disastrous

tactics ever to succeed. The dissidents retained their liturgical independence of Constantinople by remaining outside the pale of orthodoxy.

But though the direct attempt of Constantinople to enforce its own liturgy failed entirely to bring about liturgical uniformity in the East, the general tendency, of which this was only a political perversion, to adopt a Syrian liturgy of the Jerusalem-Antioch type, has since operated throughout the East by voluntary 'Syrianisation'. The Egyptian monophysite version of S. Mark was heavily revised with borrowings from S. James and S. Basil in the fifth or sixth century. Later (? in the ninth century) it was replaced altogether, except on the Friday before Palm Sunday, by two alternative Syrian liturgies, a version of S. Basil (older than the present Byzantine text in some respects), and a liturgy addressed to the Son ascribed for some reason to S. Gregory.[1] (There is no reason to suppose it has anything to do with him.) So the tradition which had come down at Alexandria from the apostolic age through Athanasius and Cyril was laid aside at Alexandria by the Copts. The Greeks after heavily Byzantinising it for a while, abandoned it altogether at the end of the twelfth century in obedience to Balsamon. Only the three dioceses of Uniat Copts now use S. Mark (or S. Cyril as they call it) even once a year.

The East Syrian rite of Addai and Mari has likewise acquired a considerable number of Antioch-Jerusalem characteristics at various times since the fifth century; and two alternative liturgies of the ordinary Antiochene type, ascribed to Nestorius and Theodore of Mopsuestia, have been brought into use. The Armenian rite has been affected both by the Byzantine version of the Syrian rite and by the Syrian rite of S. James itself, to the extent of becoming practically a rite of the Syrian type; though it still retains a few interesting native features, and some Latin borrowings it picked up in Crusading times.

The Byzantine rite itself,[2] clearly of Antiochene-Syrian derivation, continued to develop along its own lines down to the seventh century and did not become absolutely rigid until the ninth century. (Two complete revisions of the lectionary, for instance, can be traced in the seventh and the eighth centuries, none since). After that date only continual minor verbal changes in the prayers of the liturgy, and the accumulation of supplementary devotions during and before the preparation of the elements, can be

frame of mind could be given from Byzantine authors from the sixth century onwards. The result in this case was the final disuse of the Greek rite of Alexandria by the Greek church of Alexandria.

[1] There is reason to think that other liturgies than that of Alexandria continued in use in some Egyptian country churches, both in Greek and Coptic, as late as the eighth–tenth centuries (at least on occasion), but no complete texts have survived.

[2] The liturgy of S. John Chrysostom is something of a puzzle. It is not the ancient Constantinopolitan rite of the days of Chrysostom himself, as his citations shew. (I incline to think traces of this survive in the E. Syrian Liturgy of Nestorius.) S. John Chrysostom is probably a late sixth century composition put together at Constantinople on the Antiochene model. S. Basil appears to have come originally from Asia Minor, though it has been in some things 'Antiochenised'.

traced. It is now used with only the slightest verbal differences throughout the orthodox world in a variety of translations; and once there ceased to be a Byzantine emperor looming behind it, its prayers and ceremonies and customs (*e.g.* the *ikonostasion*) have increasingly affected the rites and churches of the dissidents, especially in modern times.

We in the West are accustomed to speak of the 'unchanging East' and its 'immemorial rites'. It is as well to be clear that this is a state of things which only begins in the seventh century. Before that date the East had shewn more tendency to innovate in the liturgy than the West, particularly in the fourth and fifth centuries; and its rites, if they shew fewer signs of later development than those of the West, underwent much more drastic changes in that period than has been generally realised. What caused them to cease to develop in the seventh and to grow rigid after the ninth century is a matter for discussion. It is worth noting that this rather sudden ossification is a phenomenon which is found at about the same period in the whole artistic and mental life of the world that looked to Constantinople. But so far as the liturgy is concerned I believe that the use of the term 'arrested development' is unjust and untrue. It is only a case of 'completed development'. Without some fresh principle, such as the effect of the calendar on the prayers gave to the Western rites, the Eastern rites simply had no further possibilities of growth along their own lines. They were complete and satisfying expressions of the eucharistic action and its meaning according to the tradition of the churches which used them. There was nothing more to be said, nothing to be added. And into the closed world of Byzantium no really fresh impulse ever came after the sixth century. The Byzantine state had exhausted its own traditions by the ninth century, and then became mummified and finally disappeared. The Byzantine church survived it because it is the church, though the Phanar, 'the royal church' of Constantinople itself, has done little since to make that survival either fruitful or dignified. Orthodoxy is a far greater and more christian thing than Byzantinism—rich in faith and holiness and above all in martyrs. Until this last twenty years it was still possible (though unfair) to call it a 'sleeping church'. But that sleep began not with the rule of the Turks in 1453, but in the ninth century, perhaps even earlier, in the sixth after Justinian. It will be fascinating to see what it makes of its magnificent patristic heritage in the modern world when it has been everywhere set free from its old entanglement with autocracy. One thing it will assuredly keep is the Byzantine rite by which all orthodoxy worships, and has saved itself from extinction by worshipping. This is the joint creation of Greek christian theology and the old Hellenic poetic spirit, working together on a Syrian rite. Along with the *Digest* of Justinian it is the greatest legacy of Byzantine thought to the world.

## B. The Development of the Western Rites

The Western development is more complicated and diverse and continued for much longer. It will occupy the remainder of this chapter, and can most conveniently be set out by following up separately the various regional developments which come to their synthesis in the tenth century, and then continuing from that. But there are certain essential general observations which must be borne in mind all through, if we are to understand the matter.

The importance and interest of the special developments of the Gallican and Mozarabic rites have been much obscured in modern study. This is due partly to the fact that they have been for so many centuries virtually museum pieces, and it is correspondingly difficult to enter into their particular spirit. Partly also it is due to less excusable mistakings of their history and significance, the most serious of which is the persistent attempt to find for them a non-Western origin. These rites certainly contain Eastern elements (like the *Aios* and the *Kyries* and the *Sanctus*), just as the Roman rite contains Eastern elements (like the *Kyries* and the *Sanctus* and the *Agnus Dei*), and for the same reason—the deliberate piecemeal borrowing, now of one item, now of another, from Eastern and especially from Syrian sources. The Gallican and Mozarabic rites contain rather more of these items than the Roman only because Rome rather less readily admitted innovations from any source. But in all the Western rites these Eastern borrowings are relatively late and of superficial importance, matters of decoration rather than of substance. Structurally and in their fundamental spirit and origin these French and Spanish rites are as Western as any in Italy. Such structural differences as they exhibit from the Roman rite are due to slightly different arrangements of those lesser prayers of the 'second *stratum*', which only began to be introduced one by one into any of the Western rites about or after A.D. 400.

The question has often been debated as to the relation of these rites with those of Rome and Africa. Attempts have been made to shew that Africa used the 'Gallican' rite, or alternatively that it used the Roman. It has been held that the so-called 'Gallican' rite is really the original form of the Roman, faithfully preserved in the provinces when the mother-church (secretly and without record) turned its own rite upside down; or alternatively, that the churches of France and Spain originally used the pure Roman rite and that the whole of the Gallican and Mozarabic liturgical development in a novel and rootless local experiment of the dark ages. I can only say that this whole way of regarding the matter has come to seem to me not only mistaken but perversely unhistorical. And I suspect that it is not unconnected (however unconsciously) with partisan positions, for and against, on the modern problem of 'Rome'. In reality it is wholly unwarrantable to read back into the fifth and sixth centuries—or for the matter of that with any rigour into the seventh or even the eighth centuries, though the conception was developing about then—anything like the modern conception of 'rites' as defined and separate entities, ranged alongside one another in conscious difference and even in rivalry. Who is going to tell us whether the compilers of the *Bobbio Missal* or the *Missale Francorum* on the one hand, or the various Frankish 'Gelasian' missals on the other, supposed their books with their heterogeneous contents to be books of the 'Gallican' or the 'Roman' rites? Even with modern scientific methods of classification it is difficult, sometimes impossible, to decide; and what is quite clear is that the compilers themselves never even asked themselves the question. In the fifth and even sixth century, as in the fourth, there were still no 'rites' in our modern sense, but only 'the liturgy', which everyone knew to be the same thing everywhere. Every local church had its own traditional way of doing it, which it was free to revise or augment or improve as it saw fit, from its own inventions or by borrowings from elsewhere. There were tentative efforts after local uniformity, like those of the Councils of Milevis and Vaison; but they were still occasioned by local circumstances, and limited and temporary in their real effect on what went on in practice at the altars in the churches. In every church contemporary fashions and novelties had their own attractions in each generation. Local tradition still played a preponderating part. In the long run *racial* temperament and characteristics (rather than geographical distinctions) made their different and immensely powerful influences felt on the wording of prayers and above all on the character of devotion and rites. In the circumstances this was inevitable; there were as yet no artificial national unities in the West, and Europe was in the melting pot. We know little enough about the African rites. But to an impartial view even the scanty evidence available indicates that they were neither 'Roman' nor 'Gallican' but *African*—the local development of the pre-Nicene African tradition, enriched by borrowings from other churches, not only Western but Eastern, but the whole moulded by the mind and spirit of the African local churches. The passage from the African sixth century prayer cited by Fulgentius (*p.* 297) indicates that it was *not* variable like the contemporary French and Spanish prayers. But it certainly is not 'Roman' any more than it is 'Gallican', though it is quite easily recognisable as Western'.

And it was the same elsewhere. All the Western rites have their roots in the old pre-Nicene tradition, which as regards the Shape of the Liturgy was oecumenically the same. As regards the contents of the prayer the Western rites as a group have preserved the old conceptions of the eucharist more faithfully in some things than those of the East, which underwent more radical changes during the fourth century. Certain peculiarities common to the whole of the West (*e.g.* the 'naming' in connection with the offertory) make their appearance in the fourth century, and grow into real distinctions from the Eastern rites during the fifth and sixth centuries. (This is partly the result of *different* innovations being made simultaneously in the East.) All this is a consequence of the need for adapting the eucharist to a public worship. Most important of all for the future, the new Western principle of varying the prayers according to the calendar makes its appearance in the fifth century and is applied by the various Western churches in rather different ways, or perhaps it is truer to say, to a varying extent. In the course of the sixth–seventh century, when political confusion is great and intercourse between the Western churches much interrupted, these local Western differences in the application of a common principle harden into real distinctions, obvious to all and disconcerting to some minds, *e.g.* to that of S. Augustine of Canterbury.[1] The Roman 'rite', the Milanese and Beneventan 'rites', the Gallican 'rite', the Mozarabic 'rite', in our modern sense, are all substantially products of this period—it might even be said of the single sixth century. But in A.D. 600 men were not yet conscious of them as separate things, but still thought of them rather as different ways of doing the same thing. Each is the outcome of a local tradition and a local *population* living a local history; each is subject to particular influences from outside, as well as to local developments, working diversely upon the roughly similar basis all had inherited from the fixed rites of the fourth century, under the new influence of the ecclesiastical year and the calendar.

### The Development of the French and Spanish Rites

Viewed thus, as the native and characteristic products of the French and Spanish churches of the fifth and sixth centuries from their old liturgical tradition, the Gallican and Mozarabic rites come into their own, by coming into real life. They are the living response of French and Spanish *christianity* to the sordid and desperate times when Europe had collapsed and civilisation was struggling for a tolerable existence and the Faith had somehow to redeem to christian goodness whole populations of uncouth and violent men and women. As such these rites have an exciting interest. And it is possible, I think, to shew that though they did not formally persist much beyond the dark ages which gave them this particular form, they yet handed on a permanent element to that synthesis of Western liturgy which is the slow work of the seventh to the tenth centuries.

The outstanding peculiarity of these rites is their treatment of the eucharistic prayer, in which, except for the text of the sanctus and the paragraph containing the narrative of the institution, the whole eucharistic prayer is varied, or 'proper', on every liturgical occasion. Both in France and Spain this prayer consists always of five paragraphs:

[1] *Cf. p.* 576.

1. The *Contestatio, Illatio* or *Immolatio*, or as we should say, 'preface'.

2. The *Sanctus*, sung by the people.

3. A short paragraph, linking sanctus and consecration, known as the *Post-Sanctus*.

4. The institution-narrative, said in silence and known therefore as *Mysterium* or *Secreta*.

5. A prayer for the communicants, later changed to one for the offerings, as communions became infrequent, known as *Post-Mysterium, Post-Secreta*, or *Post-Pridie*.

Let us take examples. Here is the prayer of the eighth century *Missale Gothicum* (French) for the feast of the Epiphany:

*Contestatio:* 'It is truly meet and right, just and right,[1] that we should always and everywhere give thanks unto Thee, O Lord holy, Father almighty, everlasting God; Who didst lift up Thy voice unto us from heaven above Jordan's banks like the sound of thunder: to point out the Saviour of the world, and shew Thyself the Father of the eternal Light, Thou didst open the heavens and bless the air and purify the waters, and shew Thine only Son by the Dove of the Holy Ghost. On this day the waters received Thy blessing and took away our curse; that they might offer to the faithful the washing away of all sins, and by regeneration make sons of God unto life eternal of those whom fleshly birth had brought forth to life in time. For those on whom death had laid hold by disobedience, life eternal recapturing them from death recalls to the heavenly realm. Wherefore with rightful exultation we join to the praises of the Angels our voices as we worship Thy glory in this wonderful sacrament on this day's feast and offer unto Thee the sacrifice of praise for the Epiphany of Jesus Christ our Lord and for the source of our own calling unto Thee (*i.e.* baptism) through Him our Lord, through Whom the Angels praise, the Dominations adore, the Powers fear Thy majesty. The heavens and the powers thereof and the blessed Seraphim in common exultation tell Thy praises. With whom we pray Thee bid that our voices also be admitted, with suppliant praises saying:

'Holy, holy, holy, etc.

*Post-Sanctus:* 'Truly holy, truly blessed is our Lord Jesus Christ Thy Son, Who in token of His heavenly birth bestowed upon the world this day these wonders of His majesty: that He showed the worshipful star to the Wise Men, and after the passing of years turned water into wine, and by His own baptism hallowed Jordan's flood; even Jesus Christ our Lord:

*Mysterium:* 'Who on the day before He suffered . . . (There follows the institution).

*Post-Mysterium:* 'O Lord, we pray Thee, look with favour on these sacri-

---

[1] *Vere dignum et iustum est, aequum et iustum est*, as in the fourth–fifth century Italian prayer cited on *p.* 540.

fices before Thee; wherein no more gold and frankincense and myrrh is offered, but that which by these same gifts is declared, is (now) offered, sacrificed and taken. Through Jesus Christ our Lord Thy Son: Who with Thee and the Holy Ghost etc.'[1]

This prayer illustrates a fairly common occurrence in the French prayers, the working in of prayers from the Roman rite into Gallican masses, as a rule in a rather different connection. The end of this Gallican preface for the Epiphany (from 'through Whom the Angels praise . . .') is taken from the Roman 'common' preface (not that 'proper' to the Epiphany); and the Roman offertory prayer for the Epiphany has been used for the Gallican *post-mysterium*.

Here, again, is a 'pure' Gallican prayer for use on any 'green' Sunday from the seventh century *Masses of Mone*, the oldest Gallican collection extant:

*Contestatio:* 'It is meet and right that we should ever give thanks unto Thee, O God in Trinity, Whose power created us by Thy Word, and deservedly condemned our offences, Whose love delivered us by Thy Son, and called us to heaven by baptism and repentance: Unto Whom (all Angels and Archangels deservedly give ceaseless praises saying:)[2]

'Holy, etc.

*Post-Sanctus:* 'O God Who willest that we should not only offer to Thee the hymn but also the deservings of heavenly spirits, and should have no less the holy offices than the songs of the Angels: Grant that we who in setting forth Thy praises take to ourselves the united strains of the heavenly Powers, may also by amending our evil ways take to ourselves the love of the heavenly life, now that we are about to say those words of our Lord Jesus Christ which He left us for the memorial of His passion: through Jesus Christ our Lord . . .

*Mysterium:* 'Who on the day before . . .

*Post-Secreta:* 'O God of Abraham, God of Isaac, God of Jacob, God and Father of our Lord Jesus Christ, do Thou mercifully smiling down from heaven receive this our sacrifice with most indulgent love. May there descend, O Lord, the fulness of Thy majesty, Godhead, piety, power, blessing and glory upon this bread and upon this cup: and may it be unto us the eucharist Christ ordained[3] by the transformation of (*i.e.* into) the Body and Blood of the Lord: that whosoever among us, and howsoever often, shall partake of this bread and this cup, we may take unto ourselves a memorial (*monumentum*) of faith, sincerity of love, and untroubled hope of resurrection and unending immortality in the Name of

---

[1] *Missale Gothicum, ed.* Mabillon, *de Lit. Gall., pp.* 209 *sq.*
[2] This common Gallican form indicated by a cue in *Mone* is supplied from *Missale Gothicum.*
[3] So I translate *legitima eucharistia,* a phrase about which there has been some discussion; *cf. legitima oratio, ap.* Tertullian, *de Oratione* x.

the Holy Ghost Who proceedeth from Thee and Thy Son[1] in the communion of all saints, in the remission of all our sins. We believe, O Lord, that Thou wilt grant these things which we ask with unwavering faith. Through.'[2]

It should be said that the compiler has carried the principle of variability to the length of equipping this prayer with an alternative *contestatio* besides the one here given—a variation of a variation—though this is not uncommon in the Gallican books. The frequent incoherence of the Gallican prayers is illustrated by the *post-secreta* here.

Finally here is the eucharistic prayer of the Spanish rite for the feast of S James (later the patron of Spain) which in the ninth century was kept on December 30th, the day after S. John:

*Illatio:* 'It is meet and right that we should always give thanks unto Thee, O Lord holy, Father eternal, everlasting God, through Jesus Christ, Thy Son, our Lord: in Whose Name Thy chosen servant James healed the impotent man that cried unto him when he was being dragged to death, and by this miracle so moved the heart of him who mocked him that he brought him to attain to the glory of martyrdom when he had been instructed in the mysteries of the faith. So James himself fell slain by beheading for the confession of Thy Son: attaining in peace unto Him for Whom he bore this death. For He is Thy only-begotten Son Who gave His life as a ransom for many. Through Whom, O God the Father, do Thou bid that our sins be forgiven. Unto Whom all Angels and Archangels deservedly give ceaseless praises saying:

'Holy, etc.

*Post-Sanctus:* 'Truly holy, truly blessed is our Lord Jesus Christ the Son, Whom James leaving Zebedee his father so followed loving Him most dearly as to be chosen unto life, clean in conscience and approved in doctrine: at the last so commending his wisdom by his works that he died by beheading for Him Whom he knew had laid down His own life for himself and for all men.

'*Mysterium:* Even Jesus Christ our Lord Who . . .'[3]

---

[1] . . . *in tuo Filiique tui Spiritu Sancto nomine.* There is something wrong with the text.

[2] This is Mass vi. according to Wilmart's rearrangement of the leaves of the MS. It is found as fragments of iv. and ix. in the editions of Mone (*pp.* 23 *sq.* and 35) and Forbes (*pp.* 10 *sq.* and 26).

[3] It is a curious fact that while the prayer after the *mysterium* is always called the *post-pridie* in the MSS. the word *pridie* does not occur in the institution-narrative of the Mozarabic rite, which begins 'Who in the night He was betrayed . . .' The text of this paragraph is almost always omitted in the MSS., but Dom Férotin found it twice, once in the *Liber Ordinum* (eleventh century) *ed.* Férotin, *col.* 238 and once in another eleventh century MS. (*Lib. Moz. Sac.*, *p.* xxv.) in a slightly different form. It looks as though the wording of the institution-narrative in the Mozarabic rite had been changed at some point from the Western form *Qui pridie* to the Eastern '*In the night*'. The Roman form now used was inserted in A.D. 1500.

*Post-Pridie:* 'O God, bow down our necks under Thy yoke: that we may so bear Thy burden which is light unto them that love Thee with all desirable, devotion, as James Thine Apostle was joyfully dragged to execution with a rope around his neck; that sanctifying these things which we offer unto Thee, Thou wouldst bless us by the partaking of this Host (*or* Victim). Through . . .'[1]

It is obvious that the Mozarabic and Gallican rites are, as regards the eucharistic prayer, variants of a single rite—scarcely even that, for the same technical terms, liturgical tags and phrases, even the same formulae, recur constantly in both. The distinction between them comes in the addition of two prayers of the 'second *stratum*', the 'collect' and 'thanksgiving', which the Spanish churches were behind the French in adopting. (We may probably see in this a result of the more direct contacts of the French with the Italian churches in the later sixth century.)[2] But as regards the eucharistic prayer the Mozarabic and Gallican rites may be treated as being a single collection of variable prayers.

Nor, structurally, does there seem to be much difficulty in tracing the origin of this form of canon. It goes back plainly enough to the general fourth century fixed type of Western prayer, as revealed *e.g.* in Mai's Italian prayers (*p.* 540). The preface and sanctus have replaced the 'thanksgiving series', with an allusion to the liturgical commemoration of the day in the place of the old general 'thanksgiving' for the redeeming work of Christ. But the opening is the same, and most Gallican *contestationes* (like most Roman prefaces) are careful to retain at some point the *per Quem* ('through Whom'), which is a notable feature of the Western 'thanksgiving series' as early as the prayer of Hippolytus. The *post-sanctus* is still the precise equivalent of 'the link' (Hippolytus *e*) between the 'thanksgiving series' and the institution narrative. But now it links the inserted sanctus with the institution. This latter is followed by a prayer for the communicants of precisely the same general type as that in Hippolytus (*k*) and the *Supplices Te* of the Roman canon. All that is missing from the Hippolytan outline is the *anamnesis* paragraph (*h*). But as we have seen, all the evidence

[1] *Liber Mozarabicus Sacramentorum*, ed. Férotin, *coll.* 73 *sq.* It is right to add that some of the Mozarabic *post-pridie* prayers contain an invocation of the Holy Ghost upon the elements of the Syrian type, and there has been much discussion as to whether this was an original feature of the rite. Such invocations were certainly known in the seventh century in Spain, but the consensus of specialists on the Mozarabic rite both in England and abroad seems to be that they are a later borrowing from the East. (*Cf.* W. S. Porter, *Journal of Theol. Studies*, October, 1943.) A blessing of the elements in vague terms of the kind in the last clause of the prayer above is a usual feature of both Gallican and Mozarabic prayers, but this rather than a fully developed 'invocation' of the Eastern type is all that can be called 'normal' in these rites. (This is probably a fairly late specimen of a Mozarabic prayer. It is not an unrepresentative specimen, and the older ones are all inconveniently long for insertion.)

[2] Perhaps also the authority of S. Isidore's list of the prayers as being seven and only seven in number in the Mozarabic rite prevented the addition of these two for some centuries.

suggests that this was still a local Roman peculiarity in the third and fourth centuries.[1]

If we look back to the eucharistic prayer cited by S. Ambrose in *de Sacramentis* as the contemporary Milanese and Roman canon, we find that after the *laudes* ( = 'thanksgiving series') and the asking of 'prayers for kings, for the people' ( = the 'Names')[2] it runs as follows:

1. 'Make for us this oblation approved, ratified, reasonable, acceptable, seeing that it is the figure of the Body and Blood of our Lord Jesus Christ:

2. 'Who the day before He suffered . . . (there follows the institution).

§ 'Therefore making the *anamnesis* of His most glorious passion and resurrection from the dead and ascension into heaven,

§ 'we offer to Thee this spotless offering, reasonable offering, unbloody offering, this holy cup and bread of eternal life:

3. 'And we ask and pray that Thou wouldst receive this oblation at Thine altar on high by the hands of Thine angels, as Thou didst vouchsafe to receive the offerings of Thy righteous servant Abel, and the sacrifice of our patriarch Abraham, and that which Thine high-priest Melchisedech offered unto Thee. (That as many of us as shall receive by this partaking of the altar the most holy Body and Blood of Thy Son may be filled with all heavenly benediction and grace)'.[3]

The paragraphs marked § are already present in substance in the local Roman prayer of Hippolytus *c.* A.D. 200. For the rest, it seems easy to recognise in 1, 2, 3 'the link', the institution and the prayer for the communicants of the Gallican *post-sanctus, mysterium* and *post-mysterium*, and of Hippolytus *e, f* and *k*. The main differences between the Franco-Spanish and Italian developments are 1. That the Italian prayers place 'the Naming' in the second paragraph of their eucharistic prayer (this is probably a fourth century innovation)[4] whereas the Franco-Spanish rites place it at the offertory (probably the original Western position). 2. That the Roman prayer (if not other Italian prayers also) retains an old pre-Nicene peculiarity in inserting the *anamnesis* clauses (§ §) between the institution and

---

[1] *Cf. p.* 264. It is right to note that Cyprian, *Ep.* 63, 17, 'We make mention of *His passion* in all our sacrifices' taken in conjunction with Fulgentius, *Fragm.*, xxviii. (cited *p.* 297), 'Commemorating *the passion* of our Lord Jesus Christ, we ask that . . .' suggests that the African tradition was to make an *anamnesis* of the passion only, at the point where Rome commemorated the passion and resurrection. This is hardly certain, but it is worth remembering in considering the African rite in relation to other Western rites.

[2] S. Ambrose, *de Sacr.*, iv. 4, 14.

[3] S. Ambrose, *de Sacr.*, iv. 5 and 6 (21–7). On the last clause *cf. p.* 229. The previous clause ('And we ask—unto Thee') is very similar to clauses found in various Syrian prayers (*e.g., Ap. Const.*, viii, Brightman, L. E. W., *p.* 17, *ll.* 15 *sqq.*) and probably represents a fourth century Roman borrowing. It was already present in the Roman canon *c.* A.D. 385 when it is cited by the Roman 'Ambrosiaster', *Quaest. V. et. N.T.*, 109.

[4] *Cf. p.* 501.

prayer for the communicants.[1] But apart from this all the Western prayers have the same structure.[2]

When the evidence is set out, no one could easily suppose that the Gallican eucharistic prayers as they stand represent any very ancient survival. They are too completely affected in their contents by the sanctus

[1] The history of the Roman canon does not seem very difficult to make out in its main lines, once we discard theories about 'dislocation' and 'diptychs' and the 'primitive Roman epiclesis'. The preface and sanctus replaced the old 'thanksgiving series' in the fifth century. *Te igitur* and *Hanc igitur oblationem* are connected with 'the naming', introduced at this point in the fourth century. *Communicantes* was introduced by Gelasius (A.D. 492–6) to conform to the Jerusalem custom of 'naming' the saints. *Quam oblationem* is the survival of the pre-Nicene 'link'. There follow, institution, *anamnesis* and prayer for the communicants (*Qui pridie*, *Unde et memores*, *Supplices Te*, this last somewhat rearranged). The commemoration of the dead is originally a special insertion at funerals; *Nobis quoque* was introduced by Gelasius at the same time as *Communicantes* and for the same reason (*cf.* P. B. Whitehead, *art. cit. Speculum* III, 1928, *p.* 152). *Per Quem haec omnia* is the old blessing of fruits, etc., found attached to the eucharistic prayer at Rome in Hippolytus; *Per Ipsum* is the closing doxology. All the *variable* prayers in the canon are thus fifth century additions, of the period when the Gallican eucharistic prayer was beginning to be variable; *i.e.*, the prevailing Western fashion of the fifth century nearly carried the day at Rome also. The solid core of unvarying matter (from *Quam oblationem* to *Supplices Te*) corresponds in structure to the Gallican 'link', institution and prayer for the communicants (with the addition of the old Roman *anamnesis*). Thus at Rome the Western structure of the prayer *c.* A.D. 200 has survived the attentions of the 'improvers' of all the centuries and two major revisions (by Gelasius and Gregory) with only trifling alterations of order (in the *Supplices Te* and *Supra quae*). I believe that this account of the matter can be fully substantiated from the evidence, though it has not yet been done.

[2] These last three paragraphs and the relevant footnotes are intended to raise—tentatively and merely by way of recognition that it exists—the question of the *origin* of the whole group of Latin liturgies, Italian, Franco-Spanish and African. Is there *one* original type behind them all? If so, what was its original geographical centre? To what extent, if any, are these originally translated rites? These and other connected questions will form one of the major topics of discussion among scientific liturgists at some point during the next generation, and the solution of the problem will considerably affect the presentation of the early history of the liturgy in general. None of these questions is yet answerable; little 'pointers' of evidence are only just beginning to be noticed. But the questions ought to be being asked, and I fear that they are not. Hitherto the scientific approach to the early history of the Latin liturgies has usually seemed to stop short at an upward limit *c.* A.D. 500 with a curious abruptness. (In the case of many writers it might be truer to say that it stopped at S. Gregory a century later still.) Before that, all is left in confusion and obscurity, illuminated only by random and unconfessed guessing. It is my hope that in this chapter and the two which precede it some other investigator may find sufficient hints to enable him to push the whole problem back to the later fourth century and perhaps to carry it back from there, though for my own part I hardly see my way at present behind that point. It will be noted that I have assumed that the 'second half' of Hippolytus' *Greek* Roman prayer in the third century corresponds (at least roughly) with the articulation of the eucharistic prayers in use among contemporary *Latin* groups at Rome. The assumption seems to me justifiable, but it is an assumption. At present we know next to nothing about these groups except that they existed. They do not seem to me to be necessarily identifiable with the partisans of his rival Callistus; and though the structural evolution of their Latin prayers (I think) was along the lines revealed by his Greek one, it does not follow that it proceeded at exactly the same pace or under the impulse of exactly the same ideas. There are obscure traces in the canon of *de Sacramentis* of a combination of or compromise between Hippolytan and other (? African) ideas.

and the influence of the calendar, neither of which, as we have seen, make their appearance in the Western rites till the fifth century. The preface and the 'link' are dominated by both these influences, and even the prayer for the communicants is frequently overwhelmed by the allusion to the day (*cf.* the mass of S. James on *p. 555*). Their fidelity to tradition consists in arranging their new contents on the old Western scheme. Only the institution narrative itself, now regarded as too sacred and too important as the consecration formula to be lightly varied, has survived unchanged from before the acceptance of the new fashion of variability. For the rest, the very fact that a fresh composition had to be found for every liturgical day in the year prevents us from hoping to discover any surviving trace in the Gallican prayers of the actual wording used in Gaul and Spain in the fourth century before variability came in. At the best a church could only keep its traditional prayer as one variant, for days which had no particular liturgical associations, *e.g.* 'green' Sundays. But all the Gallican collections extant provide a whole set of alternatives for these, none of which fail to conform to the later Gallican type. The French and Spanish local eucharistic prayers of the fourth century and earlier seem to have transmitted only their structure, not their wording, to their successors.

The date when the Spanish and French eucharistic prayers first became variable with the calendar cannot be satisfactorily fixed. It is clear that when Pope Vigilius in answer to the enquiries of Bishop Profuturus of Braga (Portugal) described the fixed Roman canon with variable insertions on certain great feasts in A.D. 538,[1] he was already aware of a difference of practice in this between Rome and the Spanish churches, though he does not press the point. S. Isidore of Seville attributes the composition of 'prayers well adapted for various feasts and masses in an elegant style and lucid phrasing' to Peter, bishop of Lérida *c.* A.D. 500.[2] Though this does not specifically refer to the eucharistic prayer as such, Isidore, who used the Mozarabic rite, would doubtless not have considered a mass which did not include a complete 'proper' eucharistic prayer 'well adapted' for a feast. There is no reason to suppose Peter was the first author of Spanish variable prayers, but the names of the earlier authors have not been recorded.

In Gaul we seem to have such an earlier record. Musaeus, a presbyter of Marseilles (d. *c.* A.D. 460) is said 'to have compiled at the request of his bishop Saint Venerius lections from the holy scriptures suitable for the feast days throughout the year; and also responsories from the psalms and versicles and responses (*capitula*) fitting the seasons and lections; which book is so far considered a necessity by the lector in the church, that it relieves him of all fuss and worry and does away with delay, and at the same time instructs the people and gives fitting honour to the feast. And he also composed and dedicated to the bishop S. Eustace, the successor of the aforesaid man of God, a remarkable and fairly long Book of Sacraments,

[1] Vigilius, *Ep.* ii.    [2] S. Isidore, *de Viris Illustribus*, M.P.L., lxxxii, 1090.

divided into sections for the sequence of offices and seasons, and for the text of the lections and the arrangement and chant of the psalms; but displaying his usual earnestness both in prayer to God and the acknowledgment of His goodness'.[1] Musaeus had some reputation as an exegete, but this part of his work was clearly liturgical. The book composed for bishop Venerius (d. *c.* A.D. 452) seems to be for the office, and it has been questioned whether the *volumen sacramentorum* dedicated to his successor was not a book of instructions or homilies rather than a 'sacramentary'. It seems sufficient answer to point out that *Liber Sacramentorum* is the official heading of the *Gelasian Sacramentary* compiled *c.* A.D. 475–510. Gennadius also tells us that Voconius, bishop of Castellanum in Morocco *c.* A.D. 460 wrote another *volumen sacramentorum,*[2] probably an African sacramentary, but there is no indication in this case that the prayers were arranged according to 'the sequence of the offices and seasons' (and presumably varied with them) as in the work of Musaeus.

Eustace seems to have become bishop *c.* A.D. 452 and Musaeus died *c.* A.D. 460. Once again, as in the case of the Milanese 'proper' prefaces, we are pointed to the period about or soon after A.D. 450 as that of the introduction of variable prayers in the Western rites. Musaeus may not have been the first author of such prayers in Gaul, but he is the first to be recorded. And Gennadius writing *c.* A.D. 495 gives a fairly full account of even the lesser ecclesiastical writers of southern Gaul in the fifth century. It seems hardly likely that he would have passed over ecclesiastics who had made any considerable name for themselves as liturgical authors in a new *genre* during this period. Musaeus need not be regarded as personally responsible for the invention of variable prayers in general, or even of only those of the Gallican rite. The idea seems to be too widespread too suddenly in the latter half of the fifth century to have had any single inventor. Probably it was in the air, a consequence of the new ecclesiastical year which had now dominated the whole celebration of the liturgy for more than a generation as a fixed and accepted institution of church life. The new fashion, coming in sporadically and haphazard, may well have been the occasion for Musaeus' orderly and systematic compilation much more than the consequence of it, even at Marseilles itself. And other South French churches doubtless made their own terms with it at about the same time, though they could not command the services of a well-known scholar to refurbish their liturgical traditions, and their obscure and tentative compilations have in consequence left no trace. Even Musaeus is not said to

---

[1] Gennadius, *de Script. Eccles.,* lxxix. As the text presents some obscurity at the end I give the passage relating to the 'Book of Sacraments': *Sed et ad personam S. Eustasii episcopi, successoris predicti hominis Dei, composuit sacramentorum egregium et non parvum volumen per membra quidem pro opportunitate officiorum et temporum, pro lectionum textu psalmorumque serie et decantatione discretum: sed supplicandi Deo et contestandi beneficiorum eius soliditate sui consentaneum.*

[2] Gennadius, *ibid.,* lxxviii.

have written variable *eucharistic* prayers, though the word *contestandi* inevitably recalls the Gallican term *contestatio* for the variable preface. In any case once the first paragraph of the prayer had been made to vary with the liturgical feast, the idea of varying other paragraphs of the prayer in accordance with it need not have been long in presenting itself to someone. The admission of merely alternative texts (not dependent on the calendar) of the whole prayer earlier in the century had already undermined the fourth century idea of a single fixed eucharistic prayer unvarying on all occasions. All things considered, I think we may safely date the general acceptance in France and Spain of variable eucharistic prayers in the latter half of the fifth century, with perhaps a period of preliminary and tentative beginnings in the ten or twenty years before that.

It hardly admits of question, from the mere identity of structure, that the Gallican and Mozarabic rites spring from a single source and are indeed only a single rite. Whether it originated in Gaul or Spain there are no decisive means of telling (though my own guess would be in favour of Gaul). The oldest surviving French MS. (the Reichenau palimpsest containing the *Masses of Mone*) is dated *c.* A.D. 650. The oldest Spanish MSS. are only of the ninth century, but what is recognisably the Mozarabic rite is described by S. Isidore of Seville in his *de Ecclesiasticis Officiis* in the early seventh century. Spanish tradition usually ascribed the rite itself to his compilation. But whatever lies behind the tradition, mention of Peter of Lérida as the author of some of the prayers more than a century earlier shews that Isidore's work can have been no more than a revision and reorganisation, akin to that carried out by S. Gregory in the Roman rite in the same period.

The great mutability of the eucharistic prayer in these rites was against the building up of any very stable tradition. When the laity expected to hear an entirely different set of prayers every time they went to church, they were not likely even to know whether this year's set, *e.g.* on Ascension Day, was the same as last year's, since only the celebrant had a book. The permanent tendency of the clergy to innovate in the text of the liturgy was thus released from the usual check of the layman's attachment to a familiar form, except so far as concerned the structure of the prayer and certain obvious cues, before the sanctus and the concluding 'Amen'. Thus though we can be sure that the special characteristics of this *type* of prayer were in general accepted by the churches of Spain and Southern Gaul by *c.* A.D. 500, it is not safe to take it for granted with our present knowledge that the *texts* which we have are necessarily much older than the extant MSS. which contain them. None of the seventh century texts of the *Masses of Mone* are found again in the eighth century Gallican books. Elipandus, bishop of Toledo in A.D. 794 cites from the masses found in the ninth century Mozarabic *Liber Sacramentorum* for such important days in the calendar as Maundy Thursday, Ascension Day and others, and he ascribes each mass by name to its author. All those he mentions are bishops of Toledo after A.D. 650.[1] He is writing officially on behalf of the whole Spanish episcopate to the bishops of Gaul. His statements can hardly be made at haphazard; and if the attributions of the authorship of the various masses had not then been certainly known at Toledo, it is strange that the prayers should have been fathered on comparatively recent writers, and not on Isidore or some other great name of the more remote past, for Elipandus is anxious to impress. Of course, these seventh century bishops' 'authorship' may have consisted in no more than a mere revision of older work and the attachment to it of their own names. Yet little more than a superficial investigation of the Mozarabic and Gallican prayers is needed to shew that they come not only from many hands, but from more than one period of taste and latinity. Some may well be as old as the later fifth century (e.g. the Mozarabic masses for S. Martin) but others are undoubtedly from the ninth century, after the Moorish conquest. It may be that one day we shall be able to distinguish more easily than we can at present the earlier from the later in the main bulk of these prayers.

It remains to say something of their distribution and history. The Mozarabic rite was codified as the rite of the see of Toledo, whose archbishop is still 'Primate of the Spains'. But the ecclesiastical greatness of Toledo dates only from the conversion of the Visigothic kings from Arianism in the late sixth century; and it was only in A.D. 633 that its rite was made the standard for the whole of Spain and the Visigothic dominions in the South of Gaul. Previous to that the various provinces had tended to adopt the rite of the local metropolitan.[2] No doubt most of these were of the Mozarabic type, and some of the prayers of the Toledan missal were undoubtedly drawn from these older provincial and local 'propers'.[3] But the national council of the independent Suevic kingdom of Galicia held at Braga in A.D. 565 had ordered the use of the Roman rite. The use of the Toledan Mozarabic rite was enforced in Galicia as a political measure by the Visigoths when they conquered it, and it thus became the national rite of Spain.

It remained such down to and after the moslem conquest in the early eighth century. In the eleventh century the fringe of independent christian principalities in the North and West began to adopt the now general Western rite. This was partly under the impulsion of French monks from Cluny who were unaccustomed to the Mozarabic, partly because, engaged as they were on a perpetual crusade for the reconquest of their country, the Spanish princes and peoples themselves were more conscious of their own

[1] ap. M.P.L., cl. 1328 sq.
[2] Cf. e.g., Can. 1 of the Council of Gerona, A.D. 517, for the province of Tarragona.
[3] Cf. p. 380.

unity with the rest of the christian West. The Mozarabic remained the rite of the christians living under the yoke of the Caliphs of Cordova. But as the tide of christian reconquest advanced during the middle ages, so, too, did the Roman rite, which had now become the badge of freedom. By the end of the fifteenth century the Mozarabic rite had all but died out, being used only in some of the parish churches of Toledo and occasionally in the cathedral, and in some scattered churches elsewhere on a few occasions in the year. It was rescued from extinction by Cardinal Ximenes in A.D. 1500, who provided for its continuance in a somewhat Romanised form in seven Toledan parish churches and a specially endowed and staffed chapel in the cathedral.

The question of the diffusion of the Gallican rite is more difficult. Every single extant liturgical MS. of the Gallican rite can be traced back either to Burgundy or the country to the south-west of it (the Narbonnaise and Acquitaine) *i.e.* either to the region of France most accessible to Visigothic Spain and in intimate relations with it, or to the actual original nucleus of the Visigothic state. This is a fact not to be lost sight of in considering whether Gaul or Spain is the birthplace of the rite; but too much should not be made of it since the evidence of Gregory of Tours makes it probable that in the sixth century this rite was used also at Tours, which lay outside the Visigothic sphere after A.D. 496.

The problem arises as to the rite used in the North and East of France. The earliest MS. which has reached us from the church of Paris is a copy of the Roman *Gelasian Sacramentary* written *c.* A.D. 700, probably at S. Denis. And there is no doubt that the use of the Roman rite, at all events in certain churches, goes back in the North and East to a period a good way before A.D. 700 and probably before 600. This region *may* have used something like the Gallican rites of the South of France before that date. But we have seen that the Gallican rites really only begin to grow up in the South in the later fifth century. It is conceivable, therefore, that the Roman Gelasian book was the first compilation of variable prayers to succeed the old fixed rites in the North There is no evidence either way.[1] We have also seen that Ireland used a form of the Roman rite soon after A.D. 600 and perhaps earlier. The Anglo-Saxon churches did the same from the landing of Augustine (A.D. 596). The real sphere of the Gallican rite after A.D. 600 seems therefore to have been confined to the centre and south of Gaul. Burgundian missions had begun to carry the Gallican rite to South Germany in the seventh century, just as Augustine found the Burgundian bishop Liudhard before him at Canterbury using the Gallican rite in the private chapel of Queen Bertha, who had been a Burgundian princess before she married the king of Kent. But the definitive conversion of both

---

[1] But it is perhaps relevant that a direct dependence on the surviving relics of the Western empire in Italy lasted longer in the North and East (to the death of the prefect Syagrius in A.D. 486) than in the rest of Gaul.

England and Germany was effected by missions using the Roman rite, and the Gallican never took root in either country.

In France itself it fell into great decay during the eighth century, though it held on in the South and South-West until the time of Charlemagne c. A.D. 800, who formally abolished it. It is possible, however, that it did not finally die out in scattered churches for another fifty years or so after his time. Thereafter it survives only in certain sporadic ceremonies continued in many French churches, and as a pervading influence in the Romano-French liturgical books which resulted from Charlemagne's reform.

⎸The Gallican rite as a rite had therefore an effective life of some 400 years, from the fifth century to the ninth. The Mozarabic rite lasted for another two centuries in Spain, and took another three or four to fade into the position of an isolated local peculiarity in a handful of churches. In each country their disappearance coincides with the transition from the barbarian centuries to the new Europe and the beginnings of the resurgence of civilisation.

## The Development of the Italian Rites

It is not possible to present the local Italian development of the liturgy from the fourth to the eighth centuries in complete isolation from development in Gaul during the same period, owing to the nature of the extant evidence. North of the Alps the renaissance of civilisation under Charlemagne c. A.D. 800 not only allowed the preservation of some evidence from before that period, but it brought about a recovery of civilised living which was never altogether lost again, even in the troubled period which followed under his weaker successors. But the later ninth and tenth centuries were in some ways the darkest of all in Italy, and this has seriously affected the extent to which older Italian MSS. have survived. It thus comes about that our earliest copies of Italian liturgical texts happen for the most part to have been written in France. They have undergone a certain amount of adaptation for use in the Frankish churches, though the underlying Italian basis can be disentangled, at least in outline, with a little trouble, and it is with this that for the moment we are chiefly concerned.

I choose the term 'Italian' rather than the usual one 'Roman', deliberately. From the fourth century to the sixth or seventh, the Roman rite is only the most important local rite amid a number of other Italian local rites, varying in the phrasing of their prayers but all having much the same general character. Even in the present very fragmentary state of the evidence they form a recognisable sub-group within the general group of the Western rites. Just so in the same period the Alexandrian rite is only the most important of a group of Egyptian local rites, the Antiochene one of a group of Syrian rites, and so on. It must be repeated that the 'second period' from the end of the fourth to the seventh–eighth centuries is a confused period, when we must allow for two opposing tendencies at work on the liturgy all over christendom. The abiding influence of provincial and even parochial peculiarities handed down in local churches from the third century is crossed by the new tendency of whole regions to assimilate all their local rites to that of the provincial capital or the nearest oecumenically important see—of Egyptian country churches to approximate to the rite of Alexandria, and so on. And the rites of the two holy cities of the East and the West, Jerusalem and Rome, exercise a special and separate influence on those of other churches, that of Jerusalem being the more far-reaching. We have to remember that the process of 'borrowing' by one rite from another is not merely local in its effects; it can and does take place between churches geographically remote from each other—as Rome and Gaul and Africa and Spain all borrowed independently and differently and at different times from Syria. Yet out of these cross-currents the great historic rites slowly crystallise during the fifth–sixth centuries along the main lines each had formed for itself in the fourth–fifth centuries. The end of the universal empire with its easy communications and the break-up of the old oecumenical communion of the churches lie in the background of this hardening of local differences in the performance of 'the liturgy' into separate 'rites'.

Italy is no exception to this universal trend of liturgical history from the fourth to the seventh centuries, from local diversity to provincial and then regional uniformity. We can trace it in Spain by the aid of such enactments as those of the Council of Gerona in A.D. 517 and of the fourth Council of Toledo in A.D. 633.[1] The process was slower in Gaul and Italy only because in those countries there was as yet no effective national government to bring about a sense of regional unity over-riding the old provincial loyalties, which shewed themselves (amongst other ways) in the adherence to old local and provincial rites.

At the end of the fourth century Italy, like other regions, was full of local rites. The text of these has perished, but Mai's Arian author provides us with invaluable evidence that they existed. The fact, too, is admitted, resentfully enough, by Pope Innocent I in the opening of his letter to Decentius c. A.D. 415.[2] In the fifth century the tendency towards regional

[1] Cf. p. 561.
[2] 'If celebrants would only keep strictly to the institutions of the church as they have been handed down from the blessed apostles, there would be no contradictions and no differences in the ceremonies they observe and the prayers they say. But when every one believes that what ought to be followed is not what has been handed down but whatever he thinks fitting, there arise thence obvious differences in belief and worship between different churches and places; and this is a cause of scandal to the people; who, because they do not know what the ancient traditions were which have been corrupted by human presumption, either think the churches do not agree together, or that contradictory teachings were given by the apostles or apostolic men'. *Mutatis mutandis*, how often have we Anglicans not heard the same wail of the bureaucrat? And their remedy is always Innocent's 'Do what I do' (even though it be quite a recent innovation, as his particular fancies were).

uniformity operates by the gradual spontaneous adoption in the Italian provincial churches of the outline or Shape of the Roman Liturgy and of the text, perhaps with local modifications, of the Roman eucharistic prayer. This had already happened at Milan *c*. A.D. 390 in S. Ambrose' time, and may very well have been his doing. Other Italian churches may have been slower than Milan to do so. At all events, no Italian eucharistic prayer other than slightly variant forms of the Roman one, has come down to us from the sixth century and after.

But in the fifth century there arises also the new influence of the calendar on the liturgy, and the tendency towards local diversity concentrates itself upon the variable 'lesser' prayers (collect, offertory prayer, etc.), just then being incorporated one by one into the structure of the Western rites. Local diversity is given full play in the elaboration of the 'propers' in the sixth century. Thus in the fifth–sixth centuries the Italian local rites are built up, with the same framework and a number of different sets of variable prayers.

In the case of the local Roman rite we possess monuments of two stages in this process, the *Gelasian Sacramentary* (hereafter called Gel.) and the *Gregorian Sacramentary* (hereafter called Greg.) which may be dated for practical purposes *c*. A.D. 500 and *c*. A.D. 600 respectively. We have besides a third document of great value but more doubtful origin, known as the *Leonine Sacramentary* (hereafter called Le.).

### The Gelasian Sacramentary

Though Gel. originates as a book of the Roman rite *c*. A.D. 500 the earliest complete copy of it we possess was written in France, probably at S. Denis, *c*. A.D. 700. Fragments of other copies and other evidence make it certain that this MS. is representative of many then in use in Northern and Eastern France and in England. It is certain, too, that this had been the case since *c*. A.D. 650, and probable that copies of Gel. had crossed the Alps well before A.D. 600, perhaps as early as *c*. A.D. 550. Edmund Bishop, who was the first to illuminate this period of the history of the Western liturgy, always insisted that this unique surviving MS. was only a typical copy of what amounted to a 'Frankish edition' of Gel. made for use in France *c*. A.D. 650, which he christened 'the Gel. of the seventh century'. In this Frankish revision a number of French customs and prayers were added to the imported Roman book, which are as a rule quite easily detected. The text of the Roman canon of Gel. was revised to accord with the current Roman text, as fixed by S. Gregory *c*. A.D. 595. (It is possible that these Frankish changes and additions in the 'Gel. of the seventh century' were made in more than one stage, but the total result was the same.) But with these exceptions Bishop claimed that this Frankish 'Gel. of the seventh century' represented in substance the book used at Rome itself from *c*.

A.D. 500 to *c*. A.D. 600, the book whose revision by S. Gregory produced Greg. *c*. A.D. 600.

It is doubtful if the matter is quite so simple as that. Frere[1] has since pointed out that after the Frankish accretions have been removed from the 'Gel. of the seventh century', the resulting book lacks some elements of the strictly *local* Roman rite, and incorporates feasts and prayers which suggest an origin not at Rome itself but in the country to the south of it, round Capua or Cumae. Mr. J. T. Sinclair[2] has carried the argument further by pointing out the very considerable divergence in the prayers of the 'proper' between Gel. and Greg. and the difficulty of considering Greg. as a direct revision of Gel. in this respect. It seems possible that we must interpose a further stage between the Frankish 'Gel. of the seventh century' and the Roman book of *c*. A.D. 500, which undoubtedly lies somewhere behind it. About A.D. 525 the current Roman book may well have been adopted in substance by some South Italian church, where the local propers were substituted for many of the proper prayers then used at Rome. And by some accident it was a copy (or copies) of this sixth century 'Italianised' edition of Gel. which was carried across the Alps soon after A.D. 550 and became the basis of the Frank sh edition of Gel.—the 'Gel. of the seventh century' —made *c*. A.D. 650.

This 'Italian' edition of Gel. *c*. A.D. 525 in fact illustrates very well the probable course of development in other Italian local rites in the sixth century. We know of another such compilation in this period. Bishop Maximian of Ravenna (A.D. 546–556) in a single 'large volume' 'drew up missals for the whole cycle of the year and of all the saints. As for the "quotidian " (*i.e.* what we should call "green") and lenten seasons, and whatever concerns the rite of the *ecclesia*, you will without difficulty find it there.'[3] Another such compilation (as I believe) from N. Italy is found in the *Leonine Sacramentary*, of which something must now be said.

---

[1] *Studies in the Early Roman Liturgy*, I, 1930, *pp.* 42 *sqq.*
[2] *Art. cit.*, *Theology*, xxxii (1936), *pp.* 144 *sqq.*
[3] Agnellus of Ravenna, *Liber Pontificalis Ecclesiae Ravennatis* in *Mon. Germ., SS. Rerum Langobardicarum*, *p.* 332 (cited E. Bishop, *Lit. Hist.*, *p.* 59, *n.*); Agnellus had personally examined the volume. It was evidently arranged in two books, a *temporale* and a *sanctorale*, as the 'Italianised Gel.' is drawn up in three, *temporale*, *sanctorale* and 'votives'. The Roman tradition as found in Greg. (and Le.) was to have a single book, fusing *temporale* and *sanctorale* and putting miscellaneous items at the end. It may have been the more convenient arrangement in separate divisions which caused the 'Italianised Gel.' to be taken as the basis of the Frankish 'Gel. of the seventh century' instead of the 'pure Roman Gel.' The 'Italian' tradition of separating the saints' day prayers from those of the seasons ultimately prevailed even in Roman MSS. (except for the saints in Christmas week; *cf.* the arrangement of collects, epistles and gospels in the Book of Common Prayer)—but only after the tenth century.

*The Leonine Sacramentary*

The seventh century MS. in the library of Verona cathedral in which this is found is now unique, but there is evidence that other copies were once in circulation in N. Italy, S.E. France, and even Spain. It is a somewhat disorderly compilation, originally containing a collection of variable prayers for the eucharist throughout the liturgical year, though a good deal of this MS. has perished and the collection is very incomplete. The 'propers' of the seasons and saints' days are mingled with each other in the Roman (as opposed to Italian) way. Masses for occasions like funerals and the provision for the 'green' seasons are mixed up with those for feasts in a very confused fashion. Some MSS. of this document evidently contained a pre-Gregorian text of the Roman canon[1] and perhaps an ordinary also; but this section of the extant MS. has gone, if it ever contained it. What is most remarkable about the book is that it gives a large number of alternative sets of variable prayers for use on the same feast, in some cases as many as ten or twenty complete sets for a single day. This is unique among books of the Roman rite, though it is as such that Le. must be classed.

Various theories have been put forward as to its origin. It has been represented as a mere collection of materials, not an official liturgical book at all, put together by a private compiler. But it is difficult in this case to see why it should have been so widely and carefully copied. This view seems to rest upon the suppositions (a) that the present MS. is the compiler's own copy, (b) that it was always unique, and (c) that it never contained the canon; all of which are unfounded. We know that other copies existed and were not confined to Italy. The scribe of the extant MS. has carefully noted variant readings in some of the prayers drawn from more than one MS., so it already had a certain circulation. And other copies certainly, and probably this one, were equipped with a text of the canon. The book was intended for practical use in church.

On the other hand Le. has been regarded as a copy of a book of unique authority, the mass-book of the fifth century Popes themselves, into which were collected the prayers which successive Pontiffs—occasionally exercising their still living episcopal prerogative of extemporising the prayers of the liturgy—composed afresh when they felt so moved, to celebrate various feasts each year. This theory seems impossible from the contents of the book. It contains matter not only from old Roman sources, but from the *non*-Roman source in the 'Italianised edition' of Gel.; there are also a few Gallican and some Milanese prayers, and some which are now found in no rite, but are known to have been in circulation in North Italy in the seventh century. And, most surprising of all, there are clear indications that its compiler knew the authentic text of the *Gregorian Sacramentary* compiled

[1] See Dom R. H. Connolly, *Downside Review*, xxxvi (1917), p. 58.

*c.* A.D. 595.[1] What, however, gives Le. its special importance is that among the sources upon which it has drawn is a genuinely Roman book of the period before Gregory's reform, which is not the 'Italianised Gel.' Possibly there is material from more than one such pre-Gregorian Roman *stratum* in Le. Duchesne has pointed out that such historical allusions as can be identified in the prayers seem to belong to the first half of the sixth century rather than to the fifth,[2] and this is true of the bulk of the material. But there are one or two items (*e.g.* the ordination prayers) of which it might be said that there is still a probability that they go back to the fifth century, perhaps even to the age of S. Leo himself (*c.* A.D. 450) though I am not aware that this could be proved.

But the supposed connection of Le. as a book with S. Leo, or with the Papal liturgy of the fifth century, must be abandoned. It was put together in the first half of the seventh century in some country church in N. Italy (a monastery seems more likely than a secular church on some counts) from a large variety of materials, amongst which was a Roman book of *c.* A.D. 550 (not 450). Le. is thus in some ways a N. Italian parallel to the S. Italian 'Italianised Gel.' though put together much less skilfully and about a century later in date of compilation. They are both specimens of the Roman rite adapted for use in various ways in Italian provincial churches, with the addition or substitution of other 'propers' drawn from various sources—from obsolete as well as current Roman books, and probably from other Italian local rites whose texts have vanished.

### Italian Local Rites

The finished products of such 'Italian' local developments are found in such rites as those of Milan and Benevento,[3] when these are first revealed to us by extant MSS. of the ninth century and after. It is probable that

---

[1] *Cf.* the cases noted by E. Bishop, *Lit. Hist., p.* 94, *n.*—which do not stand alone.
[2] Duchesne, *Origins, ed. cit., pp.* 137 *sq.*
[3] The Beneventan local rite has only come to light in this century, and its texts are still incompletely published. H. M. Bannister, *Journal of Theol. Studies,* vi., *pp.* 603 *sqq.,* drew attention to one point in it as early as 1905. The credit for discovering that it was a complete local rite belongs to Mgr. Benozzi, Archbishop of Benevento (formerly a monk of Monte Cassino) who being unable to find time to publish it himself drew the attention to it of Dom Andoyer of the French Abbey of Ligugé. Such texts as are available are to be found: Dom Andoyer: *L'ancienne liturgie de Bénévent* in *Rév. du Chant Grégorien,* 1912–14 and 1919–21; Dom R. J. Hesbert: *Les dimanches de carême dans les MSS. Romano-Bénéventaines* in *Eph. Lit.,* xlviii (1934), *pp.* 3 *sqq.; L'Antiphonale Missarum de l'ancien rit Bénéventain, ibid.* lii (1938), *pp.* 28, 125, etc. (incomplete); *La tradition Bénéventaine* in *Paléographie Musicale,* t. xiv. (incomplete). Both these publications have been interrupted by the present disturbances on the Continent, as the original articles of Dom Andoyer were in 1914. Briefly, the history of the rite seems to be that all the local propers are older than *c.* A.D. 800, when local composition ceased; new masses were taken over after that from the Roman rite when required. The old collection of local propers, which dropped out of use in the thirteenth century, was replaced by the corresponding texts from the Western missal then coming into general use in S. Italy.

these are only chance survivors of a number of such rites, all 'Roman' in the
Shape of their Liturgy and the text of their canon since the fifth century,
but with their own sixth century propers. These local rites received their
final codification in the sixth and seventh centuries, much as the local
Roman rite received its final codification from S. Gregory and his seventh
century successors. Some of them may still have continued in use after
the ninth century, but ultimately failed to transmit their MSS. after they
fell into disuse during the middle ages. It is to be noted that within the
Beneventan rite itself there are local variations, MSS. from Bari not being
altogether identical with those from Benevento.

Both Milan and Benevento have complete local traditions of the proper,
not only for the eucharist but for the office; and these local traditions
included their own proper chants as well as the texts. Some of the melodies
in each case are in substance the same as the corresponding Roman ones,
but in each church some of these borrowed melodies have been re-written.
In other items, sometimes the text, or the music, or both, have been
borrowed by Benevento from Milan (or *vice versa*), and these borrowings
too have been freely adapted. But much in the proper of each rite is peculiar
to itself, either the product of local talent or borrowed from yet other
sources no longer extant. There must have been in circulation in Italy a
very large *corpus* of variable prayers, (collects, prefaces, etc.) all of them
'Roman' in general type, but many of them of provincial manufacture and
never included in the strictly local Roman books. They make their appearance in these various Italian rites, not always assigned to the same day.
Some of them, preserved by chance on scraps, are never found in any
extant rite;[1] some are found in more than one form. If we say that Italy as a
whole, including Milan but excluding the Greek colonies in the South, had
come to use the 'Roman' rite before the seventh century, we must be careful to recognise what a wide local variety such a term then covered. And
some of these rites incorporated not only non-Roman, but also non-Italian
material. The *Bobbio Missal* for instance, though it uses the Roman canon
and has a largely Roman Shape of the Liturgy and was used at an Italian
altar, is quite fifty per cent. Gallican in its contents. The Milanese rite has
adapted to its Roman framework quite a lot of Gallican material. It is a
remarkable fact that the only pure and unabbreviated text of the Gallican
preface of S. Martin—a French saint if ever there was one—is found not in
the professedly Gallican books but in the 'Roman' Milanese missal. On two
days in the year Milan even admitted Gallican 'patches' into its local text
of the Roman canon.

[1] Of the forty 'Roman' collects copied without heading or rubric on the back of a
roll of the eighth–ninth century from Ravenna (publ. by A. Ceriani, *Il rotolo episto-
grafa del principe Antonio Pio di Savoia*, Milan, 1883) only one appears in any
known sacramentary, Le. Of seventeen others, scribbled in seventh century shorthand on a scrap from Bobbio, most but not all are also found in Le. (publ. by G.
Mercati in *Studi e Testi*, vii (1902), *pp*. 35 *sqq*.)

*The Gregorian Sacramentary*

It is upon this background of a whole group of closely related Italian rites, all being more or less simultaneously enriched and revised in the same period, that we must see S. Gregory's purpose in his revision of the local rite of Rome *c.* A.D. 595. It is true that this had vastly greater repercussions on the later liturgical history of the whole West than any revision of the Milanese or Ravennate rite could have had. But that could hardly have been foreseen at the time. The Roman rite was then much further from being the rite of the whole West than the rite of Alexandria was from being that of all Egypt, or the rite of Antioch from becoming that of all the remaining orthodox churches of Syria. In Gregory's time all Spain and half Gaul used a quite different development of the general Western type of the fourth century, and Burgundian missions were just beginning to carry this to England and Germany. In Latin Italy we have seen with what freedom the Roman rite was adapted by the local churches; and in the East and South of the peninsula and Sicily were the Greek Byzantine colonies, much more Eastern than Roman in rite,[1] though these were just then less important than they had been and would be again. And in so far as the Roman rite was already used outside Italy, it had spread in the 'Italian edition' of Gel. and not in the authentic Roman text. Nor had Pope Gregory himself any idea of setting up his own text as a standard necessarily to be accepted elsewhere. He advised Augustine at Canterbury to take what seemed best out of both the Gallican and Roman rites, and form a new mixed rite for the Anglo-Saxon church;[2] he advised the bishop of Milan to continue old Milanese customs; he recognised without *arrière pensée* that the customs of Ravenna are in some things not those of Rome, and insists that they shall be maintained. He is no exponent of that theory of the 'purity' and self-sufficiency of rites which modern liturgists have invented for themselves, but just an old-fashioned believer in the ancient liberty of local churches to order their own rites—within the bounds of orthodoxy and a decent conformity with tradition—and enrich them with the best they can find elsewhere if they are so minded. And this liberty he proceeded to exercise with the local rite of his own church when he embarked on its revision.

We have already discussed his changes in the Shape of the Liturgy—the insertion of the *Kyrie* hymn (imitated from the Gallican rite?) as an alternative to Gelasius' litany, and his insertion of the Lord's prayer in its Jerusalem position after the canon. He made certain verbal changes in the text

[1] Some used the Roman rite in Greek, some the Byzantine rite, others *S. James* and yet others *S. Mark*. Some appear to have used all four liturgies indifferently, since they are found copied in one MS.
[2] Bede, *Eccl. Hist.*, I, 27.

of the canon,[1] adding a whole clause to the *Hanc igitur* paragraph[2]—the last official addition to the wording of the Roman eucharistic prayer. But it was rather on the texts of the proper and the chants that he seems to have bestowed his chief pains. A series of brilliant and discerning studies by a group of Belgian liturgists has of late years made plain something of the minute care and delicate sense of the music of words with which the great Pope personally revised the individual collects and other lesser prayers for the whole cycle of the year.[3] The invalid and harassed Pope bore the burdens not only of Rome and Italy but of all Europe in the years when the skies were darkening for the final fury of the barbarian storm. It must have been some relief to turn for an hour from the horrors of the Lombard wars to a task so congenial to one who never ceased to be a monk at heart.

A careful examination of his work reveals that many of the prayers he revised left his hands not indeed new, for he keeps closely to the old style and matter, but with an added quality. If what Frere called 'the poised word of Leo' gave to the Roman collects their penetrating thoughtfulness and that pointed form they never lost till the Franciscans of the middle ages took to writing collects, it is Gregory as often as not who gave them their

[1] The best discussion of the early variants in the text of the Roman canon is still that of E. Bishop, *Lit. Hist.*, *pp.* 77 *sqq.*, though further materials will be found in the critical text *ed.* by Dom B. Botte, *Le canon de la Messe Romaine*, Louvain, 1935. Bishop's conclusions stand, that S. Gregory's text has come down in two main recensions: *A*, an early seventh century text, of which the only extant witnesses have relations with Ireland; this is in the main 'Gregorian', but contains three or four 'pre-Gregorian' readings; [*i.e.*, it has the appearance of an attempt to conform the pre-Gregorian text, as used in Ireland, to S. Gregory's revision, not quite meticulously carried out.] *B*, a text current in Italy in the seventh century, but attested rather later than *A* in extant MSS. [This is probably an accident.] Both *A* and *B* texts were current in France in the later seventh century. The present text in the Roman missal is related to *B* more closely than to *A*, though not quite verbally identical. [Bishop excludes the Milanese text from consideration. It seems to be a later re-working of *B* with some older Milanese readings.]

[2] It is to be noted that this destroyed the original connection of this para. with 'the Naming', which had been maintained, at least occasionally, in the sixth century (*cf.*, *e.g.*, *Gelasian Sacramentary*, ed. Wilson, *p.* 34). In Le. the *Hanc igitur* appears to have come before *Communicantes*, instead of after it (*cf. Leonine Sacramentary, ed.* Feltoe, nos. 24, 25), which is what one would expect from comparison with the prayer cited on *p.* 540. It is possible that S. Gregory was responsible for the change in the order of *Hanc igitur* and *Communicantes*; and probable that he expanded and re-arranged the two lists of saints in *Communicantes* and *Nobis quoque* (*cf.* V. L. Kennedy, *The Saints of the Roman Canon*, Rome, 1938). Altogether this amounts to a rather more extensive revision of the canon than he is generally credited with.

[3] See Dom B. Capelle, *La main de S. Grégoire dans le sacrementaire Grégorien*; *Rév. Ben.*, xlix (1937), *pp.* 13 *sqq.*; G. Callewaert, *L'œuvre liturgique de S. Grégoire*: *Le temps de la Septuagésime et l'Alleluia*; *Rév. d'hist. ecclés.*, xxxviii (1937), *pp.* 306 *sqq.*; G. Verbeke, *S. Grégoire et la messe de S. Agathe*; *Eph. Liturg.*, lii (1938), *pp.* 67 *sqq.*; G. Callewaert, *Texte liturgique composé par S. Grégoire*; *ibid.*, *pp.* 189 *sqq.*; Dom B. Capelle, '*L'Aqua Exorcisata*' *dans les rites romains de la dédicace des églises au VIème siècle*: *Rév. Ben.*, l. (1938), *pp.* 306 *sqq.*; G. Callewaert, *S. Grégoire, Les Scrutins et quelques Messes Quadragésimales*; *Eph. Liturg.* liii. (1939), *pp.* 191 *sqq.*; to these may be added, Dom B. Capelle, *Note sur le lectionnaire romain de la messe avant S. Grégoire*; *Rév. d'hist. ecclés.* xxxix (1938), *pp.* 556 *sqq.*, throwing light on his revision of the lections.

lovely simplicity. Again and again he drops or adds half a clause or changes
a word or two, and the result is luminous, where the old form for all its
sonority and force must have been hard to follow when *heard*. It is a token
of the sympathy of the Pope who wrote *The Pastoral Care* with those
whom he so often calls the *plebs sancta Dei*—'the holy common folk of
God', of that sensitive and apostolic spirit that was moved to such practical
purpose by the sight of heathen slave boys from Northumbria for sale in
Rome—whom so many others saw, and nothing followed from the seeing!
'Gregory our father, who sent us baptism', as the English called him.

But apart from the details of his revision—which are fascinating—there
is a much greater aspect of his liturgical work, which is an aspect of the
greatness of his own mind. Edmund Bishop once expressed the hope that
the day would come when historical understanding would have been
sufficiently cultivated 'to see how Gregory discarded earlier practices, now
out of date and almost meaningless, and modernised the rite. On the other
hand—and this is much more important and may to some appear more
attractive—it will be possible to appraise the religious implications of the
Gregorian book and understand what is, I venture to think, an almost
astounding as it is a unique survival and conservation of old and simple
ideas in regard to some matters which most deeply touch the christian life.'[1]

Liturgical studies have not progressed altogether satisfactorily in England since Edmund Bishop's death—twenty-six years ago to-day as I write
this—largely, perhaps, because we have so much neglected the lessons that
he taught, of which the most important was that the study of liturgy is
primarily a study of *people praying*, and not of the history of regulations.
But whether it be yet recognised or not, this is the true importance of the
*Gregorian Sacramentary* in the history of European religion. It does not lie
in any archaeological meticulousness. Gregory, though he was conservative, could be quite ruthless with mere antiquarian details. Its quality lies
in its deliberate and faithful adherence to certain old and simple ideas
about the eucharist, just because they were both simple and true, which
every other rite in christendom has to a greater or lesser extent overlaid
with later and more complicated ones. If the Roman rite to-day, in comparison with some other rites, still pays for this particular kind of primi-
tiveness with a sort of abruptness, it nevertheless retains under all its
carolingian and mediaeval ornament the pre-Nicene and even apostolic
directness of concentration upon the eucharistic action to the exclusion of
all else. Just so the New Testament accounts of the institution neglect the
circumstances—the emotions of those who were there, and even the supper
itself—to rivet attention on the creative acts of Christ before and after
supper, which alone constitute the eucharist.

With Gregory's revision the local evolution of the Roman rite at Rome
is virtually over. About a dozen masses were added in the century after his

[1] *Lit. Hist., p.* viii.

death, partly pieced together from old texts, partly new. And a complete outfit of prayers for the lesser Sundays—for which he had omitted to provide, in the antique fashion—was taken over almost unchanged from the 'Italian edition' of Gel. by some seventh century Pope. But by and large the *Gregorian Sacramentary* as S. Gregory left it, with its practical thoughtfulness, its deep roots in tradition, its unemotional sobriety, remained the final contribution of the old local church of Rome to that general synthesis of Western liturgy which is the accompanying sign of the rise of the new Europe in the West. The old Europe of Diocletian and Theodosius had been based on a political unity, resting on the civil authority of the emperors invested with a sort of spiritual sanction by their deification. The new Europe was based on a spiritual unity, expressed in the spiritual leadership of the popes, invested (in theory) with a sort of temporal sanction by their coherence with the revived Western empire. Rome, the city of Augustus and of Peter, was the link that bound the new world to the old. The best of the traditions from the old world of organised human living, both by liturgy (in the life of the spirit) and by law (in the life temporal) were transmitted in her name to the new. The first of these transmissions was chiefly the work of Gregory, the second of Justinian, the last respectively of the classical popes and emperors, men born out of due time. After them—between them and the new Europe—comes the real deluge, the most destructive of those barbarians and the most sterile of those Byzantines, whose first waves had already combined to ruin the old Europe during the fifth century.

### The Western Synthesis

The later fourth century had seen the general 'Western' outline of the liturgy take shape within the framework of the old universal tradition. The fifth witnessed its adaptation to a public worship and the rise of the influence of the calendar. In the sixth the various regional developments of this common Western basis in Gaul and Spain and Italy (and, no doubt, in Africa, though we know little about it) each come to such maturity as is possible along their own separate lines. This is a rough account of the stages of the process, but it holds broadly true right across the West. In the seventh century and after there comes a change of direction. It is in one sense the period of the *nadir* of christendom, of the darkest barbarism in the West and of quick recession before Islam in the East. But in the West it is also the time of the first faint stirrings of new life. Tentatively in the seventh century, clearly in the eighth and after that consciously and deliberately, the period from the seventh century to the tenth is the period of a new liturgical synthesis in the West, which marks a new synthesis of European *life*. It was achieved not at Rome but in the new creative centre of Western thought, in Gaul.

Just as the old Roman Gel. book, first compiled c. A.D. 500, had crossed
the Alps and been brought into use in some churches in Gaul between
A.D. 550 and 600, so the new Roman Greg. book, compiled c. A.D. 600, also
crossed the Alps at a date variously placed between A.D. 640 and 690. The
effects of its arrival are obvious on all French liturgical MSS. written after
c. A.D. 700, not only on French versions of the Roman rite, but on the
books of the Gallican rite themselves. The *Missale Gothicum* has borrowed
some Greg. prayers, and it was written c. A.D. 700. (It has also more from
Le. and some from Gel.) The *Missale Gallicanum* has borrowed more; and
the *Missale Francorum* has so many that Duchesne felt obliged to treat it as
substantially a Roman book with some Gallican survivals, though its
compiler probably thought of it as an ordinary South French book, not an
'Italian' one. The *Bobbio Missal* has not only borrowed from the Greg.
propers but supplanted the very principle of the Gallican variable canon by
the fixed Roman one. Only the *Masses of Mone* (copied c. A.D. 650) have no
Roman borrowings.[1]

The impact of the new Greg. on the Roman rite as used in Gaul is
equally clear. The unique MS. of the old Frankish 'Gel. of the seventh
century'[2], copied c. A.D. 700, has already a Greg. text of the canon and has
been adapted to Greg. in certain other details, even though the book as a
whole is still decidedly a Gel. not a Greg. book. In the course of the century (probably rather after A.D. 750) there appeared a more thoroughgoing adaptation of the old Frankish Gel. book, which Edmund Bishop
christened the 'Gel. of the 8th century'.[3] The name is not perhaps the best
that could have been chosen; it conceals the fact that this book is much
more than a fresh edition of the Frankish 'Gel. of the 7th century'. Its
foundation is no longer its Gel. but its Greg. element, though it retains
from the Frankish 'Gel. of the 7th century' many of the prayers and ceremonies which the latter had inherited from the 'Italianised Gel.' of the
sixth century, as well as most of the properly French additions Gel. had
received in the course of some two centuries' use in France. The result is
not merely a 'Gelasianised Gregorian' book, less austere and sober in tone
han Greg. as S. Gregory had left it. It can only be described as an ingent-
ous combination of French taste and feeling with the old Roman sense of

[1] The Spanish books are much more free than the French ones from Roman
borrowings. The ninth century *Lib. Sacr.* has a few, all, so far as I have noticed,
from Le. (*e.g.* coll. 519–520.) The eleventh century *Lib. Ord.* has more, and the
influence of Greg. is obvious (*e.g.* coll. 227 *sqq.*). The earliest extant Spanish books
of the Roman rite are of the tenth–eleventh century (two from San Millan, noted by
Férotin, *Lib. Sacr.*, coll. 911 *sq.*, and also *B.M. Addit.* 30, 847, from Silos). They
appear to be based on Greg. as adapted in France, the 'Gel.-Greg. of the tenth
cent.' (see below); but none of them have been edited.
[2] This is the book *ed.* by H. A. Wilson as *The Gelasian Sacramentary*, Oxford,
1894.
[3] Dom P. de Puniet has suggested that it was put together in Burgundy, *Eph. Liturg.*,
xliii (1929), *p. 96.*

form. The Western synthesis is being effected in the eighth century, though it is not yet complete.

### The Reforms of Charlemagne

The surviving MSS. of this 'Gel. of the 8th century' differ a good deal as to the proportions in which they blend their Gel. and Greg. and other elements.[1] Even in those churches in Gaul which used the Roman rite (covering by *c.* A.D. 750 probably a good half of the country) there can have been little uniformity, 'Gel. of the 7th century', 'Gel. of the 8th century' and probably 'pure' Greg. books variously adapted being found in use even at different altars in the same church. As for the Gallican rite, that was falling rapidly into decay all through the eighth century, as the increasingly wholesale substitution of Roman and Spanish prayers in the later Gallican MSS. indicates. The French church was in a very disordered and corrupt condition, which reflects itself in its liturgical life.

The man who reorganised the churches of Gaul was the great emperor Charlemagne (A.D. 768–814) who, layman though he was, took a more than clerical interest in the details of liturgical worship and ceremonies. This was a subject upon which his views were decided and obstinate, and not free from the passion and narrowness which so often mark the amateur. His orderly mind was offended as much by the ceremonial and liturgical diversity of the churches in his dominions as by the disorder and disorganisation of episcopal administration which were its underlying cause. He determined on a liturgical 'fresh start', on the basis of a universal adoption of the authentic Roman rite.

There was more in this scheme than the mere prejudice of an autocrat with a hobby. Rome with its imperial legend was in one sense the goal of all his policy, but in another it was from the first its foundation. His dynasty was already the traditional ally of the Popes, and it was as the heir of the traditions of the empire that Charlemagne stood before the West long before he was crowned as Roman emperor by the Pope in S. Peter's on Christmas Day A.D. 800. If there was to be a uniform rite in his realms it could only be some form of the Roman rite, as a matter of practical politics, quite apart from the magic of the name of Rome in those particular decades. The Roman rite in a Frankish dress already served half the churches of Gaul, and those the Frankish ones in the heart of his empire. Even the Gallican books contained a steadily increasing proportion of Roman material. But Charlemagne's dominions included more than Gaul. Italy and Rome itself would never change from their indigenous tradition, as Gaul was in process of doing. East of the Rhine and in the Low

---

[1] Perhaps the most representative are the *Sacramentary of Gellone*, ed. by Dom P. de Puniet and that of *Angoulême*, ed. by Dom Cagin. That nearest to the original is probably the MS. now at Padua, *ed.* by Dom Mohlberg.

Countries, also within Charlemagne's grasp, the Roman rite was already in full possession. If he looked to the North or the East or the South-East of his Eastern frontier, all that was christian was already, more thoroughly Roman in liturgy than any other part of Europe north of the Campagna. We must go back a little to explain how this had come about.

### The English Influence

When the Roman missionaries under S. Augustine arrived at Canterbury in A.D. 596, they found a small Burgundian mission under Liudhard using the Gallican rite. Augustine himself was consecrated to the episcopate by Aetherius, bishop of Arles, where again he may have found the Gallican rite in use. He must have encountered it more than once on his passage through Gaul. He wrote to S. Gregory in some perplexity, both at the existence of these differences of rite, and as to the policy he was to adopt in the infant Anglo-Saxon church in face of them. Augustine, saint though he was and our English apostle, seems occasionally to exhibit more than one trait of the typical Italian *monsignore*. There is his occasional timidity combined with a real devotion to duty; there is his serious and humble realisation of the responsibilities of his office, combined with an almost childish touchiness about the deference due to his official position. But nothing is more characteristic than this perturbation of mind at the discovery that there were quite good catholics who did not use the Roman rite at all, let alone the authorised current edition of the *curia*. At all events, Augustine did not take the Pope's large-minded advice to draw on the best in both rites, but introduced at Canterbury the new *Gregorian Sacramentary* which had just been introduced at Rome. On this we have the testimony both of Archbishop Egbert of York and S. Aldhelm of Wessex.[1] Whatever may be the truth in the much-disputed question as to the survival of any organised remains of Romano-British christianity in Eastern Britain, nothing can be more certain than that the new archbishopric of Canterbury inherited—and intended to inherit—from the old Romano-British church of S. Alban and Bishop Fastidius neither jurisdiction nor succession of orders, neither tradition of doctrine nor anything in its liturgy. Under a succession of archbishops who were all either missionaries from Italy (this includes the Greek S. Theodore) or Saxon disciples trained in their school, the Anglo-Saxon church was 'Roman of the City' in its rite, in its calendar, in the dedications and fittings of its churches,[2] in its church music[3] and in ecclesiastical details generally. Even in the North, where the Roman missions for the most part only reaped a harvest sown by Celtic missions from Iona, the same state of affairs came to prevail after the Synod of Whitby in A.D. 664. S. Wilfrid of York and Ripon is a declared ultra-

---

[1] Cited and discussed by E. Bishop, *Lit. Hist.*, *pp.* 42 and 104 *sq.*
[2] Bede, *Eccl. Hist.*, I, xxix; IV, xviii; etc.    [3] *Ibid.*, II, 20.

montane; S. Benedict Biscop is an enthusiastic importer of Roman books and ecclesiastical paraphernalia generally;[1] the Venerable Bede is an avowed partisan of Roman ways against the errors of the *Britones*.[2]

But was there in fact a 'British' rite akin to the Gallican, as has often been assumed? The Irish church in the seventh century used a form of the Roman, and the influence of Ireland was then predominant among the Celtic churches. We hear of no questions raised between the Welsh and Anglo-Saxon churches about the rite of the eucharist, but only about baptism and the tonsure and the date of Easter; though both sides were in a frame of mind not to pass over any questions that could be raised. We have no direct evidence either way. But whether the British churches used a form of the Gallican or the Irish-Roman rite, it made no difference to their relations with the Anglo-Saxons. Their clergy would not eat or sleep in the same house with a Saxon cleric. And from the eighth century onwards a kind of loathing of the *Scotti* and all their doings and all their ways seems to have swept over the English, in which racial bitterness and ecclesiastical prejudice were probably nicely blended. The canons of the national synod of Celcyth in A.D. 816 excluded all 'Scottic' ecclesiastics from any form of ministration whatever in English churches. They forbade English bishops to ordain them or to accept their orders, the English clergy to tolerate their ministering in English parishes, and the English laity to receive baptism or holy communion at their hands or even to hear mass when they celebrated it. It was the English reply to the former Welsh refusal on racial grounds to assist in the evangelisation of their invaders. Irish influence on English religion—and in the field of private extra-liturgical devotion the Irish contribution to English religion is not inconsiderable—is either earlier than this in date or else represents something which has filtered indirectly into England by way of the Continent.

Every item of liturgical evidence we possess from the Anglo-Saxon church without exception reveals the use of the Roman rite, either in the form of the Greg. sacramentaries brought by S. Augustine, or in copies of the Frankish 'Gel. of the 8th century' introduced across the channel later on. And it was to Anglo-Saxon missions, bringing with them as a matter of course the Roman rite by which the English worshipped, that Holland and Frisia, parts of Flanders, Central and in part Southern Germany all owed their conversion during the eighth century; and by such missions that the conversion of Scandinavia and North Germany was begun in the ninth century. Right down to the end of the middle ages the impress of the first Anglo-Roman liturgical books brought from England by these missionaries on the calendars and missals of Sweden, Norway, Denmark, Holland, Hesse, Thuringia and Bavaria is never effaced.

The success of the Roman mission at Canterbury had in effect outflanked the Gallican rite, though such a result had been far from Gregory's

[1] *Ibid.*, IV, 18.    [2] *Ibid.*, V, 22.

thoughts. It was a further unforeseen result of his initiative that the eighth century English missions to the other Teutonic peoples made the Roman rite, probably for the first time, the rite of the actual majority of Western christians. Not only so, but the continual and cordial relations of the new Anglo-German churches with the Papacy ensured that the Roman rite as they practised it should take a much purer form than it had hitherto done in Gaul or even in North Italy. This in turn reacted after a while on the more free and easy use of it among the Franks. When the English archbishop of Mainz, Boniface the apostle of Germany—perhaps the greatest missionary Europe had seen since S. Paul—was repeatedly called in *c.* A.D. 750 by the Frankish churches to assist as Papal legate in their own reform, one of the points to which he turned his attention was the Frankish liturgy. It is possible that the Frankish 'Gel. of the 8th century' is partly a result of his initiatives.

But the time was not yet ripe for reconstruction in Gaul. There was no effective primatial centre, like Toledo in Spain, to take the lead; there was no national unity between the half-German Franks, the Celtic Bretons, the Latin *méridionaux* and the half-Spanish Goths of the South-West, to create such a centre. (To this day there are at least five prelates in France who bear the title of *Primat de Gaule.*) The new Caroling dynasty was not yet firmly enough set upon the throne to take the lead in reform in the absence of a leader from the church. Boniface, a foreigner, distracted by the incessant calls of his German missions, could not supply that lack. He found the bishops recalcitrant to all reform; and he seems to have felt that the Frankish king Peppin, the father of Charlemagne, had neither the organising ability nor the steadiness of purpose for enforcing it. The task was left for Peppin's son and another Englishman to carry through between them. It was as well, for the licentiousness and illiteracy of the eighth century French bishops which were the real obstacle to every reform were too deep-seated to be cured by anything but death and a whole generation of new and better appointments. The spasmodic efforts of Boniface made no lasting improvement for the moment, but they pointed to the path which would have to be taken a generation later.

### The Work of Alcuin

It was therefore by no arbitrary personal whim of Charlemagne that the reform of the liturgy followed the path it did, but as the natural fulfilment of a movement to which everything had been converging for more than 200 years. If there was to be a unification of rites, the basis must be the Roman rite in some form, since it was already spontaneously used in the large and growing majority of the churches concerned. And it had the further advantage of having received an admirable latinity and a standardised text from S. Gregory's revision, now canonised by the passage of two centuries of reverence. Charlemagne's difficulty was not to introduce the Gregorian reform into the French churches, but to secure an authentic and standard text among the multitude of copies already in use, all unofficially altered and emended to suit French ways. Charlemagne therefore applied to the Pope Hadrian I, for an authentic copy of Greg. as early as 781. The Pope was a busy man, and irritatingly uninterested in the great project of securing perfect conformity throughout the West to the rite of his own see. No book arrived, and Charlemagne was forced to repeat his request. At last, somewhere between 785 and 791 the long-awaited copy came. After all this delay the book the Pope had sent turned out to be unusable as it stood for Charlemagne's purpose. Not only had the text been carelessly copied, but the book itself must have seemed to the emperor strangely defective. It contained no proper provision for the 'green' Sundays or even for those of Eastertide; next to no 'votives' for weekdays when the liturgical cycle ordered no feast or fast; practically nothing for funerals or weddings, for the profession of nuns or the reconciliation of penitents, or other occasional needs.[1] The old-fashioned Roman rite *c.* A.D. 600 had not felt the need of these things, and this was a copy—freshly but not very carefully made—of the *Gregorian Sacramentary* as it had left S. Gregory's hand, with a few seventh century additions. It is perhaps regrettable that history records no expression of Charlemagne's opinion of the Pope or his book when the latter was presented to him after getting on for ten years of expectation.

The Roman model was thus itself in need of some touching up by Charlemagne's standards. Fortunately Charlemagne had at hand the very man for the work in the person of Alcuin, an Englishman, the first scholar of his age and Charlemagne's wisest adviser in all that concerned the department of education and literature.[2] Alcuin carefully revised the text of Pope Hadrian's MS. with the aid of older copies of Greg. already circulating in France, producing a good critical text. He added the masses for the missing lesser Sundays, presumably also from these MSS. (They had already been added to current MSS. of Greg. even at Rome itself, from the old pre-Greg. 'Italianised edition' of Gel. during the seventh century.) He supplied a number of items not found in Hadrian's MS. to make the book 'workable' for contemporary church life in France.

But he went further. His scholar's sense of broad questions, and the shrewd Englishman's knack of knowing men which comes out so often in his letters, told him instinctively that the severity of the Roman book as it

---

[1] The text of Hadrian's book has been edited from two Cambrai MSS. by H. Lietzmann, *Das Sacram. Greg. nach dem Aachener Urexemplar*, Münster, 1921.

[2] It is an interesting and little-known fact that Alcuin is ultimately responsible for the modern form of our printed letters, which are derived from the script specially evolved for legibility in the *scriptorium* of his monastery at Tours. It is an instance of the practical bent of his scholarship.

stood would prove too bare for the Franks, or indeed for the Northern peoples generally. Accustomed to elaborate symbolical ceremonies and the more rhetorical and flowery style of the Gallican and 'Frankish Gel.' prayers, the people and clergy of the North were likely to view the simplicity of Greg. as baldness, its sobriety as dullness and the pregnant brevity of its prayers as cramping to their own more exuberant and affective devotional style. As it stood they would never bring themselves to make it the framework of their own devotion. And so Alcuin added to the authentic Greg. book a 'Supplement' as long as the book itself, containing prayers and rubrics for certain extra ceremonies and occasions dear to the Northern piety. In this was to be found a considerable collection of the best things in the 'Frankish Gel.' books of the seventh and eighth centuries, supplemented by some prayers drawn from Gallican sources and others from the Mozarabic rite of Spain, adapted for use in the framework of the Roman rite. It was all chastened a little in style and expression by Alcuin's careful revision. But it formed a corpus of Frankish or Northern devotions whose origin is as unmistakable in its warmth and colour as is that of the Gregorian book in its quite different way.

Between Greg. and its new Supplement Alcuin set a 'Little Preface' (known as the *Praefatiuncula Hucusque*, from its first word), explaining how the book is to be used. All that precedes the preface, the work (with small exceptions) of the great Gregory, is to be used by everybody, entirely and without any variation—'anyone will reject it in any particular only at his own peril.' (There is an intimation of Charlemagne in the background behind Alcuin here.) But though Greg. is thus made universally compulsory, Alcuin goes on to explain that the use of his own Supplement—about which he is disarmingly humble—in any or all of its contents is entirely optional. Those to whom these prayers are dear and familiar—*cui animo sedent*, an understanding phrase!—will draw on them as they please. Others, the purists of the new *régime*, will use the Greg. book in its authentic form without these tolerated frills. And both parties are to follow their own preference *placabiliter*—'without bickering'.[1] Alcuin the Englishman had a tolerably good notion of the way to work a compromise.

Such was the liturgical reform of Charlemagne—the introduction of a book in which the framework and about forty per cent. of the contents were genuinely Roman, while the rest came from Gallican and 'semi-Gallicanised' sources. And the church was left a good deal of freedom to determine by actual use the proportions in which the two elements were finally to be mingled. It was the decisive moment in the Western synthesis.

---

[1] Alcuin's book is that *ed.* by H. A. Wilson as *The Gregorian Sacramentary*, H.B.S., 1915.

*The End of the Gallican Rite*

One immediate result was the end of the Gallican rite as a rite wherever it still survived. Charlemagne peremptorily forbade its use. It was followed two centuries later by the slower decline of the sister Mozarabic rite in Spain. It is always with a certain regret that one comes to 'the end of an auld sang', when a tradition for which and by which many men and women have lived fades irremediably into the dead past. More especially ought this to be so for a christian in the case of a liturgical tradition sprung from the soil and native to the minds and hearts of a population, which has formed for God whole generations of men and women, nameless and unremembered for the most part, but still praying men and women and bone of our bone 'in Christ'. Every liturgy has been the road to God and their eternal destiny of so many of the *plebs sancta Dei*—and the footsteps of the great multitude of the unknown saints are holy in the dust even on long-forgotten paths.

In the case of the Gallican rite this regret will perhaps be tempered for the student by the Gallican documents themselves, which plainly indicate that the end was not very far off when Charlemagne so abruptly hastened it. The barbarous boisterous Merovingian Latin in which they were composed would never have suited the clerks of the Carolingian renaissance, no Ciceros in reality but very proud of their culture, and certainly incomparably better educated than their predecessors only fifty years before. These clumsy old prayers have indeed a moving kind of poetry of their own, rather like that of the surviving fragments of the Frankish epics. But quite apart from their barbarisms of syntax and accidence, they bear very plainly written in their substance the marks of their own times, and could never have served another. They voice the desperate cries of an age horror-stricken by its own unending turmoil, and yet quite unable to check the violence of its lusts and brutalities. 'Let not our own malice within us but the sense of Thy longsuffering (*indulgentiae*) be ever before us; that it may ceaselessly keep us from evil delights and graciously guard us from the disasters (*cladibus*) of this life'.[1] Doubtless that is a prayer which christians can never wholly omit without peril. But one feels that in these ever-repeated entreaties from the heart of the dark ages the struggle with evil and calamity is so close and so terrible that there is never time or breath to stand for a moment and look at the holiness and beauty and redeeming wisdom of God, which is—after all—the end of religion. The whole energy of the christian life is taken up in the negative battle with sin. Perhaps it was an instinctive feeling for the need of a more balanced and serene contemplation of the economy of redemption, such as many of the old Roman collects provide, which led in the better times of the eighth century to the

[1] *Contestatio* of Mass XX in the *Miss. Francorum*, ed. Mabillon *de Lit. Gall.*, 1729, p. 324.

large-scale adoption of Roman prayers in books which professed to follow the Gallican rite.

This increasing and voluntary self-Romanisation of the Gallican rite is in fact the clearest confession of its own inadequacy to serve the needs of the time. And it laboured under other disadvantages. Men were beginning to *think* again, penetratingly, philosophically, theologically. And the Gallican prayers, though they contain gems of poetry, have for the most part a fatal verbosity, a tendency to substitute words for meaning, which on occasion degenerates into sheer vapidity. This would prejudice educated men, who were still a small minority. But there was another disadvantage which affected the rank and file of the clergy. The Gallican style was florid; its prayers were longer than the terse Roman prayers; it needed a different eucharistic prayer for every day in the year. A full Gallican book was bound to be longer than a full Roman one, with its unchanging canon which only had to be copied once. When every liturgical MS. for use at the altar had to be copied by hand, and country priests were still apt to need a portable altar book in their large and scattered parishes, this must have told heavily against the survival of the Gallican rite in the long run.

### The Adoption of Alcuin's Missal

But though we may admit that it had no future and that Charlemagne adopted the only practical course in basing his reform on Greg., there is less to be said for his method of carrying it out by the use or the threat of his secular authority. This was in line with the theocratic view of royal and imperial authority which he sedulously fostered, and which was in fact an inheritance from the fourth century post-Constantinian Roman empire. But even so his imperious Act of Uniformity might have been difficult to enforce, but for the tact and wisdom of Alcuin in compiling his permissive Supplement of familiar Frankish prayers. Even as it was, it is doubtful how far the emperor was obeyed in actual practice at the altars of the Frankish realm, despite the straitness of his command and the eager compliance of his bishops. It is noteworthy that at the Abbey of S. Riquier near Abbeville in Picardy the inventory of A.D. 831 reveals that there were in use in the church nineteen Gelasian missals, three Gregorian books and only one copy of the authorised 'Gregorian and Gelasian missal recently arranged by Albinus' (*i.e.* Alcuin). The inventories of half-a-dozen village churches near Rheims *c.* A.D. 850 have chanced to survive. Of these, all were 'Roman' not 'Gallican' in rite, but three used Greg. only (with or without the supplement?). Two had both Greg. and Gel. missals. One had still only a copy of Gel.[1] Allowing for the inevitable delays of an age when MSS. could only

[1] E. Bishop, *Lit. Hist.*, pp. 47–8. It is proper to say that I have drawn largely in this section on both the conclusions and evidence of Bishop's essays on *The Gelasian Mass Book* (*op. cit., pp.* 39 *sqq.*), and *The Liturgical Reforms of Charlemagne* (*Down-*

be slowly provided by hand, fifty years is a long time for the carrying out of a heartily desired change. There are, too, quite a number of MSS. of the 'Gel. of the 8th century' in ninth century script, books which ought never to have come into existence, if orders were being strictly obeyed. The evidence is too scanty for generalisation. But it looks as though there had been for a while a certain amount of passive resistance by the clergy.

One thing is quite certain from the MSS. themselves—the popularity of Alcuin's supplement in Gaul. While the Greg. book without the Supplement, or any part of it, still continued to be copied in Italy in the late ninth and even tenth century—in itself a significant indication of the different devotional ethos to be found north and south of the Alps—there are, I think, only two copies from ninth century Gaul of the unsupplemented Greg. text, despite its much shorter length and the consequent temptation to copyists and purchasers to be content with the compulsory part alone. Alcuin's careful delimitation between the official rite and the optional appendix soon disappeared. First the text of the preface, and then all distinction between Greg. and the Supplement, were omitted from new copies. It means that the optional additions were everywhere wanted and everywhere in use in Gaul. As the ninth century progresses these additions are inserted into the body of the text of Greg. at the appropriate places, and the Roman and Frankish elements become inextricably fused into a single book. In the troubled times that came again after Charlemagne's death the eye of authority upon the scribes and clergy was distracted, and even at court the fashion changed a little from 'pure' Roman to Roman à la française. In late ninth and tenth century MSS. a considerable number of old 'Frankish Gel.' items which Alcuin had omitted have found their way back into the mass-book and even a few more of the forbidden Gallican prayers. The missal thus greatly supplemented begins to spread into England and Italy in the tenth century, and had silently ousted the Roman 'pure' Greg. books at Rome itself before the eleventh century was over. This seems to have taken place insensibly, probably in the course of the eleventh century reform of the Papacy. This was largely conducted by German Popes, who must have brought with them the liturgical usages and books to which they were accustomed from beyond the Alps.

### The Western Missal

With these 're-Gelasianised Gregorian' books of the tenth century the Western synthesis is complete, after a process of 300 years. They are the direct origin of the missals[1] that served the whole West (with diminishing

---

side Review, xxxvii (1919), pp. 1 sqq.), though I have modified Bishop's views in certain respects from my own study. But there is no other full and scientific approach to the matter than Bishop's discussions.

[1] And also of much in the Pontifical and Ritual.

exceptions) for six centuries, and of that which serves half of all christendom to this day. The decisive point in the history is the work of Charlemagne, or rather, as I believe, the special idea of Alcuin. If the emperor saw that the old Roman framework of the rite with its old and simple ideas could alone provide a satisfactory basis for unity, it was the insight of Alcuin which understood how its spirit must be made less rigid if it was to contain the fulness of Western devotion. And it was his wisdom which left to the churches—the christian people and clergy in their unofficial multitudes—a large measure of freedom to decide for themselves by the experience of practical use how far this process was to go. In the event it went further than even he expected. Alcuin was indebted to predecessors for ideas as well as materials. Seventh century books like the *Bobbio Missal* and the 'Frankish Gel.' had been fumbling after what he did; the 'Gel. of the 8th century' and the *Missale Francorum* come nearer to it. Alcuin's merit lies in two things, the skill with which he selected his materials, and the relative freedom which he left to the church at large to continue the process of selecting and blending along the lines he had laid down.

It is a mistake to call the final product 'Roman', in the sense that the *Gregorian Sacramentary* is Roman. To compare the book that Hadrian sent to·Charlemagne with the book the Franco-German church sent back to Rome three centuries later is to understand that the Mozarabic and Gallican were not the only old local rites which were obliterated by the new Western missal. Amongst others this killed also the old local rite of Rome. It is true that the Greg. element which Charlemagne and Alcuin made its basis is never eliminated thenceforward from the Western missal; that structurally the Western mass is thenceforward Roman and not 'Gallican'; that a recognisable proportion of the variable prayers are still as Roman in spirit and feeling as when they left the pen of Gregory; that the name *Missale Romanum* attaches to the whole. But the old Roman element has been overlaid and very greatly enriched in its grasp by a larger quantity of material from other churches.

Into the Western missal have gone important elements brought to the West in the fifth and sixth centuries from the rites of Jerusalem and Antioch, Constantinople, Egypt and Africa; and others, mostly of rather later date (sixth–ninth centuries), from Italy, Spain, Ireland and Gaul. Treasures from all over christendom were poured into a Roman vessel, which had kept better than others the simple classic shape. But they were mostly not Roman, and they were not collected by a Roman. The real scene of the synthesis was the palace chapel of Charlemagne at Aachen, built by Frankish labour from German stone pieced together with old Italian and Byzantine and Syrian marbles and columns brought from Ravenna and from Rome. And England's contribution to the Western synthesis was the Blessed Alcuin of York, the final begetter of the Western rite.

*Mediaeval and Post-Mediaeval Developments*

The Western rite never shewed any signs of reaching that immobility which finally sets in in the Byzantine rite in this very period. But the wisdom of Alcuin is shewn by this, that there are no more changes of shape or principle in the Western liturgy, but only a continual and vivacious development within the principles he had fixed. Even the most remarkable of the 'derived rites' of the Middle Ages—Paris, Carthusian, Trier, Sarum, Autun, Dominican, Rouen, Hereford, Carmelite and the forty or fifty others—are none of them new 'rites' in the technical sense, still less different rites from the Western rite, as *e.g.* the old Alexandrian, Antiochene and Roman rites had really been different rites from one another. They are only local dialects, some of them hardly more than 'accents', of the one universal 'Western' rite which the work of Alcuin had created.[1] Their variants lie in details of ceremonial, which are sometimes quite striking, and in the texts of the propers and the priest's private prayers.

The old freedom to compose and use local propers was hardly affected by Charlemagne's reform. In practice the freedom to replace the texts of the propers of seasons by new compositions was not much used, but for the saints' days the formation of local propers continued unabated throughout the middle ages. It gave rise to 'sub-dialects', as it were, within the derived rites themselves, so that the prayers for the saints' days in a Norwich-Sarum book are not entirely the same as those of a Salisbury-Sarum one. Even within the centrally controlled rite of the modern post-Tridentine church, liberty is still found for a supplement of propers for each diocese and abbey of the Latin rite—some 1,500 in all—thus continuing the old freedom of the propers, which the Popes had naturally always respected as an inheritance from the second and third century, and which Alcuin had wisely retained. The old practice of borrowing feasts and texts between different local churches, too, continued unaffected, so that *e.g.* the English feast of the Conception of our Lady appears at Lyons, carried thither by an English canon of Lyons, Gilbert, later bishop of London, even before it had been officially authorised by the Norman bishops of England; and the new Belgian feast of the Holy Trinity invented by Stephen of Liége was providing the dedication of new English cathedrals like Norwich and Chichester before it was accepted (or apparently heard of) at Rome. The writing of new 'votives' for all sorts of devotional *attraits* and necessities of secular life also continued throughout the middle ages and beyond. It was a form of piety which Alcuin himself had found attractive—the mass in the present missal 'in time of war', amongst others, seems to be his compilation from older materials—and some of the mediaeval votives (*e.g.* 'the Five

---

[1] Adrian Fortescue says somewhere that to speak of the 'Roman, Sarum and Gallican rites' is like speaking of 'English, Yorkshire dialect and French' as three different languages.

Wounds of our Lord Jesus Christ' and 'against the pagans') are fine
compositions.

The insertion of new feasts not only of modern saints but of our Lord
(*e.g.* 'the Precious Blood of our Lord Jesus Christ' by Pius IX and 'Christ
the King' by Pius XI) has slowly been centralised in the hands of the curial
Congregation of Rites in the post-Tridentine church. The French dioceses
continued to do this for themselves (in the old Frankish way) down to the
French revolution; and the system of curial control as a whole never became
fully effective until the nineteenth century. Yet even thus limited, the freedom of the propers and the special influence of the calendar on the Western
rites (which had brought in the variable prayers not only of the propers but
the votives) have continued to prevent that fossilisation of the liturgy which
inevitably beset the Byzantine rite once it had perfected its two alternative
sets of celebrant's prayers. No doubt when unwisely exercised these qualities can degenerate into the fostering of cults which are mere devotional
side-issues at the best, distracting popular interest from the grand facts of
redemption to some aspect of them which happens to have become a pious
fashion at the moment. But christian good sense has a way of re-asserting
itself in the end over all sacristy pieties. The history of Western catholicism
is littered with discarded devotions of all kinds, most of which found their
representation in the missal for a while until popular interest waned and that
mass was removed. These are the inevitable effects of a living contact of
the liturgy with the prayers of the christian people in each age. The people
have a certain right to be vulgar; and the liturgy, even while it must teach
them, has never a right to be academic, because it is their prayer. The ease
with which the Western system of variable prayers can enable it to respond
to the people's special interests and devotions at any time may have its
dangers. But it has given the Western rite a closer and more intimate grasp
of human life than any other.

From the time of S. Gregory's revision of the local Roman rite *c.*
A.D. 595 to that of S. Pius V undertaken at the request of the Council of
Trent nearly 1,000 years later no Pope ever officially touched the Roman
ordinary. After Alcuin's revision just before A.D. 800 there was never a
further official edition put out for general use before the Pian missal. All
that vast general conformity of the whole West to the same outline of the
rite during 700 years was in reality a largely *voluntary* conformity to something which met the church's needs, and yet allowed of sufficient local freedom. It is true that Popes from time to time put forth Bulls promulgating
new feasts and new masses. But the initiative in adopting these was in
practice, if not in theory, a local one. Thus the feast of Corpus Christi was
promulgated for the whole church by Urban IV in 1264, but the majority
of churches even in Italy had not yet adopted it fifty years later, though it
was by then just beginning to be taken up by churches in the North.[1] Often

[1] The decade 1320–1330 sees its beginning in many important dioceses.

enough the mediaeval promulgation of a new feast or mass takes the form of a 'grant' of it to particular churches or countries or orders which had asked for it. Almost always they had been observing it on their own authority for some while previously, and now wished to confirm their practice with the highest sanction they could find. Even the feast of Corpus Christi, the most important Papal initiative in the liturgy during the whole middle ages, had been kept at Liége nearly twenty years before Urban IV 'instituted' it.

### Uniformity

There is thus remarkably little foundation for the idea which has been assiduously propagated of late years in England that 'the catholic priest, at least if he has any tincture of the true catholic and priestly spirit, would rather say the most jejune and ill-arranged rite, which was that imposed upon him by authority, than the most splendid liturgy devised by himself.'[1] Either the whole church from the second century to the sixteenth was devoid of 'any tincture of the true catholic and priestly spirit', or such statements are comprehensively mistaken. Even in the first century the use of the liturgical eucharist apart from the supper must have spread by mere borrowing from church to church, as is proved by the verbal identity everywhere in the pre-Nicene church of the dialogue before the *eucharistia* (unless we are to imagine that there then existed some central liturgical authority whose dictates were obeyed without variation everywhere). And after that in every century every liturgy borrowed where it chose, without the intervention of 'authority' in the matter at all, till we come to the edicts of Byzantine emperors and Charlemagne. It is true that in every church the rite was from time to time codified in a revision by the local bishop—a Sarapion, a Basil, a Gregory. But it is also true that their work never endures as they leave it. The same process of unauthorised alteration and addition and borrowing begins again, as it began again within fifty years of the imposition of Alcuin's authorised rite. The proof is written in almost every liturgical MS. in existence. The primitive bishop had control of the text of the prayers because their recitation was his special 'liturgy'; he was the normal celebrant. When he passed on that 'liturgy' to individual presbyters, in practice if not in theory the same control tended to pass to the new normal celebrant, however objectionable in principle the fact may now seem to us. The presbyter was largely ruled by tradition—as the bishop had been. But I have a not altogether inconsiderable experience of ancient liturgical MSS. Setting aside mere copyists' errors, I do not remember any two professing to give the same rite which altogether agree on the text of the celebrant's prayers.

[1] Cited from *The Church Times*, Jan. 22, 1937, by the Rt. Rev. Dr. G. K. A. Bell, bishop of Chichester, in his Charge, *Common Order in Christ's Church* (1937), p. 49.

We have heard a lot in England of late years of the bishop's *jus liturgicum*. The term is entirely unknown to the canon law or to any writer in any country before the later nineteenth century, when it comes into use among a certain group of Anglican ecclesiologists, who invented it as a means of lifting the dead hand of parliamentary statutes off Anglican worship. So far as the primitive bishop had any such right he had it not so much as bishop but as celebrant. When he ceased to be the normal celebrant it passed as a practical fact to other people. If any one were to say that from the sixth century to the eleventh it was habitually exercised much more by the copyists of liturgical MSS. than by bishops, it would not be easy to bring factual evidence to refute him. And *in practice* there is no doubt that it was exercised by the parish priest, 'doing the liturgy' for his flock under the guidance of tradition from such MSS. as he had, which he did not feel much scruple about adding to or altering with his own hand.

This state of things was coming to an end from the thirteenth century onwards. The more centralised religious orders (Cistercians, Mendicants, etc.) tried hard from the first to secure uniformity in all their churches, though the old ways died hard and their general chapters complain a good deal about the growth of variations. The older Benedictines and Augustinians kept up the old local freedom and allowed each house its own missal. In the same period the parish churches began to come to a general conformity with the cathedral of their own diocese, though there were still more traditional peculiarities of ceremonial and calendar in the parish churches of the fifteenth century than a modern catholic would expect. There was a tendency in the fourteenth and fifteenth centuries for diocesan rites which had acquired a certain reputation for their completeness or 'up-to-dateness' to be adopted by their neighbours, as the Sarum rite was adopted by many South English dioceses (in the secular churches) and even in some Irish ones. But even here, when a diocese took over the general arrangement of the rite from a neighbour, it usually made some modifications of its own, and always retained its own local propers of the saints, and often added new ones. Often, too, it kept much of its own traditional ceremonial.

What ended the continuing relics of the old local freedom in the West were, 1. the invention of printing, and 2. the energetic measures taken by the Papacy within its own communion after the Council of Trent and (more especially) by the secular governments of the protestant powers in the same period, to enforce uniformity down to the last comma.[1] The Papacy respected the old freedom of the propers everywhere, and exempted

[1] The most extraordinary instance of this is in Sweden, where on each Sunday every pastor in the country must preach on the same text, chosen and published beforehand, by the Minister of Public Worship. A series for the whole year is put out by his authority every December.

from the scope of the new decrees all local customs which could be proved to be more than 200 years old.

In the East, Byzantine centralisation had always striven for exact uniformity under the aegis of the secular power. Among the Eastern dissidents, however, where the liturgy was still recited from MSS. and not from printed books until quite recent times, borrowing of prayers and customs and even whole liturgies, across the barriers which separated them from the orthodox and from one another, continued at least to the end of the nineteenth century.[1]

There is no need to argue from these facts that the restoration of the old local freedom in its fulness is either possible or desirable. But we shall never understand the history of the early liturgy or even that of the early middle ages, if we try to view it in the light of the drive of the Western churches for uniformity since the sixteenth century. However much ecclesiastical administrators like Innocent I and Charlemagne may have lamented the fact, the churches in the earlier ages did not desire uniformity. And those who have taken part with any understanding in the worship of provincial and country churches in France and Spain and Italy and Germany—or in the parish churches of England—may wonder whether they really care very much about it now.

### The Mediaeval Presentation of the Liturgy

It is easy enough for the student to see the connection between the way in which the eucharist is celebrated in the *Ordo Romanus Primus c.* A.D. 700 and the way the primitive bishop-celebrant performed the eucharist—say, in the time of Hippolytus. Due allowance made for the change of scale, they are both in broad outline the same 'way' of doing the rite. And once the main clue—the changed position of the bishop's throne—has been understood, it is not difficult to see the connection between the rite and ceremonial of the *Ordo Romanus Primus* and a modern pontifical mass sung by a bishop. There have been both simplifications and complications in the ceremonial since the eighth century, but there is a real and obvious derivation of the modern rite of the bishop from the early mediaeval one, and of the latter from the pre-Nicene ceremonial and way of doing things. It is a good deal more difficult to trace the connection of the modern Western 'simple said service'—whether it takes the form of a Roman low mass or an Anglican eight o'clock celebration or a Wesleyan communion service—with the kind of eucharist described by Hippolytus *c.* A.D. 200 and traceable in Clement's epistle *c.* A.D. 96, with the considerable amount of *corporate* action and movement these writers imply.

[1] *Cf. e.g.*, the adoption in the seventeenth century of the Monophysite *S. James* by certain Malabar churches which traditionally used the Nestorian *Addai and Mari*; the increasing Byzantinisation of the modern Coptic rite, and so on.

The 'simple said service' does derive from the primitive ceremonial, like the pontifical mass, and this through the type of thing described in the *Ordo Romanus Primus*. But there are a further two stages interposed between our practice and that of the primitive church, which have no place in the evolution of the pontifical rite. These are: (1) High mass—a sung eucharist celebrated by a single presbyter, assisted by a deacon and subdeacon and various assistants. (2) Low mass—a eucharist *said* by a single presbyter, assisted by a single minister or even just answered by a congregation. The evolution through these two stages took place during the middle ages. The former is common to East and West alike in its main outlines. The latter is entirely confined to the Latin West.

There was nothing new about presbyters celebrating the eucharist when the middle ages began. They had been deputising for the bishop as celebrants ever since the second century. After the middle of the fourth century, as christianity spread to the countrysides and churches in towns multiplied, perhaps the actual majority of christians on any given Sunday morning might have been found to have assisted at a eucharist celebrated by a presbyter (or concelebrated by several) without the presence of their bishop. But in this period the idea of the bishop's 'stational' eucharist as the central liturgical observance of his whole flock was still strong. There are signs that in some of the little Italian city-bishoprics with their very small area the tradition was still a living reality in the sixth century. Even at Rome with its multitude of churches it was not wholly lost sight of before the 'captivity' at Avignon in the fourteenth century. North of the Alps, where much larger 'tribal' dioceses were the rule from the start (outside Provence) the position was always different. The bishop's liturgy was indeed the central observance in his own see-town; but elsewhere the mass of the 'parish priest' assumed from the first the place which the bishop's liturgy had held in the pre-Nicene church.

It is not quite easy to make out the outward circumstances and ceremonial of these eucharists celebrated by presbyters from the second and third century onwards, because all descriptions of the eucharist down to the early ninth century continue to make the traditional assumption that the bishop is the normal celebrant, and the pontifical eucharist the norm of the rite. But without exception all the evidence I have been able to gather—it is considerable in quantity but very fragmentary—suggests that outwardly, in ceremonial and performance, there was no difference whatever in the fifth century between the rite as celebrated by a presbyter and that of a bishop. The celebrant presbyter performed his liturgy from a chair behind the altar like the bishop, with the assistance of a number of deacons, etc., and of concelebrants if other presbyters were present. Except for the *pallium* or *orarion* there were still no special episcopal—or for that matter ecclesiastical—ornaments like the later mitre and gloves. There was in fact nothing to make any ceremonial difference between the rite of the bishop and that of the presbyter. A ceremonial on these lines, with a presbyter-celebrant and assistant presbyters and four or more deacons, continued in use in some French cathedrals on certain days down to the French revolution.[1]

The first great change in Western ceremonial, the bringing of the celebrant round from behind the altar where he faced the people, to before it where he had his back to them, appears to have begun, almost accidentally, in Gaul and the Rhineland during the eighth–ninth century. It was due to certain architectural and devotional changes of fashion. The placing of bodies or relics of the martyrs *under* the altar, in imitation of Rev. vi. 9, goes back certainly to the fourth century, probably to pre-Nicene times. In Merovingian France the usual Western desire to 'see' led to the relics being placed *upon* the altar in costly reliquaries, a cause of some inconvenience on the small square altars of the period. Ultimately they were placed on pedestals behind it, blocking the celebrant's access to his old position.

His consequent coming round to the front involved certain changes of ceremonial. The bishop kept his throne, the symbol of his teaching office; but it was now placed on the gospel side between the altar and the people, to give him easy access to his new position at the front of the altar while making it possible for him still to see and address the people from his throne. He continued as of old to conduct the synaxis sitting on his throne, but in this new position, only going to the altar at the offertory. The presbyter, having as such no teaching office, abandoned the use of the chair and began to conduct all that part of the synaxis which concerned him at the altar itself, only retiring to a seat on the epistle side to listen to such parts of the synaxis as formed the special 'liturgy' of the lesser ministers—the lections and chants. Thus was developed one obvious difference between the eucharist as celebrated by a bishop and by a presbyter—that the bishop as in pre-Nicene times continued to preside over the synaxis from his throne, though its position had been altered in many churches; the presbyter now conducted the synaxis, so far as concerned his own 'liturgy' in it—the prayers—from the altar itself like the eucharist.[2] And because presbyter celebrants were now far more numerous than episcopal ones, from the people's point of view this became the normal thing, and the bishop's ceremonial a peculiar and exceptional thing.

In a work by Alcuin's pupil, Rabanus Maurus, we get for the first time a description of a celebration by a single presbyter, assisted by a deacon and sub-deacon and other ministers, but much less elaborate than the old corporate rite of a bishop with the whole clergy and laity of his church.[3]

[1] A version of it was also the Lincoln use on festivals in mediaeval England.
[2] The frequent journeyings of the ministers to the *sedilia* in the first part of high mass are apt to seem to many people rather unnecessary. But historically it is the saying of any of this part of the rite at the altar which is the innovation, and the sessions at the *sedilia* which represent the continuance of ancient custom.
[3] Rabanus Maurus, *de Institutione Clericorum*, I, 23.

This is presented as being now the normal way of performing the rite, which every cleric ought to know. As he describes it, it is clearly a deliberate simplification of the bishop's rite of the *Ordo Romanus* made for the ordinary parish church. But it is equally clearly the essential outline of that rite which the middle ages called high mass. The modern Roman ceremonial has preserved it very much as Rabanus Maurus describes it in the ninth century. Some of the mediaeval French rites complicated it a good deal with symbolical ceremonies of the kind always dear to the Gallican mind, and also with a good deal of what appears to the modern taste mere fuss.[1] But these are only the characteristics of the Roman and Gallican types all through history. What is important is that high mass, whatever its particular brand of ceremonial, is in essence an early mediaeval simplification of the old bishop's rite, for the public liturgy conducted by a *single* presbyter. High mass is the 'public' half of the consequences of a very important change which had been going on slowly for centuries in the West without attracting any attention at all. *Concelebration* by a number of presbyters with or without a bishop *was falling out of use.* By the thirteenth century, though S. Thomas Aquinas fully recognises the principle,[2] it had become a survival confined chiefly to ordinations, when the newly ordained priests still concelebrate with the bishop to this day in the West.

The old corporate eucharist was not normally celebrated daily in pre-Nicene times. The fourth century had greatly increased the frequency of celebrations by its elaboration of the calendar. A daily celebration, like the daily offices, had been introduced in Africa in S. Augustine's time, though not all Western churches had yet followed this example. Rome especially was slow to adopt a *daily* eucharist as such, keeping the rite for those days on which the calendar provided a special commemoration, feast or fast. There was not even an official eucharist on quite every day in Lent at Rome until the seventh century. (The East has remained at this stage officially down to this day, though a daily liturgy was not unknown in monastic churches, and even some secular churches, in Russia before 1914.) But even this daily liturgy, where it had come in, is still in the fifth century a single corporate concelebration by the bishop and all his presbyters assisted by all the deacons, etc., though naturally the majority of the laity could not be present at so full a rite on weekdays. Some individuals are known to have celebrated daily in the fifth and sixth centuries as a matter of devotion (just as some of the laity communicated daily). But these are chiefly bishops, who doubtless celebrated publicly for their churches.[3]

The real change comes with the breakdown of the bishop's 'stational'

---

[1] A Dominican high mass is the nearest modern survival of these rites, being a simplification of the thirteenth century rite of Paris. It can be witnessed *e.g.* at Haverstock Hill or Blackfriars, Oxford.

[2] *S. Th.*, III, lxxxii, 2.

[3] A useful collection of the early evidence on daily celebration is found in *Sacrificial Priesthood* by Fr. Joseph Barker, C.R., London, 1941.

liturgy as an effective system, which occurs in different regions at different times. As churches multiplied, presbyters more and more become not con-celebrants with their bishop or occasional deputies to celebrate the 'sta-tional' liturgy in his absence, but permanent delegates who are the normal celebrants for a detached congregation in a 'parish church', which the bishop only occasionally visits. Once the 'liturgy' of the christian eucharis-tic 'high-priesthood' has become a regular part of the presbyter's office as such, as it had always been a part of the bishop's, the same devotional ten-dency which had led to a daily corporate eucharist for the communion of the laity and the daily exercise of the various 'liturgies' of all the orders, inevitably led the earnest presbyter to wish to celebrate daily that he might exercise his 'liturgy' fully.

The practice develops most markedly in the Frankish churches, partly because the 'stational' system had never been fully effective in the large Frankish dioceses with their many rural churches, partly because a larger proportion of monks in the Frankish monasteries of the seventh century seems to have been in priest's orders than was commonly the case else-where. Presbyters are much more numerous than bishops everywhere. The desire of many individual presbyters to fulfil their own 'liturgy' frequently cannot be met if each is to have the full assistance needed for high mass. The solution is 'low mass'—the simplification of high mass in order to multiply possibilities of celebrating by discarding all assistance but that of a single minister to answer the priest. The reference to 'morning masses' as opposed to the 'public mass' by the Council of Vaison suggests that something like this was already well known in the South of France in A.D. 529.

A second cause is the desire of individuals or groups among the laity to have the eucharist offered for a special reason. There had always been occasions which the church reckoned desirable for the eucharist which did not properly concern the whole church, e.g. weddings and funerals. If the eucharist is that act by which Jesus of Nazareth brought Himself and all His circumstances finally under the realised Kingship (or into the King-dom) of God,[1] then it is right that those who are His members should seek to bring themselves and particular circumstances which affect their whole individual life (e.g. marriage, sickness) under that Kingship, by a deliberate entering into His act. Even though the whole church is not concerned with them in this, they do so as members of His Body, with and through the authorised representative of that Body. The rise of the Western variable prayers had opened to the liturgy a great opportunity of direct association with and consecration of the joys and sorrows and cares of daily life. The old Gel. books to a special extent, and all the Western rites of the sixth century to some extent, had provided a large number of 'votives', special sets of variable prayers 'for travellers', 'for the sick', 'against judges acting

[1] Cf. p. 75.

unjustly', 'for the amending of a quarrel', and so on—for just such semi-private occasions and needs, to be used on days when the calendar prescribed no special observance.

Partly in gratitude for the special prayers of the clergy in this way, partly to secure them, the laity presented alms and endowments to monasteries and parochial churches, and the clergy repaid their generosity with such offerings of the eucharist for the special intentions of the benefactor. One result is the Frankish addition to the original Roman text of the canon of the clause *'for whom we offer or* who offer for themselves'.[1] Here we have the seemingly innocent root of the whole unsatisfactory system of mass-stipends, and also of something much more important. When the priest offers the eucharist with and in the midst of the laity concerned (as the Roman text presupposes) he is still fulfilling a 'liturgy' in a corporate action, even when the occasion is 'private' and does not concern the whole church. But when he offers it for absent benefactors (as the Frankish text presupposes) the conception has shifted—or is liable to shift—a good deal. The eucharist is becoming something which the priest does *for*, not *with*, the laity, even though they are 'with' him in spirit and he does it at their request.

We are in fact getting near the practical divorce of those complementary ideas of the corporate offering and the priesthood of the priest, whose combination is essential to any organic doctrine of the church as well as of the eucharist. Without it the eucharist is turned into something which a priest alone can do simply in virtue of his personal possession of holy orders, without sufficient regard had to the fact that the eucharist is the corporate act of the church. To this, indeed, his 'order' is necessary; but it is only one 'order' within a hierarchical unity which is incomplete without the co-operation of the other 'orders' in the organic Body of Christ. The addition of a theory which assigned a value and efficacy to this special sacerdotal offering separate from (though dependent on) that of Calvary (as *e.g.* that the sacrifice of each mass by a priest did away venial sin, as the sacrifice of Calvary did away mortal sin) was all that was needed for the whole conception to become obviously different.

### Lay Religion in the Dark and Middle Ages

We have to add, moreover, the further disturbance of the primitive understanding of the rite brought about by the general cessation of lay communions, for which the mediaeval Latin church cannot be held altogether responsible. It had begun in the East in the fourth century, in deference to the new Syrian devotional emphasis on the 'fear' and 'awe' attaching to the consecrated sacrament. It spread to the churches of Gaul in the fifth century, where it occasioned frequent remonstrances, but in

[1] *Cf. p.* 501. (Frankish addition italicised.)

vain. S. Paul's word 'eateth and drinketh judgement (*krima*) unto himself' (1 Cor. xi. 29) interpreted, perhaps over-pessimistically, as 'condemnation', led to an over-emphasis on the *achieved* high state of sanctity required of the christian communicant rather than the earnestness of his desire to achieve it, and 'the food of men wayfaring' came to be looked upon rather as the reward of the saints, so far as the laity were concerned.

It was a turn of spirituality which had in the end many grave consequences, but it had at least a partial explanation in the state of the times. The population of the empire in the fourth century may have been exhausted and corrupt, but it was at least still intelligent. Where an individual's will and moral sense could be touched through his mind he could be brought to an understanding of the responsibilities of the christian communicant. The increasing collapse of civilisation in the fifth century presented the church with the problem of hordes of immigrant barbarians who though vigorous were for centuries manifestly incapable of even the intellectual exercise necessary to build a stone building larger than a hut, and also of whole populations of Roman provincials already more or less christian but rapidly sinking back to the intellectual level of their conquerors. The almost incredible childishness of thought and language to which a man of real ability like S. Caesarius of Arles found it necessary to descend in explaining the creed to adult catechumens early in the sixth century is very revealing when compared with the intelligent sort of simplicity with which men like Augustine and Ambrose had found it possible to discharge the same duty a century or so before.

The barbarians followed their chiefs submissively into the fold of the church, which was thereby enabled to continue to work for a christian society. But that did not in fact make them responsible christians. Their mass-movements into christianity or from Arianism to orthodoxy did not betoken any sort of change of heart. Instead, many of them began to add the vices of the decadent provincial populations with which they were now mingling to the unthinking brutalities of the healthy savage. It is only when one has studied the depressing literature of the *Penitentials* or manuals for confessors; or the horrible domestic annals of the Merovingian princes with their monotonous record of parricides, adulteries, casual murders and unending civil wars; or the history of the Lombard wars; all of which present us with a practical view of the human material with which the church then had to work—it is only then that one understands the reason for the rigorist spirit in which the church of the dark ages approached the question of preparation for communion. It may have been the wrong line to adopt, but the alternative is not easy to contemplate. The sordidness of conduct in those times has to be studied to be believed.

One may, of course, blame the church for accepting these mass-conversions in the fifth and sixth centuries. Certainly the standard of instruction and of sincerity required was much lower than it had been in the fourth.

But again one must remember that the church's own resources for giving instruction had been immensely decreased by the very catastrophes which increased the need of it. The decline of the schools in the West was one of the first consequences of the barbarian invasions; there was no longer a large well-educated class from which an intelligent clergy could be recruited. Such intellectual life as remained the church had now to provide for the world, instead of—as in the fourth century—the educated world providing a constant stimulus and material for the church. The conversion of the barbarians could not, indeed, have been brought about by intellectual processes; it had to be the work of sheer faithfulness and goodness by men of God, like Martin and Patrick and Remigius and Boniface, who were wise but not learned. To have refused the mass-conversions when they came would have been not only impossible but wrong. The barbarians were everywhere the masters of the situation. To have excluded them from the church if they were willing to enter it would have been to close the only door to any bettering of the conditions.

The fifth century church is, I think, more open to attack in principle than that of the fourth on the ground of accepting easy conversions, but not more so if the practical facts of the situation are taken into account. In both cases it is very hard to see how the situation could have been differently handled than it was. But the consequences were serious. All through the dark and middle ages there is an immense drab mass of nominal christianity in the background, looming behind the radiant figures of the saints and the outstanding actions of the great men and women who make up the colourful foreground of the history—a mass of ignorance, squalor and poverty on which no one made any deep impression before S. Francis. A noble and faithful pastoral work must, indeed, have been done by the nameless and rustic clergy of the dark ages and the early mediaeval parish priests. Otherwise the civilisation that flowered in a S. Thomas, a Dante, a S. Louis could never have sprung from the conditions of the sixth century, and the faith would never have been transmitted as it was. The people came to church in the dark ages, or most of them did, and morals and manners were in the course of centuries to some degree tranquillised. But down to the end of the middle ages this great lay mass, the product of the mass-conversions, was never fully absorbed by the church.

Perhaps when it got to church there was not enough preaching. The Reformers thought not, though there was certainly more than the Reformers said there had been, particularly after the thirteenth century. But there is an aspect of the remains of mediaeval sermon literature which I have never seen mentioned, though it seems to stand out from almost every collection I have read. There is very little of this comparatively large class of literature which is concerned with instruction. In nearly all of it the note of moral exhortation is sounded clearly and continually. There are attempts to arouse the people's emotions by descriptions of the passion and various other incidents of the life of our Lord like the nativity, some of which are very moving. But always the end is to move the *will* to goodness, to moral endeavour. The good conduct inculcated is described plainly and practically enough. But there is hardly ever an attempt to make the people *understand* their religion, to instruct them 'apologetically', so to speak, in the faith. No doubt, the faith was not publicly questioned; there was no need for defence. But this lack of the element of instruction in preaching meant that the mediaeval layman's religion was necessarily a very ignorant religion. One may say that the clergy were leaving the people in their ignorance and superstitions; or one may say that in putting this emphasis on right conduct with a population still for the most part unlettered and very barbarous the clergy were putting first things first. It is a fact that the sudden stop put to any preaching but protestant polemics in the reign of Edward VI led to an open and general collapse of morals in England, which the Reformers themselves lamented in no measured terms. It is also a fact that the people's astonishing ignorance of the real teaching of the traditional catholicism was one of the Reformers' most powerful weapons against the old religion. Here I believe are the proofs both of the virtue and the weakness of mediaeval preaching and of the church's traditional method of dealing with the nominal christian mass.

### Lay Communions

It is only when we bear in mind this situation of a very large proportion of the laity from the fifth century onwards that the history of lay communion becomes really intelligible. So we find in the sermons of S. Caesarius of Arles *c.* A.D. 500–530 a curious contradiction. He makes strong appeals to the laity to come more often to communion, but there are other indications that he really does doubt whether a lot of them ought to. He has vigorous denunciations of open evil living among those who do come to communion; there is a continual firm insistence on the need of penitence before communicating—and it is a practical penitence which will do something towards amendment of life at once. The Council of Agde (A.D. 506) at which he presided, felt bound to be content with the statement that those who will not communicate at least at Christmas, Easter and Pentecost 'are not to be accounted catholics'. Even this standard was found to be too high, and later Gallican councils are content with the rule of once a year at Easter. At Rome itself the tradition of a general communion of the people on all Sundays and great feasts persisted in the eighth century,[1] and even in the eleventh century Roman clergy brought up in the urban tradition like Pope Gregory VII were still encouraging the laity to frequent communion. With the retention of the people's communion, Rome still retained

[1] Bede, *Ep.* II

the rite of the people's offering of bread and wine, and the general sense that the eucharist was a corporate rite.

Elsewhere in the West holy communion became practically a clerical and monastic monopoly after the fifth century. The position improved in the twelfth century, and frequent communion for all was at least recognised as theoretically desirable by thirteenth century theologians like S. Thomas[1] and S. Bonaventura,[2] though with some hesitation as to those for whom it is helpful. Again one feels the difficulty arising from the recognition of the great mass of nominal christianity which comes to church. From that time on, monthly, weekly and in some cases daily communion for devout layfolk is by no means unknown. But it is clear from a good many incidents in the lives of the saints that right down to the sixteenth century the mere fact of frequency was apt to arouse suspicion of extravagance or illuminism. It remained true, broadly speaking, of even later mediaeval religion, that the priest as such was normally the only communicant.

The seriousness of this disappearance of lay communion was increased by the fact that partaking of communion had always been so closely linked in the West with the right of *offering*. When the layman ceased to communicate, he ceased as a matter of course to have an active part in the offertory; and when the partial recovery of lay communion came in the twelfth-thirteenth centuries, the custom had lapsed, and the layman's offering of bread and wine at the offertory was not recovered. Thus along with the increased emphasis on 'consecration' (the 'liturgy' of the celebrant alone) there went a parallel movement by which the layman lost all active participation in the rest of the rite, the offertory and the communion—his 'liturgy'. He became a mere spectator and listener, without a 'liturgy' in the primitive sense at all.

### Later Mediaeval Eucharistic Devotion

If we put together all these things—the isolation of the priesthood of the priest from the corporate offering; the false theory of a separate value of the sacrifice of the mass from the sacrifice of Calvary; the elimination of the layman's 'liturgy' of offering and communion, which makes the holy communion (in practice) a part of the celebrant's 'liturgy' and nobody else's; the reduction of the laity's part in the rite to 'seeing' and 'hearing' (the latter being reduced very much in importance through the use of Latin, which placed an over-emphasis on 'seeing' the consecrated sacrament);—and in consequence of all these, the placing of the whole devotional emphasis in the rite on the consecration and conversion of the elements—if we put all these things together, we can see what the mediaeval liturgical development is doing. It is steadily building up the material for all the doctrinal controversies about the eucharist in the sixteenth century. And I believe

[1] S. Th., III, lxxx, 10          [2] In IV Sent., dist. xii, ptm. ii art. 2, q. 2.

that it can be shewn that in all their mistakes the Reformers were the victims—as they were the products—of the mediaeval deformations they opposed.

At all events this was the mediaeval Western presentation of the rite: 1. On occasions, pontifical mass, a form recognisably derived from the way of doing the eucharist practised in the pre-Nicene church. 2. High mass, an eighth–ninth century simplification of 1. which retained much of the old corporate character, being sung and allowing of the fulfilment of the separate 'liturgies' of all the 'orders', deacon, subdeacon, acolytes and laity as well as of the celebrant, in a single corporate act of worship. Nothing but custom prevented it from being the occasion of a general communion, though the custom was not often broken except in some monastic churches. Throughout the middle ages this was the official norm of the rite, its proper 'public' presentation—usual in well-equipped parish churches on all Sundays and holidays, and offered daily in cathedral and collegiate churches, in religious houses and even some large parish churches.[1] 3. Low mass— the devotional expedient of the individual presbyter for fulfilling his own 'liturgy' in the Body of Christ fully and frequently. As such it provided adequately for the fulfilment of no 'liturgy' but his own. The service was said in a low voice, and answered by a server, who was rather a convenience to enable the priest to perform the rite than an adequate substitute for the corporate concurrence of all the other 'orders' of the church in the action, which however in theory he did represent.

Nevertheless low mass was performed publicly, the laity could attend it —and it was short. Human nature being what it is, it was never unpopular. And it had certain advantages. It did—probably for the first time—make it possible for busy layfolk to be present at the eucharist on week-days if they wanted to. And they found in it a real way of assisting their own devotion. The quiet of low mass afforded the devout an excellent opportunity for using mentally the vernacular prayers which they substituted for the Latin text of the liturgy as their personal worship, which the corporate rite of high mass with its singing and music tended to distract.

Let us be quite clear what this last development really means. The old corporate worship of the eucharist is declining into a mere focus for the subjective devotion of each separate worshipper in the isolation of his own mind. And it is the latter which is beginning to seem to him more important than the corporate act. The part of the individual layman in that corporate action had long ago been reduced from 'doing' to 'seeing' and 'hearing'. Now it is retreating within himself to 'thinking' and 'feeling'. He is even beginning to think that over-much 'seeing' (ceremonial) and 'hearing' (music) are detrimental to proper 'thinking' and 'feeling'. While the catholic doctrines of the priesthood and the conversion of the elements were

---

[1] In England especially, special bequests were often made by parishioners to make this possible.

retained, the remnants of the corporate action still provided an objective centre which was identical for all present. But it needed only a continuation of the shift of emphasis for the eucharistic action itself to come to be regarded as a mere *occasion for* or accompaniment to the individual's subjective devotion and thoughts. This shift of emphasis was growing in the fifteenth century,[1] and it reached full development in the sixteenth. We call it 'the protestant conception of the eucharist'.

The logical development would have been to remove the external action altogether, and so leave the individual's mental appreciations of and reactions to the passion and the atonement in complete possession of the field. But official protestantism (apart from the Quakers) felt unable to do this, at all events for a long time. The tradition that the eucharist was the culminating point of christian worship was too strong to be overthrown at once. The New Testament represented our Lord as having instituted this action for His followers, and great attention had to be paid to that fact.

The Reformers themselves therefore tried hard to retain a central importance and meaning for the eucharist in christian worship. But in every case they failed to carry their followers with them. Throughout the churches of the Reformation the eucharist rapidly assumed the position of an occasional addition to a worship which ordinarily consisted only of praises, prayers, exhortation and reading, somewhat similar to that which the primitive church had considered suitable for the catechumens at the synaxis.

But it is noticeable that in orthodox protestantism in the sixteenth and seventeenth centuries the general purpose and aim of this normal 'edifying' worship is concentrated on stimulating devout emotions and reactions in the minds of the worshippers to the thought and memory of *the passion and the atonement*, to the practical exclusion of all other aspects of the christian redemption. Anyone at all well acquainted with the fifteenth century devotional books for the use of the layfolk at low mass will find himself in a quite familiar atmosphere. It is too strong to say that protestant worship in its orthodox period represents no more than the layfolk's devotion at mass with the eucharistic action altogether removed. But that is only an exaggeration of a real and observable resemblance and derivation. And this derivation is even more clearly observable in the *devotional* ethos of the protestant eucharistic rites. Such a statement may well appear disconcerting to the modern catholic and protestant alike, conscious as they are of great doctrinal differences. Yet I believe this is true, as I have often had occasion to note in looking over devotional literature from the unreformed fifteenth and the very reformed sixteenth and seventeenth centuries. We will not labour the point here, but give what may be a sufficient illustration of the fact in a separate note, to which I venture to draw special attention.[2]

[1] *Cf. p.* 249.          [2] See *Additional Note, p.* 605.

Protestantism has in fact always been in a difficulty what to do with the eucharist, and whether or how to give it that central position in worship which it obviously held in the life of the primitive church. To criticise or even analyse the worship of one's fellow-christians is an invidious business, and I pray that I may write without offence. But it seems to me that the difficulty arises precisely out of the only meaning which protestantism *could* assign to the eucharist which did not contradict its own basic principle of 'justification by faith alone'—*viz.* that the service is a very specially solemn and moving *reminder* to all who attend it with faith of the passion and atonement of Christ, and so a valuable means of eliciting devout feelings of gratitude, love, confidence and union with Him in those who make use of His ordinance. To partake of the sacrament after His example is the most solemn pledge of re-dedication to God's service which His followers can give.

The difficulty with this view is that the eucharist thus simply duplicates the function of the normal *non*-eucharistic protestant worship. But this is complicated by a communion in bread and wine which, despite its traditional and recognised solemnity and sanctity, is difficult to relate specifically to the psychological reactions of the individual. After all, recollection of the passion and redemption, and loving aspirations of confidence and faith and union with our Lord, are commonplaces of every sincere christian's spiritual life, in no way limited to the performance of the eucharist. We all of us pledge ourselves afresh to the service of God 'in Christ' a dozen or a hundred times a day. Such devout thoughts often come more readily and are felt more intensely in the silence of solitary mental prayer than in the inevitably distracting presence of a number of other people. Of course, corporate worship in general supplies certain aids and values which solitary devotion cannot give. But unless the eucharistic action in itself *effects* something specific and *sui generis* both in the church which performs it corporately and in the individual who takes part, it is difficult to see why the eucharist should necessarily be preferred to other forms of corporate worship. Where its whole value and purpose is held to lie in the subjective effects it stimulates in the psychology of the individual, there is a good deal to be said for celebrating it infrequently. The added solemnity may increase its psychological effect, while a frequent repetition may lead to either over-familiarity or psychological strain. Given the general suspicion of any external forms and actions in worship common to all forms of puritanism, christian and non-christian alike; given, too, the particular reasons which protestantism had for denying any effect or value *ex opere operato* to this particular action; given the dogma of 'justification by faith *alone*'—there was every reason to expect that the eucharist would not be able to maintain either a predominance in protestant public worship or a central and unique place in the spiritual life of protestant individuals.

Its New Testament sanction and traditional position[1] as the centre of
christian devotion secured for it a long continuance in high reverence,
though infrequent practice, in most protestant churches. But when the
original protestant insistence on the atonement by the Blood of Jesus had
finally worn itself out in the nineteenth century, the eucharist with its
emphasis on 'the Lord's death' became irrelevant to the general tone of
protestant piety, which was openly replacing the doctrines of 'imputed
righteousness' and 'salvation by the Blood of the Lamb' (with their old-
world implications of sacrifice and atonement) by a new theory of ethical
progress to be achieved by following the example of Christ's life, which was
really derived from the nineteenth century theory of evolution.[2]

The way was thus cleared for that largely non-eucharistic piety of
modern popular protestantism, in which the eucharist is an occasional and
entirely optional appendage to a normal worship of 'edification'. A little
conversation with most protestant laity, or even many ministers, will make
it clear that in their eyes it is no longer the fact of being a communicant (or
even of having been baptised) which constitutes a man a 'member' of their
churches, but more or less regular attendance at this *non*-eucharistic worship, supplemented by the requirement in the case of some bodies that he
shall have undergone certain subjective experiences and taken certain
interior decisions constituting 'conversion'. 'Going to communion' is
reckoned by them a *consequence* of these things, not these things of 'going
to communion', as among catholics. All this seems a consistent development from the adoption of the principle of 'justification by faith alone'.
What I am concerned to insist upon is that though it is at the opposite pole
from the ideas about the eucharist of the primitive church, its *devotional*
roots go back behind the Reformation to the practice of mediaeval Western
eucharistic piety.[3] What the Reformation did was to take the mediaeval
layman's *practice* of piety at the eucharist, centre it on the communion of
which he had been deprived, and then transform the mediaeval practice
into the protestant theory of what the eucharist must be.

It was not accidental that all the Reformers took as their model for the
performance of the eucharist, not the primitive corporate action with its
movement and singing, but the mediaeval Western development of low

---

[1] Probably the latter operated more powerfully on the protestant churches than
they realised. Clear New Testament sanction (Mark vi. 13; James v. 14) did not, for
instance, avail to save the rite of unction in protestantism anywhere.
[2] The exact process by which the doctrine of 'justification by faith alone' thus
finally issued in a doctrine of 'justification by works' and 'it doesn't matter what a
man believes provided he does what's right' would make a most interesting study.
[3] This is the chief reason why the East has never spontaneously produced anything similar to protestant ideas either in worship or doctrine, and never seems able
to arrive even at a clear understanding of what protestantism is about. The latter is
a movement which grows out of the special characteristics of mediaeval Latin
catholicism, by way both of reaction and development. Without that particular
background it must remain largely unintelligible to the patristic Eastern tradition.

mass—the 'simple said service' performed by a single minister, at which the people had only to look and listen and silently pray. When the English puritan divines spoke of 'the minister being appointed for the people in all publick services appertaining unto God, and the Holy Scriptures both of the Old and New Testaments intimating the people's part in publick prayer to be only with silence and reverence to attend thereunto'[1], they spoke, however unconsciously, out of a tradition built up by eight centuries of low masses.

### Mediaeval Liturgy

Yet it would not be just to judge the mediaeval Western liturgy by the *régime* of low masses alone. They were a devotional by-product, even an unavoidable one, though one with momentous consequences. Rather our judgement must be based on the complete round of the liturgy as it was meant to be performed, not so much in a religious house[2] as in one of the great secular churches set in the midst of a busy city, like old S. Paul's or Notre Dame de Paris or the Duomo of Milan or the Dom of Cologne. There the day began with quite a large staff of clergy and clerks rising before dawn for the long office of mattins and lauds, to praise God on behalf of the citizens before the city's day could be spoiled by sin. All through the day the public recitation of the Hours of the office followed one another to the *Nunc dimittis* of compline, voicing prayer and penitence and praise on behalf of the whole population working in the streets around the church—making the sign of the cross continually over the city's daily bread. But the centre of it all was the mass. The thirty or forty low masses going on continually through the earlier hours of the morning were offered for the special intentions of individuals, and they made it possible for any who wished to join in the central act of christian living before daily work began. The chapter high mass, offered corporately and solemnly every day in the name of every christian soul in the diocese, lifted to God and brought under His kingship the cares and joys and troubles and work of the whole christian people as members of Christ.

It may have been a great burden of worship for those who offered it to bear easily, especially with the additions of the Office of our Lady and the Office of the Dead which the ninth and tenth centuries had unconsideringly added to the daily round. Few mediaeval visitations failed to reveal

---

[1] *Exceptions* of the Puritans at the Savoy Conference, §3 (Cardwell, *Hist. of Conferences, etc.*, 1840, *p.* 305). I owe this quotation to the kindness of the Rev. E. C. Ratcliff.

[2] The monk always remained something of an individualist, a man who had chosen for himself a life of personal communion with God. Though his corporate worship was offered for and with the church, it was essentially directed towards, and the product of, that personal inward life. The canon of a secular church had a different function. His *business* was public worship as such. He was maintained by society to carry on public worship for the public, as society's representative.

evidence of routine and formalism and sometimes downright irreverence in such corporations. Yet there is this to be said: Society at large supported these quite considerable bodies of men in leisure for continual public worship, because it was then convinced that God *ought* to be assiduously praised and thanked for the redemption of the world through our Lord Jesus Christ. Of course, where the substance of worship is held to lie in the sincerity of the individual's interior response to God and his own *consciousness* of that response, the whole conception of such a 'worship by representatives' will seem meaningless or worse. Protestantism has been consistent in its general abandonment of a liturgical worship offered on behalf of society. Its public worship is held not as representative of society, but as an opportunity for each of the individuals in society to attend and be 'edified' for himself in company with the others. But mediaeval men had not a purely subjective notion of worship; it was still for them, as for the primitive church, largely something 'done'. Nor had they arrived at the notion of society as essentially composed of isolated individuals. On their own grounds they too were consistent in what they did.

It is a historical mistake to idealise and romanticise the middle ages. The ordinary mediaeval man lived in a world which was horribly uncomfortable and dangerous, very poor in material resources, and also very sinful. And he knew all that quite well. But his literature, from the popular literature of the ballads up to the great works of genius, reveals a world that was hopeful nevertheless, and had a great zest for living. Our own world is also uncomfortable and dangerous; it is much better equipped with material resources, though it has made poverty its nightmare. And it is reluctantly returning to the conviction that it is sinful. But it is hardly what one would call hopeful, and it has a fear of living. This is because our world has forgotten or has ceased to believe that it has been redeemed.

It is probable that the conventional religion of most men in the 'Ages of Faith' went not much deeper really than the conventional irreligion of most men to-day. Yet religion did penetrate all human life then with a hopefulness and a purpose beyond its human littleness which it is very hard to imagine in our secularised society. That continual solemn and public rendering of society's worship and thanksgiving for redemption in the choirs of christendom by day and night did keep the fact of redemption before men's thoughts continually. Any setting aside and maintenance of large delegations of men for the *business* of public worship, to *do* it on behalf of their fellows continually (as others, *e.g.*, judges, mathematical dons, soldiers, etc., are set aside and maintained for other apparently uneconomic functions) does in itself glorify God and edify men and sanctify life, because it publicly acknowledges in the most obvious way the claim of the spirit over the body and of God over all the temporal living of men. But the mediaeval public liturgy of the West did more. By making the corporate eucharist its daily centre it asserted to the world in an unique way the dogmatic fact that in and through Jesus of Nazareth *alone* those claims are completely fulfilled. The mediaeval devotional approach to the eucharist was seriously defective in more than one way. But so far as its public use of the liturgy is concerned—what else is this but the meaning of S. Paul's 'Ye do proclaim the Lord's death'?

## ADDITIONAL NOTE

### Mediaeval Eucharistic Devotions for Layfolk and the Protestant Conception of the Eucharist

THE point outlined on *p.* 600 may quite well appear paradoxical, and could only be decisively proved by a somewhat elaborate survey of the literature. But it may be illustrated—sufficiently, I hope, to set others to work to examine the matter for themselves—by two books which happen, by no pre-arranged selection, to be within reach of my hand as I sit and write.

The first is a little collection of fifteenth century English mass-devotions for layfolk, entitled *Langforde's Meditations in the Time of Mass* (edited by J. Wickham Legg in his Volume of *Tracts on the Mass*, H.B.S. 1904, *pp.* 19 *sqq.*). There is no need to give the whole work, or to retain the fifteenth century spelling. We know nothing of 'B. Langforde' save that he was an Englishman, and presumably a priest, who was anxious to give his people 'Meditations for ghostly exercise in the time of mass'. For him in 'the process of the mass is represented the very process of the passion of Christ'. 'Let this' (*i.e.* the mass) 'be your *daily meditation*, to stir you to the diligent and compendious remembrance of the passion of Christ'. 'Our intent is to move souls to the devotion of the mass and to the loving remembrance of the passion of Christ.' Here are specimens of his method:

'At the offertory when the priest doth take the chalice and hold it up and forms the oblation:

'Have meditation how our Lord, the Saviour of all mankind, most willingly offered Himself to His eternal Father, to be the sacrifice and oblation for man's redemption; and offer yourself to Him in return both body and soul, which He so dearly bought. Rendering in recognition of the same to His grace by devout meditation all the thanks of your heart, that it would please His goodness to be the ransom for your trespass and sins.'

(At the beginning of the canon:)

'Have you in hearty meditation the process of our Lord's Maundy with all the ceremonies of meekness which His grace did in His own Person shew for our information. In the which Maundy He did feed His disciples with His precious Body and Blood, consecrated under the form of bread and wine. So every man and woman that is in grace both the living†and the dead†may be refreshed by that blessed sacrament. For not only it reneweth and feedeth by grace and augmentation of the same the souls of them that living do duly†honour†it†but also it is remission of pain an indulgence to all the souls that be in purgatory† . . . Therefore with pure heart and contrite soul in all your whole affection and love honour this blessed sacrament to the profit of your own soul, your friends and all Christian souls, both quick†and dead†. . . .'

(After the elevation:)

'Call to remembrance and imprint inwardly in your heart by holy meditation the whole process of the passion from the Maundy (last supper) unto the point of Christ's death; first the prayer in the garden where in great agony He sweated blood and water . . .' Then follows a detailing of the sufferings of the passion, charmingly phrased—'with a garland of sharpe thornes crownyd and a reed for a septur of golde'—and all obviously directed to arousing the emotions of the layfolk using it. This 'is a meditation of sweetness unspeakable to them that inwardly can consider it, and in the same to remember . . . the great mercy and tender charity of Him that did vouchsafe to suffer that confusion for our sakes. This I commend to your memory, trusting that ye will give thanks to our Lord therefor with all your heart . . . the Son of God suffered for us all the night before, labouring in watch, pain and abstinence, in great silence, patience and meekness, like a lamb among lions, wolves and dogs, labouring all that long time in the winepress of His blessed passion. I tarry the longer and make repetition of this foresaid meditation, because it should not lightly pass over, but rather be graved in the soul of man and imprinted in his heart . . .'

(At the Our Father) 'in which prayer are vii petitions contained', . . . 'remember the vii words of great mystery which our Lord did speak hanging quick upon the cross in His great agony, distress and pain of death ; and specially follow the example of that holy word in the which He prayed for His enemies, . . . See now that you likewise forgive all enmities, displeasures, wrongs and occasions for the love of Him that thus meekly and mercifully did forgive His trespassers. Then shall you be His disciples, then shall you be the chosen vessels apt to receive His grace, and both meet and able to receive the fruit of this most blessed sacrament . . .'

(At the Pax:)

'Remember the peace betwixt God and man which our blessed Saviour did merit for us in His blessed death, reconciling us to His Father in heaven, God omnipotent. . . . Wherefore remit all enmities, whether they be ministered of superiors or inferiors, and evenly dispose you at this time of the mass in a charitable, contrite and clean heart to receive our Lord spiritually, and so by Him to receive all these great benefits rehearsed . . .'

(At the Agnus Dei:)

'Have in meditation with perfect remembrance and your whole mind, considering the most tender mercy and love of our sweet Lord and Redeemer Jesu ... to suffer in our nature most shameful, terrible and cruel death, and all to win our love. Which precious death is signified at this time of the mass in the oblation of the blessed Body and Blood of our most merciful Saviour ministered to us under the savour and taste of bread and wine.... For like as bread and wine be those things which most conveniently sustain and relieve the necessities of the body, so our blessed Lord will give unto us under the qualities and taste of bread and wine His blessed Body and Blood as most convenient and wholesome food, to restore and relieve all the necessities of soul and body unto everlasting glory ...'

We may leave it at that, with this anticipation of the Anglican Catechism to emphasise the point. First, excepting perhaps the three little phrases I have obelised, is there anything in these manly, devout and thoroughly evangelical meditations of the unreformed fifteenth century which the sternest protestant that ever came out of Ulster could conscientiously refuse to use? Do they not rather anticipate many of the actual phrases of our own *liturgy* as well as our eucharistic devotional books? Secondly—and this is important—all this admirable devotional exercise is suggested by and accompanies the eucharistic action, *but it is no part of it*. It goes on entirely within the individual worshipper's own mind. Meanwhile the liturgical action, performed exclusively by the priest and server, proceeds in front of the layman in complete detachment from him. What preoccupies his devotion is the *different* thought of the passion as it historically happened, and his own subjective reactions to that. He does not even join in the Lord's prayer as such; it only reminds him of the seven words from the cross! Except as the occasion for the meditation, the liturgy might just as well not be happening at all. I submit that a churchful of worshippers each silently contemplating the passion and atonement in his or her own mind, and each forming devout affections upon that, while a priest and server offer the eucharist inaudibly and in another tongue, is very near a different thing altogether from the corporate action of the primitive eschatological rite. The prayers of the liturgy treat of many aspects indeed of christian truth besides the passion, but the devotion of the worshippers takes no account of them. They do not communicate, but make a 'spiritual communion'—which all ascetic authors tell us not only can but *should* be repeated frequently during the day in all sorts of circumstances, not only at the liturgy. What has the liturgy here to do with the layman's worship? Only at one point in 'Langforde' does it impinge actively upon his exercises—at the elevation—when he is told '*If it like you* ye may say ... this little orison', and there follows a short act of adoration. 'In the second elevation at *your pleasure* ye may say thus ...' and there follows a salutation to 'the precious Blood of our redeemer, the pledge of our eternal inheritance.... Blessed be my Lord God Jesus Christ from Whose side thou wast shed for the redemption of the world'. The whole meditation is concerned with the atonement, but at the one point where this might be closely connected with the progress of the liturgy, the connection is left entirely optional! Yet in fact the introduction of the ceremony of the elevation had originally come about in order that it might be possible for the laity to *see* the consecrated sacrament, and at least then relate their private devotions to the supposedly corporate action. If this tradition of subjective individual devotion to the passion and atonement were to be maintained, and the catholic doctrines of the priesthood and the conversion of the elements were to be removed, what need could there be for maintaining the performance of the eucharist as the centre of christian worship? It would surely be inevitable that some form of worship more closely directed to the stimulation of devout affections on the passion would be found more suitable. So it was—after the Reformation.

The other document which happens to be to hand is *The Reformed Liturgy* which Baxter and his fellow puritans put forward at the time of the Savoy Conference as a preferable alternative to that of the Book of Common Prayer.[1] It is of portentous length; even the prayer for the king occupies forty-six lines. And in accordance with puritan principles the part of the people is markedly 'only with silence and reverence to attend thereunto'. Even the Nicene Creed (for which 'sometimes' the Athanasian is to be substituted) is to be recited by the minister alone, and the Ten Commandments are to be recited without any intervening responses by the people. The minister also says the 'Confession of Sin' for the people (three and a half pages) preceded by the recitation of fourteen texts 'for the right affecting the People and moving them to a penitent believing Confession'—('Uncomfortable Words'?). Instead of an absolution it is followed by the Lord's prayer (said by the minister alone), and nine more texts as 'Comfortable Words' and a further series of eighteen texts (some of three or four verses) that they may 'Hear what you must be and do for the time to come if you would be saved.'

In that part of the rite which corresponds to the eucharist proper of the primitive church, the congregation never once open their mouths except to receive holy communion. It begins with a long 'Explication of the Nature, Use and Benefits of this Sacrament' addressed to the congregation, to be used at the discretion of the minister, which is of interest for our purpose:

'The Lord's Supper, then, is an holy sacrament instituted by Christ, wherein bread and wine being first by consecration made sacramentally, or representatively the Body and Blood of Christ, are used by breaking and pouring out to represent and commemorate the sacrifice of Christ's Body and Blood upon the Cross . . . and they are received eaten and drunk by the church to profess that they willingly receive Christ Himself to their justification, sanctification and glorification; and to signify and solemnise

---

[1] Baxter, *Works*, ed. Orme, 1830, vol. xv., *pp. 451 sqq.*

the renewal of their covenant with Him and their holy communion with Him and with one another . . . we offer and deliver to Him ourselves as His redeemed sanctified people to be a living acceptable sacrifice . . .

'The holy qualifications to be before provided, and in receiving exercised, and after receiving, are these:

'1. A true belief in the articles of the Christian faith . . . (Trinity and Incarnation.)

'2. The sense of our sinful and undone condition . . . so as humbly to loathe ourselves for our transgression.

'3. A true desire after Christ for pardon . . .

'4. A thankful sense of the wonderful love of God . . .

'5. The exercise of holy love and joy in the sense of this unspeakable love; if these two be not felt before we come, yet in and after the sacrament we must strive to exercise them.

'6. A love to one another and forgiving wrongs to one another . . .

'7. The giving up ourselves in covenant to God . . .

'8. A patient hope for the coming of Christ Himself and of the everlasting kingdom . . .

'The benefit of the sacrament is not to be judged of by present experience and feeling, but by faith . . . whatever we feel at present, we may and must believe that we sincerely wait not on Him in vain'.

This is followed by a long 'Exhortation' in a fervent strain, '. . . See here Christ dying in this holy representation. Behold the sacrificed Lamb of God, that taketh away the sins of the world! It is His will to be thus frequently crucified before your eyes. O how should we be covered with shame and loathe ourselves, that have both procured the death of Christ by sin and sinned against it! And how should we all be filled with joy, that have such mysteries of mercy opened and so great salvation freely offered to us! O hate sin, O love this Saviour . . .' and so on for two pages. Then follows a further two-page prayer of contrition and for pardon and that we may *feel* all these emotions: 'O love us freely and say unto our souls that Thou art our salvation . . . receive us graciously to the feast Thou hast prepared for us, cause us to hunger and thirst after Christ. . . . Give us to know Thy love in Christ which passeth knowledge . . . let us rejoice with joy unspeakable and full of glory . . . speak and seal up peace to our sinful wounded souls . . .', and so on. I do not think it will be denied that all this is primarily directed to evoking emotions in those present, and that the object is simply a meditation on the passion. It is a purely subjective devotion, just like that of Langforde's *Meditations*; and the emotions aimed at are the same and have the same object. The difference is that while Langforde's devotions are intended to accompany an objective liturgy, Baxter's have replaced it and become themselves the liturgy.

After this we come to the eucharistic action itself.

'*Here let the Bread be brought to the Minister and received by him and set upon the Table and then the Wine in like manner . . . let him bless them, praying in these or the like words:*

'Almighty God, Thou art the Creator and the Lord of all things. Thou art the Sovereign Majesty we have offended: Thou art our most loving and merciful Father, Who hast given Thy Son to reconcile us to Thyself, Who hath ratified the New Testament and Covenant of Grace with His most precious Blood; and hath instituted this holy Sacrament to be celebrated in remembrance of Him till His coming. Sanctify these Thy creatures of bread and wine which according to Thy institution and command we set apart to this holy use, that they may be sacramentally the Body and Blood of Thy Son Jesus Christ. Amen.

*'Then (or immediately before this Prayer) let the Minister read the Words of the Institution saying:* 'Hear what the Apostle Paul saith: For I have received of the Lord . . . (1 Cor. xi. 23-6).

*'Then let the Minister say:*

'This bread and this wine being set apart and consecrated to this holy use by God's appointment, are now no common bread and wine but sacramentally the Body and Blood of Christ.' [There follows a brief prayer for 'the pardon of our sins and Thy quickening Spirit without which the flesh will profit us nothing'.]

*'Then let the Minister take the bread and break it in the sight of the people saying:*

'The Body of Christ was broken for us and offered once for all to sanctify us: Behold the sacrificed Lamb of God, that taketh away the sins of the world.

*'In like manner let him take the Cup and pour out the Wine in the sight of the Congregation, saying:*

'We were redeemed with the precious Blood of Christ, as of a Lamb without blemish and without spot.'

[There follows a short prayer for a good communion addressed to the Holy Ghost.]

*'Then let the Minister deliver the Bread thus consecrated and broken to the Communicants, first taking and eating it himself as one of them, when he hath said:*

'Take ye, eat ye, This is the Body of Christ which is broken for you, do this in remembrance of Him.

*'In like manner he shall deliver them the Cup, first drinking of it himself, when he hath said:*

'This cup is the New Testament in Christ's Blood, which is shed for you for the remission of sins, drink ye all of it in remembrance of Him.'

It is interesting to find that the eucharistic action takes just two pages of print out of the thirty-four occupied by the whole rite. It is, from the traditional standpoint, better arranged than Cranmer's,—offertory, consecration, fraction and communion following one another connectedly, with only brief devotional prayers between, though both the dialogue and the whole 'thanksgiving' element, the original nucleus of the rite, have completely disappeared. But the contrast with the primitive rites comes out unmistakably in the facts, 1. That it is very far indeed from being a corporate action of the church. It is on the contrary designedly and thoroughly something which the minister alone does for the church; and something to which, so Baxter and his fellows contended, each minister must have it in his sole discretion whether he would *admit or refuse admission* to any individual. 2. That this eucharistic action, so far from being an entering into the eternal action of Christ, and as such addressed to God, is now a separate repetition of His action, addressed by the minister to the congregation, to stir up in them those interior resolutions and affections which have become the primary purpose of worship. Whatever relics of primitive language and form may remain, the primitive conception of the rite has wholly vanished. But (to me, at all events) any contrast of *type* with the mediaeval low mass is much less evident. As at a low mass said by the priest alone, the people meditate on the passion in silence, till the sacerdotally-consecrated victim is brought to their notice, by the priest with his action at the elevation, by the puritan with the words of his declaration. The communion of the people has been restored; the essential core of low mass has been put into a new setting of emotional prayers and exhortations. But Baxter's rite remains essentially low mass in all that distinguishes it from the primitive presentation of the rite. And even the 'devotional' setting fulfils precisely the purpose of the mediaeval layfolk's devotions. All that has happened is that now instead of being a private and silent accompaniment to the rite, these devotions have been made into the public and spoken substance of the rite.

Baxter's *Liturgy* concludes with a prayer of thanksgiving of a page and a half,—'with our thanks and praise (we) present ourselves a living sacrifice to be acceptable through Christ'—and an Exhortation: 'Dear brethren, we have been here feasted with the Son of God at His table, upon His Flesh and Blood in preparation for the feast of endless glory. You have seen here represented what sin deserveth, what Christ suffered, what wonderful love the God of infinite goodness hath expressed to us ... O carry hence the lively sense of these great and excellent things upon your hearts ...' and so forth; then comes a psalm followed by a blessing.

Looking at the proposals as a whole, the modern Anglican may well be puzzled as to what the puritan objections to the use of the Anglican Prayer Book in the seventeenth century really amounted to. Their 'Exceptions' put forward in 1660, though they make somewhat finical objections to some of the rubrics of its eucharistic rite, contain no sort of objection to its eucharistic doctrine.[1] And this, their desired alternative rite, is clearly

[1] The nearest they come to it is on the 'Prayer of Humble Access', in which the clause 'that our sinful bodies may be made clean by His Body and our souls washed

based on that of Cranmer against which they were protesting. To an Anglican it must read like a pathetically unpractical and verbose attempt to do again exactly what Cranmer had already done with much greater judgement and literary skill. But that is a thought which suggests that the contrast is not to be drawn between Baxter and Cranmer, but between both and Hippolytus or Sarapion, a question which requires separate consideration.

through His most precious Blood' moved them to the objection that 'these words seem to give a greater efficacy to the Blood than to the Body of Christ'. This is reasonable. The idea that the sacrament was instituted under both kinds, the Body for our bodies and the Blood for our souls, though it is grounded upon no warrant of holy scripture, is a fairly common speculation among mediaeval theologians (*cf.* e.g. Paschasius Radbert, *de Corp. et Sang. Dni*, 11; S. Thomas Aq., *S. Th.*, III, lxxiv, 1, etc.). Cranmer held strongly to this notion (*cf. p.* 644). But there is no particular reason why people should be made to *pray* mediaeval speculations in a Reformed church.

# CHAPTER XVI

## THE REFORMATION AND THE ANGLICAN LITURGY

IT was after prolonged hesitation that the addition of this chapter to the book was decided on, and then only in deference to the advice of others. I am still sensible of two objections to doing so. One is that to place this chapter at this point in the book is inevitably to give the impression that the work of Archbishop Cranmer is in some sense the climax of all christian liturgical development, whereas in the whole story it is no more than an incident, and that of no central interest to the subject of liturgy as a whole. A Coptic christian, if one were to read this book, might feel that the process (which I have barely mentioned) by which the Antiochene liturgies of the *Egyptian S. Basil* and *S. Gregory* replaced the old Alexandrian liturgy of *S. Mark* at Alexandria was more worthy of study; and it could not be denied that the extinction of a genuinely ancient tradition going back continuously to apostolic times is of much more interest to the scientific study of liturgy than the replacement of the late derived rites of Sarum and Hereford and the rest. In the one case a tap-root of all liturgical history which has contributed to all other rites in their origins and in their present structure (*e.g.* the preface and sanctus) is severed; in the other a top branch with some rather luxuriant flowers is cut off, while the tree remains unaffected.

The appending of this chapter, viewed from the strictly scientific standpoint, is therefore a disproportion. But I think it is a sufficient answer to this to say that the book seems less unlikely to be read by Anglicans than by Copts. An author and his readers are quite entitled to pursue their special interests, though they will be wise to remind themselves of their relative proportions in the subject as a whole. The Anglican rites, in their various forms, to-day serve perhaps 20,000,000 people, of whom perhaps 5,000,000 are practising communicants. The Latin rites serve (nominally) some 250,000,000; the Eastern rites perhaps 45,000,000 in all (excluding Russia); there are probably between 100,000,000 and 150,000,000 members of the various protestant bodies. No doubt in each case we must make very large deductions from these nominal totals, as in the case of the Anglicans, to come at the real number of worshippers. But they remain impressively larger than ourselves. If we are candid we shall remember this.

The second objection is less easily disposed of. Ever since the sixteenth century we Anglicans have been so divided over eucharistic doctrine, and we are to-day so conscious of our divisions, that there is scarcely any statement that could be made about either the eucharist or our own rite which would not seem to some of one's fellow churchmen to call for immediate contradiction on conscientious grounds. It is quite understandable. These things go deep behind us. Two archbishops of Canterbury have lost their lives and a third his see, in these quarrels. One king has been beheaded and another dethroned; many lesser men have suffered all manner of penalties from martyrdom downwards on one side and another. These things have left their traces, tangling and confusing our own approach to the matter in all sorts of irrelevant ways. Besides the conscious inheritance of different intellectual and doctrinal positions from the past, and inextricably mingled with it, is another inherited world of unconscious misunderstandings, prejudices, assumptions, suspicions, which are only accidentally bound up with theological terms and which yet come into play instantly and secretly and quite irrationally with their use. To spring the word 'transubstantiation' on the company without preparation in certain circles (or the names 'Tyburn' or 'Barnes' in others) is to invite a reaction which springs much more from emotion than from reason. It is unfortunate from my present point of view that these feelings gather most strongly and most intricately around the person of Archbishop Cranmer and his liturgical changes. It is recognised on all hands that these divisions in English religion go back to his work, even if he did not precipitate them. Nor can these difficulties be altogether avoided by adhering simply to naked historical fact. Where present controversies are bound up so closely with questions of history, it is difficult in the extreme to be sure that one has seen the facts oneself without prejudice, and almost impossible to convey them to the reader in the exact proportion that one understands them without their being interpreted by his prejudices without his knowledge.

I am not sure that in my own mind I have satisfactorily answered this objection to adding this chapter. By far the most important part of the book (in my own judgement) lies in what precedes. But just because what follows is likely to be of more personal interest to most of my readers, and this chapter is necessarily placed where it is, the first fifteen chapters are likely to be taken for mere prolegomena to this one, which of all judgements on the book I would most desire to avoid. Yet to omit the chapter seems impossible. It would be a tacit slight to a liturgy which for me is bound up with the memories of my own first communion and ordination and first celebration, and of ministrations since to thousands of good christian people. And it would in effect deprive the book of practical usefulness to those whom I most desire to serve, the Anglican clergy and lay people in our present serious liturgical embarrassments. It has therefore been added after being re-written in whole or in part several times in an effort to avoid hurting those whom I am anxious to help, for I know for myself how easy it is to be hurt by the way these things can be treated. As it stands it is an attempt to regard the Anglican liturgy and its making with that sort of historical interest which might be taken in it by, let us say, a well-educated Syrian Monophysite. I ask that it shall be taken as such, for whatever light such a

dispassionate approach may throw on our problems, and not as an attempt
to argue for or against any particular proposals whatever as to practice.

## The Post-Medieval Crisis

It will be obvious, I think, that in most of this book we have been moving
over ground very little trodden by the disputants on either side in sixteenth
century England. Many of the texts we have studied were not then known,
and the bearing of most of those that were known was then not clearly
understood. The real background of these sixteenth century controversies
is not the New Testament, isolated texts from which were wrested by both
sides; still less was it the practice of the primitive church, of which both
sides were about equally ignorant. It is the mediaeval Western rite, as it was
in use *c*. A.D. 1500, the only liturgy which either party had ever *used*. This
alone explains both what it was that one party sought to change, and the
awkward and unsatisfactory formulation of the traditional position which
the other side felt bound to defend. And just as we shall not understand
the circumstances and the meaning to S. Gregory's own mind of his
revision of the local rite of Rome *c*. A.D. 600 unless we see it on the background of the similar codifications of other Italian local rites being undertaken at about the same time; so we must see Cranmer's liturgical changes
as one of a number of related attempts to do the same thing for the same
reasons elsewhere. It is an incident in the general post-mediaeval liturgical
crisis provoked in the West by what the mediaeval liturgical practice itself
had come to be, or perhaps it is truer to say, had come to mean to those
who worshipped by it.

Let us set down the changes of conception to be noted between the pre-
mediaeval and the mediaeval conceptions of the eucharist, noting as we
do so how far back the roots of the sixteenth century difficulties go, and
how hard it is to separate the several difficulties from one another, even
for purposes of discussion—let alone reform.

1. The notion of the eucharist as a corporate action has been transformed.
The celebrant's irreplaceable 'liturgy' of saying the *eucharistia* had always
been *an* essential element in the rite. It is for Justin 'the food which has
been "eucharistised" ' which 'is the Flesh and Blood of that Jesus Who was
made Flesh'. The old four-action shape of the rite in which this formed one
part still persisted intact in the Western rite *c*. 1500. But at low mass the
whole action has been transferred to the celebrant. He alone offers at the
offertory; he alone—as always—says the prayer. Instead of the fraction
being performed by the deacons and concelebrants as in Hippolytus, it is
now done by the celebrant alone; and in popular understanding there had
been attached to it the unprimitive meaning of the 'breaking' of our Lord's
Body in the passion, and therefore a connection with immolation, so that
it had assumed the character not only of a sacerdotal but of a directly

sacrificial act. Normally the celebrant alone communicated. The whole liturgical action from beginning to end has thus passed to him. We have seen the very gradual and accidental process by which this had come about, but its completion was nevertheless a very considerable change. In a new sense it could be said that the individual priest 'offered' the eucharist, or it could at least be popularly supposed that he did.

2. To each of such individual sacerdotal offerings there could be attached in popular understanding a separate efficacy and value of its own, each dependent on that of Calvary, but separable from one another. Thus ten masses were necessarily and determinably worth more than five. And since each offering was the celebrant's own offering, something which he alone could do, though he did it in virtue of his personal possession of holy orders, it rested with him to apply the efficacy of each mass to particular souls or causes as he willed. Again we can trace the slow and gradual stages by which the primitive ideas had reached this development. But again the change which results is of a very considerable importance.

3. Not only had the part of the laity at low mass been reduced to one of passivity—seeing and hearing only—but the use of Latin reduced the function of hearing to small usefulness for most people, though the aesthetic effect of the music at high mass remained to stimulate religious emotion, even when the texts were not understood. Here again there is a long history behind the situation c. A.D. 1500, which it is worth while to consider a little more fully, though it does not affect the serious consequences of the situation as it stood then.

It is sometimes forgotten by the advocates of a vernacular liturgy that our Lord as a palestinian jew never attended a strictly vernacular service in His life. Alike in the temple and the synagogue the jewish services in Palestine were in the liturgical Hebrew, which was not understood by the people without special instruction. Though the lections in the synagogue were *targum*ed or translated in the second century A.D., there is no evidence that this was the case in our Lord's day; and according to S. Mark it was the liturgical Hebrew, not the vernacular Aramaic, which rose to His lips in prayer at the supreme moment of His passion.[1] Though neither side seems to have noted this fact in the sixteenth century, the mediaeval church had the most warrantable of all precedents for using a language 'not understanded of the people' in the liturgy, if it had cared to plead it. Outside Palestine, however, jewish services in the first century were usually held not in Hebrew, but in Greek, the general vernacular of the Levant. It was this precedent which eventually carried the day in the christian church. A few Hebrew words like Amen, Hosanna, Alleluia, remained in use in christian worship to remind christians of its Hebrew origin. But the church agreed with S. Paul that 'if I pray in an unknown tongue my spirit prayeth, but my understanding is not fruitful; I will pray with the spirit, and I will

[1] Mark xv. 34.

pray with the understanding also',[1] and used the vernacular. The local church of Rome had begun as a Greek-speaking body; the majority of its members were Greek-speaking Levantines living in the foreign quarters of the city. But it began to use Latin in its liturgy, probably in the latter half of the second century, as the faith spread among the Latin-speaking inhabitants; though the use of Greek went on side by side with Latin down to the fourth—perhaps even the fifth century. Elsewhere in the West, e.g. in Africa, Latin had been used by the church from the second century.

In the fourth-fifth centuries, when Greek was ceasing to be spoken in the West but Latin was still a *lingua franca* in which e.g. all public notices were posted up from Northumberland to Casablanca and from Lisbon to the Danube, it was natural that all christian rites should be in Latin in the West. In the fifth century the barbarian settlements brought a variety of teutonic dialects into the different Western provinces, and a cross-division of language everywhere between the new masters and the old populations. Even among the latter the rapid decline of civilisation brought an inability to keep up the old cultured but complicated language. All through the sixth and seventh centuries the barbarians and provincials were mingling and profoundly affecting each other's speech. Languages were everywhere in flux and European speech was a chaos of local *patois*. The composition of vernacular rites was impossible; there is not even a vernacular literature worth speaking of anywhere in the West from this period. The church still stood for all that was left of the old tradition of civilisation, and could only conserve that in so far as it was protected from contemporary influence in a Latin armour.

The revival of civilisation which begins in the eighth century came about by the recovery of just those traditions of the past which were most favourable to the renewed use of Latin. It culminates in Charlemagne's 'restoration of the Roman empire', and his imposition throughout his dominions of the Roman rite. Neither policy was calculated to elevate the position of the vernacular languages which are just beginning to take a recognisable form in the ninth century. But the adoption of the 'local Roman' *Gregorian Sacramentary* as the core of the universal Western rite had an important result, quite apart from things ecclesiastical. It placed at the basis of all Western culture the only tradition of the use of Latin in which the language had evolved without break from the classical tongue of Cicero and Virgil, through the expressive and supple silver Latin of the third and fourth centuries, to the 'ecclesiastical Latin' of the age of Leo and Gregory, without any serious admixture from outside.

The culture which sprang from the work of Charlemagne, but which finally made sure of life only in the eleventh century, was not a formal restoration of the classical imperial culture such as the sixteenth century artificially essayed, but it was its true descendant in many ways. As such it

[1] I Cor. xiv. 14.

was emphatically an international culture—or at this stage when nations were still embryonic, it is truer to say an inter-regional culture—whose natural instrument was a common language. And since religion was at the very heart of this new culture, Latin (which by now was not so much common to all regions as not particularly limited to any of them) was still used in church.

This excluded the great mass of the people from intelligent participation in the church services. But we have to remember that they were excluded no less from participation in the revived secular culture of the times. There is always in the background of mediaeval history the great half-civilised, half-christian mass of the population, living dumbly, obediently, laboriously, squalidly, leaving singularly little trace in the record, while the history which is told in books goes on in front of it. Even when the new national monarchies of the thirteenth and fourteenth centuries were slowly forming their peoples into separate unities, the international forces in educated society and the dialectal differences and linguistic poverty of this great mass of the people in each country were still much too great for national vernacular liturgies to have been a practicable proposition. We have all heard the story of the fourteenth century Englishman who said 'eyren' and was not understood by the fourteenth century Englishwoman to be asking for 'eggys'. It was not before the end of the fifteenth century, and in some regions hardly then, that vernacular languages first became even capable of being instruments for vernacular liturgies.

It is not until this situation is understood that we are in a position to appraise the measures taken to meet it in the sixteenth century either by the old religion or the new. The mediaeval church was not altogether blind to the difficulties occasioned by the use of Latin. Real efforts were made in the fourteenth and fifteenth centuries to provide vernacular devotions for the layfolk to use during mass. Most unfortunately these do not seem anywhere to have taken the form of translations of the prayers actually used at the altar, which would have enabled the laity to participate more intelligently in the rite itself. Instead, the laity were given compilations of supplementary prayers, devotions and aspirations (of which Langforde's *Meditations* are an excellent specimen) to occupy their thoughts while the liturgy itself went on in Latin independently of them. And as Latin theology by comparison with earlier ideas had restricted the significance of the sacrifice of Christ to the passion, without sufficient regard had to the resurrection and ascension, these lay eucharistic devotions, scriptural in essence though they were, were quite naturally dominated by the thought of Calvary. (This is something which, as we have already seen, survived the Reformation.)

This substitution of other prayers for those of the liturgy itself even in lay manuals of devotion was very unfortunate. No doubt the expense and labour of hand copying books had much to do with it. A translation of the missal would be a comparatively long book; a set of devotions for the length of a low mass was short, and could serve for every day in the year. But given the impossibility of supplying translations of the rite to the laity as is done among modern Roman Catholics, the situation at the end of the middle ages was rendered still more difficult by the facts (1) that the great half-submerged mass of the population was just beginning to be articulate, and (2) simultaneously with this, members of the educated classes and the clerical body itself were publicly questioning the rightness of the mediaeval formulation of the liturgy in entirely new ways.

Even with all the resources of modern publishing and printing to provide adequate and cheap translations for the laity, it is no secret that some contemporary Roman Catholic liturgists and clergy regard it as an open question whether the Roman church will not even yet be forced to make more use of the vernacular in parish churches, if the bulk of the laity are to participate fully in the liturgy, despite the convenience of a common rite for an international church. This is not our business, though we may note in passing that the arguments by which the retention of Latin for the liturgy is now defended are the precise opposite of those which originally brought about the introduction of a Latin rite at Rome. But in the crisis at the end of the middle ages the use of the liturgy in the now sufficiently evolved vernaculars would have been of incalculable service to the old religion. It would have released the evangelising power of the liturgy itself upon the masses, just awakening to think. Probably nothing else would have sufficed adequately to meet their need of instruction just then. As it was, this potent instrument was left entirely to the Reformers, and the masses' ignorance of their own religion left them much more receptive to the new teaching.

There were many on the catholic side who saw this clearly. But the church in the early sixteenth century was shewing every sign of staleness and inner moral crisis, and was in no position to face voluntarily the change in long-established conventions which would have been involved. By the time the Counter-Reformation had sufficiently restored the church's freedom of action the question of the vernacular had become a partisan issue, which could no longer be decided on its own merits. The great catholic need had become that of unity and the closing of the ranks against the new negations. For this the old liturgy, purged of local diversities and late mediaeval accretions, and in the same language everywhere, was too valuable an instrument to lose. The result was the reformed Roman Missal of Pius V, 'imposed' on the whole Roman obedience by an unprecedented legislative act of the central authority. (Even in this crisis, though, the fact that the real basis of liturgy is *custom*, not law, was recognised by allowing all 'customs' contrary to the use of this missal which could shew a continuous usage for 200 years and more.) This is the basis of the modern Roman Catholic rite; it is little else than the tenth century 'Gelasianised-Gregorian'

missal with unimportant additions. By thus imposing a rigid liturgical discipline in a purified and militarised mediaeval church, the post-Tridentine
Papacy avoided the necessity of solving the liturgical crisis which faced the
sixteenth century church as a result of the appearance of new conditions
in society at the close of the middle ages. It is possible, however, for an
outsider to hold that the inevitable question was only postponed, and not
really avoided.

4. The thwarting of lay participation in the rite by 'hearing', which was
involved in the use of Latin, threw an exaggerated emphasis on the mediaeval layman's participation by 'seeing'—the only other share in the rite
left to him. But low mass left little more for the layman to watch than the
priest's back and occasional movements of his hands. There was virtually
no ceremonial. In the *Ordo Romanus Primus* every stage of the rite is
accompanied by a good deal of 'publicity' and movement. The gospel is
chanted from the *ambo*, with a preliminary procession with lights and incense; the offertory occupies all the clergy and all the people, each taking
their own part in a great co-ordinated action; the eucharistic prayer had
anciently been chanted aloud by the pontiff in the midst of his clergy and
people all listening attentively with bent heads; the fraction had been a
preparation by all the clergy for the eucharistic feeding of the multitude,
while the acolytes came up to receive the *fermentum* to carry away to absent
members of the one Body; the communion had been the huge corporate
communion of a whole population. In low mass all this had been reduced to
its simplest elements. It was all still done—but almost entirely in silence or
in a very low voice, by one man, without moving from the altar. Quite
naturally and inevitably the layman's participation in the rite by 'seeing'
concentrated itself on the one moment in the rite when he did see—the
elevation, specially introduced in the eleventh century in order that he
might see. And seeing he adored.

Cranmer describes the consequences of this concentration of devotion
on 'seeing' and the elevation thus: 'What made the people to run from their
seats to the altar, and from altar to altar, and from sacring (as they called it)
to sacring, peeping, tooting and gazing at that thing which the priest held
up in his hands, if they thought not to honour the thing which they saw?
What moved the priests to lift up the sacrament so high over their heads?
Or the people to say to the priest "Hold up! Hold up!"; or one man to say
to another "Stoop down before"; or to say "This day have I seen my
Maker"; and "I cannot be quiet except I see my Maker once a day"? What
was the cause of all these, and that as well the priest and the people so
devoutly did knock and kneel at every sight of the sacrament, but that they
worshipped that visible thing which they saw with their eyes and took it for
very God?'[1]

---

[1] Cranmer, *A Defence of the True and Catholic Doctrine, etc.*, iv. 9; *Remains*, ed.
Jenkyns, Oxford, 1833, *p.* 442.

Cranmer is not an unbiased witness, and there is a touch of his chaplain Becon's scurrility on his pen here. But even if he parodies it, the type of eucharistic devotion he recognisably describes differs in important respects from that which had led Ignatius of Antioch to insist that 'the eucharist is the Flesh of our Saviour Jesus Christ'.[1] In the primitive conception the consecration by the celebrant's prayer is subordinate to the whole eucharistic action as an essential part to the whole. In the mediaeval devotional conception the whole eucharistic action (carried on by the priest alone) is simply a means to bring about the consecration, for the purpose of individual adoration by each person present. Seen thus, the whole meaning of the liturgy is altered, and with it the meaning of consecration, even though the dogmatic foundation that 'the eucharist is the Flesh of our Saviour Jesus Christ' remains the same.

For my own part I cannot doubt that this change of conception is partly due to the unnatural emphasis placed on 'seeing' as the mediaeval layman's chief means of participation in the rite. It can hardly be accidental that the anxious preoccupation of the West which has continued ever since with the problem of the exact metaphysical relation of the physical realities of the bread and wine to our Lord's Body and Blood begins in the ninth century.[2] This is the period when the nascent vernaculars of Europe are beginning to be independent languages and the Latin of the church services is becoming finally incomprehensible to the mass of the people. The pre-Nicene and patristic centuries had taken this problem in their stride, as has the later Eastern tradition, in which the conception of the eucharist as a corporate *action* (not for the layman something seen or heard) has never been lost, despite the form which its liturgical presentation as a 'mystery' has taken.

5. Finally, and this seems to me the most momentous distinction of all between mediaeval Western and primitive eucharistic thought, the eschatological conception of the primitive rite has been almost entirely lost to view.

We have seen that Western eucharistic thought had for centuries concentrated chiefly upon that part of Christ's redeeming action (into which the church enters at the eucharist) which lies wholly within history and time in the past, the passion upon Calvary. The resurrection and ascension (which are the transition from time to the eternal—or rather perhaps from history to the metahistorical) and the eternal action of the High-priest at the heavenly altar had never been entirely excluded from the scope of the eucharist in Western theological discussion. The very language of the Western canon—'Making therefore the *anamnesis* of the blessed passion . . . and also of His blessed resurrection . . . and also of His glorious ascension. . . .'

[1] Ignatius, *Smyrn.*, vi.
[2] The *de Corpore et Sanguine Domini* of Ratramnus; c. A.D. 840, is the first treatise on this problem in theological history.

—'Bid these things to be borne by the hands of Thy holy angels to Thine altar on high in the sight of Thy divine majesty, that as many of us as by this partaking of the altar shall receive . . .'—such language as this could not allow the clergy who used it altogether to forget the older and wider understanding of the rite. But the people did not hear or understand the canon. The altar was seen by them through the arches of the screen, above which towered the great Rood with its realistic crucifix, perpetually focussing attention on the facts that the Son of Man had *died* and *here* was the living memorial of His passion. It is no wonder that lay devotion concentrated on this theme. Nor was it only lay devotion. Those prayers of private preparation and thanksgiving for the priest to use which are found in all mediaeval missals—which many of us still use profitably—the 'Seven prayers ascribed to S. Ambrose' (by John of Fécamp), 'Another prayer of S. Ambrose', 'A prayer of S. Thomas Aquinas', and the others, these are all preoccupied with the passion. 'O High-priest and true Pontiff Jesus Christ, Who didst offer Thyself to God the Father upon the altar of the Cross', is the burden of them all. Of course they *presuppose* the resurrection and the ascension. But I have failed to find one single explicit mention of these two events, not only in these usual prayers but in any private devotion suggested for celebrants in any print of a mediaeval missal available in the Nashdom library. This is, I think, a sufficient indication of the direction which even clerical devotion took in considering the eucharist in the later middle ages. It is entirely preoccupied with relating the eucharist *to the passion*.

The immense formative influence of such devotional exercises on the theological conception which even a learned cleric might hold of the rite has only to be considered to be understood. And the clergy taught the people. The total effect of the mediaeval view is to emphasise the past historical reference in S. Paul's words that in the eucharist 'ye do proclaim the Lord's death', to the neglect of the eschatological implications of what follows, 'till He come'. Thus when we find—as we shall—that Cranmer's rite of 1552 has not one single mention of the resurrection and ascension outside the creed, we shall recognise what we are dealing with. It is the undiluted tradition of mediaeval extra-liturgical devotion in which he had always lived, but transferred by him from the sphere of private devotion to become the very substance and meaning of the liturgy itself.

Again there is a long history behind the mediaeval development. The beginnings of the translation of the meaning of the eucharist from eschatology to history go back to the fourth century, even to the late third. The mediaeval Latin church only gradually carried out the process over the whole range of its eucharistic theology and devotion, and even so only achieved this translation in defiance of the language of its own liturgy, composed before the eschatological understanding had been lost. (There could not be a more significant instance of the power of the liturgical tradition to conserve a wider and more balanced conception than the rationalisations of the learned tradition of theology.) Yet the mediaeval tradition, both in its scholastic and devotional expressions, retained a clear understanding that the eucharist is in itself an *action*, or more properly an entering into the redeeming action of Christ, even though the earthly action was now wholly taken over by the celebrant.

It was just here that the practical confining of the redeeming action of Christ (into which the eucharist enters) to Calvary led to serious and unnecessary difficulties. Being wholly within history and time, the passion is wholly in the *past*—the only moment of redemption which is so wholly confined to the past. The church at the eucharist can only be conceived to enter into a wholly past action in one of two ways, either purely *mentally* by remembering and imagining it; or else, if the entering into it is to have any objective reality outside the mind, by way of some sort of *repetition* or iteration of the redeeming act of Christ. Thus the way was not so much laid open as forced upon the church to that general late mediaeval notion of some *fresh* sacrifice of Christ, and His immolation again at every eucharist. There was no other way by which the reality of the eucharistic action could be preserved on the mediaeval understanding of it; yet the unbroken tradition of liturgy and theology alike insisted on this reality. And since the eucharistic action was now viewed as the act of the priest alone— though the liturgy itself continued to state a different view ('We Thy servants together with Thy holy people offer unto Thee . . .'), there was no escaping the idea that the priest sacrifices Christ afresh at every mass. However hard they tried to conciliate this view of the matter with the doctrine of the Epistle to the Hebrews of the one oblation for sins, perfect and complete (so far as history and time are concerned) on Calvary, the mediaeval theologians, and the party of the old religion at the English Reformation, never quite got away from the necessity of defending the reality of the eucharistic sacrifice as in some sense an iteration of the sacrifice of Christ at the hands of the priest, even though they insisted that it was not a *new* sacrifice.

The Reformers, on the other hand, likewise carrying on the mediaeval insistence on the passion as the whole redeeming act into which the eucharist enters, took the other alternative. Since the passion is wholly in the past, the church now can only enter into it purely mentally, by *remembering* and imagining it. There is for them, therefore, no real sacrifice whatever in the eucharist. The external rite is at the most an acted memorial, *reminding* us of something no longer present. There is nothing but a 'figurative' meaning in such phrases as 'to eat the Body and drink the Blood' of Christ, which are, as Cranmer so often insisted, no longer here but in heaven. At the most we are then especially moved by the tokens or pledges of a redemption achieved centuries ago to rejoice and believe that we *have been* redeemed long ago on Calvary, and to renew our allegiance and gratitude to our Redeemer. We have 'communion' with Him when we take the bread and wine as He bade us do 'in remembrance' of Him, because the mere obedience stimulates devout emotions and aspirations, and thus deepens our purely mental union with Him which we have by conscious faith.

All that constitutes the eucharistic action on this view is the individual's reception of the bread and wine. But this is only a 'token'. The real eucharistic action (if 'action' is not a misleading term) takes place mentally, in the isolated secrecy of the individual's mind. The eucharistic action is thereby altogether deprived of its old corporate significance; it is practically abolished even as a corporate act. The external action must be done by each man for himself; the real eucharistic action goes on separately, even if simultaneously, within each man's mind.

The old conception had been of the church in its hierarchic unity entering into Christ's action, by the co-operation of all its various 'orders' (each having its own 'office', as S. Paul conceived it), and so in His action 'becoming what it is' eternally—His Body. The new conception is of a strictly *personal* mental reflection upon His action in the past. We cannot enter into it, since as a matter of history the passion is unique and finished.

Even the external rite is no longer a *corporate* rite integral to the performance of the real eucharistic action, but a common preparation for it, designed only to prepare each communicant subjectively to perform it for himself. Because of this, and for order's sake and ecclesiastical discipline, it may be well to commit the holding of the service to the professional preacher, who has a hortatory and disciplinary office in the society of christians. The partaking of the eucharist has always been a social act. But in strict necessity there is no need of this. Since the real eucharistic action consists in the individual's own personal mental remembrance of the passion, and is not an act of the universal Body of Christ throughout time and space, there is no more need for a priest commissioned to act for the whole Body, or indeed possibility of such a priesthood. There is no possibility of pleading the eucharist for one another, or for the dead in Christ; though we may pray together *at* it (not *by* it) as we intercede at other times. And since the action is purely mental, the external means to the action—the bread and wine—need only be a 'token'. There is no need to suppose that 'the eucharist is the Flesh of our Saviour Jesus Christ', as the primitive church had held. In strict necessity there is no need even of the taking of the bread and wine, which is only a Christ-ordained stimulus to the real eucharistic action, the devout remembering of His passion by the justified and believing soul dwelling upon the thought that He has saved it.

All this is a strictly logical and inevitable development from the protestant basis, and the proof of this is that it was the development everywhere followed by later protestantism, in spite of the hesitations of the Reformers. They would gladly have saved more of the primitive and mediaeval devotional estimation of the eucharist, if they could. But I ask attention for the fact that it is the logical development along one line of something which in itself is Latin and mediaeval, the practical restriction of the significance of the eucharist to the passion, as the historical element in the redeeming act, seen apart from its supra-historical elements in the resurrection, ascension and eternal priesthood. Given that restriction, there is no way of entering into Christ's action but by a repetition of it however guarded, or by a mere mental remembering of it, however vivid and devout. Fifteenth-century catholicism, in effect, took the one line; protestantism, to safeguard the sovereign efficacy of the sacrifice of Christ, took the other. As regards the eucharist[1] they are not complementary in their ideas, but strictly alternative developments of the same idea. The one can never comprehend the other.

## The Reformation

No estimate of the situation in the early sixteenth century will do justice to the Reformers which does not take account of this *impasse* to which the Western liturgy had been reduced by the later mediaeval tradition of simultaneously laying the whole devotional emphasis on the perfect atonement of Calvary, and yet exposing itself to the idea of trying to repeat or supplement this by the action of the priest in the mass. On the other hand the liturgical work of Alcuin was still intact; it had scarcely even been obscured by later accretions. The implications of the actual text of the liturgy might be ignored in current teaching and practice, but it still enshrined not the mediaeval teaching but those old and simple ideas about the eucharist which Gregory had preserved and Alcuin had faithfully handed on before the mediaeval mis-development began.

We can see now that what was required was a careful reconsideration by the church of the questions of what the eucharistic action is and how it is performed; and that all that was needed to find a way out of the *impasse* was a return to the liturgy itself and to its teaching. This would have offered an appeal behind both the mediaeval absorption of eucharistic devotion in the passion and the mediaeval teaching about the 'sacrifices of masses'. Most unfortunately neither side took this line at all. Instead, each of them clung to one horn of the mediaeval dilemma. The Reformers retained and even emphasised the mediaeval restriction of the significance of the eucharist to the passion without its eternal consequences. The Counter-Reformation restated the mediaeval teaching about the sacrifice in a more defensible form, and fortunately with such vagueness as to permit of the reopening in quite modern times of aspects of the matter which

---

[1] And I think in other directions also, *e.g.*, the doctrines of 'irresistible grace' and 'justification by faith alone' are strictly alternative to fifteenth century semi-pelagianism and what amounted to 'justification by dodges'.

the mediaeval teaching obscured or ignored.[1] The advantage of the Counter-Reformation was that it conserved the text of a liturgy which dated in substance from long before the mediaeval development. With this it preserved those primitive statements which indicated the true solution of the mediaeval difficulty, even though it was a long while before the post-Tridentine church made much use of them for the purpose. The protestants on the contrary discarded the whole text of the liturgy, and especially those elements in it which were a genuine monument of that primitive church they professed to restore. They introduced in its place forms which derived from and expressed the mediaeval tradition from which their own movement sprang.

There are, I think, ample explanations and excuses for this unfortunate confusion in the Reformers' aims and ideas. 'Eschatological' primitive christianity and the 'established' church of the post-Constantinian world are even in terms contradictories; and the difference between them was probably never so intense as at the end of the fifteenth century—the period in which the Reformers were growing up. These men were, like most of us, very largely creatures of their own training. As one reads their works it is obvious that they were never able to clear their own minds of the late mediaeval scholastic and devotional outlook. At every end and turn their thought is dominated by this, with its abstractness and rigorous logic on the one hand, and its intense emotional concentration on the *history* of the Redeemer on the other. This was the only mental world they had ever known, and its limitations were hardly even beginning to be revealed. The first known edition, *e.g.*, of Justin Martyr was only issued in 1551, of the liturgy of S. *James* in 1560, of the *Apostolic Constitutions* in 1563. Such documents might have made both sides aware that they were arguing from much too narrow a basis in taking the mediaeval Western tradition alone. But they did not appear until after the Reformation had got under way. Passions were already inflamed; positions had been taken up and consecrated by the blood of martyrs on both sides. The new documents only provided weapons for the attack and defence of doctrines elaborated without reference to them. In the really vital period, the generation from *c.* 1515–1550 when the breach was made, though the disputants made perpetual use of patristic arguments, they were obliged to rely on the texts inherited from the middle ages, corrupt—or at the best uncritical—in the case of the Western fathers, defectively translated in the case of the Greeks. The very important Syriac fathers were then all but unknown. Patristic

---

[1] To see how far the modern Roman church has moved beyond the Counter-Reformation's purely defensive position in the direction of the primitive doctrine of the sacrifice one has only to note the emphasis with which *e.g.*, de la Taille's *Mysterium Fidei*, 1921, *pp.* 304–5 repudiates the notion of Bellarmine and de Lugo of some 'real destruction' of Christ in the eucharist. Yet they themselves had represented a big modification of current mediaeval teaching. And the progress has gone a good deal further in some quarters since 1921.

texts were frequently cited only from the collections of extracts found compiled for quite different purposes in the canon law, and were used polem-
ically in obvious ignorance of their context and with false attributions. No
scholar with a modern knowledge of patristics who reads, *e.g.*, Cranmer's
*Defence of the True and Catholic Doctrine*, followed by Gardiner's attack on
it in his *Explicacyon*, followed again by Cranmer's *Answer*, can fail to be
aware that though Gardiner convicts his opponent of more actual abuse of
patristic evidence than Cranmer was able to bring home to him, both
parties are equally thorough in their interpretation of the patristic and
primitive church solely in the light of their own post-mediaeval situation.
It is the same frame of mind which made their contemporaries paint the
centurion on Calvary in early sixteenth century armour and S. Clement of
Rome in a cope and mitre. In art this is harmless and even good interpretation. But in the vital doctrinal discussion, where accurate historical interpretation might have provided the only possible solution apart from
schism, it was fatal. The lack of historical perspective, due to the mediaeval
ignorance of history, was perhaps the greatest single contributory cause in
the intellectual field of the sixteenth century break-up of Western christendom. It is one more example—history abounds with them—of the danger
of attempting to solve the practical problems of the present without a
thorough understanding of their causes in the past.

But the causes of the breach at the Reformation were not only intellectual and theoretical. If we would be just to the Reformers we must remember the practical situation. They looked out upon a church plagued
with a multitude of real superstitions, some gross and wholly evil in their
effects, some merely quaint and fanciful, but all equally irrelevant to the
christian religion. Their existence is not the invention of protestant propaganda; they were lamented and denounced by enlightened catholics quite
as loudly as by protestants, and the abating of them occupied much of the
attention of the Council of Trent. Again there is a long history behind the
post-mediaeval situation. They had been accumulating for more than a
thousand years—in grosser forms during the dark ages, in more poetic
ones from the middle ages proper. Their existence was largely the revenge
of the half-assimilated mass of the population upon the church for its
exclusion from intelligent participation in public worship. They were
certainly not the product of, or in most cases even connected with, the
mediaeval doctrine of the eucharist. But they all presented themselves by
this time under the aegis of the old religion. And the church under such
pontiffs as Julius II or such pastors as Cardinal Wolsey seemed utterly
disinclined to take any measures to disembarrass herself of them, if not
incapable of doing so. The consciousness of their ubiquity, and what looked
like their cynical tolerance by ecclesiastical authority, was enough to
exasperate to the highest degree earnest and intelligent men who were
wrestling with the loftiest problems of christian thought. If men could then

have foreseen the spirituality of John of the Cross and Teresa, the zeal of Ignatius, the charity of Francis de Sales and Vincent de Paul, they might have possessed their souls in more patience. As it was they were driven to despair of any effective evangelisation without a root-and-branch change of religion.

Further we must allow for the effect on the minds of good and sincere men of the great practical abuses in the government and machinery of the church. The Borgia and Medici popes did not look much like Vicars of Christ. The bishops, great lords much occupied politically or triflers wasting time upon the dilettantism of renaissance scholarship, were not often reassuringly like successors of the apostles. The church itself was disguised. The Avignon Papacy had come to depend upon a lay bureau-cracy of lawyers for the efficient conduct of the increasing business of a centralised ecclesiastical administration. The bishops throughout Europe now similarly administered their dioceses through squads of lawyers in minor orders. The Body of Christ was thus given the appearance of a vast human machine for salvation by sacraments, operated by very human men for very human motives, in the name and by the mechanism of an absentee Christ. And the machine had grown so complicated by successive patchings up and tyings together to keep it going somehow that it was no longer efficient for its real purposes. Its whole power and energy were absorbed in keeping itself going.

If one studies the visitation records of the early decades of the sixteenth century, the impression they make is probably less one of widespread cor-ruption than of a general torpor and an utter lack of spontaneity—at all events so far as England is concerned. The machine has taken charge of the church's life, and is still turning, but that is all there is to be said. Scandals are not notably numerous but they are inveterate, and the machine cannot prevent or eradicate them. The parochial clergy, often abysmally ignorant and ordained without training or testing, were in large part not pastorally efficient. The religious orders, for the most part respectably pious, were ridden by routine. Probably conditions in England were better—perhaps much better—than in many regions abroad.

All this had nothing to do with the mass or the liturgy itself. But the whole creaking, obsolescent, unchangeable ecclesiastical machine existed to get that liturgy performed, lived by performing it, was still justified in its own eyes and those of the multitudes because it performed it. It was natural enough that men who rebelled against the whole bureaucratic and mechanical conception of religion should assume that by sweeping away the mass they would end that conception with it. At least in England they were to find that the two were very little connected. When the mass had gone the whole Avignon system of administration, staffed by the same officials, operating by the same methods and regulations, acting through the same courts, remained in full working order. It was the shock of this discovery which produced the second wave of the English Reformation, the puritan movement and ultimately the puritan revolution. But that is a later story.

At the time of the Reformation proper all was by no means corrupt in the old religion, and there is no need unduly to darken the picture. To take the case of England alone, Cardinals Fisher and Pole offer examples of a sanctity and beauty of character unmatched among their opponents (unless by Hugh Latimer) and rare among highly placed ecclesiastics in any age. Thomas More was as holy a layman, as respected a Speaker of the Commons and as efficient a Chancellor, as England has ever known. There were zealous parish priests quite ready to die for the faith of their flocks, like John Hales, the vicar of Isleworth, and John Larke of Chelsea Old Church. The martyred Carthusians drew from their monastic life the strength to endure sweetly and patiently and with striking courage a course of treatment whose calculated cruelty matches any achievement of the Cheka and the Gestapo with all their modern advantages. Yet when all has been said of this kind that can be said, the fact remains that for whatever reason the life of the church as a whole was running at a very low level and seemed unable to recover its vigour. I believe that the real reason lay in the liturgical life of the church, which was frustrated in its deepest meaning by the mediaeval misunderstanding. If this be the real cause, both the puzzling violence of the Reformers against the mass as it was presented to them, and the radical nature of their innovations in the liturgy and the strange misdirection of their aims become much more comprehensible. But however this may be, we must reckon with the fact that the Reformers just as much as their opponents were conceiving of the problem they set themselves to solve only within the contemporary post-mediaeval situation. Both sides alike are the products and the victims of that long Western development, which since the end of the thirteenth century had somehow increasingly gone astray.

The first public attack on the mass was made by Luther in a sermon in April 1520, without stating any very definite objections.[1] But in his pamphlet *On the Babylonish Captivity* in October of the same year[2] he enunciates a first sketch of the later protestant thesis, attacking (1) the practice of communion under one kind alone, (2) the doctrine of transubstantiation, (3) the doctrine of the eucharist as a propitiatory or meritorious sacrifice. It may be remarked once more that each of these features of the contemporary idea of the eucharist has a long and not altogether simple history of development behind it.[3] But Luther is not at all concerned with origins but only

[1] *Werke* (ed. Weimar, 1888), vi., *pp. 349 sqq.*  [2] *Ibid., pp. 502 sqq.*
[3] (1) The second century church had practised communion under one kind alone from the *reserved* sacrament; in the third century, and probably earlier, communion was given to infants at the liturgy from the chalice alone. But communion under both kinds separately was normal at the liturgy everywhere until the seventh–ninth century, when the barbarous behaviour of the times caused so many profanations that various devices were tried to protect the contents of the chalice, *e.g.* the use of a

with what was then going on in christian worship in Saxony. At this stage he was content with polemics without suggesting changes in practice. He

spoon (in the East) or a metal tube (in the West), intinction, and so forth. None of these were very satisfactory, but this did not much matter because lay communions were very rare. They increased in frequency in the West in the thirteenth century, and the practice grew up in consequence of communicating at the liturgy in the form which had always been customary from the reserved sacrament, under the species of Bread alone. It seems to have originated as a matter of convenience, and official directions to do so only begin towards the end of the thirteenth century, when the innovation was already firmly established. It remained the normal Western custom down to the sixteenth century. It is to be noted that Luther is responsible for that misrepresentation of the custom as 'the denial of the cup to the *laity*', which imports a note of caste-prejudice. It was as much 'avoided by' as 'denied to' the laity originally; and the Western discipline 'denies the cup' to the clergy (from the Pope down) just as much as to the laity when they do not happen to be celebrating, but only communicating.

(2) 'Transubstantiation' is a philosophical explanation of *the way* in which the truth of our Lord's words at the last supper, 'This *is* My Body' is to be reconciled with the truth, obvious to the senses, that the experienced physical realities of bread and wine persist in the elements. It was defined, somewhat vaguely, by Can. 1 of the Lateran Council in A.D. 1215 as the result of three hundred and fifty years of controversy about the matter in the West. Nobody—or scarcely anybody—then denied either truth; it was a question of their rational reconciliation in a single statement. The definition of the Lateran is an attempt to state, in terms of metaphysics rather than theology, the relationship between the persisting physical realities in the elements and the Body and Blood of our Lord, in such a way as not to deny either that all the physical qualities of the bread and wine remain (which would overthrow the nature of a sacrament and contradict universal sense-experience) or that—as our Lord said—'This *is* His Body' (which would overthrow the significance of the eucharistic action and contradict universal spiritual experience). The definition left many points open to discussion and perhaps conserved both truths better than it reconciled them. Its acceptance was made obligatory, as defining the area within which future discussion could proceed without denying either truth, much as the Chalcedonian definition of our Lord's Divine and Human Natures in One Person had done. As a *metaphysical* reconciliation of two accepted facts it was always theoretically open to restatement in a different set of philosophical terms (*e.g.* in terms of a dynamic metaphysic instead of the static Aristotelian categories) and in the sixteenth century good catholics like Bishop Tunstall of Durham were found who regretted that the term 'transubstantiation' had ever been imported into the discussion. Some Lutherans and some Anglicans have at times attempted such a restatement which shall not be open to the strictly metaphysical objections which can be urged against transubstantiation and yet equally conserve both parts of the truth, though none of these attempts can be said to have achieved their object altogether satisfactorily. (I do not know that any thoroughgoing attempt has ever been made to state the truth along the lines of a theology of the eucharistic action instead of in terms of the metaphysical correlation of the elements with the Body and Blood.) The real objective of the protestant attack on transubstantiation was not the metaphysical statement of the relation between the elements and the Body and Blood, though it was delivered with metaphysical weapons, but the primitive christian belief that, as Ignatius said, 'the eucharist *is* the Flesh of our Saviour Jesus Christ, which Flesh suffered for our sins'. This rests ultimately on our Lord's words as reported by S. Paul and the evangelists. The problems raised by the purely metaphysical controversy played an immense part in sixteenth century propaganda, but these are really only a continuation of academic controversies which had raged in the fifteenth century. Like those which concerned communion under both kinds they inflamed popular partisanship (and still do) but they are quite secondary to the real issues as these affect the liturgy, which is why they are relegated to a foot-note here.

(3) The question of the eucharistic sacrifice is sufficiently treated of above (*pp.* 111.*sqq.*, 273 *sq.*).

did not even discourage the laity from receiving under one kind, or priests from continuing to say the Latin mass, or even from receiving mass-fees, providing they had no intention of sacrificing but only of reciting the prayers of which the liturgy is composed.[1]

The first to see the full consequences of the protestant thesis and carry them into effect in public worship was not Luther but his follower Carlstadt, whose 'evangelical mass' in the Castle chapel at Wittenberg (in Luther's absence) on Christmas day 1521 is the beginning of a revolution. Carlstadt saw and proclaimed that a 'religion of the spirit' can find no place for external actions as *causes* in the realm of grace. They can only be 'tokens' of a reality inwardly accomplished independently of them. Unable to rid historic christianity of the external acts of baptism and the eucharist —as he once confessed would be desirable—because of the New Testament evidence, he had to be content with robbing that evidence of any intelligible meaning. Confronted by the indignant Luther with the words of institution he explained that our Lord had distributed bread to the disciples, and then—pointing to His own physical Person—had declared '*This* is My Body. Do this (*i.e.* distribute bread) in remembrance of Me.' Within a month of that first protestant Christmas he had already denied the efficacy of infant baptism, and in protest against it was rebaptising adults who had been baptised in infancy. If justification is by conscious faith alone, as Luther was teaching, then since infants cannot have conscious faith, their baptism had been no valid 'token' of a spiritually received incorporation into Christ. (Yet to insist on *re*-baptising because of this was in fact to attribute to the 'token' an importance which on this theory it could not possess.) Luther was horrified. Before the end of January there was a riotous pillaging of churches and smashing of altars and images in Wittenberg in what was to become the approved protestant fashion. A few weeks later the peasants of the countryside were massacring their feudal oppressors in the name of the new religion. The political anarchism of the Anabaptists had begun. These developments brought discredit on the new ideas in Germany for a while, and momentarily checked their progress—not least in Luther's own mind. But the inherent drive of the protestant idea was too strong to be stifled in contemporary conditions by the hesitations of the man who had made himself its first mouthpiece. Its development was merely transferred elsewhere.

Oecolampadius of Basle and Zwingli of Zurich arrived at much the same conclusions as Carlstadt at about the same time, and taught them with much greater discipline and reasonableness. Zwingli was a priest and a *monsignore*, who had formerly been chaplain to Pope Leo X. He had also managed to combine this with a commission in the army as an officer of Swiss mercenaries, in which capacity he took part in the battle of Marignano in 1515. (He did not lose his love of fighting after becoming a

[1] *Werke*, vi., *pp*. 526 *sqq*.

Reformer, but was killed in full armour at the battle of Cappel in 1531.) In 1519 he was accused of Lutheranism, and carried through a revolution in his native city which from a semi-political became an ecclesiastical movement. His doctrine of the sacraments, like that of his colleague of Basle, leaves them no force or efficacy of their own whatsoever. They are bare signs or ceremonies by which a man assures *other people* rather than himself of his saving faith in Christ's redemption.[1] Baptism does not make sons of God nor remit sins; the baptism of Christ is in all respects the same as the baptism of John.[2] In the eucharist there is but plain bread and wine, a *reminder* of the salvation achieved long ago on Calvary. In his *Fidei Ratio* issued in the year before his death Zwingli states his belief on this matter thus: 'I believe that in the holy eucharist . . . the true Body of Christ is present by the contemplation of faith, *i.e.* that those who give thanks to the Lord for the benefit He has conferred upon us in His Son, recognise that He took upon Him true flesh, in that flesh truly suffered, truly washed away our sins by His blood, and thus everything wrought by Christ for them becomes as it were present by the contemplation of faith.'[3] In other words, the eucharistic action consists in a vivid mental remembering of the passion as the achievement of 'my' redemption in the past.

The same idea is expressed with great clearness in liturgical form in an exhortation after communion in the Zurich rite which he drew up in 1525. 'Now remembering, dear brothers and sisters, what we have just done according to our Lord's command, namely that with thankful remembrance we have borne witness to our belief that we are all miserable sinners, but by His Body given and His Blood poured forth [*i.e.* on Calvary] we have been cleansed from sin and redeemed from everlasting death . . . we ought sincerely to pray to God to grant us all to hold with firm faith within our hearts this remembrance of His bitter death, and bear it ever within us, and thereby die daily to all wickedness.'[4] As he explained the words of institution—' "This is", that is, "signifies", "My Body". Which is as though to say, it is as if a wife were to shew a ring left by her husband'— ('engraved', he adds on another occasion 'with his portrait')—'and say "Look, this is my husband".'[5] Except that Oecolampadius reaches his conclusion by interpreting 'My Body' as 'the symbol (*figura*) of My Body' instead of 'is' as 'signifies', he does not appear to differ in any particular from Zwingli.

A greater man than either of these was Jean Calvin, a Frenchman who settled at Geneva. We are not here concerned with the majestic but unbalanced supernaturalism of his theology as a whole, which is the most

[1] *de Vera et Falsa Religione*, ii. *ed.* Schuler *u.* Schulthess, p. 198.
[2] *Ibid., p.* 121.
[3] Cited in Kidd, *Documents of the Continental Reformation, p.* 474.
[4] E. Wolfensberger, *Die Zürcher Kirchengebete, p.* 57.
[5] *de Vera et Falsa Rel., p.* 293.

THE REFORMATION AND ANGLICAN LITURGY 633

complete and satisfying to the mind of all the expositions which protestantism has received. Calvin is at one with Zwingli in denying any but a
figurative sense to the words of institution,[1] but for the characteristic
reason that to think otherwise would be an unworthy abasement of the
glorified Christ in heaven.[2] Nevertheless Calvin will not agree with Zwingli
that communion is *merely* a 'bare sign'. There is a presence of Christ at the
eucharist—he does not hesitate to call it a 'Real Presence', and once to say
that 'It is not by the imagination and thought that Jesus gives us His Body
and Blood in the supper', 'but the *substance* of them is truly given unto us'.[3]
But such traditional language must not mislead us as to his real meaning.
'The reign (of Christ) is in no way limited to any places in space, and in no
way determined by any bounds that Jesus Christ should not show His
power wherever He pleases, in heaven or on earth, that He should not
declare Himself present *by His power and virtue*, that He should not ever
aid His own, breathing living life into them, sustaining them, strengthening
them, giving them vigour, and ministering to them no less than *if* He were
present in Body; in fine, that He should nourish them with His own Body,
the participation whereof He makes to flow into them *by the power of His
Spirit*. Such, then, is the mode of receiving the Body and Blood of Jesus
Christ in the sacrament'.[4]

This, then, is his final meaning—that in the eucharist Jesus bestows His
Spirit on the spirit of the individual who believes in Him as Redeemer and
partakes of the bread and wine as He had commanded. There *is* an efficacious significance of its own in the act of the individual's communion, to
which the whole eucharistic action has been reduced. But for all the greater
warmth and reality which Calvin's doctrine thus imparts to the notion of
the eucharist over Zwingli's, he does not meet the difficulty that what our
Lord had said He was giving was not His Spirit, but His *Body*. The last
supper is not Pentecost, even if one leads to the other.[5] The real eucharistic
action is for Calvin individual and internal, not corporate. It is one more
example of the intractability of the scriptural sacraments to the protestant
theory, and the impossibility of adapting to a 'religion of the spirit' and
pure individualism the institutions of a 'religion of incarnation' which presupposes the organic community of the renewed Israel. Modern protestantism has solved the difficulty by leaving the sacraments on one side,
and—when pressed by the scriptures—by inventing nameless Antiochenes
who misled S. Paul, and by denying that our Lord instituted or intended
to institute the sacraments at all. The Reformers did not feel able thus to
set aside the evidence of the scriptures, though they were unable to fit the
external sacramental actions at all comfortably into their theological and
devotional scheme of christianity.

[1] *Institutes*, IV, xvii, 20.    [2] *Ibid.*, 19.    [3] *Ibid.*, 19.    [4] *Ibid.*, 18.
[5] This doctrine is not the same as that primitive idea that in the eucharist we
receive 'Spirit' by means of the Body (*cf. p.* 266).

It was, in fact, this difficulty of the New Testament evidence about the eucharist which broke up the early unity of the Reformation. Luther had been scared by the violence which followed Carlstadt's bold applications of his own teaching. It is significant that the only rampart he could ever find against such logical deductions from that theoretical teaching consisted precisely in the acceptance at its full value of the New Testament evidence. As he declared years afterwards in a letter to the protestants of Strassburg, he had never felt able to deny the plain and simple meaning of the words of institution as the scriptures reported them, though he would have been glad to add this further barrier of separation between himself and the papists. In fact he seems never to have wavered in his determination to defend their literal sense, and declared in 1534, 'The papists themselves are obliged to praise me for having defended the doctrine of the literal sense (of these words) much better than themselves. And in fact I am persuaded that, even were they all to be compounded into one man, they could never maintain them as strongly as I do.'[1] The *Confession of Augsburg*, the primary Lutheran confession of faith, in its tenth article, declares that the Lutheran churches 'teach that the Body and Blood of Christ are truly present in the Lord's supper and that they are distributed to the communicants, and blame those who teach the contrary.' The sixth article of Luther's *Articles of Smalkeld* in 1537 says that 'The Bread and the Wine at the supper are the true Body and true Blood of Christ, and not only good christians but the wicked themselves receive them.' Violent controversies accompanied by the most unpleasant abuse took place between the German and Swiss reformers on this topic, but always the argument revolved around this question of the meaning of the scriptural evidence. Luther insisted that it must mean what it plainly said. Zwingli and Calvin replied that if it were to be accepted in this sense it must overthrow the whole protestant conception of the sacraments and with that the cardinal doctrine of justification by faith alone. It may be suspected that, as so often happens in controversies, both sides were right in what they affirmed.

Luther, however, did not cease to be a protestant. Nothing could exceed the violence of his language against the mass: 'Yea, I declare that all the brothels (though God has reproved these severely) all manslaughters, murders, thefts and adulteries have wrought less evil than the abomination of the popish mass.'[2] Though he insisted on the external reality of the Body and Blood in the eucharist on the ground of the scriptural evidence, he insisted that there is no sacrifice. All that is offered to God is the prayers of the rite. The Body and Blood of Christ are not offered to God but *to men*— to the communicants. There is still a eucharistic action, even an action of Christ in the eucharist—but the church does not enter into it. Her part is

[1] See this, and the other passages cited by K. G. Goetz, *Die heutige Abendsmahls-rage in ihrer geschichtlichen Entwicklung*, Leipzig, 1907, pp. 50–55.
[2] *Werke, ed. cit.*, xv., pp. 773 sq.

only to prepare herself for it and to *receive it*. We can see here the effect of Luther's perpetual primary assumption about the end of religion, that it is not the worship of God but the comfort of man.[1]

Understood thus, the Lutheran eucharist does not contradict the cardinal protestant doctrine of justification by faith alone, despite its retention of belief in the objective reality of the communicants' reception of our Lord's Body and Blood by good and bad alike. For Luther the eucharistic action is not creative of the church, nor does the church enter into it corporately. It has been reduced to the act of communion alone, which each must do for himself. Indeed, it is not clear how far the term 'action' can properly be applied even to Luther's conception of the communion (except as a purely physical description of what the communicant does with his hands and mouth) for Luther always views it as something *passive*, as a 'reception'. And even so, he insistently denies that reception of communion *causes* grace (though it does 'cause' damnation in the man who receives without justifying faith). Grace is caused by the faith of the individual in his having been redeemed by Christ on Calvary. (Faith for Luther is always not faith *in Christ* as redeemer, but faith *in my redemption* by Him.) The gift to us by Christ of His own true Body and Blood only *rewards* our confidence (already achieved) that our sins have been remitted through the imputation to us of His righteousness. Participation in His Body and Blood does increase that confidence, because it proves to us that we have been redeemed by our own increased consciousness of our own confidence in Christ. (The whole process is self-regarding and self-generated as Luther presents it.)

It is perhaps not surprising that Luther's doctrine of the objective reality of our reception of our Lord's Body and Blood in the eucharist slowly declined in precision within the Lutheran churches.[2] It is based simply on the literal understanding of the words of institution, and is logically unrelated and unnecessary to the Lutheran doctrine as a whole. It kept its place in the Lutheran doctrinal confessions, but it received and could receive no adequate expression in the Lutheran liturgies. When the bulk of

---

[1] *Cf.* his distinction between 'the hidden God' of reason, the contemplation of Whom 'casts one into a horrible despair', and of Whose will 'it is hard to think without a secret anger against God' (*Werke*, xl. *a.*, *pp.* 77, 78), *i.e.* God in Himself Who is the object of worship; and on the other hand, God in relation *to us*, God redeeming *us* in Jesus Christ, Who justifies the sinner, and *as such* is lovable. Hence his immense emphasis on faith as the *consciousness* of being justified by the merits of Christ, the comforting sense of which he never tires of expatiating on, and the *experience* of which is for him in itself the whole process and purpose of our union with God.

[2] Luther's metaphysical explanations of *how* the Body and Blood are related to the bread and wine are not carefully elaborated but thrown out in passing, rather by way of a repudiation of transubstantiation than as a seriously thought out alternative. They are usually called in England 'consubstantiation', but Luther never seems to have used that term himself, and I cannot find it in any of the official Lutheran confessions. I do not think this side of his teaching—the metaphysical definition—was ever taken very seriously either by himself or by his followers.

the German Lutherans were united with the German Calvinists in the
Prussian State Church in the early nineteenth century, it was in the result
the Calvinistic eucharistic doctrine which prevailed, though the question
was formally left open for every communicant to decide for himself.

Such were the new ideas which threw the continental churches into a
ferment in the twenties and which were filtering into England in the thirties
of the sixteenth century. Cranmer personally encountered them in more
than one form in Germany after 1530, while he was qualifying for the
archbishopric of Canterbury as a member of the diplomatic service—and
on occasions of the secret service—of king Henry VIII.

Secular historians both in Germany and elsewhere nowadays tend increasingly to ascribe the violence of the Reformation explosion to a mere
outbreak of the recurrent *furor teutonicus* against European civilisation.
It is true that interesting parallels can be drawn. When the old common
ordering of civilisation in the West had got into an unhealthy and weak
state *c.* A.D. 400 it was ruined by a German disruption of its political basis
through the barbarian settlements. When the West had painfully rebuilt its
common order and unity on a new spiritual basis, which had again got into
an unhealthy and weak state *c.* A.D. 1500, it was again ruined by another
German outbreak against its spiritual basis in the Reformation. When
Western European unity had again been rebuilt upon a common economic
basis, which had grown similarly unhealthy in the early twentieth century,
it has once again been ruined beyond hope (or fear) of restoration in its old
form by another twofold paroxysm in what looks like the permanent weak
spot in the organism of the West. Luther furnishes curious parallels with
Adolf Hitler—the same 'somnambulism'; the same sense of surrender to
mysterious impersonal forces, 'grace' and 'nature' as he labels them,
irresistibly thrusting the passive human soul to a predestined fate; the
same rather frantic brand of oratory, glorying in antinomies and self-con-
tradiction; the same contempt for reason and exaltation of intuition and
impulse, which have proved able to stupefy the German mind in other
periods also (*cf., e.g.,* Caesar, *Gallic War,* I. 44).

Such views are fashionable among historians at the moment. To me
personally, for what the opinion is worth, the parallels seem unduly selective to be true. And they will prove gravely misleading by their over-
simplification if they bring with them any acceptance of the view of history
as a process of 'racial determinism', which is only another form of the
Nordic *Herrenvolk* nonsense preached by Hitler himself. History is not
simply the result of biological factors, even though biological factors do
continuously enter into it by providing the men who make history. What
makes up the whole process is an immensely complex interplay of the biological and economic setting with cultural forces and temporarily prevalent
human ideas, the whole moulded in the end by certain voluntary actions of
individual men and women. His mixture of Albanian and British blood did

not *cause* Constantine to accept christianity, with all the tremendous consequences still flowing from that action of his; nor did the economic and cultural situation of the time compel him to it, any more than it compelled his colleague Licinius to persecute the church. The situation of the empire and the current towards monotheism in the fourth century did form the setting for their different choices of action. But there is nothing to suggest that the result would have been the same if their choices had been reversed. Cultures would have been different if Mohammed or Descartes or Marx had never lived; history would have been different if Constantine or Charlemagne or Napoleon had acted otherwise than they did on certain occasions when it was in their power to act quite differently; even though the situations in which they chose their actions were not of their own making.

So it is with the Reformation, which is an immensely complex movement in which one can discern many factors at work—the low state of the church; the new nationalism; the greed of the territorial aristocracy; the agitation in the submerged masses; new cultural developments breaking up the structure of mediaeval society and the fixed framework of mediaeval thought; and half-a-dozen more. Among these the apparently permanent tendency of many men of German race to introspectiveness and *verloren-sein*[1] may have its place, and would account for much of the hysteria and the violent tendencies—anarchistic in practice and even nihilistic in thought—with which it was often accompanied in Germany. Even so, we must remember that much the same emotional reactions were exhibited by some French Huguenots and some English puritans. Nevertheless in the last analysis it was the work of men, good, bad and indifferent in all parties. Leo X and Tetzel, Luther and Melanchthon, Saint Cajetan and Pfefferkorn, Calvin and Henry Tudor, Cranmer and Wolsey, Charles of Hapsburg, John Larke and Joan Butcher, Stephen Gardiner and Ulrich Zwingli and Anne Boleyn and all the rest—each must bear his or her own share of merit or responsibility for the ultimate results, right down to the nameless hinds who cut faggots or would not say Amen to the parson's new prayers, or just stood and laughed while the Carthusians were dragged by on hurdles through the kennel to Tyburn. Only God can assess all that with both justice and mercy.

Yet behind all the violence and the controversy and the inescapable but polluting alliances with secular motives and secular powers (which form the grimy compromise of ideas with human living in any given historical situation) one can, I think, discern the force of a single idea carrying the whole protestant movement forward with an impetus sufficient to overcome the strength of tradition, the resistance of sincere opponents and critics and even the mistakes and faults of the Reformers themselves. (I do not think anyone has ever claimed personal *sanctity* as the outstanding

[1] Sense of being lost and consequent blind panic—a symptomatic German word for a peculiarly German state of mind.

characteristic of Luther, Calvin, Zwingli—or Cranmer.) That idea was the conception of a personal relation of each individual soul to God. It was a true idea, though it was presented by the Reformers in so unbalanced a way as to assume all the characteristics of a half-truth. But it was not a new idea, or even one which it is fair to say that the mediaeval church had neglected except in one particular direction. One need only look, to take one instance, at what the mediaeval church had made of the primitive institution of penance, to be sure of that. The old pre-Nicene public penance for post-baptismal mortal sin—the 'single plank in shipwreck' that a man might undergo only once in a life-time, was directed chiefly to maintaining the *corporate* christian standards at a high level. The mediaeval church turned it into the auricular confession that we know, with all its psychological and other benefits to the individual, precisely in order to assist and develop the personal relation of the individual soul to God. The mystical writers of the thirteenth, fourteenth and fifteenth centuries, who had an immense influence, are full of this idea of the individual's relation to God, as the patristic authors had never been. The devotional tradition of the later middle ages is far more individualistic than that, *e.g.*, of the pre-Nicene church. Why then did the idea develop such intense emotional force in the period of the post-mediaeval liturgical crisis?

It is not neglected truths, but those which are at once fully acknowledged and frustrated of their proper expression, which take the most drastic psychological revenges. As I see it, it was precisely because this truth of the spiritual life was at once emphasised in fifteenth century teaching and devotion, and denied all practical expression in its proper field, the liturgy —which is the 'vital act' of the church's life—that it generated such explosive force. In the end it attacked the liturgy, which in its contemporary presentation opposed a direct barrier to its expression, with an unreasoning fury which on any other explanation is difficult to account for. It swept this ruthlessly away. And it proceeded to sweep after it just those elements of catholic tradition which stood in the path of its most extreme and unbalanced expression—the idea of the church as the sphere of redemption, the sacraments as effectual signs of grace, and with these the doctrines of the apostolic ministry and the communion of saints. It left intact other things like the orthodox doctrines of the Trinity and the atonement. Yet these were in fact no more (and no less) 'scriptural' than the doctrines it rejected. The formulation of them which protestantism retained rested just as much on 'ecclesiastical tradition' as that of the doctrines it discarded so vehemently. These latter are, from the point of view of modern scholarship, actually easier to trace in the pre-Nicene centuries than a fully Athanasian orthodoxy about the incarnation and the Trinity.

The real safeguard of the doctrines retained by protestantism in the sixteenth century was not the Bible, but the fact that they did not impinge upon the full sweep of the overmastering idea of the individual's relation to God, as the discarded doctrines might do. Even in sixteenth century protestantism it was not a direct relation to God which was in question; there was always Christ as the only mediator by His passion. The one-sided *devotional* emphasis of the fifteenth century on the atonement was fully maintained and even increased by the Reformers. As soon as the immediate post-mediaeval conditions which had lent this idea such vehemence passed away, protestantism lost all its expansive force. It fell back into reliance upon an institutionalism of its own and the support of secular society, as a new 'tradition' and a settled order of things. It retained a vigorous inherited opposition to catholicism, but it had only a diminished content of positive ideas derived from the christian past with which to oppose the onset of the new commercial secularism and the disintegrating effects of its own inherent individualism.

The attempt is being made to restore to it in various ways some of the catholic values it discarded, though it is difficult to see how this can be done effectively without a negation of the basic protestant idea. On the other hand, the modern attempt, seen *e.g.* in the writings of Barth and Brünner, to return to that motive idea of the protestant reformation in all its dazzling simplicity, though it has invigorated the thinking of many protestants, does not seem to have revivified either the protestant thesis or the energies of protestantism as a whole. Protestantism still has many able scholars, to whom it is a delight and a privilege to pay tribute. But that barrenness of what may be called creative or seminal thoughts which for more than a generation has alarmed philosophical protestants as a symptom of internal decay, still continues unbroken. (One has only to consider the contribution of English protestant dissent to christian thinking in England during the last five years to understand what I mean.)

Meanwhile, though the East has now had many opportunities of sympathetic contact with able and holy protestants, it has shewn no sign of discovering any contribution in protestant thought which it can usefully assimilate. Do not all these facts suggest that apart from the particular situation which gave it such terrific emotional force at the close of the Western middle ages, the protestant idea has never had in itself sufficient content to embrace either the whole essence of the christian religion or the whole complexity of human life? The asking of such a question by one who rejects the protestant account of christianity may be ascribed by some to mere prejudice, but it can honestly be said that it does not spring from any lack of sympathy with the Reformers or their followers. I ask it only because I believe that the history of protestantism itself indicates that they were the chief and most permanent sufferers by the accumulated mistakes of the mediaeval Latin church.

*Archbishop Cranmer*

From the day that Thomas Cranmer became archbishop of Canterbury in 1533 he seems to have believed sincerely that any ideas he might have for remedying the acknowledged crisis in the old religion ought to be strictly subordinated to those of that firm if somewhat eccentric supporter of things as they were, king Henry VIII. His business was to build up a strong and effective Royal Supremacy, by which the king might take such constructive action as seemed to him good after seeking counsel from his ecclesiastical advisers. The archbishop might have his own ideas, but it was for the king alone to decide how far they should be put into practice. King Henry died in January 1547. The accession of a minor, while it increased the archbishop's difficulties by weakening the sanctions behind any action which might be taken, also increased his opportunities of securing that it should be what seemed to himself the right action. In such circumstances the initiative and the responsibility for solving the problems now generally recognised as urgent clearly lay with him.

To secure an adequate acquaintance with the facts of the situation a general ecclesiastical Visitation of the whole country by Royal Commissioners in the name of the new Supreme Head of the English Church was ordered, and energetically carried out during the autumn. From some date late in the autumn we have the first diagnosis by the archbishop himself of the problems which confronted him and the first cautious sketch of the remedies he proposed to employ. The one took the form of a *questionnaire* addressed to his brother bishops, the other of his own answers to it.

'Queries concerning the mass:

'1. Whether the sacrifice of the altar was instituted to be received of one man for another, or to be received of every man for himself?

'2. Whether the receiving of the said sacrament of one man do avail and profit another?

'3. What is the oblation and sacrifice of Christ in the mass?

'4. Wherein consisteth the mass by Christ's institution?

'5. What time the accustomed order began first in the church, that the priest alone should receive the sacrament?

'6. Whether it be convenient that the same custom continue still in this realm?

'7. Whether it be convenient that masses satisfactory should continue, that is, priests hired to sing for souls departed?

'8. Whether the gospel ought to be taught at the time of the mass, to the understanding of the people being present?

'9. Whether in the mass it were convenient to use such speech as the people may understand?'[1]

---

[1] *Cranmer's Works,* ed. Jenkyns, II, *pp.* 178 *sq.* (There are two further questions on reservation.)

It is interesting to set beside Cranmer's own answers those returned by a group of six bishops who made a joint reply from the conservative side:

### Cranmer

1. The sacrament of the altar was not . . . instituted to be received of one man for another, but to be received of every man for himself.

2. The receiving of the said sacrament by one man doth avail and profit only him that receiveth the same.

3. The oblation and sacrifice of Christ in the mass is so called not because Christ indeed is there offered and sacrificed by the priest and the people (for that was done but once by Himself upon the cross) but it is so called, because it is a memory and representation of that very true sacrifice and immolation which before was made upon the cross.

4. The mass by Christ's institution consisteth in those things which be set forth in the Evangelists Mk. xiv; Lk. xxii; 1 Cor. x and xi.

### Boner etc.

1. I think that the sacrament of thanks was not . . . instituted to be received of one man for another, but of every man for himself.

2. I think that the receiving of the said sacrament doth not avail or profit any other, but only as all other good works done of any member of Christ's church be available to the whole mystical body of Christ, and to every lively member of the same, by reason of mutual participation and spiritual communion between them. And also it may be profitable to others as an example . . .

3. I think it is the presentation of the very Body and Blood of Christ being really present in the sacrament; which presentation the priest maketh at the mass in the name of the church unto God the Father, in memory of Christ's passion and death upon the cross, with thanksgiving therefore and devout prayer that all christian people, and namely they which spiritually join with the priest in the said oblation and of whom he maketh special remembrance, may attain the benefit of the said passion.

4. I think it consisteth principally in the consecration, oblation and receiving of the Body and Blood of Christ with prayers and thanksgivings; but what the prayers were, and what rites Christ used or commanded at the first institution of the mass, the scripture declareth not.

5. I think the use that the priest alone did receive the sacrament without the people began not within six or seven hundred years after Christ.

5. I know no further order or commandment of the church; but what time the devotion of the people was so greatly decayed that they would not come to receive the sacrament, then the priests were compelled to receive it alone.

6. I think it more agreeable to the scripture and primitive church, that the first usage should be restored again, and that the people should receive the sacrament with the priest.

6. I would wish that at every mass there would be some to receive the sacrament with the priest: nevertheless, if none will come to receive it, I think it lawful and convenient that the priests of this realm of England may say mass and receive the sacrament alone.

7. I think it not convenient that satisfactory masses should continue.

7. I think that such of the schoolmen as do write of masses satisfactory, do define them otherwise than is declared in this question; nevertheless, I think it is not against the word of God but that priests praying in the mass for the living and the dead, and doing other things in the church about the ministration of the sacraments, may take a living for the same.

8. I think it very convenient, that the gospel concerning the death of Christ and our redemption should be taught to the people in the mass.

8. I think it not necessary to have a sermon at every mass, but the oftener the same is done to the edifying of the people (so that the service of their vocation be not defrauded) the more it is to be commended.

9. I think it convenient to use the vulgar tongue in the mass, except in certain secret mysteries, whereof I doubt.[1]

9. To have the whole mass in English, I think it neither expedient nor convenient.

The parties are less agreed than they might seem at first sight, for they differ over questions 3 and 7, which are really the key questions. The six bishops' answer on 7 misses the real point, which Cranmer's does not reveal. In 3 everything turns on the meaning of the word 'memory', which subsequent events shew that the two parties were already using in different

[1] *Ibid.,* pp. 179 *sqq.*

senses, though that is not obvious here. One notes in both answers to this question the mediaeval restriction of the sacrifice of Christ entirely to His passion and death; this is taken for granted by everybody (and the mediaeval devotional tradition is emphasised again, unconsciously but strongly, in Cranmer's answer to No. 8). One notes, too, the mediaeval 'sacerdotalist' form of the bishops' answer to No. 3. For both parties alike the sacrifice of Christ is irremediably in the remote past. Along this line the *impasse* between entering into His action as mere mental *remembering* and something which has at least the appearance of repetition by the priest is inevitable, even though it is still concealed by the use of the word 'memory' by both sides.

There were further exchanges of questions and answers in the next few weeks, which brought out Cranmer's thoroughgoing disbelief in any effective doctrine of the 'communion of saints' on earth, such as is stated in the bishops' answer to 2; and, on the other side, the reluctance of the bishops to innovate against the 'uniformity of all churches' in liturgy. However, a parliamentary statute in the previous December had already required the bishops to draw up a form for communion under both kinds. Despite the rather wrangling tone the exchange of views between them had begun to take, the bishops unanimously put out the *Order of Communion* in March 1548 under the authority of this statute, without having formally submitted it to Convocation.[1]

This consisted of (*a*) an 'exhortation' to the parishioners to prepare for communion, to be pronounced by the priest some days beforehand; and (*b*) an English form for administering communion to the laity, to be inserted into the customary Latin mass, which was otherwise to be recited as it always had been without variation.

(*a*) The former is, apart from stylistic verbal variations, the exhortation 'Dearly beloved, on ——day next I purpose, etc.' still contained in the present Prayer Book. Apart from a paragraph about the restitution of stolen goods or lands (inserted in 1549 but omitted in 1552 in deference to the protests of the new proprietors of old church lands and never since replaced) this has been retained throughout the history of the Anglican rite. In it the eucharist is described as 'the most comfortable sacrament of the Body and Blood of Christ, to be taken of them *in the remembrance* of His most fruitful and glorious passion: by the which passion we have obtained remission of our sins, and be made partakers of the kingdom of heaven, whereof *we be assured and ascertained* if we come to the said sacrament with repentance, faith and intention of amendment'. If the reader will return for a moment to the Zurich documents cited on *p.* 632, he will find them illuminating as to the doctrine behind this statement. The exhortation went on to the paragraph contained in substance in the same exhortation in

[1] On the preliminary discussions see H. A. Wilson, *The Order of the Communion* 1548 (H.B.S., 1908), *pp.* x. *sqq.*

the present Prayer Book, that any one still troubled in conscience after private self-examination and contrition, shall 'come to me or some other discreet and learned priest, taught in the law of God' and make his confession and receive absolution. This is nowadays quite legitimately cited as evidence that the English Church has *retained* the sacrament of penance. But when it first appeared the emphasis must have been felt to lie all the other way. Confession to a priest had hitherto been the invariable preparation of the laity for their infrequent communions. This exhortation suggests that it should now become exceptional, and goes on to require that those who do not use it shall not be judged by their fellows any more than those who do by those who do not. Under the appearance of impartiality this was an official defence of an innovation.

(*b*) The form for administering communion also consists of items still found in our present Prayer Book. After the priest's communion (made according to the Latin rite) he turns to the people to say what is still substantially our 'Long Exhortation', though it has since undergone more alterations than the preliminary exhortation just treated of. There follows our 'Short Exhortation'—'Ye that do truly—' (in which the people's confession is described as made 'to Almighty God *and to this holy church here gathered together in His Name*', shortened to 'before this congregation' in 1552, and omitted in 1662); then the Confession in its present form. The Absolution was changed a little, apparently to improve the coherence of its wording, in 1549; but even in 1548 it is already substantially as it is now. There follow the present 'Comfortable Words', and then, all kneeling, the priest says the 'Prayer of Humble Access' in its present form, except that after 'so to eat the flesh of Thy dear Son Jesus Christ and to drink His Blood' it runs '*in these holy mysteries, that we may continually dwell in Him* . . . The words italicised were removed in 1552. After this comes the communion of the people with the forms: 'The Body of our Lord Jesus Christ . . . preserve thy *body* unto everlasting life', 'The Blood of our Lord Jesus Christ . . . preserve thy *soul* unto everlasting life', reflecting the mediaeval speculation that the bread is for the communicant's body and the chalice for his soul, also found in the Prayer of Humble Access (*cf. p.* 612). After this the priest is to 'let the people depart' with 'The peace of God . . .' (without the addition of 'And the blessing of God . . .' first added in 1549, when 'The peace' was transferred to the end of the whole eucharistic rite). Presumably in 1548 the people only 'departed' to the nave to await the rest of the Latin rite.

This *Order* is partly a fruit of Cranmer's embassy abroad. An unsigned letter from one of his suite (now thought to have been Sir Thomas Eliot) about 1530 describes how they found that at Nuremberg 'after the levation the deacon turneth to the people, telling them in the Almaigne tongue a long process how they should prepare themselves to the Communion of the Flesh and Blood of Christ. And then may every man come that listeth with-

out going to Confession'.[1] Other passages in the letter make it clear that
'Mr. Cranmer' had been very interested; and it is certain that the Branden-
burg-Nuremberg *Kirchenordnung* drawn up by Cranmer's father-in-law
Osiander was at least consulted by him in drawing up the preliminary
exhortation for giving warning of communion.[2] The general confession in
Cranmer's *Order* has, however, made more direct use of Hermann of
Cologne's *Consultatio*, rather more than fifty per cent. of its wording being
taken over bodily from this Lutheran document, together with about fifty
per cent. of the absolution (though the changes in this case are not unimportant) and three of the four 'Comfortable Words'.[3] But while these
Cologne prayers are meant to be said before mass begins, Cranmer has
transferred them for use immediately before communion; and the Nuremberg matter, employed in the original immediately before communion,
has been used by Cranmer for the preliminary occasion some days before.

It has been worth while to set out the facts about this *Order*, which was
in use only for some fifteen months, a little more thoroughly than is
usually done, because it casts a good deal of light on the archbishop's own
mind. It is no small part of the evidence both for Cranmer's personal
honesty and for his fixity and consistency of mind that he felt able to
employ this same set of communion devotions from the first to the last of
his liturgical experiments with only one verbal change which can be supposed to be of any doctrinal importance—the omission in 1552 of the
words '*in these holy mysteries*' from the phrase about eating the Body and
drinking the Blood of Christ in the 'Prayer of Humble Access'. In this
connection the statement of sacramental doctrine in the preliminary exhortation is of outstanding interest.

It was obvious, of course, that the *Order of Communion* could only be an
interim arrangement; and the Royal Proclamation by which it was put out
said as much. It was superseded by the first Prayer Book at Pentecost 1549,
which in outline mostly followed the old Latin rite and contained much
that was reminiscent of the old prayers of the missal. The new English
prayers of the *Order of Communion* were placed in exactly the same position
in the new English rite of 1549 that they had occupied in the Latin one the
year before.

It is usual to interpret this rite as evidence of a half-way stage in Cranmer's doctrinal development, a stage when he held an approximately
Lutheran position of belief in some reality of connection between the consecrated elements and our Lord's Body and Blood, though it is plain that

[1] *Original Letters etc.* (ed. H. Ellis), III, ii. 192.
[2] H. E. Jacobs, *The Lutheran Movement in England etc.*,[1] (1892), pp. 240 sqq.,
thinks that Cranmer also used the Cassel *Ordnung* of 1539 and the earlier Nuremberg *Order* of Volprecht (1524). He appears to me to exaggerate the resemblances
of the English *Order* to these two documents.
[3] The two documents are printed side by side in H. A. Wilson's *ed.* of *The Order
of Communion* H.B.S., 1908), pp. 49 sqq.

the rite of 1549 does not view the rite as a sacrifice. His judges at his trial charged him with having taught three different doctrines at various times (Papist, Lutheran and Zwinglian).[1] Most of his contemporaries, friendly and hostile, agreed that he had passed through a Lutheran stage, an opinion followed by most modern historians. His own repeated and passionate claim both at his trial and earlier that he had never 'taught but two contrary doctrines' (*i.e.* transubstantiation and one other)[2] have been set aside, not seldom with an echo of the jibe of his opponent, Dr. Henry Smith: 'O Lord, what man is so mad as to believe such mutable teachers, which change their doctrine at men's pleasure as they see advantage or profit? They turn and will turn, as the wind turneth'.

As a matter of strict historical justice this judgement seems to me altogether unfair to the man. And since its perpetuation does a great deal to confuse the meaning of the rites he produced, I propose to investigate the matter. Cranmer had all the former don's sense of the precise meaning of words, and all the former diplomat's willingness to propound a contentious idea in a not too disturbing way. But from the death of Henry onwards, when he seems to have accepted responsibility for the changes he thought it necessary to introduce, he was always quite straightforward as to the doctrine which he himself held, and by which he conceived it his duty to frame the new liturgy. If his own repeated statements of doctrine be examined minutely, there is, with the possible exception of a single sentence in his earliest doctrinal work,[3] no flicker of inconsistency from 1547 right down to his final disputations at Oxford in 1554–5. Three phrases in the Prayer Book of 1549 were (perhaps designedly) ambiguous, though perfectly compatible with the explanations which he gave of them while the book was in use, and with the final 'Explication' of his doctrine which he put in at his trial in 1554.[4] The meaning of the Prayer Book of 1549 was certainly 'explained' much more clearly in that of 1552, but the preamble of the Act which introduced 1552 (which is of Cranmer's penning) openly declared that this was the purpose of the new Book.

What then was this doctrine which both his liturgies expressed, and which is already found in the first Exhortation of the *Order of Communion* in 1548? During that last grim five minutes in S. Mary's at Oxford Cran-

---

[1] Cranmer, *Miscellaneous Writings* (Parker Soc. Ed.) II, p. 218. (This ed. will be cited as Parker I and II.)

[2] Parker II, *pp.* 225 *sq. Cf.* I, 190; II, 374, etc.

[3] The passage in question occurs in his translation of Justus Jonas' *Catechism*, a 'high' Lutheran work, where Cranmer says that '*in* the sacrament *we receive* truly the Body and Blood of Christ'. (The original in Jonas is *quod vere corpus et sanguis eius sit*, which is not the same thing.) Cranmer himself repeatedly defended this phrase as consistent with his teaching elsewhere, *cf.*, *e.g.*, *Defence*, iv. 8 (*Works*, ed. Jenkyns, vol. 2, *p.* 440), but I find it difficult to agree with him that it is so. It seems to be originally a piece of carelessness. In all other cases he has carefully eliminated from his 'translation' all traces of the original's Lutheran doctrine of the reality of the Body and Blood in communion. Here he has failed to do so thoroughly.

[4] Parker I, *pp.* 396 *sqq.*

mer declared: 'As for the Sacrament I believe as I have taught in my book against the bishop of Winchester', by which he means his *Answer unto a Crafty and Sophisticall Cavillation devised by Stephen Gardiner*, published in 1551. But this takes the somewhat tortuous form of a reply to a reply to his own *Defence of the True and Catholic Doctrine of the Sacrament* (1550), which Gardiner had attacked in his *Explication*. Cranmer modifies no single point of his doctrine as expounded in the *Defence* in the course of the *Answer*, but defends it sentence by sentence. I propose, therefore, to work chiefly from the *Defence*; partly because it gives his teaching in a positive form, partly because being published in 1550 while the Book of 1549 was in use, it forms, as it were, his own commentary on the meaning of the first Prayer Book as well as the second, and serves to establish their consistency.

In the preface to the *Defence* he says plainly, 'What availeth it to take away beads, pardons, pilgrimages and such other like popery, so long as the two chief roots remain unpulled up? . . . The rest is but branches and leaves . . . but the very body of the tree, or rather the roots of the weeds, is the popish doctrine of transubstantiation, of the real presence of Christ's Flesh and Blood in the sacrament of the altar (as they call it), and of the sacrifice and oblation of Christ made by the priest for the salvation of the quick and the dead.'[1] And again at the end of the book he is equally explicit: 'And as for the saying or singing of mass by the priest as it was in time passed used, it is neither a sacrifice propitiatory, nor yet a sacrifice of laud and praise, nor in any wise allowed before God, but abominable and detestable; and thereof may well be verified the saying of Christ, That thing which seemeth an high thing before men is an abomination before God . . . But thanks be to the eternal God, the manner of holy communion, which is now set forth within this realm (*i.e.* 1549) is agreeable with the institution of Christ, with S. Paul and the old primitive and apostolic church, with the right faith of the sacrifice of Christ upon the cross for our redemption, and with the true doctrine of our salvation, justification and remission of all our sins by that only sacrifice.'[2] One may regret that he should call an 'abomination before God' that rite of the eucharist which had been the heart of religion for every holy man and woman there had ever been in England since Augustine landed—which had sanctified the lips and fed the soul of Bede and Dunstan, which Alcuin had adorned and Edmund and Audrey and Edward had heard and loved. But that was in the manner of the times. What is quite certain is that he himself did not consider his own book of 1549 to be only a vernacular translation or adaptation of that 'abomination', or even a half-way house to it; but something radically different from it and essentially consistent with the doctrine of 'justification by faith alone'.

The key-point in Cranmer's doctrine is his definition of what is meant by 'spiritually eating the Flesh' and 'drinking the Blood' of Christ, phrases

---

[1] *Defence*, Preface, *Works*, ed. Jenkyns, II (1533), *p.* 289.
[2] *Defence*, V, 15, 18, *pp.* 459, 468.

which he uses in a peculiar sense of his own, though he is careful to explain that sense, and returns to it again and again. But unless and until that definition is grasped the reader is perpetually misleading himself (as the judges quite evidently did at his trial) by reading into Cranmer's use of these words something which is not intended to be there. The plainest passages are these (italics in every case are mine):

A. *Cranmer's doctrine concerning eating the Flesh and drinking the Blood of Christ.*

(1) *Defence*, III, 2 (*p.* 357). The papists 'say that every man, good and evil, eateth the Body of Christ: We say, that both do eat the sacramental bread and drink the wine, but none do eat the very Body of Christ and drink His Blood, but only they that be lively members of His Body.[1] They say that good men eat the Body of Christ and drink His Blood only at that time when they receive the sacrament: We say that *they eat, drink and feed of Christ continually,* so long as they be members of His Body . . . They say that the fathers and prophets of the Old Testament did not eat the Body nor drink the Blood of Christ: *We say that they did eat His Body and drink His Blood although He was not yet born* nor incarnated.'

(2) III, 10 (*p.* 378). (The words of Jn. vi. 'He that eateth My flesh etc.') ' . . . are not to be understand[ed] that we shall eat Christ with our teeth grossly and carnally, but that we shall spiritually and ghostly with our faith eat him, being carnally absent from us in heaven; and *in such wise as Abraham and other holy fathers did eat Him* many years before He was incarnated and born . . . *for they spiritually by their faith were fed and nourished with Christ's Body and Blood,* and had eternal life by Him before He was born *as we have now* after His ascension . . .'

*Ibid.* (*p.* 381). 'The eating of Christ's Flesh and drinking of His Blood is not to be understand[ed] simply and plainly as the words do properly signify, that we do eat and drink Him with our mouths; but it is a figurative speech spiritually to be understand[ed], *that we must deeply print and fruitfully believe in our hearts, that His Flesh was crucified and His Blood shed for our redemption.* [*Cf.* Langforde's *Meditations, p.* 606.] *And this our belief in Him is to eat His Flesh and drink His Blood,* although they be not here present with us, but be ascended into heaven. *As our forefathers before Christ's time did likewise eat His Flesh and drink His Blood,* which was so far from them that it was not yet born.'

(3) III, 15 (*pp.* 404 *sq.*). 'The true eating of Christ's very Flesh and drinking of His Blood' is ' . . . an inward, spiritual and pure eating with heart and mind; *which is to believe in our hearts that His Flesh was rent and torn for us upon the cross and His Blood shed for our redemption,* and that the same Flesh and Blood now sitteth at the right hand of the Father, making continual intercession for us; and *to imprint and digest this in our minds,* putting our whole affiance and trust in Him as teaching our salvation and offering

[1] There could not be a plainer repudiation of *Lutheran* doctrine in this matter.

ourselves clearly unto Him, to love and serve Him all the days of our life. This is truly, sincerely and spiritually to eat His Flesh and to drink His Blood.'

(4) IV, 2 (*pp.* 426 *sq.*). 'But as the devil is the food of the wicked, which he nourisheth in all iniquity and bringeth up unto everlasting damnation: so is Christ the very food of all them that be lively members of His Body, and them He nourisheth, feedeth, bringeth up and cherisheth unto everlasting life. And every good and faithful christian man feeleth in himself *how* he feedeth of Christ, eating His Flesh and drinking of His Blood. *For he putteth the whole hope and trust of his redemption and salvation in that only sacrifice which Christ made upon the cross,* having His Body *there* broken and His Blood *there* shed for the remission of sins. And this great benefit of Christ the faithful man earnestly considereth it in his *mind*, chaweth and digesteth it with the stomach of his heart, spiritually receiving Christ wholly into Him, and giving again Himself wholly into Christ. *And this is* the eating of Christ's Flesh and drinking of His Blood, the feeling whereof is to every man the feeling how he eateth and drinketh Christ, which none evil man nor member of the devil can do.'

There are a considerable number of other passages which might be cited, but I think these will suffice to make it clear that whenever Cranmer speaks of 'spiritually eating the Body and drinking the Blood of Christ' we must understand that *he means by this,* '*thinking with faith that Christ died for my sins on Calvary*', and nothing else but this. His judges quite failed to grasp this fact at his examination, and were at cross-purposes with him throughout the proceedings in consequence.

I am fairly sure that the first reaction of every modern Anglican will be to ask, Then what in the world has this 'spiritual eating and drinking of Christ's Body and Blood' to do with receiving holy communion, if Abraham and Moses 'did likewise eat His Flesh and drink His Blood'? Cranmer's answer to such a question would be '*Specifically, nothing at all!* To suppose that it has is precisely one half of the popish doctrine I am combating. That is not the purpose of the Lord's supper at all, though to those who, as I say, "eat drink and feed on Christ *continually*, so long as they be members of His Body", the supper as well as any other time may be an occasion for it. But the supper itself has another purpose which I describe very lucidly in the 5th book of my *Defence*.'

B. *Cranmer's doctrine concerning the true use of the Lord's supper.*

(1) V, 9 (*p.* 455). 'Popish masses are to be clearly taken away out of christian churches, and the true use of the Lord's supper is to be restored again, wherein godly people assembled together may receive the sacrament every man for himself, *to declare that he remembereth what benefit he hath received by the death of Christ, and to testify that He is a member of Christ's Body, fed with His Flesh and drinking His Blood spiritually*' [*i.e.* in the sense defined above].

(2) V, 10 (*p.* 455). 'Christ did not ordain His sacraments to this use that one should receive them for another and the priest for all the lay people; but He ordained them for this intent, that every man should receive them for Himself, *to ratify, confirm and stablish his own faith* and everlasting salvation.'

(3) V, 13 (*p.* 459). '. . . His holy supper was ordained for this purpose, *that every man eating and drinking thereof should remember that Christ died for him, and so should exercise his faith, and comfort himself by the remembrance of Christ's benefits;* and so give unto Christ most hearty thanks and give himself also clearly unto Him.'

(4) III, 15 (*p.* 419). 'The show-bread of the law was but a dark shadow of Christ to come; but the sacrament of Christ's Body is a clear testimony that Christ is already come, and that He hath performed that which was promised, and doth presently comfort and feed us spiritually with His precious Body and Blood [*i.e.* whenever we trust in His passion] notwithstanding that corporally He is ascended into heaven.'

Again I think the modern Anglican, with his mind set on some sort of idea that 'the spiritual eating of Christ's Body and Blood' must somehow have *some* connection with receiving holy communion, will feel impelled to ask 'What then is the meaning of "consecration", and of our own "prayer of consecration" '? Again Cranmer is perfectly plain and explicit in his reply.

C. *Cranmer's doctrine concerning Consecration.*

(1) III, 15 (*p.* 413). 'Consecration is the separation of any thing from a profane and worldly use unto a spiritual and godly use . . . Even so when common bread and wine be taken and severed from other bread and wine to the use of the holy communion, that portion of bread and wine, although it be of the same substance that the other is from the which it is severed, yet it is now called "consecrated" or "holy" bread and holy wine. *Not that the bread and wine have or can have any holiness in them,* but that they be used to an holy work and represent holy and godly things. And therefore S. Dionyse calleth the bread holy bread and the cup an holy cup, *as soon as they be set upon the altar to the use of the holy communion.*[1] But *specially they may be called* holy and consecrated when they be separated to that holy use by Christ's own words, which He spake for that purpose, saying of the bread, This is My Body, and of the wine, This is My Blood. So that commonly the authors before those words be spoken do take the bread and wine but as other common bread and wine; but after those words be pronounced over them, then they take them for holy bread and wine.'

(2) He returns to this point (*ibid., p.* 414): 'Not that the bread and wine can be partakers of any holiness or godliness or can be the Body and Blood of Christ; but that they *represent* the very Body and Blood of Christ, and

---

[1] Ps.-Dionysius, *de Ecclesiast. Hierarch.* 3. (As a matter of fact Ps.-Denys calls them that before they are set on the altar.)

the holy food and nourishment we have by Him [*i.e.* through believing that He died for our sins]. And so they be called by the names of the Body and Blood of Christ, as the *sign, token and figure* is called by the name of the very thing which it showeth and signifieth.'

(3) What he means by this is perhaps more clearly put in a previous passage: II, 11, where, discussing a (spurious) passage in S. Cyprian, Cranmer says: 'And yet the bread is changed, not in shape nor substance but in nature, as Cyprian truly says, not meaning that the natural substance of bread is clean gone, but that by God's word there is added thereto another higher property, nature and condition, far passing the nature and condition of common bread, that is to say, that *the bread doth shew unto us*, as the same Cyprian saith, *that we be partakers of the Spirit of God* and most purely joined unto Christ, and spiritually fed with His Body and Blood [in Cranmer's sense] so that now the said mystical bread is both a corporal food for the body and a spiritual food for the soul.'

(4) III, 2 (*p.* 356). 'We do affirm according to God's word, *that Christ is in all persons that truly believe Him*, [*i.e.* at any time, not only in holy communion] *in such sort that with His Flesh and Blood He doth spiritually nourish and feed them* and giveth them everlasting life, and doth *assure* them thereof, as well by the promise of His word, as by the sacramental bread and wine in His holy supper, which He did institute for the same purpose.'

There could be no plainer statement than this that in Cranmer's idea the spiritual feeding on Christ is something dependent solely on 'belief' in Him, and independent of receiving holy communion, which is, as he says, one among several assurances thereof. But here is a further passage which is specially interesting for the light it throws on Cranmer's understanding of the 'Prayer of Humble Access':

(5) III, 15 (*p.* 406). 'For although (S. Hilary) saith that Christ is naturally in us (by holy communion), yet he saith also that we are naturally in Him. And nevertheless in so saying he meant not the natural and corporal presence of the substance of Christ's Body and ours; for as our bodies be not after that sort within His Body, so is not His Body after that sort within our bodies; but he meant that Christ in His incarnation received of us a mortal nature and united the same unto His Divinity, and so we [*i.e.* humanity] be naturally in Him. And the sacraments of baptism and of His holy supper, if we rightly use the same, do most assuredly *certify* [*i.e.* not 'make'] us that we be partakers of His godly nature, having given unto us by Him immortality and life everlasting, and so is Christ naturally in us. And so we be one with Christ and Christ with us not only in will and mind, but also in very natural properties.'

S. Hilary assuredly did not mean this, as a glance at the context will inform anyone, and as was pointed out at his trial Cranmer has misquoted him. But the mistakes seem to have been made in all good faith, and from our present point of view all that matters is the renewed insistence that the right use of the Lord's supper only 'certifies' us of something which proceeds independently of it. But it may be asked, if 'consecration' is so meaningless, what is the function of priesthood in the rite at all? Surely anyone can 'separate' bread and wine 'to an holy use'? Again the answer is plain:

D. *Cranmer's doctrine concerning the Ministry.*

(1) V, 11 (*p.* 456). ' . . . the difference that is between the priest and the layman in this matter is only in the ministration; that the priest, as a common minister of the church, doth minister and distribute the Lord's supper unto other, and other receive it at his hands. But the very supper itself was by Christ instituted and given to the whole church, not to be offered and eaten of the priest for other men, but by him to be delivered to all that would duly ask it.

'As in a prince's house the officers and ministers prepare the table, and yet other as well as they eat the meat and drink the drink; so do the priests and ministers prepare the Lord's supper, read the gospel and rehearse Christ's words; but all the people say thereto, Amen; all remember Christ's death, all give thanks to God, all repent and offer themselves an oblation to Christ, all take Him for their Lord and Saviour and spiritually feed upon Him, *and in token thereof* they eat the bread and drink the wine in His mystical supper.

'And this nothing diminisheth the estimation and dignity of priesthood and other ministers of the church, but advanceth and highly commendeth their ministration. For if they are much to be loved, honoured and esteemed, that be the king's chancellors, judges, officers and ministers in temporal matters; how much then are they to be esteemed that be ministers of Christ's words and sacraments, and have to them committed the keys of heaven, to let in and shut out, by the ministration of His word and gospel?'

It will be noticed that Cranmer here does not actually say *whose* 'ministers of Christ's word' the clergy are. He is justified in not raising this quite different question at this point, but it is as well to clear it up in order to understand his ideas as a whole.

(2) There still exist, partly in Cranmer's own hand, drafts signed by himself of certain *Questions and Answers concerning the Sacraments* drawn up in the autumn of 1540, of which the following are relevant:[1]

*Q.* 9. 'Whether the apostles lacking a higher power, as in not having a Christian king among them, made bishops by that necessity, or by authority given them by God?'

*Ans.* 'All Christian princes have committed unto them immediately of God the whole cure of all their subjects, as well concerning the administration of God's word for the cure of souls, as concerning the ministration of things political and civil governance. And in both these ministrations they must have sundry ministers under them, to supply that which is

---

[1] Parker II, *pp.* 116 *sq.*

appointed to their several offices. The civil ministers under the king's majesty in this realm of England be those whom it shall please his highness for the time to put in authority under him: as *e.g.* the lord chancellor, lord treasurer, ... etc. The ministers of God's word under his majesty be the bishops, parsons, vicars and such other priests as be appointed by his highness to that ministration, as *e.g.* the bishop of Canterbury, the bishop of Durham, the bishop of Winchester, the parson of Winwick, etc. ... All the said officers and ministers, as well of the one sort as the other, be appointed, assigned and elected in every place, by the laws and orders of kings and princes. In the admission of many of these officers be divers comely ceremonies and solemnities used, which be not of necessity but only for a good order and seemly fashion: for if such offices and ministrations were committed without such solemnity, they were nevertheless truly committed. And there is no more promise of God, that grace is given in the committing of the ecclesiastical office, than it is in the committing of the civil office.

'In the apostles' time, when there were no christian princes, by whose authority ministers of God's word might be appointed, nor sins by the sword corrected, there was no remedy then for the correction of vice or appointing of ministers, but only the consent of ⟨the⟩ christian multitude among themselves, by an uniform consent to follow the advice and persuasion of such persons whom God had most endued with the spirit of counsel and wisdom ... and so sometime the apostles and other unto whom God had given abundantly His Spirit, sent or appointed ministers of God's word; some time the people did choose such as they thought thereunto; and when any were appointed or sent by the apostles or other, the people of their own voluntary will with thanks did accept them; not for the superiority, impery or dominion that the apostles had over them to command as their princes or masters, but as good people, ready to obey the advice of good counsellors ...'

*Q.* 11. 'Whether a bishop hath authority to make a priest by the scripture or no? And whether any other, but only a bishop, may make a priest?'

*Ans.* 'A bishop may make a priest by the scripture, and so may princes and governors also, and that by the authority of God committed to them ...'

*Q.* 12. 'Whether in the N.T. be required any consecration of a bishop or priest, or only appointing to the office be sufficient?'

*Ans.* 'In the N.T. he that is appointed to be a bishop or a priest needeth no consecration by the scripture, for election or appointing thereto is sufficient.'

*Q.* 14. 'Whether it be forfended by God's law ... that the king ... should make bishops [in case of necessity] or no?'

*Ans.* 'It is not forbidden by God's law.'

*Q.* 16. 'Whether a bishop or priest may excommunicate and for what crimes? And whether they only may excommunicate by God's law?'

*Ans.* 'A bishop or priest by the scripture is neither commanded nor forbidden to excommunicate, but where the laws of any region giveth him authority to excommunicate, there they ought to use the same in such crimes as the laws have authority in; and where the laws of the region for-biddeth them, there they have none authority at all: and they that be no priests may also excommunicate, if the law allow them thereunto.'

The ministers of the eucharist are thus acting as such simply as officials of the secular government of the christian state in Cranmer's opinion. Such was his idea in 1540 and he insisted on defending the same opinion at his trial in 1554, declaring that 'Nero was head of the church' in his day, 'that is in worldly respect of the temporal bodies of men, of whom the church consisteth; for so he beheaded Peter and the apostles. And the Turk (*i.e.* Sultan) too is head of the church of Turkey.'[1] It is therefore not likely that we shall find anything which may be fairly interpreted in terms of a differ-entiation of 'order', as the primitive church understood it in Cranmer's liturgies of 1549 or 1552, still less anything corresponding to the idea of a priestly 'oblation'. Nevertheless, as we have seen (D. 1) Cranmer does admit *an* idea of oblation in the eucharist, which he calls 'a sacrifice of laud, praise and thanksgiving.' He defines carefully the sense in which it is so.

E. *Cranmer's doctrine concerning the Sacrifice of Praise and Thanksgiving.*

(1) V, 3 (*pp.* 448 *sq.*). 'One kind of sacrifice there is, which is called a propitiatory or merciful sacrifice, that is to say, such a sacrifice as pacifieth God's wrath and indignation, and obtaineth mercy and forgiveness for all our sins, and is the ransom for our redemption from everlasting damnation. And although in the Old Testament there were certain sacrifices called by that name, yet in very deed there is but one such sacrifice whereby our sins be pardoned and God's mercy and favour obtained, which is the death of the Son of God our Lord Jesus Christ; nor never was any other sacrifice propitiatory at any time, nor never shall be.

'Another kind of sacrifice there is, which doth not reconcile us to God, but is made of them that be reconciled by Christ, to testify our duties unto God, and to shew ourselves thankful unto Him; and therefore they be called sacrifices of laud, praise and thanksgiving.

'The first kind of sacrifice Christ offered to God for us; the second kind we ourselves offer to God by Christ.

'And by the first kind of sacrifice Christ offered us also unto His Father; and by the second we offer ourselves and all that we have, unto Him and His Father. *And this sacrifice generally is our whole obedience unto God, in keeping His laws and commandments.*'

This does not appear to be at all closely connected with the eucharist, but he is somewhat more explicit later on.

(2) V, 13 (*p.* 459). 'In this eating, drinking and using of the Lord's sup-per, we make not of Christ a new sacrifice propitiatory for remission of sin. But the humble confession of all penitent hearts, their knowledging of

<hr>

[1] *Ibid., p.* 219.

Christ's benefits, their thanksgiving for the same, their faith and consolation in Christ, their humble submission and obedience to God's will and commandments, is a sacrifice of laud and praise, accepted and allowed of God no less than the sacrifice of the priest.'

It would appear, therefore, that the sacrifice and oblation in the eucharist consists for Cranmer in the emotions and ideas of those present at the eucharist, and not in anything appertaining to the rite itself.

It is, I think, only just to add to these doctrinal passages a devotional one, which Cranmer places at the end of his positive exposition of his views before embarking on controversy.

*F. Cranmer's esteem for the Eucharist.*

I, 16 (*p.* 307). 'All men desire to have God's favour; and when they know the contrary, that they be in His indignation and cast out of His favour, what thing can comfort them? How be their minds vexed! What trouble is in their consciences! All God's creatures seem to be against them, and do make them afraid, as things being ministers of God's wrath and indignation towards them. And rest and comfort can they find none, neither within them nor without them. And in this case they do hate as well God as the devil; God as an unmerciful and extreme judge, and the devil as a most malicious and cruel tormentor.

'And in this sorrowful heaviness, holy scripture teacheth them, that our heavenly Father can by no means be pleased with them again, but by the sacrifice and death of His only-begotten Son, whereby God hath made a perpetual amity and peace with us, doth pardon the sins of them that believe in Him, maketh them His children, and giveth them to His firstbegotten Son Christ, to be incorporate into Him, to be saved by Him, and to be made heirs of heaven with Him. And in the receiving of the holy supper of our Lord, *we be put in remembrance of this His death,* and of the whole mystery of our redemption. In the which supper is made mention of His Testament [*i.e.* Covenant] and of the aforesaid communion of us with Christ and of the remission of our sins by His sacrifice upon the Cross.

'Wherefore in this sacrament, if it be rightly received with a true faith, we be assured that our sins be forgiven, and the league of peace and the Testament [*i.e.* Covenant] of God is confirmed between Him and us, so that whosoever by a true faith doth eat Christ's Flesh and drink His Blood [*i.e.* meditate on the passion] hath everlasting life by Him. Which thing when we feel in our hearts at the receiving of the Lord's supper, what thing can be more joyful, more pleasant or more comfortable unto us?'

I take leave to set beside this a few words from those meditations which the priest Langforde placed before his parishioners as the substance of their non-communicating eucharistic devotion: 'Call to your remembrance and imprint inwardly in your heart by holy meditation the whole process of the passion . . . which is a meditation of sweetness unspeakable to them that inwardly can consider it.' *Plus ça change*—? Was it really worth all that tremendous upheaval of English religion in order to add what Cranmer insisted is only a 'token' communion in bread and wine to the layman's meditation on the passion? Yet *devotionally*, and so far as the layman is concerned, does the change really amount to much more than this, that whereas under the old *régime* the liturgy and the eucharistic action went on while the layman meditated on the passion, but independently of him, now that meditation on the passion is publicly conducted and has actually become the liturgy and the eucharistic action, to which he himself must now listen, and he must receive the bread and wine? Doctrinally the change is, of course, very much greater.

By a somewhat forced use of the phrase 'to eat the Body and drink the Blood of Christ' when he means 'to remember the passion with confidence in the merits of Christ', he succeeds in preserving a good deal of traditional catholic language, though he is quite fair in being explicit as to what he does mean by this phrase, and that the traditional language must not be understood in anything like its traditional sense. He can make good use, too, of Lutheran material, and I rather suspect that its customary *schwär-merei* appealed to one side of his very sensitive nature. He can clothe his negations with the comparative warmth of the Calvinist's idea of eucharistic devotion. But for my own part, surveying all the exposition of his teaching in his own words given here, I am quite unable to distinguish the substance of his doctrine from that of Zwingli.[1]

### Cranmer's Liturgical Work

We are now in a position to understand the meaning—and the brilliance —of Cranmer's liturgical work. It must be remembered that the *Defence* from which all the above passages except D. 2 (dated 1540) have been drawn, was published in 1550, while the first Prayer Book was still in use. It is in fact his own commentary on that rite, which is referred to at the end of the treatise as embodying this doctrine. There can be no doubt that though 1549 was unpopular with the laity as a novelty, and suspect among the theologians, many clergy did use it as a 'vernacular mass' without much misgiving. Looking at it now, with the *Defence* before us, it is easy enough to see how subtly it had been worded: 'Having in remembrance His blessed passion . . . rendering unto Thee most hearty thanks for the innumerable benefits procured unto us by the same, entirely desiring Thy fatherly

[1] This was clearly understood at the time. 'The Archbishop of Canterbury entertains right views as to the nature of Christ's presence in the supper. . . . He has some articles of religion to which all preachers and lecturers in divinity are required to subscribe, or else a license for teaching is not granted them; and in these his sentiments respecting the eucharist are pure and religious and similar to yours in Switzerland' (Hooper to Bullinger, Dec. 27, 1549; *Original Letters*, Parker Soc., ed. Robinson, I, xxxvi, *p.* 71).

goodness mercifully to accept this our sacrifice of praise and thanksgiving: most humbly beseeching Thee to grant that by the merits and death of Thy Son Jesus Christ . . . we and all Thy whole church may obtain remission of our sins and all other benefits of His passion. And here we offer and present unto Thee, O Lord, our self, our souls and bodies, to be a reasonable, holy and lively sacrifice unto Thee: humbly beseeching Thee that whosoever shall be partakers of this holy communion may worthily receive the most precious Body and Blood of Thy Son Jesus Christ: and be fulfilled with Thy grace and heavenly benediction . . . and although we be unworthy through our manifold sins to offer unto Thee any sacrifice: yet we beseech Thee to accept this our bounden duty and service, and command these our prayers and supplications by the ministry of Thy holy angels to be brought up into Thy holy tabernacle before the sight of Thy divine majesty not weighing our merits but pardoning our offences . . .'. This is the rite's own expression of what the eucharistic action is. Every word of it, as Cranmer shewed in the *Defence*, was certainly compatible with, and for the most part clearly expressed, his own Zwinglian doctrine. Yet his opponents were consoling themselves with the thought that it expressed, awkwardly and not at all fully but still sufficiently, the traditional ideas with which they themselves used this rite. He could even allow a verbal reminiscence of the old second century oblation at the heavenly altar to remain, by deftly substituting 'prayers' and 'tabernacle' for the 'oblations' and 'the altar on high' of which Irenaeus had spoken.

There are in 1549 only three phrases which are difficult to interpret fairly along the lines of Cranmer's teaching in the *Defence*: (1) In the canon, before the institution: 'Hear us, O merciful Father, we beseech Thee, and with Thy Holy Spirit and Word[1] vouchsafe to bless and *sanctify* these Thy gifts and creatures that *they may be unto us the Body and Blood* of Thy most dearly beloved Son . . .' (2) Also in the canon: 'humbly beseeching Thee that whosoever shall be *partakers of this holy communion may worthily receive the most precious Body and Blood* of Thy Son and be fulfilled with Thy grace and heavenly benediction, and made one Body with Thy Son Jesus Christ, that He may dwell in them and they in Him.' (3) In the prayer of humble access, immediately before communion: 'Grant us . . . so to eat the flesh of Thy dear Son Jesus Christ and to drink His blood *in these holy mysteries* that we may continually dwell in Him.'

Gardiner felt able to cite these three passages, together with the words

[1] This is often said to be an imitation of the Eastern 'invocation'. It may be so, but both the form and position of the prayer are quite different from those of any Eastern rite known in Cranmer's time. The clause is clearly representative of the *Quam oblationem* of the old canon in position and meaning, combined perhaps with a reminiscence of the dictum of Paschasius Radbert (*de Corp. Dom.* 12) that the sacrament is consecrated in the Word of the Creator and the power of the Holy Spirit. Under the name of Augustine this had got into the mediaeval catenae and was frequently cited as a commonplace by scholastic authors.

of administration and the kneeling recitation of the prayer of humble access before communion (as implying adoration)[1] as setting forth the teaching 'that they receive with their bodily mouth the Body and Blood of Christ.' Cranmer retorted sharply that any such suggestion was 'a plain untruth'.[2] Looking at the matter in the light of the *Defence*, it is possible to see how he would have explained these passages to himself. He is right in claiming that Gardiner's use of them rests only on inference, and moreover inference which the rest of the rite does not support but goes some way to contradict. But it was a reasonable inference from these passages taken alone as they stood. He was evidently startled to find how completely the rite had been misinterpreted in a catholic sense, and in 1552 took pains to alter every point in 1549 to which Gardiner had appealed.

There is substantial evidence that Cranmer from the outset regarded 1549 like 1548 as a mere *ballon d'essai*, and made no secret of the fact from those around him.[3] It may well be that in compiling a temporary form Cranmer was not scrupulous to avoid all ambiguity. But the Book of 1549 had a bad reception on all hands. His foreign friends were not impressed by it. The English laity mocked at it as 'naught but a Christmas game' and rose in rebellions over half the countryside, which were only suppressed with considerable slaughter by the use of foreign mercenaries.[4] Even after these *dragonnades*, as the Second Act of Uniformity lamented in 1552, the laity 'do wilfully and damnably abstain and refuse to come to their parish churches' where 1549 was still in use. The clergy, unconvinced of the merits of the Book by the hanging of priests for non-compliance, were deliberately misinterpreting it and making it as much like a mass as they dared.[5] Five bishops had had to be deprived of their sees for obstructing its enforcement, and others were known to be unenthusiastic. To a man who sincerely believed that the mass was 'an abomination before God', while his own 'very godly order' was 'agreeable to the Word of God and the primitive church, very comfortable to all good people, and most profitable to the estate of this realm' it might very well seem that those refusing the latter would 'answer before God for such evils and plagues wherewith Almighty God may justly punish His people for neglecting this good and wholesome law' (*i.e.* the Act of Uniformity of 1549).

---

[1] It is to be remembered that there was no kneeling by the priest in the mediaeval rite at this point. It would be all the more striking, therefore, as an innovation in 1549, and lend itself to this misunderstanding.
[2] Parker I, *p.* 53.
[3] See the evidence cited by F. M. Powicke, *The Reformation in England*, Oxford, 1941, *pp.* 89 *sq.* (It is much to be wished that the reading of this wise essay might be made compulsory among the clergy. Doubtless most of us would still remain 'high' and 'low' churchmen on the traditional lines, but a good deal of the mythology which makes us so would be destroyed.)
[4] The protestant John Ab Ulmis puts the number of executions at 'about 5,000' since June, writing in August 1549 (*Orig. Letters*, II, clxxxix, *p.* 394).
[5] *Cf.* Hooper, *Orig. Letters*, I, xxxvi, *p.* 72.

And so there came the second Act of Uniformity with the second Prayer Book annexed, in 1552, because 'there hath arisen in the use and exercise of the foresaid common service (1549) in the church ... divers doubts for the fashion and manner of the ministration of the same, *rather by the curiosity of the minister and mistakers than of any other worthy cause:* therefore ... the king's most excellent majesty with the assent of the lords and commons in parliament assembled and by the authority of the same hath caused the aforesaid order ... to be faithfully and godly perused and made fully perfect'; and anyone, lay or cleric, worshipping otherwise than by the new Book in any manner whatsoever, is to be imprisoned for six months for the first offence, a year for the second, and for life upon a third conviction. The time for ambiguity had gone by and the Book of 1549, 'explained and made fully perfect' in that of 1552, is to enforce the truth upon the obstinate English people.

The rite of 1552 does in fact express with great accuracy the doctrine, which Cranmer once said that he had learned from Ridley,[1] which we have already studied. What had largely assisted the general misunderstanding of 1549 was its retention of the traditional Shape of the Liturgy. Cranmer realised that this was a mistake if he wanted the new belief to be adopted; and in 1552 he made radical changes in this in order to bring out the doctrinal implications of 1549. But the wording of the prayers of 1549 needed no such drastic treatment. Rearranged in their new order they served with remarkably few changes to express the full Zwinglian doctrine—in itself a reasonable vindication of Cranmer's claim that this had been their most obvious meaning all along.

Such changes as 1552 made in the part of 1549 which corresponded to the ancient synaxis seem to have been designed rather to give fair warning of the stand the English church was now definitely to be regarded as taking up, than to express particular doctrinal notions in themselves. Many if not most of the Lutheran *Ordnungen* had retained the introit psalm in some form, as had 1549. The Zwinglians and Calvinists had abandoned it, and 1552 abolished it too, leaving the Lord's prayer and 'collect for purity' as the only introduction to the rite. (These were a relic of the old 'preparation' of the ministers before the altar, being among the latest mediaeval additions to these prayers.) The old *Kyrie*-hymn and *Gloria* were replaced by the Ten Commandments, whose use at this point seems to have been suggested by the *Ritus Ministerii* of the Alsatian Calvinist Pullain, published at London in 1551. This has also supplied the wording of the final response, 'And write all these Thy laws in our hearts, we beseech Thee'. The primitive greeting and its response are omitted before the collects, probably in accordance with the usual protestant theory that it is the business of the minister alone to carry on the service, while the people are only

[1] Parker II, p. 218. (The date of his conversion to Zwinglianism would appear to be 1546.)

to answer Amen and listen. The collect for the day is always to be followed by a collect for the king as Supreme Head of the church.[1]

The Roman sequence of collect and lections is retained, but the chant of the gradual psalm between epistle and gospel, which had come down from apostolic times and indeed from our Lord's own worship in the synagogues of Galilee, had already been abolished in 1549 and was not restored in 1552. It had been used in the late Sarum ceremonial to 'cover' the mixing of the chalice by the deacon and subdeacon. Cranmer's determination to exclude any possibility of an offertory from the rite is probably the motive for its abolition. The collocation of collects with epistle, and of gospel with creed and sermon, are the only sequences in the structure of the old Sarum rite which recognisably survived in 1552.

After the sermon in 1552 followed the intercessions (which had formed the first part of the canon in 1549). These may have been placed here in deference to primitive precedent. But there is no suggestion of this reason in Cranmer's writings, and it is not easy to see how from the materials available at the time he could have been aware that the primitive intercessions had come at this point. It is to be noted that the intercessions follow the sermon in most Swiss protestant rites, including that of Pullain which Cranmer was studying when he compiled 1552. Their primitive position in our rite may thus be only a happy accident, which was somewhat marred in 1662 when an offertory was awkwardly re-inserted before them, thus confusing Cranmer's scheme of the rite as a whole. The intercessions in 1552 followed the protestant model in being a long monologue by the celebrant to which the people replied Amen; and not a corporate exercise in which all 'orders' play a co-operative part, as in the primitive rites. In 1552 this prayer corresponds fully with the bidding for 'the church militant here in earth'—(introduced for the first time in 1552)—all mention of the departed and the saints (retained in 1549 when this prayer formed part of the canon) being excluded. The somewhat hesitant prayer about the dead introduced in 1662 (which just succeeds in being a prayer *for* them) made Cranmer's bidding and the title 'prayer for the church militant' no longer applicable. But they were retained in 1662 as already customary. Here again 1662 spoils the finish of Cranmer's workmanship.

There is no mention of an offertory of bread and wine before this prayer in 1552—or at any other point in the rite. Cranmer's treatment of the offertory is very interesting, and an excellent indication of his skill in expressing his ideas liturgically, though it has not been appreciated as it

[1] The placing of the collect for the king *before* that of the day is the work of 1662, following Laud's Scottish book. It seems to be due not so much to the exuberant loyalty of the Laudian school as to a desire to avoid turning over pages at this point. The emphasis on the regal office is felt to be a little jarring by most people, especially when, as for instance on Good Friday or Easter Day, it actually takes precedence of the redemption of the world in the thought of the church. Cranmer had too much liturgical sense to make a mistake of that sort.

deserves through the constant attempts to interpret his liturgy by ideas which he did not hold. Like Luther he believed that any form of offertory 'stank of oblation'. The difficulty was to avoid having one in some form. In 1549 Cranmer had substituted a presentation of money by the people themselves, not at the altar but into a box in the chancel. This avoided any idea of a priestly oblation in connection with the money. The communicants remained in the chancel, having filed up to put their money in the box, and with this rough guide to their number the priest was to 'take so much bread and wine as shall suffice for the persons appointed to receive the holy communion, laying the bread upon the corporas or else in the paten, or else in some other comely thing prepared for that purpose: and putting the wine into the chalice, or else in some fair or convenient cup prepared for that use (if the chalice will not serve)[1] putting thereto a little pure and clean water: and setting both the bread and wine upon the altar'. Immediately after this follows the dialogue, preface, sanctus and eucharistic prayer. 1549 has thus no offertory prayer of any sort anywhere in the rite. It is one of its most significant changes from the old Shape of the Liturgy.

It is probable that the substitution of the offering of money for that of bread and wine in the particular form adopted in 1549 is an imitation of current Lutheran practice,[2] though something of the same kind is found sporadically throughout the middle ages as a relic of the old Western offertory by the people. This, however, hardly solved Cranmer's problem. We have seen that the solemn placing of the bread and wine upon the altar in itself constituted the primitive 'oblation' of them to God, and that any form of accompanying prayer is a later development. In the Western rite the *secreta* or offertory prayer had always been said in silence, so that though Cranmer had altogether omitted any such prayer or suggestion of offering in 1549, the rubric about putting the bread and wine upon the altar cited above did in fact leave the offertory *looking* exactly as it had always done, from the point of view of the people. If they were to be taught an entirely different idea, something more was required.

Cranmer found this in 1552. The placing of the alms in the 'poor men's box' was retained, but they were now to be collected first by the churchwardens, who were then to place the money in the box. There is evidence that the trooping up of the people to put money in the box one by one had caused a good deal of amusement among the laity, used to remaining stationary in the mediaeval worship. It may be this which was particularly referred to as 'the Christmas game'. The intercessory prayer 'for the church militant' was placed in 1552 immediately after this monetary substitute for the offertory, and a clause was inserted in its first paragraph, 'we

[1] Mediaeval chalices, from which the celebrant alone communicated, were small. They might not prove large enough for a general communion in both kinds in 1549.
[2] Brightman, *The English Rite*, I, *p.* lxxxi, gives the evidence.

humbly beseech Thee most mercifully *to accept our alms* and to receive our prayers'. The alms had not been offered or even handled by the priest; there could be no danger of their being thought of as an 'oblation' in the old sense. But this clause emphasised them as the only material content of the 'offertory'. The elaborate rubric about placing the bread and wine upon the altar found at this point in 1549 is altogether omitted in 1552.

This cannot be accidental, but when the elements are to be placed on the altar is not specified. Probably Cranmer intended them to be placed upon the altar privately before the service began. There is evidence that this was sometimes done in Elizabethan times, but perhaps practice varied. Some may have continued the custom of 1549. But in the seventeenth century Bishop Andrewes was accustomed to place them on the altar after the prayer of humble access, immediately before the consecration, and this does not seem to have been considered one of his special innovations. Baxter's puritan liturgy sets them upon the altar at what may be taken for the same point in the rite. As the elements were not referred to or required before the consecration in the rite from 1552 to 1662, it was a natural inference that just before it was the proper point at which to introduce them. The rubric before the prayer of consecration in 1662 itself—'When the priest . . . hath so ordered the bread and wine that he may with more readiness and decency break the bread etc.'—looks like a trace of previous practice which has survived the re-introduction of an offertory before the prayer for the church militant. In any case, the omission of the placing of bread and wine upon the altar at the position of the old offertory in 1552 cannot but have been deliberate.

The treatment of the offertory received instead an altogether new development in 1552 which, as an ingenious piece of liturgical workmanship, deserves admiration. We have seen (E. 2) that while Cranmer denied any offering of Christ to God in the eucharist, he insisted that 'the humble confession of all penitent hearts, their knowledging of Christ's benefits, their thanksgiving for the same, their faith and consolation in Christ, their humble submission . . . to God's will and commandments, is a sacrifice of laud and praise.' It is precisely these 'elements' which the rite of 1552 brings before God *in the position of the old 'offertory prayer'*, between the offering of alms and the dialogue and preface.

The constant omission in these days of the 'Long Exhortation', which is an integral part of Cranmer's structure of the rite, has mutilated his idea. But one has only to look at its last paragraph coming immediately before the 'Short Exhortation' and Confession to see its point in conjunction with what follows: 'And above all things, ye must give most humble and hearty thanks to God the Father, the Son and the Holy Ghost, for the redemption of the world by the death and passion of our Saviour Christ, both God and Man, Who did humble Himself even to the death upon the cross for us miserable sinners which lay in darkness and in the shadow of death, that

He might make us children of God and exalt us to everlasting life. And to the end that we should always remember the exceeding great love of our Master and only Saviour Jesu Christ, thus dying for us, and innumerable benefits which by His precious bloodshedding He hath obtained to us, He hath instituted these holy mysteries, as pledges of His love and ⟨? a⟩ continual remembrance [*i.e.* reminder] of His death, to our great and endless comfort. To Him, therefore, with the Father and the Holy Ghost, let us give as we are bound continual thanks: submitting ourselves wholly to His holy will and pleasure, and studying to serve Him in true holiness and righteousness all the days of our life. Amen.'

These are precisely *the elements* of Cranmer's 'sacrifice of praise and thanksgiving'. One notices how naturally this exhortation reverts to the tone and even the phrasing of such mediaeval devotions as Langforde's. But what is much more important is that it states every element which Cranmer considered to be part of the eucharistic sacrifice, and it states the meaning of the rite as Cranmer understood it with perfect precision. It is the continual mental 'remembering' of His passion and death which constitutes 'eating the Flesh and drinking the Blood of Christ'; and it is the stirring up of our penitence, our thankful acknowledgement of His benefits, our faith and consolation in His passion, and our intention of amendment, which constitute the only eucharistic action and offering. *This we forthwith make by the confession and by listening to the 'comfortable words'*.

Upon this substitute for the offertory and offertory prayer there follow at once, in the traditional way, the dialogue (shorn of its 'The Lord be with you' and response)[1] and the preface (shorn of the Seraphim, who are certainly its oldest constituent element)[2] and sanctus. After this follows the prayer of humble access said kneeling. In its present position this comes between the preface (all that remains of the apostolic *berakah*, the primitive consecration prayer itself) and the consecration. It seems to have been transferred to this point, before the consecration, in order to prove unmistakeably that Gardiner's inference from its 1549 position (said kneeling before the communion) as betokening some connection between the consecrated elements and the Body and Blood of Christ, was unjustified. We are to interpret it by Cranmer's repeated statement that 'the true eating and drinking of the said Body and Blood of Christ is with a constant and lively faith *to believe that Christ gave His Body and shed His Blood upon the cross for us,* and that He doth so join and incorporate Himself to us that He is our head and we His members and flesh of His flesh and bone of His bones, having *Him dwelling in us and we in Him.* And herein standeth the whole effect and strength of this sacrament. And this faith God worketh

---

[1] Perhaps Cranmer dropped this because Cyprian did not happen to quote it in his *de Orat.* 31, where he cites the rest. But we now know that it is much older than Cyprian.

[2] *Cf.* Origen, *in Is.*, I, 2; *de Princip.*, I, iii. 4.

inwardly in our hearts by His Holy Spirit, and confirmeth the same outwardly to our ears by hearing of His word and to our other senses by eating
and drinking of the sacramental bread and wine in His holy supper'.
(*Defence*, I, 16, *p.* 306.) Placed before the consecration, this prayer is
meant to serve as a safeguard against any traditional ideas as to the force
or meaning of consecration.

The prayer which follows was first called 'The Prayer of Consecration'
in 1662. In 1552 it is intended only as 'the separation' of the bread and
wine 'from a profane and worldly use unto a spiritual and godly use. . . .
Not that the bread and wine have or can have any holiness in them, but
that they be used to an holy work, and represent holy and godly things'
(C. 1). 1549 had already, with one exception, said all that Cranmer wished
to say on this point, with its unmistakeable emphasis on 'His one oblation
once offered, a full perfect and sufficient sacrifice, oblation and satisfaction
for the sins of the whole world', long ago—on Calvary—and its relegation
of the eucharist to a 'perpetual *memory*'—a cleverly chosen word—'of that
His precious death, until His coming again' (where 'again'—not in S.
Paul—emphasises that as the passion is in the past, so the 'coming' is in
the future, not in the eucharist). The only change needed was in the
words 'with Thy Holy Spirit and Word to bless and sanctify these Thy
gifts and creatures of bread and wine, that they may be unto us the Body
and Blood of Thy most dearly beloved Son Jesus Christ.' These might well
be interpreted to mean that the gift of the Body and Blood was in some
sense connected with the bread and wine. They certainly, by the word
'sanctify', implied that the bread acquired some 'holiness'. Cranmer has
gone beyond 'explanation' to 'fully perfecting' 1549 in the change he made
here in 1552: 'Grant that we receiving these Thy creatures of bread and
wine [*i.e.* which remain so, unsanctified, at the moment of reception]
according to Thy Son our Saviour Jesus Christ's holy institution *in remembrance* of His death and passion may be partakers of His most blessed
Body and Blood'. It was Cranmer's whole point that 'remembrance of His
death and passion' *is* the partaking of His most blessed Body and Blood,
'in such wise as Abraham and other holy fathers did eat Him' (A. 2). Then
follows the citation of Christ's own words separating the bread and wine
to a spiritual use (*cf.* C. 1). In 1552 there is no Amen of the people after their
recital. They are not a prayer of the church but a ministerial act, the 'preparing of the supper' (*cf.* D. 1).

It is further to be noted that both 1549 and 1552 omit that provision for
a further consecration if there should be insufficient of the sacramental
species for the number of communicants, a provision which the *Order of
Communion* in 1548 had been careful to make. There is some evidence that
some continued to follow the directions of 1548 as late as 1550 'if the wine
has happened to fail in the cup.'[1] But the practice was greatly disliked by

[1] Strype, *Memorials of Thomas Cranmer*, II, lxi, *p.* 899.

all those who followed the Swiss school, which held that the recitation of the words was for the *hearers*, not for any effect upon the sacramental elements. The words having been heard once, there was no point in repeating them, but rather a tendency to superstition. This seems to have been Cranmer's own opinion,[1] and there can be little doubt that the omission of the direction to repeat them over fresh bread and wine in both 1549 and 1552 was entirely deliberate.

Immediately upon the separation of the elements to their sacramental use, that use is made of them. Without pause even for an Amen or the Lord's prayer, 'Then shall the minister first receive the communion in both kinds himself and next deliver it to other ministers if there be any present, that they may help the chief minister—[Note the agreement with the terminology of D. 1]—and after to the people in their hands kneeling. And when he delivereth the bread he shall say, Take and eat this in remembrance that Christ died for thee and feed on Him in thy heart with thanksgiving. And the minister that delivereth the cup shall say, Drink this in remembrance that Christ's Blood was shed for thee and be thankful'.—It is the perfect summary of Cranmer's teaching as to what the eucharistic action and the eucharist are.

Immediately after the communion follows the Lord's prayer. No one seems to have found a quite convincing reason why Cranmer changed its position from before to after communion, unless it was a determination to leave nothing unchanged in the ancient structure of the rite, which seems too childish to be probable. My own suggestion is that it was from a desire to keep the whole of what he conceived as the external action uninterrupted—the setting apart of the elements for their holy use followed at once by their use. But that is merely a conjecture. What is certain is that all those later interpretations of this change which depend on the close association of communion with receiving the Body and Blood of our Lord —as that having now received the Son we can say of right 'Our Father', and so forth—can have had no place in the mind of the author of the *Defence*.

There follows either what we now call the 'prayer of oblation' or the 'thanksgiving'. Regrets have often been expressed that these were made alternatives, but Cranmer was quite right to do so from his own point of view. Each of them in reality duplicates matter which he had otherwise sufficiently provided for in the fixed elements of the rite, and it was probably only for the sake of constructional finish that a prayer was provided here at all. He had the same instinct as the primitive church that the climax of the rite is communion, which he would probably have expressed by saying that the sacrament terminated in the 'use' of it. But he desired to emphasise his new conception of the eucharistic oblation, and the concluding section is therefore devoted to this theme.

[1] *Defence*, iii, 15, p. 414.

The old concept of the oblation was that Christ offers His perfect oblation of Himself to the Father, and that the earthly church as His Body enters into His eternal priestly act by the eucharist. Cranmer deliberately sought to substitute for this the idea that *we* offer to God '*ourselves*, our souls and bodies'. Even in 1549 this had formed the whole content of the prayer of oblation when it stood within the canon, to the exclusion of the old notion. But we have seen that in 1552 Cranmer had provided for this offering of ourselves by placing the exhortations, confession, etc. in the position of the old *offertory* prayer. The prayer of oblation was thus rendered superfluous. But to repeat the oblation in a position detached from the canon (where it could not lend itself to any misunderstanding such as had arisen about its meaning in 1549) would serve a useful purpose in emphasising its difference from the old notion. Its clause ' . . . desire Thy fatherly goodness . . . mercifully to accept this our sacrifice of praise and *thanksgiving*' sufficiently expressed the notion of 'thanksgiving' to serve the purpose of an optional variant for the invariable 'thanksgiving prayer' of 1549.

At the same time, this so-called 'prayer of oblation' was carefully adapted to its new position. In 1549 its central clause had run: 'Humbly beseeching Thee that whosoever shall be partakers of this holy communion *may worthily receive the most precious Body and Blood of Thy Son Jesus Christ:* and be fulfilled with Thy grace and heavenly benediction, *and made one Body with Thy Son Jesus Christ,* that He may dwell in them and they in Him'. This lent itself much too easily to the idea that the reception of holy communion was connected with 'feeding on Christ' in a sense different from that in which Abraham and Moses had done so. In 1552 it was altered to read ' . . . that all we which be partakers of this holy communion may be fulfilled with Thy grace and heavenly benediction', where the omissions leave no doubt of the intention with which they were made.

The continual modern proposals to replace this prayer after the prayer of consecration as it stands, without any regard to Cranmer's careful changes of wording for its present position, are very strangely conceived. It is possible to hold that in its present position it is 'ourselves' as already communicated—as 'accepted in the Beloved'—which are supposed fit to be offered to God. If the prayer were put back *before* communion in its present wording, it would not only be an obvious piece of Pelagianism to offer 'ourselves . . . to be a reasonable, *holy* and lively sacrifice'; but, taken in conjunction with the lack of any explicit offering of the sacrifice of Christ in our rite, it would lay a most unfortunate emphasis on its substitution of the oblation of the sons of men for that of the Son of Man. Such was Cranmer's own purpose, admittedly. But it is hard to suppose that it is that of those who constantly repeat this proposal. Fortunately for his reputation Cranmer was not under this delusion that the words of a prayer have no meaning, and that prayers are interchangeable as they stand between different parts of a rite.

The thanksgiving occupies in 1552 the same position in which it had served invariably in 1549. But again Cranmer made changes to bring out its meaning, which can better be seen if the two forms are set side by side.

| 1549 | 1552 |
|---|---|
| 'We most heartily thank Thee for that Thou *hast* vouchsafed to feed us *in* these holy mysteries with the spiritual food of the most precious Body and Blood of our Saviour Jesus Christ, and *hast* assured us *duly receiving the same* of Thy favour and goodness towards us, and that we be very members incorporate in *Thy*[1] mystical body . . .' | 'We most heartily thank Thee for that Thou *dost* vouchsafe to feed us *which have duly received* these holy mysteries with the spiritual food of the most precious Body and Blood of Thy Son our Saviour Jesus Christ, and *dost* assure us *thereby* of Thy favour and goodness towards us, and that we be very members incorporate in *Thy*[1] mystical body . . .' |

We have to remember that when Cranmer wrote 1549 he already believed that the 'spiritual feeding on the most precious Body and Blood of our Saviour Jesus Christ' is nothing else but the purely mental remembrance of the passion with faith. The 1549 form of this prayer, with its '*hast*' and '*in* these holy mysteries', greatly obscured this idea, and at least implied that the 'spiritual feeding' had a close connection with receiving holy communion. The '*dost* vouchsafe' of 1552, in conjunction with what follows, makes it much clearer that the 'spiritual feeding' is intended to be thought of as *independent* of the 'due reception of these holy mysteries', *viz.* it depends simply on the remembrance with faith of Christ's passion.[2] 'Thereby' in 1552 refers to the 'due receiving'; and this 'due receiving' (not the 'spiritual feeding') *is* the 'assurance' of God's favour and goodness towards us.[3] It is all very delicately expressive of Cranmer's personal teaching; but we fail to appreciate its craftsmanship unless we remember continually that in his idea 'to eat the Body and drink the Blood of Christ' spiritually is nothing else but 'to believe in our hearts that His Flesh was rent and torn for us upon the cross and His Blood shed for our redemption' (A. 3); or as Zwingli put it, we bear witness by receiving the bread and wine 'to our belief that we are all miserable sinners, but by His Body given and Blood poured forth [in the passion, not the eucharist] we have been cleansed from sin and redeemed from everlasting death.'[4]

After these alternative prayers in 1552 follows the *Gloria*, transferred to this position from before the collects, where it had stood in 1549 as the

---

[1] This rather strange '*Thy* mystical Body' in a prayer addressed to the Father, found in both 1549 and 1552, was not corrected to 'the mystical body of Thy Son' till 1662, one of the few verbal improvements in the rite then effected.
[2] *Cf.* A. 1 above.  [3] *Cf.* F. 1 above.  [4] *Cf. p.* 632.

'hymn' of the synaxis common to all rites. This ensures that an element of the 'sacrifice of praise and thanksgiving' (in Cranmer's sense) shall terminate the liturgy, whichever of the post-communion prayers has been used. The conjecture that it was placed here to represent the 'hymn' of Mark xiv. 26 by an uncritical piece of scripturalism seems impossible. All the reformers were aware that this 'hymn' was a 'psalm', and Tyndale's Bible actually uses the word. Rather we must see here, with that acute but unread scholar W. Lockton, the influence of Zwingli's rite on his more liturgically gifted English disciple. 'The idea of our Lord as the Lamb of God, and the Lord's supper as the christian passover, is a feature of the Zurich service'.[1] At Zurich, when the elements had been replaced on the table after the communion, they said either the jewish passover *Hallel* (Ps. cxiii.) or a sort of christian *Hallel*: 'He is the Lamb of God, the pardon of our sins, the one and only pledge of mercy'.[2] Any idea that Cranmer intended to provide an opportunity for 'intra-liturgical devotions' by the adoration of the consecrated elements replaced upon the altar is a sheer perversion of his whole teaching. For him 'consecration' was related only to the *use* of the sacrament in communion.

After that it had no meaning whatever. The singing or saying of the *Agnus Dei* between consecration and communion might easily have ministered to the 'high' Lutheran doctrine that our Lord is truly and substantially present at least in the 'use' of the sacrament. But the *Agnus Dei* (retained in its old position in 1549) was removed in 1552 for this very reason—or rather, it was with misplaced ingenuity fused with the *Gloria* by the interpolation of a third 'O Lamb of God . . .' into the pre-Nicene text of that hymn.[3] Once the 'use' of the sacrament was done, there could in his mind be no further danger of 'adoration' in connection with it. Did not Zwingli himself and the Zurich church replace the remains of the sacrament upon the table?

The alternative to doing this was something to which all the Reformers of the Swiss school both in England and abroad took the utmost exception —the consumption of the remains of the sacrament and the ablution of the vessels at their primitive place, immediately after the communion, before the rite proceeds to its conclusion. This implied in their eyes that 'the bread and wine have or can have some holiness in themselves', as Cranmer put it. Commenting on that rubric of 1549 which directed the minister at

---

[1] W. Lockton, *The Remains at the Eucharist*, Cambridge, 1920, p. 184.
[2] E. Wolfensberger, *Die Zürcher Kirchengebete*, p. 55.
[3] The variant of the *Gloria* found in the *Codex Alexandrinus*, sometimes cited in extenuation of Cranmer's rather vandalistic treatment of its text, seems irrelevant. (1) *Cod. Al.* does not agree with Cranmer's text. (2) It was not then known. (3) There is no other MS. evidence for its variant. I fear we must just agree that Cranmer tampered with a text older than the Nicene Creed by a solitary error of literary judgement, in an endeavour to emphasise a specifically Zwinglian feature of his rite.

the offertory to take only '*so much* bread and wine as will suffice for those appointed to communicate', Bucer had written to Cranmer that from this direction 'some make for themselves the superstition that they consider it unlawful, if anything of the bread and wine of the communion remain over when it is finished, to allow it to come to common use; as if there were in this bread and wine of itself anything of divinity or even sanctity outside the use at communion. And so men must be taught that ... outside that use of the communion which the Lord instituted, the bread and wine, even if they have been placed on the table of the Lord, have nothing in them of sanctity more than have other bread and wine.... These things it is fitting that the people be taught as in word so also in deed, as diligently as may be.'[1] Cranmer took the point, and taught diligently. There were no instructions in 1549 as to what was to be done with the remains of the sacrament, which had given occasion to many to continue to take the ablutions at the Sarum (and primitive) place, after the communion. In 1552 they were ordered to be replaced upon the table, Zurich fashion. And after the blessing there appeared a new rubric: 'If any of the bread or wine remain, the Curate shall have it to his own use.' This does not refer, as does the 1662 rubric—'remain *unconsecrated*'—to any reserve provision, but to the only bread and wine mentioned in 1552, '*the* bread and wine'. This having been 'separated to a godly use' for which it was not needed, was forthwith free again for common uses, since it 'can have no holiness in itself'.

The 1552 rite, like 1549, concludes with an expanded form of blessing, in place of the primitive dismissal. Coming after communion, as the ancient church understood communion, a solemn blessing would have been an anticlimax. It is significant that a final blessing only begins to make its appearance in the various liturgies as non-communicating attendance becomes the normal custom of the laity. It was adopted sporadically in the West during the middle ages; but it makes its first official appearance as the invariable termination of the Roman rite (so far as I can discover) only in the printed missal of 1474. Sarum still officially ended with the primitive *Ite missa est* and *Deo gratias* right down to 1549; though the blessing after this was probably customary in some English churches. But when the eucharistic action had been so radically altered in conception as it had been by Cranmer, a concluding blessing acquired great appropriateness. Both in 1549 and 1552 it has its present form, in which the blessing proper is preceded by 'The peace of God, etc.', which had come after the communion in the *Order* of 1548.

Such was the rite of 1552, and such the reasons which led its author to frame it as he did. If it were a matter of pure history there we might leave it. But the modern Anglican cannot quite leave it there, for 1552 still supplies the whole structure of his present liturgy and some ninety-five per

[1] M. Bucer, *Scripta Anglicana, Censura,* iv. Works, p. 464

cent. of its wording. We do not, of course, receive it because it is Cranmers,'
but as twice revised (in 1559 and 1662) and as the rite of the Church of
England. Yet the fact remains that our rite is as it is because Cranmer
thought as he thought. I am free to confess that it is only painfully and with
reluctance that I have brought myself to face candidly some of the facts
here set out, and I cannot but fear that they will bring equal distress to
others. Yet once they have been fully understood, there is more to be said
which is equally true, and more relevant to our situation as Anglicans in the
twentieth century. All history, secular as well as religious—and not least
the secular history of the twenty years since Versailles—shews not only the
folly but the danger of attempting to solve the difficulties of the present
without a clear understanding of their causes in the past. We cannot hope
either to understand the course of Anglican liturgical history since 1552 or
to find an adequate solution of our present liturgical troubles, if we persist
in cherishing illusions about the source from which they spring. It could
not reasonably be maintained that Anglicanism as such has ever been
Zwinglian in doctrine. But a great part of Anglican history is taken up with
difficulties caused by the fact that the Anglican rite was framed with
exquisite skill to express this doctrine which the Anglican church has always
repudiated, tacitly since 1559, explicitly since 1563.

Putting aside these issues for the moment, what should be our judgement of the rite of 1552 simply as a piece of liturgy-making? Obviously, it
has little formal relation to the primitive rites we have been studying. The
basis of Cranmer's understanding of the eucharist seems to have been the
idea, to which he reverts insistently, that our Lord 'instituted a holy supper' to be held in memory of His death. In fact, as we have seen, our Lord
'instituted' nothing. What He did was to give a new meaning to a double
action before and after supper. But the action was so slightly connected
with the supper that the church in the first generation found itself compelled to discard the supper lest the new meaning of the action should be
obscured. And the meaning of the action in the earliest recorded version of
our Lord's statement of it was not specifically connected with His death at
all—'Take, eat, this is My Body which is for you. Do this for the *anamnesis*
of *Me*'; 'This cup is the New Covenant in My Blood. Whenever you drink
(the cup of blessing) do this for the *anamnesis* of *Me*'. The apostolic
church read into this, and rightly, a reference to His sacrificial death, but
to much more also. It is '*Me*', the whole Christ, not only the Victim of
Calvary, which the eucharist 're-calls'.

In consequence of this initial misunderstanding both of what constitutes
the eucharist and of its purpose, Cranmer has radically misconceived the
eucharistic action and consequently changed the Shape of the Liturgy by
which that action is performed. What remains of the old 'four-action
Shape' in 1552? (1) There is no offertory in bread and wine at all; it has
been deliberately discarded. (2) Whether the 'eucharistic prayer' remains

it is not easy to say. The notion of 'consecration' has been deliberately watered down to that of 'setting apart to a holy use', and attached to the words of institution, which the middle ages had come to regard as *the* essential of the rite. But what of the *eucharistia*, that 'thanking' which is the apostolic nucleus of the prayer, and the solemn concluding doxology, the 'glorifying of the Name' of God? Of the first there remains a clear trace in the preface. But only during four weeks in the year, when a proper preface is provided, is it in any sense an *anamnesis* of the Person and Work of Christ, as in the primitive rites. For the rest of the year He is not so much as mentioned in it. And even this survival has been altogether removed from any connection with the consecration by the interpolation after the sanctus of the 'prayer of humble access', through the exigencies of that unfortunate controversy with Gardiner. And the doxology, that 'blessing of the Name' without which for the first century jew and the primitive christian no blessing could be a blessing, has similarly been removed from the prayer to beyond the communion—at the end of the prayer of oblation or of thanksgiving. (3) The fraction, ordered in 1549, has disappeared in 1552, apparently because Bucer warned Cranmer that it was an opportunity for 'superstition'. (4) There remains the communion, which Cranmer himself insists is only a *token* act—'Take and eat this *in remembrance* that Christ died for thee.'

The real eucharistic action for Cranmer does not lie in these things at all, but is something purely mental and psychological—'This is the eating of Christ's Flesh and drinking of His Blood, *the feeling* whereof is to every man *the feeling how* he eateth and drinketh Christ' (A. 4), which he insists means 'believing that Christ died for me'. As a strictly mental 'action' (if that be a permissible term) it has of course ceased to be anything at all of a 'corporate' action. Even its external 'token', the partaking of the bread and wine, must be done 'every man for himself', as Cranmer insists. Not even the carrying on of the rest of the rite, 'the preparing of the supper' as he calls it, is corporate. That is the business of the minister, to which the people are only to listen. From being the action which creates the unity of the church as the Body of Christ, the eucharist has become precisely that which *breaks down the church into separate individuals*. (The consequences of this, slowly gathering force over 400 years, are very manifest in Anglican religion to-day, and constitute one of our most serious problems.) Behind the whole idea lies Cranmer's perpetual use of the phrase 'to *feed on* Christ', for 'to have faith in Him as Redeemer'. It is noteworthy that this precise expression does not occur anywhere in the New Testament. The nearest to it—'he that cheweth (*trōgōn*) My Flesh and drinketh My Blood' (John vi. 54, 56, 58)—is found in a chapter of which the exegesis is notoriously difficult. It is plain that the symbolism of the eucharist is colouring the evangelist's thought throughout its length, but I venture to think it is certain that only *vv.* 51–8 are intended to refer directly to the eucharist *as a rite*, while the remainder of the chapter is dealing with the much wider question of faith in Christ's Person and Office in terms of eucharistic symbolism. Such at least is the consensus of exegesis, both ancient and modern. Cranmer's root mistake lies in misunderstanding this distinction.

But in thus comparing Cranmer's rite with those of the primitive church we are not truly acting fairly, even though he himself repeatedly challenges the comparison, because we are placing him against a standard of which he knew, and could know, virtually nothing. Not until centuries after his time did the historical material necessary for the interpretation of the primitive eucharist begin to be available; much of it was unknown or not understood even in 1900. The true background of Cranmer's work is, as I have said, the contemporary post-mediaeval liturgical crisis, and the *Kirchenordnungen* of the German and Swiss Reformation which sought to solve it. The rite of 1552 takes its natural place among these, and only when seen thus can its qualities and those of its creator be fully and fairly appreciated. Compared with the clumsy and formless rites which were evolved abroad, that of 1552 is the masterpiece of an artist. Cranmer gave it a noble form as a superb piece of literature, which no one could say of its companions; but he did more. As a piece of liturgical craftsmanship it is in the first rank—once its intention is understood. It is *not* a disordered attempt at a catholic rite, but the only effective attempt ever made to give liturgical expression to the doctrine of 'justification by faith alone'. If in the end the attempt does not succeed—if we are left with a sense of the total disconnection of the token communion in bread and wine with that mental 'eating and drinking of Christ's Flesh and Blood', *i.e.* remembering of the passion, which is for Cranmer the essential eucharistic action—that must be set down to the impossible nature of the task, not to the manner of its performance. Cranmer was in the end baffled like all the Reformers by the impossibility of reconciling the external rite of the eucharist and the scriptural evidence of the last supper with the idea that 'we spiritually and ghostly with our faith eat Christ, being carnally absent from us in heaven, *in such wise* as Abraham and other holy fathers did eat Him many years before He was incarnated and born . . .' (A. 2). The communion in bread and wine is and must be permanently irrelevant to that conception, simply because Abraham did not receive it. Modern protestantism has avoided the difficulty by allowing the eucharist to slip into the background, and explaining away or ignoring the New Testament. Cranmer faced it, even if he did not solve it.

It may be inevitable that 'high' churchmen who feel conscientiously bound at all costs to save the character of our present rite should try to do so at the expense of its original author, by accusing him of moral cowardice and dissembling, of being 'blown about with every wind of vain doctrine', of unwilling deference to the Council and to foreign refugees, and so on. They must, I suppose, take this for an 'attack' on Cranmer and his work, and nothing I can say will prevent it. If to believe the man's own earnest and repeated claim to have been both sincere and consistent be an attack, then I have attacked him. But I wonder which Cranmer would have preferred, to be 'attacked' by me, or to have his belief in the eucharistic oblation of Christ—which he passionately repudiated—established by the suggestion that he deceived protestants and catholics alike as to his real opinions out of cowardice? At least he did not die like a coward, nor were his public repudiation of any part or lot in the setting up of the mass again at Canterbury *after* Mary was upon the throne but before his own arrest, and his public refusal to say mass before the Queen, dissembling acts.[1] The last words he was heard to speak in S. Mary's at Oxford were 'Never before this time (*i.e.* in his recent recantations) have I dissembled.'

He is in truth a tragic and ironical figure, but not a weak one. After his condemnation they came to him with the argument that, the Queen having accepted Papal supremacy and all that went with it and commanding him to do the same, he was bound by a subject's allegiance and all his own teaching to accept it too. It was the very trap that he had helped to spread for Fisher and More. Ever since he had been archbishop he had laboured to build up the Royal Supremacy as unquestionable, unanswerable, established by God, rightly overriding all oaths, all conscience, all teaching, all loyalties, all rights, all laws, all faith, that might impinge upon its sweep. To build this he had formally perjured himself in accepting his see of Canterbury; to maintain it he had connived at the greatest spoliation of the church that had ever yet happened; for this he had shed blood, or consented to its shedding, in case after case where, rightly or wrongly, he believed the victims innocent. All rebellion against the King's sovereign will was always for him the sin of Judas.[2] The Royal Supremacy was the one potent instrument by which he had achieved his own mission of changing the religion of England. And now it had broken in his hand. At first he was non-plussed, but after a little he answered firmly enough, that 'The Queen could not command him to anything against his conscience.' He had joined the other martyrs against his own life's work!

Zwinglian and papist, he had burned them both at different times, along with miscellaneous Arians and Eutychians and Anabaptists, for their creeds—reluctantly (for he was by nature gentle) but persistently enough—right down to Van Morey, not long before King Edward died. And now he was coming to join them himself. One wonders if the thought of them all passed through the old man's mind as he hurried of his own accord out of S. Mary's along the Turl to where the stake stood in the Broad outside Balliol—Lambert the Zwinglian and Friar Forrest—and the gentle Fisher,

[1] Parker I, *p.* 428.
[2] See his letter to Henry VIII in defence of Cromwell after the latter's arrest: 'If the noble princes of memory, King John, Henry II and Richard II had had such a councillor about them, I suppose that they should never have been so traitorously abandoned and overthrown as those good princes were' (Parker II, *p.* 401). A royalism which could idealise King John into a 'good prince' needs fanaticism.

and More the witty chancellor, and old abbot Whiting—but they were in King Henry's time, and for a matter of treason, like the Carthusians—whether the Boleyn girl were a lawful queen or a whore—Both!—That would have ruined him if he had not condemned her, though he had almost thought her innocent—and Seymour the Admiral, and his brother and murderer Seymour the Protector—he had abandoned them both in turn, though he had thought them innocent too—but their cases were desperate, and his own mission could not be compromised in fighting lost battles—and those hundreds of yokels strung up in 1549—and little Jane Grey and that ruffianly Northumberland—the cur professed himself a papist on the scaffold, that had been the raveningest protestant in England! —A safer religion for a bad man to die in?—and the sturdy decent Latimer—and Nicholas Ridley, who had shewn him, Thomas, how the truth lay about the sacrament—(Not much further now!)—They had all died, almost every one he had ever known—and thousands more unknown—and many others still to die—in these quarrels about the bread and the Body—that could never have blazed so fiercely in England or spread so far but for his work.—If he had used his position as archbishop altogether otherwise, to reform the old religion, not to make a new prevail?—Impossible! If a man saw the truth so clear, it was a duty to impose it—if the king were willing. —Would English christians always be rent henceforward?—(Here was the stake at last)—This was what it all came to in the end—the bread had nothing to do with the Body—That was what he was dying for—

### The Anglican Settlement

The Church of England has never accorded to Cranmer that position which Lutheranism gives to Luther, Calvinism to Calvin, Zwinglianism to Zwingli. He is not personally a source of Anglican doctrine. (In point of fact few modern Anglicans have read him.) This was soon made clear in Elizabeth's reign when the new religion was restored, even though the Elizabethan Prayer Book of 1559 was the Book of 1552 with only five changes.[1] Of these only one affected the rite of the eucharist; to the words of administration of 1552, 'Take and eat this in remembrance that Christ died for Thee . . .', 'Drink this in remembrance . . .', were now prefixed those of 1549, 'The Body of our Lord Jesus Christ . . .'. 'The Blood of our Lord Jesus Christ . . .'. Thus at one stroke—whether intentionally or not—the 1559 liturgy itself reopened the whole question which Cranmer's rite was intended to close decisively.

[1] The so-called 'Black Rubric' or 'Declaration on Kneeling' (at communion) was never part of 1552, but had been interpolated by authority of the Privy Council while the book was printing. 1559 in restoring 1552 naturally omitted this extraneous addition, though the omission is usually reckoned a sixth alteration. It is not so included, however, by Archbishop Whitgift in his account of the changes to Burleigh (Strype, *Annals*, I, 1, *p.* 143).

The Convocation of 1559 had nothing to do with making this change, which was probably due to the Queen herself. But it had already given ample proof of its rejection of Cranmer's teaching by passing five articles —afterwards subscribed by the universities—to be presented to Parliament. The first three run thus:

'1. That in the sacrament of the altar, by virtue of the words of Christ duly spoken by the priest is present *realiter*, under the kinds of bread and wine, the natural Body of Christ conceived of the Virgin Mary, and also His natural Blood.

'2. That after the consecration there remains not the substance of bread and wine, nor any other substance but the substance of God and Man.

'3. That in the mass is offered the true Body of Christ and His true Blood, a propitiatory sacrifice for the living and the dead.'

The other two are concerned respectively with 'the authority of handling and defining concerning . . . faith, sacraments and discipline ecclesiastical' as belonging 'only to the pastors of the church whom the Holy Ghost hath set in the church to that purpose, and not to laymen'; and with affirming the pastoral authority of the successor of Peter as Christ's Vicar. But that the first three articles (with which alone we are here concerned) are not to be set aside as a mere final ebullition of Marian popery is shewn by the Convocation of 1562, which first gave authority to Cranmer's *xlii Articles* of 1553. Before it did so it omitted three of them, including one which gave expression to Cranmer's doctrine of the non-participation of the wicked in the Body and Blood of Christ (*cf.* A. 4)[1]. And in what is now our *xxviiith Article* it deliberately substituted the statement that 'the Body of Christ *is* given, taken and received in the supper only after an heavenly and spiritual manner' for Cranmer's statement that 'a faithful man ought *not* either to believe or openly confess the real and bodily presence (as they term it) of Christ's Flesh and Blood in the sacrament of the Lord's supper.'

In 1571 at the revision of these *xxxix Articles* Bishop Cheney of Gloucester protested against the retention of the word 'only' in this Article. (It is to be noted that he was no Marian conformist, but had had to hide for his life in that period.) He also said that Bishop Guest of Rochester, who was absent from the debate, shared his objection. But Guest wrote to Cecil: 'I suppose you have heard how the bishop of Gloucester found himself grieved with the placing of this adverb "only" . . . because it did take away the presence of Christ's Body in the sacrament. . . . Whereas I told him plainly that this word "only" in the aforesaid Article did not exclude the presence of Christ's Body from the sacrament, but only the grossness and sensibleness in the receiving thereof; for I said unto him, that though he take Christ's Body in his hand, received it in his mouth, and that corporally, naturally, really, substantially and carnally, as the Doctors do write, yet did he not for all that see it, feel it, smell it or taste it. And,

---

[1] This was re-inserted in 1571.

therefore, I told him I would speak against him herein, and the rather because the Article was of my own penning. And yet I would not for all that deny anything that I had spoken for the presence'.[1] Bishop Guest's interpretation of his own doctrinal Article is fully as relevant as Archbishop Cranmer's interpretation of his own liturgy in determining the sense of Anglican eucharistic belief.

That liturgy was certainly not regarded as self-interpreting in the reign of Elizabeth, e.g. in 'Johnson's Case'. We have seen that the Prayer Books of 1549, 1552 (and consequently 1559) had no rubric for the contingency of a second consecration if the sacramental species proved insufficient, such as had found a place in the *Order* of 1548. We have seen, too, that the omission was intended by Cranmer to enforce the Zwinglian view of 'consecration' and the purpose of the recital of the institution. In 1573 Robert Johnson, then chaplain to the Lord Keeper, Francis Bacon, was arraigned by the High Commission for not reciting the institution a second time on such an occasion, and administering bread and wine unconsecrated to a number of communicants. Though the letter of the current Prayer Book was entirely in his favour, and he expressly cited Cranmer in his own defence, he was condemned to a year's imprisonment, during which he died.

Yet we must note that such things do not necessarily betoken a return to specifically catholic doctrine. Some of them at least are equally compatible with the 'high' Calvinist view of the eucharist. What they do shew is that there was a steady and increasing rejection of those particular ideas which Cranmer's liturgy had been so carefully designed to express. Hooker himself, though he is not altogether consistent, and his general doctrine of 'receptionism' is further removed from catholic than from Calvinist teaching, is yet more irreconcilable with Cranmer, whose main point is that 'eating the Body and drinking the Blood of Christ' is not connected at all with receiving the bread and wine; (otherwise it would not be analogous to the 'eating the Body of Christ' by the Old Testament patriarchs, who did not receive the bread and wine at all). The rejection of this dissociation of receiving holy communion from the effect traditionally ascribed to it was general in Elizabeth's reign. Overall's statement that 'the Body and Blood of Christ are verily and indeed taken and received by the faithful in the Lord's supper' was added to the Catechism in 1604 on the petition of the puritans themselves, and was nowhere challenged. It represents a direct negation of the basic underlying idea of Cranmer's rite.

It is, of course, recognised that the reaction against this was widespread in the seventeenth century. But it does not seem to be clearly understood that it has a twofold source. On the one hand the Elizabethan tendency to appeal to the primitive church (revealed e.g. in the canon of 1571 ordering preachers to teach nothing 'but that which is agreeable to the doctrine of

[1] *Calendar of State Papers (Domestic)*, lxxviii. 37.

the Old Testament and the New and that which the catholic fathers and ancient bishops have gathered out of that doctrine') issues in the comparatively small school of men like Bilson, Montague and Andrewes, who taught the full patristic doctrine. But Calvinism, which in the person of prelates like Archbishop Whitgift of Canterbury was exceedingly influential in the Elizabethan church, was in this particular matter equally opposed to Cranmer's personal ideas. And Calvinism issues in that much larger school of seventeenth century divines who combined a firm belief in the Apostolic Succession with either the Calvinist view of a 'spiritual presence' or the new 'receptionism' of Hooker.[1] The seventeenth century puritans did not share the episcopalian ideas of the Laudian school, or their views of the importance of sacraments compared with edification. (This springs from their different idea of the church.) But as regards their actual doctrine of the eucharist they are not far removed from most of their opponents, and they shared their opposition to Cranmer's Zwinglianism. If Baxter's *Reformed Liturgy* be compared with Cranmer's it will be found abjectly inferior to it alike as a literary composition and from the standpoint of practical 'usability'. But it is nevertheless a whole stage nearer to the catholic tradition, in its conception of the eucharistic action and in its close attachment of the eating of the Body and drinking of the Blood of Christ to the reception of the consecrated species. This is inevitable, since an essentially Calvinist theology lies behind Baxter's clumsy rite, while the beauty of Cranmer's is clothed upon the negations of Zwingli.

It may be asked why, if the Church of England rejected Cranmer's theology, it has retained for nearly four centuries a rite which so skilfully and unmistakeably embodied that theology not only in its wording but in its very structure? To a sympathetic historical understanding, however, the real question would rather seem to be, How in the circumstances to which Cranmer had decisively committed her, the English church could possibly have got rid of his liturgy?

It was, indeed, not for nothing that Cranmer had been prepared for his labours as archbishop by his appointment as Henry's ambassador to the catholic Emperor Charles V and simultaneously his secret negotiator with Charles' opponents, the German protestant princes. Cranmer was no mean diplomat. If the retention of office—and his head—continuously through all the dangerous years from before the first breach with Rome to the death of Edward be any indication, Cranmer was indeed the wariest politician of all who sat at the table of the Privy Council. Every man there knew all the

[1] Mr. C. W. Dugmore's essay *Eucharistic Doctrine from Hooker to Waterland* (London, 1942) is important as demonstrating that the majority of seventeenth century 'high church' Anglicans did not hold anything like the Tractarian doctrine of the 'Real Presence' (though they used the term freely) but rather the 'high' Calvinist doctrine, or else Hooker's new heresy. The unity of the seventeenth century 'high church' movement was much more a unity of sociological than of theological doctrine in more than one respect.

time that some of his colleagues were seeking his own ruin and death with every move of the game, and that the simplest or seemingly most everyday question of administration or policy might cover a sudden order to the Tower, or be twisted to that end. (It is no wonder that symptoms of hysteria are plain among the little gang who were the real rulers of England through this period; they lived for the most part at a terrible tension.) Cranmer was there throughout, and though he had his difficult moments he never fell under the axe like his allies Cromwell and Somerset, nor was removed to prison like his opponents Wriothesley and Gardiner. Yet pliant as he seemed he was no cipher, but the only one among them all who achieved his ends, and even established them for centuries to come.

After Cromwell's sudden fall everything seemed to be against his achieving success, but he worked on, patiently, cautiously, devotedly, never losing sight of his end and using any means that came to his hand. Henry's lusts; the morbid fanaticism of the clever, sickly boy Edward; Somerset's strange fancy of himself as the 'Lord's Elect'; Northumberland's unscrupulous ambition—all these served his purpose. Even Gardiner's unskilful intrigues against him and Hooper's short-sighted opposition to his politic concentration on essentials were turned to strengthen his own position. In the end Mary's twisted vengefulness gave him the halo of martyrdom and made the future of his schemes secure. (It is a remarkable fact that in every case his purposes were served better by the weaknesses and faults of his associates, whether friends or enemies, than by the good points of their characters.) Baffled again and again, by the conservative instincts of Henry, by the quarrelsomeness of the Reformers, by the instability of the political situation under Edward, he had yet achieved a short-lived success before Edward died, and he laid firm foundations for the restoration of his own work after his death. He had the instinct which is the supreme gift of the politician, that of knowing just how much 'too far' it is at any given moment really safe to go. It is quite untrue that he was pushed by others further than he meant to go in the direction of theological change, though he was on occasion over-ruled by the Privy Council and made to sanction moves which he thought unwise.[1] Yet one has only to examine, for instance, Bucer's *Censura* of 1549 to see that Cranmer has used it with really good judgement in framing his second Prayer Book. He has ignored some of Bucer's most cherished suggestions, but in other things (*e.g.* in omitting all mention of the saints and the departed) 1552 has gone right beyond what Bucer regarded as wise. Yet in almost every case Cranmer's instinct as to how far he could go was justified by the event. The changes he

---

[1] *E.g.*, in the addition of the 'Declaration on Kneeling' to 1552, and in the attempt to set up Lady Jane Grey in opposition to Mary. The first was something entirely in accord with his own teaching; the second would certainly have coincided with his own hopes; but he opposed both because they were certain to be rejected by the country at large. And his instinct was right in both cases.

devised are nominally in force at the present day, with slight (though very important) modifications. But unless we understand that from 1547 onwards Cranmer is just as much an 'extremist' as Ridley or Hooper or Bucer, we fail to do justice either to the sincerity of the author of the *Defence* or to the remarkable skill and wisdom with which he guided events to a result at which the small and short-sighted Zwinglian party could never have arrived but for him. It was by the exercise of this unostentatious political skill that Cranmer carried through his purpose in most unpromising circumstances; and by the same skill that he fortified his personal ideas in possession of the English field.

He was well aware that left to itself the English church would by a great majority refuse to endorse them. He could only succeed by enlisting behind them another force which for its own ends could be trusted to see that they prevailed. As primate he was the pivot of the ecclesiastical machinery of England, but that was useless for his purposes. Cranmer put his faith in something other than the church—in the new centralised monarchy, now drawing to itself most of the resources of a renaissance despotism out of the ruins of the Lancastrian experiment in constitutional government. Thomas Cromwell had seen that a church wielding independent authority over conscience was the only force which such a despotism had to fear in the condition of the times; and had set himself to bring the church under royal control as 'Vicar General' of the new 'Supreme Head of the Church'. The fact that the primate himself was an ardent supporter of such control, out of principle and conviction, made the task easy. Cromwell was discarded by Henry before the work was completed, but only the fact that Cromwell's disciple Cranmer was still primate made it safe for the king to dispense with him. The work would go forward the more safely and with less danger of opposition in the hands of an archbishop.

The 'Royal Supremacy' to churchmen nowadays connotes little more than a picturesque historic loyalty and a good deal of exasperating legal red tape, together with a peculiar method of selecting bishops. But few churchmen would feel called upon to change their beliefs about—say—the desirability of reading the Bible[1] and their way of saying their bedside prayers[2], merely because the ideas of the reigning monarch on these things were reported to have changed. Yet it was precisely this conception which after Cromwell died was made a terrible reality in England, while Cranmer was the king's foremost ecclesiastical adviser. Men died—publicly and in

[1] Lest it be thought I exaggerate, the Act of 1543 'for the advancement of true religion' forbade any man under the degree of a yeoman to possess a copy of the *authorised* translation of the Bible to read to himself. No woman, if she were not a noblewoman, might read it. Ever since 1534 Convocation had been trying to encourage Bible reading, with the king's approval. Now the king had changed his mind, not liking the result. Cranmer spoke and voted for the Act of 1543 in the Lords.

[2] The 'King's Primer' issued in 1545 was intended to regulate *private* prayers and specifically orders 'none other to be used throughout all his dominions'.

horrible ways—for not conforming to every fresh change of the royal conscience. It was made treason to speak against the Royal Supremacy, even in private conversation; and spies and *agents provocateurs* were employed in men's houses to delate them. It was even made treason to feel unable to swear when required that one believed the new dogma, even while taking no overt step by word or deed to oppose it. All preaching was forbidden, except to those clergy specially licensed by the archbishop, and he saw to it that they were all propagandists for the Supremacy. It was the nearest approach to the *régime* of the Gestapo that England has ever enjoyed.

It is laid down in the gospel that men should render unto Caesar the things that are Caesar's and unto God the things that are God's. The whole quarrel of paganism with the church was always about this, that she would persist in believing that there was one sphere where Caesar's word could not make law. It does seem that our world is slowly coming to the conclusion that this is as a matter of practical fact the abiding defence of all human freedom. But Cranmer passionately disbelieved this. He was faithful throughout his career to his conception of the clergy as the *king's* 'ministers of religion' to his subjects, as his judges were the king's 'ministers of justice' to them. The clergy administered the king's laws and commands in things spiritual as his other officers administered his law and commands in things temporal. This theory he put into writing as early as 1540[1] and still defended at his trial fourteen years later. The Royal Supremacy was the last point on which he hesitated to give way when he came to his pitiful recantations after his condemnation.[2] We find him still desperately arguing with Queen Mary about it by correspondence in 1555.[3] In all resistance to the royal religion he saw the sin of Korah and Dathan.[4]

Put in this way, of course, it was an entirely novel theory. But when one examines the practice of the end of the middle ages, does he not rather sweep away—just as in the contrast of the old liturgy with the late mediaeval tradition of supplementary lay devotion—relics of a much older state of things no longer in accord with the reality of late mediaeval practice, and boldly make the latter the whole basis of his new theory? *Was* Cardinal Morton more a minister of the church than of the king? Did not Cardinal Wolsey at the end confess that he had *not* served his God as he had served his king? Is not Cranmer himself in this also the product of the late mediaeval practice when he resolved the growing tension between contemporary practice and the primitive theory by abolishing the latter, and declared that to render unto Caesar *is* to render unto God, and that the two cannot be opposed?

It was, therefore, upon conviction no less than from expediency that he acted when he made the imposition of the new religion altogether the act of

[1] *Cf. p.* 652.   [2] Parker II, pp. 563 *sqq.*   [3] Parker II, *pp.* 447 *sqq.*
[4] *Cf.* his *Answer to the* 15 *Articles of the Devon Rebels* (*ibid., pp.* 163 *sq.,* esp. *pp.* 184 *sq.*) written in a white heat of unfeigned indignation.

the state, and not of the church. The *Order of Communion* in 1548 was authorised by an act of Parliament and put out by royal proclamation. It was compiled by 'sundry of His Majesty's most grave and well learned pre· lates'—the king's ministers in such things—and others who were by the King's Majesty 'caused to assemble themselves . . . and agreed upon such order'. In 1549, as Professor Powicke says, 'it is generally agreed that the first Prayer Book of Edward VI was not even submitted to Convocation',[1] but came out from the king in Parliament. In 1552 the general question of the need of a revision of 1549 was on the agenda of Convocation, but seems never to have been discussed. It is certain that Convocation had no voice in the process, and it was sent home before the text of the new book was made public for the first time in Parliament in March. In 1553 the *xlii Articles*, which rounded off the liturgical changes with a doctrinal statement, professed to have the authority of 'the Synod at London', to which they had never even been submitted. It is hard to be patient with Cranmer's explanation that this was done because they were published while Convocation was in session. And even this lame shift seems to have been untrue. They had behind them only the personal approval of Cranmer.

The introduction of the new religion—we need not scruple to use a term which was robustly used by those concerned—thus had about it all the characteristics of a *coup d'état* so far as the constitutional machinery of the church was concerned. There can hardly be a doubt that Cranmer as archbishop could have blocked this procedure from the start, if he had wanted to. We must be just to him. The beginnings of the revolution go back behind him into the middle ages, to the day when the English state first undertook to punish heresy by the law of the land, in Richard II's time, and more definitely in 1415. The change made by Cranmer is that now the state, or rather the king declares what is heresy, instead of accepting the definition of it from the church. From 1530 onwards the crown manifests an increasing tendency to act along these lines,[2] and the reason is not just plain Erastianism. The growing crisis in the old religion did legitimately concern the state, inasmuch as church and state were inextricably entangled by a thousand years of previous history. Cranmer added to this his own conscientious royalism, but royalism of that brand was in the air of Tudor England. Gardiner savagely defended the execution of Fisher at the time,[3] and Tunstall and Boner spoke as loudly for the Royal Supremacy as Cranmer himself in its early years. But it is still the fact that

[1] *The Reformation in England*, 1941, *p.* 81. This was formerly questioned, but the evidence is against such a submission.
[2] *e.g.* the royal proclamations concerning Dedication and Patronal festivals and other liturgical observances in 1534, 1536, 1541; the 'purged' edition of the Sarum Breviary in 1541 and its imposition by the Crown on all clerics (through Convocation) in 1542, etc.
[3] See Prof. Powicke's brilliant analysis of Gardiner's development, *op. cit., pp.* 96 *sqq.*

the primate, the successor of Becket and Langton and Edmund Rich, whose throne was the traditional bulwark of the liberties of the English church and people against absolutism, not only acquiesced in but did all in his power to forward the procedure by which those liberties were set aside. This alone made their ignoring possible, with all its far-reaching consequences. Cranmer would gladly have accepted the responsibility for that, and he must bear it. He used the occasion to the furthest possible extent to impose upon the church, not a reform which others saw to be desirable, but his own conscientious convictions.

Amongst the consequences two stand out plainly. The first is that he engaged the whole interest of the new centralised authority of the state, and especially of that thriving class the lawyers, to maintain his work. The second is that he imposed upon his theological opponents the necessity of working through the same procedure as himself. Changes embodied in parliamentary statutes could only be undone by other parliamentary statutes. The Marian restoration of the old religion was forced to take the same indefensible revolutionary means as had been employed to overthrow it. As Jewel was quick to point out to the papist Harding, who had jibed at the Elizabethan 'parliament religion', 'Your fathers and brethren had of late, in the time of Queen Mary, a parliament-faith, a parliament-mass, and a parliament-pope'.[1] Mary restored Gardiner and Boner and Tunstall to the sees of which they had been deprived by the crown under her brother, and removed their intruded successors. And however she might declare this a matter of right and charge the intruders with heresy, it had an air of Cranmer's theory that bishops held office of the Crown and only 'during the royal good pleasure'. It was not the Convocations but the Parliament which legally restored the Latin mass, even though the clergy and people had everywhere anticipated its action.

The Marian restoration was an episode. However popular it might be—and it was popular at the beginning—it was brought about, like the changes before and after it, by the personal will of a Tudor monarch acting through the usual constitutional machinery of the secular state. Its effective force was in fact that very Royal Supremacy which Mary detested and repudiated. When she died and the Supremacy passed to her sister it was the same story. Convocation was not consulted as to the liturgical changes that ensued; it was sent home in a hurry before they were made, lest it comment upon them. The third Act of Uniformity of 1559 was withdrawn for a season after its first introduction, while the government worked upon a dubious House of Commons. It was got through the Commons at a second attempt, and through the Lords by a majority of one, against the vote of every single spiritual peer present. Such was the power of a Tudor government that this faint endorsement sufficed. The passive opposition of the Marian bishops to the restoration of the Prayer Book was overcome as the

[1] *Works* (Parker Soc. 1850), iv., p. 904.

passive opposition of Cranmer and Ridley and Latimer to the restoration of the Latin mass, and the passive opposition of Boner and Tunstall to the Edwardian book had been overcome, by their removal from their sees by the authority of the Crown. But in all this there is no consultation of the church. It is a repetition of Cranmer's—and of Mary's—*coups d'état*.

The modern Anglican may lament these facts or he may accept them. The point is that the Elizabethan Englishman, of whatever persuasion, was in precisely the same position. With the ecclesiastical machinery firmly in the grip of whatever government happened to be in power, the church had before it the choice between complete disruption and acquiescence. Leaderless and voiceless, the population, both those favourable and those unfavourable to the changes, necessarily acquiesced. The recusants went on attending their parish churches for years, and took a decade to come to a sense of the real situation. Even then they were handicapped by the possibility that the succession of the next heir, Mary Queen of Scots, would once more reverse the position by governmental means. All but the most convinced stood aside and waited for that when in 1569 a hesitant recourse to arms was made, too late, by the catholics of the North. A gradually increasing proportion of their fellow-countrymen had been passing from acquiescence to acceptance. Administrative measures had quietly changed the composition of the Privy Council, the judicial Bench, the Commission of the Peace, as well as the Episcopate. The slow dying out of the Marian priesthood with its memories of the old *régime*—there were only 360 recusant priests at work in England when Elizabeth died, including the new missionaries from abroad—left a new generation which had never known any other rite than the Prayer Book. A discreet use of fines and imprisonments, reinforced later by executions, steadily weakened the recusant body. By spasmodic penal action and continuous social ostracism it was kept negligible for two centuries—except for a short period in the seventeenth century when once more the Royal Supremacy threatened to revive it. In the nineteenth century the government lost its interest in the matter.

If such was the immediate disarray into which the action of the government cast the recusants, who after all could look abroad for leadership and organisation (though they received little enough of either till Dr. Allen came upon the scene) the situation of conformists like Archbishop Parker and Bishop Guest was in some ways even more difficult. They would gladly have welcomed something better than the settlement made by the government for political reasons. But their whole mind and instinct shrank from the disruption that successful defiance of the government must bring. Besides, by what means and in the name of what principle were they to defy it? No doctrinal settlement had been arrived at at all so far. The liturgical settlement so narrowly imposed by Parliament was barely tolerated by the 'extreme left' now returning from its Marian exile abroad, but the Book of 1549 satisfied no one. It was no use pressing for that. It represented (and was then understood to represent) the same ideas as 1552; but the protestants and the recusants alike refused to use it; and the rite of 1552 was the one the government was committed to enforcing. Within the limits left for any action by the church, such men could and did do a good deal to influence the settlement, as the revision of Cranmer's *Articles* and the appeal to the primitive church and the 'catholic fathers' testify. But with the liturgical changes already made by the action of the state they had no chance whatever to interfere, even if they had had an alternative ready to propose.

There were others who found themselves within a church not altogether to their liking. Puritanism, as it came to be called, was a strong and lively element, and one to which insufficient justice has generally been done by Anglican historians. For my own part I cannot help thinking that among our pragmatic countrymen it represented fundamentally much more the desire of good men to deal with those practical abuses of the ecclesiastical machine which had clamoured for amendment in 1534 and which the English Reformation had left entirely unamended and in some cases protected and strengthened, than the continental protestant theology with which it was almost accidentally associated. The incipient presbyterian and congregationalist movements under Cartwright and Browne did express, however awkwardly and inadequately, a desire for a less bureaucratic and above all a more *religious* organisation and life of the church *qua* church. They had a real sense that the church is not, and ought not to appear, a department of the state but a divine society with a supernatural life of its own. In their own ways they were 'high church' movements, and it is the saddest pity that the ancestors of the 'Anglo-catholics' could not possibly have recognised the fact.

It is just here that the disastrous results of the actual procedure of the English Reformation made themselves most plainly apparent, in making the maintenance of the whole settlement as it stood—the new liturgy, the primitive ordinance of episcopacy, the haphazard and ramshackle doctrinal basis (which was only added afterwards) and the incoherent mediaeval organisation, all together—a matter for secular law and the lawyers. It gave the whole structure a rigidity, and an unreality in the sphere of *religion*, which were profoundly unchristian and uncatholic, even when they were protecting primitive christian and catholic conceptions from ignorant assault. Both under Edward VI and Elizabeth and in the seventeenth century the government was vigorously episcopalian in sentiment—but only for its own ends. A score or so of bishops appointed by itself were a deal easier to control and to work through than dozens of locally elected presbyteries and independent *classes*. Puritans were often exasperating and cranky people. Their objections to the use of the Prayer Book were many of them captious and childishly pedantic, and some of them (from my own standpoint) plainly heretical. Yet one does not need to have read the whole story through their eyes to see how the fact that it was always a secular law and a secular authority with which they were confronted and repressed poisoned the whole situation within the church. A few of the Elizabethan episcopalians (*e.g.* Bilson) might argue for the divine authority of episcopacy from the scriptures and the fathers. The great majority preferred to insist on the more obvious fact that it had legal authority from the Queen to compel the puritans to conform to the government's settlement of religion, to which they objected on conscientious grounds. Nor did this offensively erastian handling of the puritan problem cease in the seventeenth century when the 'high' view of episcopacy had come to prevail. On the contrary it was intensified by all but one or two of the Laudian divines, and received perhaps its most odious expression of all in Bishop Parker's *Discourse of Ecclesiastical Politie*, published in 1670.[1]

And so the Elizabethan church got under way somehow, with its extraordinary medley of theological influences, its ubiquitous mediaeval survivals, its Avignon museum of church courts worked by lay lawyers wielding spiritual censures with temporal consequences to enforce financial payments, its criss-cross of episcopal jurisdiction, royal injunctions, parliamentary statutes, spasmodic influence from the Privy Council and the King's Bench, and the over-riding extra-legal authority of the High Commission. It had a liturgy on which it had never been consulted, and no doctrinal standards whatever to start with, save the declaration of Parliament in the Act of Supremacy that no one is to judge 'any matter or cause to be heresy, but any such as heretofore been . . . adjudged to be heresy by the authority of the canonical scriptures or by the first four general councils . . . or such as hereafter shall be ordered, judged or determined to be heresy by the High Court of Parliament of this realm.' All this meant—and was intended to mean—that conformity to the official liturgy and not to belief, of which liturgy is of necessity only an expression, had to be taken as the Anglican basis. Anglicanism might—and did—persecute. But it persecuted in the name of the law of the state and not in the name of truth, except in the rare cases of Arians, etc., who came under the censures of the 'first four general councils'. Of these about a dozen were burned in the next fifty years. (The last is Legatt, burned at Smithfield in 1612, though the writ *de haeretico comburendo* was not formally abolished for yet another fifty years.) On the other hand Anglicanism retained an episcopate and the threefold ministry, for whatever reasons, and with it the possibility of an organic conception of the church; it made an appeal to the practice and teaching of the primitive church, though the consequences of this were hardly understood at the time; and it had a sort of blind instinct for order. It rested really on the fact that Englishmen had to have a church of some

[1] Brilliantly answered from the puritan side by Marvell's *Rehearsal Transprosed*, which is still amusing.

kind, and this was the only kind of church which their government was prepared to let them have.

Actual church life and practice in Elizabeth's reign is not a subject on which churchmen now can look back with a great deal of pride. Every mediaeval abuse in the ecclesiastical machine—pluralism, non-residence, simony, ignorance among the parochial clergy—was still rampant. More than one of the bishops were publicly scandalous, and the general standard of clerical life and devotion was probably a good deal lower than at any other period in our history, not excepting the eighteenth century, which in this respect has been somewhat unfairly abused. Churchgoing was enforced on the laity by the government through the justices of the peace by a system of delations and fines. Secular historians are agreed that down to 1588 a waning majority of Englishmen passively desired the old rites; but the threat of a Spanish invasion to restore them did not assist their popularity. By then a new generation was growing up which had not known the mass. It was the threat of the permanent continuation of the Latin rite in England as a rival to the state liturgy by the new influx of seminary priests and Jesuits ordained abroad which produced the savage new Treason Act of 1581. Under colour of secular politics this made the saying or hearing of mass subject to the ghastly penalty of being half-hanged and cut down alive, and then castrated, disembowelled and finally having the heart plucked from the still living body (which was to be dismembered after death) in the case of priests and laymen; or the atrocity known as *peine forte et dure* in the case of women, *i.e.* being slowly squashed to death with heavy weights. (Margaret Clitheroe took an hour to die in this way at York, for hearing mass.) 189 persons, mostly priests, suffered in this way during the latter part of Elizabeth's reign, to whom must be added thirty-two Franciscans starved to death in prison. 277 had been burned in the much shorter reign of Mary, but the Church of England about levelled the evil score in the seventeenth century. For protestant dissenters the gaol rather than the scaffold was employed, except in the case of those who had the fancy to be Arians or Nestorians.

It is a horrible story all round, and it is not surprising to find that it did not strengthen the hold of organised religion in general on the hearts of the people. There is much scattered but convincing evidence that the great decline in English churchgoing begins in the sixteenth century, not in the eighteenth, as is often supposed. The Reformation found the great mass of the people regular and even somewhat enthusiastic churchgoers. With an inexcusable suddenness, between a Saturday night and a Monday morning at Pentecost 1549, the English liturgical tradition of nearly a thousand years was altogether overturned. Churchgoing never really recovered from that shock. Measures of compulsion kept the churches reasonably full in the reign of Edward VI and the earlier half of Elizabeth's. But voluntary, and above all weekday, churchgoing—on the popularity of which in

England most fifteenth century travellers had remarked—virtually disappeared. Ridley, no prejudiced witness in favour of the old religion, declares: 'It was great pity and a lamentable thing to have seen in many places the people so oathesomely and irreligiously come to the holy communion and to the Common Prayers . . . in comparison of that blind zeal and indiscreet devotion which they had aforetime to these things whereof they understood never one whit'.[1] The same complaint can be paralleled from Latimer, Hooper, Bucer, Bullinger, and every leader connected with the Reformation under Edward VI save Cranmer himself. It is repeated in Acts of Parliament and Royal Proclamations and in private letters and other documents, in a way which leaves no doubt of its substantial truth. There appears to have been no legal compulsion to church in the reign of Mary and little need for it; though there are cases of punishment for interrupting services or otherwise obstructing the restoration of the old worship. But the complaints about non-attendance begin again in the reign of Elizabeth, along with the renewal of measures of compulsion. The truth is that the great mediaeval half-christianised bulk of the population had a tradition of mass-going, and perhaps not much more. Admittedly, that is by no means all that the New Testament understands by christianity. Yet it did bring them to church, and this offered an unparalleled opportunity for teaching them something more. Instead of this they were suddenly compelled to accept not only a totally different conception of worship, but *two* new rites in rapid succession, followed again by two further revolutions in the next six years, each accompanied by conscientious public murders on a nation-wide scale. Is it any wonder that in the general upheaval, the overthrow of traditional sanctities, the bewildering succession of liturgies, the *habit* of churchgoing broke down? And so the greatest opportunity for the effective evangelisation of England that there has ever been was very largely wasted. God alone can justly distribute the blame between reckless innovators and *mumpsimus*-minded conservatives. But that the methods employed—the enforcement by penal statutes of a novel liturgy and a novel theology, on which the church had never even been consulted—were wholly unsuitable for evangelisation will hardly be denied.

All this is not perhaps the conventional Anglican picture of the Reformation—certainly it is not that on which I was brought up. But it seems, nevertheless, to have been what happened, and its consequences are with us all in the English church to-day. Anglicans are apt to be a little sensitive about 'continuity', and it may be as well to make it clear that I do not see how anything in this chapter can be thought to shed new light on that question from either side. As regards the first four years of the reign of Elizabeth, one has only to ask 'What is supposed to be continuous with what?' to throw the whole subject into inextricable confusion for Anglicans and Romanists alike. Granted the formal continuance of the succession in

[1] *Works* (Parker Soc. 1841), *p.* 60.

the case of Archbishop Parker (a matter which can reasonably be left to the available historical evidence to settle) the legitimacy of the existence of Anglicanism to-day, which is presumably what is really in question in this controversy over 'continuity', surely has to be considered on a wider basis, and defended or attacked by more formidable arguments than can be found either in the personal beliefs of Archbishop Cranmer or the singular makeshift of the first years of the Elizabethan settlement.

The Elizabethan church began with no doctrinal basis whatever but the Prayer Book, imposed by a single vote in the House of Lords. Such basis as was reached afterwards was the work of Convocation, supervised by the Queen and the Privy Council and her miscellaneous advisers. The revival of Convocation under Elizabeth is real enough in a way when compared with its treatment under Henry VIII and Edward VI, though it was kept under strict control. It passed the *Articles* in 1563, but it was not allowed to enforce subscription to them even on the clergy. All that was enforceable was the Oath of Supremacy and the Prayer Book, which were imposed by Parliament. The statute of 1571 which did compel the clergy to subscribe to the Articles, significantly imposed it only for certain Articles out of the xxxix, which Parliament selected. Elizabethan Convocations passed quite a number of canons, but they did not by any means all receive the assent of the Crown, and these could not be, and were not, enforced. Convocation and the church which it represented had no power or possibility of touching such part of the Settlement as the government had imposed through Parliament, though it was given scope to administer it independently, under the watchful eye of the Crown.

It is the same story in the seventeenth century. The changes to be made in the Prayer Book after the Hampton Court Conference in 1604 (none of which affected the rite of the eucharist) were decided upon by the king personally, put into form by a group of bishops and privy councillors on the spot, and put out by letters patent. The changes were not of great importance, and nobody raised the least objection to the procedure.[1] The canons of 1604 enacted by Convocation (chiefly through the efforts of Bancroft) received the royal assent. But because they were important and had not been enacted in Parliament, the courts—including the church courts—refused to enforce them on the laity. Bancroft's whole scheme for the reform of the gross practical abuses which had disfigured the Elizabethan church was crippled by the lawyers because it had behind it only the authority of the Convocations.

But, it will be said, at least in 1662 the rights of the church were respected. The 1604 Prayer Book was first revised by the Convocations and only then given legal force by the king in Parliament through an Act of Uniformity. The situation certainly was different in 1662, in that there were now really

[1] See the letter of Toby Matthew, Bishop of Durham, to the Archbishop of York. Cardwell, *Hist. of Conferences*, pp. 161 *sqq.*

three, not two factors in the situation: the church, represented by the Convocations; the newly restored royal executive; and the Parliament which was no longer a royal instrument, but the most powerful factor of the three. The two weaker tried to support one another against the third, and the sequence of events is interesting.

The king returned in May 1660, and the liturgy of 1604 was at once restored in his chapel and in many churches. But the king would not allow Convocation to meet till May 1661. The Savoy Conference between representative episcopalians and presbyterians was already sitting, under a commission from the king to discuss changes in the Prayer Book. It did not break up until July 24th. Convocation filled up its time with preparing new offices for Restoration Day and the baptism of adults, but was forced to adjourn on July 30th, so that it could not begin its consideration of the existing Prayer Book of 1604 until its next group of sessions, on November 21st. Meanwhile the House of Commons as early as the 25th of June had shewn some anger at the possibility that Convocation might make changes in 1604. It proceeded to set up a committee to study 1552 and to 'provide for an effectual conformity to the liturgy of the church for the time to come'. Apparently the Cavalier squires who formed the majority of members were about equally anxious as Cavaliers that no concessions should be made through the Savoy Conference to the lately triumphant puritans, and as squires that no countenance should be given to the 'innovations' of the late Archbishop Laud (though he had made none in the English Prayer Book) who had been violently unpopular with the squirearchy for his opposition to enclosures. They do not appear to have liked the Book of 1552, for by the 9th of July they had passed through all its stages in the lower house a 'Bill for the Uniformity of Public Prayer and the Administration of the Sacraments', to which the Book of 1604 without change was annexed. This was at once sent to the Lords, but Parliament adjourned on July 30th before the Lords had considered it. It did not meet again till November 20th, the day before Convocation began its revision of 1604. The Convocations took just a month over their revision (Nov. 21st to Dec. 20th—a contrast with the twenty-five years occupied in this century!). Despite pressure from the Commons to proceed with the Bill enforcing 1604, the Lords at the request of the king agreed to await the result of Convocation's work. But on the 14th of February, before receiving the new Book from Convocation, they gave a first reading to the Bill restoring 1604, and a second reading on the 17th, after which it was sent to a select committee. It was a fairly strong hint to Convocation. The unrevised Book of 1604 required only one more reading in the Lords to be presented for the Royal Assent—which could hardly have been refused—and so to become law.

Meanwhile the Book as revised by Convocation had been sent to the Privy Council, where certain changes seem to have been made, of which the only one of importance was the restoration of the 'Black Rubric' or 'Declaration on Kneeling' at communion. This had been added by the Privy Council in 1552 and omitted in 1559 and 1604; it was now reinserted with the change of the denial of 'any *corporal* presence of Christ's actual flesh and blood' in the sacrament, for the '*real and essential* presence' denied in 1552.[1] The re-insertion of this 'Declaration' had already been demanded by the puritans and refused by the bishops at the Savoy Conference; it had deliberately not been reinserted by Convocation. The new Book was received by the Lords, who gave it a third reading without change on April 9th, and sent it down to the Commons.

There it provoked a commotion by the number of its changes from 1604 —some 600—and a close comparison of the two Books was instituted. It was found that though numerous they were almost all only verbal or stylistic. Even so, it was only by 96 votes to 90 that the Commons decided not to vote on them one by one; and they did pass a resolution that they had 'a full right' to reconsider any changes Convocation had made. Meanwhile Convocation had accepted the situation gracefully. On March 5th, the Bishops of S. Asaph, Carlisle and Chester were deputed by both Houses to review 'the emendations or other alterations made in the Book of Common Prayer by the House (*sic*) of Parliament' and assent to them. No changes made in Parliament were then before them, for neither House had yet voted on the Book (and in fact none were made there at all, but only in the Privy Council). The commission can only have been prospective. No doubt the proprieties were saved, even as regards the 'Black Rubric', by the affirmative votes of these three bishops in the House of Lords. But Convocation could hardly have found a more discreet way of recognising that in respect of the liturgy its function amounted in practice to not much more than those of a drafting committee for Parliament. There was no idea in 1662 (as was proposed in 1927-8) of sending the Book back to the Convocations after it had been given statutory authority by the king in Parliament to receive 'spiritual authority' from the clergy.

It has often been remarked that in their revision the Convocations seem to have disregarded the king's suggestion that 1604 should be compared 'with the most ancient liturgies which have been used in the church in the primitive and purest times'. At all events they put forward no recommendations for such changes in Cranmer's Shape of the Liturgy as must have been suggested by comparisons of this kind. Yet such changes had been made in practice on his own authority by Bishop Overall (*d.* 1615), and had been officially imposed in Scotland by Laud's Scottish Book of 1637; some of the most prominent revisers in 1662 are known to have desired

---

[1] C. W. Dugmore, *op. cit., pp.* 74 *sq.* is not convincing that no change of meaning was intended by the change of wording in 1662; he has not noticed that the Declaration was only added after the Book had finally left Convocation, which had refused the puritan request for its replacement.

them in the English rite. But the king had also charged them to avoid 'as much as may be all unnecessary alterations of the forms and liturgy wherewith the people are already acquainted'. It was impossible to carry out both instructions; and Convocation received from Parliament before, during and after its revision such plain intimations that it would be allowed to make none but the slightest changes in 1604 (which as regards the eucharist is 1552, except for the single change in the words of administration made in 1559) that it was not worth while to propose or discuss them. To have done so would undoubtedly have resulted forthwith in Parliament's re-enacting 1604 without change.

In revising the rite of the eucharist, therefore, Convocation in 1662 had to content itself with registering the general reaction against Cranmer's Zwinglianism which had taken place in the course of a century, by changes in terminology—'consecrated bread and wine' for 'bread and wine', and so forth; and by ordering greater decency of practice, e.g. that when the consecrated elements were replaced upon the altar after communion it should be done 'reverently', and that they were to be covered with a linen cloth, and reverently consumed after the blessing, not taken home by the parson for secular use.

Two changes in the rite were made, however, almost surreptitiously, which made it easier to interpret Cranmer's rite along the lines of the 'four-action shape' of the liturgy. They restored both the offertory of the elements and the fraction, which Cranmer had deliberately omitted.

By ordering that the 'alms' before the 'prayer for the church' should be offered by the priest at the altar and not placed in the 'poor men's box' by the churchwardens, 1662 restored the idea of an 'offering' of something material at this point of the rite, which Cranmer had been so careful to eliminate. And they implemented this by adding the two words 'and oblations' to the clause of the following 'prayer for the church'—'We beseech Thee ... to accept our alms *and oblations*'. But they went further. By directing that the bread and wine were to be placed upon the altar immediately after the alms and before this prayer was said, they made it possible to understand these words 'and' oblations' as referring to the eucharistic bread and wine. This interpretation of the words is hardly more than an inference, though it is one which is commonly made nowadays, and which was made by Bishop Simon Patrick of Ely early in the eighteenth century. But it seems to have been proved beyond reasonable question that by 'oblations' the revisers themselves in 1662 meant only 'financial contributions for the support of the clergy' as distinct from 'alms' for other charitable objects.[1]

It was certainly desirable to restore the offertory, and a good thing though not an absolute necessity to have a prayer referring to it. But the position in which it was thought necessary to place it in order to smuggle it

[1] See J. Dowden, *Further Studies in the Prayer Book*, London, 1908, pp. 176 sqq.

through Parliament under cover of the collection had a serious disadvantage. It greatly confused the clear outline of the rite as Cranmer had left it from the point of view of construction, even though it made it somewhat easier to read a catholic interpretation into Cranmer's wording. The offertory of bread and wine placed *before* the 'prayer for the church' (representing the old intercessions of the synaxis) is thus thrust back out of the eucharist proper into the synaxis. This is only an archaeological point, of no importance in itself. But the offertory is thus separated from the consecration by the whole length of the intercessions (the longest prayer in the rite) and the long and short exhortations, the confession, absolution and comfortable words, before we reach even the eucharistic dialogue and preface. And this again is separated from what the revisers of 1662 were the first to call the 'prayer of consecration' by the intervening 'prayer of humble access'. This long sagging gap between offertory and consecration is one of the chief constructional weaknesses of our present rite, dissociating the church's offering from its acceptance. One result has been the neglect of the meaning of the offertory in our devotional tradition, with the consequent distortion of the eucharist into something in which we get rather than give. Cranmer's replacement of the offering of bread and wine (inseparably connected with the idea of *self*-offering by the people's oblation at the altar) by his *new* expression of self-offering in the exhortations, confession, etc. is also obscured by the disconnection of the offering of the elements from the exhortations, confession etc., by the intervening intercessions. I do not think most people now regard these devotions as a self-oblation at all, as Cranmer intended. They are treated as misplaced 'communion devotions' or, by some bishops, misplaced 'consecration devotions'. Nothing could have been further from Cranmer's mind. The muddle is completed by treating the so-called 'prayer of oblation' as though it were a misplaced 'second half' of the eucharistic prayer instead of a 'thanksgiving for communion', as he clearly intended.[1] If the current attempts to found christian sociological doctrine on the eucharistic offertory are to receive any satisfactory expression or even meaning in our rite, something will have to be done to clear up this structural confusion which the well-meaning re-introduction of an offertory of the elements at so awkward a position in 1662 has created.

[1] I have never seen any official consideration of the fact that our present 'prayer of oblation' was in content originally intended for an *offertory* prayer (*cf. p.* 731 *n.*). Instead of this we have the perpetual episcopal harping on the idea of placing it after the prayer of consecration, despite the fact that Cranmer after trying it there, rightly saw that it was entirely unsuitable for such a position, and deliberately removed it. He was an admirable liturgist. If you share his theology you had much better use his liturgy as he left it, for a better expression of that theology will not be achieved by tinkering with his rite. If you do *not* share his theology, you will not achieve the expression of a different doctrine merely by shuffling the parts of his rite as they stand, because the *words* of a prayer have a meaning. (As an offertory prayer the prayer of oblation would not actually need the change of a word, though

1662 also restored the fraction, as the puritans desired, along with the other manual acts. The seventeenth century puritans as Calvinists attached great importance to the fraction,[1] whereas Zwinglians objected to it strongly, in accordance with their special idea of dissociating the reception of the bread and wine altogether from the 'eating and drinking of Christ's Flesh and Blood'. In replacing the manual acts the revisers were therefore in accord with the general anti-Zwinglian movement of the time, and also protesting against Cranmer's notion that the recitation of the institution was directed to the *hearers* only and had no reference to the elements. On the other hand, by including the fraction in the prayer instead of placing it at its primitive position before communion, they obscured its meaning and confused the outline of the rite. Probably they were influenced to do so not so much out of fear of protestant opposition—Baxter's rite has it after the prayer before the communion, in the primitive position—as in order not to arouse the attention of Parliament to the fact that they had here made a change of some importance from 1604.

The revision of 1662 thus tried to consolidate the general reaction from the ideas expressed by Cranmer in his liturgy, while retaining the whole substance of his liturgy unchanged. It is no wonder that from the point of view of liturgical construction the resulting rite is incoherent, and appears to be a confused succession of parts without a logical design as a whole. That is because the Carolines were obliged to try to interpret in terms of patristic theology a rite which was designed to express a wholly different idea. What I am concerned to point out is that the unsatisfactory result is not due to Cranmer, whose original rite expressed the real meaning of its author about as clearly and beautifully as a rite can do. Nor can it be fairly blamed on the revisers when the limitations under which they knew they were obliged to work are considered. It was the procedure of 1662 which was at fault. The truth is that under cover of a formal consultation of the church the essential process of the Edwardian, Marian and Elizabethan settlements was followed once more in that under Charles II, though with a considerable shift in the balance of the secular power imposing it.

The king himself seems never to have shared the sentimental delusion of the Cavalier Parliament that after 'the late troubles' the state's organisation, political and religious, could be restored exactly as it had been in his father's golden days. Even if it had been possible, he cherished other ideals. But Parliament did intend this, and throughout insisted on making the Restoration settlement of the church so far as possible a return to the *status quo*. The return to the 1604 liturgy was part of a reactionary policy intended to apply to every aspect of life. As the Act of Uniformity declares: 'Now in

'to be *made* a reasonable and lively sacrifice' would avoid the suggestion of Pelagianism; and 'ourselves, our *lives and labours*' would more fully express self-oblation than 'ourselves, our souls and bodies', which is tautologous.)

[1] *Cf. p.* 610.

regard that nothing conduceth more to the settling of the Peace of this Nation . . . than an Universal agreement in the Public Worship of Almighty God; and to the intent that every person within this Realm may certainly know the rule to which he is to conform in public worship . . . Be it enacted by the King's most Excellent Majesty, by the advice and with the consent etc. . . . that all and singular Ministers in any Cathedral Collegiate or Parish church or chapel or other place of public worship within this Realm . . . shall be bound to say and use . . . the said Book annexed and joined to this present Act.'

What is too little regarded among us now is that all this is something which is not merely intended to control the clergy. It is part of a system for *'every person within this realm'*. It was intended that no judge should sit upon the Bench, no member take his seat in Parliament, no don lecture in law or physic at the University, no officer hold a commission in the Army or Navy, no village schoolmaster teach his class, no town councillor discuss a rate—before they, too, had each given proof of 'conformity' to the settlement. The lay citizen might be fined for non-attendance at his parish church, by justices who had to take the declaration of assent before they could be of the commission of the peace, just as the clergy must do before they could hold an ecclesiastical preferment. The layman could be punished for attending an unlawful conventicle at which other forms were used, just as the clergy could be legally punished if they contravened the Act in taking the services. It is a real attempt to restore that immense system of state-control of conscience which Cromwell and Cranmer had dreamed of, and which Laud had maddened his opponents by putting into force a generation before. The only change from Cranmer's ideal is that the controller of conscience is no longer in anything but name the personal monarch. It is now the totalitarian Parliament, which had exercised so decisive an influence in the retention of Cranmer's liturgy without substantial change.

The attempted restoration was no longer possible. The royal executive, to say the least, had no desire to persecute recusants. Protestant dissent was organised, and too powerful to be coerced. The Clarendon Code under which the dissenters groaned was at least a recognition that their organised existence must be tolerated. Before a generation had passed the whole system had broken down. The 'high churchmen' of Queen Anne's reign (when the term first comes into use) and the 'high Tory' squires might rage at the way 'Dissenters and Sectaries are suffered to pull down the church'. What was really crumbling was the state's attempted control of conscience, and with it Cranmer's notion of the church. A century before or after 1720 the Church of England might have been invigorated by the process. As things were it was enfeebled, because the state had reduced the church to utter dependence on itself, and then lost interest in it without abandoning it to its own devices. Convocation, the traditional organ of the church's own life, had been put to silence; but the church could no longer rely on the Hanoverian Crown and the Whig Parliament to some extent to supply the loss by their interest in its life and needs, as the Tudor Crown and the Stuart Parliaments had done. The eighteenth century church is often reproached for its worldliness and for reliance on its remaining social privilege and state establishment. But what else was left it to rely on? The state had ordered its liturgy, and removed it altogether from the church's control by freezing it rigid, down to the last comma, in the form of a secular statute. The state had left it church courts, and then insisted that they should administer not canon law but new parliamentary statutes, wherever the two might differ. The state had retained the episcopate, and insisted that it must choose its members with a primary regard for the state's needs, not those of the church. There was no single form of expression necessary to the corporate life of any society which the eighteenth century state did not completely usurp in the case of the Church of England. Of course the church grew to be parasitic upon the state. In the particular case of the liturgy, it is seen in the way in which eighteenth century churchmen increasingly based the worship of the church not on her own doctrinal interpretation of it but on the mechanical fulfilling of the Act of Uniformity, as 'the incomparable liturgy with which the wisdom of our legislature had endowed us', as Archbishop Herring of Canterbury (1747–57) termed it. And as soon as Cranmer's liturgy was thus left to be self-interpreting, it had its natural consequence in the eighteenth century Neo-Zwinglian movement in Anglicanism.

By the nineteenth century the Church of England had become an instrument virtually useless to the state for the control of conscience, not because the state had lost its hold on the church, but because the church had lost its hold on the majority of the people. The alliance of church and state remained from the past as a strong but entirely static tradition, with which the increasingly secularised state refused to encumber itself in fresh ways as its own activities and interests continually expanded to meet modern conditions. The effective links between church and state were now the lawyers, with their ideals of uniformity, of immutable administration according to precedent, and of the perpetual authority and exact execution of every statute left unrepealed by the legislature. Cranmer had placed them in control of the church's life in the quite different circumstances of the agricultural England of the sixteenth century. It is highly disputable whether the experiment can be considered a success at any period. The first Act of Uniformity produced rebellions almost on the scale of a civil war. The second produced chaos, and determined the country to endorse the Marian refusal to face the new problems presented for religion by post-mediaeval conditions in any constructive way at all. The third resulted in the organisation of the English recusant body, and the fourth in the organisation of English protestant dissent. I am not contending that the English church has not a right to a determined faith and worship. Of course it has.

But the whole method of arriving at them adopted in the sixteenth century seems to have been unsuitable and wrong in itself, though there may be two opinions about the possibility of any other method at the time. What is not disputable is that the perpetuation of it after the Industrial Revolution and right down to the present day as a special *régime* within the established church is a grotesque anachronism. Its whole *raison d'être* in the elaborate system of state control of conscience, of which it had still formed a part even at the Restoration, has disappeared piecemeal in the meanwhile.

As things stood at the beginning of the nineteenth century, though the 'Evangelical Revival' might restore the personal piety of individuals within the existing system, the church as a church could not undertake new tasks to meet changed conditions, or even hope to recover the ground lost in its pastoral activities since the beginning of the Industrial Revolution. The only way to an effective recovery of corporate life lay in an appeal *beyond* the Church of England itself and what the state had made of it, to the primitive and undivided church. Fortunately the right to make that appeal had been claimed, ineffectually enough as it seemed at the time, by the Elizabethan Convocations. It had been repeated at intervals since by the Carolines and the Non-jurors.

This way the Oxford Movement took, and for all its inconvenient and unsatisfactorily archaeological character, the appeal was surprisingly successful. It was opposed continuously by the nineteenth century state, clinging for what it was still worth to the tradition of control, and inspired by the tenacious memories of the lawyers. It was opposed, too, as was natural, by the most part of the state-appointed bishops; and, as was deplorable but inevitable, by all that was still living in the genuinely religious tradition of protestantism which had grown up in England since the sixteenth century. Among the general English public it was opposed by the national tendency to conservatism and that peculiar English taste for preserving monuments of the past as purposeless ruins scrupulously kept ruinous by the care of a government department. And yet, by the beginning of the twentieth century, the English church as a whole, not merely the professed followers of the Oxford Movement, was beginning to be convinced that it had a divine life of its own, quite distinct from that of even a christian state. In reality this was a denial of the whole basis upon which Cranmer had carried through the English Reformation. Old habits of thought might persist illogically along with it for a while, but sooner or later it would necessitate a thorough reconstruction of the life of the English church on a different basis.

As these things happened in England and in the English church, this was not at all the standpoint from which matters were approached. Just as in the sixteenth century, so in the twentieth, attention was centred on practice not theory, and the core of christian practice is the liturgy. A parliamentary agitation for the more exact performance of the statutory liturgy by the clergy brought about a Royal Commission, whose report in 1906 carefully analysed the symptoms but only hinted at the real cause of the disorders. (1) 'The law of public worship in the Church of England is too narrow for the religious life of this generation', and the church possessed no sufficient powers to adjust its law to the needs of its life. (2) 'The machinery for discipline has broken down', inasmuch as too large a number of churchmen now refused to accept the decisions of the present erastian church courts as binding in conscience to allow that machinery to work. In other words, by 1906 a large proportion of churchmen no longer accepted the principle of parliamentary control of faith and worship even within the established church. The rest of the population had long ago abandoned that principle for themselves. Presumably the system was at an end.

Nothing, however, seems to have been further from anyone's thoughts at the time; and nobody seems to have questioned publicly the suitability in the circumstances of the procedure of 1662, with Convocation as a drafting committee and Parliament in final control. Perhaps no other procedure would have stood any chance of acceptance at that moment, though that shrewd man of affairs Archbishop Davidson had his misgivings from the start as to the outcome,[1] while bravely continuing to do his best to meet the difficulties as they arose during the next twenty-five years. Royal Letters of Business were issued to the Convocations in November 1906 authorising them to present a 'Report' to the Crown on 'the desirability and the form and contents . . . of any modifications of the existing law relating to the conduct of Divine Service and to the ornaments and fittings of churches'. The very terms of this document shew how completely Cranmer's conception of the clergy as 'the king's ministers of Christ's Word'—the department of public worship—still governed the whole situation in the minds of the lawyers, and was at least acquiesced in by the bishops. There was a general intention among the latter, 'First, that there should be a minimum of change; and next, that there should be no change that in any sort of way could honestly be said to touch doctrine at all.'[2] This was the policy of 1662. The work along these lines was in sight of completion in the summer of 1914, when war postponed its final stages.

When it was being carried forward again early in 1918 the bishops seem to have drifted into a quite new attitude towards their task, without ever definitely bringing themselves to face the fact that they had done so, and that it might have awkward consequences. They were no longer occupied with revising details of the existing statutory rite with a view to making its legal enforcement more practicable. They were trying to improve the Church of England's eucharistic rite considered simply as a rite, from the

---

[1] *Randall Davidson*, by Dr. G. K. A. Bell, I, *pp. 650 sqq.*
[2] Dr. G. F. Browne, then Bishop of Bristol, summarising the progress of revision in Feb. 1914.

point of view of liturgy not of law. They could not, of course, forget the over-riding necessity of steering the result through Parliament. This probably affected their proposals in 1927 to a larger extent than they made public, while its effect upon the changes between 1927 and 1928 was admitted and obvious. Nevertheless they began in 1918 to take the very course which the revisers of 1662 had refrained from adopting, as certain to be disallowed by Parliament. The bishops attacked their new task with very little knowledge of the theoretical and historical questions involved (though the appointment of Bishop Frere to Truro in 1921 secured that adequate information was at all events available on the bench), with no scientific appreciation of how to set about constructing a liturgy, and in some cases without much interest in the subject of worship for its own sake. Consequently, they seem never to have envisaged their new rite sufficiently as a whole; and they never succeeded in clearing their minds as to what they meant their liturgy to do, *i.e.* as to what that eucharistic action is which the liturgy performs. They were obviously much hampered by trying to produce something upon which they could agree among themselves while maintaining unresolved a great diversity of eucharistic theology.

Two years were occupied in this new approach to their task without attracting much public attention, and it is just conceivable that if the results had been presented to Parliament in 1920 they would have been enacted. But the Enabling Act of 1919 had just set up what was destined to turn out to be another disappointing instalment of the reconstruction of the church, in the shape of the National Assembly of the Church of England. To this body Parliament had delegated some of its legislative powers in the affairs of the church, but in all major matters it could only forward measures for the approval or disallowance (but not the amendment) of Parliament. Whatever may be the relation of Convocation to Parliament, there can be no doubt that Parliament was given, explicitly and deliberately, a veto over the measures of the Church Assembly; and that the church whether wisely or not had knowingly accepted that fact when the Assembly was set up. Nevertheless, Archbishop Davidson had formally pledged himself in the House of Lords that the Assembly should be consulted on Prayer Book Revision. The fact that the revision of the Prayer Book ultimately came before Parliament from the Assembly, not Convocation, gave Parliament an unassailable right, if it wanted one, to reject it.

Nevertheless, seven more years were spent in getting the endorsement of this not very impressive body for the bishops' new proposals, since it insisted with the ardour and unwisdom of youth in doing what amounted in the end to the same work all over again for itself. The delay was fatal. The debates in the Assembly roused party feeling to great exasperation in the church and gave time for the launching of outside campaigns of various kinds which attracted much public attention.

The revision had assumed the form not of amendments to 1662 but of a complete alternative rite, incorporating most of the material of 1662 with some additions or alterations, but designed to be used where desired *instead of* 1662. The bishops had rashly wandered into a position where they could be represented as having produced a new and different rite as their answer to Parliament's instructions to observe the old one better. It was precisely the position avoided in 1662, and the result was what it would have been in like case. The Lords passed the Book of 1927, as the Lords might have passed a more heavily revised Book in 1662; but the Commons rejected it, as the Commons would undoubtedly have done then. A fresh attempt to pass what amounted to the rejected book toned down to appease the prejudices of the Commons was again rejected by a slightly larger majority in 1928. This left 1662 without change as the only statutory liturgy, as it is to the present day. Just so in 1662 the Commons were prepared to re-enact the existing Book of 1604 without change, if Convocation had attempted to make any but minor revisions. And as 1662 is substantially the rite of 1604, 1559, and 1552, it can reasonably be said that Parliament has stood throughout for one thing, the settlement which Cranmer originally imposed on the church by its means.

. . . . .

If this book should meet with a reader who is not an Anglican, he may easily find a lack of relation between this chapter and the rest of the book. If it does not interest him, I am sorry. But the fact is that I am an Anglican, and therefore could not omit it; and it does not impair whatever usefulness to his liturgical studies there may be in what precedes it. And if the Anglican reader is distressed by some things in it, I am sorry. But the fact is that I am distressed, too; and therefore I could not omit it, though I would have been glad to do so. The book which precedes it is solid work, and from the general standpoint of the subject is—so far as I can judge—more important. I would ask him to forget this last chapter and return and judge the book only by what precedes it, were it not that I believe that he will find that some things (at least) in this last chapter follow necessarily for him from what has gone before.

ADDITIONAL NOTE:

## THE PRESENT LITURGICAL POSITION IN THE CHURCH OF ENGLAND

THE foregoing chapter tells a story one might have supposed sufficiently well known in most of its aspects for its practical lessons to be understood and applied by Anglicans in the present notorious liturgical difficulties of the Church of England. Yet a survey of the official proposals to remedy those difficulties during the last forty years reveals an inattention to their root causes and real nature so marked and continuous as almost to suggest a deliberate policy. By a natural consequence the attempted remedies have mostly aggravated the disorder. It is now agreed on all hands that the resulting state of affairs is no longer merely an inconvenience and a scandal but has become a serious handicap to the life and work of the English church. We have to face the facts that though the Church of England has an official liturgy more rigidly and minutely prescribed in its details than that of almost any other church in christendom; and though its observance is fortified by a most complicated and formidable system of courts and legal penalties, such as no other religious society in history has ever found necessary to secure the observance of its rites, yet the Church of England to-day presents a liturgical disorganisation such as is found in no other christian body, and exhibits a liturgical diversity not commonly found in bodies which do not profess to have any set liturgy at all.

A long course of mishandling has made this a very sore subject for any Anglican to touch, and I have no wish at all to wound the consciences of others or to appear disrespectful to authority. Yet some plainness of speech seems to be necessary if this matter is to be dealt with at all, and I quite expect to be freely criticised in my own turn. I write about it only as a private person who has tried to give what study and thought he can to it from a somewhat detached position, with the aid of opportunities for observation afforded by preaching in a good many churches in different parts of the country, and after two years' practical experience of this difficulty while serving a parochial church, in which circumstances made it somewhat specially obvious, at the beginning of this war. For what the opinion is worth, I should say that the finding of an effective remedy is becoming a matter of real pastoral urgency. But I cannot conceive of any way in which the present state of affairs could be much amended unless and until its neglected causes are understood and taken into account, first of all by the bishops, but also in a general way by the church at large. What is necessary is an approach to the whole question along quite different lines from those we have hitherto tried.

Before preparing this Note I read or re-read and carefully analysed some forty episcopal Charges and kindred documents which adverted to the problem between 1929 and 1939. So far as I understand these pronouncements, the official view of the cause of the evil is that it is due: (1) To the culpable irresponsibility of large sections of the clergy, and particularly of the 'high church' clergy, in making changes in the legal liturgy at their own discretion; (2) To the action of Parliament in 1927–8, when it rejected a revised liturgy which had taken the bishops more than twenty years to devise, and thus frustrated the only remedy for the liturgical situation which had any chance whatever of success. (Before considering this diagnosis it is right also to report that no one of these documents admits that the episcopate bears any special responsibility for the development of such a situation; and that only two suggest that the episcopate as such might have a more creative function on the eucharistic worship of the church than securing that 'the law', ecclesiastical or civil, is carried out.)

It is no doubt easy for those without experience of the thorny responsibilities of Anglican bishops to criticise their utterances. But this view of the causes of our troubles seems so superficial as to be almost entirely untrue. It is, of course, a fact that many of the clergy do alter the official liturgy considerably, but the practice is by no means confined to any one school of thought. There must be some powerful cause at work to induce them to do this so generally as they do, for they are not as a whole an irresponsible body of men. It is nowadays a frequent observation even with unbelievers that the English parochial clergy have a high professional standard.[1] So far as my reading carries me, they nowadays perform their always difficult and in these days often thankless duties with a steady devotion at least equal to that displayed by their predecessors at any previous period in the history of the English church, and incomparably better than in some periods which pass for 'reformed'. And I have found from my own observation that it is often those clergy, of all schools of thought without exception, who are most zealous and attentive to their pastoral duty who are now least concerned to observe the statutory rite with any exactness; while it is, on the whole, the less energetic and devout (again of all schools of thought) in whom the bishops would find least to complain of in this respect. There is surely something here which deserves careful consideration rather than the shrill accusations of 'disloyalty' with which it has too often been treated by the authorities.

As for the action of Parliament in 1928, it really altered nothing in the whole situation—except the bishops' own respect for the law of the land. It is true that Parliament then re-asserted firmly, but not without warrant or altogether unexpectedly, the principle of its own final control of the liturgy, and especially the eucharistic rite, of the established church. This was the unmistakeable tenor of the two debates in the Commons. But there was nothing new in this. It was the principle established by Cranmer himself, the principle for which Parliament had always stood since his day. In 1552 and 1559 Parliament had imposed Cranmer's rite without consultation with the church. In 1662 it had made it clear that it would tolerate no considerable changes in that rite by the bishops or Convocation. The decision of 1928 was not a 'snap' vote; it was reached by an increased majority after a year's reflection. But all the same, it was a quite unreal decision, in the sense that it had no effect. Parliament voted that the church

[1] See e.g. the remarkable tribute paid to them by Dr. C. E. M. Joad, *God and Evil* (London, 1942), p. 353. The parochial clergy are entitled to set such appreciations from those outside the church (and even outside christianity) against the criticisms and persistently ungenerous treatment which they receive from some members of the Church Assembly.

should use only the legal rite of 1662, exactly and without change. The church continued to use it as it had been doing before 1928, with a multitude of unofficial changes. It is true that the new rite of 1928 did not come into use. But that had nothing to do with Parliament's refusal to sanction it. Neither the bishops nor the church at large paid any attention to that. The rite of 1928 did not come into use only because the church—the worshipping clergy and people—after due consideration found it did not like it enough to use it instead of all the other variants of 1662.

The real causes of the present situation go much deeper than 1928, which was only an incident, and in retrospect a curiously futile incident from the point of view of all concerned. The bishops since then have not been facing a new situation at all, or one unexampled in past history, but one which has been recurrent in different connections in the English church at intervals ever since the sixteenth century, and which is due to a difficulty inherent in the whole position of the Establishment as Cranmer left it. In the late summer of 1549 officials and supporters of the government were already complaining loudly that the clergy and people were not properly carrying out the clear directions of the legislature as to the way in which they were to worship God. At this stage the complaint was chiefly what it was before 1928, that the legal liturgy was being assimilated, so far as the worshippers dared do so, to the old mass. Under Elizabeth a 'long term' policy was tried with such conservatives. It took a long while to get the legal liturgy observed at all exactly in some places, especially in the North. But when the performance of and attendance at the old rites was finally made a matter of high treason, those whose theological aversion to the legal liturgy and attachment to the old one could not be broken even by the savage penalties then imposed were at least driven from the publicity of the churches to worship in secret.

Even so, the result was not that general 'Uniformity' of public worship on the legal model which the government intended, though the variations now came from a different source. The conservatives had been driven out of the churches, but the puritans were still inside them; and they were equally averse to the use of many things in the parliamentary liturgy, though on different grounds. The politically nominated bishops tried to do their duty by enforcing 'conformity' on all alike. The seventeenth century theological controversies between Anglicans and puritans rather disguise from us the real issues between them in these Elizabethan troubles. A specifically Anglican theological position was only in process of evolution in the generation of Jewel and Hooker. Some of the bishops themselves were then as thoroughly Calvinist in doctrine as any puritan, while others, e.g. Guest, could probably have brought themselves to use the actual language of the Roman missal without much theological scruple. What they were all enforcing was not dogma but law. What the bishops upheld against papist and puritan alike was the right of the state to enforce a single form of public worship in the practice of all its citizens regardless of their different private beliefs.

This was no doubt partly due to the application of accepted mediaeval principles of society. But before the Anglican Reformation was fifty years old it had been demonstrated that the system was simply unworkable on the basis of a purely national church. There was too much room for confusion between the national church *qua* church and the political behests of the national government acting altogether outside its proper sphere. A sincere man's worship expresses his own belief and is moulded by it—or it dies of unreality. Mere political enforcement of a form by the state brings neither a practical conformity to the law nor theological agreement, but the decay of religion. If worship is a matter only of law, a conviction of difference of belief will send men out of the church rather than join in its worship, as happened with the Elizabethan papists. Where theological differences are still only instinctively and incipiently felt, men may still remain uneasily within the state church, but they will feel bound to alter its worship to express their own beliefs, as happened with the Elizabethan puritans. Bancroft before he became a bishop wrote indignantly of the puritans that 'every man useth and refuseth what he listeth' of the Prayer Book, and that many bishops connived out of sympathy, or from 'their desire to be at ease and quietness to think upon their own affairs.'[1]

Bancroft was of the new Anglican school which thought in terms of doctrine, and which was apt to speak contemptuously of the Elizabethan bishops. But these neo-Anglicans had this much justification, that they knew as no other generation since has known or could know that the elaboration of a properly Anglican doctrinal position was accomplished only just in time to save the English church from complete disintegration by decay. One has only to study the unemotional, purely factual, reports on the growing disorganisation of church life and the general emptiness of the churches, and the increasing neglect of all worship, which reached the Privy Council in a steady stream from the Judges of Assize and the emissaries of the Ecclesiastical Commission from all over the country in the 80's and 90's of the sixteenth century,[2] to be well aware that the Church of England itself is no exception to the rule that worship *must* express belief, or it dies. It was the new Anglican doctrinal basis which gave the motive and the inspiration for that thorough reorganisation of the church under Bancroft and his contemporaries, which deserves to rank beside the Reformation under Cranmer and the Renewals of the nineteenth century

---

[1] *A Survey of the Pretended Holy Discipline* (1593), p. 249.
[2] They have to be extracted from the *Calendar of State Papers* (*Domestic*) and similar collections (*e.g. The Cecil Papers* calendared by the Historical MSS. Commission). So far as I know no published work has ever done full justice to the lamentable picture they draw or to the unanimity with which they draw it. But there are some fairly startling extracts in Bishop Frere's essay on *The Church under Queen Elizabeth and James I.*

in the history of Anglicanism. The title which R. G. Usher chose for his account of it—*The Reconstruction of the English Church*[1]—involves no exaggeration of its scope, though the work then accomplished has unaccountably been underestimated in most of our manuals of church history. The theological reconstruction due to Jewel and Hooker and their successors owed little doctrinally to Cranmer himself, just as the practical reconstruction by Bancroft in many things ran directly counter to Cranmer's measures. The fact that this new creation of an Anglican position was forced to take over Cranmer's liturgy because the state and not the church had absolute control of worship was an element of weakness in this reconstruction which would make itself felt in the future in more than one way.

I do not propose to follow the case further here. It is sufficiently plain that the modern Anglican episcopate of the nineteenth and twentieth centuries has been confronted by something not unlike the Elizabethan situation. And they have met it with much the same policy as their Elizabethan predecessors. They fell back at first on the expedient of trying to make Anglicans of very diverse doctrinal beliefs about the eucharist all use the same statutory liturgy in the same way, while allowing them to retain their respective theologies. It was the Elizabethan predicament. Theology and thought were free, but the liturgy was to be rigidly stereotyped by the legislation of the state, which controlled the practice of public worship in church through its courts and judges, and appointed the bishops who administered the relevant statutes. But there was this difference in the nineteenth century from the earlier situation. The state was no longer effectively totalitarian in the sphere of religion; the earlier dissenters had taught it that its power had limits in that direction. The mere fact that worship could now legally be offered outside the Establishment in other ways than the law prescribed had made the nineteenth century state much less directly interested in the enforcement of its own laws about worship even within the Establishment. In the sixteenth and seventeenth centuries it was a primary object of policy, and the state had exerted its full power to this end, so that those who would not use the legal liturgy were at least driven out of the church. In the nineteenth century there were limits beyond which the state and public opinion would not go. Public opinion was still for a while prepared to tolerate rioting in defence of the statutory liturgy; the state by a miscalculation found itself imprisoning recalcitrant clergymen, and quickly withdrew from that embarassing position. But no one was prepared to go to the length of torture or the death penalty to enforce the use of the Book of Common Prayer. These had been found necessary under Elizabeth, and their disuse had led to the establishment of dissent outside the church. When riots and prosecutions failed to check innovation there was no effective remedy for what amounted to dissent within the church. So it came about that those whose theological beliefs led them in

[1] 2 vols., London, 1910.

the nineteenth century to vary the statutory way of worship were able to remain, somewhat uncomfortably, within the church, and still to express their beliefs in this way. They suffered the same sort of harassing from their bishops for their conduct as had the Elizabethan puritans for the same conduct; and many of them developed much of the 'Martin Marprelate' attitude towards bishops in consequence, despite their warm belief in the doctrine of Apostolic Succession. But the half-heartedness of the state in support of its own ecclesiastical statutes prevented their position in the church from being made quite impossible. And once more, many of the bishops connived, either out of sympathy or from 'their desire to be at case and quietness to think upon their own affairs'.

It is impossible not to sympathise with the Victorian and Edwardian bishops. When one has said all that is true about the theological tradition which had never quite been broken from Elizabethans like Guest and Bilson through the Carolines and Non-Jurors and later eighteenth century high churchmen to men like Hugh James Rose, it must still be admitted that much of the teaching which followed from the Oxford Movement amounted to a drastic revolution so far as the normal current Anglican theology was concerned. The same is true also of the consequences of the subsequent 'liberal' upheaval in theology. Between them these movements made a thorough reconstruction of the 'official' Anglican theological tradition about the eucharist, which descended from Hooker through Waterland, a necessity. It was fantastic to suppose that movements of theological thought of this magnitude would not be reflected in public worship. They followed inevitably. The 'catholicising' changes were the earlier and the more obvious. But this was only because the Oxford Movement began earlier than its rival, and its disciples were more interested in worship as such than were the 'liberals.' Once the latter had made good their right to exist within the Establishment, their changes in the conduct of public worship were no less far-reaching than those of the 'ritualists', though they often took the less conspicuous form of omission, rather than interpolation and the introduction of ceremonial novelties. But both movements have followed exactly the same course in this matter of changes in the legal liturgy, though the 'Anglo-catholics' led the way, and have always been more vigorously reprobated by the authorities.

One must feel pity for the bewildered inmates of Victorian episcopal palaces, when the introduction by certain clergy on their own initiative of things like vestments, candles and incense provoked not a storm but a hurricane. Of course they promptly lost not only their sense of proportion, but much of their sense of justice. Yet, again, when one has finished disputing about the historical meaning and force of the 'Ornaments Rubric' and the Elizabethan 'Advertisements', or the precedents afforded by Caroline ceremonial, it remains true that these things in themselves were as much a revolution in the normal current Anglican practice of worship as were the doctrines they implied in current Anglican theology. An equivalent series of innovations in the worship of any other christian body in any age made in the same way, would provoke just the same uproar as this created in the nineteenth century Church of England. But anywhere else it would certainly also have provoked effective ecclesiastical prohibition and extirpation. Had the Church of England been free to control her own worship in the 60's and 70's of the last century, bishops and laity would undoubtedly have been at one in passing immediately a series of canons as thoroughly restrictive of all liturgical innovations as those which the Church of Ireland passed in the same period. But the state control of worship intervened in this matter as in all others. A legalistic interpretation of the state's own law of public worship was found to cover and even to require many of these things. Once this had been established in the state courts the bishops were entirely helpless to suppress them; though even the ecclesiastical lawyers boggled at the idea of enforcing their use in every church in England, which the letter of the law now seemed to demand. In spite of much episcopal discouragement and disapproval the ceremonial innovations (or restorations, if you will) have spread steadily and have had to be officially tolerated by the church, probably against the desire of most practising churchmen, simply because the state's control of worship prevented their prohibition.

These innovations were originally introduced as accompaniments to the statutory liturgy, left unaltered in its text and order, and they are still sometimes so used to-day. But it was in the logic of the situation that the innovators should not stop there. It is not ceremonial adjuncts but the Shape of the Liturgy which performs the eucharistic action; and it is the wording of the prayers which expresses its meaning. This is what is the essence of the matter. Though in all good faith the followers of the Oxford Movement interpreted Cranmer's rite as doing and meaning what they themselves did and meant, they had come to conceive that action and its meaning in a way which his rite was originally intended directly to contradict. Because worship always expresses and is in turn moulded by belief, they came in course of time—often reluctantly and little by little—to substitute other forms for his. This sort of innovation certainly was not covered by the state's law of worship. On the contrary, it directly challenged it. The bishops, or most of them, did their duty and tried to uphold the law. But because they could neither control theology nor change the law of worship in minor matters so as to save its main principles, the attempt was hopeless from the first. The rapid spread of such 'illegalities' in public worship (and they were most of them directly and plainly illegal so far as the law of the land was concerned) led directly to the agitation in Parliament which resulted eventually in the proposed new rite of 1927–8. This was intended as the *ne plus ultra*—the extreme limit of innovation, the Prayer Book of King Canute. Yet it was itself so drawn up that its champion, Bishop Frere, was once constrained to remark, 'You could drive a coach and horses through it in almost any direction, if you had a good lawyer.' With its innumerable permissive alternatives—its rubrics allowed for more than 300 different variations of the one office of Morning Prayer on any given Sunday—it was itself something very like a confession that the whole conception of a uniform statutory liturgy was a mistake.

The present situation, therefore, merely continues a state of affairs which the bishops had allowed to develop for at least a generation before 1928; or rather, had been forced to allow to develop by their inability to adapt the law of worship to the progress of theological change. It is no longer a matter of ceremonial diversity. It is the eucharistic rite itself, the order and text of its parts and prayers, which many of the clergy with some lay support are anxious to see changed with or without authority. In the last fifty years they have increasingly taken to doing this for themselves according to their own very various ideas. This is not the place to judge of the original rightness or otherwise of their course of action, which is now admittedly the cause of much confusion and a certain amount of friction in the church. But as regards the present position it may be remarked that so long ago as 1906 a Royal Commission appointed to enquire into breaches of 'the present law of public worship' reluctantly reported that it 'is too narrow for the religious life of this generation'. As regards the eucharist that law is still exactly the same, and it has not grown more serviceable in the last forty years. It is now clear, too, that the officially prescribed remedy, the proposed rite of 1928, will never solve the difficulty, whatever its merits or demerits—if only because the greater part of those clergy and laity whom it was especially designed to satisfy sincerely regard those particular proposals not only with contempt but with a sort of rancour. Without expressing any opinion on the justice of this attitude, its existence is a fact which must be accepted; and it puts those proposals outside practical consideration. It was the failure—comprehensible enough, but still the failure—of the bishops and the 'representative laity' in Church Assembly and Parliament to make a proper provision for 'the religious life of this generation' in the liturgy, which has finally thrust it upon the parochial clergy to do something to meet their people's continuing needs. All orders in the church, bishops, clergy and laity, have contributed in different ways to bring about the present situation. The church is weary of controversy on the matter, but quite unwilling—and unable—to coerce determined minorities. Though the bishops and the Assembly failed to find a rite which Parliament would pass or the church would use, the mind of the church as a whole has very reluctantly, but with a quiet finality, accepted the fact that changes in the rite there will have to be. It is still quite uncertain what they are to be or on what principles they should be framed.

The present situation has been called one of 'liturgical anarchy', which is one way of looking at it; though in itself the description is an interested exaggeration of the real facts by the advocates of an old-fashioned adminis-trative absolutism of bishops which is now impossible even if it were desirable. It is true that the situation is very uncomfortable, because it is essentially a period of 'liturgical experiment', during which a large variety of unofficial proposals are being sifted by the only practical test for such things—use in the worship of ordinary congregations. Many people would repudiate such an interpretation of what is happening; but that is in fact what is going on, however much the ecclesiastical bureaucrat or the conser-vative worshipper may dislike the process. It is a wholesome and necessary stage, though a very inconvenient one, in discovering the real mind of the church. As the events of the past twenty years have shewn, there is no sufficient substitute for it in the proceedings of official committees. There have been periods of this kind before in the history of the church, both universally and in England. An English communicant who had lived through the fifteen years between 1547 and 1562 and been forced in that time to worship by five different rites, mostly accompanied by the torture or execution of recalcitrants, might feel that we have managed more sensibly between 1927 and 1942.

This is not to say that the present situation is satisfactory, even if some-thing like it be temporarily unavoidable. There must some time come an end to experiment and a stage of settled results. The serious thing about the present situation is that we are doing nothing whatever to profit by it, and so to transform it. It is the clergy in the parishes who are making the experiments with their parishioners, without much guidance, and often without a clear understanding of what they are doing and of the results they are reaching, or of the tests and principles by which to judge those results. There is a natural tendency to force cut-and-dried solutions upon individual congregations—the Roman rite in English, various combina-tions of this with 1662, the so-called 'Interim rite' (*i.e.* the prayers of 1662 in the order of 1549) or the rite of 1549 itself, or even *ad hoc* compilations by the vicar, as in one midland church. This is because those who make the experiments are not specialists equipped to explain to their people the technical principles underlying eucharistic worship, but busy parish priests, who must to some extent adopt methods ready made. The contri-bution of the bishops (with one exception) to this process of 'liturgical experiment' has been curiously unpractical and probably quite undesigned. They obstructed it at the outset with all their power, in pursuance of the long discredited Elizabethan policy of uniformity of liturgy as a cure for diversity of doctrine. When that had failed once more, they took up the project of making a revision of the rite themselves, but only after their long delay in adopting it had made it certain that the church would require a more drastic revision than Parliament would pass. Having produced the unloved baby of 1928 and seen it disowned by Parliament, they then seriously weakened the remaining authority of 1662 by their attempts to get 1928 accepted by the church. When that hope failed also, they spent two years in something rather like sulking, and in ignoring the whole problem. Finally they have reverted to trying to enforce the legal liturgy of 1662, not by the courts and the secular law, but by their own 'spiritual authority' (exerted by methods not entirely divorced from financial pressure and the distribution of patronage) with 1928 used almost as a threat for those who will not conform to 1662. The unfortunate result of this series of somersaults of policy unaccompanied by any clear development of principle has been at each stage to prevent the church from beginning to come to any common mind on the matter at all, or from setting out to gather the fruits of the experience gained by the experiments in the parishes.

The only new element in the situation brought about by the parliamentary decision of 1928 was this: it set the bishops for the first time at open odds with the state's law of public worship. As soon as Parliament's decision was known the bishops unanimously agreed to the following statement, published by the then Archbishop of Canterbury: 'It is a fundamental principle that the Church—that is the Bishops together with the Clergy and Laity—must in the last resort, when its mind has been fully ascertained, retain its inalienable right, in loyalty to our Lord and Saviour Jesus Christ, to formulate its Faith in Him and to arrange the expression of that Holy Faith in its forms of worship'. Readers of the New Testament may be startled by this statement. Our Lord did not say ' . . . And unto God in the last resort the things that are God's.' But even with this qualification, this was still the bravest thing on the subject which had been said by English bishops since 1559. As his biographer has said, coming from a man of Archbishop Davidson's personal antecedents it was the more remarkable. In July 1929 the Upper House of Canterbury resolved that ' . . . the bishops in the exercise of that legal or administrative discretion which belongs to each bishop in his own diocese, will be guided by the proposals set forth in the Book of 1928, and will endeavour to secure that the practices which are consistent neither with the Book of 1662 nor with the Book of 1928 shall cease'. In other words, the bishops quietly claimed that by their own action they could reverse the repeated decision of Parliament, and do precisely what they would have done if Parliament had passed the Book.

The bishops have hardly been given credit for the courage this required. It was a very bold claim indeed, and it would be interesting to discover the source in English law of this '*legal* discretion' of a bishop to set aside the force of a parliamentary statute 'in his own diocese' or anywhere else. Nothing had been heard of it by the Royal Commission of 1906[1] or by anyone else before 1929, though its existence might have greatly eased the awkward position of the bishops ever since about 1900. However,

---

[1] There is perhaps just a hint of it in Archbishop Davidson's evidence before the Commission (*Report*, Minutes of Evidence, 13230).

Parliament soon discovered that it had no means of calling their bluff short of disestablishment, which it was not prepared to face, any more than were the bishops. The House of Commons could only adopt a policy of dignified ignorance of what was going on. The legal position after 1928 remained precisely what it had been in 1900; and even now from time to time the ecclesiastical courts still give expensive exhibitions of their irrelevance to the present life of the church by acting upon it. But it was certain thenceforward that Parliament would never again be in a position to control Anglican worship by fresh legislation.

The bishops thus successfully recovered from the humiliation inflicted on them by Parliament, by asserting their own right to control the liturgy over its head. But they suffered another and much more vexatious discomfiture when they tried the same lofty tactics on the church. Had they taken their courage in both hands and brought their Book into use in 1927 when it was first rejected by Parliament, it would almost certainly have been widely used, at all events for a time, until its defects as a liturgy had become obvious. But 1927 was toned down to 1928 to meet the prejudices of Parliament, and when it had again been rejected it began to present a somewhat shop-soiled appearance. The rite of 1928, despite much semi-official encouragement and extravagant episcopal praise,[1] has never come into use among any but a *coterie*, and is now further than ever from general acceptance.[2] This was not because Parliament had forbidden it, but because the church declined to use it. The refusal was gradual, but in the end it was definite. By about 1935 it was becoming clear that neither Parliament nor the bishops were going to have the final control over the future of Anglican worship. The liturgy would have to take a form that the church was prepared to use.

It is difficult to analyse the motive which impelled this widespread disesteem for 1928. It cannot have been an increased respect for the law as recently re-affirmed by Parliament or a return of affection for 1662, for both were increasingly disregarded. The church at large, laity and clergy alike, had never been more than lukewarm about the rite of 1928 in itself. But most churchmen had been a good deal incensed by the action of Parliament about it at the time, and might have been expected to follow the bishops' bold defiance of the veto, if only to shew this disapproval. Yet the impression slowly grew that the action of Parliament, however improper from the church point of view, was in reality a deliverance. So far as I understand it, the rejection was much more instinctive than reasoned. The church came to feel obscurely that the new rite had been compiled by

---

[1] One bishop in a debate in Convocation in January 1942 described it as 'the finest liturgy available for use in any church in christendom'. Brightman, who had actually studied every liturgy in every language in christendom, has left on record a quite different appreciation.

[2] A careful survey made unofficially by one bishop places the number of churches in which it is now used at under 100.

wrong methods under the wrong influences; and was not what it wanted, because it did not really express its mind.[1]

The difficulty was to know what the church did want. It would not use either 1662 or 1928 as they stood.[2] But no other official alternative was in sight, and various unofficial proposals failed to rally support. It is impossible not to sympathise with the bishops in the increasing administrative difficulties caused by the liturgical confusion which resulted. But it is consistent with sympathy, and I hope with respect, to say that the policy which they next adopted soon ceased to present any appearance of being constructive. The only remedy they could envisage seems to have been the continuance of the *ancien régime* of authoritarianism in liturgy which had finally broken down thirty years before, but now with themselves as the 'authority' in the place of Parliament. They continued to extol the merits of 1928 long after it had become obvious that the church would not have it, and to put it forward as having some sort of 'spiritual authority'. In fact the procedure they had devised for giving it this had never been carried out, to avoid a final affront to Parliament. They endeavoured also to cast a fresh mantle of 'spiritual authority' over the statutory liturgy of 1662, by representing it as the rite which the church prescribed through their own admonitions. Most of them were prepared to authorise small decorative changes in this rite by their own authority in defiance of the statute (but *not* in the illegal liturgy of 1928, which they tried to get used just as it stood). Some of them even laid formal claim to be that 'lawful authority' which is referred to in the statutory 'Declaration of Assent' (taken by the clergy to the legal liturgical formularies) as empowered to alter or supplement the legal Prayer Book. The re-publication of the assurances given by the then bishops during the debate in the House of Lords in 1865, when the present terms of that Declaration were framed, would in itself have sufficed to refute any such claim; though no one seems to have thought of doing this.

All this looked very like self-stultification. If such minor decorations had been all that was needed to get 1662 used again as it stood by the church, why had the bishops risked the dangerous experiment of presenting to Parliament the much more comprehensive proposals of 1927-8? And if they believed their own proposals as such had 'spiritual authority' and represented the mind of the church, why not have tried to enforce them in their original (1927) form, which had had larger majorities in Convocation and the Assembly than 1928, instead of in the form which had avowedly been altered in the hope of satisfying Parliament in 1928?

[1] For a courteous but devastating exposure of its amateurish workmanship see Dr. W. K. Lowther Clarke's recent work: *The Prayer Book of 1928 Reconsidered*, London, 1943.

[2] Dr. George Bell's charge *Common Order in Christ's Church* (1937) reveals that no priest out of more than 400 parishes in his diocese used 1662 exactly as the law prescribed, and only two used 1928 as printed.

The bishops were in fact in a most unenviable position. By producing 1927 they had virtually subscribed to the opinion that 1662 no longer adequately met the needs of the church or represented its mind, and was consequently unenforceable. But the tacit rejection of the new Book by the church coming after its rejection by the state left them bankrupt of any policy at all on the liturgical problem. In default of a constructive solution, they fell back on the issuing of 'regulations' of their own, of highly disputable legal or canonical force, merely in the search for something which would 'work'. This was to cease to regard the question from the christian point of view of the interests of worship as such, and to treat it instead in the Whitehall manner, as an administrative problem. The result was at once apparent in a series of mild commotions in each diocese where the attempt was made to enforce such 'regulations', which the clergy resented and disobeyed while the laity were puzzled and disedified. (Anyone can understand the deplorable feelings aroused in many of the clergy by the policy of the bishops in the years before the war who remembers the state of extreme exasperation to which the courteous, energetic and well-meaning officials of the Ministry of Health and other Government Departments reduced many of the citizens of London in September 1940, by attempting to deal with an unprecedented situation within the framework of Departmental Regulations, drawn up—of necessity—without full foreknowledge of what would happen. The situation in London in 1940 was transformed by a new Regional Commissioner, who framed his measures by the situation as it stood and allowed the Departmental Regulations to look after themselves. It has not yet been transformed in the church.)

The question of 'authority' in the liturgy is really only one aspect of the larger question of 'authority' in the christian religion generally, and this the bishops were not in a good position to face. The English church disavowed the authority of the Pope in the sixteenth century; in the nineteenth century under the impulse of theological liberalism it had largely lost sight of the authority of the Bible, in the old sense; in the twentieth it had almost ceased to enforce the authority of its own doctrinal formularies, first upon the 'liberals' and then upon the 'Anglo-catholics.' The bishops had not much left to fall back upon in the way of authority save themselves. Yet it is hardly possible to maintain that the English Reformation was conducted in order to set up a papacy in commission among the episcopate, on the model of that 'Cyprianic' theory of the episcopate which probably owes more to Archbishop Benson than to S. Cyprian. In any case the bishops were precluded from going far along this line by the advances they were simultaneously making to non-episcopal dissent, which involved pitching the note of Apostolic Succession rather low. You cannot convincingly demand conscientious submission to your divinely-given authority in liturgical matters from one set of people, while explaining publicly to another that the total rejection of that authority not only in liturgy but in everything else as well, does not at all impair their position as 'real ministries in Christ's church'.

As regards the liturgy the practical 'authority' in the Church of England since 1559 had always in reality been that of the state. The church at large had been increasingly rejecting this authority in practice for more than a generation before 1928. The bishops themselves had publicly turned their backs upon it in 1929—but without providing an adequate substitute. They were now compelled to fall back on their own resources. They would not assert that they had an apostolic authority inherent in their office. They claimed instead that they had a far-reaching administrative authority over the church, simply as bishops of the 'historic episcopate'. Without entering into the history of episcopacy in the primitive church, it is enough to say that it would be exceedingly difficult to prove that bishops have always had or even claimed to have any such authority in the post-reformation Church of England. And in claiming it now our bishops had not the support of that moral authority which might have been given them by being the church's own choice as the fittest men for their exceedingly difficult office. They are still appointed by the state, not always on grounds which are immediately obvious to churchmen. It is little wonder if in the face of such complicated handicaps the bishops largely failed to 'restore order' by brandishing their croziers during the ten years following 1928.

A 'Round Table Conference' of unwieldy size, representative character and diversified prejudices was gathered at Lambeth in 1938 to evolve a liturgy which the bishops could enforce. After wasting some months without providing itself with any very definite agenda it was anaesthetised by the present war. It was an open confession that what the bishops were now seeking was not a good liturgy but a workable measure for police purposes. Yet it served to shew that the bishops had learned that the church must at least have some say in framing the rite which they were still hoping to discover in order to enforce it; and that they had wisely determined not to make use for this of the Church Assembly any more than of Parliament, if they could help it.

In 1941 the present Bishop of Oxford made some carefully constructed proposals for a new Anglican canon, based on considerations only of what is theologically and liturgically desirable in eucharistic worship, and not on the principle of 'enforcement' at all. They were put forward simply on their intrinsic merits, not as an administrative device. They at once attracted widespread interest and support, not so much by their contents, which were open to certain important theological and liturgical criticisms, as by the new approach which they revealed to the whole question. But the bench as a whole was still obsessed with the idea of imposing a solution in the sixteenth century manner, and grasped at the hope that they had at last found something which would 'work'. The question was taken up officially, prematurely and in a way certain to wreck any prospects the scheme might have had. The carefully balanced proposals were first crudely eviscerated behind the scenes, in complete disregard of the scholarly considerations on which their author had originally framed them. In this mutilated form (Jan. 1942) they were passed by 14 votes to 7 in the Upper House of Canterbury, the Bishop of Oxford being absent. The debate unfortunately displayed an ignorance of the history of the Prayer Book and a degree of misinformation about the general subject in hand which compared unfavourably even with those in the same House before the passage of 1928.[1] The Lower House of Canterbury in the following May tactfully saved the reputation of the Upper House by voting consideration of the pathetic wreckage sent down to them 'inopportune'.[2] There the matter now rests, except that at least five bishops have since told us that we shall have to have more 'uniformity' after the war. It would appear that Hegel was right in his depressing remark that the only thing one learns from history is that men never learn from history.

It is a most humiliating and saddening story for all who love the Church of England. One by one each single piece of the imposing machinery available—Assembly, Parliament, Bishops, Convocations—has proved itself incompetent to provide for the Church of England a tolerable method of doing that which is the very centre of its life for every christian church. Yet I venture to think the real meaning of the story is something rather different from what it appears on the surface, and much more hopeful. The cause of the whole difficulty is that the English church has recovered a consciousness of its own organic life in an almost miraculous manner, and has in consequence rejected that Tudor absorption into the English state which was the very basis of the Anglican liturgical settlement. That settlement has now collapsed along with its basis. There are still Erastians, and the lawyers still in many things exercise that day-to-day control of the church's life which is the most practical consequence of a statutory Establishment. But the church as a whole has unmistakeably rejected the Erastian principle, and there is no important Erastian party even among the state-appointed bishops. Almost all defenders of the present statutory liturgical settlement defend it as being good and true in itself, not merely because it is the state's. The failure to find a solution of our liturgical difficulties is due chiefly to the attempt to find something different from the sixteenth century solution while persisting in using sixteenth century methods. A more hopeful approach would be opened up by a candid acknowledgement that the rejection of the basis of Cranmer's liturgical settlement—the religious authority of the state—places the church back in

[1] I am prepared to substantiate this if necessary with a detailed commentary giving page and line references to the *Chronicle of Convocation*. I only refrain from doing so here out of a reluctance to name some of those who spoke.

[2] It deserves to be placed on record as an instance of single-mindedness that one proctor in May 1942—(Gazala! Tobruk!)—proposed that Parliament should be approached about the position of the prayer of oblation.

the position in which it found itself about A.D. 1534, before Cranmer's settlement began to be imposed.

Our present liturgy had its origin in a period of liturgical crisis very like the present, in which the church was dimly conscious that its liturgical life no longer met its contemporary needs. What was required was that the church should very carefully reconsider (1) exactly what the eucharistic action *is* and (2) how that action is to be 'done' in the liturgy. Questions of vestments, posture, etc. are not secondary, but tertiary, to this. I hesitate to say anything which might even seem to disparage the blessed truth that we 'take Christ's Body in our hands, receive it with our mouths, and that corporally, naturally, really, substantially and carnally', as the author of our xxviiith Article affirmed that it meant. Nevertheless, even this, if we take our Lord's words in their earliest record—'This is My Body which is for you; do this—' seems to be only the *means* to the fulfilment of the action He commanded. That alone is primary.

The pity is that in the generation of the sixteenth century when the crisis demanded solution, the church never adequately did reconsider the primary question at all, because it was never allowed to. Its attention was made to centre on the secondary question of the Presence, in the mediaeval fashion, and on the tertiary questions of language (which has, however, great practical importance), ornaments and postures. Cranmer with a few personal friends alone had an effective share in the consideration of the primary question of the action. I have set out above in his own words the conclusions to which he came on that. He imposed upon the church the expression of those personal conclusions in a liturgy, without discussion, without possibility of amendment, without even asking a formal assent, by the sole force of the temporal power, with heavy penalties exacted from clergy and laity alike for worshipping otherwise or even for absenting themselves from its performance. I do not suppose there is an Anglican alive to-day who really believes that receiving holy communion is the token of exactly the same thing as Abraham's faith that in his seed all the nations of the earth should be blessed. The Church of England has officially rejected the most characteristic of Cranmer's doctrinal notions on the eucharist ever since 1559.[1] But it has continuously had to use a liturgy which was quite brilliantly designed to express those particular notions.

It would be untrue to suggest that this is entirely the fault of the state, and that the church has always chafed against it. For long periods the Church of England has not only acquiesced in but sincerely appreciated that liturgy; I have tried to point out that there is a good deal in it to

---

[1] Perhaps the nearest approach to Cranmer's ideas among contemporary theologians is made by Dr. E. W. Barnes, Bishop of Birmingham (*Should Such a Faith Offend?* 1927, *pp.* 319 *sqq.*). But Dr. Barnes is capable of expressing his ideas positively (*e.g. ibid., pp.* 209 *sq.*) and Cranmer would certainly have rejected some of his positive statements (*e.g.* some on *p.* 223) as the thin end of the Pope's wedge.

appreciate. But it is true to say that since 1559 the church has put her own glosses upon it, and I should not be where I am if I did not believe that it is patient, however awkwardly, of a different interpretation from its author's. It obviously contains—it could hardly help doing so—all the essential minimum which the mediaeval church had come to consider as necessary to 'validity', though it is not likely that Cranmer went out of his way to secure this. In calling the present rite the 'statutory liturgy', I am not trying to make insinuations even indirectly against its origins, but simply taking account of its present sanction. The church put it forward in 1662 in preference to 1604, and Parliament with some hesitation allowed it. But the claim that our present rite (which is in substance and outline Cranmer's rite of 1552) has a 'spiritual authority' which our reformed rite had never previously had, because it had never before 1661 been formally passed through Convocation, seems somewhat unreal when one considers the actual circumstances in which Convocation worked on that occasion.

The very conception of such a 'spiritual' equivalent for 'statutory authority' as the sanction of a rite does not in itself seem to be older than the sixteenth century, and rests on an analogy with secular law. It was adopted by the Post-Tridentine Roman church in the same period as among ourselves, and is still in full force in the Roman Canon Law. But one has only to think of Pope Gregory's advice to Augustine of Canterbury to make his own choice of what seemed to him best from the current Roman and Gallican uses, to be aware of the former recognition of a quite different principle as the sanction of the liturgy, not only at Rome and Canterbury but all over christendom. This particular kind of 'spiritual authority', given by a sort of *legislative* enactment by the church, could only be attributed to 1662 out of all the rites ever used in England. If we abandoned this sixteenth century legalist conception, we should be free to set aside the embarrassing question of the moral freedom or otherwise of Convocation from undue pressure in 1662. And we could also place the use not only of 1662 but of 1559 and 1552 and 1549 on the same footing as every other rite which had ever been used in England since the landing of S. Augustine. It has the authority of 'acceptance by the church and use for her sacramental purpose'. That is a different sort of authority from the authority of any statute passed by a legislator, ecclesiastical or secular. But it was at one time the only sort of authority recognised by the liturgy. One can cite certain exceptions; there are liturgical edicts put out by Byzantine emperors; there is the initiative of Charlemagne, though this was largely emptied of its statutory character by Alcuin's method of carrying it out. But from the beginning until the sixteenth century, broadly speaking the sanction in liturgy was not 'law' but 'custom'.

In its nature the authority of custom is a self-enforcing thing. If a large number of people cease to observe a custom, then it just 'dies out'. Even the most obsolete law requires a definite act of the legislator to repeal it before it ceases to bind. A custom dies by ceasing to be observed. And its authority while it lives is a voluntarily accepted and natural thing, not a compulsive and artificial one. The peculiar appropriateness of such an authority for 'the glorious liberty of the children of God' in their worship of love needs no emphasis. Its safeguard against degeneration into licence in the liturgy is the fact that worship expresses belief, or it dies of unreality; and the faith behind all catholic liturgies is fundamentally the same, even though it has not always been explained in the same terms or even in the same way. It is here, in the sphere of what are essentially intellectual propositions—in eucharistic theology—that identity of phrasing and meticulous definition have their proper function in maintaining identity of belief. While that is maintained the diversity of liturgies—which reflects differences of history, culture and taste—is not only allowable; it is human, desirable, inescapable, the reflection of the catholicity of the living church. We have seen the train of causes by which the English church in the six-teenth century was obliged to reverse this rational scheme of things, so that eucharistic theology was left vague and diverse, while the liturgy was minutely prescribed. We are paying the penalty for that now that the liturgical sanction of secular law has broken down. A clear common theology would have issued simply and naturally in a new common custom.

The stability of any custom in the last analysis always rests upon its own intrinsic reasonableness. It is merely a way of doing something which many people need to do frequently or regularly in some way. If it becomes evi-dent that another way does the same thing more conveniently or somehow better than the customary way, then the custom will change—slowly, per-haps, for men are creatures of habit—but certainly in the end. It is just this which has been happening to our liturgy. Whenever the Elizabethan appeal to the primitive church has been pressed seriously, by the Carolines, or the Non-Jurors, or the Oxford Movement, those who made it have always manifested a certain discomfort in using Cranmer's rite; and this despite their own preconceptions of its meaning, and while strenuously maintaining that it supported their own position. We cannot have it both ways. Either Cranmer was or was not desirous and capable of expressing his own conception of the eucharistic action in his liturgy. But if you under-stand that action as the primitive church understood it, you will feel a dis-accord with a rite excellently composed to express a quite different con-ception of it. A scholar may read into it most of its omissions and interpret its own statements by patristic theology. But even the peculiar shape and structure of Cranmer's rite are in themselves significant, and were meant to be so.

The Carolines and the Non-Jurors were largely academic in their influ-ence. The Oxford Movement turned to the parishes and taught the parish priests and the laity in great numbers to think of the eucharistic action as the patristic authors had thought of it, and as Cranmer quite certainly did not. And as soon as the liturgy began to be conceived of no longer as a Schedule annexed to an Act of Parliament, to be obeyed in that mechanical and exact fashion in which Acts of Parliament are intended to be obeyed, but as the vital act of the church to be done according to her mind, then our liturgical custom began to change—as customs in such circumstances inevitably do change. There is nothing abnormal in this; it has happened a hundred times and more in the liturgies of other churches, gradually and naturally. The process was only made painful and troublesome in our case by the fact that our liturgy was embalmed in a parliamentary statute, of which not a comma *can* be changed gradually and naturally, but only by the parliamentary process. What we have been watching in the Church of England for the last fifty years is a struggle between two opposite conceptions of liturgy—between the idea of liturgy as primarily an act of conformity to the terms of an external law (whether that law be of the church or of the state) and the idea of liturgy as expressing *belief* first of all, and conforming to the church's custom because the belief it expresses is that of the church. The first is the idea of liturgy accepted by the West in the sixteenth century, and still maintained to-day by Roman Canon Law. The other is the idea which governed the whole development of liturgy in the primitive and patristic period, and which is still formally retained in the East. Even the Royal Commission of 1906 already recognised that it was the latter principle which was gaining the upper hand in the modern Church of England.

The whole development of the classic liturgies is by continual liturgical experiment. Every church had its 'customary' way of doing the liturgy, which was 'customary' only because it adequately expressed that church's mind and belief as to what the eucharistic action is and means. Whenever an idea which seemed to enrich that conception was encountered, whether in the teaching and devotional experience of that church itself, in the rites of other churches or in the works of theologians, it could be and was incorporated into the customary rite. If, after the only trial of which such things are capable, a period of actual use at the altar, it was found that it did more fully express the eucharistic action, it was absorbed into the local eucharistic experience as something which had become that church's own, and permanently incorporated into the local liturgical tradition. If it did not serve, then ultimately it fell out of use again.

The depth and breadth and allusiveness of the classical rites comes just from this, that their real author is always the worshipping church, not any individual however holy and gifted, any committee however representative, or any legislator however wise. The results in every tradition were codified from time to time by men with a gift or a taste for this sort of work. But all the time such men were working within a tradition, with materials supplied them by the immense eucharistic experience of the whole worshipping church of the past, of other churches as well as their own. And when their work was done, the church came after them again, commenting, adding, altering, omitting, improving, sometimes spoiling, enriching, adjusting perpetually to her own contemporary mind and life and needs. We have seen what the church did with the work, for instance, of Gregory or of Alcuin after their time. It was right that it should. No one man is great enough or good enough to fix the act of the Body of Christ for ever according to his own mind and understanding of it. The good liturgies were not written; they grew.

About the beginning of the sixteenth century it did look as though something of this kind needed to begin again. The eucharistic practice of the church no longer fully expressed her contemporary mind and life and needs; but a fairly brief period of liturgical experiment might well have enabled it to do so. Instead, one man's personal and quite unrepresentative opinion, come to before ever the first changes were tried out in practice, was clamped upon the Church of England in a fixed form, which it was never afterwards free to alter. Now that stage is over, and the opportunity missed in the sixteenth century has come again. In spite of all the well-intentioned efforts of the bishops to prevent it, a good deal of the necessary 'liturgical experiment' has been carried out by the clergy in the last forty years. But it has had to be done with so little guidance from authority that most of the results have been unco-ordinated and many have not been observed. We need a new 'custom', with the stability and self-enforcement that any satisfactory custom has in itself. Can we reproduce deliberately and consciously and in a reasonably short space of time—say five to ten years—that process by which *the church* produced the great liturgies naturally and instinctively in a period of centuries? This is what would be meant by *scientific* 'liturgical experiment'. I believe there are encouraging signs that we could do this with success if we had a mind to, but there are three difficulties which would have to be avoided; and also one pre-requisite absolutely necessary to be provided, which would require a good deal of courage on somebody's part.

The difficulties are these: 1. The old relation to the state, the Establishment, persists—'indefensible in theory and intolerable in practice', as Dr. Henson has said. But it is there, and it would have to be reckoned with, in the form of courts and the statutes they could still try to enforce if they were invoked, even though there is little prospect of fresh legislation by Parliament about the liturgy. Yet it does not seem to be the business of the church to challenge the state directly to sever this relation, but to try still to work within it so far as is consistent with fidelity to her own mission.

2. There is a complete lack of regular machinery suitable for the purpose of making liturgical changes. The Assembly would talk itself frantic for some years about a new liturgy, and could only present it for Parliament's approval at the end of that. The debate in the Upper House of Convocation in January 1942 demonstrated conclusively that the bishops as a body are

not equipped for composing a liturgy, and the initiation of measures in the Lower House is a cumbrous procedure. In any case the initiative in such a matter ought to lie with bishops. Bodies of the size of either house are quite unsuitable for drafting a liturgy, and can only proceed by way of 'party' debates on anything submitted to them. And at present there is no proposal to lay before them.

3. There is a section of the church, numbering perhaps a quarter of its members, the 'Evangelical' party, whose set and fixed practice, if not principle, is opposition to the *recognition* of any sort of change in the *status quo* in the church. (They themselves have changed considerably both in teaching and practice since the time of Charles Simeon. It is not so much change as the acknowledgement of it that they dislike.) The nineteenth century bishops were so preoccupied with opposing the Oxford Movement that they took no steps to prevent what the Elizabethan bishops in their own day more wisely foresaw must be a danger to the cohesion of the church—the formation of a puritan *imperium in imperio* within the church, permanently impenetrable behind a financial rampart to any ideas current in the rest of the church. By the system of Evangelical schools, Evangelical halls at the Universities, Evangelical theological colleges and Evangelical patronage trusts, it is now quite possible for a boy to be educated and grow up, take a degree, be ordained and serve a ministerial lifetime, without once encountering directly any theological idea unacceptable to the founders of the party in the period of the Crimean War. To the framing of any new liturgy the Evangelicals would offer the most determined and conscientious opposition, not so much because they value the old one (which many of them disregard in different ways as flagrantly as any Anglo-catholic) as because it would mean admitting a change of some kind from what was customary a century ago. They would certainly decline to use any new liturgy which would satisfy the rest of the church, and they ought not in charity to be asked to do so. But this would not prevent their obstructing the official compilation of any new rite. The idea of composing a liturgy with the assistance and to the satisfaction of those who sincerely object to its coming into existence and who firmly intend never to use it is so Alice-in-Wonderland that it can hardly be discussed. But any proposal to be workable must bear this difficulty in mind.

Can anything be done within the limits of these conditions to enable the Church of England to declare its own mind and at least find the basis of a new custom?

Suppose that a group of bishops—say seven—too many to be ignored by their brethren, too few to provoke the law officers of the Crown to extremes —were at an opportune moment to put out a book with a preface somewhat as follows:

'This book contains a liturgy—a complete Ordinary, with a workable minimum of Propers for the ecclesiastical year. We do not put it forward as representing the maximum of the Act of Uniformity which the "Anglo-catholics" can be forced to obey or the minimum which will content the "Evangelicals"; nor yet as the best that Parliament can be expected to pass or as the only compromise at which the Church Assembly can arrive. We put it forward simply on its own merits, and as being in itself, we believe, a good liturgy.

'That is to say, it performs the eucharistic action as it has traditionally been understood from the beginning of the church, simply and coherently and reverently, and its structure is logical and expressive of the action of the rite. It is written in English which is everywhere dignified and simple, and, so far as we can make it, attentive to the melody and rhythm of words. The prayers express the meaning of the eucharist soberly and clearly, according to the ancient universal tradition of christendom. We have assured ourselves that everything in it has sufficient precedent to make it a suitable and reasonable thing in itself for christians to want to do at the eucharist. None of the rubrics are framed prohibitively. They just describe clearly how this rite is meant to be performed, which is what rubrics are for.

'But we wish to make it clear that this rite has no more "authority" (in the current meaning of that term) than have a great many other things which are now done in many parish churches. If the clergy were to use it, the fact that we have put it forward would not protect them from the lawyers. In our own dioceses we shall tolerate its use so far as it lies with us to do so, as we already tolerate a considerable number of other deviations from the statutory rite. But we shall not say to ordinands and presentees, " Either '1662 and none other' or 'My new regulations' ", for we recognise that "My new regulations", like 1928 or any other deviation from 1662, are just as illegal in the Church of England as the Sarum rite. We desire to make it clear that any clergyman who brings it into use in dioceses other than ours without the connivance of his own bishop does so entirely on his own responsibility, and that we shall decline to be embroiled with our brethren in his defence. The clergy will understand that the situation which already prevails in respect of the legal liturgy is in no way altered by the publication of this book.

'It may be that some will desire to use it in church, but will dislike or disagree with some phrases or arrangements or prayers in the rite. In that case we beg them not to hesitate, but to *alter* it with the same freedom that they would use if it were in the Book of Common Prayer. Nevertheless we think that they should refrain from altering the passage printed in large type on *p.* (*so-and-so*), which has been generally regarded as very important if not essential to the rite. For the rest, they will use their discretion—whatever we may say. We would only suggest that before making alterations they should consider exactly what it is that they dislike in our form, and why they dislike it. When they have made their alterations to their own satisfaction, let them consider again whether their amendments express clearly and fully what they themselves desire to express. If after a practical trial for, say, six months, they still think their amendment a real improvement on our composition, they would do us a kindness by sending a copy of it (with page and line reference) together with a short statement of why they prefer it, to the Rev. —— ——, who has kindly undertaken to collect such suggestions for our study. There is no trap in this; you need not even attach your name and address. We are interested only in the quality of your changes. It is quite possible that you have found the word or the idea or the phrase that we were unable to think of. It is precisely because we do not believe that we have any monopoly of liturgical skill or taste that we are acting as we are.

'It will be noted that we are issuing this book in two forms. One is of a large size, interleaved with blank pages in the Ordinary and with a hundred more blank pages at the end. This will make it easier to insert improvements legibly, so that others who may use that copy will observe them. The blank pages will conveniently record suggestions for the completion of the Proper. The other format is of the normal size of a prayer book, and is also interleaved in the Ordinary. If an incumbent were to decide to break the law by using this rite in church, he would probably find it convenient to use the larger size at the altar; in that case we should greatly hope that copies of the smaller size would be in the hands of the congregation. And we most earnestly suggest that if he thinks of amendments in the Ordinary, he should publicly and clearly explain to his people just what changes he is proposing to make, and tell them where to write them in on the appropriate blank pages. We believe that it is very important that the laity should understand clearly just what is being done, and should be able to follow it easily for themselves from their books. We should hope that the rite would not be introduced until it had been in their hands for a month or two, and had been simply and clearly explained to them from the pulpit. And we think that a parish priest would be well-advised to pay some attention, after perhaps a year of practical use, to any observations and criticisms concerning both our composition and his own improvements, which his regular congregation may make. For our own part we shall receive gratefully and humbly any constructive suggestions that the laity as well as the clergy may care to send to the same address.

'Even as it stands we believe that this is a good liturgy. We think so because . . . (and here would follow a careful and simple *rationale* of the rite, framed in such a way as to assist the clergy to explain it to their people in a course of three simple sermons. The preface might conclude:)

'This liturgy, therefore, we have put before the church for the church's own consideration and amendment and, if others think it right, practical testing. If there seems to be sufficient interest, we shall put forward an amended edition in the same way in three years' time, incorporating every improvement offered to us which approves itself to our mind. If thereafter at any time an occasion should present itself, we might be prepared to take whatever action seemed appropriate to secure it some measure of official recognition. But at present we have no intention whatever of doing this, until the worshipping church shall have had time to declare itself in respect of our work fully and freely, in the only way in which its mind can be made plain, *viz.* by adopting or ignoring this book in its public worship.

'We are aware that we shall be criticised severely for acting most irregularly in this, and we regret sincerely any disturbance or distress of mind we may have caused to anyone by so doing. But we are clear in our conscience that what we seek is only the good of the church, that it may worship more understandingly and faithfully according to its own mind. "It is a fundamental principle that the Church—that is the Bishops together with the Clergy and the Laity—must, when its mind has been fully ascertained, retain its inalienable right, in loyalty to our Lord and Saviour Jesus Christ, to formulate its Faith in Him and to arrange the expression of that Holy Faith in its forms of worship" '. (The source of this quotation, and if it were thought necessary, the extent and meaning of the omission, could be explained in a footnote.) 'We start from this "fundamental principle", and we mean only to give it a practical application. It is in the power of the church at large to shew that it approves or condemns what we have done, and in either case we shall have to accept its judgement. That is the way that every church in christendom has always come by its liturgy, by a process of using or not using forms which were put before it for its judgement under the guidance of its bishops. We shall be well contented if the Church of England is enabled to do the same. Our only concern has been to secure that the material put before it shall in itself be both suitable and good.'

This has not, perhaps, the authentic ring of the current episcopal style of drafting; and no doubt the preface could be framed on less realistic lines and still fulfil its purpose. But before I am told from all sides that this is an outrageous suggestion, I would ask those who feel outraged to consider in cold blood the only alternatives: Either 1. The present position will continue indefinitely. Personally, I should be inclined to consider this an outrageous suggestion. The church is very weary of it and it is a real hindrance to her life and work. Or else 2. Some official action will be taken to end it, which means that some untested proposal will have to be passed somehow through some of the existing machinery. Recourse to Parliament is outside practical possibilities, at all events for the present. Official action now could therefore only take one of these forms:

*a.* The bishops might agree among themselves to put a liturgy into force by their 'administrative authority' alone. This is the method employed to bring 1928 into use, and acted upon ever since. It has not improved the situation. The events of the last ten years suggest very strongly that the day has gone by when the church will accept a rite as satisfactory only because the bishops say so—and, really, the blame for this does not lie altogether with the church. Whether the new rite were 1928 or a different one, is there the slightest reason to suppose that recourse to 'administrative authority' will secure less disorder now than it has in the past? This would in practice amount precisely to perpetuating the present situation by the present methods.

*b.* The bishops could try to use Convocation to give 'authority' to a liturgy, but the events there in January and May 1942 are not exactly encouraging. Granted that affairs then were not diplomatically managed; granted, too, that the proposals as they were brought forward were openly conceived of as an administrative device for 'restoring order' and not as a more desirable way of worshipping God, which one hopes was sufficient in itself to chill the enthusiasm of 'stewards of the mysteries of God'; yet only fourteen bishops could be found to vote for these insignificant changes,[1] while seven voted against them out of a total of thirty members of the Canterbury Upper House. And the Lower House would not give concurrence. Even if the latter vote had been reversed, exactly how much chance of securing general obedience would *any* proposal have which was passed in Convocation over the head of so considerable a minority as this? And what other proposal at present could rally that overwhelming support in Convocation necessary to secure it the moral authority of general consent, which alone will in the long run give us a stable and self-enforcing custom? As things stand, if a new rite cannot secure a large measure of *voluntary* acceptance, how is it to be enforced? If the decayed folly of the ecclesiastics' courts is to be invoked, they can only pronounce the new rite itself to be .legal. If moral pressure is to be exercised by godly admonition (and 'black-listing') and synodical action, large minorities can usually resist any amount of moral pressure for an indefinite length of time. It is to be remembered that those resisting would feel supported by genuine theological conviction.

*c.* Some *ad hoc* body like the 'Round Table Conference' might be summoned to evolve a liturgy. If it is to be sufficiently representative for its support to carry any weight whatever with the church, it will be a replica of the Assembly. In this case the work might as well be done by the official body, since its name is already known to most churchmen, and such prestige as it enjoys ought to be capitalised behind the new proposals. If on the other hand the *ad hoc* body consisted solely of scholars competent to act as a drafting committee, it is dubious how far its proposals would be adopted by the present bishops, if the whole bench were consulted. And conscientious scholars would certainly refuse to be made responsible for proposals

[1] The actual form of the proposals was that previously treated with such incisive contempt by the late Bishop Frere in *The Anaphora, p.* 199, *n.* 1. The Upper House appears to have been unanimously unconscious of the fact that its new panacea had been three times discussed and rejected as futile between 1908 and 1918.

of which they did not approve. Once more the whole weight of enforcement would rest on the bishops.

*d.* No doubt, the Church Assembly could—if it would—pass some resolution supporting some episcopal proposals without proceeding to prepare a measure for Parliament. But under any conceivable circumstances that means a 'party' debate and a majority vote. There is a real objection to such a proceeding in the Assembly at present, which would apply just as much to debates in Convocation or a representative conference. As things stand to-day they would probably never consider the real point at all. The debate would inevitably circle around the old mediaeval and sixteenth century quarrels over what is called the 'Real Presence'—a term which has been used by gross materialists ('Capharnaites'), Thomists, Lutherans, High Calvinists and even some Zwinglians, to describe each their own doctrines. Whatever its history in the past, its fatal imprecision has done more to confound our modern Anglican discussions, and in some respects to embitter them, than the use of any single other historic phrase.[1] Whenever in history this question has been raised in this form the same *impasse* has been reached. Ignatius *c.* A.D. 115 is already reproaching those who deny 'that the eucharist is the Flesh of Christ' as the enemies of grace; while from his own polemics it seems clear that they retorted that his notions were 'unspiritual'. The primary question in the *construction* of a liturgy is the Shape, and the meaning of the whole eucharistic action which that performs. But nothing could prevent a public discussion from concentrating on the secondary question of the liturgical phrases describing the nature of the 'Presence', unless the church at large had had time to assimilate by practical experience the idea of another approach to the matter altogether—obedience to our Lord's command to 'do this', in which the consecration is only one co-ordinated element in the rite, and the consecration of the sacrament is a means to the end, not an end in itself. The upshot of any such debates now could only be another 1928, with all Cranmer's verbal Zwinglianisms retained intact, and the good liturgical workmanship which he put into 1552 destroyed by some rearrangement. Nothing else could secure a majority. There is really something very profane about the idea that we can only come before God with circumlocutions which it has been agreed to misunderstand differently. And would such a rite be *used* in the end, any more than 1928 was? Events since then suggest quite forcibly that what the church is looking for is a liturgy, not an ingenious diplomatic arrangement.

Those who hanker for some official action at present and a liturgy which has 'authority' may be right, but in any case they will have to find a new

[1] It has not been necessary to use it at any point in this book. It would be an immense help in discussion if it could be altogether debarred from use among us for a while, and thus everyone be made to state at every stage in his arguments precisely what he does mean as to the relation of the consecrated elements to the Body and Blood of Christ.

means of arriving at it. The official proceedings before 1927 roused party feeling in the church to a dangerous degree. There are now other subjects to be discussed in the near future, like those which touch upon reunion, which look like straining charity among us quite enough by themselves. If these are to be dealt with in an atmosphere already heated by party quarrels over the liturgy, the strain might well reach breaking-point. Yet we cannot simply postpone action indefinitely. If we may still assume that anything like the modern Church of England with its present balance of forces will survive after the next few years, we ought now or in the reasonably near future to be laying the foundation of a new general custom in the liturgy, at least in its main lines.

Admittedly the suggestion I have made would have its disadvantages, but no inevitably fatal results could follow. 1. This mode of action does not directly challenge Parliament at all. If the state could accept in silence the public over-riding of its veto by the entire episcopate in 1929, it is hardly likely to take drastic action over the unofficial proceedings of seven bishops. If the latter timed the production of their book for a moment when Parliament was preoccupied with the 'Four-Year Plan' or the Peace Treaty, it need not even be noticed. If those churchmen who still desire parliamentary control of the liturgy were to try to invoke the state, what action could Parliament take which it cannot take now against open episcopal toleration of 1928 or any other deviation from 1662? There is always disestablishment, of course. But presumably those who desire the continuance of parliamentary control of worship would be the last of all churchmen to take action which was likely to result in that.

2. Such a way of proceeding as I suggest would avoid all the dangers obvious in any use of the existing machinery at present, without preventing the use of any of it whenever it might seem suitable. It would ensure that the proposal, if it did get put forward officially in the end, would only risk bringing those dangers upon the church if it were really likely to solve the problem. There would be no repetition of 1928, when the church was divided, relations between church and state were strained, and the work of the church was greatly distracted from its proper object, all over a proposal which turned out to be no solution at all in the end. Those who disliked the unofficial proposals of a group of bishops as they stood could criticise them objectively on their merits, without being placed in the invidious position of an 'opposition' to the hierarchy. In the meanwhile the church at large, the worshipping priests and people—and not only the bishops and the 'experts' and those indefatigable people who attend committees—would have a fair chance to make up their own minds as to whether they wanted the new rite, and to amend it—as they probably could do if they were given the chance. Only if the proposal won considerable voluntary acceptance and interest—as I believe it would, if people knew that they had a chance to join in its revision and perfecting in a

practical way—would it be worth while to bring it forward for official acceptance. That is to say that the absolute *sine qua non* for any successful 'official' proposal in present circumstances would be secured before this ever became an 'official' proposal at all. If the church did not like it, it would not be used. In that case it would never be brought forward for official adoption, and there would be no controversy. We should be no worse off, and a certain amount of material would have been collected, which might come in useful later on in other ways.

3. Those who desire no change at all in the liturgy would not be involved at all. They would take no part in a 'liturgical experiment' which might be creating the new form an official liturgy would one day take. They would contribute nothing to it and have no influence upon its content; but that would be their own business. They could do so like anybody else at any moment, if they wanted to. But they would be no worse off than at present, if they did not contribute. And they would retain all their present power and right to oppose or obstruct any change whatever, if and when it were proposed to give it any official sanction. These people know quite well that in many churches the statutory liturgy is not used at all exactly as things are now; many of them do not use it at all exactly themselves. They could not reasonably object to what was going on *more* than they object to what is going on now.

Besides these three difficulties to be avoided by any method of solving our present liturgical troubles, it was suggested that there was one prerequisite to be provided, which has not been defined. It is that the liturgy proposed should be in itself, and from the point of view of construction and workmanship, really a *good* liturgy. No new rite could have the immense advantage possessed by 1662 of being thoroughly familiar to the clergy and worshippers; and it would lack the prestige and that sort of *patina* which come from the mere antiquity of the classic rites. It could therefore only secure voluntary adoption by its own intrinsic merits, by the fact that it performed the eucharistic action in conformity with the general christian tradition more intelligibly and satisfactorily than either 1662 or any of the present competing deviations. This does not mean that it would have to adopt academic foibles alien to the general mind and tradition of the English church (as 1928 adopted a pseudo-oriental 'invocation'). It ought not to be impossible to find a good and sensible rite inspired by our own eucharistic tradition, which was also theologically and liturgically sound in construction. That is what the church is looking for. Lacking those qualities, any proposals will ultimately share the fate of 1928. They must expose themselves to fair criticism simply for what they are, and as a practicable liturgy to be used in the ordinary parish church. Unless they are defensible as such, they will not be adopted. It would be the quality of the proposal as a *good* Anglican liturgy which would settle the fate of any such 'liturgical experiment'.

And that is as it should be, for that is precisely what we are trying to find.

This is not to say that it would necessarily have either to reject or to keep all our present sixteenth century material. Cranmer was a great liturgical artist, even though he was a Zwinglian; and the phrases of the present rite are very dear to thousands upon thousands of our people from habit and intimate personal associations. These people have an absolute right to be most tenderly considered, and a wise revision would remember that. But because he was so unrepresentative of later Anglicanism in his eucharistic doctrine, a mere shuffling of the parts of Cranmer's rite as they stand would not fulfil the purpose adequately. The question of the way in which his material would have to be used needs more, and—if I may say so without presumption—more intelligent, consideration than it seems to have received.

As a matter of practical observation, a re-arrangement of the order of the old prayers seems to cause almost as much disturbance to most lay-people as the introduction of wholly new prayers, since they cannot follow it in their existing books. The remedy lies in giving them books in which they can follow, in careful explanation and, above all, in presenting them with a rite whose real advantages over that to which they are accustomed they can, with explanation, come to see for themselves. If a plebiscite of regular communicants could be taken, I believe that an actual majority would probably still be found for 'no change'; almost certainly it would if Easter communicants were consulted. Just so in 1560 a majority of English churchpeople would probably have voted for the Latin mass. Apart from the element of sheer conservatism, this is not now (and was not then) necessarily because they are unaware that a change is needed, or because they hope that no change will come. But they have no clear proposal before them which gives them guidance in a way they can trust and understand, and they cannot judge for themselves as to the form such changes ought to take.

There are significant signs that a new liturgy which concentrated on being a *good* liturgy first of all, would evoke a surprising amount of interest and support. Even in the terrible months when France was falling and the Battle of Britain being won the Bishop of Oxford's proposals secured the immediate attention of thousands not only of the clergy but of the laity all over the country. I am not trying to recommend these particular proposals, but only the method by which they were put forward and the sort of con-siderations upon which they were based. The obvious ignoring of such considerations in the mutilation they underwent and the hasty official attempt to turn them into one more 'regulation', at once killed the outside interest in them stone dead, and led straight to the fiasco in Convocation. Is it too much to hope that the significance of this has not been lost where it is most necessary for it to be appreciated? The clergy and the church have for a long while now proved very refractory to 'regulation' and the *droit administratif* of a state-appointed episcopate. They might respond much better to guidance based on principles capable of convincing explanation, and not founded simply on expediency and an obsolete statutory position. In that way, and probably now in no other way, the bishops might recover the initiative in the liturgical difficulty which ought to be theirs, and which was theirs for a moment in 1929, and which by their own policy since they have lost. And the rest of the church ought by now to appreciate that without such guidance from the bishops it will not find for itself a stable and self-enforcing custom. You cannot by-pass the episcopate in the working of an episcopal church.

It may be objected that the method of proceeding suggested here would not 'make to cease' those 'variations in the liturgy' which are the cause of the present confusion, and might even increase them. It could hardly do more to increase them than has been done by the methods of the last twenty years. It is the conception of the organisation of christian worship as being the same thing as the maintenance of discipline by police methods which has been half our trouble. But there is perhaps room here for a certain distinction between 1. variations in the liturgy as celebrated in different parish churches and 2. variations in the liturgy from time to time as celebrated in the same church. We have heard much of the former; it naturally comes more often to the notice of bishops. But in most cases it is 2. which causes more disturbance and confusion to the laity.

A priest anxious to teach his people a fuller and more meaningful idea of eucharistic worship usually sees before him the alternative of making a number of small successive changes one by one, or else a very considerable change all at once. If he adopts the latter course, he probably alienates his people altogether, and certainly acts very unfairly towards them. If he adopts the former course of being considerate to his people and trying to teach them as he goes, he runs a risk of confusing and puzzling them much more than the clergy usually understand, even when he has their confidence and they are genuinely trying to follow him. The people do not see the total effect of all the changes he has yet in mind to make, or appreciate it, as he does. They do not know quite where the changes are leading or where the process is to stop or what will be altered next. (Nor, unfortunately, has the parish priest always an entirely clear idea about these things himself.) All they get is a series of incomplete notions of the eucharistic action, to each of which they must readjust themselves afresh. And they cannot follow in their books! Perhaps we have under-rated the value to the liturgical spirit in worship of what is represented by that ever-repeated cry. If we had a good liturgy, easily intelligible by coherent principles, recommended as such by a group of bishops—a thing which still carries a good deal of weight with the laity—and, above all, available to be put before them as a whole from the start in books, it would certainly do a great deal to help them in their difficulties, even while they understood that the rite had no 'authority'. It is not its authority nearly so much as its comprehensibility which worries the majority of the laity in the matter of a rite. And by having as it were a definite programme of change to set before them, any priest who adopted it would largely eliminate the need for successive variations in his own church.

This does not deal with the question of variations from church to church—a trouble which we shall not easily end, in any case. Unless we are to re-introduce the whole principle of 'Uniformity', which was never entirely enforceable and is now quite impracticable, there will still be those who will reject any new liturgy. While claiming to continue to use 1662 they will deviate from it in all sorts of ways. That is the penalty for taking twenty-five years to compile the abortive rite of 1928. The use of congregational rites does undoubtedly foster a tendency to congregational heresies. The liturgy ought not to be the means to a particular congregation's self-expression, but its expression of the act and faith of the whole church. But the argument for Anglican Uniformity as it is often presented is strikingly reminiscent of the Roman Catholic argument for having mass not only in the same identical form but in the same syllables from China to Peru. It complacently assumes that the mass is celebrated primarily for the benefit of the travelling public. As a matter of fact the proportion of strangers in any given congregation is usually infinitesimal. We have to start from the situation as it is. Our laity on the whole seem less disturbed by—or perhaps more resigned to—this sort of variation in the rite between different churches, than are our bishops. Perhaps this is only because they encounter it less frequently. Bishops rarely worship in the same church two Sundays running; the vast majority of our communicants worship habitually in the same church week by week, and can grow accustomed to its ways—if they remain the same. From the point of view of the clergy and laity, this latter is the more urgent problem. If something could be done to relieve this in the way suggested, it would in time certainly have some effect towards bringing more uniformity into the rites of different churches.

It is, I hope, permissible to have suggested a method by which we could make a different approach to our liturgical problem, which would allow the liturgy under the guidance of the bishops to respond to the mind of the worshipping church. Good liturgies are not written; they *grow*. Having said this, it would obviously be impossible for a private person to offer even a sketch of such a liturgy as is here suggested. But perhaps I may be allowed to suggest instead a hint as to the kind of rough test a private person might employ for any such proposal which was put before him. I have learned it only from practical study of the classical rites of christendom.

As we have seen, it is the business of the eucharistic prayer to state the meaning of the eucharistic action. The place above all others where it is virtually *impossible* to avoid stating plainly the meaning given to that action in any particular rite is in the 'second half' of the prayer, that which follows the words of institution. We have seen that Cranmer's eucharistic theology ascribed no discoverable meaning at all to the eucharistic action itself. In his idea, Abraham and Moses, who did not perform the eucharistic action at all, still 'ate the Body and drank the Blood of Christ', just as we do. That is why the abrupt cessation of his prayer at the words of institution, with no 'second half' at all, is so significant and so interesting. I know of no evidence that Cranmer, any more than the ancient liturgists, had consciously noted this constructional principle. It was simply that the facts themselves took charge, and because his conception gave no assignable meaning to the eucharistic action, he *could* not find a content for the 'second half' of his prayer. In 1549 he had tried putting the contents of our present 'prayer of oblation' there, but had rightly removed them in 1552 as quite unsuitable. He had always known that the primitive and patristic church had associated the offering of 'ourselves, our souls and bodies' only with the offertory.[1] But in 1549 he had deliberately removed any sort of offertory prayer, and in 1552 he had removed the offertory itself. Since he wished to retain the idea of an offering of 'ourselves', the only thing to do was what he did. The relics of the phrasing of the 'prayer of oblation' were carefully rebuilt into a 'thanksgiving' and placed at the appropriate point as an alternative to the existing thanksgiving prayer of 1549.

Now that 1662 has replaced an offertory in bread and wine we are much embarrassed by the remnants of Cranmer's scheme. Any Anglican revision would probably try to remedy the lack of a 'second half' of the eucharistic prayer. But if this new 'second half' were found to consist of the 'prayer of oblation' in either its 1549 or 1552 form without considerable changes, we should find upon analysis that it still *did not state any meaning of the eucharistic action proper* at all. It would be a fair indication that Cranmer's Zwinglian conception of the rite had still dominated the new revision, and that the substitution of the oblation of the sons of men for that of the Son of Man still continued. Cranmer's 'prayer of oblation' virtually puts 'These are our bodies' in the place of 'This is My Body'—and that is not the eucharist. If this were the belief of those who used the new liturgy it would no doubt serve their turn. There would be no more to be said, except that it is not the meaning given to the eucharistic action itself by the primitive church, though it is associated with one part of it—the offertory. The important thing to remember is that it is *the action as a whole* which is the essence of the rite; and that the way it fulfils this and the meaning it attaches to it is the ultimate test of a rite's suitability for its purpose.

---

[1] See *The Book of Ceremonies* drawn up *c.* 1540, which had at least Cranmer's sanction (though it was never published). 'Then followeth the offertory, whereby we be learned to prepare ourselves by God's grace to be an acceptable oblation to him to the intent we may be partakers of the blessed sacrifice which Christ offered for us upon the cross' (*The Rationale of Ceremonial*, ed. by Sir C. Cobb, Alcuin Club Coll. XVIII, London, 1910, *p.* 22). *Cf. p.* 117.

A new Anglican rite might gain or lose support by all sorts of features. But the simplest and most practical constructional test of its merits, viewed simply as a liturgy—a way of doing the eucharistic action—would be by an analysis of the 'second half' of its eucharistic prayer. It is there that the *meaning* of the eucharistic action will be stated, if it is stated at all.

Yet when the revisers and the bishops and the liturgists have all done their best for our rite, there would still have to be the work of the church upon it, not only to improve it, but to *use* it and pray it and give it meaning in its own life. Perhaps we all, bishops and priests and people alike in the Church of England, need to examine our consciences rather seriously. We have discussed the liturgical problem for forty years or more. Meanwhile one person in every eighteen or nineteen in England is an Easter communicant of the Established Church, of whom perhaps two-thirds are adults, the majority of these being over fifty years of age. Perhaps one in fifty of the adult population is a really regular communicant. According to the last published figures, the diocese of London (with an income from all sources of close on £1,000,000 a year) had rather less than 150,000 Easter communicants out of 4,500,000 inhabitants. According to Mr. Seebohm Rowntree's social survey of York during the last forty years, Anglican church attendance there has dropped by twenty-seven per cent. during that period. Churchgoers forty years ago by no means coincided with the total population. But what makes the figures look really catastrophic is that the population of York has increased by about fifty per cent. during that period.[1] The same sort of figures are available from all over the country. From A.D. 1660 to 1760 we had a virtual monopoly of public worship in England. The penalised Roman Catholics and the socially uninfluential dissenters did not between them make up ten per cent. of the population. By no means ninety per cent. were Anglican worshippers; probably not fifty per cent. But at least it was we who had the opportunities.

We have an immense advantage over the dissenters in that we have a liturgy, and over the Roman Catholics in that it is in the vernacular. We still retain certain facilities given us by the Establishment, which makes possible a parochial system covering the whole country. We still have the old buildings, with all the force of the feeling for the old 'parish church' and the sense of themselves as 'parishioners', which are still strong in many provincial districts, even among those who never enter a church. But we are not managing to give the English people any idea of the meaning of the eucharist in christian life. We are still the National Church, but we are allowing our christian people to become increasingly non-communicant— a nation of catechumens. One has only to listen to broadcast addresses on such an occasion as a 'National Day of Prayer' to realise that 'petition' for

---

[1] Dissenting attendances have dropped forty per cent., Roman Catholics have increased twenty-six per cent. in the same period.

his own interests is the furthest we expect the ordinary man to go in his religious practice. That is the christianity of the catechumen.

One cause for this popular ignoring of the eucharist among uninstructed but *praying* English people may be that our eucharistic worship is very divorced from real life. By omitting all the 'votives' for the emergencies of human living Cranmer aimed at getting rid of the old 'intentions' in the offering of the 'sacrifices of masses'. But one result has been to make our eucharistic worship look like an affair of pure 'piety', suitable for the naturally devout but quite unconnected with all earthly affairs. This at least we ought to remedy. The late Archbishop of Canterbury speaking on the Social Teaching of Christianity in the Albert Hall on September 26th, 1942, said that holy communion is the consecration of human life to God, and the offering of bread and wine—not wheat and grapes, as he emphasised—is the offering of human labour upon God's gifts. One listener could not help reflecting, not only how true this is (when seen in relation to the rest of eucharistic doctrine) but also that it is a truth never brought out in our liturgy, and difficult even to read into it as it stands. Do we not expressly call them 'these *Thy creatures* of bread and wine'?

The admirable lead in christian social teaching now being given us by authority has been desperately needed for a generation and more. Coming so belatedly it is not going to save us from a great wave of secularism in the coming years. Unless balanced by a deepening of spirituality, it might lead only to a secularising of religion within the church itself. There is always the same danger in different forms that men's schemes for bringing in a King-dom of God on earth will take the place of the gospel of how God brought it in, by a human dying and a coming again from the dead to the right hand of power. (It was this same good intention in another form which brought about the fifteenth century mechanisation of the Western church.) How else shall we better be kept in mind that the Kingdom is God's, with the power and the glory of it, than by the 're-calling' of Calvary and Easter and Ascension? But it would help us more to do this if our rite mentioned the two latter just once! Where shall men begin to learn what it means truly to live in community better than at communion, in the act which creates the perfect divine-human society? But our 'prayer for the church militant' suggests that the first duty of a christian government is to 'punish'!

I mention these as specimens of the sort of things any thoughtful revision would try to amend. There are plenty of others. We shall certainly not convert England merely by inventing a new liturgy, especially if we quarrel about it. Yet at least we ought to see to it that our liturgy gives those who do attend it not a merely Tudor sociology, but the fulness of the christian ideas which we long to give to the rest of our fellow-countrymen.

I think it was Lord Morley who, in discussing the difference between a statesman and a politician, said that the latter is dangerous because he approaches great questions as though they were not truly great. If we and our bishops again approach the revision of our eucharistic liturgy in the spirit of ecclesiastical politics, we shall do the English church a terrible, perhaps an irreparable, harm. It is not a matter of academic niceties or devotional fancies or of administrative convenience. A church which sets out to revise its liturgy has taken in hand something which will affect its own supernatural life at its very source. It is difficult for bishops and those invaluable clergy and laity who give their time to administrative committees to realise that all their labour, necessary as it is, passes over the heads of the clergy and the laity in the parishes, remote, uninteresting and almost unheard of. For these people, whose salvation is the very *raison d'être* of the church—for whom Christ died—it is not administration but *worship* which constitutes their only contact with religion. Every parish priest knows that, however successful the work of his parish, however much money is raised for missions, however vigorous the social interest, however large the Sunday school and efficient the day schools and flourishing the Scouts and Guides and all the rest of it, it is always the nucleus who are regularly with him at the altar week by week or month by month on Sundays who are the real mainspring of the work. It is these people who provide the prayers and most of the effort and the gifts and the zeal which make the impact of the church in that place possible. This is inevitable, for it is not organisation but the eucharist which is always creating the church to *be* the Body of Christ; to do His will, and work His works, and adore His Father 'in His Name', and in Him to be made one, and by Him in them to be made one with God. That is the consummation of human living and the end of man.

# CHAPTER XVII

## 'THROUGHOUT ALL AGES, WORLD WITHOUT END'

THERE are hopeful symptoms at the present time of a renewal of interest in the study of liturgy in this country. But if this revival is to be healthy and the study is to make genuine progress, there are certain observations which it seems important that somebody should make plainly and openly at this stage. I have no commission or desire to pontificate on the subject as a whole; but it may be useful from more than one point of view to sum up my own book, both what it is and what it is not intended to be and to achieve, in the light of these general considerations.

This book is not, and is not intended to be a technical 'History of the Liturgy', though no doubt it could serve some of the purposes of one for a beginner in the subject. But such a History to be scientifically adequate would need a different sort of treatment, and in any case I do not know enough to undertake such a task. Indeed it is more than doubtful whether even a group of specialists in combination could put together a really satisfactory History of the Liturgy at just the present stage of liturgical studies. The old accepted outline of the subject began to fall to pieces under critical investigation soon after the beginning of this century. The last generation saw the production of more than one general theory—such as those associated with the names of G. P. Wetter and H. Lietzmann and others, or (in a different way) of Walter Frere—all designed to replace the old *dogmes d'école* by something which took more scientific account of new knowledge. Attention has naturally been chiefly concentrated among non-specialists upon those parts of these theories which sought to cast new light upon liturgical origins. But you cannot in fact revolutionise your view of origins without considerably affecting your treatment and understanding of the later course of liturgical history as a whole. And for the christian church, and ultimately for every member of it however unlearned, that is in the end not an academic but a *practical* matter as regards the eucharist. Slowly but certainly it will affect first what they think and then how they pray in the central and vital act in fully christian living, the corporate celebration of the eucharist.

All these theories have been presented with learning and some of them with brilliance. They have opened up new questions, many of which are not yet ripe for solution. The scientific study of liturgy has still to come to a final reckoning with some of their results, and in a number of matters to readjust its perspectives considerably in accordance with new evidence. But it is already clear that none of these modern theories—whether revolutionary or restatements of old theses—will serve as it stands for the groundwork of that scientific reconstruction of which liturgical study is now acknowledged to stand in need. When that comes it will be analogous to the work of Wellhausen in the critical study of the Old Testament; whatever may be the final stability of its immediate theses, after it the subject will be studied differently from before. All other branches of church history have already undergone a similar transformation at the hands of scholars of every doctrinal allegiance. There is no reason to doubt that the history of the liturgy will have to undergo the same process.

The innumerable footnotes of this book probably bear sufficient witness to the fact that these recent attempts at a new synthesis have been before me in the writing of it. But I have also tried continually to keep in mind the fact that I had not set out to produce a technical manual, but a book for the intelligent christian—perhaps mainly the intelligent ecclesiastic—and him especially of my own communion, who is anxious to acquire a practical acquaintance with the subject as it now stands, in order to make what use of it he can in solving the formidable and occasionally desperate practical problems presented by living the life of the Body of Christ in our own times. This has involved reducing technical minutiae to the minimum consistent with a full and intelligible presentation of the subject (and also, where it seemed helpful, some repetition). But I think I can assure him that everything important in the work of the last generation of scholars which is at all likely to survive into the findings of the next has here been taken into account. If these recent theories make no great shewing in this book, that is because they have already been generally rejected by competent scholars as satisfactory basic explanations. The new facts for which they were intended to account have been included. The book is, indeed, mainly a description of the facts, because I do not think the time has yet quite come for theorising, except in the very broadest outlines.

I ought also to point out that this has involved skirting several important questions,[1] about which there seems to me to be an insufficiency of established facts for anything but speculative and inconclusive discussions, which would be out of place in a book of this kind. These matters will all have to be more closely investigated by somebody before anything like a definitive History or Manual can be written. These dark patches are scattered irregularly all over that part of the subject which is concerned with the first eight centuries. The vital period of course is that of 'origins' —say down to c. A.D. 125. Here I have tried to shew that the available evi-

---

[1] Those which I should most have enjoyed discussing at length are (1) the tradition of Asia Minor (cf. pp. 289 sq.): (2) the origin of the Latin liturgies (cf. p. 557, n. 2) whether the type is African or Italian in origin, and the influences which moulded it; and (3) the nature of the complexity which we cover by using the blessed word 'Antiochene' and the diverse elements, Anatolian, 'hellenistic' Syrian, 'semitic' Syrian (and others?) which are to be discerned behind its fourth–fifth century amalgam, and the various ideas these represent. There are, of course, other important omissions in the book which will strike the expert reader, but these seem to me the most serious.

dence does enable us to establish a few—a very few—certainties, which are just enough to enable us to reconstruct the later history, when it begins to be discernible, upon foundations which do not rest only on a bog of guess-work. As regards the rest of the pre-Nicene period, the later second and third centuries, we have still very much less information than we could wish. Yet I cannot help thinking, for what the opinion is worth, that as regards both the East and the West the essential outlines of the history of the *Shape* of the Liturgy are a good deal clearer from the second—or even the end of the first—century onwards down to the end of the fourth, than they are in the three centuries which follow. The jewish evidence, with the jewish-christian evidence of the New Testament, enables us to make out something of the period of 'origins'. After that our real key-point of knowledge is still the fourth century, about which we are comparatively well informed, because then the christian church comes out into the after-noon daylight of the ancient civilisation. We have to work backwards from that into the pre-Nicene period of secrecy, and forwards from it into the night of the dark ages after the collapse of civilisation.

The first process is usually both safer and easier than the other. The pre-Nicene church lived and thought and worshipped within the world of the imperial-hellenistic civilisation, even when it stood consciously embattled against it; and that world is still there in the fourth century. There is thus a real homogeneity of background between the fourth century and the period before it, even though we have to take account of the considerable changes in christian ideas brought about by the changed political situation of the church after Constantine. But between the fourth century and the growing secular chaos of the period which follows there is no such con-tinuity of framework and background. We are apt not to allow enough for the tremendous break-up of ideas in the confusion of the barbarian cen-turies, just because the literary sources for the period come from those ecclesiastical circles which were trying manfully to conserve all that could be saved of the old civilised way of thinking. Even in the liturgy, where continuity is on the whole more complete than in any other sphere of European culture,[1] these conservative efforts were in one essential respect unsuccessful. The forms of the liturgy were preserved, on the whole with a surprising fidelity. But the *thought* of the mediaeval Latin and Byzantine churches about the eucharist, their 'devotional' approach to it and the way the ordinary priest and worshipper regarded it and prayed at it, these things were in certain important respects quite different from those which the fourth century had inherited from the pre-Nicene church.

[1] The only possible comparison is in the realm of law, where the work of Justinian did transmit the principles of imperial jurisprudence (with a Byzantine *nuance*) to the middle ages. But here there is hardly continuity. The Western study of Roman law in the twelfth century was largely a deliberate revival. And in practice the Teutonic law which had grown up in the interval held some of its ground, and even affected the theories of the civil lawyers to some extent.

Both the cause and the process of this breach of continuity lie in the dark ages.

It is unnecessary and in any case quite useless to deplore these changes made necessary by the history of the dark ages. There is no more reason to set up the fourth century (or for that matter the first) than the thirteenth or the sixteenth as the ideal for those who have to be christians in the twentieth. But it is very important that we should understand these changes, for they have abiding results now upon ourselves. It is not really surprising that Western protestants and Western catholics to-day should each somehow find it easier to learn from the Easterns than from one another, in spite of the wide difference of tradition between East and West. This is because modern Western catholicism and modern Western pro-testantism are in essentials mutually exclusive logical developments of *the same* 'Western' pattern of thought, as it emerged from the dark ages. Each is instinctively seeking a complement; and each is instinctively aware that in the other it will find not a complement but an alternative, and so turns more hopefully for what it needs to the East. But what seems hitherto to have prevented the East from being able to fulfil this dimly felt need of the whole West in a satisfying way is precisely certain elements of the Eastern tradition which arose in the same period *c.* A.D. 400–*c.* 800. They might be defined as what Byzantium added to Orthodoxy. It is one more proof that 'Catholicism'—'Wholeness'—is something more than and prior to the interplay of divergent local christian traditions.

It was in the dark ages that 'Catholicism' in this sense was first resolved into *divergent local traditions of thought*,[1] and the practical expression of this is in the history of the liturgy. But we know very little about the pro-cess. We have from literary sources an adequate knowledge—compara-tively speaking—of the rites of the fourth century; and we have the rites which have evidently developed from them, as these begin to appear in surviving liturgical MSS. from about A.D. 700 onwards. Everything in between has to be worked out painfully and inductively from this earlier and later evidence. The result is that we know solidly very little about the *causes* of liturgical history in this period, and not a great deal about its actual course. Admittedly this is not quite so vital as the pre-Nicene history. Yet it is a most important period, during which the Eastern and Western groups finally draw apart, and develop each their own ethos. The evidence from this period is in some directions actually less in quantity than from the pre-Nicene church; and it is both more complicated to handle and harder to piece into a comprehensible story. This is probably partly because we know less of the cultural and devotional influences which shaped the changes then taking place. But, partly at least, it represents a

---

[1] The pre-Nicene local traditions of the eucharistic prayer are very divergent in expression, but so far as I understand them they are all different attempts to express the same things. This is not true in the same way of later differences.

more complicated course of development than in pre-Nicene times.[1] I do not know how it may appear to other students, but to me the fifth and sixth centuries appear to offer more individual questions to which we do not seem to have as yet even the outline of a definitive answer than any other period.

Few of these unsolved problems of liturgical history in any period seem likely to prove permanently insoluble, if we know where to look for the evidence. But this is often to be found in the 'background' of the period as much as in the obviously liturgical material. In the earliest period of all, the period of origins, the christian material has a jewish background as well as a Greek one, and it is the former which is much the more important and enlightening. It is even true to say that the christian evidence cannot be interpreted apart from it. I am aware that this is a conclusion which still fails to commend itself in all quarters. Nevertheless, surveying what is known of the apostles of the New Testament—not excluding Saul the pharisee—as well as the earthly life of Jesus of Nazareth, I am at a loss to understand how anything which is 'apostolic' in the sense of being aboriginal in the christian religion could be expected to be anything but jewish in its historical affiliations. The Old Testament (the only 'bible' of Jesus and the primitive church) with the jewish apocalyptic and devotional

[1] One great help towards disentangling this period, at least so far as concerns the East, would be a new and entirely recast edition of Brightman's *Liturgies Eastern and Western*. The book has done yeoman service. But it is something of a reflection on English liturgists that we still have to use as our chief source-book one published forty-six years ago, which itself was only a revision of Hammond's book of the same title, published sixty-five years ago. As it stands it is an accurate but uncritical print of the mediaeval texts of some of the most important Eastern rites as these are found in the best MSS. available seventy years ago. But excepting the Byzantine rite there is no liturgy in *L.E.W.* of which (in whole or in part) better and older MSS. are not now available; and several documents of first-class importance (*e.g.* Sarapion) are not included at all. I have used *L.E.W.* to give references because it is likely to be the book most generally available for checking my statements. But it ought to be said that it is no longer satisfactory for the purposes of students. What is wanted is a critical text of the rites (giving MS. variants, as in Swainson's *Greek Liturgies*, 1884) and indicating by a difference of type (*i*) those parts of them known to be older than A.D. 400; (*ii*) those which date from *c.* A.D. 400–800; (*iii*) mediaeval and modern accretions. The mere process of arranging the book for publication in this way would probably enable the editors to clear up more than one of the obscurities now besetting the history of the Eastern rites *c.* A.D. 400–800 (especially in the case of the Egyptian liturgies).

Nor should it be forgotten that the book as it stands is only a torso, of which the second and third volumes were never compiled, and never could be according to the author's scheme. (No materials for them, even, seem to exist among Dr. Brightman's papers.) But within more practicable limits than he seems to have contemplated, a second volume of inaccessible Latin liturgical documents or Latin texts still in need of scientific editing, and a third volume of *Critica Liturgica* of various kinds, could render the same sort of service to students that the old book has rendered so faithfully in the past. No one now alive is competent to undertake the whole task. It would have to be the co-operative work of a number of specialists under a small dietorial committee, and would need a good deal of pains and trouble. But no other publication would in the long run so effectively assist the general progress of the study.

literature of the period between the two Testaments (some knowledge of which is discernible in parts of our Lord's own teaching, and some of which is significantly quoted as 'scripture' both by New Testament writers and some of the second century fathers) and also the literature of earlier rabbinism—all this can teach us much about the oriental world out of which christianity came. The hellenistic world into which it came *created* nothing in the religion of the New Testament, though hellenistic judaism began to influence its presentation in the second, perhaps even in the first, decade after the passion. But pagan hellenism at the first encounter found it already fully equipped with ideas and institutions of its own, and in this earliest period furnishes at the most analogies, and those as a rule not very close ones.

In the second and third centuries christianity became almost exclusively a religion for gentile converts. Though the marks of its judaic origin were never lost, the hellenistic background now becomes increasingly important. Only in Syria and the regions immediately to the North and East of it the native semitic or half-semitic background preserves in the local churches there a closer contact in some respects with the thought of the original judaeo-christian *milieu*. This differentiates them increasingly from the more and more hellenised churches of the Greek and Latin West. This cross-division of pre-Nicene christianity into 'semitic' and 'hellenistic' churches, which runs along a different line from that which later separated Greek and Latin christendom, is likely to prove of considerable importance in the elucidation of the evidence before A.D. 400. It seems to require more investigation than it has yet received, in which the special influence of the *Greek* Syrian churches in the hellenised cities as transmitting agents in both directions ought not to be overlooked. There is room for a good deal of adaptation to have happened in the course of this process.

As regards the latter part of the pre-Nicene period, of course, we shall always be mainly dependent on specifically christian material. Failing the discovery of new documents, the most promising line of advance seems to lie in a meticulous investigation of all the extant fourth and fifth century local traditions of the eucharistic prayer, coupled with an assiduous comparison with the writings of the pre-Nicene fathers. Just because liturgy is apt to be more conservative than theology, the later liturgical prayers often illuminate the earlier fathers and are in turn illuminated by them in a very remarkable fashion. This is one of the most pressing tasks now confronting students of liturgy, but it will be a laborious and detailed business, and one full of pitfalls, which will have to be left to the experts.

After this we are in the fourth century. From then onwards we are dealing with a nominally christian world, in which christian ideas and assumptions mould secular cultures as much as the latter influence christianity. In the 'second period' therefore (A.D. 400–800) and to a growing extent from A.D. 325–400 the christian liturgical material offers information of some importance to the social historian, which has not yet been fully exploited. In return, the answers to liturgical problems are sometimes found to lie in the material of the social or even political historian rather than in that which is usually supposed to be the concern of the liturgist.

This great variation in the necessary background for the scientific study of liturgy in the various periods is, of course, quite natural when one considers the matter. But it offers a practical problem in the adequate training of students for this field of research. It is difficult to become really knowledgeable in such different directions, and this will probably lead to the sort of specialisation which is not desirable. Yet that some more scientific methods of training are now necessary seems obvious. After leading the world in the generation before the last, English liturgical studies—with the honoured exception of three or four names—have been steadily falling below the best work in Belgium, Germany and France for the last twenty years. This is partly from want of workers, but mainly from want of method. No subject can have a greater appeal for its own sake to christians than the record of what has always been the essential *life* not only of the church corporately, but of all the individual saints and sinners who have gone to God before us in the Body of Christ—the tradition of christian worship, unbroken since the Upper Room. No subject could have a more practical bearing on the problems of christian living at the present time, if only it is properly approached. Yet the number of young recruits to such studies in England in the last ten years has been infinitesimal. The apprenticeship required is somewhat exacting, necessitating the acquiring of languages as well as very wide historical reading. But not everyone need start by setting out to become an expert fitted for research. The real difficulty is that there are now practically no reliable 'Introductions' or 'Beginner's Manuals'. The modern ones are encumbered with dubious theories; the older ones are obsolete in their information, and are also as a rule not only academic but slightly repellent in their whole approach to the subject.[1]

The study of liturgy is not rightly to be regarded as a branch of canon law or christian administrative history; it cannot be properly treated as the mere study of a series of changes in 'regulations' about christian worship. It is here that I see the chief reason why English liturgical studies have made such disappointing progress since the death of Edmund Bishop. We have forgotten that the study of liturgy is above all a study of *life*, that christian worship has always been something done by real men and women, whose contemporary circumstances have all the time a profound effect upon the ideas and aspirations with which they come to worship. We must grasp the fact that worship cannot take place in an ecclesiastical Avalon, but to a large extent reflects the ever-changing needs and ideas of the worshippers. So it gives rise all the time to new notions by the

[1] I venture to repeat the recommendation of Dr. Srawley's book, *cf. p.* 208, *n.* 1.

interaction of these urgent contemporary ideas in the minds of those worshipping by ancient inherited forms. Thus arises the ever-shifting emphasis of christian devotion and 'devotions', which plays around the liturgy, interpreting it afresh to every generation and to every race. This is a psychological study of the utmost fascination, which requires insight and human sympathy as well as wide knowledge. It is an integral and most instructive part of the study of liturgy. Yet except for some essays by Edmund Bishop and some by Dom Wilmart (if we may borrow a French monk of Farnborough to adorn the ranks of English scholarship) it has been almost unrepresented in English work since the death of Neale. Until we take it more seriously we shall not understand the history of the liturgy, and we shall not put such dry knowledge of it as we may gain to any valuable use. In particular the immense eirenic possibilities latent in the understanding of how differences of christian practice first arose will remain unexplored. Yet these differences of practice are psychologically far more sundering to the laity of the different christian bodies than the differences of doctrine which they represent. It is quite true, as T. A. Lacey once said, that, in the broad meaning of the terms, 'It is theology which unites us and religion which divides us'.

Every science progresses not so much by the haphazard accumulation of facts (though established facts are always valuable) as by the asking and eventual answering of certain key questions. Liturgical studies have failed to advance largely because we have been asking the wrong questions. In so far as this book goes any way towards being a 'History of the Liturgy', such usefulness as it may have lies in its attempts to ask some of the right questions. They are not emphasised as new, but liturgical students will be aware how many of them have not been asked before, or at all events have not been put quite in the same way. I have tried to give the answers on the basis of all the evidence I know, indicating candidly where it seems to me that the material available still reduces us all to guess-work. It would be too much to hope that in a work involving many hundreds of small points of evidence my handling of them will in every case commend itself to specialists. Much, too, which is relevant to the right answers I have no doubt missed. Others will supply that, once the right questions have been raised. We know more to-day, much more, than Mabillon and Martène and Cardinal Tomasi and Forbes and all the rest of the older liturgists, polymaths though they were in their time. The difference is not only in sheer quantity of information, though our resources of facts are much greater than theirs, even if we do not always make better use of them. But we have also profited by their work to answer questions which they raised and could not answer, and the new answers have in turn produced new questions and new knowledge. If it stimulates others to ask the really revealing questions more aptly and more persistently than they are asked here, this book will have contributed usefully to the subject.

This may appear a somewhat hesitating recommendation of a book professing to give historical information. Emphatically, I should not claim that it is exhaustive or definitive as a history, though I am soberly confident that the broad outlines of the history of the liturgy as it is incidentally sketched here will not be greatly modified when the results of modern study come to be assessed, perhaps in a generation's time. Details will be corrected; considerable gaps will be filled in; some things will appear in a different proportion. But we are beginning to know enough now to be sure that at least we are working on right lines. Yet I repeat that this is designedly not a 'History of the Liturgy' but something preparatory to it—a study of how the normal Shape of the Liturgy came to have the form it has.

Every rite which goes back beyond the sixteenth century is to a large extent the product not so much of deliberate composition as of the continual doing of the eucharistic action by many generations in the midst of the varying pressures of history and human life as it is lived. The immense local variety of rites represents the immense variety of cultures, races and local circumstances in which the one Body of Christ has incarnated itself by 'doing this' in the course of two thousand years. During that time several great civilisations and empires and innumerable lesser social groups have risen and flourished and passed away. Many of them have left a mark in their time on the local liturgy as it survived them, in the wording of a few prayers or in some gestures and customs, on the cut of a vestment or some furnishing of the sanctuary. But under all this superficial variety there is the single fixed pattern common to all the old churches of the East and West, which was not everywhere wholly destroyed among the churches of the Reformation. This is always the same, not by any imposed law or consciously recognised custom that it should be so, but through the sole force of the fact that this way of doing the eucharist alone fulfils every need of every church in every age in the performing of the eucharistic action with its essential meaning.

The outlines of that ritual pattern come down to us unchanged in christian practice from before the crucifixion, the synaxis from Jesus' preaching in the synagogues of Galilee, the eucharist proper from the evening meals of Jesus with His disciples. The needs of a christian corporate worship gradually brought about their combination. The needs of a christian public worship have added to these inheritances from our Lord's own jewish piety only an 'introduction' of praise and a brief prayer of thanksgiving. The whole has a new meaning fixed for all time in the Upper Room. But the form of the rite is still centred upon the Book on the lectern and the Bread and Cup on the table as it always was, though by the new meaning they have become the Liturgy of the Spirit and the Liturgy of the Body, centring upon the Word of God enounced and the Word of God made flesh.

At the heart of it all is the eucharistic action, a thing of an absolute simplicity—the taking, blessing, breaking and giving of bread and the taking, blessing and giving of a cup of wine and water, as these were first done with their new meaning by a young Jew before and after supper with His friends on the night before He died. Soon it was simplified still further, by leaving out the supper and combining the double grouping before and after it into a single rite. So the four-action Shape of the Liturgy was found by the end of the first century. He had told His friends to do this henceforward with the new meaning 'for the *anamnesis*' of Him, and they have done it always since.

Was ever another command so obeyed? For century after century, spreading slowly to every continent and country and among every race on earth, this action has been done, in every conceivable human circumstance, for every conceivable human need from infancy and before it to extreme old age and after it, from the pinnacles of earthly greatness to the refuge of fugitives in the caves and dens of the earth. Men have found no better thing than this to do for kings at their crowning and for criminals going to the scaffold; for armies in triumph or for a bride and bridegroom in a little country church; for the proclamation of a dogma or for a good crop of wheat; for the wisdom of the Parliament of a mighty nation or for a sick old woman afraid to die; for a schoolboy sitting an examination or for Columbus setting out to discover America; for the famine of whole provinces or for the soul of a dead lover; in thankfulness because my father did not die of pneumonia; for a village headman much tempted to return to fetich because the yams had failed; because the Turk was at the gates of Vienna; for the repentance of Margaret; for the settlement of a strike; for a son for a barren woman; for Captain so-and-so, wounded and prisoner of war; while the lions roared in the nearby amphitheatre; on the beach at Dunkirk; while the hiss of scythes in the thick June grass came faintly through the windows of the church; tremulously, by an old monk on the fiftieth anniversary of his vows; furtively, by an exiled bishop who had hewn timber all day in a prison camp near Murmansk; gorgeously, for the canonisation of S. Joan of Arc—one could fill many pages with the reasons why men have done this, and not tell a hundredth part of them. And best of all, week by week and month by month, on a hundred thousand successive Sundays, faithfully, unfailingly, across all the parishes of christendom, the pastors have done this just to *make* the *plebs sancta Dei*—the holy common people of God.

To those who know a little of christian history probably the most moving of all the reflections it brings is not the thought of the great events and the well-remembered saints  but of those innumerable millions of entirely obscure faithful men and women, every one with his or her own individual hopes and fears and joys and sorrows and loves—and sins and temptations and prayers—once every whit as vivid and alive as mine are now. They have left no slightest trace in this world, not even a name, but have passed to God utterly forgotten by men. Yet each of them once believed and prayed as I believe and pray, and found it hard and grew slack and sinned and repented and fell again. Each of them worshipped at the eucharist, and found their thoughts wandering and tried again, and felt heavy and unresponsive and yet knew—just as really and pathetically as I do these things. There is a little ill-spelled ill-carved rustic epitaph of the fourth century from Asia Minor:—'Here sleeps the blessed Chione, who has found Jerusalem for she prayed much'. Not another word is known of Chione, some peasant woman who lived in that vanished world of christian Anatolia. But how lovely if all that should survive after sixteen centuries were that one had prayed much, so that the neighbours who saw all one's life were sure one must have found Jerusalem! What did the Sunday eucharist in her village church every week for a life-time mean to the blessed Chione—and to the millions like her then, and every year since? The sheer stupendous *quantity* of the love of God which this ever repeated action has drawn from the obscure christian multitudes through the centuries is in itself an overwhelming thought. (All that going with one to the altar every morning!)

It is because it became embedded deep down in the life of the christian peoples, colouring all the *via vitae* of the ordinary man and woman, marking its personal turning-points, marriage, sickness, death and the rest, running through it year by year with the feasts and fasts and the rhythm of the Sundays, that the eucharistic action became inextricably woven into the public history of the Western world. The thought of it is inseparable from its great turning-points also. Pope Leo doing this in the morning before he went out to daunt Attila, on the day that saw the continuity of Europe saved; and another Leo doing this three and a half centuries later when he crowned Charlemagne Roman Emperor, on the day that saw that continuity fulfilled. Or again, Alfred wandering defeated by the Danes staying his soul on this, while mediaeval England struggled to be born; and Charles I also, on that morning of his execution when mediaeval England came to its final end. Such things strike the mind with their suggestions of a certain timelessness about the eucharistic action and an independence of its setting, in keeping with the stability in an ever-changing world of the forms of the liturgy themselves. At Constantinople they 'do this' yet with the identical words and gestures that they used while the silver trumpets of the Basileus still called across the Bosphorus, in what seems to us now the strange fairy-tale land of the Byzantine empire. In this twentieth century Charles de Foucauld in his hermitage in the Sahara 'did this' with the same rite as Cuthbert twelve centuries before in his hermitage on Lindisfarne in the Northern seas. This very morning I did this with a set of texts which has not changed by more than a few syllables since Augustine used those very words at Canterbury on the third Sunday of Easter in the summer after he landed. Yet 'this' can still take hold of a man's life and work with it.

It is not strange that the eucharist should have this power of laying hold of human life, of grasping it not only in the abstract but in the particular concrete realities of it, of reaching to anything in it, great impersonal things that rock whole nations and little tender human things of one man's or one woman's living and dying—laying hold of them and translating them into something beyond time. This was its new meaning from the beginning. The Epistle to the Hebrews pictures our Lord as saying from the moment of His birth at Bethlehem, 'Other sacrifice and offering Thou wouldest not, but a Body hast Thou prepared for me; Lo I come to do Thy will, O God'.[1] On the last night of His life it was still the same: 'This is My Body'—'And now I come to Thee'.[2] It was the whole perfect human life that had gone before and all His living of it that was taken and spoken and deliberately broken and given in the institution of the eucharist.

The next morning the offering was completed. His offering cost the Offerer Himself. The death was real. Even now, and for ever upon the throne of the universe, it is still true that for three days the Son of Mary was *dead*. God is real, and is really worshipped only with a real sacrifice, which exacts a real offering that is 'devoted', wholly handed over to God. That is the meaning of 'sacrifice'—to 'make' a thing *sacrum*—to pass it over altogether into the possession of God. It may be doubted whether either theologically or historically 'destruction' as such is necessarily of the essence of such a notion, as de Lugo and most other post-Tridentine theologians, both catholic and protestant, seem to have conspired to teach. The destruction of the victim may be an accompaniment of many forms of sacrifice, but the older christian tradition, both mediaeval and patristic, was more accurate as well as more inclusive in its definition, perhaps because it was broader based, on pagan as well as scriptural *data*. (Rightly so, for sacrifice is something as wide as worshipping humanity, a rite of natural as well as revealed religion.) 'Sacrifices are properly so called when *anything is done about things offered to God*', says S. Thomas.[3] 'A true sacrifice is any act that is done in order that we may cleave in an holy union to God . . . for though it is done or offered by man, yet *a sacrifice is a thing belonging to God* (*res divina*) so that the old Romans used this term also for it', says S. Augustine.[4] There is no need to cite more.

On this showing it is not the 'destruction' of the victim, but the completeness of the offerer's surrender of it and the completeness of God's acceptance of it which together make up the reality of sacrifice. Its essence lies in the action of persons rather than in the fate of a thing. The destruction of the victim, if such there be, is incidental to its transference from man to God, a means to the end of releasing it irrevocably from the power of its human possessor into that of God. So when the old Roman Republic vowed to the gods its supreme offering, a *ver sacrum*, all male offspring

[1] Heb. x. 5.　　　　　　　　　　　　　　　　[2] John xvii. 13.
[3] *circa res Deo oblatas aliquid fit* (*S. Th.* II-II. lxxxv, 3, ad. 3).　　[4] *de Civ. Dei*, x. 6.

born between March 1st and May 1st were 'devoted', the young of all live-
stock to sacrifice by immolation, but the boy babies born that spring to
life-long and irrevocable exile (so soon as they could fend for themselves)
that the city and their own families might never profit from their life and
strength. All alike were 'sacrificed'—'made *sacrum*'—even though the children still lived. What is necessary to sacrifice, however it be accomplished,
is the complete surrender of the victim by man and its complete acceptance
by God.

It may be that the form taken by the surrender of the human victims of
the *ver sacrum* is only the more merciful relic of a sterner ritual, by which
in older ages the boys had been actually destroyed along with the offspring
of the cattle, though there is no certain evidence of this. But in any case
human sacrifice has occurred among mankind as the most precious of all
sacrifices, and whatever horror it may now evoke, it was not always done
for merely horrible or ignoble reasons. It is among the most deep-rooted
of all human ideas (as anyone who cares to analyse much current war-
propaganda can see for himself). Unless we are willing to stultify something which is the very centre of the presentation of christianity in the New
Testament, the Messianic Sacrifice, we must acknowledge that here, too,
Christ came not to destroy but to fulfil. But here there could be no room
for mercy! The surrender of a human Victim *self*-offered in sacrifice must
culminate in 'Father, into Thy hands I will lay down from Myself (*para-
thēsomai*) My Spirit.'[1] Short of that, the surrender of the Victim by the
Offerer cannot be complete. There must be 'destruction' here (but not
necessarily in the eucharistic *anamnesis* of this) if there is to be reality of
sacrifice, even though it be incidental. In such a case God's acceptance of
sacrifice does not empty its destructiveness of reality; it reverses the destruction into fulfilment. The Victim is 'made *sacrum*'—passes wholly into
the power of the Living God.

The resurrection is not Jesus' survival of death; all men do that in any
case. It is the reversal of His death. The Divine acceptance of Calvary
is in Easter and Ascension, and in what follows from them in the World
to Come. For the latter we have only picture-language—the 'entering
in' of the eternal High-priest to the heavenly altar; the bestowal of
the crown and dominion of the everlasting kingdom; the 'coming' of one
like unto the Son of Man upon the clouds of heaven to the Ancient of Days.
These and other scriptural pictures are so many attempts to represent that
real entrance of the temporal into the eternal, which is just as much a consequence of the incarnation as the irruption of the eternal into time. There
is about them all a 'once-for-all' quality in consequence of which there is
(paradoxically) something new but permanent in eternity, just as there is
something new but enduring in time. It is this *double and mutual repercussion of time and eternity upon each other* in that act of God which is the

[1] Lk. xxiii. 46.

redemption of the world by Jesus of Nazareth, that is the essence of primitive christian eschatology. And of this the supreme expression from the beginning is the eucharist.

It is not myth or allegory which is at the heart of what the eucharist 're-calls' and 'proclaims' before God and man, but something rooted in a solid temporal event, wrought out grimly and murderously in one Man's flesh and blood on a few particular square yards of hillock outside a gate, *epi Pontiou Pilatou*—'when Pilate was governor', as they used to say in Judaea. That is history, with no admixture whatever of the eternal. And what follows, too, which is also 'proclaimed' in the eucharist, is history likewise, though it withdraws progressively beyond it. Between sunset on Saturday and dawn on Sunday the death was reversed. The New Testament finds no human words to describe what happened then in itself, but it had direct historical effects, which are described. A stone was rolled away, some soldiers fell unconscious, a woman cried aloud in a garden, two fishermen raced through the dawn to look at grave-clothes, and so on. These are historical events in space and time, and so on one side are all the things that happened during the forty days. The Ascension, on the other hand, is hardly describable in terms of earthly events at all. 'As they were looking'—that is factual, historical—'He was lifted up and a cloud received Him from before their eyes'.[1] That is obviously acted parable. The assumption of a Man into the Shechinah, with what that involves, is beyond historical description, even though there is in it some meeting-point of history and eternity. And after that there are only symbols, drawn from admittedly inadequate earthly pictures of priests and kings and the like.

All this together is 're-called'—made present and operative in its effects (*anamnesis*) in the eucharist; we need not go over the primitive liturgical texts again (*cf. pp.* 242 *sq*). We are here concerned only with the primitive understanding of what those effects are. But first we must note that just as the Messianic sacrifice has its meaning set for it beforehand at the last supper (*cf. p.* 76 *sq*) which is wholly within time, so it issues in Pentecost, which is the consequence within time of the eternal acceptance and efficacy of that sacrifice.[2] Just so the eucharist has its basis and pledge in the offertory of wholly earthly elements, and issues in that return of the eternal within the temporal in communion, in which the primitive church saw the gift of *pneuma* (divine 'Spirit') by means of the 'Body' to each of its members.

There is matter in this for deeper consideration than can be given it at the end of a long book, though it is relevant to all that the apostolic church thought about the eucharist. Here we limit ourselves strictly to the question of the eucharistic action and its effects, as these were understood in the earliest period. We shall not fully grasp its meaning until we learn to take much more seriously than our post-renaissance individualism is apt to do

[1] Acts i. 9.    [2] Acts ii. 33

the biblical and patristic teaching on the solidarity of the human race as one entity. As the early church saw it, that race fell in Adam, that 'was the son of God',[1] by disobedience, and was restored by obedience in Jesus, the new Adam, that was 'the Son of God'.[2] The New Testament everywhere takes this solidarity for granted and does not argue the matter.[3] The later fathers, confronted with Greek individualism, sometimes found themselves compelled to discuss it at some length.[4] Their unanimous conclusion was that the principle of this human unity lies in that mysterious 'image of God' in which man was created. One and the same 'image' is implanted in each man, yet there is but a single 'image' in them all. It is this 'image' which makes of each man a 'living soul', or as we should say a spiritual being. It was this 'image' which by his disobedience was defaced but not expunged in Adam, God's created son; and retained by His obedience to the uttermost in the second Adam, God's begotten Son, Who is personally 'the image and glory of God'.[5]

Whatever we may make of the particular terms in which the apostolic and pre-Nicene church expressed these ideas, they represent something which is essential to the primitive and scriptural doctrine of redemption, which nineteenth century presentations of christianity were the poorer for obscuring. If we would understand the mind of the primitive church about the eucharist and enrich our own conceptions by it, it is especially important that we should recognise how thoroughly and generally these ideas concerning the 'image of God' in mankind were accepted in the church. So when Hippolytus wishes to speak compendiously and in passing of the redeeming work of Christ, he speaks of God in Christ 'presenting to Himself that image of Himself which had gone astray'.[6] When Irenaeus reaches the conclusion and climax of the most considerable christian treatise which has survived from the second century, he conceives it thus:—There is but one God and Father, 'And again there is one Son, Who fulfilled the Father's will, and *one human race wherein the mysteries of God are fulfilled*; Whom the angels desire to look into, but they cannot penetrate the wisdom of God, whereby His creature (man) is perfectly conformed to and incorporated in the Son; that His own Son, the Word, the first-begotten, should descend into the creature which He had formed, and be laid hold of thereby; and the creature in turn, laying hold upon the Word, should ascend to God, mounting above the angels, and *should become according to the*

---

[1] Luke iii. 38.    [2] Luke iv. 3.    [3] *E.g.* 1 Cor. xv. 45–9; Rom. v. 19, etc.
[4] These ideas are worked out most fully, perhaps, by Gregory of Nyssa, *Of the Creation of Man* (M.P.G., xliv.) who goes to the length of denying the legitimacy of speaking theologically of 'men' in the plural; there is only 'mankind' (*cap.* viii.). But I do not think there is a single Greek father before the fifth century whose works have survived in any quantity in whose teaching these ideas have not left plain traces, and they are common in some of the Latins, *e.g.* Augustine. Some Greeks (*e.g.* Methodius of Olympus, *Banquet*, iii. 4 *sqq.*) speak of our Lord as *physically* Adam *redivivus*.
[5] 1 Cor. xi. 7.            [6] Hippolytus, *Ap. Trad.*, i. 1.

*image and likeness of God*.[1] For him, this doctrine of 'the image' is christianity 'in a nutshell', as we say. In the most serene of his treatises, before the long distraction of the Arian heresy began, Athanasius states the classical teaching on the incarnation and redemption thus: 'Therefore the Word of God came in His own Person, in order that, as He was the image of the Father, He might be able to re-create *the man* (*sing.*) made after the image'.[2]

Such a view closely associates the redemption with the creation of the world, as we have seen that the early eucharistic prayers all do by their 'thanksgiving series'. But with this view of redemption there necessarily went a doctrine of sin and atonement which has at least a rather different emphasis from our own. We Westerns all tend to lay the chief stress on the internal disorder caused by sin in the individual sinner's own soul, and view redemption mainly as the healing of each sinner's own wounds. Our doctrine of the work of Christ is, in technical language, 'soteriological', rather than 'cosmological', which has its own effects upon our eucharistic doctrine. Though this aspect of the matter was not ignored by them, the pre-Nicene writers had a plain sight also of a larger truth. Because any sin is the defacing of God's image which is one and the same in all men, any and every sin is a general shattering of the perfection of that image throughout mankind, and so an atomising of something which God created to be a unity. *Ubi peccata sunt, ibi est multitudo*, says Origen: 'Where there is sin, there is dispersion, there schisms, there heresies, there dissensions. But where there is goodness, there is unity, there is union, whence came that "one heart and one mind" of all the faithful (in the apostolic church). And to put the matter plainly, the principle of all evils is dispersion, but the principle of all good is drawing together and reduction from disordered multitudes to singleness'.[3]

No doubt the presentation of the idea here and in most of the fathers is Platonic, with its opposition of 'the one' and 'the many' as the principles of good and evil. But in its substance their thought is entirely scriptural, deriving ultimately from the Old Testament by way of the New. When S. John explains the final jewish prophecy of the old dispensation, pregnant now with all the meaning of the new, that 'one Man should die for the People' (*laos*)[4], he finds no other explanation of the Messianic sacrifice than this: 'that Jesus should die for the nation (*ethnous*) and not for the nation only, but that He might *gather together into one* the children of God that are scattered abroad'. Westcott remarks of this last phrase (*dieskorpismena*) that it 'marks a broken unity and not only wide dispersion (Matt. vi. 31; Acts v. 37). Such is the state of mankind in relation to its divine original.

---

[1] Irenaeus, *adv. Haer.*, v. 36, 3, conclusion. *Cf.* Origen, *de Princip.* II, vi. 3; *in Gen. Hom.* I, 3; *etc., etc.*
[2] Athanasius, *de Incarnatione*, xiii.      [3] Origen, *in Ezech. Hom.*, ix. 1.
[4] John xi. 50.

*Cf.* Isa. xlix. 6; lvi. 8'. The jews are no longer exclusively the *laos*, 'the people of God'; they have become absorbed, along with the gentiles 'made nigh (to them) by *the blood* of Christ' into that all-embracing restored unity of the new *laos*, 'in Christ Jesus, Who is our peace (with one another) Who *hath made both one*, and hath broken down the middle wall of partition (which divided the 'court of the gentiles' from the 'court of the men of Israel' in the Jerusalem temple) having abolished in *His flesh* the enmity (between us) for to make *in Himself* of the twain *one new man*'.[1] This healing of the deadly breach between jew and gentile in the ancient world (as rancorous and deep as that between Teuton and Slav in our time) is for S. Paul but one application of 'the mystery' of God's secret plan 'to *gather together in one* all things in Christ, both which are in the heavens and which are on earth; even in Him.'[2]

This is 'atonement', and it is also 'communion'. Contemplated upon such a background, not only the doctrine of original sin—that inescapable basic fact of human life—but the truth of its abolition 'in Christ' take on a clearer meaning. And so does the eucharist, in which the defiled 'image of God' is restored in men by the reception afresh of the one archetypal image, and mankind renewed and 'gathered into one' is presented to the Father 'in Christ' as the 'one new man', His recovered 'son'. So the purpose of God in man's creation to His glory is fulfilled in the eucharist. 'Glory be to God on high, and in earth peace to men of good will!' The more one studies the most ancient eucharistic prayers (the 'thanksgiving series'), the more it is plain that this is the fundamental theme of them all. This, so the ancient church believed, is not represented but *effected* at the eucharist. This is the 'coming' of the kingship of God among men, even within time, with its 'judgement' and its power, so that those who are not present to accept it or are present unworthily are condemned.[3] Here at the supper 'is the Son of Man glorified and God is glorified in Him '[4] Here those for whom He has appointed a kingdom, as His Father has appointed unto Him, eat and drink at His table in His kingdom, and sit on thrones judging.[5] Now He drinks again of the fruit of the vine,[6] yielded by the branches He Himself nourishes by the care of His Father the husband-man,[7] in the day that He drinks it new with us in His Father's kingdom.[8] So 'the people of the saints of the Most High' which God has willed 'to be conformed to the image of His Son, that He might be the first-born among many brethren',[9] come as one man, 'like the Son of Man', upon the clouds of heaven to the Ancient of Days and being offered draw near to Him, and there is given to them 'in Christ' the kingdom that shall not be destroyed.[10]

This is the whole life of the church and of the christian expressed,

[1] Eph. ii. 13 *sqq.*    [2] Eph. i. 10.    [3] 1 Cor. xi. 32.    [4] John xiii. 31.
[5] Luke xxii. 29, 30.    [6] Mark xiv. 25.    [7] John xv. 1 and 2.
[8] Matt. xxvi. 29.    [9] Rom. viii. 29.    [10] Dan. vii. 13 *sqq.*

fulfilled, done, in an action; for as Goethe (I think) says somewhere, 'the highest cannot be spoken, it can only be acted'. The more we can learn to think of our own worship at the eucharist not in terms only of assistance at a pleading or recollection of a redemption two thousand years ago, nor yet in terms only of 'my communion' (however true these partial understandings may be), but in terms of the 'pan-human' fulfilment of the Messianic sacrifice, the nearer we shall be to entering into the mind of the apostolic church about the eucharist and the further from most of our present controversies.

'There is one human race in which the mysteries of God are fulfilled.' It has been said that the problem of our generation will be the *motive* of civilisation. But in fact that is the problem in one form or another of all generations, the theory of human living. It has only been made more acute for us by the progressive apostasy of the liberal tradition in Europe for the last three centuries. The dream of the self-sufficiency of human power has haunted the hearts of all men since it was first whispered that by slipping from under the trammels of the law of God 'Ye shall be as Gods', choosing your own good and evil.[1] The shadows of that dream renew themselves continually in fresh shapes even in the minds and wills of those who serve God's kingship. Where that kingship is unknown or consciously denied that dream rules men, who are in the apostle's terrible phrase 'free from righteousness'.[2] In its crudest form, in the politics of our day, the pagan dream of human power has turned once more into a nightmare oppressing men's outward lives. That will pass, because it is too violent a disorder to be endured. But elsewhere and less vulgarly, as a *mystique* of technical and scientific mastery of man's environment, it is swiftly replacing the old materialism as the prevalent anti-christianity of the twentieth century. In this subtler form it will more secretly but even more terribly oppress the human spirit.

In the eucharist we christians concentrate our motive and act out our theory of human living. Mankind are not to be 'as Gods', a competing horde of dying rivals to the Living God. We are His creatures, fallen and redeemed, His dear recovered sons, who by His free love are 'made partakers of the Divine nature'.[3] But our obedience and our salvation are not of ourselves, even while we are mysteriously free to disobey and damn ourselves. We are dependent on Him even for our own dependence. We are accepted sons in the Son, by the real sacrifice and acceptance of His Body and Blood, Who 'though He were a Son, yet learned He obedience by the things which He suffered; and being made perfect, He became the author of eternal salvation unto all them that obey Him; called of God an Highpriest after the order of Melchisedech'.[4]

[1] Gen. iii. 5.                    [3] Rom. vi. 30.
[2] 2 Pet. i. 4.                    [4] Heb. v. 8 *sq.*

*Let us all with awe and reverence draw nigh to the mysteries of the precious Body and Blood of our Saviour. With a pure heart and faith unfeigned let us commemorate His passion and re-call His resurrection. For our sakes the only-begotten of God took of mankind a mortal body and a reasonable and intelligent and immortal soul, and by His lifegiving laws and holy commands hath brought us near from error to the knowledge of the truth. And after all His dispensation for us, He the firstfruits of our nature was lifted up upon the cross and rose from the dead and was taken up into heaven. He hath delivered to us His holy mysteries that in them we might re-call all His grace towards us. Let us then with overflowing love and with an humble will receive the gift of eternal life, and with pure prayer and manifold sorrow let us partake of the mysteries of the church in penitent hope, turning from our transgressions and grieving for our sins and looking for mercy and forgiveness from God the Lord of all . . .*

*Let us receive the Holy and be hallowed by the Holy Ghost.*

℟. of the People

*O Lord, pardon the sins and transgressions of Thy servants.*

The Deacon

*And in union and concord of minds let us receive the fellowship of the mysteries in peace with one another.*

℟. of the People

*O Lord, pardon the sins and transgressions of Thy servants.*

The Deacon

*That they be to us, O my Lord, for the resurrection of our bodies and the salvation of our souls and eternal life with all those who have been well-pleasing in Thy sight now and for ever and world without end.*

*Proclamation of the Deacon at the Fraction in the Liturgy of Addai and Mari*

# INDEX

Present conditions have prevented the inclusion of the full Bibliography and Indices I had planned, but I trust that this select Index of topics, used with the Table of Contents, will enable students to find their way easily enough about the book. It might be possible to issue something more scientific in pamphlet form later.

Only the more important references are given for most entries here.

Ablutions (ritual) of persons, 124; of vessels, 139, 668, 691
Abyssinian (Ethiopic) rites, 110, 530
acolytes, 35, 408, 417 sq.
Adamantius, 279
*Addai and Mari, Liturgy of SS.*, (East Syrian), 126 sq., 135, 177 sqq., 201, 206, 217 n., 220, 227, 233, 253, 263, 265, 275, 300, 445 sq., 452, 470 n., 476, 505 sq., 528, 547. *See also* Edessa
administration of communion, 136, 310, 514 sqq., 643 sqq., 665
'advent' (of euch. consecration), 168, 253, 276, 279, 289
Advent (season), 359, 362, 364, 457
African rites, 85, 108, 122, 131, 156, 180, 296, 453, 463, 468, 473, 485, 492 sq., 498 sqq., 508, 510, 517, 531, 535, 539, 549 sq., 556 n., 559, 592, 736 n.
agape, 19 sq., 23, 81 sqq., 96 sqq., 99 sqq., 325, 382, 419
Agde, council of, 597
*Agnus Dei*, 226, 523, 544, 668
aios, aius, see *trisagion*
Alcuin, 364 sq., 367, 378, 579, 584
Alexandria, church of, 9, 44, 156, 407, 544
— rite of, 9 n., 43, 136, 171 sq., 197, 200, 218 sqq., 439, 458, 502, 504 sq., 537 sq. *See also* Egypt
*alia* (Mozarabic), 488
alleluia, 40, 471
altar, 21, 23, 281 sq., 310, 412, 419 sq.
— cloths, 104, 282. *See also* corporal
— cross, 411 sqq., 419 n.

altar lights, 412, 415 sqq., 419 sqq.
— viewed as 'tomb', 282 sqq.
'alternative' euch. prayers, 531, 535 sq., 540
*ambo*, 23, 418
Ambrose, S., 122, 131, 228, 277 n., 374, 460, 495, 500, 539, 556. *See also* Milan
Amen, 128 sqq., 665
*anamnesis*, 161, 171, 181 sq., 190, 217, 227, 234, 242 sqq., 245, 264, 274, 349, 393, 555 sq., 670
Ancyra, council of, 111
Anglican rite (English), 18, 37, 49, 110, 128, 133, 212, 238, 349, 355 n., 362, 367, 430, 470 n., 525, 640–734
— (Scottish), 210, 660 n.
— (U.S.A.), 294
Anglo-saxon church, rite of, 366 n., 377, 476 n., 562, 575 sqq.
Annunciation, 358, 377, 384
*antiminsion*, 104
Antioch, church of, 9, 46, 156, 173, 302, 328, 401 n., 427
— rite of, 109, 122, 126, 176 sq., 187–207, 204, 281 sq., 289 n., 291 sq., 450 sqq., 465, 478, 502, 513, 736 n.
Apocalypse, 28, 314
apocryphal lections, 470
*apologiae*, 524 sqq.
*Apostolic Constitutions*, rite of, 126, 130, 133, 135, 139, 176 n., 205, 210, 228, 264, 280 n., 289, 291, 449, 470 n., 476 n., 477 sq., 481, 495, 513
apostolic age, rite of, 5, 209 sq., 214
Armenian rite, 135, 286, 291, 358 n., 362, 445, 450, 530, 547

Ascension day, 340, 358, 363
ashes, imposition of (Ash Wednesday), 355
Asia Minor, rites of, 115, 123, 168, 224 *sq.*, 276, 282 *sqq.*, 287, 289 *sq.*, 449, 455 *n.*, 545, 547 *n.*
Assumption, 376
audibility, 14, 482
Augustine, S., of Hippo, 241 *n.*, 247 *sq.*, 321, 375, 380, 386, 388, 392, 439, 441 *n.*, 473, 492, 495, 517, 746
—— of Canterbury, 343, 551, 562, 576 *sq.*
Autun, use of, 520, 585

Bancroft, Archbishop, 703
baptism, 17 *sq.*, 23, 41, 170, 260, 275, 305, 339, 348, 356 *n.*, 418, 485 *sq.*, 529 *n.*, 631 *sq.*
*Basil, Liturgy of S.*, 115, 135, 176, 204 *sq.*, 208, 229, 287 *sq.*, 291, 495, 516, 529, 547
—— (Egyptian), 547, 613
barbarians, conversion of, 595 *sqq.*, 617 *sq.*
Baxter, R., Reformed Liturgy of, 608 *sqq.*, 677
*Benedictus*, 449 *n.*, 456, 464 *n.*, 465, 467 *sq.*
*Benedictus es*, 467
Benevento, rite of, 551, 568
*berakah*. See thanksgiving, jewish
*Biasca, Sacramentary of*, 460
bishop, 'liturgy' of, 1, 6 *sqq.*, 28, 31 *sqq.*, 40, 60 *sq.*, 82 *sqq.*, 99, 104 *sqq.*, 111, 128, 131, 141 *sqq.*, 389, 428, 445, 528, 536, 587 *sq.*
— primitive notion of, 21, 29 *sq.*, 269, 370
'black rubric' (Anglican), 674 *n.*, 678 *n.*
blessing at departure, 479, 482, 512 *sqq.*, 522, 644, 669
— of bread, 52, 54, 55 *n.*, 82 *sqq.*, 272
—— catechumens, 42, 478
—— communicants, 512 *sqq.*, 517 *sqq.*
—— cup, 52, 57, 78, 82 *sqq.*
—— fire, 23, 87
—— food, 51

blessing of lamp, 23, 85 *sqq.*, 418
—— oil, 319, 512
—— wine, 52, 83 *sqq.*, 90 *sq.*
*Bobbio Missal*, 363, 462 *n.*, 466 *sq.*, 468 *sq.*, 470 *n.*, 550, 569, 574
borrowing of rites and prayers, 6 *sqq.*, 171, 176, 208 *sqq.*, 230 *sqq.*, 291, 304 *sqq.*, 353, 361, 379 *sqq.*, 452 *sqq.*, 494, 527, 536, 564, 585 *sq.*, 587. See also local churches
Braga, use of, 9 *n.*, 561
Bucer, M., 669 *sq.*, 678
'Byzantinisation', 9 *sqq.*, 176 *sqq.*, 474, 494, 548
Byzantium, church of, 9, 175 *sq.*, 449 *n.*, 474, 543 *sq.*, 546 *sq.*
—, rite of 9 *n.*, 109, 126, 139, 156 *n.*, 241, 284 *sqq.*, 287, 289, 362, 445 *sqq.*, 450 *sqq.*, 456, 471, 476, 486, 502 *sqq.*, 515 *sqq.*, 529, 546 *sq.*, 570 *n.*, 589

Caesarius of Arles, S., 123, 467, 520, 595, 597
calendar, African, 335 *n.*, 357, 375, 378
—, Byzantine, 351 *n.*, 362, 364, 376 *sq.*, 384 *sq.*
—, effects of, 370, 492, 527, 529, 537, 545, 551
—, Gallican, 351 *n.*, 358 *n.*, 359 *n.*, 375, 377
—, Gothic, 384 *sq.*,
—, Jerusalem, 350 *sqq.*, 357 *sq.*, 375 *sqq.*, 384 *sq.*
—, organisation of, 333-385
—, post-Nicene, 347 *sqq.*
—, pre-Nicene, 335 *sqq.*
—, Roman 335 *n.*, 346, 351, 357 *sqq.*,
—, Spanish, 359 *n.*, 383 369 *sqq.*, 375 *sqq.*, 384, 440
Calvin, -ism, 632 *sq.*, 676 *sq.*
Capua, lectionary of, 362
Carlstadt, 631
Carmelite use, 585
Carthage, council of, 180, 535
Carthusian use, 420, 585
*catecheses*, 354
catechumens, 41 *sq.*, 46 *n.*, 82 *sqq.*, 391 *sq.*, 436 *sqq.*, 443, 478
— exorcism of, 340, 354
— preparation of, 354, 356 *n.*, 391, 595 *sq.* See also blessing, dismissal

celebrant, 'liturgy' of, 7, 15, 31 *sqq.*, 42 *sqq.*, 269, 318 *sq.*, 415, 477 *sq.*, 528, 587 *sq.*, 615 *sqq.*
—, position of, 482, 591
Celestine I, Pope, 401, 414, 449, 452
Celtic rites, 110, 468 *sqq.*, 508, 562, 577
ceremonial, 141, 350, 397 *sqq.*, 430 *sq.*, 446, 494, 589–94, 599.
'ceremonious worship', 312, 351 *sqq.*, 398, 430, 494
*chaburah, –oth*, 50 *sqq.*, 60, 76 *sqq.*, 95, 232, 425
Chair, S. Peter's, 368, 370, 378
chanted prayers, 141, 483 *n.*
chants, 39 *sq.*, 360, 365, 453, 492 *sq.*, 513 *sqq.*
Charlemagne, 9, 364, 474, 487, 545, 563, 575–85, 617
*cherubikon*, 121, 285
chrism, 23, 46 *n.*, 125
Christmas, 357 *sq.*, 359 *n.*, 363, 370, 419, 456 *n.*
Chrysostom, S. John, 122, 126, 176, 204 *sq.*, 239, 243 *sq.*, 264, 281, 291, 293 *sqq.*, 449, 480, 502, 513
*Chrysostom, Liturgy of S. John*, 135, 156 *n.*, 229, 287, 289, 291, 516, 529, 547 *n.*
Church, 19 *sqq.*
— buildings, 17 *sq.*, 19, 32 *sq.*, 306, 309
—, 'organic' conception of, 27 *sqq.*, 246 *sq.*, 271
Circumcision, 358, 377
Cirta, church of, 24 *sqq.*, 141, 311, 314
Clement of Alexandria, 169 *sq.*, 226 *n.*, 245, 252
—— Rome, 1, 27, 33, 102, 111 *sq.*, 252, 371 *n.*, 589
'clericalisation' of euch., 7 *sq.*, 12 *sqq.*, 45, 318 *sq.*, 442 *sq.*, 522, 615 *sqq.*
collect, 360, 363, 367, 372, 447, 458, 461, 464 *sq.*, 468 *sq.*, 490 *sq.*
communicants, 18, 172, 436, 499 *sqq. See also* offerers, blessing
—, prayer for in euch. pr., 158, 170 *sq.*, 186, 190 *sqq.*, 203, 297

communion, 46 *n.*, 48 *sq.*, 81 *sq.*, 135 *sq.*, 227 *sq.*, 230, 242, 483, 511 *sqq.*, 616, 665
— chant, 492 *sq.*, 513 *sq.*, 516
— devotions, 511 *sqq.* 526 *n.*, 645
— effects of, 160, 169. *See also* Spirit
*completuria*, 519
concelebration, 34, 105, 126, 590 *sqq.*
confessors, 373 *sqq.*
confirmation, 17 *sqq.*, 23, 41, 83, 107, 125, 260, 339, 348, 436
consecration, 14 *sq.*, 230, 238 *sqq.*, 243, 293 *sqq.*, 620 *sq.*, 664, 668. *See also* moment, petition
— effects of, 167 *sq.*, 169, 244 *sqq.*
— under one kind, 62, 239 *n.*
consubstantiation, 635 *n.*
*contestatio*, 552, 560
contributions in kind, 51, 78, 97 *n.*, 104, 132
corporal, 104
corporate action, 1 *sq.*, 7, 15, 45, 59, 141, 151, 154, 247, 254, 268 *sq.*, 318, 357, 397, 436, 442, 483 *sq.*, 592 *sqq.*, 600, 615 *sq.*, 624, 660
Corpus Christi, 358, 586
court christian, 91, 105 *sq.*
Cranmer, Archbishop, 128, 183, 248 *n.*, 365 *n.*, 367, 472, 612 *sqq.*, 620, 627, 636, 640–674, 677–682
— liturgies of, 643 *sqq.*, 656–672
creed, 474, 477, 485 *sqq.*
cross, 310, 410 *sqq. See also* altar
—, Exaltation of, 358
— processional, 410
crucifix, 33, 424. *See also* rood
'cup of blessing' (jewish), 52, 57, 60, 62, 78 *sqq.*, 95, 101
Cyprian, S., 115 *sq.*, 253, 400, 498, 556 *n.*
*Cyril, Liturgy of S. See Mark, Lit. of S.*, Alexandria, rite of
Cyril of Jerusalem, S., 104, 124, 135, 137, 171, 187–207, 217 *n.*, 253, 277 *sqq.*, 300, 306 *n.*, 348 *sqq.*, 442, 493, 499, 513 *sqq.*, 538

Daily eucharist, 592 *sq.*
— offices, 324, 328 *sqq.*

'day, prayer of the', 477, 488 *sqq.*, 492

Damasus I., Pope, 329, 452, 532 *sqq.*

Dan. vii. 13., 261, 265, 271

deacon, functions of, 1, 23, 29, 42 *sqq.*, 82 *sqq.*, 85 *sqq.*, 104 *sq.*, 106, 111, 120, 131, 136, 141 *sq.*, 282 *sqq.*, 401 *n.*, 437, 446, 481, 513, 518 *sqq.*

deaconess, 405

dead, prayers for, 170 *sqq.*, 192, 498 *sqq.*, 507 *n.*, 510, 660

*depositio*, 369 *sqq.* *See* calendar, Roman

*deprecatio Gelasii*, 453 *sq.*, 455 *n.*, 461, 468

'derived rites' (mediaeval Western), 585 *sqq.*

devotional tradition, 432, 513, 742

——, Anglican, 12 *sqq.*, 45 *sq.*, 525, 526 *n.*

——, Eastern, 12 *sq.*, 14, 18, 432, 524

——, Gallican, 432, 580 *sqq.*, 592

——, Mediaeval Latin, 13 *sq.*, 18, 45 *sq.*, 248 *sq.*, 433, 525, 585, 592, 599 *sq.*, 603 *sq.*, 605 *sqq.*, 618 *sqq.*, 638

——, Protestant, 249 *sq.*, 600 *sqq.*, 623 *sq.*, 638 *sqq.*, 659

dialogue, eucharistic, 52 *sq.*, 79 *sq.*, 126 *sqq.*, 663

*Didache*, 48 *n.*, 90 *sqq.*, 105, 167, 342

*Didascalia Apostolorum*, 93, 106, 122, 142, 253 *n.*, 277 *sq.*, 291, 416

'Dionysius the Aeropagite'. *See* pseudo-Denys

diptychs, 498 *sqq.*, 510

dismissal, at euch., 81, 514, 516, 520 *sq.*

—— synaxis, 41 *sq.*, 437, 473, 478

domestic character of euch., 16 *sqq.*, 23 *sq.*, 141, 306, 314, 348, 372

Dominican use, 334 *n.*, 585, 592 *n.*

doxology, 130, 172, 185, 216, 221

'drug of immortality', 169

Dura-Europos, 26 *n.*, 141, 314, 422 *n.*

Easter, 338 *sqq.*, 349, 357 *sq.*

Eastern rites, general character of, 45, 288, 524, 530, 542, 546 *sqq.*

*ecclesia*, 19 *sqq.*, 28 *sqq.*, 96 *sqq.*, 99, 310, 326, 336, 347

Edessa, rite of, 171, 177 *sqq.*, 362, 439, 446, 530. *See Addai and Mari, Lit.*

Egypt, rites of, 7 *n.*, 43, 49 *n.*, 110, 123, 128, 133, 139, 162 *sqq.*, 217 *sqq.*, 226, 276, 446 *sqq.*, 451 *sq.*, 504 *sq.*, 512 *sq.*, 542, 547. *See Mark, Lit.*

*eileton*, 104

elevation, 14, 482, 484, 620

Elvira, council of, 421 *sq.*, 476 *n.*, 499, 501

Ember days, 342 *sq.*, 467, 471

emperor, prayers for, 43

emperor-worship, 147, 307, 386, 423 *sq.*

entrance-chant, 367 *n.*, 414, 449 *sq.*, 452 *sqq.*, 461 *sqq.*, 463 *sq.*, 465 *sq.*, 659

'Entrance, Great', 120, 284 *sqq.*, 289, 416, 483

entrance-procession, 397, 414, 438, 448 *sqq.*

Ephraem Syrus, S., 280, 428, 444

*epiklesis*. *See* invocation

Epiphany, 355, 357 *sq.*, 359 *n.*, 529 *n.*, 552 *sq.*

epistle lection, 360, 471

eschatology, 4, 127, 129 *sq.*, 138 *sq.*, 181, 185 *sq.*, 255 *sqq.*, 305, 314, 335 *sqq.*, 340, 345, 359 *sq.*, 369 *sq.*, 394, 512, 541, 621 *sq.*, 626

Etheria, 329, 334, 348 *sqq.*, 419 *n.*, 427, 437, 441 *n.*

eucharist as 'Canaan', 80, 136

eucharist apart from supper, 81 *sq.*, 95 *sqq.*

*eucharistein*, 79, 92 *sqq.*

*eucharistia*, 79 *sq.*, 99, 128, 215 *sq.*, 222

eucharistic action, 2, 12, 623, 632, 671, 743 *sq.*

— prayer, 7 *sq.*, 48, 78 *sqq.*, 156–237, 239, 271 *sqq.*, 304, 511, 517, 528, 551 *sq.*, 615, 730 *sq.*

—— addressed to Son, 180, 535

—— B.V.M., 530 *n.*

*eulogion*, 82 *sqq.*, 436

excommunication, 436 *sq.*, 499

exorcised bread, 82 *sq.*

exorcism, 170, 340, 354

extempore prayer, 6 *sqq.*, 128, 528

Faithful, prayers of, 42 *sqq.*, 171, 473, 478 *sqq.*, 491 *n.*
fans, 282, 415 *n.*
fast, fasting, 82, 335 *n.*, 341 *sqq.*, 353 *sqq.*
feasts of B.V.M., 375 *sqq.*
—— our Lord, 357 *sqq.*, 360, 371, 586
—— the saints, 343 *sqq.*, 347, 359, 369 *sqq.*, 585
*fermentum*, 21, 105, 134, 285
*Filioque*, 487, 544
'four-action Shape', 48 *sq.*, 78 *sqq.*, 101, 103–140, 232, 670 *sq.*
fraction, 48, 80, 131 *sqq.*, 319, 511 *sqq.*, 615, 671, 693
Frankish churches, rite of, 550, 562, 565–84
'Frankish Gel.', 550, 565–84
Fulgentius, S., 296 *sq.*, 401 *n.*, 473, 550, 556 *n.*
funerals, 320, 369, 372 *sq.*, 416 *sq.*, 427 *n.*, 523, 593
furnishings of churches, 24 *sqq.*, 141, 310
fusion of synaxis and euch., 37, 171, 437 *sqq.*

Gallican lectionary. *See* Luxeuil
— rite, 23 *n.*, 123, 128, 131, 156 *n.*, 180, 264, 276, 360 *n.*, 363, 380 *sq.*, 411, 429, 446, 465 *sqq.*, 471, 476 *n.*, 490, 520, 530 *sq.*, 542, 549 *sqq.*, 575, 581
——, origins of, 459 *sqq.*, 558 *sqq.*
Gardiner, Bishop, 627, 657 *sq.*, 678
*Gelasian Sacramentary*, 363, 365, 375, 377, 401 *n.*, 441 *n.*, 453 *n.*, 457, 491, 501 *n.*, 532, 535 *n.*, 536 *sq.*, 559, 562, 565–83
'Gelasianised-Gregorian' missals, 574, 619
'*Gelasianum* of 7th cent.', 550, 565–584
—— of 8th cent.', 574 *sq.*, 577 *sq.*
Gelasius I, Pope, 7 *n.*, 451, 453, 508, 532 *n.*, 535
'Germanus of Paris', Epistles of. *See* pseudo-G.
Gerona, council of, 561 *n.*
*Gloria in excelsis*, 452 *sqq.*, 456 *sq.*, 464 *sq.*, 468, 659, 667 *sq*

Good Friday, 36, 39 *n.*, 42, 348 *sqq.*, 363, 440, 510
gospel lection, 39, 338, 360, 417 *sq.*
gradual, 23, 360, 367 *n.*, 471, 660
greeting, 38, 103, 458, 465, 468, 513
*Gregorian Sacramentary*, 364, 375, 377 *sq.*, 440 *n.*, 455 *n.*, 457, 468, 491, 565 *sqq.*, 570 *sqq.*
Gregory I, Pope, 131, 226, 365, 400, 404, 429 *n.*, 453 *sq.*, 461 *n.*, 468, 491, 508, 565 *sqq.*, 570 *sqq.*
*Gregory, Egyptian Lit. of S.*, 180, 547, 613
Guest, Bishop, 675 *sq.*

*Hallel*, 88 *sq.*, 668
*hanc igitur*, 372 *sq.*, 557 *n.*, 571
hand-washing, 51 *sqq.*, 56, 104, 124, 140
harmonies of gospels, lit. use of, 470
'hearing' in euch. devotion, 12 *sqq.*, 599, 616 *sq.*
'heavenly altar', 229, 243 *sq.*, 289, 304
— High-priest', 244, 251, 279 *sq.*, 292, 304
hellenisation, hellenism, 173, 740. *See* mysteries
Hereford, use of, 522, 585, 613
high mass, 590 *sqq.*, 599, 603
Hippolytus, S., 30 *sq.*, 33, 36, 82 *sqq.*, 110, 126, 133, 138, 157, 210, 216, 235, 245, 263, 323 *sq.*, 346, 749
——, rite of, 7 *n.*, 110, 131, 136, 221 *sqq.*, 234, 275 *sq.*, 297, 300, 511, 537, 555, 589. *See* Roman rite, Greek
'historical' conception of worship, 305, 335, 347 *sqq.*, 358 *sq.*, 368, 370 *sqq.*, 394, 622 *sq.*
Holy Saturday, 23, 39 *n.*, 348, 363, 418, 440, 454, 493 *n. See* paschal vigil
Holy Week, 343, 348 *sqq.*, 354, 440 *n.*
house-churches, 18, 22 *sqq.*, 27, 141, 147
*Hucusque*, 580
'humble access, prayer of' (Angl.), 611 *n.*, 644, 657 *sq.*, 663, 671
hymn of the synaxis, 445, 451 *sqq.*, 461 *sqq.*, 465 *sq.*, 470, 659

Ignatius of Antioch, S., 21, 99, 113, 132, 137, 244, 369, 621
*ikon, ikonostasion*, 15, 424, 481. *See* images, screen
*illatio*, 552
images, cultus of, 422 *sqq.*, 431
Immaculate Conception (B.V.M.), 377, 433, 585
*immolatio*, 552
imposition of hands at offertory, 105, 125 sq.
incarnation and euch., 277
incense, 310, 314, 350, 424 sq., 444 *sqq.*
Innocent I, Pope, 109, 118 n., 439, 496, 500, 539, 564
insignia of office, 410 *sqq.*
institution narrative in euch. pr., 158 *sqq.*, 167 sq., 181 sq., 189 sq., 201, 226 sq., 232 *sqq.*, 275, 281, 293, 551, 554 n.
—— as consecration, 239 sq.
— under both kinds for body and soul, 611 sq., 644
intercessions at euch., 170 sq., 192 *sqq.*, 498 *sqq.*, 510
—— synaxis, 37 sq., 170 sq., 318, 437, 440, 498 *sqq.*, 509, 528, 660
introduction at synaxis, 443 sq., 469
invitation to communion (*sancta sanctis*), 134, 514
invocation in euch. pr., 168, 182 sq., 197, 205, 213, 241, 275 sq., 290, 292 *sqq.*, 657 n.
—— of Holy Spirit, 191 sq., 198 sq., 277 *sqq.*, 281 *sqq.*, 350, 555 n.
—— Name, 169 sq.
—— Word, 167 sq., 276
—— viewed as 'resurrection', 283 sq., 288 *sqq.*
invocation of saints, 345 *sqq.*, 455 n.
—— of Sunday, 530 n.
Irenaeus, S., 31, 40, 113, 117, 137, 244, 749
Irish rite. *See* Celtic
'Italian Gel.', 566, 573 sq., 579
Italian rites, 437 n., 462, 468, 487, 500, 540, 556, 563 *sqq.*

*James, Lit. of S.*, 9 n., 126, 135, 175–207, 286, 291, 428, 437., 442, 450, 456, 466, 476 n., 503, 546 sq., 570 n., 626. *See* Jerusalem, rite of

Jerusalem, church of, 10, 61 *sqq.*, 65, 69 sq., 176, 328, 334, 348 *sqq.*, 399, 427, 481, 487, 544
—, rite of, 9 n., 24 n., 46, 58 n., 61 *sqq.*, 109, 130, 171, 176–207, 280, 291, 339, 362, 437, 438 n., 440 n., 448 sq., 476 n., 499, 564. *See James, Lit. of S.*
John, gospel of S., on euch., 50, 132, 137, 160, 266, 671, 750
—, *Leucian 'Acts'* of, 61 n., 224
'Johnson's Case', 676
*Judas Thomas, 'Acts' of*, 61 n., 224
*jus liturgicum*, 588
Justin Martyr, S., 20, 36, 108, 111, 116, 150, 159 sq., 216, 222 sq., 233, 244, 354, 626
Justinian, emperor, 109, 450, 463, 548, 573, 737 n.

*Kiddush*, 54 n., 88
kind, communion under one, 629 n.
Kingdom of God, 75 *sqq.*, 390, 393, 593
*kirchenordnungen*, 645, 659, 672
kiss of peace, 103, 105 sq., 107, 226
kneeling at communion, 13
*Kyrie eleison*, 9 n., 452 *sqq.*, 461 sq., 464, 468, 478

*Laïkos*, 480
laity, 1, 41 sq., 172, 480 sq. *See* lay
Langforde's *Meditations*, 605 *sqq.*
'language of fear', 200 sq., 352, 436, 480 sq., 594
Laodicea, council of, 449
'last gospel' (Jn. i. 1–14), 526
last supper, 50 *sqq.*, 70 *sqq.*
Latin rites, origin of, 557 n.
— use of in services, 599, 616 *sqq.*
lauds, 329 sq.
lay communion, frequency of, 18 sq., 249 sq., 319, 594 *sqq.*
— devotion, 45 sq., 250, 323 sq., 380, 513, 594 *sqq.*, 618, 687
— oblation at offertory, 120, 319, 436, 476, 598
lections, 39 sq., 338, 360 *sqq.*, 470 *sqq.*
lector, 23 *sqq.*, 35, 558
*legitima eucharistia*, 553 n.
Lent, 340, 343, 353 *sqq.*, 361, 371 n., 440 n., 471, 518, 529

Leo I, Pope, 7 n., 355, 357, 373 n., 375, 401 n., 439 sq., 473, 533, 568, 571, 745

Léon, Antiphoner of, 463

Leonine Sacramentary, 373 n., 532, 567 sq., 569 n.

'liberals', 55, 60 sq., 65 sqq.

Liber Mozarabicus Sacramentorum, 463 n., 518, 554 n., 561 sq., 574 n.

Liber Ordinum, 519, 554 n., 574 n.

Liber Pontificalis, 342, 411, 452, 535

lights, 350, 416 sqq.

Lincoln, use of, 591 n.

'link' (clause in euch. pr.), 226, 300, 555, 557 n.

itany, 46, 411, 450, 452 sqq., 461 sq., 462 n., 477 sqq., 510

'liturgy' (function in worship), 1, 7, 21, 32 sqq., 35, 40, 111 sq., 117, 124, 268 sq., 365, 393, 432, 480, 500 n., 587 sq., 592 sq., 599

liturgical history, theories of, 4 sqq., 209 sqq., 532 sqq., 734 sqq.

'living sacrifice', 166, 222

local churches, liturgical independence of, 5 sqq., 8, 156 sq., 171, 176 sq., 185, 208 sqq., 230 sqq., 304, 354 sqq., 474, 536, 540, 550, 563 sq., 568, 570, 585 sq., 588

Lord's prayer, 94, 108 sq., 130 sq., 140, 196, 226, 350, 513 sqq., 517, 665

Lord's supper. See agape

low mass, 14 sq., 484, 538, 589, 593, 599, 602, 615

lucernarium, 87, 419

Luke, gospel of S., on euch., 48 n., 54, 56, 61 sq., 68

Luther, M., 629 sqq.

Luxeuil, lectionary of, 363

Lyons, use of, 9 n., 414, 585

Macon, council of, 123, 476 n.

Mal. i. 11., 91, 111, 427

manifestation, 255, 268, 289

manual acts, 131 sqq., 134 n., 515 sq., 693

manuscripts, liturgical use of, 528, 582, 587 sq., 589

Mark, gospel of S., on euch., 48 sq., 57 sqq., 63 sqq., 68, 73, 98, 132, 268

Mark, Liturgy of S., 135, 165, 204 n., 217 sqq., 226, 229, 291, 428, 447, 451, 473, 504 sq., 510, 544, 546 n., 547, 613. See Alexandria, rite of; Egypt

Maronite rite, 175, 176 n., 180

marriages, 320, 593

martyrdom, 20, 143, 307, 386, 686

martyrs, 145, 149, 152 sq., 333, 343 sqq., 361, 363, 369 sqq., 380 sqq., 388, 392, 419, 421 sqq.

Masses of Mone, 264, 363, 521, 553, 560, 574

Matthew, gospel of S., on euch., 48 sq., 68, 73, 98, 132, 227, 268

Maundy Thursday, 36, 348, 440 n., 441, 454

Messianic sacrifice, 73 sqq., 259., 349, 746 sqq.

Milan, rite of, 10, 109, 122, 131, 229, 329, 334, 360 n., 363, 446, 460 sqq., 490, 497, 500, 539, 556, 565, 568 sq., 571 n.

Milevis, council of, 536, 550

milk and honey, 80, 136

Missa (Moz.), 488

missal. See Western

Missale Francorum, 363, 550, 574, 581

— Gallicanum Vetus, 574

— Gothicum, 267, 363, 497, 552, 574

mixed chalice, 104

'mixed cup' (jewish), 57

moment of consecration, 168, 240 sqq., 299 sq., 301 sq.

monasticism, 40, 316 sq., 319 sqq., 354

monogenes, 447, 450

Mopsuestia, rite of, 109, 134 n., 264, 282 sqq., 289, 449. See Theodore of

Mozarabic (Spanish, Visigothic) rite, 109, 127, 156 n., 180, 297, 363, 380, 405, 462 sqq., 476 n., 487 sqq., 496, 499 sq., 501 n., 509, 518 sqq., 532, 542, 549 sqq., 554, 561 sq.

music, 365, 427, 493, 569, 599

munera, 500 n.

mysteries, pagan, 61, 65, 72, 153, 398, 405, 409, 413, 415 *sq.*, 430 *sq.*, 483

'Name, glorifying of the', 52 *sq.*, 80, 169, 185 *sq.*, 275, 671
— power of the', 170, 219, 226 *n.*, 230, 274, 291, 512 *n.*
names, recitation of, ('Naming', the), 477, 497 *sqq.*, 550, 556
Naples, rite of, 362, 377 *n.*
Narsai, 286, 419 *n.*, 439, 476 *n.*, 493 *sq.*, 506
*natale, natalitia,* 369
*Nestorius, Liturgy of Mar,* 547 *n.*
New Covenant, 57 *sq.*, 67, 69, 74 *sqq.*, 80, 271 *sqq.*
New Testament and euch., 3 *sqq.*, 48 *sqq.*, 572, 602, 615, 634
—— liturgy, 3 *sqq.*, 49 *sq.*, 133, 233
Nicaea, I, council of, 485
non - communicating attendance, 436, 442, 513, 516, 520, 522, 594 *sqq.*, 669

'Oblation, prayer of' (Anglican), 657, 665 *sq.*, 731 *sq.*
Oecolampadius, 631 *sq.*
offerers, *offerentes,* 104, 115, 436, 499 *sqq.*, 500 *n.*, 501 *n.*, 598, 623
offertory, 46, 48 *sqq.*, 78, 104, 110–123, 227, 244, 247, 283, 319, 438 *n.*, 500, 660 *sqq.*, 692
— chant, 285 *sqq.*, 492 *sq.*
— prayers, 118, 367, 477, 495 *sqq.*, 500, 511, 660 *sqq.*, 691 *sq.*
— procession, 120, 282, 290, 438 *n.*, 476
office, divine, 323 *sqq.*, 328 *sqq.*, 349, 408 *sq.*, 603
Old Testament lections, 39 *n.*, 338, 470 *sq.*
*oratio,* 473, 489
— *super populum,* 461 *n.*, 518, 521
— *super sindonem,* 491
*Order of Communion* (Anglican), 643 *sqq.*, 676, 681
*Ordo Romanus primus,* 131, 404 *n.*, 411, 418, 455 *n.*, 457, 589, 592
—— *secundus,* 414 *n.*, 455 *n.*
—— (others), 440 *n.*, 441 *n.*
*oremus,* 489

Origen, 165, 197, 200, 253, 260 *n.*, 346, 750
Orleans, council of, 520
Orthodoxy Sunday, 358

Palm Sunday, 348, 440 *n.*
Paris, use of, 334 *n.*, 585
*Pascha* (Passover), 274, 335, 337 *sqq.*, 348 *sqq.*, 358 *sq.*, 360, 529 *n.*
paschal candle, 23
— vigil, 39 *n.*, 325, 338 *sq.*, 348 *sq.*, 419, 439, 454
Paschasius Radbert, 612 *n.*, 657 *n.*
Paul, S., on euch., 1, 48 *sq.*, 55 *sq.*, 57 *sqq.*, 63 *sqq.*, 73, 96 *sqq.*, 107, 132, 137, 236, 242, 248, 254, 266, 268, 595, 605, 622, 749
*Paul, 'Acts' of,* 346 *n.*
*Paul and Thecla, 'Acts' of,* 61 *n.*
*pax. See* kiss
penance, penitents, 26, 147, 356 *n.* 437, 478, 638
Pentecost, 335, 341, 350, 359, 360, 529 *n.*
*Persian Liturgy, fragments of a,* 179 *n.*
petition for consecration, 168 *sq.*, 228 *sq.*, 253, 299 *sqq.*
Philocalian calendar. *See* calendar, Roman
*pneuma* received in euch. *See* 'Spirit'
pontifical mass, 589, 599
*post-mysterium,* 552
*post-pridie,* 552, 554 *n.*
*post-sanctus,* 552, 555 *sq.*,
*post-secreta,* 552
*praefatio,* 473, 488 *sqq.*, 535
Prayer Book, First (Anglican), 420 *n.*, 470 *n.*, 645, 656–658, 681
——, Second (Anglican), 409, 470 *n.*, 659–672, 681
——, Revisions of (Anglican), 660, 667 *n.*, 674–733
preface and sanctus, 165 *sq.*, 180 *sq.*, 188, 196 *sq.*, 200, 218 *sqq.*, 300, 367, 500, 527, 537 *sqq.*, 555, 663
preparation of elements, 121, 285, 289 *sq.*, 524
—— ministers, 482, 524, 659
preparatory devotions, 13 *sqq.*, 524
*Presanctified, Liturgy of the,* 36, 440, 442, 529

presbyters, functions of, 1, 28, 33 *sqq.*, 104 *sq.*, 128, 135, 270, 310, 587, 590 *sqq.*, 615 *sqq.*
'president' of supper (jewish), 50 *sqq.*, 60, 84, 268
*prex* ( = euch. pr.), 498; ( = litany), 468 *n.*
private prayer, 317, 323, 326, 599 *sq.*, 607 *sqq.*
propers, 360 *sq.*, 537, 541, 585
*prophetia. See Benedictus*
*prosphora, prospherein*, 111, 172, 244, 436, 499
*prospherontes. See* offerers
Protestant Reformation, 10, 597, 623, 625 *sqq.*
— rites, 10, 608 *sq.*, 623, 659 *sqq.*
psalmody, 39 *sq.*, 326, 330, 334 *n.*, 360, 445, 492 *sq.*
pseudo-Denys (Dionysius), 445, 476 *n.*
pseudo-Germanus of Paris, 459 *sqq.*, 465 *sqq.*, 494, 521
public worship, 16 *sqq.*, 304 *sqq.*, 314 *sqq.*, 331, 397, 437, 439, 604
Purification, 358, 376, 384
puritans, puritanism, 312 *sqq.*, 317, 326, 494 *sq.*, 601, 603, 608 *sqq.*, 630, 684 *sq.*

*Quam oblationem*, 169, 299, 557 *n.*, 657 *n.*

Rabanus Maurus, 591
Ravenna, rite of, 566, 569 *n.*
relics, 344 *sqq.*, 371, 376 *sq.*, 419, 423, 591
*requiem. See* funeral
reservation, 21, 36, 105, 139 *sq.*, 151, 310, 324, 326, 440 *sq.*
Rogation days, 411, 455
Roman law on christianity, 143 *sqq.*, 306 *sqq.*
Roman rite (*a*), Greek, 158 *sq.*, 216, 222, 235, 264, 528 *n.*, 545, 570 *n.*, 617. *See* Hippolytus, rite of
—— (*b*), Latin, 23 *sq.*, 39 *n.*, 42, 108, 115, 120, 128, 131 *sqq.*, 171, 201, 208, 226, 265, 355, 360 *n.*, 363 *sq.*, 365 *n.*, 429, 437, 440, 446, 452 *sqq.*, 464, 470 *sq.*, 487, 490 *sqq.*, 496, 500, 505

*sqq.*, 513 *n.*, 518, 533 *sqq.*, 542, 549 *sqq.*, 555, 557 *n.*, 565–74, 586, 619
'Romanisation', 10 *sq.*, 474, 494, 497
Rome, church of, 7 *n.*, 9, 21, 84, 101, 112, 126, 532 *sqq.*, 543, 573, 575
rood, 33, 622

Sacramentalism (jewish), 72
sacramentary, 365
sacrifice, 238, 242, 272 *sq.*, 746 *sq.* *See* 'living', Messianic, 'unbloody'
sacrificial interpretation of euch., 59, 77, 111 *sqq.*, 162, 166, 185, 190 *sqq.*, 199 *sqq.*, 227, 229 *sq.*, 238 *sqq.*, 270 *sq.*, 273 *sqq.*, 393, 623, 625, 646, 746 *sq.*
*sacrum*, 746 *sq.*
saints, cultus of, 344 *sq.*, 372 *sqq.*, 380 *sqq.*, 419, 421, 438 *n. See* invocation
— days, 335 *n.*, 343 *sqq.*, 351 *n.*, 361, 363, 369 *sqq.*, 585
— named in euch. pr., 351, 373, 499, 508, 678
*Sanctum*, 134, 285
*sanctus*, 165 *sq.*, 197, 221, 467 *n.*, 537, 551, 663
Sarapion, S., rite of, 7 *n.*, 42, 162 *sqq.* 217 *n.*, 220, 222, 242, 275, 289, 319, 446, 472, 495, 499 *sqq.*, 511, 528, 536
Sarum, use of, 334 *n.*, 364 *n.*, 366 *n.*, 522, 585, 613, 660
Savoy Conference, 603, 689
*secreta* ( = institution narrative in euch. pr.), 483 *n.*; ( = offertory pr.), 118, 367, 661
schism, 10, 60, 272
screen, 15, 481, 482 *n. See* ikonostasion
scriptures, surrender of, 24 *sq.*
'second half' of euch. pr., 225 *sqq.*, 231 *sq.*, 234, 275 *sq.*, 511
'second stratum' in liturgical history, 9, 435–522, 534
'seeing' in euch. devotion, 14 *sqq.*, 615 *sq.*, 620 *sq.*
separation of euch. and agape, 50, 77 *sq.*, 82, 84 *sqq.*, 95 *sqq.*
sequences, 472

sermon, 40 *sq.*, 318, 338, 472, 596 *sq.*, 642, 660
— prayer after the, 472
'seven-action Shape', 48 *n.*
sin-offering, 125
'Spirit' received in euch., 137 *sq.*, 183 *sq.*, 201 *sq.*, 262, 266 *sq.*, 298, 633
'Spirit' = Presence, 183 *sq.*, 289, 299, 472
— = Word, 254 *n.*, 276, 299
'station', 342 *sq.*
stational liturgy, 21, 371, 420, 457, 538, 592 *sq.*
*Stowe Missal*, 110, 468, 508
subdeacons, 24 *sq.*, 35
Sunday, 154, 336 *sq.*, 354 *sq.*, 359 *sq.*, 368
supper-ritual (jewish) 50 *sqq.*, 83 *sqq.*
Supplement (Alcuin's), 580, 582 *sq.*
*supplices Te*, 229, 555, 557 *n.*
symbolic actions, 124, 133, 397 *sq.*, 417 *sq.*, 432
synagogue service, 16, 36 *sqq.*, 360, 616, 743
synaxis, *syneleusis*, 17 *sq.*, 20, 36 *sqq.*, 170 *sq.*, 318, 324 *sq.*, 361, 393, 434, 440, 443 *sqq.*, 591, 659, 743
Syrian influence in West, 465 *sq.*, 509, 523, 538, 541, 549, 556 *n.*
Syrian rites, 9 *n.*, 15, 46, 122, 128, 131, 139 *sq.*, 173–207, 224, 438 *n.*, 451 *sqq.*, 509, 513, 530, 537, 542, 547

'Ten-action Shape,' 48 *n.*
Tertullian, 84 *sq.*, 115, 150 *sq.*, 245, 255 *sq.*, 342, 345, 369, 553 *n.*
'thanksgiving', jewish, 52 *sqq.*, 60, 78 *sqq.*, 83 *sqq.*, 96, 124, 215 *sqq.*, 226, 232, 272, 274, 291
— (liturgical post-communion), .81, 367, 512 *sqq.*, 519, 521, 667
— devotions, post-liturgical, 516, 524 *sqq.*
— 'series' in euch. pr., 157, 159, 178, 189, 204, 215 *sqq.*, 224 *sq.*, 274, 300, 511, 537 *sq.*, 539 *sqq.*, 555, 671

Theodore of Mopsuestia, 38 *n.*, 118 *n.*, 282 *sq.*, 289, 298, 416, 480. *See* Mopsuestia
Theodotus, 170, 226 *n.*, 230, 253 *n.*
'third *stratum*' in liturgical history, 10, 522 *sqq.*
Thmuis, rite of. *See* Sarapion
Thomas Aquinas, S., 248, 612 *n.*, 746
throne, 23, 28, 41, 591
'titles', *tituli*, 21, 371
Toledo, councils of, 404, 487, 519, 561
—, rite of, 9 *n.*, 362, 561. *See* Mozarabic
Tours, rite of, 467, 562
tract, 471
tradition, 2 *sqq.*, 41, 49 *sq.*, 133, 286, 443, 531
Transfiguration, 358
transubstantiation, 199, 630 *n.*
Trinity Sunday, 358, 362, 364 *n.*, 585
*trisagion*, 449 *n.*, 451 *sqq.*, 463, 465 *sqq.*, 468 *n.*

*Umbella*, 415
'unbloody sacrifice', 166, 222
uniformity, 9 *sq.*, 121, 230 *sqq.*, 536, 538, 550, 564, 580 *sqq.*, 587, 659, 693 *sq.*, 702 *sqq.*

Vaison, council of, 9 *n.*, 461, 466, 509 *n.*, 538, 550, 593
variable prayers, 360, 517, 527 *sqq.*, 558 *sqq.*, 586
veil, sanctuary, 15, 480
veneration of the Cross, 348, 440 *n.*
vernacular, use of, 10, 599, 616 *sq.*
vespers, 46, 323, 329 *sq.*, 419, 424 *n.*
vestments, 350, 398 *sqq.*
vigil, 325 *sq.*, 328
virgins, Egyptian rule for, 93 *sqq.*
votive masses, 537, 579 *sq.*, 585, 593

Water, chalice of, at baptismal euch., 136
wineless eucharists, 48 *sq.*, 58 *n.*, 61 *sqq.*
Western missal, 583 *sq.*
Western rites, divergence of, 549 *sq.*
——, general character of, 288, 524, 531, 543, 549 *sqq.*, 585

Western rites, origins of, 477, 492,
    517, 550, 555, 557 *n.*, 573
———, synthesis of, 551, 573 *sqq.*, 583
Westminster, use of, 522, 525 *n.*
words in relation to worship, 312,
    397 *sq.*, 424 *n.*

*Würzburg capitulary*, 362, 471

Zante, 9 *n.*
*Zeon*, 515
Zürich, 631 *sq.*, 668
Zwingli, 631 *sqq.*, 656, 659, 668